Lecture Notes in Computer Science 8512

Commenced Publication in 1973
Founding and Former Series Editors:
Gerhard Goos, Juris Hartmanis, and Jan van Leeuwen

Masaaki Kurosu (Ed.)

Human-Computer Interaction

Applications and Services

16th International Conference
HCI International 2014
Heraklion, Crete, Greece, June 22-27, 2014
Proceedings, Part III

Springer

Volume Editor

Masaaki Kurosu
The Open University of Japan
2-11 Wakaba, Mihama-ku, Chiba-shi
Chiba 261-8586, Japan
E-mail: masaakikurosu@spa.nifty.com

ISSN 0302-9743 e-ISSN 1611-3349
ISBN 978-3-319-07226-5 e-ISBN 978-3-319-07227-2
DOI 10.1007/978-3-319-07227-2
Springer Cham Heidelberg New York Dordrecht London

Library of Congress Control Number: 2014938357

LNCS Sublibrary: SL 3 – Information Systems and Application, incl. Internet/Web and HCI

Typesetting: Camera-ready by author, data conversion by Scientific Publishing Services, Chennai, India

Printed on acid-free paper

Springer is part of Springer Science+Business Media (www.springer.com)

Foreword

The 16th International Conference on Human–Computer Interaction, HCI International 2014, was held in Heraklion, Crete, Greece, during June 22–27, 2014, incorporating 14 conferences/thematic areas:

Thematic areas:

- Human–Computer Interaction
- Human Interface and the Management of Information

Affiliated conferences:

- 11th International Conference on Engineering Psychology and Cognitive Ergonomics
- 8th International Conference on Universal Access in Human–Computer Interaction
- 6th International Conference on Virtual, Augmented and Mixed Reality
- 6th International Conference on Cross-Cultural Design
- 6th International Conference on Social Computing and Social Media
- 8th International Conference on Augmented Cognition
- 5th International Conference on Digital Human Modeling and Applications in Health, Safety, Ergonomics and Risk Management
- Third International Conference on Design, User Experience and Usability
- Second International Conference on Distributed, Ambient and Pervasive Interactions
- Second International Conference on Human Aspects of Information Security, Privacy and Trust
- First International Conference on HCI in Business
- First International Conference on Learning and Collaboration Technologies

A total of 4,766 individuals from academia, research institutes, industry, and governmental agencies from 78 countries submitted contributions, and 1,476 papers and 225 posters were included in the proceedings. These papers address the latest research and development efforts and highlight the human aspects of design and use of computing systems. The papers thoroughly cover the entire field of human–computer interaction, addressing major advances in knowledge and effective use of computers in a variety of application areas.

This volume, edited by Masaaki Kurosu, contains papers focusing on the thematic area of human–computer interaction (HCI), addressing the following major topics:

- Interacting with the web
- Mobile Interaction

- HCI for health, well-being and sport
- Mobility, transport and environment
- Interacting with games
- Business, sustainability and technology adoption

The remaining volumes of the HCI International 2014 proceedings are:

- Volume 1, LNCS 8510, Human–Computer Interaction: HCI Theories, Methods and Tools (Part I), edited by Masaaki Kurosu
- Volume 2, LNCS 8511, Human–Computer Interaction: Advanced Interaction Modalities and Techniques (Part II), edited by Masaaki Kurosu
- Volume 4, LNCS 8513, Universal Access in Human–Computer Interaction: Design and Development Methods for Universal Access (Part I), edited by Constantine Stephanidis and Margherita Antona
- Volume 5, LNCS 8514, Universal Access in Human–Computer Interaction: Universal Access to Information and Knowledge (Part II), edited by Constantine Stephanidis and Margherita Antona
- Volume 6, LNCS 8515, Universal Access in Human–Computer Interaction: Aging and Assistive Environments (Part III), edited by Constantine Stephanidis and Margherita Antona
- Volume 7, LNCS 8516, Universal Access in Human–Computer Interaction: Design for All and Accessibility Practice (Part IV), edited by Constantine Stephanidis and Margherita Antona
- Volume 8, LNCS 8517, Design, User Experience, and Usability: Theories, Methods and Tools for Designing the User Experience (Part I), edited by Aaron Marcus
- Volume 9, LNCS 8518, Design, User Experience, and Usability: User Experience Design for Diverse Interaction Platforms and Environments (Part II), edited by Aaron Marcus
- Volume 10, LNCS 8519, Design, User Experience, and Usability: User Experience Design for Everyday Life Applications and Services (Part III), edited by Aaron Marcus
- Volume 11, LNCS 8520, Design, User Experience, and Usability: User Experience Design Practice (Part IV), edited by Aaron Marcus
- Volume 12, LNCS 8521, Human Interface and the Management of Information: Information and Knowledge Design and Evaluation (Part I), edited by Sakae Yamamoto
- Volume 13, LNCS 8522, Human Interface and the Management of Information: Information and Knowledge in Applications and Services (Part II), edited by Sakae Yamamoto
- Volume 14, LNCS 8523, Learning and Collaboration Technologies: Designing and Developing Novel Learning Experiences (Part I), edited by Panayiotis Zaphiris and Andri Ioannou
- Volume 15, LNCS 8524, Learning and Collaboration Technologies: Technology-rich Environments for Learning and Collaboration (Part II), edited by Panayiotis Zaphiris and Andri Ioannou

- Volume 16, LNCS 8525, Virtual, Augmented and Mixed Reality: Designing and Developing Virtual and Augmented Environments (Part I), edited by Randall Shumaker and Stephanie Lackey
- Volume 17, LNCS 8526, Virtual, Augmented and Mixed Reality: Applications of Virtual and Augmented Reality (Part II), edited by Randall Shumaker and Stephanie Lackey
- Volume 18, LNCS 8527, HCI in Business, edited by Fiona Fui-Hoon Nah
- Volume 19, LNCS 8528, Cross-Cultural Design, edited by P.L. Patrick Rau
- Volume 20, LNCS 8529, Digital Human Modeling and Applications in Health, Safety, Ergonomics and Risk Management, edited by Vincent G. Duffy
- Volume 21, LNCS 8530, Distributed, Ambient, and Pervasive Interactions, edited by Norbert Streitz and Panos Markopoulos
- Volume 22, LNCS 8531, Social Computing and Social Media, edited by Gabriele Meiselwitz
- Volume 23, LNAI 8532, Engineering Psychology and Cognitive Ergonomics, edited by Don Harris
- Volume 24, LNCS 8533, Human Aspects of Information Security, Privacy and Trust, edited by Theo Tryfonas and Ioannis Askoxylakis
- Volume 25, LNAI 8534, Foundations of Augmented Cognition, edited by Dylan D. Schmorrow and Cali M. Fidopiastis
- Volume 26, CCIS 434, HCI International 2014 Posters Proceedings (Part I), edited by Constantine Stephanidis
- Volume 27, CCIS 435, HCI International 2014 Posters Proceedings (Part II), edited by Constantine Stephanidis

I would like to thank the Program Chairs and the members of the Program Boards of all affiliated conferences and thematic areas, listed below, for their contribution to the highest scientific quality and the overall success of the HCI International 2014 Conference.

This conference could not have been possible without the continuous support and advice of the founding chair and conference scientific advisor, Prof. Gavriel Salvendy, as well as the dedicated work and outstanding efforts of the communications chair and editor of *HCI International News*, Dr. Abbas Moallem.

I would also like to thank for their contribution towards the smooth organization of the HCI International 2014 Conference the members of the Human–Computer Interaction Laboratory of ICS-FORTH, and in particular George Paparoulis, Maria Pitsoulaki, Maria Bouhli, and George Kapnas.

April 2014

Constantine Stephanidis
General Chair, HCI International 2014

Organization

Human–Computer Interaction

Program Chair: Masaaki Kurosu, Japan

Jose Abdelnour-Nocera, UK
Sebastiano Bagnara, Italy
Simone Barbosa, Brazil
Adriana Betiol, Brazil
Simone Borsci, UK
Henry Duh, Australia
Xiaowen Fang, USA
Vicki Hanson, UK
Wonil Hwang, Korea
Minna Isomursu, Finland
Yong Gu Ji, Korea
Anirudha Joshi, India
Esther Jun, USA
Kyungdoh Kim, Korea
Heidi Krömker, Germany
Chen Ling, USA
Chang S. Nam, USA
Naoko Okuizumi, Japan
Philippe Palanque, France
Ling Rothrock, USA
Naoki Sakakibara, Japan
Dominique Scapin, France
Guangfeng Song, USA
Sanjay Tripathi, India
Chui Yin Wong, Malaysia
Toshiki Yamaoka, Japan
Kazuhiko Yamazaki, Japan
Ryoji Yoshitake, Japan

Human Interface and the Management of Information

Program Chair: Sakae Yamamoto, Japan

Alan Chan, Hong Kong
Denis A. Coelho, Portugal
Linda Elliott, USA
Shin'ichi Fukuzumi, Japan
Michitaka Hirose, Japan
Makoto Itoh, Japan
Yen-Yu Kang, Taiwan
Koji Kimita, Japan
Daiji Kobayashi, Japan
Hiroyuki Miki, Japan
Shogo Nishida, Japan
Robert Proctor, USA
Youngho Rhee, Korea
Ryosuke Saga, Japan
Katsunori Shimohara, Japan
Kim-Phuong Vu, USA
Tomio Watanabe, Japan

Engineering Psychology and Cognitive Ergonomics

Program Chair: Don Harris, UK

Guy Andre Boy, USA
Shan Fu, P.R. China
Hung-Sying Jing, Taiwan
Wen-Chin Li, Taiwan
Mark Neerincx, The Netherlands
Jan Noyes, UK
Paul Salmon, Australia
Axel Schulte, Germany
Siraj Shaikh, UK
Sarah Sharples, UK
Anthony Smoker, UK
Neville Stanton, UK
Alex Stedmon, UK
Andrew Thatcher, South Africa

Universal Access in Human–Computer Interaction

Program Chairs: Constantine Stephanidis, Greece, and Margherita Antona, Greece

Julio Abascal, Spain
Gisela Susanne Bahr, USA
João Barroso, Portugal
Margrit Betke, USA
Anthony Brooks, Denmark
Christian Bühler, Germany
Stefan Carmien, Spain
Hua Dong, P.R. China
Carlos Duarte, Portugal
Pier Luigi Emiliani, Italy
Qin Gao, P.R. China
Andrina Granić, Croatia
Andreas Holzinger, Austria
Josette Jones, USA
Simeon Keates, UK
Georgios Kouroupetroglou, Greece
Patrick Langdon, UK
Barbara Leporini, Italy
Eugene Loos, The Netherlands
Ana Isabel Paraguay, Brazil
Helen Petrie, UK
Michael Pieper, Germany
Enrico Pontelli, USA
Jaime Sanchez, Chile
Alberto Sanna, Italy
Anthony Savidis, Greece
Christian Stary, Austria
Hirotada Ueda, Japan
Gerhard Weber, Germany
Harald Weber, Germany

Virtual, Augmented and Mixed Reality

Program Chairs: Randall Shumaker, USA, and Stephanie Lackey, USA

Roland Blach, Germany
Sheryl Brahnam, USA
Juan Cendan, USA
Jessie Chen, USA
Panagiotis D. Kaklis, UK
Hirokazu Kato, Japan
Denis Laurendeau, Canada
Fotis Liarokapis, UK
Michael Macedonia, USA
Gordon Mair, UK

Jose San Martin, Spain
Tabitha Peck, USA
Christian Sandor, Australia
Christopher Stapleton, USA
Gregory Welch, USA

Cross-Cultural Design

Program Chair: P.L. Patrick Rau, P.R. China

Yee-Yin Choong, USA
Paul Fu, USA
Zhiyong Fu, P.R. China
Pin-Chao Liao, P.R. China
Dyi-Yih Michael Lin, Taiwan
Rungtai Lin, Taiwan
Ta-Ping (Robert) Lu, Taiwan
Liang Ma, P.R. China
Alexander Mädche, Germany
Sheau-Farn Max Liang, Taiwan
Katsuhiko Ogawa, Japan
Tom Plocher, USA
Huatong Sun, USA
Emil Tso, P.R. China
Hsiu-Ping Yueh, Taiwan
Liang (Leon) Zeng, USA
Jia Zhou, P.R. China

Online Communities and Social Media

Program Chair: Gabriele Meiselwitz, USA

Leonelo Almeida, Brazil
Chee Siang Ang, UK
Aneesha Bakharia, Australia
Ania Bobrowicz, UK
James Braman, USA
Farzin Deravi, UK
Carsten Kleiner, Germany
Niki Lambropoulos, Greece
Soo Ling Lim, UK
Anthony Norcio, USA
Portia Pusey, USA
Panote Siriaraya, UK
Stefan Stieglitz, Germany
Giovanni Vincenti, USA
Yuanqiong (Kathy) Wang, USA
June Wei, USA
Brian Wentz, USA

Augmented Cognition

Program Chairs: Dylan D. Schmorrow, USA, and Cali M. Fidopiastis, USA

Ahmed Abdelkhalek, USA
Robert Atkinson, USA
Monique Beaudoin, USA
John Blitch, USA
Alenka Brown, USA
Rosario Cannavò, Italy
Joseph Cohn, USA
Andrew J. Cowell, USA
Martha Crosby, USA
Wai-Tat Fu, USA

Digital Human Modeling and Applications in Health, Safety, Ergonomics and Risk Management

Program Chair: Vincent G. Duffy, USA

Design, User Experience, and Usability

Program Chair: Aaron Marcus, USA

Distributed, Ambient and Pervasive Interactions

Program Chairs: Norbert Streitz, Germany, and Panos Markopoulos, The Netherlands

Juan Carlos Augusto, UK
Jose Bravo, Spain
Adrian Cheok, UK
Boris de Ruyter, The Netherlands
Anind Dey, USA
Dimitris Grammenos, Greece
Nuno Guimaraes, Portugal
Achilles Kameas, Greece
Javed Vassilis Khan, The Netherlands
Shin'ichi Konomi, Japan
Carsten Magerkurth, Switzerland
Ingrid Mulder, The Netherlands
Anton Nijholt, The Netherlands
Fabio Paternó, Italy
Carsten Röcker, Germany
Teresa Romao, Portugal
Albert Ali Salah, Turkey
Manfred Tscheligi, Austria
Reiner Wichert, Germany
Woontack Woo, Korea
Xenophon Zabulis, Greece

Human Aspects of Information Security, Privacy and Trust

Program Chairs: Theo Tryfonas, UK, and Ioannis Askoxylakis, Greece

Claudio Agostino Ardagna, Italy
Zinaida Benenson, Germany
Daniele Catteddu, Italy
Raoul Chiesa, Italy
Bryan Cline, USA
Sadie Creese, UK
Jorge Cuellar, Germany
Marc Dacier, USA
Dieter Gollmann, Germany
Kirstie Hawkey, Canada
Jaap-Henk Hoepman, The Netherlands
Cagatay Karabat, Turkey
Angelos Keromytis, USA
Ayako Komatsu, Japan
Ronald Leenes, The Netherlands
Javier Lopez, Spain
Steve Marsh, Canada
Gregorio Martinez, Spain
Emilio Mordini, Italy
Yuko Murayama, Japan
Masakatsu Nishigaki, Japan
Aljosa Pasic, Spain
Milan Petković, The Netherlands
Joachim Posegga, Germany
Jean-Jacques Quisquater, Belgium
Damien Sauveron, France
George Spanoudakis, UK
Kerry-Lynn Thomson, South Africa
Julien Touzeau, France
Theo Tryfonas, UK
João Vilela, Portugal
Claire Vishik, UK
Melanie Volkamer, Germany

HCI in Business

Program Chair: Fiona Fui-Hoon Nah, USA

Andreas Auinger, Austria
Michel Avital, Denmark
Traci Carte, USA
Hock Chuan Chan, Singapore
Constantinos Coursaris, USA
Soussan Djamasbi, USA
Brenda Eschenbrenner, USA
Nobuyuki Fukawa, USA
Khaled Hassanein, Canada
Milena Head, Canada
Susanna (Shuk Ying) Ho, Australia
Jack Zhenhui Jiang, Singapore
Jinwoo Kim, Korea
Zoonky Lee, Korea
Honglei Li, UK
Nicholas Lockwood, USA
Eleanor T. Loiacono, USA
Mei Lu, USA
Scott McCoy, USA
Brian Mennecke, USA
Robin Poston, USA
Lingyun Qiu, P.R. China
Rene Riedl, Austria
Matti Rossi, Finland
April Savoy, USA
Shu Schiller, USA
Hong Sheng, USA
Choon Ling Sia, Hong Kong
Chee-Wee Tan, Denmark
Chuan Hoo Tan, Hong Kong
Noam Tractinsky, Israel
Horst Treiblmaier, Austria
Virpi Tuunainen, Finland
Dezhi Wu, USA
I-Chin Wu, Taiwan

Learning and Collaboration Technologies

Program Chairs: Panayiotis Zaphiris, Cyprus, and Andri Ioannou, Cyprus

Ruthi Aladjem, Israel
Abdulaziz Aldaej, UK
John M. Carroll, USA
Maka Eradze, Estonia
Mikhail Fominykh, Norway
Denis Gillet, Switzerland
Mustafa Murat Inceoglu, Turkey
Pernilla Josefsson, Sweden
Marie Joubert, UK
Sauli Kiviranta, Finland
Tomaž Klobučar, Slovenia
Elena Kyza, Cyprus
Maarten de Laat, The Netherlands
David Lamas, Estonia
Edmund Laugasson, Estonia
Ana Loureiro, Portugal
Katherine Maillet, France
Nadia Pantidi, UK
Antigoni Parmaxi, Cyprus
Borzoo Pourabdollahian, Italy
Janet C. Read, UK
Christophe Reffay, France
Nicos Souleles, Cyprus
Ana Luísa Torres, Portugal
Stefan Trausan-Matu, Romania
Aimilia Tzanavari, Cyprus
Johnny Yuen, Hong Kong
Carmen Zahn, Switzerland

External Reviewers

Ilia Adami, Greece
Iosif Klironomos, Greece
Maria Korozi, Greece
Vassilis Kouroumalis, Greece
Asterios Leonidis, Greece
George Margetis, Greece
Stavroula Ntoa, Greece
Nikolaos Partarakis, Greece

HCI International 2015

The 15th International Conference on Human–Computer Interaction, HCI International 2015, will be held jointly with the affiliated conferences in Los Angeles, CA, USA, in the Westin Bonaventure Hotel, August 2–7, 2015. It will cover a broad spectrum of themes related to HCI, including theoretical issues, methods, tools, processes, and case studies in HCI design, as well as novel interaction techniques, interfaces, and applications. The proceedings will be published by Springer. More information will be available on the conference website: `http://www.hcii2015.org/`

General Chair
Professor Constantine Stephanidis
University of Crete and ICS-FORTH
Heraklion, Crete, Greece
E-mail: `cs@ics.forth.gr`

Table of Contents – Part III

Interacting with the Web

Mobile Interaction

HCI for Health, Well-Being and Sport

Mobility, Transport and Environment

Interacting with Games

Business, Sustainability and Technology Adoption

Interacting with the web

CORPUS: Next-Generation Online Platform for Research Collaborations in Humanities

Yuan Jia[1], Xi Niu[1], Reecha Bharali[1], Davide Bolchini[1], and André De Tienne[2]

[1] School of Informatics and Computing, Indiana University
[2] Institute for American Thought
1535 W. Michigan Street, 2ES 0010 902 W New York Street, Indianapolis, IN 46202
{jiayuan,xiniu,rbharali,dbolchin,adetienn}@iupui.edu

Abstract. Two major research resources for humanities scholars are manuscripts and scholarly editions (rigorously reconstituted standard texts of seminal writers and thinkers). However, most of these resources either have not been digitized or are not easy to access online [1]. Consequently, scholars frequently need to spend unnecessary time and effort to find and manage different versions of materials (physical or digital) from different sources. To solve this problem, we propose an online platform called CORPUS – a **C**ollaborative **O**nline **R**esearch **P**latform for **U**sers of **S**cholarly edition – to support scholarly research online in an efficient manner. CORPUS aims to integrate different types of research materials in the humanities (manuscripts, scholarly editions, online publications, and personal notes) and aggregate different versions of the same texts. In addition, it enhances collaboration among scholars while also providing them with a peer-review-based incentive to share and publish their research work.

Keywords: Contextual Inquiry, Digital Humanities, User Study, Design, and Prototype.

1 Introduction

The role of scholarly editions is central to the humanities: they seek to reconstitute and establish the texts of seminal writers and thinkers with rigorous exactitude in order to provide researchers with an authoritative standard text they can trust. The majority of such editions exist only in print and the source manuscripts have either not been digitized or are hard to access online. This forces scholars to spend unnecessary time and effort to conduct research on different versions (physical and digital) of materials from different sources (online, library or other organizations) [1, 5].

To solve this problem, we developed CORPUS (Collaboration Research Platform for User of Scholar Edition), which is a novel collaborative online platform aiming at supporting the research process of scholars in humanities in a much more efficient and effective way. CORPUS has two unique goals:

1. Integration. to integrate different types of research materials in Humanities—manuscripts, scholarly editions, online publications and personal notes—together to support scholars' need for their research work;

M. Kurosu (Ed.): Human-Computer Interaction, Part III, HCII 2014, LNCS 8512, pp. 3–12, 2014.

2. Collaboration. enhance collaboration among scholars to make their research work richer and more effective.

The project started with understanding the domain of the digital humanities in general. The researchers tried to understand current online projects, present available literature on the subject and naturalistic interview techniques with editors to understand the available techniques. With this background, the next step was to look into the requirement gathering stage. The method of contextual inquiry with intensive interview was used to understand how scholars conduct their research work in their working environments. There were 10 scholars involved in the early round of interviews at the Institute of American Thought (IAT), Indianapolis. The interviews were transcribed and the qualitative data were collected and analyzed by the Human Computer Interaction Design Technique of Affinity Diagram. As an output, current working models (Flow Model and Physical Model) were generated. These models helped in defining the goal of CORPUS, with various design opportunities found from the breakdowns in the model. Based on the data gathered from interviews and the breakdowns in the model, a conceptual vision of CORPUS was proposed to be used in the following study. To validate the issues identified and the appropriateness of the conceptual vision, a detailed interview was again conducted with the users. In this stage of contextual interviews, the users were shown the conceptual vision and asked about detailed feedback about each feature. After both contextual interviews Stage 1 and 2, the list of requirements for CORPUS was generated.

In the following stages, we designed an interactive prototype, which showcased the key elements of CORPUS as an online dissemination platform. Many of the features were what the contextual inquiry had proposed including the design ideas from the researchers. At the end of this study, a formal evaluation was conducted, and the feedback was received and used into the improvement of the platform.

2 Related Works

A few existing projects also support scholars' digital research work in the Humanities. However, some of them either offer less flexibility for browsing source manuscripts online [2,3,4], or are limited to transcribing source materials through crowd sourcing methods [5].

For example, the Mark Twain Project produces scholarly editions, fully annotated version. The project mainly supports searching and browsing Mark Twain manuscripts and productions. All comments are organized in the form of metadata. It only deals with the manuscripts of Mark Twain and has limited functionalities when it comes to working with those scholarly editions and manuscripts. The main limit of the Mark Twain Project is that users are not allowed to store what they have read and re-find them later. It is a collection that users can only browse. Also, there is no support for annotating or managing users' own annotation.

In addition, none of the existing projects helps scholars browse scholarly editions digitally. Furthermore, some other projects are unable to design their system from a scholarly perspective, such as the Escidoc project [2]. It encourages scholars from various organizations to share their unfinished works or preliminary data with one another. However, it discounts the fact that some scholars may not be willing to share their own unpublished works with other scholars. In contrast to those existing projects, CORPUS supports interactive access to and browsing of research materials (not only manuscripts but also scholarly editions) and all the design features were generated from scholars' points of view.

3 Understanding Users

To understand the context of scholars' research work process in Humanities, a User Centered Design (UCD) method – contextual inquiry is selected in this study. Contextual techniques are designed to gather data from customers in the field, where people are working or living. Contextual Inquiry is a field data-gathering technique that studies a few carefully selected individuals in depth to arrive at a fuller understanding of the work practice across all customers. The conversation between a participant and an interviewer about the participant's work (rather than about the system design) creates a shared understanding. The core premise of Contextual Inquiry is very simple: go where the customer works, observe the customer as he or she works, and talk to the customer about the work.

In this study, two stages of Contextual (See Table1.) Inquiries were conducted on 10 participants in the Institute for American Thought (IAT) in Indianapolis, IN, U.S.A.. The aims for both of the stages are listed below:

Stage One. To understand the contexts of the current workflow, and generate the conceptual vision for CORPUS.

Stage Two. To get feedback for the vision of CORPUS and to generate detail functions of CORPUS.

Table 1. Two stages of User Study

	No. of Scholars	*Mode of Interview*
Interview Stage 1	10	On Site
Interview Stage 2	10	On Site/ Skype

3.1 The Results from the First Stage of the Contextual Inquiry

In the first stage, all the contextual interviews were transcribed. A collaborative analysis method called – Affinity Diagram – was used to analyze the qualitative data gathered from these interviews. Then the current working models were generated to describe the workflow and physical environments during scholars' research work process in Humanities. At the end this stage, a conceptual vision of CORPUS was created for the next stage in this study.

Affinity Diagram. The affinity process was introduced as one of the "seven quality processes" from Japan (Brassard, 1989; as known as the K-J method in Kawakita, 1982). Affinity diagram organizes the individual notes captured during interpretation session into a hierarchy revealing common issues and themes. It shows the scope of the customer problem: it reveals in one place all the issues, worries, and key elements of work practice relevant to the team's focus. It also defines the key quality requirements on the system. The hierarchical structure groups similar issues so that all the data relevant to a theme is shown together, creating stories about the customer relevant to the design problem.

Figure1. shows the hierarchical structure of the 3 main themes found, followed by the sub-categories, including 1) the types of materials scholars need; 2) the sources of collecting the materials; 3) How to work on the materials; 4) the ways of storing the materials, and 5) how to collaborate with other scholars.

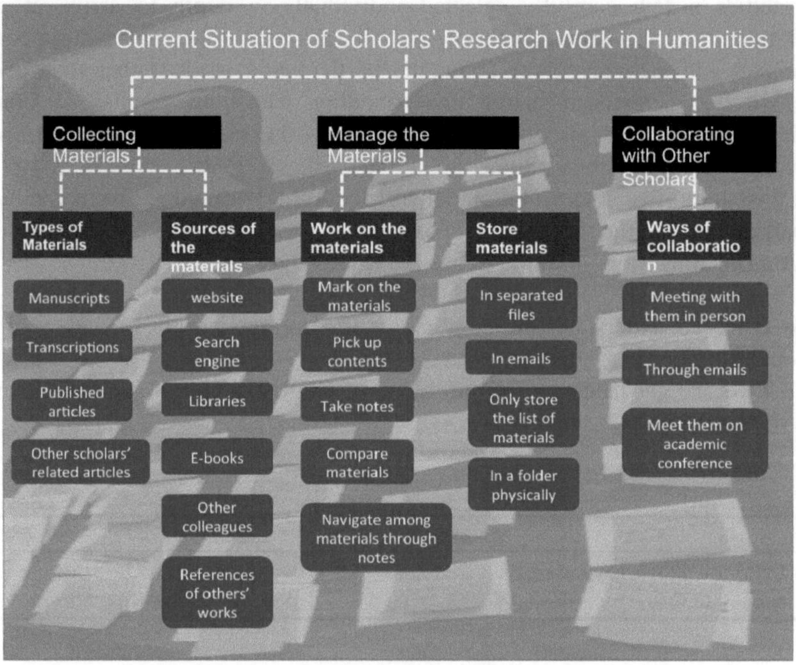

Fig. 1. The main themes adapted from the Affinity Diagram

Current Working Models. From the data analysis from the affinity diagram, scholars' current working models – flow model and physical model – were generated. The models helped understand how the users work in their environment and where the current problems exist. The shock symbol in the models shows the design opportunity found by researchers in the models; which were further used in defining user requirements and taking design decisions for building the prototype.

Flow Model. Figure2. shows the flow model of the scholars' research work in Humanities. From the model, we can see that scholars in Humanities often spend unnecessary efforts on collecting the materials they need from four main sources: the libraries, some specific organizations, websites and other scholars in the related field. For example, most of them had the experience of traveling to the libraries/organizations in other cities or countries to study materials. The materials usually contain manuscripts, letters, the authors' published books/papers, other scholars' publications, and other online materials such as news, blog articles. Researchers are always transcribing those manuscripts or letters to the authors' intended text at the beginning of their research process. Then they come up with their own works out of the process of reading, comparing, and managing those materials. In this whole process, the communication among scholars is also very important. Researchers seek to know what happens in their research field by attending research conference, workshops or sending emails.

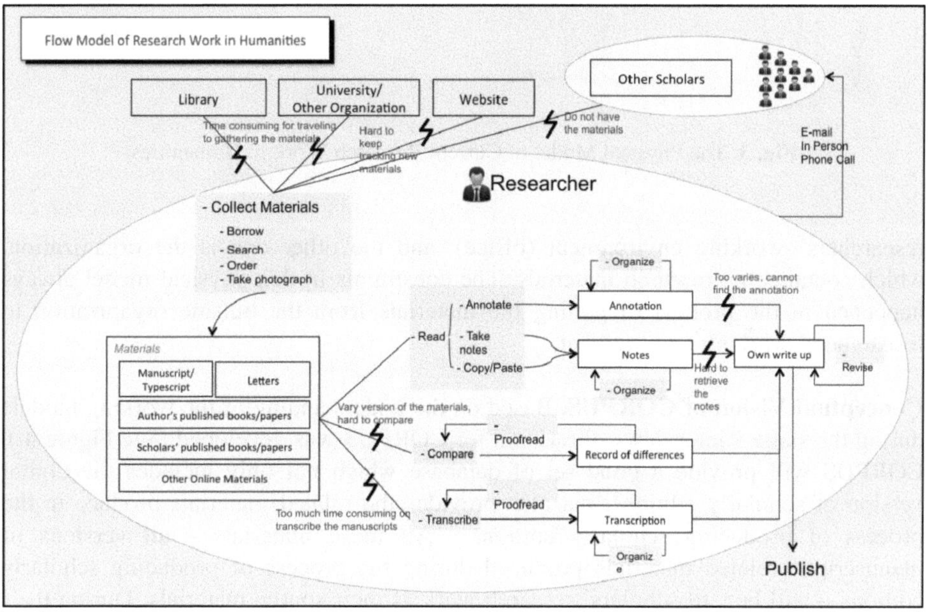

Fig. 2. The Flow Model of Current Research Work in Humanities

Physical Model. Any product or system must live with the constraints of the physical environment as it exists. If it ignores those constraints, it creates problems for its user. The studying of users' workplace ensures that the system accounts for the physical environment. The physical environment constraints what people can do, but within those constraints people do have some control over their environment. Studying the workplace offers important clues to the way people structure and thinks about work. In this study, two types of physical environments are involved. The first one is the

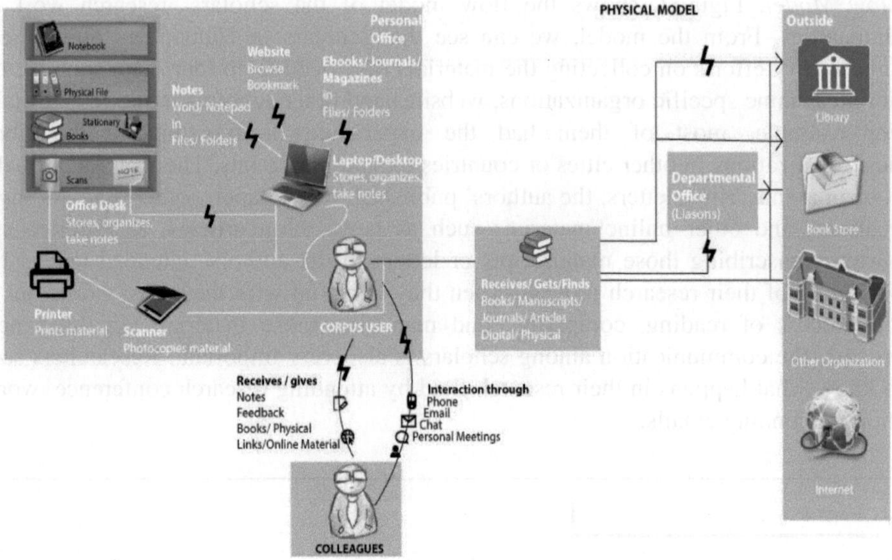

Fig. 3. The Physical Model of Current Research Work in Humanities

researchers' working environment (office), and the other one is the organization, which contains the research materials. The constraints in this physical model always happened in the process of getting the materials from the outside organization to researchers' working environment.

Conceptual Vision of CORPUS. Based on the understanding of the working models during the stage 1 interviews; the vision for CORPUS was developed (See Figure 4.). CORPUS will provide a good set of database which not only includes the digital version of scholarly editions, but also provides the related materials produce in the process of producing scholarly editions. All these materials – all versions of manuscripts, related materials produced during the process of producing scholarly editions – will benefit scholars' research work as their source materials. During their working process, CORPUS enable the scholars to browse materials' content, browse other scholars' reviews of the materials, create their own content and reviews, discuss research problems they have and also support their collaborative contributions. The works scholars created will go through an online peer-review process before they publish on CORPUS.

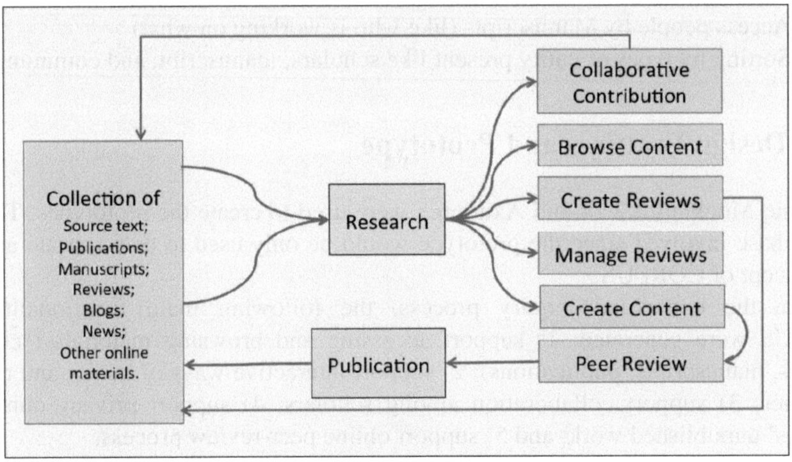

Fig. 4. The Conceptual Vision of CORPUS

3.2 The Results from Second Stage of the Contextual Inquiry

In the second stage, the vision of CORPUS was shown to the same 10 scholars to get feedback. The contextual interviews in this stage were transcribed, and an affinity diagram was also created. Base on the analysis of the affinity diagrams, working models and the vision of CORPUS, we generated a detail user requirements list for CORPUS platform as a final output of the user study process. It contains:

1. Access to the digital-version of the manuscripts Browse the manuscripts and its information Access related research materials online:

a. Publications or online news related to the research topic

b. Publications related to the manuscripts

2. Access/Browse the citation of the materials Share/access the transcription of the manuscripts

3. Navigate among related manuscripts Navigate among related publications

4. Navigate between manuscripts and related publications

5. Take notes/annotations of the manuscripts or other materials Access the notes/annotations

6. Navigate among the notes and materials

7. Retrieve and manage personal work

a. Materials: manuscripts, related publications, transcripts, notes, and external links

b. Contacts: other scholars' emails

c. Own research work

d. Transcriptions: my shared transcription, others transcriptions (need to review if I am an editor)

e. Basic setting: privacy, personal info

7. Automatic Search Notifications

8. Track New Materials that are being added.

9. Navigate through Scholar profiles

10. Access people by Manuscripts (like who is working on what)
11. Sorting by types of entity present like scholars, manuscript, and communities.

4 Design Features and Prototype

Balsamiq Mockups 2.2.14 and Axure 6.5 were used to create the prototypes. There is no database involved since the prototype would be only used to demonstrate and test the concept of CORPUS.

From the contextual inquiry process, the following main functionalities of CORPUS were generated: 1) support accessing and browsing materials (scholarly editions, manuscripts, publications); 2) support interactive ways of taking and retrieving notes; 3) support collaboration among scholars; 4) support privacy control of scholars' unpublished work; and 5) support online peer-review process.

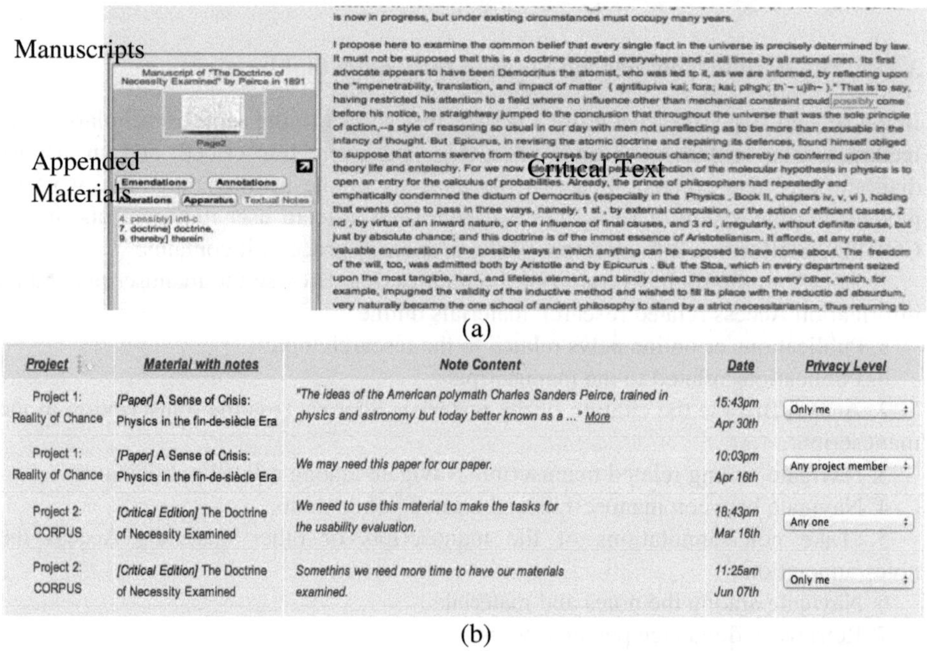

Project	Material with notes	Note Content	Date	Privacy Level
Project 1: Reality of Chance	[Paper] A Sense of Crisis: Physics in the fin-de-siècle Era	"The ideas of the American polymath Charles Sanders Peirce, trained in physics and astronomy but today better known as a ..." More	15:43pm Apr 30th	Only me
Project 1: Reality of Chance	[Paper] A Sense of Crisis: Physics in the fin-de-siècle Era	We may need this paper for our paper.	10:03pm Apr 16th	Any project member
Project 2: CORPUS	[Critical Edition] The Doctrine of Necessity Examined	We need to use this material to make the tasks for the usability evaluation.	18:43pm Mar 16th	Any one
Project 2: CORPUS	[Critical Edition] The Doctrine of Necessity Examined	Somethins we need more time to have our materials examined.	11:25am Jun 07th	Only me

Fig. 5. Screenshots of Interactive Prototypes: (a) viewing scholarly editions (b) collaborations through projects

4.1 Viewing Scholarly Editions / Manuscripts

In CORPUS, two interactive browsing views for research materials were supported: scholarly edition view and manuscript view. Scholarly edition contains critical text (editor-enhanced text) and appended materials (emendations, textual notes, alterations, etc.). In the paper world, most scholars will ignore the appended materials because they want to avoid going back and forth between the critical text and the appended materials. In scholarly edition view, a synchronized way of reading the two is possible, and it overcomes the constraints of traditional linear reading on papers (see (a) in Figure1). In the manuscript view, scholars are able to browse the manuscripts, their corresponding scholarly edition and other related materials (other versions of manuscripts, publications, online news, and videos).

4.2 Managing/Retrieving Notes

According to the results from the contextual inquiry process, scholars took notes to mark important points in the literature or leave comments on a particular part of the materials. However, the approach and media they took notes on are various, including email, hard/ digital copy of materials, physical notebook or separate digital files. CORPUS proposes a novel way of managing and retrieving research notes: link research notes and their corresponding materials automatically. Scholars can always look into notes by accessing materials or by browsing their personal notes list (See Figure 2).

4.3 Collaboration through "Project"

Forums are a popular way to support communications in Humanities [1, 5], however, from our contextual inquiries, scholars are not often communicating with one another in forums. Instead, they contact each other only when they have a common interest in their research work. Thus, CORPUS decided to support collaboration among scholars in the form of "projects" – giving scholars the choices to group themselves together by self-defined project topic. They are able to share materials with notes, discuss research problems, and review each other's work collaboratively.

4.4 Privacy Control

Privacy concerns were also taken into consideration during the design process. Scholars have three levels of privacy control (private, project member, and public) on all their materials, projects, notes and personal works.

4.5 Online Peer-Review Process

CORPUS also offers online peer-review certifications that scholars can use as evidence of professional worth for instance in P&T (promotion and tenure) dossiers or grant applications.

5 Evaluation

After developing the interactive prototype of CORPUS, a formal usability evaluation was conducted with the same 10 participants in IAT. Six tasks were designed based on the key functions. The evaluation focused on testing the utility and usability problem of CORPUS, so both quantitative and qualitative data were collected. Some usability problems were found out, and improvements were made accordingly.

The evaluation results show that the participants favored three functionalities most: "managing and retrieving notes", “collaboration through projects”, and “viewing manuscripts”. The participants reported that the “viewing scholarly editions” is a little difficult to understand at the beginning, but getting better after a short time of learning.

From the qualitative comments, the “managing and retrieving notes” feature was reported to be very useful when it integrates with the “project” feature. The participants thought “note sharing” could be very helpful when they work with other scholars as a project group. One of the scholars said: “I was looking on this book today, and I was trying to make notes on this particular paragraph. And I also want to do the same thing but with different books. This notes-sharing function would be really needed. I would share these notes with others and ask them to please check it if I used the wrong date—that kind of thing.”

6 Discussions and Future Work

Compared to existing studies, CORPUS focuses on supporting scholars’ collaborative research work process in Humanities, and all the features of the system are designed according to the User-Centered System Design theory. Several functions are unique, such as browsing critical editions digitally and interactively, integration of the notes and their corresponding materials, supporting collaborative research work through notes and project management, support online peer-review process on this platform.

In the future, we want to promote and market CORPUS as a new concept of publication platform and a fairly comprehensive solution for researchers in Humanities to conduct their research work digitally.

References

1. Borgman, C.L.: The digital future is now: A call to action for the humanities. Digital Humanities Quarterly 3(4) (2009)
2. The Mark Twain Project, `http://www.marktwainproject.org`
3. The ESCIDOC Project, `https://www.escidoc.org`
4. The Collected Letters of Bertrand Russell, `http://russell.mcmaster.ca/brletters.htm` - overview
5. Wilensky, R.: Digital library resources as a basis for collaborative work. Journal of the American Society for Information Science 51(3), 228–245

B2C Websites' Usability for Chinese Senior Citizens

Liang Kang and Hua Dong

College of Design and Innovation, Tongji University, Shanghai, China
Janiskang@outlook.com, donghua@tongji.edu.cn

Abstract. As E-commerce develops fast in Chinese market, so grows the need for online shopping of Chinese senior users. However, The senior users are still the niche market and they tend to be excluded from the "target users". To design a usability test on existing B2C websites based on the Chinese context, we integrated the User Centered Design into the whole process. A preliminary study with 48 Chinese seniors helped to get insights into the Chinese senior users, which directly guided the development of the usability test protocol. Then we conducted usability tests with 16 participants selected from the preliminary study. According to the results of the usability test, the overall usability performance of the mainstream Chinese B2C websites is concluded and whether the "user-driven usability test" has brought a different perspective is discussed.

Keywords: Usability test, E-commerce, Chinese senior citizens, B2C websites.

1 Introduction

To provide a thoroughly Chinese context-based usability test on existing B2C websites, we integrated the User Centered Design into the whole process of usability testing. The reason for selecting B2C websites rather than C2C websites is that they have a simpler dealer-consumer relationship and they provide more reliable products, thus it is more suitable for seniors to understand and easier for them to try [1].

There already exist various versions of guidelines and principles for senior usability as a result of massive usability tests, especially in western countries. The Nielsen-Norman Group has been conducting extensive research on senior usability. To evaluate usability, they give participants tasks, watch them work, and analyze their behavior. Online shopping is part of the tasks. Their report includes design recommendations based on the behavioral research. The report offers 46 guidelines in the first edition, which increases to 106 ones in the second edition. They have also developed a methodology on how to conduct usability studies with seniors[2].

Additionally, usability studies continuously demonstrate older users frustrations with completing specific tasks. In a study completed by Chadwick-Dias, McNulty, and Tullis, Participants over the age of 55 had significantly longer task duration time than those under the age of 55. Their study suggests that older adults tend to

M. Kurosu (Ed.): Human-Computer Interaction, Part III, HCII 2014, LNCS 8512, pp. 13–20, 2014.

be more cautious when interacting with a website such as clicking on a link and spent more time reading information before clicking. The study also demonstrates that "older users were often confused as to where they were within the context of the Web site" [3].

However, since East Asians and Westerners perceive the world and think about it in very different ways[4], it is hard to expect that the research results from Westerners can totally apply to East Asians. In China, though there are studies on e-commerce websites usability, the target users are mainly young people. In 2007, Li Chen conducted a usability study on online shopping sites for the elderly, in which the researcher did the requirement analysis of the elders, including user definition, user characteristics, user online shopping requirements and behavior features.[5] However, there is no significant relevance between the content of the usability test and the elders' requirement analysis: the main elements such as websites and the tasks to be tested are determined by the researcher.

2 Method

To ensure the results reflect Chinese seniors' needs, the usability test should combine their requirement analysis with the whole usability test process. In our study, we first conducted a preliminary study with 48 Chinese seniors, which helped to get insights into the Chinese senior users; the result determined the elements of the usability test protocol. Under the guidance of the developed usability test protocol, we conducted usability tests with 16 participants selected from the preliminary study.

2.1 User-Driven Usability Test – An Overview

In the process of a typical User-Centered Design, the phase of user profiling (including user requirements collection/analysis) supplies rich contextual information and meanwhile determines the goal as well as the direction of product design [6]. Accordingly, in this study, a preliminary study helps to collect the Chinese seniors' requirements, so as to develop the usability test protocol on the basis of user needs. Figure 1 presents the process of our user-driven usability test. The main feature is that the research participants make the decision of testing tasks and decide the weight of evaluating factors.

2.2 Collecting and Analyzing User Requirements

In total 48 participants, most from Yangpu and Changning districts in Shanghai, were asked to fill in a questionnaire which consisted of a basic online shopping survey, weighting of online shopping tasks, and if the participant agreed to take part in subsequent tests, a technology screening test. In the basic online shopping survey, participants were asked about which B2C websites they knew, what kind of products

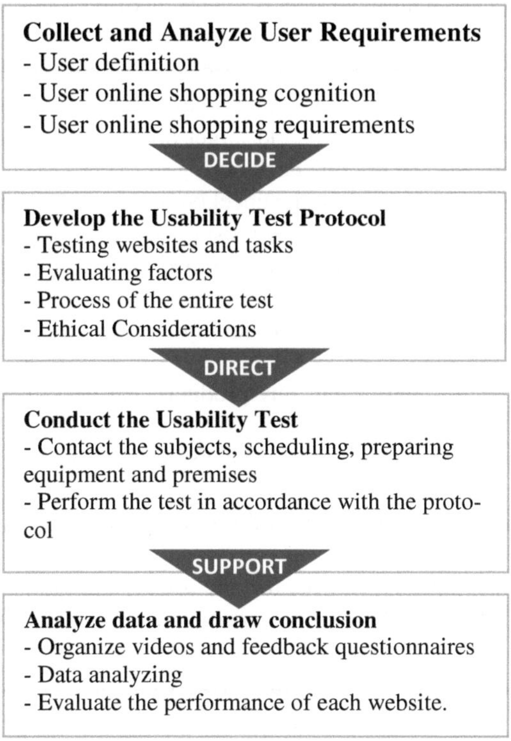

Fig. 1. The process of user-driven usability test

they would like to purchase online but research offline, and what kind of products they preferred to do category research online.

Nielsen has concluded the online shopping tasks as: a) known-item purchase; b) category research; c) bargain hunting; d) browsing for inspiration [7]. To get insights into what kind of tasks the elders would consider important to complete alone, we developed the four types of online shopping tasks to six more detailed tasks with concrete examples (see A-F in the item 2 in Table 1).

In addition, considering that the checkout process has its own uniqueness and is not included in Nielsen's four types of tasks, we added a separate question asking the seniors whether they thought it was necessary to complete the checkout process by themselves or it was just enough knowing how to find the target products and add it to the shopping cart. The participants were asked to choose three tasks they wished to complete alone out of all. The complete shopping tasks for weighting are presented in Table 1. In the technology screening test, the participants were asked to tick all descriptions that match their attitudes towards online shopping and high-tech devices.

Table 1. Questionnaire to identify seniors' needs in online shopping

1. Which is your attitude towards check out process during online shopping?

A. It is enough to know how to find target products and add it to the shopping cart. My children can help me do the check out.

B. it was necessary to complete the checkout process by myself.

2. Which 3 of the tasks are tasks you wish most to complete alone?

A. Search for a product that I already researched in real stores and see its price online, such as a Sony TV.

B. Search for a daily necessity that my family usually buy, e.g. a box of Milk (24 packs).

C. Category research: identify and buy products that best match my needs: price, brand or customer rating.

D. Detailed comparison of different products, such as screen size, operating system, producers and so on.

E. Bargain hunting, e.g. looking for a discounted radio during the Spring festival offers.

F. Browsing for inspiration, see what the site is offering without specific target.

G. (not available if A is ticked in the former question) Check out and pay the online order.

2.3 Developing the Usability Test Protocol

Each part of the preliminary research contributed to the development of the usability test protocol. From the result of the online shopping questionnaire, we chose 3 websites to be tested and decided the length of each test. From the weighting of online shopping tasks, we obtained insights into what tasks the seniors wanted most to perform online. For example, to do category research like comparing cellphones of different brands or to just quickly find the cellphone they already "researched" offline in the stores. From the technology screening test, candidates were classified by different levels of technology familiarity, which would help in future usability test. The development of protocol also took into consideration the ethic perspective of conducting usability tests with senior citizens such as how to lead the seniors to think aloud while performing the test.

2.4 Conducting the Usability Test and Analyzing Data

Under the guidance of the developed usability test protocol, we conducted usability tests with 16 participants selected from the preliminary study. 14 of them have not tried online shopping once, the other two can go shopping online by themselves. The test was divided into three sections: in each section the participants were asked to perform the one of the three tasks on the three websites one by one. After completing the task on a website, the participants filled in a SUS (System Usability Scale) questionnaire to rate the performance of the tested site. After each section, a list of different factors was given to the participants to assign each factor a weight in a range from 1 to 7. To avoid ambiguous description from the participants, we adopted the prepared lists of factors instead of oral interviews. The collected lists helped identify the relevant weighting of different factors for further data analysis.

Combining the data analysis of the SUS questionnaire and the recordings, we evaluated the performance of each website and get insights into each task. Finally, whether the "user-driven usability test" has brought a different perspective is discussed.

3 Results and Discussion

From the results of the preliminary research, the three best known B2C sites are identified:

- Yihaodian (Yhd.com), an online supermarket
- Jingdong (Jd.com), an online department, famous for home appliances and digital products
- Suning (Suning.com), an online mall for home appliances and digital products

As for online shopping tasks, only 22.9% of the elders thought it was necessary to complete the checkout process all alone, most seniors would just prefer to pick products independently. Figure 2 presents the seniors' preference on all the listed tasks. The 3 most desired tasks are: a) searching for specific items they have researched offline; b) doing category research to help identify and buy products that best match their needs; c) bargain hunting. Furthermore, seniors chose home applications, food & drinks and households as the products they would like to do research offline. And they also chose digital products as the products they preferred most to do research online. Therefore, according to the results of the questionnaire as well as the difficulty of each task, the final testing tasks, are described below:

- **Task 1.** Search for a specific item on the website, e.g. Sony Digital Camera Tx66.
- **Task 2.** Find cellphones with specified price and brand/network/functions, sort the result according to their sales, and then add the one with the highest ratings to the shopping cart from the top three sales.
- **Task 3.** Browse the website and try to find a satisfying bargain, then put it to the cart.

In order to get more accurate feedback, Task 1 and Task 2 are revised into 3 similar tasks, i.e. Task 1 asked the seniors to search for a) digital camera; b) a type of popular biscuit; or c) home use heaters. These tasks were randomly assigned to the participants.

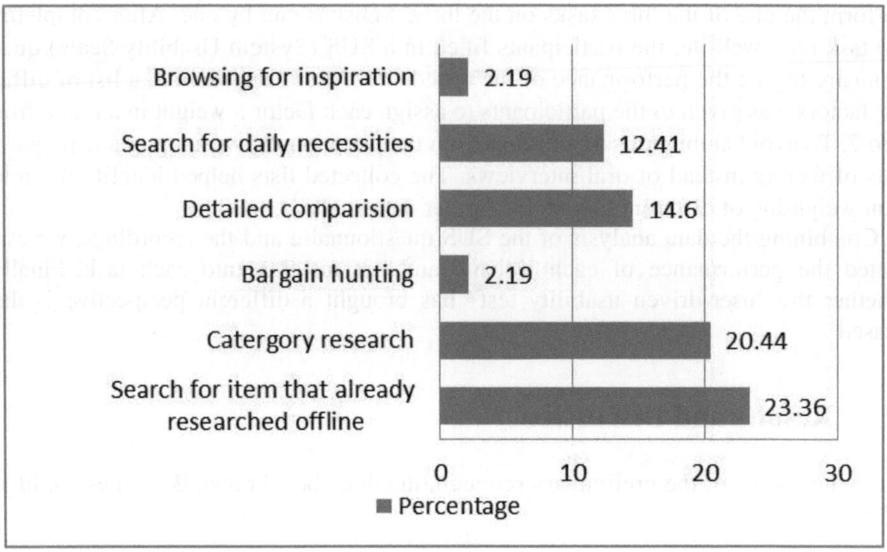

Fig. 1. Tasks seniors wished most to complete alone

During Task 1, the seniors were asked to search for a specific item with an exact model number and specifications, i.e. "Sony Dsc-Tx66 Digital Camera, Red". 15 participants completed this task. But unexpectedly, Only 3 of the 16 participants tried to use the search box, others all preferred to look for the relevant category through navigation, and then tried to search for the target in the entire product list. After the test most of the seniors expressed their difficulties in inputting Chinese characters with keyboard. The barrier of the Chinese input method made the user read all the text in the navigation. Another reason is that websites such as Suning.com has a light grey search box which is not obvious enough; there is only a magnifier icon beside the search box without any text indicating "search".

Task 2 was relevantly more complicated, only 7 participants succeeded in setting the right filters to find required products, and 5 succeeded to sort them in price order. Notably, the seniors who tried the search box in Task 1 tended to rely on the search box. They input "cellphone 1000-1500 yuan highest sales" directly in the search box and expected the websites to match their requirements automatically. Of course no websites satisfied such needs, but Jd.com had a relevantly better performance for it could match "cellphone 1000-1500yuan" to cellphones with price between 1000-1500 yuan. However, when the seniors tried to filter the cellphones on Jd.com, they often got confused. The cellphone category page of Jd.com is full of "hot deals" and promoting advertisements (ads), the seniors could not see any of "cellphones" they filtered in the first screen. What was worse, when they tried to find "cellphones" on the page, e.g. clicking the label "1500-2000 yuan", the page just refreshes and still stays at the top. No hints were given to the users that all the cellphones between1500-2000yuan were under the hot deal, ads and filters. On the contrary, Suning.com had a simple and clear category page without picture ads or hot deals, but the problem was that the filters were of light color and many seniors just ignore it.

Another point was, some seniors tried to use the search box while they were in the cellphone category page. They input "Samsung" and click search, expecting the websites to present them with the specific Samsung cellphone, but the result was all kinds of products that belongs to Samsung: Laptops, Cameras and even Fridges.

Task 3 has the least restrictions, all the participants managed to find something they would like to buy. When bargain hunting, the participants tended to ignore the dazzling slider ads but still read navigation and text link first. This makes Yhd.com the highest rated because it highlights "Spring Festival Offers" in the navigation and the participants could easily found bargains. The seniors also suggested that they did not want to click the picture ads announcing "up to 50%" or "buy one get one" because they considered these ambiguous promotional words as lies. Besides, the participants did have the concept that "group purchase" offered cheap and good deal, over 60% of them tried to browse the "group purchase" channel through navigation.

4 Discussion and Conclusion

According to the result of Task 1, the surprisingly high rate of the seniors using navigation to "search" suggested the importance of navigation design. Clear and smart navigation design would help the senior customers a lot. This might differ from countries using alphabetic languages since Chinese seniors have more trouble in inputting characters. It can be also concluded from the task 3, in which people tends to find bargains through navigation instead of the colorful and large slider ads.

Moreover, when seniors are browsing the category page, they wanted to know which of the products are now on sale. A "sale" label might help. Or furthermore, add a filter label "now on sale" so that users can find all the discounted products.

Apart from this, texts prove to be more accessible and reliable than pictures or icons for seniors without much online shopping experience. Adequate text hints help seniors to figure out different functions of an unfamiliar website while dazzling large animation and flash annoy and confuse seniors.

Comparing to previous work, the user-driven usability test offered a different perspective: Test what the user care. It might offer a better understanding when evaluating a general performance of websites, because "the user" is no longer a "persona" but strongly integrated into each phase of the study. And selecting test candidates from people who were involved in preliminary research made the participant have a greater sense of participation. Most of the participants tried to complete the task actively and patiently, even some tasks are quite difficult for non-experienced users. One of the participants expressed that it was great to try these tasks so that they could try online shopping when they went back home.

5 Future Research

There could be various directions for future user-driven usability test on Chinese senior citizens. First of all, due to the scale and time issue, the Task 1, 2 and 3 were performed at the same time. The experience from former tasks affected the users' decision-making in latter. For example, seniors who are expressed by the filter functions in Task 2 would try it again in Task 3 bargain hunting, ignoring the other way to searching for an ideal product. Therefore separate tests with different participants for each task may bring results with subtle difference.

Another research direction is to pay a return visit to the participants, to see whether such an active learning experience would result in continuous attempts and to test if the revised prototypes which adopted the suggestions above really work for the users.

Furthermore, our study has offered the result of user-driven usability test on Chinese seniors. In the future if possible, a comparative research on young users would help to know better the difference between the needs of Chinese seniors and young people and to verify if senior-friendly websites could also benefit Chinese young people.

References

1. Ling, Z.: Exploring the trend of Chinese B2C e-commerce's development. J. E-Commerce 31, 22–23 (2011) (in Chinese)
2. Pernice, K., Nielsen, J.: Usability For Senior Citizens: Design Guidelines Based on Usability Studies with People Age 65 and Older. Nielsen Norman Group, http://www.nngroup.com/reports/senior-citizens-on-the-web/
3. Chadwick-Dias, A., McNulty, M., Tullis, T.: Web usability and age: how design changes can improve performance. In: The 2003 Conference on Universal Usability, Vancouver, Canada, pp. 30–37. ACM, New York (2003)
4. Nisbett, R.E., Masuda, T.: Culture and point of view. Proceedings of the National Academy of Sciences of the United States of America 100, 11163–11170 (2003)
5. Chen, L. : Usability Design Research Of Online Shopping Site For The Elderly. D. Shanghai Jiao Tong University (2007) (in Chinese)
6. Dong, J., Salvendy, G.: Human-Computer Interaction: User Centered Design and Evaluation, pp.16-20. Tsinghua University Press (2003) (in Chinese)
7. Ecommerce Usability Improvements, http://www.nngroup.com/articles/ecommerce-improvements

Intelligent Interface for Web Information Retrieval with Document Understanding

Rahul S. Khokale[1] and Mohammad Atique[2]

[1] Department of Computer Science & Engineering, PIGCE, Nagpur, India
[2] P.G Department of Computer Science & Engineering, Sant Gadge Baba Amravati University, Amravati, India
softrahul@gmail.com, mohammadatique@sgbau.ac.in

Abstract. Web Based Information Retrieval (WBIR) is becoming an integral part of the daily activities of computer users. In the present computing world, people are highly accustomed to the use of web for acquiring any kind of information. However, retrieval of useful documents with high degree of relevance is an important problem. There is a need of an intelligent interface for WBIR to alleviate efforts of information seekers. In this paper, an intelligent interface for web based information retrieval with document understanding is proposed. The aim of intelligent interface for WBIR is to control the underlying information retrieval system, by directly interacting with the user, and allowing him to retrieve relevant information without the help of human intermediary. The interface helps users to formulate query by using Natural Language Processing (NLP) techniques. Also, it is capable of retrieving documents with respect to order of relevance.

Keywords: Web Based Information Retrieval, Document understanding, Natural Language Processing, Intelligent Interface.

1 Introduction

Search on the web is a daily activity for many people across the world. Search and communication are most popular uses of the computers. The field of computer science is most involved with research and development in information retrieval. The process of searching specific information among a large number of information items is known as Information Retrieval (IR).According to Salton, "Information retrieval is a field concerned with the structure, analysis, organization, storage, searching, and retrieval of information."

The Internet and the Web offer new opportunities and challenges to information retrieval researchers. With the information explosion and never ending increase of web pages as well as digital data, it is very hard to retrieve useful and reliable information from the Web. Materials from millions of web pages from organizations, institutions and personnel have been made public electronically accessible to millions of interested users. The Web uses an addressing system called Uniform Resource Locators

M. Kurosu (Ed.): Human-Computer Interaction, Part III, HCII 2014, LNCS 8512, pp. 21–31, 2014.

(URLs) to represent links to documents on web servers. These URLs provide location information. Like titles of books in traditional libraries, no one can remember all URLs on the Web. Web search engines allow us to locate the internet resources through thousands of Web pages. It is almost impossible to get the right information as there is too much irrelevant and out dated information. Information retrieval systems provide useful information in libraries to researchers.

The Web can be viewed as a virtual library. Information retrieval is an important and major component of the Internet. The World Wide Web plays an important role in knowledge discovery. General search engines such as, Google, AltaVista, Excite are considered as the powerful search engines so far. Most of the current search engines are based on words, not the concepts. When searching for certain information or knowledge with a search engine, one can only use a few key words to narrow down the search. The result of the search is tens or may be hundreds of relevant and irrelevant links to various Web pages.

In spite of the voluminous studies in the field of intelligent retrieval systems, effective retrieving of information has been remained an important unsolved problem. Implementations of different conceptual knowledge in the information retrieval process such as ontology have been considered as a solution to enhance the quality of results. Furthermore, the conceptual formalism supported by typical ontology may not be sufficient to represent uncertainty information due to the lack of clear-cut boundaries between concepts of the domains [1].

In the case of database management systems, standard 'syntactic' solutions based on structured nature of the data is used for retrieving required data from the database. Whereas, for web information retrieval that approach is not suitable as it deals with unstructured nature of data, hence a new approach at 'semantic' level is needed. Moreover, often the user has to face some problems, for instance to express a need regarding an unknown field. For overcoming these difficulties, the user of an IR system is usually supported by an human expert, an Intermediary, that acts as an interface between the user and the IR system [2].

This solution is effective, but the growing diffusion of databases creates a new scenario: the human intermediary is not always available and the user has to interact directly with the system. Of course, the system has to be modified and an artificial intermediary between the IR system and the user is needed, and this brings into the scenario the discipline of Human Computer Interaction (HCI). Moreover, for designing and implementing such artificial intermediary, artificial intelligence techniques seem to be promising as the problems at hand are ill defined. The obtained system is named Intelligent Interface (IIs) to an IR system or II for IR [2].

The field of IIs for IR is thus the intersection of three fields IR, human computer interaction and artificial intelligence [2].

2 Related work

Many researchers have been given contribution towards the efficient and effective information retrieval on web. We have discussed some of the techniques used for information retrieval as below:

Intelligent information retrieval approach based on two degrees of uncertainty fuzzy ontology was proposed to enhance the performance of retrieval system [1]. By implementing linguistic variables, uncertainty level in domain's concept has been modeled, and ontology relations have been modeled by fuzzy theory consequently. Then, the combined these uncertain models and proposed a new ontology with two degrees of uncertainty both in concept expression and relation expression. The generated fuzzy ontology was implemented for expansion of initial user's queries in Software Maintenance Engineering (SME) domain [1].

Searching for relevant information on the world-wide web is often a difficult and frustrating task. The information one is looking for, is hidden among thousands of documents returned by a search engine. One way of making search for relevant information easier, is to create better interfaces to the search engines; interfaces that facilitate quick and efficient browsing through the multitude of returned documents. A new multimodal interface was presented. It was situated in an Intelligent Environment, for retrieving information from the web. The work brings together progress made in three research areas: multi-modal interfaces, interfaces for information retrieval, and intelligent environments [3]. The name of this interface is FIRE (Friendly Information Retrieval Engine). The FIRE, a multimodal interface for information retrieval deployed in the Intelligent Room at the MIT AI Lab. FIRE differs from most of other interfaces for information retrieval in that it combines a couple of interaction modalities to improve the search process[3].

A web search engine searches for information in WWW. A vertical Search provides the user with results for queries on that domain. Meta Search Engines send the user's search queries to various search engines and combine the search results. The authors introduce intelligent user interfaces for selecting domain, category and search engines for the proposed Multi-Domain Meta Search Engine. An intelligent User Interface is also designed to get the user query and to send it to appropriate search engines. Few algorithms are designed to combine results from various search engines and also to display the results [4].

Decision-making theories aiming at solving decision problems that involve multiple criteria have often been incorporated in knowledge-based systems for the improvement of these system's reasoning process. However, multi criteria analysis has not been used adequately in intelligent user interfaces, even though user-computer interaction is, by nature, multi criteria-based. The actual process of incorporating multi criteria analysis into an intelligent user interface is neither clearly defined nor adequately described in the literature. It involves many experimental studies throughout the software life-cycle. Moreover, each multi criteria decision-making theory requires different kinds of experiments for the criteria to be determined and then for the proper respective weight of each criterion to be specified. In this research, the authors address the complex issue of developing intelligent user interfaces that are based on multi criteria decision-making theories. In particular, they present and discuss a software life-cycle framework that is appropriate for the development of such user interfaces. The life-cycle framework is called Multi-criteria based Intelligent User Interface (MBIUI). Given the fact, that very little has been reported in the literature about the required experimental studies, their participants and the appropriate life-cycle phase during which the experimental studies should take place; MBIUI provides useful insight for future developments of intelligent user interfaces that incorporate multi criteria theories.

One significant advantage of MBIUI is that it provides a unifying life-cycle framework that may be used for the application of many different multi criteria decision-making theories. In this paper, the authors discuss the incorporation features of four distinct multi criteria theories namely: TOPSIS, SAW, MAUT, and DEA. Furthermore, they give detailed specifications of the experiments that should take place and reveal their similarities and differences with respect to the theories [5].

3 Proposed Work

Intelligent interface can adapt to the needs of different users, it can learn new concepts and techniques, it can anticipate the needs of the users, it can take initiative and make suggestions to the users, and it can provide explanation of its actions. Typically, an intelligent interface should employ some kind of intelligent technique. The following list is a fairly complete list of the kinds of techniques that today are being employed in intelligent interfaces:

- *User Adaptivity*: Techniques that allow user-system interactions to be adapted to different users and different usage situations.
- *User Modeling*: Techniques that allow a system to maintain knowledge about a user.
- *Natural Language Technology*: Techniques that allow a system to interpret or generate natural language utterances, in text or in speech.
- *Dialogue Modeling*: Techniques that allows a system to maintain a natural language dialogue with the user, possible in combination with other interactions mean (multimodal dialogue).
- *Explanation Generation*: Technique that allow a system to explain its results to a user.

In this paper, an intelligent interface for web based information retrieval with document understanding [7][8] is proposed. The aim of intelligent interface for WBIR is of controlling an underlying information retrieval system, directly interacting with the user, and allowing him to retrieve relevant information without the help of human intermediary. The interface helps users to formulate query by using Natural Language Processing (NLP) techniques[11]. It retrieves documents with respect to order of relevance. The architecture of our proposed system is depicted in Figure 1. The terms which are used in this paper are defined as follows.

Definition 1 (Intelligent Interface): *It is software which interacts with user and web information retrieval system. It consists of knowledge base (K) and inference engine (E). It is denoted as I = (K,E).*

Definition 2 (Web Information Retrieval System): *It is a system which takes user query as an input and retrieves web pages or Uniform Resource Locators (URLs) relevant to the user query. Let Q be the set of user queries, i.e.* $Q = \{Q_1, Q_2, \ldots, Q_m\}$ *and D be the set of documents to be retrieved i.e.* $D = \{D_1, D_2, \ldots, D_n\}$. *The web information retrieval system can be viewed as a transformation function f which maps Q to D. i.e.* $f: Q \rightarrow D$.

Definition 3 (Document Understanding): *It is defined as a process of summarization of document or extracting the main content of the document. The document can be a web page, email, book, news stories, word file, PDF file etc.*

Definition 4 (Precision & Recall): *The efficiency of search facility is measured using two metrics Precision and Recall. Let* D_1 *be the number of documents retrieved and* D_2 *be the number of relevant documents.*

$$Precision = \frac{D1+D2}{D1} \quad (1)$$

$$Recall = \frac{D1+D2}{D2} \quad (2)$$

3.1 Architecture of Intelligent Interface

The Intelligent Interface consists of Graphical User Interface (GUI), User Modeling, Knowledge Base (KB) and Inference Engine (IE). The Architecture of proposed intelligent interface is depicted in Figure 1.

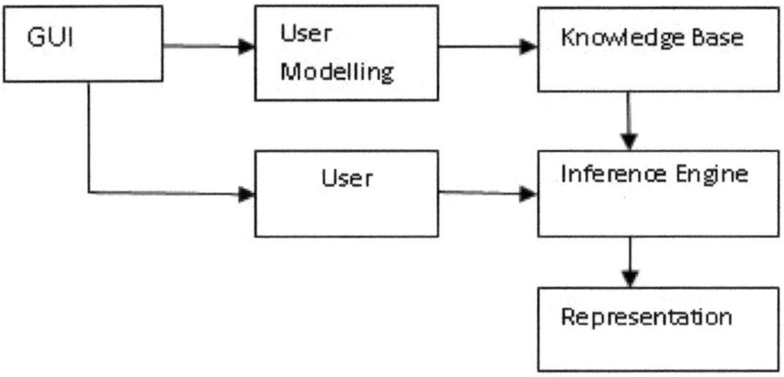

Fig. 1. Architecture of Intelligent Interface

Using the GUI, user can formulate his or her query that is then presented to the Inference Engine. Information about the user is acquired through GUI which is required for user modelling and also for knowledge representation for knowledge base

(KB). User modelling means representing the necessary information about the user, which plays an important role in web information retrieval process. The Knowledge base (KB) is the repository of facts and rules represented using predicate logic. Inference Engine applies inference rules to generate appropriate requirement of the user. For user modelling, the system maintains information about various attributes of user such as name, gender and age and also the attributes of the information which he/she is seeking for. This process is shown in Figure 2.

The important part of the knowledge base is knowledge representation[12]. We have represented the entities 'user' and 'information' by using predicate logic. The structure of predicate logic is defined as:

```
User(name, age, sex)
Information(document, type, content)
```

e.g. "John is a 40 years old man seeking information for algorithms of data mining in the form of PDF file".

This fact can be represented as:

```
user( "john", 40, "male")
information("document", "PDF", "data mining algorithms")
```

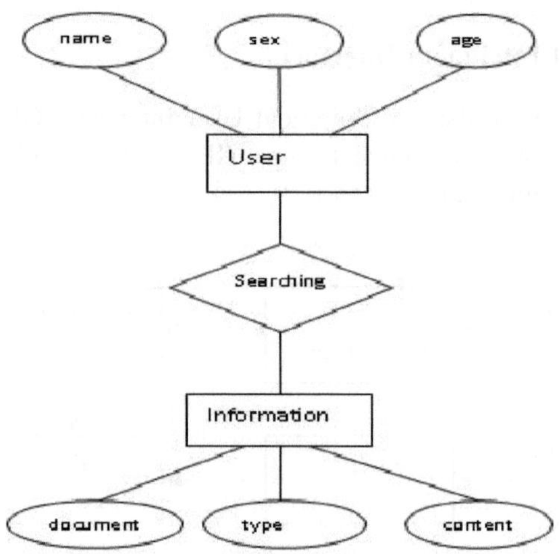

Fig. 2. User Modeling

Intelligent interface[9] helps user to formulate his query. The original query can be written in natural language form[10]; the system interacts with inference engine through knowledge base and tries to produce an optimal query which will ensure that the results of retrieval process may be more relevant. The Inference engine is based on inference rules and ability to infer the facts.

Consider following user query,

"I want to know how many tigers are living in the Kanha National Park".

Our intelligent interface will process this query after applying appropriate natural language processing and artificial intelligence algorithms and will produce the optimum query as:

"Number of tigers in Kanha National Park wiki"

Document understanding[7][8] plays an important role in web information retrieval. In this paper, we have tried to use document understanding as a tool to decide the document relevance. It is shown in Figure 3.

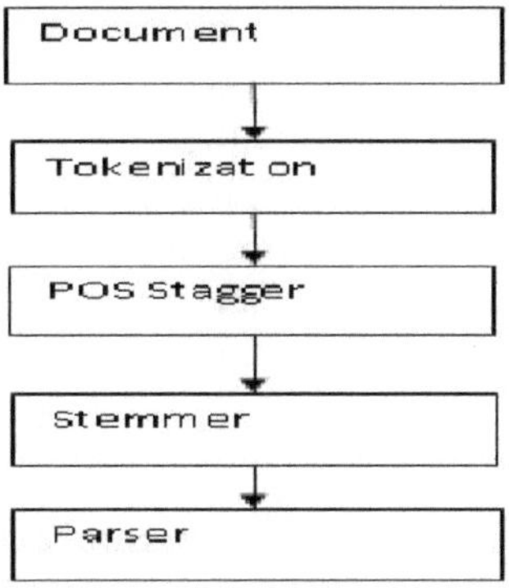

Fig. 3. Document understanding

Tokenization is a primary step of machine translation. In this phase, the input sentence is decomposed into tokens. These tokens are given to Part-of-Speech Tagger (POS Tagger) function to tag the tokens with their respective type.

e.g. Sentence : *"India has won the match by six wickets"*

Tokens : *"India" "has" "won" "the" "match" "by" "six" "wickets"*

A POS Tagger is a piece of software that reads text in some language and assigns parts of speech to each word (and other token), such as noun, verb, adjective, etc., although generally computational applications use more fine-grained POS tags like 'noun-plural'.

Consider the input string: *"Boy is very good"*
The output of POS tagger for this sentence will be:

Boy → noun
is → verb
very → adjective
good → noun

Stemmer is very useful to find stem i.e. root word of any word. Consider the input string:

"Beautiful ladies are also extremely healthy and egoist"

The stemmer will find stem for each of the words in the given sentence.

Table 1. Result of stemming

word	stem
beautiful	beauty
ladies	lady
are	are
also	also
extremely	extreme
healthy	health
and	and
egoist	ego

3.2 Proposed Intelligent Interface for Web Information Retrieval

In this paper we have proposed the intelligent interface for web based information retrieval [6] with document understanding. The architecture of this entire system is as shown in Figure 4. There are eight components of this system:

- Intelligent Interface
- Query representation
- Web documents
- Document representation
- Indexing
- Comparison
- Retrieved documents
- Relevance feedback

Working of Intelligent interface is already discussed above. Its objectives are:

- To produce the most relevant documents as per user interest.
- To enhance the effectiveness of document search on the internet.

The effectiveness of the search process is highly depending upon the type of query submitted to the system. As discussed above, the user may write his or her query in natural language form as he or she is more comfortable with. Our system will try to help user to formulate the query. The utility like WordNet is used to determine the thesaurus and synonyms of the words.

In query representation process, the natural language query is processed by inference engine and it is represented as Boolean query which will be forwarded to search engine. Information on the internet is available as documents. These can be web pages, emails, PDF files etc. Web documents are represented as HTML or XML pages. The web crawler searches for desired information by crawling through network of web servers. The web pages are organized into logical sequence called inverted index. The web page which has highest page score or highest page rank will come first and so on. Page score for each of the documents will be determined by following page rank algorithm:

1. Initialize the PageScore()=0
2. Enter the User Query for which documents are to be searched;
3. Let W= {*w1*, *w2*,.................,*wN* } be the number of words belong to User Query
4. Web crawler starts with a list of URLs to visit called *Seeds* and downloads the respective page from the Internet at the given URL.
5. A Web crawler parses through the downloaded page and retrieves the links to other pages. Each link in the page is defined with an HTML anchor tag.
6. Each link is added *Queue*.
7. Calculate the Page Score as follows:

For each *wi* ∈ W, do
if *wi* is present in the document;
PageScore()=PageScore() + 1;
else
PageScore() is unchanged;
end

8. return PageScore()
9. exit

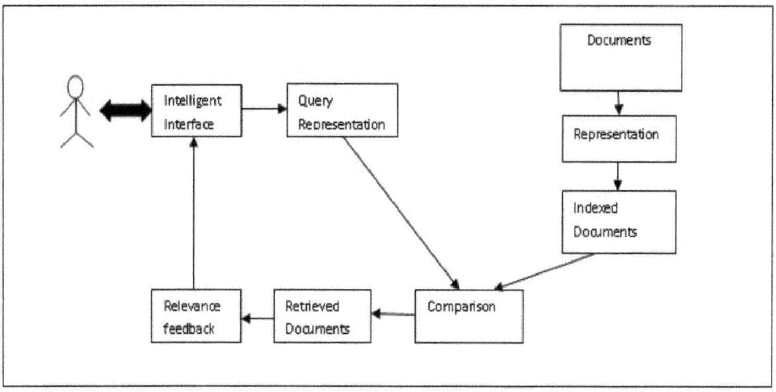

Fig. 4. Web Information retrieval using intelligent interface

Table 2. Result without interface

corpus	Average precision	Average Recall
Simple queries	0.90	0.42
Compound queries	0.67	0.26

Table 3. Result with interface

corpus	Average precision	Average Recall
Simple queries	0.95	0.48
Compound queries	0.82	0.32

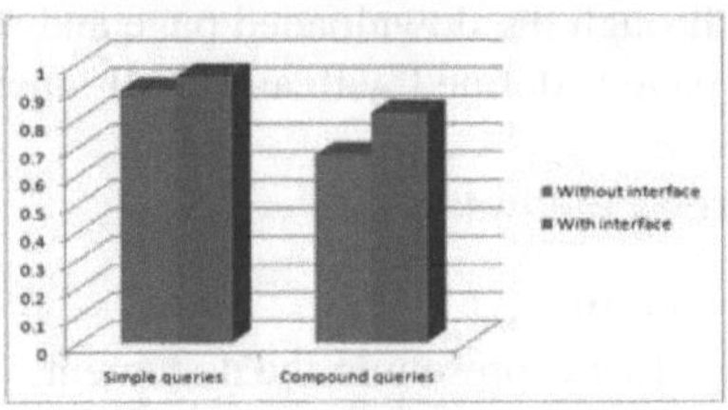

Fig. 5. Comparison of average precision

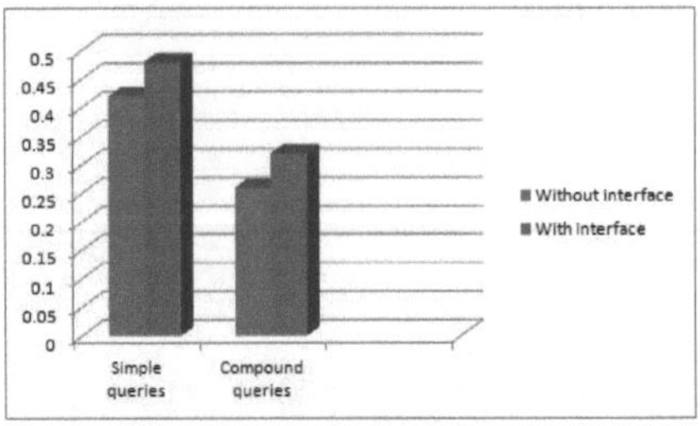

Fig. 6. Comparison of average recall

4 Results and Conclusion

We have chosen a corpus consisting of one hundred simple keyword queries and one hundred compound queries. The performance of our system is evaluated on the basis of two metrics: average precision and average recall. Comparison of result of retrieval without interface and with interface is presented in Table 3 and 4 and plotted in Figure 5 and 6 respectively.

References

1. Hourali, M., Montazer, G.A.: An Intelligent Information Retrieval Approach Based on Two Degrees of Uncertainty Fuzzy Ontology. Advances in Fuzzy Systems, vol. 2011, pp. 1–11. Hindawi Publishing Corporation
2. Mizzaro, S.: Intelligent Interfaces for Information Retrieval: A Review (May 1996)
3. Gajos, K., Kulkarni, A.: FIRE: An Information Retrieval Interface for Intelligent Environments. In: International Workshop on Information Presentation and Natural Multimodal Dialogue, IPNMD 2001, Verona, Italy (December 2001)
4. Minnie, D., Srinivasan, S.: Meta Search Engine With An Intelligent Interface For Information Retrieval On Multiple Domains. International Journal of Computer Science, Engineering and Information Technology (IJCSEIT) 1(4) (October 2011)
5. Kabassi, K., Virvou, M.: A Knowledge-Based Software Life-Cycle Framework for the Incorporation of Multicriteria Analysis in Intelligent User Interfaces. IEEE Transactions On Knowledge And Data Engineering 18(9) (September 2006)
6. Dhingra, V., Bhatia, K.K.: Towards Intelligent Information Retrieval on Web. International Journal on Computer Science and Engineering (IJCSE) 3(4), 1721–1726 (2011)
7. Rabiah, A.K., Sembok, T.M.T., Halimah, B.Z.: Improvement of document understanding ability through the notion of answer literal expansion in logical-linguistic approach. WSEAS Transactions on Information Science and Applications 6(6) (June 2009)
8. Aiello, M., Monz, C., Tororan, L., Worring, M.: Document Understanding for a Broad Class of Documents. International Journal on Document Analysis and Recognition
9. Albusac, J., Vallejo, D., astro-Schez, Remagnino, P., Morcillo, C.G., Jimenez, L.: Monitoring Complex Environments Using a Knowledge-Driven Approach Based on Intelligent Agents. IEEE Journal of Intelligent Systems 25(3), 24–31 (2010)
10. Radev, D., Lapata, M.: Natural Language Processing and the Web. IEEE Journal Intelligent Systems 23(5), 16–17 (2008)
11. Klink, S., Kieninger, T.: Rule Based Document Structure Understanding with a Fuzzy Combination of Layout and Textual Features. International Journal of Document Analysis and Recognition 4, 18–26
12. Duman, H.: An Intelligent Agent Approach for Visual Information structure Generation. IEEE Journal of Intelligent Systems 24(3), 23–29 (2009)

Data Preloading Technique using Intention Prediction

Seungyup Lee[1], Juwan Yoo[1], and Da Young Ju[2]

[1] School of Integrated Technology, Yonsei University, South Korea
youb007@gmail.com, j.y@yonsei.ac.kr
[2] Yonsei Institute of Convergence Technology, Yonsei University, South Korea
dyju@yonsei.ac.kr

Abstract. Various smart devices provide fast response time and ubiquitous web-environment to users for better user experiences (UXs). However, high device performance that users perceive is not always promised because there should be limited network bandwidth, and computation capabilities. When the network and computation capabilities are overloaded, users experience buffering and loading time to accomplish a certain task. We, therefore, propose data preloading technique [1], which predicts user intention and preloads the web and local application data to provide better device performance in spite of poor network conditions and outdated hardware. We also design intention cognitive model to predict user intention precisely. Four user intention prediction algorithms, which are applicable to various conventional input methods, are described and compared each performance in both user's and device's aspects.

Keywords: Preloading algorithm, intention prediction, hovering state, input device.

1 Introduction

Technology has been dramatically developed for a few years to realize the ubiquitous computing environment. Hardware and software technology have been developed for the better performance but they are not so systemically connected to each other that the usability of the smart devices is limited to their network conditions and hardware capabilities. For example, when a user wants to watch a web video clip with a smartphone, the response time is highly dependent on the network environment and the processing power of user's device. Although the various user interface technologies are proposed for the users, they are not able to overcome the limitations of the network conditions and hardware capabilities in these days. Three related key techniques are described at next chapter as follows: (i) research developing new interaction methods with hovering state using various input devices, (ii) prefetching and preprocessing studies to shorten web-latency, (iii) predicting user intention using the cursor movement.

M. Kurosu (Ed.): Human-Computer Interaction, Part III, HCII 2014, LNCS 8512, pp. 32–41, 2014.

2 Related Works

2.1 Interaction Methods in the Hovering State

As touchscreen-based smartphones and tablet PCs become popular and are commonly used, not only the touch screen but also various types of input devices, e.g. digitizer, stylus pen, are commonly embedded in the smart devices. These input devices provide rich user experiences (UXs) with a variety of developers' ideas. Especially, gesture interaction technology leads this trend by tracking the hovering state of users' fingers and stylus. Some researchers propose the 3-D interaction technology using cameras [5], IR sensors [3][4], light sources [6], electromagnetically induced type device [7][8], etc. However, most of them focus on GUI (Graphical User Interface) effects not predicting the user intention and consider only one input method, which is not compatible to the other input methods. These researches are limited to tangible interface technology, which provide the intuitive interaction method.

2.2 Prefetching and Preloading Research

Prefetching is now a common technology for web applications. It downloads the web page that is likely to be accessed in the near future depending on some criteria [9-11]. Furthermore, the prefetching is an effective way to improve perceived performance and user experience especially in the mobile environment [12]. Preprocessing and pre-rendering are similar concepts to the prefetching in that they carry out some tasks prior to receiving the real input or requests. We integrate these concepts to the preloading concept, as we do not confine our data preloading technique in a certain application area. The data preloading technique can be adapted to prefetch web-data, pre-rendering image data and pre-do something when there is a detectable hovering state.

Most of prefetching and preloading researches analyze DOM (Document Object Model) [18] with the past log data of the users' queries. These query data is so originated from only for keyboards that compatibility of the preloading applications are confined to specific area. However, as already mentioned, the input devices are getting more various, the preloading interface should sufficiently be needed to be studied for these input devices. Others [13][14] suggested web prefetching method only using the mouse direction, but this method lacks behavioral analysis to predict user intention.

3 Intention Prediction Model

3.1 Data Preloading User Interface

The conventional loading method loads the web (or local) application data right after the input signal from the user, because there is no intention prediction step. However, the data preloading technique predicts the user intention and preloads the web and local application data for providing a better device performance to mitigate the network conditions and hardware capabilities. Fig. 1 illustrates how the data preloading technique and the conventional loading method are different and shows that each method works sequentially according to the user input action. A server starts to transfer the web application data to the device (or the device starts to process the local application data) when the target area of the web content is likely to be touched or clicked. When a user performs the touch or click action, a screen of the device just displays the preloaded data. It is theoretically obvious that the data preloading technique can shorten the response time and accomplish the better user experience.

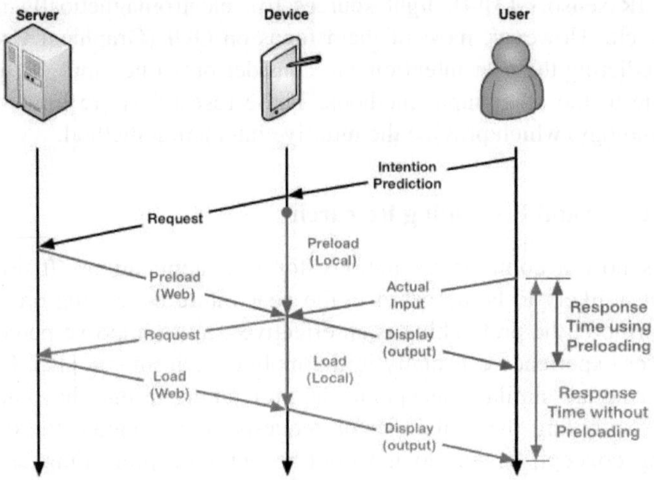

Fig. 1. Comparison between proposed method and conventional interface

For more widely acceptable application to existing consumer electronics, we propose two types of data preloading technique for providing rich experiences to users. The first type is data preloading technique for indirect control which enables to perform the general pointing tasks with indirect input method [2], e.g. mouse and trackpad, in PC and laptop environment. The second type is data preloading technique for direct control [2], which is specialized for direct input methods such as touch screen with IR sensor [3][4] and electromagnetic induction type digitizer that enable to track the "hovering state" of finger or digitizer.

3.2 Intention Cognitive Model

Intention Metaphor. We design intention cognitive model of user as shown in Fig. 2. The intention model consists of three elements: a user, a device and user interface. Then the user interface is divided into three layers: user layer, intention layer and prediction layer. When a user interacts with a certain device, the user passes the cognitive process to provide input action at the user layer. After the cognitive process, the actual input is provided to the device with input device (ID). The input device is a kind of bridge which connects the user and device. At this point of view, we can assume that the input device is a metaphor of user intention. Thus, we can comprehend the user intention by analyzing the input device movement at the prediction layer. Task analysis module tracks the input device for collecting appropriate data such as coordinates and time. Prediction module receives dataset of input device and identifies the user intention. With the results of prediction module, preloading module makes decision and gives an order to the device before the actual input is provided.

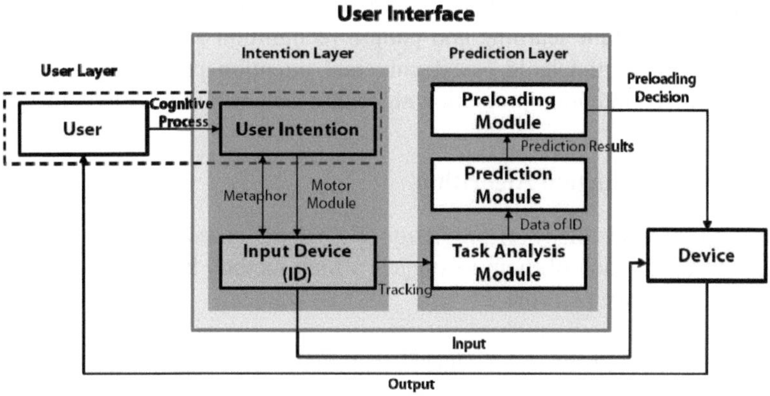

Fig. 2. User intention model

With the input device as a metaphor of user intention, we assume two basic hypotheses as follows:

- H1. The position of the pointer indicates the intention of the user.
- H2. The closer between the position of the pointer and the target, the stronger intention to click (or touch).

The first hypothesis is based on the human motor theory after the visual input [15-17]. The movement of the pointer to the target means execution of cognitive decision. It is also obvious that the position of the pointer tends to be almost physically corresponded to the target right before the real input action such as the second hypothesis.

Table 1. Data preloading technique categorization

Input Methods	Characteristics
Indirect Control	• Continuous trajectory • Almost PC devices (High Spec) • Applicable to threshold –based and machine learning algorithms
Direct Control	• Discontinuous Trajectory • Almost mobile devices (Low Spec) • Only applicable to threshold-based algorithms

Analysis of Input Data. After designing intention cognitive model, we analyze characteristics of two data preloading techniques and apply to task analysis module. Table 1 demonstrates crucial characteristics which should be considered to develop user intention prediction algorithms. Data preloading for indirect control can employ various machine learning ad pattern recognition algorithm because indirect input device is always in trackable state with continuous trajectory. Moreover, the indirect input methods are usually attached high computing power device, such as desktop PCs, it is affordable to compute heavy algorithms. On the other hand, as the direct input devices have discrete trajectory and are usually equipped with mobile devices, it is hard to apply machine learning and pattern recognition algorithms. We, therefore, develop and propose threshold-based universal intention prediction algorithms and indirect-specialized intention prediction algorithm according to our hypotheses.

3.3 Intention Prediction Algorithm

We propose five types of novel prediction algorithms based on the two basic hypotheses and compare each of them to suggest which method is appropriate in a certain circumstance as shown in Table 2.

Table 2. User Intention prediction algorithms

Name	Operation	Type
Preloading All (**PA**)	Preloads all targets below the pointer.	Universal
Time-threshold Prediction (**TT**)	Preloads when a pointer stays on a target for a certain period more than threshold time.	Universal
Velocity-threshold Prediction (**VT**)	Preloads when a pointer is on a target with a certain velocity under threshold.	Universal
Distance-threshold Prediction (**DT**)	Preloads when distance between a target and a pointer is smaller than threshold.	Universal
Temporal Prediction (**TP**)	Prelaods using Neural Network.	For indirect

The PA is a reference method, which always preloads data when a pointer passes through the targets. There is no consideration for computational load and battery life of devices because it is always running at the background process. The TT, VT, and DT preload the target below the pointer when the pointer exceeds a certain predetermined time, velocity and distance threshold. The threshold is determined by mean values of pointing devices' past movement data right before the input requests. These methods totally follow H1, which the position of the pointer reveals intention of a user, and are designed for universal that are independent to input method types. The TP detects expecting click time when the real input is likely to be provided by the user and fires a preloader which is a container for downloading data. This algorithm is employed with neural network algorithm based on already tracked continuous position data of the pointer while using indirect input device, so that it is only for indirect control. We develop the TP by extracting two features from tracked continuous data of indirect control: 1) Average velocity of the pointer, and 2) Instant velocity of the pointer. The average velocity is computed by total movement distance divided by an interval from an input to next input signal. The instant velocity is the velocity when mouse-event occurs. With these two features, a neural network algorithm is trained and finds optimized weights to predict the temporal state when the input signal is likely to be provided.

4 Evaluation of Proposed Model

4.1 Prototype Development

We implement web multimedia application [19] which preloads video player and multimedia streaming data as a prototype as shown in Fig. 3. The multimedia web application, e.g. Youtube, is the most dependent application on the network capability or the hardware specification. Many international users who use these multimedia web-services experience buffering state from a few seconds to minutes every day especially on their mobile devices. We, therefore, prototype the multimedia web application which is the most appropriate one to show the effectiveness of data preloading technique. The prototype is developed with javascript for securing OS compatibilities and using mouse-event function API. Samsung Electronics' LC-BX2440AFDKR 24 inches monitor which has 1920X1080 pixels and Chrome web browser have been employed to collect the data and experiment. Samsung Electronics Slate Tablet PC, which has intel core i5, 11.6 inches display and an electromagnetic-induced digitizer, are used for data preloading technique for direct control.

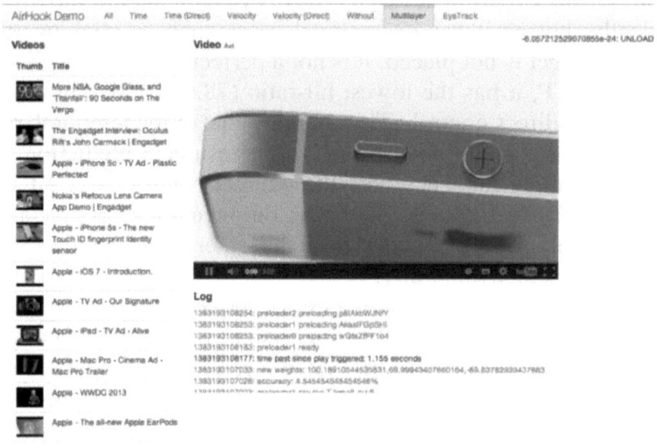

Fig. 3. Prototype by proposed algorithm

4.2 Experimental Design

We have collected 24 participants (18 males and 6 females), who have average 27.5 years old, when they are using mouse and a digitizer at a prototype website. The YouTube-like prototype website is consisted of various video contents. Fig.3. illustrates the layout of prototype website. The video contents lists are placed at the left-side and the video plays at the right-side of the website. The users randomly click (or touch) the video in the list and watch them from about 5 minutes to 10 minutes.

Then we preform three kinds of experiments to each preloading algorithm to evaluate the effectiveness of data preloading technique as follows:

- Hit-ratio: Measures whether the preloaded data in a preloader is selected by actual input action of a user.
- Availability: Number of preloading commands during click-to-click interval.
- Response Time: Duration from clicking a video target to playing the video contents.

With these three experiments, we validate which preloading algorithm is appropriate to the indirect and direct input control compared with Without Preloading (WP).

5 Results

The experimental results are shown in Table 2 and Table 3. Hit-ratio measures whether the preloaded data in a preloader is selected by actual input action of the user. If preloaded data is not selected to play, the preloading command misses the intention prediction. Of course, as TT, VT, DT and PA are pointer-based methods, they have very high score in this experiment results. In PA case, it should have 100% hit-ratio result theoretically, but as it has exceptional cases such as clicking (touching) the blank area that the target is not placed, it is not a perfect 100% (99.53%). On the other hand, in the case of TP, it has the lowest hit-ratio (78.65%) among the other prediction algorithms for indirect control. This implies that only temporal prediction has limitation to predict user intention accurately. The results of prediction algorithms for direct control have similar tendency with the indirect control case: TT (94.32%), VT (95.91%), DT (78.7%), PA (96.62). As the hit ratio cannot be a standalone measurement which certain algorithm is better than the others, we mentioned the score of prediction algorithms with availability.

Availability measures the number of preloading commands during click-to-click interval. This means that the data preloading system is how available for using time. This also indicates the sensitivity of system, required computational loads and network bandwidth while a certain prediction algorithm is running at the background. For instance, if the availability is too low, there can be a circumstance that the preloading command does not appropriately operate at the adequate time. On the other hand, if the availability is too high, data preloading system loads to the user's device so that this shortens the battery life and decreases the network downloading speed because of preloading the unnecessary data. Thus, availability should be placed theoretically at the middle point which is not too high either too slow.

Table 3. Experimenatl results of data preloading technique for indirect control

Prediction Method	Hit-ratio (%)	Availability	Response Time (ms)
PA	99.53%	11.28	953.67
TT	97.74%	4.36	856.72
VT	89.04%	3.71	893.32
DP	96.48%	15.05	941.52
TP	78.65%	10.63	1015.78
WP	-	-	2035.84

Table 4. Experimenatl results of data preloading technique for direct control

Prediction Method	Hit-ratio (%)	Availability	Response Time (ms)
PA	96.62%	6.76	6214.41
TT	94.32%	2.64	3682.65
VT	95.91%	3.63	3895.47
DT	78.70%	12.11	8423.84
WP	-	-	6565.39

For indirect control, DP (15.05) is the most available and sensitive prediction algorithm and it requires more computation power and network bandwidth than TP (10.63) and PA (11.27). However, TT (4.35) and VT (3.7) have very low availability compared with DT, TP and PA. For direct control, DT (12.1) is the most sensitive prediction algorithm that is same as indirect control case. It is paradoxical that DT, which is almost for mobile device, needs much powerful processors and more network bandwidth than TP, which is designed for indirect control device such as desktop PCs.

The response time is a duration from the time when a user clicks (or touch) a target video content to the time when the video starts to play. All prediction methods of data preloading technique for indirect control significantly shorten the response time than WP case. In the absence of data preloading, the average response time is about 2035.84 ms and 5620.17 ms for each indirect control and direct control case. The result shows that the response time of all prediction algorithms for indirect control are dramatically improved from 50.7% (TP) to 57.9% (TT). On the other hand, the result of direct control case shows that each prediction method has quite different performance. TT is the fastest prediction method in shortening the response time having a similar advance (43.9%) with indirect control case, and VT (40.7%) follows the next. However, DT (-26.4%) records the worse response time than WP, and PA (5.3%) has almost no improvement at all.

DT records the worst prediction algorithm through all experiments. For direct control, nothing is better than PA and even WP. This is very crucial because PA is the reference prediction algorithm which always on the preloading state whenever the mouse event occurs. We conclude the reason DT scores the worst as PA preloads one target below the pointer at once, whereas DT preloads the several data at once when the targets come into pre-determined distance threshold.

In user's point of view, as the perceived response time is the significant factor to determine device performance, we propose several user intention prediction algorithms according to response time results. All prediction algorithms of indirect case are highly recommended, which is usually a desktop computer that has strong computing power. On the other hand, the direct control devices, e.g. smart phones and tablet PCs, are recommended to employ time and velocity threshold prediction methods selectively. Furthermore, DT should be avoided to apply to direct control.

6 Conclusion

In this paper, we introduce novel data preloading techniques that predict the user intention, and preload the web or local application data for providing a better device performance to mitigate the limits of the conventional interface, network and hardware technologies. The two types of data preloading technique, for indirect control and direct control, are proposed to cover the various existing input devices, such as a mouse, stylus pen and digitizer. Five user intention prediction algorithms (preload-all, time, velocity, distance-threshold, temporal prediction algorithm) are developed according to intention cognitive model and hypotheses. We evaluate hit-ratio, availability and response time of user intention prediction algorithm and compare the results for each prediction algorithm to recommend which prediction algorithm is appropriate to certain types of input device. The time and velocity threshold-based methods have shown much higher performances than distance threshold method in direct control, which are widely used for mobile devices. On the other hand, data preloading technique for indirect control, which is targeted to apply to the conventional desktop PCs, runs all prediction algorithms more powerful even using complicated prediction algorithm such as TP. However, we do not consider the various external variables such as layout design, gender and ages of users. Thus, we will study the effects of these variables for future work.

Acknowledgements. This research was supported by the MSIP (Ministry of Science, ICT and Future Planning), Korea, under the "IT Consilience Creative Program" (NIPA-2014-H0201-14-1001) supervised by the NIPA (National IT Industry Promotion Agency).

References

1. Yoo, J.Y., Lee, S.Y., Ahn, C.T.: Air Hook: Data preloading user interface. In: IEEE International Conference on ICT Convergence (ICTC), pp. 163–167 (2012)
2. Shneiderman, B., Plaisant, C.: Interaction devices: Designing the User Interface, 5th edn., pp. 331–337. Pearson (2010)

3. Suh, S., Yi, K., Choi, C., Park, D., Kim, C.: Mobile LCD device with transparent infrared image sensor panel for touch and hover sensing. In: IEEE International Conference on Consumer Electronics, pp. 213–214 (2012)
4. Mizumata, T., Sakamoto, R.: A pinch up gesture on multi-touch table with hover detection. In: ACM SIGGRAPH ASIA 2010 Posters, p. 27 (2010)
5. Hirsch, M., Lanman, D., Holtzman, H., Raskar, R.: BiDi Screen: A Thin, Depth-Sensing LCD for 3D Interaction using Light Fields. ACM Trans. on Grap. 28, 159 (2009)
6. Dohse, K.C., Dohse, T., Still, J.D., Parkhurst, D.J.: Enhancing Multi- user Interaction with Multi-touch Tabletop Displays Using Hand Tracking. In: International Conference on Advances in Computer-Human Interaction, pp. 297–302 (2008)
7. Moffatt, K., Yuen, S., McGrenere, J.: Hover or tap?: supporting pen- based menu navigation for older adults. In: ACM SIGACCESS Conference on Computers and Accessibility, pp. 51–58 (2008)
8. Grossman, T., Hinckley, K., Baudisch, P., Agrawala, M., Balakrishnan, R.: Hover widgets: using the tracking state to extend the capabilities of pen-operated devices. In: ACM SIGCHI Conference on Human Factors in Computing Systems, pp. 861–870 (2006)
9. Jiang, Y., Wu, M.Y., Shu, W.: Web prefetching: Costs, benefits and performance. In: International Workshop on Web Content Caching and Distribution, Colorado (2002)
10. Jiang, Z., Kleinrock, L.: Web prefetching in a mobile environment. IEEE J. Per. Comm. 5, 25–34 (1998)
11. Jiang, Z., Kleinrock, L.: An adaptive network prefetch scheme. IEEE J. Selec. Are. Comm. 16, 358–368 (1998)
12. Matsudaira, K.: Making the mobile web faster. Commun. ACM 56, 56 (2013)
13. Kundu, A., Guha, S.K., Mitra, A., Mukherjee, T.: A new approach in dynamic prediction for user based web page crawling. In: ACM International Conference on Management of Emergent Digital EcoSystems, pp. 166–173 (2010)
14. Kundu, A.: Dynamic Web Prediction Using Asynchronous Mouse Activity. In: Computational Social Network, pp. 257–280. Springer (2012)
15. Helsen, W.F., Elliott, D., Starkes, J.L., Ricker, K.L.: Temporal and Spatial Coupling of Point of Gaze and Hand Movements in Aiming. J. Mot. Behav. 30, 249–259 (1998)
16. Smith, B.A., Ho, J., Ark, W., Zhai, S.: Hand eye coordination patterns in target selection. In: Symposium on Eye Tracking Research & Applications (2000)
17. Salvucci, D.D., Anderson, J.R.: Intelligent gaze-added interfaces. In: ACM CHI 2000: The SIGCHI Conference on Human Factors in Computing Systems (2000)
18. World Wide Web Consortium, Document Object Model (DOM), http://www.w3.org/DOM/2005
19. Data Preloading Technique Prototype, http://airhook.yonsei.ac.kr

Textual Emotion Communication with Non-verbal Symbols in Online Environments

Eunice Njeri Mwangi, Stephen Kimani, and Michael Kimwele

Department of Computing
School of Computing and Information Technology (SCIT)
Jomo Kenyatta University of Agriculture and Technology
P.O. Box 62000-00200 Nairobi, Kenya
njeri.eunice@gmail.com, stephenkimani@googlemail.com,
mikekimwele@yahoo.com

Abstract. Recently computer mediated communication became a popular way of interaction. Unfortunately nonverbal elements are normally absent in these online communications. This paper describes the results of a study carried out to determine the use of textual symbols/patterns to provide nonverbal cues and to express emotions in online text based environments. The focus is on the use of online textual symbols/patterns of vocalics (e.g. the use of capitals and use of punctuation "!" and "!!s!" or "?" and "???", length of response e.t.c), and those of chronemics (e.g. time to respond to an email or to a chat message) to communicate emotions in text. The study forms a basis for the development of an affect recognition model that is able to recognize emotions from written language and especially in environments where informal styles of writing are used.

Keywords: Emotions, non-verbal symbols (Vocalics & Chronemics), Textual symbols, Computer Mediated communication (CMC), social presence, affective computing, emotion recognition from text.

1 Introduction

Social interaction among people is an important part of every society .In face to face communications, people often rely on nonverbal cues such as body language, facial expressions, gestures, physical proximity, and dress to communicate meaning and establish relationships. Recently computer mediated communication became a popular way of interaction, especially among young students in the universities. Unfortunately nonverbal elements are generally missing in these online communications. According to [2] nonverbal cues provide 93% of the meaning exchanged in the interaction, 35% from tone and 58% from gestures, expressions and other physical cues. Such cues are essential for human cognition and influence different aspects of peoples' lives. For online communications to be successful consideration of social factors such as emotions is essential [7-8];In this regard, social presence has emerged as a major design principle and a core construct in studying computer-mediated communication (CMC) [1].

M. Kurosu (Ed.): Human-Computer Interaction, Part III, HCII 2014, LNCS 8512, pp. 42–48, 2014.

Research in the field of artificial intelligence (AI) is increasingly focusing on developing systems that incorporate emotions [9]; Emotions are essential to several natural processes that are modeled in AI systems. A wide range of modalities for identifying emotions have been considered including affect in speech, facial display, posture, and physiological activity e.t.c. [9]. A great deal of social interaction happens online and in textual form (emails, facebook chats, and blogs e.t.c) thus textual information is gaining increased attention as an important modality for identifying emotions. Emotion recognition can be applied to numerous areas such as online learning environments, personality analysis and modeling e.t.c. A number of researchers in the field of affective computing have tried to develop techniques for sensing users' affective states. However, there are other interesting and challenging aspects that still need to be investigated in regard to online communication and emotions. The aspect investigated in this study is the use of textual symbols to provide nonverbal communication elements and to express emotions in online text based communications. This study is based on the assumption that online users have developed their own ways of complementing these nonverbal cues to communicate their emotions during online interactions particularly in environments where people tend to use an informal style of writing.

The objectives of the study include:

i. Explore use and meaning of certain non verbal textual symbols/patterns used in text to communicate emotions in online environments
ii. Investigate the informal style of communication used by online users to communicate emotions e.g. use of slang language, use of onomatopoeia
iii. Identify the patterns/symbols frequently employed by online users to express emotions in online textual based communications
iv. Develop a mapping of these non verbal textual symbols/patterns to particular basic emotional states

2 Features of Online Communication

The focus of this work is on emotion recognition from text and specifically on the use of non verbal codes of vocalics and chronemics in online environments to communicate emotions. In face to face communications vocalics includes tone of voice, loudness of voice, shouting, and vocal pauses [5]. According to [9] users can also communicate nonverbal vocalic cues via CMC using capital letters and repeated punctuation. Chronemics non verbal code pertains to time. Communication occurrence and duration are considered as chronemics cues that can be conveyed through computer mediated means [3].Such cues include time stamps on e-mails or text messages, chat messages.

The communications exchanged in applications such as Facebook chats, Google chats and WhatsApp e.t.c. cover everyday topics ranging from home to school to work, as well as friendly interactions. These environments are good for emotion study, as they are likely to be rich in emotion content. A great number of students engage in such communications, hence it was easy to find examples of patterns /textual symbols of investigation for this study from their online chat interactions. Below are sample messages exchanged by university students during their online interactions.

Sample Messages

M1: I GET MY TRANSCRIPT TODAY!!!

M2: I am going home!!!

M3: You mean you would do such a thing to me??????

M4: LEAVE ME ALONE

M5: Are you serious!!!!!!!

M6: WHAAATT!!!

M7: Yeah. That sucks. Sorry

M8: Eeww!!! That was boring

M9: Oh!!! That's cool

The above messages demonstrate the evolving language used in online communications; from the messages, students use onomatopoeia, for example, words such as Eeeww,Yeah, Oh, slang language ,capitalizations and exclamation marks while communicating. The repetition of these sound words is open to a variety of interpretations, or possibly misinterpretations.

3 Communicating Emotions in Online Environments

This section describes the purpose of the study, setup and findings:

3.1 Study Purpose and Setup

The study focus was on the use of online non verbal textual symbols of vocalics (e.g. the use of capitalizations and use of punctuation "!" or "!!s!" or "?" or "???" and"……"), and online chronemics (e.g. time to respond to an email) to communicate emotions. Informal styles of writing e.g. use of slang language, onomatopoeia (repetition of sounds) were taken into consideration. The online questionnaire was administered targeting university students who have interacted and used text messaging environments such as text chats. The questionnaire was sent to 61 participants. A total of thirty(30) student respondents from the university(17 Male(57%),13 Female(43%)) took part in the study. All of them were computer literate.

3.2 Demographics and Background Information

As indicated in Table 1, the sample was dominated by young ((60 %, 21-25 years old).93% of the participants indicated they use computers for study purposes and all participants had an internet experience of more than a year. Other variables of importance included gender, and education.

Table 1. Demographic Information of Participants

Variables	Items	Percentage (%)
Gender	Male	57
	Female	43
Age	< 20	17
	21-25	60
	26-35	23
	36+	0
Education	Certificate student	0
	Degree student	77
	Masters Student	20
	Phd Student	0
Computer Usage	Work	50
	Games	47
	Study	93
	Communication	70
	Hobby	30
Internet Experience	Less than 1 Year	0
	1-5 yrs	47
	6-10 yrs	47
	More than 10 yrs	7

In order to identify the modes students frequently used while communicating: the participants were asked to rate the frequency of use of various modes of communication. The modes of focus were discussion forums, Emails, text chat, Wikis, blogs, Social book marking, News Feeds, Micro blogs, Journaling, Instant messaging. Emails, Text chats, Instant Messengers and Micro blogs were the modes frequently used as indicated in Table 2.

Table 2. Modes of Communication Frequency of use

Modes of Online communication						
Mode	Less Often	Quite often	Often	Very often	Don't use at all	Maximum No of Responses
Emails	1	5	4	20	0	20
Text only chats	2	2	11	14	0	14
Discussion Forums	13	4	5	2	3	13
Wikis	7	7	5	7	3	7
Blogs	12	1	7	6	3	12
Micro Blogging	12	3	5	5	5	12
News feeds	4	5	8	11	2	11
Instant messenger	5	5	7	13	0	13
Voice chat	9	5	7	3	5	9
Online conferencing	8	4	1	2	10	10
Social Book Marking	11	5	5	6	2	11
Journaling	12	4	6	3	5	12
Frequency of Use	13	7	11	20	10	

3.3 Online Non Verbal Symbols and Emotions

Based on the chat messages exchanged by students ,the study focused on the following textual symbols: Multiple exclamation marks (!!!!!!),Multiple question marks (???????),Multiple full stops (……),Discourse markers such as but ,Capitalization, Abbreviations or shorthand such as brb (be right back),ASAP ,Length of the response(very short, short, long, very long), Slang language "LOL", Onomatopoeia e.g. "whizz", "aaarrr", and the response time. 90% of respondents agreed to have felt and communicated emotions while interacting in online environments.

Figure 1 below shows the forms that students frequently used to communicate their emotions.

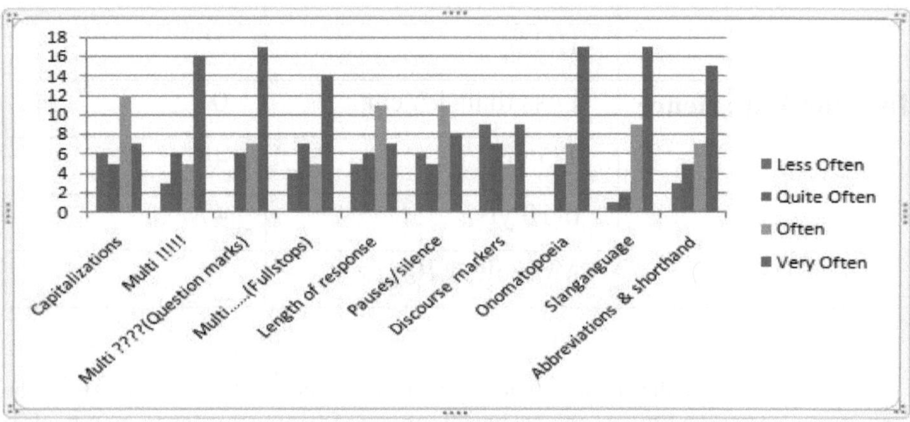

Fig. 1. Frequency of use of non verbal textual symbols

Slang language, Exclamation marks and onomatopoeia were the most frequently employed patterns of communication by students to express emotions. 53% indicated they very oftenly use Exclamation marks!!! to communicate their emotions. Other forms that were frequently used included: repetition of!!!!!! And abbreviations

3.4 Mapping Non Verbal Textual Symbols and Emotions

The study identified a mapping of the identified symbols to the six (basic) emotions as described by Ekman (1999) happiness, sadness, anger, fear, surprise and disgust. The figure below illustrates how the respondents mapped various symbols/patterns to basic emotion states.

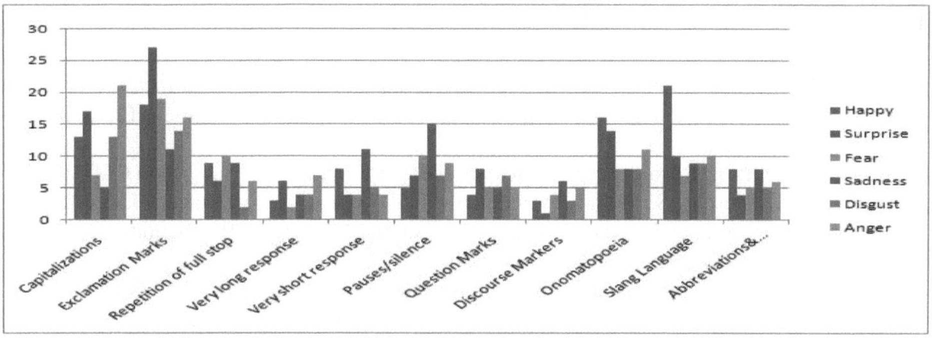

Fig. 2. Mapping between non Verbal symbols and Emotions

Slang language, exclamations and onomatopoeia were the forms mostly associated with the happy emotion with 70% of the participants mapping Slang Language with the happy emotion.60% also mapped exclamation marks to Happy. 53% of the participants mapped onomatopoeia with happy emotion. Pauses, short and very short response were the forms mostly mapped with the sad emotion with 50%, 37%, and 37% respectively. Exclamation marks, pauses /silence were the forms mostly associated with fear with 63% and 33%respectively. 70% participants mapped Capitalization with anger. 90% participants associated exclamation marks with surprise.57% of the participants also associated capitalization with Surprise. Disgust inclined towards anger with capitalizations and exclamations being more used by participants to indicate it.

4 Conclusion and Future Work

The study described in this paper indicates a mapping between various textual symbols and basic emotions. The study forms a basis for the development of an affect recognition model, as practical technique to augment social presence in computer-mediated communications.

Affect models can be applied to several areas such e-learning systems, personal modeling and consumer analysis e.t.c. Most applications of automatic emotion recognition deal with real world text. Such text often contains noise, such as misspellings, onomatopoeic elements and slang. Online communication is rapidly changing and people employing so many cues/patterns to communicate their feelings/emotions in online environments and hence deeper research is needed to investigate online communication of emotions in text based environments.

For training machine learning systems and for the evaluation of any automatic learning system, it is pre-requisite to have an annotated data. Most of existing corpora are not appropriate for training systems to recognize emotions in environments where informal styles of communication are used. The described study forms a basis for the development of a corpus of text that can be used in emotion recognition research taking into consideration the evolving nature of language in online conversations.

References

1. Biocca, F., Harms, C., Burgoon, J.K.: Toward a more robust theory and measure of social presence: Review and suggested criteria. Presence: Teleoperators & Virtual Environments 12(5), 456–480 (2003)
2. Bovee, C., Thill, J.: Business communication today. Prentice Hall, Englewood Cliffs (2000)
3. Doering, N., Poeschl, S.: Nonverbal cues in mobile phone text messages: The effects of chronemics and proxemics. Paper presented at Annual Meeting of International Communication Association Conference, San Francisco, CA (2007)
4. Ekman, P.: Facial Expression and Emotion. American Psychologist 48, 384–392 (1993)
5. Hall, J.A.: Womenís and menís nonverbal communication. In: Manusov, V., Patterson, M.L. (eds.) The Sage Handbook of Nonverbal Communication, pp. 201–218. Sage Publications, Thousand Oaks (2006)
6. Ma, C., Prendinger, H., Ishizuka, M.: Emotion Estimation and Reasoning Based on Affective Textual Interaction. In: Tao, J., Tan, T., Picard, R.W. (eds.) ACII 2005. LNCS, vol. 3784, pp. 622–628. Springer, Heidelberg (2005)
7. Neviarouskaya, A., Prendinger, H., Ishizuka, M.: Textual Affect Sensing for Sociable and Expressive Online Communication. In: Paiva, A.C.R., Prada, R., Picard, R.W. (eds.) ACII 2007. LNCS, vol. 4738, pp. 218–229. Springer, Heidelberg (2007)
8. Picard, R.W.: Affective computing. MIT Press, Boston (1997)
9. Walther, J.B.: Virtual dialogs: Relational communication in chat reference encounters. Paper Presented at Annual Meeting of International Communication Association Conference, New York, NY (2005)

A Preliminary Study of Relation Induction between HTML Tag Set and User Experience

Azusa Nakano[1], Asato Tanaka[1], and Masanori Akiyoshi[2]

[1] Faculty of Applied Information Science, Hiroshima Institute of Technology, 2-1-1 Miyake, Saeki-ku, Hiroshima, Hiroshima 731-5193, Japan
[2] Faculty of Engineering, Kanagawa University, 3-27-1 Rokkakubashi, Kanagawa-ku, Yokohama, Kanagawa 221-8686, Japan

Abstract. This paper addresses a preliminary study for relation identification between the HTML tag set and user experience. Today's Web technologies such as "HTML5" and "Ajax" enable content providers to design rich Web pages, sometimes complicated and not ease-of-use. On the other hand, "user experience" is getting more and more significant as everyone from young to elder people uses the Web. The design principle seems not to be established from "user experience" viewpoints, because it includes user practical activities. Therefore our approach is to collect user operations and user impressions as to the target Web pages, then induce relation between user impression and such collected data by mining technologies. This paper reports a preliminary experimental results towards such systematic analysis.

Keywords: Web interface, user experience, relation induction.

1 Introduction

This paper addresses a preliminary study for relation identification between the HTML tag set and user experience, which is considered to be difficult to identify simply by analyzing the collected user enquete as to Web design. Web design is drastically changing along with related technologies, for instance, "HTML5", "Ajax" and so forth. Moreover "user experience" includes a user's practical activities as indicated in the term, which seems to be slightly different from user impression. This means that the design guideline is complex so that it considers concrete user operations and evaluation.

We here address the systematic approach towards the Web design evaluation from "user experience" viewpoints. To achieve this goal, we introduce mining function approach to identify relation between the HTML tag set and user experience. As to "user experience", a user's operations such as "mouse move", "mouse scroll" and "mouse over" on the browser screen and "mouse click" on the hyper link are stored with time stamp, and his/her impression concerning the target Web pages is collected by enquete including several aspects of Web design and usability. If we could identify some sequential mouse operations as patterns, this may indicate specific features for "user experience". Also we focus

M. Kurosu (Ed.): Human-Computer Interaction, Part III, HCII 2014, LNCS 8512, pp. 49–56, 2014.

on enquete from subjective evaluation as to this specific features. Then relation identification will be systematically done by association rule mining between these two data set.

Based on the above-mentioned approach, this paper describes entire framework for this systematic identification and preliminary experimental results by using data collection system and executing a sequential pattern mining technique. Section 2 describes previous research on this field. Section 3 describes the framework for relation identification between the HTML tag set and user experience. Section 4 describes results on data collection and sequential pattern mining. Section 5 describes the findings and future work.

2 Related Work

Usability is argued from various viewpoints such as psychology, system functionality, user performance and so forth. The work in [1] reports the experimental results when executing task-based usability testing and guideline-base inspection as to the broad-reach Web portals. The paper tries to clarify the result of consistency along with the testing and inspection, using questionnaire-based data, but does not handle the concrete operational data concerning the target interface. From a user viewpoints to design the Web interface, the work in [2] discusses the interface from "semiotics" viewpoints and makes re-design of Web signs, which mainly handle the static design under "semiotics". This approach is slightly different from "user experience" aspect that we focus. The work in [3] directly handles "user experience" aspect when a user executes information search on the Web, which implements interactivity-oriented interfaces for the search. This indicates interactiveness provides effective and convenient way to a user, but limits to the keyword search task. The work in [4] discusses more closely as "user experience" from emotional aspects of Web design. Of course a user emotional is significant that affects "user experience", but mostly focuses on the guideline evaluation.

3 Relation Induction Framework

3.1 Proposed Framework

As mentioned in Section 1, our proposed relation induction framework utilizes user operational log and subjective evaluation on the Web interface. Fig. 1 indicates the overview of our proposed framework, which consists of "data collection system" and "data mining system".

The "data collection system" collects minute user operations for executing pre-defined task and enquete after accomplishing the task. The "data mining system" includes two mining subsystems; one is a sequential pattern mining and the other is an association rule mining.

The requirement of "data collection system" is to collect user operations on the Web page without being aware of it. So it should be embedded ordinary

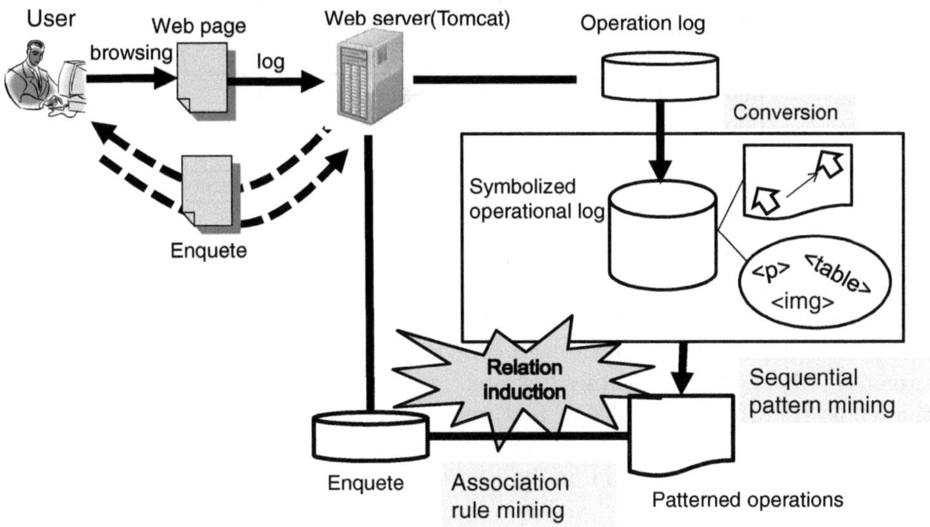

Fig. 1. Overview of Relation Induction Framework

Web browser to monitor and record the operations. Also the requirement of "data mining system" is to derive interpretative relationship between the HTML tag set and user evaluation. The HTML tag set is mostly categorized into two; one is structural tags and appearance tags. The former are tags for "itemization", "hyper link", "table" and so forth. The latter are tags for "colorization", "font", "layout" and so forth, which are basically recommended to use "⟨span⟩" in "HTML5". From capturing user operation viewpoints, the structural tags are seem to be significant, since those correspond to target components of user operations on the Web pages. Then our "data mining system" focuses on structural tags.

3.2 Data Collection System

Table 1 shows log items with time stamps; "mouse move" that are mouse x-y position, "mouse scroll" that is scrolling increment, "mouse click" that is operated on the hyper links, and "mouse over" on HTML tags that correspond to the Web components for the target task. Popular target tasks when a user uses Web pages are considered to be as follows; "information search " and "goods ordering". "Information search" means the situation that a user needs to know something and search information under browsing. "goods ordering" involves some procedures after deciding buying goods, for instance, input a user name and address, choose a payment method, designate the delivery time and so forth. Since we think the latter has less flexible operations than the former and the evaluation related to the former task indicates wide variety, we simply focus on the relation induction towards "information search" task.

Table 1. Log Items using Mouse Event

Type of mouse event	Collected data
mouse move	x position and y position
mouse scroll	vertical increment
mouse click	target url
mouse over	target tag in the HTML source

The Web browser strictly limits the local access to storage resources such as HDD, so our system sends whole log data to the server by using Ajax technology. Fig. 2 shows the procedure of this data transferring, a part of Javascript code and collected data. To use Javascript code including Ajax, we need to modify the target HTML source for adding "⟨script⟩" tag. Therefore our system downloads the whole HTML related files at first and inserts the "⟨script⟩" tag.

As indicated in Fig. 2, the actual collected log data using "!" as delimiter involves a user operations on one page as one line "string" data. Time stamps represent UTC.

3.3 Data Mining System

Characterizing Mouse Move. The time-series data of mouse events and transitions among Web pages are analyzed by using a sequential data mining technique, which induces a certain patterned user operation. To apply this mining, our system first converts relative mouse positions into absolute positions to identify mouse move such as "upward". Fig. 3 shows this conversion and the following fomula denotes this calculation where y_i^{abs} does absolute i-th y position, y_i^{rel} does relative i-th y position, and y_k^{scroll} does k-th vertical scroll increment.

$$y_i^{abs} = y_i^{rel} + \sum_{k=1}^{i} y_k^{scroll}$$

Mouse move notation such as "upward" is necessary to extract patterns by sequential pattern mining. So we set eight directional mouse move notation as shown in Fig. 4. At this point, we do not discriminate the mouse move among the same directions, that is, ignoring the amount of pixel move, for instance, 10 pixel downward and 100 pixel downward are considered to be the same notation "downward". The symbolized mouse moves are given to numbers as indicated in Fig. 4.

Extracting Mouse Patterns. The purpose of pattern mining is to extract a certain set of mouse operations embedded in when looking into one Web page and a certain set of transitions embedded in when traversing among several Web pages. The former is more significant because when searching information in the Web page, such specific operations may reflect users impression after finishing the browsing tasks. Of course the latter may also reflect users impression, especially whole evaluation-related impression. It is slightly easy to identify the latter, because a user actions towards links embedded in the Web page are mostly common under given tasks. Therefore this paper focuses on the former when users browse one Web page.

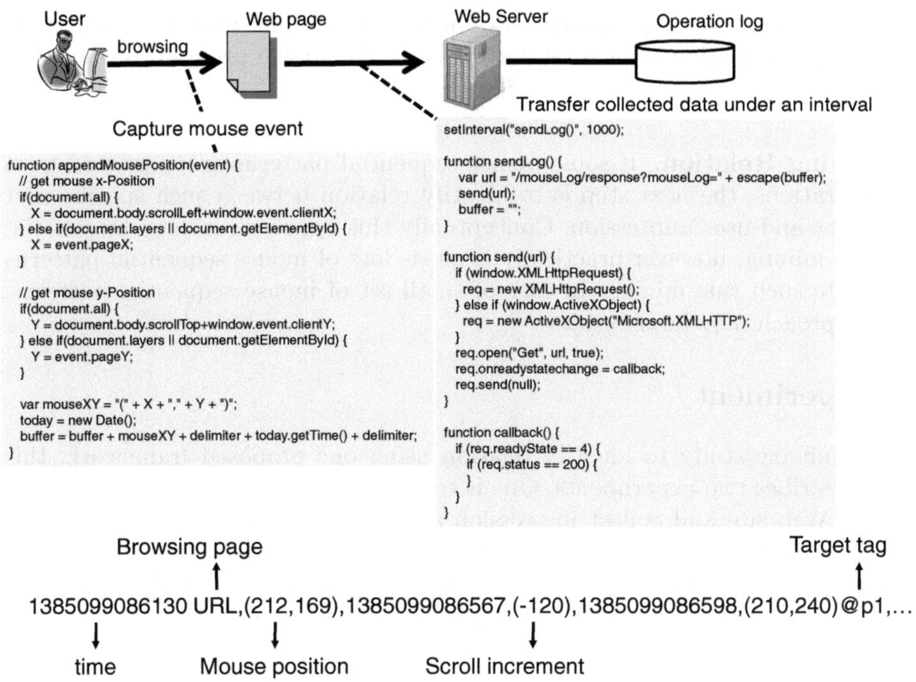

Fig. 2. Data Collection System Procedure

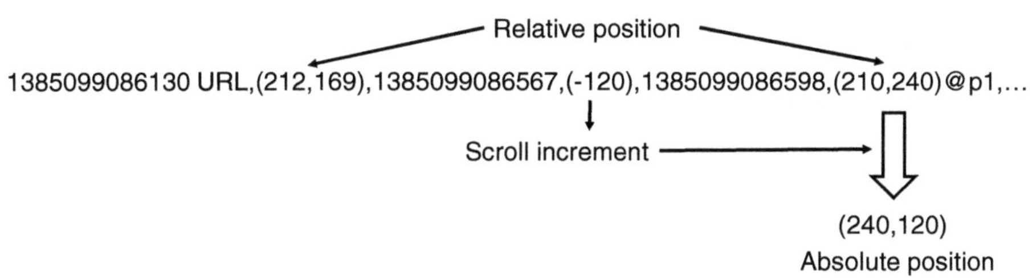

Fig. 3. Mouse Position Conversion

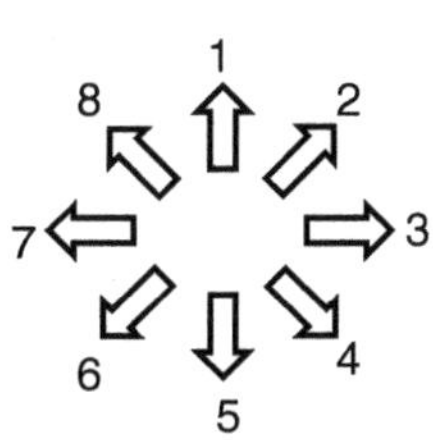

Fig. 4. Symbolized Mouse Move

There exist several sequential pattern mining algorithms, and our requirement is to extract adjoining sequential patterns exactly, so the program proposed in [5] is used.

Identifying Relation. If some mouse sequential patterns are extracted from user operations, the next step is to identify relation between such specific user operations and user impression. Conceptually this approach is done by association rule mining, however practically it needs lots of mouse sequential patterns to execute such rule mining. In case of small set of mouse sequential patterns, other approach may be necessary.

4 Experiment

As preliminary study to identify relation using our proposed framework, this paper describes two experiments. One is to use three Web sites with three tasks for each Web site and collect impression after finishing each site. The other is to use one Web sites with three tasks for each Web site and collect impressions after each task. Figure 5 shows one sample screenshot of experimental Web pages; Guide for graduate school entrance examination, which is used in both experiments. As indicated in Figure 5, this Web page has "⟨p⟩" HTML tag to depict some information. So after downloading this Web site entirely, target component IDs in the Web page are set.

Tasks set for this Web page are to grasp "[task1] difference between undergraduate school and graduate school", "[task2]subjects of entrance examination" and "[task3]how to study for entrance examination". The questions in enquete are as follows with "yes/no" response.

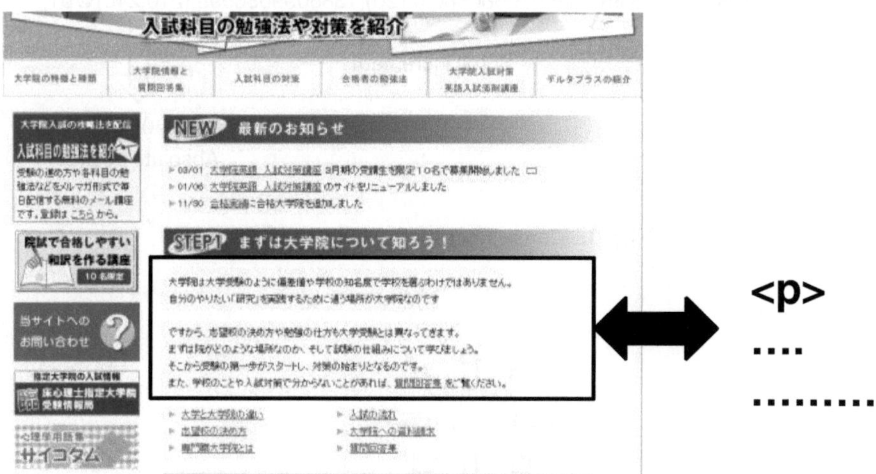

Fig. 5. Screenshot of Experimental Web Page

Q1: Do you feel the unity concerning "color" and "design" ?
Q2: Do you feel ease-of-use appearance concerning "menu", "character(font)", "graphics" ?
Q3: Do you collect information you look for ?
Q4: What do you think is hard to understand in this Web page ?
Q5: Do you feel sense of intimacy ?

Seven testers browse the three Web sites for the experiment 1, and nine testers do the one Web site for the experiment 2. The following are results on the common Web site "Guide for graduate school entrance examination" in both experiments

In the experiment 1, there exists mouse move pattern " $\Rightarrow$, $\Uparrow$, $\Downarrow$, $\Uparrow$ ". Table 2 shows the number of "yes" from the enquete.

Table 2. Question and response number

question	number of "yes"
Q1: ... the unity ...	7
Q2: ... ease-of-use appearance ...	6
Q3: ... collect informaton ...	5
Q4: ... hard to understand ...	5
Q3: ... sens of intimacy ...	3

In the experiment 2, there exist mouse move patterns as indicated in Table 3.

Table 3. Sequential patterns in each task

task	mouse pattern
difference between undergraduate school and graduate school	$\Downarrow$, $\Rightarrow$, $\Downarrow$
subjects of entarance examination	$\Rightarrow$, $\Downarrow$, $\Rightarrow$
how to study for entrance examination	$\Rightarrow$, $\Uparrow$, $\Downarrow$

Table 4 shows the number of "yes" from the enquete.

Table 4. Question and response number in each task

question	number of "yes"		
	task1	task2	task3
Q1: ... the unity ...	9	8	8
Q2: ... ease-of-use appearance ...	7	7	7
Q3: ... collect informaton ...	4	0	2
Q4: ... hard to understand ...	4	6	4
Q5: ... sens of intimacy ...	1	1	1

As indicated in the results of sequential pattern mining towards mouse operations, we can get simple mouse move pattern that cannot explicitly relate to a certain meaningful move operation. This is caused by one reason that symbolized mouse move notations are generated under ignoring amount of pixel move. For instance, "downward" notations differ between the displayed page a user can gaze at a glance and the scrolled page. Other reasons are still under investigation.

5 Summary

This paper report a preliminary study for induction of relation between HTML tag set and user experience, which uses a user concrete mouse operations by capturing mouse events and corresponding HTML tag of "mouse over". The experimental results using actual Web pages show the problems to be tackled for applying mining techniques. In addition to mouse operations, a user eye movement needs to be added to capture a user intentional operations.

References

1. Granic, A., Mitrovic, I., Marangunic, N.: Usability evaluation of web portals. In: 30th International Conference on Information Technology Interfaces(ITI 2008), pp. 427–432 (2008)
2. Islam, M.N.: Towards Designing Users' Intuitive Web Interface. In: Sixth International Conference on Complex, Intelligent and Software Intensive Systems (CISIS), pp. 513–518 (2012)
3. Jianquan, L., Hanxiong, C., Furuse, K., Ohbo, N.: Using an interactive interface to support Web search for improving user experience. In: First International Conference on the Applications of Digital Information and Web Technologies(ICADIWT 2008), pp. 210–215 (2008)
4. Hussin, S.N., Mohd Lokman, A.: Kansei website interface design: Practicality and accuracy of Kansei Web Design Guideline. In: International Conference on User Science and Engineering (i-USEr), pp. 30–35 (2011)
5. Hirate, Y., Yamana, H.: Generalized Sequential Pattern Mining with Item Intervals Academy Publisher. Journal of Computers(JCP) 1(3), 51–60 (2006)

Analysis of Demographical Factors' Influence on Websites' Credibility Evaluation*

Maria Rafalak[1], Piotr Bilski[2], and Adam Wierzbicki[1]

[1] Polish-Japanese Institute of Information Technology, (PJIIT), Warsaw, Poland
[2] Institute of Radioelectronics, Warsaw University of Technology, Warsaw, Poland
{maria.rafalak,awierzbicki}@pjwstk.edu.pl,
pbilski@ire.pw.edu.pl

Abstract. The paper presents results of an experiment conducted in 2013 via Amazon Mechanical Turk Platform (www.mturk.com) aimed at creating a classifier predicting online content credibility evaluation misjudgement tendencies. The rough sets based module processes demographic variables describing each participant and predicts his/her misjudgement tendency. Data collection method, data-set preparation are described in detail. Next the rough set methodology is introduced explaining the process of training and validating using available data. Experimental results are presented in detail showing the classification accuracy for various configurations of rough-sets algorithms. The analysis of importance of subsequent demographic variables on prediction efficiency is discussed as well. The paper is concluded with future prospects and future applications of implemented methodology.

Keywords: Demographic variables, rough sets, classification, artificial intelligence, credibility assessment.

1 Introduction

Internet has undeniably become a vital part of our everyday lives. Among many versatile functions that it serves, probably the most important aspect of Internet use is the functionality of information search. Currently www technologies allow for free and simple content transfer between users. In *Web 2.0* paradigm, every user is the author of potentially important information. The credibility of such data is often dubious and should be treated with precaution. This also refers to the opinions and judgments made about the Internet content. The tendency to overestimate the web pages' credibility and usefulness of their information was discovered recently. There is the psychological effect causing better judgment (higher grades) than the page actually deserves. The examples are the online movie database (www.imdb.com), book community *Books Crossing*, music review systems or *Amazon* – online retailer [1]. The reason for this behaviour is unknown, but the bias, i.e. the constant shift towards the positive opinions was confirmed. People

* Research supported by the grant "Reconcile: Robust Online Credibility Evaluation of Web Content" from Switzerland through the Swiss Contribution to the enlarged European Union.

M. Kurosu (Ed.): Human-Computer Interaction, Part III, HCII 2014, LNCS 8512, pp. 57–68, 2014.

rarely verify information found online with other sources like books or newspapers [2, 3]. As the number of websites grows exponentially, the tool for distinguishing the relevant content from the unimportant one is required. The topic of this paper is the analysis of the websites assessment made by Internet users related to their demographic characteristics (such as age, sex, education, living location or political views). Based on these features the authors determine the users' tendency to over- or underestimate the credibility of selected websites.

1.1 Definition of Credibility

Credibility can be understood as a personal belief that certain piece of information can be trusted. It is worth noticing that using concept of truth is purposely avoided here. Adopted definition refers to subjective conviction of individual making judgment rather than construct of objective truth. Existence of the latter, from our point of view, remains in the sphere of philosophical inquiries.

Research trends dedicated to credibility of online content so far have concentrated on two big issues: technical characteristics of websites (such as i.e. design, functionality or thematic area) and individual differences of users. Such factors as familiarity with the topic [1, 2], the first impression effect [3,4] or preferred heuristics in making evaluations [5] are claimed to moderate final credibility judgments of online content.

Defining credibility evaluations as subjective implies that identical stimulus is likely to elicit different reactions depending on characteristics of a person making judgment. One of the recently most popular theoretical frameworks giving foundations for scientific investigation of credibility evaluations is *Prominence - Interpretation Theory* (*P-I*) proposed by Fogg [4]. In general, according to *P-I* final credibility evaluation depends heavily on particular elements user notices on the website (prominence) and the meaning he/she attaches to them (interpretation). Among the factors affecting *prominence* Fogg lists user's task, motivation, experience, type of website content (informational vs transactional) and individual differences (literacy level, cognitive abilities, psychological traits etc.). *Interpretation* depends on users' knowledge, assumptions, goals and context of making evaluation. The process of noticing website element and interpreting it has an iterative character of subjectively defined stop criterion and leads to formulating website's overall credibility evaluation.

Basing on factors influencing final judgments Fogg [4] distinguishes four types of credibility: *presumed*, *earned*, *reputed* and *surface credibility*.

Presumed credibility reflects general assumptions and stereotypes held in evaluator's mind i.e. those connected with site identifiers (.gov, .org, .edu, etc.). *Surface credibility* is connected with general impression about the website including its design, usability and presence of advertisements. *Earned credibility* refers to experience user has with the website including its responsiveness. Finally, *reputed credibility* stands for seals of approval, links to other reputed websites etc. This distinction is not disjunctive and which of those factors are taken into account by user depends strongly on individual differences.

1.2 Credibility Evaluation Aid

There are two main approaches of giving Internet users guidance about how to assess website credibility. The probably most intuitive way are checklists which are specially designed lists of statements, questions or phrases supposed to sensitize user on not credible content. One of the main advantages of this approach is teaching a habit to search for certain website elements that may suggest whether the source should be trusted. This method however is time consuming and requires some effort from user. Following tools may serve as an example of checklist approach: *University of Maryland Library checklist*[1] , *Berkeley checklist*[2], *Health On the Net*[3], *Widener University checklist*[4] and *Discern*[5].

Second option for giving users clues about credibility of online content bases on crowdsourcing approach. Recommender or rating systems gather votes from websites' reviewers and combine them into a credibility rating. Users registered in such systems are able to vote and view websites ratings. This approach does not consume user's time unless they wants to make a contribution. Following tools may serve as an example of crowdsourcing approach: *ReConcile*[6], *MyWot*[7], *Factlink*[8], *Hypothes.is*[9].

1.3 Positive Bias in Credibility Evaluations

Adopting crowdsourcing approach in website credibility estimation is not free of drawbacks. It has been noted that wisdom of crowd can sometimes lead to overenthusiastic credibility evaluations. Vassilis Kostakos [6] in his paper showed that rating systems of such popular online services like *Amazon*, *BooksCrossing* or *Imdb* are negatively skewed. The same pattern has been distinguished in restaurant [7] or music review systems [8]. As opposed to online auction systems giving reviews does not imply any reciprocity. This is why phenomenon of overenthusiastic positive evaluation in this context cannot be explained in terms of strategic reasoning as suggested by [9]. The mechanism explaining users' online behaviour is yet to be determined.

1.4 Our Study General Idea

Studying credibility evaluations is a challenging task as by definition the construct is subjective and easily influenced by many factors. Polish-Japanese Institute of Technology is currently working on creating an online platform (www.reconcile.pl) that

---

[1] http://www.lib.umd.edu/binaries/content/assets/public/usereducation/evaluating-web-sites-checklist-form-fall-2012.pdf

[2] http://www.lib.berkeley.edu/TeachingLib/Guides/Internet/EvalForm.pdf

[3] http://www.hon.ch/

[4] http://www.widener.edu/about/campusresources/wolfgram library/evaluate/original.aspx

[5] http://www.discern.org.uk/

[6] http:// www.reconcile.pl

[7] https://www.mywot.com/

[8] https://factlink.com/

[9] http://hypothes.is/

would support evaluation of web content. This system is designed to take into account both credibility evaluations of registered users and websites' characteristics. However, it is feared that specific misjudgement tendencies presented by the users (i.e. positive bias) may reduce the effectiveness of credibility estimations given by the system. In order to avoid such effect we aspire to create a mechanism that would identify users with tendencies to overestimate or underestimate websites' credibility and in the future enable to correct their votes in the reconcile system.

We hypothesize that individual differences which according to Fogg's *P-I theory* [4] determine prominence of particular website elements and influence credibility evaluation, may be connected with demographic background of users. Demographic variables such as sex, age or education are easily accessible in many systems as they usually need to be defined in registration forms. Therefore proving the usability of demographic data in predicting specific credibility misjudgement tendencies would be beneficial not only for *reconcile* project but for all automated systems designed to aid credibility evaluations.

2 Experiment Design

Experiment was conducted via *Amazon Mechanical Turk* online platform (www.mturk.com) in the first quarter of 2013. Participants were asked to evaluate credibility of presented websites on five point Likert scale (where 1-very poor, 5-very high). Websites were assigned to participants at random. Every participant could decide how many websites he/she wanted to evaluate, getting monetary reward for every vote (0.35-0.55 /evaluation, depending individual total evaluation number). In order to eliminate the effect of websites' design on credibility evaluations we decided to create big website corpus so that individual characteristics of websites' could be neglected in final data analysis. Websites selected for the experiment (N = 4699) represented five broad topics: 'medicine', 'personal finance', 'healthy lifestyle', 'politics, economy, ecology', 'entertainment'. Websites' external credibility index (www.mywot.com) was monitored. The index can take values from 0-100 range. Mean reference credibility index in the experiment website corpus was 72.

Participants were recruited from registered mTurk American users with at least 75% approved assignments. Apart from giving credibility evaluations they shared some basic demographic information including: sex, birth year, education, political views, state of residence, and wage level.

We decided to use artificial intelligence method, namely rough sets, to build a classifier aimed at predicting specific misjudgement tendencies.

3 Data-Set Preparation

Over two thousand mTurk users (N = 2075) took part in our study (986 males, 1419 females). Median age of participants was 27 (minimum age 16, maximum age 90). On average every person evaluated three websites.

In order to prepare data-set to the rough set analysis the following steps have been applied to the original dataset. As the reference website credibility index (www.mywot.com) varies from 0 to 100 the distribution of websites' reference credibility has been transformed to standardized distribution ($M = 0$; $SD = 1$).

According to the experiment design every participant evaluated declared number of randomly assigned websites. Therefore for every person we calculated median of evaluations given on five point Likert scale. Next we transformed this distribution of median values to standardized distribution ($M = 0$; $SD = 1$).

For every *website-participant* pair we calculated the following difference:

$$\textit{standardised median evaluation of person} - \textit{standardised credibility index} .$$

For every participant we calculated median of the abovementioned difference. After examining the distribution of those median values we assigned respondents to three distinct categories: *under-raters* (*UR*; showing tendency to underestimate websites' credibility), *over-raters* (*OR*; showing tendency to overestimate websites' credibility), *average-raters* (*AR*; giving adequate judgments about websites' credibility). We arbitrarily decided that people obtaining scores below or equal the first quartile of the abovementioned distribution (Q_1 = - 0.944) were be classified as *under-raters* (*UR*; $N = 515$), people obtaining results over or equal third quartile (Q_3 = 0.859) were classified as *over-raters* (*OR*; $N = 1041$) and all other participants were qualified as *average-raters* (*AR*; $N = 519$). We chose such cut points in order to distinguish users with most extreme misjudgement tendencies.

4 Description of the Data Analysis Method

Rough Sets (*RS*) are the standard classification tool of large data sets, used widely in the biology [10a] and, financial [10,11] engineering [12] sciences. Their advantage is considering the measurement uncertainty (such as missing data or incorrect values of attributes), which is typical in real-world applications. As opposed to the classical theory of sets (where the object can belong to only one set), in *RS* it is possible to have objects belonging to multiple sets "in some degree", which expresses the complexity of real-world problems.

The basis for the analysis of data is the decision table, i.e. the structure $\boldsymbol{D_T}$, containing the information system $\boldsymbol{I_S}$ (1) supplemented with the information about the category of objects $\boldsymbol{d}$.

$$\boldsymbol{I_S} = (\boldsymbol{U}, \boldsymbol{A}) \tag{1}$$

It is the pair consisting of the set of objects **A** represented by their attributes (here demographic variables), while **U** is the universe, i.e. the set of all possible objects (Internet users).

This way the original data set, described in section 3, can be treated as $\boldsymbol{D_T}$ (2), where with objects are described by the *under-*, *average-* or *over-rater* category $\boldsymbol{d}$, based on the analysis presented in section 3.

$$\boldsymbol{D_T} = (\boldsymbol{I_S}, \cup \{d\}) = (\boldsymbol{U}, \boldsymbol{A} \cup \{d\}) \tag{2}$$

The *RS* operation uses the indiscernibility relation, findings groups of attributes describing examples, which makes objects non-distinguishable from each other. The equivalence relation between objects describes the redundancy existing in the decision table, which is the requirement for extracting knowledge from the available data.

The application of *RS* as the classification module requires extracting knowledge from the training data *L* and verification of the generalization abilities using the validating set *V*, both having the form (2). This approach falls into the supervised learning scheme, where the desired output *d* of the classification module for the selected set of input data is known. The *RS*-based module produces the classification hypothesis c for each object oi from *V*, which is confronted with *d*. It is crucial for *L* and *V* to be disjunctive, therefore each object (participant) should belong to only one set. The classification quality is measured by the following sample error es, calculating the fraction of incorrectly classified objects by the module with respect to the number of objects in *V*:

$$e_s(\mathbf{V}) = \frac{\left| o_i \in \mathbf{V} : d(o_i) \neq c(o_i) \right|}{|\mathbf{V}|} \cdot 100\% \tag{3}$$

The alternative measure of the classification quality, also used in our research, is the supplement 1-e_s(*V*). Because the *RS* algorithms are parameterized, the training process must be repeated multiple times for different configurations, until their optimal set (minimizing the error (3)) is found. The training of *RS* ad knowledge extraction operation is presented in Fig. 1. The subsequent operations are parameterized by vectors $\boldsymbol{p_d}$ (for discretization) and $\boldsymbol{p_r}$ (for reduction). Their content depends on the particular applied algorithm.

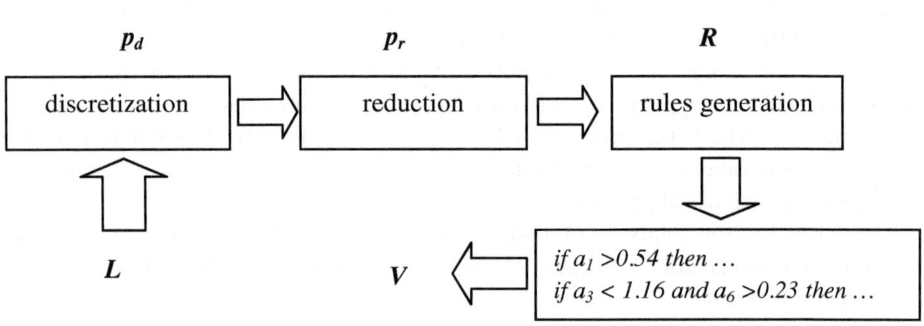

Fig. 1. Training scheme of the RS-based classification module

The following steps are implemented here:

1. Discretization of selected attributes from $\boldsymbol{D_T}$ to exchange their continuous values with the discrete numbers of intervals. The latter are described by the index of the attribute and threshold values. There are many discretization algorithms available, such as *Boolean Reasoning*, *Equal Frequency Binning* (*EFB*), *naive* or *semi-naive approaches*. It was proven in [13] that the discretization has the decisive impact on

the classification efficiency of *RS*, therefore the proper algorithm and its parameters have to be carefully selected. The characteristic feature of the demographic data is their discrete nature. Such attributes, as sex or level of education, have only a few different values, therefore are not suitable for this operation. The only attribute, which had to be discretized was the birth year of analysed participants. Although it is also discrete, the cardinality of its values range makes it quasi-continuous. The most important discretization parameter $\boldsymbol{p_d}$ is the number of intervals, dividing the continuous range of attribute values. In multiple applications *EFB* approach was considered the most useful, but the optimal number of intervals had to be selected heuristically. Other methods, especially naïve and semi-naïve algorithms generate too many intervals, leading to the classification deterioration, disregarding the reduction method.

2. Calculating reducts, i.e. the subsets $\boldsymbol{R}$ of attributes describing categories $\boldsymbol{d}$ as accurately as the whole information system. Because usually multiple reducts can be found in the set, it is desired to find as many of them as possible. The reduct is represented as the binary vector of the length equal to the number of attributes in $\boldsymbol{D_T}$ (1), with ones on the positions corresponding to the particular attributes. For example, the reduct containing attributes No. 2,3 and 5 (out of six) has the form:

$$\{0,1,1,0,1,0\}$$

   Searching for reducts is the *NP-hard* problem [14], therefore no exact algorithms can be used for this purpose. Instead, approximate methods are employed, which find as many reducts as possible in reasonable time. The most popular ones are *genetic*, *Johnson's* and *Holte's* algorithms, differing in the method of searching through the space of possible atrributes' combinations. Because the analyzed sets have six attributes, it is possible to generate all combinations using the exact approach. In our experiment we tested approximate methods as well. The parameters vector $\boldsymbol{p}_r$ refers mainly to the genetic reduction, where the size of the population, mutation and cross-over probability can be determined.

3. Generating rules. Based on the discrete reducts $\boldsymbol{R}$, all structures of the following form are created:

   If premises then decision

   The premises part contains the set of conditions that must be met by the particular attributes to fire (activate) the rule. As the consequence, the decision $\boldsymbol{c}$ about the object category is made. The conditions check if the value of the selected attribute is above or below the particular threshold, separating neighbouring intervals. The *RS* produce large sets, with hundreds or even thousands of rules.

4. The rules are next used to make decision about the category of users from **V**. The classification is based on the voting mechanism, with multiple rules pointing at the same category. During the analysis, each rule is analysed. If the premises part is fulfilled, the rule is fired. After analysing all rules in the set all activated are grouped according to the categories they point at. The category supported by the maximum number of active rules is the output of the *RS*-based module.

The scheme from Fig. 1 is repeated multiple times for various sets of parameters $\boldsymbol{p_d}$ and $\boldsymbol{p_r}$ in searching for the minimal value of $e_s(V)$ [15,16]. Also, the problem in our research was relatively small number of available objects (compared to the number of all Internet users). Therefore the division of all objects into the learning and testing set was of the great concern. To make sure the knowledge extracted during the training process would be useful in the analysis of new users, the cross-validation procedure was applied. It consists in repeated dividing the original data set into $\boldsymbol{L}$ and $\boldsymbol{V}$, training and validating the module for the subsequent versions and averaging the result. The *Repeated-Random Sub-Sampling Validation* (*RRSSV*) was used. The following steps were implemented:

1. Random selection of n objects (without replacement) from the set $\boldsymbol{D_T}$ (containing all available participants) and storing them in the set $\boldsymbol{V}$. Remaining examples form the set $\boldsymbol{L}$. Here n is determined to cut the predefined fraction of objects from $\boldsymbol{D_T}$. For instance, if there are 1500 users in $\boldsymbol{D_T}$, n can be set to 500. This way one third objects belongs to $\boldsymbol{V}$ and 1000 – to $\boldsymbol{L}$.
2. Training and validating the RS-based module using the scheme from Fig. 1.
3. Repeating the procedure from step 1 k times, creating different $\boldsymbol{L}$ and $\boldsymbol{V}$ from $\boldsymbol{D_T}$.
4. Calculation of the averaged sample error (or its supplement) as the mean of the n results.

The alternative to *RRSSV* is the *k*-Fold validation, which is susceptible to the position of objects in the original decision table, therefore was not used here. We implemented $n = 5$ repeats of the training/validating procedures, which is the compromise between the time of computations and the quality of results.

Although the cross-validation assumes the selection of objects from $\boldsymbol{D_T}$ to $\boldsymbol{L}$ and $\boldsymbol{V}$ with the uniform distribution, we decided to additionally implement the probabilities depending on the distribution of subsequent categories in the original data set. Because the number of average-rating people was assumed twice as high as the number of under- and over-rating, the chance of selecting the former to $\boldsymbol{V}$ was 0.5, while the latter – 0.25. In the experimental section both approaches are compared. This is justified if the assumed fraction of under- and over-rating users in the real world is the same as in the analysed set.

5 Experimental Results

Data processing was implemented using Rosetta software [17]. The tests of the *RS*-based module included optimization of discretization $\boldsymbol{p_d}$ and reduction $\boldsymbol{p_r}$ parameters to minimize the sample error $\boldsymbol{e_s}$. Also, the significance of the particular attributes for the distinguishing between the separate categories was checked. The mean classification accuracy (supplement to (3)) was below 50 percent, which reveals low correlation between the demographic variables and the evaluation of webpages by users. Probably introduction of psychological variables would increase the number of correct classifications. The method of selecting objects to $\boldsymbol{L}$ and $\boldsymbol{V}$ has strong impact on the results. The uniform distribution of objects gives about 40 percent accuracy, while the distribution reflecting the frequency of subsequent categories in $\boldsymbol{D_T}$ gives almost 48 percent. In contrast, the fully random category selection gives about 35 percent. The results for particular combinations of discretization /reduction algorithms are in Table 1. The abbreviation *US* stands for the *Uniform Selection* of objects to the validating set, while *NUS – Non-Uniform Selection.* Abbreviations *EFB9*, *EFB10*, *EFB12* stand for *equal frequency binning* discretisation of "birth year" variable into 9, 10 and 12 intervals respectively.

All discretization and reduction methods presented in section 4 were tested. Results confirm the conclusions from previous research [13] about the usefulness of particular methods. The most effective discretization approach is *EFB*, although the optimal number of intervals must be individually adjusted in each case. For the "birth year" attribute the number of intervals ensuring the best classification results varies between 8 and 12. The influence of the number of intervals on the outcome (assuming the genetic reduction) is in Fig. 2. Increasing the number of intervals increases the classification accuracy to some point, although their too large number leads to the similar effect as in the naïve discretization. Finding the optimal number of intervals is always the problem, requiring the repeated computations for the varying number of intervals.

Table 1. Classification accuracy for selected combinations of discretization/reduction algorithms

discretization / reduction	EFB9		EFB10		EFB12		Naive		Semi-naive	
CV Object selection	US	NUS	US	NUS	US	NUS	US	NUS	US	NUS
Genetic	38.31	46.26	40.0	45.57	40.48	47.50	39.27	45.30	31.08	37.18
Johnson	32.53	40.24	33.73	35.18	28.91	37.10	31.08	36.62	30.0	33.46
Holte	51.08	65.06	51.08	65.06	51.08	65.06	51.08	65.06	51.08	65.06

The optimal discretization/reduction combination is *EFB/genetic algorithm.* The *Holte's* reduction tends to generate majority of rules pointing at the most frequent category. Therefore although the percentage of correctly classified objects is not lower than for genetic and *Johnson*'s reduction, it can't be used in practice. Various values of genetic reduction (i.e. crossover and mutation probabilities and the population size) were tested. Crossover probability was tested in range between 30 and 80 percent. Mutation probability was between 0.05 and 0.3. Analysed population size varied from 50 to 200. No changes in parameters modified the results. Increasing them causes longer optimization time, but does not lead to the improvement of the classification efficiency. This means the algorithm quickly finds the optimal configuration, but no improvement is possible, even after expanding the search space and introducing more solutions analysed simultaneously. In any case, the genetic algorithm is still supreme over other methods.

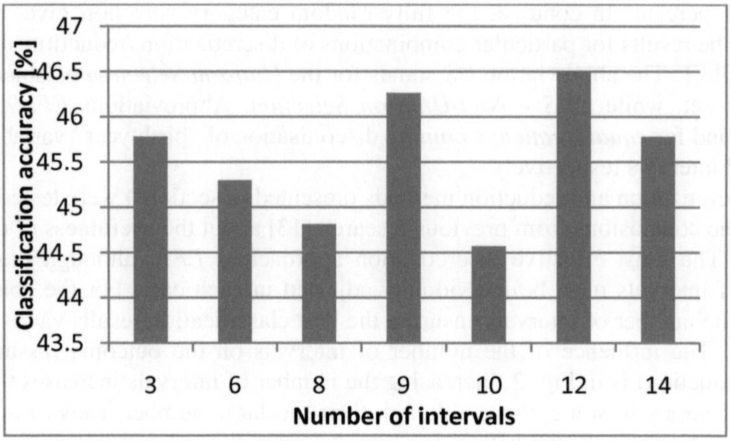

Fig. 2. Influence of the number of EFB intervals on the classification efficiency (genetic reduction, improved object selection for RRSSV)

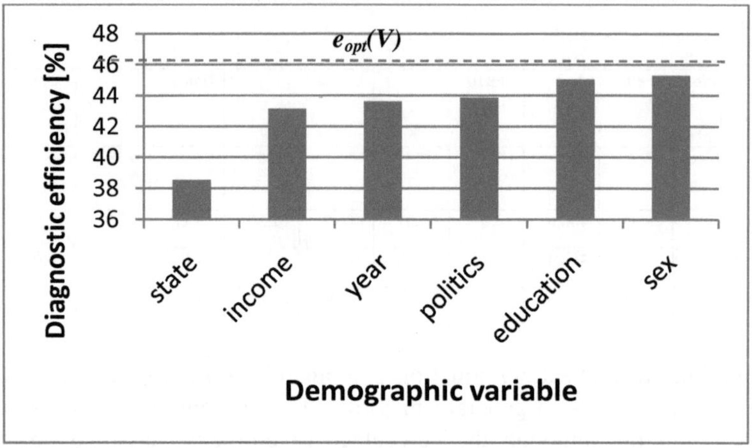

Fig. 3. Importance of the demographic variables for prediction of the user's web page credibility assessment

The mechanism of reducts generation allows for minimizing the number of attributes correlated with the categories. If the particular attribute is not present in any reduct, its elimination should not degrade the classification efficiency. All demographic variables appear to be important. The experiment consisted in eliminating the selected attribute from the set and checking the classification accuracy on the reduced table (using the genetic reduction method). Fig. 3 shows attributes in the descending order (the ones to the right being the least important). The greatest deterioration is for the set after eliminating the "state" attribute, while the smallest – for the "sex" variable. The dotted line determines value of the $e_{opt}(V)$, i.e. the maximum classification accuracy, obtained by the optimal combination of discretization and reduction methods.

6 Discussion

The rough set based prediction strongly depends on the applied discretization and reduction algorithms. Experiments show that finding dependencies between demographic variables and Internet user's tendency to *over*- or *under*-estimate webpage credibility is difficult. The obtained efficiency, although better than random category selection is still on unsatisfactory level. The solution to increase the classification accuracy would be the addition of psychological variables – probably better correlated with decision making presented in this paper. Also implemented strategy for the object selection to the validating set during the cross-validation gives promising results. However its usefulness is based on the assumption that category distribution in the analysed data-sets conforms to the actual distribution among Internet users. Results of conducted data analysis suggest that "education level" and "sex" are demographic variables most strongly influencing final results of *rough set* classifications of misjudgement tendencies in evaluating online content. We hypothesize that "education level" may be a factor connected with user's expertize, which strongly influences credibility evaluations [18]. It is likely that "education level" may be also connected with intelligence and in this sense have moderating effect on making judgements.

When it comes to "sex" we hypothesize that obtained result might indicate individual differences in psychological traits level. Differences between men and women in intensity of certain psychological traits is documented in literature. We suspect that level of risk taking [19, 20] or general trust [21] might be worth examining in the context of credibility evaluation in future studies. Therefore we prepare to replicate this study and include psychological measures together with expertise level. To sum up, application of artificial intelligence methods in the context of credibility evaluations so far have focused mainly on examining websites' characteristics. We suggest that in order to fully explain the phenomenon of trust in online content *human factor* should be included in such studies. In [22] it was shown that predicting personality traits from online behaviour (Facebook likes) can be successful. Using artificial intelligence methods to predict credibility evaluation misjudgement tendencies would be a powerful tool applicable in consumer studies or crowdsourcing systems.

References

1. Lucassen, T., Schraagen, M.: The inuence of source cues and topic familiarity on credibility evaluation. Computers in Human Behavior 29(4), 1387–1392 (2013)
2. Rimmer, T., Weaver, F.: Different questions, different answers? media use and media credibility. Journalism & Mass Communication Quarterly 64(1), 28–44 (1987)
3. Morris, M., Counts, S., Roseway, A., Ho, A., Schwarz, J.: Tweeting is believing?: understanding microblog credibility perceptions. In: Proceedings of the ACM 2012 Conference on Computer Supported Cooperative Work, pp. 441–450. ACM (2012)
4. Fogg, B.J.: Prominence-interpretation theory: explaining how people assess credibility online. In: CHI 2003 Extended Abstracts on Human Factors in Computing Systems, pp. 722–723 (2003)

5. Metzger, M., Flanagin, A., Medders, R.: Social and heuristic approaches to credibility evaluation online. Journal of Communication 60(3), 413–439 (2010)
6. Kostakos, V.: Is the crowd's wisdom biased? a quantitative analysis of three online communities. In: Computational Science and Engineering International Conference, vol. 4, pp. 251–255. IEEE (2009)
7. Weijia, D., Jin, G., Lee, J., Luca, M.: Optimal Aggregation of Consumer Ratings: An Application to Yelp.com. Harvard Business School Working Paper 13, 42 (2012)
8. Salganik, M.J., Dodds, P.S., Watts, D.J.: Experimental Study of Inequality and Unpredictability in an Artificial Cultural Market. Science 311(5762), 854–856 (2006)
9. Bolton, G., Greiner, B., Ockenfels, A.: Engineering trust: reciprocity in the production of reputation information. Management Science 59(2), 265–285 (2013)
10. Hvidsten, T.R., Komorowski, J.: Rough Sets in Bioinformatics. In: Peters, J.F., Skowron, A., Marek, V.W., Orłowska, E., Słowiński, R., Ziarko, W.P. (eds.) Transactions on Rough Sets VII. LNCS, vol. 4400, pp. 225–243. Springer, Heidelberg (2007)
11. Tay, E.H., Shen, L.: Economic and Financial Prediction Using Rough Sets Model. European Journal of Operational Research 141(3), 641–659 (2002)
12. Sikora, M., Sikora, B.: Rough Natural Hazards Monitoring, Rough Sets: Selected Methods and Applications in Management and Engineering. In: Advanced Information and Knowledge Processing, pp. 163–179 (2012)
13. Bilski, P., Wojciechowski, J.: Rough-Sets-Based Reduction for Analog Systems Diagnostics. IEEE Transactions on Instrumentation and Measurement 60(3), 880–890 (2011)
14. Tan, S., Cheng, X., Xu, H.: An Efficient Global Optimization Approach for Rough Set Based Dimensionalty Reduction. International Journal of Innovative Computing, Information and Control 3(3), 725–736 (2007)
15. Pawlak, Z.: Rough sets. International Journal of Parallel Programming 11(5), 341–356 (1982)
16. Pawlak, Z., Grzymala-Busse, J., Slowinski, R., Ziarko, W.: Rough Sets. Communications of the ACM 38–11, 88–95 (1995)
17. Öhrn, A., Komorowski, J.: ROSETTA: a rough set toolkit for analysis of data. In: Proceedings of the Third Joint Annual Conference on Information Sciences, Durham, NC, pp. 403–407 (1997)
18. Metzger, M., Flanagin, A.: Credibility and trust of information in online environments: The use of cognitive heuristics. Journal of Pragmatics 59, 210–220 (2013)
19. Jianakoplos, N., Bernasek, A.: Are women more risk averse? Economic Inquiry 36, 620–630 (1998)
20. Dwyera, P., Gilkesonb, J., List, J.: Gender differences in revealed risk taking: evidence from mutual fund investors. Economics Letters 76(2), 151–158 (2002)
21. Buchana, N., Crosonb, R., Solnickc, S.: Trust and gender: An examination of behavior and beliefs in the Investment Game. Journal of Economic Behavior & Organization 68(3-4), 466–476 (2008)
22. Kosinski, M., Stillwell, D.J., Graepel, T.: Private traits and attributes are predictable from digital records of human behavior. Proceedings of the National Academy of Sciences (PNAS) (2013)

Drivers for the Actual Usage of Cloud Services: An Examination of Influencing Factors for Digital Natives

Mark Stieninger and Dietmar Nedbal

University of Applied Sciences Upper Austria, Steyr, Austria
{mark.stieninger,dietmar.nedbal}@fh-steyr.at

Abstract. Cloud Computing has been gaining significant relevance throughout the business as well as the private environment. With several factors responsible for this adoption, this paper explores the influence of the perceived usefulness, perceived ease of use, trust, costs and age on the actual usage of Cloud services. The focus is set on the group of digital natives whereat attitudinal differences amongst them are examined in a survey. Correlation analyses show that the factors perceived usefulness, perceived ease of use, trust and age influence the actual usage of Cloud services, whereas the factor costs has no statistically significant relationship with the actual usage.

Keywords: Cloud Computing, cloud services, digital natives, technology acceptance model, influencing factors, technology adoption.

1 Introduction

For the last couple of years Cloud Computing has been one of the fastest growing business segments of the IT industry [1, 2]. Areas of application can be found both in the business and in the private environment. For companies it is becoming more and more crucial to keep costs low to remain competitive in the globalized economy. As the ratio of IT expenditures plays a vital role, the investigation of novel opportunities to lower them is of high interest for them. Cloud Computing is one of those opportunities [3, 4]. The increasing adoption of Cloud Computing is also reflected in revenues gained by Cloud Service Providers (CSPs) [5]. Nevertheless, the attitude towards Cloud Computing among companies as well as individuals is still quite divergent. According to a recent study, the number of supporters and opponents is growing in a comparable way. The waverers are taking up position little by little, likewise on both sides [6]. The reasons for this are manifold and the influencing factors are still subject of investigation in both research and economy [7]. One of the factors influencing the individual's attitude towards Cloud Computing might derive from the gap regarding accessibility and skills to use these technologies, the so-called "digital divide" [8]. This leads to the situation that individuals who grew up in the digital age and use these technologies in their daily life are often more technologically adept [9].

M. Kurosu (Ed.): Human-Computer Interaction, Part III, HCII 2014, LNCS 8512, pp. 69–79, 2014.

Within this paper the authors focus on the investigation of influencing factors for the actual usage of Cloud services among people who grew up in the digital age, termed as the "digital natives" [10]. The research objective was to examine the attitudes of individuals within this age group towards the use of Cloud Computing services under consideration of their age and several other factors.

The remainder of this paper is arranged as follows: Section two deals with the clarification of essential terms used within the paper to establish a consistent understanding. Section three outlines the research methodology leading to the conduction of a survey. Section four covers the results of the survey and discusses the findings. Finally, the paper is concluded in section five.

2 Definition of Key Terms

This section provides an overview of the key terms which is dealt with in this paper in order to establish a consistent understanding. The focus is set on the more recent and complex terms Cloud Computing, followed by the concept of the digital divide and the related terms digital natives and digital immigrants.

2.1 Cloud Computing

Both academic and applied research provide a variety of definitions for Cloud Computing [11, 12]. The definition provided by Mell and Grance from the National Institute of Standards and Technology (the so-called NIST definition) [13] is the most popular one which most other definitions refer to [11]. According to the NIST definition, "*Cloud computing is a model for enabling ubiquitous, convenient, on-demand network access to a shared pool of configurable computing resources (e.g., networks, servers, storage, applications, and services) that can be rapidly provisioned and released with minimal management effort or service provider interaction. This cloud model is composed of five essential characteristics, three service models, and four deployment models.*" [13] The first mentioned essential characteristics are:

- *on-demand self-service*: automatic provision of computing capabilities
- *broad network access*: services are provided over the network and available for different platforms
- *resource pooling*: dynamic allocation of services from a shared pool for multiple tenants
- *rapid elasticity*: rapid or even automatic provisioning and releasing of resources depending on the actual demand
- *measured service*: automatic management and monitoring of resource usage by consumer and provider

The three types of service models are [13]:

- *Software as a Service (SaaS)*: applications and software are provided.
- *Platform as a Service (PaaS)*: basic infrastructure is provided, including an operating system
- *Infrastructure as a Service (IaaS)*: basic hardware and networking resources are provided.

The NIST definition furthermore recognizes the following deployment models [13]:

- *private cloud*: the provided services are exclusively available for one organization.
- *community cloud*: exclusive allocation of services to a defined group of users.
- *public cloud*: services are provided for general public.
- *hybrid cloud*: a combination of two or more of the other models which work independently but are connected to enable portability of data, applications etc.

Even though further aspects have been identified in literature [11, 12], the NIST definition is considered as sufficient and accurate enough to provide a common understanding of the term Cloud Computing in the context of this paper.

2.2 Digital Divide, Digital Natives and Digital Immigrants

In the digital age the use of information technology (IT) is increasingly a basic requirement for access to all kind of information and for participation in social and economic life. The term "digital divide" hereby describes "*the perceived disadvantage of those who either are unable or do not choose to make use of these technologies in their daily life*" [8]. Discussions about the digital divide, its background and its impact are taking place in political as well as in academic communities [14]. A digital divide can emerge from different origins like:

- the gap between industrialized countries and developing countries [15]
- the gap between rich and poor countries [16]
- the gap between individuals, households, businesses and geographic areas at different socio-economic levels with regard to both opportunities to access IT and their use of the internet for a wide variety of activities [17]
- the disparity in access across classifications of race, gender, age, income and education to telephone, personal computers and the internet [18]
- the gap between the media-savvy, multitasking younger Web 2.0 generation and others that need to familiarize themselves with these technologies, also called the Digital Divide 2.0 [19].

Another approach for a conceptualization of the digital divide is the differentiation between *digital access divide*, *digital skill and use divide* and *digital outcome divide*, each of them divisible into the three levels individual, organizational and global [20, 21].

As this brief literature review has shown, there exist multiple definitions and forms of digital divides. For the purpose of this research the focus is on the disparity in access across individuals of different ages which are roughly defined as digital natives and digital immigrants. This paper examines amongst others the factor *age* as a possible reason for differences in the actual usage of Cloud services. These age groups are commonly split into the digital natives and the digital immigrants. Digital natives are defined as people who were born into the digital age, after 1980, and therefore grew up having access to networked digital technologies and strong computer skills and knowledge [10, 22]. Digital immigrants are defined as people who were born before 1980 and therefore came in contact with digital technologies later in their lives [22]. The classification into these two groups has also been subject of criticism. Wang et al. for example suggest the application of "*a continuum rather than a rigid dichotomy between digital natives and digital immigrants*" [14]. Within this paper the authors investigate particularly the group of digital natives.

3 Research Methodology

The modus operandi of the undertaken investigation comprised four main steps. (i) In the first step suitable factors influencing the actual usage of Cloud services were identified. The factors *perceived usefulness, perceived ease of use, trust* and *costs* as well as *age* were chosen for examination. (ii) Five hypotheses aiming at the before mentioned factors were formulated. (iii) A quantitative survey was carried out to test these hypotheses. (iv) The data gained from the survey was subject to correlation analyses followed by an interpretation of the results.

3.1 Influencing Factors

Well established theories on the adoption of technological innovations formed the basis for identifying influencing factors on the usage of Cloud services. For the context of this research, factors from the perspective of the individual's perception were of primary interest. For this reason the two main factors *perceived ease of use* and *perceived usefulness* provided by Davis' Technology Acceptance Model [23] were selected. Davis' model illustrates factors influencing the behavior of individuals towards novel technologies. The chain of factors starts with the external stimulus *system design features* which influences the cognitive responses *perceived ease of use* and *perceived usefulness*. It is these two factors which directly influence the affective response *attitude towards using* and thereby the behavioral response *actual system use*. Additionally, the factors *trust* and *costs* are subject of investigation as they also were already identified as important factors concerning the adoption of Cloud Computing [7]. Finally, as already mentioned, the research also examined the *age* as a driver for the adoption of Cloud services.

3.2 Formulation of Hypotheses

In the second step of the investigation five hypotheses were formulated addressing the five factors *perceived usefulness*, *perceived ease of use*, *trust*, *costs* and *age*:

1. The greater the perceived usefulness of Cloud services, the higher their actual usage.
2. The greater the perceived ease of use of Cloud services, the higher their actual usage.
3. The greater the trust in Cloud services, the higher their actual usage.
4. The higher the costs involved in using Cloud services, the lower their actual usage.
5. The younger the individual, the more likely is the actual usage of Cloud services.

These five hypotheses were the main subject of examination within the subsequent survey.

3.3 Testing of Hypotheses and Conduction of the Survey

In order to test the hypotheses a quantitative survey was conducted. To measure the factors several questions were formulated. These predefined questions were included into a tool for online surveys (SoSci Survey). The invitation link was spread via e-mail and additionally via social media among the Austrian population. The survey was executed in German language and open for the period of 10 days (Aug. 18-28, 2013). Limiting its scope to the Austrian population helped to avoid interfering influences for example from geographical or cultural factors which could have appeared by broadening the target group. In the course of the survey a total of 32 questions were asked, two of which aiming at hypothesis H1 [u1, u2], four of which aiming at hypothesis H2 [e1-e4], two aiming at H3 [t1, t2], two aiming at H4 [c1, c2] and one question aiming at H5 [a1]. Further questions were asked concerning the general attitude towards technology, availability and image. The following questions were asked concerning the particular hypotheses:

- [u1] Are Dropbox, Google Docs, iCloud or similar services useful or could they be useful for your daily tasks? (H1)
- [u2] Do you think that Cloud services are able to increase your performance in a certain task? (H1)
- [e1] Storing data in the Cloud does not cause any effort, almost by itself. (H2)
- [e2] I know how to store my data in the Cloud. (H2)
- [e3] Accessing my data is facilitated by Cloud services because they are available everywhere. (H2)
- [e4] Utilization of Cloud services is more complicated than storing data locally. (H2)
- [t1] How secure do you think is data stored in the Cloud (Dropbox, Google Drive, etc.) against access by third parties? (H3)
- [t2] How secure do you think is private data stored in the Cloud (Dropbox, Google Drive, etc.) against data loss? (H3)
- [c1] Do you think a backup of your computer or smartphone in the Cloud is cheaper than a local backup? (H4)
- [c2] Do you think it is cheaper to recover data after a hardware failure from the Cloud than from a local storage? (H4)
- [a1] What is your year of birth? (H5)

Furthermore the participants were asked about their actual usage of Cloud services:

- [au] Do you use Cloud services like Dropbox, iCloud, Amazon EC2, Google Docs, Google Drive etc.?

The participants were asked to choose their answer on a 4-point Likert scale (Cf. frequency tables 1 - 3 in the next section). For the birth year [a1] they had radio buttons to choose from and for the actual usage [au] they had to choose between three options ("no", "yes – one", and "yes – multiple"). The answers to these questions were subject of correlation analyses. The results of the survey are presented in section 4 followed by their interpretation and discussion.

4 Results and Discussion of Findings

4.1 Overview and Frequency Analyses

The survey provided a total of 246 completed questionnaires. 44 participants were born before 1980 and thus classified as digital immigrants; the remaining 202 were digital natives. Focusing on the group of digital natives only, received inputs by participants born before 1980 were not included in further examinations. Details concerning the distribution of years of birth are shown in Fig. 1.

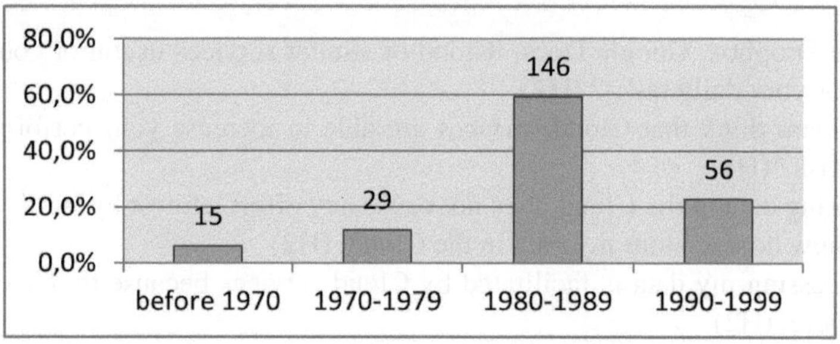

Fig. 1. Frequency distribution of years of birth

The frequency analyses shown in the following tables provide an overview of the responses. To avoid non-reliable responses the participants were also given the choice of "no opinion" or "cannot answer", therefore the number of valid cases varies.

Table 1. Frequency analyses (perceived usefulness and costs)

		[u1]		[u2]		[c1]		[c2]	
		frequency	%	frequency	%	frequency	%	frequency	%
Valid	yes	105	52,0	74	36,6	25	12,4	56	27,7
	rather yes	61	30,2	70	34,7	69	34,2	69	34,2
	rather no	22	10,9	32	15,8	53	26,2	29	14,4
	no	7	3,5	6	3,0	30	14,9	17	8,4
	total	195	96,5	182	90,1	177	87,6	171	84,7
Missing	no opinion	7	3,5	20	9,9	25	12,4	31	15,3
Total		202	100,0	202	100,0	202	100,0	202	100,0

Table 2. Frequency analyses (perceived ease of use)

		[e1] frequency	[e1] %	[e2] frequency	[e2] %	[e3] frequency	[e3] %	[e4] frequency	[e4] %
Valid	agree	81	40,1	136	67,3	134	66,3	14	6,9
	somewhat agree	89	44,1	42	20,8	48	23,8	50	24,8
	somewhat disagree	12	5,9	2	1,0	3	1,5	56	27,7
	disagree	2	1,0	13	6,4	0	0,0	62	30,7
	total	184	91,1	193	95,5	185	91,6	182	90,1
Missing	cannot answer	18	8,9	9	4,5	17	8,4	20	9,9
total		202	100,0	202	100,0	202	100,0	202	100,0

Table 3. Frequency analyses (trust)

		[t1] frequency	[t1] %	[t2] frequency	[t2] %
valid	secure	5	2,5	62	30,7
	rather secure	77	38,1	104	51,5
	rather insecure	84	41,6	21	10,4
	insecure	26	12,9	9	4,5
	total	192	95,0	196	97,0
missing	no opinion	10	5,0	6	3,0
total		202	100,0	202	100,0

Table 4. Frequency analyses (actual usage)

		[au] frequency	[au] %
valid	yes, multiple	121	59,9
	yes, one of them	61	30,2
	no	19	9,4
	total	201	99,5
missing	cannot answer	1	,5
total		202	100,0

Within the next step the collected data was analyzed with regard to correlations. The results of the correlation analyses are shown in the following subsection.

4.2 Results of the Correlation Analyses

To unveil influencing factors on actual usage of Cloud services, several correlation analyses were conducted. Kendall's tau-b was chosen as correlation coefficient as raw data was of ordinal level. The answers to the questions [u1, u2, e1-4, t1, t2, c1, c2, a1] presented in subsection 3.3 were tested concerning correlations with the answers to question [au].

Table 5. Results of the correlation analysis concerning the actual usage [au]

		[u1]	[u2]	[e1]	[e2]	[e3]	[e4]	[t1]	[t2]	[c1]	[c2]	[a1]
[au]	r	**,371****	**,285****	,115	**,244****	,093	**-,188****	**,136***	**,140***	-,020	-,004	**,180****
	p	,000	,000	,050	,000	,099	,003	,021	,018	,384	,479	,004
	N	195	182	184	193	184	182	191	195	177	171	201

r = Correlation coefficient (Kendall's tau-b), p = Significance level, N = Number of valid cases
**. The correlation is significant at a level of 0,01 (both sides).
*. The correlation is significant at a level of 0,05 (both sides).

The Influence of Perceived Usefulness on Actual Usage. As Table 5 shows, both questions aiming at the perceived usefulness of Cloud services show a significant statistical correlation with the actual usage of Cloud services. Therefore hypothesis H1 (the greater the perceived usefulness of Cloud services, the higher their actual usage) is supported by the survey result. Usefulness for daily tasks and the ability to increase performance have a positive influence on the actual usage of Cloud services.

The Influence of Perceived Ease of Use on Actual Usage. Concerning the perceived ease of use, the two questions [e2] and [e4] showed a significant correlation with the actual usage. The knowledge how to store data in the Cloud [e2] positively contributes to an actual usage. The negative correlation of [au] with [e4] reveals that the more complicated it is to use Cloud services the less is their actual usage. This means that the ease of use of Cloud services also influences the actual usage in a positive way. Hypothesis H2 (the greater the perceived ease of use of Cloud services, the higher their actual usage) is supported too.

The Influence of Trust on Actual Usage. The factor trust was addressed from two perspectives within the survey: Question [t1] aimed at trust in the meaning of privacy and security against access by third parties whereas question [t2] aimed at trust in the reliability of Cloud services and data safety concerning protection against data loss. As the frequency analysis revealed, the participants of the survey are by the majority quite positive about the safety of data stored in the Cloud whereas privacy and data security is still a more critical issue. Additionally, the correlation analysis showed that increased trust – regardless from which of the two perspectives – induces increased usage of Cloud services. Thus, trust is an important factor for the actual usage and hypothesis H3 is supported.

The Influence of Costs on Actual Usage. Questions concerning the factor costs did not show significant statistical correlation with the actual usage of Cloud services. Hypothesis H4 is not supported by the survey result which leads to the conclusion that costs have no significant influence on the actual usage of Cloud services.

The Influence of Age on Actual Usage. Concerning the factor age the conducted correlation analysis revealed that within the group of digital natives, it is the individuals born before 1990 who adopt Cloud services more intensely than those born after 1990. Hence, the initially proposed hypothesis H5 (the younger the individual, the more likely is the actual usage) was not supported. Instead, the correlation analysis revealed that older digital natives show a higher usage of Cloud services than younger digital natives. This result shows the importance of a more fine grained investigation into the group of digital natives to reflect an accurate view of the differences among multiple age groups. This supports the suggestion of Wang et al. stating that it is not sufficient to solely differentiate between the groups of digital natives and digital immigrants [14].

Table 6. Key statements of the survey

Percent	Statement
86.6 %	declared themselves as interested in technology.
86.6 %	concern themselves with the topic Cloud Computing.
90.1 %	use at least one Cloud service.
40.6 %	think private data stored in the Cloud is secure against access by third parties.
82.2 %	think private data stored in the Cloud is secure against data loss.
46.6 %	think Cloud backups of computers or smartphones are cheaper than local backups.
61.9 %	think recovering data after a hardware failure causing data loss can be cheaper from a Cloud storage than from local storages.
82.2 %	think Cloud services are useful for their daily jobs.
71.3 %	think Cloud services increase their performance.
84.2 %	declared that storing data in the Cloud does not cause any effort.
31.7 %	think it is easier to store data locally.
88.1 %	know how to store data in the Cloud.
90.1 %	think Cloud services make access to data easier through ubiquitous availability.

5 Conclusion

This paper investigates factors influencing the actual usage of Cloud services among individuals. Five factors were derived from scientific literature dealing with the adoption and diffusion of innovations. A quantitative survey was conducted to reveal insights whereat the focus was set on the age group born after 1980, the so-called digital natives. The results indicate that the factors perceived usefulness, perceived ease of use, trust and age influence the actual usage of Cloud services, whereas the factor costs has no statistically significant relationship with the actual usage. Concerning the age it could be assessed, that individuals within the age group of those born before 1990 are actually more willing to use Cloud services than those born after 1990. The following Table 6 summarizes the managerial results of the survey.

The results also suggest that the classification into the two groups of digital natives and digital immigrants is not sufficient in the context of technological innovations like Cloud Computing. The considered age group of digital natives within this examination provides opportunities for researchers to undertake future investigations at a larger scale. Furthermore, the inclusion of a broader range of possible influencing factors might lead to a more complete set of factors relevant for the adoption of Cloud services among individuals.

Acknowledgement. Parts of this work emerged from the research project OptiCloud. This project is funded by the European Regional Development fund (EFRE, Regio 13) as well as by the Federal State of Upper Austria.

References

1. Dillon, T., Wu, C., Chang, E.: Cloud Computing: Issues and Challenges. In: 2010 24th IEEE International Conference on Advanced Information Networking and Applications (AINA), pp. 27–33. IEEE Computer Society (2010), doi:10.1109/AINA.2010.187
2. Sun, W., Zhang, X., Guo, C.J., Sun, P., Su, H.: Software as a Service: Configuration and Customization Perspectives. In: IEEE Congress on Services Part II, pp. 18–25 (2008)
3. Weinhardt, C., Anandasivam, A., Blau, B., Borissov, N., Meinl, T., Michalk, W., Stoesser, J.: Cloud Computing – A Classification, Business Models and Research Directions. Business & Information Systems Engineering 1(5), 391–399 (2009)
4. Hayes, B.: Cloud computing. Commun. ACM 51(7), 9–11 (2008), doi:10.1145/1364782.1364786
5. BITKOM - Bundesverband Informationswirtschaft, Telekommunikation und neue Medien e.V.: Umsatz mit Cloud Computing steigt auf fast 8 Milliarden Euro, Hannover (2013)
6. KPMG AG Wirtschaftsprüfungsgesellschaft: Cloud Monitor 2013. Cloud Computing in Deutschland - Status quo und Perspektiven (2013)
7. Stieninger, M., Nedbal, D.: Diffusion and Acceptance of Cloud Computing in SMEs: Towards a Valence Model of Relevant Factors. In: Proceedings of the 47th Hawaii International Conference on System Sciences. Hawaii International Conference on System Sciences, pp. 3307–3316 (2014)
8. Cullen, R.: Addressing the digital divide. Online Information Review 25(5), 311–320 (2001)
9. Nedbal, D., Auinger, A., Hochmeier, A., Holzinger, A.: A Systematic Success Factor Analysis in the Context of Enterprise 2.0: Results of an Exploratory Analysis Comprising Digital Immigrants and Digital Natives. In: Huemer, C., Lops, P. (eds.) EC-Web 2012. LNBIP, vol. 123, pp. 163–175. Springer, Heidelberg (2012), doi:10.1007/978-3-642-32273-0_14
10. Palfrey, J.G., Gasser, U.: Born digital. Understanding the first generation of digital natives. Basic Books, New York (2008)
11. Stieninger, M., Nedbal, D.: Characteristics of Cloud Computing in the Business Context: A Systematic Literature Review. Global Journal of Flexible Systems Management (2014)
12. Yang, H., Tate, M.: A Descriptive Literature Review and Classification of Cloud Computing Research. Communications of the ACM 31(1), 35–60 (2012)

13. Mell, P., Grance, T.: The NIST definition of cloud computing, 800-145. National Institute of Standards and Technology (2011), http://csrc.nist.gov/publications/PubsSPs.html#800-145 (accessed January 23, 2013)
14. Wang, E., Myers, M.D., Sundaram, D.: Digital Natives and Digital Immigrants: Towards a Model of Digital Fluency. In: ECIS 2012 Proceedings (2012)
15. Neumair, S.M., Schlesinger, D.M., Haas, H.D.: Internationale Wirtschaft: Unternehmen und Weltwirtschaftsraum im Globalisierungsprozess. Oldenbourg Wissenschaftsverlag (2012)
16. James, J.: From origins to implications: key aspects in the debate over the digital divide. J. Inf. Technol. 22(3), 284–295 (2007), doi:10.1057/palgrave.jit.2000097
17. OECD: Understanding the Digital Divide (2001)
18. Colby, D.: Conceptualizing The "Digital Divide": Closing The "Gap" By Creating A Postmodern Network That Distributes The Productive Power Of Speech. Communication Law and Policy 6(1), 123–173 (2001), doi:10.1207/S15326926CLP0601_04
19. Vie, S.: Digital Divide 2.0: "Generation M" and Online Social Networking Sites in the Composition Classroom. Computers and Composition 25(1), 9–23 (2008), doi:10.1016/j.compcom.2007.09.004
20. Wei, K.-K., Teo, H.-H., Chan, H.C., Tan, B.C.Y.: Conceptualizing and Testing a Social Cognitive Model of the Digital Divide. Information Systems Research 22(1), 170–187 (2011), doi:10.1287/isre.1090.0273
21. Riggins, F.J., Dewan, S.: The Digital Divide: Current and Future Research Directions. Journal of the Association for Information Systems (6) (2005)
22. Prensky, M.: Digital Natives, Digital Immigrants Part 1. On the Horizon 9(5), 1–6 (2001)
23. Davis, F.: User Acceptance of Information Systems. The Technology Acceptance Model (TAM), Michigan (1987)

Proposals for an Assessment Method of Accessibility and Usability in Web Software

Edson Corrêa Teracine[1] and Fabíola Calixto Matsumoto[2]

[1] Centro de Tecnologia da Informação Renato Archer,
Divisão de Segurança de Sistemas de Informação, Campinas, São Paulo, Brazil
[2] Centro de Tecnologia da Informação Renato Archer,
Centro Nacional de Referência em Tecnologia Assistiva, Campinas, São Paulo, Brazil
{edson.teracine,fabiola.calixto}@cti.gov.br

Abstract. Nowadays, applications hosted in the Internet face the challenge to serve a wider range of end users with a potential variety of disabilities that has to be taken into account in the process of Web designing and programming. In this context, the research and development of assessment methods to validate software accessibility have grown in importance. The present document shows a comparative study of methods applied for assessment of the characteristics accessibility and usability in a complementary way, in order to collaborate with the improvement of assessment methods in the implementation of accessibility in Websites and Web applications.

Keywords: Assessment Methods of Accessibility and Usability of Software, Assessment of the Characteristics Accessibility and Usability in Web Software.

1 Introduction

This study has started from the observations made during assessments and production of accessible Websites, considering the currently available methods for validating and verifying the characteristic accessibility in Web applications.

Aiming at overcoming the limitations identified, new perspectives are proposed by the integration of complementary methods of assessment of accessibility and usability found in the literature.

The reminder of this paper is as follows: Section 2 presents standards and assessment methods elected for the study; Section 3 contains methodology and precepts adopted to conduct the comparative analysis of methods; Section 4 shows propositions and specifications made for the integration of methods and the proposals for an assessment method of accessibility and usability in Web software; Section 5 concludes the paper.

2 Assessment Methods of Web Accessibility and Usability

In the context of the considered methods of assessment and validation of accessibility, the need to identify standards which represent a general source of reference for most of the currently available methods was defined. This leads to considering the Web

M. Kurosu (Ed.): Human-Computer Interaction, Part III, HCII 2014, LNCS 8512, pp. 80–89, 2014.

Content Accessibility Guidelines - WCAG 2.0 [1] as the actual reference standards for accessibility policies in the Web and for this study. At the same time, the presentation of a conceptual approach level, which represents a fundamental premise for integrating the methods under comparison, is adopted as an important selection criterion.

The adoption of a complementary vision to the characteristic accessibility considering usability attributes for an effective complementation justifies the attention upon software product quality [2] and the inclusion of MEDE-WEB – Quality Assessment Method of Websites version 2005 [3] in the study, opening both the possibility of new aspects to be assessed and the important points of contact between the characteristics (accessibility and usability).

The following standards and assessment methods of accessibility and usability in the Web are considered to perform the comparative study:

- Web Content Accessibility Guidelines WCAG 2.0 [1];
- Method of Model of Accessibility in Electronic Government – Model e-Mag [4];
- Method of WebAIM's WCAG 2.0 Checklist for HTML Documents – CHD [5];
- MEDE-WEB – Quality Assessment Method of Websites version 2005 [3].

2.1 Web Content Accessibility Guidelines – WCAG 2.0

According to W3C [1], Web Content Accessibility Guidelines WCAG 2.0 consists of a set of accessibility guidelines created by WAI (Web Accessibility Initiative) with the goal of making Web content more accessible to a broad group of people with disabilities, in addition to Web users in general.

WCAG is structured in layers of guidance, including principles, guidelines, success criteria, sufficient and advisory techniques, and represents the conceptual reference model for the treatment of accessibility in the Web worldwide, used for many of the currently existing assessment methods.

For the purpose of the comparative study, only WCAG's layers of guidance until success criteria, which are testable statements for the implementation of related guidelines, will be considered in order to not deal specifically with practical examples of Web development technologies (programming languages or codes). Therefore, the layer of techniques will not be a subject of this study, to establish a basis for comparison only on a conceptual level.

2.2 Method of Model of Accessibility in Electronic Government – Model e-Mag

The Electronic Government (e-GOV) [4], as an initiative of the brazilian Government, created the Model of Accessibility in Electronic Government e-Mag version 3.0 (Model e-Mag) as a result of the study of accessibility rules and comparison of standards adopted by different countries.

According to e-GOV, Model e-Mag assumes three steps to perform the process of developing an accessible site:

1) the application of Web standards; 2) the application of accessibility guidelines; 3) the performance of accessibility assessment. In the present study, the checklists offered by Model e-Mag for the assessment of accessibility in the Web are considered.

Model e-Mag has as its reference the WCAG's hierarchical structure, layers of guidance and concepts, being in a direct relation to them.

For the comparative study, checkpoints of e-Mag's method will be considered just in their "Item" topics just to keep the focus on a conceptual level, excluding any particular technological solution approach for Web programming and development ("What to evaluate" topics).

2.3 Method of WebAIM's WCAG 2.0 – CHD

The Web Accessibility In Mind (WebAIM) [5] is a collaborative community that aims to help make Web more accessible to individuals with disabilities.

The recommendations proposed by the method CHD are based on WCAG's specifications, following the same structure with its respective layers of guidance, but with a particular interpretation of WCAG's guidelines and success criteria, with suggestions for fulfilling these criteria.

2.4 Quality Assessment Method of Websites version 2005 – MEDE-WEB

MEDE-WEB is a method created in the Centro de Tecnologia da Informação Renato Archer (CTI) [3], specifically by the team of researchers from Division of Process and Software Quality Improvement.

According to CTI, MEDE-WEB can be used in conducting the process of assessment and verification of the characteristic usability in Websites, through the application of assessment items that express specific quality requirements, verifiable in a Web software product in use. The degree of fulfillment of requirements, which characterize certain quality attributes, is what determines the quality level of the assessed product. To do so, components or integrating elements of a Website and aspects applicable to each component are considered in a hierarchical structure, as in the example shown in Figure 1:

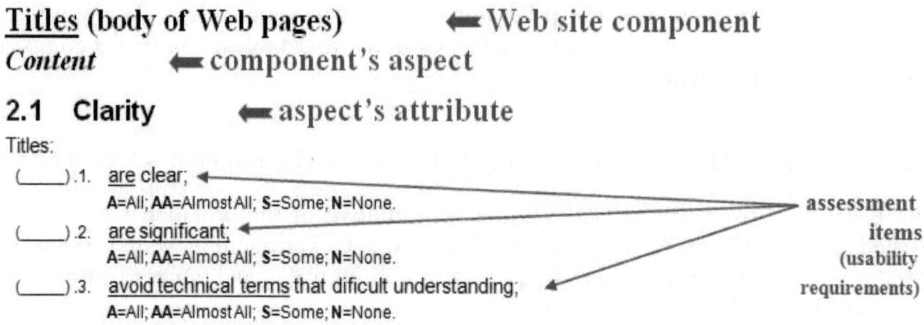

Fig. 1. Example of MEDE-WEB Assessment Items and Usability Requirements

However, as already mentioned, there are common points between the characteristics accessibility and usability of software, presented by MEDE-WEB on many of its assessment items.

3 Methodology of Comparative Analysis of Assessment Methods of Accessibility and Usability in Web Software

The methodology of comparative analysis aims to identify the layers of guidance presented in the studied methods, as well as their application and correlations in the hierarchical degrees of the structure of layers. And, at the same time, to consider the necessary adjustments for the construction of a new proposal of guidance, from the raised observations.

The layers of guidance based on WCAG 2.0, as well as their correspondence with each other considering the methods, are shown in Table 1:

Table 1. Layers of Guidance of the Methods

Layers of Guidance of the Methods			
A	**B**	**C**	**D**
• *WCAG Layer of Principles* • *CHD Layer of Pinciples*	• *WCAG Layer of Guidelines* • *CHD Layer of Guidelines*	• *WCAG Layer of Success criteria* • *e-Mag Layer of Recommendations* • *CHD Layer of Success criteria*	• *e-Mag Layer of Checkpoints (Items)* • *CHD Layer of WebAIM Recommendations*

4 Proposals for an Assessment Method of Accessibility and Usability in Web Software

Proposals will be presented for a new model of approach and assessment method of the characteristics accessibility and usability in Web environment by integrating the methods studied and the adoption of new points of view in the treatment of accessibility and usability requirements.

4.1 New Hierarchical Structure of Layers of Guidance

The need of integration of the assessment methods, in the purpose of creation of proposals for a new model, assumes the revision and adaptation of the layers of guidance already identified in a new structure of layers. The presented reinterpretation of the layers in which accessibility is handled by the methods studied has the aim of creating a common field to enable such integration. The redefinition of layers in a new configuration is shown schematically in Figure 2:

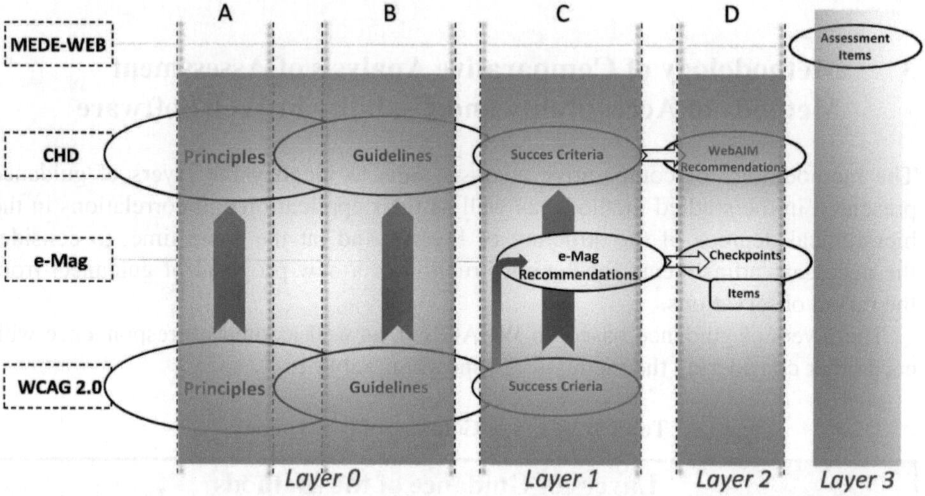

Fig. 2. Layers of Guidance of the Methods and Integration in a New Structure (Layers 0 to 3)

Specifications are shown in Table 2 for the new proposed structure of layers of guidance, based on the methods studied:

Table 2. Layers of Guidance - Integration of the Methods

Layers of Guidance – Integration of the Methods				
Layer of Guidance Number and ***Name***	Layer 0 ***Layer of Principles***	Layer 1 ***Layer of Guidelines***	Layer 2 ***Layer of Checking***	Layer 3 ***Layer of Requirements***
Definition	Patterns, principles and general precepts that characterize an accessible information	Guidelines testable and applicable to Web environment that make their content accessible	Specifications of accessibility requirements that allow to implement and validate ***Guidelines*** **[Layer 1]**	Specifications in a more detailed degree that differentiate and extend, through usability requirements, the accessibility requirements of ***Checking*** **[Layer 2]**
Corresponding to the level of	• *WCAG Principles* • *WCAG Guidelines* • *CHD Principles* • *CHD Guidelines*	• *WCAG Success criteria* • *CHD Success criteria* • *e-Mag Recommendations*	• *e-Mag Checkpoints (Items)* • *CHD WebAIM Recommendations*	• *MEDE-WEB Assessment Items*

The new created structure of layers reflects a hierarchy already presented by WCAG 2.0 in the approaching of information regarding the characteristic accessibility, but from the wider layer (Layer 0) to an even more specific one (Layer 3), representing the latter an innovation in the methodologies of accessibility assessment studied here.

The incorporation of assessment items pertaining to usability requirements presented by MEDE-WEB enables an additional detailing from the Layer 3 of the new hierarchical structure (Layer of requirements), in a new proposition for an assessment method of accessibility and usability in Web software, as shown in Figure 3:

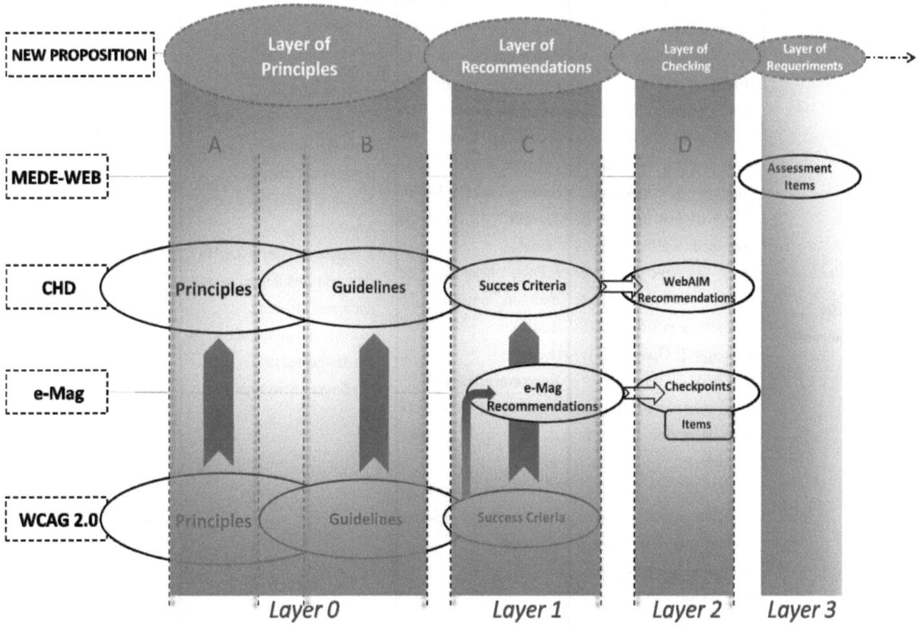

Fig. 3. New Hierarchical Structure of Layers of Guidance

In Table 3, "titles" component of Web pages is applied into and interpreted within the new structure of layers of guidance of the proposed model:

Table 3. Application of the New Hierarchical Structure of Layers of Guidance

Application of the New Hierarchical Structure of Layers of Guidance				
Layer of Guidance Number **and** ***Name***	Layer 0 ***Layer of Principles***	Layer 1 ***Layer of Guidelines***	Layer 2 ***Layer of Checking***	Layer 3 ***Layer of Requirements***
Titles **Component**	**Principle 1: Perceivable** (*WCAG*) Information and user interface components must be presentable to users in ways they can perceive. (*CHD*) Web content is made available to the senses - sight, hearing, and/or touch **Guideline 1.3: Adaptable** Create content that can be presented in different ways (for example simpler layout) without losing information or structure. **Principle 2: Operable** (*WCAG*) User interface components and navigation must be operable. (*CHD*) Interface forms, controls, and navigation are operable **Guideline 2.4: Navigable** Provide ways to help users navigate, find content, and determine where they are.	**(*WCAG* and *CHD*)** **Success criteria 1.3.1: Info and Relationships** Information, structure, and relationships conveyed through presentation can be programmatically determined or are available in text. **Success criteria 2.4.10: Section Headings (Titles)** Section headings are used to organize the content. (*e-Mag*) **Recommendation 2:** Organize HTML code in a logic and semantic way **Recommendation 3:** Use heading layers correctly	**(*e-Mag*)** **Checking point (Item):** Titles present a logic order in text? Are they described correctly? **(*CHD*)** **WebAIM's Recommendation:** • **(Success criteria 1.3.1)** Semantic markup is used to designate headings... Semantic markup is used appropriately. • **(Success criteria 2.4.10)** Beyond providing an overall document structure, individual sections of content are designated using headings, where appropriate.	**(*MEDE-WEB*)** **Assessment Items:** **2. TITLES (body of pages)** ***Content*** **2.1 Clarity** Titles: (____).1. are clear; A=All; AA=Almost All; S=Some; N=None. (____).2. are significant; A=All; AA=Almost All; S=Some; N=None. (____).3. avoid technical terms that difficult understanding; A=All; AA=Almost All; S=Some; N=None. (____).4. avoid defined and undefined articles in their beginnings (such as.: The, A, Any, etc.); A=All; AA=Almost All; S=Some; N=None. (____).5. are concise (transmit as much information with a minimum of words possible). A=All; AA=Almost All; S=Some; N=None.

4.2 Accessibility and Usability Requirements in the New Structure - Layers 2 and 3

The "titles" component can be analyzed within the new hierarchical structure by identifying the respective accessibility and usability requirements treated by the methods of Model e-Mag and MEDE-WEB, shown in a synthetic way in Table 4:

Table 4. Accessibility and Usability Requirements - Layers 2 and 3

Accessibility and Usability Assessment Methods *AUTHORS X PROPERTIES*		
AUTHORS*/Methods** / ***PROPERTIES	***e-GOV*** Model e-Mag **(Layer 2)**	***CTI*** MEDE-WEB **(Layer 3)**
TITLES		
Accessibility and Usability requirements	Logical order in text	
	Correct description	
		Clear
		Significant
		Avoid technical terms
		Avoid articles
		Concise
		Consistent
		Different font sizes
		Easy-to-read colors
		Easy-to-read styles
		Avoid underlining

According to the proposals for a new assessment model, the treatment of such requirements is performed in two of the layers of guidance presented by the new hierarchical structure (Layer 2: Layer of checking and Layer 3: Layer of requirements) in a larger and more detailed set of assessment items, with the inclusion of the usability requirements of the latter (Layer 3).

Finally in Table 5, a new set of accessibility and usability requirements identified for other Web page components is shown in Layers 2 and 3 of the new structure:

Table 5. Web Components X Accessibility and Usability Requirements

Accessibility and Usability Assessment Methods ***AUTHORS X PROPERTIES***		
AUTHORS/*Methods** / ***PROPERTIES	***e-GOV*** Model e-Mag **(Layer 2)**	***CTI*** MEDE-WEB **(Layer 3)**
LINKS		
Appropriate, meaningful and succinct description	X	X
Explicit indication of the result of access		X
Presentation of explanatory balloons		X
Balloons identify result to be accessed		X
Correct targeting	X	X
Opening on page	X	
Appropriate location		X
Appropriate external contents		X
Indication of exiting to external sites		X
Default description for the same content accessed		X
Use of underlining		X
Legible presentation		X
BUTTONS		
Proper function	X	
Presentation of description	X	
Adequate description	X	
Representative on the content to be accessed		X
Keep the same purpose in different pages		X
Appropriate location for better understanding		X
Expected content targeting		X

5 Conclusions

The proposals for a new assessment method by the integration presented are justified in the existing complementarity between the methods studied and the new contributions emerged during the comparative process.

This represents from the point of view adopted in the study an innovation and proposition for the revision and extension of concepts applied to information considered to be accessible, without restrictions or prioritizations of any kind to the public profile of end users, even though observing and complying the specificities of its different components groups and the impossibility of answering all the needs by a unique standardized assessment approach.

The current study opens new opportunities for the exploration of the characteristic usability on the horizon of Web accessibility assessment.

References

1. W3C - World Wide Web Consortium; WAI - Web Accessibility Initiative: Web Content Accessibility Guidelines - WCAG 2.0 (2008), http://www.w3.org/ http://www.w3.org/TR/WCAG20/ (acesso em June 2013)
2. Guerra, A.C., Colombo, R.M.T.: Tecnologia da Informação: Qualidade de Produto de Software, PBQP Software - Ministério da Ciência e Tecnologia, Secretaria de Política de Informática, Brasília (2009)
3. Centro de Tecnologia da Informação Renato Archer - CTI/MCT: LAPS - Laboratório de Tecnologia de Avaliação de Qualidade de Produto de Software; LAQS - Laboratório de Avaliação de Qualidade de Software: MEDE-PROS - Método de Avaliação da Qualidade de Produto de Software, versão 2006 e MEDE-WEB - Método de Avaliação da Qualidade de Websites, versã (2005)
4. Governo Eletrônico (e-GOV) - Ministério do Planejamento, Orçamento e Gestão, Secretaria de Logística e Tecnologia da Informação; Ministério da Educação, Secretaria de Educação Profissional e Tecnológica: e-Mag Versão 3.0 - Modelo de Acessibilidade em Governo Eletrônico (2011), http://www.governoeletronico.gov.br/, http://emag.governoeletronico.gov.br/emag/ (acesso em July 2013)
5. WebAIM - Web Accessibility In Mind: WebAIM's WCAG 2.0 Checklist for HTML Documents – CHD., http://webaim.org/standards/wcag/checklist/ (Acesso em ago. 2013)

The Correlation between Visual Complexity and User Trust in On-line Shopping: Implications for Design

Kai-Ti Tseng and Yuan-Chi Tseng

YCT Cognition & Experience Design Lab, Department of Industrial Design
National Cheng Kung University, No. 1 University Road, Tainan, Taiwan
grace0733@gmail.com, yctseng@mail.ncku.edu.tw

Abstract. Perceived visual aesthetics of a web site positively affects a user's credibility assessment of the site and less visual complex web page is associated with more favorable attitudes toward the page. Here we further investigate whether the visual complexity of a web site affects its aesthetic preference and as a consequence is associated with the users' credibility. Two experiments with on-line payment scenario were conducted. Experiment 1 shows users trust pages with higher text-based complexity more. Experiment 2 shows perceived image-based complexity is negatively correlated with credibility. Our results show text-based complexity and image-based complexity have different effects on the credibility of on-line shopping site. Designers can decrease image-based complexity of a web site to increase users' aesthetic preference and trust. This work can serve as the fundament to develop an automatic evaluation tools to predict the users' trust and preference of a web page based on the visual complexity computation.

Keywords: Credibility, Aesthetics, Complexity, E-commerce, Visual Design.

1 Introduction

Literature has shown beautiful web sites are often perceived as more trust [1] and more usable [1-6]. For example, User's credibility on a web site can be influenced by the first impression of its aesthetics [7]. Balance, harmony, contrast and dominace, are the major aesthetic elements underlies credibility of a web site [7]. Fogg and colleagues [8] asked 2,684 participants to rank the degree of credibility and collected the reasons behind their ranks. They found that when people evaluate the credibility of a web site, the design look is mentioned more often (46.1%) than any other features, such as information design/structure (28.5%), information focus (25.1%), company motive (15.5%), usefulness of information (14.8%), accuracy of information (14.3%) and so on. Robins and Holmes [9] compared 20 web sites which have identical contents but two levels (low and high) of aesthetics and suggested that the level of the aesthetics of a web page is highly correlated with the degree of the judgments of credibility of the page and, as a consequence, it affects the user's willingness to stay in the current page or move on to another web page. They also found that before any type of complex conscious cognitive analysis occurs, credibility judgments are

M. Kurosu (Ed.): Human-Computer Interaction, Part III, HCII 2014, LNCS 8512, pp. 90–99, 2014.

already made based on the perceived visual design elements, such as the combination of colors, layout, overall aesthetic treatment, fonts, use of bulleted lists, or presentation of tabular data. These findings show the critical role of aesthetics and design in the credibility of a web site.

Trust is particularly an important issue in e-commence. Ang and Lee [10] claimed that "If the web site does not let a consumer to believe that the merchant is trustworthy, no purchase decision will be made". The level of trust of online shoppers towards the web sites is one of critical factors affecting the consumers' online purchase decision [10-12]. To build a trustworthy web site has become the primary key for online shops. All successful web pages should make people feel confident, joyful, or arouse some positive emotion [8]. The visual design is not just about "what is communicated but rather about how information is communicated" [13, 14]. However, how to design a beautiful on-line shopping web site which arouses users' positive emotions and credibility during the interaction is not easy for designer.

Wang and Emurian [15] suggests that the trust between on-line shoppers and shops can be influence by the visual design of e-commerce interface. Alsudani and Casey [7] used a more theoretical and systematical framework to investigate how visual elements of a web site influence its credibility and offers some guidelines about affective design factors on credibility which helped web page designers to evaluate the design factors on the credibility. Wang & Emurian [15] have also proposed 14 design features which can induce user trust. They created a web site following these features so as to demonstrate how designers can apply these design features on the web site, particularly when they want to increase the user trust. However, although these 14 design features, such as the use of three-dimensional and half-screen size clipart, the symmetric use of moderate pastel color of low brightness and cool tone and so on, could become the constraints limiting visual design space, designers still do not know whether their design match the guidelines without user testing. While design process should allow web site designers more space to express their ideas, creativity and personal styles or allow a company to express their traditional value and identity via the details, aesthetics and the styles of visual designs, it should be accelerated by more efficient and effective evaluation tools or process.

Studies have also shown that the visual complexity is highly correlated with the visual aesthetics [16, 17, see 18 for a review]. For example, Michailidou, Harper and Bechhofer [16] found the correlation between visual complexity and aesthetics and layout. In a series studies, Tuch and colleagues [18-20] show that users prefer web sites with lower visual complexity. They [18] found the less complex web design is associated with psychophysiological responses, such as lower experienced arousal, more positive valence appraisal, higher heart rate and lower facial muscle tension and with cognitive responses, such as shorter visual search time and higher recognition rate after one week. This study shows that the visual complexity has effects on human emotion and cognition. More recently, they found less complex web page results in higher emotion, fewer eye movements and larger finger pulse amplitude [19].

Moreover, Researchers have proposed several ways to calculate visual complexity based on the text and images occupied in the space [21, 22], on the boundary [21, 23], on the number of colors used in the web page [22], or on the number of leaves resulting from a quadtree decomposition of the image [24]. For example, Zheng and colleagues [24] found that web sites that have higher number of leaves calculated by the quadtree decomposition of the image often are perceived as unprofessional and complicated. More recently, also based on the computation of spatial distribution of the resulting leaves of the quadtree decomposition, Reinecke and colleagues [25] found the perceived complexity is highly correlated to the calculated visual complexity and the visual complexity negatively affect the visual aesthetic preference. Therefore, there is a chance for us to evaluate the visual complexity and aesthetics by calculating the visual complexity on the web page.

Based on the abundant evidence has showed that aesthetics play an important role in credibility [1, 7-9, 26, 27] and aesthetics is affected by the visual complexity [16-20], here we aim to further investigate whether the visual complexity of a web site affects its aesthetic preference and, as a consequence, influence the users' credibility. We found the credibility and text-based complexity is positively correlated and credibility and image-based complexity is negatively correlated. The results of this study can further be applied to develop an automatic evaluation tool based on the computation of visual complexity [25]. The automatic evaluation tool can help designers to assess the level of visual complexity of visual designs and then predict the level of the credibility earlier in the iterative design cycle to reduce the cost of user testing.

2 Experiment 1

In Experiment 1 the correlations between variables, such as calculated complexity, user perceived complexity, and trust in an on-line shopping web page were investigated. The major factor which affected the visual complexity in the Experiment 1 is the amount of text using in the page. Therefore, the visual complex in Experiment 1 is the text-based complexity.

2.1 Method

A real life scenario was created to simulate the payment activity in an on-line web page. Participants were provided experimental tokens to pay the product on the experimental web page. They were asked to select one of the five experimental pages to pay and finish the buying. However, they were informed in advance that four of the five web pages are scams. If participants paid in the scam web site, the tokens would be taken away. Only one of the web sites rewarded the product on the web site. The scam and the reward web sites were randomly assigned. This design motivated participants to choose an interface that they trusted most. Participant's selection time and score (1 to 100) of the perceived visual complexity and credibility were collected and analyzed. After all the stimuli were shown, participants were also interviewed to understand the possible different strategies and decision reasons underlying their choice.

Participants. Twenty participants, including 13 males and 7 females, were recruited from the community of National Cheng Kung University. They were asked to pick a web page to finish a simulated shopping and evaluate the credibility, preference, and perceived visual complexity. Adult participants aged over 20 were chosen. The female average age is about 21.7 and the male average age is about 22.3.

Apparatus. ACER Aspire S3-391 was used to run the samples during the experiments, products picture were downloaded from Apple.com. Adobe Photoshop CS5 and Adobe Illustrator CS5 were used for Web page design preparation. The score of the perceived visual complexity and credibility of a web page was evaluated on paper sheets.

Stimuli. We designed five on-line shopping web pages having different amount of text information (see figure 1). All design features of the web page were based on the trust-inducing features proposed by Wang and Emurian [15]. Five levels of the text-based complexities of the created web pages were adjusted by the Quadtree decomposition method. The computation code is provided by Reinecke and colleagues [25].

(a) (b) (c) (d) (e)

Fig. 1. The experimental web pages of Experiment 1. The calculated visual complexity score by the Quadtree decomposition method [25] is: (a) 2.23, (b) 3.70, (c) 5.99, (d) 7.90, (e) 9.88, respectively.

Procedure. The 5 levels of text-based complexities were arranged in a counterbalanced manner. First, a sample web site picture was shown to allow participants familiar with the experiment. After providing the introductions, participants started the experiment. Participants had unlimited time to examine sample web pages until they selected the sample page that they trusted most to finish the buying. The score of the credibility and the perceived visual complexity were then collected by paper sheets. First, participants ranked the sample web pages and then gave each of them a score of the visual complexity and a score of the credibility. Participants were also asked their subjective reasons underlying the choice.

2.2 Results and Discussion

First of all, the calculated visual complexity is positively related with users' perceived complexity (R^2=0.59, $p< .001$). This result validates that the visual complexity of Experiment 1 was successfully calculated by the program of Reinecke and colleagues [25]. Figure 2 shows that the calculated text-based visual complexity of a web page is positively related with users' credibility (R^2=0.363, $p< .001$). Figure 3 illustrated that the correlation between credibility and perceived complexity is also positively correlated (R^2=0.501, $p< .001$). This result indicates that the more text information on an on-line shopping web page, the more trust from the users. Although the more text information increases the complexity of a web page, but it provides user more useful information about the web page and, as a consequence, more trust toward the web page.

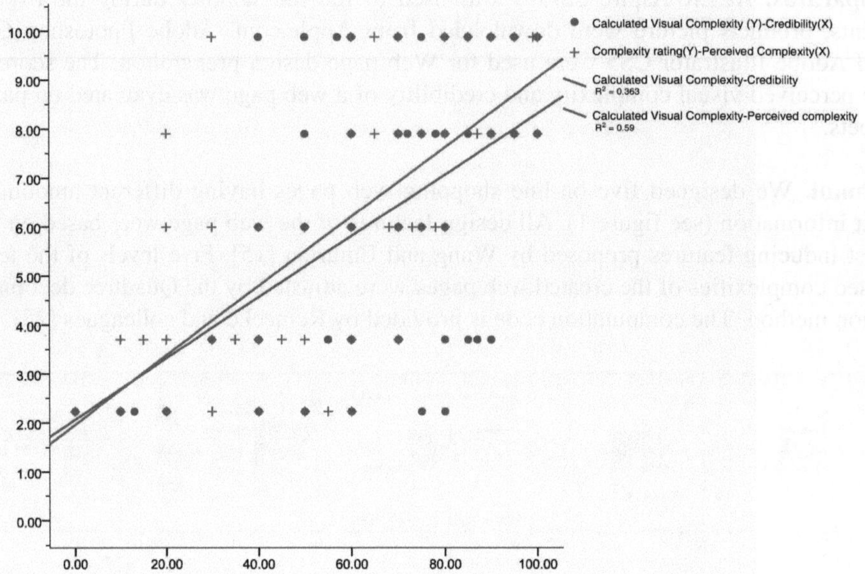

Fig. 2. Experiment 1. The calculated visual complexity is correlated with the credibility (red line, R^2=0.363, p< .001), and with the perceived complexity (green line, R^2=0.59, p< .001).

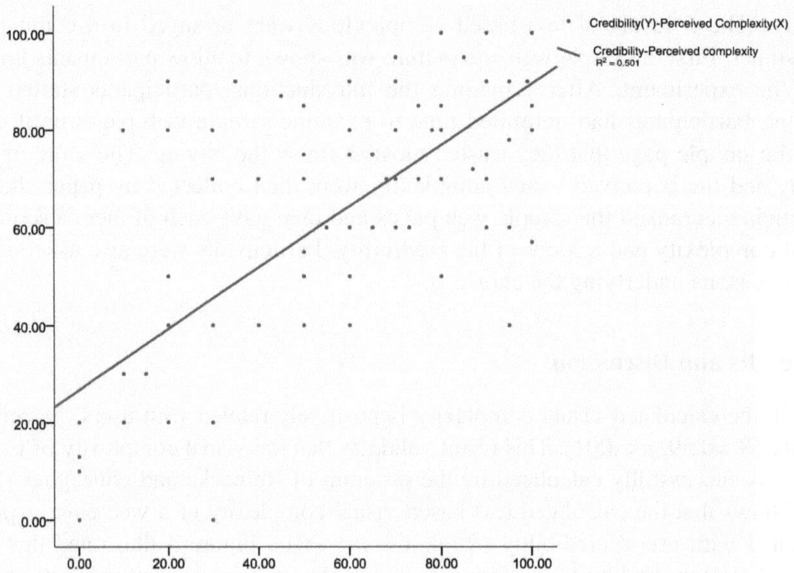

Fig. 3. Experiment 1. The correlation between credibility and perceived complexity (green line) (R^2=0.501, p< .001).

3 Experiment 2

3.1 Method

The five different complex web pages in the Experiment 1 were majorly manipulated by different amount of text information. To investigate the correlation between image complexity and credibility, the 5 levels of image-based complexities were manipulated by adjusting the image elements used in the web pages in the Experiment 2. The different levels of image-based complexities were evaluated by the Quadtree decomposition method used in [25] (see Figure 4).

Except for the 5 experimental web pages, the other settings in the method of the Experiment 2 were kept the same as Experiment 1. The 20 participants in the Experiment 2 were also the same as the Experiment 1.

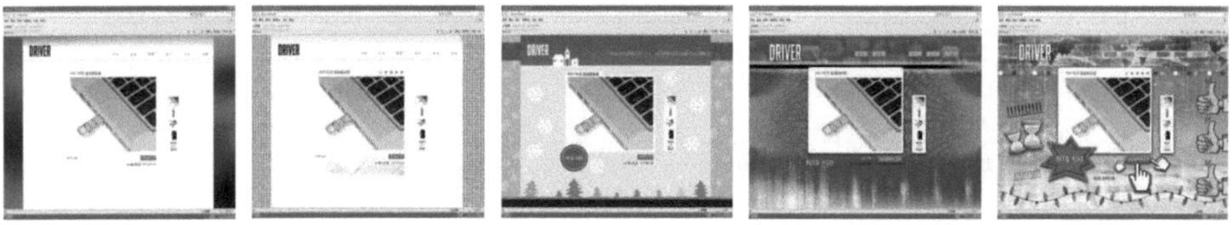

(a) (b) (c) (d) (e)

Fig. 4. The experimental web pages of Experiment 2. The calculated visual complexity score is: (a) 2.68, (b) 4.15, (c) 5.42, (d) 6.66, (e) 5.49, respectively. Comparing to Experiment 1, the lower score here is because the calculated visual complexity score by Quadtree decomposition method used in [25] is hard to increase only by adding images in the web page.

3.2 Results and Discussion

First, the visual calculated visual complexity is positively related to user perceived complexity (R^2=0.333, p< .001). Again, this result validates the codes of the computation of visual complexity used in this Experiment. Figure 5 shows that calculated visual complexity of a web page is negatively related with user perception of credibility (R^2=0.053, p< .05). This indicates that the amount of image content in an on-line shopping web page has an effect on the credibility of the page. The users' attitudes toward the trust of a web page increase as the decrease of the level of its image complexity. Moreover, visual complexity score of a web page is negatively correlated with the aesthetic preference (R^2=0.093, p= .002). This result is consistent with the previous findings of Tuch and colleagues [18-20].

Figure 6 shows that the correlation between variables. The correlation between credibility and aesthetic preference is positive (R^2=0.671, p< .001), while the correlation between aesthetic preference and perceived complexity, and the correlation between credibility and perceived complexity is negative (R^2=0.161, p< .001, R^2=0.099, p= .001, respectively). These results show that the image complexity reduces the users' aesthetic preference and credibility judgment.

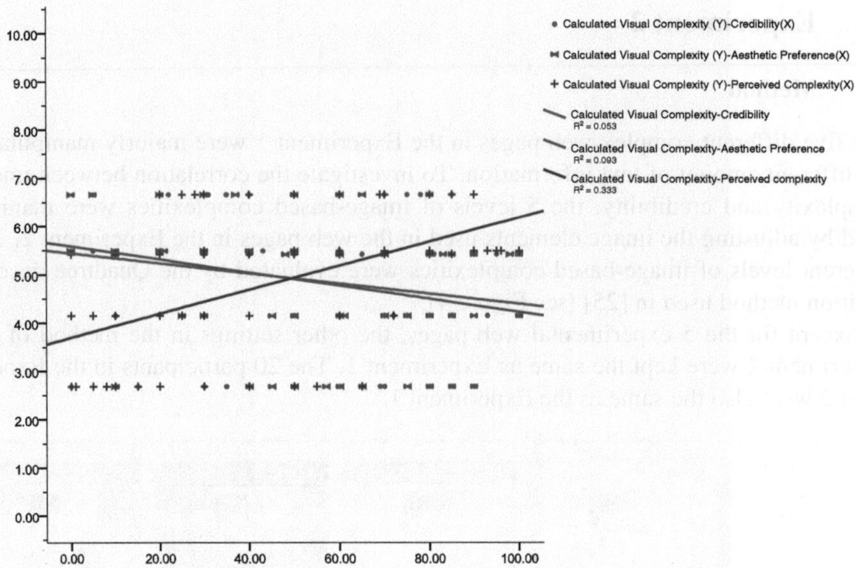

Fig. 5. The calculated visual complexity is negatively correlated with the credibility (orange line, R^2=0.053, p< .05), and with the aesthetic preference (purple line, R^2=0.093, p= .002), and positively correlated with the perceived complexity (green line, R^2=0.333, p< .001)

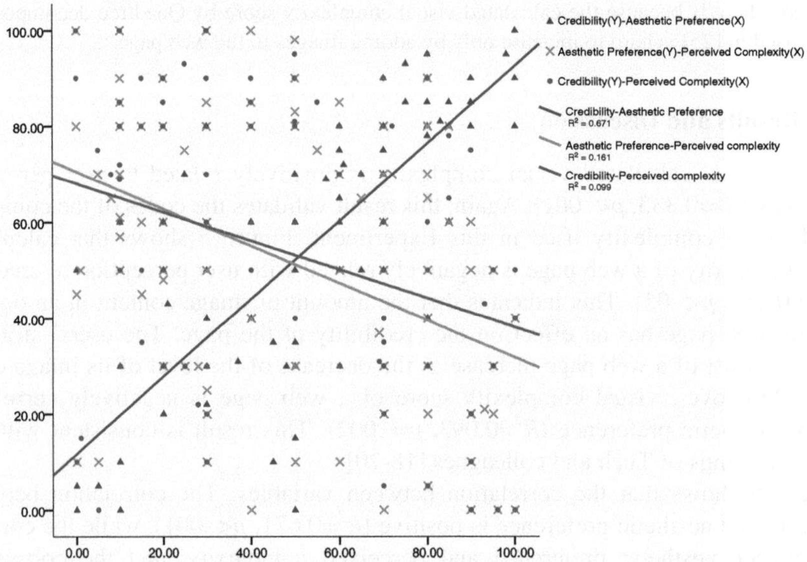

Fig. 6. Experiment 2.The correlation between variables, such as credibility and aesthetic preference (blue line, R2=0.671, p< .001), aesthetic preference and perceived complexity (yellow line, R2=0.161, p< .001), and credibility and perceived complexity (green line, R2=0.099, p= .001).

4 General Discussion

The present two experiments investigate the correlation between visual complexity of a web page and user's credibility perception. The results of the both experiments show the perceived complexity is highly correlated to the calculated complexity which is based on the number of leaves by the quadtree decomposition of an image [24, 25]. This result validates the methodology of the computation of the visual complexity used in previous work [24, 25]. However, when we prepared the visual materials for the Experiment 2, the image-based complexity is not easy to increase by only adding the image elements without increasing the text information. Therefore, the computational model used in [25] seems to be more appropriated to calculate text complexity rather than image complexity. More investigation of the complexity computation is needed in the future.

Our main finding was that the credibility perception is highly correlated with the visual complexity of the on-ling shopping web page. The results of Experiment 1 show that the amount of text information is positively correlated with the credibility perception. In Experiment 1 the visual complexity of the stimuli was increased by adding related shopping information in the page (see figure 1). This result indicates that the more related shopping information in an on-line shopping web site, the more trust the users may have. Moreover, the more text information web sites in the Experiment 1 look more similar to the popular on-line shopping site in Taiwan, according to the participants' answers in our interviews. In Fogg and colleagues study [8], information focus and usefulness of information is mentioned 25.1% and 14.8% respectively when evaluating the credibility of a web page. Focus and useful text information seems a factor to increase the trust. The future study can focus on understanding how the relevant level of the text information (e.g. the degree of focus and usefulness) affects the credibility perception.

Experiment 2 shows that the amount of image elements is negatively correlated with the aesthetic preference. The negative correlation between visual complexity and aesthetic preference is in line with the previous works by Tuch and colleagues [18-20] which shows that the lower visual complex web page gains the more positive emotion and aesthetic judgment from the users. The evidence of Experiment 2 also shows that the credibility perception is positively correlated with the aesthetic preference. This finding is in line with previous results [1, 7-9, 26, 27] showing that aesthetics play an important role in the credibility perception. People trust a more beautiful on-line shopping web site more than less beautiful one. More interestingly, we found for the first time that the visual complexity is negatively correlated with the credibility perception. Experiment 2 correlates the visual complexity and credibility: image-based visual complexity decreases the aesthetic preference and, as a consequence, is negatively associated with the credibility perception.

The different results of visual complexity on the credibility in the Experiment 1 and Experiment 2 show that the text-based complexity and image-based complexity have different effects on the credibility perception. The text-based complexity may provide more related shopping information which allows people feel confident toward a on-line shopping web site. It seems that a web site having more useful and focus information is a more trustworthy web site [8]. The image-based complexity may confuse the user when searching useful information and result in less trust.

The reasons underlying the difference effects between text-based complexity and image-based complexity on the credibility is interesting for further study in the future.

Recent study [25] shows a possible way to predict the aesthetic preference of a web page based on the computation of its visual complexity, because the high correlation between visual complexity and aesthetic preference [1, 7-9, 26, 27]. The present study further establishing the relationship between visual complexity and credibility provides the fundament to develop an automatic evaluation tool to predicts user preference and trust. This tool can help designers to check visual layout earlier in the design cycle and reduce cost of iterative user testing. This work strongly suggests that the image-based complexity is the major factor which influence user's preference and trust. This work also provides the web page designers flexible guidelines to increase the trust of a web page by adjusting visual design elements while maintaining the content information.

Acknowledgments. We thank K. Reinecke for help with the codes of the computation of visual complexity in this study. This research was supported by a grant, NSC 102-2410-H-006-019, from the National Science Council, Taiwan.

References

1. Lindgaard, G., Dudek, C., Sen, D., Sumegi, L., Noonan, P.: An exploration of relations between visual appeal, trustworthiness and perceived usability of homepages. ACM Transactions on Computer-Human Interaction (TOCHI) 18(1), 1 (2011)
2. Hartmann, J., Sutcliffe, A., Angeli, A.D.: Towards a theory of user judgment of aesthetics and user interface quality. ACM Transactions on Computer-Human Interaction (TOCHI) 15(4), 15 (2008)
3. Lindgaard, G., Fernandes, G., Dudek, C., Brown, J.: Attention web designers: You have 50 milliseconds to make a good first impression! Behaviour & Information Technology 25(2), 115–126 (2006)
4. Reinecke, K., Bernstein, A.: Improving performance, perceived usability, and aesthetics with culturally adaptive user interfaces. ACM Transactions on Computer-Human Interaction (TOCHI) 18(2), 8 (2011)
5. Tractinsky, N.: Aesthetics and apparent usability: empirically assessing cultural and methodological issues. In: Proceedings of the ACM SIGCHI Conference on Human Factors in Computing Systems, pp. 115–122. ACM (1997)
6. Tractinsky, N., Katz, A., Ikar, D.: What is beautiful is usable. Interacting with Computers 13(2), 127–145 (2000)
7. Alsudani, F., Casey, M.: The effect of aesthetics on web credibility. In: Proceedings of the 23rd British HCI Group Annual Conference on People and Computers: Celebrating People and Technology, pp. 512–519. British Computer Society (2009)
8. Fogg, B.J., Soohoo, C., Danielson, D.R., Marable, L., Stanford, J., Tauber, E.R.: How do users evaluate the credibility of Web sites?: a study with over 2,500 participants. In: Proceedings of the 2003 Conference on Designing for User Experiences, pp. 1–15. ACM (2003)
9. Robins, D., Holmes, J.: Aesthetics and credibility in web site design. Information Processing & Management 44(1), 386–399 (2008)
10. Ang, L., Lee, B.-C.: Influencing perceptions of trustworthiness in Internet commerce: A rational choice framework. In: Proceedings of Fifth CollECTer Conference on Electronic Commerce, pp. 1–12 (2000)

11. Jarvenpaa, S.L., Tractinsky, N., Saarinen, L.: Consumer Trust in an Internet Store: A Cross - Cultural Validation. Journal of Computer - Mediated Communication 5(2) (1999)
12. Teo, T.S.H.: Attitudes toward online shopping and the Internet. Behaviour & Information Technology 21(4), 259–271 (2002)
13. Arnheim, R.: Visual thinking. University of California Pr. (1969)
14. White, A.W.: The elements of graphic design. Skyhorse Publishing Inc. (2011)
15. Wang, Y.D., Emurian, H.H.: Trust in e-commerce: consideration of interface design factors. Journal of Electronic Commerce in Organizations (JECO) 3(4), 42–60 (2005)
16. Michailidou, E., Harper, S., Bechhofer, S.: Visual complexity and aesthetic perception of web pages. In: Proceedings of the 26th Annual ACM International Conference on Design of Communication, pp. 215–224. ACM (2008)
17. Pandir, M., Knight, J.: Homepage aesthetics: The search for preference factors and the challenges of subjectivity. Interacting with Computers 18(6), 1351–1370 (2006)
18. Tuch, A.N., Bargas-Avila, J.A., Opwis, K., Wilhelm, F.H.: Visual complexity of websites: Effects on users' experience, physiology, performance, and memory. International Journal of Human-Computer Studies 67(9), 703–715 (2009)
19. Tuch, A.N., Kreibig, S.D., Roth, S.P., Bargas-Avila, J.A., Opwis, K., Wilhelm, F.H.: The role of visual complexity in affective reactions to webpages: subjective, eye movement, and cardiovascular responses. IEEE Transactions on Affective Computing 2(4), 230–236 (2011)
20. Tuch, A.N., Presslaber, E.E., Stöcklin, M., Opwis, K., Bargas-Avila, J.A.: The role of visual complexity and prototypicality regarding first impression of websites: Working towards understanding aesthetic judgments. International Journal of Human-Computer Studies (2012)
21. Bucy, E.P., Lang, A., Potter, R.F., Grabe, M.E.: Formal features of cyberspace: Relationships between Web page complexity and site traffic. Jasis 50(13), 1246–1256 (1999)
22. Ivory, M.Y., Sinha, R.R., Hearst, M.A.: Empirically validated web page design metrics. In: Proceedings of the SIGCHI Conference on Human Factors in Computing Systems, pp. 53–60. ACM (2001)
23. Bauerly, M., Liu, Y.: Effects of symmetry and number of compositional elements on interface and design aesthetics. Intl. Journal of Human–Computer Interaction. 24(3), 275–287 (2008)
24. Zheng, X.S., Chakraborty, I., Lin, J.J.-W., Rauschenberger, R.: Correlating low-level image statistics with users-rapid aesthetic and affective judgments of web pages. In: Proceedings of the SIGCHI Conference on Human Factors in Computing Systems, pp. 1–10. ACM (2009)
25. Reinecke, K., Yeh, T., Miratrix, L., Mardiko, R., Zhao, Y., Liu, J., Gajos, K.Z.: Predicting users' first impressions of website aesthetics with a quantification of perceived visual complexity and colorfulness. In: Proceedings of the SIGCHI Conference on Human Factors in Computing Systems, pp. 2049–2058. ACM (2013)
26. Fogg, B.J., Marshall, J., Kameda, T., Solomon, J., Rangnekar, A., Boyd, J., Brown, B.: Web credibility research: a method for online experiments and early study results. In: CHI 2001 Extended Abstracts on Human factors in Computing Systems, pp. 295–296. ACM (2001)
27. Robins, D., Holmes, J., Stansbury, M.: Consumer health information on the Web: The relationship of visual design and perceptions of credibility. Journal of the American Society for Information Science and Technology 61(1), 13–29 (2010)

Mobile Interaction

Digital Love Letter: A Handwriting Based Interface for Non-instant Digital Messenger

So Jung Bang, Yoonji Song, Jae Dong Kim, Kiseul Suh, Chung–Kon Shi, Graham Wakefield*, and Sungju Woo*

Graduate School of Culture Technology, KAIST, Daejeon, Korea
{sojungb,keyofsky,jaedong27,kiseul.suh,chungkon, grrrwaaa,woo1016}@kaist.ac.kr

Abstract. The instant messenger has developed as an important communication media platform. However, because of the nature of instant communication, instant messenger services place many limitations on communicating with nuance. We believe that the easy nature of digital communications tends to weaken serious aspects of personal communication such as patience and commitment. On the basis of critical perspectives, we designed the digital messenger 'Digital Love Letter' (DLL)': a mobile messenger in which the expressive *process* of interaction is more important than the final output. The main concept of DLL is to share the process of communication using a non-instantaneous and non-multitasking interface, so that users can share their time with some similar nuances to face-to-face communication. Both writing and reading messages require concentrated attention. Thus, this paper suggests a new system of digital messenger, that is also a new method of computer-mediated communication (CMC).

Keywords: Affective Messenger, Computer Mediated Communication (CMC), Social Presence, Instant Messaging.

1 Introduction

Instant messaging (IM) has become an effective and convenient means to communication over a distance. This digital technology has made it easier for us to contact others immediately and instantly, however messaging services predominantly focus on quick information delivery. Even when messages can be complemented with diverse emoticons and attached files, there are many limitations on communicating with nuance.

Many scholars have criticized communication mediated with digital technology because the instant nature of digital communication tends to weaken serious aspects of personal communication such as patience and commitment.

George Myerson [1] critically analyzed mobile phone communication using the philosophical paradigms of Heidegger and Habermas. In Heidegger's approach,

* Corresponding authors.

M. Kurosu (Ed.): Human-Computer Interaction, Part III, HCII 2014, LNCS 8512, pp. 103–113, 2014.

communication is about the listener's understanding. For Habermas, to communicate means to make the speaker's desires understood, not to pursue their immediate fulfillment. That is to say, communication is not a one-way information transmission, but a shared *effort* toward mutual understanding; a *process* of reaching in which two parties share their existence.

Sherry Turkle [2] suggested that multitasking and rapid responses in online interactions can make us obsessive about our numerous connections. Quick connections mediated with digital technology become a measure of self-esteem. Walter Kirn [3] also describes the everyday "dumbing down" effects of online multitasking, with reference to fMRI studies.

Instant messaging has developed into a dominant means of communication in modern society, so these criticisms should not be disregarded. We suggest addressing some of the drawbacks of instant connection based communication by realizing, with digital technology, aspects of emotional interactions requiring effort and concentration.

There have been many previous studies aimed at improving the richness of emotional interaction through digital technology. Affective Computing aims to realize emotional interaction through digital technology, but it is predominantly focused on improving interactions between humans and computers such as the automatic recognition of human emotional information [4]. There have been digital messaging services based on affective computing which help to convey emotion effectively [5], however, the systems to detect and deliver emotion are mainly limited to measuring physical responses, that are not necessarily directly associated with specific emotional states. These types of automatic interfaces can also reinforce the problems of effortless aspects of digital communication.

Human Computer Interaction (HCI) has become concerned with critical theory and reflective thought [6]. Philip Agre [7] advocated the development of "critical technical practices" in which technology development becomes a way to reflectively explore attitudes towards and premises about technology and humanity.

On the basis of the above critical perspectives and theories we designed the mobile messenger 'Digital Love Letter' (DLL),' which presents an original reflection on digital technology and interpersonal communication. It is a mobile messenger with a handwriting-based interface in which the expressive process of interaction is more important than the final output. The main concept of DLL is to share the process of communication using a non-instantaneous and non-multitasking interface, so users can share their time in a similar way to real world communication: with empathy. The central concept is that both writing and reading messages requires concentrated attention.

We performed an experimental study to see how people interact with each other through DLL. The concept of 'social presence' (see section 2.2) was used to evaluate this system. Social presence is a theoretical model used to analyze computer-mediated communication (CMC). This is usually explained as "the degree of salience of the other person in the interaction", but is also interpreted as empathy and mutual understanding in psychological involvement.

2 Related Work

2.1 CMC with Emotion

Computer-mediated communication (CMC) is increasingly used to maintain relationships, so people need to communicate emotionally through digital technology. Although researchers have offered a plethora of definitions of emotion, they are generally centered on a mental process related to affective states such as sadness, anger, fear, happiness, joy, and love. The term affect comes from the Latin word '*affectus*', which means passion or emotion. Affective information is complementary to cognitive information, which has a rational basis [8], [9]. Despite origins in rational thinking, technological developments increasingly allow affective communication through electronic and digital devices, so many authors regard emotion as an important factor in CMC.

Riordan, M [10] examined how people choose specific channels for socio-emotional communication over others. Three channels such as email, instant messaging (IM) and face to face (FTF) were assessed. Two types of positive emotions and negative emotions were assessed depending on channel choice. This study showed that the prominent reason for choosing FTF over email or IM was the existence of more emotional cues. It appeared that people rely on nonverbal and emotional cues when they communicate. However, Derks, D [11] suggested that there is no indication that CMC is a less emotional or less personally involving medium than in F2F. The conclusion was that emotions are abundant in CMC.

Hancock, J [12] analyzed how people express and detect emotions during text-based communication. It was found that disagreement, negative affect terms, punctuation and verbosity, were used by most communication partners to distinguish between positive and negative emotion in a textual communication context. Pfeil, U [13] investigated how empathy is expressed and facilitated in an online community for older people (SeniorNet). The qualitative content of 400 messages from an online message board about depression was analyzed. It was shown that empathy is an important aspect of online communication. Harris, R [14] also studied message cues in CMC that promote the transfer of affective information. Emotion words, linguistic markers and paralinguistic cues were shown to be factor for higher perceptions of emotions in CMC.

2.2 Social Presence

Interactive media systems for inter-communication can be evaluated through social presence. Social presence has been defined as the "sense of being with another in a mediated environment". It is increasingly known as an important factor for understanding effects of interactive media [15]. Hwang, H [16] analyzed the gratification utility of instant messaging from a social presence standpoint. This study showed that social presence plays an important role in communication through instant messaging services. It also shows that communicative competence is positively related to CMC through social presence [17].

There have been many proposals for the measurement of social presence. Short, J [18] proposed measuring social presence according to four dimensions: personal-impersonal, sensitive-insensitive, warm-cold and sociable-unsociable. High social presence is correlated to factors of how personal, sensitive, warm or sociable the presence is. Biocca, F [19] approached social presence with a networked-oriented measure, grouped with three areas: co-presence, psychological involvement and behavioral engagement. Co-presence is mutual awareness, psychological involvement is mutual understanding with empathic senses, and behavioral engagement refers to interdependent action. Nowak, K [20] differentiated co-presence from social presence, in that co-presence refers to the perceived sense of being with each other, while social presence refers to a broader concept that concerns the consequent salience of the interpersonal relationship. Nevertheless it was found that dimensions of co-presence and social presence were highly and significantly correlated.

2.3 Affective Messenger

There have been many attempts to design technology and systems for communicating emotional information through media, including delivering emotion through instant messaging aided by affective computing interfaces. Some authors have designed tactile interfaces to convey emotional contents. 'TCONs' [21] is a device that includes tactile output and input systems: vibrating motors, pin actuators, heat oil, pressure sensor, button and LEDs. The aim of this research was to support expression with an intuitive, tangible way through a Digital Messenger. 'iFeel_IM!' [22] is a system that integrates a 3D virtual world with affective computing haptic interfaces. It used automated emotion recognition from text messages, and haptic feedback, providing nonverbal communication through physical sensors. 3D avatars are visualized with automated emotion sensing by affective haptic devices, which include *HaptiHeart*, *HaptiHug*, *HaptiButterfly*, *HaptiTickler*, *HaptiTemper*, and *HaptiShiver*. 'HIM' [23] is also made by haptic instant messaging framework. They designed '*hapticons*' and haptic IO devices to augment the communication of text messages.

Besides haptic interfaces, emotion detection by computers has been used for mobile messaging systems, such as 'eMoto'. With eMoto users can compose messages through emotion related input, influenced by body gestures, and it renders a background of colors, shapes and animation [24]. 'Conductive Chat' [25] is an instant messaging system that incorporates user's skin conductivity levels, including emotional arousal, into a dialogue interface. 'FAIM' [26] is a 3D avatar based messaging system for empathic communication. It is a messaging application that shows each person as a 3D character who can express emotion through facial expression.

There are also non-academic, commercial online messengers that help people communicate privately and intimately. 'Snapchat' is a photo messaging application that allows users to set a time limit for how long recipients can view messages. 'Paintchat' is an online chat room that participants can draw together in real time with their partner.

3 Digital Love Letter

We authored the mobile messenger application 'Digital Love Letter' (DLL) for smart phone and tablet PC using the HTML5 standard. The interface was made to show users the whole, gradual *process* of writing the message in real time, so users do not just deliver information, but can focus on sharing the communication as it unfolds in time. In order to block one-way communication and multitasking, users cannot send a message if the receiver is not actively ready to receive it. Messages are not stored in the application, so users can only view a message once. The purpose of these constraints is to make an environment requiring patience and commitment. Users can also send an image and write or draw with their fingers to facilitate nuance through multi-layered communication. The client interface also offers an optional style with a blurred background images, emulating the personal, ephemeral atmosphere of drawing on a steamed-up window created from someone's breath. When the sender draws lines, the original, underlying image appears vividly (Fig.2).

The usage process outline is:

1. A sender turns on the mobile messenger application 'Digital Love Letter'.
2. The sender chooses a receiver and awaits the receipt.
3. The receiver accepts the connection.
4. The sender takes or chooses an image and writes or draws on the image.
5. The receiver sees every process that a sender writes or draws.

The server application for DLL was developed using Flask, a Python-based web framework, while the client used HTML5 and JavaScript. We designed 'DLL' using web technologies to operate on any mobile device.

As a user draws lines in the client web application, the application sends each frame update at regular intervals to the server using a web protocol. The server stores the every frame until their partner's client web application request it from the server. If the receiving client receives the images, it will be displayed in the web application (Fig.1).

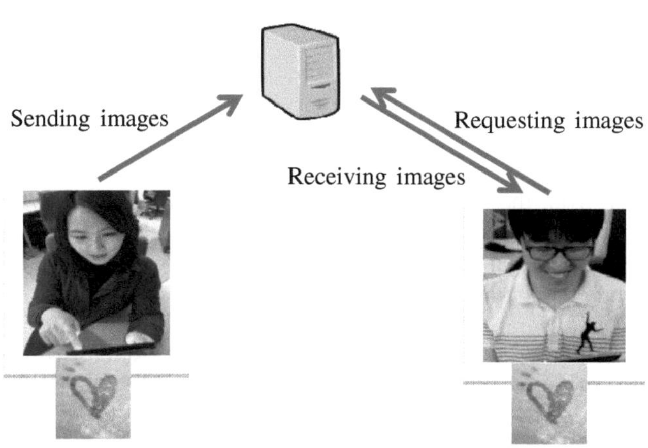

Fig. 1. System Architecture

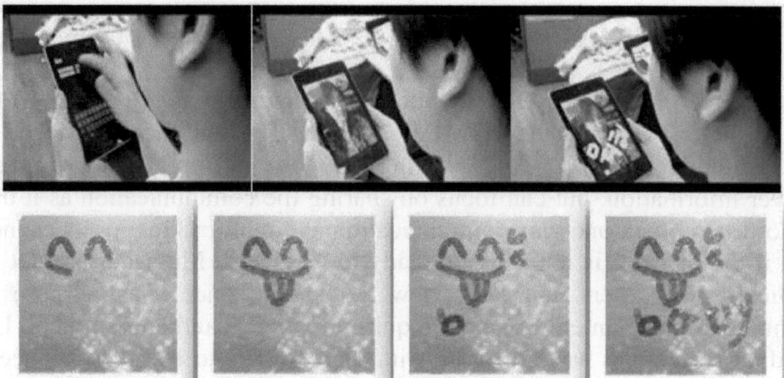

Fig. 2. Time-lapse screenshots

4 Experimental Study

4.1 A Preliminary Test

We performed a preliminary test with thirty people (17 female, 13male; 5 undergraduate students, 20 graduate students, 5 full-time employees). We let them use the 'Digital Love Letter' once or twice with randomly-assigned partners in a testing room, followed by a survey. The survey included 10 items of multiple-choice and 3 items of short form answers. We asked people how they commonly communicate through digital technology and compared it with the way of communication through the DLL prototype. Through questionnaires, the differences between non-instant and instant communication mediated by computers were analyzed. The most commonly reported method of communicating emotion in other messaging services was through the use of emoticons and participants were asked to compare that with their emotion communication experience using DLL. Most people responded that sharing of the writing process is the main attraction and dominant feature of DLL compared to other messengers. The feedback on the overall experience of using DLL was generally positive.

5 User Study

5.1 System Setting

Based on feedback from the experimental study we developed the hypothesis that an interface that shows the process of writing in real time will result in users having a higher perception of social presence. To test this hypothesis we developed a secondary user study using variations of the DLL system.

We compared two types of handwriting-based messenger writing interfaces that utilize a simplified interface with a black pen on a white screen (Fig.3). The first variation was the visually simplified version of type DLL, which still shares the process of writing with a partner in real time. The second variation, which we called 'Digital Letter' (DL),' was designed such that the process of writing is not shared, so the receiver only sees the final output image.

Our hypothesis is that the average score of the sense of co-presence in the DLL will be higher than that of the DL (Hypothesis 1). Also, DLL will result in a higher sense of psychological involvement in user experience than DL (Hypothesis 2).

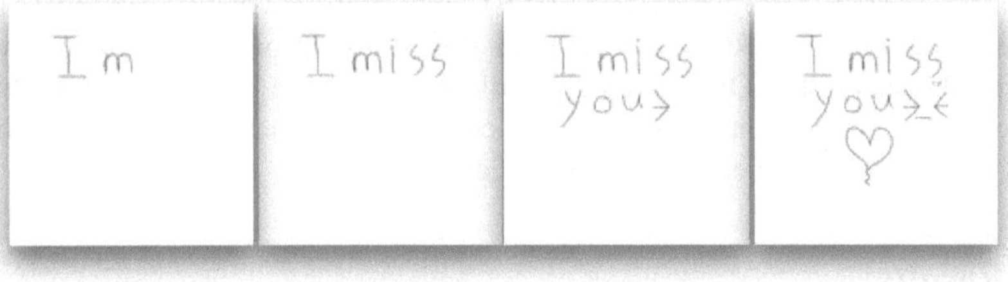

Fig. 3. Process time-lapse for the simplified application variations used in the second user study. In the first variation (DLL), the receiver also sees the whole process of writing as it unfolds. In the second variations (DL), the receiver receives only the final image, none of the intermediate stages.

5.2 Procedure

We conducted a user study with couples that identified themselves as being in a romantic relationship, to evaluate private and intimate communication through DLL. Ten couples were recruited using a university online message board and given monetary compensation. All participants were university students, ranging between 21 and 27years of age. Two couples had been in relationship for three or more years, two couples for two to three years, and six couples for one to two years. Participants used the DLL and DL variations for ten minutes each, with their partner in a separated room, and were asked to complete the questionnaire about co-presence and psychological involvement of social presence. The task they were given was to express love to their partner by drawing affectionate figures or writing some short text. We let them suppose they were not within close range of each other. Five couples were asked to use the DL first and the other five couples to use the DLL first. The participants were requested to fill the questionnaire after they used our messenger. When one experimental session was finished, we did an interview with the couple together.

5.3 Measurement

The co-presence measurement developed by Nowak, K [20] was used to measure participant's perceptions of social presence. The twelve items of the co-presence questionnaire were measured by 5-point Likert scale (Strongly agree=5, Strongly disagree=1, Cronbach`s alpha=.85). The psychological involvement measurement of social presence included two sub factors: empathy and mutual understanding. The psychological involvement questionnaire had twelve items estimated by seven-point Likert scale (Strongly agree=7, Strongly disagree =1, Cronbach`s alpha =.91) [19]. All participants were asked to complete the questionnaire of the co-presence and the psychological involvement after they finished the task with DL and DLL.

5.4 Usability Test

The usability of DLL was measured through The Post-Study System Usability Questionnaire (PSSUQ) with a seven-point Likert scale. The PSSUQ includes three sub scales: System Usefulness (SYSUSE), Information Quality (INFQUAL) and Interface Quality (INTERQUAL) [27]. In this study Information Quality was not measured because the DLL prototype did not include support information or documentation. Participants were asked to complete the questionnaires regarding the usability when they finished the testing process.

6 Results

6.1 Social Presence

We conducted a paired t-test with data from eighteen participants. Answers from two of the original twenty participants were deemed unreliable due to inconsistency in inverted questions. It was found that there was a statistically significant difference of perception of co-presence between DL (M=3.94, SD=.96) and DLL (M=4.38, SD=.91) ; two-tailed paired t test, $t(17)=3.01$, $p<0.01$. Therefore, hypothesis 1 was supported. However, no significant difference was found for sub factors of psychological involvement between the two groups. Hypothesis 2 was not supported.

Table 1. Comparison of co-presence between DL and DLL. Co-presnece is measured by 5-point Likert scale (stronly agree=5, strongly disagree=1).

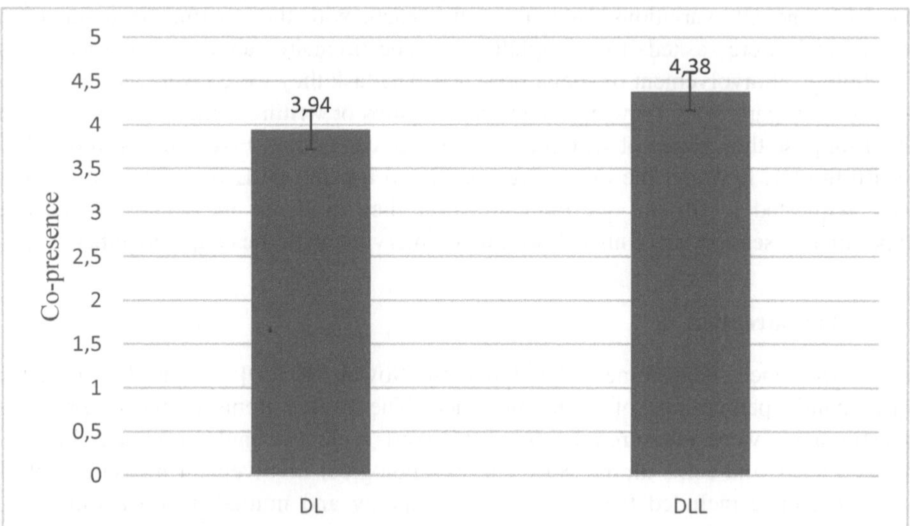

6.2 Usability Test

We measured the satisfaction of the participants through The Post-Study System Usability Questionnaire (PSSUQ) with a seven-point Likert scale. High scores are better than low scores due to the fixation used in the 7-point scales [27]. Results showed that overall satisfaction score was 5.03 and System Usefulness (SYSUSE) score was 5.34 and Interface Quality (INTERQUAL) score was 4.43.

Table 2. Usability test

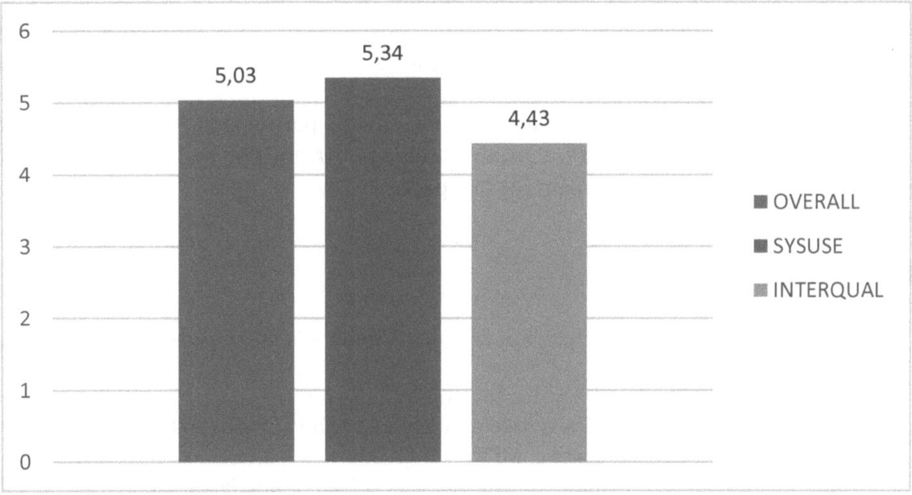

7 Discussion and Conclusion

We made the digital mobile messenger DLL with a handwriting-based interface that shares the process of communication non-instantaneously and without multi-tasking. The DLL application, where messages are not stored for later retrieval, requires concentrated attention from users while they write and read messages. We tried to reflect on the digital messaging service and CMC through this system from a critical perspective.

We compared a DLL prototype with DL, where the process of writing could not be shared, via a co-presence and social presence questionnaire. The difference of co-presence between DL and DLL was significant, but a significant difference in psychological involvement was not found. We also did a usability test through PSSUQ. The overall satisfaction and system usefulness score was found to be high but the interface quality score was relatively low, suggesting an area of improvement for future versions.

It was found that sharing the process of writing on a messaging service was effective to perceive co-presence. However, there were limitations on measuring psychological involvement such as empathy and mutual understanding precisely because the experiment duration was too short to build emphatic and mutual communication. The reasons of low interface quality score were revealed through the users' interviews. The user interface was not designed aesthetically to support sensorial communication. Thus, there are many necessary improvements for the interface design, including an erasing function and diverse colors.

Many participants showed different attitudes when functioning as a sender to being a receiver. They felt burdened by the fact that their partner could see their entire writing process, because they had to be more cautious and conscious. In contrast, they showed much interest in seeing their partner's writing process and even tended to enjoy observing their partner's hesitations and difficulties. In future research, we plan to differentiate emotional response between sender and receiver through a longitude experiment with a more developed DLL design.

Acknowledgments. We would like to thank all the participants of the study and thanks to Prof. Chongwook Park, Patrick Hutchings, Arram Bae and Jimin Rhim who provided insights and improvement for this paper.

References

1. Myerson, G.: Heidegger, Habermas and the Mobile Phone (Postmodern Encounters) (2001)
2. Turkle, S.: Can you hear me now. Forbes. com 5(7), 7 (2007)
3. Kirn, W.: The autumn of the multitaskers. Atlantic Monthly, 66–80 (2007)
4. Picard, R.W.: Affective computing. MIT press (2000)
5. Wong, M.: Emotion assessment in evaluation of affective interfaces. Neuron 65(3), 293 (2006)
6. Dourish, P., Finlay, J., Sengers, P., Wright, P.: Reflective HCI: Towards a critical technical practice. In: CHI 2004 Extended Abstracts on Human Factors in Computing Systems, pp. 1727–1728. ACM (April 2004)
7. Agre, P.: Toward a Critical Technical Practice: Lessons Learned in Trying to Reform AI. Social science, technical systems, and cooperative work. Beyond the Great Divide 131 (1997)
8. Konijn, E.A., Van Vugt, H.C.: Emotions in mediated interpersonal communication. Mediated Interpersonal Communication 100 (2008)
9. Brave, S., Nass, C.: Emotion in human-computer interaction. The human-computer interaction handbook: fundamentals, evolving technologies and emerging applications, pp. 81–96 (2002)
10. Riordan, M.A., Kreuz, R.J.: Emotion encoding and interpretation in computer-mediated communication: Reasons for use. Computers in Human Behavior 26(6), 1667–1673 (2010)
11. Derks, D., Fischer, A.H., Bos, A.E.: The role of emotion in computer-mediated communication: A review. Computers in Human Behavior 24(3), 766–785 (2008)
12. Hancock, J.T., Landrigan, C., Silver, C.: Expressing emotion in text-based communication. In: Proceedings of the SIGCHI Conference on Human Factors in Computing Systems, pp. 929–932. ACM (April 2007)
13. Pfeil, U., Zaphiris, P.: Patterns of empathy in online communication. In: Proceedings of the SIGCHI Conference on Human Factors in Computing Systems, pp. 919–928. ACM (April 2007)

14. Harris, R.B., Paradice, D.: An investigation of the computer-mediated communication of emotions. Journal of Applied Sciences Research 3(12), 2081–2090 (2007)
15. Tu, C.H.: The impacts of text-based CMC on online social presence. The Journal of Interactive Online Learning 1(2), 1–24 (2002)
16. Hwang, H.S., Lombard, M.: Understanding instant messaging: Gratifications and social presence. In: Proceedings of PRESENCE 2006, pp. 50–56 (2006)
17. Hwang, Y.: Is communication competence still good for interpersonal media?: Mobile phone and instant messenger. Computers in Human Behavior 27(2), 924–934 (2011)
18. Short, J., Williams, E., Christie, B.: The social psychology of telecommunications (1976)
19. Biocca, F., Harms, C., Gregg, J.: The networked minds measure of social presence: Pilot test of the factor structure and concurrent validity. In: 4th Annual International Workshop on Presence, Philadelphia, PA (May 2001)
20. Nowak, K.: Defining and differentiating copresence, social presence and presence as transportation. In: Presence 2001 Conference, Philadelphia, PA (2001)
21. Shin, H., Lee, J., Park, J., Kim, Y., Oh, H., Lee, T.: A tactile emotional interface for instant messenger chat. In: Smith, M.J., Salvendy, G. (eds.) HCII 2007. LNCS, vol. 4558, pp. 166–175. Springer, Heidelberg (2007)
22. Neviarouskaya, A., Tsetserukou, D., Prendinger, H., Kawakami, N., Tachi, S., Ishizuka, M.: Emerging system for affectively charged interpersonal communication. In: ICCAS-SICE, pp. 3376–3381. IEEE (August 2009)
23. Rovers, A.F., van Essen, H.: HIM: a framework for haptic instant messaging. In: CHI 2004 Extended Abstracts on Human Factors in Computing Systems, pp. 1313–1316. ACM (April 2004)
24. Sundström, P., Ståhl, A., Höök, K.: In situ informants exploring an emotional mobile messaging system in their everyday practice. International Journal of Human-Computer Studies 65(4), 388–403 (2007)
25. DiMicco, J.M., Lakshmipathy, V., Fiore, A.T.: Conductive Chat: Instant messaging with a skin conductivity channel. In: Proceedings of Conference on Computer Supported Cooperative Work (November 2002)
26. Fabri, M., Moore, D.J., Hobbs, D.J.: Empathy and enjoyment in instant messaging. In: Proceedings of 19th British HCI Group Annual Conference (HCI 2005), Edinburgh, UK, pp. 4–9 (September 2005)
27. Lewis, J.R.: IBM computer usability satisfaction questionnaires: psychometric evaluation and instructions for use. International Journal of Human-Computer Interaction 7(1), 57–78 (1995)

Evaluation Based Graphical Controls: A Contribution to Mobile User Interface Early Evaluation

Selem Charfi, Houcine Ezzedine, and Christophe Kolski

L.A.M.I.H. – UMR CNRS 8201
UVHC, Le Mont Houy, 59313 Valenciennes Cedex 9, France
{Selem.Charfi,Houcine.Ezzedine,
Christophe.Kolski}@univ-valenciennes.fr

Abstract. In this paper, we present a set of graphical controls intended for the coupling between the design and the evaluation of mobile user interfaces. It is a contribution to user interface early evaluation. The presented controls include mechanisms aiming to inspect their consistency according to a predefined set of ergonomic guidelines. We also report on the proposed approach current implementation, and an example of application.

Keywords: User interface evaluation, mobile user interface, early evaluation, graphical control, ergonomic guideline, usability.

1 Introduction

The era in which we live is surely the information one. It is marked by the propagation of Information Technologies. Thus, many interactive devices are designed to enable users to manipulate different kinds of information. Among these devices, mobile devices are the most used ones. As a consequence, mobile software designers are faced with many challenges. In this work, we focus on the information display on these devices. In fact, the user interface is the mobile software part ensuring communication between applications and users. Thus, it has to be validated for better use and for ensuring intuitive use. Many works were proposed to provide better interaction between mobile devices and their users: guidelines, design patterns, evaluation methods, etc. [11] [13].

In this paper, we propose a set of graphical controls for designing user interfaces through Integrated Development Environments (IDE) using the WYSIWYG[1] principle. These controls support an *auto-evaluation* process. This evaluation is made as checking the consistency of the control according to selected guidelines. These guidelines are selected by the evaluator and are coded externally from the controls. Then, they are not hard coded into the evaluation engine. The adopted evaluation process is applied by early evaluation phases.

---

[1] *What You See Is What You Get.*

M. Kurosu (Ed.): Human-Computer Interaction, Part III, HCII 2014, LNCS 8512, pp. 114–123, 2014.

The remainder of the paper is organized in the following way: first, we briefly survey the related work. Then, we present our contribution. Next, we present an overview of our proposal current implementation and an example of application in order to evaluate feasibility, time, and cost. Finally, this paper ends with a conclusion and research perspectives.

2 Related Work

2.1 Mobile User Interface Evaluation

In the last decade, the mobile devices quickly changed from a simple phone device (i.e. ensuring calling and receiving calls) to a complex system operating many features (e.g. internet browsing, GPS, and entertainment). Researches about mobile devices' interfaces have been an evolving area. Consequently, a new need is growing [11]. It concerns methodologies and tools ensuring the evaluation of mobile user interfaces [14]. Mobile application developers, evaluators and users converge to the fact that usability is an important and an indispensable quality factor of the mobile devices [10] [12]. As a consequence, many works supporting such evaluation are elaborated. Most of classical evaluation methods can be applied to mobile user interface evaluation such as heuristic evaluation, cognitive walkthroughs, Think Aloud Protocol, and usability testing [8]. Beck et al. affirm that 44 out of 114 scientific papers (recent papers related to HCI field) opt to traditional evaluation methods and that only 6 of them exploited new methods for mobile user interface evaluation [1].

As mobile phones have been evolving in an increasing pace, many recommendations, style guides and guidelines are proposed by mobile device industries such as "*BlackBerry SmartPhones: UI Guidelines*"[2] and "*iOS Human Interface Guidelines*"[3] by *Apple*. They are mainly intended to assist designers to conceive ergonomic user interfaces and then to improve the provided interaction. They can also be used for user interface evaluation by validating these interfaces according them.

2.2 Available Tools for Mobile User Interface Evaluation

As interest in automatic support for the evaluation of mobile interfaces is rapidly growing, recent works are proposed to support and improve this evaluation. They have mainly introduced methods for gathering and/or analyzing data for the evaluation such as the case of "Experience Sampling Method" [7] and "Diary Studies" [21]. The proposed methods are implemented as tools like Momento [3], the tool proposed by Carta et al. [2], MultiDevice RemUsine [19], and MyExperience [9].

Generally these tools gather usage information about the interaction between the user and the interface. Some tools exploit questionnaire as a complementary evaluation method. Others, such as MultiDevice RemUsine, adopt a remote evaluation in order to enable the users to use the phone in real context and to not bother

[2] `http://tinyurl.com/4t7lydl`

[3] `http://tinyurl.com/oyu4mx3`

them during interaction sessions. Furthermore, remote evaluation enables users to use the mobile devices in their familiar environments to gain more *natural* behavior [19]. Other tools exploit log files to gather usage information. The data analysis is a difficult task due to the fact that the use context varies a lot from a user to another. In addition to that, for the same user, the context can constantly change. Some works are conducted in order to support the evaluation of context based applications (e.g. The Topiary System [17]).

2.3 Early Evaluation

Most of the proposed mobile user interface evaluation methods and tools are applied during the last phase of the mobile application life cycle. The common principle consists in first designing the graphical user interface, implementing the software interface, and finally evaluating it. In this case, effort, time, and resource loss are detected. In fact, after the evaluation process, in the case of design error detection, the designer has to correct the interface (and even to re-design it). To avoid such loss, it is recommended by several authors to proceed to the evaluation process (or take into consideration the evaluation specificities and requirements) since early mobile application life cycle phases. It is the case of early evaluation. This evaluation is defined by Tarby and his colleagues as coupling between the evaluation and the design phases [22]. Thus, we propose to proceed with the evaluation process since first mobile application life cycle phases.

2.4 Motivation

Our goal is to support the evaluation since early design stages and then to reduce evaluation cost and to facilitate it to evaluators. Rather than using complex features for the evaluation, we opt for an easy to use approach to support designers to create ergonomic mobile user interfaces.

In general, existing evaluation tools for mobile user interfaces focus on the ensured interaction between the user and the interface. Nevertheless, the mobile phones are very personal devices and each user interacts differently than others due to the variant contexts: quite or noisy environment, alone or accompanied by other persons, etc. Then, we opt to heuristic evaluation for the reason that it does not approximate the conditions under which user use the mobile device [20]. Furthermore, it is easier and less costly than user tests. These choices are also augmented by the fact that mobile phone application development is relatively short compared to consumer appliances [15]. Kallio and Kekalainen [14] reported that the mobile application life cycle is limited considering the rapid change in mobile technology and the extensively competitive market [14]. Thus, there is a great demand in mobile industry marked by low time constraints and minimal efforts requirements for evaluation approaches and methods [11] [14]. Our proposal concerns to couple between the design and the evaluation phases into a fast and inexpensive phase.

In addition to that, one of the main goals of the present proposal is to make the evaluation as automated as possible. It is mainly due to the fact that automation enables evaluation to save considerable time comparing to manual and semi-automated evaluations. It increases then the possible frequency of evaluation sessions [4].

3 Proposal of Graphical Controls Intended for the Design and the Evaluation of Mobile User Interfaces

3.1 The Proposed Approach

The proposed approach consists in assisting the designer for implementing user interface. It is applicable for WYSIWYG principle based IDE to conceive consistent interfaces according to ergonomic guidelines specified by the evaluator, Fig. 5. Every time the designer adds a new control to the user interface, he/she is notified by this control about its coherence according to the selected guidelines (by the evaluator). The notification message is generated by the new control following its self-inspection according to these guidelines. The proposed controls support such evaluation specificities. They also support usual controls' functionalities and provide the same layout. They, first, inherit from the IDE proposed controls. Then, they consider evaluation specificities by integrating specific mechanisms. These mechanisms enable the control to inspect its coherence according to a set of ergonomic guidelines (EG) and then to notify the designer about eventual inconsistencies [5].

3.2 Ergonomic Guidelines Modeling

To proceed to the evaluation, the selected guidelines have to be expressed into XML files following a specific format. We opt for a simplistic modeling of the guidelines. A guideline is defined though: an ID, a name, a reference, an associated error, an associated recommendation, an evaluated aspect, an associated operator (i.e. superior, inferior, equal, different, different from, in, count, and between), and recommended value(s). A guideline is considered by the control as a logical expression:

```
If (control_value EG_Operator (EG_Value1; EG_Value2))
{ } // These is not any design problem related to the control.
Else // A design problem is detected.
{
 Error = Error + EG_Error;
 Recommendation = Recommendation + EG_Recommendation ;
// Show the detected design problem through a notification message
}
```

Fig. 1. Depicts an example of an ergonomic guideline expressed through XML notation. This guideline is: "*Given the unpredictability of color screens and of users, the choice can be very complicated. In general, do not use more than three primary colors for information* "[23].

```
- <Guideline>
    <EG_ID>#ER15</EG_ID>
    <EG_Name>Font Colors </EG_Name>
    <EG_Controls> Button, TextBox, Label, RadioBox, ComboBox</EG_Controls>
    <EG_Aspects>Font.Color</EG_Aspects>
    <EG_Operator>In</EG_Operator>
    <EG_Value1>Black, Red, Green, Blue</EG_Value1>
    <EG_Value2>Null</EG_Value2>
  - <EG_Error>
      Design error related to information display colors
    </EG_Error>
  - <EG_Recommendation>
      Given the unpredictability of color screens and of users, the choice can be very complicated. In general, do not use more than three primary colors
      for information
    </EG_Recommendation>
  - <EG_Reference>
      Watzman, S.: Visual design principles for usable interfaces. In Sears A., Jacko J.A. (Eds.), The Human Computer Interaction Handbook, CRC
      Press, 263-285 (2002).
    </EG_Reference>
  </Guideline>
```

Fig. 2. An example of ergonomic guideline expressed through XML notation

To model a guideline, the evaluator can specify it into XML file manually or can use a dedicated tool for this modeling, Fig. 3.

This tool enables evaluators to: add new guidelines; modify existing guidelines; view existing guidelines, and modify the configuration (save path and file name).

3.3 Proposed Evaluation Process

As depicted in Fig. 4, the design/evaluation process requires two stakeholders: a designer for the conception of user interfaces, and an evaluator for the selection of guidelines. Note that, according to Law and Hvannberg [16], the effectiveness of the evaluation process closely depends on the selected guidelines. Thus, the evaluator has to select adequate guidelines to cover the largest possible specter of the user interface design problems. The selection of ergonomic guidelines is an important phase established at the first step. Then, the selected guidelines are modeled through a dedicated tool into XML files as described in the previous sub-section, Fig. 3. Next, the designer conceives the user interface by dragging and dropping the proposed graphical controls from the tool panel to the user interface. Every time a control is added to the interface, it loads the selected guidelines into memory and inspects it-self according to these guidelines. The control includes algorithms to proceed to the inspection. Therefore, it draws itself on the interface and updates the evaluation file (i.e. a text file) and the interface configuration file. A notification message is generated and shown to the designer including the detected inconsistencies(s) and the related recommendations. The designer re-iterates this sub-process until finishing the interface design. At the end, the evaluator reviews the design/evaluation report.

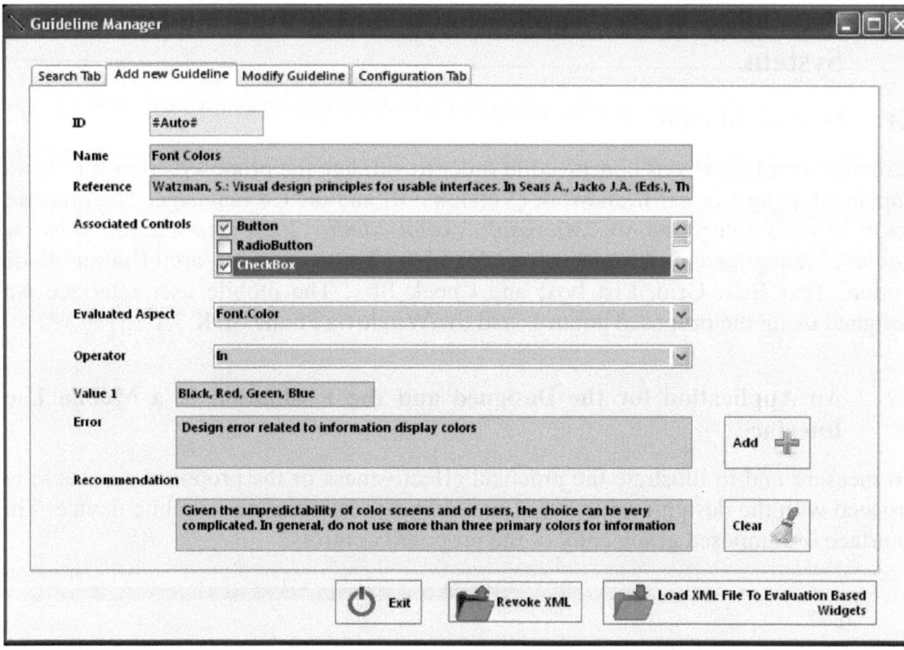

Fig. 3. A screen shot of the Guideline Manager User Interface

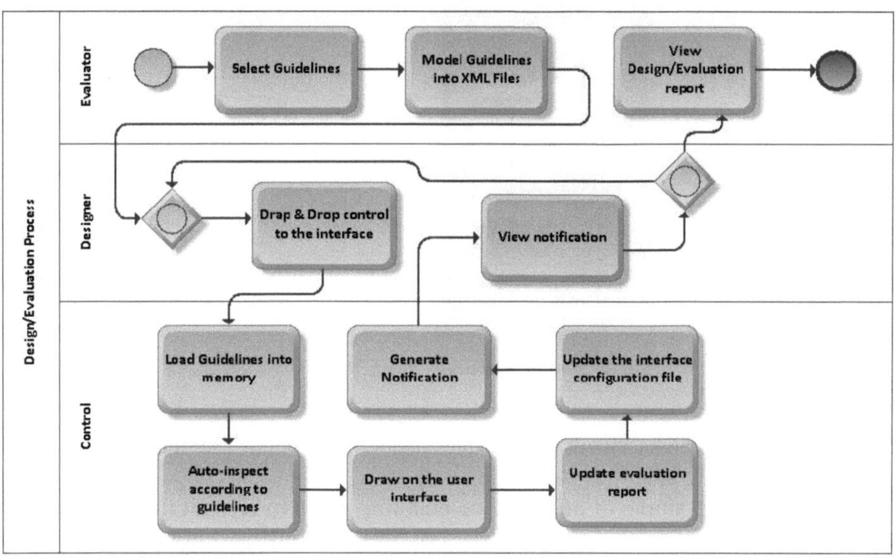

Fig. 4. The proposed Design/Evaluation process modeled through BPMN[4]

[4] Business Process Model and Notations.

4 Feasibility Study: Application to an Information Diffusion System

4.1 Implementation

A research prototype was conceived in order to validate the proposed approach. It was implanted using *Dot net* framework (Version 3.0) and the *C#* language. The proposed controls were integrated to "*Microsoft Visual Studio 2010 Express for Windows Phone*" [5] integrated development environment. These controls are: Button, Radio Button, Text Box, Grid, List box, and Check Box. The mobile user interface was designed using the proposed controls and the Windows Phone SDK 7.1[6].

4.2 An Application for the Designed and the Evaluation of a Mobile User Interface

To measure and to illustrate the practical effectiveness of the proposed approach, we proceed with the design/evaluation of an interface operating on a mobile device. This interface is composed graphically of the proposed controls.

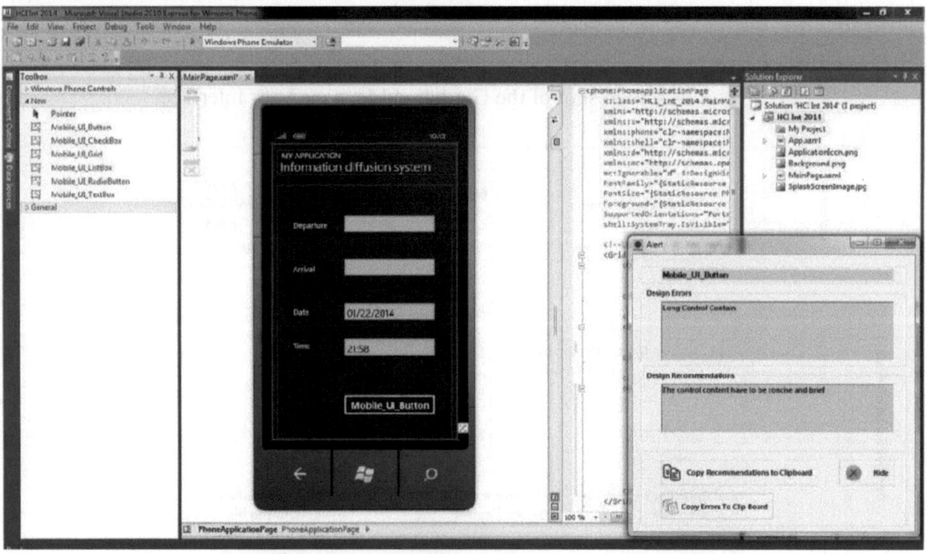

Fig. 5. A screen shot of the design/evaluation of a mobile user interface

We choose the example of an interface enabling users to consult the time schedule of vehicles on a transportation network. For this feasibility study, we select a set of ten guidelines related to: character size, color, and font; size, and number of the pictures and icons; text length; widget dimensions; the number of used colors; global interface density, and background color.

5 `http://tinyurl.com/mlyokg4`

6 `http://tinyurl.com/onnbvtv`

Every time the design adds a control to the user interface, a notification message is shown on the screen to report ergonomic inconsistencies (the detected error(s) and the related recommendation(s), Fig. 6.

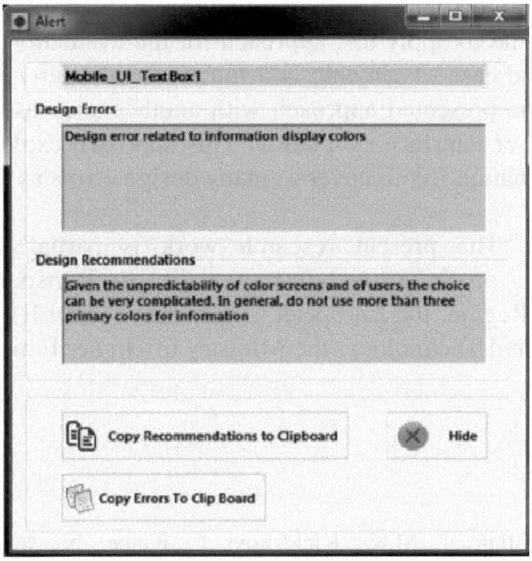

Fig. 6. An example of a notification message

5 Conclusion and Future Work

In the present paper, we first presented an overview of the existing works about mobile user interface evaluation. Then, we presented our approach for mobile user interfaces early evaluation. The approach consists of a set of graphical controls that inspect themselves according to ergonomic guidelines that are not hard coded into the evaluation engine. Then, we reported its current implementation, and an example of application.

The main advantage of this approach is the fact that is it applicable during the first stages of the mobile application life cycle. Furthermore, as illustrated in the previous section, it is relatively easy and simple to apply. In addition, the proposed evaluation process is automated. It requires only the evaluator for selecting guidelines and the designer for the conception of the user interface. Moreover, the provided results are not costly in terms of effort, required resources, and materiel cost. However, the provided evaluation is made locally and does not consider the overall user interface; it is made control by control. The proposed approach does not indicate clearly the quality of the conceived interface; it only indicates about the detected ergonomic inconsistencies. In addition, the detected problems are related to the low severity rate of ergonomic problems (in the sense of Nielsen design error classification [18]); the detected design errors are mainly related to cosmetic errors' category. Furthermore, the proposed guideline modeling supports only some guidelines and cannot be applied to all guidelines (e.g. for instance: "A control font color has to be different from the control fore color." cannot be modeled through the proposed guidelines modeling.).

As perspectives for future research, we first intend to integrate *intelligent* mechanisms into the guidelines that they can adapt themselves following the selected guidelines. Such task needs to find a way to resolve the problem of guidelines contradiction. Second, we intend to apply this approach for the evaluation of post-WIMP user interfaces, such is the case of tangible and touch-sensitive user interface. Third, we intend to combine the presented approach with another one based on graphical controls dedicated for user interface evaluation. This approach exploits the user interaction data for the evaluation [6], to cover as many design errors as possible.

Acknowledgements. The present research work is partially supported by the International Campus on Safety and Inter-modality in Transportation (CISIT), the Nord-Pas-de-Calais Region, the European Community (FEDER), the Regional Delegation for Research and Technology, the Ministry of Higher Education and Research, and the CNRS.

References

1. Beck, E.T., Christiansen, M.K., Kjeldskov, J., Kolbe, N., Stage, J.: Experimental evaluation of techniques for usability testing of mobile systems in a laboratory setting. In: Viller, S., Wyeth, P. (eds.) Proceedings of OZCHI 2003 Conference, pp. 106–115. CHISIG, Brisbane (2003)
2. Carta, T., Paternò, F., Santana, V.: Support for Remote Usability Evaluation of Web Mobile Applications. In: SIGDOC 2011, Pisa, Italy, October 3-5, pp. 129–136. ACM, New York (2011)
3. Carter, S., Mankoff, J., Heer, J.: Momento: Support for Situated Ubicomp Experimentation. In: CHI 2007, pp. 125–134. ACM, New York (2007)
4. Charfi, S., Ezzedine, H., Kolski, C., Moussa, F.: Towards an automatic analysis of interaction data for HCI evaluation: Application to a transport network supervision system. In: Jacko, J.A. (ed.) Human-Computer Interaction, Part I, HCII 2011. LNCS, vol. 6761, pp. 175–184. Springer, Heidelberg (2011)
5. Charfi, S., Trabelsi, A., Ezzedine, H., Kolski, C.: Graphical Controls Based Environment for User Interface Evaluation. In: Winckler, M., Forbrig, P., Bernhaupt, R. (eds.) HCSE 2012. LNCS, vol. 7623, pp. 360–367. Springer, Heidelberg (2012)
6. Charfi, S., Trabelsi, A., Ezzedine, H., Kolski, C.: A User-Oriented Test environment based on User-Interface evaluation graphical controls. In: 12th IFAC/IFIP/IFORS/IEA Symposium on Analysis, Design, and Evaluation of Human-Machine Systems, Las Vegas, USA, August 11-15, pp. 494–504. IFAC (2013)
7. Consolvo, S., Walker, M.: Using the Experience Sampling Method to Evaluate Ubicomp Applications. IEEE Pervasive Computing 2(2), 24–31 (2003)
8. Duh, H.B.L., Tan, G.C.B., Chen, V.H.: Usability evaluation for mobile device: a comparison of laboratory and field tests. In: Proceedings of the 8th Conference on Human-Computer Interaction with Mobile Devices and Services (MobileHCI 2006), pp. 181–186. ACM, New York (2006)

9. Froehlich, J., Chen, M., Consolvo, S., Harrison, B., Landay, J.A.: MyExperience: A System for In Situ Tracing and Capturing of User Feedback on Mobile Phones. In: Proceedings of the 5th International Conference on Mobile Systems, Applications and Services (MobiSys 2007), San Juan, Puerto Rico, pp. 57–70. ACM, New York (2007)
10. Hartson, H.R., Andre, T.S., Williges, R.C.: Criteria for evaluating usability evaluation methods. International Journal of Human-Computer Interaction 13(4), 373–410 (2001)
11. Ji, Y.G., Park, J.H., Lee, C., Yun, M.H.: A usability checklist for the usability evaluation of mobile phone interfaces. International Journal of Human-Computer Interaction 20(3), 207–231 (2006)
12. Jokela, T., Iivari, N., Matero, J., Karukka, M.: The standard of user-centered design and the standard definition of usability: analyzing ISO 13407 against ISO 9241-11, pp. 53–60. ACM, New York (2003)
13. Jones, M., Marsden, G.: Mobile Interaction Design. John Wiley and Sons Ltd. (2006)
14. Kallio, T., Kekäläinen, A.: Improving the effectiveness of mobile application design: User-pairs testing by non-professionals. In: Brewster, S., Dunlop, M.D. (eds.) Mobile HCI 2004. LNCS, vol. 3160, pp. 315–319. Springer, Heidelberg (2004)
15. Klockar, T., Carr, D.A., Hedman, A., Johansson, T., Bengtsson, F.: Usability of mobile phones. In: Proceedings of the 19th International Symposium on Human Factors in Telecommunications, Berlin, Germany, December 1-4, vol. 4, pp. 197–204 (2003)
16. Law, E.L., Hvannberg, E.T.: Analysis of strategies for improving and estimating the effectiveness of heuristic evaluation. In: Proceedings of the Third Nordic Conference on Human-Computer Interaction, pp. 241–250. ACM, New York (2004)
17. Li, Y., Hong, J., Landay, J.: Topiary - Design Challenges and Principles for Wizard of Oz Testing of Location-Enhanced Applications. In: Pervasive Computing, vol. 6(2), pp. 70–75. IEEE Press (2007)
18. Nielsen, J.: Engineering Usability. Morgan Kaufmann Publishers Inc., San Francisco (1993) ISBN 0125184050
19. Paternò, F., Russino, A., Santoro, C.: Remote evaluation of mobile applications. In: Winckler, M., Johnson, H. (eds.) TAMODIA 2007. LNCS, vol. 4849, pp. 155–169. Springer, Heidelberg (2007)
20. de Sá, M., Carriço, L.: An Evaluation Framework for Mobile User Interfaces. In: Gross, T., Gulliksen, J., Kotzé, P., Oestreicher, L., Palanque, P., Prates, R.O., Winckler, M. (eds.) INTERACT 2009. LNCS, vol. 5726, pp. 708–721. Springer, Heidelberg (2009)
21. Sohn, T., Li, K.A., Griswold, W.G., Hollan, J.D.: A diary study of mobile information needs. In: Proceedings of the SIGCHI Conference on Human Factors in Computing Systems, CHI 2008, Florence, Italy, pp. 433–442. ACM, New York (2008)
22. Tarby, J.C., Ezzedine, H., Kolski, C.: Trace-based usability evaluation using aspect-oriented programming and agent-based software architecture. In: Seffah, A., Vanderdonckt, J., Desmarais, M.C. (eds.) HCSE. Human-Computer Interaction Series, pp. 257–276. Springer, London (2009) ISBN 978-1-84800-906-6
23. Watzman, S.: Visual design principles for usable interfaces. In: Sears, A., Jacko, J.A. (eds.) The Human Computer Interaction Handbook, pp. 263–285. L. Erlbaum Associates Inc. (2003)

Smartphone Input Using Its Integrated Projector and Built-In Camera

Sergiu Dotenco, Timo Götzelmann, and Florian Gallwitz

Nuremberg Institute of Technology, Germany
{sergiu.dotenco,timo.goetzelmann,florian.gallwitz}@ohm-university.eu

Abstract. Touch input on modern smartphones can be tedious, especially if the touchscreen is small. Smartphones with integrated projectors can be used to overcome this limitation by projecting the screen contents onto a surface, allowing the user to interact with the projection by means of simple hand gestures. In this work, we propose a novel approach for projector smartphones that allows the user to remotely interact with the smartphone screen via its projection. We detect user's interaction using the built-in camera, and forward detected hand gestures as touch input events to the operating system. In order to avoid costly computations, we additionally use built-in motion sensors. We verify the proposed method using an implementation for the consumer smartphone Samsung Galaxy Beam equipped with a deflection mirror.

Keywords: Mobile computing, user interfaces, small screen, fat finger problem, touch input, fingertip detection, projector smartphone, DLP projector.

1 Introduction

In the last few years, the size of touchscreens increased rapidly. Today, mobile devices are available in various sizes and form factors. There is a smooth transition between smartphones and tablet computers with a touch sensitive user interface. Modern devices often feature screen sizes up to 5 inches. These so called *phablets* have even larger screens. However, as the smartphones are typically carried in bags or pockets, their size is subject to physical constraints. Often, the size of the smartphone and its handiness are inversely proportional.

As the size of smartphones generally faces physical limitations, the size of the touch input area is affected by this limitation as well. A user study in ergonomics by Colle and Hiszem [3] has shown that a correlation between the size of the touch input area and the user input performance exists. A typical example is the input using a virtual keyboard which can be very tedious, since the space reserved for individual keys is limited.

Despite the use of high resolution displays combined with precise capacitive touchscreens and sophisticated algorithms that can filter out unwanted input events, the problem of limited screen space remains unsolved. The input using a virtual keyboard is even more problematic for small devices.

M. Kurosu (Ed.): Human-Computer Interaction, Part III, HCII 2014, LNCS 8512, pp. 124–133, 2014.

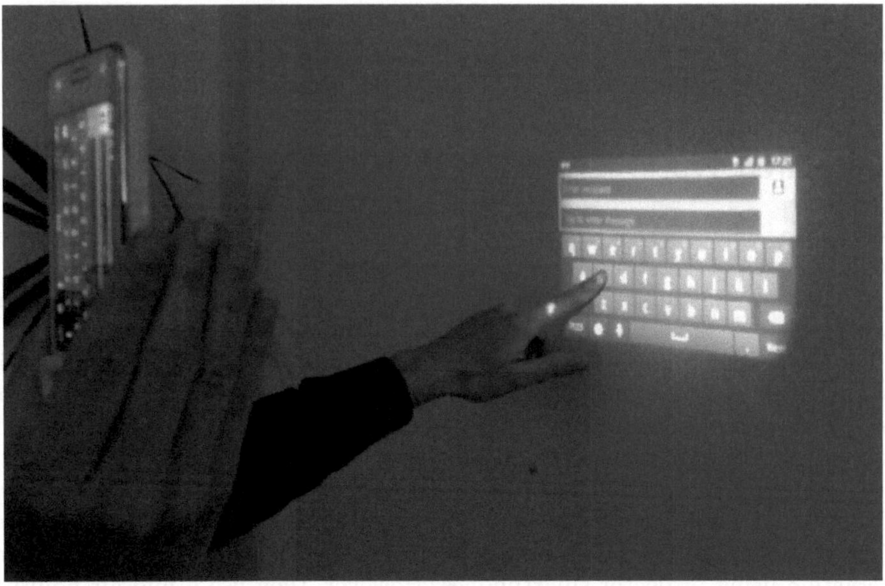

Fig. 1. In our approach, we use a smartphone with an integrated projector and a built-in RGB camera. The user holds the smartphone in one hand and projects the screen content onto a planar surface, while the camera is used to detect the projected screen and the user's interaction with it. The detected hand motion and gestures are forwarded to the smartphone's operating system as touch input events.

To increase the input area of any smartphone, a portable, small-sized projector attached to the smartphone could be used to project the screen contents onto a planar surface. Smartphones with an integrated projector, however, are clearly more flexible. Although, there are only few smartphones on the market that have an integrated projector, such as the Samsung Galaxy Beam, Apple Inc. as one of the major smartphone vendors has also shown interest in integrating a projector into their iPhone product line [5].

As a possible solution to the addressed problems, we propose a novel approach that allows users to interact with a projection of a smartphone screen, and explore the feasibility of using standard hardware in consumer smartphones to overcome the size limitations of typical smartphone touchscreens. We assume that integrated projectors will be a standard feature of smartphones in the future, as cameras are today. This would also allow to develop devices with very small screens or even devices without actual screens. Holding the device in one hand, the user will then project smartphone's user interface onto a surface. The other hand can be used to interact with the projection. Simultaneously, the camera captures the user interaction and forwards detected gestures to the system. This process is illustrated in Fig. 1.

The remainder of this paper is organized as follows. Fig. 1 presents the related work. In Fig. 1 we introduce our approach. Fig. 3 provides implementation details. In Fig. 3 we evaluate the approach. Finally, the conclusions are given in Fig. 4.

2 Related Work

Today's consumer market offers already a few smartphones with an integrated projector, such as Samsung Galaxy Beam, Sharp SH-06C, and Intex V.Show IN 8810. But more manufacturers are likely to follow suit, most notably Apple Inc. showing interest in such devices by filing a related patent application [5].

The challenge of interacting with a projection has been tackled previously in several ways. Mistry et al. [12] introduced a wearable gesture interface. Using a small wearable projector and a mobile camera, they proposed a method for interacting with an abstract ten digit keyboard. Their system recognizes finger input using a marker based technique. Harrison et al. [9] showed impressive results using a wearable interface combined with stereo cameras and depth sensors. Winkler et al. [16] conducted a study in which they point out the potential of interaction using projector smartphones. However, they use a mid-air pointing technique, and rely on an external tracking system and infrared markers attached to user's finger. Specifically for the virtual keyboard input, the concept study [7] investigated the freehand interaction with a projected keyboard.

3 Our Approach

Our approach is intended to work on smartphones with a built-in RGB camera and an integrated projector. Using the smartphone, the user projects the screen contents onto a planar surface while holding the smartphone in one hand, and simultaneously interacting with the projected screen using the other one, as seen in Fig. 1). In the first step of our method, we detect the screen projection using the built-in RGB camera. Then, we determine the perspective transformation matrix using the quadrilateral corners of the projected screen. Later, this allows to map the coordinates from the image domain to those of the smartphone display. Detecting the screen projection is performed only if the attitude of the smartphone changes, e.g., due to hand jitter, as opposed to performing the detection in every video frame. This allows to avoid costly and unnecessary computations. Finally, we use the skin color segmentation method by Rahman et al. [14] to detect the hand of the user and the tap gesture, which we defined as a closed hand.

3.1 Detecting Screen Projection

Since the built-in RGB camera will generally capture an area much bigger than that of the projected screen, the projection has to be located in the captured video frames. After that, projection screen coordinates can be mapped to those

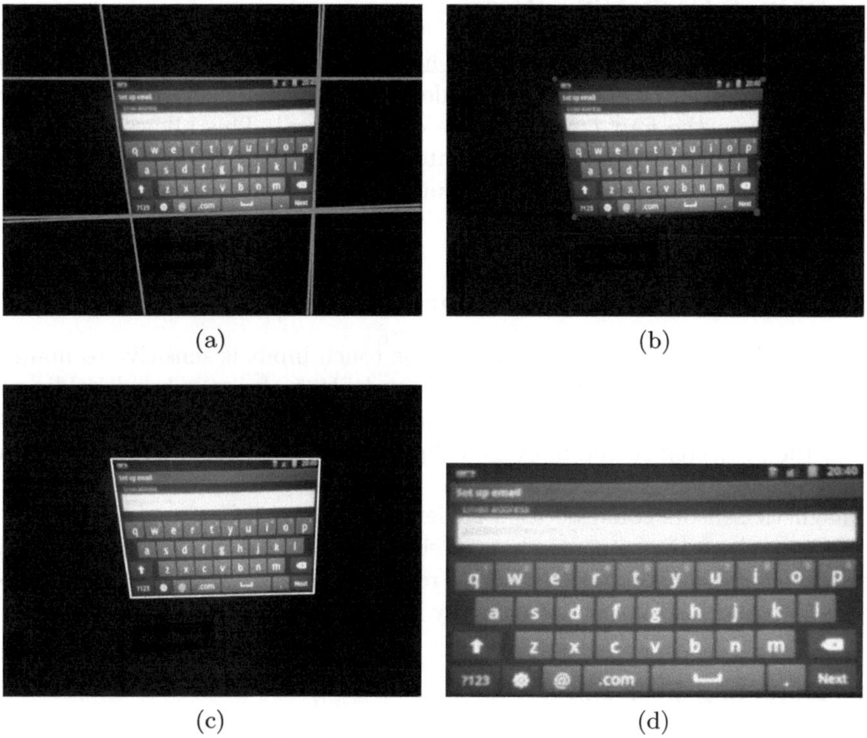

Fig. 2. Steps involved in detecting the projection screen and its perspective rectification: (a) line detection using probabilistic Hough transform, (b) intersections (shown as circles) between the lines, (c) quadrilateral that resulted from selecting four intersection points nearest to the image edges, (d) rectified perspective

of the touchscreen. As soon as the projected screen has been detected, the perspective of the projection screen can be rectified and the fingertip position (in display coordinates) can be determined.

In order to detect the projected screen, we assume that the area surrounding the projection is much darker than the actual projection. Here, we threshold captured video frames according to their luminance using a suitable threshold value. Ideally, this operation will result in a quadrilateral shaped blob that corresponds to the projected screen. To remove small defects in the blob, we apply morphological erosion and dilations. We then proceed with the extraction of the edge map using the Canny edge detector [2], and finally apply the probabilistic linear Hough transform to detect lines and to obtain the quadrilateral from line intersections points. The four line intersection points that build the quadrilateral are chosen such that they are close to the corresponding edges of the video frame. This ensures that the quadrilateral with the largest area will be obtained.

3.2 Perspective Rectification

In general, the user will not be able to hold the smartphone exactly orthogonal to the projection surface. We therefore determine the perspective transformation matrix M from the four corners of the quadrilateral. This allows us to rectify the perspective distortion, and to locate the fingertip position in touchscreen coordinates. Fig. 2 illustrates the steps involved in the detection of the projected screen.

3.3 Avoiding Costly Computations

Detection of the projected screen as well as touch input is sensitive to marginal changes of the smartphone attitude. Natural jitter of user's hand holding the smartphone, however, is generally unavoidable. Still, to omit unnecessary detection of the projected screen in every video frame, we perform the detection only if the attitude of the smartphone changes significantly. Alternatively, gravity and geomagnetic sensors could be used to detect motion.

In cases where the attitude changes significantly (e.g., by $1°$), the projection screen is detected again. Otherwise, we reuse the previously determined perspective transformation matrix M to rectify the video frames.

3.4 Detecting User Input

To detect the hand, we use skin color segmentation. For gesture recognition, we additionally assume that just one finger is used for interaction with the projected screen (e.g., the index finger). For a tap, the user has to close the hand. The tap will be performed at the fingertip position detected previously.

Fingertip Detection. As the computational resources on a typical consumer smartphone are limited, we use a computationally inexpensive method for fingertip detection. We start with the segmented skin areas, followed by the extraction of their contours. After that, the contour with the largest area is selected. We then reduce the number of points in the selected contour using the Douglas-Peucker algorithm [4]. As long as the resulting contour consists of only few points, we extract the corresponding convex hull, and determine the combination of convex points with the largest Euclidean distance. We used a threshold of 20 points which suffice to approximate the contour of a hand or a finger. Contours consisting of more points are unlikely to represent the contour of a hand. The candidate fingertip position is the point with the largest distance to the video frame border (see Figs. 2 and 2). Finally, we combine the candidate point with its nearest neighbors, and compute their arithmetic mean as the fingertip position.

This approach does not require the whole hand to be visible, since no shape information is used to match the hand or the fingertip.

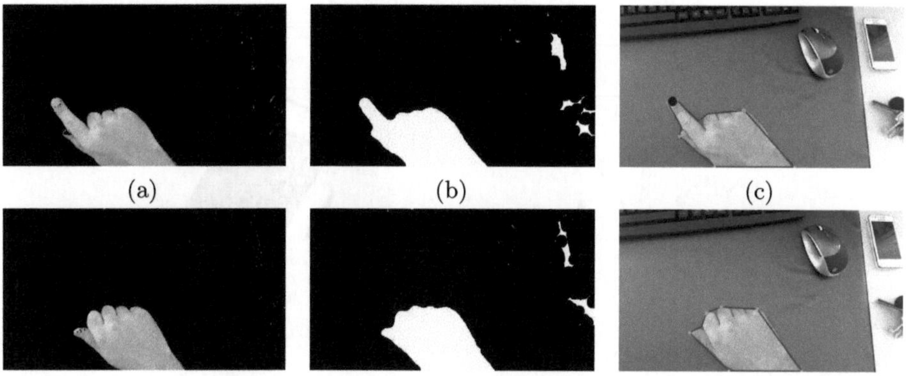

(a) (b) (c)

(d) (e) (f)

Fig. 3. Illustration of single steps performed in order to detect the hand gesture in a toy video sequence. (a) (d) Skin color segmentation, (b) (e) thresholding followed by morphological dilation and erosion, (c) (f) the selected contour. The blue circle in (c) indicates the position of the detected fingertip.

Tap Gesture Detection. To distinguish between an open hand with a pointing finger and closed one, we extract convexity defects of the convex hull (see Figs. 2 and 2). If the maximum depth of all convexity defects is above a certain threshold, we detect the hand as open. Otherwise, the hand is considered to be closed, and a tap at the previous fingertip position is executed.

4 Implementation

We implemented the proposed approach for the Android operating system, which according to a market survey by Gartner [6] at present dominates the global smartphone market. The approach, however, could easily be implemented for other systems such as Apple's iOS, Symbian, Blackberry OS, Windows Phone 7, etc., as long as the smartphone is equipped with a camera and a projector.

In our implementation, we used the OpenCV library [1]. For performance reasons, we implemented the image processing functionality in native code. An Android service was used to capture the video frames, to execute projection screen and fingertip detection, and to react to attitude changes. We used an image resolution of 640×480 pixels for captured video frames. Detected tap gestures were forwarded to a test application by our Android service. Once a finger tap has been detected, tactile feedback is given by the vibration actuator.

5 Qualitative Evaluation

We performed a qualitative evaluation of our prototype implementation. As prototype system we used Samsung Galaxy Beam (Model GT-I 8530), a consumer smartphone with an integrated projector.

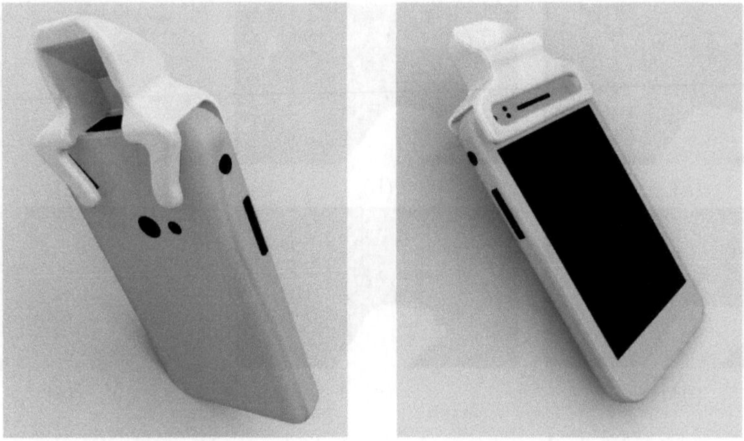

(a) Back view (b) Front view

Fig. 4. Mirror mechanism for Samsung Galaxy Beam which reflects the projection in the direction of the back-facing camera

One major issue that concerns most consumer projector smartphones is that the projector is often mounted perpendicularly to smartphone's back-facing camera. To overcome this problem, we built a mirror mechanism using rapid prototyping. This mirror can be clipped at the top of the smartphone, which allows to reflect the projection into the direction of the camera. The mirror mechanism is shown in Fig. 4. A stereolithography file (STL) that can be used to 3D print the mirror mechanism can be obtained from our website [8].

As our approach is sensitive to illumination conditions, the test setup required setting up an environment with properly balanced illumination. On the one hand, the environment has to be rather dark in order to achieve a high contrast between the projection surface and the area surrounding the projection. On the other hand, the environment should not be too dark, because in this case the hand will not be illuminated properly anymore, resulting in incorrect hand skin segmentation.

The illumination conditions not only concern the environment itself, but also the smartphone screen contents. Specifically, dark colored user interface elements, whose projection covers the hand or even the pointing finger, can tamper the skin color, producing incorrect detections. This problem also applies in case of extremely bright portions of the user interface.

Despite implementing the algorithms in native code, our projection screen detection achieved only a rate of 0.9 frames per second (FPS) ($\approx$ 1110 ms per frame). In combination with the fingertip detection, the frame rate decreased to around 0.5 frames per second ($\approx$ 1000 ms). This is generally too slow for fast and smooth input.

6 Conclusion and Future Work

We presented a novel approach for joint use of a built-in smartphone camera and an integrated projector. We discussed the requirements arising from the freehand use of a smartphone camera and a projector. Motion sensors were integrated into our framework to avoid unnecessary detections. Actuators were used to give feedback to the user once a finger tap has been detected.

Overall, our implementation showed the feasibility of the proposed method. However, the implementation needs to be optimized in order to work reliably under varying illumination conditions and different projection surfaces. Determining the optimal parameters for our implementation is still ongoing work.

The algorithms for projected screen detection, perspective rectification, and the recognition of the user input are sensitive to illumination conditions. Additionally, mobile projectors such as the built-in projector of the smartphone Samsung Galaxy Beam achieve only 15 lumens, requiring the smartphone to be used in a rather dark environment. In our implementation, parameters had thus to be adjusted manually to suit illumination conditions. Since smartphones are often equipped with light sensors, they could be used to automatically adjust the parameters.

The finger detection in our experimental implementation relies on a simple methodology. The detection rate and accuracy could be improved by placing markers on fingertips. However, markerless systems are clearly be more flexible. Alternatively, the fingertip could be located using Hough circle detection. Each time the recognized circle of the fingertip vanishes, it could be recognized as a tap. Several sophisticated approaches were proposed that can be integrated to solve this challenging problem (e.g., [10, 11, 13]).

As opposed to detecting and rectifying the perspective of the projected screen after its detection, the projection itself could be perspectively corrected in advance using the technique suggested by Raskar and Beardsley [15]. This would allow to pre-warp the projection, ultimately eliminating the need in rectifying the perspective. Alternatively, motion and geomagnetic sensors available in many smartphones could be used to determine the perspective transformation. This could be done by initially placing the smartphone on the projection surface, allowing to measure its inclination and distance between the surface and future smartphone position.

To improve the detection of the fingertip without relying on skin color models, the display contents could be subtracted from the projection surface. This approach, however, would have to take different lightning conditions into consideration. Also, the accuracy of the detected fingertip position could be increased by removing radial distortions of the smartphone camera.

Compared to desktop systems, there are special necessities for testing the usability for mobile devices [17]. For the concept of the joint use of smartphone's camera and projector, it will neither be sufficient to apply desktop usability measures nor to solely apply usability measures for mobile systems. For this novel type of interaction, distinct usability measures have to be found. Our current aim is to carry out user studies to optimize the proposed input method.

References

1. Bradski, G.: Programmer's toolchest – the OpenCV library. Dr Dobb's Journal-Software Tools for the Professional Programmer 25(11), 120–126 (2000)
2. Canny, J.: A computational approach to edge detection. IEEE Transactions on Pattern Analysis and Machine Intelligence 8(6), 679–698 (1986), http://dx.doi.org/10.1109/TPAMI.1986.4767851
3. Colle, H.A., Hiszem, K.J.: Standing at a kiosk: Effects of key size and spacing on touch screen numeric keypad performance and user preference. Ergonomics 47(13), 1406–1423 (2004)
4. Douglas, D.H., Peucker, T.K.: Algorithms for the reduction of the number of points required to represent a digitized line or its caricature. Cartographica: The International Journal for Geographic Information and Geovisualization 10(2), 112–122 (1973)
5. Fai, A.Y.S.: Projected display shared workspaces. Patent US 20110197147 A1 (2011)
6. Gartner: Gartner says worldwide sales of mobile phones declined 3 percent in third quarter of 2012; smartphone sales increased 47 percent (2012), http://www.gartner.com
7. Götzelmann, T.: Concept of the joint use of smartphone camera and projector for keyboard inputs. In: Proceedings of the 3rd International Symposium on Computing in Science & Engineering, ISCSE 2013, pp. 52–57. Gediz University Press, Gediz (2013a)
8. Götzelmann, T.: Deflection mirror for projector smartphones (stl file for 3d printers) (2013), http://www.in.th-nuernberg.de/professors/goetzelmann/BeamerPhoneDeflectionMirror.stl
9. Harrison, C., Benko, H., Wilson, A.D.: Omnitouch: Wearable multitouch interaction everywhere. In: Proceedings of the 24th Annual ACM Symposium on User Interface Software and Technology, UIST 2011, pp. 441–450. ACM, New York (2011), http://doi.acm.org/10.1145/2047196.2047255
10. Hasan, M.M., Mishra, P.K.: Real time fingers and palm locating using dynamic circle templates. International Journal of Computer Applications 41(6), 33–43 (2012)
11. Jiang, X.-H., Li, J.-W., Wang, K.-Q., Pang, Y.-W.: A robust method of fingertip detection in complex background. In: International Conference on Machine Learning and Cybernetics (ICMLC), vol. 4, pp. 1468–1473 (2012)
12. Mistry, P., Maes, P., Chang, L.: Wuw - wear ur world: a wearable gestural interface. In: CHI 2009 Extended Abstracts on Human Factors in Computing Systems, CHI EA 2009, pp. 4111–4116. ACM, New York (2009)
13. Oka, K., Sato, Y., Koike, H.: Real-time tracking of multiple fingertips and gesture recognition for augmented desk interface systems. In: Fifth IEEE International Conference on Automatic Face and Gesture Recognition, pp. 429–434. IEEE (2002)

14. Rahman, N.A.B.A., Wei, K.C., See, J.: RGB-H-CbCr Skin Colour Model for Human Face Detection. In: Proceedings of the MMU International Symposium on Information & Communication Technologies (2006)
15. Raskar, R., Beardsley, P.: A self-correcting projector. In: Proceedings of the 2001 IEEE Computer Society Conference on Computer Vision and Pattern Recognition, vol. 2, pp. II-504–II-508 (2001)
16. Winkler, C., Pfeuffer, K., Rukzio, E.: Investigating mid-air pointing interaction for projector phones. In: Proceedings of the 2012 ACM International Conference on Interactive Tabletops and Surfaces, ITS 2012, pp. 85–94. ACM Press, New York (2012)
17. Zhang, D., Adipat, B.: Challenges, methodologies, and issues in the usability testing of mobile applications. International Journal of Human-Computer Interaction 18(3), 293–308 (2005)

Touchscreen Mobile Phones Virtual Keyboarding for People with Visual Disabilities

Agebson Rocha Façanha[1], Windson Viana[2], Mauro Cavalcante Pequeno[2], Márcia de Borba Campos[3], and Jaime Sánchez[4]

[1] Instituto Federal de Educação, Ciência e Tecnologia do Ceará, Brasil
agebson@ifce.edu.br
[2] Universidade Federal do Ceará, Brasil
{windson,mauro}@virtual.ufc.br
[3] Pontifícia Universidade Católica do Rio Grande do Sul, Brasil
marcia.campos@pucrs.br
[4] Universidad de Chile, Chile
jsanchez@dcc.uchile.cl

Abstract. This paper presents the design and initial evaluation of a Braille virtual keyboard which allows text input on touchscreen devices such as smartphones and tablets. The virtual keyboard, called LêBraille, is a metaphor of the Braille writing system that uses audio and vibration feedbacks to promote accessibility for people with visual disabilities. We integrated this keyboard into two mobile applications and implemented an initial usability evaluation with nine people with visual disabilities. The evaluation comprised activities including a comparison of text input in three types of keyboards (physical keyboard, alpha numeric virtual keyboard, and LêBraille). Initial results indicates that writing activities can be as fast as a virtual keyboard depending on the Braille expertise of the user and the degree of blindness, however, the writing pace with a virtual keyboard is lower than the writing pace with a physical keyboard.

Keywords: Accessibility, Mobile Computing, and Braille.

1 Introduction

Touchscreen interfaces on smartphones and tablets have brought a new interaction challenge for users with visual disabilities [9,11]. After all, these devices have a glassy surface with several visual elements accessed through capturing the movements and gestures on the screen. Also, these interfaces have fewer points of reference and low tactile feedback to guide the interaction. Third-party applications developed for these platforms are more demanding from a visual perspective; they are based on gesture navigation and possess an adaptive layout, which changes the interface according to the device position (i.e., device screen rotation). In addition, physical keyboards are replaced by virtual versions. These characteristics make the interaction with these devices more complex for people with visual disabilities and often require strong cognitive efforts from them, such as the memorization of the positions of

M. Kurosu (Ed.): Human-Computer Interaction, Part III, HCII 2014, LNCS 8512, pp. 134–145, 2014.

virtual keyboard keys [9,10,11,12]. Therefore, there is a growing demand for visual accessibility of these devices, since people with visual disabilities claim for adaptations that allow them to have access to such technological innovations [10,12].

A very well-known layout by people with visual disabilities is that of the six cells in the Braille system. Braille is one of the main resources available for communication and social inclusion for people with disabilities into society. However, it is noted that currently there is a trend towards less use of Braille in digital technologies, when compared with the use of haptics and sound technologies 1.

In this context, our research is focused on the design of a software application, the LêBraille virtual keyboard, which allows writing on touchscreen devices using a Braille metaphor. We aimed at examining this layout as alternative for QWERTY and Perkins based keyboards [14], and also to promote a much wider use of Braille in digital technologies. In this paper, in particular, we present the design and development of the LêBraille virtual keyboard, its integration into two mobile applications (SMS and Twitter clients), and an initial usability evaluation with nine users with visual disabilities. The final version of the LêBraille virtual keyboard and its evaluation are the main contribution of this paper.

The remainder of this paper is organized as follows: Section 2 presents related work on text input on mobile devices. The LêBraille Virtual keyboard, and its design and development processes are described in Section 3. Section 4 presents the usability evaluation of the mobile applications. Finally, we conclude the paper with final considerations and future work in Section 5.

2 Related Work

Research on the development of assistive technologies for mobile devices is relatively recent. In fact, the presence of audio, communication, and sensor features on these mobile devices offer a unique and personal platform to the development of new services (e.g., entertainment, navigation, and communication) aimed at people with visual disabilities which have attracted the attention of many researchers [1,8].

The challenge of text input on such devices has been one of the research objects [1,9]. Examples of such researches are: Eyes-Free Text Entry [9], NavTouch [11], No-Look Notes [10], NavTilt [12], BrailleType [1], BrailleTouch [14], Mobile Messenger for the Blind [8], and TypeInBraille [15].

NavTouch [11], NavTilt [12], and BrailleType [1] have been developed by researchers at the University of Lisbon, Portugal. NavTouch, for example, is software used for text entry that interacts with the user through directional movements (right, left, up and down) and sound features. NavTilt differs from traditional approaches of text input based multitapping by having a gesture-based 3D interaction and a new organization of the alphabet; the aim is to allow text input using only one hand. BrailleType is an evolution of these previous experiences. It proposes a method of text input through the touch-based graphical representation of the Braille alphabet. The system was developed for Android in which the letters are encoded in a matrix of six points with audible feedback through the SVOX voice synthesizer.

In our approach, we propose to reuse the well-known layout of six cells of the Braille system. Eyes-free [9] NavTouch [11], No-Look Notes [10], NavTilt [12], however, they are applications more centered on the production of new keyboard layouts. In fact, our proposal for text input resembles in some principles to the project BrailleType 1, which was designed concurrently with our project. We use the same keyboard metaphor, both applications execute on Android platform, and our target device is the smartphone. In this paper, we go one step further by including the development of two applications that promote the use of our Braille-based keyboard.

3 The LÊBRAILLE Virtual Keyboard

LêBraille is a mobile service for the Android platform that aims to include the use of Braille on new technologies. It uses gestures on the screen, gestures using the device, audio feedback, and nuances of Braille to facilitate text input on touchscreen devices. Besides to propose an alternative data entry on touchscreen devices, we expect that our research can also be used for practical training of the Braille alphabet. For the development of the virtual keyboard and the mobile applications we adopted an extension of the co-design methodology proposed by Millard et al. [13]. This methodology integrates techniques of software engineering, agile development methodologies, and methods for the design of graphical user interfaces in order to compose an iterative development process. Fig. 1. illustrates the general stages of the methodology. We decided to adopt a development in three sprints described below.

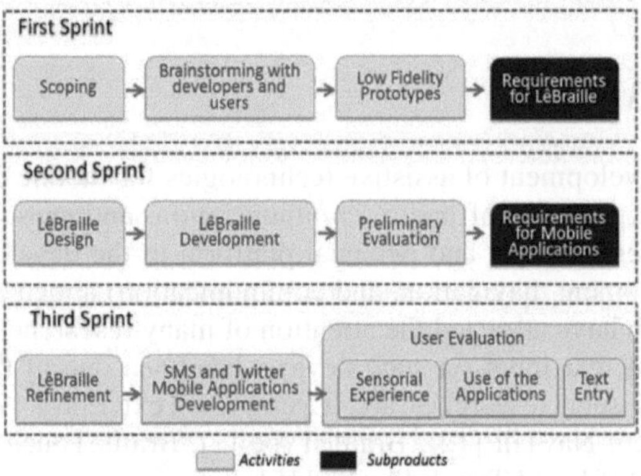

Fig. 1. Sprint-based process for the development of our approach

The first stages of the methodology include the study and design of applications made during the discussion meetings with a small group of users. These early stages were included in the **first two sprints**. At first, we held storyboarding meetings with three developers on mobile systems, which had notions of accessibility, and two persons who are blind[1]. The main objective was to understand the needs and expectations in the interaction with these interfaces. Based on these observations, we developed a

[1] They were two men, one aged 25 and another aged 43. Both were blind from birth, possess advanced knowledge on Braille, intermediate knowledge on computers, and had little or no experience in the use of touchscreen interfaces.

low-fidelity prototype virtual keyboard based on the Braille System. During the meeting, a discussion on the choice of prototype platform was initiated. We opted for the Android platform, since it is a more open platform, despite being, at that time, a fledgling operating system regarding accessibility compared to Apple's iOS.

Following the methodology mentioned, we developed a high-fidelity prototype of the virtual keyboard. We conducted a brainstorming process with a group of 5 people with visual disabilities, who had heterogeneous profiles (knowledge of Braille, age, gender). This experience was important for structuring the research and allowed for a better definition of the scope and the limitations of the study. This very preliminary research pilot study including practical activities is reported in a previous study [2].

Taking this initial evaluation and considering other experiments described in the literature [3,4,5,8], we have identified some key requirements to improve visual accessibility in applications that run on touchscreen devices [1]. Some of these requirements were applied in the design of mobile applications in this study, such as:

- Always provide feedback for all actions in the interaction elements.
- Preferably, use motion-based interaction, because the actions performed through gestures reduce the barriers imposed by the interface.
- When using the interaction elements, the application must include an exploration mode of the screen, since the interaction elements must be identifiable with both tactile and audio feedbacks.
- The elements of interaction including the interfaces should be presented in a list layout or in a two columns layout, avoiding table layouts. Then, the device sides can be used as reference points.
- Alert messages and pop-ups must fulfill the entire screen with options to exit and return to the previous screen.
- Use of timeout in an element selection should be avoided. It can confuse users, especially novice users who need more time to interact with the application.
- If it is not possible to design an interface adapted to the screen rotation, it is better to set a layout orientation (preferably vertical, top to bottom).
- The use of colors that provide a minimum contrast between background and foreground is required.

Based on the requirements to improve visual accessibility and the feedback from the usability of the initial experiment [2], we redesigned a more complete version of the virtual keyboard LêBraille. The virtual keyboard LêBraille was based on the operation of the Braille system. The arrangement of interface elements follows the structure of a Braille cell; the buttons correspond to the formation of Braille points. Once touched, the device emits a sound corresponding to the selected cell.

During the interface design, we chose to merge the use of buttons and gestures. Thus, the system can be used by people who are blind, by people with low vision, and sighted people that understand the Braille system. The keyboard LêBraille interacts with speech synthesis software configured as standard on the mobile device (e.g., Pico, SVOX, eSpeak). For this study, we used a native function of the Android platform (android.speech.tts.TextToSpeech). The language used by the TTS software is automatically configured by device operational system. LêBraille can be invoked by any other text application using inter-process communication based on Intents. Fig. 2 presents an overview of the system commands.

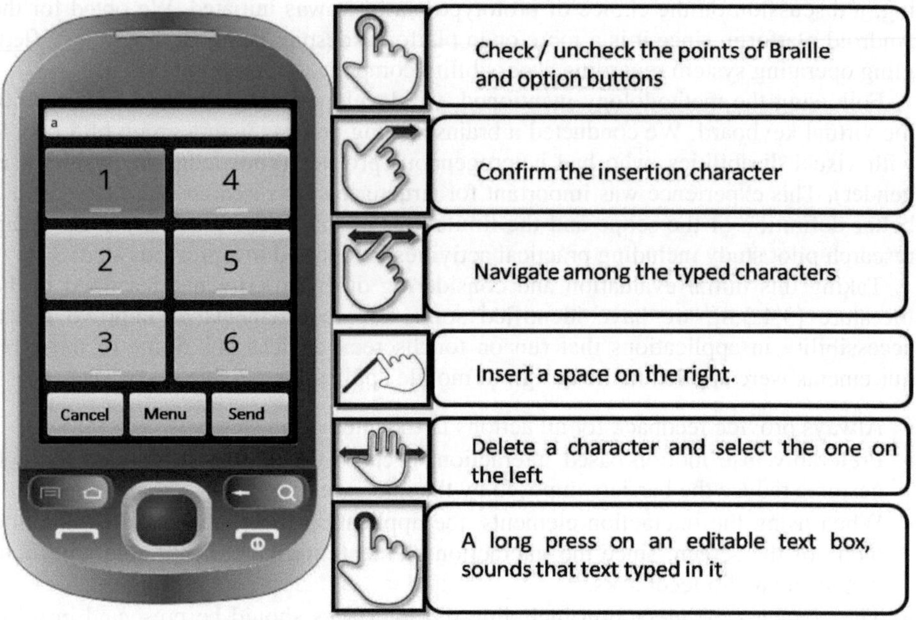

Fig. 2. LêBraille commands and recognized gestures

We developed two mobile applications to encourage interaction and communication between people with visual disabilities through services that provide the tasks of sending and receiving messages. These applications offer access to the social networking platform Twitter (LêBrailleTWT) and to the SMS messaging service (LêBrailleSMS). Both applications use the virtual keyboard LêBraille to allow for writing messages on a touchscreen device. The mobile applications developed are illustrated in Fig. 3 and Fig. 4. They have universal design of their graphic interfaces. Thus, non-blind people (e.g., special education teachers) can also practice the Braille by using text-based communication services provided by these applications.

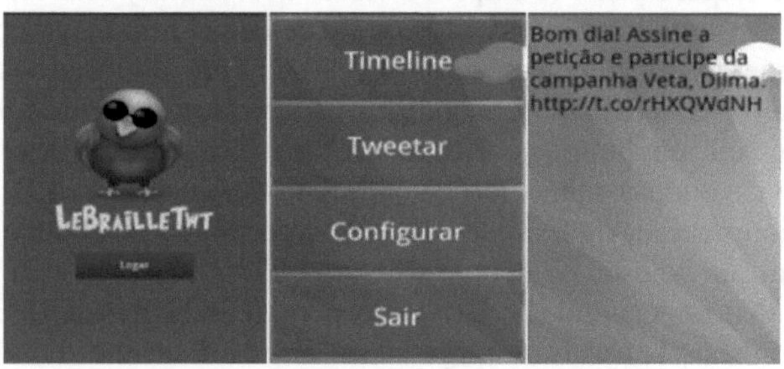

Fig. 3. Twitter mobile client screenshots

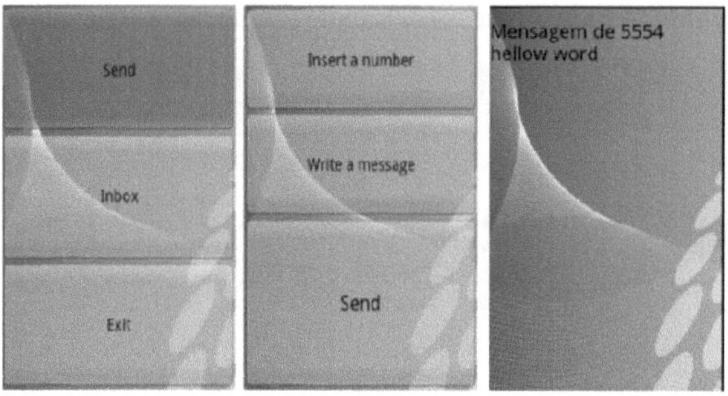

Fig. 4. SMS mobile client screenshots

Both applications access the device accelerometer to recognize some gestures. They also communicate with the Internet and the mobile phone network to perform its functions. For example, LêBrailleTWT performs a REST request to the Twitter Web-Service in order to make communication (e.g., list and read the 20 most recent posts and tweet a message). LêBrailleSMS, in turn, invokes a method of sending text messages via the Android SDK. The virtual keyboard is also used to enter the recipients' phone number and maintain the same interface, since it is possible to enter numbers using Braille. LêBrailleSMS provides both the sending and receiving messages in an accessible way, having a structure comprising navigability, gestures and commands similar to LêBrailleTWT application. A video illustrating the use of LêBrailleTWT is available in http://www.youtube.com/watch?v=IY8cgd-jh8g. It shows one user that is reading his Tweets and is writing a message with the LêBraille virtual keyboard. He writes the phrase "Web Accessibility" in Portuguese.

4 Usability Evaluation

After designing and developing the mobile applications, a usability evaluation was performed and also the speed of writing using LêBraille was measured.

4.1 Sample

For the usability evaluation, we use the focus groups methodology[2] [6], in order to obtain an initial validation of the mobile systems with a test group of nine users. Four different sessions were implemented: i) a test knowledge of Braille, ii) an analysis of the Twitter client and the writing speed of the virtual keyboard, iii) an analysis of the interface for sending and receiving SMS messages from the application, and finally, iv) a comparative writing test with other types of keyboards.

Each session had an average duration of two hours. The sessions were held in the period from March 2012 to April 2013. The sample was non-probabilistic, selected for convenience according to [7]. Users with visual disabilities were older than 18 years, with prior knowledge of Braille and computer practice. The detailed profile of each participant is shown in Table 1.

[2] Focal group methodology is sampling process that seeks to obtain qualitative information given the perceptions reported by participants during discussion meetings.

Table 1. Profile of the users sample for the usability evaluation

	User 1	User 2	User 3	User 4	User 5	User 6	User 7	User 8	User 9
Age	27	25	34	26	22	45	41	28	26
Gender	M	M	M	M	F	M	M	F	M
Degree of Blindness	Blind	Blind	Blind	Low Vision	Blind	Blind	Blind	Blind	Blind
Cause of Blindness	Acquired (8 years)	Birth	Acquired (6 years)	Birth	Birth	Birth	Birth	Birth	Birth
Knowledge of Braille	Intermediate	Advanced	Intermediate	Intermediate	Advanced	Advanced	Intermediate	Intermediate	Advanced
Computing Skills	Advanced	Intermediate	Intermediate	Intermediate	Intermediate	Intermediate	Intermediate	Intermediate	Advanced

4.2 Materials

We developed wood model prototypes that simulate some interfaces of the mobile applications. The goal was to familiarize users with the systems layout, through the appropriation of their repertoire of commands, gestures and actions. A wood prototype example is illustrated in Fig. 5. During the experiments with LêBraille we used a Galaxy 5 I5500B device including a 2.8 inch screen and the Android 2.2 system.

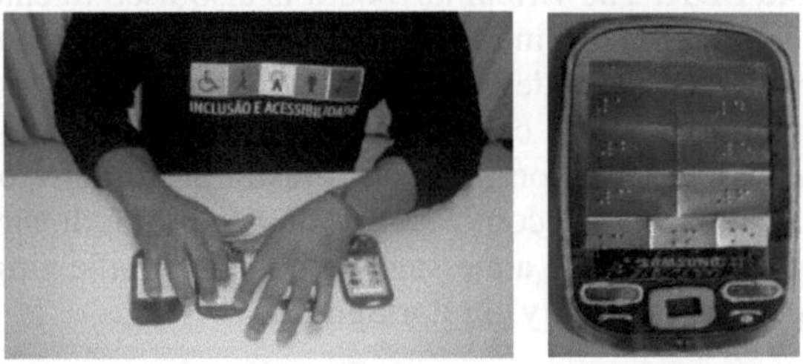

Fig. 5. Sensorial experimentation with wood prototype models of the virtual keyboard

The session aiming to compare speed of writing was implemented with a Nokia E5 device and the Galaxy 5 I5500B device. Nokia E5 possesses a physical QWERTY keyboard. A virtual QWERTY keyboard with audio feedback was installed on the Android device since we were unable to use the default virtual keyboard of the platform. All sections were recorded by videotaping and at end of each session we asked users to fill out a questionnaire.

4.3 Instruments

A questionnaire was administered in order to discover, analyze and validate, through observations of the user group, requirements for improving the mobile applications. The questionnaire was created guided by the following metrics:

I. *Organization and Presentation*. Indicate levels of user´s acceptance. This is determined by the way of presenting the technology being tested. Therefore, involves the overall organization, structure, presentation strategy, consistency and completeness.
II. *Motivation*. Measures the ability of technology to impact, motivate and arouse interest. It is also related to user´s acceptance
III. *Design*. Measures the quality of the design presented in the application interface.

IV. *Audio Style*. Refers to the understanding, quality, and style of the audio provided by the application.
V. *Navigation*. Measures the easiness of the user in browsing pages and its content.
VI. *Content*. Relates to the subject matter covered by the technology being tested.
VII. *Speed*. Determines the speed of access to the page or application contents.
VIII. *Objectives*. Quantifies if the approach achieves its purposes and goals.
IX. *Special Education*. Measures whether the technology can be applied in the education of people with visual disabilities.

4.4 Procedure

Before the initial interaction with the mobile applications users had undergone practical tests to prove their skills with the Braille system. They transcribed the same phrases used during testing with the mobile applications. The time for writing these phrases was measured. During session II and III three activities were proposed with increasing levels of difficulty. They aim to achieve better quantitative results of validation and acceptance of the virtual keyboard and mobile applications.

For activity I, we asked users to navigate in the Twitter client application, to read tweets and re-send some tweets (retweet). Then, a practical challenge was proposed for each participant. The challenge was to tweet the complete alphabet through the text input interface. The goal of this challenge was to evaluate the writing pace using LêBraille which so far had not been evaluated by Braille literate users.

Activity II was to post a message to Twitter. This message followed the reports of Socialmediatoday[3], which cite the average words per tweet. Thus, we proposed writing (via LêBrailleTWT) a proverb[4] that fits the specifications mentioned. Each user had a time period to conduct a random posting to remember the steps of submission. After this time, the activity began.One of the objectives of the activity II was to evaluate the average writing time with the virtual keyboard LêBraille. In the fourth section, we asked users to write the same sentence of the activity II using two other types of keyboards: a QWERTY virtual keyboard and a physical QWERTY keyboard. The comparative results of these interactions are described in the next section. Activity III consisted in sending a SMS (via LêBrailleSMS). The user could select the message, but it should contain at least 10 words and the last word should be the user name as message identification. This message was sent to the mobile phone number of one researcher. The main objective of this activity was to obtain qualitative information from the perceptions reported by participants during the performance tests using the SMS application.

4.5 Results

Graphic 1 shows the results of the writing challenge in the activity I. The graphic presents the time results of each participant to conclude the challenge using LêBraille, slate and stylus. When using LêBraille, the average time to writing and posting of

---

[3] `Socialmediatoday.com/joshgordon/253668/content-marketing-lessons-top-10-retweets-2010`

[4] "Antes de dar comida a um mendigo, da a ele uma vara e o ensina a pescar".

messages was 05 min and 23 sec. The coefficient of variation was 39.26. The comparison with the writing time using the slate and stylus indicate speed difference between the two approaches, which may be explained by navigational difficulties due to lack of experience of the user with the application and the challenge to use touchscreen interfaces to write text. Some users showed better results (3 min and 20 s), such as the user 4 that has low vision and users 5 and 6 that had advanced skills on Braille.

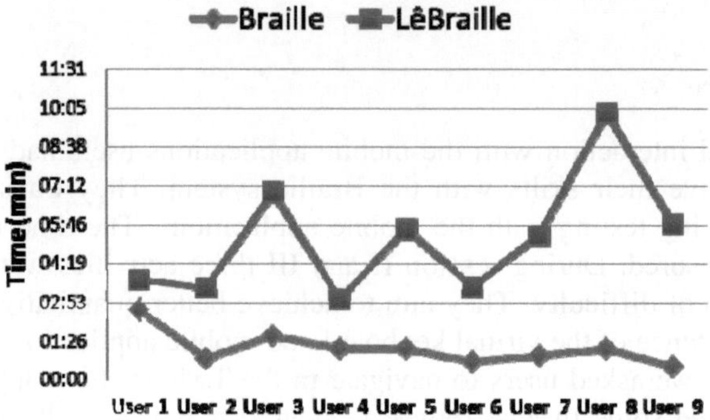

Graphic 1. Time for writing the alphabet using LêBraille with the slate and stylus

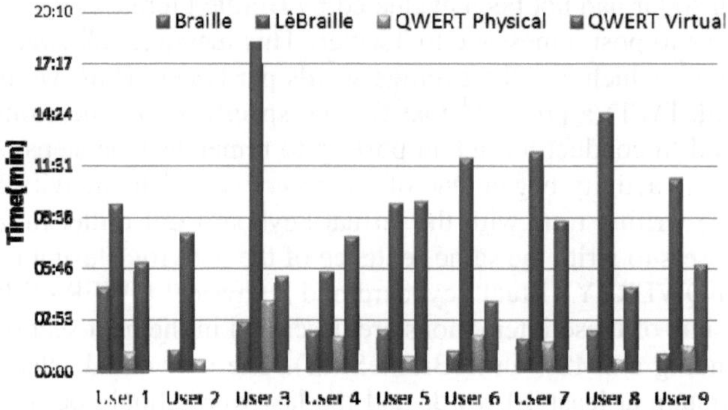

Graphic 2. Time to writing the proverb on the four systems

Graphic 2 illustrate the writing time of the proverb on the four systems experimented: Braille, LêBraille, a QWERTY virtual keyboard, and a QWERTY physical keyboard. The average time for writing and posting on Twitter with LêBrailleTWT was 11 min and 36 sec and the coefficient of variation was 33.99. This suggests a relatively high time. Regarding the comparison between the writing approaches, it is clear the better performance of data input using physical returns as Braille and QWERTY keyboard with physical buttons. Even for some users using the physical keyboard had a better performance compared to the use of Braille. This makes us believe the increasing use of computers as a means of communication to the detriment of Braille.

Of the nine users who conducted the experiment, three of them had better performances using the LêBraille than using the QWERTY virtual keyboard. User 2, although trying for three times on different days, could not finalize the proposed activity with the QWERTY virtual keyboard. According to him, the task was not completed because of failing to adapt to the interface, since there was a lot of information on the screen and it requires much effort and precision for locating the keys. The user 4 with low vision also excelled in the experiment. He had the best performance using LêBraille. According to him, this occurs because of the contrast provided by the interface. Regarding user 5, which practically had equivalent performance between the two virtual solutions, we noticed that he is a user with advanced skills in Braille and good notions on computer uses.

For some users, such as users 3 and 8, the intermediate domain of Braille and computer use had influences on the inefficient performance in relation to the use of Virtual Qwert. It is important to note that the use of the physical QWERTY keyboard in the same section may have helped them to remind and tie the QWERTY layout. Despite this fact, it should be said that through the evaluation criteria used in the questionnaire administered, all members approved the Twitter application and the virtual keyboard in the categories described in section 3.3.

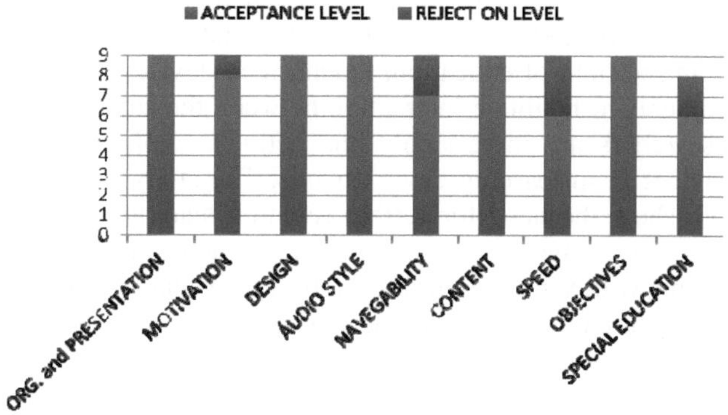

Graphic 3. Results of the Evaluation Questionnaire for the SMS application

Graphic 3 show the results of the application of the same questionnaire for the SMS application. The results were obtained after completion of the third activity (i.e., access the inbox messages and send an SMS message to a specific mobile phone). Most users, 88.8%, confirmed that the proposed technology is interesting, has an impact and motivates them. Also, 77.7% of users reported the ease of browsing the pages and content, and 66.6% of users considered acceptable the speed to access the content. Over 66.6% accepted the idea of combining SMS with LêBraille to be used as a tool to support Braille learning (one user chose not to answer).

5 Discussion and Conclusions

Mobile devices have a major role in today's information society. If the trend of the ubiquity of touchscreen devices without physical keyboard is confirmed, the research for new ways to allow text input and the design of mobile applications with multimodal interfaces (i.e., haptics, gesture, audio recognition) should be encouraged to avoid interaction issues with these devices by people with disabilities.

In this paper, we present an initiative in this context, focused on the issue of text input on touchscreen devices. Different from other studies more centered on the production of new keyboard layouts, we propose to reuse the layout of six cells of the Braille system. People with visual disabilities were able to accomplish the writing activities with both the LêBraille virtual keyboard and the mobile applications developed in this study. All three activities implemented were able to be performed by the users: tweet the alphabet, tweet a proverb, and send SMS with a phrase the user's choice. In some cases, the writing pace was as quick as or faster than with an alpha numeric virtual keyboard. However, for all users, the speed of writing in both virtual keyboards approaches (a QWERTY virtual keyboard, and the LêBraille) was much slower than the activity with a physical keyboard.

When analyzing the results of writing paces we should also take into consideration that the users had contact with the applications only during the experimentation sessions. This occurred since the Android system in its version 2.3, even with the use of screen reader TalkBack, did not provide full autonomy to the user with visual disabilities to operate the device. Thus, it is essential to implement a long term usability evaluation considering a bigger sample and diverse contexts of use in order to monitoring whether there is a significant time reduction to write and send messages or tweets.

Furthermore, in the field of education, touchscreen devices are being inserted into learning environments to facilitate interaction between the student and the content to be learned. Researchers are increasingly and actively exploring ways to integrate touchscreens devices in m-learning environments. The study presented here, as well as in [1,9,10,11], show the need for further research leading to the development of new mobile accessible technologies. Therefore, these new studies should promote the inclusion of students with visual disabilities in these new classrooms practices.

As future work, we envision developing educational games that use the LêBraille virtual keyboard to serve as a tool to stimulate student writing. These games can be used in non-formal school literacy activities of people with visual disabilities, or even, for training sighted people who want to learn or practice Braille in a playful way.

References

1. Oliveira, J., Guerreiro, T., Nicolau, H., Jorge, J., Gonçalves, D.: BrailleType: Unleashing Braille over Touch Screen Mobile Phones. In: Campos, P., Graham, N., Jorge, J., Nunes, N., Palanque, P., Winckler, M. (eds.) INTERACT 2011, Part I. LNCS, vol. 6946, pp. 100–107. Springer, Heidelberg (2011)
2. Façanha, A.R., Viana, W., Pequeno, M.C.: Estudo de interfaces acessíveis para usuários com deficiência visual em dispositivos móveis touch screen. In: XVI Congreso Internacional de Informática Educativa (TISE 2011), Santiago Chile (2011)
3. Kane, S.K., Wobbrock, J.O., Ladner, R.E.: Usable gestures for blind people: understanding preference and performance. In: Proceedings of the SIGCHI Conference on Human Factors in Computing Systems (CHI 2011), pp. 413–422. ACM, New York (2011)
4. Kane, S.K., et al.: Access overlays: improving non-visual access to large touch screens for blind users. In: Proc. of the ACM Symposium on User Interface Software and Technology (UIST 2011), pp. 273–282. ACM, New York (2011)
5. WCAG. Web Content Accessibility Guidelines (WCAG) 2.0. (2008), http://www.w3.org/TR/WCAG/

6. Lunt, P., Livingstone, S.: Rethinking the focus group in media and communications research. Journal of Communication 46(2), 79–98 (1996)
7. Levy, P.S., Lemeshow, S.: Sampling of Populations: Methods and Applications, 4th edn. Wiley Series in Survey Methodology (2008)
8. Sánchez, J., Aguayo, F.: Mobile Messenger for the Blind. In: Stephanidis, C., Pieper, M. (eds.) ERCIM Ws UI4ALL 2006. LNCS, vol. 4397, pp. 369–385. Springer, Heidelberg (2007)
9. Tinwala, H., MacKenzie, I.S.: Eyes-free text entry on a touchscreen phone. In: Proceedings of the IEEE Toronto International Conference – Science and Technology for Humanity – TIC-STH 2009, pp. 83–89. IEEE, New York (2009)
10. Bonner, M.N., Brudvik, J.T., Abowd, G.D., Edwards, W.K.: No-look notes: accessible eyes-free multi-touch text entry. In: Floréen, P., Krüger, A., Spasojevic, M. (eds.) Pervasive 2010. LNCS, vol. 6030, pp. 409–426. Springer, Heidelberg (2010)
11. Guerreiro, T., Lagoá, P., Nicolau, H., Gonçalves, D., Jorge, J.A.: From Tapping to Touching: Making Touch Screens Accessible to Blind Users. IEEE MultiMedia 15(4), 48–50 (2008)
12. Lucas, D., Nicolau, H., Guerreiro, T., Jorge, J.A.: NavTilt: Interface Gestual para Cegos. In: Proceedings of the 4th National Conference on Human-Computer Interaction (Interacção 2010), Aveiro, Portugal (2010)
13. Millard, D., Howard, Y., Gilbert, L., Wills, G.: Co-design and Codeployment Methodologies for Innovative m-Learning Systems. In: Multiplatform E-Learning Systems and Technologies: Mobile Devices for Ubiquitous ICT-Based Education. IGI Global (2009)
14. Frey, B., Southern, C., Romero, M.: Brailletouch: Mobile Texting for the Visually Impaired. In: Stephanidis, C. (ed.) Universal Access in HCI, Part III, HCII 2011. LNCS, vol. 6767, pp. 19–25. Springer, Heidelberg (2011)
15. Mascetti, S., Bernareggi, C., Belotti, M.: TypeInBraille: a braille-based typing application for touchscreen devices. In: The Proceedings of the 13th International ACM SIGACCESS Conference on Computers and Accessibility (ASSETS 2011), pp. 295–296. ACM, New York (2011)

Comparison Test of Website Use with Mobile Phone and Laptop Computer

Martin Maguire and Min Tang

Loughborough Design School, Loughborough University
LE11 3TU, UK
m.c.maguire@lboro.ac.uk

Abstract. The study compared user performance and subjective ratings between a mobile phone and laptop computer for accessing the internet. Twenty four participants were required to carry out two equivalent sets of 5 tasks, one set of tasks with a mobile phone and the other set with a laptop. It was found that the task times for the mobile phone were higher than those of the laptop for all tasks but only significantly different for two of the task pairs. The most important reason for this result seemed to be the difference in size of the screens on each device. Participants were also asked to rate the difficulty of each task performed on both laptop and phone. Interestingly, participants did not rate the difficulty of using the mobile phone significantly higher than for the laptop. This seemed to be because of lower expectations when using the mobile phone, good dexterity in zooming in and out of the screen, and spending less time reviewing each page on the phone than on the laptop before moving on another page.

Keywords: Usability evaluation, Website, Mobile phone, Laptop.

1 Introduction

Mobile phones are not just a device for calling and texting people but have become a necessary and indispensable tool in our daily lives. In combination with the internet, mobile phones already have the functions of a personal computer but in a handy portable size. However the relatively small screen and keyboard size of a mobile phone can make an ordinary webpage or ecommerce website difficult to use [1]. Smart phones can display most websites without modification, however the user is often unable to read the text or see useful content without pinch-zooming. Responsive websites can adapt to the device or operating environment although the technology still faces challenges to overcome such as non-fluid advertisements [2]. This study explored the difference between mobile phone and laptop when using them to perform search tasks on the internet. The project was also inspired by the need for Loughborough University information to be easy to obtain via a mobile device which is often student's preferred way of accessing the internet.

2 Aims and Method

This aim of the study was to compare a mobile phone and a computer laptop for accessing the internet. In addition, it was intended to record the user's experience of

M. Kurosu (Ed.): Human-Computer Interaction, Part III, HCII 2014, LNCS 8512, pp. 146–154, 2014.

the Loughborough University website and ideas for a reduced mobile version of the home screen.

The project used performance testing to compare the difference between the laptop (with a 13.3 inch screen and physical keyboard) and mobile smart phone (with a 4 inch screen and touch screen keyboard). Although a laboratory test has some limitations compared to a field study [3], this style of evaluation is more straightforward for conducting a controlled comparative study.

The testing recorded time to complete five tasks with each device and used a paired t-test used to determine if there was a significant difference between times for the mobile phone and laptop. The five tasks used with each device were designed to be equivalent to make the two sets equivalent in difficulty. The order of presentation of the tasks and device was varied between participants to avoid order effects.

A questionnaire was also developed to collect participants' subjective ratings, opinions and suggestions for tailoring the Loughborough University website to access via mobile phone.

The participants included members of staff and students (PhD and postgraduate students) from Loughborough University; thus they were familiar with the website and could give more useful suggestions about its improvement. A total of 24 persons aged from 25 to 55 years old took part in the study with a median age of 35. Ten participants were female and 14 were male. Most of the testing was carried out in the Loughborough University Design School, although for the convenience of two of the participants, it was carried out in their own homes.

For each task a time limit of 5 minutes was set so if the participant did not complete it within this time, the task was stopped and the time not included in the statistical analysis. The participants also gave a rating about how easy or difficult they found that task (from 1=very difficult to 7=very easy) and the overall satisfaction about using the website on this device (from 1=very unsatisfying to 7=very satisfying). The ratings were also analysed with the Wilcoxon test to see if the difference between the two devices was significant. All the task pairs in this study were designed

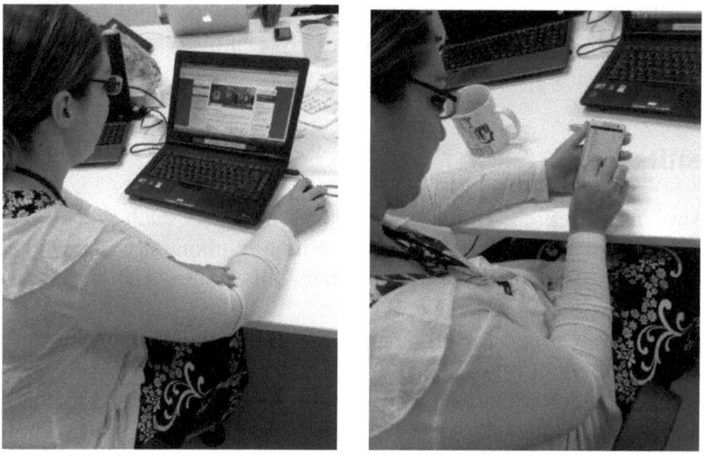

Fig. 1. Participant within the study

to be equivalent in terms of number of steps and level of difficulty. At the end of the post-test questionnaire, each participant was asked to sketch the design for a reduced home screen for Loughborough University to make it suitable for a mobile phone.

The instructions for the two sets of tasks were as follows:

- **Task Set A**
  - Task 1: Go to the Design School web page and find information about postgraduate course on Ergonomics (Human Factors). Find and read out the entry qualifications.
  - Task 2: Use the Design School gallery and find out who is the contact person for the SAMMIE (workspace modelling) system.
  - Task 3: You wish to go to from the University Library to Loughborough town centre on Monday morning by bus during university holidays. Find the information about what time you could choose.
  - Task 4: Find the opening hours and map location of Faraday Dining Hall during term time.
  - Task 5: Find information about the Polar Film Festival Event (venue location and ticket price) taking place at the University.
- **Task set B**
  - Task1: Go to the School of Business and Economics web pages and find information about postgraduate course on Economics and Finance. Find and read out the entry requirements.
  - Task 2: Use the Design School research pages and find out how many members of staff are in the User Centred Design Research Group.
  - Task 3: Where you should go and what is the card replacement cost is if you lost your University ID card?
  - Task 4: Find accommodation information about John Phillips Hall: map location and occupancy information and what date can new postgraduates come into the hall.
  - Task 5: Find information about the RSPB (Royal Society for the protection of birds) Talk - The Long Journey North by Danny Green (venue location and ticket price) taking place at the University.

3 Results

The chart shown in Figure 2 is a boxplot of task times for each pair of 5 tasks. It can be seen that all the five median values for the mobile phone are higher than their corresponding task for the laptop. The six outlier values shown as numbered points on the chart were excluded from the test.

The range of times taken for task pair 1 and 2 is smaller than the ranges for task pair 3, 4 and 5. The main reason for this might be the clarity of the searching operation and the interference of related information. In task pair 1 and 2, the required information to find is simple and clear so did not cause too much confusion for the user. But in task pairs 3, 4 and 5, there were related information showing on other pages which did not provide the right answer, which may have caused participants to spend

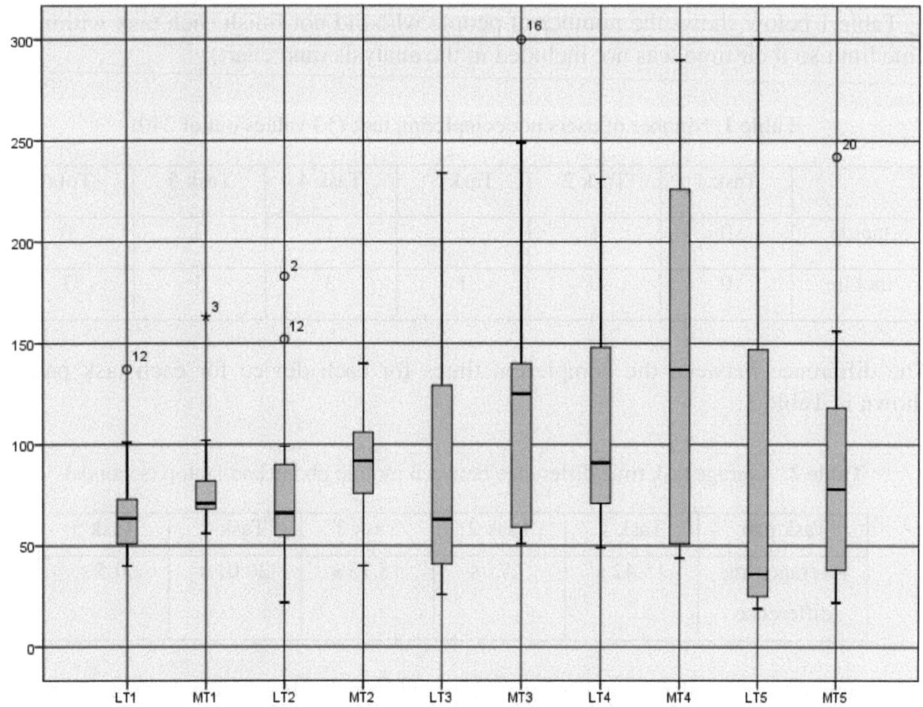

Fig. 2. Boxplot of completion times

too much time searching on the wrong page. And in task pairs 3, 4 and 5, there were more than one way to find the right information and some of them were more complicated than others, so this needed more time to complete the task.

The results of the t-test, showed that for task pair 1 and 2, the completion time of laptop is significantly quicker than mobile phone at the significance level p=0.01, but in task pair 3, 4 and 5 there is no significant difference between the laptop and mobile phone. Comparing this result with the boxplot (Figure 2), in task pair 1 and 2 the operation of completing the task is clear and did not have too much information to distract the user. So the difference in mean time might reflect the different operation of these two devices. But in task pair 3, 4 and 5, there was more than one way to do the task and some other related information showing on other pages which was not needed for the task which may have made participants spend too much time searching information on the wrong page. Therefore, these factors may have affected the completion time and the test results. Moreover, when people used the mobile phone to search for information they tended to just scan the text in the website instead of reading details information. So if they went to the wrong page, they quickly browsed the page and then returned to the home page to find another path. But using laptop to perform the task, because the larger screen which could show enough text and make it easy to read, participants always liked to read the detailed information on the page they already found when they did not find the right answer of the task. This difference on the two devices may have influenced completing times.

Table 1 below shows the number of people who did not finish each task within the time limit so their time was not included in the analysis (and chart).

Table 1. Number of users not completing task (13 values out of 240)

	Task 1	Task 2	Task 3	Task 4	Task 5	Total
laptop	0	1	1	1	3	6
mobile	0	0	1	3	3	7

The difference between the completion times for each device for each task pair is shown in Table 2:

Table 2. Average task time difference between mobile phone and laptop (seconds)

Task pair	Task 1	Task 2	Task 3	Task 4	Task 5
Average time difference	15.42 s	7.71 s	18.75 s	26.01 s	0.5 s

Participants were also asked to provide a subjective choice of which device was harder to use for each task, either mobile phone or laptop. The results are shown in Table 3. For task pair 3, a clear majority thought that the mobile phone was harder to use than the laptop. However for the other task pairs there were no clear differences between the choices and for task pairs 2 and 5 more participants thought that the mobile phone was easier to use than those who thought the phone was harder. A Wilcoxon non-parametric test was used to test the difference in the choice of more difficult device between the laptop and mobile phone. None of the task pairs showed any significantly differences between the choice of mobile phone or laptop as the easier or harder device to use.

Table 3. Subjective rating of which device was easier or harder for each task pair

Task pair	Task 1	Task 2	Task 3	Task 4	Task 5
Mobile harder	9	6	14	10	8
Mobile and laptop same	10	8	2	5	4
Mobile easier	5	10	8	9	12

Also within the questionnaire, participants gave comments about the two devices for accessing the internet. Some participants reported that even though the mobile phone is more handy and easy to carry when they go out and want to search for some information, most participants still prefer the laptop for accessing the internet which was seen as generally more convenient. Comments about specific features of the devices are summarised below:

Screen Size. 75 percent of participants reported that the screen size was a key problem when using the mobile phone to search for information since during the searching process. They needed to zoom in and out multiple times in order to read the information detail and also browse the whole website. One of the participants suggested that a "word wrap" function may make it easier to read specific text. The "word wrap" function is provided on the Blackberry mobile phone and some HTC mobile phones. So when the user zooms in to the website to read the detailed information, the text will re-format automatically so the user won't need to move left and right across the screen but just scroll the page up and down.

Miss Clicking. In the questionnaire, almost 30 percent of the participants stated that it was not so convenient when they wanted to click a specific link on the touch screen. This problem also related to the relatively small size of the screen, so that users frequently clicked the wrong button or link on the web page. Possibly a touch screen stylus could solve this.

Keyboard. 25 percent of participants reported that the keyboard on the mobile phone was harder to use than that on laptop, especially the male participants who generally had larger fingers than the female which hampered typing on the touch screen keyboard. Some smart phones which have both a real keyboard and a touch screen may improve on this situation.

4 Discussion

The analysis of task performance shows that across all the five task pairs, performance with the laptop was greater (or faster) than with the mobile phone. This was in general due to the smaller size of the mobile phone screen and consequently smaller size of information, web-links and touch-screen keyboard.

4.1 User Behaviour with the Smaller Screen

The mobile phone's smaller screen could just show some part of the website while the laptop could show the whole width of a home page on screen. Therefore, if people wanted to find particular information with mobile phone, it would take longer to look around and scroll across the screen to find the information. Moreover, for older participants who might have poorer vision, to read the text in the small screen, they had to zoom into the text. However, once they enlarged the text font they could not see the whole information of the website. So to then check the whole page, they had to decrease the font size. This problem meant that participants had to repeatedly enlarge and decrease the font size when they were looking for specific information with the mobile phone, which increased the completion time of each task.

4.2 Wider Spread of Performance Results with Mobile for Map Task

For task pair 4, the spread of performance times was noticeably broader with the mobile phone than the laptop. As the smaller mobile phone screen was only able to show part of the map, participants needed to zoom in and out to find where the building was. However with the mobile phone participants sometimes scanned information less thoroughly than on the laptop and if they thought they might be on the wrong page (or part of the map) and could not find the information they wanted, they just returned to the search page and started the task again. For this reason some participants might have found the location of the building for task 4 on the mobile phone as quickly as on the laptop.

4.3 Difference between Task Performance Times and Subjective Perception of Difficulty

From the average time difference (Table 2), it shows that when using the mobile phone all tasks took longer than using a laptop. But in terms of difficultly rating, Table 3 shows that participants did not necessarily consider using the mobile phone harder to use than the laptop and the Wilcoxon test showed no significant difference in participants' selection of either device as being easier or harder. There might be several reasons for this. Firstly, even though using a mobile phone may take longer to finish the task, it does not mean that it is perceived as harder to use than a laptop. Even if the user spent more time using a mobile phone to search for information, if the process was going smoothly, they may have thought that mobile phone was as easy to operate. Secondly, the outlier values shown in the boxplot in Figure 2 may have disproportionately affected the average time differences. Because of these outliers, the results show that the mobile phone took longer than the laptop to complete each task when people may not have felt that the mobile phone was harder to use than laptop. Thirdly, participants may have not liked to admit or consider that a task was harder for them when they realised that they just missed some information that they felt they should have seen or recognised that there was an easy way to complete the task. Thus they may have given a more positive rating.

5 Suggestions for Mobile Phone Website Designs

After the user trial each participant was invited to design a reduced home screen for Loughborough University to be suitable for a mobile phone. Although smart phones already have relatively large screens for phones, the information of a typical website is still too much to display for comfortable use. Thus a reduced mobile phone version home screen might be useful and necessary.

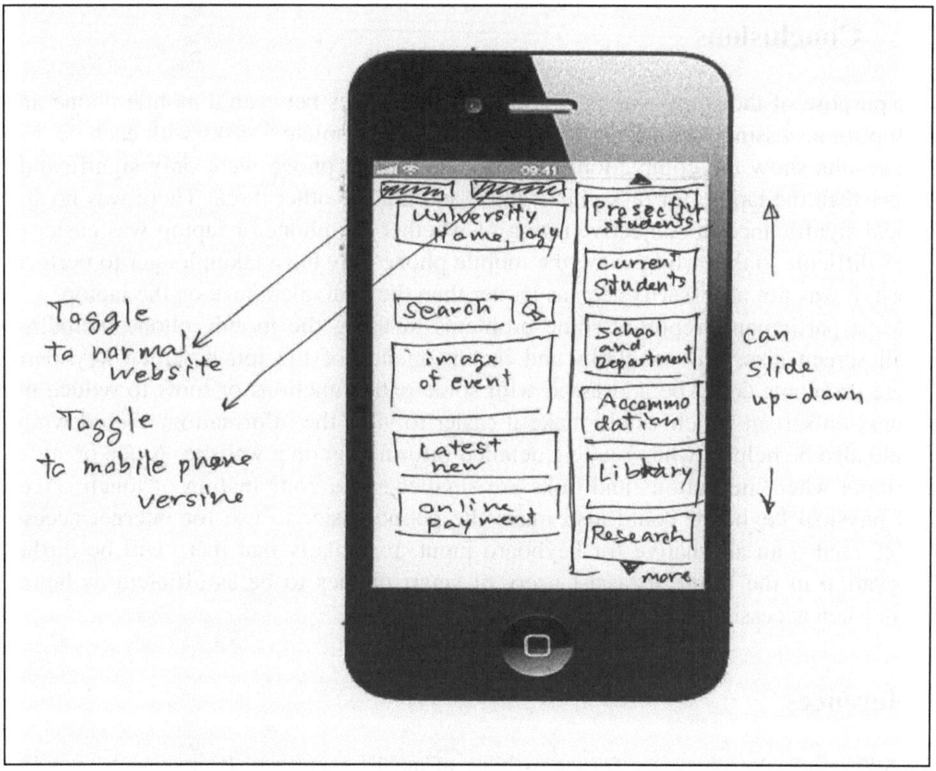

Fig. 3. Example of a redesigned home screen for mobile phone

From the sketches made by the participants, most people chose to include a search bar, school and department tabs or links, and current student and staff functions on their mobile home screen. An example sketch is shown in Figure 3. This shows a mobile version which incorporates a split screen with fixed, generally useful, options on the left and a scrolling list of more specific options on the right. Tab buttons are also provided at the top of the screen to allow the user to swap between the normal full screen version and the mobile version as they wish.

6 Contextual Aspects of Study

This study had certain characteristics that could have affected the results. Firstly, as all the participants were from Loughborough University Design School they might have already used the School webpages before, so the completion times may have been affected by their previous experience. However this was not a noticeable effect during the study. Secondly, although the shortest path for each task made each task pair equivalent, there were different ways to complete some of the tasks, so the number of steps followed varied depending on the route followed which may have affected the equivalence of the task pair for a particular participant.

7 Conclusions

The purpose of the study was to explore the differences between a mobile phone and laptop for accessing the internet by asking users to complete 5 tasks with each device. The results show the completion times for the mobile phone were only significantly longer than the laptop for task pair 1 and 2 and not the other three. There was no statistical significance in subjective rating of whether the phone or laptop was easier or more difficult so that while using the mobile phone may have taken longer to perform a task, it was not necessarily seen as harder than the equivalent task on the laptop.

Most participants reported some problems in using the mobile phone including: small screen size, missed clicks and inconvenience of the touch screen keyboard. These problems could be addressed with some extra functions or tools to reduce the content on screen which would make it easier to view the information. "Word wrap" would also be helpful when reading detailed information on a website. A pen or stylus for input when the buttons and links are smaller and a combination of touch screen and physical keyboard could also make the phone easier to use for internet access. Voice is also an alternative for keyboard input. It is likely that there will be further innovation in the future to assist users of smart phones to be as efficient as laptop users when accessing the internet.

References

1. AlShaali, S., Varshney, U.: On the usability of mobile commerce. International Journal of Mobile Communications 3(1), 29–37 (2005)
2. Responsive web design. Wikipedia (2014), http://en.wikipedia.org/wiki/Responsive_web_design
3. Nielsen-Norman Group: The definition of user experience (2014), http://www.nngroup.com/about-user-experience-definition

A Study of Emoticon Use in Instant Messaging from Smartphone

Tae Woong Park[1], Si-Jung Kim[2], and Gene Lee[1]

[1] University of Central Florida, Industrial Engineering and Management Systems, Orlando, Florida, USA
taewoong.park@knights.ucf.edu, glee@ucf.edu
[2] University of Central Florida, School of Visuial Arts and Design - Digital Media, Orlando, Florida, USA
sjkim@mail.ucf.edu

Abstract. Instant messaging (IM) has become one of the most popular modes of instantaneous electronic communication mediums throughout the world for users. A unique feature of IM on the smartphone is its choice of text-based, graphical or animated emoticons that express emotion and intentions. Many studies have been conducted on computer mediated communication (CMC), IM and emoticons, but little is known specifically about the study of emoticons in IM on the smartphone. The goal of this study was to understand how emoticons are used in IM on the smartphone and to investigate the inconsistent results of previous research. Thus, this study explored the frequency and variety of emoticon usage as well as the user traits based on emoticon types, relationships between users, availability of computer keyboards, and user emotional states in IM on the smartphone. The corresponding suggestions provided by this study would help to increase the understanding of emoticon usage and the designing of future emoticons in IM on the smartphone.

Keywords: Emoticon, Emotion, Instant Messaging (IM), Smartphone, Computer mediated communication (CMC).

1 Introduction

Traditional social interaction is face-to-face but today it is no longer the primary way for communicating with one another as there are many other alternative computer mediated communication (CMC) methods such as e-mail, text message and instant messaging (IM). A text-based CMC has a long history of sending text messages over networks and has been available since the 1960s. In the last decade, e-mail has been the prevalent communication tool of internet users [1]. Text messaging, such as IM, has been the prominent way of communication throughout the world [2]. IM is a popular mode of instantaneous electronic communication as well. Nardi and Whittaker suggested that IM is used mainly for four functions: (1) quick questions and clarifications, (2) organization and scheduling of work tasks, (3) organization of spontaneous social meetings, and (4) keeping in touch with friends and family [4]. Currently, there

M. Kurosu (Ed.): Human-Computer Interaction, Part III, HCII 2014, LNCS 8512, pp. 155–165, 2014.

is IM software available via the internet such as Kakao Talk, AOL Instant Messenger, Google Talk, MSN Messenger, Yahoo Messenger and Facebook. As CMC replaces some face-to-face interaction, text-based communication methods, such as IM, are limited in expression and prone to misunderstandings. Face-to-face conversation depends on back channels such as the tone of voice, body language and interpretation of the listener's expressions, but text-based communication loses these back channels completely [5]. The back channel in face-to-face communication may serve different functions: (1) providing information; (2) regulating interaction; and (3) expressing intimacy [6]. Thus, CMC, such as IM, lacks the conventional non-verbal dimensions of human communication such as facial expressions, gestures, body positions, personal distance, vocal variety, and eye contact [7].

Consequently, finding ways to enrich the text-based communication is important. CMC users have found ways to increase the richness of CMC. The emoticon was created for this purpose. The use of the emoticons was well documented in a variety of sources in the CMC literature. There were a number of slightly varying definitions regarding emoticon. Antonijevic defined emoticons as emotional icons and visual representations of facial expressions used in CMC in order to represent the mood and/or emotion of the user [8]. The visual cues, such as emoticons, have been remarked as being the primary way to express emotion in CMC and are ways to replace non-verbal communications when not face-to-face [9, 10]. Text messages without emoticons result in incorrect interpretation of the nature of the message and the senders' emotion or attitude [11]. Another study showed that children perceived higher degrees of social presence and greater intrinsic motivations when they were exposed to animated emoticons compared to when they were exposed to traditional emoticons [12]. The first person documented to have used the emoticons :-) (happy) and :-((sad) was Scott E. Fahlman using a series of symbols to indicate mood in the body of an e-mail to prevent miscommunications from happening on September 19th, 1982. Recently, graphical emoticons have been introduced in IM and email and examples are shown in Table 1[1].

Table 1. Text-based and Graphical emoticon examples [1]

Emotion	Emoticon	
	Text based	Graphical
Happy	:-)	
Sad	:-(	
Cry	;~(	
Laughing	:-D	
Wink	;-)	

Since the introduction and consequential booming of the smartphone, smartphone users frequently send and receive instant messages with emoticons via IM in one's everyday life. A unique feature of IM on the smartphone is allowing usage of text based emoticons as well as graphical and animated emoticons. Smartphone users convey meaning using emoticons to represent individual identity, presence, awareness and feelings.

Although many studies have been conducted on general CMC, IM and emoticons, most studies have focused on emoticon use in order to better understand the effect of emoticons on interpreting messages, but little is known specifically about the study of emoticons in IM on the Smartphone. The smartphone is being adopted at an exceptional rapidity, but little is known today about how people use these devices. In 2009, smartphone diffusion in the United States was 25% and 14% of worldwide mobile phone shipments were smartphones. In 2011, smartphone sales already exceeded desktop PCs. Falaki and Mahajan investigated the view of what users use their smartphones for and the communication dominates as a result of this study [13]. In conclusion, the use of IM on the smartphone is likely to increase at a rapid rate.

2 Purpose of Study

2.1 Research Questions

This study is an exploratory study with the survey research questions. First of all, this study is intended to identify the general characteristics of emoticon use. It was expected that the trait of emoticon use in IM on the smartphone would show a different tendency than in IM on the computer.

There are many emoticons used in IM, but emoticon users do not use all emoticons. Danet showed that the best known ones are a :-) (smile), ;-) (wink), and :-((frown) [14]. Garrison and Remley investigated that use of three emoticons, :-) (happy/smile), :-P (playfulness) and ;-) (wink) run to 73% and the :-) (happy/smile) was the most used emoticon (35%) in his data set [3]. Tossell and Kortum showed that the top three emoticons are :) (happy), : ((sad), and :D (very happy) and these made up 70% of the total amount of emoticons sent across all participants [2]. In this line of reasoning, this study investigated what specific style of emoticons is the most commonly used in IM on the smartphone (Question 1).

With the introduction of various media in CMC, graphical emoticons, as well as text-based emoticons, became very popular. Furthermore, as animated emoticons became more widely supported, countless animated emoticons were created and continue to be created today. This study examined whether users prefer text-based :-), graphical  or animated emoticons (actually moving) when users send emoticons with instant messages on their smartphones (Question 2).

CMC users often incorporate emoticons as visual cues to augment the meaning of textual electronic messages [15]. It appears that users of CMC attempt to compensate for the lack of the traditional nonverbal cues by the usage of emoticons [16]. Though emoticons are defined as a means to express one's emotion, some people would like to conceal emotion when in a negative emotional state or to make a warm and bright atmosphere in an IM. To attain this intention, one sends a text message with a :-) (happy emoticon) [22]. In this line of reasoning, this study examined the main intention or reasoning for the use of emoticons in IM on the smartphone (Question 3).

In the Tossell's study, the authors collected real communications data from individuals' smartphones over a 6-month period. In general, SMS messages were not used very much overall, with only 4% of all messages containing at least one emoticon [2]. Ling analyzed 882 messages using phone interviews to collect data and showed that only 6% of these messages contained emoticons [17]. On the contrary, in other survey-based research, Qiao showed that 88% of a Chinese sample used emoticons. Findings also showed that Chinese highly used emoticons in SMS for humor and as a substitute for non-verbal communication [18]. Because of these previous inconsistent results, this study examined how many emoticons were included in IM on the smartphone (Question 4).

Thus, the primary research questions related to emoticon use were presented as follows: (1) What specific styles of emoticons do most people like? (2) Out of the three types of emoticons (text-based, graphical and animated emoticons) which do most people prefer? (3) What is the main reason or intention most people send emoticons? (4) How many emoticons do most people send in an instant message on the smartphone?

2.2 Hypotheses

Next, this research was attracted to investigating existing research of emoticon use because other studies have had inconsistent results. On the basis of the results of our prior research questions', we analyzed the aspect or attitude of emoticon users, considering various factors related to the use of IM from a user's smartphone with specific research hypotheses. In particular, how the availability of a computer keyboard, gender, user's emotional state, and the relationship of those texting affects the frequency of emoticon use.

The computer keyboard is still one of the most commonly used input devices today. It allows rapid entry of text by experienced users. It is easy to enter textual data using the computer keyboard when one uses instant messenger on the computer. Today, it is commonplace to see users who are tapping their fingers on the small virtual keyboards of their smartphones but people feel an inconvenience or irritation when one uses instant messenger on the smartphone. In addition, smartphone users are often experiencing a difficulty in typing characters exactly on minute keys due to their thick thumbs [19]. In this line of reasoning, do people send emoticons in IM from smartphones in the same manner one sends emoticons with a computer keyboard? Individuals at least feel the need to convey some of their emotions or points with emoticons rather than long text. It is faster to use emoticons than words to convey certain expressions based on the result of question 3. Therefore, this study expected that people would use more emoticons on the smartphone than on the desktop or laptop with an established standard keyboard (Hypothesis 1).

There were a few studies regarding gender difference. There are other studies that have had inconsistent results. In particular, there was disagreement within the research about the effect of gender on the frequency of emoticon usage. In one study, across all mediated communication methods, there were no statistical gender differences [20]. In another study, Derks and Bos [21] also showed that females use more non-verbal communication in face-to-face encounters. In the same manner, males sent less emoticons in text messages compared to females [2]. Luor and Wu found that the intention of using emoticons was not statistically significant in terms of gender, but data suggested that females used more emoticons [22]. However, these studies only considered the gender of the sender and not the relationship with the gender of the receiver. This study investigated how often males and females use emoticons in instant messages with both genders. In terms of gender, females will send more emoticons in instant messages to males than to females and males will send more emoticons in instant messages to females than to males (Hypothesis 2).

An interaction was found between valence and the kind of context; in negative or task-oriented contexts people used the least emoticons [20]. When chatting in IM on the smartphone, it was interesting to know whether people would send more emoticons in a positive emotional state than in a negative emotional state (Hypothesis 3).

The frequency of nonverbal emotions in face-to-face interaction increases when the interacting partner was considered to be a friend [23]. Text messages are mostly private communications with friends [24]. In this line of reasoning, when chatting privately as well as officially in IM, it was interesting to know whether horizontal relationships (equal-equal, e.g., friends) would result in greater emoticon usage than vertical relationships (superior-inferior, e.g., supervisor) (Hypothesis 4).

To sum up, this study tested the following four research hypotheses related to emoticon use: (1) There will be more emoticon usage on the smartphone than on the computer. (2) Users will send more emoticons in instant messages to users of the opposite sex, than to the same sex. (3) People will send more emoticons in good emotional state than in bad emotional state. (4) Horizontal relationships will result in greater emoticon usage than vertical relationships.

3 Research Methods

3.1 Participants

A total of 53 people participated in this survey. This study investigated the feature of emoticon use among people who use IM on the smartphone. The participants consisted of 29 males (54.7%) and 24 females (45.3%). There are four participants in the 10-20 years age range, 48 participants in the 30-40 range, and one participant in the over 50 range. Over 48 of the participants (90.6%) were 30-40 years old.

3.2 Independent and Dependent Variables

For four primary research questionnaires, this study applied descriptive statistics. On the other hand, for testing the research hypothesis, the Mann–Whitney U test was conducted to compare user's attitudes with respect to several hypotheses and a single Likert scale question was written as 5 point scale ranging from "Strongly Disagree" on one end to "Strongly Agree" on the other and "Neither Agree nor Disagree" in the middle. This is a non-parametric test, and is therefore well suited to our Likert scale data because we cannot presume that the population of the collected data fits a normal distribution. Specifically, four independent variables were considered to test the research hypotheses: availability of the computer keyboard (a computer keyboard and a smartphone keyboard), gender (male and female), emotional states (positive and negative) and human relationship (vertical and horizontal). Dependent variables of this study were user's attitudes about frequency of emoticon use.

3.3 Procedures and Questionnaire

A web survey research was conducted to see how emoticons are used in IM on the smartphone. After designing the survey research, it was sent to participants via Internet and tracked during two weeks in October 2012. A set of questionnaires were developed that has three sections: basic information of participants, primary questionnaire and research hypotheses about emoticon use. Participants received a questionnaire, which he/she filled out individually. For research questions, each of these was measured by multiple items in the questionnaire. The respondents were permitted to react by given a text message, by selecting the frequency and by picking emoticons from a list of thirty-seven emoticons. For research hypotheses, the respondents were asked to indicate their level of agreement with a given statement by way of an ordinal scale. This survey took approximately 15 minutes of his/her time.

4 Results and Discussion

4.1 Results

The results of four primary research questions related to emoticon use were presented as follows: First, there are many emoticons used in IM, but emoticon users did not use all emoticons. Participants showed a great dependency on just five of all possible 37 emoticons to be used and implemented, and utilized only 14 different emoticons in total. For users' first choice of emoticons, the five emoticons used mostly by the participants were chuckle (, 32.1%), smile (, 20.8%), beam (, 15.1%), wink (, 7.5%), and crushed (, 5.7%). As the findings show, emoticon styles that most users preferred were similar to a smiling face in the survey.

Second, although graphical emoticons as well as animated emoticons became very popular, out of the three types of emoticons (text-based, graphical and animated emoticons), text-based emoticons were more preferred (39.6%) compared to the other two, graphical (34.0%) and animated emoticons (26.4%).

Third, we have identified the main reason and intention most people send emoticons in IM on the smartphone. They were as follows: (1) Emoticons can help the receiver understand more accurately and clearly (35.0%), (2) To make a warm and bright atmosphere in IM (22.5%), (3) Using emotions is easier than to write text messages in IM (18.8%), (4) It is fun to use emoticons in IM (15.0%), (5) Using emoticons is popular now in IM (6.2%) and (6) The other response (2.5%). These results mean that emoticon use was considerably correlated to enforcing richness of information exchange. To make the conversation smooth and bright is not the first reason.

Lastly, when people IM from start to finish on a smartphone, the frequency of emoticons were as follows: Most participants tend to use at least one emoticon when they are texting. The frequency of emoticon use analysis showed that only three participants (5.7%) are not using emoticons when texting. The other distribution of the emotion use is that one emoticon is used (37.7%), two to three emoticons are used (28.3%), four to five emoticons are used (3.8%) and over six emoticons are used (24.5%).

In the second place, this study tested the research hypotheses related to emoticon use: First, will emoticons be used more on the smartphones rather than on the non-mobile devices such as laptop and desktop? There was a difference between the frequency of emoticons on the smartphone and on the computer. There was more emoticon use on the smartphone than on the computer ($U = 389.5$, $p < .01$, one-tailed) Thus, hypothesis 1 was confirmed.

Second, there were statistical gender differences. Users sent more emoticons in IM to users of the opposite sex, than to the same sex (same sex Mdn = 1, opposite sex Mdn = 2, $U = 2207.5$, $p < .01$, one-tailed). This means that hypothesis 2 was confirmed.

Third, interestingly, there was a difference between the frequency of emoticon use in good emotional states and the frequency of emoticon use in bad emotional states. The participants tend to use emoticons in their good emotional states more than in their bad emotional states ($U = 709.5$, $p < .01$, one-tailed). Hypothesis 3 was confirmed.

Lastly, there was a difference between the frequency of emoticons on the horizontal relationships between friends and on the vertical relationships between supervisor and worker. People send more emoticons on the horizontal relationships than on the vertical relationships ($U = 765.5$, $p < .01$, one-tailed). Hypothesis 4 was confirmed.

4.2 Discussion

The present study about emoticon use showed interesting results. Participants showed a great dependency on just five emoticons. Most users preferred emoticons that were similar to a smiling face. This implies that participants would like to express their positive feelings with others rather than expressing their negative emotional feelings. It identified that people prefer more emoticons to represent a smiling face than emoticons to represent a scowling face (Question 1). This result corresponds with research from Lee and Wagner which showed that people displayed more emotions in positive contexts than in negative contexts [25]. Although, IM on the smartphone is more accessible to express negative emotions, people are reluctant to use negative emoticons even in this kind of electric communication. On the other hand, people who do not use emoticons in IM replied that: (1) Sending emoticons in IM from a smartphone is annoying. (2) Using emoticons in IM interrupts the communication. (3) Emoticons make chatting conversations less serious.

The text-based emoticons were preferred over graphical and animated emoticons (Question 2). The main reason was that it is easy to type the emoticons directly on the smartphone keyboard without needing to find particular emoticons. In other words, emoticon users wanted the speed to type emoticons and convenient access to emoticons. However, people who prefer graphical emoticons presented different opinions and emotions or feelings that he/she can express more exactly and diversely than through text-based emoticons. Also, he/she replied that animated emoticons are more actively appealing but not professional. On the other hand, people who prefer animated emoticons gave his/her opinions that they can communicate emotions and feelings more strongly by them than through graphical or text-based emoticons.

The results were analyzed regarding the main reason and intention most people send emoticons. Emoticon use was considerably correlated to enforcing richness of information exchange (Question 3). Senders want receivers to understand instant messages well, so he/she sends emoticons to prevent miscommunication. Next, some emoticon users sent emoticons to induce a warm environment before stating IM.

Tossel and Kortum showed that over 158,098 text messages were sent and received by his 21 participants and only 4% contained emoticons [2]. In contrast to his findings, this study showed that the frequency of emoticons use was varied when people IM from start to finish on a smartphone. Particularly, this study showed that participants send messages including zero emoticons (5.7%). The difference of results can be outcome of cultural or nationality differences between the two countries. It can be concluded that people who used three or fewer emoticons have an intention such as an expression of emotion, richness of communication and a bright warm mood. Over four emoticons users showed that emoticon use could become habitual and less conscious in IM.

As the result of the research hypotheses test, hypothesis 1 was confirmed. People use more emoticons on the smartphone than on the desktop computer or laptop. Speed and accuracy of communication are important considerations in the design of interactive systems. Although the layout of the letters on a smartphone keyboard is similar to a computer keyboard, the arrangement of a smartphone's keys is not optimal for typing. This resulted in more text messages displaying several emoticons because people have not become accustomed to virtual keyboards of smartphones.

Hypothesis 2 was confirmed as well. Users sent more emoticons in IM on the smartphone to users of the opposite sex, than to the same sex. This result was found from the receiver's sex. Some studies showed that females are more intensive emoticon users than males. Luor and Wu already showed that females had a higher frequency of using emoticons to express their emotions when using IM compared with males [22], but the above studies need to be analyzed in terms of the receiver's sex.

Hypothesis 3 was confirmed as well. People sent more emoticons in good emotional states than in bad emotional states. This result supports the finding that we described earlier that most participants preferred to use positive emoticons rather than negative emoticons. This study concluded that emoticons are not used as frequently in negative moods as most users preferred emoticons representing smiling faces. Clearly, the emoticons that are used to express negative emotions are not frequent in a negative situation.

Hypothesis 4 was confirmed as well. People send more emoticons on the horizontal relationships (equal-equal) than on the vertical relationships (superior-inferior). It is more appropriate to show one's emotions and feelings towards friends or colleagues than towards supervisors or seniors. The expression of emotions in IM from a smartphone, by use of emoticons, is similar to the expression of emotions in face-to-face communication. Most people want to be very sincere and professional to his/her supervisors or elders. Although, emoticons are not actual non-verbal behavior, this fact was showed in electronic communication.

5 Conclusion and Future Work

This study intended to uncover the user's trait associated with emoticon use in IM on the smartphone. The overall conclusion of this study is that traits of emoticon users in IM on the smartphone are similar to in face-to-face communication. The primary of emoticon use was to help them communicate accurately. Emoticons are being used to represent their emotions or feeling as well as to make their conversations smooth and represented in positive mood. In addition, emoticons are being used more between the different genders rather than the same gender. Also, emotions are being used more among the same horizontal relationships rather than among the vertical relationships. It is our belief that the characteristics of emoticon use that we found from this study would contribute to the understanding of emoticon use in IM on the smartphone and further that they would serve as a base for developing and improving the next levels of emoticon. The next step of this research is to conduct another user study with a diverse group of participants that will provide more characteristics of emoticon use.

References

1. Huang, A.H., Yen, D.C., Zhang, X.: Exploring the potential effects of emoticons. Information & Management 45(7), 466–473 (2008)
2. Tossell, C.C., et al.: A longitudinal study of emoticon use in text messaging from smartphones. Computers in Human Behavior 28(2), 659–663 (2012)
3. Garrison, A., et al.: Conventional Faces: Emoticons in Instant Messaging Discourse. Computers and Composition 28(2), 112–125 (2011)
4. Nardi, B.A., Whittaker, S., Bradner, E.: Interaction and outeraction: instant messaging in action. In: Proceedings of the 2000 ACM Conference on Computer Supported Cooperative Work. ACM (2000)
5. Dix, A., et al.: Human Computer Interaction, 3rd edn. (2004)
6. Harrison, R.P.: Nonverbal Communication. Human Communication As a Field of Study: Selected Contemporary Views, 113 (1989)
7. Rogers, E.M., Allbritton, M.M.: Interaction Communication Technologies in Business Organizations. The Journal of Business Communication 32(2), 177–195 (1995)

8. Antonijevic, S.: Expressing Emotions Online: An Analysis of Visual Aspects of Emoticons. In: EEO Conference Papers: International Communication Association 2005 Annual Meeting, New York (2005)
9. Walther, J.B., D'Addario, K.P.: The Impacts of Emoticons on Message Interpretation in Computer-Mediated Communication. Social Science Computer Review 19(3), 324–347 (2001)
10. Riva, G.: The Sociocognitive Psychology of Computer-Mediated Communication; The Present and Future of Technology-Based Interactions. Cyberpsyc Hology & Behavior 5, 581–598 (2002)
11. Lo, S.K.: The nonverbal communication functions of emoticons in computer-mediated communication. CyberPsychology & Behavior 11(5), 595–597 (2008)
12. Tung, F.-W., Deng, Y.-S.: Increasing social presence of social actors in e-learning environments: Effects of dynamic and static emoticons on children. Displays 28(4-5), 174–180 (2007)
13. Falaki, H., et al.: Diversity in smartphone usage. In: Proceedings of the 8th International Conference on Mobile Systems, Applications, and Services. ACM (2010)
14. Danet, B., Ruedenberg-Wright, L., Rosenbaum-Tamari, Y.: Smoking dope at a virtual party: Writing, play and performance on Internet Relay Chat. Network and Netplay: Virtual Groups on the Internet (1997)
15. Rezabek, L.L., Cochenour, J.J.: Visual Cues in Computer-Mediated Communication: Supplementing Text with Emoticons. Journal of Visual Uteracy 18(2), 201–215 (1998)
16. Krohn, F.B.: A generational approach to using emoticons as nonverbal communication. Journal of Technical Writing and Communication 34(4), 321–328 (2004)
17. Ling, R.: Mobile communications vis-à-vis teen emancipation, peer group integration and deviance. The Inside Text, 175–193 (2005)
18. Qiao, Q.: The adoption and use of SMS among Chinese teenagers (2010)
19. Kwon, T., Na, S., Park, S.-H.: Drag-and-Type: A new method for typing with virtual keyboards on small touchscreens. In: 2013 IEEE International Conference on Consumer Electronics (ICCE). IEEE (2013)
20. Derks, D., Bos, A.E.R., Grumbkow, J.V.: Emoticons and social interaction on the Internet: the importance of social context. Computers in Human Behavior 23(1), 842–849 (2007)
21. Derks, D., Bos, A.E.R., Von Grumbkow, J.: Emoticons and online message interpretation. Social Science Computer Review 26(3), 379–388 (2008)
22. Luor, T., et al.: The effect of emoticons in simplex and complex task-oriented communication: An empirical study of instant messaging. Computers in Human Behavior 26(5), 889–895 (2010)
23. Wagner, H., Lee, V.: 10. Facial Behavior Alone and in the Presence of Others. The social context of nonverbal behavior, p. 262 (1999)
24. Häkkilä, J., Chatfield, C.: 'It's like if you opened someone else's letter': user perceived privacy and social practices with SMS communication. In: Proceedings of the 7th International Conference on Human Computer Interaction With Mobile Devices & Services. ACM (2005)
25. Lee, V., Wagner, H.: The effect of social presence on the facial and verbal expression of emotion and the interrelationships among emotion components. Journal of Nonverbal Behavior 26(1), 3–25 (2002)

Appendix

Table 2. Graphical emoticons of Kakao Talk

Emotion	Meaning	Emoticon	Meaning
	Sulk		Cute
	Devil		Bubble
	Puke		Cool
	Embarrassed		Cry
	Blush		Pish
	Surprised		Alien
	KiKi		Sleepy
	Wink		Satisfied
	Frustrated		Confused
	Worried		Sleeping
	Relieved		Crushed
	Grumpy		Sneer
	Angry		Alien-girl
	Tipsy		Hesitant
	Oh, my goodness		Curious
	Smile		Sick
	Hurray		Tongue
	Scared		Beam
	happy		

Mobile Users Are More Vigilant Than Situated Users

M. Giles Phillips

subforum.org, Boston, MA 02113
giles@alum.mit.edu

Abstract. With the rapid growth of mobile device usage, daily life offers much empirical evidence that users frequently and persistently interact with mobile devices while doing other things. These users might be highly engaged within a mobile experience or unfulfilled by their real world experience; but significantly, their frequent usage could also be a form of vigilant behavior. This research seeks to understand whether or not mobile usage leads to an increased prevalence of user vigilance, first by establishing criteria that can be used to determine if a specific session of use is vigilant, and then applying these criteria to analyze observed sessions of use for two distinct cohorts: mobile users and situated users. In the analysis, it was found that everyday vigilant usage scenarios are fairly prevalent, and also that mobile users were 3 times more vigilant than situated users. These initial findings need further validation, but may prove significant to interaction design: optimizing a software interface to better support vigilant usage requires an opposing set of considerations when compared to traditional consumer product design. These design considerations are discussed, in addition to the limitations of the study, and guidance for future work.

Keywords: Mobile, User Interface Design, Vigilance, Attention.

1 Introduction

Vigilance is a state of watchfulness, the compulsion for which maps directly to the perceived consequence of missing out on possible observations. Most prior research into vigilance in the realm of HCI has focused exclusively on situated (terminal, desktop PC or laptop PC) usage with specific tasks that involve watchfulness, in order to understand the physiological impact of a sustained vigilance state when interacting with machines [5],[7],[9]. The key findings of this work have been how exhaustion and attention decline affect usage – and consequently performance – for sustained vigilance tasks such as radar operation [5], anesthesia monitoring and operation [18], and intrusion detection [15].

This narrow focus seems to imply that vigilant scenarios only exist within a small subset of human-computer interactions, namely, situated tasks performed by trained professionals or operators. However, a broader survey of scholarship into attention among people and mammals suggests that vigilance is more general – it is a context-specific state that often coincides with other tasks or distractors [4], [12], [13], [19]. For example, a grazing animal must balance two tasks that are necessary for survival: intermittently eating and watching vigilantly for any approaching predators [4]. Or, a rushing commuter, who is navigating, must also be watchful while crossing the

M. Kurosu (Ed.): Human-Computer Interaction, Part III, HCII 2014, LNCS 8512, pp. 166–177, 2014.

street. Now, imagine this commuter has a mobile phone in his pocket, buzzing for attention. Would he wait until he exited the crosswalk before checking to see who had texted? If he thought the message was important, he might not. In our interactions with computers, just as with our interactions in the physical world, vigilance is inclusive of, but is not limited to, specific and situated tasks [10]. After all, the true measure of vigilance is not that usage is sustained, but that attention is sustained. In the day-to-day reality of an average consumer, like the commuter in the crosswalk, HCI vigilance scenarios may frequently and intermittently overlap their other activities.

But how prevalent are these vigilant scenarios, really? And are mobile devices, with their nagging, their beeping, and their omnipresence, creating more vigilance scenarios than earlier technologies did? This research seeks to answer these questions. Background is provided on prior research into vigilance, how it is supported by technology, as well as prior scholarship into mobile and social media usage. A specific study is then described, detailing goals, criteria used for determining if a particular session of use is vigilant or not, participants, and methodology. A quantitative analysis of the study findings is presented, followed by a qualitative analysis of user interviews. A discussion of design considerations is subsequently provided. Finally, key achievements and future work are described in the conclusion.

2 Background

2.1 Why Does Vigilance Occur?

The instinctual basis for entering into a vigilant state is the preservation of self or society [3]. It's easy to see how this applies to a radar operator huddled over the radar screen in a WW2 aircraft. But it's a little more difficult to see how vigilance might relate to everyday device usage by normal users. To understand everyday vigilance, consider a common example: the social networking behaviors of teenagers.

For many teens, social network usage is associated with self-preservation because their interactions within that system are a basis for socialization and, partially, the formation and preservation of their identity, their sense of self [16]. In developing these social interactions, a teenager must break her natural methods for real-time communication into the discrete unidirectional communiques that these technologies enable: things like messages, status updates, and photo uploads. These communiques are signals that the teen uses for social encoding, impression management, and identity performance [1-2]. In so doing, the teen extrapolates socialization from her natural and immediate embodied experience, and pushes it into exogenous, serialized and persistent media that she must then watch over. This phenomenon could be described as a serialization of socialization, and the resultant compulsion to be watchful forces the teenager to be vigilant.

2.2 How is Vigilance Supported?

Certainly, an active social network user might spend a few hours a day logged into the system on her laptop, monitoring things. This usage is not entirely vigilant, but the interface employs a number of visual and audible alerts to direct the user's attention to something that they might need to see. The user will watch for these alerts, in case she needs to respond to something. This is an everyday example of vigilance, occurring in a situated usage scenario.

Now consider mobile devices, which have quickly become a primary means of communication as we move through our daily physical lives [6], [11]. An active social networker will not stop monitoring the network when she closes her laptop; rather, she will use her mobile device to monitor things. However, the nature of her engagement with the device is quite different. By design, mobile devices must be held, carried, and tended to. While the average user engages with their mobile device for about an hour each day, this usage is broken up into numerous one-minute sessions [14]. Like the desktop experience, mobile devices employ notifications and alerts to capture attention. But with mobile devices, those alerts often pull the user's attention away from the physical world, and into the mediated world. This is less often the case with a situated user, who is already engaged in the mediated. As such, the growth of mobile devices and their utility as a communication tool has brought rise to a form of vigilance that spans intermittent sessions of device usage. In this form of vigilance, a state of watchfulness over the mediated experience is sustained and balanced within the physical world, via endogenous and exogenous cues [10].

In the everyday case of social networking, vigilant usage scenarios have emerged as a result of the inextricable role that technology plays in the establishment and maintenance of the self. Mobile devices enable this vigilance to persist as networkers navigate the physical world, pushing them into a state of divided attention. And yet, vigilant scenarios appear to be much more ubiquitous than a teenager constantly checking her social network. As Sherry Turkle notes: "It is the more mundane examples of attention sharing that change the fabric of daily life. Parents check e-mail as they push strollers. Children and parents text during family dinners." This is neither boredom, nor simple device addiction – it is a compulsion invoked by the perceived importance of socialization. She further explains, "Although we can't keep up with [our mobile device], we feel responsible for it. It is, after all, our life." [16].

3 Study

3.1 Study Goals

This research seeks to demonstrate that mobile usage leads to increased user vigilance, first by establishing criteria that can be used to analyze whether or not a usage session is associated with vigilance, and then applying these criteria to observed sessions of use for two distinct cohorts: mobile users and situated (terminal-based, laptop or desktop) users. Both cohorts were comprised of participants who were actively communicating through social networks and other mediated channels like text messages and emails. It is important to note that sustained usage was not assumed to be a criterion for vigilance. The vigilance tasks could be of any duration or relative complexity.

3.2 Criteria for Vigilance in a Session of Use

Because of the diversity of users and their relationship to computing devices and software, it is difficult to describe any general usage scenario as categorically vigilant or not. For a user who is deeply engaged in a social network, monitoring that network might become an important aspect of socialization - important enough to trigger vigilant attention. However, a casual user of that same social network may feel no need to monitor things – their usage may be entirely non-vigilant. In order to observe the prevalence of vigilance among day-to-day computer usage scenarios, we must establish a set of criteria against which an individual observed session of use can be evaluated as vigilant or not. For this study, the following criteria were used:

1. **High Task Importance.** First, the importance of completing the associated task must be recognized by the user as being higher than average. This follows the simple logic that self-preservation is important; if a task is associated with self-preservation, then it must also be important. In this study, users were asked to rank the importance of individual usage scenarios directly, and their ranking of task importance was performed antecedent to task completion. As such, one limitation of this study is that it did not necessarily capture false alarms, scenarios where users thought something might have been important and took action to engage with their device, but ultimately decided the task was not important [8]. In this study, participants may not have described false alarms as important, although vigilant attention may have invoked their session of use.
2. **Endogenous or Exogenous Cueing.** Secondly, the scenario must have been invoked by an exogenous or endogenous cue. In other words: the user was either responding to some type of alert or notification, or the user had experienced a desire to check for some form of update or response. This criteria differentiated vigilance tasks from planned tasks (like work or homework), direct inquiries (like research and web browsing), and boredom activities (like playing games or surfing the internet). As vigilance is a state of sustained watchfulness over potentially intermittent sessions of use, cues are essentially the events that invoked the user's engagement with the device. Exogenous cues are those that are specifically designed to capture the user's attention: a smartphone buzzing when you receive a text message, or your email client displaying a visual alert when you receive a new email on your laptop [20]. Endogenous cues are invoked by the mind of the user and manifest as the compulsion to direct attention to the device; for example, checking to see if you'd received a response to an email you sent, after having been away from the computer [20]. Or, looking to see how many responses you received to an update that you posted in a social network.
3. **Dire Consequences for Failure to Complete Task.** The user should perceive that failure to complete the associated task would have dire consequences. This follows the logic that if you do something out of self-preservation, then you believe that you would be harmed in some way if you failed to do the task. Along with the other criteria, this helps establish that the task is associated with a scenario of sufficient gravity to validate vigilance. In order to capture this criterion, users were asked to speculate what would have happened if they had not done the task, and if their failure to perform the task would have created any problems for them.

For this study, any observed session of use that met the first two criteria – that the task was important to the user, and that some form of endogenous or exogenous cue invoked the task – was considered to be a vigilance scenario. A subset of these vigilance scenarios was then further analyzed to determine if it met the third criterion: that there would be dire consequences for the users if they failed to complete the task.

3.3 Study Participants

Two user groups were established and their device usage was monitored for vigilance. One user group was comprised of situated users, and the other group was comprised of mobile users. Users who were interested in taking part in the study filled out a brief application form that focused upon their relationship with their computing devices. In order to be selected to serve as a participant in the study, applicants need to meet the following criteria:

- They must own or have access to a mobile device or a computer.
- The user must have a profile on at least one social network.
- That profile must have been created at least 6 months ago.
- The user must check on the status of his or her social network at least once a day.
- The user must have completed an initial 20 minute interview over the phone.

Based upon these criteria, applicants were screened and 8 participants were selected for each of the two user groups, resulting in a total of 16 participants. (Figure 1)

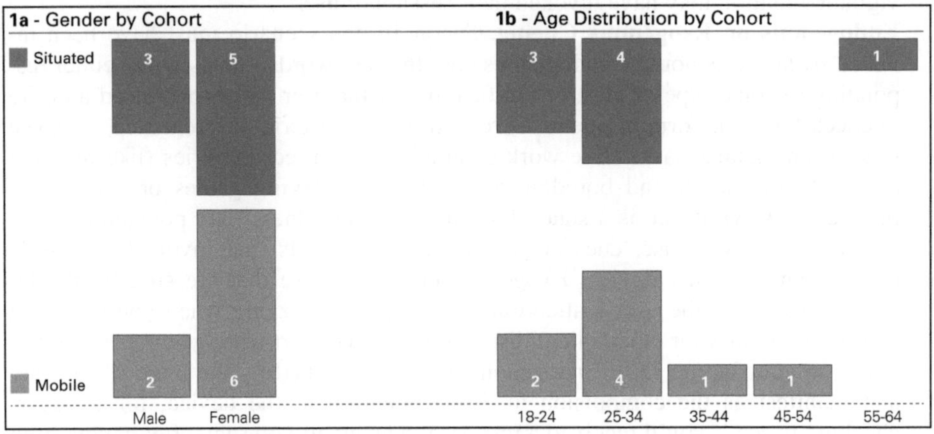

Fig. 1. Gender and Age Distribution by Cohort

3.4 Study Methodology

The study consisted of two distinct phases. The first phase was a phone interview within which users were asked to describe their technology usage patterns and their relationship to their devices. Users were asked to describe their social network engagement in some detail, including the reasons that they typically access their network. They were also asked about other prevalent modes of communication: email and text messages.

The second phase of this research, which commenced immediately upon completion of the interview portion, was a longitudinal study. Participants were asked to maintain a daily journal, where they described a specific session of use that occurred on that day, using an online journal form. This component of the study lasted for approximately two weeks, until each participant completed 14 journal entries. If a participant missed a journal entry on any particular day, he simply resumed on the following day. The test moderator emailed each participant every day with a reminder and link to the daily journal form. The email was sent at random times of day over the course of the study, and all 7 days of the week were included in the study.

The journal entries were concise - up to 6 questions, and designed to take approximately one minute to complete. Each entry was focused upon a single session of device usage. The order of response options was randomized for all multiple choice questions. Over the course of the study, a set of core questions persisted for all 14 entries, and a number of questions were introduced for a fewer number of entries, resulting in 3 distinct journal entry types, as shown in Figure 2. This created an element of diversity into the participant's experience, but also enabled the collection of additional data points without making the daily journals too long.

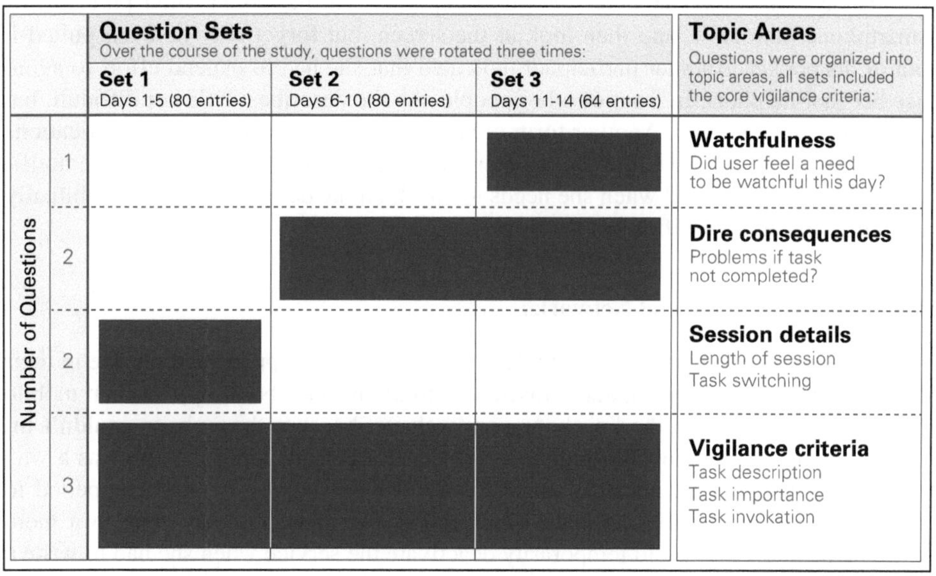

Fig. 2. Journal Types: Question Distribution by Topic Area

4 Qualitative Analysis

A number of observations were made regarding the usage of mobile and situated devices during the participant interviews.

4.1 Separation Anxiety for Mobile Users

Many mobile users described a feeling of anxiety when without their phones. Several described that the last time they had left home without their phone, they immediately returned home to retrieve it. One user noted that she'd "feel lost" without it, because it lets her know what's going on around her. Another user described feeling "kind of scared" when she'd lost her mobile phone. A student recalled the time she'd broken her mobile: she immediately stopped studying for her exam and went to get the phone replaced. Another user summarized the experience of being without her phone: "it is the worst. I feel like I am not connected to the world. You feel lost." In describing the importance of his device, a young professional made a profound observation about his mobile phone: "when not at my desk, it's my only form of communication."

Situated users had less separation anxiety. One desktop user described frustration and boredom when a hurricane had knocked out Internet connectivity. Computers were also associated with livelihood for some situated users. As one participant noted: "[My computer] is critical. I have to have it. It is how I make my living."

4.2 Habituated Usage Patterns

A number of mobile users also revealed different aspects of how they had become habituated to use their devices. One user reported that he would often pull out his smartphone, unlock it, and then look at the screen, but forget why he even pulled it out of his pocket. Another participant indicated that she had to expend effort to avoid use her mobile phone in front of other people. As she describes: "it's not difficult, but I have to think about it". Another form of habituation involved the use of notifications to know when to open the device. One participant described that she "trusts the notifications" to tell her if and when she needs to check on the device, and would habitually open the device if a notification was received.

4.3 Suppressing Social Networks

Active social networkers employed a few workarounds to suppress the service in their everyday life. One participant refused to install the Facebook app on her mobile phone and instead used the Facebook.com website, because the website couldn't invoke alerts or notifications through the phone. For her, avoiding the app was a way to suppress the service, because otherwise she'd be distracted by, and compelled to respond to the alerts. For another user, suppressing Facebook was done in a more extreme fashion: she would temporarily deactivate the service when she had to write a paper or during exam week – "because [Facebook is] counterproductive."

5 Quantitative Analysis

A total of 224 journal entries were recorded: 14 entries for each of the 16 participants. Each journal entry described a single session of device usage for the day the entry was submitted; as such, the journal captured user descriptions of 224 distinct sessions of use. It is important to note that users were not directly asked if they were being vigilant or not; rather, they were asked a number of questions related to the type of tasks they were doing, the relative importance of these tasks, and what events prompted their session of use. The responses within each journal entry were then analyzed according to the vigilance criteria in order to determine whether the corresponding session of use appeared to be vigilant or not. The two test groups were then compared. For the mobile group, 43.8% of the recorded sessions were vigilant. For the situated group, 14.3% of the recorded sessions were vigilant – see Figure 3. Thus, it was observed that mobile users are about 3 times more likely to be vigilant than situated users.

Users were also asked to speculate about the consequences if they had not completed the tasks involved. This was accomplished through a pair of questions that were together included in 144 of the 224 journal entries, the first asking if failure to complete the task would have been a problem, the other asking for speculation about what would have happened if they'd failed to complete the task. Users associated negative or dire consequences with failure to complete their task for 95.2% of the vigilant sessions captured, shown in Figure 3b. This high correlation validates that the usage sessions were vigilant.

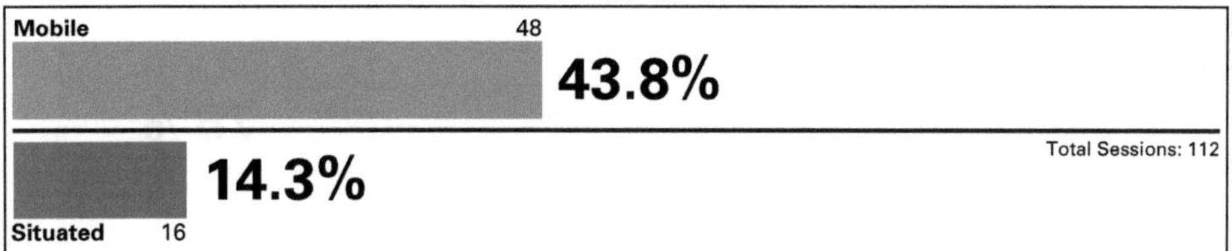

Cohort	Total Sessions	Vigilant Sessions	Number of vigilant sessions on days where users recorded consequences	Vigilant sessions associated with dire consequences by users	Correlation of vigilance and dire consequences
			3b. User's Perception of Dire Consequences		
Mobile	112	48 *43.8%*	31	30	96.8%
Situated	112	16 *14.3%*	11	10	90.9%

Standard Deviations

- 2.6 vigilant sessions among mobile participants
- 1.5 vigilant sessions among situated participants

Fig. 3. Percentage of Sessions That Were Vigilant

Mobile users had a higher standard deviation of 2.6 vigilant sessions per user compared to 1.5 for the situated users, indicating greater variance in the vigilance of mobile users. One possible explanation is that mobile devices are a newer technology than laptops and PCs, and thus there may be more experimentation among mobile users. Secondly, because mobile devices are carried upon the person, they support a greater diversity of usage scenarios, whereas situated usage was more often correlated with planned work. Thirdly, there may simply be more variation among mobile users in the perceived importance of monitoring the device.

Mobile users reported that they felt the need to be watchful over their device on 78% of the days observed, while situated users felt the same need on 44% of the days observed. (See Figure 4) Watchfulness was established by directly asking users whether they felt the need to be watchful or not, each day. Measuring watchfulness was useful a number of ways. First, to account for unobserved usage sessions that may have been vigilant. Because each daily journal asked users only to describe their most recent, or most notable session of use on a particular day, it captured only a subset of all sessions that the user actually conducted each day. Self-reported watchfulness was much more commonly observed than vigilance was: the ratio of watchfulness to vigilance was 78:43.8 (57%) for mobile users and 44:14.3 (32.5%) for situated users. This may suggest that a significant number of vigilant sessions occurred outside of the sessions described in the journal entries. Secondly, self-described watchfulness was used as a measure of quality control of the vigilance criteria: vigilant sessions should always correlate to days where the user described a need to be watchful. This was found to be the case: across both mobile and situated user groups, it was observed that 95.5% of the sessions that were found to be vigilant occurred on days where the user described a need to be watchful over his or her device.

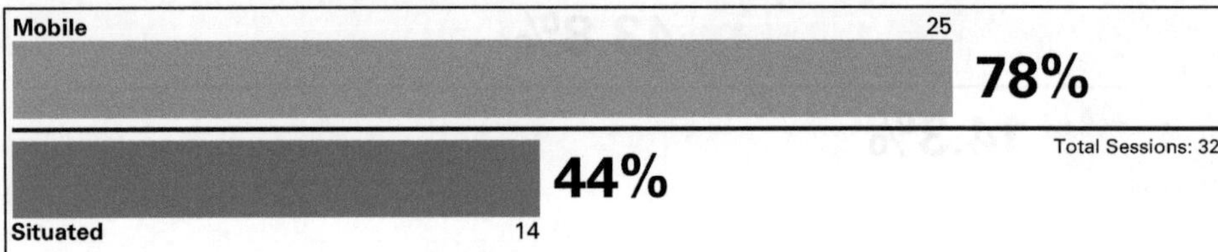

Cohort	Total Sessions	Watchful Sessions	Number of vigilant sessions on days where users recorded watchfulness	Vigilant sessions occuring on days where users felt the need to be watchful	Correlation of vigilance and watchfulness
			4b. Correlation to Vigilance		
Mobile	32	25 *78%*	15	15	100%
Situated	32	14 *44%*	6	5	83%

Fig. 4. Percentage of Days Where Users Felt the Need to be Watchful

6 Discussion

While more work must be done to substantiate these findings, the analyses suggest that vigilance scenarios are prevalent in everyday consumer interactions. But how effectively is vigilant use being supported by today's consumer experiences? Users who are trying to balance device watchfulness with their physical experiences need to spend as little time interacting with the device as possible [10]. We must design for *disengagement*, and make it easy for them to put the device down. Successful designs will enable users to easily watch for signals that need their attention, quickly and efficiently enact a response, and return back to the real world with minimal interruption:

6.1 Vigilance Design Principles

- **Vigilance First.** Vigilance compelled the user to start their task, and as such, the initial interface should be optimized for vigilant use. Users should be presented with only enough information to know if they need to take further action or not. All actions should be enabled via efficient, optimized paths within the application flow. The interface should eliminate or deemphasize all distractors (unrelated content, secondary actions, advertisements.)

- **Encourage Disengagement.** Alerts should be minimized and vigilance should be supported via the shortest possible session of use. When the vigilant task is completed, the session should terminate. Shorter sessions create less interruption and distraction from the real world experiences that the user is balancing.
- **Make Habituation Easy.** Interactions should be standardized and not novel. Users should be able to easily form habitual usage patterns that require less cognitive focus to process and perform. This also means that users may be more resistant to changes in the interface design if habituated usage patterns are disrupted.

6.2 Challenges Lay Ahead

The clear challenge with these principles is that by reducing engagement, they likely compete with the business goals and Key Performance Indicators of the company that is designing the software. Most consumer applications are designed in an effort to deepen user engagement. Vigilance requires a paradigm shift. Designers have been taught to value the attributes of an engaging user experience - immersion, focused attention, and lengthy sessions of use – often above all others. This is because a user's attention is of considerable value to most organizations that build web products. For one, the user's session can be monetized with advertisements that interrupt views or are displayed alongside content, and the more time the user spends within the product, the more opportunities there are to show him ads. Many such organizations track the length of sessions of use or the number of typical interactions that they see from users, in order to raise the amount of money they can charge for ad impressions. A site with engaged users can charge much more than a site with disengaged users.

Another challenge is that vigilance is likely not the only scenario that everyday consumer products must support. Vigilance emerges only after the software or service is used enough that the user begins to feel the need to be watchful. Outside of any moment of vigilance, the user may be more casual and exploratory, even immersed or deeply engagement. Consumer products most support both extremes.

Users also need to completely disengage at times when they expressly do not wish to be vigilant. As demonstrated by the participant who deactivated her social network in order to study for her test, suppression is a critical form of control. This may involve a different mode in the interface, or settings that suppress alerts or notifications.

7 Conclusion

This study had several limitations requiring additional research in order to validate the findings. With a small population size of 16 participants, the results are not statistically reliable. A similar study should be performed with an increased population size, increasing the total number of journal entries for analysis. With a larger population, distinct cohorts could also be defined, enabling analysis of vigilance behavior based upon age range or other demographic criteria. Another key limitation of this work was that it relied upon self-reporting rather than instrumentation or direct observation. This reduces the quality of the data by introducing the possibility of subjectivity, biases, and errors on the part of the participant. While interviews and self-reporting will likely be useful methods for future work, other research methods like instrumented environments for observational research, instrumentation of user devices, and instrumentation of software and services would be useful quantitative methods that would help hybridize the general methodology and validate the findings. More work is needed to fully define principles that can be effectively utilized during the design process, in order to better support vigilant user scenarios. The discussed design principles should be further defined and their effectiveness evaluated. Towards this end, user studies could be used for specific interfaces, evaluating how effectively vigilance scenarios are supported through workflows or tasks presented to users.

This study suggests that vigilance is an important and common usage motivator for everyday consumers, and also that mobile devices have increased the prevalence of vigilant use. This research further supports the observation that everyday users might be quite vigilant in their device usage. Vigilance in HCI is not limited to specific situated tasks performed by trained professionals or operators; rather, vigilant use applies to a broad spectrum of tasks performed by consumers. In short, it is more important to support vigilance in a world full of mobile users. This has profound implications for software, because optimizing the interaction design of a software product to better support vigilant usage requires a different, and at times opposing, set of considerations than traditional consumer product design does.

Acknowledgments. Thank you to Dr. Sherry Turkle for providing valuable insights and discussion related to this work. Thank you to Damon Dimmick for assistance in planning and conducting user interviews.

References

1. Boyd, D.: Why Youth (Heart) Social Network Sites: The Role of Networked Publics in Teenage Social Life. In: Buckingham, D. (ed.) MacArthur Foundation Series on Digital Learning - Youth, Identity, and Digital Media Volume, pp. 119–142. MIT Press, Cambridge (2007)
2. Boyd, D.: Social Network Sites as Networked Publics: Affordances, Dynamics, and Implications. In: Papacharissi, Z. (ed.) Networked Self: Identity, Community, and Culture on Social Network Sites, pp. 39–58 (2010)
3. Edmunds, M.: Defense In Animals: a Survey of Anti-predator Defenses. Longman, New York (1974)
4. Lima, S.L., Bednekoff, P.A.: Back to the basics of antipredatory vigilance: can nonvigilant animals detect attack? Animal Behaviour 58(3), 537–543 (1999)
5. Mackworth, N.H.: The breakdown of vigilance during prolonged visual search. Quarterly Journal of Experimental Psychology 1, 6–21 (1948)

6. Youth Are Moving to Mobile Devices for Their Communication Needs: R You Here? American Press Institute,, http://www.americanpressinstitute.org/wp-content/uploads/2013/09/NIE_youth-moving-to-mobile.pdf
7. Parasuraman, R.: Sustained attention: a multifactorial approach. In: Posner, M., Marin, O. (eds.) Attention and Performance XI, pp. 493–511. Lawrence Erlbaum, Hillsdale (1985)
8. Parasuraman, R. (ed.): The Attentive Brain. The MIT Press, Cambridge (1998)
9. Parasuraman, R., Caggiano, G.: Neural and genetic assays of mental workload. In: McBride, D., Schmorrow, D. (eds.) Quantifying Human Information Processing, pp. 123–155. Rowman and Littlefield, Lanham (2005)
10. Phillips, M.G.: Designing for Vigilance during Intermittent Use. In: 3rd Annual ACM Web Science Conference, pp. 243–246. ACM, New York (2012)
11. Mobile Factbook, Portio Research Limited (2013), http://www.portioresearch.com/media/3986/Portio%20Research%20Mobile%20Factbook%202013.pdf
12. Quenette, P.-Y.: Functions of vigilance behaviour in mammals: A review. Acta Oecologica 11(6), 801–818 (1990)
13. Robinette, R.L., Ha, J.C.: Social and Ecological Factors Influencing Vigilance by Northwestern Crows, Corvus Caurinus. Animal Behaviour 62, 447–453 (2001)
14. Sch, J., Hecht, B., Matthias, B., Fachhochschule, M.: Falling Asleep with Angry Birds, Facebook and Kindle - A Large Scale Study on Mobile Application Usage. Measurement 11, 47–56 (2011)
15. Schultz, E.E., Proctor, R.W., Lien, M., Salvendy, G.: Usability and Security: An Appraisal of Usability Issues in Information Security Methods. Computers & Security 20(7), 620–634 (2001)
16. Turkle, S.: Alone Together. Basic Books, New York (2011)
17. Warm, J.S., Parasuraman, R., Matthews, G.: Vigilance Requires Hard Mental Work and Is Stressful. Human Factors 50, 433–441 (2008)
18. Weinger, M.B., Slagle, J.: Human Factors Research in Anesthesia Patient Safety. J. Am. Med. Inform. Assoc. 9, S58–S63 (2002)
19. Wickens, C.D.: The structure of Attentional Resources. In: Nickerson, R. (ed.) Attention and Performance VIII, pp. 239–257. Lawrence Erlbaum, Hillsdale (1980)
20. Wright, R.D., Ward, L.M.: Orienting of Attention. Oxford University Press, Oxford (2008)

Heuristic Evaluation of Mobile Usability: A Mapping Study

André de Lima Salgado and André Pimenta Freire

Federal University of Lavras
Computer Science Department
Campus Universitário, Caixa Postal 3037, Lavras, MG, Brazil
andre@bsi.ufla.br,
apfreire@dcc.ufla.br

Abstract. The mobile devices market has grown substantially, along with significant developments in mobile interactive technologies. Devices such as tablets, smartphones and others have increasingly become more popular and helped improve the way people interact and exchange information. The aim of this paper is to perform a systematic mapping of the literature regarding the use of heuristic evaluation methods applied on mobile applications. The aims of this research were twofold: analysing what are the most used sets of usability heuristics on usability evaluations of mobile devices, providing a common base to improve mobile design and usability evaluation; analysing details of how usability inspections of mobile applications have been conducted. The results show that different heuristics have been reported in research papers to evaluate usability of mobile devices. The study identified a total of 9 different heuristics sets means of the literature mapping. The traditional set of heuristics proposed by Nielsen and Molich was still the most used set of heuristics in heuristic usability evaluations of mobile devices, but the proposal of new specific heuristics for mobile interfaces has grown substantially.

Keywords: mobile usability, heuristic evaluation, usability inspection.

1 Introduction

There has been a substantial growth in the mobile devices market, along with significant developments in mobile interactive technologies [4] [27]. Devices such as tablets, smartphones and others have increasingly become more popular and helped improve the way people interact and exchange information. According to Monetate Ecommerce Quarterly [21], e-commerce businesses are seeking for ways to deliver relevant messages to mobile consumers because the traffic from smartphones has increased in a very fast pace.

Mobile devices have some specifics characteristics, they can be used while walking, within different weather situations and it can be easily used at different places [2].

M. Kurosu (Ed.): Human-Computer Interaction, Part III, HCII 2014, LNCS 8512, pp. 178–188, 2014.

Within this context, the development of mobile applications has been an important segment in the software industry [4]. Given the key role played by usability as a quality attribute in software development [13], it has become extremely relevant to research appropriate methods to evaluate and improve the usability of mobile applications.

Although having become more ubiquitous, the usability of many mobile applications still remains a challenge to be addressed [4] [10]. According to Billi et al. [5], mobile devices have a number of limitations, such as small screen, limited input capabilities, limited computational resources, limited power supply (batteries), and large heterogeneity in models. Nayebi et al. [22] state that there is a need for more specific and systematic measurement methodologies for evaluating mobile usability.

Heuristic evaluation (HE), proposed by Nielsen and Molich [24], has been championed as a useful low-cost inspection method to professionally evaluate software usability. HE methods are extensively used to evaluate usability of conventional desktop software. This method requires that evaluators inspect some specific interface elements, being guided by pre-defined tasks and compare the interface with a list of heuristics aiming to find usability problems. However, considering the specificities and all differences between mobile and desktop technologies, adopting methods and acquired knowledge in the evaluation of desktop applications directly in the evaluation of mobile applications may not be necessarily straightforward [27].

The use of ordinary desktop-oriented heuristics in HE methods may not always be appropriate to evaluate all types of mobile interfaces, and may not embrace mobile-specific interface characteristics [7]. Heo et al. [10] argue that even with the large number of heuristics for usability evaluation of software systems, they are still not sufficient to appropriately reveal many mobile usability issues, and Bertini et. al. [2] afirm that specific heuristics are need because the traditional ones implicitly embody assumptions about static desktop location and use.

In order to help investigate the current state of the art to develop into these gaps, this paper aims to perform a systematic mapping of the literature regarding the use of heuristic evaluation methods applied on mobile applications. The goal of this research is to analyse what are the most used sets usability heuristics on usability evaluation of mobile devices, investigate how HE methods have been applied and to map the different heuristics that have been used on mobile usability evaluations to provide a common base to improve the design and evaluation of the usability of mobile applications.

The method employed was based on systematic reviews of the literature, by means of reviews and quantitative and qualitative analyses of data reported in literature, combining the results with meta-analytic techniques to increase the likelihood of discovering effects that smaller studies are not able to detect [17].

2 Literature Mapping Process

2.1 Description

Reviewing the literature to systematically collect studies related to a specific theme is a work of precision. The review process of the present study was made based on Kitchenham's [16] stages of a systematic review. As proposed by Kitchenham [16], this mapping process is based on three main phases: *Planning the Review*, *Conducting the Review* and *Reporting the Review*.

Within the *Planning the Review* phase, two stages are included:

1. Identification of the need for a review.
2. Development of a review protocol.

The *Conducting the Review* phase consists of five other stages:

1. Identification of research.
2. Selection of primary studies.
3. Study quality assessment.
4. Data extraction and monitoring.
5. Data synthesis.

The final phase, *Reporting the Review*, emcompasses the review of the whole mapping process, the analysis of all of the results and the publications of the work.

2.2 Mapping Review Protocol

The mapping review protocol includes all methods that are to be done by means of the systematic review. Without this protocol, there is a substantial chance that the mapping process be driven by researcher expectations [16]. The points of the Mapping review protocol are highlighted as following.

Objective: this mapping study has the main goal of finding what are the heuristics used to evaluate usability of mobile devices.

Research Question: "What are the main aspects of heuristic evaluations of mobile usability reported in literature?".

Source search method: sources will be searched by web engines using a search string.

Keywords: usability, heuristics, heuristic evaluation, mobile, android, iOS.

Sources List: publications of all types that were indexed by ACM Digital Library, IEE Xplore, SpringerLink and Science Direct.

Inclusion and exclusion criteria: publications considered in this mapping must be available in electronic format through the mentioned sources list and be written in english. Beside this, publications need to inform, at least, about the keywords mobile, heuristic and usability inside the summary.

Quality assessment criteria: publications need to inform about heuristics or heuristics sets used in usability evaluation of mobile devices. Each publication should also inform enough details about the procedure to perfom the inspection in order to verify whether it could be classified as a heuristic evaluation.

2.3 Conducting the Review

Ater the Mapping review protocol was completed, the mapping process was conducted by one research and supervised by another one (both authors of this paper).

The *identification of research* stage was conducted from October 16th, 2013, to November 7th, 2013. To execute all searches through chosen sources lists search engines, the following search string was used: "usability" AND ("heuristic evaluation" OR "heuristics") AND ("mobile" OR "android" OR "iOS"). A total of 2172 publications were identified through all source search engines listed. From these results, 26 are from ACM Digital Library, 10 from IEEE Xplore, 1335 from SpringerLink and 801 from Science Direct.

From the initial set of 2172 search results, the selection of primary studies (described previously) was performed to execute a first filter. This filter is a faster way to decrease the number of publications that do not overlap the mapping purposes. The *selection of primary studies* have occurred and 26 studies were accepted, 3 from the ACM Digital Library, 7 from IEEE Xplore, 13 from SpringerLink and 3 from Science Direct.

For a final filter, the study quality assessment criteria were applied. The goal of this phase was to analyse all results that provide evidence of using heuristics to mobile usability evaluation, in order to compose the final body of results of this systematic mapping. After the *study quality assessment* stage, 19 studies were included in the mapping process, being 3 from the ACM Digital Library, 5 from IEEE Xplore, 10 from SpringerLink and 1 from Science Direct.

All of the 19 studies were revised and the *data extraction and monitoring* phase was performed to collect information about the types of heuristics used in the evaluation and the process used to perform the heuristic evaluations in the studies. At this stage we used a database containing the full list of all identified heuristics, and other details about the method used to evaluate (such as whether the heuristic evaluations were performed according to the method proposed by Nielsen and Molich [24] or if it used some variation of the method) and the number of evaluators.

Finally, in the *data synthesis* of this mapping study, we analysed the main aspects observed in the literature about heuristic evaluation of mobile usability. This study reviewed a total of 2172 publications about the theme, and after using two filters, we obtained 19 results that have provided us a large list of heuristics used to evaluate usability of mobile devices. This list was reviewed by two coders, and after analysing heuristics with similar descriptions, a list of 29 distinct heuristics was obtained (see full list in the Appendix).

3 Results and Discussion

The results presented in this paper are the synthesis of the analysis of 19 publications that provide information about heuristic evaluation of mobile applications. We present in this section the results of the data analysis and summary of the findings. Section 3.1 presents the evolution of research works performing heuristic evaluations of mobile usability, Section 3.2 presents a summary of the identification of distinct heuristics and heuristics sets used in the research works surveyed, and Section 3.3 presents an analysis of the methodological aspects of how the heuristic inspections were performed.

3.1 Evolution of Research Studies Using Heuristic Evaluation of Mobile Usability

The results including in this systematic mapping spanned a period ranging from 2004 to 2013. Figure 1 shows the number of research studies published in each year grouped by the database where they were sourced from.

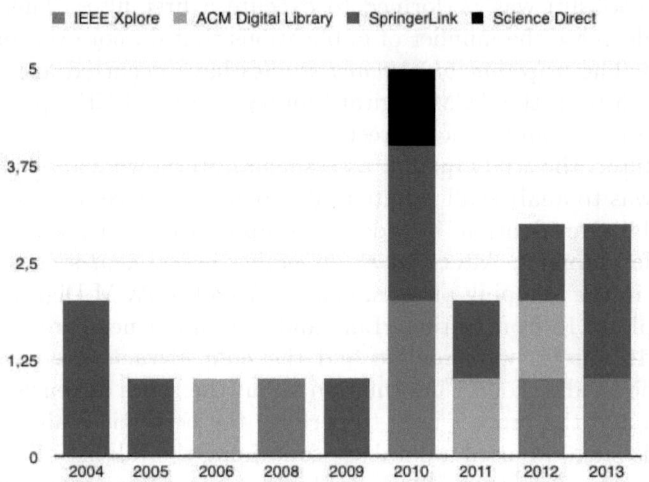

Fig. 1. Number of mapping results, divided by sources and year of publishing

It is possible to observe that the number of publications reporting the use of heuristic evaluation of mobile applications peaked in 2010. However, other research studies have still been published in the following years, which shows this is still a relevant research topic.

3.2 Sets of Usability Heuristics Used in Surveyed Studies

Identifying which heuristics are reported by research studies was an important goal of this systematic literature mapping. We aimed to collect and map the heuristics used in each paper and to verify whether significantly more new heuristics have emerged, or whether classic desktop-oriented heuristics are also applied in the evaluation of mobile applications.

In an initial analysis, we identified a total of 106 heuristics, belonging to 9 different sets. Following the initial identification, the authors coded similar heuristics in order to identify a set of distinct heuristics. This resulted in a set of 29 distinct heuristics. The full list of the distinct heuristics identified is listed at the Appendix, containing the identification of each heuristic and which research studies considered it in the evaluation.

Table 1 summarises nine sets of heuristics identified as a set proposed by given authors. Table 1 also shows citations of research studies that mentioned using each set. It is possible to note that the heuristics purposed by Nielsen and Molich [24], one of the classic and most popular sets of heuristics to evaluate desktop software, were the most used to perform heuristic evaluation of mobile applications in the studies surveyed.

As broken down in the Appendix of this paper, heuristics worded exactly as defined by Nielsen and Molich's heuristics or heuristics very closely related to them were the most used in the surveyed studies. Other heuristics not cited by as many studies included domain-specific heuristics, especially those related to games.

Table 1. Heuristics sets and surveyed studies that reported using them

Heuristic set	Referenced by studies
Nielsen and Molich [24]	[11], [31], [1], [28], [7], [26], [30], [12], [15], [14],
Heuristics for evaluating game usability [18]	[32], [29]
Mobile usability heuristics [3]	[3], [5], [6]
MATcH [27]	[27]
MMRGs [9]	[8]
Heuristics for Designing Mobile Applications [19]	[19]
UI Design Heuristics [20]	[20]
Heuristic Evaluation - A System Checklist [25]	[6]
Touchscreen-based mobile devices heuristics	[11]

Despite the differences in technologies, these results show that old principles traditionally used in HCI also apply to mobile usability, considering the specificities of those devices.

3.3 Methodology Used in Usability Inspections with Usability Heuristics

The analysis of the results also provided data about the evaluation method used, or suggested to future use, on each research study. According to the definition from Nielsen and Molich [24] of HE, we devided the research studies into those which followed the HE method more strictly according to the original definition and others which somehow used a heuristics to perform other types of usability inspections (such as using heuristics in checklists and questionnaires). In this cases, the evaluation was taken asking evaluators to follow a static questionnaire, or a checklist, in order to find usability problems (which does not follow the definition of Nielsen and Molich [24] of HE). According to the results, 13 research studies followed Nielsen and Molich's [24] original method, and 6 studies showed heuristics used in different methods.

From the 13 studies that followed a stricter definition of heuristic evaluations as defined by Nielsen and Molich, 11 informed the number of evaluators involved on the HE. Of these 11 studies, one cited an HE performed by just two evaluators; four mentioned HE using three evaluators; five shoed HE performed by four evaluators and one reported an HE being performed by five evaluators. Figure 2 summarizes the number of studies that employed each number of evaluators. Most evaluations employed between 3 and 4 evaluators.

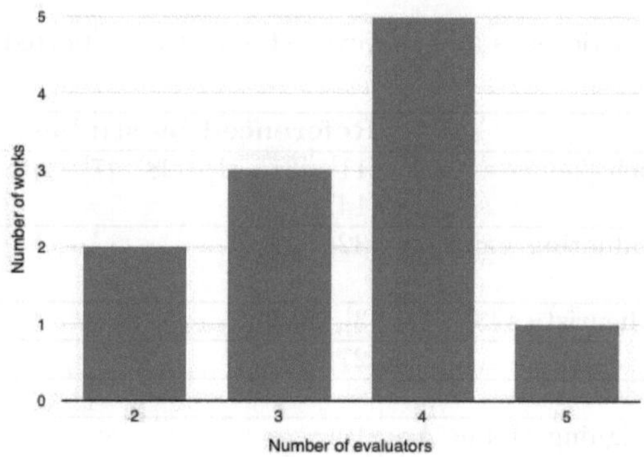

Fig. 2. Number of evaluators employed in HE studies

We also analyzed the severity scales used by different research studies. A total of 9 research studies categorized the severity of problems using the scale proposed by Nielsen, ranging from 1 - cosmetic, 2 - minor, 3 - major and 4 - catastrophic. Two studies used Likert-scales and one study categorized severities in low, medium or critical. The other studies did not provide details about the severity rate scale used.

4 Conclusion and Future Work

This work aimed to perform a systematic mapping of the literature regarding the use of heuristic evaluation methods applied on mobile applications. According to the results, this theme has been a relevant topic and that since 2010 the interest on it has been bigger than previous years.

The results also showed that a considerable number of heuristics sets has been used, a total of 9 heuristics sets were reported in the literature and the classic heuristic set proposed Nielsen and Molich [24] was the most used set to evaluate usability of mobile applications. In most part of results, HE are taken following Nielsen and Molich [24] definition of HE method and the most common numbers of evaluators during HE of mobile usability are 3 and 4. Despite the large adoption of Nielsen and Molich [24] set of heuristics, some works proposes the use of heuristics along questionnaries and checklists, contradicting the Nielsen and Molich [24] definition of HE.

As future work, we intend to deepen the analysis of the heuristics surveyed in practice applying them in empirical studies with evaluators performing heuristic evaluations of mobile applications.

Acknowledgments. Thanks to ALCANCE Research Group, the Federal University of Lavras, CNPq, FAPEMIG and to MSc. Elisa Boari de Lima for all their support to this research.

References

1. Barricelli, B.R., Devis, Y., Abdelnour-Nocera, J., Wilson, J., Moore, J.: MANTRA: mobile anticoagulant therapy management. In: 2013 7th International Conference on Pervasive Computing Technologies for Healthcare (PervasiveHealth), pp. 278–281. IEEE (2013)
2. Bertini, E., Catarci, T., Dix, A., Gabrielli, S., Kimani, S., Santucci, G.: Appropriating heuristic evaluation for mobile computing. Human-Computer Interaction and Innovation in Handheld, Mobile and Wearable Technologies 20 (2011)
3. Bertini, E., Gabrielli, S., Kimani, S.: Appropriating and assessing heuristics for mobile computing. In: Proceedings of the Working Conference on Advanced Visual Interfaces, pp. 119–126. ACM (2006)
4. Biel, B., Grill, T., Gruhn, V.: Exploring the benefits of the combination of a software architecture analysis and a usability evaluation of a mobile application. Journal of Systems and Software 83(11), 2031–2044 (2010)
5. Billi, M., Burzagli, L., Catarci, T., Santucci, G., Bertini, E., Gabbanini, F., Palchetti, E.: A unified methodology for the evaluation of accessibility and usability of mobile applications. Universal Access in the Information Society 9(4), 337–356 (2010)
6. Conde, A., et al.: An Intelligent Tutoring System Oriented to the Integration of People with Intellectual Disabilities. In: Demazeau, Y., Dignum, F., Corchado, J.M., Bajo, J., Corchuelo, R., Corchado, E., Fernández-Riverola, F., Julián, V.J., Pawlewski, P., Campbell, A. (eds.) Trends in PAAMS. AISC, vol. 71, pp. 639–647. Springer, Heidelberg (2010)
7. Fetaji, M., Fetaji, B.: Comparing developed MLUAT (mobile learning usability attribute testing) methodology with qualitative user testing method and heuristics evaluation. In: Proceedings of the 12th International Conference on Computer Systems and Technologies, pp. 516–523. ACM (2011)
8. Gielkens, C., Wetzel, R.: A framework for usability evaluation of mobile mixed reality games. In: Herrlich, M., Malaka, R., Masuch, M. (eds.) ICEC 2012. LNCS, vol. 7522, pp. 401–404. Springer, Heidelberg (2012)
9. Gielkens, C.: A framework for usability evaluation of mobile mixed reality games. Faculty of Science Theses (2012)

10. Heo, J., Ham, D.H., Park, S., Song, C., Yoon, W.C.: A framework for evaluating the usability of mobile phones based on multi-level, hierarchical model of usability factors. Interacting with Computers 21(4), 263–275 (2009)
11. Inostroza, R., Rusu, C., Roncagliolo, S., Jimnez, C., Rusu, V.: Usability Heuristics for Touchscreen-based Mobile Devices. In: 2012 Ninth International Conference on Information Technology: New Generations (ITNG), pp. 662–667. IEEE (2012)
12. Huang, C.H., Wang, C.M.: Usability Analysis in Gesture Operation of Interactive E-Books on Mobile Devices. In: Marcus, A. (ed.) Design, User Experience, and Usability, Pt I, HCII 2011. LNCS, vol. 6769, pp. 573–582. Springer, Heidelberg (2011)
13. ISO, I., FCD, I.: 25000, Software Engineering-Software Product Quality Requirements and Evaluation (SQuaRE)-Guide to SQuaRE. International Organization for Standardization, Geneva (2004)
14. Karahoca, A., Bayraktar, E., Tatoglu, E., Karahoca, D.: Information system design for a hospital emergency department: A usability analysis of software prototypes. Journal of Biomedical Informatics 43(2), 224–232 (2010)
15. Karampelas, P., Akoumianakis, D., Stephanidis, C.: Usability inspection of the WardInHand prototype. In: Universal Access in Health Telematics, pp. 197–208. Springer, Heidelberg (2005)
16. Kitchenham, B.: Procedures for performing systematic reviews. Keele, UK, Keele University 33 (2004)
17. Kitchenham, B.A., Charters, S.: Guidelines for performing systematic literature reviews in software engineering (2007)
18. Korhonen, H., Koivisto, E.M.: Playability heuristics for mobile games. In: Proceedings of the 8th Conference on Human-Computer Interaction with Mobile Devices and Services, pp. 9–16. ACM (2006)
19. Longoria, R.G., McGee, M., Nash, E.: Heuristics for Designing Mobile Applications. In: Designing Software for the Mobile Context, pp. 109–134. Springer, London (2004)
20. Marcus, A., Abromowitz, S., Abulkhair, M.F.: Heuristic Evaluation of iCalamityGuide Application. In: Marcus, A. (ed.) DUXU 2013, Part III. LNCS, vol. 8014, pp. 130–139. Springer, Heidelberg (2013)
21. Monetate: More Bad News for Email?. Ecommerce Quarterly (EQ3) (2013)
22. Nayebi, F., Desharnais, J.M., Abran, A.: The state of the art of mobile application usability evaluation. In: 2012 25th IEEE Canadian Conference on Electrical & Computer Engineering (CCECE), pp. 1–4. IEEE (2012)
23. Nielsen, J., Budiu, R.: Mobile usability. Pearson Education (2012)
24. Nielsen, J., Molich, R.: Heuristic evaluation of user interfaces. In: Proceedings of the SIGCHI Conference on Human Factors in Computing Systems, pp. 249–256. ACM (1990)
25. Pierotti, D.: HE Checklist. Xerox Corporation, http://www.stcsig.org/usability/topics/articles/he-checklist.html (last accessed on February 7, 2014)
26. Po, S., Howard, S., Vetere, F., Skov, M.B.: Heuristic evaluation and mobile usability: Bridging the realism gap. In: Brewster, S., Dunlop, M.D. (eds.) Mobile HCI 2004. LNCS, vol. 3160, pp. 49–60. Springer, Heidelberg (2004)
27. Salazar, L.H.A., Lacerda, T., von Wangenheim, C.G., Barbalho, R.A.: Customization of usability heuristics for mobile phones. In: Companion Proceedings of the 11th Brazilian Symposium on Human Factors in Computing Systems, pp. 37–38. Brazilian Computer Society (2012) (in Portuguese)

28. Schönfelder, R., Schmalstieg, D.: Augmented reality for industrial building acceptance. In: Virtual Reality Conference, VR 2008, pp. 83–90. IEEE (2008)
29. Soomro, S., Wan Ahmad, W.F., Sulaiman, S.: Evaluation of Mobile Games Using Playability Heuristics. In: Zaman, H.B., Robinson, P., Olivier, P., Shih, T.K., Velastin, S. (eds.) IVIC 2013. LNCS, vol. 8237, pp. 264–274. Springer, Heidelberg (2013)
30. Varsaluoma, J.: Scenarios in the Heuristic Evaluation of Mobile Devices: Emphasizing the Context of Use. In: Kurosu, M. (ed.) HCD 2009. LNCS, vol. 5619, pp. 332–341. Springer, Heidelberg (2009)
31. Wahab, N.A., Osman, A., Ismail, M.H.: Engaging children to science subject: a heuristic evaluation of mobile learning prototype. In: 2010 Second International Conference on Computer Engineering and Applications (ICCEA), vol. 2, pp. 513–516. IEEE (2010)
32. Zaibon, S.B., Shiratuddin, N.: Heuristics evaluation strategy for mobile game-based learning. In: 2010 6th IEEE International Conference on Wireless, Mobile and Ubiquitous Technologies in Education (WMUTE), pp. 127–131. IEEE (2010)

Appendix:

#	Heuristic	Referenced by studies
1	Visibility of system status	[11], [31], [1], [28], [7], [26], [30], [12], [15], [14], [3], [5], [27], [6], [32], [29], [20]
2	Match between system and the real world	[11], [31], [1], [28], [7], [26], [30], [12], [15], [14], [3], [5], [6], [27], [20], [32], [29]
3	User control and freedom	[11], [31], [1], [28], [7], [26], [30], [12], [15], [14], [27], [20], [6]
4	Consistency and standards	[11], [31], [1], [28], [7], [26], [30], [12], [15], [14], [32], [29], [3], [5], [6], [27], [20], [9], [19]
5	Error prevention	[11], [31], [1], [28], [7], [26], [30], [12], [15], [14], [20], [6], [8]
6	Recognition rather than recall	[11], [31], [1], [28], [7], [26], [30], [12], [15], [14], [32], [29], [27], [8], [20], [6]
7	Flexibility and efficiency of use	[11], [31], [1], [28], [7], [26], [30], [12], [15], [14], [32], [29], [3], [5], [6], [27], [20]
8	Aesthetic and minimalist design	[11], [31], [1], [28], [7], [26], [30], [12], [15], [14], [3], [5], [27], [19], [20], [6], [8], [32], [29]
9	Help users recognize, diagnose, and recover from errors	[11], [31], [1], [28], [7], [26], [30], [12], [15], [14], [32], [29], [8], [20], [6], [3], [5]
10	Help and documentation	[11], [31], [1], [28], [7], [26], [30], [12], [15], [14], [32], [29], [8], [20], [6]

#	Heuristic	Referenced by studies
11	Audio-visual representation supports the game	[32], [29], [8]
12	Pleasurable and Respectful Interaction with the User	[32], [29], [6]
13	Provide constant and appropriate feedback	[32], [29], [8], [20]
14	Ease of input, screen readability and glanceability	[3], [5], [6], [8], [19]
15	Aesthetic, privacy and social conventions	[3], [5], [6]
16	Physical interaction and ergonomics	[11], [27]
17	Information legibility and density	[27], [20]
18	Keep your navigation model simple	[27], [19]
19	Every round trip counts	[8], [19], [20]
20	There is a need	[19]
21	Provide unobstructed views that are appropriate for the users current situation	[8]
22	Real world navigation takes into account the type of game and is logical	[8]
23	Safeguard the players legal safety	[8]
24	Think modular	[19]
25	Allow for desktop based communication	[19]
26	Fight the hype	[19]
27	Direct manipulation/See and point	[20]
28	Modelessness	[20]
29	Perceived stability	[20]

Where Is Mobile Projection Interaction Going? The Past, Present and Future of the Mobile Projected Interface

Yun Zhou, Tao Xu, Bertrand David, and René Chalon

Université de Lyon, CNRS,
Ecole Centrale de Lyon, LIRIS, UMR5205
{chouyun920}@gmail.com,
{tao.xu,bertrand.david,rene.chalon}@ec-lyon.fr

Abstract. With the rapid development of portable projection technologies and the miniaturization of sensors, the magnitude mobile projector system provides an alternative access to mobile interaction and communication. In this review, we survey and discuss the mobile projected interactions that enable seamless integration of techniques into real world tasks. We first briefly describe the background of emerging projection interaction from past to present. Then we conduct a statistic literature review by collecting data from top tier conferences in the field of Human-Computer Interaction. We next present our two applications corresponding to the new affordances of mobile projectors. We finally conclude with a discussion of the challenges, ranging from hardware issues, social issues, device and sensor fusion in the context, input gesture design and usability, as well as the opportunities provided by mobile projected interfaces.

Keywords: Mobile projectors, Ubiquitous computing, Mobility, Affordance, Projection interaction, Context, Literature review, Pico-projector.

1 Introduction

As one of the methods for demonstrating information and displaying images, projection techniques have been used by humans for hundreds of years. Previous use of projectors or projector-like prototypes was limited to displaying images and showing stories. In recent years, with the development of sensors, devices, and projection techniques, the projector is not only used to project visual images but is also leveraged to interact. Furthermore, miniaturization of projectors provides more opportunities for researchers to explore interaction modalities and interfaces that are different from traditional ones, and also enables creation of mobile projection ubiquitously. Also, projectors have distinct properties from other displays, namely scalabilities and mobility. These properties can be used to inform novel interaction design, but also raise new challenges and social issues for researchers. Besides, the context concepts and relative technologies introduce implicit inputs and outputs to ubiquitous computing. The context collected by visual markers and other sensors could be made available to computers and used to assist interaction.

M. Kurosu (Ed.): Human-Computer Interaction, Part III, HCII 2014, LNCS 8512, pp. 189–198, 2014.

In this paper, we provide an overview and panoramic snapshot of mobile projection interaction. This paper starts by discussing projection interaction from the past few years to the present, and then sets the definition of mobile projection, also distinguishing it from large display projection and table range projection. We then conduct a literature review with top tier conference sources. We collect data in the first step, and discuss the results from collected and classified data in the second step. In the section of new affordances, we discuss the affordances and present our two applications corresponding to each affordance. Finally, we walk through the challenges and social issues to be addressed, and also propose some potential suggestions and solutions.

2 Projection Interaction from Past to Present

In this section, we briefly review the history of projection from past to present, and identify nomadic projection interaction and mobile projection. We do not discuss the former use of projection, but only focus on development in recent decades.

The projector is the display device for presenting visual images as well as projecting graphical user interfaces. In recent years, projector miniaturization has led to the emergence of mobile devices with embedded projector or palm-size projectors. Projector components start to be embedded in household digital cameras and mobile phones. Besides its role as an auxiliary accessory, the actual pico-projector as a standalone device has the ability to connect with other devices and to project images of high quality. Also, pico-projectors are small enough to be worn on the body, held in the hand or put into the pocket.

Before the emergence of mobile projectors, the interactions of large-size projectors were explored by researchers. Projection interaction has experienced fixed large display interaction in a room or in public, table range projection interaction, limited to the scope of the desk, and mobile and personal projection interaction either with small-size embedded or standalone projectors.

Fig. 1. Large display projection [25], table range projection [13], mobile projection [9]

Paper Windows [11] describes a projecting window prototype that can simulate manipulation of digital paper displays. The user can thus perform tasks by interacting with paper documents using his fingers, hands and stylus. The Quickies [20] system is designed to augment sticky notes as an I/O interface. The DisplayObjects [1] proposes a workbench allowing the user to interact with projected information on the physical object. These studies all investigated either large display interaction or table range interaction.

One of the possible solutions for enabling ubiquitous projection interaction is nomadism, where the user is not equipped with any wearable or mobile devices. An alternative solution is mobility, where the user is equipped with wearable or mobile devices. We identify fixed large display interaction and table range interaction as nomadic interaction, and mobile and personal projection interaction as mobile interaction. In this paper, we focus on mobile projection interaction rather than nomadic projection interaction studies such as IllumiRoom [12].

3 Literature Review

A literature review was conducted to review mobile projection interactions. We focused on papers published from 2009 to 2013 since mobile smart phones and pico-projectors are prevalent during this period. We reviewed the most relevant conference sources that included topics covering mobile projection applications, related innovative interaction modalities, and evaluations. The literature review was conducted in two steps: literature search and literature content analysis. The aim of the first step was to collect articles related to mobile projection research including titles, keywords, abstracts, introductions and contributions. The aim of the second step was to characterize the previous studies and explain how these innovative interaction modalities support mobile projection interaction.

3.1 Reviewing Process

The first step in the literature review was to collect the topic-related publications from the identified sources. We first considered the premier forums and conferences as our target sources and identified the following conferences as the most relevant sources: the ACM Conference on Human Factors in Computing Systems (CHI), the ACM User Interface Software and Technology Symposium (UIST), the ACM Conference on Computer Supported Cooperative Work and Social Computing (CSCW) and the ACM Conference on Human-Computer Interaction with Mobile Devices and Services (MobileHCI). The literature review was limited to publications between 2009 and 2013 due to the emergence of pico-projectors and the prevalence of mobile smart phones. To achieve the aims of the literature review, two research processes were conducted: literature search and literature content analysis.

The sources included different types of publications such as full papers, short papers, doctoral consortium, and demos. We focused our study not only on full papers but also on other forms of work in these conferences. Table 1 shows the numbers of publications that were collected from each source between 2009 and 2013. (N/A means it is not applicable for the year of publication.)

We examined 5 main factors including the title, the abstract, the keywords, the introduction, and the contribution. If the keywords contained the words "pico projector", "mobile projector", "mobile projection", "handheld projector" or "handheld projection", the publications were directly kept. If the keywords did not contain such words, the abstracts were examined in a further step. The abstract of each remaining

Table 1. The number of publications collected from each source

sources	*2013*	*2012*	*2011*	*2010*	*2009*	*Total*
CHI Proceedings	2	1	3	2	1	9
CHI EA	0	2	3	3	2	10
UIST Proceedings	1	2	2	1	0	6
UIST Adjunct	0	0	2	0	N/A	2
CSCW Proceedings	0	1	0	0	N/A	1
CSCW Companion	0	0	N/A	N/A	N/A	0
MobileHCI Proceedings	1	1	3	1	0	6
MobileHCI Companion	N/A	3	N/A	N/A	N/A	3
Total	4	10	13	7	3	37

paper was tested to see whether the paper revolved around the topics of mobile projection interaction: for example, the paper proposed a mobile projection application or conducted an evaluation of mobile projection devices. However, publications that focused on large display projections or table fixed projection interactions were removed. We collected 37 papers from sources, and extracted research topics and subjects from these papers, then classified the papers by topics. The titles, keywords, abstracts, introductions, and contributions were all kept and used in the second step of Analysis and Results.

3.2 Analysis and Results

We revolved around the question of what topics and subjects have been explored in this step. We extracted 11 topics from the introductions and contributions of these publications. Then we calculated the numbers of publications of related topics. Most publications dealt with multiple topics. Table 2 shows the topics and the numbers of relative publications.

We found that 13 papers referred to the topic of personal and mobile projection in augmented reality. We selected these papers by searching for the words "augmented", "augmentation" and "augment". We also examined the contents of papers to verify whether the paper related to this topic. For example, iLight can recognize objects and augment information directly on them [15], while PenLight is a system that visually augments paper documents, giving the user immediate access to additional information and computational tools [23]. Two studies considered social effects and social issues [26] [7]. The research [26] explores how people will want to use projector technology, how they will feel when using it, and what social effects the researcher can expect to see. Results from this investigation showed that users are willing to project content, even when in social spaces and with other people around. One contribution indicated that projector phones should support careful control over projected content so that users have no problems maintaining privacy. Also, mobile projection has gradually evolved into the topic of social interaction. The study [17] concluded that integration of projection technology into wearable devices such as smart phones might thus become a promising future opportunity for better suited projection surfaces, with real potential application areas including people with specific diseases who have problems remembering social information, speed dating, business meetings or conference networking. Four papers [9] [19] [10] [17] focused on worn projector interactions, including discussing the position for fixing the wearable devices. Fixing points on the body varied from the shoulder, the head, and the arm, even including a shoulder bag attached to the body. With the emergence of commercial projector phones, six papers such as [14] [6] [18] [21] [4] explored the related research. Besides wearable pico-projectors, mobile phones integrated into the projector have also been used to display, overlay or augment the image to assist interactions. Utilization of hands and fingers as input techniques has already been studied for a long time now. In the mobile environment, pens, hand gestures, and even the projector itself have been leveraged to input. Seven studies such as [24] [6] [22] [27] [5] explored novel input devices, methods and navigations, combined with mobile projection. Nine studies on multi-user interactions and eleven studies on multi-device interactions were investigated. These studies covered issues such as how multi devices co-work spontaneously, what are the roles of multi users, and how to transfer media items among devices. Studies concerning exploration of innovative interfaces (5 papers) and applications (5 papers) based on mobile projection interaction were also important topics in the papers reviewed. The user interface with ubiquitous computing considers a broader range of inputs than the desktop interface. In the mobile situation, it leverages not only explicit inputs including human gestures, voices, gaze, etc., but also covers implicit input of context data from various sensors [3]. Although only one paper focused on mobile projection with implicit context input [2], this is a potential topic and will be considered further in the near future.

Table 2. The topics and numbers of relative publications

Topics	*Numbers of Publications*
personal and mobile projection in augmented reality	13
social effects with mobile projection interaction	2
social interaction using mobile projectors	3
worn projector interaction	4
mobile projector-phone interaction	6
input of mobile projection interaction	7
multi user interaction and collaboration	9
interfaces of mobile projection	5
new application areas of mobile projection	5
mobile projection with implicit context	1
multi display interaction	11

4 New Affordances

Compared with transitional desktop interaction and large display projection as well as table projection interaction, we found that the mobile projector possesses the new affordances of mobility and scalability. We discuss these two new affordances in this section, explaining our two research actions into these two new affordances, including interaction design, a brief introduction on development, and the evaluation results.

4.1 Mobility

Existing mobile projection interaction research focuses more on investigation into stationary settings, which cannot satisfy the requirements of interaction in sophisticated daily life especially when people are walking or moving. To investigate effective hand gesture input and projection output in mobile settings, we propose a wearable camera-projector system with pinch gesture and hover gesture [30]. We stabilize the camera-projector device unit on the ear: its projection image can move with head motion and closely follow eyesight. We employ the pinch gesture for pointing, drag-drop action and painting. To investigate how the user might interact with this system in both stationary and mobile settings, we compare the interactions of hover gesture and pinch gesture, and also evaluate projection output in three situations such as standing, sitting and walking. We discuss interaction time, the average selection time, and interaction errors, as well as users' preferences. These findings imply the importance of interaction based on hand gestures input and projected output in a mobile situation rather than only in a stationary state. Results from our experiments have shown that the pinch gesture undergoes less influence than the hover gesture in mobile settings. Mobility impacted both gestures. Also, the drag-drop action is more stable to interact than the pointing action when the user is walking. The ear side position is a good position to display, but we need to improve stability and lower weight. The manual focus would influence interaction with the scalable interface. Also, mobility highlights four limitations: lack of coordination, jitter hand effect, tired forelimbs, and the extra attention paid, which need to be considered to inform mobile projection interaction design.

4.2 Scalability

While studying mobile projection interaction, we found that the projector possesses the property of scalability, with which it can display different sizes of the interfaces according to surface size and the distance between the projection surface and projector. Unlike the screen with non-scalability, if we provide the same content and layout to the different size interfaces, usability will decrease. This problem occurs commonly with the adaptive interface: usability will be lower if we transfer directly the same elements and layout from the web browser on a traditional desktop screen to the small screen of mobile devices. The difference between scalability and adaptability is that the former exists in one device, while the latter exists in several devices. With the aim of solving the aforementioned problem of scalability, we propose an approach to provide the appropriate interfaces by detecting the distance between the surface and the pico-projector [31]. We also performed a scalability evaluation. We found that the nearer interface can provide a phone-like experience, higher efficiency for selection, a comfortable visual reading field and fewer disturbances for privacy, while the farther interface can offer a larger display experience and the possibility of sharing. To maximize the performance of scalability to improve design, more factors should be considered such as colors, textures and sizes of surfaces. Thus, besides planar surfaces, non-planar projective surfaces and daily colored surfaces, such as the surface of the cup, which is curved in the horizontal direction and has different colors than white only, should be considered. In addition, the projected augmented information requires perception of the surface and form of the object in the context.

5 Challenges

The challenges of mobile projection interaction such as finding the appropriate projection place, social issues, hardware limitations, accessing problems, and input issues will be discussed in this section.

The first challenge is that it is hard for users to find an appropriate place to project the interface, due to the arbitrary surface and the mobile situation of users. Daily surfaces in the real environment are sophisticated and have different colors and textures, resulting in problems for augmentation on the projected interface. Unlike a high quality mobile phone screen, a daily surface usually cannot provide a uniform size, easy-to-project texture, or suitable color. In addition, when people are moving about or in the bus, it is difficult to find a planar surface such as a wall or table to project. Thus, a palm or a book could be an alternative solution. Moreover, protection of privacy is a very important issue.

Secondly, users are willing to share their projection interaction experience with other people, thus giving rise to social issues such as projecting in public. Ju-Chun Ko et al. [16] explore the rights for people to project and be projected in public spaces, and provides some possible solutions. The issues of applying these projected user interface techniques in real life have been discussed. A formative field study in [8] has been explored to investigate users' reactions to public projection. The results indicated that personal projection attracts a large amount of attention, is dependent on the social context, and has been accepted socially. With further exploration of this emerging field, more social issues will be considered and studied.

Thirdly, the insufficient abilities of projector hardware such as low brightness, insufficiently small size, and manual focus adjustment, decrease users' experience of interaction. Current pico-projector products have a low lumens; brightness varies from 15 lumens to 200 lumens, far removed from the requirement to support interaction under normal illumination. Thus, most research work with the pico-projector is performed in a darker environment. While this limitation is likely to be alleviated in a few years, with the emergence of more mature technology, mobile projection interaction today cannot be performed in a true ubiquitous environment. Another problem revolves around where and how researchers can embed and fix the projector. If the projector is as small and light as a button, it is also easy to fix on the body. However, the current pico-projector still has the size of a mobile phone. When people are moving, it will cause problems of jittered hands and tired arms due to the size and weight of the projector. Therefore, projector miniaturization techniques should be considered as an essential issue.

Fourthly, regarding wearable projector systems, accessing time and methods continue to be a big issue. How the user could start and restart the wearable interface quickly and simply just like starting a smart phone is a problem not yet solved. Also, the solution for hibernating and quickly closing the system has not yet been found.

Fifthly, performing efficient recognition of hand gestures as input and looking for the appropriate usability evaluation metrics of inputs are issues still to be dealt with. Even if we endeavor to support interaction in a realistic mobile environment, the restriction still exists. On the one hand, the real background in our daily life is multicolored, which will lead to incorrect recognition of the colored markers located on the fingers. Similarly, in a sophisticated background or a darker environment, efficiency of bare hand recognition will decease to a greater or lesser extent. On the other hand, there are no standard and unified usability evaluation metrics on how to evaluate mobile inputs such as pens, gestures, and other sensors. The current evaluation mainly focused on a specific mobile projection application, but was not aimed at the generic attributes of applications.

Sixthly, the literature review statistics show that the context has not been really considered with mobile projection design. However, it is important to provide the user with information and context collected from the environment. In other words, the projected interface should also be able to obtain in-environment information. For example, the environment can be contextualized beforehand by markers, and the markers can be pasted on the appliance, wall, book, or door, etc. In this way, public and professional guiding information can be used for contextualization. Taking ARToolKit tags as an example, the webcam recognizes the unique pattern of the marker and then provides the related information. In this way, the implicit input of context data from various sensors can be leveraged to assist interaction in the context.

6 Conclusion

This paper has discussed previous and ongoing research on mobile projection interaction. It began with an introduction to projectors and related interactions. Then, a brief description ranging from large projectors to personal projector interaction was viewed, and nomadic and mobile projection interaction was discussed and described. Later, a systematic review of previous studies on mobile projection interaction was presented. Also, the methodology for reviewing the literature was covered, including the literature review process, and the results of research questions concerning this emerging field. Moreover, new opportunities and challenges were discussed based on issues of affordances for mobile projectors, social issues and the use of context data. Our aim is to present a clear and global view of the past, present and future of mobile projection interaction, and foster improvement and innovation of design and development with mobile projectors.

References

1. Akaoka, E., Ginn, T., Vertegaal, R.: DisplayObjects: prototyping functional physical interfaces on 3d styrofoam, paper or cardboard models. In: TEI 2010: Proceedings of the 4th International Conference on Tangible and Embedded Interaction, pp. 49–56 (2010)
2. Åkerman, P., Puikkonen, A.: Prochinima: using pico projector to tell situated stories. In: MobileHCI 2011: Proceedings of the 13th International Conference on Human Computer Interaction with Mobile Devices and Services, pp. 337–346. ACM (2011)
3. Baber, C.: Ubiquitous Computing Fundamentals (2010)
4. Baur, D., Boring, S., Feiner, S.: Virtual projection: exploring optical projection as a metaphor for multi-device interaction. In: CHI 2012: Proceedings of the 2012 ACM Annual Conference on Human Factors in Computing Systems, pp. 1693–1702. ACM (2012)

5. Chan, L.W., Wu, H.T., Kao, H.S., Ko, J.C., Lin, H.R., Chen, M.Y., Hsu, J., Hung, Y.P.: Enabling beyond-surface interactions for interactive surface with an invisible projection. In: UIST 2010: Proceedings of the 23nd Annual ACM Symposium on User Interface Software and Technology, pp. 263–272. ACM (2010)
6. Cowan, L.G., Li, K.A.: ShadowPuppets: supporting collocated interaction with mobile projector phones using hand shadows. In: CHI 2011: Proceedings of the SIGCHI Conference on Human Factors in Computing Systems, pp. 2707–2716. ACM (2011)
7. Dachselt, R., Jones, M., Häkkilä, J., Löchtefeld, M., Rohs, M., Rukzio, E.: Mobile and personal projection (MP 2). In: CHI 2011 Extended Abstracts on Human Factors in Computing Systems, pp. 21–23. ACM (2011)
8. Greaves, A., Akerman, P., Rukzio, E., Cheverst, K., Hakkila, J.: Exploring user reaction to personal projection when used in shared public places: A formative study. In: MobileHCI 2009 Workshop: CAM3SN (2009)
9. Harrison, C., Benko, H., Wilson, A.D.: OmniTouch: wearable multitouch interaction everywhere. In: UIST 2011: Proceedings of the 24th Annual ACM Symposium on User Interface Software and Technology, pp. 441–450 (2011)
10. Harrison, C., Tan, D., Morris, D.: Skinput: appropriating the body as an input surface. In: CHI 2010: Proceedings of the 28th SIGCHI Conference on Human Factors in Computing Systems, pp. 453–462 (2010)
11. Holman, D., Vertegaal, R., Altosaar, M., Troje, N., Johns, D.: Paper windows: interaction techniques for digital paper. In: CHI 2005: Proceedings of the SIGCHI Conference on Human Factors in Computing Systems, pp. 591–599 (2005)
12. Jones, B.R., Benko, H., Ofek, E., Wilson, A.D.: IllumiRoom: peripheral projected illusions for interactive experiences. In: CHI 2013: Proceedings of the SIGCHI Conference on Human Factors in Computing Systems, pp. 869–878. ACM (2013)
13. Kane, S.K., Avrahami, D., Wobbrock, J.O., Harrison, B., Rea, A.D., Philipose, M., LaMarca, A.: Bonfire: a nomadic system for hybrid laptop-tabletop interaction. In: UIST 2009: Proceedings of the 22nd Annual ACM Symposium on User Interface Software and Technology, pp. 129–138. ACM (2009)
14. Kaufmann, B., Ahlström, D.: Studying spatial memory and map navigation performance on projector phones with peephole interaction. In: CHI 2013: Proceedings of the SIGCHI Conference on Human Factors in Computing Systems, pp. 3173–3176. ACM (2013)
15. Kim, S., Chung, J., Oh, A., Schmandt, C., Kim, I.-J.: iLight: information flashlight on objects using handheld projector. In: CHI 2010 Extended Abstracts on Human Factors in Computing Systems, pp. 3631–3636. ACM Press, New York (2010)
16. Ko, J.C., Chan, L.W., Hung, Y.P.: Public issues on projected user interface. In: CHI EA 2010: Proceedings of the 28th of the International Conference Extended Abstracts on Human Factors in Computing Systems, pp. 2873–2882 (2010)
17. Leung, M., Tomitsch, M., Vande Moere, A.: Designing a personal visualization projection of online social identity. In: CHI 2011 Extended Abstracts on Human Factors in Computing Systems, pp. 1843–1848. ACM (2011)
18. Löchtefeld, M., Gehring, S., Jung, R., Krüger, A.: guitAR: supporting guitar learning through mobile projection. In: CHI 2011 Extended Abstracts on Human Factors in Computing Systems, pp. 1447–1452. ACM (2011)
19. Mistry, P., Maes, P., Chang, L.: WUW-wear Ur world: a wearable gestural interface. In: CHI EA 2009: Proceedings of the 27th International Conference Extended Abstracts on Human Factors in Computing Systems, pp. 4111–4116 (2009)
20. Mistry, P., Maes, P.: Quickies: Intelligent sticky notes. In: IET 2008: 4th International Conference on Intelligent Environments, pp. 1–4 (2008)

21. Robinson, S., Jones, M., Vartiainen, E., Marsden, G.: PicoTales: collaborative authoring of animated stories using handheld projectors. In: CSCW 2012: Proceedings of the ACM 2012 Conference on Computer Supported Cooperative Work, pp. 671–680. ACM (2012)
22. Song, H., Guimbretiere, F., Grossman, T., Fitzmaurice, G.: MouseLight: bimanual interactions on digital paper using a pen and a spatially-aware mobile projector. In: CHI 2010: Proceedings of the SIGCHI Conference on Human Factors in Computing Systems, pp. 2451–2460. ACM (2010)
23. Song, H., Grossman, T., Fitzmaurice, G., Guimbretiere, F., Khan, A., Attar, R., Kurtenbach, G.: PenLight: combining a mobile projector and a digital pen for dynamic visual overlay. In: CHI 2009: Proceedings of the SIGCHI Conference on Human Factors in Computing Systems, pp. 143–152. ACM (2009)
24. Willis, K.D.D., Poupyrev, I., Shiratori, T.: Motionbeam: a metaphor for character interaction with handheld projectors. In: CHI 2011: Proceedings of the SIGCHI Conference on Human Factors in Computing Systems, pp. 1031–1040 (2011)
25. Wilson, A.D., Benko, H.: Combining multiple depth cameras and projectors for interactions on, above and between surfaces. In: UIST 2010: Proceedings of the 23nd Annual ACM Symposium on User Interface Software and Technology, pp. 273–282. ACM (2010)
26. Wilson, M.L., Robinson, S., Craggs, D., Brimble, K., Jones, M.: Pico-ing into the future of mobile projector phones. In: CHI EA 2010: Proceedings of the 28th of the International Conference Extended Abstracts on Human Factors in Computing Systems, pp. 3997–4002 (2010)
27. Xiao, R., Harrison, C., Willis, K.D., Poupyrev, I., Hudson, S.E.: Lumitrack: low cost, high precision, high speed tracking with projected m-sequences. In: UIST 2013: Proceedings of the 26th Annual ACM Symposium on User Interface Software and Technology, pp. 3–12. ACM (2013)
28. Zhou, Y.: Context-based Innovative Mobile User Interfaces. Ecole Centrale de Lyon. pp. 105–129 (2012)
29. Zhou, Y., David, B.T., Chalon, R.: PlayAllAround: Wearable One-hand Gesture Input and Scalable Projected Interfaces. In: ERGO-IHM 2012: Ergonomie et Interaction Homme-Machine, ACM Digital Library (2012)

Do Gender and Age Matter? A User Study on Differences in Photo Collection Management

Angelina de C. A. Ziesemer, Francine B. Bergmann, Isabel H. Manssour, João B. S. de Oliveira, and Milene S. Silveira

Faculdade de Informática — PUCRS
Avenida Ipiranga 6681, Prédio 32 – 90619-900,
Porto Alegre - RS, Brazil
{angelina.ziesemer,francine.bergmann}@acad.pucrs.br,
{isabel.manssour,joao.souza,milene.silveira}@pucrs.br

Abstract. The low cost and ubiquitousness of digital cameras allow users to collect large amounts of photos. Although storage is not usually a problem, selection of content for presentation requires time and work. Thus, we intend to investigate how users currently deal with the tasks of organizing and presenting their photos. A survey was conducted with 100 participants pointing out their preferences and differences related to age and gender in this subject. The research methodology, the experiment and the statistical results are discussed in this paper.

Keywords: photo albums, digital photos, user experience.

1 Introduction

Due to digital photography and the availability of cameras in mobile phones, it is now possible for thousands of photos to be taken in a single year by any individual [17]. Some of the factors that contributed to this are the cost per shot, the immediate results and the large storage capacity of these cameras. Before digital cameras, several issues limited the amount of photos taken and the common practices adopted used to be a small number of photos saved in paper form and the best of them usually selected to create photo albums.

Several authors [7, 8, 11, 14, 19] studied how people handle photo collections and their studies show an evolution in the practices adopted during the transition from non-digital photos to digital ones. Results present a good insight about user behavior, but this has also changed as the tools, the accessibility of the internet, the advent of social networks and available technologies to share, manage, visualize and store photos also have changed.

In order to comprehend how users have changed their photo management habits and whether their behavior has association to age or gender, this work reports a quantitative and qualitative analysis of the data collected from participants of a survey where major research questions are: (a) How people manage and

M. Kurosu (Ed.): Human-Computer Interaction, Part III, HCII 2014, LNCS 8512, pp. 199–207, 2014.

share their photos and photo albums nowadays? (b) Is there association among gender and/or age on how people manage their photos and photo albums? The results from this study show that there are differences in photo management behavior with respect to participants' gender and age. The main differences found are related to how users store their photos, the main digital devices used to take photos, how they share photos and how they prefer to present them.

Our main contributions in this paper are: (1) A statistical analysis to verify age association to photo management behavior. We found that participants differ significantly in storage behavior, to share photos on social networks and in the habit of creating digital photo albums when age was used as explanatory variable. (2) Moreover, we observe the results using gender as explanatory variable: we found gender association related to printing and photo album creation.

Results from this study can direct digital photo tools to customize environments according to users gender or age and consequently improves the users experience. The remainder of this paper is organized as follows: related works are presented in the next section, followed by study methodology and the results obtained from the survey. The final considerations are discussed in the last section.

2 Related Works

It is possible to observe that as technology evolves people adopt distinct behaviors to take, share, store and organize their photos.

Regarding albums in general, Jin et al. [9] stated that the management of printed photos in an album is easier than with digital photos. They also showed that people typically have more than ten printed albums in their homes and claims that digital photos do not have the same sentimental appeal as the traditional albums.

Khalid and Dix [10] as well as Malinen [13] discuss about sharing photos through online media, such as websites like Flickr[1] and photologs, highlighting that they are appropriate to preserve stories of a group, being a resource for maintaining social relationships with those who are near and far away, and functioning as a kind of "virtual photo album".

Among the studies that address tools, there are those that serve as organizers/archives of photos, showing the pictures like a photo album. Yagawa et al. [21] present a personal file system that allows users to entertain themselves while their archive and retrieve multimedia data. Following this, the article by Jin et al. [9] describes a device that stores and manages digital images also imitating a photo album. The device provides a natural interface, as if the user were turning the pages of a real photo album, using only motion gestures on a touch screen. The work was based on the assumption that emotional satisfaction is more important than efficiency in this kind of task, and it must be also easy to learn by any kind of people. Abdel-Mottaleb and Chen [1] showed a similar

[1] https://www.flickr.com

system that allows navigation based on the arrangement face and representing events with a set of composite images.

Also, as the use of mobile devices increases, there are applications being developed particularly for those users that use these devices, to deal with photo collections. Xiao et al. [20] has developed an application for iPhones (called iPhotobook), which allows the creation and edition of photo albums (or photo books). The application automates selection, grouping, editing and layout of images by the user, which would be difficult to accomplish without the help of a larger screen, and then presents an alternative solution to the problem of creating photo books on mobile devices.

In this paper, we intend to verify if there is gender or age association regarding photo management behavior. In the next section we present the methodology used to answer our research questions proposed in this work.

3 Study Methodology

Personal collections of digital and non-digital photos have changed in the way that users organize, visualize, present and share them. Our study was designed to gather information about how users manage their photo collections and the major research questions are:

- How people manage and share their photos and photo albums nowadays?
- Is there association among gender and/or age on how people manage their photos and photo albums?

To gather these information we made available an online survey and asked people to complete it during two weeks. A total of 100 individuals completed the survey, 43% female and 57% male, having ages from 18 to 24 years (26%), 25 to 30 (29%), and more than 30 years (45%). Most of the data obtained from the survey is composed by categorical variables and due to this we use non-parametric tests to analyze the sample. Also, there are some qualitative variables that gave us insight into the participant motivations for use digital albums.

4 Study Results and Implications

We focus the analysis on those questions that could describe user behavior and how they are used to manage their photo collections. Due to the nature of the data we use Chi-square tests to verify the association among gender and age (as explanatory variable) to the behaviors gathered by this survey.

4.1 Dealing with Digital Photos

The access to digital cameras favored the growth of digital photo collections to the disadvantage of non-digital forms, as stated by [5,12,15]. Some of the factors that contributed for this are the cost per shot, the immediate results and the large storage capacity of these cameras.

We started our survey asking participants about occasions when they are more likely to take photos: participants answered that in general they take photos on events (68%) or trips (71%) and their photos are organized mainly by events and/or date.

Organizing photos by date and events is a common approach adopted by most of photo management systems, but it is not enough for helping users keep their photos organized. Due to the storage facility for keeping digital photo collections, the organization of them become laborious as the number of photos taken increases. There are distinct approaches for helping users to manage their photo and the most recent include location information, content-based organization, tags/annotations, context information and facial recognition ("who is in the photo") [3,4].

Regarding the devices used to take photos, participants reported that their preferred are the digital camera and the camera from mobile phone. Moreover, the use of cameras from mobile phones showed a particular association to users having less than 30 years ($X^2 = 7.23$, p-value $= 0.026$), they are more likely to use it as main device to take photos than users older than 30 years. Cameras from mobile phones have huge potential for helping users to categorize and organize photos since they allow for a range of tools that use network information and the context of photo in the moment it was taken.

Further, concerning photo storage, 45% of the participants are used to choose those photos which should be kept and which not and 32% answered that they usually keep all their photos. We found an association between age and photo storage behavior (Table 1): people younger than 25 are more likely to keep all their photos ($X^2 = 6.46$, p-value $= 0.039$), while those who are 25 or more are more likely to choose the photos that they want to keep ($X^2 = 11.75$, p-value$=$ 0.002). Nowadays, people are not only taking more pictures due to the advent of digital cameras, but they are also storing more it since devices, image hosting website and social networks allow for users more and more space to keep content.

Table 1. Age association

Behavior	< 24	25 to 30	> 30	Overall	Chi-square
Keep all their photos	50%	22%	26%	32%	$X^2 = 6.46$
Choose photos to keep	20%	63%	51%	45%	$X^2 = 11.75$

The web has also changed the way people share and present their digital photos. Most participants (79%) still use their computer screen or TV to present their digital photos for friends, but they are also sharing it more and more through social networks (SN) (37%) and image hosting websites (34%). Moreover, participants also pointed social networks as the main tool used to publish a complete digital photo album.

In the next section we report the results from this survey related to photo collections management through digital photo albums.

4.2 Dealing with Digital Photo Albums

Digital photo albums may organize photos according to events, dates or places and users use it to preserve the context of the media, their experience and to share moments or subjects. Most participants reported that they like to create photo albums and we did not find any association to this subject related to gender. They reported that social media networks (49%) are the main tool used to create and share digital photo albums, followed by Picasa[2] (28%) and Flickr (15%). Moreover, we found that users with more than 30 years are less likely (33%) to publish digital photo albums on social networks (X^2 = 8.68, p-value = 0.01).

Most users of social networks as tool to publish digital albums were participants with less than 24 years (67%). This behaviour related to age can be associated to the fact that in general teenagers tend to be more active in social networks and this trend declines as age increases [6]. Also, image hosting websites as Flickr and Picasa have evolved into a social environment where users can explore, tagging and bookmarking other users/friends content, thus improving user interaction and management possibilities.

Despite the popularity of digital photo albums and the use of social networks to share it, in this survey participants reported that a printed album is the best way to present a photo collection and we found that this is preferred mainly by female participants (X^2 = 4.69, p-value = 0.03).

In the next section we present the results from this survey related to printed photos and how participants deal with it.

4.3 Printing Digital Photos

Even with digital photos, users still believe that printed photos are the best way to present a photo collection. A previous research [8] observed that despite users are continuous using and sharing digital photos, physical prints are again in fashion. Also, sharing photos in person was described by participants of other study [7] as the most common and pleasant way to exchange memories. This leads to a mixture of reminiscence and conversation in which a story is told collaboratively by those who participate in the sharing.

In this survey, most participants (52%) said that they eventually printed photos. We found that there is an association between gender and the reasons to print photos: female participants are more likely (X^2 = 6.16, p-value=0.01) to print photos mainly from special events, and consequently male are more likely to never print photos (X^2 = 9.74, p-value=0.00). Frohlich et al. [7] stated that few people spent time organizing their digital photos, a phenomenon also discussed by Platt [18]. This author mentions that people "throw" their photos into a folder similarly to the shoe box where printed photos are often stored.

[2] `http://picasaweb.google.com`

So, even when printed photos are the preferred way to present a photo collection, users are still struggling to organize it in a efficient and easy way.

Next, we report how users deal with their traditional albums and digital photo albums created for posterior printing.

4.4 Printing Digital Albums

As the number of digital photos shared in social networks and image hosting website increases, printed photo collections are still the preferred way reported to present a set of photos. Participants in general like to create photo albums particularly women ($X^2 = 7.77$, p-value $= 0.00$) and those older than 25 ($X^2 = 9.55$, p-value $= 0.00$) although, only 24% of them reported that they are used to create traditional photo albums. We also found a gender association in this case ($X^2 = 6.58$, p-value$=0.01$), female participants are more likely to create traditional photo albums than male users (Table 2).

Table 2. Gender association

Behavior	F	M	Overall	Chi-square
Enjoy to create photo albums	77%	50%	62%	$X^2 = 7.77$
Used to create photo albums	36%	14%	24%	$X^2 = 6.58$

As the popularity of digital photos increases, distinct tools to manage this kind of content have emerged. We also asked participants whether they are used to create digital albums for printing. This kind of photo album in general is created using specific tools available by companies that provide photo printing services. Most participants answered that they never tried to create this kind of photo album before. Moreover, from those participants who had tried, they found it very laborious.

We asked how they would prefer to create digital photo albums: female and male respondents did not differ significantly in their responses, the preferred answer was to create a photo album manually page by page ($X^2 = 2.79$, p-value $= 0.09$) and the second preferred way reported was with a tool that could create and organize their photos automatically ($X^2 = 0.51$, p-value $= 0.47$). The less popular way voted by the participants was related to the use of templates to help users create their digital photo album. Surprisingly, most participants who answered before that creating a photo album is laborious, also prefer to create a photo album page by page. In our previous work [2], we performed an experiment asking users to create a digital photo album for posterior printing using a tool that organizes automatically the photos and results showed that users enjoyed the possibility of generating automatic layout, but those users used to full-featured tools demand more liberty to create a photo album.

Next, we report results from a open question asked to understand their motivations for use digital albums.

4.5 Users' Report about Digital Albums

In order to achieve a deeper understanding about user behavior regarding digital albums, users were asked – in a open question – why and when they would use this kind of album. Most users highlighted that they could use them to preserve special moments (as trips, graduations, birthdays and/or special dates). They report some answers as:

"When I have many photos, to keep them organized and remember the name of places, people and events. I also use albums for professional reasons, show work already done and acclimatised, always with their captions and explanations, in order that even the layman understand the subject."

"I would use to keep special moments."

Another motivation was to ease the presentation of photos to friends and family and to people that are distant (even to show them anywhere, anytime). Also, some users could use this kind of album to organize their photos, as they have reported:

"To store them in a organized way."

"For better organization and quality of presentation."

"I use once a year, to organize and store the best photos."

In general users use it because digital albums are easy to share and present photos for friends anywhere. Also, as users create a new photo album, the notion of event also emerges from it.

5 Final Considerations

This work describes a comparative study about users photo management behavior regarding participants age and gender. The results show that new phenomena are emerging as the technology and applications for photo sharing and photo storage also emerges: users are more and more using cameras from mobile phones and sharing content via social networks. Okabe [16] reported that most photos taken by camera phones are not sent or shown to others, but are captured as a personal visual archive. However, nowadays there are many applications developed for social photo sharing and we believe it is also changing users' behavior to manage their photos as we have seen in the results from our experiment.

Results from this paper show that the use of mobile phones as main device to take photos has an association with age, we found that younger participants are more likely to use this device as the main way to take photos. Moreover, these same younger participants are more likely to store more photos than older ones.

Also, social networks were the preferred way reported by participants as tool for sharing photo albums and this behavior also showed to be associated to participants age. However, even with the popularity of digital albums in social media and social networks, participants still prefer printed photo albums for presenting purpose. Moreover, we found that female participants are more likely create a printed photo album than male participants.

We believe that since social networks are more and more popular, there is room for sites like Flickr, Facebook[3], Instagram[4] and Picasa to make available printing services to ease this task that was reported as very laborious for most participants.

Thereafter, as smartphones, users and behaviors change, new possibilities and issues associated with photo sharing and visualization constantly challenge developers and application designers. As further research we believe that could be an interested point of view to explore particularly how camera phone users share and storage their photos once this devices and applications are quickly evolving.

Acknowledgments. This paper was achieved in cooperation with Hewlett-Packard Brasil Ltda. using incentives of Brazilian Informatics Law (Law n. 8.2.48 of 1991).

References

1. Abdel-Mottaleb, M., Chen, L.: Content-based photo album management using faces' arrangement. In: 2004 IEEE International Conference on Multimedia and Expo, ICME 2004, vol. 3, pp. 2071–2074 (2004)
2. Bergmann, F.B., Manssour, I.H., Silveira, M.S., de Oliveira, J.B.S.: Automatic layout generation for digital photo albums: A user study. In: Kurosu, M. (ed.) HCII/HCI 2013, Part III. LNCS, vol. 8006, pp. 117–126. Springer, Heidelberg (2013)
3. Cooray, S.H., O'Connor, N.E.: Enhancing person annotation for personal photo management applications. In: Proceedings of the 2009 20th International Workshop on Database and Expert Systems Application, DEXA 2009, pp. 251–255. IEEE Computer Society, Washington, DC (2009)
4. Cui, J., Wen, F., Xiao, R., Tian, Y., Tang, X.: Easyalbum: An interactive photo annotation system based on face clustering and re-ranking. In: Proceedings of the SIGCHI Conference on Human Factors in Computing Systems, CHI 2007, pp. 367–376. ACM, New York (2007)
5. Cunningham, S.J., Masoodian, M.: Identifying personal photo digital library features. In: Proceedings of the 7th ACM/IEEE-CS Joint Conference on Digital Libraries, JCDL 2007, pp. 400–401. ACM, New York (2007)
6. Elahi, N., Karlsen, R.: User behavior in online social networks and its implications: a user study. In: Proceedings of the 2nd International Conference on Web Intelligence, Mining and Semantics, WIMS 2012, pp. 61:1–61:4. ACM, New York (2012)
7. Frohlich, D., Kuchinsky, A., Pering, C., Don, A., Ariss, S.: Requirements for photoware. In: Proceedings of the 2002 ACM Conference on Computer Supported Cooperative Work, CSCW 2002, pp. 166–175. ACM, New York (2002)
8. Henze, N., Boll, S.: Snap and share your photobooks. In: Proceedings of the 16th ACM International Conference on Multimedia, MM 2008, pp. 409–418. ACM, New York (2008)

[3] `https://www.facebook.com/`

[4] `http://instagram.com`

9. Jin, Y.K., Choi, S., Chung, A., Myung, I., Lee, J., Kim, M.C., Woo, J.: Gia: Design of a gesture-based interaction photo album. Personal Ubiquitous Comput. 8(3-4), 227–233 (2004)
10. Khalid, H., Dix, A.: The experience of photologging: Global mechanisms and local interactions. Personal Ubiquitous Comput. 14(3), 209–226 (2010)
11. Kirk, D., Sellen, A., Rother, C., Wood, K.: Understanding photowork. In: Proceedings of the SIGCHI Conference on Human Factors in Computing Systems, CHI 2006, pp. 761–770. ACM, New York (2006)
12. Lee, B.N., Chen, W., Chang, E.Y.: Fotofiti: web service for photo management. In: Proceedings of the 14th Annual ACM International Conference on Multimedia, MULTIMEDIA 2006, pp. 485–486. ACM, New York (2006)
13. Malinen, S.: Photo exhibition or online community? the role of social interaction in flickr. In: 2010 Fifth International Conference on Internet and Web Applications and Services (ICIW), pp. 380–385 (2010)
14. Obrador, P., de Oliveira, R., Oliver, N.: Supporting personal photo storytelling for social albums. In: Proceedings of the International Conference on Multimedia, MM 2010, pp. 561–570. ACM, New York (2010)
15. O'Hare, N., Gurrin, C., Lee, H., Murphy, N., Smeaton, A.F., Jones, G.J.: My digital photos: where and when? In: Proceedings of the 13th Annual ACM International Conference on Multimedia, MULTIMEDIA 2005, pp. 261–262. ACM, New York (2005)
16. Okabe, D.: Emergent social practices, situations and relations through everyday camera phone use. In: International Conference on Mobile Communication and Social Change, Seoul, Korea (2004)
17. Plantié, M., Crampes, M.: From photo networks to social networks, creation and use of a social network derived with photos. In: Proceedings of the International Conference on Multimedia, MM 2010, pp. 1047–1050. ACM, New York (2010)
18. Platt, J.C.: Autoalbum: Clustering digital photographs using probabilistic model merging. In: IEEE Workshop on Content-Based Access of Image and Video Libraries 2000, vol. 2000, pp. 96–100. Press (2000)
19. Rodden, K., Wood, K.R.: How do people manage their digital photographs? In: Proceedings of the SIGCHI Conference on Human Factors in Computing Systems, CHI 2003, pp. 409–416. ACM, New York (2003)
20. Xiao, J., Lyons, N., Atkins, C.B., Gao, Y., Chao, H., Zhang, X.: iphotobook: Creating photo books on mobile devices. In: Proceedings of the International Conference on Multimedia, MM 2010, pp. 1551–1554. ACM, New York (2010)
21. Yagawa, Y., Iwai, N., Yanagi, K., Kojima, K., Matsumoto, K.: The digital album: A personal file-tainment system. In: ICMCS, pp. 433–440 (1996)

HCI for Health, Well-Being and Sport

Tool to Help the Communication for Autists

Janaina Cintra Abib[1, 2], Luciana Rodrigues[3], and Reginaldo Gotardo[2, 4]

[1] Federal Institute of São Paulo – Araraquara/SP – Brazil
[2] Federal University of São Carlos – São Carlos/SP - Brazil
[3] Centro Universitário Barão de Mauá – Ribeirão Preto/SP – Brazil
[4] UNISEB; Cross Reality – Ribeirão Preto/SP – Brazil
janaina@ifsp.edu.br, lu_arodrigues@yahoo.com.br,
reginaldo@crossreality.com.br

Abstract. Communication is the main skill to interact in society, regardless of ability or level of cognitive development. Through the process of communication people can share feelings, desires, actions, thoughts and experiences. The communication process does not need to be expressed only through verbal language, but can happen with gestures, glances, body movements, signs and symbols. People with disabilities can use different forms of communication and some technological resources to facilitate the communication process. Inclusion of computational tools in school´s environment facilitates social relations between autistic and others in their learning environment enabling the use of appropriated educational software and communication techniques becoming part of natural process of social interaction. The goal of this research is the development of a medium fidelity prototype software to facilitate the learning and communication of students with autism in school, understanding their differences in learning, processing and organize information and everything should be conducted through the establishment of a daily routine.

Keywords: communication process, autists, communication tool.

1 Introduction

Computer is a valuable tool in the teaching-learning process of children with pervasive developmental disorder (PDD). These students process thoughts in images, they have difficulties in changing their routine activities, they need structured and organized environment to learn and they lack perception, comprehension and communication abilities; so this tool can make social relation between autist and real world easier [6]. The computer allows the learning through educational software properly used, because they can create situations which provide intellectual, social and affective development in individuals with or without the disorder.

This paper aims at using the computer as a tool to make the Reading, the socialization and the Independence easier for students with pervasive developmental disorder (PDD), through software that will be developed to make the learning process easier. PDD is understood as individuals who present global and severe damage in several areas of development: mutual social interaction abilities, communication abilities or

M. Kurosu (Ed.): Human-Computer Interaction, Part III, HCII 2014, LNCS 8512, pp. 211–220, 2014.

behavior, interests and activities stereotypes ([4], our translation). Students with PDD, like the autists, present a different way of learning, organizing and processing information, since everything must be taught following a routine to solve problems.

It is important to consider the 5 categories in which the PDD is divided according to the Diagnostic and Statistical Manual of Mental Disorders (4th Edition- Revised Text - DSM IV – TR) organized by the American Psychiatric Association and by the Classification of Mental and Behavioral Disorders (CID4 – 10) elaborated by the World Health Organization [8]:

- Rett`s Syndrome: this affects only girls. It is characterized by the progressive loss of motor and neurological functions after a period of apparently normal development during the first months of life;
- Autistic Disorder: it is characterized by alterations in communication and social interaction abilities, as well as restricted and stereotyped activities and interests;
- Asperger`s Syndrome: individuals with this syndrome are considered high-level autists and the autist manifestations are presented more moderately;
- Childhood Disintegrative Disorder: a very rare disorder which is manifested after a normal development period followed by regression of previously acquired abilities, specially communication and language skills.
- Pervasive Developmental Disorder Not Otherwise Specified: there is severe and invasive damage to the development. It is evidenced when Autistic Disorder, Asperger`s Syndrome, Rett`s Syndrome and Childhood Disintegrative Disorder hypothesis are excluded.

The development of educational software will provide a great help for individuals with PDD since the communication will allow wider accessibility and quality of life, making their general development easier.

This research approached the main characteristics of the autism; the importance of the inclusion and the technology as a facilitator in the learning-teaching process through an educational software. As bibliography, books from researchers in education, technology and special education were used. However, the development of the software counted with some programming tools like: Netbeans, Databank manager, edition software and image treatment.

The paper is organized as follow. Contextualization and motivations are presented in section 2. Section 3 presents the FECAUT prototype. Finally, the section 4 presents the conclusions and future works.

2 Contextualization and Motivation

Today, before talking about autism, it is necessary to clarify the Pervasive Developmental Disorder (PDD). The terminology PDD is a psychiatric classification from the Diagnostic and Statistical Manual of Mental Disorders – DSM-IV-TR, elaborated by the American Psychiatric Association. This manual contains the classification and the phenomenological description of mental disorders through neurobiological conceptions. The following categories of PDD are in this manual: Autistic Disorder, Rett`s Syndrome, Childhood Disintegrative Disorder, Asperger`s Syndrome and the

Pervasive Developmental Disorder Not Otherwise Specified (including the Atypical Autism). The Classification of Mental and Behavioral Disorders (CID – 10) elaborated by the World Health Organization (WHO) is also mentioned, and eight categories of Pervasive Developmental Disorder are included in this classification: Autism disorder, Atypical autism, Rett`s Syndrome, Another Childhood Disintegrative Disorder, Overactive disorder associated with mental retardation and stereotyped movements, Asperger`s Syndrome, Another Pervasive Developmental Disorders and Pervasive Developmental Disorder Not Otherwise Specified.

Therefore, by observing the categories, it is possible to see that current Special Education Policies are based on the DSM-IV-TR to talk about individuals with Pervasive Developmental.

After these concepts, Autism, a Greek word meaning "by itself", can be defined according to Orrú [7] as a term used in psychiatry to understand human behavior related to the individual himself.

According to ASA - American Society for Autism, autism is defined as:

> *[...] an inadequacy in the development which manifests itself in a serious way along all life. It attacks about twenty in ten thousand new bourns and it is four times more common among boys than girls ([13], our translation).*

The World Health Organization (WHO), according to the International Classification of Disease (CID – 10), states:

> *[...] the autism is treated as a Pervasive Developmental disease, in which there is an abnormal development and/or psychological damage pattern manifested before 3 years old. The child`s abnormal abilities would be related to three areas: social interaction, communication and restrictive and repetitive behavior" ([10], our translation).*

The DSM - IV – Diagnostic and Statistical Manual of Mental Disorders, elaborated by the American Psychiatric Association, makes use of six criteria or more to diagnose the syndrome.

The causes are already known. In the past, it was believed that the hardness and rejection by the mother caused autism, but it was considered a myth because this syndrome is not triggered by emotional reasons as some academics used to defend.

Moraes and Oliveira [9] state that, according to ASA, many are the causes and they can be related to diseases like phenylketonuria when they are not treated, viruses during the first three months of pregnancy including cytomegalovirus, rubella, toxoplasmosis, anoxia, traumatism during birth. Genetic heritage and research also show evidences in the syndrome outbreak after the MMR vaccine.

According to Mello [1], autism is a syndrome defined by alterations before the age of three and it is characterized by quantitative deviation in communication, social interaction and imagination. Communication difficulties can be verbal or nonverbal and includes gestures, facial expressions, body language, language rhythm and modulation. The difficulty in social interaction means the difficulty of relating with others, lack of capacity to demonstrate feelings and emotions and the difficulty in discriminating people.

The individual with autism can also cry or laugh uncontrollably, they may not interact with the outside world, they may not recognize real danger like height and depth and they can even hurt themselves. They also present difficulty in using their imagination and it can be exemplified by obsessive and ritualistic behavior, literal comprehension of the language, lack of acceptance in changing and difficulty in creative processes [1]. All these characteristics can make the educational as well as the social inclusion process difficult, since the communication is very restricted in these individuals.

The word autist was first used by Prouller in 1906, in psychiatric literature. At that time he studied individuals with dementia which he called schizophrenia. In1943, the Austrian Doctor Leo Kanner described 11 cases of children in his article Autistic Disturbance of Affective Contact. As a common characteristic, this group was not able to relate with people and, in 1947 he created the terms Primary and Secondary Autism. In 1944, another Austrian doctor Hans Aspeger wrote an article entitled Autistic Psychopathy in Childhood, in which he described children with characteristics very similar to Kanner´s, but it took a long time to be read because it was written in German [1].

During ages people with any kind of disorder were considered unable to perform any activity and they were excluded from social environment.

The starting point people`s education related to the necessity of some kind of special education was in 16th century, when professional in health area joined in order to teach those who till then believed to be unable to learn [10].

It is necessary to remember that before the 16th century, there was a phase of exclusion and negligence; these people were mistreated and even sacrificed as they were considered demons. In 18th and 19th centuries this rejection is substituted by protection and these people receive help from professionals, but without an educational tone, they continued excluded from society, but then they had specific places to live like asylums and other institutions [14].

In 1600 in the first school for physically disabled people was opened with “Santa Casa da Misericórdia”, in São Paulo. Two centuries later, in 1854, the first teaching institution for disabled was created. It was called “Meninos Cegos” (Blind Boys) and was supported by the royalty, and in1891 its name changed to Benjamin Constant Institute. In 1931, Helena Antipoff opened “Sociedade Pestalozzi”, and created the term “exceptional” to refer to the disabled ones and she believed it was possible to have teachers able to deal with these students. The first qualified professionals came out of this institution in 1948 [5].

In the 19th century, an integration phase took place and students with difficulties to follow an ordinary class were oriented to attend special classes in the same school. In the end of the 20th century, a new framework is proposed in which the school adapts to the children needs and attends all the students with special educational difficulties in the regular classroom. Autist people have always had specialized institutions and have always related with children with the same difficulties.

According to Orrú [7] children submitted to this position in the classroom cannot overcome their difficulties because they relate with children who have the same characteristics. Thus, the best environment for an individual with autism to learn is the regular classroom, relating with other individuals with other characteristics.

According to Mello [1], before including an autist in the regular school environment, he must have a specialized attendance so the individual can know himself, and know about his abilities in order to prepare him for the inclusion. According to the author a multidisciplinary team must support each child according to their specific needs.

Then, Mantoan [11, 12] states that the school inclusion changes the teacher and makes him recognize the different cultures, the social, intellectuals and affective manifestations.

According to Martins [10], since the constitution of 1988 there was the guarantee of some rights to disabled people like the social integration, qualification and rehabilitation besides specific educational attendance. The constitution guarantees education for all, so as each individual can develop and became a conscious citizen, so these individuals cannot learn in segregated environments [11, 12].

Salamanca Statement summarized the position of 92 countries about the reception of the diversity. In this inclusion process, the school must guarantee modifications in the course, physical and environmental organization which ensures the continuity and quality in the teaching-learning process of these students.

In Brazil, the National Educational Bases and Guidelines Law (Law 9394/96) – in chapter V articles 58 and 59 foregoes specialized service to people with special needs, adjustment of course and qualified teachers.

All these studies motivated us to think about a free tool that helps the communication of autistic children in school environments, allowing them to communicate and express their needs, and facilitating their socialization.

3 FECAUT to Supporting Communication

The tool to aid autistic child (in Portuguese "Ferramenta de Auxilio à Criança Autista" - FECAUT) was developed to help autistic children in their teaching-learning process, improving the communication and reading skills, socialization and the independence of the autistic in classroom, using technologies and audiovisual resources.

The prototype was developed using techniques of medium fidelity prototyping and it was evaluated using usability inspection techniques. Initial prototypes were produced on paper based on low-fidelity prototype, to collect and validate functional requirements.

According to Gomes and Silva [3], auditory and visual stimuli are used to get attention and, if they are used properly, it can help the autistic establish some day-by-day routines. Considering these aspects, we were looking for a model to develop FECAUT tool using images and sounds to improve memory development skills and to facilitate the coordination of autistic, observing how they process information.

FECAUT tool was divided into different categories with different screens for interaction. All interactions can be performed through touch and the users can also active sound´s mechanisms. Interactions are represented by images and symbols to facilitate cognitive recognition. Some controls, such as buttons, with default actions were introduced: start the tool, exit, go back/return, and others. In addition to symbols, a word or phrase that indicates the action - for these actions is also available the sound system. This mechanism helps the learning process through word´s recognition and identification. The categories of the tool are: toiletries, school supplies, games, emotions, colors and food. These categories were informed by teaches in a Brazilian school that have autistic students in their class, and in a future work we can complement the categories with others categories that may be appropriated. The categories are subdivided in items that containing the actions related to each category.

We have been using an integrated development environment to create and develop FECAUT prototype. The prototype was evaluated through inspections conducted by usability experts and, at the end of this evaluation, the requirements have been validated.

Considering the issues highlighted in studies of [3], we´ve pursued to develop FECAUT tool with the adoption of images and sounds to help and to facilitate the memorization and autistic´s coordination, observing how they process informations.

The tool has the following functionalities: On the Initial Screen (Figure 1 - Initial Screen), the user has the option to exit the tool by clicking the button <Close> (Figure 1 - A) or start using FECAUT selecting the <enter> button (Figure 1 - B), in this case the program redirects the user to the Home Screen of the tool, shown in Figure 2 - Options from Home Screen.

Fig. 1. Initial Screen

Based on the initial screen of FECAUT, the user can choose which activity he/she desires, by clicking on button that correspond to wanted action.

When the user makes this selection/action, by positioning the mouse over the button, the sound of the word written in capital letters will be reproduced. If the user pushes the button, the tool opens the next screen containing all items in the selected category.

It is important to notice that we have been followed the principles of good design, maintaining consistency between screens of the tool, proper use of metaphors, use of a good mapping and correct use of action´s objects. It can be observed, in Figure 2 - A, the <Enter> button was disabled, since the user is already using the tool and this action is no longer needed.

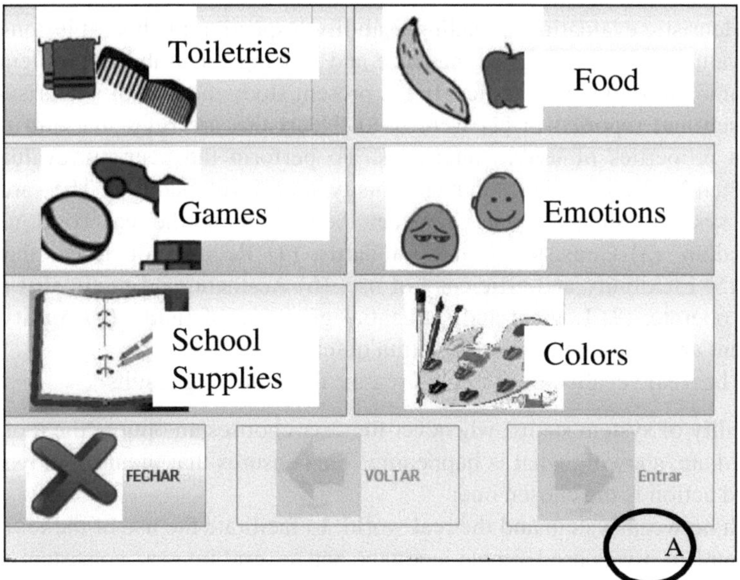

Fig. 2. Options from Home Screen

When the user chose one category, the tool displays a number of items related to the selected category. For example, the category Toilets has six items: soap, towel, hairbrush, toothbrush, toothpaste and shampoo. All icons consisting in the selected category are detailed and when the user positions the mouse over the picture a sound is played. Still, the user has the option to close the screen and return to the previous one. This process is similar for all categories of FECAUT tool.

It is recommended that parents and teachers observe the autistic child during use of the tool, if he/she is having some difficulty or not handle it. These observations are required because autistic may need help at the beginning of the use of FECAUT and also as the communication process involves the sender and also the receiver of the message, it is important that parents and teachers understand how child is using the tool to convey your wishes, feelings and needs.

3.1 Usability Inspection Applied to FECAUT

For the evaluation of FECAUT tool the validation technique was used, focusing on functionality and usability. According to Rocha and Baranauskas [2] evaluation aims to " [...] know what users wants and the problems they have been experimented, because if the designers are informed about what users want and need, they can do better products. "

To evaluate the FECAUT´s usability it was executed a usability inspection. Rocha and Baranauskas [2] define usability inspection as a technique that checks usability experts to evaluate the usability and functionality of an interface, focusing at the software. It can be done at any stage of development. Thus, this type of technique has become suitable for the work, at prototyping phase.

The Heuristic evaluation, a leading usability inspection method, it is consisting of a set of evaluators examining the interface and looking for usability problems, according to some pre-defined heuristics. In the present study the usability heuristics defined by Nielsen and reported in [2] were used. Heuristics are rules that aim to describe common properties of usable interfaces. To perform the heuristic evaluation were selected ten Nielsen heuristics that suit this type of developed tool. They are: (1) Visibility of system status; (2) Match between the system and the real world, user control and freedom, (3) Consistency and standards, (4) Recognition rather than remembrance, (5) Flexibility and efficiency of use, (6) Aesthetic and minimalist design, (7) Easy to operate; (8) Logical and sequential grouping of fields, (9) Agility in cursor movement and (10) Location information quickly.

After heuristic evaluation we could realize the following results.

- Visibility of system status: whenever the user chooses an option, the tool responses immediate, showing what is happening. This ensures that the user knows if the executed action is the chosen one;
- Match between system and the real world: to facilitate the use of the tool by people with autism it was used simple language and several images, consistent with representations of real objects;
- User control and freedom: the user can return to a previous state by clicking on the buttons that can be found on the bottom of all screens, and he/she has the feeling that controls the entire environment;
- Consistency and standards: to maintain the user´s daily routine, an important item for autistic people, a model was created to access the information by the same way anywhere when using the tool. Colors, menus and buttons were also standardized;
- Recognition rather than remembrance: FECAUT is simple to use and the user can recognize where he/she is without having to remember the path he/she have been navigating. Furthermore, the use of metaphors and patterns provides greater ease in recognition of the objects to interact;
- Flexibility and efficiency of use: This tool was developed for both the users who are accessing the system for the first time and more experienced users. But there are no keyboard shortcuts to experienced users that they can quickly perform the functions - it is a heuristics recommendation. It is also not allowed to customize the tool´s items, for example, to group categories and most used items. This heuristic was partially fulfilled because the needs of the group of users were fully met, even without the flexibility to tool´s customization;
- Aesthetic and minimalist design: The FECAUT does not contain error message, to not intimidate the user or make him feel guilty for an error or invalid selection. The interface of the tool was developed allowing the user do not make mistakes, working with enabling/disabling of the object´s action;
- Ease of operation: This tool minimizes number of click´s (actions) to perform an task, based on user´s needs who have deficits in motor coordination;
- Logical grouping and fields sequencing: FECAUT used groups of similar items, creating categories for grouping the information, making it easier to find the items by the users;

- Agility in cursor movement: To make more agile the tool´s manipulation was created buttons to interact with the tool, which have large sizes to facilitate the movement of users who do not have fine motor coordination;
- Find information quickly: The interaction´s buttons facilitate the information´s location and the user becomes independent after a period of use the tool.

FECAUT tool was developed observing the recommendations of software engineering for system development and usability engineering for interface´s development. Heuristics were used in the validation of the tool, especially for evaluated the usability, so that the tool is easy to use, easy to learn and motivates users to use it. It is required to perform an evaluation with users, both teacher and students, and it will be done in a future work.

4 Conclusion and Future Work

The communication process is essential in the school environment, especially among age children literacy to exchange information, clarify doubts and their socialization. Informal communication often helps children to perform tasks and solve problems more quickly and, therefore, it is important that autistic children are able to express themselves clearly in school environments.

This project presents the FECAUT tool that reaches the features proposed to facilitate communication, socialization and autistic´s independence in the school environment because it uses sounds, text and images for ease of symbolic thought. Given everything that was analyzed, it was found that the developed tool has no usability problems from the point of view of concepts and the tool is consistent with the Nielsen´s Heuristics, providing benefits not only for autistic children, but also for other children with communication problems, especially for children with temporary disabilities, those acquired for a short period of time. Besides this advantage, the system has practically no cost compared to existing programs on the market that have the same purpose.

As future work we have to make some improvements like inserting images in the database made by users, field research and adaptation for operation in mobile devices such as phones and tablets. Even though simple, the tool is important for the inclusion of the autistic, both in social environment as educational environment , providing knowledge and autonomy, since autistic children can indeed learn from the tool, and they are encouraged to express themselves.

Acknowledgements. We thank Rosângela M. da Silva by the proposed and developed FECAUT prototype.

References

1. Mello, A.M.S.R.: Autismo: guia prático. São Paulo: Corde, 104 p. (2007)
2. Rocha, H.V., Baranauskas, M.C.C.: Design e Avaliação de Interface Humano-Computador, p. 244. NIED, Campinas (2003)

3. Gomes, A.N., Silva, C.B.: Software Educativo para Crianças Autistas de Nível Severo. In: 4th International Conference on Design Research (2007)
4. Associação Americana De PSIQUIATRIA. *DSM-IV-TR*: Manual diagnóstico e estatístico de transtornos mentais. 4.ed.rev.Artmed (2002)
5. Sassaki, R.K.: Vida Independente: História, movimento, liderança, conceito, filosofia e fundamentos. Reabilitação, emprego e terminologia. Revista Nacional de Reabilitação (2003)
6. Ribeiro, M.L.S.: Perspectivas da Escola Inclusiva: Algumas Reflexões In: —— e BAUMEL, Roseli Cecília Rocha de Carvalho (Org.). Educação Especial do querer ao fazer. Avercamp, pp. 41– 51 (2003)
7. Orrú, S.E.: Autismo, Linguagem e Educação. Wak Ed. Rio de Janeiro (2007)
8. OMS - ORGANIZAÇÃO MUNDIAL DE SAÚDE (coord.). Classificação de Transtornos Mentais e de Comportamento da CID-10: descrições clínicas e diretrizes diagnósticas. Artes Médicas (1993)
9. Moraes, F.F.F., Oliveira, I.S.C.M.: O autismo na perspectiva de uma educação inclusiva. Disponível em, `http://www.nead.unama.br/site/bibdigital/monografias/o_autismo_na_perspectiva_de_uma_educacao_inclusiva.pdf` (Acesso em: maio 15, 2013)
10. Martins, M.R.R.: Inclusão de alunos autistas no ensino regular: concepções e praticas pedagógicas de professores regentes. Disponível em, `http://www.bdtd.ucb.br/tede/tde_busca/arquivo.php?codArquivo=692` (Acesso em: Maio 17, 2013)
11. Mantoan, M.T.E.: Inclusão escolar: caminhos, descaminhos, desafios e perspectivas.In: III Seminário Nacional de Formação de Gestores e Educadores - Educação inclusiva: direito a diversidade - Ensaios pedagógicos. Brasília: Ministério da Educação, Secretaria da Educação Especial, p.11–16 (2006)
12. Mantoan, M.T.E.: Inclusão Escolar O que é? Por quê? Como fazer? Moderna (2003)
13. Gauderer, E.C.: Autismo e outros atrasos do desenvolvimento: uma atualização para os que atuam na área; do especialistaaos pais. Ministério do Bem-Estar Social, Coordenadoria Nacional para Integração da Pessoa Portadora deDeficiência (1993)
14. Aranha, M. S.: Paradigmas da relação da sociedade com as pessoas com deficiência. In: Revista do Ministério Público do Trabalho, Ano XI, n. 21 março, pp. 160–173 (2001)

An Exergame for Encouraging Martial Arts

Connsynn Chye, Mizuki Sakamoto, and Tatsuo Nakajima

Department of Computer Science and Engineering, Waseda University, Japan
{chye,mizuki,tatsuo}@dcl.cs.waseda.ac.jp

Abstract. In this paper, we developed a game-based learning system for martial arts with the aid of a Kinect sensor, stressing the importance of providing the player with immediate feedback, clear goals and challenges that are matched to his/her skill level. We have conducted an experiment on 6 university students. The influences of punching gloves on a player's psychological processes were evident in the experiment results. As well, we found that punching gloves exhibit the potential to govern game-based learning process. We posit that the reality tool is essential in the future exergame learning system due to its virtual reality impact on a player's feeling. The game-based learning model discussed in this paper can be extended to other sports, especially those required sports equipment such as racquet, golf club, baseball bat and etc for high excitement, fun and interactive learning achievement.

Keywords: Game-based learning, augmented reality, exergaming, enclothed cognition.

1 Introduction

Parents or babysitters may be familiar with the following scenario; children threw their hands up in the air and shouted hurrah for game hours, however, the opposite happened when it comes to formal learning. This clearly shows that people are always looking forward to gameplay, because games are always related to fun, exciting and addicting. On the other hand, people tends to react reluctantly when they are told to go for training or learning, because training or learning are often associated with boring, formal or even soporific. It will be grateful if a game can be a part of our formal learning system. The idea of embedding education into entertainment started as early as a few decades ago. Edutainment was introduced in 1954 when Walt Disney began to build Disneyland. The excitement brought by entertainment and the invocation of emotions such as curiosity, joy and pride by game are similar to the key points of a successful education system. It was mentioned by Marc Prensky [16] that our traditional learning system, which worked well for hundreds of years is breaking down while the learning through Digital Games is a wave of the future. Now, game-based learning is a wave of the present.

In fact, we learned through games when we were very young. During our toddler days, every aspect of life: eat, speak, walk was games. We started to differentiate colors by color hunt game -- hunt for something red or blue or green at home, the game often ended with lots of laughter and we gained new knowledge inadvertently.

M. Kurosu (Ed.): Human-Computer Interaction, Part III, HCII 2014, LNCS 8512, pp. 221–232, 2014.

However, the game was replaced with textbooks and lecture when we enter school. Traditional textbooks and lecture were found boring for students who grown up in a pervasive technology environment, hence, educators introduced gamed-based learning in the classroom. The effectiveness of game-based learning was evident by [2], students scored significantly higher with the aid of gameplay in classroom. At present, the number of game-based learning systems is huge; the varieties are range from mathematic to science, history to politics, literature to sports and etc. The invention of highly reliability and inexpensive sensors such as Kinect and Wii had boost up the opportunities to develop game-based learning system for dynamic activities including various sports and dances that required emphasize of gesture movement.

Exergame was first introduced in the 1980s. It is a portmanteau of "exercise" and "game". However, there were on-going debates for its definition between the traditional health-related researcher and the researchers who do not have a heath-related background. In this study, we take the new definition by [14] that interpreted exergames as a combination of exertion and video games including strength training, balance, and flexibility activities while exergaming is playing exergames or any other video games to promote physical activity. In this paper, we would like to introduce an interactive digital system that promotes informal learning of martial arts, Karate. As concluded by [3], learning through games is meant to replicate children's more natural style of learning, then making them less like play and more like schoolwork will render them ineffective as educational tools. Game-based learning systems design often applies game concepts into existing education system. We suggest the other way round, which is to include martial art skill sets into existing game system design. Hence, we propose a game-based learning system that look and feel exactly like an ordinary video game that could unobtrusively teach player about martial arts during the gameplay. The ultimate goal is to have the player indirectly learn the real sport through the gameplay. As well, we explore the feasibility to utilize real sports tools in the exergame learning system.

2 Related Work

2.1 Kinect for Education

Hsu explored the potential of Kinect as interactive technology and discussed how this device can facilitate and enhance teaching and learning in [9]. She pinpointed that Kinect has the ability to create enjoyable, interesting interaction types, to boost motivation, and to promote learning via its multimedia and multi-sensor capacity. The paper concluded that Kinect has high potential despite having technical constraints such as limitation of space required. However, the paper did not present the findings about accuracy and efficiency of Kinect as an interactive tool for physical activities such as sports. A physical instructional support system was built in [13] with the aid of Kinect to provide a means of real-time direct communication. The paper emphasized on the importance of imitation learning and proposed a virtual training system for both the trainer and trainee to interact with their superimposed avatars via Kinect. Kinect sensor was used in the context of supporting tools where a human being instructor still plays an important role in this teaching-learning process.

2.2 Physical Training System

Thai boxing is inevitably known as one of the famous martial arts. Correctness of practice and proper postures were regarded as important in [15] to avoid sportsman injury. They modeled 3D avatars by motion capturing 2 actors with 42 spots on their bodies. The 3D avatars presented in this paper were lively and vivid, represented real Thai-boxing art. The results revealed that these animations helped the learners gain interest in Thai culture, although they have not personal experienced it yet. An artificial reality martial arts game installation was being discussed in [7]. In this game, the player fights with virtual enemies with kicks and punches. It was mentioned that the game worked well for entertainment and fitness application, the motion exaggeration was found fun in the game. However, most of the participants for this user study practiced more than one sports and all of them were adults. Hence, the impact and benefits of this game to the novice were unknown. It was concluded that this system can be considered to develop motion skills and fitness but it is insufficient from an educational point of view as martial arts are about mind and body, harmony and respect to fellow trainees. In [6], the authors explored the potential of motion training system that maps the user's image onto an instruction video. This training system targeted first time learners for dance and evaluated the usefulness of presenting them composite video in which beginners appear to dance like an expert. The outcome is encouraging where people like to see themselves performed well, similar to the exaggeration fun in [7].

2.3 Game Based Learning System

Csikszentmihalyi mentioned that flow is an experience people had when they "worked hard, not in order to get conventional rewards, but because the work itself was rewarding… " in [4]. The key to understanding flow is the concept of autotelic experience where people forget personal problems, lose their sense of time and of themselves, feel competent and in control. The studies of relation between flow and telepresence are being explored in [5]. The findings suggested that there is a significant correlation between flow and telepresence. The authors suggested that flow experience in virtual gameplay and learning may acquire an improved attitude of learning online. Kiili discussed about factors that contribute to flow experience in [12]. He stressed the importance of providing the player with immediate feedback, clear goals and challenges that are matched to his/her skill level in educational computer games. Killi's experiential gaming model is linked to gameplay with experiential learning to facilitate flow experience. This experiential gaming model consists of an ideation loop, an experience loop and a challenge bank. The heart is the core to sustain the motivation and engagement of the player by pumping appropriate challenges to him or her. From a motivation and learning point of view, the operation of the heart is to provide a player with challenges that are matched to his or her skill level in order to increase the likelihood of experience flow. However, Killi mentioned that it is impossible to predict how quickly a player's skills develop while gaming which makes the designing of games hard. Adaptive games can be one of the solution but adaption must be considered carefully in order to avoid bad usability, inappropriate challenges and objects that may break the harmony in the game world which bring less likelihood of experience flow. Significant grow in the publications of digital game based learning system related article from

2001 to 2010 were reported in [10]. It was found that most studies did not involve specific learning domains; instead mainly focused on the investigation of students' motivations, perceptions and attitudes toward digital games. Conventional education subjects such as "Engineering", "Language and Art", and "Science" top the list of studies. However, dynamic activities learning system were not mentioned in this paper.

3 An Exergame for Martial Arts

3.1 Design Issue

We have identified five important elements that make up a good game based learning system. Mainly, high accuracy to ensure smooth interaction between the player and the system; goal oriented for player to work towards a goal, learn and practice the right way; virtual reality is important to make a system that look and feel familiar and relevant to core subject; a system with no latency to provide immediate feedback; and the game concepts that contribute to state of flow. We have explored two sensors to fit for the above purposes. Firstly, we used a small and lightweight accelerometer sensor - TSND121[1]. Secondly, we tried with a controller less 3D infrared sensor - Kinect. TSND121 sensor is very small in size, 37mm(W) x 46mm(H) x 12mm(D) and light in weight, approximately 22g. In addition, TSND121 sensor can communicate wirelessly with PC on bluetooth connection. We tried to modify this sensor into a wearable sensor by attaching it on punching gloves. We have requested an experienced martial arts practitioner to perform a series of martial arts movement with both TSND121 sensor and Kinect sensor. It was amazing to find out that TSND121 sensor gave us high speed sampling at 1000Hz. Both sensors gave us satisfying accuracy as well as stable connection with PC. We interviewed the martial arts practitioner about his experience with both sensors. He revealed that he had great experience with both TSND121 sensor and Kinect sensor. However, he expressed his concern about

1. Attachment of multiple sensors on body that may cause the restriction on body movement.
2. Martial arts involved a series of body movement, not limited to punches and blocks but kicks and self defense steps too. A single sensor may not be able to cater for all.
3. In a conventional training scenario, a concrete target subject is preferable in precision training, to measure the distance between you and target.

From the perspectives of martial arts, a punch action does not concern only on the hands, but on the body axis as well as legs movement too. However, it will be obtrusive and impractical to request a player to put on several wearable sensors on their hands and legs including body parts such as torso before a gameplay, which may lead to dilution of virtual reality elements and limitations on body movements. On the other hand, a single Kinect sensor is able to identity 20 joint points information, in addition to its ability to track multiple user at once. Taking into consideration of the cost factor, the suitability for exergame and practicality of implementation, we have picked up a much more affordable and unobtrusive sensor, which is Kinect sensor for this study.

---

[1] http://www.atr-p.com/TSND121.html

3.2 System Architecture

From a hardware perspective, our system consists of a Kinect sensor, a PC, and a screen display. We have utilized programming tools including Xcode and Quartz Composer to implement the logics and render the graphic effects. As a big picture, the system was developed with Synapse[2] application to get the input data from Kinect sensor, the joint point information is then sent via qcOCS to Quartz Composer. Figure 1 shows the high-level architecture presentation of this system.

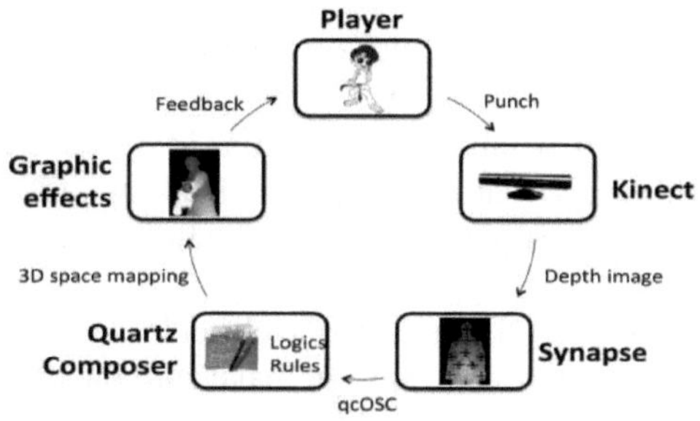

Fig. 1. System architecture

1. Player: A person needs to be at least 1 meter tall according to Kinect sensor's requirement. Kinect sensor will capture the posture of player via geometric data acquirement.
2. Kinect: A sensor to get the depth information and identify the joint points information of the player. These included head, neck, shoulders (right and left), elbows (right and left), hands (right and left), torso, hips (right and left), knees (right and left), feet (right and left).
3. Synapse: An application that sends joint points information of the player via Open Sound Control messages to Quartz Composer.
4. Quartz Composer: An application to render graphics using visual programming language. Game logics and rules are applied in Quartz Composer by 3D space mapping between player and graphics.
5. Graphic effects: Real time display as the results of mapping between player's punch and obstacle position. Sparks graphic effects are produced when the players hand position (x, y) matches the obstacle position (x, y), serve as an immediate feedback to a successful hit.

This exergame was designed to be interactive and effective game based learning system. Interactive provide a means of acting with each other, making immediate two-way communication possible between computer and player. Fig. 1 illustrated the cycle of interaction between the player and the system. It has revealed the underlying technology that plays important roles in realizing the five important element. Firstly, player's movement can be tracked by Kinect sensor at the speed of 30 frames per second that could provide a mean of high accuracy to ensure smooth interaction between the player and the system. Then, the depth information is send over to Synapse application to

[2] http://synapsekinect.tumblr.com

build the human skeleton. All joint points information will be transferred by qcOCS to Quartz Composer[3]. With Quartz Composer, we implement the game rules: obstacles in front of the players as a target subject, to provide a goal-oriented environment. We render the player's image with 3D space mapping, allowing us to create a core subject relevant virtual reality graphic effects. We have tested the cycle and found this model to be able to produce immediate graphic response to the player without any latency. All user movements are relayed and reflected immediately on display screen. Several assumptions were made when we design this game based learning system:

1. The sensor is positioned 0.6 – 1.8 meter off the floor, with nothing between player and the sensor.
2. Movements that happened within less than 0.03333 seconds are ignored. According to [11], the world fastest martial arts punch is 44 mph (70.8 km/h). Kinect sensor that operates at 30 frames per second can obtain 2 frames for the fastest punch in the world.
3. Due to the limitation of 2D display screen, obstacle will always be displayed in front of the player. In another word, we can make sure the player are always facing (180° parallel) to the display screen and hence player's hands are always visible to Kinect sensor.
4. The size of the obstacle is of the same the size as punch gloves.
5. Punching gloves is not black in color and is adjustable to fit various size of fist, it will not impact Kinect sensor's performance.

3.3 Game Setting

We developed a punching game; the game flow is shown in Fig. 2. We have taken Kiili's Experiential gaming model [12] into consideration for the system design. We have provided clear goal - hitting obstacle; immediate feedback - real-time display; and challenges - obstacle that runs into random directions.

1. Overview: Before the game start, player should stand 1.5 meter from the Kinect sensor and face to the display screen. Game can be started after player's joint point positions were identified by Kinect sensor. (1 – Punching gloves, 2 – Display screen, 3 – Kinect sensor)
2. Start: Once player were being identified, they will appear on the screen with "fire on fist" graphical effect. Top left corner of the display will show the number of hit (Number of count start from 0), while top left corner of the screen will show a stopwatch in seconds (Number of seconds start from 0). (4 – Fire on fist, 5 – Obstacle, 6 – Number of hit, 7 – Stopwatch)
3. Play: Obstacle was designed to run into random direction. Sparks are produced when the player has successfully punched the obstacle with his or her hands, indicating successful hit. (8 – Sparks on hit)
4. End: Results will be displayed when the game is over indicating the game has come to an end. (9 – Results)

---

[3] A node-based visual programming language.

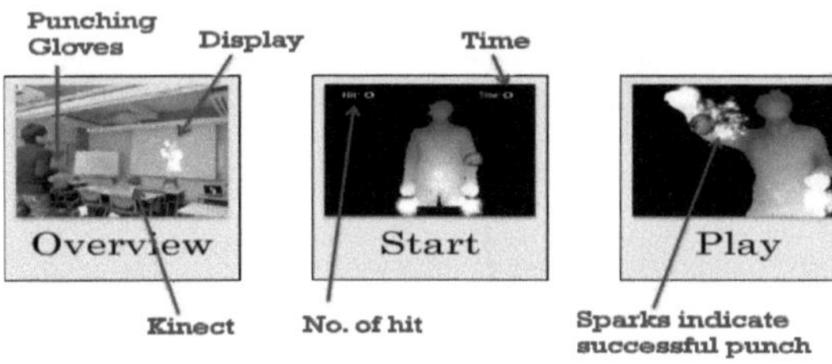

Fig. 2. Game Setting

Taking into considerations of human body physical abilities limitation, we have designed the game short. One is expected to finish the game in less than 60 seconds. Our system rely on 2-dimensional display, hence, the obstacle will always appeared in front of the player in screen projector although the Z coordinates may in fact located behind the player. According to [8], video frame rate is an important factor in producing painterly animation. Hence, we have adjusted the motion of obstacle by considering the human visual system that processes 10 to 12 separate images per second. The projection size of the player on display screen is dependent on the distance between player and kinect sensor, a player appear smaller when they are farther from the Kinect sensor compared to a player who is the same height but located nearer to Kinect sensor. We have designed the obstacle size to be about the same as fist size considering the ideal scenario, player is located 1.5 meter from the Kinect sensor. It is possible for the system to track more than one player with the present technology, however, we have not designed the system to cater for concurrent multiple player. Hence, the system is limited to have one player at a time. The intention of this design is to promote exercise and indirectly promote martial arts learning. However, the movements are limited to 1 meter in horizontal plane and less than 0.5 meter in vertical plane. The Kinect sensor works perfectly when a player is standing at 1.5 meter in front of it. Hence, forward and backward movements may deteriorate the user tracking and user detection rate.

4 Evaluation

We have conducted an experiment with this game-based learning system in the University on 6 participants aged between 22 – 26 years old. There is no specific requirement on choosing the participants apart from they have to be at least 1 meter tall and they are fit to perform physical activity with Kinect sensor. We have randomly picked up 6 university students and they were requested to interact with the system twice, once by putting on punching gloves and once with empty handed. They are being observed during the gameplay in an open space, required to fill in a one-page paper survey and a follow-up interview if necessary. All participants were given the same instruction, literally "Please track and punch the stone (obstacle) as many as 30

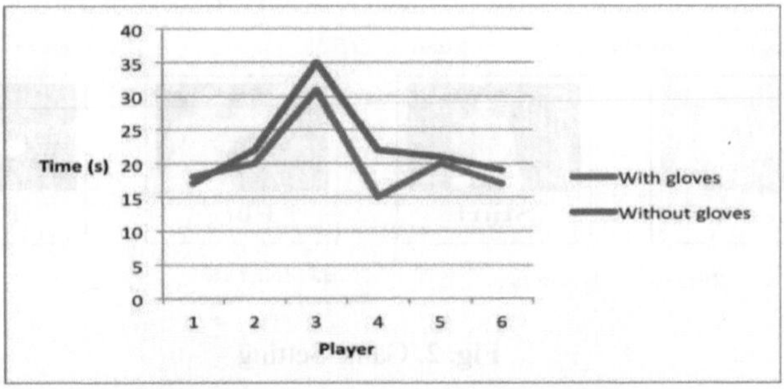

Fig. 3. Time taken to make 30 punches

times within shortest timespan as you can". All participants have the freedom to choose to play the first game with or without punching gloves and the opposite for the second game. This is to avoid prejudice about punching gloves' impact on the gameplay. We have prepared a 2 meter square clean space (without chair, table) and shut down all the windows to minimize side or back light that may obstruct Kinect sensor performance. Figure 3 presents the time taken (Note: Measurement in unit of time: Second (s).) to have 30 successful hits on obstacle for 6 participants. The user tracking works perfectly at 100% detection rate. There is a real time feedback on display screen for each user movement and we are excited to find no latency for the communication between Kinect Sensor and PC during the experiments. However, some users required significantly longer detection time than the others. Mainly caused by:

1. Low depth resolution with far distance. It was mentioned in the Kinect document that the random error of depth measurements increases quadratically with increasing distance from the sensor reaches 4 cm at the maximum range.
2. Clothing color appears to have impact on the detection rate [9]. We have difficulty to detect users in black colored shirt.

From Fig. 3, we found that there is slightly faster completion time comparing one playing with gloves and one playing without. The findings revealed that one with punching gloves outperformed himself/herself without punching gloves. While the sequence of playing with or without punching gloves were in random basis, this clearly shows that the faster completion speed is not related with the sequence of play but the attachment of punching gloves actually improved player performance in this study.

4.1 Survey

All participants were required to fill up a short survey form that is related to age, score in the game, past experience about martial arts, the impact of punching gloves to their gameplay, did the system make them exercise and did they had fun with this system.

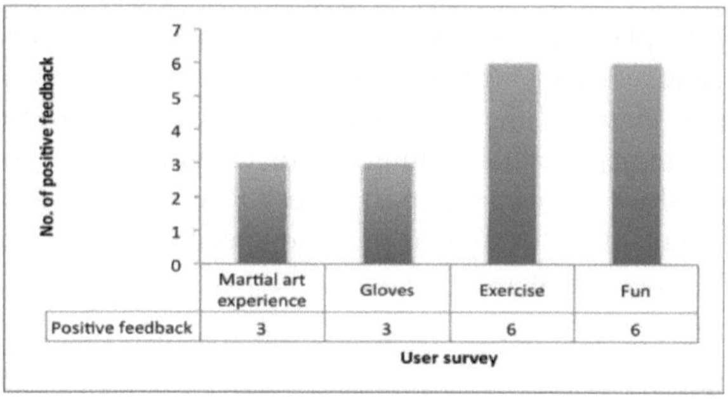

Fig. 4. Survey results

The experiment revealed that punching gloves helped to achieve better performance. This indicates that punching gloves did not limit the movement of players and players can perform better if they have punching gloves attached. Fig. 4 shows the summary of user survey results. 50% of the participants admitted they felt better to play with punching gloves. This indicate that punching gloves actually possess impact on the experiment results as well as influenced feeling of players gameplay. Provided no technical enhancement on the gloves, players gave the following comments on the gloves:

+ I feel that it was a real exercise when I put on the gloves.
+ I feel that I am doing real punching when I put on the gloves.
+ I feel that I am more excited with the game when I put on the gloves.

All participants agreed that they exercise along with the game. Kinect game is very different from conventional controllers/handheld games. Kinect sensor provides controller-free gaming that brings on full body play, it responds to how player move. In this game, player is required to "hunt down" the obstacle, they have to get off the couch and move their hands to reflect themselves punching obstacle through display. We have designed the obstacle to run in random direction, hence, one need to move not only their arms, but also the whole body including legs to track the obstacle. All participants said they had fun with the game. Players were excited to see the exaggerated effects, fire on fists and sparks effect by Quartz Composer. The authors believe that a successful game based learning system is achieved when the players reached flow state, where they worked hard to play, not in order to get conventional rewards, but because the subject itself was rewarding, fun and pleasurable. We have purposely designed the system to look and feel exactly like an ordinary video game. Slightly differ from normal game-based learning systems; we did not include common game mechanics such as achievements, infinite gameplay, levels, lottery, points, status and etc. This finding prove us right where fewer game mechanics did not dilute the fun and pleasure because the gameplay itself is rewarding and meaningful to the player. Gamifying a learning system normally involves creation of the state of flow in player and enhancement of motivation by adding game concepts in existing learning system. However, this is a very hard process, as it does not work by simply adding all game mechanics such as rewards, achievements, game currency and etc into the system without attracting the player to the core subject, let it be maths, science or sports matter. On the other hand, edifying a game system maybe simpler in the sense that adding rules and regulations on top of the game without impacting the harmony of the whole game. As illustrated in experiential gaming model, creating challenges is the heart and essence in creating flow. In our system, it is technically possible to have additional rules and tighter regulations for movements and speed can be leverage for different levels by having higher challenges.

4.2 Observation

We have observed the players throughout both gameplays. We noticed some significant reactions from the players including excitements on their face when they see fire on their hands and the happy laughter face when they have successfully get a score, of course, we saw the disappointing faces when they missed the obstacle too. This matches the results from the survey where everyone said they had fun with the system. The phenomenon of excitement brought by punching gloves may be explained with the term "Enclothed Cognition" to describe the systematic influence that clothes have on the wearer's psychological processes. In [1], Adam & Galinsky argued that the experience of wearing clothes triggers associated abstract concepts and their symbolic meanings. For example, if you wear a white coat that you believe belongs to a doctor, your ability to pay attention may increases sharply. Given the symbolic meaning of the punching gloves as fight, punch, boxing and etc. People who are actually wearing the punching gloves may feel that they have increased ability to punch, this was reflected in the experiment score results. Players scored better when they have attached punching gloves when there is no technical modification or enhancement in the punching gloves itself. We posit that putting on punching gloves may possess similar effects on cognitive processes, like what Adam & Galinsky suggested for clothes.

On top of the "Enclothed Cognition" effects, we found that punching gloves are as well governing the fist and punching action. In the cases without gloves, we found players played "creatively", they ignored the given "punch" instructions. They tend to cheat by trying to perform "swipe" instead of "punch" to get better score, higher achievements in the gameplay. On the other hand, we did not notice this trend of gameplay in the punching gloves gameplays. Instead, they "punch" hardly when they put on punching gloves. Hence, we posit that gaming tools play an important role to governance players to obey game rules and it will be very helpful to have these supportive tools in gameplay for augmented reality effect, to achieve better learning outcomes. This observation outcome may advocate the utilization of reality tool in the future exergame as an alternative way of learning sports. During observation, we have found something that is not revealed by the survey, which is the intention to replay among the players. There was a situation where a player was requested to fill in the survey form after he has completed both gamplay. He stayed back to watch the gameplay performed by another player. He has requested a replay in order to outperform another player. This can relate to Kiili's "The ideation process is most fruitful if it is performed in groups." The motivation to repeat the same tasks can be improved by introducing peers competition, a list of ranking to invoke goals setting in player's mindset. As well, the repetition of the same tasks may help to achieve perfect motion in certain sports such as martial arts and dance as practice makes perfect. Hence, game concepts such as ranking list can be a good motivator to encourage replay that may lead to indirect physical training.

5 Conclusion

The results revealed that Kinect sensor's user detection rate was promising. It's no latency feature and high accuracy detection rate, on top of it's controller-less feature to replace wearable sensors convinced us that Kinect sensor is a very useful body area network device for physical game-based learning, training or exergame. We foresee it's importance and potential huge contribution to physical game based learning system with its easy setup inherent quality. The "Enclothed Cognition" effects from the punching gloves have exceeded our expectations. Provided, punching gloves did not bring negative impact to Kinect sensor's performance, never cause latency into the system and did not bring confusion to the players. We posit that bringing real-world tools such as real golf club, real racquet, baseball bat and etc into game will boost up the augmented reality effect as well as triggers associated abstract concepts and their symbolic meanings to the players. This can potentially enhance the game experience as well as boost the learning values in a game.

References

1. Adam, H., Galinsky, A.D.: Enclothed cognition. Journal of Experimental Social Psychology 48(4), 918–925 (2012)
2. Blunt, R.: Does game-based learning work? Results from three recent studies. In: Proceedings of Interservice/Industry Training, Simulation & Education Conference (I/ITSEC), pp. 945–954. NTSA, Orlando (2007)
3. Charsky, D., Ressler, W.: Games are made for fun: Lessons on the effects of concept maps in the classroom use of computer games. Computers & Education 56, 604–615 (2011)
4. Csikszentmihalyi, M., Csikszentmihalyi, I.S. (eds.): Optimal experience: Psychological studies of flow in consciousness. Cambridge University Press (1922)
5. Faiola, A., Newlon, C., Pfaff, M., Smyslova, O.: Correlating the effects of flow and telepresence in virtual worlds: Enhancing our understanding of user behavior in game-based learning. Computers in Human Behavior 29(3), 1113–1121 (2012)
6. Fujimoto, M., Terada, T., Tsukamoto, M.: Physical Instructional Support System Using Virtual Avatars. In: Proceedings of the Fifth International Conference on Advances in Computer-Human Interactions, ACHI 2012, pp. 309–314 (2012)
7. Hamalainen, P., Ilmonen, T., Hoysniemi, J., Lindholm, M., Nykanen, A.: Martial arts in artificial reality. In: Proceedings of the SIGCHI Conference on Human Factors in Computing Systems, CHI 2005, pp. 781–790 (2005)
8. Hertzmann, A., Perlin, K.: Painterly rendering for video and interaction. In: Proceedings of the 1st International Symposium on Non-Photorealistic Animation and Rendering, pp. 7–12 (2000)

9. Hsu, H.J.: The Potential of Kinect as Interactive Educational Technology. In: Proceedings of 2nd International Conference on Education and Management Technology, vol. 13, pp. 334–338. IACSIT Press, Singapore (2011)
10. Hwang, G.J., Wu, P.H.: Advancements and trends in digital game-based learning research: a review of publications in selected journals from 2001 to 2010. British Journal of Educational Technology 43(1), E6–E10 (2012)
11. Khoshelham, K.: Accuracy analysis of kinect depth data. In: ISPRS Workshop Laser Scanning, vol. 38(1) (2011)
12. Kiili, K.: Digital game-based learning: Towards an experiential gaming model. The Internet and Higher Education 8(1), 13–24 (2005)
13. Ogawa, T., Kambayashi, Y.: Physical Instructional Support System Using Virtual Avatars. In: Proceedings of the Fifth International Conference on Advances in Computer-Human Interactions, ACHI 2012, pp. 262–265. IARIA, Valencia (2012)
14. Oh, Y., Yang, S.: Defining exergames and exergaming. In: Proceedings of Meaningful Play, pp. 1–17 (2010)
15. Phunsa, S., Potisarn, N., Tirakoat, S.: Edutainment-Thai Art of Self-Defense and Boxing by Motion Capture Technique. In: Proceedings of International Conference on Computer Modeling and Simulation, ICCMS 2009, Macau, pp. 152–155 (2009)
16. Prensky, M.: Digital game-based learning. McGraw Hill, New York (2000)

Exploring B-Learning Scenarios Using Fuzzy Logic-Based Modeling of Users' LMS Quality of Interaction in Ergonomics and Psychomotor Rehabilitation Academic Courses

Sofia B. Dias[1], José Alves Diniz[1], and Leontios J. Hadjileontiadis[2]

[1] Faculty of Human Kinetics, University of Lisbon, 1495-688 Cruz Quebrada, Lisbon, Portugal
{sbalula,jadiniz}@fmh.ulisboa.pt
[2] Department of Electrical and Computer Engineering, Aristotle University of Thessaloniki GR-54124 Thessaloniki, Greece
leontios@auth.gr

Abstract. The multidisciplinary field of human-computer interaction can be seen as an open-ended concept used to refer to the understanding of different relationships between people (users) and computers. The pedagogical planning within the blended learning environment with the users' quality of interaction (QoI) with the Learning Management System (LMS) is explored here. The required QoI (both for professors and students) is estimated by adopting a fuzzy logic-based modeling approach, namely FuzzyQoI, applied to LMS Moodle data from two undergraduate courses (i.e., Ergonomics and Psychomotor Rehabilitation) offered by a public higher education institution. In order to facilitate the understanding of the learning context and curricula organization of the both courses, the MindMup tool from the i-Treasures Pedagogical Planner (www.i-treasures.eu) is employed. The results presented can inspire LMS administrators to include the measure of QoI and reflect upon issues like system-quality, system-use and user-satisfaction into their current evaluation techniques of LMS based b-learning systems efficiency.

Keywords: Blended-Learning Scenarios, LMS Moodle, Quality of Interaction, Fuzzy Logic-Based modelling, Ergonomics and Psychomotor Rehabilitation courses, Human-Computer Interaction, Pedagogical Planning, i-Treasures.

1 Introduction

Education is a domain that is closely interconnected with the multidisciplinary field of human-computer interaction (HCI). The latter can be seen as an open-ended concept used to refer to the understanding of different relationships between people (users) and computers. HCI research examines both the improvement and evaluation of educational technologies (e.g., multimedia systems, interactive simulations, computer-assisted instructional materials) [1]. In fact, information and communications technologies (ICTs) have provided an unarguable potential for change, allowing the development of inclusive approaches regarding teaching and learning; however, there

M. Kurosu (Ed.): Human-Computer Interaction, Part III, HCII 2014, LNCS 8512, pp. 233–243, 2014.

is still insufficient knowledge regarding best practices in higher education institutions (HEIs), mainly concerning the use of online environments and communication tools [2]. Fortunately, intelligent and interactive Learning Management Systems (LMSs) appear to mobilize agents of innovation and provide flexibility and accessibility in educational contexts [3]. Additionally, a combination of traditional F2F and online learning has initiated the concept of blended (b-) learning, combining different delivery methodologies that have the potential to balance out and optimize the learning development, deployment costs and time [4].

To facilitate the realization of b-learning in practice, flexible and adaptable Course Management Systems (CMSs) are needed. LMS Moodle platform can be seen as such example, since it is a universal well-known LMS that supports b-learning [5], which belongs to the kind of LMS that is intentionally built on a particular pedagogical strategy (e.g., behaviorism, cognitivism, constructivism, connectivism), allowing management of user data, usability issues, and exhibits adaptation capabilities [6], [7]. On the one hand, the development of learning environments can be seen as an opportunity to implement/develop innovative tools, which enable the enhancement of a new quality of learning; on the other hand, the adoption of LMSs has led to the introduction of new instructional approaches and to the promotion of different educational contexts within the online environment. According to Conole et al. [8], the user's interaction with a LMS (e.g., Moodle) is actually realized within online learning environments (OLEs), which are characterized by fastness and immediacy, i.e., the ability to quickly access a vast amount of information coupled with a plurality of Web 2.0 tools. Apparently, the efficiency of the LMS depends on how effectively the users can access its multi-faceted benefits when interacting with it. However, an essential factor, in determining the efficacy of online instruction, is the users' quality of interaction (QoI) with LMSs; yet, in many cases, QoI has not been properly acquired, mainly, due to its inherent qualitative character.

2 Methodology

2.1 The *FuzzyQoI* Model

In the effort to develop a system of evaluation, e.g., the QoI of LMS users, intelligent systems can play an important role, i.e., can provide a model of the domain expert's evaluating system, using advanced features and adaptive functionality [9], [10]. Based on the latter, a Mamdani-type [11] fuzzy logic-based QoI modeling, namely FuzzyQoI scheme, was proposed by Dias and Diniz [12]. The FuzzyQoI model constitutes a Fuzzy Inference System (FIS) structure that is able to produce evaluative inferences upon input data. In particular, the latter correspond to the key-parameters and variables (metrics) of LMS Moodle involved within a b-learning environment concerning the user's interaction with the system, whereas the outputted inference forms a quantitative measure of the user's overall QoI [12]. The block diagram of the FuzzyQoI model is depicted in Fig. 1. As it is apparent from the latter, the users (professors/students at a HEI) interact with the LMS and the available 110 LMS Moodle metrics are corresponded to 12 categories that serve as inputs to the FIS structure.

In an effort to efficiently handle the 12 input variables, they are grouped in three groups and a nested sequence of five FISs (FIS1-FIS5) is used to form the proposed FuzzyQoI scheme. The first level includes FIS1, FIS2 and FIS3, which output the values of View (V), Addition (AD) and Alteration (AL), respectively. In the second level of inference, V, AD and AL are considered as intermediate variables and are used as inputs to the FIS4, which outputs the value of Action (AC). Finally, in the third level of inference, the AC is considered as intermediate variable and along with Time Period (TP) and Engagement Time (ET) rom LMS are used as inputs to the FIS5, which outputs the estimated QoI as the final output of the FuzzyQoI scheme [12]. For the construction of the knowledge base of the FuzzyQoI scheme, an expert in the field of analyzing LMS Moodle data within the context of b-learning was used, for defining the structure of the membership functions used for each FS and the corresponding IF/THEN fuzzy rules (600 in total). In particular, a three-level of trapezoid membership functions corresponding to Low, Medium and High values, respectively, are used for the FIS1-FIS4, whereas a five-level of trapezoid membership functions corresponding to Very Low, Low, Medium, High and Very High values were adopted for the final FIS5, increasing, this way, the resolution in the segmentation of the universe of discourse of the AC, TP and ET inputs and QoI output in the final FIS5. Analytical description of the FuzzyQoI model can be found in [12].

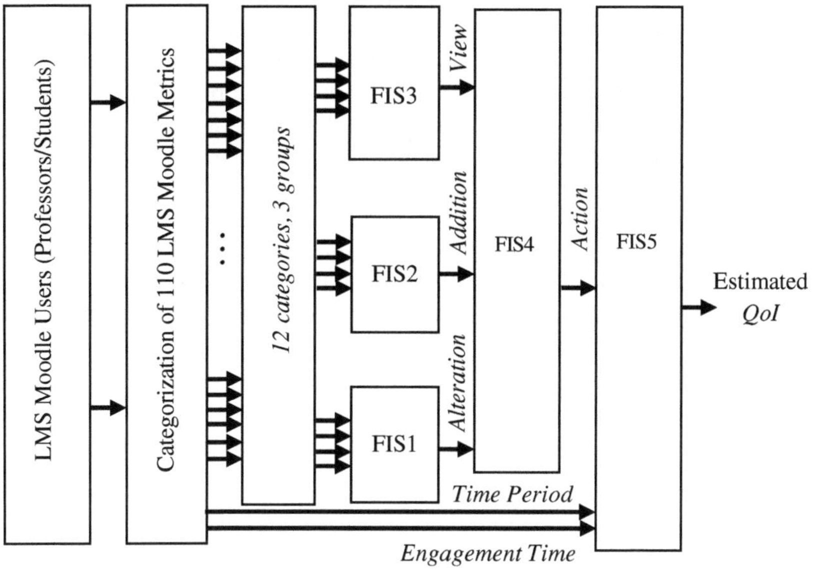

Fig. 1. Block-diagram of the FuzzyQoI model [12]

2.2 The Pedagogical Planning (PP)

The organization of educational scenarios during the LMS interaction is facilitated here with the adoption of the Pedagogical Planning (PP) [13]. The realization of the latter is achieved by adopting the MindMup tool from the i-Treasures Pedagogical Planner [14], which is a scalable cross-browser Web-based application developed in PHP, MySQL and JavaScript.

The PP is essentially a teacher-oriented online tool, yet in the way it is used here, it could serve as a combinatory tool that incorporates both designing and planning of the educational interventions and feedback from the realization of the b-learning delivered instruction. In this way, causal relations between professors' and students' at the level of their LMS-based QoI could be identified and professors' metacognitive processes could be fired towards the enhancement of their pedagogical planning and delivery.

The PP comprises of both authoring and display capabilities, with specially designed functions and interface features in both cases. In particular, target population, learning context, content domain, objectives and metrics, along with available tools (such as MindMup), are the core characteristics of the PP (www.i-treasures.eu).

3 Dataset and Related Courses Principal Components

Here, the FuzzyQoI [12], was applied to LMS Moodle data from two undergraduate courses, i.e., Ergonomics and Psychomotor Rehabilitation, offered by a public HEI (Faculty of Human Kinetics, University of Lisbon, Portugal). The data from 73 students and 13 professors, including 69247 interactions in total (40109 from Ergonomics Course and 29138 from Psychomotor Rehabilitation Course), were used and analyzed for the duration of two academic semesters, corresponding to a 51-week LMS Moodle usage time-period (August 26, 2009-August 18, 2010).

In order to identify any possible changes in the users' interaction behavior correlated with a specific time-period section, the resulted time-period sections (e.g., semesters, exams, interruptions) were used as landmarks. More specifically, the Semester 1 (S1) and Semester 2 (S2) are denoted on the graphs with the vertical solid lines located at weeks 2 and 16 (S1) and weeks 23 and 38 (S2) (see Figs. 4-7); the Interruptions are defined as: Christmas (weeks 16-18), Carnival (weeks 24-25), and Easter (weeks 30-31).

Figures 2 and 3 illustrate the PP of the both courses in the form of the MindMup output, where the principal components, i.e., scientific domains, learning objectives, learning context, LMS Moodle tools and forms of assessment, are shown in the form of connected branches.

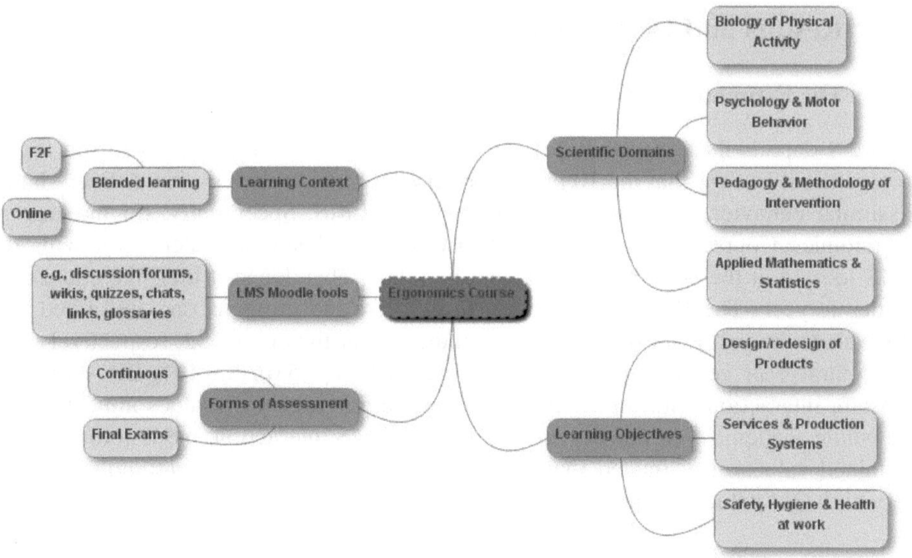

Fig. 2. The MindMup output of the PP of the Ergonomics course context

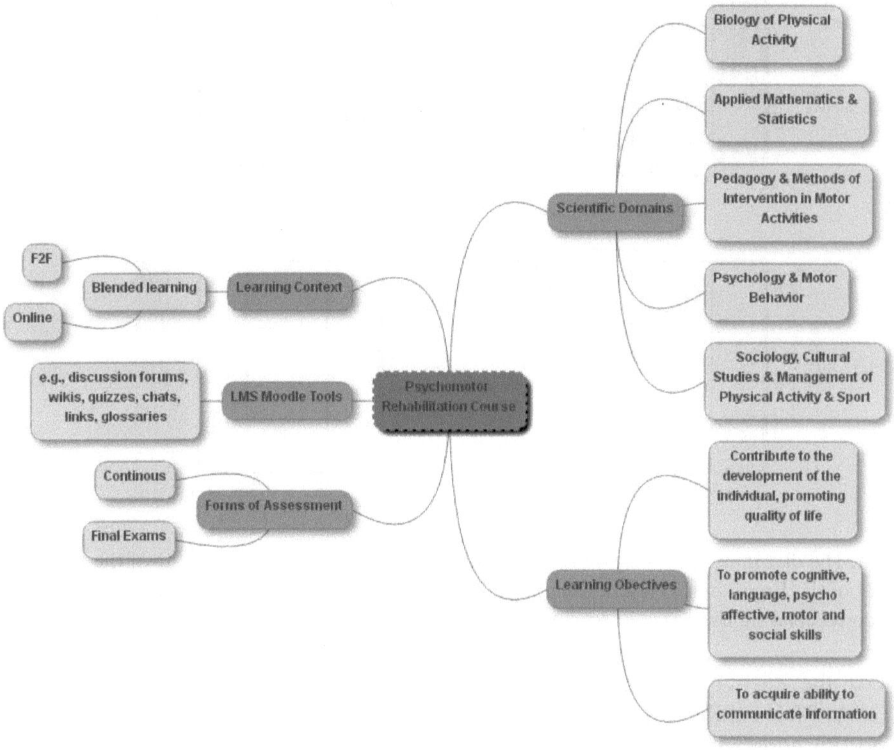

Fig. 3. The MindMup output of the PP of the Psychomotor Rehabilitation course context

4 Results and Discussion

4.1 The Estimated QoI

Figure 4 depicts the estimated QoI for all cases explored. In particular, from Fig. 4 (top panel) it is clear that the 10 professors incorporated in each course delivery had a dissimilar behavior, regarding their QoI with the LMS. Specifically, for the case of Ergonomics Course (EC), Professor #4-EC exhibited smooth interaction with the LMS located at the beginning of S1, and he totally abandoned it until the end of the academic year. The Professors #3 and #2-EC, like the previous one, exhibited low QoI values, however, located at the beginning and at the end of S2, respectively. On the contrary, in general, all the other Professors (#{1,5,6,7,8,9,10})-EC showed a constant interaction with the LMS, exhibiting her/his high QoI values almost across the whole academic year; however, based on S1 LMS interaction, more notorious and sustained values of estimated QoI was identified (i.e., reaching, continuously, high-very high QoI values for more than one week) compared to S2.

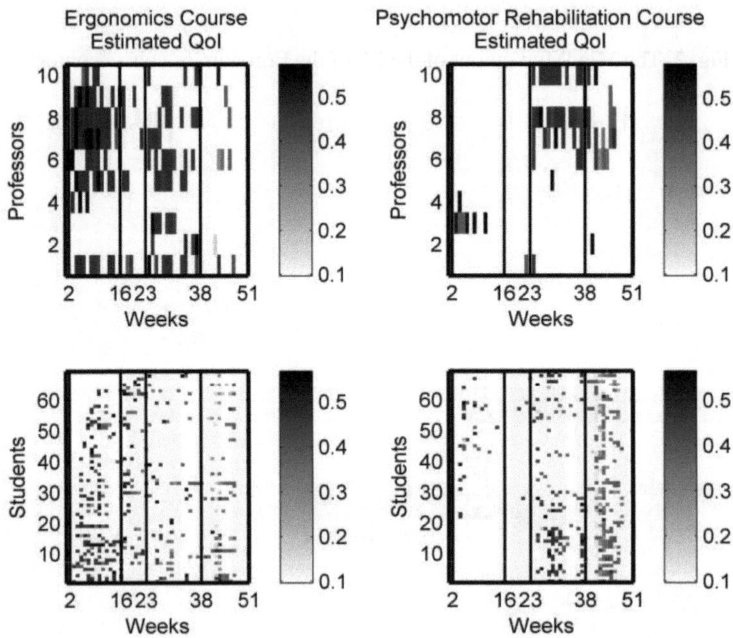

Fig. 4. The distribution of the estimated output QoI from the FIS 5 (see Fig. 1) of the FuzzyQoI model of the Ergonomics (left column) and Psychomotor Rehabilitation (right column) courses and corresponding users (professors: top, students: bottom)

For the case of Psychomotor Rehabilitation Course (PRC), some Professors (#{3,4})-PRC exhibited sparse interaction with the LMS, just located at the beginning of S1. In contrast, all other Professors (#{1,2,5,6,7,8,9,10})-PRC just initiated the LMS-based process in the S2; however, in some weeks, a high-very high estimated

QoI was identified for the Professors #7, #8 and #10-PRC, moving toward a more productive behavior, in general. Concerning the students' QoI values (Fig. 4: bottom panel), they were higher at S1 rather than in S2 for the case of EC, whereas the opposite effect was noticed for the PRC case.

Focusing at the mean estimated QoI shown in Figure 5, it is clear that the interaction with LMS for both users (professors and students) was higher in the case of the EC (top panel) than the case of PRC (bottom panel). Almost across the whole academic year, in the case of the PRC, the students showed a tendency to exhibit synchronized QoIs with the professors; however, in the case of the EC more synchronization was evident during the period of the S1.

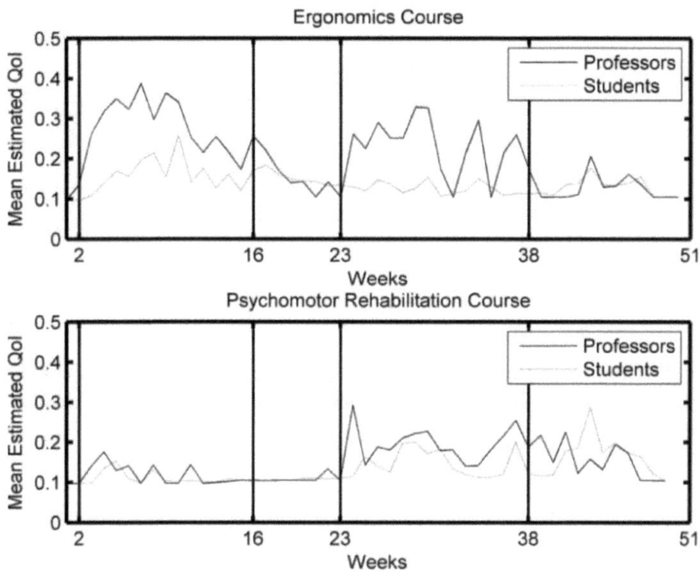

Fig. 5. The mean estimated QoI of the EC (top panel) and PRC (bottom panel) courses and corresponding users (professors: black line, students: gray line)

4.2 Deeping into the Results: Common Users

In the two courses, some common users (three professors and four students) appeared. Focusing at their QoIs it can be seen from the Figure 6 (top panel) that the three common professors had a dissimilar behavior in each course, regarding their QoI with the LMS. Focusing on Professor #1's performance in both courses, it is clear that he exhibited low interaction with the LMS in EC; however, in the S1, a more productive and sustained behavior was identified for the PRC case.

Just appearing in S2, Professors #2 and #3 seem to interact with LMS in a more effective way in PRC rather than EC. In general, regarding the students' QoI values (Figure 6: bottom panel), they exhibited low QoI values in both courses. In particular, for the PRC is possible to understand that all students interacted with the LMS at least more than one week across the whole academic year. Focusing at the mean estimated

QoIs shown in Figure 7, it is clear that the mean interaction with LMS for both courses was higher in the S2. In fact, both users, in both courses, initiated the LMS-based process at the beginning and mid of S1 with apparent motivation.

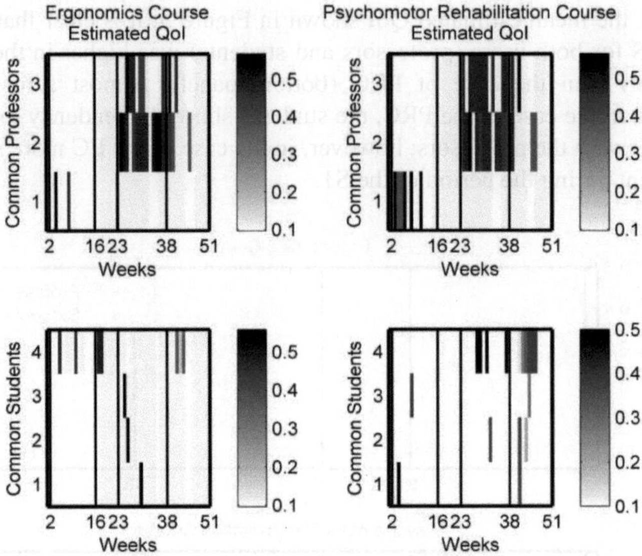

Fig. 6. The distribution of the estimated QoI of the FuzzyQoI model of the Common Users of the EC (left column) and PRC (right column) and corresponding users (professors: top, students: bottom)

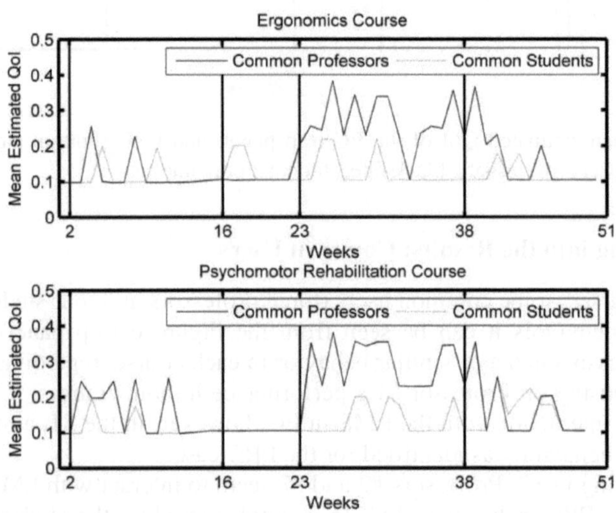

Fig. 7. The mean estimated QoI of the Common Users of the EC (top panel) and PRC (bottom panel) and corresponding users (professors: black line, students: gray line)

The results described above could be reflected to PP of Figs. 2 and 3, based on b-learning scenarios, setting the shift towards more interactive and appealing online LMS Moodle resources (e.g., quizzes, discussion forums, blogs, videos, e-portfolios), which could accompany the F2F interaction and complement the effort towards developing a more multifaceted and enriched way of learning. Practically speaking, it is apparent that the proposed approach could be extended to various educational scenarios and use-cases (within [15] and outside the i-Treasures project) posing a dynamic character to the role of LMS towards an intelligent LMS [16], assisting both teachers and students to enhance the quality of the educational environment.

4.3 Correlation Analysis Results

Stemming from the results of Figs. 5 and 7, a correlation analysis that explored any possible association between the mean QoI values of the professors' and students' of both courses (i.e., EC and PRC) was carried out. In particular, the cross-correlation R (with probability of false alarm p) along with the coefficient of determination R^2 across users/courses and between/within subjects were estimated (see Table 1).

Table 1. Cross-correlation R (with probability of false alarm p) along with the coefficient of determination R^2 across users/courses and between/within subjects. Bold values indicate statistically significant cross-correlations ($p < 0.05$). EC: Ergonomics Course; PRC: Psychomotor Rehabilitation Course.

Between subjects		
	Professors (n=10)	Students (n=69)
	PRC	PRC
EC	$R = 0.114$ ($p = 0.446$) $R^2 = 0.013$	$R = -0.0411$ ($p = 0.774$) $R^2 = 0.0017$
Within subjects		
	Common Professors (n=3)	Common Students (n=4)
	PRC	PRC
EC	$\mathbf{R = 0.8337}$ ($p = 10^{-13}$) $R^2 = 0.6951$	$R = -0.0163$ ($p = 0.9115$) $R^2 = 2.6 \times 10^{-4}$
Between subjects		
	EC	PRC
	Professors (n=10)	Professors (n=10)
Students (n=69)	$\mathbf{R = 0.5090}$ ($p = 0.0002$) $R^2 = 0.2591$	$\mathbf{R = 0.4786}$ ($p = 0.0005$) $R^2 = 0.2291$
Within subjects		
	EC	PRC
	Common Professors (n=3)	Common Professors (n=3)
Common Students (n=4)	$R = 0.160$ ($p = 0.2670$) $R^2 = 0.0256$	$\mathbf{R = 0.3068}$ ($p = 0.0320$) $R^2 = 0.0941$

From Table 1, when considering the "between subjects" analysis, two statistically significant estimates of R across users and courses, namely for professors' and students' of EC ($R = 0.5090$) and PRC ($R = 0.4786$), were found. Moreover, concerning the common users (i.e., "within subjects" analysis), a strong R value was exhibited for common professors across courses ($R = 0.8337$). In addition, only one statistically significant estimate of R was exhibited, namely across common professors and common students of PRC ($R = 0.3068$).

In general, we notice that, unlike the common students, the common professors act almost similarly regarding their mean QoI at both courses and that most of the students are in a similar pathway with the LMS behavior of professors. These trends reveal the dependencies at the LMS Moodle interaction of the OLE users, revealing the existence of a somehow "causality" between professors and students, which should be taken into account in the design and planning of the online-related resources (see Figs. 2 and 3), in an effort to maximize the effective engagement of all stakeholders in the OLE.

5 Conclusions

Overall, the results have shown the potential role of QoI to shift the educational scenarios and strategies towards a more dynamic design, yet taking into consideration the inherent tendencies and attitudes of the users' interaction within the b-learning context. Furthermore, LMS-based educational strategies could also be reflected in areas that incorporate HCI for practical paradigms, such as the educational scenarios of the use cases of the i-Treasure platform, facilitating the capturing of the intangible cultural treasures. Finally, among others, it is our expectation that the results presented here can inspire LMS administrators to include the measure of QoI and reflect upon issues like system-quality/use/satisfaction into their current evaluation techniques of LMS based b-learning systems efficiency.

Acknowledgements. This work has received funding from the EU Seventh Framework Programme FP7-ICT-2011-9-ICT-2011.8.2, under the grant agreement n° 600676: "i-Treasures" Project (www.i-treasures.eu). The authors also thank Dr. C. Ferreira at FHK for his assistance in the retrieval of the LMS Moodle data.

References

1. Myers, B., Hollan, J., Cruz, I., Bryson, S., Bulterman, D., Catarci, T., Citrin, W., Cruz, I., Glinert, E., Grudin, J., Hollan, J., Ioannidis, Y., Jacob, R., John, B., Kurlander, D., Myers, B., Olsen, D., Pausch, R., Shieber, S., Shneiderman, B., Stasko, J., Strong, G., Wittenburg, K.: Strategic directions in human-computer interaction. ACM Computing Surveys (CSUR) 28(4), 794–809 (1996)
2. Redecker, C., Ala-Mutka, K., Bacigalupo, M., Ferrari, A., Punie, Y.: Learning 2.0: The impact of web 2.0 Innovations on Education and Training in Europe. Joint Research Centre (JRC)-Institute for Prospective Technological Studies (2009), `http://is.jrc.ec.europa.eu/pages/Learning-2.0.html`

3. Pirani, Z., Sasikumar, M.: Accessibility Issues in Learning Management Systems for Learning Disabled: A Survey. In: Thampi, S.M., Abraham, A., Pal, S.K., Rodriguez, J.M.C. (eds.) Recent Advances in Intelligent Informatics. AISC, vol. 235, pp. 253–264. Springer, Heidelberg (2014)
4. Oliver, M., Trigwell, K.: Can 'Blended Learning' Be Redeemed? E-learning and Digital Media 2(1), 17–26 (2005)
5. Aberdour, M.: Open Source Learning Management System. EPIC Whitepaper (2007), http://www.epic.co.uk/content/news/oct_07/whitepaper.pdf
6. Graf, S.: Adaptivity in Learning Management Systems Focussing on Learning Styles. PhD Thesis, Vienna University of Technology, AU (2007), http://sgraf.athabascau.ca/publications/PhDthesis_SabineGraf.pdf
7. Kladich, S., Ives, C., Parker, N., Graf, S.: Extending the AAT Tool with a User-Friendly and Powerful Mechanism to Retrieve Complex Information from Educational Log Data. In: Holzinger, A., Pasi, G. (eds.) HCI-KDD 2013. LNCS, vol. 7947, pp. 334–341. Springer, Heidelberg (2013)
8. Conole, G., de Laat, M., Darby, J.: 'Disruptive technologies', 'pedagogical innovation': What's new? Findings from an in-depth study of students' use and perception of technology. Comput. Educ. 50(2), 511–524 (2008)
9. Levy, Y.A., Weld, S.D.: Intelligent internet systems. Artif. Intel. 118, 1–14 (2000)
10. Hadjileontiadou, S.J., Nikolaidou, G.N., Hadjileontiadis, L.J., Balafoutas, G.N.: On enhancing on-line collaboration using fuzzy logic modeling. Educ. Tech. Soc. 7(2), 68–81 (2004)
11. Tsoukalas, H.L., Uhrig, R.E.: Fuzzy and neural approaches in engineering. Wiley & Sons, New York (1996)
12. Dias, S.B., Diniz, J.A.: FuzzyQoI Model: A fuzzy logic-based modelling of users' quality of interaction with a learning management system under blended learning. Comput. Educ. 69, 38–59 (2013), doi:10.1016/j.compedu.2013.06.016
13. Olimpo, G., Bottino, R.M., Earp, J., Ott, M., Pozzi, F., Tavella, M.: Pedagogical plans as communication oriented objects. Comput. Educ. 55(2), 476–488 (2010)
14. Bottino, R., Earp, J., Olimpo, G., Ott, M., Pozzi, F., Tavella, M.: Supporting the design of pilot learning activities with the Pedagogical Plan Manager. In: Kendall, M., Samways, B. (eds.) Learning to live in the Knowledge Society. Springer (2008)
15. Dias, S.B., Diniz, J.A., Hadjileontiadis, L.J.: On Enhancing Blended-Learning Scenarios Through Fuzzy Logic-Based Modeling of Users' LMS Quality of Interaction: The Rare & Contemporary Dance Paradigms. In: Grammalidis, N., Dimitropoulos, K., Ioannides, M. (eds.) (Co-Chairs) IAMICH/VISIGRAPP 2014, Lisbon, Portugal, January 5-8 (2014a)
16. Dias, S.B., Diniz, J.A., Hadjileontiadis, L.J.: Towards an Intelligent Learning Management System Under Blended Learning: Trends, Profiles and Modelling Perspectives. In: Kacprzyk, J., Jain, L.C. (eds.) Intelligent Systems Reference Library, vol. 59, Springer, Heidelberg (2014b) ISBN: 978-3-319-02077-8

User Interfaces of Mobile Exergames

Tim Dutz[1], Sandro Hardy[1], Martin Knöll[2], Stefan Göbel[1], and Ralf Steinmetz[1]

[1] Multimedia Communications Lab, Technische Universitaet Darmstadt, Germany
[2] Department of Architecture, Technische Universitaet Darmstadt, Germany
{tim.dutz,sandro.hardy,stefan.goebel,
ralf.steinmetz}@kom.tu-darmstadt.de,
knoell@stadt.tu-darmstadt.de

Abstract. Exergames are video games that require the player to be physically active. They can be roughly grouped into two categories, namely indoor exergames that are usually being played in the confines of one's living room, and mobile exergames, which run on a user's smartphone and can be played outside. While indoor exergames have been able to establish themselves as a popular type of video game, mobile exergames are still far and few between. An explanation for this phenomenon may lie in the difficulty of designing user interfaces for mobile exergames. This contribution analyzes the user interfaces of various existing mobile exergames and fitness applications, and proposes a methodology for the creation of such games.

Keywords: Serious Games, Exergames, Mobile Games, User Interfaces.

1 On Indoor Exergames

The purpose of a serious (video) game is to have a positive effect on the player besides mere entertainment [1]. This is usually achieved by motivating the player through the game mechanics to perform a task that she would otherwise consider dull or tedious, such as solving mathematical formulas, or going for a run. Games that motivate their players to be physically active are called "fitness games" or "exergames" (the latter being a commingling of the words "exercise" and "game"), and there are many examples for both indoor exergames played in front of one's PC monitor or TV screen, and mobile exergames, which are played using a smartphone or another type of mobile device while the player is out and about.

In 2006, Nintendo released the game *Wii Sports* for its game console *Wii*. *Wii Sports* requires the player to perform certain movements with her arms and upper body in order to succeed in various mini-games such as tennis or golf. The player's movements are tracked by the accelerometer sensors within the wireless *Wii Remote* device, which the user has to hold in her hand(s) while playing. Because the movements required for playing the mini-games are not exactly extensive and can even be reduced further to but a flick of the hand while sitting on a couch [2], it is questionable whether *Wii Sports* actually qualifies as a full-fledged exergame, although studies have shown that frequent playing can indeed contribute to weight management [3].

M. Kurosu (Ed.): Human-Computer Interaction, Part III, HCII 2014, LNCS 8512, pp. 244–255, 2014.

Nevertheless, *Wii Sports* clearly demonstrated the demand for games that integrate physical activity into their gameplay and that promise to turn the chore of working out into a more interesting and entertaining experience: in early 2014 – more than seven years after its release – *Wii Sports* was still the commercially most successful video game up to date with almost 82 million copies sold in total [4, 5]. But while *Wii Sports* may be the most successful representative of indoor fitness games, it was neither the first, nor the last of its kind.

A very early example of this type of game is Konami's *Dance Dance Revolution* (abbr. DDR). The US release of the first DDR game dates back to 1999, and the series has spawned many new releases since. It also comes to no surprise that Nintendo tried to repeat the success of *Wii Sports* and released more exergames for its console, of which the two most successful ones are *Wii Fit*, released in the US in 2008, and its successor *Wii Fit Plus,* released in 2010. As of early 2014, the combined sales of the two games exceeded 45 million units [6, 7]. *Wii Fit* is sometimes attributed as being the first real indoor exergame [8], which probably comes from its no-nonsense attitude when compared to earlier fitness games such as *Dance Dance Revolution* or *Wii Sports*. Instead, there is a clear focus on fitness and self-improvement, reflected in aspects like virtual trainers, training plans, and performance statistics.

A core challenge of all exergames is to determine the player's activities (and to adapt the game accordingly), and to that end, both *Dance Dance Revolution* and *Wii Fit* rely primarily on sensor mats placed on the (living room) floor. Of course, the utilization of such mats implies that the player has to be fairly stationary while playing the corresponding games. In late 2010, Microsoft introduced the Kinect sensor technology for the *Xbox 360* video game console and released a more powerful second-generation Kinect sensor three years later. The Kinect sensor is capable of tracking the movements of multiple persons within a distance of a few meters without requiring them to carry any type of sensor or marker in their hands or on their body. This practically allows complete freedom of movement while playing, at least within the confines of one's living room. Microsoft's game *Xbox Fitness,* released in late 2013 for the *Xbox One,* tries to tap into that potential. Very similar to the way that Nintendo gradually changed the character of its indoor exergames over time, Microsoft picked a much more serious tone for *Xbox Fitness* when compared to earlier fitness game releases such as *Kinect Adventures!* or *Kinect Sports. Xbox Fitness* now clearly targets adult users with a primary interest in improving their physical fitness. Apparently, indoor exergaming is coming of age.

This correlates with the fact that indoor exergames and supporting technologies such as sensors mats and Kinect sensors are not only relevant to the entertainment industry. Various research groups focus on the development of indoor exergames and/or on the analysis of the effects that such games have on their players. Often, the focus of such work lies either on children [9], or on senior users [10]. An interdisciplinary team of psychologists, sport scientists, and engineers developed a theoretical model for the customization of indoor exergames to the needs of such specific groups [11]. Summing up this introductory chapter, we find that in early 2014, indoor exergames have been both an established type of video game as well as a subject of scientific interest for more than a decade.

2 On Mobile Exergames

Interestingly, the situation changes when we look at the mobile counterparts of such games. Contrary to indoor exergames such as *Wii Fit* or *Xbox Fitness*, mobile exergames are played on mobile devices – oftentimes smartphones – and usually do not rely on external appliances such as sensor mats or TV screens. In other words: all the user needs to play such games is a smartphone (and possibly a pair of running shoes). Since the introduction of Apple's iPhone in 2007, smartphones have continued to grow in popularity and more than one billion units have been sold in 2013 alone [12]. Due to this, chances are that a given person already has one of these devices available – different to, for example, the aforementioned *Nintendo Wii* gaming console.

Indeed, this is just one of the reasons why in theory, the advantages that mobile exergames have over stationary ones are manifold. The second advantage is the pervasiveness of these games, as many of them can be played wherever and whenever the player pleases, for instance during travel. In this regard, mobile exergames profit from the smartphone characteristics that differentiate such devices from classic gaming devices such as PCs or video game consoles [13]: smartphones are *mobile* (light and small enough to be carried around in a pocket or hand), *available* (rarely more than an arms-length away), and *sensitive* (capable of determining many aspects of the user's contextual situation thanks to a multitude of integrated sensors). Finally, a good amount of people seems to generally prefer the outdoors when it comes to sports, and mobile exergames go well with such activities.

However, despite these alleged benefits, we find that only a small number of mobile exergames actually exists. An early mobile exergame and a game still being played is *Geocaching*. At its core, the game is a global treasure hunt, with people hiding so-called caches, small waterproof boxes containing some type of "treasure". The coordinates of such a cache are then made publically available on the Internet by its owner and other players will use this information to navigate to the cache's position and then try to find its exact hiding place. The first caches were hidden in the year 2000 [14], and early geocachers used handheld GPS trackers to find them. Today, smartphones with integrated GPS modules and cellular phone network enabled Internet access make playing *Geocaching* easy and consequently, the game enjoys a wide popularity. In early 2014, the official *Geocaching* website knew of more than two million registered caches and more than six million registered players [14].

Figure 1 shows a few screenshots of the official *Geocaching* application by Groundspeak Inc. As one can see from the screenshots, the user starts with viewing a list of nearby caches (depending on the user's position as determined by her smartphone's GPS module). If the user selects a cache from the list, she is shown a map that helps her navigate to the cache's hiding place. Alternatively, she can also rely on a compass to orientate herself. As many caches are located in forests and away from towns, geocaching almost always involves a good amount of walking and occasionally even climbing. Additionally, many caches are hidden extremely well in hollow trees or beneath bushes and as such, the player also needs to search her environment thoroughly once she has reached the approximate hiding place. This makes *Geocaching* a mobile exergame, even if the energy expenditure (EE) of playing it will oftentimes not be higher than walking the dog.

Fig. 1. Geocaching application [14]

Geocaching is also a so-called location-based game, a game in which the physical location of the player, determined by GPS, has influence on the way that the game plays. In other words: changing one's location, usually by foot, is an integral part of these games. Various location-based services and games exist, such as *Yelp* [15] and *Foursquare* [16], but of all the location-based games and services currently available, the game *Ingress* [17] is both the most interesting and the most successful one. In *Ingress*, players initially get to choose one of two factions and are then expected go out and conquer virtual portals for their team. These portals can be found in the vicinity of distinctive real-world structures, such as statues. If a player is close enough to a portal (that is, the corresponding real-world location), she can attempt to "conquer" it for her team by pressing the according GUI buttons. Such interactions with portals will gain the player virtual items and experience which are both required to progress through the game.

Similar to *Geocaching*, *Ingress* requires players to physically move to specific locations, and it is very clear about this aspect of the game, as can be seen from the left screenshot in figure 2. The central screenshot shows the map view that allows players to locate portals in their vicinity (note the two different colors representing control areas of the factions). The right image shows the portal interaction panel that becomes available once the player gets close enough to a portal. Although *Ingress* can be interpreted as being a mobile exergame, the aspect of movement is not as relevant to *Ingress* as it is to *Geocaching*. This is because in *Ingress*, a player can theoretically acquire virtual items and experience by conquering the same portals over and over again, for instance portals that are close to her home or working place. Furthermore, the player can acquire so-called "portal keys" of specific portals which will subsequently allow her to interact with these portals even if not being in their vicinity.

Fig. 2. Ingress [17]

Although location-based games such as *Geocaching* and *Ingress* require their players to change their location while playing, this can usually be done by walking or even by using a car. Consequently, the EE of such games is oftentimes low. This cannot be said for distance-based exergames, as they require players to cover distances by running or cycling. Different to location-based games, distance-based games are not bound to specific locations for which the "real-world anchors" that connect the virtual to the real-world (such as the caches of *Geocaching* and the portals of *Ingress*) have been set up a priori. Instead, the single parameter relevant to these games is the user's speed, which can be determined by either the smartphone's GPS module or its accelerometer. We find that many of the fitness applications used by runners and cyclers to track their training performances contain elements of gamification to make workout sessions more interesting, but that only a few actual distance-based games exist.

Starting with gamification in fitness applications, a good example is the *NikeFuel* concept of the *Nike+* running application [18]. For each training session, users are awarded *NikeFuel*, with the amount depending on the intensity of their training. *NikeFuel* is supposed to be a measurement unit for one's training performance and can be used for the comparison with other users. Another approach for gamification in fitness applications is the "Story Running" mode of the *Runtastic* application [19]. These *Story Runs* are audio books that mix spoken text passages and music, to which the user listens to while running. In the story "The Carrier of Truth", for example, the player listens to an actor that comments his ongoing escape from the Alcatraz prison. The identification with this actor is supposed to motivate the user to run faster and longer than usually. However, *Runtastic's* Story Running mode is not interactive and the user simply listens to the audio book while running, during which the application's user interface displays the usual information such as a map and the player's pace.

One of the few actual distance-based games is *Zombies, Run!* [20]. The game is based on the same core mechanic as *Runtastic's* Story Running, namely a series of audio books to which the player listens to while running. In the case of *Zombies, Run!*, these stories tell of a group of people trying to survive in a post-apocalyptic world of zombies. The survivors have managed to establish a small base, but members of the community have to leave the safe walls every now and then to gather supplies such as food and medicine from the outside world. These are the "runners", and the user is one of them, being addressed to as "Runner 5" by the voice actors.

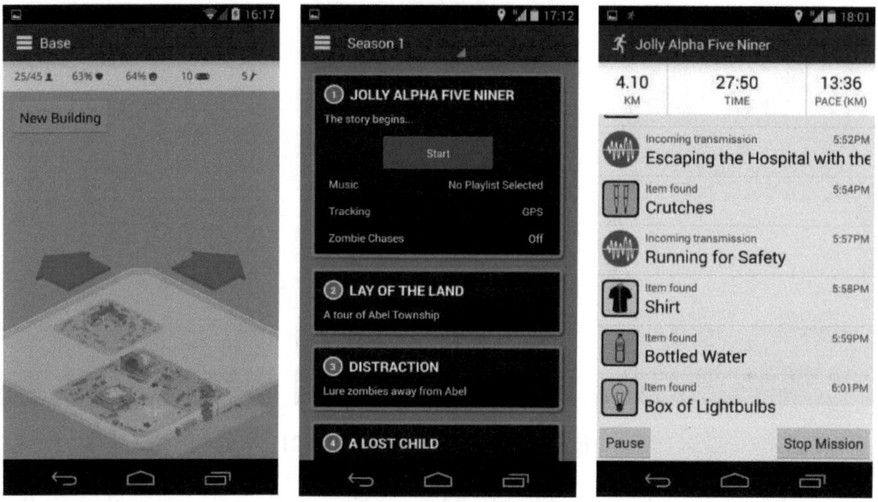

Fig. 3. Zombies, Run! [20]

While the story itself is supposed to be motivating, *Zombies, Run!* goes beyond *Runtastic's* Story Running by also providing an additional off-training game mode in which the player gets to manage her virtual community of survivors, for instance by adding new buildings to the base or improving existing ones. For all these actions, the player needs resources and she acquires those by physically running while listening to the stories. Figure 3 shows screenshots of *Zombies, Run!*, whereby the left screenshot shows the player's base (the game's off-training mode), the central screenshot the mission selection screen, and the right screenshot the application's main screen during a training session. We can see that besides a few performance statistics, such as the running distance and time, the training screen primarily shows the virtual supplies that the player has "picked up".

It is important to realize that *Zombies, Run!* is not a location-based game. The application uses the smartphone's GPS module or its accelerometer sensor to measure the distance that the player has covered, but the supplies that she gathers are not actually distributed in her surroundings – they are randomly rewarded during a training session. This means that instead of following a route through the city or the woods, the player could also run in circles on a dirt track and still gather the same amount of virtual supplies. To make the game more challenging, *Zombies, Run!* features an optional mode called "Zombie Chases". If activated by the player, virtual zombies may randomly appear during a session. The player then needs to "outrun" these zombies by increasing her speed for a certain time, or lose all virtual supplies she has gathered up to this point. During zombie chases, the approaching zombies are represented by grunts and heavy breathing which is getting louder and more intense when the player is in danger of being caught by the zombies (because she is too slow).

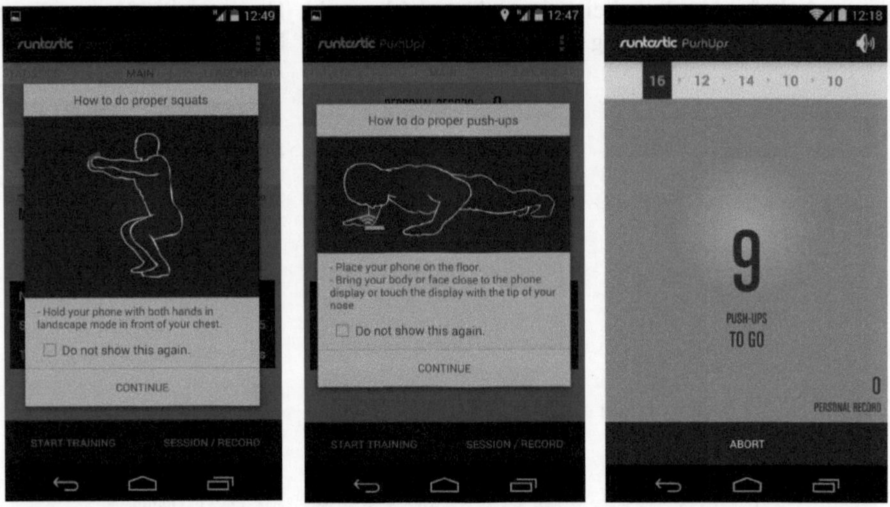

Fig. 4. Runtastic Pumpit apps [21]

All applications and games introduced up to here focus on motivating walking, running, and/or cycling activities – that is, training of the lower limbs and the cardio-vascular system. Almost no applications try to use the smartphone's integrated sensors to support upper body training. Notable exceptions are the *Runtastic Pumpit* apps that use the smartphone's sensors to determine the number of push-ups, sit-ups, pull-ups, or squats that the user has performed. To this end, the user has to hold the smartphone in a proper way, as can be seen from the instructions on the left and central screenshots in figure 4. The right screenshot shows the GUI while the user is performing push-ups.

3 A Methodology for Interfaces of Mobile Exergames

As part of our work at the Technische Universitaet Darmstadt, we have created the location-based exergame *PacStudent* [22], which is based on the famous arcade game *Pac-Man*. The game is played on a smartphone and requires players to run along predefined lanes and collect virtual gold coins while trying to evade virtual ghosts. *PacStudent* uses the smartphone's GPS module to determine the real-world location of the player and then positions the virtual player icon on the virtual map accordingly. Being a classic location-based game, the game area where the game should be played at (the virtual game's real-world anchor) must be defined upfront by the developers. Ideally, the corresponding real-world location already provides for paths or roads that can function as lanes for the game. The current version of *PacStudent* can be played at various locations at Darmstadt, Germany, among them the public park "Prinz-Georgs-Garten" which offers a nice layout of paths.

Fig. 5. PacStudent [22]

Figure 5 shows screenshots of the *PacStudent* game. To the left is the game area selection screen. The main interface of the game itself is shown on the central screenshot. The right screenshot shows the game's statistic screen. The user interface of *PacStudent* is fairly simple: the player sees a virtual map of her surroundings on the screen, along a virtual representation of herself (the black triangle that can be seen on the central screenshot), the virtual coins that she is supposed to collect (the golden ovals) and the virtual ghosts that she is supposed to evade (the red suns). Such a 2D-interface is typical for location-based games – but for this specific case, it is far from being optimal. Due to the inevitable shaking of the screen while running, the player is forced to stop every now and then in order to reorientate herself in the virtual world. Only through this, she can figure out where the ghosts and the remaining coins are at. However, while the player is standing still, the enemies keep moving and thus, the player runs the risk of being caught by one of them, simply because she is forced to pause and look at the smartphone's screen.

The aim of designing a better interface for *PacStudent* first led to an analysis of user interfaces of existing, popular mobile exergames (as detailed in chapter 2) and then to the realization that the complexity of the user interface must strongly correlate with the intensity of movement that is required for playing the game. As pointed out by Sinclair et al. [23], players must be able to focus on a narrow field of attention in order to feel entertained. If their attention lies elsewhere such as the road ahead, the game should not require too much of their concentration. Vice versa, if the player is not preoccupied with a lot of physical activity, the game interface should be able to capture the player's attention for an extended period of time. Thus, interfaces of exergames must balance the two factors complexity of interaction and intensity of movement. While this already holds true for all exergames, an additional challenge of mobile exergames is that the smartphone's that they are being played on are both input devices and output devices at the same time. This differentiates mobile exergames from most indoor exergames such as *Wii Fit*, where there is a clear separation between the input device (in this specific case the *Wii Balance Board* sensor mat) and the output device (usually a TV screen). The main effect of this is that due to the steadiness of gaze and hand that is required for interacting with small elements on the smartphone's screen, the usage of most graphical user interfaces is impracticable when the user is performing even just mildly intense physical activities. And obviously, this holds even truer for all types of activities that require both hands (such as pull-ups).

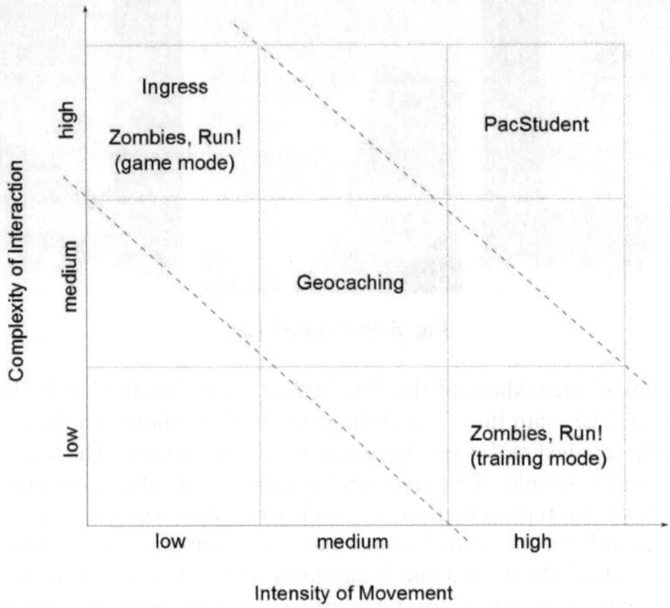

Fig. 6. The Focus Corridor

Figure 6 visualizes what we call the "focus corridor": the range of optimal combinations of user interface complexity and movement intensity for mobile exergames. Combinations "below" the corridor are likely to bore the player, as the amount of focus that is required to maintain her current level of physical activity (such as walking) is low enough to allow for complex interactions with the smartphone, but the game cannot provide for such. Accordingly, combinations "above" the focus corridor are likely to stress the player, because the intensity of her physical activity does technically hinder complex interactions with the device, but the game demands them nevertheless.

Two questions arise naturally from these considerations. The first question is how to classify the intensity of movement; the second question is how to rate the level of interaction complexity. Starting with the first question, we have already found that a difference between indoor exergames and mobile exergames lies in the fact that for the latter, the smartphone is both the input device and the output device. This influences the extent to which the player can interact with the game and consequently, we can classify the level of physical activity in the context of mobile exergames as such:

- **Low-intensity activities** in the context of mobile exergames are all types of physical activity that enable the user to have both a steady view on her smartphone's screen and a steady hand for interacting with on-screen elements. Examples for this type of activity are sitting, standing, and walking.
- **Medium-intensity activities** are all those activities that prevent either a steady gaze on the smartphone's screen or a steady hand to interact with on-screen elements. Examples are various types of activities that involve the upper-limb such as push-ups, and normal cycling (when the smartphone is mounted to the handlebar).
- **High-intensity activities** are activities that prevent both a steady gaze and a steady hand, such as running and pull-ups.

For the interaction complexity, we propose the following classification:

- **Low-complexity interfaces** in the context of mobile exergames are primarily non-graphical interfaces, such as voice output and input, as well as haptic feedback (i.e., vibration). Depending on the nature of physical activity required for playing the game, very simple graphical user interfaces such as a single large button or a large text label that encompass the entire screen may or may not be counted among low complexity interfaces.
- **Medium-complexity interfaces** for mobile exergames are comparably simple 2D graphical user interfaces with large elements. For some activities such as running, augmented reality interfaces that enhance the camera feed of the smartphone with virtual elements can also be considered medium-complexity, as they allow runners to both focus on the road ahead and to receive visual feedback from the game at the same time.
- **High-complexity interfaces** for mobile exergames are complex 2D interfaces with small elements (such as the game mode in *Zombies, Run!*) and all kinds of 3D interfaces that require the player to use multi-touch gestures (such as in *Ingress*).

A solution to cope with the challenge that the focus corridor poses may lie in the creation of mobile exergames that adapt their interface complexity to the player's intensity of movement. The two game modes of *Zombies, Run!* are a step towards this direction, but more sophisticated games that dynamically adapt their interfaces to the player's physical activity seem reasonable. For instance, Macvean and Robertson [24] have created a prototypical mobile exergame named *Collect the Coins*, which is not unlike *PacStudent* and which uses audio and vibration feedback to notify the player when it is time to stop moving and to look at the smartphone's screen again. We are looking forward to experiment with such approaches in the future and intend to create interfaces that dynamically adapt themselves to the player's activity level, thus providing for a more fulfilling gaming and training experience.

4 Conclusions and Future Work

Motivated by the aim of improving the user interface of our own location-based exergame *PacStudent*, we have analyzed the interfaces of several existing mobile exergames and then developed a methodology for the selection of user interfaces for mobile exergames in general. As a next step, we plan to implement and evaluate various types of interfaces for *PacStudent* in order to determine the respective quality of experience that they provide.

Acknowledgments. This work is partially financed by the European Commission under the FP7-ICT-Project ALFRED (grant agreement no. 611218). The authors would like to thank Chris Michel, Gerhard Saeckel, Christina Stadler, Katharina Moebus, Jan Peter Glock, Juergen Kugler, Yannick Rabow and Ewald Klippenstein for the design and implementation of the original PacStudent game as part of their studies at the Technische Universitaet Darmstadt.

References

1. Goebel, S., Hardy, S., Wendel, V., Mehm, F., Steinmetz, R.: Serious Games for Health – Personalized Exergames. In: Proceedings of the International Conference on Multimedia. ACM, New York (2010)
2. Levac, D., Pierrynowski, M.R., Canestraro, M., Gurr, L., Leonard, L., Neeley, C.: Exploring Childern's Movement Characteristics During Virtual Reality Video Game Play. In: Human Movement Science, vol. 29(6). Elsevier, Amsterdam (2010)
3. Graves, L.E., Ridgers, N.D., Stratton, G.: The Contribution of Upper Limb and Total Body Movement to Adolescents' Energy Expenditure Whilst Playing Nintendo Wii. European Journal of Applied Physiology 104(4) (2008)
4. VGChartz.com: Sales of Wii Sports, `http://www.vgchartz.com/game/2667/wii-sports/` (accessed January 24, 2014)
5. VGChartz.com: Overall Video Game Sales, `http://www.vgchartz.com/gamedb/` (accessed January 24, 2014)
6. VGChartz.com: Sales of Wii Fit, `http://www.vgchartz.com/game/7480/wii-fit/` (accessed January 24, 2014)
7. VGChartz.com: Sales of Wii Fit Plus, `http://www.vgchartz.com/game/35077/wii-fit-plus/` (accessed January 24, 2014)
8. Stross, R.: Exergames Don't Cure Young Couch Potatoes, New York. The New York Times (June 24, 2013)
9. Graf, D.L., Pratt, L.V., Hester, C.N., Short, K.R.: Playing Active Video Games Increases Energy Expenditure in Children. Pediatrics 124(2) (2009)
10. Gerling, K.M., Schild, J., Masuch, M.: Exergame Design for Elderly Users: The Case Study of SilverBalance. In: Proceedings of the 7th International Conference on Advances in Computer Entertainment Technology. ACM, New York (2010)
11. Hardy, S., Goebel, S., Gutjahr, M., Wiemeyer, J., Steinmetz, R.: Adaptation Model for Indoor Exergames. In: Wiemeyer, J., Goebel, S. (eds.) Serious Games - Theory, Technology & Practice. Proceedings of Gamedays 2011. Springer, Heidelberg (2011)

12. IDC Press Release: Worldwide Smartphone Shipments Top One Billion Units for the First Time (2013), http://www.idc.com/getdoc.jsp?containerId=prUS24645514 (accessed February 3, 2014)
13. Dutz, T., Knoell, M., Hardy, S., Goebel, S.: Calm Gaming – How Mobile Devices Could Change the Face of Serious Gaming. In: Ziegler, J. (ed.) i-Com, vol. 12(2). Oldenbourg Verlag, Munich (2013)
14. Official Geocaching Website, http://www.geocaching.com (accessed February 3, 2014)
15. Website of Yelp, http://www.yelp.com (accessed February 3, 2014)
16. Website of Foursquare, http://www.foursquare.com (accessed February 3, 2014)
17. Website of Ingress, http://www.ingress.com (accessed February 3, 2014)
18. Website of Runtastic, http://www.runtastic.com (accessed February 3, 2014)
19. Website of Nike+, http://nikeplus.nike.com (accessed February 3, 2014)
20. Website of Zombies, Run!, https://www.zombiesrungame.com (accessed February 3, 2014)
21. Website of the Runtastic Pumpit apps, https://www.runtastic.com/en/pumpit (accessed February 3, 2014)
22. Website of PacStudent, http://pacstudent.de.im (accessed February 3, 2014)
23. Sinclair, J., Hingston, P., Masek, M.: Considerations for the Design of Exergames. In: Proceedings of the 5th International Conference on Computer Graphics and Interactive Techniques in Australia and Southeast Asia. ACM, New York (2007)
24. Macvean, A., Robertson, J.: iFitQuest: A School Based Study of a Mobile Location-Aware Exergame for Adolescents. In: Proceedings of MobileHCI 2012. ACM, New York (2012)

AwareCycle: Application for Sports Visualization Using an Afterimage Display Attached to the Wheel of a Bicycle

Azusa Kadomura[1], Yoko Ichioka[1], Koji Tsukada[2], Jun Rekimoto[3], and Itiro Siio[1]

[1] Department of Computer Science, Ochanomizu University, Japan
{azusa,yoko.ichioka,siio}@is.ocha.ac.jp
[2] Department of Media Architecture, Future University Hakodate, Japan
tsuka@acm.org
[3] Initiative in Information Studies, The University of Tokyo, Japan
rekimoto@acm.org

Abstract. In this study, we define a method that allows the real-time presentation of a sportsman's physical status to an audience as the AwareSports concept. In particular, we focus on cycling to illustrate the AwareSports concept and develop an AwareCycle system to show the sportsman's status on the wheel, which has not been utilized previously as a display area for presenting the sportsman's status in real-time to the audience. We also implement an iPhone software application that is connected to the wheel component in order to monitor and display the sportsman's heart rate.

Keywords: Afterimage display, Bicycle, Cycling, Heart rate, Physical information, Sport-Augmented, Wheel.

1 Introduction

Recently, people have become more interested in watching and participating in various sports to improve their health. Alongside the popularization of mobile computing, some systems that log a sportsman's physical status (e.g., speed and heart rate) have been proposed[1, 2]. The detected information can be analyzed by users (sportsmen) and coaches to improve sports performance and strategy, as well as for motivating training. However, such information is usually presented to users (sportsmen) and their coaches. Thus, it is not utilized to provide real-time feedback to an audience. This might be beneficial because some sports are not only a means of exercise but also can be enjoyable to watch. Some services provide the sportsman's information to the audience by displaying additional information on a TV or PC screen. However, these types of projects require that the audience need to have a device (e.g., TV, PC and smartphone) for increasing the enjoyment while watching sports.

---

[1] `http://www.nike.com/jp/ja\_jp/c/nikeplus-fuelband` (Nike+ FuelBand by NIKE Inc.).

[2] `http://www.fitbit.com/jp` (fitbit by Fitbit, Inc.).

M. Kurosu (Ed.): Human-Computer Interaction, Part III, HCII 2014, LNCS 8512, pp. 256–264, 2014.

Again, sports might be more attractive to watch if the audience could observe the physical status of sportsmen during games. Thus, we focus on developing a method that facilitates the presentation of the actual physical status of a sportsman to the audience without any devices. In this study, we propose a new method for sports visualization, which represents aspects of a sportsman's physical status (e.g., position, speed, and heart rate) that cannot be determined simply by watching.

We define a method that allows the real-time presentation of a sportsman's physical status to observers as the AwareSports concept. As one possible example, we focus on cycling to illustrate this new visualization method, where AwareCycle displays a sportsman's physical status to an audience on the wheel of a bicycle, which has not been utilized previously as a sports visualization display area (Figure 1). LEDs are placed on the wheel, which allows its use as a display based on afterimage effects.

We also focus on the heart rate as a major indicator of the physical status and we implement a convenient smartphone software application that changes the contents displayed on the wheel based on the sportsman's heart rate. The heart rate is an important parameter in sports and it changes frequently [1]. For example, an analysis of various data related to each participant in the Tour de France showed that the heart rate differed markedly among subjects[3].

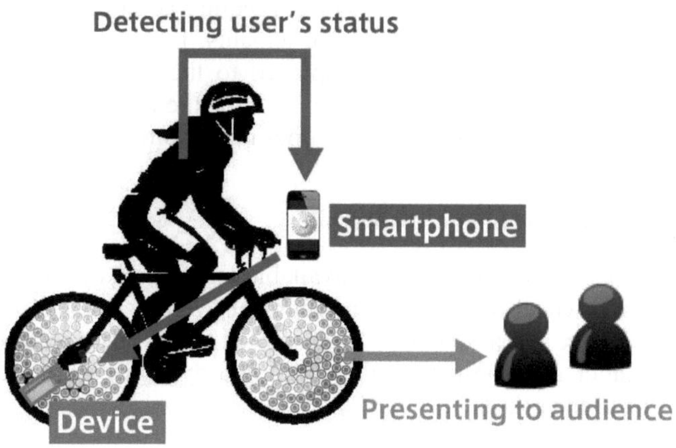

Fig. 1. Overview of the AwareCycle system

2 Related Work

2.1 Availability of Physical Information During Sports

As stated previously, human-computer interaction (HCI) studies have focused on log-based systems for detecting the physical status of sportsmen (users). They can detect and log the actions of users and then publish the data via web services. In addition,

[3] http://velonews.competitor.com/2013/07/tour-de-france/pro-power-analysis-stages-18-19-at-the-tour-de-france_296653 (Pro Power Analysis: Stages 18-19 at the Tour de France by Velonews).

some studies have employed the user's status data as a motivational tool in sport. For example, Mueller et al. proposed a system that allows long-distance joggers to listen to specific types of sound based on the heart rates of other people [2]. HeartLink [3] is a user system that collects real-time heart rate information and transmits this data online via the user's smartphone. The web audience provides feedback based on the data, which can be transformed into real feedback via vibrations of the user's smartphone. These projects are focused on providing feedback to the user (sportsman). By contrast, our method aims to display the physical status of the user (sportsman) to an audience in real time.

2.2 Methods for Presenting Sports to Audiences

Some projects attempt to make sports more enjoyable and meaningful by improving the realism of sport. Similar to our approach, some services provide information about sportsmen to an audience by displaying additional information on a TV or PC screen. Sportvision Inc.[4] is a visualization system that displays the speeds of yacht races on TV. Hallberg et al. also proposed a system that provides the real-time position status of sportsmen on the Web during cross-country races [4]. Nilsson et al. produced a system that detects the positions of players during basketball and ice hockey games using a portable PC [6]. However, these services require additional devices such as a TV or a PC to obtain the status of sports participants. In our method, however, the real-time physical status of a cyclist is displayed to the audience on the bicycle's wheel. Thus, we propose a new sports visualization method that represents the physical status of a sportsman, where the audience does not require a special device.

2.3 Application of Afterimage Displays

Similar to our method, some products are available (e.g., Monkey Light[5]) that embed an LED array on the wheel of a bicycle to augment cycling. Most of these products are intended to improve the aesthetics and design of cycles. By contrast, our wheel-type LED array can change the pattern displayed in a dynamic manner depending on the physical status of the cyclist.

3 AwareCycle

The AwareCycle system is based on the AwareSports concept and it has three main features.

3.1 Aims of the Presentation System

The visualization of a sportsman's status (i.e., the user's status) may have two main applications: (1) displaying information to the user while practicing and (2) display-

[4] `http://www.sportvision.com/` (Sportvision, Inc.).

[5] `http://www.monkeylectric.com/` (MonkeyLectric).

ing the user's status to an audience to enhance the realism of a sporting game. In the present study, we focused on the latter application, i.e., presenting the real physical status of a sportsman to an audience. Thus, we propose a new method for sports visualization.

3.2 Types of Information Displayed

In general, sports visualization comprises two main content types: (1) presenting data related to the game, such as the number of fouls in basketball and strikes in baseball; (2) presenting data on the individual status of each sportsman, such as their speed, heart rate, and level of perspiration. In the present study, we focused on the latter content. By providing information about the physical status of sportsmen during sports games, the audience may acquire original insights that enhance their appreciation while watching, such as: "*Does the lead runner still have enough strength?*" and "*Only a pro could do that! Even with a low heart rate!*" Our method can present the sportsman's status to the audience, i.e., the heart rate in the present study.

3.3 The Method of Presentation

Various methods have been developed for sports visualization. For example, some methods add information on the screen, such as by publishing the sportsman's information (e.g., position) on the Web. Thus, these methods display information on the screen of a TV or PC, so the audience must use a device such as a smartphone even if they are in the stadium. However, the major events in games may occur within the space of a few seconds and the use of a device may be a burden that spoils the enjoyment for the audience. Therefore, our proposed sports visualization method detects and displays the sportsman's status without any special device, simply by using the bicycle's wheel as a display unit.

4 Implementation

As shown in Figures 2 and 3, the system comprises the wheel part (the main circuit board, the reed switch and the battery) on the wheel that displays the sportsman's status, a heart rate monitor on the sportsman's chest, and an iPhone, which is connected to the main circuit board and the heart rate monitor via Bluetooth 4.0.

The user fixes the box that contains the main circuit board, the reed switch and the battery onto the wheel and wears the heart rate monitor on the chest. The user activates the AwareCycle's iPhone software application to connect with the main circuit board and the heart rate monitor via Bluetooth 4.0. When the user starts cycling, the reed switch on the wheel detects its rotation and the LEDs on the main circuit board attached to the wheel flash to display the user's heart rate status (Figure 4).

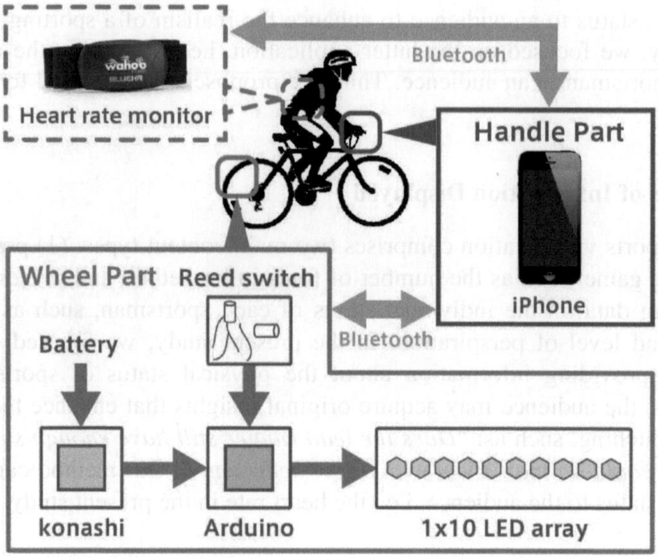

Fig. 2. System configuration

Fig. 3. Prototype system installed on an actual bicycle

4.1 Wheel Part

The main circuit board on the wheel comprises a reed switch, 10 full-color LEDs (LED array), two microcomputers (Konashi[6] and Arduino Pro Mini[7]), and a battery, as shown in Figure 5. The reed switch is fixed on the frame adjacent to the wheel by a magnet and it is used to detect the rotational speed of the wheel, thereby measuring

[6] http://konashi.ux-xu.com/ (YUKAI Engineering Inc.).

[7] http://arduino.cc/en/Main/ArduinoBoardProMini

the speed of the bicycle, and to control the LED display timing. The LED array, Konashi, and Arduino are fixed to the main circuit board. The main circuit board has multiple holes to fix to the wheel using cable ties and is housed in an ABS (acrylonitrile butadiene styrene) resin box with holes. The LED array is perceived as a circular display because of the afterimage effect created by the rotation of the wheel. Thus, full-color images can be displayed within the 24-inch diameter of the wheel (Figure 6). Konashi has a tool kit that can be controlled by the application on the iPhone and it connects to iPhone on the handle via Bluetooth 4.0. Konashi sends the sensed data (the measured rotational speed of the wheel) to the iPhone and it also sends operation commands to the Arduino Pro Mini via serial communication at the same time. Each full-color LED on the LED array can be controlled individually by Arduino pro Mini.

Fig. 4. Basic usage

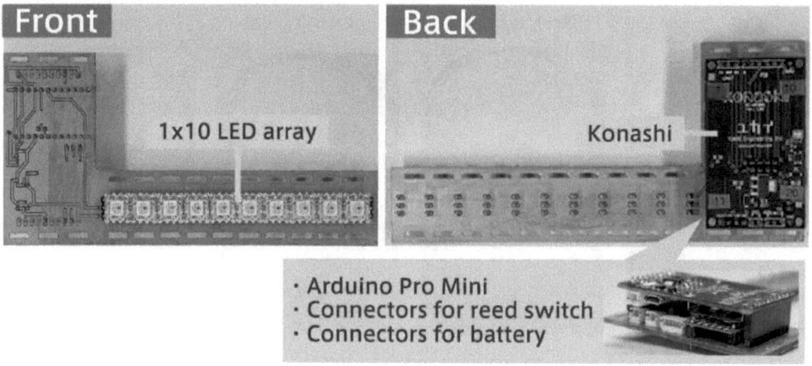

Fig. 5. Main circuit board

Fig. 6. Full-color image displayed within the 24-inch diameter of the wheel

4.2 Heart Rate Monitor

In the present study, our prototype used a heart rate monitor produced by Wahoo[8], which is worn on the chest by the user. The heart rate monitor is connected to the iPhone via Bluetooth 4.0. Using Wahoo's API, an iPhone app was written in Objective-C to allow the display of the sportsman's (user's) heart rate on the wheel.

We tested four types of visual pattern for displaying the heart rate: (A) numbers, (B) heart symbols, (C) a vertical bar graph, and (D) a horizontal bar graph (Figure 7). The each pattern changes based on the cyclist's real heart rate.

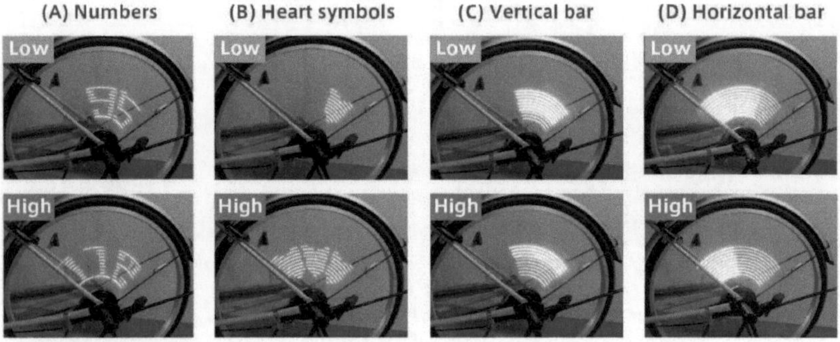

Fig. 7. Four types of visual patterns used to display the heart rate

[8] `http://www.wahoofitness.com/` (Wahoo Fitness).

5 Evaluation

To assess the performance of the AwareCycle system, we conducted an evaluation in the university grounds on a sunny day at 13:00. We recruited four subjects (women aged in their 20s) who observed the different displays on the wheel. One of the authors wore the heart rate monitor on her chest, which was connected with the AwareCycle's devices, and she cycled around the subjects 36 times (distance from the observers = radius 5 m × 12 times, radius 10 m × 12 times, and radius 20 m × 12 times). The system displayed four different visual patterns, each on three occasions. The percentages of correct answers at each distance were 80% at radius = 5 m, 81% at radius = 10 m, and 66% at radius = 20 m. This evaluation was limited but it helped us to assess the system's performance, which was better in the dark (in the evening and at night).

6 Discussion

6.1 Application to other Sports

In this study, we focused on cycling as an example of the AwareSports concept, but this method could be applied to other sports. However, the sportsman would have to wear an addition device to display their status in sports that do not utilize equipment (e.g., swimming and running). Although the application of the AwareSports concept has various limitations, we consider that the AwareSports concept has other applications in addition to cycling.

6.2 Comparison with other Visualization Methods

During the sports that do not need special equipment (e.g., swimming and running), other visualization methods, such as AR technique, are considered for displaying information. However, the methods require that the live audience watch sporting events through devices such as a smartphone. By embedding the device on the sportsman's equipment (a bicycle in the present study) and using it as a display, our system can present information to an audience without requiring any devices.

6.3 Reducing the Additional Weight Burden for the Sportsman

In the present study, the device was attached to the wheel of a bicycle. Therefore, it is possible that the speed of the cyclist would be reduced due to the additional weight of the device. Thus, to reduce the moment of inertia, we placed the heaviest part of our device at the center of the wheel. We aim to make further improvements, however, such as developing a lightweight device.

7 Conclusion and Future Work

In this study, we proposed and developed a sports visualization system, AwareCycle, which detects the physical status of a cyclist (i.e., heart rate) and displays this information on the wheel using a device attached to full-color LEDs. In our future research, we plan to improve this system by allowing the visual pattern to display further aspects of a sportsman's status and by making the device waterproof. We also plan to evaluate this device in a real environment. Our system includes a smartphone, which means that is connected to a network; thus, we aim to develop an application for multiple users. We will also explore the application of this concept to sports visualization in other sports.

Acknowledgement. This work was supported by the Japan Science and Technology Agency PRESTO Program.

References

1. Segerståhl, K., Oinas-Kukkonen, H.: Designing personal exercise monitoring employing multiple modes of delivery: Implications from a qualitative study on heart rate monitoring. International Journal of Medical Informatics, 203–213 (2011)
2. Mueller, F., Vetere, F., Gibbs, M.R., Edge, D., Agamanolis, S., Sheridan, J.G.: Jogging over a distance between Europe and Australia. In: Proceedings of the 23nd Annual ACM Symposium on User Interface Software and Technology (UIST 2010), pp. 189–198. ACM (2010)
3. Curmi, F., Ferrario, M.A., Southern, J., Whittle, J.: HeartLink: open broadcast of live biometric data to social networks. In: Proceedings of the SIGCHI Conference on Human Factors in Computing Systems (CHI 2013), pp. 1749–1758. ACM (2013)
4. Hallberg, J., Svensson, S., Ostmark, A., Lindgren, P., Synnes, K., Delsing, J.: Enriched Media-Experience of Sport Events. In: Proceedings of the Sixth IEEE Workshop on Mobile Computing Systems and Applications (WMCSA 2004), pp. 2–9. IEEE Computer Society (2004)
5. Andreas, N., Nulden, U., Olsson, D.: Spectator Information Support: Exploring the Context of Distributed Events. In: Wiberg, M. (ed.) The Interaction Society: Practice, Theories and Supportive Technologies, pp. 271–303 (2005)

Refreshing Quantification and other Ploys to Give Up the Habit

A Repertoire of Relations, Identities, and Rhetorical Devices in Smoking Cessation Applications

Ştefania Matei[1], Cosima Rughiniş[1], and Răzvan Rughiniş[2]

[1] University of Bucharest, Department of Sociology, Bucharest, Romania
{stefania.matei,cosima.rughinis}@sas.unibuc.ro
[2] University Politehnica of Bucharest, Department of Computer Science, Splaiul Independenţei 313, Bucharest, Romania
razvan.rughinis@cs.pub.ro

Abstract. In this paper we analyze 26 smoking cessation applications on Android OS focusing on how they address their implied users. We identify 'refreshing quantification' as a main method, which endorses a portrait of the users as myopic in risk perception, but heroic in their individual pursuit to reach the non-smoker identity. App-created relationships and identities give rise to a temporal order based on contemplating the past and anticipating the future. Users are guided towards an autonomy-centered identity project, which renders them accountable for success or failure in smoking cessation. Users' experience of smoking cessation is co-constructed in their interaction with the app-coach and with peers. Apps and peers offer diagnoses, advice, labels that populate the world in which the would-be ex-smokers pursue their project.

Keywords: Smoking Cessation, Implied User, Android Applications, Refreshing Quantification, Rhetorical Device.

1 Introduction

Applications designed to assist efforts at giving up smoking have become increasingly complex and diverse. They are neither strictly a manual of self-government with motivational claims directed towards renouncing a habit, nor a simple record of a behavior. Instead, they provide an identity project with moral implications through which users are transformed from the position of irresponsible consumers of cigarettes to the position of responsible, well-documented and self-controlled persons. We aim to examine this process, in light of frequent skepticism expressed about the effectiveness of behavioral change apps.

Previous research on smoking cessation programs has looked into intervention designs, short- and long-term impact, and users' experiences. Impact evaluation meta-analyses indicate that Internet interventions seem promising for long-term (6 month) results, especially if they are interactive and tailored to the individual user [1]. Mobile

M. Kurosu (Ed.): Human-Computer Interaction, Part III, HCII 2014, LNCS 8512, pp. 265–276, 2014.

text messaging interventions also seem to be effective in supporting long term cessation [2]. Still, mobile applications for smoking cessation have not yet been systematically evaluated as regards impact. Anyway, a review of 47 iPhone apps indicates that they have a low degree of conformity with clinical practice guidelines [3]; the best followed guideline refers to offering rewards and presenting the benefits of quitting, while least attended guidelines refer to recommending approved medication and counselling. Apps are often developed independently of medical expertise, thus raising the question: what are the persuasive approaches put in place to support users through a difficult personal transformation?

2 Structural Design and Implied Users

In our inquiry we start from the concept of the 'implied user' - a productive conceptual instrument in analyzing human-device interaction throughout the life of an application: starting from its creation and design and ending up with its circulation and utilization.

Either approached as a rhetorical tool for designers (a "scenic feature of the design space" [4]) or as a human prototype that is inscribed into persons through interaction with application scripts [5], the 'user' has received much scientific attention, particularly in the study of software.

In this thread of research, the 'implied user' is not assembled as a statistical or psychological aggregate of real people who use applications. In some cases it is retrieved as an assumed model of person, formulated through discourse in interaction, which designers and other participants in software development require in order to make sense of the situation, coordinate their actions, and account for their decisions [4-9]. From this perspective, users' expected behaviors are interweaved with the product development requirements [6] [7] [8].

Secondly, in other types of research, the 'implied user' is a typification embedded in the structural design of the application [9] which can be retrieved by examining the parameters, settings, functions and possible modes of operating an application, without reference to how it was designed or actually used. Empirical studies based on this perspective analyzed software programs as modes of 'performing users' by imputing them certain qualities [10].

Thirdly, in a related understanding, the 'user' does not take the form of a repository of needs and interests, but it represents a mode of behavior and habits acquired through and by using an application. In this sense, the 'user' might be addressed as an outcome of engaging with technology, therefore being a projection of the influence that an application might have in real-life situations. Even if this approach allows for the study of users on different levels, empirical research is focused mainly on evaluating and measuring the impact of software programs on human behavior [11].

Last but not least, investigations of actual use can contribute to highlight discrepancies between the implied users' and the flesh-and-bones users' forms of interaction [12].

In this conceptual landscape, we start from the perspective that the 'user' is part of a system of categories useful for organizing specific situations that appear in relation to a software application. Even if the 'user' is often assimilated with a consumer, customer, or operator, thus receiving a factual and observable form of existence, it is essentially a rhetorical construction that gains meaning through practices in which descriptions of human actions are made to be relevant in accounts that guide understanding.

In this paper we analyze 26 smoking cessation applications on Android OS (presented in Fig. 1 in the descending order of their popularity), and we inquire into their repertoire of proposed relationships, user identities, and rhetorical styles. We focus on how the implied user is configured through communication invited by the apps. The increasing diversity of the app environment should benefit from a systematic examination, offering developers information on current and possible ways of approaching users.

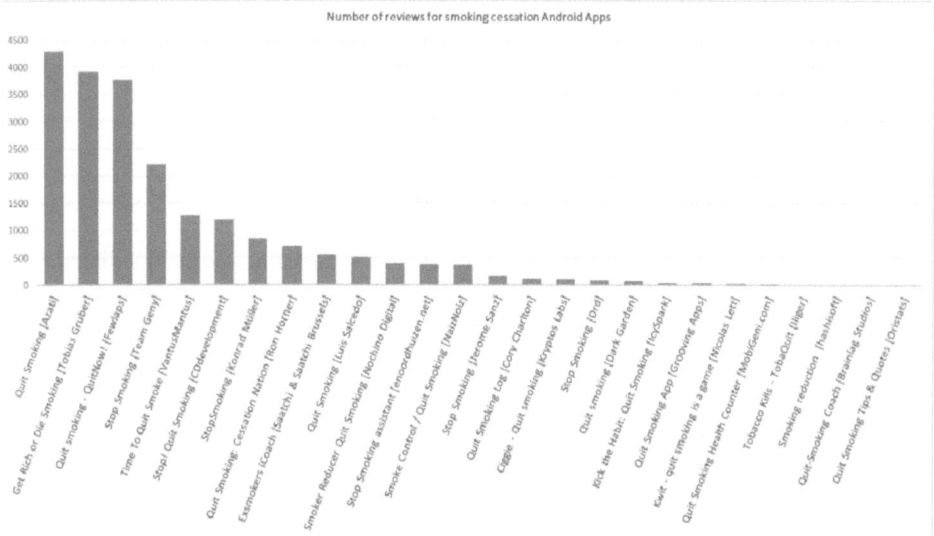

Fig. 1. Android apps for smoking cessation sorted by number of user reviews

Many mobile applications visible when searching Google Play for "quit smoking" share important features when formulating and approaching the problem they profess to solve. Users can launch the application by deciding to quit smoking: the planned date of renouncing cigarettes is inputted as the main application propellant. Users may also introduce other details about their past smoking behavior. From that moment a counter is enabled, measuring the time passed without smoking, and displaying statistics in accordance with input data. Former smokers are motivated to avoid relapse by accumulating achievements in proportion to the period spent without smoking. These digital rewards consist in the display of health benefits, in consumption proposals based on money savings, or other motivators. The applications offer various incentives: tips and tricks, gamified environments, surveys, questions of reflection, opportunities of interacting with peers, the possibility to maintain a dialogue with the application etc.

We anticipate a general conclusion: the implied user of the examined applications is a lone rider, unassisted by medicine or counseling, solely equipped with a mobile device that works as a time traveling machine. The user is engaged in an initiatory journey having to pass from a dangerous to a safe world with only one imperative: do not smoke. The mobile is an omniscient companion which gives advice and other super-natural powers that help in fighting the pitfalls encountered in the mad world of cigarettes. Cessation is framed as time travel, in which users can reach almost instantaneously each part of their life by contemplating the must-get-rid-of-it past and by envisaging a promising future. In this sense, the main application operations function as a myopia-correcting gear by bringing about a quantitative makeup of the world as a frame of reference, which may also be shared with other users, on local forums or social media. Users are addressed as knowledge seekers afflicted by short-sightedness and misperception of risks. The 'refreshing quantification' modules make visible for users those risks and benefits that they, presumably, could not see. Applications approach these cognitive limitations by transforming general and prevalent risks in individual self-inflicted threats. We argue that this dominant implied user is problematic in light of the high frequency of relapse among smokers who start to quit.

3 Relationships in the App World

Smoking cessation applications involve the users in four main types of mediated relationships, embedded in the architecture, technical features, and possibilities of engagement they propose. These relationships create links between various components of the process of quitting and represent the structural ground on which the personal transformation path develops.

Firstly, the applications propose a *relationship with oneself*, created through increased self-monitoring procedures. Apps often include a 'refreshing quantification' module that offers numerical estimates of current health risks and their future evolution, continuously updated. Users are informed about the micro-level transformations of their bodies, and the macro-level changes that will materialize in the next days, months, and years, with a rhetoric of high precision. Apps thus offer a 'microscope' and a 'telescope' to examine one's present and future body (Fig. 2a). Of course, all these numbers are not personalized estimates related to the current state of the users' body, but aggregate guesstimates that input users' succinct smoking profile into formulas relying on publicly available statistics of risks computed on large populations.

Each of the examined applications attempts to render smoking behavior visible, by requesting users to describe it through numbers in a smoking profile. Applications use quantification to objectify smoking by transposing it in something easily measurable (e.g. number of cigarettes smoked per day, number of cigarettes in a pack), and to highlight the relevance of cost (e.g. cost per pack of cigarettes). Beside these, there are other indicators that shape the awareness of smoking behavior from different points of view (e.g. time spent per cigarette, which is framed as a cost). All these indicators are used to define the position from which users are apprehended, to establish *what counts* in their transformation, and *how it should be counted.*

This first stage of quantification involves initial data input and is mandatory. Thus users are requested to think about their past smoking behavior and to objectify it in numbers. This assessment makes smoking appear uniform in time, which is not always the case. By continuing to use the application, the former smokers accept that this type of conventional quantification (number of cigarettes per day, price per pack etc.) is meaningful for describing and managing their behavior.

Moreover, by producing numerical estimates, users implicitly consent with (and legitimate) the quantitative language and representations of their worlds and actions. On the one hand, estimates provided by the application depend on the inputs offered by the user, and thus the plausibility of application metrics is a direct function of the credibility of users' initial information. On the other hand, there is also a symbolic connection: through agreeing to provide succinct generalizations of one's past behavior, users also agree to accept broad generalizations of their future. In this way, *an implicit contract is established between users and smoking cessation applications, through a common and agreed upon quantitative language of self-description.*

Secondly, the applications develop users' *relationships with a gameplay environment.* Applications may frame the quitting process as a game or offer minigames either as future rewards or as means to distract attention from craving. For example, they include in the quantification module sets of game-like achievements, which users unlock after being smoke free for a certain time (Fig. 2b).

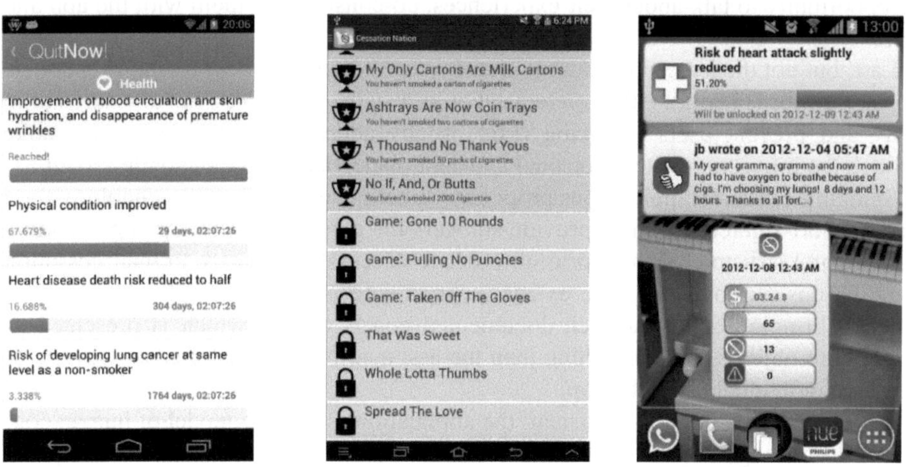

a) 'QuitNow': Present and future b) 'Cessation Nation': Gamification c) 'Stop! Quit Smoking': Forum talk

Fig. 2. Types of relationships: with self, the gameplay environment, and peers

The achievements function as evidence-based credentials [13] which account in communicating merits [14] and establishing relevant targets [15]. By using achievements, the applications provide a vocabulary of relevance as a descriptor of users' behavior . Thus they create a shared space in which a sense of purpose is continuously maintained through an infrastructure of sustained commitment.

Gameplay elements, understood as a productive media to support interaction between various actors [16], introduce users in a meaningful story developed in parallel with their embodied experience. This is a story of courageous transformation, in which users are the main protagonists in search for the ultimate "powers of non-smoking". In strongly gamified applications persistent smoking cessation is attested by a first class cup, a paramount medal, or a final congratulation message, all of them certifying the end of the difficult pursuit. As in a usual game, users are informed that they can try again and again to pass an obstacle, but through effort and self-training the success is guaranteed. By highlighting the 'ultimate achievement' in the interaction with users, a sense of purpose is integrated in an ongoing process of difficult, often painful transformation. A couple of applications also make visible the level of difficulty proposed to users: some periods or tasks are framed as being more difficult than others.

Another type of mediated relationships refers to *relationships with a community of peers*. Applications can host their own forums (Fig. 2c) which enable users to share their experiences, progress, and achievements. They can also post on Facebook or other social media. Applications integrate various forms of sociability in their design, by creating a platform of dialogue and support and by bringing together participants willing to share their experience with others. These online communities grow in parallel with other applications features, creating a "new application within the main application" which functions on its own rationale. Online communities can offer different styles of communication, advice, and frames from the dominant app logic. Users get the opportunity to talk about their experiences, co-constructing them with the app and peers.

Last, but not the least, applications create users' *relationship with a quitting couch*. Apps offer tips (Fig. 3a), either on request or as a static page. They can also attempt to delay and prevent users' smoking (Fig. 3b) by addressing their desire to smoke through the interaction with a personal assistant made visible on the mobile screen.

Smoking-cessation applications propose to function as an assistive technology for a kind of short-sightedness: they provide smokers the perceptive tools for apprehending the temporal structure of the world, in order to successfully adhere to their cessation plan. To this purpose, they use extensive procedure of framing smoking, risks and benefits, bringing about the well-documented coach version which is presented as being more objective and enriching than the assumed blurred, distorted worldview of the naive individual using the app.

By integrating a personal assistant, the applications share the model of human cognitive functioning construed in the heuristics & biases psychological literature [6], [7]. According to experimental evidence in this field, people in daily situations are poor statisticians: their estimates of risk are widely divergent from normatively correct figures, ignoring baseline values and being mostly dependent on recent incidents (the availability heuristic) and situational cues (anchoring). A related strand of psychology and economics indicates that we value our future selves less than our present selves ('time discounting' or 'hyperbolic discounting' [8]; time discounting is enhanced in cases of addiction [9]). To put it briefly, people in general and smokers in particular are expected: (1) To not know, in quantitative details, specific risks of smoking and benefits of quitting; (2) To discount future health benefits in favor of the immediate gratification of nicotine, as a biological agent, and smoking, as habit and social interaction; (3) To ignore health warnings, through various forms of rationalization and exception-based reasoning. The applications, by integrating the advice of a smoking coach, aim to provide users with access to some kind of a privileged knowledge and modes of self-regulation assumed to be superior to the usual, naïve smokers' strategies of cessation.

4 Burning the Bridge: Moral and Process Identities

Smoking cessation applications project the user in past, present and future identities. By organizing the process of transformation in different frames, the applications integrates time structures and practices which are prone to establish a dynamic of use and sustain different forms of engagement [17]. Based on temporal arrangements, the applications propose a path of socialization into a new role defined according to users' attachment to cigarettes. Apps propose judgments of right and wrong, worthy and non-worthy, thus defining users' actions as moral or, conversely, immoral. While engaging with the applications users must mitigate between their past identities and the desired ones, in order to become part of the moral order developed through design.

A frequent identity available to users is *the future non-smoker*. Users are inscribed on a quantified trajectory that connects them with the identity of the non-smoker, as specified through their health risks (Fig. 2a). Quantification is a device that simultaneously brings forward a reality of improved health and finances, and makes possible emotions of enjoyment of one's evolution, and the admiration of the impact of one's actions.

Applications also support the *transitional 'smoke-free' identity*, dealing with the difficulties of hour-by-hour abstinence. Users are cast as transitional characters, moving from a "risk-laden world" to a "safe haven" of financial and health benefits. This voyage is, though, extremely slippery, and there is no possibility of coming back to a previous estate. Each smoked cigarette reported into the application resets all metrics and brings the user back at square one. In the app world, there is no inertia of benefits: health advantages that have been so vividly materialized, through ever increasing metrics, in previous days, vanish in the smoke of one (reported) cigarette. Gradual accumulation does not entail gradual loss: metrics are used to position users in one or the other of the two worlds, but never in both. Smoking can only occur in the smoking world, from which the travel must start anew. This one-way model of users' trajectory superposes psychological risks with health risks: the psychological damage of relapses, which reaffirm addiction and decrease self-efficacy, is made visible by erasing accumulated health benefits.

Through constant updating, the future becomes incorporated in the present: each day that passes reduces in the here-and-now risks of future disease; this actuality of the future is best captured by what we term *'refreshing quantification'*, the practice of using *precision* and *updates*, in the communication of metrics, as rhetorical resources to depict changes in users' bodies. Users receive precise estimates of their health improvement – even if the app, of course, has no individual-level information about users' physical transformation.

Another recurrent moral identity is the *Lone Ranger*. Most applications promote autonomy as the core value of the smoking cessation project: users are framed as independent, individual fighters against addiction. This identity explains the absence of advice for pharmacotherapy and counseling (with the notable exception of Ex-Smokers iCoach). The examined applications share a model of their implied users: they are people who have decided to quit smoking and are determined to carry through this radical transformation. The implied users are independent individuals, technologically adept, and honest about their smoking behavior. More importantly, the implied user is the bearer of specific problems that the application purports to solve - but only under the conditions of active involvement. Therefore, moral agency is a key quality of the implied users, which makes possible their interaction with the app.

Local, app-specific identities are also available: the *Ultimate Kwitter* (Kwit – quit smoking is a game), a quest-driven gamer, or the *ExSmoker* (ExSmokers iCoach), an 'unstoppable' character, derive their force from the specifics of app use. These identities are achieved by progressing though a scenario in which users establish relationship with objects (digital or real) that might become a substitute for cigarettes.

Through multiple, synchronously evolving quests, the application communicates *consistency and intelligibility*: saved money, saved time, improved life expectancy. Unlike health risks and benefits, which are experientially distant from the user and come across as interesting scientific but possibly mistrusted 'facts', information about money saved is directly related to the immediate costs of smoking, which the users can observe and influence on their own. Controllable financial and time metrics, derived from reported expenses, compensate for the subjective uncertainty of health benefits that are estimated across large populations, in obvious ignorance of the individual health condition of the user.

Some applications quantify the money *saved* by each not-smoked cigarette, framing it as a desirable achievement and integrating both past behavior and the anticipation a future reward. This metric corresponds to users' direct experiences of spending money to buy cigarettes. Still, saved money is more abstract than spent money; saved money does not accumulate in a distinctive account, and it may be experienced, ultimately, as a fiction. In order to render this quantitative dimension of the smoke-free world more visible, some applications convert saved money into illustrative goods: "You saved $5, that's the cost of a Subway Footlong Sandwich", "You saved $10, that's the cost of a regular movie ticket". "You saved $50, that's the cost for a month's membership at the gym". In some applications, such as "Get Rich or Die Smoking", users can assemble personal wishlists of goods to purchase with the money arithmetically saved from smoking, and can share these lists on social media – thus adding an extra-layer of reality derived from others' reactions, a medium to create and share moral significance.

5 From Broadcast to Dialogue: Rhetorical Devices

Communication styles range from broadcast (generic messages, such as quitting advice or anti-smoking posters) to interactive, personalized dialogue. Customization is mainly achieved in relation to users' numerical smoking patterns (frequency, cost, duration); tips and advice are, as a rule, not customized to users' preferences or quitting stage.

The style of communication that most of the applications propose is bidirectional: both directed from users to application (when reporting the smoking habits, filing out the surveys, answering questions) and from applications to users (when giving advice, questioning habits, providing statistics or other information). In much complex applications, the communication patterns are based on feedback: users might report whether they are prepared to move on to the next stage or not, whether a tip was useful or not. Also, the apps provide feedback to users confronting a failure or enjoying a success. These possibilities of communication constitute the interactional structure for the mediated relationships and the identities discussed above.

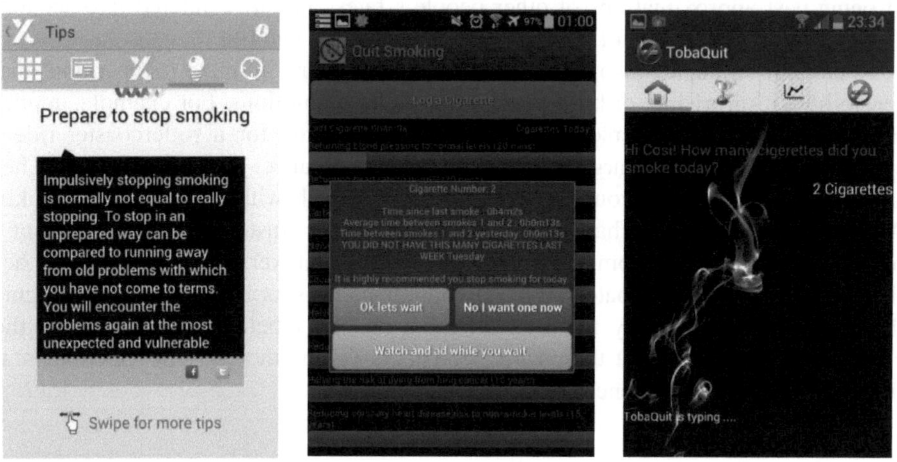

a) 'ExSmoker's ICoach': Tips

b) 'QuitSmoking': Statistical profile

c) 'Tobacco Kills': App anthropomorphism

Fig. 3. Communication and rhetorical strategies

Other modes of personalizing communication include strategies of positioning users within aggregated statistical landscapes computed with information from all other users. Some apps such as 'Quit Smoking: Cessation Nation' provide aggregated and archived data on the situation of the entire community.

Some applications open *choice spaces* for users (Fig. 3b), mostly designed for situations of craving, when users decide whether or not to smoke a cigarette in that particular moment. Therefore, the question-answer interactions that define the choice are essential not only for their motivational power, but also for the possibility of quantifying relapses and in ensuring the accurate reset of those achievements and health benefits achievements gained in the period of abstention. There are frequent relapses in the early days of quitting, due to withdrawal difficulties; many smokers quit successfully after several attempts. Several interesting questions arise: For such users, who enjoy the force of 'refreshing quantification' in bringing to life a safe world of gradually diminishing health risks for a couple of days, is this reset understood as a descriptive estimate of risks, or as a punishment for not staying true to one's promise? To what extent does this instability of health benefits undermine the credibility of the metrics, by de-materializing and conventionalizing the numbers? How do users who relapse communicate with the application in this choice space? Do they report honestly, or do they omit the occasional cigarette so that they would benefit from the motivational force of seeing the safe haven of a smoke free life? These questions invite further empirical scrutiny, in relation to evidence of high relapse rates [10], [11].

Other rhetorical tools of dialogue include both using one's first name (surprisingly rare, although preferred by users [18]) or apps that impersonate a human: "TobaQuit is typing" (Fig. 3c). Through *forms of direct address*, probabilities (reduced risks, increased benefits) become facts about oneself. Probabilities are freed from the doubt of being past approximations of other people's fates, and are rendered into accurate, actual description of transformations in one's own body and life.

Rhetorical strategies also include advice tips that are intimate (concerning one's sensibilities), surprising, or humoristic, thus eliciting emotions. For example, applications address in detail personal feelings: "Be prepared for a rollercoaster ride of emotions: denial, anger, bargaining, depression, acceptance, and complacency. These are normal emotions for your body when going through withdrawal" (Stop Smoking Assistant) or "Everything has its time, even your panic. Instead of being afraid of it: observe the feeling, it is something you can bear" (Exsmokers iCoach). Through these tips, apps not only anticipate future feelings or help users introspectively recognize their actual states, but, by focusing attention and by labeling such emotions, they create the experiences that they describe. This is yet another way in which apps actively shape users' experiences of quitting smoking.

6 Conclusions

Mobile applications for smoking cessation are a growing form of support for people who attempt to quit the habit. By an empirical analysis of Android OS applications, we observe their communication patterns and the projects through which they purport to assist learners.

In order to center users' identities on the core values of freedom and autonomy, mobile apps propose a temporal order in which the past (quantification of previous behavior), present (craving management tools) and future (personalized predictions) are addressed concomitantly. Users are encouraged to shift from one temporal realm into another in order to improve their ability to face obstacles when desiring or craving to smoke. Apps also claim to give users access to scientifically-formulated, privileged knowledge about smoking risks and cessation benefits. By transmitting this information and by a strong moral framing of smoking, apps render users morally accountable for their actions.

We observe several ways in which the experience of smoking cessation is co-constructed in interaction between users, application and peers. Apps provide users with clues of interpreting their past, present and future behavior. Beside this, they often rely on 'refreshing quantification' to construct a shared language and a shared worldview with their users, in which numbers bring to the touchscreen a better, healthier life.

Many applications frame smoking cessation as a heroic, individual pursuit: smokers are invited, without any equipment but their mobile devices, to enhance their probabilistic vision in order to carry through a lonely, one-way travel from danger to safety. Relapse is punished by return to square one: health benefits are thus moralized, functioning less as a quantitative description of one's body than as an indicator for the moral statuses of 'smoker' or 'former smoker'. Given the high prevalence of relapse, especially in early days, it is important to investigate empirically how people relate to this implied user model, and whether it could be improved.

Acknowledgments. This article has been supported by the research project "Sociological imagination and disciplinary orientation in applied social research", with financial support of ANCS / UEFISCDI grant no. PN-II-RU-TE-2011-3-0143, contract no. 14/28.10.2011.

References

1. Civljak, M., Stead, L., Hartmann-Boyce, J., Sheikh, A., Car, J.: Internet-based interventions for smoking cessation. The Cochrane Database of Systematic Reviews 7 (2013)
2. Whittaker, R., McRobbie, H., Bullen, C., Borland, R., Rodgers, A., Gu, Y.: Mobile phone-based interventions for smoking cessation. The Cochrane Database of Systematic Reviews 11, 1–24 (2012)
3. Abroms, L., Padmanabhan, N., Thaweethai, L., Phillips, T.: iPhone Apps for Smoking Cessation: A Content Analysis. American Journal of Preventive Medicine 40(3), 279–285 (2011)
4. Sharrock, W., Anderson, B.: The user as a scenic feature of the design space. Design Study 15(1), 5–18 (1994)
5. Mads, B., Brown, N., Konrad, K., Harro Van, L.: The Sociology of Expectations in Science and Technology. Technology Analysis & Strategic Management 18(3-4), 285–298 (2006)
6. Johansson, M., Messeter, J.: Presenting the user: constructing the persona. Digital Creativity 16(4), 231–243 (2005)
7. Oudshoorn, N., Rommes, E., Marcelle, S.: Configuring the User as Everybody: Gender and Design Cultures in Information and Communication Technologies. Science, Technology, & Human Values 29(1), 30–63 (2004)
8. Rooksby, J., Martin, D., Rouncefield, M.: Users as contextual features of software product development and testing. In: Group 2007, pp. 4–7 (2007)
9. Woolgar, S.: Configuring the user: the case of usability trials. In: Law, J. (ed.) A Sociology of Monsters: Essays on Power, Technology and Domination, pp. 57–102 (1991)

10. Higgins, V.: Performing Users: The Case of a Computer-Based Dairy Decision-Support System. Science, Technology & Human Values 32, 263–286 (2007)
11. Möller, A., Scherr, J., Roalter, L., Diewald, S., Hammerla, N., Plötz, T., Olivier, P., Kranz, M.: GymSkill: Mobile Exercise Skill Assessment to Support Personal Health and Fitness. In: Adjunct Proceedings of 9th International Conference on Pervasive Computing Pervasive (2011)
12. Brandt, C., Dalum, P., Thomsen, T.: 'I miss the care even though I know it's just a machine': An explorative study of the relationship between an Internet-based smoking cessation intervention and its participants. Health Informatics Journal 19(3), 233–243 (2013)
13. Rughini, R.: Talkative Objects in Need of Interpretation. Re-Thinking Digital Badges in Education. In: AltCHI 2013, ACM SIGCHI Conference on Human Factors in Computing Systems, pp. 1–10 (2013)
14. Rughiniş, R., Matei, S.: Digital Badges: Signposts and Claims of Achievement. In: Stephanidis, C. (ed.) Posters, Part II, HCII 2013. CCIS, vol. 374, pp. 84–88. Springer, Heidelberg (2013)
15. Rughini, R.: Badge Architectures in Engineering Education. Blueprints and Challenges. In: The 5th International Conference on Computer Supported Education, CSEDU 2013 (2013)
16. Rughini, R.: Gamification for Productive Interaction. Reading and Working with the Gamification Debate in Education. In: The 8th Iberian Conference on Information Systems and Technologies, CISTI 2013, pp. 1–5 (2013)
17. Rughini, R.: Time as a Heuristic in Serious Games for Engineering Education. In: The 5th International Conference on Computer Supported Education CSEDU (2013)
18. Jamison, J., Naughton, F., Gilbert, H., Sutton, S.: Delivering Smoking Cessation Support by Mobile Phone Text Message: What Information do Smokers Want? A Focus Group Study. Journal of Applied Biobehavioral Research 18(1), 1–23 (2013)

Eliciting Accessibility Requirements for People with Hearing Loss: A Semantic and Norm Analysis

Marta Angélica Montiel Ferreira[1] and Rodrigo Bonacin[1,2]

[1] FACCAMP, Rua Guatemala, 167, 13231-230, Campo Limpo Paulista, SP, Brazil
[2] CTI Renato Archer, Rodovia Dom Pedro I, km 143,6, 13069-901, Campinas, SP, Brazil
zmontefer@gmail.com, rodrigo.bonacin@cti.gov.br

Abstract. The barriers for people with hearing loss to access the Web go beyond the perceptual ones, i.e., the use of audio based content. Many people with hearing loss have difficulty writing and interpreting long or complex texts on the Web. In this study, we analyzed the semantic and normative aspects of Web content production and consumption by means of participatory studies with 29 deaf users. These studies resulted in the elicitation of 121 key problems, and the respective high level design recommendations. The recommendations aim to transform the Web into an inductor of learning. They also include design solutions that demand further research on assistive technologies

Keywords: Web Accessibility, Universal Design, Organizational Semiotics, Universal Usability.

1 Introduction

People with singular impairments have various usage barriers when navigating the web, including perceptual, cognitive, and social ones. A person with total hearing impairment can be understood as someone who is not able to understand the spoken language, regardless of amplification devices. There are multidisciplinary studies that explore alternatives for how to teach the written language to people that already know sign language. Despite advances in teaching practices, the level of comprehension of the written language amongst people with hearing loss varies from person to person.

Nowadays, although there is a large amount of visual information on the web, the predominant means of communication is still the written language. One of the challenges in the design of an accessible Web is how to understand the users' needs, what are their barriers during Web usage today, and their suggestions to remove or minimize these barriers.

Our previous studies [1], highlighted many difficulties for people with hearing loss using the Web. In these previous studies, we adapted two methods from the Problem Articulation Methods (PAM) [2]: the Semiotic framework (or Semiotic diagnosis) and the Evaluation framing (from the valuation framing) to analyze opinions and scenarios faced by internet users with hearing loss.

M. Kurosu (Ed.): Human-Computer Interaction, Part III, HCII 2014, LNCS 8512, pp. 277–288, 2014.

The focus of this paper is to investigate the semantic and normative aspects of barriers for people with hearing loss producing and consuming Web content. This investigation aims to elicit a set of requirements and recommendations for the design of Web content and application, and of assistive technology. The methodology used during the analysis is based on Gibson's [3] affordances concept expanded by Stamper in the Semantic Analysis Method (SAM) and the Norm Analysis Method (NAM) [2, 4]. The objective is to identify the affordances, as well as ontological dependencies and norms of the production and consumption of Web content.

Organizational Semiotics studies the nature, characteristics, function, and effect of information and communication in organizational contexts. An organization is considered a social system in which people behave in an organized manner by conforming to a certain system of norms [2]. Among the methods employed by the OS community is a set of methods known as MEASUR (Methods for Eliciting, Analyzing, and Specifying Users' Requirements) [2, 4]. The SAM is one of the MEASUR methods which focus on the agents and their pattern of behaviors.

In addition to the SAM, the NAM [3] is used to describe the relationships between an intentional use of signs and the resulting behavior of responsible agents in a social context. The behavioral norms express how people behave in regular patterns, e.g., for reading and writing on the Web.

In this study, the above-mentioned methods were adapted to be used in participatory practices with people with hearing loss. The study was performed using the following 4-step method: (1) *Individual Interview*, (2) *Semantic Analysis*, (3) *Norm Analysis and Problem Synthesis*, and (4) *Participatory Solutions Proposal*. Based on the findings, the article proposes high level design recommendations for enhancing accessibility for people with hearing loss, and discusses research challenges.

This paper is structured as follows: the second section defines key concepts used in this work, and presents the theoretical and methodological foundations of SAM and NAM; the third section presents the study methodology, including its context and subjects; the fourth section presents and discusses the results; and the fifth section concludes the paper.

2 Concepts and Methodological Foundations

In this section, we focus on introducing key concepts adopted in the paper, including the deaf literacy problem (subsection 2.1) and the accessibility on the web (subsection 2.2). This section also presents the theoretical and methodological foundations of SAM and NAM (subsection 2.3).

2.1 Deaf Literacy

The deafness concept (a degree of Hearing impairment) is associated with the inability to understand speech, even with amplification, i.e., the individual is impaired in processing linguistic information through hearing [5]. Face to face communication usually occurs during spoken language, however deaf people communicate primarily using gestures. Written language can be considered a second language for many, as a deaf persons' first language is usually Sign Language [6]. Studies highlight that diagnose and treatment of hearing impairment should be done during early years of child development to stimulate Neuroplasticity[1]. Early contact with sign language and other forms of expressions (e.g., written language) should be stimulated.

In practice, there are many people who are born with hearing impairment and achieve high levels of literacy skills. However, language skills vary from person to person. Furthermore, people (with or without hearing loss) are continually learning and improving their language skills due to new knowledge and experiences. According to [7], in Brazil only 7% of deaf people know how to read and write in Portuguese. One of the causes of this low literacy rate is the fact that literacy skills are frequently not taught in two languages at the same time.

In Bilingual deaf education, the students learn sign language as their first language, and written/spoken language as their second. In Brazil, Libras was recognized relatively late as a national language; nowadays, the use of Libras in education and government services is mandatory[2]. Nevertheless, according to some studies [e.g., 8], the Portuguese language is mostly an exclusive language for acquisition and knowledge sharing. In [8] the authors emphasize the need to promote the inclusion of the deaf community in the development of educational polices.

2.2 Hearing Loss and Web Accessibility

Previous studies (e.g., [1]) highlighted that the written language is a serious barrier for using the Web; for example, in situations where there are long and complex texts. Many deaf users read "word by word" trying to understand the meaning by associating each word with a sign that they already know. Another problem is the existence of many technical and typical Internet terms. The "Internet slang" (or Cyber-slang) is a barrier, because formal grammatical rules that can be learned (memorized) are commonly substituted by phonetic based constructions in the Portuguese language. Furthermore, some W3C recommendations such as the use of short and simple text are not always possible or easy to be followed by content producers.

There are various Assistive Technologies (AT) for supporting meaningful interactions on the Web. AT solutions for users with hearing loss range from simple caption editors to complex video generators, which translate the written text into sign language videos. These AT solutions are certainly an important mechanism for including people with hearing loss on the Web. However, in addition to AT, there is a need for research to be developed in the field of Web design, which will probably require new AT solutions.

Some studies argue that it necessary to promote the participation of users in the design process to provide properly accessible solutions [9]. One of the most difficult aspects is how to interact with the people that will use the interfaces in a proper way,

---

[1] Capacity of the neural system to reorganize due to learning activities or injuries.

[2] Law 10.436, April 24, 2002.
`http://www.planalto.gov.br/ccivil_03/Leis/2002/L10436.htm`

i.e., promoting the direct participation of all in the design process [10]. The development of appropriate practices and modeling methods for supporting the participatory design of accessible Web content is an open research issue.

As mentioned above, our previous studies [1] highlighted many difficulties for people with loss. The paper presented a study performed in two steps with 21 participants: (1) questionnaire and situation/scenario description, and (2) participatory evaluation of problems and barriers for using the Web. However, the study was limited to a conceptualization of the problem (by using the *Semiotic Framework*) and the identification of problems, questions, and solutions (by using the *Evaluation Framing*). This paper goes one step further by systematically studying problems related to normative aspects by using the SAM and NAM as methodological reference.

2.3 SAM and NAM Concepts

As part of MEASUR, SAM focuses on the agents and their pattern of behaviors. Some basic concepts of SAM adopted in this work are [2]:

- "Affordance", the concept originally introduced by Gibson [3] to express the behavior of an organism made available by some combined structure of the organism and its environment, was expanded by Stamper [11] to include invariants of the social world. Social affordances arise from the norms we share with people around us. Stamper argues that reality as we know it was not constructed individually; it was created by cultural development over millenniums. For example, a cup is a human artifact. Its use is not only possible because of its physical aspect but also because of its social affordances (children have learned to use it for drinking, instead of throwing it at someone);
- "An agent" is defined as something (e.g., a person, a cultural group or an organization) that has responsible behavior. Agents are affordances that can take responsibility both for their own actions and for the actions of others;
- "Role-name" is the role of the agents according to the affordances for which they are in charge. For example, the "content producer" is a person in charge of the "content";
- "An ontological dependency" is formed when an affordance is possible only if certain other affordances are available. For example, for a person to be able to stumble, he/she must first walk;
- "Determiners" are invariants of quality and quantity that differentiate one instance from another. For example, text size.

The concepts used in Semantic Analysis are represented by means of ontology charts, which have a graphical notation to represent agents (circles), affordances (rectangles), ontological dependencies (lines drawn from left to right), role-names (parentheses), whole-part relations (dot), and determiners (#).

The NAM focuses on social, cultural, and organizational norms that govern the actions of agents in the business domain. At the social level, norms describe beliefs, expectations, commitments, contract, law, culture, as well as business [2].

According to Liu [2] one way to categorize norms is according to how norms "control" human behavior (i.e., tendency of behaving in a certain way). Several norms can be identified in this way, each of which "governs" a certain aspect of human behavior. The *behavioural norms*, analyzed in this study, represent how people behave in regular patterns. People's behavior is affected by social conventions, law, standard procedures, among other aspects. The following example illustrates a behavioural norm description (using the formalism presented by [2]) in the context of this paper:

Whenever *someone is using a wiki*
if *is writing a post*
then *content producer*
is *obliged to*
to *use the correct verbal tense*

This formalism can be used to represent norms for Web content production and consumption in an organizational context; however it is worth mentioning that the behavioral norms are not understood (from the OS perspective) as a guide or handbook; they are linked to actual expected behavior agents in society. Stamper [12] emphasizes that norms can be understood as a "force field" that leads the agents to behave in a certain way; therefore norms are not concrete objects.

3 Methodology

This section presents the methodology employed in the study reported in this paper. Section 3.1 presents the subject and context where the study was performed. Sections 3.2, 3.3, 3.4 and 3.5 present, respectively, the four steps used in the study: *Individual Interview, Semantic Analysis, Norm Analysis and Problem Synthesis,* and *Participatory Solution Proposal.*

3.1 Subject and Context

The study presented in this paper was conducted in two institutions: the Deaf Service Center in the city of Macapá in Brazil - CAS (*Centro de Atendimento ao Surdo*), and the Deaf Mission (in Libras) of the Baptist Church of Macapá.

The study started in CAS with 21 participants, named Group 1 (Table 1). This group includes teachers, the director, and students. All the participants of Group 1 had high levels of hearing loss and were fluent in Libras. Nineteen participants (90%) had lip-reading skills; however they had different skill levels in the Portuguese language. Considering their educational levels, 14 participants held university degrees and 7 held high school degrees. Their ages ranged from 14 to 44 years old. All the participants declared that they use the internet frequently (more than once a week); nevertheless most of them also declared that they have serious difficulties using the internet. The participants have higher educational levels than the average Brazilian population. They also have high proficiency in sign language.

The Group 2 (Deaf Mission) was composed by 8 participants, including an interpreter. All the participants of Group 2 (Table 2) were fluent in Libras and had lip-reading skills (except for the interpreter). Six participants had high levels of hearing loss and varying skill levels in the Portuguese language. With respect to their educational levels, 3 participants held high school degrees and 4 participants were students. Their ages ranged from 12 to 26 years old. Four participants declared that they do not use the internet frequently (more than once a week). All participants (except for the interpreter) also declared that they have serious difficulties using the internet.

Table 1. Participants of the Study – Group 1

Nº	Name	Age	Educational level	Use Internet Frequently	Sign Language	Level of hearing loss	Lip reading
01	A.B.O.	28	Undergraduate (information systems)	Yes	Yes	Profound	No
02	D. S.	32	Undergraduate (information systems)	Yes	Yes	Profound	Yes
03	C. A. M. B.	40	Undergraduate (information systems)	Yes	Yes	Profound	No
04	C. C. S.	26	Undergraduate (pedagogy)	Yes	Yes	Profound	Yes
05	D. E. L.	28	Undergraduate (pedagogy)	Yes	Yes	Profound	Yes
06	F.	28	Secondary	Yes	Yes	Profound	Yes
07	G. L. C.	25	Graduate (pedagogy)	Yes	Yes	Moderate	Yes
08	J.	25	Secondary	Yes	Yes	Profound	No
09	V. R.	39	Undergraduate (pedagogy)	Yes	Yes	Profound	Yes
10	J. R. C.	32	Undergraduate (pedagogy)	Yes	Yes	Profound	Yes
11	A. –Teacher in CAS	32	Graduate (pedagogy)	Yes	Yes	Profound (hearing loss after age 8)	Yes
12	Rf. P.	26	Undergraduate (pedagogy)	Yes	Yes	Profound	Yes
13	Ro. P.	26	Undergraduate (pedagogy)	Yes	Yes	Profound	Yes
14	V. A.	28	Undergraduate (pedagogy)	Yes	Yes	Profound	Yes
15	J.A.P.B.	31	Undergraduate (pedagogy)	Yes	Yes	Profound (hearing loss after age 7)	Yes
16	M.J.N.C.B. CAS Director	44	Graduate (pedagogy)	Yes	Yes	Profound	Yes
17	T.N.C.	15	Primary school student	Yes	Yes	Severe	Yes
18	A.S.C.	23	Secondary	Yes	Yes	Profound	Yes
19	M.L.M.	16	Secondary school student	Yes	Yes	Profound	Yes
20	L.B.C.	26	Secondary	Yes	Yes	Profound	Yes
21	R.S.C.	17	Secondary school student	Yes	Yes	Profound	Yes

Table 2. Participants of the Study – Group 2

Nº	Name	Age	Educational level	Use Internet Frequently	Sign Language	Level of hearing loss	Lip reading
01	T.N.C	15	Secondary school student	Yes	Yes	Profound	Yes
02	A.S.C	23	Secondary	Yes	Yes	Profound	Yes
03	A.P	21	Secondary	No	Yes	Profound	Yes
04	J.B	12	Secondary school student	Yes	Yes	Profound	Yes
05	L.B.C	26	Adult education primary	No	Yes	Profound	Yes
06	M.L.M	16	Secondary	No	Yes	Profound	Yes
07	R.S.C	17	Adult education secondary	No	Yes	Moderate	Yes
08	D.- interpret			Yes	Yes	No	

3.2 Individual Interview

The results from the application of the PAM, present in [1], with all participants of Group 1 were used to elaborate the structure and questions of the individual interviews. After the interviews, the groups discussed the issues elicited.

The objective of the individual interviews was to clarify key aspects elicited by the participants. The individual interview was preformed initially with two teacher of CAS (participants 11 and 16 in Table 1). The answers were collected in to steps: they were asked to write their answer on paper and then to discuss with the designers.

Table 3. Individual Interview Questions

Nº	Questions
1	What are the computer devices that you have problems using?
2	Do you use internet search tools?
3	Do you use social networks ?
4	Can you easily navigate Web pages? What are your difficulties?
5	Can you understand the results presented by the search tools? Can you find what you searched for?
6	Do you enjoy the websites? Do you feel comfortable?
7	Do you consider that it is easy to learn how to interact with the websites? Do you easily remember what you found?
8	Do you frequently need help to interact with the computer?
9	Describe your experiences using computer systems.
10	Can you use discussion Forums, where you have to interact simultaneous with other users?
11	Do you have any additional comment or observation?

3.3 Semantic Analysis

The semantic analysis began by using problem descriptions synthesized from the answers from individual and group interviews. The affordances were then identified, grouped, and represented in an ontology chart.

The affordances represent the main invariants of behavior necessary to produce and consume Web content. The ontology chart also described the dependencies of each affordance, the main roles, specializations, and part-whole relationships. Each affordance was individually discussed and analyzed in the next step.

3.4 Norm Analysis and Problem Synthesis

In addition to the interviews (individual and group), 30 questions regarding grammatical rules and semantic aspects were discussed with the participants. The objective was to identify the most common errors when reading and writing Portuguese texts/posts on the Web. These errors became the basis for modeling a set of behavioral norms for the affordances modeled in the semantic analysis. These norms represent the expected behavior necessary to properly read, write, and interact on the Web.

The norm analysis focused on three types of Web activities: synchronous communication (e.g., Web chat), asynchronous communication (e.g., wiki, blogs and social network posting), and information recovery (using search mechanisms). Each norm was discussed with the participants: they were questioned about the difficulties "to obey/follow" the formal norms. After that, typical writing problems were discussed with the participants (Group 1 and 2) aiming to clarify the reasons behind their mistakes.

3.5 Participatory Solutions Proposal

For each norm discussed with the participants, possible high-level design solutions (including the use of AT) were cooperatively developed. The focus was on possible solutions that stimulate learning and the full autonomy of the users. In addition, we conducted a *StoryTelling* [13] session with Group 1; this participatory practice helped us understand the problem and visualize possible solutions. The technique was adapted to facilitate communication, which included the presence of an interpreter to support the conduction of the activities.

A *BrainDraw* [13] session was then conducted with six participants from Group 1 that declared to have higher skills using the Web. Two participants drew the solutions on paper and four participants used a computer graphics tool. The objective was to produce design alternatives from the users' point of view.

4 Results and Discussion

Figure 1 presents the ontology chart (simplified) of textual production and consumption. The main agents involved in this task are:

- *Society*: as the root agents, which means that all the agents and affordances are existentially dependent on that society;
- *Person*: Person is also a central agent and *Hearing* is a determiner of a person. The *Person* agent has two roles:
  - *Content Producer*: The person who produces *Web Content*: the *Designer* is a *Content Producer*;
  - *Content Consumer*: The person who consumes the *Web Content*;

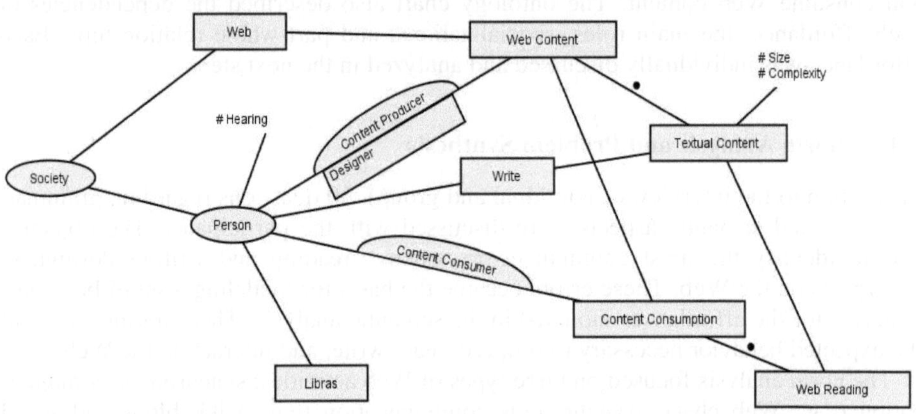

Fig. 1. Ontology Chart of Textual Production and Consumption Overview

Figure 1 also presents the main *affordances*, ontological dependencies for this task:

- *Web*: The Web is an affordance of society. The society is in charge of the Web and it is an ontological dependent of the society, i.e., the Web exists while the society exists;
- *Write*: It is an affordance of a *Person*;
- *Web Content* (production): It depends on the existence of the *Web* and the *Content Producer* (to produce and maintain it). *Textual Content* is part of the *Web Content* and depends on *Write*. *Size* and *Complexity* are examples of determiners of the *Textual Content*;

- *Content Consumption*: It is an affordance of *Content Consumer*. *Web Textual Reading* is part of the *Content Consumption* and depends on *Textual Content*;

A total of 121 norms were modeled to formalize the most expressive (according to the users' views) writing and reading rules for the three scenarios (synchronous communication, asynchronous communication, and information recovering). Table 5 illustrates examples of the norms and the respective problems that were identified by the participants as the root cause of norm violations, i.e., the problems represent the users' view of why they violate the norm. Table 5 includes only the norms for reading tasks in synchronous communication tools. Similar tables were constructed for the other scenarios.

Table 4. Norms and primary problems detected on Chart reading

Nº	Norm	Problem
1	**Whenever** using instant messages tools **if** have to read something (in Portuguese) **then** "Content Consumer" **is *obliged*** **to** understand the general meaning of Portuguese sentences	Some users have Libras as their first language , without the appropriate Portuguese education.
2	**whenever** using instant messages tools **if** have to read something (in Portuguese) **then** Content Consumer" **is *obliged*** **to** know the meaning of words (individually)	Deaf people usually know fewer words; frequently in Brazil they only know basics words.
3	**whenever** navigating the Web **if** have to read something (in Portuguese) **then** "Content Consumer" **is *obliged*** **to** know the words' synonym	Frequently this population knows only one meaning for each word, sometimes it is hard to understand a synonym, because they usually associate the words with visual signs
4	**whenever** using instant messages tools **if** have to read something (in Portuguese) **then** "Content Consumer" **is *obliged*** **to** know the words figuratively	Commonly users associated the words with the concrete meaning of the words
5	**whenever** using instant messages tools **if** have to read something (in Portuguese) **then** "Content Consumer" **is *obliged*** **to** know the verbal tense	Usually the verbal tense is not stressed in the Portuguese alphabetization for deaf people. It is not easy to associate the verbal forms to visual elements.
6	**whenever** using instant messages tools **if** have to read something (in Portuguese) **then** "Content Consumer" **is *obliged*** **to** know the word from technology	Some words introduced in the Portuguese language (from technology) have no standard signs in Libras. Frequently users employ English words during Web communication.
7	**whenever** using instant messages tools **if** have to read something (in Portuguese) **then** "Content Consumer" **is *obliged*** **to** read quickly	Deaf people read each word in isolation making it, difficult to understand the (complex) text quickly.
8	**whenever** using instant messages tools **if** have to read something (in Portuguese) **then** "Content Consumer" **is *obliged*** **to** interpret the language based on phonemes	Phoneme based words are hard to understand. Many words in internet slang are based on phonemes and there is no standard translation to Libras. Sometimes the formal grammatical rules are not obeyed to form phoneme-based sentences.

A total of 121 high level design recommendations were produced with the users. These are design solutions that must be implemented by the developers of detailed design solutions, for each specific situation or tool. Table 6 presents the design recommendations for the chat reading problems, i.e., for each norm and problem presented in Table 5 there are respective recommendations in Table 6.

Table 5. Chat design recomendations

Nº	Elicited Alternatives	Elicited Recommendations
1	Minimize the problem with examples of how to interpret the text.	Include options to explain the meaning of each term and construction of the sentence
2	Teach by showing the meaning of the words the suer does not know.	Include options that explain the meaning of the words, exemplifying them with contextualized scenarios; those scenarios can be complemented with visual elements, e.g., using either Libras or images/videos.
3	Teach by showing the meaning of the synonym the user does not know.	Include options that explain the various meanings of a word, exemplifying them with contextualized scenarios where it could be used; those scenarios can be complemented with visual elements, e.g., using either Libras or images/videos.
4	Teach by showing the figurative meaning of the words.	Include options that explain the figurative meaning of a word, exemplifying them with contextualized scenarios where it could be used; those scenarios can be complemented by visual elements, e.g., using either Libras or images/videos.
5	Minimize the problem with examples of the verbal tense.	Include options that explain the meaning of each verbal construction for a selected verb, exemplifying them by contextualized scenarios where it could be used; those scenarios can be complemented by visual elements, e.g., using either Libras or images/videos.
6	Teach by showing the meaning of the words introduced by the technology.	Include options that explain the meaning of each word introduced by the technology in a sentence, exemplifying them by contextualized scenarios where it could be used; those scenarios can be complemented by visual elements, e.g., using either Libras or images/videos.
7	Include reading assistance and automatic translations to help with quick reading	Include options that help users utilize assistances (e.g., with hints), text simplifiers and/or Libras translators.
8	Teach by showing the meaning of the sentences based on phonemes	Include options that explain the meaning of the sentences based on phonemes, exemplifying them by contextualized scenarios where it could be used; those scenarios can be complemented by visual elements, e.g., using either Libras or images/videos.

Figure 2 presents an example of the design solution proposed by the users after *StoryTelling* and *Braindraw* practices. Designers modeled the solutions based on the design alternatives produced with the participants during the *Braindraw* sessions. The design solutions illustrate the proposed recommendations. Therefore, the objective was not to develop detailed solutions to be followed, but provide examples to illustrate the recommendations.

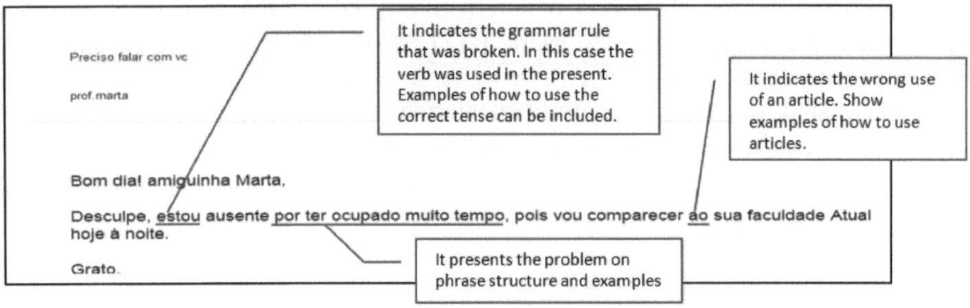

Fig. 2. Example of design solution proposed with the users

We produced a total of 46 interface prototypes with the objective of illustrating the recommendations. Some prototypes grouped the recommendations in a single interface. Considering the three scenarios, the results show that one problem can potentially be repeated in many situations and tools; simultaneously, some solutions may minimize barriers for various different problems. Some recommendations are quite simple and easily developed using existing AT, while others are complex or depend on additional research on new assistive tools.

In general, the results show the potential (as initial experiments) of using the Web to stimulate learning of the written language. These results contradict the idea of creating a separated *web* or even a translated *Web* for deaf people. In our view, the role of AT on the *Web* (*e.*g., Libras translators, text simplifiers, and dedicated devices) goes beyond providing means to expand perceptual aspects. Its role is also (in a properly design solution) to promote learning and user independency in long term.

However, this work does not present conclusive design solutions. Although some solutions were proposed by the users, more studies should be conducted with the objective of producing complete and standard design recommendations. In particular, there is a need for empirical data about the impacts of using the proposed recommendations on the *Web*. The effects on learning and users' autonomy can only be precisely analyzed after an extensive period of use by several users.

5 Conclusion

Written language is still the predominant means of communication on the Web. Many people with hearing loss have difficulties understanding and producing text-based content. On the Web these difficulties are exacerbated due to the use of technical terms, internet slang, and the demand for reading and writing quickly (especially on synchronous communication tools). In this paper, we have analyzed the barriers for users with hearing loss while using the Web. A study, using SAM and NAM as the methodological reference, was performed with 29 users and focused on the elicitation of barriers when producing and consuming *Web* content. A total of 129 norms were developed by the users. These norms represent commonly expected behaviors that are not followed due to problems users have during synchronous communication, asynchronous communication, and information recovering tasks. Participatory practices were conducted for the elicitation of alternatives, and for the high level design of recommendations according to the users' point of view. The proposed recommendations can be seen as a set of design issues to be deeply explored in the future.

As a next step, we propose the implementation of prototypes with the elicited recommendations, followed by empirical studies with the users. The results from the empirical studies can be used in an interactive process to improve the recommendations.

References

1. Ferreira, M.A.M., Bonacin, R.: Analyzing Barriers for People with Hearing Loss on the Web: A Semiotic Study. In: Stephanidis, C., Antona, M. (eds.) UAHCI/HCII 2013, Part II. LNCS, vol. 8010, pp. 694–703. Springer, Heidelberg (2013)
2. Liu, K.: Semiotics in information systems engineering. Cambridge University Press (2000)
3. Gibson, J.J.: The Theory of Affordances. In: Shaw, R., Bransford, J. (eds.) Perceiving, Acting, and Knowing (1977)
4. Stamper, R.: Social Norms in Requirements Analysis – an outline of MEASUR. In: Jirotka, M., Goguen, J., Bickerton, M. (eds.) Requirements Engineering, Technical and Social Aspects. Academic Press, New York (1993)
5. Elzouki, A.Y., Harfi, H.A., Nazer, H., Oh, W., Stapleton, F.B., Whitley, R.J.: Textbook of Clinical Pediatrics, vol. 1. Springer (2011)
6. Power, D., Leigh, G.R.: Principles and practices of literacy development for deaf learners: A historical overview. Journal of Deaf Studies and Deaf Education 5, 3–8 (2000)
7. Moura, G., Vasconcelos, L.A., Cavalcanti, A., Breyer, F., da Silva, D., Teixeira, J.M., Leão, C., Kelner, J.: Luz, Câmera, Libras!: How a Mobile Game Can Improve the Learning of Sign Languages. In: Marcus, A. (ed.) DUXU/HCII 2013. LNCS, vol. 8013, pp. 266–275. Springer, Heidelberg (2013)
8. Fernandes, E.: Surdez e Bilinguismo, 4th edn., Editora Mediação. Porto Alegre (2011)
9. Keates, S., Looms, P.O.: User –Centered design and accessibility in real-world contexts. HCI Tutorial. Springer, Heidelberg (2013)
10. Fuglerud, K.S., Sloan, D.: The Link between Inclusive Design and Innovation: Some Key Elements. In: Kurosu, M. (ed.) HCII/HCI 2013, Part I. LNCS, vol. 8004, pp. 41–50. Springer, Heidelberg (2013)
11. Stamper, R.: Signs, Information and Systems. In: Holmqnist, B., et al. (eds.) Signs of Work Semiotics Information Processing in Organisations. Walter de Gruyter, N. Y (1996)
12. Stamper, R.K.: Information Systems as a Social Science: An Alternative to the FRISCO Formalism. In: Falkenberg, E.D., Lyytien, K., Verrijn-Stuart, A.A. (eds.) Information System Concepts: an Integrated Discipline Emerging, pp. 1–51. Kluwer Academic Publishers, USA (2000)
13. Müller, M.J., Haslwanter, J.H., Dayton, T.: Participatory Pratices in the Software Lifecycle. In: Helander, M., Landauer, T.K., Prabhu, P. (eds.) Handbook of Human-Computer Interaction, 2nd edn., pp. 255–297. Elsevier Science (1997)

Can a Theory-Informed Interactive Animation Increase Intentions to Engage in Physical Activity in Young People with Asthma?

Jennifer Murray[1], Brian Williams[2], Gaylor Hoskins[2], Silje Skar[2], John McGhee[3], Dylan Gauld[4], Gordon Brown[5], Shaun Treweek[6], Falko Sniehotta[7], Linda Cameron[8], Aziz Sheikh[9], and Suzanne Hagen[10]

[1] Edinburgh Napier University, School of Life, Sport and Social Sciences, Edinburgh, Scotland
j.murray2@napier.ac.uk
[2] Nursing, Midwifery and Allied Health Professions Research Unit, University of Stirling, Stirling, Scotland
{brian.williams,gaylor.hoskins,silje.skar}@stir.ac.uk
[3] College of Fine Arts, University of New South Wales, Australia
john.mcghee@unsw.edu.au
[4] Duncan of Jordanstone College of Art and Design, University of Dundee, Dundee, Scotland
d.gauld@dundee.ac.uk
[5] Asthma UK Scotland, Edinburgh, Scotland
gbrown@asthma.co.uk
[6] Health Services Research Unit, University of Aberdeen, Aberdeen, Scotland
s.treweek@abdn.ac.uk
[7] Newcastle University, Newcastle, England
falko.sniehotta@ncl.ac.uk
[8] University of California Merced, California, USA
lcameron@ucmerced.edu
[9] The University of Edinburgh, Edinburgh, Scotland
Aziz.Sheikh@ed.ac.uk
[10] Nursing, Midwifery and Allied Health Professions Research Unit, Glasgow Caledonian University, Glasgow, Scotland
s.hagen@gcu.ac.uk

Abstract. A theoretically-informed interactive animation was developed, using themes drawn from psychology, sociology, applied health research, and narrative theory, which aimed to encourage young people with asthma to engage in physical activity. The animation was evaluated using qualitative and quantitative methods. A web-based Interactive Modelling Experiment was used to evaluate whether the animation was effective in three key areas: knowledge about asthma, inhaler use, and intention to increase physical activity. One-to-one interviews and focus groups were used to evaluate the acceptability of the animation and whether the theoretical basis was effective. Preliminary qualitative findings indicate good acceptability and perceived effectiveness. The quantitative findings are less clear, with a change in simulated activity and inhaler use being found, but with no clear association between these changes and the animation itself. Future work will be carried out to established whether these levels

M. Kurosu (Ed.): Human-Computer Interaction, Part III, HCII 2014, LNCS 8512, pp. 289–300, 2014.

of acceptability and perceived effectiveness are actually translated into behaviour change.

Keywords: Asthma, interactive animation, wIME, theory-informed, multidisciplinary.

1 Introduction

Visualisation techniques are increasing in popularity as health care interventions [1]. However, despite this increasing popularity, the majority of visual health interventions are not being developed using sound theoretical bases or even explicit theoretical [2] or design frameworks [1]. This lack of definition and explicit targeting of the underlying mechanisms upon which an intervention is based may impede the success of and evaluation of the intervention; only through understanding and defining the concepts and constructs that the intervention seeks to change and embedding these using a solid theoretical framework can the success of an intervention be measured.

In order to move away from inductive, intuitive creation of health promotion visual interventions, a four stage process for development and evaluation has been developed [1], based on the UK Medical research Council Framework for Development and Evaluation of Complex Interventions [3]. The model proposed is a staged process. To begin, a theoretical basis should be established (the conceptual content). Following this, the modelling structure/visual narrative should be developed, with the 'look' of the intervention then being created. An iterative process of development may continue until a suitable solution is reached at this point, moving between the design stages. Following this, a period of modelling checking should occur, to establish the interpretation of the intervention and its potential impact.

The current research sought to evaluate the effectiveness of an interactive animation that had been developed in line with the described framework for developing complex visual interventions for use in health care [1] and that had a strong, explicit theoretical framework informing its development and content [4]. In brief, cognitive learning theories, health behaviour/behaviour change theories, self-efficacy, narrative theories and HCI principals were embedded within the animation in order to attempt to optimise its propensity for intention and behaviour change [4]. The animation itself aims to increase intentions to (and ultimately increase) engagement in physical activity among young people with asthma (aged 12-18 years), and to increase their knowledge about their asthma and safe/proper inhaler use.

In the UK, the incidence of asthma has increased significantly [5], with approximately one in five children in the UK now being affected by asthma [6, 7]. It is known that physical activity levels among healthy young people is dropping in industrialised nations [8], and that young people with asthma are even less likely than their peers to be physically active [9], despite the evidence linking physical activity to improved asthma control/coping [10], reduced hospital admissions, reduced absenteeism from school, fewer consultations with health professionals, and reduced medication use [11].

There is therefore an urgent need to develop strategies that address the unique barriers faced by young people with asthma in order to increase physical activity and exercise, and interventions that are tailored to young people specifically. The animation that the current paper will evaluate was developed with this need as a key focus. The hypotheses for the evaluation are:

H1: The animation will increase people's simulated intentions to engage in physical activity.

H2: The animation will increase people's intentions to engage in safe/proper inhaler use.

2 Method

2.1 Design

Using a web-based Interactive Modelling Experiment (wIME), a 2x2 mixed factorial design was used to evaluate the effectiveness of the animation, with participants completing a 'baseline' online questionnaire and then completing the same questionnaire approximately two weeks later after either being shown the animation or being assigned to a control group (no animation or alternative was shown). The dependent variables were people's responses on the questionnaire. In addition, one-to-one in-depth interviews and small focus groups were used to assess the acceptability of the animation and to identify whether the theoretical basis for the animation was acceptable and effective. Framework analysis was used to analyse the qualitative data.

2.2 Participants

For the wIME, participants were recruited online, via social networking sites (e.g., Facebook, Twitter) and through specific online asthma-interest groups (e.g., Asthma UK forums). Snowballing was also encouraged, with participants being asked to distribute the link to the questionnaire to potentially interested parties. Target participants were young people with asthma (12-18years) or parents of young people with asthma. Fifty-three participants completed the initial questionnaire (pre-intervention; 24 parents, 29 young people). Twenty-six participants completed both the pre-intervention and post-intervention questionnaire (14 parents, 12 young people), indicating a 49% completion rate. Of those who participated in both questionnaires, 16 were allocated to the control condition and 10 to the animation intervention condition. The mean age of the young-people participants was 17.3 years (17.3 years animation condition; 17.2 years control condition). Seven were male and 19 were female (parents answered on behalf of their male/female child, where it was a parent who responded). Participants were randomly allocated to conditions. All participants indicated that they had asthma or were a parent of a young person with asthma.

For the one-to-one interviews, four participants were recruited via the National Health Service in Scotland. Young people with asthma were identified by an asthma nurse and were approached and informed about the study (with their parent) and invited to participate by the health professional. A 'young person' was defined as someone aged between 12-18 years, for the purposes of the current research, as this was the age group for which the animation was primarily developed/designed for. Those who were interested were then contacted by the researchers and provided with additional information. All participants were offered the opportunity to have their parents present during the interview. The focus groups consisted of health professionals and school physical education teachers. Participants were recruited through purposeful sampling, by pre-identifying potentially interested parties through mailing lists, asthma interest groups, and through contacting primary clinics directly. Two focus groups were carried out, involving eight participants in total. Interviews and focus groups lasted approximately 40 minutes to one hour in length.

2.3 Materials

The animation was developed using theory to guide the content and 'look', using a multi-disciplinary perspective and included theoretical bases drawn from applied health research, HCI, sociology and psychology. A fuller description of the theoretical development for the animation is detailed elsewhere [4]. The animation aimed to increase levels of physical activity in young people with asthma, while also increasing their knowledge about their asthma and what occurs within the lungs when they are breathless during exercise in comparison to being breathless due to their asthma, and their knowledge about inhaler use. In addition to these key areas of outcome measurement, the animation also was embedded with information to promote safety-asthma messages and self-efficacy building messages (theories that were deemed to be important based on the existent literature and previous in-depth qualitative work carried out by the research team in relation to asthma and physical activity). The animation lasts for approximately seven minutes and allows the user to select a male or female character, which type of activity the character will take part in (running, dance or football) and, at various stages, whether the character will take an inhaler or not. After the animation has been played the user has the option to re-run selecting different options to view different outcomes. For the purpose of the evaluation, to allow consistency across user experiences, users were only able to select running as an activity but could still select their character and the inhaler use options. The animation was developed to appeal to 12-18 year olds and emulated the look of a popular 3D animation style used in film. Colours, visual content, textual and speech content were carefully selected by the research team to enhance the learning opportunities and coherence. The animation's development was further informed by an online consultative user group. This group consisted of 23 people; a mixture of young people with asthma, health professionals, parents, and school staff. The group were consulted on key elements of the animation as they were under development (e.g., character design, gender and activity types to be used in the animation, narratives and storyboarding) in order to increase the animation's acceptability and resonance with key stakeholders. This process was found to be highly informative in shaping the final artefact.

The wIME was hosted on LifeGuide (www.lifeguideonline.org). A wIME is a way of carrying out exploratory work prior to conducting a full-scale trial [12]. Key elements of the intervention can be manipulated to simulate real world effects.

The benefits of IMEs to inform behaviour change research have been demonstrated [13, 14], thus the method was deemed a cost effective and suitable first step in evaluating the effectiveness of the animation. The wIME consisted of a large number of questions which fit under various sub-themes, including asthma perceptions, asthma knowledge, asthma severity, questions specific to theoretical bases for the animation (e.g., Theory of Planned Behaviour [15]), current levels of physical, intentions to engage in physical activity, inhaler use, and finally reactions to specific vignettes relating to projected inhaler use and physical activity decisions. For the purposes of the current paper, only the vignette-related responses will be discussed. It is intended that the remaining wIME findings will be published elsewhere in the future.

The vignettes were balanced in terms of gender, age of character within vignette (all fell within 12-18 year age range), asthma severity, asthma control, level of physical exertion required for the activity and inhaler use. Sixteen vignettes were created in total: eight for pre-intervention and eight for post-intervention, with eight female and eight male vignettes. Pre- and post- intervention, participants responded to four vignettes. Male participants read versions of the vignettes with a named male character and females received vignette versions with a named female character in order to increase the potential for vicarious learning, in line with e-learning and artificial intelligence 'co-learner' theories [16]. The vignettes were developed in line with empirical guidance on effective vignette development [17, 18] and were piloted and fed-back on by the consultative user group prior to their use in the evaluation. Vignettes were all of approximately equal length (approx 150 words), with all provided information being directly relevant to the study's focus, with consistent volume, type and order of presented information being present across vignettes. Each vignette asked participants to imagine that they were the character and say whether they would take their inhaler (inhaler use simulation; two questions which were summed and an average score was calculated) and whether they would engage in physical activity (physical activity simulation; two questions which were summed and an average score was calculated), and how difficult it was to make these judgements. All of the vignette based questions were answered on a seven point likert-style scale, with 1 indicating a less positive response and 7 indicatng a more positive response.

A topic guide was used to help structure and focus the interviews and focus groups. However, these were mainly participant led discussions and the discussions were therefore not highly structured. Framework analysis was used, following Published guidance [19] to analyse the data. Framework analysis is a systematic form of thematic analysis which uses clear steps for the analysis process and produces highly structured, summarised data. It has been successfully used in policy research for 25 years and is increasingly being used to analyse qualitative data collected in applied health research [19]. Key themes and sub-themes were identified both within the individual interviews and focus groups and across the whole data set, providing a descriptive overview of the whole data set. Standardised consent forms and information sheets were used in all of the evaluation processes to ensure informed consent, and interviews and focus groups were audio-recorded using a digital audio recording device.

2.4 Procedure

The wIME. Participants were recruited online, via a dedicated link to the baseline questionnaire (pre-intervention). After reading the information sheet and consenting to participation in the study, participants completed the questionnaire which assessed their current knowledge a about asthma, knowledge about inhaler use, and intention to increase physical activity. Following on from the questionnaire, the participants read four vignettes which described a young person with asthma who was engaging in a physically active task and answered questions relating to inhaler use and physical activity engagement based on the vignettes. Upon completion, participants were directed to a debriefing page where they were asked for their contact email address in order for them to be invited to participate in the second part of the study and, by means of incentive, were entered into a competition to win an iPod if they chose to take part in the second stage. After approximately two weeks, participants were emailed and invited to take part in the second stage of the study. They were provided with a link to take part in either the control condition (no animation) or the experimental condition (animation). Participants in the control condition completed the same questionnaire as in the first stage, and then were presented with four new vignettes that were designed to be balanced with/equivalent to the four that they had previously read. They again answered questions on these. They were then debriefed and were offered the opportunity to view the animation (for fairness). Participants in the experimental condition first viewed the animation and then completed the questionnaire and vignettes, and were then debriefed.

One-to-one in-depth qualitative interviews and focus groups. Participants read a standardised information sheet and completed a consent form prior to the session beginning, and all sessions took part in a suitable, private room to avoid distractions. Participants were verbally informed that the researchers were interested in their assessments of and interpretations of the animation that had been developed. The purpose of the animation was not disclosed until after the procedure (during debriefing) to avoid confounding the interpretations or biasing the participants' viewpoints. Participants were asked to view/use the animation and were told that they could work through it as many times as they wanted and that they could either comment on the animation as they were using it (i.e., 'think aloud' techniques, commonly used within clinical evaluations and for usability testing [20]; in line with methods previously used in similar contexts [1]). Following the viewing of the animation, the interviews/focus groups were carried out. These began by asking the participant(s) to explain what the animation was trying to convey, and the participants' interpretations were then used to structure the subsequent discussion(s). Following the interviews and focus groups, participants were fully debriefed.

3 Results

3.1 Results of the wIME

To test the Hypothesis that the animation would increase people's simulated intentions to engage in physical activity, a 2x2 mixed factorial ANOVA was conducted, with the between groups independent variable being the control vs animation condition and the within groups independent variable being the pre/post intervention. The dependent variable was participants' ratings for simulated intentions to engage in physical activity. The results are shown in Table 1. A main effect of time was found, $F(1,19)=23.45$, $p<0.001$, $n^2p=0.552$, indicating that when completing the questionnaire at time point two (post-intervention), participants had a greater intention to engage in physical activity (mean 3.95) than when they completed the questionnaire at time point one (pre-intervention; mean 2.89). No main effect of condition (control vs animation) or interaction was present and so this change cannot be attributed to the animation.

Table 1. Descriptive statistics for ratings of simulated intentions to engage in physical activity across the control/animation conditions and the pre/post intervention time points

		N	Mean	SD
Pre-intervention	*Control*	12	2.94	0.93
	Animation	9	2.81	0.75
	Total	21	2.89	0.84
Post-Intervention	*Control*	12	3.93	0.31
	Animation	9	3.99	0.04
	Total	21	3.95	0.23

To test the hypothesis that the animation would increase people's intentions to engage in safe/proper inhaler use, a 2x2 mixed factorial ANOVA was conducted, with the between groups independent variable being the control vs animation condition and the within groups independent variable being the pre/post intervention. The dependent variable was participants' ratings for intentions to engage in safe/proper inhaler use. The results are shown in Table 2. A main effect of time was found, $F(1,18)=81.74$, $p<0.001$, n2p=0.820, indicating that when completing the questionnaire at time point two (post-intervention), participants had a lower intention to engage in safe/correct inhaler use (mean 3.93) than when they completed the questionnaire at time point one (pre-intervention; mean 4.66). No main effect of condition (control vs animation) or interaction was present and so this change, again, cannot be attributed to the animation.

Table 2. Descriptive statistics for ratings of simulated inhaler use across the control/animation conditions and the pre/post intervention time points

		N	Mean	SD
Pre-intervention	*Control*	13	4.69	0.26
	Animation	7	4.61	0.21
	Total	20	4.66	0.24
Post-Intervention	*Control*	13	4.00	<0.01
	Animation	7	3.79	0.57
	Total	20	3.93	0.34

Finally decision difficulty relating to activity intentions and inhaler use intentions was investigated. In order to assess whether decision difficulty increased overall between the pre/post intervention conditions and across the control and animation conditions, a 2x2 mixed factorial ANOVA was carried out. No significant main effects or interactions ($p>0.05$) were found, indicating that rating decision difficulty was not different across the pre/post intervention time points or across the control/animation conditions. These findings are illustrated in Table 3.

Table 2. Descriptive statistics for ratings of decision making difficulty across the control/animation conditions and the pre/post intervention time points

		N	Mean	SD
Pre-intervention	*Control*	11	5.11	0.21
	Animation	7	5.36	0.64
	Total	18	5.21	0.43
Post-Intervention	*Control*	11	5.14	0.26
	Animation	7	4.86	0.38
	Total	18	5.03	0.33

A Pearson's correlation was carried out to identify whether there were any relationships between decision difficulty, inhaler intentions and physical activity intentions between the control and animation groups (post-intervention ratings only). None of the relationships were statistically significant ($p>0.05$). However, the relationship between decision difficulty and physical activity simulation ratings was approaching significance, $r=-0.445$, $p=0.06$, $r2=0.198$ (19.8% shared variance). This relationship is illustrated in Figure 1; as shown, it appears that as decision difficulty increases, the intention to take part in physical activities decreases.

3.2 Results of the Qualitative Evaluation

Seven key themes emerged from the data: asthma and personal experiences; asthma and medication; physical activity at school; physical activity outside school; the animation; the support of friends and family; and translating their knowledge into practice. Of particular interest in the context of the current paper are the themes: 'asthma and medication', 'the animation' and ''translating knowledge into practice.' These will be discussed further, with a fuller and more detailed description of the rest of the themes being planned for a future publication. In relation to 'asthma and medication', participants discussed their current understandings of their medication and how it works, and related this to their change in knowledge following viewing the animation. This was largely a positive change, for example: "P: And especially the bit where it showed the little capillaries inside the canister... cause I think for children... to see it, so I think that actually just puts it in their head that there is actually something in there... so I felt that was really good, especially for wee ones. Just cause... you know, cause he was quite young when he got it, so I think that was quite... maybe it was

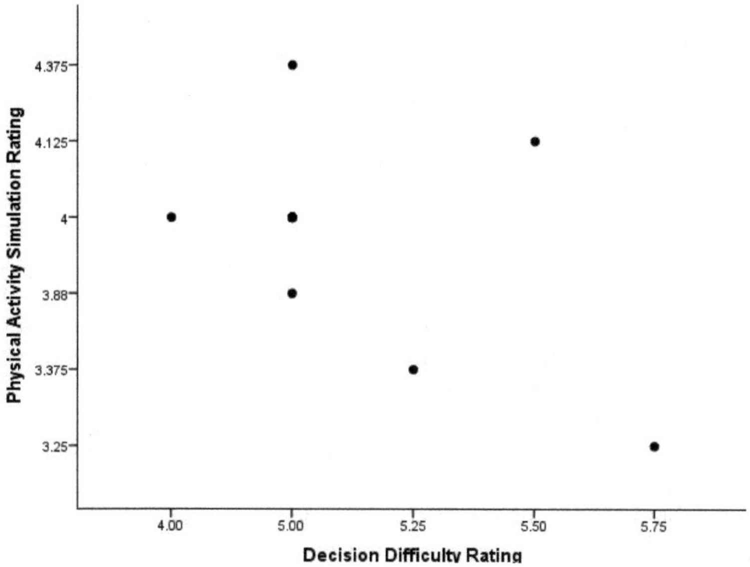

Fig. 1. Relationship between decision difficulty and physical activity simulation ratings for time point 2 (post-intervention)

more age for maybe seven or eight I think or even smaller it could be even more simplified, but I think it's very good."

In relation to 'the animation', participants responded to and directly discussed the animation and their attitudes towards it. Again, his was largely positive, with comments relating to the animation look ("P: When I saw the one with AJ, he did the one activity that I also do"), content ("INT: Was it too much information for them? P: I don't think for a 12 year old, it's quite basic, it's quite basic for Sarah's age and maybe to 18, but for kids and stuff I think it's good. It was explained, it simplified it down which was good and it showed you how... would work"), and purpose ("INT: So how helpful did you find, in your own words, how helpful did you find the animation? P: I found it quite helpful because it did explain to you well how you can do things if you have asthma, and even if you need to take your inhaler during it and you can still keep going") being viewed as acceptable and useful.

In relation to 'translating knowledge into practice', participants discussed the ways that their new knowledge about their asthma (through watching the animation) may influence their future participation in physical activity, expressing initial difficulties/concerns with this: "INT: So would you consider being more physically active, but I guess you have to talk with your GP or your health professionals and things before that, but your view of physical activity and asthma, d'you find it difficult? P: Yeah I find it quite difficult to do stuff like that but watching that, telling you what to do and stuff before sport and stuff"; and then later expressing increased motivation to engage in physical activity, "INT: Okay. And after viewing the animation, d'you think you're more motivated to be more physically active? P: Definitely."

4 Discussion

The present research aimed to identify whether a theory informed interactive animation could be used to increase intentions to engage in physical activity and improve knowledge about and intentions to use inhalers safely among young people with asthma and relevant others involved in their health care (i.e., parents, school staff, health professionals), and to identify whether the animation was acceptable to and meaningful to these groups. These aims were measured through an online evaluation (wIME), one-to-one in depth interviews and focus groups. The findings of the evaluation were mixed, and therefore indicates that further investigation is required.

The qualitative evaluations did indeed indicate that young people with asthma, parents, school staff and health professionals saw value in the animation, believing that it increased their knowledge about asthma; specifically, what happens in the lungs when a person is breathless due to asthma compared to when they are simply breathless due to being active, and increasing knowledge about inhaler use and purpose. Of particular positive note for the animation in terms of design and HCI, participants indicated that the animation's look was appealing, the level of choice in terms of characters and activities was advantageous to their immersion and experience, and that the level of information was about right (i.e., not too detailed and not too basic).

The qualitative findings are highly positive, and indicate that the animation may hold some promise. However, the quantitative findings are less indicative. Findings did indicate that the intention to engage in physical activity was greater at the second time-point (post-intervention questionnaire), but this increase was not statistically related to or accounted for by the animation itself. In addition, significant differences were found between the pre/post intervention ratings for participant's ratings of safe/proper inhaler use simulations. In this instance, participants' ratings actually decreased, indicating poorer intentions to use inhalers properly; and, again, this decrease was not associated with the animation itself. It can only be assumed that something outwith the study's measurements was influencing or mediating these intention ratings.

In order to further investigate and to clarify the discrepancy between the qualitative and quantitative findings, the research team plan to engage in a full trial to assess whether the apparent increased intentions, expressed in the qualitative evaluations, to engage in more physical activity will indeed translate to a change in behaviour. This follow on work will also include an assessment of the efficacy of including an associate individualised 'action plan' to help promote a concrete pathway to behaviour change following viewing the animation. This will be a key challenge, as it is well known within the psychological literature that even though someone may express the intention to change a behaviour, the actual behaviour change may not follow (i.e., the intentions-behaviour gap).

References

1. Williams, B., Anderson, A., Barton, K., McGhee, J.: Can theory be embedded in visual interventions to promote self-management? A proposed model and worked example. International Journal of Nursing Studies 49(12), 1598–1609 (2012)
2. Williams, B., Cameron, L.: The potential and problems of the increasing use of images in health care interventions: Are we running before we can walk? Journal of Health Services Research & Policy 14(4), 251–254 (2009)
3. Craig, P., Dieppe, P., MacIntyre, S., Michie, S., Nazareth, I., Petticrew, M.: Developing and evaluating complex interventions: new guidance. Medical Research Council, 1–39 (2008)
4. Murray, J., Williams, B., Hoskins, G., McGhee, J., Gauld, D., Brown, G.: Developing a theory-informed interactive animation to increase physical activity among young people with asthma. In: Shumaker, R. (ed.) VAMR 2013, Part II. LNCS, vol. 8022, pp. 60–65. Springer, Heidelberg (2013)
5. Anandan, C., Nurmatov, U., Schayck, O., Sheikh, A.: Is the prevalence of asthma declining? Systematic review of epidemiological studies. Allergy Asthma Proc. 65(2), 152–167 (2009)
6. Asher, M.I., Montefort, S., Bjorksten, B., Lai, C.K.W., Strachan, D.P., Weiland, S.K., et al.: Worldwide time trends in the prevalence of symptoms of asthma, allergic rhinoconjunctivitis, and eczema in childhood: ISAAC Phases One and Three repeat multicountry cross-sectional surveys. The Lancet 368(9537), 733–743 (2006)
7. Beasley, R.: The International Study of Asthma and Allergies in Childhood (ISAAC) Steering Committee. Worldwide variation in prevalence of symptoms of asthma, allergic rhinoconjunctivitis, and atopic eczema: ISAAC. The Lancet 351(9111), 1225–1232 (1998)
8. Dollman, J., Norton, K., Norton, L., Cleland, V.: Evidence for secular trends in children's physical activity behaviour. Commentary, 892–897 (2005)
9. Glazebrook, C., McPherson, A.C., Macdonald, I.A.S., J. A, Ramsay, C., Newbould, R., Smyth, A.: Asthma as a barrier to children's physical activity: implications for body mass index and mental health. Pediatrics 118(6), 2443–2449 (2006)
10. van Veldhoven, N.H.M.J., Vermeer, A., Bogaard, J.M., Hessels, M.G.P., Wijnroks, L., Colland, V.T., et al.: Children with asthma and physical exercise: effects of an exercise programme. Clinical Rehabilitation 15, 360–370 (2001)
11. Welsh, L., Kemp, J.G., Roberts, R.G.D.: Effects of physical conditioning on children and adolescents with asthma. Sports Medicine 35(2), 127–141 (2005)
12. Bonetti, D., Eccles, M., Johnston, M., Steen, N., Grimshaw, J., Baker, R., et al.: Guiding the design and selection of interventions to influence the implementation of evidence-based practice: An experimental simulation of a complex intervention trial. Social Science and Medicine 60, 2135–2147 (2005)
13. Hrisos, S., Eccles, M., Johnston, M.: An intervention modelling experiment to change GPs' intentions to implement evidence-based practice. BMC Health Services Research 8(10) (2008)
14. Yeatts, K., Sotir, M., Music, S., Herget, C.: Health consequences for children with undiagnosed asthma-like symptoms. Arch. Pediatr. Adolesc. Med. 157, 540–544 (2003)
15. Ajzen, I.: The theory of planned behaviour. Organisational Behavior and Decision Processes 50, 179–211 (1991)
16. Lee, J.R., Nass, C., Brave, S.B., Morishima, Y., Nakajima, H., Yamada, R.: The case for caring colearners: The effects of a computer-mediated colearner agent on trust and learning. Journal of Communication 57, 183–204 (2007)

17. Ashill, N.J., Yavas, U.: Vignette development: An exposition and illustration. Innovative Marketing 2(1), 28–36 (2006)
18. Heverly, M.A., Fitt, D.X., Newman, F.L.: Constructing case vignettes for evaluating clinical judgment: An empirical model. Evaluation and Program Planning 7, 45–55 (1984)
19. Gale, N.K., Heath, G., Cameron, E., Rashid, S., Redwood, S.: Using the framework method for the analysis of qualitative data in multidisciplinary health research. BMC Medical Research Methodology 13, 117 (2013)
20. Jaspers, M.W.M.: A comparison of usability methods for testing interactive health technologies: Methodological aspects and empirical evidence. International Journal of Medical Informatics 5, 340–353 (2009)

Mapping Graceful Interaction Design from Dance Performance

Nor Laila Md. Noor[1], Wan Norizan Wan Hashim[2], Wan Adilah Wan Adnan[1], and Fauzi Mohd Saman[1]

[1] Faculty of Computer and Mathematical Sciences, Universiti Teknologi MARA, Shah Alam, Malaysia
norlaila@tmsk.uitm.edu.my
[2] Faculty of Cognitive Sciences and Human Development, Universiti Malaysia Sarawak, Kuching, Malaysia

Abstract. Graceful interaction is one of the several forms of aesthetic interaction that have been proposed to enrich the quality of user experience. In this paper we discuss the refinement of the concept of graceful interaction by mapping physical dance movement into graceful interaction. We argued that graceful interaction has deep roots in organic bodily rhythms and the social conditions which help structure them. To gain a further understanding of graceful interaction we compared physical dance movement with the conception of graceful interaction. We conducted a literature analysis on pertinent aesthetic concepts used in interface design, followed by an interview with an art performance expert to gain an understanding of pertinent graceful concepts in art performance. An interpretive analysis was then conducted to produce mappings of graceful interaction concepts from art performance to graceful interaction features based on an interaction quality framework.

Keywords: aesthetic experience, movement interaction, graceful interaction design, HCI.

1 Introduction

Research in HCI has shown that aesthetic factor in interactive products affect the user's judgment about usability in terms of the user perspective of the systems usefulness and the product appeal when considering the overall quality of experience offered [1], [2], [3], [4]. The concern for user experience is not limited to the production of quality user experience but also address the effort to foster core human values such as aesthetics in movement. It has been argued that interaction that involves movement design elements in graceful interaction is a form of aesthetic interaction [5],[6]. However the concept of graceful interaction in movement has not been explored further. This paper addresses the conception of graceful interaction from the artistic perspective.

M. Kurosu (Ed.): Human-Computer Interaction, Part III, HCII 2014, LNCS 8512, pp. 301–311, 2014.

2 Aesthetics in HCI and the Research Motivation

The pioneering work of visual aesthetics in HCI of [1] has led to other aesthetic research in HCI ranging from aesthetics appeal in information display to aesthetics of interaction. The concepts and vocabulary of aesthetics have much to offer to HCI since they emphasize qualities and issues that HCI is obviously concerned with in interaction design. This includes qualities of experience, beauty, enlightenment, form and meaning, taste and judgment and many others. This section discusses the literature on aesthetics in HCI and the motivation behind this research.

2.1 From Philosophical Perspective of Aesthetics to Technological Perspective of Aesthetics

As aesthetics is more dominant in the field of arts its subjective view is discussed heavily in the literature. According to philosophers, human pursuits can be fundamentally categorized into the pursuit of truth, beauty and good and right [3]. The pursuit of beauty falls under the subject of aesthetics where its issues are mainly discussed within the realm of aesthetics philosophy of arts until Kant's Critique of Judgment established aesthetics as a discipline [4]. Philosophers differ in terms of believing whether aesthetics judgment is independent or dependent of its utilitarian or instrumental value. Following the paradigm of pragmatism, [7] while agreeing with [8] argued that aesthetics is a particular kind of experience that emerges in the interplay between user, context, culture and history and should not be seen exclusively as a feature of either the artifact or the viewer and will lead to the firm foundation from which to explore concepts such as playfulness, surprise and enchantment. The pragmatist paradigm is also adopted by [9] to understand people's interaction with technology. Within the context of IT artifact engineering the subjectivity or objectivity of aesthetics needs to be addressed [10]. Subjective concepts of aesthetics such as aesthetics perception [2], perceived visual attractiveness/appeal [9],[10] and aesthetics experience [6] have been developed and used. Objective concepts of aesthetics are discussed in [11],[12] where aesthetics ratings based on semantic differential scale were used to show the relationship between aesthetics and usability of products. However the finding from these work are currently insufficient to illustrate how aesthetic values inform the process of functional engineering design and later be used to evaluate IT artifacts aesthetic quality. Here we argue that an understanding of the artistic nature aesthetics must be appreciated before hand.

2.2 Technological Determinism and Aesthetics Cultural Values

Advocates of technological determinism are concern with how a technology tends to dictate its users' behaviours which may slowly diminished the human agency. When considering the view on technopoly, [13] insist that culture should define tools and not vice versa. This view aligns with the humanist view on the changing intensities of habits that affect the life experience [14]. Value-sensitive design is premised on a growing consensus on the needs to also include criteria that embody or at least help foster core human values [15]. This idea that revolves around how software can influence or persuade users by altering their beliefs about preferable conduct is a subject matter of value-sensitive design. Simultaneously the movement on slow technology is set to curb some of the damaging effects of excessive technologies in human life by trying to promote slower or less extreme interactions through reflection and moments of mental rest [16]. Since aesthetics is a kind of experience that emerges in the interplay between user, context, culture and history [7], it is interesting to consider how can a society retain and preserve its cultural values when its younger generation are fascinated by the technology of speed as seen for example in the use of computer games and other IT uses. For instance a society that treasures graceful mannerism may fear the erosion of this culture when their younger generation are exposed to technology that shapes them into global users thus forgetting their own cultural values. This interesting issue motivates us to explore different forms of interactions with the computer in particular on aesthetics interaction with a focus on gracefulness.

2.3 Aesthetics Experience and Aesthetics Interaction

Aesthetic experience is often associated with human experience with art performance like dancing, singing and other art performances. Aesthetic experience is defined by [17] as a particular state of mind that is characterized by a focus on a certain object which engages and fascinates a subject, whereas all other actions in the environment are excluded from consciousness. On the other hand, aesthetics interaction refer to the qualities of a design that lead to the feelings, emotions and the behaviours that result from bodily types of interactions [8]. In other words to project an aesthetic experience, an aesthetic interaction must be designed. Aesthetic interaction has been a subject of interest in the industrial design as reflected in the work of [6] and [18]. The importance of aesthetics in interaction design has been argued both from the philosophical stance and the psychological perspective [16]. As we have witnessed for a while aesthetics took a back seat to make way for usability in the early era of HCI as reflected in the work of [1],[2],[3]. The Vitruvian principle of *firmitas, utilitas* and *venustas* that originated from architecture has been argued to be the theoretical framework that can be used to understand the creation of digital space [19] where *venustas* can be addressed through concepts of beauty and delight. As the interest in experience design grows aesthetic interaction becomes an important subject matter when considering the design of aesthetics experience by product designers. Aesthetics interaction design cares about the aesthetics experience when users interact with an interactive system [20].

2.4 Motion-Based and Movement-Based Interaction

The HCI literature does not show clear distinction between the terms motion and movement except they seems to differ in terms of the context of use. Motion refers to general movement in the abstract disregard of efficiency or efficacy while movement refers more narrowly to the mechanics of how the human body moves. However in the past HCI literature the term motion and movement has been used interchangeably in motion-based and movement-based interactions. For instance in [21] the interaction is known as motion-based but in actual the motion referred to here is the human movement in Tai Chi was the subject of the study in the interaction design.

Motion is a distinct element of digital media and is being used in the design of user interfaces, interaction and experiences. Within the usability paradigm, the term motion is used for instrumental purposes, such as giving feedback or attracting user attention for instance in the navigation through mobile devices [22]. However, motion is less understood in terms of a design element for affective quality. On the other hand, movement-based interactions are interactions where movements of the human body are direct input to technology and movement interaction was initially approach from a task-based perspective. The common movement interaction is the eye movement-based interaction [23] and body movement-based interaction in games [24] that takes place either through a flow or brute force movement [25]. Though movement-based interaction allows the user to control the interface due to body movement, research on movement-based interaction has explored further into the phenomena of immersion as a form of experience design [26] as movement is not solely functional but highly experiential [27].

2.5 Aesthetic Interaction in Gracefulness

Gracefulness is discussed in Plato's Republic as a quality of attractiveness that can be observed in buildings, living things and human actions and movement [28]. Gracefulness in human encompasses posture and movement. However, according to Plato though gracefulness can be faked, true gracefulness is a reflection of a harmonious soul which is a target of quality of life endeavours [28]. In presenting the idea of simple living, [29] presented the concept of graceful living where he considered gracefulness as an achievement of the aesthetic of being as argued out by. It is seen in the rhythmic flow that follows the human pace in either a slow or fast dance or in other human action of performing task such as having a meal that is not entirely due to hunger but also requires an appreciation of the food serve. The structure of gracefulness resides in the characteristic of the person and is exhibited through specific pattern of behaviours. The dimensions of gracefulness are not isolated but exist in interacting facets. Communities in the Asian culture relate gracefulness to body movement in the dance and mannerism. These communities remain enthusiastic towards preserving gracefulness for its cultural identity. In the context of value-sensitive design, the question that arises now is whether there is a similar situation of gracefulness when interacting with computers which allow the human users to indulge in so that a coherence of action is seen in the physical world and the computer world.

In HCI, the notion of graceful interaction was first discussed in the context of speech user interface where the subject is graceful speech [30]. Graceful interaction was also explored in the context of intelligent environment to understand how the human make sense of the disappearing user interface [31]. The Laban Movement Theory was applied for the design of movement-base interaction in [32] and human full-body movement as interaction modality in [33]. Graceful interaction meant for web user interface in the context of product emotion was first proposed by [5] using the Laban Movement Theory. Later, a theoretical framework based on the Laban Movement Theory was proposed in [6] to determine possible design elements of graceful interaction. Graceful interaction in movement is argued be a possible form of aesthetic interaction and thus can be added to the typology of aesthetics interaction extending from the work of [20]. The typology of aesthetic interaction is illustrated in Figure 1 after adapting the work of [20]. Nevertheless, more effort is need to establish graceful interaction.

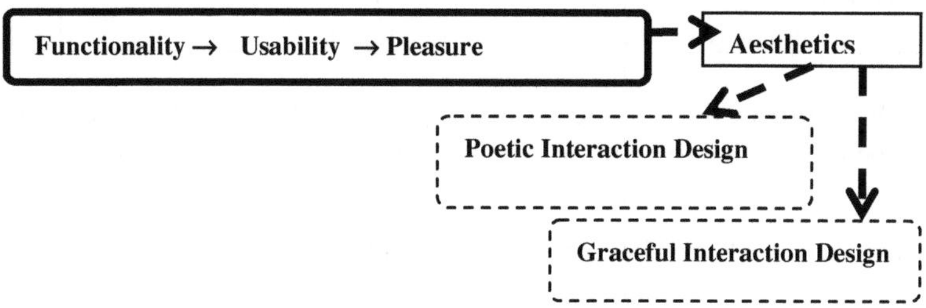

Fig. 1. Aesthetic Interaction Typology

3 A Refinement of the Conception of Graceful Interaction

An interaction model must have the capability in terms of its descriptive power, evaluative power and its generative power. Its descriptive power is the ability to describe a significant range of existing interfaces; its evaluative power is its ability to help assess multiple design alternatives and its generative power, is the ability to help designers create new designs. However to achieve that, a clear conception of the interaction model must happen first. This section describes the effort to refine graceful interaction through an artistic perspective following the method of design science. The refinement of graceful interaction concept was done through a literature review on aesthetics, an expert interview with an art performance academic who is also a choreographer and an interpretive analysis to produce mappings of art performance to graceful interaction features.

3.1 Review of Aesthetics Concepts Used in Interface Design

To gain the understanding on the relationship of aesthetics and interaction in interactive systems design, aesthetics in HCI is conceptualized in terms of the pragmatic account of human experience where feelings, emotions, and thoughts is the focus of design [5]. The literature on aesthetics is reviewed. Aesthetic concepts that have gained acceptance in interaction design are summarized in Table 1.

Table 1. Aesthetics Concepts in Interface Design

Aesthetics Concepts	Interface Design Concepts	Authors
Functionalism & Usability	Efficiency	[33]
Coherency	Coherency	[21],[34]
Emotion & pleasure	Emotion	[3]
Pragmatism	Sensing	[7]
Somaesthetics & Tangibility		[7], [9]
Provocation & Criticism	Criticism	[35]
Playfulness, Intrigue & Challenge	Playfulness	[8]

From the summary the interface concepts of coherency, emotion, sensing and playfulness appear is argued to be more aligned towards elements of gracefulness.

3.2 Interview with Art Performance Expert

In this work, the art performance of dance is used as the basis to understand movement for graceful interaction as dance performance is a form of aesthetic experience. The reason for choosing dance is because dance isolates dynamics more than any other performing art, but it also has a long tradition and a formal structure [37]. The clusters of criteria for good performance such as the flow of the movement, the choice of figures and formations used in the choreography, the complexity of the movement, the social interaction that takes place within the movement, the physical activity level of the movement and the quality of specialness or uniqueness exhibited by a movement can be used to gain an understanding of graceful interaction. This seems to have more resemblance to the interface concepts of coherence, emotion and playfulness.

An academic who is an art performance expert in dance and theatre was interviewed to gain an understanding of graceful interaction from the artistic perspective with a focus on dance. The theme, key questions asked and the response received are summarized and tabulated and shown in Table 2.

From the interview the following interpretation on beautiful dance movement that evokes emotion was made. The aesthetics of the dance performance lies in the beautiful movement of the dancers. In a beautiful dance, that dancer is able to express an emotion that can be felt by the audience. However the performer's ability to express emotion is dependent on the characteristic of the performer. It seems that beautiful dance movement can evoke emotion if the dancer is able to express the emotion he/she felt. This finding is in agreement with [17] who discussed the impact of the formal characteristics of the dance movement on the subjective experience of the dance performer that influence the success of the dance performance. Similarly, [36] discussed the criteria for good performance such as the flow of the movement, the choice of figures and formations used in the choreography, the complexity of the movement, the social interaction that takes place within the movement, the physical activity level of the movement and the quality of specialness or uniqueness exhibited by a movement. These clusters of criteria for good performance support the expert answer on defining successful performance and aesthetic in performance. A further discussion of the interpretation is presented in the following section.

Table 2. Theme, Key Questions and Response

Theme	Questions	Response
Performance Art (Dance)		
Aesthetics	What is aesthetics in the art performance context?	Beautiful in movement/ action and emotion in whatever character she/he performing (good or bad character, music, costumes, etc.)
Static vs. Dynamic	What is static in art performance?	There is no such thing as static in art performance. Although the performer is performing at only one spot of location his/ her body is still moving.
Component/ Object	Does an individual or group performance matter in aesthetics of dance?	Important element is the body of the performer. Body act as main tool in the performance since movement & emotion/expression in performance is perceived individually although it is a group performance
Factors	What are the factors that contribute to successful performance?	Performer must have emotion/ expression & movement which can be felt by audience. Overall concept (inclusive of costumes)
Performer		
Emotion	What are performer's feelings when performing?	It depends on the character of the performer.
Audience		
Background	Audience background	Knowledgeable audience/have knowledge and experience about performance
Stickiness	When audience stay longer or comes back	Back to the successful factors of performance

3.3 Mapping the Dance Performance to Graceful Interaction

The concept of graceful interaction is now mapped accordingly to the dance performance and the mapping is shown in Table 3.

Graceful interaction is interpreted as the movement of a beautiful form (dancer, costumes) that evokes emotion of the audience. By taking the view of the Interaction Quality Framework of [18] three perspectives (Table 4) of graceful interaction is discussed.

Table 3. Mapping of Dance Performance and Graceful Interaction Features

Features	Art Performance	Graceful Interaction
Interaction	Dance movement	Movement of objects/ artifacts & users
Aesthetics	Character played, costumes, music, movement flow, choreography	Visuals, sound, movement quality
Performer	Performer	Interface object; User
	Emotion of performer	Emotional appeal
Audience	Audience	User
		Other audience/ observers
Success Indicators	Staying on	Stickiness
	Coming back for more	Repeat visit
Success factors	Performer must have emotion that can be felt by audience	User emotional style
	Overall concept	Holistic design

Table 4. Mapping of Dance Performance and Graceful Interaction Features

Perspective	Art Performance	Graceful Interaction
Product	Performer	IT artifact/ interface
Person	Audience	User
Unity	Performer & Audience	Graceful interaction

The first is the product perspective, the second is the person perspective and the third is the unity perspective (unity of product and person). The interpretation is performed while taking note that the aesthetics experience that emerges from graceful interaction will be the interplay between the user, the interface object (IT artifact) and the context according to [5] and this fits with the unity perspective. This means that graceful interaction should not be seen exclusively as a feature of either the IT artifact (interface) or the user or viewer. As expected, movement appears to be important in graceful interaction and it has an emotional appeal to its audience/users and is in agreement with interface aesthetics concepts of [5], [8], [9]. The movement performed must be felt by the user. In addition graceful interaction also needs to be supported by visuals and sound (context). A graceful interaction object must have an emotional appeal through its visual, movement, sonic and environment (other parts of the interface) to give a holistic effect of graceful interaction. It can be interpreted that graceful interaction is an emergence of the user, the artifact and their unity.

4 Mapping Graceful Interaction Design Features

In terms of movement quality, the design elements of [6] that are derived from Laban Movement Analysis are next used to describe the movement feature of the interface object and the user movement quality features. The graceful interaction elements of the artifact of interaction are rhythm, tempo, sequence and direction while the user movement quality is interpreted as three main quality concepts: balance in the uniformity and diversity of movements, the attention towards the interaction (leading to stickiness) and expectation (ability to see patterns). Balance, attention and expectation can be related to interface concepts of coherence [22]. As graceful interaction involves the engagement of the user with the interface object graceful design elements can be translated accordingly and is shown in Table 5.

Table 5. Mapping of Graceful Interaction Design Elements into IT Artifact Movement and User Movement Quality

Design Elements	IT Artifact: Movement Feature	User: Movement Quality Features
Rhythm	{calm, dynamic}	Balance the uniformity and diversity
Tempo	{fast, slow}	Attention towards the interaction
Sequence	{animation, rotation, zooming} *cause-effect, ordered pattern of events*	Expectations which is the ability to see patterns
Direction	{{upward, downward}, {forward, reverse}}	Attention towards the direction of the interaction

4.1 Discussion

As discussed earlier, in pragmatist aesthetics experience emerge from the interplay between the user, the context and the culture. In our work we proposed that graceful interaction involves the unity of the user and the interaction. A movement of graceful interaction can only happen if there is an evocation of user's emotion. An important design consideration for graceful interaction is harmony of the artifact (interface) and the user/audience in the design to fulfill the unity criteria. As in the art performance, the knowledge of the audience on the performance makes a different effect on the performance. This implies the user emotional model cannot be ignored in the design of graceful interaction. However in this work we have not address the cultural context of the interaction.

5 Conclusion

In this work the conceptualization of the design method for graceful interaction is discussed based on interpretive work on the literature and expert interview. Graceful interaction features has to be integrated with the user affect model as graceful interaction is an emergent design. Future work on graceful interaction will involve empirical studies to validate the graceful interaction features and the incorporation of the user model in graceful interaction.

Acknowledgement. This work benefitted from the funding of the Ministry of Education, Malaysia under the grant 600-RMI/ERGS 5/3 (5/2011). We are indebted to the Research Centre Institute of Universiti Teknologi MARA for their support in our work.

References

1. Tractinsky, N.: Aesthetics and Apparent Usability: Empirically Assessing Cultural and Methodological Issues. In: CHI 1997 Conference Proceedings, Atlanta, March 22-27, pp. 115–122. ACM, New York (1997)
2. Liu, Y.: Engineering Aesthetics and Ergo-Aesthetics: Theoretical and Methodological Foundations. In: Proceedings of the 5th International Conference on Industrial Engineering: Theory, Application and Practice, pp. 1–12 (2000)
3. Norman, D.: Emotion and Design: Attractive Things Work Better. Interactions 9(4), 36–42 (2002)
4. Diefenbach, S., Hassenzahl, M.: The Beauty Dilemma: Beauty is Valued but Discounted in Product Choice. In: Proceedings of ACM CHI 2009 Conference on Human Factors in Computing Systems 2009, pp. 1419–1426 (2009)
5. Hashim, W.N.W., Noor, N.L.M., Adnan, W.: The Design of Aesthetic Interaction: Towards Graceful Interaction Framework. In: Proceedings of the 2nd International Conference on Interaction Sciences: Information Technology, Culture and Human, Korea, pp. 69–75 (2009)
6. Hashim, W.N.W., Noor, N.L.M., Adnan, W.: A Framework for Graceful Interaction: Applying Laban Effort Theory to Define Graceful Movement Quality. In: Proceedings of the International Conference on User Science and Engineering (i-USEr 2010), Malaysia, pp, pp. 139–144 (2010)
7. Wright, P., Wallance, J., McCarthy, J.: Aesthetics and Experienced Centered Design. ACM Transactions on Computer-Human Interaction 15(4),18(1)–18(21) (2008)
8. Petersen, M.G., Iversen, O.S., Krogh, P.G., Ludvigsen, M.: Aesthetic Interaction: A Pragmatist's Aesthetics of Interactive Systems. In: Benyon, D., Moody, P., Gruen, D., McAra-McWilliam, I. (eds.) Proceedings of the 5th Conference on Designing Interactive Systems, pp. 269–276. ACM Press, New York (2004)
9. Dyas, D., Heylen, D.K.J., Eliens, A., Nijohlt, A.: Experiencing-in-the-world: Using Pragmatis Philosophy to Design Aesthetics Experience. In: Proceedings of the 2007, Conference on Designing for User Experience, Article No. 8, pp 1–16 (2007)
10. Zhang, P.: Theorizing the Relationship between Affect and Aesthetics in the ICT Design and Use Context. In: Proceedings of the International Conference on Information Resources Management, Dubai, United Arab Emirates, May 21-23, pp. 1–9 (2009)
11. Lavie, T., Tractinsky, N.: Assessing Dimensions of Perceived Visual Aesthetics of Web Sites. International Journal of Human-Computer Studies 60(3), 269–298 (2004)
12. Monk, A.F., Lelos, K.: Changing only the aesthetic features of a domestic product can affect its apparent usability. In: Venkatesh, A., Gonzalvez, T., Monk, A., Buckner, B. (eds.) Home informatics and telematics: ICT for the next billion. Proceedings of HOIT 2007. IFIP, vol. 241, pp. 221–233. Springer, Boston (2007)
13. Postman, N.: Technopoly: The Surrender of Culture to Technology, Vintage (1993)
14. Bissell, D.: Virtual Infrastructures of Habit: The Changing Intensities of Habit through Gracefulness, restlessness and clumsiness. In: Cultural Geographies. Sage Publication (April 2013)
15. Friedman, B.: Value-sensitive Design. Interactions 3(6), 16–23 (1996)
16. Hallnäs, L., Redström, J.: Slow Technology; Designing for Reflection. Journal of Personal and Ubiquitous Computing, 161–192 (2000)
17. Ross, P.R., Wensveen, S.A.G.: Designing Behavior in Interaction: Using Aesthetic Experience as a Mechanism for Design. International Journal of Design 4(2), 3–13 (2010)
18. Vukadinović, M.: Aesthetic Experience and Emotional Identification, Art, Emotion and Value. In: 5th Mediterranean Congress of Aesthetics, pp. 393–408 (2011)

19. Rahim, W.A., Noor, N.L.M., Mehad, S.: Towards a Theoretical Framework for Understanding Website Information Architecture. In: Proceedings of the 8th International Arab Conference, Yarmouk, Jordan (2006)
20. Lin, Y.-C., Chang, H.-M., Liang, R.-H.: Designing Poetic Interaction in Space. In: Jacko, J.A. (ed.) Human-Computer Interaction, Part III, HCII 2011. LNCS, vol. 6763, pp. 559–568. Springer, Heidelberg (2011)
21. Majoe, D., Widmer, L., Guknecht, J.: Enhanced Motion Interaction for Multimedia Applications. In: Proceedings of the 7th International Conference on Advances in Mobile Computing and Multimedia, Kuala Lumpur, Malaysia, December 14-16, pp. 13–19. ACM (2009)
22. Hwang, J., Kim, I.G., Kang, D., Ahn, S.C., Kim, H.: Motion-based Interaction for Mirror World in Mobile Devices. In: Proceedings of the HCI International, pp. 1–4 (2009)
23. Jacob, R.J.K.: The Use of Eye Movements in Human-Computer Interaction Techniques: what you look at is what you get. ACM Transactions on Information Systems (TOIS) - Special Issue on Computer—Human Interaction 9(2), 152–169 (199)
24. Lundgren, S., Bergström, K., Och Björk, S.: Exploring Aesthetic Ideals of Gameplay. . In: Proceedings of DiGRA 2009: Breaking New Ground: Innovation in Games, Play, Practice and Theory, London, September 1-4, pp. 1–8 (2009)
25. Nijholt, A., van Dijk, B., Reidsma, D.: Design of Experience and Flow in Movement-Based Interaction. In: Egges, A., Kamphuis, A., Overmars, M. (eds.) MIG 2008. LNCS, vol. 5277, pp. 166–175. Springer, Heidelberg (2008)
26. Pasch, M., Bianchi-Berthouze, N., van Dijk, B., Nijholt, A.: Immersion in Movement-Based Interaction. In: Nijholt, A., Reidsma, D., Hondorp, H. (eds.) INTETAIN 2009. LNICST, vol. 9, pp. 169–180. Springer, Heidelberg (2009)
27. Levinshon, A.: Designing for Movement Experience. In: Proceedings of the CHI 2011, Vancouver, Canada, May 7-12 (2011)
28. Burnyeat, M.F.: Culture and Society in Plato's Republic, The Tanner Lectures on Human Values, December 10-12. Harvard University (1997)
29. Segal, J.M.: Graceful Simplicity: The Philosophy and Politics of the Alternative American Dream, pp. 159–167. University of California Press (2003)
30. Hayes, P.J., Reddy, D.R.: Steps toward Graceful Interaction in Spoken and Written Man-Machine Communication. International Journal of Man-Machine Studies 19(3), 231–284 (1983)
31. Wiberg, M.: Graceful Interaction in Intelligent Environments. In: Proceedings of the International Symposium on Intelligent Environments, Cambridge, April 5-7 (2006)
32. Loke, L., Larsenn, A.T., Robertson, T.: Labanotation for Design of Movement-based Interaction. In: Proceedings of the Second Australasian Conference on Interactive Entertainment, Sydney, Australia, pp. 113–120 (2005)
33. Alaoui, S.A., Caramiux, B., Serrano, M.: fzrom Dance to Touch: Movement Qualities for Interaction Design. In: Proceedings of CHI, Vancouver, BC, Canada, May 7–12 (2011)
34. Overbeeke, C.J., Djajadiningrat, J.P., Hummels, C.C.M., Wensveen, S.A.G.: Beauty in Usability: Forget about Ease of Use! In: Green, W.S., Jordan, P.W. (eds.) Pleasure with Products: Beyond Usability, pp. 9–18. Taylor & Francis (2002)
35. Bardzell, J.: Interaction Criticisms and Aesthetics. In: Proceedings of CHI2009, pp. 2357–2366 (2009)
36. Olav, W., Bertelsen, O.W., Pold, S.: Criticism as an Approach to Interface Aesthetics. In: Proceedings of Nordic CHI 2004, pp. 23–32 (2004)
37. Øritsland, T.A.: A Theory of Discursive Interaction Design. Norwegian University of Science and Technology, Trondheim (1999)
38. Dart, M.M.: Contra Dance Choreography - A Reflection of Social Change (1995)

Understanding the Interaction Support for Mobile Work in an Emergency Room

Sergio F. Ochoa[1], Alvaro Monares[1], Nicolás Ochoa[2], Ramón Hervás[3], and José Bravo[3]

[1] Computer Science Department, Universidad de Chile, Chile
{sochoa,amonares}@dcc.uchile.cl
[2] Medical School, Universidad de Chile, Chile
nico8asa@ug.uchile.cl
[3] MAmI Research Lab, University of Castilla-La Mancha, Ciudad Real, Spain
{ramon.hlucas,jose.bravo}@uclm.es

Abstract. Typically mobile and ubiquitous software applications provide services to mobile workers to help them increase their performance, effectiveness and eventually the satisfaction while doing their jobs. These services are directly related to the characterization of the activities to be supported. Based on such a characterization the designers of these solutions can envision the services that should be provided by the new system. Few guidelines are available to characterize mobile activities from an IT support point of view, therefore the designers have to guess the services to be embedded in these solutions. This paper provides a first step to address such a problem, identifying the context variables that characterize the mobile activities. Moreover, an ontology of activity characteristics and some design guidelines are provided to determine which supporting services can be used to address activities according to their characteristics. This proposal was conceived based on the empirical observation of the work performed by the medical personnel at an emergency room of a public hospital. Further analysis is required to generalize this proposal, in order to address mobile work in other scenarios.

Keywords: Ubiquitous computing, mobile computing, mobile work, activity characterization, context-aware information delivery, design guidelines.

1 Introduction

Advances in mobile technology and wireless communication have opened a space for the development of new computing paradigms, such as mobile and ubiquitous computing. These paradigms consider a user that is on the move carrying a computing device (e.g. smartphone) as support of his/her activities.

Software applications involved in these computing paradigms typically adapt their services and user interfaces according to users' current context. Such a context could consider, e.g., the level of noise and light in the work environment, the availability of Internet access, and the type of mobility and position of the user. Due the user is on

M. Kurosu (Ed.): Human-Computer Interaction, Part III, HCII 2014, LNCS 8512, pp. 312–322, 2014.

the move when interacts with these systems, his/her current work context changes accordingly. Therefore the adaptation of services and user interfaces must be done by the applications during runtime. This means that these systems must also sense or infer the users' current context in order to detect changes and trigger accordingly the new adaptations to the services or user interfaces. This service adaptation affects the performance, effectiveness and satisfaction of mobile workers. Typically, more suitable services and user interfaces allow mobile workers to improve their performance, effectiveness and satisfaction; therefore this is a goal that follows most designers of mobile and ubiquitous applications.

Although researchers of this area and also the industry have done important efforts to determine the context variables are useful to characterize mobile activities, and also to relate software services to activities according to their characteristics, the problem is still open. Therefore, the designers of these solutions depend on their own expertise to determine the supporting services to be embedded in the new system. The system is usually discarded by the user if the services identified by the designer are not suitable to support the activity.

This lack of visibility that the designers have about the services to be embedded in mobile and ubiquitous solutions is common in the development of collaborative systems, and this problem is known as the iceberg effect [1]. However, such a problem can be successfully addressed using appropriate design guidelines.

In order to help address the problem, this article reports the results of a user study in which we use used *mobile structured observations* to shadow mobile workers (mainly physicians, nurses and medical interns) during their regular activities at an emergency room (ER) of a public hospital. The interaction among mobile workers and also between them and the information supporting the tasks, were particularly observed and recorded. The study involved four sessions of direct observation at the ER. Each session lasted three hours and involved two observers. Various informal meetings and two focus groups were performed with the health professionals participating in the study, in order to analyze, discuss and clarify the information obtained from these observations.

The analysis of this information allowed us to determine an initial set of context variables that characterize these activities and influence the mobile workers' performance, effectiveness and satisfaction while doing these tasks. Although the study results only consider the mobile activities in an emergency room, the proposed characterization could also be applicable to other dynamic work processes, like construction inspections, search-and-rescues or emergency responses.

This characterization also helps analyze the interaction support required by mobile workers to perform their activities and collaborate among them. Thus, designers can determine in a more informed way, which are the supporting services that can be required by the new system. Examples of these services are awareness mechanisms, notifications, and capturers of the user attention. The article also presents some design guidelines showing how to identify the services required to support mobile activities, according to the characteristics of the work to be done.

Next section presents the related work. Section 3 describes the user study performed in the ER. Based on the study results, Section 4 presents an initial set of context variables that characterize the mobile activities, the values that these variables can assume, a preliminary ontology of activity characteristics, and also some design guidelines indicating how the proposed ontology can used to determine the supporting services required by a mobile or ubiquitous application. Section 5 presents the conclusions and the future work.

2 Related Work

There is no consensus about the meaning of context in context-aware computing [2]. This is because the variables describing the work context depend on each particular problem or task to be addressed. This situation has promoted the development of several research lines in context-aware computing and also particular definitions for each of them. In case of HCI, during the late nineties Rodden et al. [3] stated that the use of context allows determining more accurately the information and services that must be put available to the users, and thus it is possible to improve the human-computer interaction. Several applications adopted such an approach, for example the mobile geographic information system proposed by Abowd et al. [4], which provides contextualized information to the users depending on their current location. There is also a long list of location-aware mobile and ubiquitous systems that self-adapt their users interfaces, e.g. to support tourism, entertainment, healthcare and recently social applications [5, 6, 7, 8].

The user location seems to be one of the context variables most used by mobile applications to adapt the services to mobile users during runtime. A recent study performed by Herskovic et al. [9] on mobile users presence awareness, which involved engineering students, indicates that users location and status are highly useful context variables according to these users. In a posterior and more general study, which also involved a literature extensive review, these researchers identified a more important set of context variables that affects the collaborative activities [10]. Based on that, they proposed a method to determine the suitability of the awareness services supporting mobile activities according to their features (i.e. according to the values of the context variables describing the mobile activity).

Romero and Calvillo-Gámez [11] conceptualize the optimal user experience (or flow) in movement-based interaction while perform mobile activities, and they highlight the relevance of four key components: effortless attention, the context where interaction takes place, the alignment between the task being supported and the application, and the body and its role in the interaction with the system. In the same direction (i.e. user's experience) Duarte and Carriço [12] investigated the reactions and behavior of users exposed to certain awareness mechanisms in videogames using mobile devices. That study shows that the awareness information given to a user could promote stress and anxiety, or it can support the task; therefore choosing the right awareness mechanism to deliver the information seems to be mandatory.

The context information is also used by applications that provide ambient intelligence. In these computing paradigms the use of the context variables becomes richer and mandatory. For example the Portable Help Desk proposed by Garlan et al. [13]

provides spatial and temporal awareness information (e.g. the nearest printer, cafeteria or resource) to users of handheld devices. This software has an audio and a graphical interface, and the use of a particular interface will depend on the user's current mobility. Sukthankar [14] proposes also a context-aware application that uses multiple projectors to simultaneously illuminate an ambient and provide information to users. Depending on the user position and orientation, these projectors deliver the information through the most appropriate projector.

While Breiner et al. [15] propose a model-based framework for generating context-aware user interfaces for ambient intelligence systems. The proposal provides guidelines for creating new models and mechanisms for adapting the user interface during runtime according to changing user needs. Although the framework is interesting, it considers the users characteristics as the only context dimension to adapt the system interfaces.

Concerning the analysis of the activity features to determine possible services to be required in mobile and ubiquitous applications, Guerrero et al. [16] characterize the activities also considering the environment in which they are performed. That characterization only considers three dimensions: comfort of the work place, mobility level of the user, and level of data input that is required by the activity. Based on it, the authors recommend suitable devices to be used as support of that mobile activity.

In the same reasoning line, Alarcon et al. [17] proposes a framework of contextual elements to be considered during the conception, analysis and design of mobile collaborative applications. That framework helps designers to identify non-functional and also some functional requirements of these systems, according the context of the activity to be supported. Tentori and Favela [18] propose a set of coarse-grained activities (monitored, distributed and dynamic activities) that nurses regularly perform as part of their hospital work. However, this characterization is too general, and it does not allow us to identify the services required by the applications supporting these activities.

Although these proposals are useful, they are not particularly suitable to address the problem stated in section 1. Therefore, the designers of mobile and ubiquitous applications will be exposed to the iceberg effect [1] every time that they try to determine the supporting services to be embedded in their solutions. Next section describes the user study that helped us to find the context variables characterizing the mobile activities and find the services required to support them.

3 The User Study

This user study was done in an emergency room (ER) at a public hospital in Santiago, Chile. Such an area was composed of a large space with "pods" for patient treatment, and a small area for patient registration. That area was covered by a Wi-Fi network with access to Internet. Next we describe the study area, the regular activities performed in such an area, and the type of monitoring done to the mobile workers participating in the study.

3.1 Setting of the Study Area

The emergency room was an area of 20 meters by 11 meters approximately composed of small pods for basic healthcare attention. Figure 1 presents a diagram that shows the space distribution. These pods (26 in total) were isolated by curtains. One of them was used as control room, in which a nurse updates the patients records annotating the main treatments and health procedures indicated for these people. That nurse also recorded the time at which the patient gets in and out the ER.

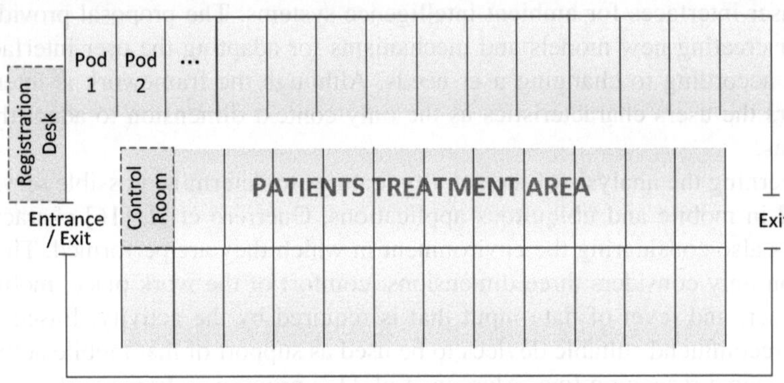

Fig. 1. Space distribution at the emergency room

One emergency physician, two physicians (usually surgeons and internists), four nurses and three medical interns were part of the permanent staff assigned to such an ER. Depending on the activity in that place and the patients' health conditions, additional medical personnel from the hospital can also support the emergency room activities. In this study we observed and interview only people of the permanent staff, particularly two physicians, three nurses and two medical interns.

3.2 Activities and Roles at the Emergency Room

People working in an emergency room represent a team, which goal is "*to stabilize the patient's condition by treating the acute problem and discharging the patient*" [19]. In such a team there are several roles; for instance emergency physicians, internists, medical interns, nurses and paramedics. According to the role that each person can play and the current needs at the ER, activities are assigned to them.

An activity involves one or more tasks, which can be performed in sequence, parallel or mix of them. Example of these activities can be the process to medicate the patients (by the nurse) according to the indications of a physician, or the diagnosis performed by an internist every time that a new patient arrives to the ER. Usually, these team members perform more than one simultaneous activity during a work shift.

The work in an ER is highly dynamic and bit chaotic. However, the activities are coordinated and monitored by an emergency physician, who usually has an important experience managing ERs. The information being shared among the medical personnel is handwritten on a paper record that is kept in the pod of the patient. If the patient is moved from one pod to other, the paper record is also moved with the patient. Typically, the results of a patient's health studies (e.g. X-Rays) are carried by hospital personnel to the attention pod of the patient. Then, when the professional monitoring the patient arrives to the pod, he reviews the studies' results and decides the next actions depending on his/her role. For instance, an emergency physician can keep, adjust or change the treatment; however a medical intern or a nurse must contact the emergency physician to know how to proceed.

Periodically the emergency physician in charge of the ER makes a diagnosis of the current situation to determine if the activities are under control, extra support is required or changes in the activities assignment must be done. As we can see from this brief description, the work in the ER involves an ample variety of activity types, which allows us to identify a rich set of context variables that characterize them.

3.3 Monitoring Process

The activities performed by the medical personnel were observed once a week, in sessions of three hours. Four sessions were involved in this study. Two observers participated in the process; each of them followed the activities of one professional during the observation period. After each session, the observers (who were knowledgeable on mobile work) analyzed individually the collected information, and then discussed their eventual findings and conclusions. Such information was then checked with the health professionals that were observed, whom eventually had to explain the meaning of their actions or behavior in order to help us understand the situation.

After the four sessions, we performed two focus groups with the participants to validate the initial findings and determine the eventual suitability of mobile and ubiquitous computing services as support of their work. Next section describes how such information was processed to obtain the characteristics of the mobile activities.

4 Characterization of Mobile Activities

The process to identify the context variables that affect the mobile work in an emergency room was initially influenced by the authors' previous studies on firefighters activities during urban emergency responses [10, 17, 20]. These studies allowed us to determine an initial set of context variables, which was then modified according to the mobile workers behavior observed in the emergency room.

The procedure to identify these variables considered several steps: (1) identify the activities, (2) determine their main characteristics, (3) validate these characterizations and (4) determine the main variables affecting the activities performance. Fifteen activities were analyzed and characterized. Then, the context variables with similar meaning were grouped. In some cases, the activity characterization allowed us to extend the set of values that can be assumed by the context variables. In the rest of this section we describe these variables and an initial ontology that represents the relationships among these variables.

4.1 Context Variables Affecting Mobile Activities

Although this set of context variables could be then extended, it is complete enough to characterize mobile activities and help designers to determine the services required to support them. Next we present the context variables that characterize the mobile activities and influence the performance of the workers at the emergency room.

Mobility level. The level of mobility required by a person (who plays a role) to accomplish the activity determines the value of this variable (i.e. characteristic of the activity). The values that can be assumed by this context variable are the following: *stationary, nomadic* and *mobile*. This mobility classification is aligned with the taxonomy proposed by Kristoffersen and Ljungberg [21]. In *stationary* activities the mobile worker performs the tasks in a small physical area, staying stationary or having very low mobility. Examples of this activity type are the examination of patients or the process of getting a blood sample. In both activities the workers must stay in the patient pods during a time period until they finish. *Nomadic* activities typically involve a set of stationary tasks, in which the worker must walk from one location to another to accomplish them. An example of this activity type is the round performed by the nurses to monitor the health conditions of the patients. A *mobile* activity requires that the worker is on the move almost permanently to accomplish it. Examples of mobile activities are the transportation of patients to the imaginology area (e.g. for X-Ray) or look for a specialist through the hospital facilities to get an expert opinion. Our observations during the study indicate that mobile workers need to be stationary (at least temporally) to read information or make annotations. Moreover, they can read information while walking only if it is short, simple and direct. In other case, they ignore the information or decide to stop to read it.

Location-dependence. Some activities can be done only in specific places, while others can be performed almost in any place. The location dependence variable determines such a feature for a mobile activity; therefore, it can assume one of the following values: *location-dependent* or *location-independent*. By *location-dependent* activities we mean those that should be performed in particular locations (it can be one or various locations). For instance, an X-Ray image should be analyzed in an X-Ray illuminator and the medication process of a patient must be done at the patient's pod. The *location-independent* activities, e.g. a medical inter-consult between two physicians, can be done almost in any place. The observations recorded in the study indicate that location-dependent activities usually impose physical limitations to mobile workers and negatively affect their performance. In some cases, the use of mobile computing and wireless communication technology can transform a location-dependent activity in a location-independent one. For instance, an X-Ray (image in high resolution) can be retrieved and analyzed by the physician in his tablet PC, avoiding thus going to get the physical image and then find a X-Ray illuminator to read it.

Coupling. The activity coupling establishes the level of interdependence between an activity and others being performed during the same time period. This characteristic can also be understood as the coordination level required by an activity. The values that can be assumed by this context variable are: *loosely-coupled, tightly-coupled* or *uncoupled*. An activity is *loosely-coupled* if it is weakly dependent on each other. Typically, the people performing these activities function autonomously and collaborate on-demand during short time periods [22]. A *tightly-coupled* activity (partially or fully) depends on some other activity that is usually being performed in parallel. The actions made by a worker provide feedback to others, whom can change their next actions or behavior based on such information. Examples of tightly-coupled activities are those performed by a nurse that is supporting to a physician during a medical procedure. The next actions of the nurse typically depend on the current actions of the physician. Two activities are *uncoupled* if there is not relationship between them. This type of coupling is usually present between people working in different areas; e.g. the activities performed by a nurse at the ER are uncoupled from those performed by a nurse working in the intensive care unit.

Information-dependence. This characteristic is similar to the location-dependence, but it indicates how mandatory is to count on external information to accomplish the activity. An *information-dependent* activity (e.g. the diagnosis of a physical traumatism) requires counting on supporting information (e.g. an X-Ray image). Contrarily, an *information-independent* activity (e.g. the interview to a patient) can be done without external information support. Finally, the *information-supported* activities (e.g. the prescription of drugs for a flu) use external information if it is available (e.g. the medical record indicating the drug allergies of such a patient).

Data input. This variable indicates the level of data input that is required to perform the activity. The data input levels can be *low* (e.g. checking boxes in a form), *medium* (e.g. annotating how to administrate the drugs during a treatment) and *high* (e.g. writing the medical history of a patient).

Context-Awareness. This characteristic indicates if an activity is dependent of the work context in which it is performed. The possible values that this variable can assume are *context-aware* or *context-independent*. The first ones are typically those with some level of coupling (i.e. loosely or tightly-coupled) and the second ones are those that do not have coupling with other activities.

A mobile work activity can be characterized using combinations of these features. If a single value cannot be assigned to these variables, it probably means that multiple tasks with different features are part of the activity. In that case, the activity being analyzed must be decomposed in tasks until a single feature can be assigned to them.

4.2 Ontology of Mobile Activities Characteristics

Figure 2 shows an initial ontology of mobile activities characteristics. These characteristics, and the relationships among them, can be used by the designers of mobile and ubiquitous applications to determine mandatory services, transversal services and eventual limitations of the system. For instance, if the activity to be supported is loosely or tightly-coupled, the designer will have to consider context-aware services and the usage of external information to support mobile workers. Moreover, if that activity requires high mobility, then the mobile worker will have to use a small device, which usually imposes restrictions for data input mechanism (e.g. through virtual or physical keyboards).

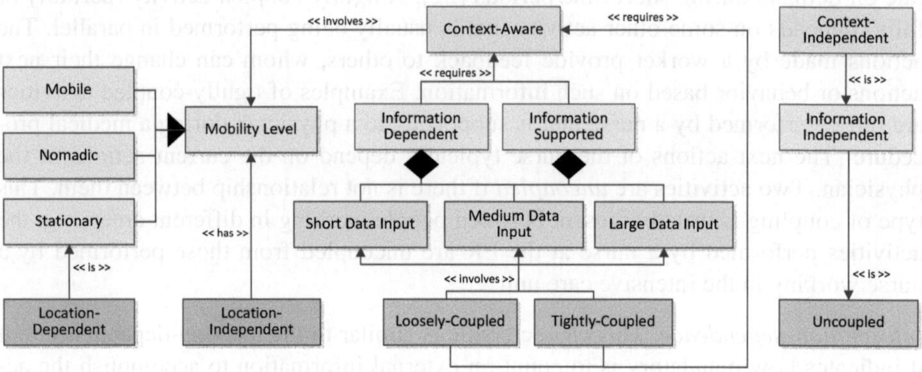

Fig. 2. Ontology of mobile activities characteristics

Although the designer can identify several system requirements only analyzing this ontology, the most important contribution of this ontology is as instrument to help designer identifying mandatory supporting services. However, this can be done once these services are linked to the characteristics of the activity. Next section exemplifies how to match services with activity features.

4.3 Design Guidelines

It is well-known that awareness mechanisms are used to support loosely and tightly-coupled activities. Therefore, services implementing these mechanisms are usually required by context-aware applications that support these activity types. Presence and location awareness services are required to support activities involving face-to-face interactions among mobile workers. Sensing services are required in applications that are context-aware. Data transfer and synchronization services are mandatory if the activity is information-dependent or supported. Location awareness services are required to support location-dependent activities. If the activity is mobile or nomadic, a capturer of the user attention (also known as CUA) should be used before delivering information to the worker; thus, the application increases the probability that such a person effectively put his attention on it. Clearly, the lack of these services in systems supporting activities with these characteristics, will determine the system limitations. These limitations must also be identified by the designer before implementing the solution.

These are just examples about the type of design inferences that the designer can do using the proposed ontology and linking supporting services to activities characteristics. Although this is a first step towards the problem solution, this analysis shows that addressing it following this approach is highly promising.

5 Conclusions and Future Work

Today, the efficiency and effectiveness of mobile activities can be improved or enhanced using supporting technology. Mobile and ubiquitous applications are typically used to reach these goals. As any other collaborative system, the development of these applications is affected by the iceberg effect [1]; therefore their software designers have to guess an important part of the supporting services that these applications have to provide to the end-users (i.e. the mobile workers).

Trying to help address such a problem, this article proposes a set of characteristics of mobile activities that can be used to help identify many of these services and also the potential limitations of the new systems. These activity characteristics were obtained from a study of the work done by physicians and nurses in an emergency room of a hospital.

Moreover, we propose an ontology of activity characteristics and some design guidelines to ease the services identification process. The ontology specifies the relationships among the possible values that can be assumed by the activity characteristics (i.e. the context variables). The design guidelines illustrate about how to use the ontology to infer the supporting services that will be required by the new application.

The next step considers determining the services that are mandatory, according to the characteristics of the activity to be supported. Moreover, we want to replicate the study presented in this paper, probably in the urban emergency responses performed by firefighters, as a way to extend and validate the proposed activity characteristics and also the ontology.

Acknowledgements. This work has been partially supported by Fondecyt (Chile), grant N° 1120207, and European projects UbiHealth (FP7-PEOPLE-2012-IRSES, European Commission, Grant: 316337) and Personal IADL Assistant (PIA) Project Number: AAL-2012-5-033.

References

1. Herskovic, V., Ochoa, S.F., Pino, J.A., Neyem, A.: The Iceberg Effect: Behind the User Interface of Mobile Collaborative Systems. Journal of Universal Computer Science 17(2), 183–202 (2011)
2. Dey, A.: Understanding and Using Context. Personal and Ubiq. Computing 5(1), 4–7 (2001)
3. Rodden, T., Cheverst, K., Davies, N., Dix, A.: Exploiting context in HCI design for mobile systems. In: Proc. of the 1st W. on HCI with Mobile Devices, Glasgow, Scotland (1998)
4. Abowd, G., Dey, A.K., Orr, R., Brotherton, J.: Context-awareness in wearable and ubiquitous computing. Virtual Reality 3(3), 200–211 (1998)
5. Calvary, G., Coutaz, J., Thevenin, D., Limbourg, Q., Bouillon, L., Vanderdonckt, J.: A Unifying Reference Framework for multi-target user interfaces. Interacting with Computers 15(3), 289–308 (2003)
6. Rocchi, C., Stock, O., Zancanaro, M., Kruppa, M., Krüger, A.: The Museum Visit: Generating Seamless Personalized Presentations on Multiple Devices. In: Proc. of the International Conference on Intelligent User Interfaces (IUI 2004), Funchal, Portugal, pp. 316–318 (2004)

7. Beach, A., Gartrell, M., Xing, X., Han, R., Mishra, S., Seada, K.: Fusing Mobile, Sensor, and Social Data To Fully Enable Context-Aware Computing. In: Proc. of the 11th ACM Workshop on Mobile Computing Systems and Applications, Annapolis, USA, pp. 61–66 (2010)
8. Hervás, R., Bravo, J., Fontecha, J., Villarreal, V.: Achieving Adaptive Augmented Reality through Ontological Context-Awareness applied to AAL Scenarios. Journal of Universal Computer Science 19(9), 1334–1349 (2013)
9. Herskovic, V., Neyem, A., Ochoa, S.F., Pino, J.A., Antunes, P.: Understanding Presence Awareness Information Needs Among Engineering Students. In: Proc. of the 16th IEEE International Conference on Computer Supported Cooperative Work in Design, Wuhan, China, May 23-25 (2012)
10. Antunes, P., Herskovic, V., Ochoa, S.F., Pino, J.A.: Reviewing the Quality of Awareness Support in Collaborative Applications. Journal of Systems and Software 89, 146–169 (2014)
11. Romero, P., Calvillo-Gamez, E.H.: Towards an embodied view of flow. In: Proc. of 2nd Workshop on User Models for Motivational Systems. CEUR Workshop Proc., vol. 740, pp. 100-105, Girona, Spain (2011)
12. Duarte, L., Carriço, L.: The influence of performance-oriented widgets on interactive behavior while playing videogames. In: Proc. of the 8th Int. Conf. on Advances in Computer Entertainment Technology, Article No. 54, Lisbon, Portugal (2011)
13. Garlan, D., Siewiorek, D.P., Smailagic, A., Steenkiste, P.: Project Aura: Toward Distraction-Free Pervasive Computing. Pervasive Computing 1(2), 22–31 (2002)
14. Sukthankar, R.: Towards Ambient Projection for Intelligent Environments. In: Proc. of CVIIE 2005, Lexington, USA, pp. 162–172 (2005)
15. Breiner, K., Meixner, G., Rombach, D., Seissler, M., Zühlke, D.: Efficient generation of ambient intelligent user interfaces. In: König, A., Dengel, A., Hinkelmann, K., Kise, K., Howlett, R.J., Jain, L.C. (eds.) KES 2011, Part IV. LNCS, vol. 6884, pp. 136–145. Springer, Heidelberg (2011)
16. Guerrero, L., Ochoa, S.F., Pino, J., Collazos, C.: Selecting Devices to Support Mobile Collaboration. Group Decision and Negotiation 15(3), 243–271 (2006)
17. Alarcon, R., Guerrero, L., Ochoa, S.F., Pino, J.: Analysis and Design of Mobile Collaborative Applications Using Contextual Elements. Computer and Informatics 25(6), 469–496 (2006)
18. Tentori, M., Favela, J.: Activity-Aware Computing for Healthcare. IEEE Pervasive Computing 7(2), 51–57 (2008)
19. Burgess, N.: What is it Like to Work in an Emergency Room? Hospital Jobs Online (2014), `http://www.hospitaljobsonline.com/career-center/healthcare-careers/what-is-it-like-to-work-in-an-emergency-room.html` (last visit: February 2, 2014)
20. Monares, A., Ochoa, S., Herskovic, V., Santos, R., Pino, J.A.: Modeling Interactions in Human-centric Wireless Sensor Networks. In: Proc. of the 2014 IEEE International Conference on Computer Supported Cooperative Work in Design (CSCWD 2014), Hsinchu, Taiwan (2014)
21. Kristoffersen, S., Ljungberg, F.: Mobility: From stationary to mobile work. In: Braa, K., Sorensen, C., Dahlbom, B. (eds.) Planet Internet, Lund, Sweden, pp. 137–156 (2000)
22. Pinelle, D., Gutwin, C.: A groupware design framework for loosely coupled workgroups. In: Proc. of the European Conf. on Computer Supported Cooperative Work, pp. 119–139 (2005)

Sweat Sensing Technique for Wearable Device Using Infrared Transparency

Masa Ogata[1], Masahiko Inami[2], and Michita Imai[1]

[1] Graduate School of Science and Technology, Keio University, 3-14-1 Hiyoshi, Kohoku, Yokohama 223-8522, Japan
{ogata,michita}@ayu.ics.keio.ac.jp
[2] Graduate School of Media Design, Keio University, 4-1-1 Hiyoshi, Kohoku, Yokohama 223-8526, Japan
inami@inami.info

Abstract. Wearable devices that are worn on the hand and display information are rapidly becoming pervasive. However, acquiring and displaying a user's own data, such as the amount of sweat flowing and the required amount of water for a particular activity, on a wearable device remains difficult. We propose a technique that senses the amount of sweat flowing from the human body. The technique, which is implemented in a wearable device, utilizes infrared transparency via a sponge that can hold the sweat. We selected sponge as the material to hold the sweat because it enables repeated measurement of the amount of sweat flowing from the human body. Consequently, we also outline the development and testing of a prototype device that actualizes the proposed technique and discuss its efficacy and feasibility.

Keywords: Sweat, Wearable device, Sensing, Photo transparency.

1 Introduction

Sporting activities are beneficial to human health for numerous reasons [12], [16]. Human beings maintain control over their health and improve their ability to keep their temperature stable when they exercise. Exercise also provides spiritual stability and physical flexibility. In recent times, particularly in urban areas, people tend to spend longer hours doing office work and sitting on chairs while working. Besides office workers, persons who work at home, and self-employed persons who use computers and sit on chairs need suitable exercise. This trend and change in the work environment increases the need for exercise. Therefore, humans have to obtain and allocate sufficient time for exercise. Hence, sporting activities including light exercise such as walking are becoming popular. Light exercise is beneficial for calorie consumption even if one exercises at night. From elementary school to high school, physical education is included as part of the education curriculum. Exercise is regarded as an elemental curriculum for developing a basic part of humanity and physical foundations.

M. Kurosu (Ed.): Human-Computer Interaction, Part III, HCII 2014, LNCS 8512, pp. 323–331, 2014.

Although there are many benefits for engaging in sporting activities, caution needs to be exercised in several areas. People can experience temporary disorders from over-exercise and are injured if they are not careful. One of the reasons for experiencing illness and disorder during exercise activities is hydration; which is associated with excessive sweating and heat disorder. Thermal fatigue is also caused by dehydration. Sweat contains water and electrolytes. Prolonged heating and sweating of the human body induces water loss. In extreme cases, it can result in loss of electrolytes from the body via vomiting. It is well known that water leaves the body via our breath, urine, and sweat. During physical activities, the perspiration that automatically flows to cool the body is the largest amount of water that leaves the body. Sweat is emitted from all parts of the body except for the palm of the hands and the soles of the feet. Consequently, it is possible to detect and measure the state of sweat on various parts of the body. A number of researchers have conducted studies associated with sweat detection [2], [3], [4], [13]. Some of these studies attempt to determine the pH level of the sweat. However, to the best of our knowledge, detection of the amount of outgoing sweat with a wearable device that can be removed easily has not been proposed. Of the many applications supported by wearable devices, functions that are specialized for sporting activities appear to be most in demand. Initially, wearable devices were conceptualized for entertainment use, such as listening to music while running. However, concomitant with miniaturization and improvements in sensing technology, it became possible to measure and sense health status and condition during sporting activities and to quantify and visualize the data. Notwithstanding, research into new technologies and techniques for sensing during sporting activities is needed to enhance the lives of human beings.

In this paper, we propose a durable sweat sensor that uses photo reflective sensing via a sponge material that holds the water. The sensor and sensing techniques are implemented in a wearable device that a user uses during sporting activities and is easy to put on before starting the activities. Infrared has already been used in several related studies [9], [10] and has proved useful for decoding many kinds of units such as distance, density, pressure, and transparency via certain materials. By incorporating it into a sweat sensor device, it will help to augment sporting activities, which are elemental for human beings. With miniaturization, improved markets, and the increasing pervasiveness of mobile devices, wearable devices are increasingly being developed and gaining in popularity. Some of the applications available for wearable devices also focus on sports and exercise use. The functions implemented in wearable devices augment human activities in sports. For example, armband-type devices such as Fitbit Flex [5] provide data collection for health care, record time-series data by mobile application, and provide recommendations. Wearable cameras that enable users to capture various sights during their sporting activities, such as skiing, swimming, and cycling, are also available. Further, a variety of wearable devices are available for every type of sport.

2 Related Work

2.1 Augmenting Sport with Technologies

Higuchi et al. [7] conducted a study in which they used a camera aboard an unmanned aerial vehicle (UAV) to capture a user's rear view. The research focused on using the third person view afforded by the UAV to allow the user to see his/her own body image and thereby improve his/her training technique. Tracking is done by detecting the color of the user's clothing and continuously tracking thereafter.

Swimoid [14] is an underwater robot for swimmers that provides a display on top of the robot showing the user's body. The robot is automatically controlled and moves in concert with the user's position in the water in order to keep the display in view of the user. This enables swimmers to recognize their own body movements and swimming form via the display, which is captured and processed while using a colored band on the user's body to aid in tracking.

Kurihara et al. [8] augmented kinesthetic sensation using a mechanical structure. Their idea improves the user experience during push-up activities by effecting vivid sensations according to the user's movements. Mechanical feedback against the arm movement produces a rotary switch feeling. They plan to develop a virtual reality application based on this idea.

2.2 Activity Sensing

In addition to sports, human activity is supported from several perspectives nowadays. Sensing the everyday status of human activity is beneficial for self-monitoring by a patient or remote monitoring by doctors. Guo et al. [6] invented a disappearing sensor that is installed in the textile of cloth and is unseen by users and third parties. Their idea is to use conductive textile to sense the breath rating from reading the voltage change during breathing. Installing the sensor in cloth is a simple design and technique to measure the activity. From our perspective however, because sensing sweat should be continuous and the sweat amount changes over time, we have to select a device that can be attached to the body and removed conveniently, besides being easy to clean.

Velloso et al. [15] created a weight lifting application that achieved qualitative activity recognition by predicting the user's activity from data sent from several accelerometer sensors attached to the body and barbells. They implemented the system in such a way that it can deduce the user's status using both model-based and sensor-based techniques.

Bächlin et al. [1] developed an assistance system for swimmers by providing actuating LED in their goggles, a vibration motor, and audio feedback. Sensing is achieved using several accelerometers to capture the continuous swim performance. They configured suitable feedback and conducted experiments with the developed device using 22 participants.

2.3 Sweat Sensing

A chemical method for sensing sweat has been proposed by Benito-Lopez et al. [3]. Their proposed method focuses on detection of the pH balance in sweat using ionic liquid polymer gel. Their expected application is also for wearable systems utilized in sporting activities. The sensor is small enough to be attached to the human body; the purpose however, is not to detect the amount of sweat but to determine the ingredients secreted in sweat.

Salvo et al. [13] proposed a method for measuring the rate of sweat. They used a gasket with two humidity sensors and compared the difference between the sensors to deduce the sweat rate. The two sensors are placed at different distances from the surface of the skin. The gasket is glued to a layer on the skin to keep it at a distance from the skin surface. Their work improves the cost and size of such wearable devices besides rendering the sensing technique inexpensive and easy to use for wearable applications.

Coyle et al. [3], [4] proposed a wearable chemosensor that analyzes body fluids using the chemical reaction of a pH indicator. Their test device is designed for continuous sensing during experimental activities in the laboratory. It is wearable and small enough to be attached to the waist and wrapped in textiles. Sensing is accomplished by color sensing of a pH indicator and an absorbent material behind the pH indicator allows sweat to go through the pH indicator and new sweat liquid to flow into it.

3 Sweat Sensing Infrared Transparency

Sensing the status of sweat is an important factor of human health in sporting activities. Because our focus is on wearable methods, we selected photo sensors and infrared LEDs to detect the amount of sweat stored in the sponge. The sponge is placed between the LED and photo sensor and the sensor detects the infrared emitted from the LED and measures the amount of water in the sponge. The sensor, LED, and sponge are positioned and, for this implementation, placed in a pipe (Fig. 1). The pipe has a hole that allows water to enter and permeate the sponge.

The infrared ray goes through the sponge and is diffused by the structure of the sponge. Sponges that primarily comprise plastic polymers have non-uniform structures. When diffused reflection occurs, the amount of infrared going through the sponge decreases. Thus, the amount detected at the photo sensor will also decrease. Water functions as a transparency material in the sponge. It easily transmits the rays and reduces diffused reflection by decreasing the reflection ratio of the sponge. Consequently, it decreases the number of rays leaving the sponge, which further results in a corresponding increase in the number of rays received at the photo sensor.

Our method leverages the above characteristics of rays in sponge and water. Using this technique, the amount, and percentage of water stored in the sponge can be measured. Infrared rays are usually used to detect water by actually absorbing them in the water. To make the sensor small, the water is turned into a transparent material and helps the rays to be transmitted into the sponge.

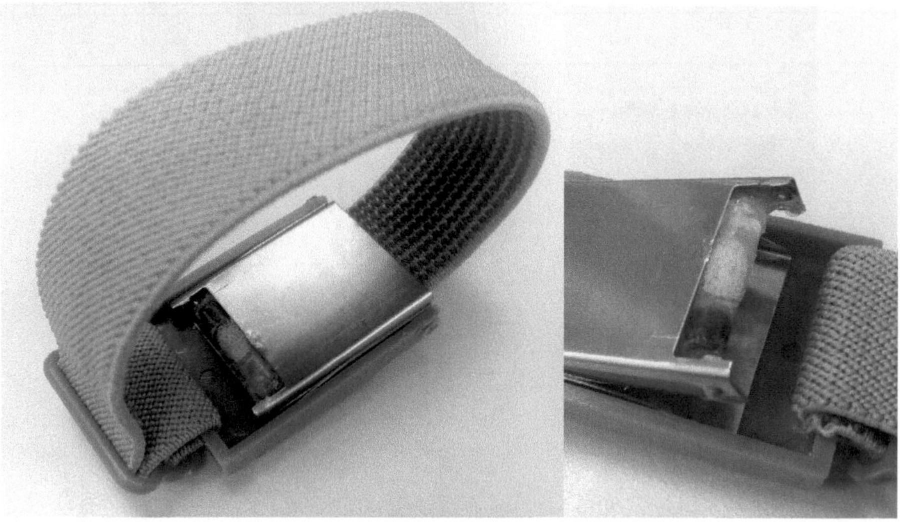

Fig. 1. Prototype of our wearable device with sweat amount sensor using infrared transparency. A tube is installed on the underside of the armband and makes contact with the skin. The tube contains a photo diode, an infrared LED, and a piece of sponge. The electronic devices are combined using glue and insulated.

3.1 Hardware

The hardware consists of an armband and sensing components including an LED, a photo diode, a piece of sponge, and a tube. The device is designed to be worn and used during sporting activities. To make the device waterproof, the sensor is stored in the tube and bonded with glue. By using armband, the sensor can gather the sweat flowing on the body and measure the amount of sweat flowing over time. The diameter of the tube is 4.5 mm, and the length of the sensor tube is 16 mm.

3.2 Experimental Results

We tested the sensing technique actualized using the above hardware. The circuit was developed using simple components: photo diode, infrared LED, tube, sponge, resistors, and a microcontroller connected to a PC. We utilized the following procedure to ensure correct measurement of the amount of water:

1. Prepare wet sponge.
2. Place sponge in the tube.
3. Measure the transparency.
4. Remove a very small amount of water by sucking it up using a square of absorbent paper.
5. Repeat Steps 3 and 4 until all the water is completely removed.

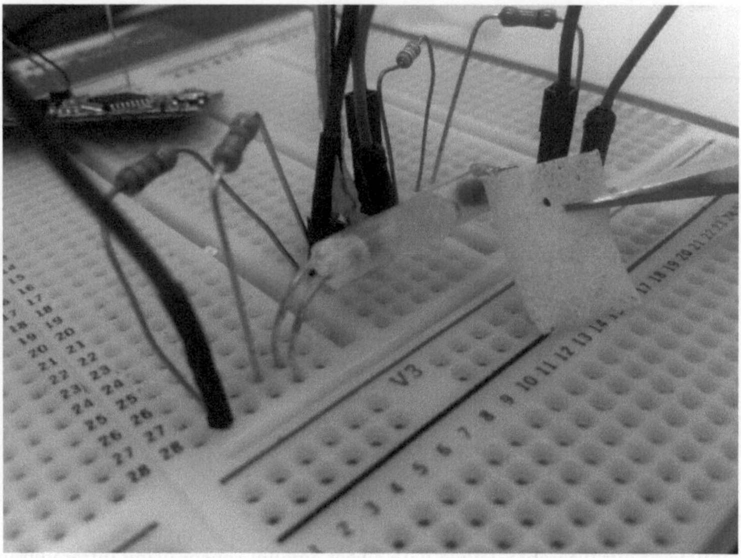

Fig. 2. Circuit and configuration of the experimental apparatus. We used a 95 Ω resistor on the LED side and a 76 kΩ resistor on the photo diode side to facilitate precise control of the infrared ray emitted.

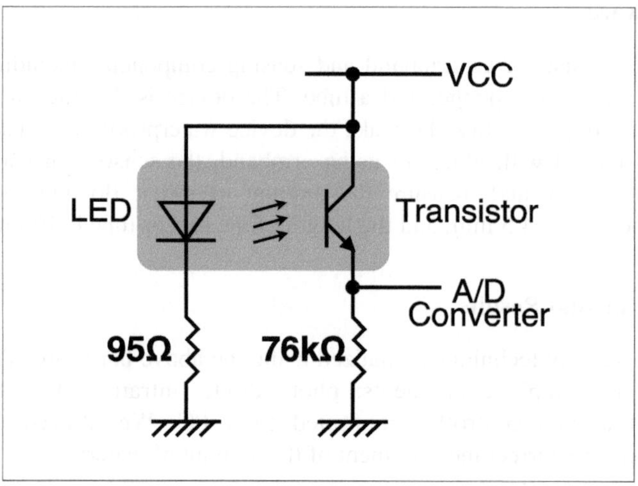

Fig. 3. Configuration of the photo sensor and diode electric circuit. The values of the resistors are not simply taken from the labels on the resistors but from actual measurements using a tester. The A/D converter is one of the functions of the microcontroller that converts the analog voltage value to a digital number.

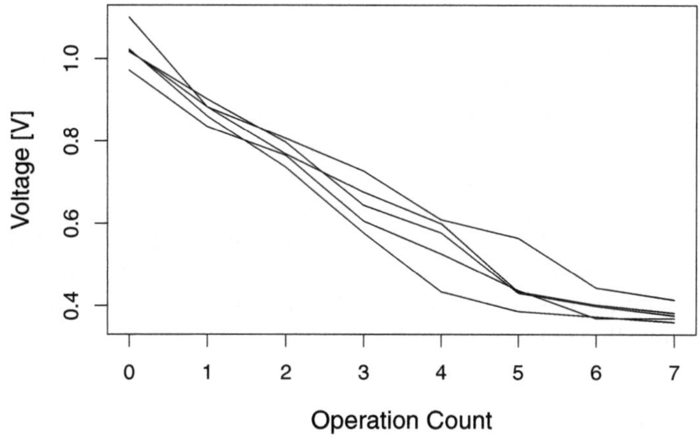

Fig. 4. Plots of voltage versus operations (five curves). Index zero on the x-axis represents the original state of the sponge. The values on the x-axis signify the number of operations, in which a small amount of water is absorbed by the paper, completed. The value on the y-axis is converted to voltage level from the digital value. The highest voltage of the microcontroller was 3.3 V.

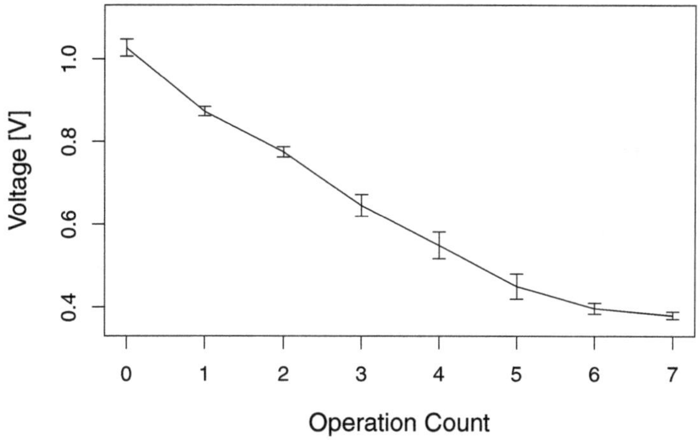

Fig. 5. Mean graph of Fig. 4 and standard deviation of five operations. Each standard deviation is indicated as a vertical line over the mean point.

To ensure that the measurement of the amount of water in the sponge was done correctly, we used tissue paper squares, each 10 mm in size. We counted the number of operations it took in each experiment for the water to be completely removed. The paper squares were sufficiently small and easily absorbed a small amount of water from the sponge. We put the paper on the sponge by means of a pair of tweezers and removed it when the paper had been evenly saturated. The configuration of the apparatus and the operation are illustrated in Fig. 2. The circuit used is depicted in Fig. 3.

Figures 4 and 5 show the results obtained in the experiments plotted on a graph. It can be seen that the plots of the third through to the fifth operation have larger standard deviations than the other operations. It appears that, during the activity of water removal using the paper, the sponge had uniform water and air distribution in it, which resulted in the larger deviations at intermediate counts. However, the mean value of each operation and deviation are sufficiently separated and the plots drawn decrease monotonically with water absorption.

4 Discussion

4.1 Limitations

To facilitate wearability, we used a small tube that can be utilized during sporting activities to detect the sweat in our design. Therefore, there are some limitations, and incomplete tasks that must be addressed before our device can be considered for actual use. First, the sponge needs to be stored inside the tube instead of sticking out from the tube as it does currently. The second issue is that of the battery. Because we are using both a LED and a diode, more electricity is required than with a simple wearable sensor. By reducing the electricity used by these apparatuses, the amount of energy, and therefore the size of the battery required can be kept small. Finally, the sponge can be improved by selecting and comparing among many types of materials, sizes, and textures.

4.2 Future Work

Using a sponge is actually only one method of implementing this system; it can be improved by experimenting with other materials and mechanisms. Further, the hardware configured with the sponge and tube can be used with other types of wearable devices such as those worn around the neck.

5 Conclusion

In this paper, we proposed a technique for detecting and measuring the amount of sweat flowing from the human body during sporting activities. We used a sponge to hold the sweat for detection over time and to facilitate the sensing of the sweat with a wearable device. The idea of photo transparency is to leverage the random reflection caused by the structure of the sponge to measure the amount of water it contains. We developed and tested a prototype device with a tube containing an LED, a photo diode, and a sponge via several water absorption operations. We found that the changes in photo transparency decreased monotonically with water absorption and that the device is sufficiently convenient for sensing sweat and small enough for wearable use.

References

1. Bächlin, M., Förster, K., Tröster, G.: SwimMaster: A Wearable Assistant for Swimmer. In: 11th International Conference on Ubiquitous Computing, pp. 215–224. ACM (2009)
2. Benito-Lopez, F., Coyle, S., Byrne, R., Diamond, D.: Sensing Sweat in Real-Time Using Wearable Microfluidics. In: 7th International Workshop on Wearable and Implantable Body Sensor Networks, Singapore,, pp. 31–33 (2010)
3. Coyle, S., Benito-Lopez, F., Byrne, R., Diamond, D.: On-Body Chemical Sensors for Monitoring Sweat. In: Lay-Ekuakille, A., Mukhopadhyay, S.C. (eds.) Wearable and Autonomous Biomedical Devices and Systems for Smart Environment. LNEE, vol. 75, pp. 177–193. Springer, Heidelberg (2010)
4. Coyle, S., Morris, D., Lau, K.T., Diamond, D., Di Francesco, F., Taccini, N., Trivella, M.G., Costanzo, D., Salvo, P., Porchet, J.A., Luprano, J.: Textile Sensors to Measure Sweat PH and Sweat-rate During Exercise. In: 3rd International Conference on Pervasive Computing Technologies for Healthcare, pp. 1–6. IEEE (2009)
5. Fitbit, `http://www.fitbit.com/`
6. Guo, L., Berglin, L., Li, Y.J., Mattila, H., Mehrjerdi, A.K., Skrifvars, M.: 'Disappearing Sensor'-Textile Based Sensor for Monitoring Breathing. In: 2011 International Conference on Control, Automation and Systems Engineering (CASE), pp. 1–4. IEEE (2011)
7. Higuchi, K., Shimada, T., Rekimoto, J.: Flying Sports Assistant: External Visual Imagery Representation for Sports Training. In: 2nd Augmented Human International Conference, p. 7. ACM (2011)
8. Kurihara, Y., Kuniyasu, Y., Hachisu, T., Sato, M., Fukushima, S., Kajimoto, H.: Augmentation of Kinesthetic Sensation by Adding Rotary Switch Feeling Feedback. In: 3rd Augmented Human International Conference, p. 28. ACM (2012)
9. Ogata, M., Sugiura, Y., Makino, Y., Inami, M., Imai, M.: SenSkin: Adapting Skin as a Soft Interface. In: 26th Annual ACM Symposium on User Interface Software and Technology, pp. 539–544. ACM (2013)
10. Ogata, M., Sugiura, Y., Osawa, H., Imai, M.: iRing: Intelligent Ring Using Infrared Reflection. In: 25th Annual ACM Symposium on User Interface Software and Technology, pp. 131–136. ACM (2012)
11. Pacelli, M., Loriga, G., Taccini, N., Paradiso, R.: Sensing Fabrics for Monitoring Physiological and Biomechanical Variables: E-Textile Solutions. In: 3rd IEEE-EMBS, pp. 1–4 (2006)
12. Ratey, J.: Spark: The Revolutionary New Science of Exercise and the Brain. Little, Brown and Company (2008)
13. Salvo, P., Di Francesco, F., Costanzo, D., Ferrari, C., Trivella, M.G., De-Rossi, D.: A Wearable Sensor for Measuring Sweat Rate. IEEE Sensors Journal 10(10), 1557–1558 (2010)
14. Ukai, Y., Rekimoto, J.: Swimoid: a swim support system using an underwater buddy robot. In: 4th Augmented Human International Conference, pp. 170–177. ACM (2013)
15. Velloso, E., Bulling, A., Gellersen, H., Ugulino, W., Fuks, H.: Qualitative Activity Recognition of Weight Lifting Exercises. In: 4th Augmented Human International Conference, pp. 116–123. ACM (2013)
16. Weinberg, R.S., Gould, D.: Foundations of Sport and Exercise Psychology. Human Kinetics (2006)

Collaborative Digital Sports Systems That Encourage Exercise

Ayaka Sato[1], Anna Yokokubo[2], Itiro Siio[2], and Jun Rekimoto[1,3]

[1] The University of Tokyo, 7-3-1 Hongo, Bunkyo, Tokyo 113-0033, Japan,
ayakasato@acm.org
[2] Ochanomizu University, Tokyo, Japan
anna.yokokubo@is.ocha.ac.jp, siio@acm.org
[3] Sony Computer Science Laboratories, Tokyo, Japan
rekimoto@acm.org

Abstract. Although the importance of health and exercising as a way to maintain fitness and physical wellbeing is widely recognized, it is often difficult for people to persist with a regular workout schedule. In this paper, we propose a solution to this problem through "Collaborative Digital Sports." This is a digital sports environment where participants are given a shared goal. Through the use of body motion sensors and video projection feedback, this environment works as a fitness playground that requires physical movements by participants. This environment is adaptable to the fitness levels of the participants, as its sensor-feedback loop is digital and unencumbered by real sports equipment. Based on this concept, we designed and implemented two collaborative digital sporting activities. The "Group Jump Rope Orchestra" is a simulated jump rope environment where people are required to synchronize jumping over a projected rope as it periodically swings by. The "How Many Legged Race!?" is a variation of the three-legged race that can accommodate any number of participants as they synchronize their steps. We tested these sports environments with numerous participants and discovered that the cooperative nature of these digital sports helps motivate the players and fosters a shared sense of caring among them.

1 Introduction

Fitness is an effective exercise to maintain and enhance health. However, exercising alone can be tedious and demotivating, and hence difficult to continue with on a regular basis. In contrast, competitive team sports, such as soccer and basketball, demand that each player exhibit responsibility and make a serious effort. However, players need a certain degree of training and skill in order to enjoy sports.

We thus propose "Collaborative Digital Sports," an environment that aims to keep users motivated to exercise. This environment effectively combines digital technology with the social aspect of team sports to enable users to stay motivated to work out, and also nurtures camaraderie among them. In this paper, we describe two instances of collaborative digital sports systems and report on feedback from the participants.

M. Kurosu (Ed.): Human-Computer Interaction, Part III, HCII 2014, LNCS 8512, pp. 332–340, 2014.

2 Collaborative Digital Sports

We define Collaborative Digital Sports as composed of the following three elements:

1. Encourages collaboration among participants
A collaborative sport is a competitive physical activity that requires that all participants work together. The collaborative element encourages participants to make an effort, stay committed to the activity and not give up because they are part of a team.

2. Easy to play
Complicated rules make it difficult for people to participate in any activity. We have kept the rules of the sports and the required movements simple, so that anyone can play.

3. Adaptable
In order to keep participants motivated, we make use of digital technology so that the parameters of the sports – the skill level of the sport, the number of participants, etc. – can easily be adapted to the situation. We believe that this flexibility in the design of our digital sports prevents participants from abandoning the activity on account of boredom or lack of skill, and also enhances their enjoyment.

We have implemented two examples of collaborative digital sports systems in accordance with the aforementioned elements. The first sport is "The Group Jump Rope Orchestra", which is modeled on the game jump rope and orchestral music. The second sport is "How many legged races!?", which is a variation of the well-known three-legged race. Both sports involve teamwork.

3 Example 1: Group Jump Rope Orchestra

Group Jump Rope Orchestra is a collaborative digital sport system that is a mixture of the game jump rope and the dynamics of an orchestra. In this sport, the participants jump over a virtual rope that is projected onto two screens, one on the floor under the participants' feet and the other on the wall, as shown in Fig.1. Their collective activity causes orchestral music to play.

Elements of Group Jump Rope. Group Jump Rope is a sport that involves two players holding a long rope and swinging it together, and any number of players in between them trying to jump over the rope so that it passes under their feet and over their heads. The game becomes more challenging as the number of players increases. In order to succeed at it, all participants have to adapt to a shared pace and rhythm. This instills a sense of unity and collective satisfaction in them.

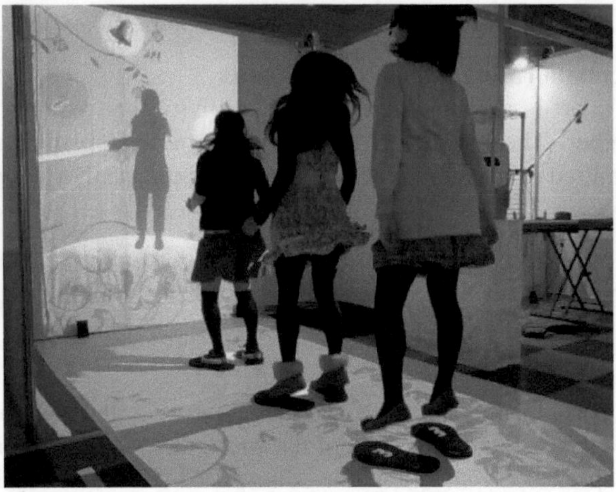

Fig. 1. The Group Jump Rope system. A virtual rope is projected on two screens at the front and the floor. Participants jump when the rope passes under their feet.

Orchestral Elements. An orchestra consists of a large group of musicians playing different instruments. The music becomes grander as the number of musicians and instruments increases. In order to sound harmonious, all musicians need to play their respective parts in accordance with the directions of the conductor.

The first of our two digital sports combines the elements of Group Jump Rope and an orchestra.

3.1 System Configuration

The system consists of two screens, two projectors, pressure sensors embedded in foot-shaped sponges, two speakers, phidgets (USB I/O module), and a PC (Fig.2). Two animations are projected on two screens, one each on the floor under the players' feet and on the wall facing them. The front screen shows a girl swinging a rope, while the image of a rope swinging in correspondence with the movement of the girl's arm is projected on the screen on the floor. The pressure sensors embedded in the foot-shaped sponges on the screen on the floor detect whether the participants are jumping at the right time. The sensors are connected to the phidgets[1] and the PC, which produce relevant animations and sounds. The PC – a MacBook Pro – runs the Adobe Flash Builder software.

[1] Phidgets: `http://www.phidgets.com/`

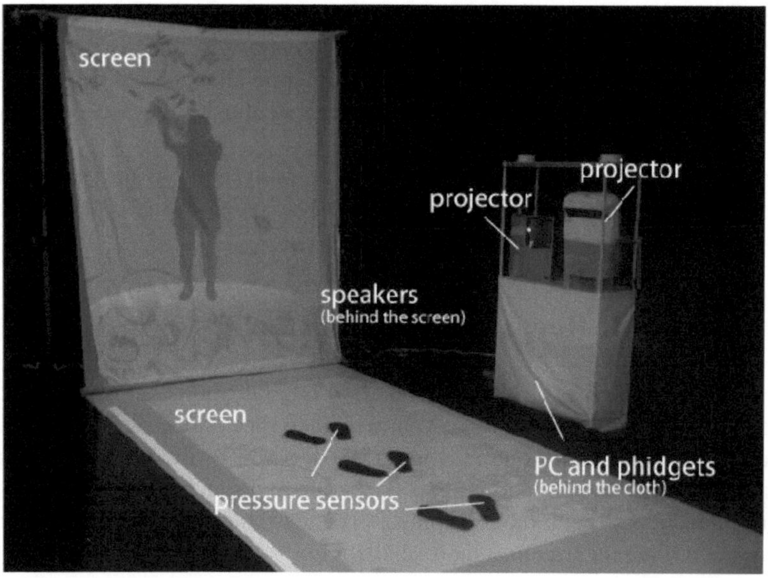

Fig. 2. System configuration for Group Jump Rope Orchestra

3.2 Usage and Feedback

The virtual rope makes a sound as it "brushes" the floor, at which time the players are supposed to jump over it. When one player jumps at the correct time and avoids the rope, the sound of one orchestral instrument – a violin, say – is played. When another player does the same, the sound of another instrument is played. When all players jump at the correct time, all instruments in an orchestra are played. A new participant can join the game at any time. Pictures of the musical instruments being played are

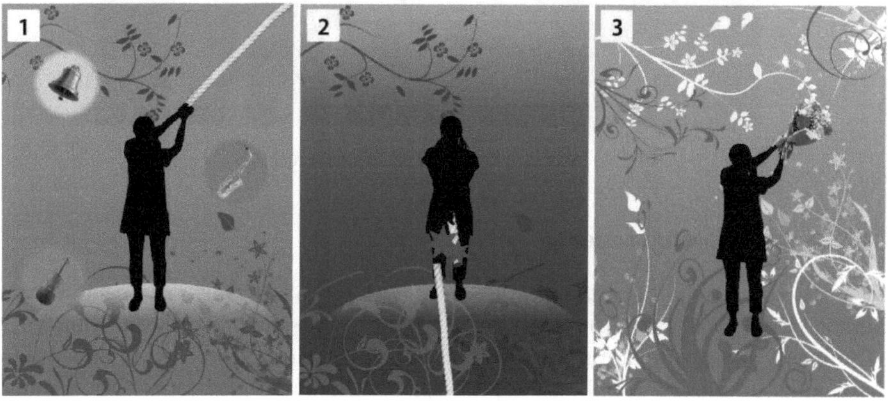

Fig. 3. The front screen animations: (1) Pictures of musical instruments appear according to the number and the role of the participants. (2) When someone fails to clear the rope, the music stops, a discordant sound is played and the animation changes. (3) When the musical piece is successfully played to completion, applause is heard and the animation changes.

projected onto the front screen according to the number of players and the instrument "played" by each player (Fig.3-1). If a player fails to clear the virtual rope, the music stops, a discordant sound is played and the animation changes as shown in Fig.3-2. If the participants manage to play an entire piece of music, the sound of applause is played and the animation changes, as in Fig.3-3.

Participants of the Group Jump Rope Orchestra system have a variety of musical compositions and animations to choose from. The speed of the rope can also be adjusted.

4 Example 2: How Many Legged Race!?

"How many legged race!?" is a Collaborative Digital Sport that combines the three-legged race and digital technology. A three-legged race is one in which a team of two people runs together, with one person's right leg tied to the other person's left leg. This sport requires that the participants cooperate and synchronize their steps to move forward quickly. As the number of players per team increases, to a maximum of four in our system, the race becomes more challenging.

Fig. 4. Overview of How Many Legged Race!?

4.1 System Configuration

This system consists of a screen, a projector, two pressure sensors per participant, a Gainer (USB I/O module)[2] and a PC (Fig.5). A screen is set in front of the participants and a simulation is projected. When all participants step in concordance, the simulation moves, enabling the participants to take a video tour of the simulated environment while racing. The software runs on Flash and the values of the pressure sensors are obtained through Gainer.

[2] Gainer: http://gainer.cc/

Fig. 5. System configuration of the "How Many Legged Race!?" system

Use of sensor values. The values from eight pressure sensors, in case four players are involved, are used to detect two factors: the number of participants and the harmony of each team's step. As shown in Fig.6, if sensors 1 and 2 are pressed, the system detects one player; if sensors 3 and 4 are pressed, the system detects two players, and so on. A new player can join in at any time. In contrast with the Group Jump Rope Orchestra system, the speed of the players' movement is not determined by the system in this sport. Participants can move at the pace of their choice so long as all players in a team move at the same speed and step in concert. Unlike the actual three-legged race, teammates in this digital incarnation do not actually have adjacent feet tied together, and so can easily join into or drop out of the game. However, each player still needs to move as if one of her feet were tied to that of her partner's. For instance, when there are two players on a team, they should take steps 1 and 4, and 2 and 3 in concert. When a team consists of four players, they should take steps 1, 4, 5 and 8, and 2, 3, 6 and 7 in concert.

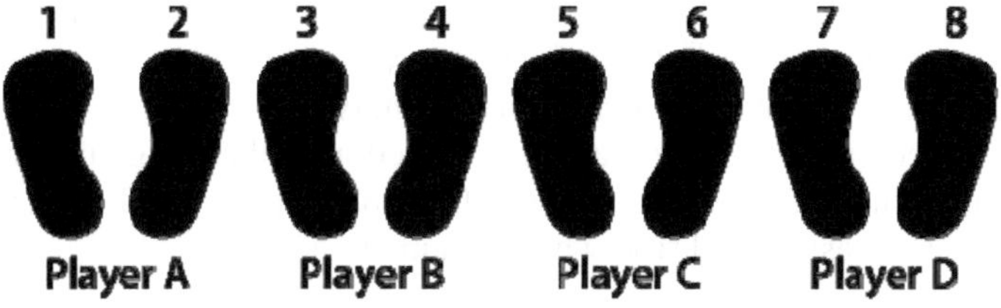

Fig. 6. (1) The number of players and (2) whether they are stepping correctly are both detected from the values of pressure sensors

4.2 System Usage

The system launches when participants step on the foot-shaped contours and start walking or running. The participants can see if their steps have been detected on the screen before them. The screen also indicates participants' speed. When a team's stepping is concordant, the virtual video on the screen progresses; and when a team's steps are discordant, its indicated speed decreases, all the way to a complete stop if the team does not correct its step. The players can control the speed of progression of the movie by stepping quickly. The greater the number of players per team, the faster its speed.

5 User Experience

We tested these two sports systems with numerous participants at exhibitions and through demonstrations at conferences. In this section, we report the feedback from a wide range of participants.

The Group Jump Rope Orchestra system was exhibited for three days at the finals of the International Virtual Reality Contest[3] (IVRC), held at National Museum of Emerging Science and Innovation (Tokyo, Japan) from August 23-25, 2010. It was also demonstrated at Entertainment Computing conference in Japan in 2010, and at the ACE in the same year [5]. We will report the results of our IVRC exhibition, where visitors of all ages took an interest in the system.

A number of children visited our exhibit and began playing Group Jump Rope Orchestra even before being instructed, and seemed to enjoy it a lot. They returned to our exhibit several times to play the sport over and over again. It seemed that people were more motivated to play with others than alone. A few children were initially scared to play the game but enjoyed it a lot once they tried it. People who were initially poor at the sport improved markedly with time, and even asked us to raise the skill level.

The How Many Legged Race!? was shown for six days at an exhibition at the University of Tokyo from June 10-15, 2010. It was also demonstrated at the Virtual Reality Conference in Japan in 2011. Most reactions to the system were similar to those to the Group Jump Rope Orchestra. Most participants were calling out "one, two, one, two..." as they took steps in order to keep step with each other. It appeared that this practice made them feel more motivated and friendly.

We also noticed that safety was a major attraction of these digital sports. The danger of serious injury often inhibits people from playing physical sports. Our digital sports have no such associated risk, which is a major advantage.

6 Related Work

Many studies have been conducted on supplementing sports with digital technologies. PingPongPlus adds visual effects to a ping-pong table by sensing ball-impact timing

[3] IVRC 2010: `http://ivrc.net/2010/`

and position using acoustic sensors [1]. Although the visual appearance of the game is altered, the game remains unchanged. In contrast, Eureka Computers introduced "E-Sports Ground," where a projection on a floor becomes a major part of the sport [2]. Since a player's motion is recognized by 3D sensors (such as Kinect), it is possible to design digital sports without using physical instruments. For example, players can "kick" a projected virtual ball. Our collaborative sports also use digital projection and sensors and introduce the idea of collaboration to foster camaraderie and keep players motivated.

Rope Revolution combines physical rope motion with digital projection [3]. Similar to our Group Jump Rope Orchestra, Rope Revolution supports multiple players on the same field. Combining physical equipment with digital sports would provide greater engagement between player and sport, but it might also limit sport design flexibility. For instance, with the use of a real rope, it becomes more difficult to change its speed according to the player's skill. We choose a fully digital solution for our sports systems because of its flexibility and cost-effectiveness. We also think that our collaborative sports scenarios are sufficiently real to prompt players to actually use their body movement.

"Jogging Over a Distance" supports communication between and among joggers [4]. Combining GPS and 3D audio, it supports pace-awareness between runners, so that collaborative or competitive running is possible even when runners are geographically separated. At present, our systems only support co-located collaboration, but we also think that our design can be extended to accommodate distributed collaboration.

7 Discussions

7.1 Tradeoff between Reality and Flexibility

In our design, we have chosen purely digital environments where the feedback to participants is in the form of image projection and sound effects and no sporting equipment is used. At the same time, we could also design a similar environment with a hybrid of real and virtual objects, as in the case of Rope Revolution [3].

We think that there is a tradeoff between the two approaches. On the one hand, participants using physical instruments, such as an actual rope or a real racket, might experience the sport more realistically and would be able to engage it more seriously. They might also be able to better use their bodies with the real instrument, such as spinning the rope or swinging the racket. On the other hand, such physical instruments might limit the flexibility of the sporting design. For instance, when the motion of the simulated rope is directly correspondent to a real rope, it might become difficult to control its speed according to the skill-level of the participants. In addition, fully digital sporting environments might be less expensive than real ones. We also expect that giving players a common goal would help them take the sport more seriously, even when the environment does not have a physical instrument.

7.2 Possibility of Distributed Collaborative Digital Sports

In our current systems, the participants are expected to gather at the same place and work out. We are now considering extending this to a distributed version, where people can remotely participate in the same sports field even when they are geographically separated. For example, a distributed version of Group Jump Rope Orchestra would connect players to their remote teammates by showing their body motions as projected silhouettes. Other communication channels, such as audio, would also be used. In addition to normal voice communication among participants, this audio channel would also convey nonverbal information, such as the sound of their footsteps. We expect that the existence of a common goal would help keep players motivated to play, even in a distributed environment.

8 Conclusion

In this paper, we proposed "Collaborative Digital Sports", a digital sports environment where participants are given a shared goal. We designed and implemented two example systems based on the concept of Collaborative Digital Sports, and tested with numerous participants at exhibitions and conferences. The feedbacks from these places confirmed that these systems motivated participants. We believe that there still is a potential for this Collaborative Digital Sports such as adjusting levels on each participant, and using in distant places.

References

1. Ishii, H., Wisneski, C., Orbanes, J., Chun, B., Paradiso, J.: PingPongPlus: design of an athletic-tangible interface for computer-supported cooperative play. In: Proc. of CHI 1999, pp. 394–401 (1999)
2. E-Sports Ground, http://www.eurekacomputer.jp/
3. Yao, L., Dasgupta, S., Cheng, N., Spingarn-Koff, J., Rudakevych, O., Ishii, H.: Rope Revolution: Tangible and Gestural Rope Interface for Collaborative Play. In: Proc. ACE, Article No. 11 (2011)
4. Mueller, F., Vetere, F., Gibbs, M.R., Edge, D., Agamanolis, S., Sheridan, J.G.: Jogging over a distance between Europe and Australia. In: Proc. UIST 2010, pp. 189–198. ACM Press (2010)
5. Sato, A., Yokokubo, A., Siio, I.: The Group Jump Rope Orchestra - An Interactive System to Present a Sense of Togetherness. In: Proc. ACE 2010 (2010)

Design Implications to Systems Supporting Informal Caregivers' Daily Life

Susanne Schinkinger and Hilda Tellioğlu

Vienna University of Technology, Austria
{susanne.schinkinger,hilda.tellioglu}@tuwien.ac.at
http://media.tuwien.ac.at
Favoritenstrasse 9/187, A-1040 Vienna, Austria

Abstract. This paper is about studying informal caregivers to understand their exhausting life. Our aim is to define design requirements for any kind of information and communication technology to support them. Based on ethnographic studies we gathered information about our users' needs, possibilities, constraints, and challenges. After a brief introduction to the related research on current technology solutions we introduce our methodology. Then we present two of our user cases in detail. We point out areas in which we can really provide technology support for our users. We also describe what qualities and features the technology should have to meet these requirements. We summarize our findings before we conclude the paper.

Keywords: User interfaces, ethnography and field work, interaction design, informal caregivers.

1 Introduction

Informal caregivers provide 80% of all care in the European Union. They are at a higher risk for both psychical and physical morbidity [5] [7]. Caring at home results in heavy physical, psychological, or emotional burden. These "hidden patients" [11] have an increased risk of mortality compared to their non-caring counterparts.

The daily life of informal caregivers is characterized as interplay between routine work, spontaneous interruptions mainly caused by care receiver, and lack of time. Activities of a normal day are usually pre-defined. Certain care needs to be carried out on a daily base by the caregiver or someone external like home care or physiotherapist. Because everything is determined by the needs of the care receiver, the course of the day is heteronomous. Heteronomy is caused besides the routine care processes, on the one hand, by the care receiver, especially when urgent help is needed or some kind of activity wanted that is out of the daily routine. On the other hand, it is caused by external service providers especially when they do not deliver their services on time. Delays have negative impact on the time resources of caregivers. The lack of time leads to social exclusion. They cannot meet their friends, spend time with others they like, or do something what

M. Kurosu (Ed.): Human-Computer Interaction, Part III, HCII 2014, LNCS 8512, pp. 341–350, 2014.

they like. Very often they are not even able to leave their home because of their care responsibilities. This makes keeping contact with other family members or friends almost impossible. The level of burden increases when informal caregivers still have a job, are old, or have a health condition.

Within the project TOPIC[1] we apply ethnographic methods like participatory observations, in-depth interviews, cultural probes to understand the life situation of several informal caregivers [1]. Additionally, we study different technological solutions available on the market to find the right match for carers' requirements. Most of the technological solutions provided nowadays aim to support professional care and to solve single problems in care processes. We think about integrated platforms and improvements of interaction interfaces to technologies, their handiness and easy use to make them attractive and acceptable for elderly informal caregivers. In this paper, we want to illustrate life situations of two caregivers and how we analyze their needs and requirements to technological solutions. We believe that it is the only way to meet their requirements and provide them a real help to overcome the challenge of care giving and having a life of their own.

In the next section we briefly present the related research on current technology solutions for informal caregivers. After introducing our methodology we describe two of the caregivers we studied in our project to underline their requirements to technology by showing their daily care situation. We also describe what qualities and features the technology should have to meet these requirements. We summarize our findings before we conclude the paper.

2 Related Research

Some studies claim that technological solutions must offer high usability and short response times by being well designed and easily understandable [2] [8]. Additionally, they have to provide different interaction modalities like speech recognition, large screen displays, handwriting recognition with support on touch screens to adapt the system to a specific user group who has certain usability and functional needs [4]. Dynamic profiling enables the specification of a user group's preferred functions and interaction styles. Especially for elderly people who are not used to deal with information and communication technology, the system might provide a guide with voice and/or text prompts for navigation and for orientation like offering the possibility to see which parts of the system the user already visited [2] [8].

Video-based learning is very useful for informal caregivers who cannot leave their homes due to their care responsibilities [2]. With such a support like courses on first-aid instructions or languages they can define the point of time and the length of the learning sessions in which they can attend a course.

---

[1] TOPIC: The Online Platform for Informal Caregivers, www.topic-aal.eu, a European project by the AAL Joint Programme. We acknowledge our project partners, our team colleagues A. Fabiano Pinatti de Carvalho and Ivan Breskovic, and all users involved in our project.

Communication through video can be seen as an important enhancement to telephony, not only in a work context. In ambient environments video-based communication can ease smooth exchange among informal caregivers [8]. Besides friends and other family members [8] [10] informal caregivers regularly need to communicate with professionals like therapists, general practitioners, or hospice staff [10]. Being an additional asset video communication increases the security perceived by caregivers and reduces their isolation and anxiety.

Shared calendars and whiteboards are used usually for communication at work or at work-related environments [4] [3]. Calendars represent work and make work that is carried out or only planned visible to others. At the same time, they are reminders of work [9]. Interestingly calendars mirror the balance achieved (or never kept) between occupational work and care work, and the time spent for recreation and recovery. Besides providing work awareness, calendars support task coordination between different persons in care context. An overview can be provided for the primary caregiver, showing who among the other potential caregivers (e.g., other family members) is available at a certain point of time. If they are also willing to provide care, a message sent by the caregiver can easily trigger asking for help [3] [4].

An online address book with data of all relevant local services was claimed for several solutions – especially when more than one person is caring for a particular family member [4] [10]. The possibility of participating in an "online discussion" group is normally very much needed considering the health and care situation of informal caregivers [8].

Two requirements are very important to all technological solutions provided for informal caregivers: Users need a platform which integrates all offered services in one [3] so that they have easy access and ambient integration. The second requirement is privacy [6]. It is about their home and their private environment including often very sensitive data.

3 Methodology

To understand the life situation and identify the needs of informal caregivers we have employed a user centered design approach supported by ethnographically informed studies within the TOPIC project.

For the pre-study, we were working with 10 informal (1 male, 9 female) caregivers in different situations: Five informal caregivers are caring for their spouse, three of them for their parent and two for their child. Two informal caregivers are not living in the same household as the care receiver. Our youngest informal caregiver is 55 and the oldest is 80 years old – the average age is about 64 years. Two informal caregivers are still working, but will retire within the next two years.

While working with these 10 informal caregivers, we were using different methodological tools: We started the contact with the informal caregivers with an interview about their situation at their homes. Then we arranged 3 to 4 more appointments at their home to conduct participatory observation during their daily routines. At one of these appointments we also brought a box with cultural probes with us and handed over to the informal caregiver: We gave them an introduction and asked them to use the probes for two weeks. During all these appointments we also talked a lot with them and also with their care receivers if possible. At the end of the observations we arranged an additional appointment for an in-depth interview, where we wanted to clarify things we didn't understand so far and asked the informal caregivers about their opinion to some of our design ideas.

The cultural probes consisted of 1 diary, 1 actimoClock (to visualize the kind of work they have to do during the day), emoticon stickers (for the diary and the actimoClock) (Figure 1), picture cards (different photos of care situations where they had to describe their associated feelings), a polaroid camera to take photos for documentation, and a social map. Additionally, the box included two kinds of questionnaires the informal caregivers had to fill in – one about the care in which we wanted to gather some (sociodemographic) information about the informal caregiver, the care receiver, and the care situation, and the Zarit Burden questionnaire [12] to get to know the stage of their burden.

In the following we want to present our two cases: Ms. Kreativ (creative) and Mr. Sorgsam (caring). After a short description of the persons we want to illustrate their requirements and try to discuss possible technologies that are, we think, useful to meet these requirements.

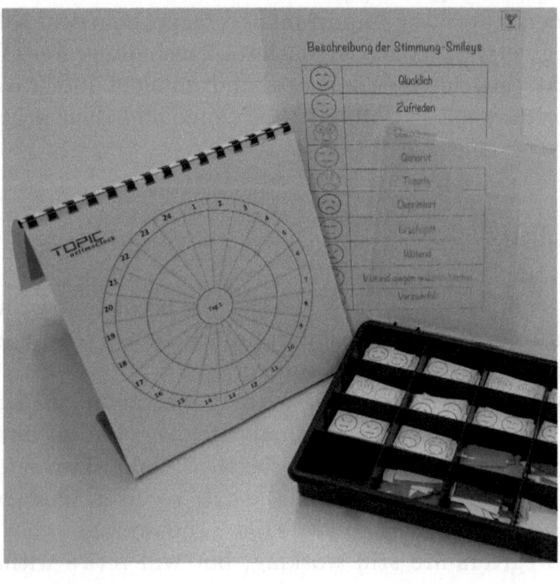

Fig. 1. Cultural probes we used in TOPIC: actimoClock, emoticons, box with stickers

4 The Case: Ms. Kreativ

Ms. Kreativ[2] is 56 years old and retired since two months. She cares for her mother who is living in the same household for more than two years now. Ms. Kreativ is feeling burdened in caring for her mother, not because of her own health situation but also because she and her mother have always disagreements and fights over almost everything. She is interested in knitting, reading, baking, and doing handicrafts (Figure 2). She needs these activities to relax and recover. From time to time she goes to the fitness center although it is hard for her to overcome hers weaker self. Ms. Kreativ is suffering from Crohn's disease and has high blood pressure.

Fig. 2. The Advent calendar made out of toilette paper rolls by Ms. Kreativ

Ms. Kreativ is not married and has a daughter who already moved out and is living together with her boyfriend in another district of the city. They meet each other from time to time: They go shopping, go to a coffee shop for a chat, or meet at home. Ms. Kreativ also has a brother and a nephew with a little son. The nephew helps once in a while with driving Ms. Kreativ's mother to the doctor. Ms. Kreativ's father died when she was a child. She suffers from his early death and often thinks of him. Now and then Ms. Kreativ meets her friends or colleagues in a coffee shop. She likes it a lot, but after retirement she has not enough money to spend for going out.

Ms. Kreativ doesn't feel well very often. She does not want that her mother is aware of her sadness or depression. She doesn't want to talk to her mother about her problems. She says that she needs to talk to somebody to feel better. Many of her friends are still working and therefore do not always have time for her – especially during the day. She cannot invite her friends to visit her because when her mother is around which is always the case, she cannot talk about her problems. And meeting in a coffee shop is too expensive for her. With *a (text, audio, or video) chat system* she could easily find some of her friends who are

[2] Pseudonyms are used to assure confidentiality to the participants and imprint one of the strong characteristics of the person in question.

online at that particular moment and available to talk. Sometimes it would be enough for her to see that someone she knows is there. The awareness about the presence of such a friend can be implemented with *an ambient system*, like *a colored cube* changing its color when somebody is available to contact.

Besides keeping contact to her friends and being aware of their presence even without actively communicating with them, Ms. Kreativ can also use the chat system to contact professionals, like nurses, psychologist, to ask her urgent questions or to get support from them to deal with her (mental) problems. She also wants to participate in *self-help groups over video communication.* Unfortunately she cannot join their face-to-face meetings that are normally held evenings when she has to prepare dinner and care for her mother. If she is connected online, she can attend the group meetings from home.

Ms. Kreativ's mother is 74 years old and had a stroke some years ago. She suffers from diabetes and therefore has to inject insulin on a regular basis. She is overweight and in danger of falling. She forgets many things (e.g., PIN code of the bank account) and it happens from time to time that she is not able to find the way back home when she is outside. Then she calls Ms. Kreativ for help. Once Ms. Kreativ's mother went for a walk just around the house block, fell down, and couldn't stand up. Luckily she was able to reach her *mobile phone* and call for help.

Ms. Kreativ's mother likes being mobile and going out, but she is doing this less and less often because she is feeling insecure. Locating her mother when she is outside can solve this problem and provide the security both need. A system capturing the *GPS coordinates of the mobile phone* of Ms. Kreativ's mother can keep track of her location if needed. In case of an emergency, e.g., if Ms. Kreativ's mother is lost, she can look for her, either go and pick her up or guide her home over the phone.

Another solution is a kind of *Smart Watch*, which Ms. Kreativ's mother has to wear when she is outside. Beside locating her geographic position, a Smart Watch can connect both by means of a video communication. For instance, when Ms. Kreativ's mother falls and is not able to reach her mobile phone, she easily can call her daughter by using the watch and tell her what is going on.

Since her retirement, Ms. Kreativ feels often bored and is afraid of letting herself go. She is thinking about attending some courses at the community college. She is interested in improving her English and computer skills. But she is not sure if she is able to pay for these courses with the less money she gets monthly for her retirement. So it would be a good solution for her, if some other informal caregivers who have good English skills can offer a kind of *an online course.* This means, that all interested people arrange an appointment where they can meet online via a video communication tool. So nobody has to leave home and their care receiver, and can improve their (English) skills.

5 The Case: Mr. Sorgsam

Mr. Sorgsam[3] is a 65-years-old retired electrician, who provides care to his 68-years-old partner. He has been caring for her for more than two years. Besides the interest in plants and electronics he had health conditions including surgery because of heavy smoking. He tries to take care of himself by spending 3 weeks a year for recovery, partly covered by his health insurance, partly self-covered.

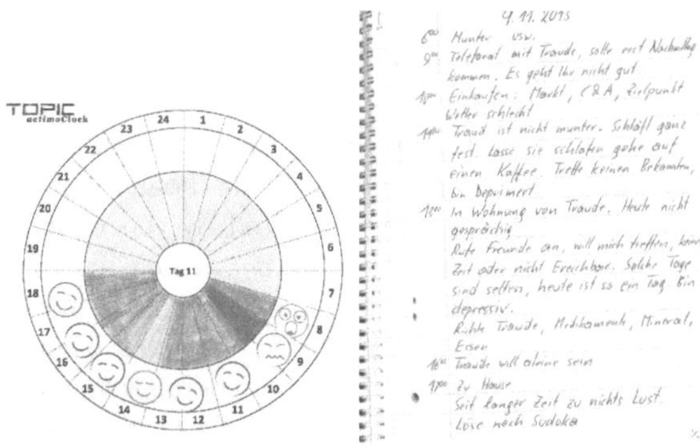

Fig. 3. The actimoClock filled by Mr. Sorgsam showing his (care) activities and his mood around the clock and a diary entry showing his daily schedule. Besides shopping one can read how concerned he was about his partner.

Mr. Sorgsam has a partner since 40 years, two sons with her and a grandchild. Unfortunately he does not meet his sons enough. They do not answer his contact requests via phone or SMS, or sometimes only with a relatively long delay. Even one of the sons lives very close to his mother's apartment, he does not visit her. Not meeting his sons makes Mr. Sorgsam very often sad and desperate.

Mr. Sorgsam lives in 30-45 min distance to his spouse. Besides accompanying and taking care after his partner (Figure 3), he has friends who he meets regularly, mostly in his favorite coffee shop. He does not share the care situation of his partner with all his friends, but only with a few. Anytime he spends the time without his partner he feels strange, because he constantly thinks of her and her well-being and wonders whether everything is all right with her at that moment.

One of the most important issues for Mr. Sorgsam is to be sure that his spouse is well and nothing is wrong in her environment. His concerns are well-explained: Mr. Sorgsam's partner suffers from chronic obstructive pulmonary disease (COPD), asthma, chronic bronchitis, arthritis, rheumatism, and osteoporosis. Hence, she is at a high risk of falling and getting seriously injured. Due to her health condition and not sharing the home with her, Mr. Sorgsam wants

[3] Pseudonyms are used to assure confidentiality to the participants and imprint one of the strong characteristics of the person in question.

to be informed about her situation and wellness the whole time. Technology can help in this matter:

- A *bidirectional video communication channel* can potentially help to maintain contact with her spouse when he is away. He can contact her, talk to her, hear her voice, ask her whether she needs something. His spouse lies in bed the most of the time and watches TV. Even during the night the TV is on. He has also a big display that he does not use because he is not interested in watching TV. Equipped with the right additional technology these both TV screens can be monitors of the video connection between both of them. So, Mr. Sorgsam would feel much better if he could observe and talk to his partner via this video channel.
- Besides the general status of his partner, Mr. Sorgsam is very alarmed about possibilities for accidents or problems of her health condition like difficulties in breathing. Her lung disease impacted by the weather conditions and humidity can cause serious troubles for her which alarms Mr. Sorgsam. If she is not close to the telephone she cannot call his spouse or answer the phone when she is called. This happens sometimes when she is not in her bed. With *a monitoring system based on several sensors* Mr. Sorgsam can be made aware of her health situation and her environment any time as needed. In this context it is very important to think about configuration of such a monitoring system by her spouse and by him. Especially it must be possible to switch off the system and notify Mr. Sorgsam that the system is shut down by her and there is no need for concern because everything is fine. Furthermore we have to answer the question when the system needs to be switched on again and by whom. What happens if she has something and that is why she cannot turn on the device? Is there any possibility to configure regular short term activation of the system to make a single image or a short clip to inform Mr. Sorgsam that she is doing fine? How would be the notification mechanism for him at the background without disturbing him or making him nervous while waiting until he gets the next message? How can he be sure that the system is running correctly?

Mr. Sorgsam cannot always spend time with her spouse because sometimes her health condition does not allow that. These are the times when he wants to talk to someone else, either one of his friends or someone who professionally can help him. *A chat system* can make this possible: He does not need to go to the coffee shop, he can stay at home and talk to a friend.

Mr. Sorgsam needs additional technical support in managing care: Home care service is scheduled on a daily base. Unfortunately the supporters very often do not arrive at the scheduled time. Mr. Sorgsam needs to know when they will really be in the flat of his spouse in order to meet them or talk to them and clarify certain care activities or arrange additional ones like going to a pharmacy or buying something for her. This would help reduce stress and save time. A telephone call is unfortunately with the home care support personnel not possible. *A distributed time schedule system* could help to enable these temporal arrangements. With an additional feature for messaging the system would make his communication with home care service people possible, independent of their arrival time.

Mr. Sorgsam is very keen on recording the changes of the health situation of his spouse and of himself. *A health care recording system* for non-professional use scan help him to keep track of such changes, e.g., by noting the blood pressure, temperature, medicine she takes, problems she has in breathing or moving, etc. He also wants to know how his and her health situation is progressing.

Mr. Sorgsam writes down regularly the money he spends for her spouse because she wants to know the exact payments related to her income. This activity can surely be easily supported by *a book-keeping application.*

6 Some Results and Conclusions

The paper presents some ideas based on the analysis of our findings in our ethnographic case study: First of all, we could describe why certain technologies are needed for informal care, like (text, audio, video) chat systems, ambient systems like colored cubes, self-help groups over video communication, mobile phones, GPS coordinates, Smart Watches, online courses, bidirectional video communication channels, monitoring systems based on several sensors, distributed time schedule systems, health care recording system for non-professional use, book-keeping systems. The integration of these different systems at one platform is important to provide a single point of access to all services implemented. This means usually a central storage of data. A distributed means of data management can be done by replication mechanisms, without increasing the response time and the effort for its maintenance. Through different peripheral devices or ambient solutions the data retrieval must be fast, adapted to the specific domestic environment, and easy to trigger.

The location of the devices plays a crucial role in their effectiveness and acceptance by their users. Some must be in a common area; some tend to be used privately. Portability at home and surrounding enable users mobility and flexibility which is crucial for informal caregivers.

Robustness and fault tolerance of the systems need to fulfill the safety related critical requirements of the care setting, especially when the system sends alarm signals in case of falls or emergencies. The software should allow interruptions, e.g., when an emergency occurs, and allow resuming without any problems, when the emergency is over.

The platform and its services should offer multiuser access, especially for other family members or professionals involved. It should also offer the possibility to adapt the user interface to the different needs like bigger font, guiding with voice, etc. Next to that, the platform and its services should provide a multimodal interaction like video, audio, text, speech recognition.

Monitoring services like camera surveillance systems or GPS tracking are very useful but should offer the possibility to be turned off. Since it should always be considered that the care receiver, who will be monitored, can be still mature and decide whether s/he wants to be monitored or not.

Not only because of the average age of informal caregivers (58 in Austria) but also of the care receiver (78 in Austria), the usability should fit for all ages. Tablets and smartphones are not the only systems that fit best our users' requirements and abilities. We have to think about other innovative embedded solutions like sensors, tangibles, or wearable systems.

Our future work in TOPIC will focus on designing, developing, and evaluating different types of systems for our users. Our special attention will be usability, integrity, robustness, reliability, privacy, and configurability of such systems.

References

1. Breskovic, I., de Carvalho, A.F.P., Schinkinger, S., Tellioğlu, H.: Social Awareness Support for Meeting Informal Carers' Needs: Early Development in TOPIC. In: Korn, M., Colombino, T., Lewkowicz, M. (eds.) Adjunct Proceedings of the 13th European Conference on Computer Supported Cooperative Work (ECSCW 2013), Paphos, Cyprus, Department of Computer Science Aarhus University, pp. 3–8 (2013)
2. Chambers, M., Connor, S., Diver, M., McGonigle, M.: Usability of Multimedia Technology to Help Caregivers Prepare for a Crisis. Telemedicine Journal and e-Health 8(3), 6 (2002)
3. Chen, Y., Ngo, V., Park, S.Y.: Caring for Caregivers: designing for integrality. In: CSCW 2013, San Antonio, TX, USA (2013)
4. Chiu, T., Massimi, M.: A Digital Support Device Designed to Help Family Caregivers Coordinate, Communicate and Plan the Care of People with Brain Injury AMIA (2006)
5. Chwalisz, K., Kisler, V.: Perceive Stress: A Better Measure of Carer Burden. Measurement and Evaluation in Counseling and Development 28, 88–98 (1995)
6. Consolvo, S., Roessler, P., Shelton, B.E., LaMarca, A., Schilit, B.: Technology for care networks of elders. IEEE Pervasive Computing 3(2), 8 (2004)
7. Coon, D., Evans, B.: Empirically Based Treatments for Family Carers Distress: What Works and Where do We Go From Hear. Geriatric Nursing 30(6), 426–436 (2009)
8. Czaja, S., Rubert, M.P.: Telecommunications Technology as an Aid to Family Caregivers of Persons With Dementia. Psychosomatic Medicine, Journal of Biobehavioral Medicine 64(3), 8 (2002)
9. de Carvalho, A.F.P., Schinkinger, S., Breskovic, I., Tellioğlu, H.: Technology for Work-Life Balance in Terms of Informal Care Work. In: ECSCW 2013 Workshop "CSCW at the Boundary of Work and Life", Paphos, Cyprus, pp. 1–6 (2013)
10. Demiris, G., Oliver, D.P., Courtney, K.L., Day, M.: Telehospice Tools for Caregivers. Clinical Gerontologist 31(1), 17 (2008)
11. Schulz, R., Beach, S.R.: Caregiving as a Risk Factor for Mortality: The Carer Health Effects Study. Journal of the American Medical Association 282, 2215–2219 (1999)
12. Braun, M., Scholz, U., Hornung, R., Martin, M.: The burden of spousal caregiving: A preliminary psychometric evaluation of the German version of the Zarit Burden. Interview Aging & Mental Health 14(2), 159–167 (2010)

A Multi-disciplinary Approach in the Development of a Stroke Rehabilitation Tool

Marie Sjölinder[1], Maria Ehn[2], Inga-Lill Boman[3], Mia Folke[2], Pär Hansson[1], Disa Sommerfeld[4], Stina Nylander[1], and Jörgen Borg[3]

[1] SICS Swedish ICT, Box 1263, 164 29 Kista, Sweden
[2] Robotdalen/Mälardalens Högskola, Box 883, 721 23 Västerås, Sweden
[3] Department of Clinical Sciences, Karolinska Institute and Department of Rehabilitation Medicine, Danderyd Hospital, Stockholm
[4] Karolinska University Hospital, Department of geriatric medicine/Danderyd Hospital, Karolinska Institutet, 182 87 Danderyd

{Marie,par,stny}@sics.se, maria.ehn@robotdalen.se, ingalill.boman@ds.se, mia.folke@mdh.se, {Disa.Sommerfeld,jorgen.borg}@ki.se

Abstract. This work describes a method used in the development of a stroke rehabilitation tool. The method was based on three key elements. The first key element was iterations between the use of broad groups with different professionals/stakeholders and small hands-on working groups with users from the same profession. The second key element was movement between understanding differences between different organizations and professionals and understanding of specific needs within the different organizations. The final key element was including implementation aspects from the very start of the work.

Keywords: Design methods, participatory design, multi-disciplinary approach.

1 Introduction

Stroke is one major cause of acquired brain injury and of prolonged, complex disabilities. High quality rehabilitation is important for maintaining the patient's function, independence and quality of life. The need of coordinated rehabilitation efforts for stroke victims is extensive. In Sweden, several caregivers are involved in the process of stroke rehabilitation and there is no national consensus in the process. Generally, there is a need for strengthening the co-operation between different caregivers and increasing the patient's access to adequate rehabilitation, especially in the later phases of the rehabilitation [1].

Today's sensor-based and interactive communication technology opens new possibilities for continuous interaction between therapists and patients as well as between different caregivers in the rehabilitation process. Strengthening the social interaction between patient and therapist is one key aspect for increasing the patient's motivation for motor training. However, there is also a need for increasing the

M. Kurosu (Ed.): Human-Computer Interaction, Part III, HCII 2014, LNCS 8512, pp. 351–362, 2014.

patient's motivation for training autonomously. One approach for doing this is to provide the patient with a stimulating gaming environment that is built upon evidence-based practice for training.

We have developed a technical tool supporting motor training of stroke patients in their home. The goal was to develop a prototype that can lead to a future product that will be commercially available and used by health care organizations. Our technical approach has been to combine interactive communication technology with a gaming environment. This environment should provide controlled exercises that, through real-time evaluation by sensor technology, give the patient feedback during training with the aim to carry out the exercises correctly. The hardware of the system consisted of a technical setup in the patient's home (including a computer connected the internet, a large screen, Kinekt sensor) and a setup at the rehabilitation clinic (including a computer connected to the internet, a normal screen, web-camera and head set). The software in the system consisted of software for planning and follow-up of training, video-communication and home-training program. Each specific exercise contained a basic level with the aim to guide the patient in performing a motion correctly; and more advanced levels, including a gamification environment, to increase the motivation of the patient to continue practicing. The patient's body was tracked by the Kinekt sensor and presented on the screen as a stick figure. Hence, feedback was given to the patient upon the motion performed by the stick figure (see figure 1).

Fig. 1. The system and the stick figure providing feedback regarding movements

Based on this process we have synthesized a method for user-centered development of motor training technology. The method developed in this work had key elements in terms of: i) Iterations between the use of broad groups with patients, different health professionals and stakeholders; and small hands-on working groups with users from the same profession; ii) Movement between understanding differences between different organizations and professionals, and understanding of specific needs and ways to apply technology in the different organizations; iii) Include implementation aspects from the very start of the work. The method was applied in three main steps: 1) Broad investigation of user needs – addressing key elements ii and iii; 2) Requirements on technology in different group settings – addressing key elements i, ii and iii; and 3) Addressing the needs in each specific organization – addressing key element ii.

2 Method

The work described in this paper was based on the participatory design framework with different participants and stakeholders with different knowledge contributing and sharing knowledge in an equal way [2].

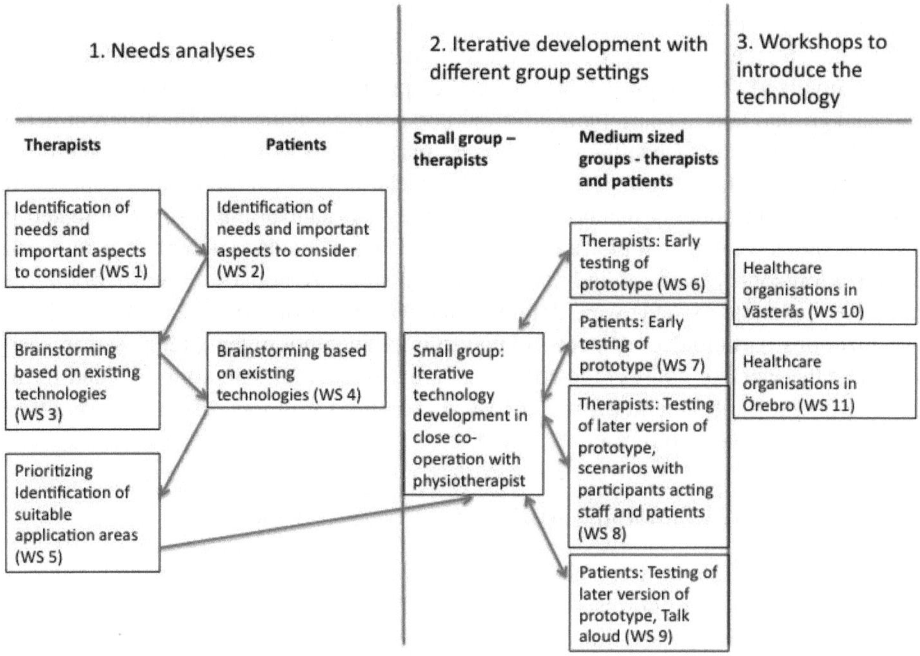

Fig. 2. The workshops and the progress of the work

Within the participatory design framework several methods are suggested to gather needs and to design systems. Here, we held both small group specific workshops, and larger ones with mixed user groups/stakeholders [3]. The needs and requirement phase (see figure 2: 1) consisted of workshops/focus groups to gather information about the different user groups' situation and needs for support. After that brainstorming sessions based on existing technology were held. The technologies that were used were solutions that we perceived could address needs or parts of needs described in the first workshops. The aim with showing different technologies was to have a starting point for the discussions [4] and to provide concrete examples of technology that could be used. After the brainstorming sessions we conducted a workshop to prioritize among all the ideas and suggested concepts. All ideas were categorized beforehand in main categories and sub categories. During the workshop the participant ranked the main categories and discussed which aspects in each category that was most important to address.

The workshops in the needs and requirements phase consisted of open discussions with a focus on the topic related to the specific issue to address (requirements, functionality and design). In the prioritizing the discussions were more structured with specific issues to address. The workshop approach was chosen since it is way of gather people with different perspectives and competences in an equal way. All the stakeholders and the user groups were involved in the beginning of the project and continued to participate during the entire process to ensure common goals and how these were met during the project [3].

The development (see figure 2: 2) was conducted iteratively with the different user groups involved. The approach was to gather participants with different knowledge and background and to share their different perspectives. Patients with different needs and different groups of healthcare personnel participated as well as project members including researchers from healthcare and technology development. People with knowledge in introducing technology in health care organizations also participated in the workshops. In the final phase (see figure 2: 3) participants from each participating organization/county was invited to a local workshop. A holistic view involving all relevant stakeholders [5] was applied, and people from different parts of the organizations participated. Aspects related to implementation were addressed in early stages of the work to address the specific context in each organization [6], and in the larger workshops at the end of the process we summarized these discussions and took the conclusions one step further.

2.1 User Needs and Requirements

Initially, five workshops were held. In these workshop needs, requests and demands concerning technical solutions supporting home-based motor training were gathered. The participants in three of the workshops (ws 1, 3 and 5) were physiotherapists and occupational therapists from five different care giving organizations (Västerås Municipality, Västmanland County Council, Örebro Municipality, Örebro County Council and Danderyd Hospital).

The participants in the two other workshops (ws 2 and 4) were stroke patients recruited from the department of Rehabilitation Medicine and the department of Geriatric Medicine at Danderyd Hospital. The inclusion criteria were good cognitive- and communicative skills and experience in post stroke motor training. In one of the two workshops with stroke patients, spouses of stroke patients also participated. The spouses were also recruited via the department of Rehabilitation Medicine and the department of Geriatric Medicine at Danderyd University Hospital.

The first workshop (ws 1) with the therapists covered needs within different groups. The results provided a starting point for understanding the needs in the following workshop (ws 2) with the patients. The results from both these workshops served as a basis for planning and gather example technology to the brainstorming sessions (ws 3 and 4). The brainstorming was first held with the therapists, and here as well we used the understanding we had got from this workshop to prepare the brainstorming for the patients. Finally, in the fifth workshop the therapists prioritized between the different ideas from the brainstorming session (ws 5).

Workshops with Therapists. The aims with these workshops were to obtain a general understanding of stroke rehabilitation process and how the stroke rehabilitation process differed between different Swedish County Councils. We also wanted to obtain a general understanding of the co-operative work with patients by physiotherapists and occupational therapists. Further, we were seeking a general understanding of the therapists' opinions regarding needs and requirements on technology. Finally, we also wanted to understand the participants' attitudes towards using distance technology in their work with patients.

The three workshops started with a broad perspective in gathering user needs, moving towards limit the number of suggestions and finally ending up with a list with possible technological solutions that had been prioritized. The workshops mainly comprised structured group discussions lead by the researchers. The themes for the three workshops were:

- Workshop 1: Identification of important aspects concerning technology assisted home based training.
- Workshop 3: Brainstorming based on hands-on trying of different existing technologies.
- Workshop 5: Identification of application areas suitable for technology-assisted home-based motor training. The rehabilitation tasks from the previous workshops were grouped into different prioritized application areas and a list of requirements for each task was established.

Workshops with Stroke Patients. Two workshops were held with stroke patients. Both workshops mainly consisted of structured whole group discussions led by the researchers. The first workshop (ws 2) focused on important aspects regarding home based training in general. Discussions were held about the patients' experiences from participating in stroke rehabilitation efforts and their view of important aspects to consider when developing technology for home based training. The second workshop (ws 4) narrowed down the scope to requirements on technology. The theme for the workshop was a brainstorming session based on existing technology. The stroke patients were introduced to the same technologies that were demonstrated to the therapists. Discussions concerning functionality and relevance for stroke rehabilitation were held with patients and their significant others.

The aim with the workshops were to obtain a general understanding of the patients' needs for technology in rehabilitation, and to understand patients' experiences and attitudes towards using distance technology and technological tools in their rehabilitation. Finally, we wanted to obtain a general understanding of important factors related to future use of the technology in the patient homes. In the second workshop significant other to persons with stroke also participated with the aim to get a general understanding of their situation and attitude towards technology in rehabilitation.

2.2 Iterative Development in Different Group Settings

When the concept had been selected, the iterative development was conducted moving between small hands-on groups consisting of physiotherapists and with medium sized groups (4-15 participants) groups consisting if of either patients or therapists from several organizations.

Small Group: Iterative Development with Physiotherapist. The small group consisted of two physiotherapists from a rehabilitation clinic specialized in motor training of stroke patients. The technical development in the project was carried out in continuous, close co-operation with physiotherapists from Danderyd University Hospital. All developed exercises were constructed on basis on needs collected in the project and the exercises were designed in collaboration with the participating physiotherapists.

The work was structured into four consecutive phases:

(1) Development of rehabilitation exercises (the content, design, feedback and gamification)
(2) Collection of feedback on developed exercises
(3) Production of a system surrounding the exercises
(4) Final adjustments for increasing usability of user interfaces and gamification environments

Medium Sized Group: Feedback on the Prototype. Two workshops (ws 6 and 7) were held to get feedback on an early version of the prototype, one with therapists and one with patients. In the first workshop that was held with therapists (ws 6), the participants could try the exercises. Whole group discussions were held concerning the usability of the technology in stroke rehabilitation and important aspects related to using the technology in different rehabilitation operations. In the next workshop (ws 7) the early version of the prototype was shown to the patients. On a voluntary basis, patients could try the exercises. A common discussion was held in the group concerning how the patients experienced their use of the system and their reflections on the technology.

After further development a later version of the prototype was the focus in two workshops (ws 8 and 9), as before, one workshop with therapists (ws 8) and one with patients (ws 9). In the workshop with the therapists, the participants took part in a role-playing acting therapist and patient. The task resulted in feedback upon the exercises and on the video communication. In this workshop participants from the same care giving organization also were grouped to discuss questions related to implementation in their organization. In the workshop where the patients participated around the later version of the prototype they could, on a voluntary basis, try the system one at the time. During the testing session, the participants were instructed to "talk aloud" (to gather thoughts and impressions in the moment) and after that a discussion was held between the patients and the researchers.

2.3 Addressing the Specific Situation in Each Organization

As a final step, large workshops (11-23 participants) were held within the different health care organizations. In these workshops (ws 10 and 11), the aim was to involve all relevant categories of participants such as representatives from patient organizations, health professionals and mangers within the healthcare organizations.

The aim in this phase was to take the results one step further based on the needs within the specific organizations and to start hands-on work with the implementation of the technology. The workshops started with a demonstration of the technology and its functionality followed by common discussion concerning aspects related to value and risks. After that, the participants were divided in three groups and worked more focused on specific topics: (i) User needs with respect to the technology based on the perspective among representatives from patient organization; (ii) User needs with respect to the technology (exercises and video-communication) based on the perspective among health professionals; (iii) Aspects related to future use of the technology in rehabilitation with health care personnel. Feedback regarding the technology and its functionalities was collected both through discussions and by written questionnaires.

3 Results and Conclusions

The outcome of this work consists of methodological results from the work with gathering user needs and with the iterative development. We also present results regarding the larger workshops that addressed the needs in each specific organization.

3.1 User Needs and Requirements from Patients and Therapists

This section describes the results from the investigation of user needs, the brainstorming sessions and the prioritizing between the different ideas. Finally the setting of the workshops is analyzed.

Broad Investigation of User Needs. The advantage of grouping people from different professions was that we obtained a consensus on the functionality of the tool that had high potential of adding value for various rehabilitation organizations and patients. The challenge though was to manage the different perspectives in terms of what they wanted to use the technology for. On the other hand, one aspect of participatory design is to highlight differences between user groups and to take different perspectives into consideration [7]. One lesson learned was that we, in the early phase as well, should have introduced small group specific workshops to be able to gather more details [4]. However, the way we did this led to interesting and fruitful discussions, and we ended up with ideas that all of the participants felt meaningful even though it might have been more pragmatic to have discussions with each group at a time, and then gather different perspectives on the selected solutions.

The patients that participated were of good health and with good cognitive- and communicative skills. Hence, the situations, needs and requirements of all stroke patients were not reflected in this group of participants. However, the aim was to include participants with experiences of stroke rehabilitation and an interest in motor training with support from technology. In the beginning of the development the participants had to have enough knowledge and interest to be able to provide ideas and suggestions into the brainstorming context.

Even though we had inclusion criteria for participating, we tried to include participants of different ages and with different rehabilitation needs. The aim was to gather different perspectives and different needs. However, when doing so there is also a risk of getting too deep into individual needs. In this work though, the discussion became a common one with all participants contributing to the ideas that was suggested.

Brainstorming Based on Existing Technology. In the following two workshops, one with therapists and one with patients, we showed examples of existing technology. We included a wide range of complementary communication technology and we also included additional products in the process upon the participants' requests. We found it highly valuable to use concrete technical products to base the discussion around. It is a challenge though to introduce something new without affecting the way the participants think. On the other hand, the aim with the activity was to provide knowledge about technical possibilities and limitations, and demonstrating different technologies is one way of doing it [8].

Prioritizing. In the phase were we had to prioritize and limit the number of possible solutions it became clear that the two groups of professionals prioritized differently and had difficulties in agreeing on which aspects that were most important to address. First, since everything was based on their own ideas they felt that everything was of equal importance. Secondly, the physiotherapist and the occupational therapists argued for the importance of the solutions that supported their aspects of the work with the patients. Our conclusion from this part of the work was that it might be more effective to involve professionals in the work with prioritize. For example, professionals who have knowledge about needs and challenges within the entire health care organisations. This could also reduce the risk of something important being missed.

Organization around the Workshops. One important aspect in setting up the workshops was to create an atmosphere were the participants felt comfortable in contributing with their needs and ideas. Mutual learning and sharing of knowledge is an important aspect of the design process when different categories of people participate [8]. We included different professionals from the project to create a feeling of that everyone in the room were there, based on his/her own experience/knowledge and that the aim was to share this with each other. It could also be an advantage to have professionals within the area to participate in sessions like this. Stroke can affect emotions, and when talking about how the disease had affected every day life it could be beneficial to have someone in the room that has experience in stroke and emotional reactions.

Our general impressions from the workshops were that we met our intention to create an informal atmosphere where every one should feel comfortable in contributing succeeded. The fact that the participants said that the enjoyed the workshops and that they wanted continue being a part of the work also supported that we had achieved in creating a good atmosphere. It is also an important aspect of the design process to have motivated users that enjoy being a part of the development. This will contribute to a better product that is based on important and relevant user needs.

3.2 Iterative Development Based on Work in Different Group Settings

In this phase we worked iteratively hands-on with two physiotherapists and with medium sized groups of therapists and patients that discussed the progress of the prototype.

Small Group: Iterative Development with Physiotherapist. The technical solution that was developed consisted of four main categories of exercises. When the software for the specific exercises had been developed, the physiotherapists could try the exercises on their own between the scheduled meetings with the technical developers. This enabled the physiotherapists to evaluate the prototype more thoroughly and give feedback based on their own testing of the exercises. Based on feedback from the physiotherapists, modification of existing exercises and development of new exercises was performed between the meetings.

When two exercises were developed, workshops were held with patients and therapists in the medium sized groups. The aim of these two workshops was to ensure that the technical development was on track with regard to the initial analysis of user-needs and demands. Once all four exercises approached finish, discussions were held concerning design and content in a web-based user interface for planning and follow-up of training. When all key elements of the technical functionality were on place, the physiotherapists tested the technologies' usability and the motivational aspects in the games. Final adjustments in the design were done in order to increase the usability and overall user experience.

The physiotherapists were essential in the work concerning concretization of exercises for all four rehabilitation tacks in several ways: Firstly, their knowledge in evidence-based rehabilitation exercises for the different rehabilitation tasks laid the ground for the movements to practice in each exercise. Secondly, their experiences from using other technical tools and computer games in stroke rehabilitation were highly valuable when designing an environment that should be suitable for patients' needs and cognitive abilities. Since the group consisted of only two persons, the work was highly dependent on their availability and interest. On the other hand, a relationship could be established over a longer time, which enabled an atmosphere that encouraged open discussions including critical feedback.

Medium Sized Group: Feedback on the Prototype. To get feedback on an early version of the prototype two workshops were held (ws 6 and 7), one with the therapists and one with the patients. When the feedback had been taken into consideration and the system had been developed further two new workshops (ws 8 and 9) were held, again one with the therapists and one with the patients. As mentioned before, it was important to constantly move between the possibilities that the hands-on work provided and by placing this work in a broader context.

Workshops with therapists: In the first workshop where an early version of prototype was shown (ws 6), an important part was to explain the basis for how we have prioritized during the technical development. Since some technical functionality, earlier suggested by the participants, had not been included in the prototype. When this had been explained, the group discussions led to general feedback on the chosen system. In the second workshop (ws 8), the participants worked in small groups with group members from the same health care organization. The work gave feedback on concrete details concerning technical functionality. We experienced that the participants were more comfortable and gave more constructive feedback in this group composition.

Workshops with stroke patients: The patients were engaged in the testing of the technology and they gave several suggestions for improvements. They thought trying the prototype was a positive experience, and they asked for possibilities to use the system in their homes. This questioned raised the issue about how to explain to the patients that a product is quite far ahead. Even though much information was given about this, it could be difficult convey the information that it will take some time before the technology will be a product. Especially since some stroke patients are very motivated to work hard to be able to recover as soon as possible.

3.3 Addressing the Specific Situation in Each Organization

The aim with these workshops (ws 10 and 11) was to address the needs in each specific organization and to understand their particular way of working with stroke patients. It was also important for the ongoing introduction of the technology to make a larger part of the personnel engaged and interested. Further, these workshops provided us with the possibility to gather data about the system from a larger group than in the previous workshops. Participants filled in questionnaire regarding attitudes towards the usage and the functionality of the system.

Regarding the larger workshops we gained a better understanding of how to adapt the workshop approach after group when several different occupations participated. As with the medium sized workshops, when the group was split into smaller groups with more hands on tasks, the engagement became stronger and more interesting discussions came up. One topic that was addressed in smaller working groups was about introducing new technology in their organization. This was a good opportunity to do this since the large workshops consisted of many different professions within the same organization.

4 Discussion

The method developed in this work had one key element in terms of iterations between the use of broad groups with patients, different health professionals and stakeholders; and small hands-on working groups with users from the same profession. The shifting between these groups was found to be very useful: the small group facilitated close cooperation in the technical development and the broad group confirmed that the prototypes reflected user needs in this group. Another key element was to understand variations between organizations and professionals as well as specific needs within different organizations. With respect to this, the medium sized workshops provided knowledge about how different the rehabilitation process could be between organizations and parts of the country. The large workshops at the end of the process provided input regarding specific aspects related to implementation in the different organizations such as transfer of patients between different caregivers. The final key element was to include implementation aspects from the very start of the work. This was done by including discussions about these aspects in the medium sized workshops that had participants from different professions. Project members in terms of researchers and professionals in introducing technology in health care organizations were also working with these issues throughout the project.

The work presented here takes its inspiration from established methods for design such as participatory design [2], user-centred design [9], and value sensitive design [10]. These methods all underline the importance of putting users centre stage, involving users and other stakeholders in the design process, and base system design and development on user needs, as well as iterating designs and implementations.

As the reader can see, we have to a large extent adopted these methods and underlying philosophies in our work in the phases of user needs investigation, technology requirements, and organizational needs. What we have added is an iteration of perspectives in switching between large, diverse groups of stakeholders and small groups of one profession, between the perspective of the variety of different organizations and the specific needs and opportunities in single organizations. This has helped us to keep the design space quite wide through the process and not narrow in on a single solution too early, as well as ensured that as many needs as possible have been catered for in the system design.

Another contribution is our inclusion of technology in all phases and iterations of the work. It might be argued that bringing technology in at an early stage hinders the design process and narrows the design space since finished technology limits our thinking. However, we argue that the inclusion of technology throughout the whole design and development process has helped in two ways. First it has showed the possibilities of state-of-the-art consumer technology such as the Kinect, which was quite unknown to many of the stakeholders in terms of possibilities and capabilities. Second, it has helped balancing the workshops not to go off into too futuristic scenarios nor settling for solutions way below the capabilities of the technology.

We believe that the way of working hands-on, both with brainstorming around existing technology and in the development of new solutions is fruitful, especially when doing so in a reciprocal way moving between hands-on work and feedback from other group constellations as well as between organizational and individual perspectives.

References

1. Hägglund, Stroke Patients' Needs for Access to Care Process Related Information (2012)
2. Schuler, D., Namioka, A.: Participatory design: principles and practices. L Erlbaum Associates, Hillsdale (1993)
3. Scandurra, I., Hägglund, M., Koch, S.: From user needs to system specifications: Multi-disciplinary thematic seminars as a collaborative design method for development of health information systems. Journal of Biomedical Informatics 41, 557–569 (2008)
4. Luck, R.: Using artefacts to mediate understanding in design conversations Building Research & Information 35(1), Special Issue: Visual Practices: Images of Knowledge Work, 28–41 (2007)
5. van Gemert-Pijnen, J.E., Nijland, N., van Limburg, M., Ossebaard, H.C., Kelders, S.M., Eysenbach, G., Seydel, E.R.: A Holistic Framework to Improve the Uptake and Impact of eHealth Technologies. J. Med. Internet Res. 13(4) (2011)
6. Fleuren, M., Wiefferink, K., Paulussen, T.: Determinants of innovation within health care organizations - Literature review and Delphi study. International Journal for Quality in Health Care 16(2), 107–123 (2004)
7. Bjerknes, G., Bratteteig, T.: The memoirs of two survivors - or evaluation of a computer system for cooperative work. In: Proceedings for the Second Comference on Computer Supported Cooperative Work, Portland, Oregon, September 26-28. ACM (1988)
8. Mörtberg, C., Bratteteig, T., Wagner, I., Stuedahl, D., Morrison, A.: Methods that Matter in Digital Design Research. In: Exploring Digital Design: Multi-disciplinary Design Practices, pp. 105–144. Springer (2010)
9. Shneiderman, B.: Designing the User Interface. Addison Wesley (1997)
10. Friedman, B. (ed.): Human Values and the Design of Computer Technology. Center for the Study of Language and Information (2004)

Snappy App: A Mobile Continuous Performance Test with Physical Activity Measurement for Assessing Attention Deficit Hyperactivity Disorder

Zoe Young[1,3], Michael P. Craven[2,3], Maddie Groom[1,3], and John Crowe[2,3]

[1] The University of Nottingham, Institute of Mental Health, Division of Psychiatry and Applied Psychology, Jubilee Campus, Nottingham, NG7 2TU, United Kingdom
{zoe.young,maddie.groom}@nottingham.ac.uk
[2] The University of Nottingham, Electrical Systems & Optics Research Division, Faculty of Engineering, University Park, Nottingham NG7 2RD, United Kingdom
{michael.craven,john.crowe}@nottingham.ac.uk
[3] NIHR MindTech Healthcare Technology Co-operative, The Institute of Mental Health, Jubilee Campus, Nottingham, NG7 2TU, United Kingdom

Abstract. A Continuous Performance Test (CPT) was incorporated into a smartphone application (App) to measure three symptom domains associated with Attention Deficit Hyperactivity Disorder (ADHD); attention, impulsivity and hyperactivity. The App was pilot tested on 11 healthy adults over three testing sessions. No differences in performance were found between testing sessions suggesting good test consistency. A decrement in performance over time was only found for one measure of attention and on one testing session. The CPT showed some sensitivity to ADHD-related symptoms where self-reported impulsive behaviour was related to the CPT measures of impulsivity and activity. User acceptability was good although some design improvements were suggested. Further pilot testing of the App in a clinical population is needed.

Keywords: Attention Deficit Hyperactivity Disorder, Continuous Performance Test, m-Health, Ecological interfaces, New technology and its usefulness, Psychological application for user interface, Qualitative and quantitative measurement and evaluation.

1 Background

Attention Deficit Hyperactivity Disorder (ADHD) is a neurodevelopmental syndrome that is characterised by three core behaviours; inattention, hyperactivity and impulsivity and often persists into adulthood [1,2,3]. It is typically thought that between 3 and 5% of school aged children have the disorder (National Institute for Health and Clinical Excellence) [4].

It has been suggested that ADHD stems from multiple causes, such as genetics, biological and psychosocial influences [5], and results in a range of pathological behaviours [6,7]. There is no single gene that is considered to underpin ADHD.

M. Kurosu (Ed.): Human-Computer Interaction, Part III, HCII 2014, LNCS 8512, pp. 363–373, 2014.

Instead, it is thought to arise from the combination of multiple genes, each gene having a small effect [5,8]. ADHD often overlaps with other disorders and can have negative long-term consequences including increased risk of school failure, unemployment and mental health difficulties [1, 9].

Given the variation in symptoms and behavioural consequences of ADHD, diagnosis, symptom monitoring and response to medication often relies on subjective interpretation of information gained through clinical interview and standardised rating scales. More recently, psychometric tests are used in the assessment process to provide objective measures of patient's symptoms. Such measures of cognitive function also offer the potential to objectively measure response to medication, and could potentially hasten the process of treatment optimisation [10].

One such standardised test is the continuous performance test (CPT) which is a neuropsychological test that measures attention and impulsivity during a sustained task. Typically, a CPT is a computer based programme which involves rapid presentation of visual or auditory stimuli. Participants are asked to respond when a given target occurs but remain passive to non-targets [11]. A commonly used CPT is one where a sequence of letters is displayed such that a response is required for a display of the letter X only after the letter A (visual AX-CPT). Missing responses (Omission Errors), incorrect responses (Commission Errors) and reaction time (RT) are recorded. This CPT is preferable to using the X-CPT in adults where ceiling effects are often found [2]. These kinds of objective tests are commonly used to assess attention [10] and are considered to be the most sensitive assessment of medication effects [12]. Studies have shown a clear separation on CPTs between people with ADHD and controls, with ADHD participants showing poorer performance on measures of attention and impulsivity [13,14]. Nevertheless, controversy remains as to whether CPTs are capable of distinguishing between ADHD and other disorders [2].

Hyperactivity is one of the core symptoms of ADHD and is usually measured by subjective standardised rating scales. Some objective measures of attention now incorporate motor activity measures using actigraphs [15] or infra-red motion analysis [10,16,17] to give a fuller picture of the range of symptoms associated with ADHD. Such cognitive tests with motion analysis can reliably differentiate children [10,17] and adults with ADHD [3] from controls and can provide a good measure of treatment response, with the potential for speeding up treatment optimisation [10].

Such measures are confined to clinic visits, which are time consuming and costly, therefore a cost effective way of remotely and objectively monitoring symptoms without patients having to attend clinic would be useful. The aim of this pilot study is to see whether a CPT can be incorporated into a smartphone application whilst also measuring motion activity throughout the course of the task.

With the recent rise in the use of smartphones and the advances in technology, mobile software applications (Apps) are now being used in healthcare. Although software applications with relevant features are available on other devices such as personal computers and laptops, smartphones (and some smaller tablets) have the advantage of being portable and are more often than not in the owner's possession. This allows the user to stay in touch with people (whether they be friends, family or healthcare professionals) and access information or receive support via the internet at any time of day and from virtually any location [18]. Smartphones are now the second most popular device for accessing the internet, second only to laptops [19].

The concept of using Apps in mental health is relatively new so many available products have not yet been researched experimentally. In general, the regulatory environment for Apps is in development (e.g. FDA guidance in the USA was finalised in September 2013). In England, a recent review of the NHS Choices apps library was focussed on safety, and consequently there is still little information regarding reliability and validity of the content of most Apps currently on the market. Available Apps for ADHD range from those that give information about the diagnosis and treatment of ADHD, to various ADHD tests, task management and reminders. There is a huge variety in the content of Apps for ADHD with a limited number having been produced by, or in consultation with, healthcare professionals. And even fewer have been researched experimentally [20].

In the current pilot study the AX-CPT test has been incorporated into a smartphone application for Android phones and subsequently as a web App that also runs on other platforms (e.g. iPhone). In addition to the CPT, the App captures 3-Dimensional movement data from accelerometer and gyroscope sensors in the phone (if present). This data is used to measure the amount of physical activity during the course of the CPT, measured by the amount the phone moves. The test combined with the sensor readings therefore provides information on each of the three ADHD behaviours (attention, impulsivity and hyperactivity). Following data capture, mean Omission Errors and Commission Errors, mean Reaction Time (RT) and standard deviation of RT (RT variability) on the CPT is analysed to provide an index of sustained attention (Omission Errors, RT, RT variability and changes in these over the course of the task) and impulse control (Commission Errors). Activity across different time sections of the task is also analysed. This data can then be used to establish whether it may be possible to extract a meaningful and reliable measurement of activity in a clinical population sample.

Subjectively measured impulsivity is measured and compared with performance on the CPT, to determine whether the test is sensitive to variation in these ADHD-related traits in healthy individuals. It is known that these behaviours vary in the general population and that ADHD is at the extreme end of this continuum. The purpose of the study was to pilot the App in the general (non-clinical) population.

2 Method

Participants

Participants were students and staff from the University of Nottingham (N=11, 1 male). All participants visited the Division of Psychiatry and Applied Psychology, University of Nottingham, where they completed a practice version of the AX-CPT on their own smartphone under the supervision of a researcher. Each participant completed the full task three times when prompted by the App (over a period of 10-14 days).

Software

The App to implement the visual CPT-AX test was initially designed using the Eclipse IDE (Integrated Development Environment) for Java developers, for an Android platform with an operating system v2.2 and above. The alarm function on the phone was employed to prompt users to take the test at predetermined times. Subsequently a web App was developed in JavaScript to implement the same functions (except without the Alarm). Fig. 1 shows a screenshot of the App (Android version).

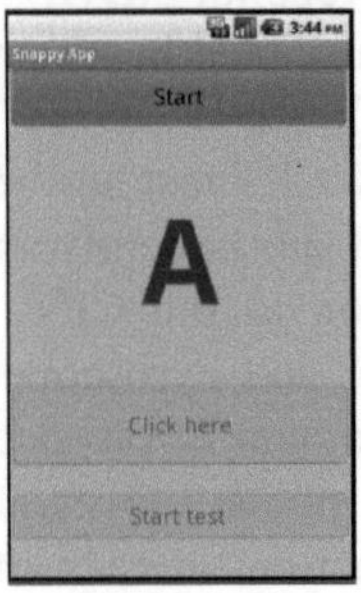

Fig. 1. Snappy App screenshot, Android smartphone implementation

Measures

Continuous Performance Test (CPT). A set of sequences containing the correct statistics for the AX-CPT were encoded to be presented in a pseudo-random manner. Within each sequence, presentation probabilities were p(A)=0.2 and p(X)=0.2 of which 50% follow A, p(H)=0.2 of which 50% follow A, and 8 other letters (B, C, D, E, F, G, J, L) with p=0.05. The website *random.org* was used to create a randomised sequence of numbers that were then assigned to the letters and AX pairs, with manual swaps where necessary to avoid creation of additional AX pairs.

Letters were presented at 1.65 second intervals with a duration of 150 milliseconds (ms), and the same presentation of 100 letters was presented four times resulting in a test lasting a total of 11 minutes, similar to the protocol of van Leeuwen et al. [11]. Sensor data was collected asynchronously down to 0.01 second intervals but the number of samples was dependant on sufficient movement of the phone. Accelerometer data including gravity was captured for each of the X, Y, Z axes (in units of m/s^2) and gyroscope orientation data for each of the Alpha, Beta and Gamma angles (in degrees) to give a measure of Activity.

CPT test and sensor data was captured for each of the 400 presentations of the letter sequence (over the 11 minutes) and, as well as recording the raw sensor data, the sums of clicks and errors from the CPT were computed for each of the four time segments and the mean and sample standard deviation was computed for RT and for the magnitudes of the accelerometer and gyroscope sensor readings for each of the same four time segments (samples of which were first averaged over the presentation period). This computation within the App was performed to speed up the analysis, although it was also possible to return to the raw data if required.

UPPS-P Impulsive Behaviour Scale. Impulsive-type behaviour was measured by the UPPS-P scale [21, 22]; a 59-item self-report questionnaire that assesses five subscales (Negative Urgency, (lack of) Premeditation, (lack of) Perseverance, Sensation Seeking, and Positive Urgency) in adolescents and adults (age 12 and up) in the general population. Participants are asked to answer the questions based on their experiences over the last six months and rate their behaviour and attitudes on a 4-point scale (1=Agree strongly to 4=Disagree strongly). The questionnaire gives a total impulsivity score plus a score for each of the five subscales. In order to put each subscale into the same metric, mean scores are calculated for the items on each subscale, from 1 to 4, where 1 indicates a low level of self-reported impulsivity and 4 indicates a high level. Negative Urgency refers to the tendency to experience strong impulses under conditions of negative affect. Positive Urgency refers to the tendency toward rash action in response to very positive mood. (Lack of) Premeditation is the tendency to fail to think and reflect on the consequences of an act before engaging in that act. (Lack of) Perseverance reflects difficulties remaining focused on a task that may be long, boring, or difficult. Sensation Seeking encompasses two aspects: the tendency to enjoy and pursue exciting activities and openness to trying new experiences.

Participant feedback questionnaire. Participants were asked to rate the App on a number of features in order to feed into further amendments to the App design in preparation for a clinical study. The questionnaire aims to determine whether participants found the task accessible and to seek suggestions to improve the task through eight items: four of which should be answered on a 5-point scale (1=Strongly agree to 5=Strongly disagree), two of which are option boxes and the final two are free text.

3 Results

Descriptive data is shown in Table 1. Mean Omission Errors, Commission Errors, RT, RT variability and Activity (from Accelerometer and Gyroscope data) were calculated across participants for each testing session. Scores were also collapsed over the three tests to give an overall mean for each CPT measure. Activity data was not available for all participants so this measure was analysed separately.

Differences between Testing Sessions

To see whether there was a difference in performance on the CPT between test sessions on each of the factors (Omission Errors, Commission Errors, RT and RT variability), a mixed design ANOVA with test session as the within subjects factor was conducted. No main effect of test session was found for any measure (all $p > .05$) suggesting that there were no practice or deterioration effects between test sessions.

Table 1. Sample characteristics for age, CPT measures and UPPS-P Impulsive Behaviour Scale including effects of testing session on CPT performance

	Overall	Test 1	Test 2	Test 3	*F*	*p*
N	11	11	11	11		
Sex (male/female)	1/10	1/10	1/10	1/10		
Age	34.03 ± 8.35	34.03 ± 8.35	34.03 ± 8.35	34.03 ± 8.35		
CPT						
Omission Errors	0.53 ± 0.48	0.45 ± 0.37	0.50 ± 0.43	0.64 ± 0.80	0.70	.51
Commission Errors	0.58 ± 0.93	0.41 ± 0.65	0.70 ± 1.01	0.61 ± 1.23	1.41	.27
Reaction Time *(ms)*	525.46 ± 94.88	524.37 ± 88.43	529.93 ± 101.69	522.07 ± 103.02	.20	.82
Reaction Time Variability *(ms)*	38.67 ± 12.71	32.28 ± 9.90	38.85 ± 23.77	44.87 ± 26.19	1.01	.38
Accelerometer (n=6)	10.57 ± 1.62	10.73 ± 1.99	10.46 ± 1.33	10.53 ± 1.53	1.08	.38
Gyroscope (n=4)	86.87 ± 38.58	61.24 ± 44.98	111.29 ± 65.66	88.06 ± 37.92	1.52	.29
UPPS-P Total	123.27 ± 20.12					
Negative Urgency	2.18 ± 0.74					
Premeditation	2.03 ± 0.33					
Perseverance	1.88 ± 0.38					
Sensation Seeking	2.64 ± 0.61					
Positive Urgency	1.73 ± 0.64					

±(standard deviations) All *p* values are non-significant

Analysis of Time on Task Measures

Mean Omission Errors, Commission Errors, RT and RT variability were calculated for each of the three tests and each test was broken into the four time periods of 100 letter presentations (TP) in order to compare performance patterns over time. We looked at the four TP for the factors; Omission Errors, Commission Errors, RT and RT variability by running a series of 1x4 mixed design ANOVA with TP as the within subject factor and repeated for each of the 3 tests. No main effect of TP was found for any measure on Test 1 or Test 2 (all $p > .05$) indicating that there were no changes in performance over time. A main effect of TP on Omission Errors was found for Test 3 only [F (3, 10) = 4.02, $p < .05$]. This effect was explored further and a linear pattern was found for Omission Errors, i.e. a decrement in performance during the course of the task, reflected in increased Omission Errors from TP 1 through 4 [F (1, 10) = 6.41, $p < .05$], with the significant difference being between TP 1 and TP 3 ($p < .05$).

Activity

Activity data were captured for four out of 11 participants due to their mobile phones having this capability. Two gave accelerometer data and four gave both accelerometer and gyroscope data. Activity levels were ultimately measured by taking the mean activity level in specific time windows using the accelerometer data only, due to the gyroscope data not readily providing a meaningful mean score for the purposes of this analysis (due to inconsistent transitions from ~0 to ~360 degrees) and also since a minority of the phones produced this data. Corrections were not made for movements triggered by making a response to the target stimulus, since these movements were of short duration compared to the presentation time period over which the mean was calculated. Activity was compared separately due to the different number of participants providing this. Activity levels were compared between test sessions by way of a 1x3 mixed design ANOVA with test session as the within subject factor. No main effect of test session was found (p> .05) suggesting participants' motor activity was consistent across testing sessions. Activity levels were also compared during the course of each test session by a series of 1x4 mixed design ANOVAs with TP as the within subjects factor. This was repeated for each of the 3 test sessions. No main effect of TP was found on any test session (all p> .05) indicating that motor activity during the course of each test was consistent.

Symptom Ratings

Correlations were calculated to determine whether the test is sensitive to variation in subjectively rated impulsive behaviour traits (Table 2). Mean scores were used for each of the five UPPS-P subscales and overall mean was used for Omission Errors, Commission Errors, RT, RT variability and Activity. Significant correlations were found between Commission Errors and one UPPS-P subscale: (Lack of) Perseverance (r= .84 n= 11 *p*= .001). Activity was significantly correlated with Positive Urgency (r=.86 n=11 p< .05). Omission Errors were significantly correlated with RT variability (r= .74 n= 11 *p*< .01) and as expected RT was significantly correlated with RT variability (r= .79 n=11 *p*< .01) (Table 3).

Table 2. Correlations between the CPT measures and UPPS-P Impulsive Behaviour Scale

	UPPS Total	Negative Urgency	Premeditation	Perserverance	Sensation Seeking	Positive Urgency
Omission	.133	.270	.024	.392	-.498	.261
Commission	.474	.539	-.436	.839**	-.162	.482
RT	-.291	-.146	-.294	-.147	-.197	-.166
RT variability	.201	.321	-.271	.244	-.151	.263
Activity	.769	.769	-.153	.753	.183	.835*

**. Correlation is significant at the 0.01 level (2-tailed).
*. Correlation is significant at the 0.05 level (2-tailed).

Table 3. Correlations between the CPT measures

	Omission	Commission	RT	RT variability	Activity
Omission	--				
Commission	.273	--			
RT	.556	-.204	--		
RT variability	.742**	.138	.793**	--	
Activity	.527	-.322	.382	.237	--

**. Correlation is significant at the 0.01 level (2-tailed).
*. Correlation is significant at the 0.05 level (2-tailed).

Participant Feedback

A summary of the participant feedback questionnaires found that:

- 11/11 participants found the task easy.
- 6/11 found the phone comfortable to hold whist doing the task (4/11 were neutral).
- 8/11 participants did not find the task stressful.
- 10/11 participants reported that they were asked to complete the task at a convenient time.
- 5/11 participants would prefer to complete the task between 11am and 1pm.

A summary of suggestions for improvements to the task were as follows:

- Replace the white screen with a coloured one.
- Provide a scoring or ranking system.
- Make the letters a larger font size.
- Provide help options.
- Choose own username.
- Text reminder after an hour if the task hasn't yet been completed.
- Ensure the time is not visible on the screen of the phone whilst completing the task.

4 Discussion

Attention, impulsivity and activity levels were consistent across testing sessions suggesting there were no effects of practice or deterioration across testing sessions. One measure of attention; Omission Errors varied over time on Test 3 only, indicating a decrement in performance over time. Further testing sessions with a larger sample are needed to determine whether this waning of attention is due to familiarity with the task as this effect was only evident in Test 3. All other performance measures remained consistent over the course of each test session. Differences in performance over time were not expected in the current sample since previous research has found no effects of time on task for healthy participants. However, decrements in performance over time are seen in ADHD participants on RT variability and Commission Errors [e.g. 16, 23].

The CPT showed some sensitivity to ADHD-related traits in healthy individuals. Subjective symptom ratings were compared with the CPT measures to find that Commission Errors were correlated with (lack of) Perseverance, suggesting that the CPT is successfully measuring one aspect of impulsive behaviour. Activity levels were correlated with Positive Urgency suggesting that the CPT is reflecting hyperactive-impulsive behaviour. Interestingly, Omission Errors and RT were the only CPT measures that were correlated (except for RT and RT variability which we would expect to be highly correlated). As both of these measures are thought to reflect attention we would also expect them to be correlated if the task is successfully measuring attention. The finding that RT was not related to any of the symptom ratings is consistent with previous research findings where the variability of RT over time seems to be a much more robust measure [23]. These findings have implications for future App development, and if shown to be a sensitive measure of ADHD symptoms, could prove to be a cost-effective and portable adjunct to clinical assessment.

Overall, participants rated their experience of using the App positively. In future studies, gathering feedback from a clinical sample will determine whether their user experiences differ.

Limitations

Activity measures were only available for 6 out of the 11 participants due to their phones not having accelerometer capabilities. With such a small sample of activity data it is difficult to draw any conclusions about activity levels. However along with the correlation between Activity and Positive Urgency, trends toward a significant correlation were found between Activity and two of the UPPS-P impulsivity measures (UPPS-P Total score and Negative Urgency). It is possible that with more participants statistically significant relationships could be found for objectively measured activity levels and subjectively rated ADHD-related symptoms. We must however note that UPPS is used for a measure of impulsivity, one element of ADHD, but that its validity and reliability as a measure of ADHD signs/symptoms is yet to be properly established.

This sample was drawn from a University so is restricted to University staff and students. This could potentially limit the variability in results. For the purposes of pilot testing the App this is not a significant concern, however if the App is further tested, a more diverse sample should be used. The sample also had many more female than male participants, which again should be rectified on further testing of the App to avoid any gender bias in the results.

Future work will take participant feedback into account to make improvements on the current App. Attempts will be made to provide a summary score for overall performance on the test and for each symptom domain; attention, impulsivity and hyperactivity. We will then seek to test the App in a clinical population of both children and adults, alongside a larger normative comparison group. Since CPTs are considered to be the most sensitive assessment of medication effects [12], there is potential for this App to be used remotely to monitor changes in ADHD symptoms while practitioners are initiating treatment. This could provide practitioners with more information regarding patient's symptoms and medication efficacy. Only through testing in a clinical sample can we determine whether the App is sensitive to ADHD symptoms.

Acknowledgements. The research reported in this paper was conducted by the National Institute for Health Research MindTech Healthcare Technology Co-operative (NIHR MindTech HTC) and funded by the NIHR. The views expressed are those of the author(s) and not necessarily those of the NHS, the NIHR or the Department of Health. MC and JC acknowledge additional support for the App development work through the Multidisciplinary Assessment of Technology for Healthcare (MATCH) programme (EPSRC Grant EP/F063822/1). The authors also wish to acknowledge the valuable input of other collaborators in both MindTech and MATCH during the Snappy App development.

References

1. Faraone, S.V., Biederman, J., Spencer, T., Wilens, T., Seidman, L., Mick, E., Doyle, A.E.: Attention-deficit/hyperactivity disorder in adults: an overview. Biological Psychiatry 48(1), 9–20 (2000)
2. Riccio, C.A., Reynolds, C.R.: Continuous performance tests are sensitive to ADHD in adults but lack specificity. Annals of the New York Academy of Sciences 931(1), 113–139 (2001)
3. Lis, S., Baer, N., Stein-en-Noss, C., Gallhofer, B., Sammer, G., Kirsch, P.: Objective measurement of motor activity during cognitive performance in adults with attention-deficit/hyperactivity disorder. Acta Psychiatrica Scandianvica 122, 285–294 (2010)
4. NICE: Attention Deficit Hyperactivity Disorder: The NICE Guideline on Diagnosis and Management of ADHD in Children, Young People and Adults. National Clinical Practice Guideline Number 72. National Collaborating Centre for Mental Health: The British Psychological Society & The Royal College of Psychiatrists (2008)
5. Faraone, S.V., Biederman, J.: Neurobiology of attention-deficit hyperactivity disorder. Biological Psychiatry 44, 951–958 (2008)
6. Ogundele, M.O., Ayyash, H.F., Banerjee, S.: Role of computerised continuous performance task tests in ADHD. Progress in Neurology and Psychiatry 15, 8–13 (2011)
7. Weinberg, W.A., Brumback, R.A.: The myth of attention deficit-hyperactivity disorder: the diagnostic utility of clinic-based tests. Journal of Clinical Child Psychology 21, 394–402 (1992)
8. Swanson, J.M., Flodman, P., Kennedy, J., Spence, M.A., Moyzis, R., Schuck, S., Murias, M., Moriarity, J., Barr, C., Smith, M., Posner, M.: Dopamine genes and ADHD. Neuroscience and Behavioural Reviews 24, 21–25 (2000)
9. Biederman, J., Faraone, S., Milberger, S., Guite, J., Mick, E., Chen, L., Mennin, D., Marrs, A., Ouellette, C., Moore, P., Spencer, T., Norman, D., Wilens, T., Kraus, I., Perrin, J.: A prospective 4-year follow-up study of attention-deficit hyperactivity and related disorders. Archives of General Psychiatry 53, 437–446 (1996)
10. Vogt, C., Williams, T.: Early identification of stimulant treatment responders, partial responders and non-responders using objective measures in children and adolescents with hyperkinetic disorder. Child and Adolescent Mental Health 16, 144–149 (2011)
11. van Leeuwen, T.H., Steinhausen, H.C., Overtoom, C.C., Pascual-Marqui, R.D., van't Klooster, B., Rothenberger, A., Sergeant, J.A., Brandeis, D.: The continuous performance test revisited with neuroelectric mapping: Impaired orienting in children with attention deficits. Behavioural Brain Research 94, 97–110 (1998)
12. Riccio, C.A., Waldrop, J.J.M., Reynolds, C.R., Lowe, P.: Effects of stimulants on continuous performance test (CPT). Journal of Neuropsychiatry and Clinical Neurosciences 13, 326–335 (2001)
13. Tinius, T.P.: The integrated visual and auditory continuous performance test as a neuropsychological measure. Archives of Clinical Neuropsychology 18(5), 439–454 (2003)
14. Doehnert, M., Brandeis, D., Imhof, K., Drechsler, R., Steinhausen, H.-C.: Mapping Attention-Deficit/Hyperactivity Disorder from Childhood to Adolescence—No Neurophysiologic Evidence for a Developmental Lag of Attention but Some for Inhibition. Society of Biological Psychiatry 67, 608–616 (2010)
15. Brocki, K.C., Tillman, C.M., Bohlin, G.: CPT performance, motor activity, and continuous relations to ADHD symptom domains: A developmental study. European Journal of Developmental Psychology 7(2), 178–197 (2010)

16. Teicher, M.H., Ito, Y., Glod, C.A., Barber, N.I.: Objective measurement of hyperactivity and attentional problems in ADHD. Journal of the American Academy of Child & Adolescent Psychiatry 35(3), 334–342 (1996)
17. Vogt, C., Shameli, A.: Assessments for attention-deficit hyperactivity disorder: use of objective measurements. The Psychiatrist 35(10), 380–383 (2011)
18. Rosser, B.A., Eccleston, C.: Smartphone applications for pain management. Journal of Telemedicine and Telecare 17(6), 308–312 (2011)
19. Ofcom: International Communications Market Report (2013), http://stakeholders.ofcom.org.uk/binaries/research/cmr/cmr13/UK_4.pdf (accessed February 5, 2014)
20. Luxton, D.D., McCann, R.A., Bush, N.E., Mishkind, M.C., Reger, G.M.: mHealth for mental health: Integrating smartphone technology in behavioral healthcare. Professional Psychology: Research and Practice 42(6), 505–512 (2011)
21. Cyders, M.A., Smith, G.T., Spillane, N.S., Fischer, S., Annus, A.M., Peterson, C.: Integration of impulsivity and positive mood to predict risky behavior: Development and validation of a measure of positive urgency. Psychological Assessment 19, 107–118 (2007)
22. Whiteside, S.P., Lynam, D.R.: The Five Factor Model and impulsivity: using a structural model of personality to understand impulsivity. Personality and Individual Differences 30(4), 669–689 (2001)
23. Epstein, J.N., Erkanli, A., Conners, K., Klaric, J., Costello, J.E., Angold, A.: Relations between continuous performance test performance measures and ADHD behaviors. Journal of Abnormal Child Psychology 31(5), 543–554 (2003)

Mobility, Transport and Environment

TellEat: Sharing Experiences on the Move

Elisa Chiabrando[1], Roberto Furnari[1], Silvia Likavec[1], Francesco Osborne[1], Claudia Picardi[1], and Daniele Theseider Dupré[2]

[1] Università di Torino, Italy
{chiabran,furnari,likavec,osborne,picardi}@di.unito.it
[2] Università del Piemonte Orientale, Alessandria, Italy
dtd@di.unipmn.it

Abstract. In a context where, due to the proliferation of mobile devices, virtual social environments on the Web are taking up a very concrete role in the way people experience their surroundings, the Future Internet seems to be headed toward a mixture of Social Web, Semantic Web and Augmented Reality. As a part of a larger project that aims at building a social network of both people and things, we designed and developed TellEat, an iPhone-based application that allows users in mobility to share facts concerning people or objects that participate in the social network, and to discover pertinent events that have been told by others. In this paper we discuss both the client application, with the interaction model and interface metaphors that have been designed to make the experience as playful as possible for users, and the server-side services that provide the necessary knowledge and reasoning mechanisms. We also present the results of preliminary tests with users.

1 Introduction

Communication and technology are moving out from offices and home environments into the outside world. Due to the proliferation of mobile devices, people have uninterrupted Internet connection and constant access to information in virtually any situation. As a consequence, virtual social environments (as for example social networking services) on the Internet are taking up a very concrete role in the way people experience and interact with their surroundings. In other words, the perception of what *is real* starts to include elements of the virtual world, blurring the distinction between "the real" and "the virtual".

Within this context, the bridging of the Social Web, the Semantic Web [12] and Augmented Reality [1] has become a feasible and interesting option. The Social Web brings together people, creates and maintains relationships, facilitates the sharing of contents. The Semantic Web organizes and gives a structure to the information provided by users, allowing for better search and retrieval mechanisms, and allowing for inferences on user-provided content based not only on the relationships between users (as in basic social networking services) but also on semantic relationships between the objects that the users discuss or comment about. Augmented Reality provides enhanced interaction with physical objects, by endowing them with Web-based counterparts accessible through

M. Kurosu (Ed.): Human-Computer Interaction, Part III, HCII 2014, LNCS 8512, pp. 377–388, 2014.

mobile devices at the same time as their physical self is. This allows users to discover additional information about their physical environment, but also to act upon it as they would do in a social networking service: tagging, commenting, posting content, and recommending to other users.

The PIEMONTE[1] project has investigated and implemented the notion of a *social web of intelligent things*, where augmented physical objects actively participate in a social network by creating relationships among themselves or users, and by sharing knowledge. Friendships between objects are established by reasoning on their semantic relations, represented by a domain ontology, and by mining users' activity in the social network. This framework is being implemented and tested in the field of traditional gastronomy, with the goal to promote the cultural heritage of the involved territory (the Piedmont region in the north-west of Italy). As a part of this project, the WantEat suite of applications [7] has been developed. The mobile application in WantEat allows users to browse the enhanced social network starting from the objects they have at hand, navigating their relationships and thereby discovering the territory they come from, or are visiting. With WantEat, users can perform social actions (tagging, rating, etc.) on objects they are browsing.

Within this framework, we proposed an approach to foster collective storytelling [14], devising a structured language and representational form to describe users' story fragments, investigating measures that capture similarity [6] and pertinence relations between them, and studying linking patterns that can be used to thread fragments into story-like narratives.

Starting from these ideas, we designed and developed TellEat, an iPhone™-based application that allows users to provide the system with a fact, concerning people or objects in the WantEat network, and to discover pertinent events told by others. A significant effort has been devoted to developing interface metaphors and an interaction model suitable for the underlying representational language, while at the same time being intuitive and playful enough to be used in mobility. In addition, preliminary tests have been conducted in order to compare the inferences made by our algorithms with those made by humans.

The rest of the paper is organized as follows. Section 2 describes the general design of TellEat in the context of WantEat, followed by the description of the user interface with the interaction model designed for the Apple iPhone™ (2.1) and the server-side architecture (2.2). Section 3 provides the results of the preliminary tests carried out with users. In section 4 some relevant literature is discussed, while section 5 points to future developments.

2 TellEat

The TellEat application has been developed as an add-on to the WantEat suite, which we briefly describe. The key ideas behind the WantEat suite are: (i) building and maintaining a social network of both people and things, (ii) allowing

[1] PIEMONTE Project - People Interaction with Enhanced Multimodal Objects for a New Territory Experience 2009-2013, `http://piemonte.di.unito.it/`

users to interact with things belonging to the social network in augmented reality, and (iii) turning things into hubs that connect users with a larger world. WantEat implements these notions in the domain of regional food and wine products. Users can have access to an object's augmented life thanks to *WantEat Mobile*, a client application for smartphones, including the Apple iPhone™. By framing labels, logos or signs with the smartphone camera [11], users can get in touch with a thing's avatar, and interact with it in the usual Web 2.0 fashion, providing ratings, tags or comments. They can also browse the "wheel" of an object's relations, explore its social network and obtain information on the object's territory. The social network connects producers, restaurants and shop owners, as well as products (cheeses, wines, vegetables, etc.) and places (shops, farms, restaurants, market stalls, etc.). Friendships between objects are established by reasoning on their semantic properties (e.g. two recipes with similar key ingredients), or by mining users' activity in the social network (e.g. two restaurants often bookmarked together) and user-generated content (e.g. a wine often mentioned in the comments on a cheese).

The goal of TellEat is to provide users with an additional way to share information with the system and other users. TellEat enables users to tell to the system what they did with a certain object. For example, they may have sipped a wine, brought it to a dinner party, or used it in a recipe. As a "reward" for telling something to TellEat, users get back a list of facts told by other people that the system reckons to be pertinent to the fact inserted by the user. This means that users can tell facts with the intent of querying the system for similar things happening to their friends.

Conceptually, TellEat is composed of the following modules (a more detailed description of the architecture and its implementation is given in 2.2).

- A **client app** for the Apple iPhone™, that allows users to interact with the system and share their contributions in a playful way.
- A **fact repository**: as described in [14], we represent facts in OWL, as instances in an ontology. Conceptually, each fact is a pair (p, F) where p is a chosen verb, representing the action, and F is a set of pairs (r_i, f_i), representing the actors and their roles in the action. For each of these pairs, r_i is a role label chosen among who, what, where, when, how, why; f_i is the role filler which can either be an entity in the domain ontology of WantEat (person, thing, place, etc.) or a custom label defined by the user.
- A **pertinence module**, which evaluates the pertinence between a newly inserted fact and those existing in the repository. The measure of pertinence we use is introduced in [14] and is based on the friendship between involved people, on the colocation between facts (co-occurrence in space and time), and on semantic similarity between the mentioned entities, computed using the distance based approach proposed in [6].

2.1 The Client App: Interaction Model and User Interface

In order to build a fact (p, F) users need to provide the verb p and as many role fillers as they like for each of the six available roles. The choice of the verb is restricted to the verbs present in our ontology; role fillers can be either entities (objects, places, people) that are present in the WantEat social network, or custom entries made of a label, a short description and an optional image.

For our interaction model we decided to use the metaphor of a letter: the fact is represented by an envelope, containing paper sheets for the different roles, in different colors, and with a stamp showing the chosen verb.

The user starts by selecting a verb, and then moves on to provide fillers for the roles; it is always possible to go back at any time if needed.

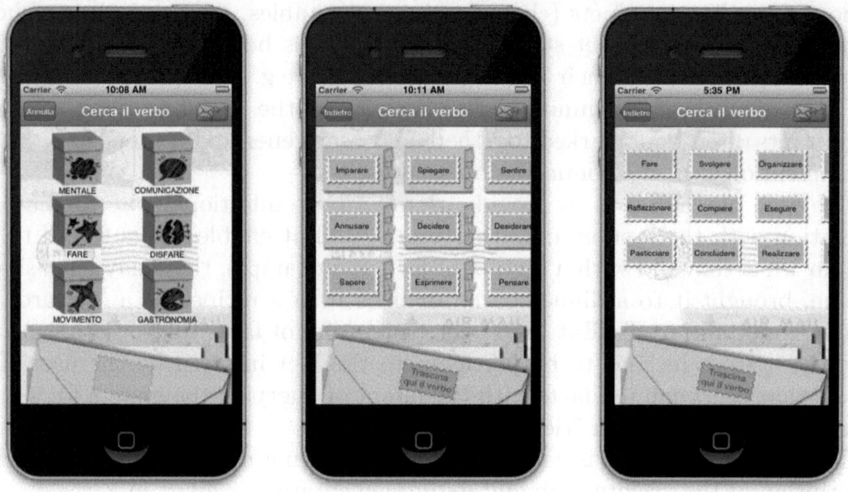

(a) (b) (c)

Fig. 1. (a) Verb categories (first level). (b) Key verbs (second level). (c) Verb variations (third level).

Figure 1 shows the phases of the verb selection process. Rather than showing the ontology structure, which would make it difficult for the user to find the desired verbs, the user interface shows verbs organized according to a three-level folder structure: the first level (Figure 1(a)) contains broad categories (e.g. *speech actions*); the second level (Figure 1(b)) contains key verbs for the category (e.g. *speak* or *talk*); the third level (Figure 1(c)) contains subtler variations of the verbs from the second level (e.g. *whisper*). A verb is selected by dragging the corresponding stamp on the envelope.

Once the verb has been chosen, the role filler selection phase takes place, as shown in Figure 2. Six paper sheets in different colors, one for each role (Figure 2(a)), appear from behind the envelope. This view serves as an overview of the given fact, where the user can see the verb and its roles at a glance; the sheets can be moved on the screen to better explore their contents. This view is also used to show to a user someone else's facts.

(a) (b) (c)

Fig. 2. (a) An empty phrase, (b) Suggestions in the envelope, (c) Creation of a new object

In order to *edit* a sheet's content, the user has to tap on it. The main screen for the role filler selection process is represented in Figure 2(b). Role fillers are represented as stickers (containing a picture or a label). A set of suggested role fillers is placed in the envelope (exploiting the recommendation service provided by WantEat); the user can either pick one of them, or search something in the WantEat domain. The search window provides also the option of inserting a custom label and/or picture and/or a short description (see Figure 2(c)) in case the desired object is not present in WantEat. However, in this case the object is not tied to the ontology and will not be interpreted by the system.

When the user has finished editing the fact, he/she can submit it by clicking on the send button at the top right of the screen. She will then get back a list of pertinent facts, which she can view one by one.

2.2 Server-Side Architecture

In order to achieve its goals, TellEat exploits services of WantEat and additional modules.

Figure 3 shows the server-side architecture, where services and modules that are TellEat-specific are distinguished by a thick black border. The figure also distinguishes three different interaction threads, numbered 1, 2 and 3, between the client application and the server.

Interaction 1 happens when the client application needs the available verbs. Since these are stored as an added part of the domain ontology, TellEat's *Coordination Manager* dispatches the query to the Fact Repository Module, that

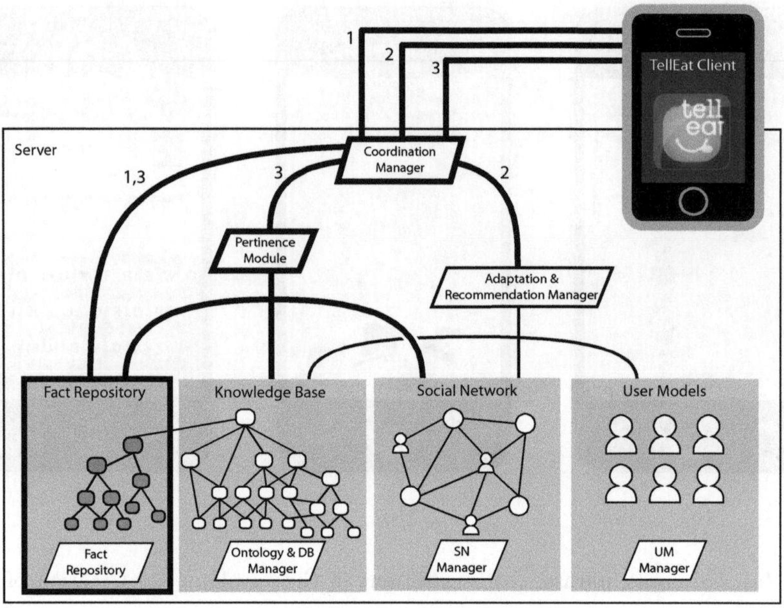

Fig. 3. Server-side architecture of TellEat

in turn queries the *Ontology & DB Manager* for the list of available verbs, and maps them to the three-level hierarchy in the client.

Interaction 2 happens when the client has to suggest role fillers to the user. This is achieved by using the support from the *Adaptation & Recommendation Manager in WantEat, as well as by taking into account other things, such as a role type, other facts inserted by the user, etc.*

Interaction 3 happens when the client submits a newly inserted fact. In this case, the fact is sent for storage to the *Fact Repository* module. After the fact has been inserted, its pertinence with other stored facts is computed by the *Pertinence Module.* Facts with a pertinence value above a certain threshold are then sent back to the client, to be shown to the user.

Fact Repository. Facts in TellEat are represented both as instances of a verb in the OWL verbs ontology and as records in a relational MySql database, storing other information as creation date, ownership, notes, custom labels and pictures. The Fact Repository provides a homogeneous access interface to the facts synthesizing a uniform representation from these two heterogeneous data sources. In particular the D2RQ tool is used to view a part of a relational database as a set of OWL individuals [2] to provide a uniform virtual data source that can be directly queried in SPARQL.

Pertinence Module. The pertinence module computes the pertinence between facts according to the measure presented in [14]. We give a short overview of the key ideas. In calculating pertinence between two facts, the following is taken into account:

- different facts use different predicates taken from the predicate ontology to express their content;
- each fact has only one predicate since every fact can be decomposed into more facts with only one predicate;
- each predicate has a set of associated values for different role fillers;
- each role might have 0 or more role fillers;
- the semantic similarity between two predicates or two role fillers is calculated using a measure presented in [6];
- co-location estimates the possibility for the actors to meet while performing the described actions.

Summing up, given two facts f and g, the *pertinence* of the fact g for the fact f is given by:

$$\text{PERT}(f,g) = \alpha_0 \text{SP} + \Sigma_{i=1}^{m} \alpha_i \text{SRF}_i + \beta \text{COLOC} \quad (1)$$

where SP is *semantic similarity of predicates*, $\text{SRF}_i, i = 1, \ldots, m$ are *semantic similarities of role fillers* (m is the number of role fillers for f), COLOC is the *colocation* and $\alpha_0, \ldots \alpha_m, \beta \in \mathbb{R}$ are weights. To reduce redundancy, when calculating the similarity of role fillers, we consider only the pairs with maximum similarity values for each role filler. This allows to take into account only meaningful conceptual distances, not any type of vague resemblance between role fillers. In the special case where similarity is being calculated for two users, we use their social network relationship. The pertinence calculation can be enhanced by introducing weights for certain roles depending on the verb.

3 Evaluation

3.1 Goals of the Experiment

In this section we describe a simple preliminary evaluation which we conducted in order to evaluate the performance of our pertinence measure. Our main goal was to find out if the facts retained pertinent to a given fact by the system, are also viewed as pertinent by the users, since this would mean that the suggestions of our system could be interesting for users.

3.2 Description of the Experiment

We recruited a total of twenty subjects among our contacts and colleagues, according to an availability sampling strategy.[2] All were native Italian speakers. The test consisted of 5 identical steps. In each step, the subject of the test

[2] Even though non-random samples are not statistically representative, they are often used in psychology research and usability testing, during early evaluation phases.

was given one primary fact and a list of seven secondary facts. We chose the secondary facts from a range of facts having different values of pertinence with the primary fact according to our system. For example, for the primary fact
"*At the party, Sonia and Lea shared a piece of cake made with Fuji Apples.*",
the secondary facts could have been
"*Sonia brought a cake made with Fuji Apples to a party.*",
as well as
"*Dan tastes a cheese in his local store.*" or
"*Fred buys a book for his girlfriend's birthday.*".
Also, the secondary facts were always presented in the random order. For each of the secondary facts, the subject was asked to assign the values on the 4-point scale from 0 to 3 (0 meaning not pertinent at all, 3 meaning very pertinent) depending on their perception of the pertinence of the secondary fact with the primary fact. Hence, each subject had to evaluate a total of 35 facts.

3.3 Results and Discussion

Given the subjective nature of pertinence evaluation by the users (context awareness, subjective importance of different roles, etc.) in a social context, the correct detection of the pertinent facts by the system is more important and interesting than the classification of non-pertinent facts. In a social system users expect to see positive results and the links between them.

To this aim, we decided to set a threshold value of PERT = 2.0 above which the secondary facts are considered pertinent, hence interesting, for users. This meant that for different primary facts the system offered between 1 and 4 pertinent secondary facts. These facts were considered pertinent by the users in 75% of the cases. When we raised the threshold to PERT = 2.25, the percentage of the facts perceived pertinent by the users was 76%.

This shows a satisfactory level of performance of our pertinence measure. On the other hand, while performing the evaluation, we learned a whole lot about human behavior in assessing pertinence between events. Some of the users were looking for cause-effect relationships, some were giving higher importance to friendship relationships between protagonists, some were valuing more the events etc. These findings provided us with valuable directions for future research and for fine tuning our application.

4 Related Work

A framework that tries to support users in mobility is described in [16]. Their "Story-To-Go" engine guides users through places of interest in a city. User-provided images and metadata, that are available at a certain location, are grouped together into so called hypespots which can be used in building a story. For each hypespot, a set of possible story directions is generated, which forms the building blocks for a future story. When the user starts a story, the story engine presents the related material covering different hypespots which fit into a reasonable time frame and cover reasonable search space.

Similarly, [10] proposes a storytelling application that can be used by people with aphasia (communication disorder caused by brain disease or injury). The prototype was implemented on a Tablet PC with an attached webcam. Their multimodal interface enables users to take photos, make drawings and record sounds in order to create their stories and express their feelings.

These applications focus on suggesting narrative possibilities, rather than truly providing information to users. Our proposal, in contrast, has at its center a single narrative fragment, and it can be seen as an evolution of Facebook[3] status messages or comments. Although we are also ultimately interested in building stories from narrative fragments, we want fragments to be as similar as possible to what people communicate with each other over social networks.

InStory [8] is a project whose goal is the implementation of a client-server platform for mobile storytelling, information access and gaming activities. The client device is able to store users' positions and their actions and send the information to the server database. Moreover, the same users can upload different types of data (text, images, etc.) to integrate them with the system data and particularly, the story created by the system. In our framework the users have more possibility to express themselves and to add details, which can be used to connect together the stories of different people.

MIST [18] is a multimedia storytelling platform where various media types are combined into non-linear stories. The users can create, edit or read stories. Stories consist of elements containing structural information or media specific descriptions. Links between story elements are made using media files and their descriptions. MIST does not support the collaborative storytelling paradigm (each user can only create his/her own story). In [5] an extension of MIST, called PESE is proposed which takes into account Web 2.0 technologies. A user model is conceived where users with different roles can perform different media operations. In this framework many handheld clients can connect to a centralized server and subscribe to various stories at the same time.

INSCAPE [9,19] is an authoring environment for designing, creating and experiencing interactive stories and simulations. Users can design interactive storyboards, edit and visualize the story structure, create 2D and 3D scenes and characters, incorporate various multimedia, such as sounds, pictures and videos, and publish the stories on the Internet. Topological graphs are used to visualize stories where nodes are objects of the story and edges are interactive transitions or conditional relationships. We are devising a similar approach to connect facts into a story. However, INSCAPE is aimed at a different audience, and it provides a representation for story fragment atoms quite different from ours.

In [4] narrative presentation for lifelog archives containing large amount of data in different formats such as SenseCam diaries, photos, videos and text documents is described. According to the authors, the most used means to describe someone's experience is the visual content, while the other modalities are used to support the visual content. They also conclude that the nature of the story and the author's personal view of the story have a considerable impact on the

[3] `http://www.facebook.com/`

fragments used for representing the story and the final outcome. In our framework the story fragments are also collected from heterogeneous sources and the users can freely chose and combine the available elements.

PoliCultura [3] is a project targeted at Italian school children which should enable the students of different age groups to design and construct interactive stories over a longer period of time. *1001stories* is a web-based authoring-delivery environment which enables children to combine images, text and mp3 files into interactive stories. The authors present their work as a platform encouraging *collective narratives*, but it seems that it is more similar to a system supporting *collaborative narratives*, where many authors collaborate in constructing a story. On the other hand, in our framework we try to enable real *collective narrative* construction where authors can work independently of each other when contributing their facts to the system and conceiving a story.

CultureSampo [13] is a semantic web portal for finnish cultural heritage. It incorporates multiple, nation wide collaboratively maintained ontologies for different domains and multiple metadata schemas. The semantic model is based on events and narratives and it provides the tools for collaborative content and ontology creation.

NetworkING [17] is a novel system for generating narratives in a medical drama domain based on the virtual characters' social network and the existing relationships among them. The user can change these relationships using a visual interface and generate new narratives. The experimental results prove that these changes do impact the diversity of produced narratives and less importance can be given to plot structure. The authors use Levenshtein string distance, similar to our pertinence measure, to compare the generated narratives.

5 Conclusions and Future Work

In this work we further develop the ideas presented in [14]. In particular, we describe the TellEat application, that allows mobile users of the Semantic Social Web to share narrative fragments called *facts*. In addition, we focus on an interaction metaphor and an interface design that provide users with a playful and intuitive way to build their own narrative fragments. The narrative fragments we are interested in are those that describe users' experiences with respect to the entities in the domain that the semantic framework describes, and that concern the theme of the Social Networking Application. Our work was in particular targeted to a Social Application about food and wine as a part of the cultural heritage of a territory.

Ultimately, the goal of our proposal is to allow automatic interpretation and correlation of the information provided by users. This idea can be expanded in several directions:

- Facts could be used in a similar way to tags, to describe or comment on specific resources (e.g. to describe the contents of an image). In this case, interpretation and correlation of facts may play a significant role in search and retrieval of information (e.g. queries of the form "People drinking wine").

- Automatic extraction of story fragments from phrases expressed in natural language could facilitate and accelerate their gathering process.
- An intelligent repository of facts may exploit the user model present in the social network to show the users only the facts provided by other people that may be of interest to them (this can indeed be done with similar techniques as those adopted in recommendation systems [15]).
- In the type of social network we are considering, where objects are active social members, each object may collect the narrative fragments where it plays a role and use them to build a personal memory and a personalized presentation to the world.
- Since different users may have different perception of pertinence for facts, finding out what influences their choices and impressions and how to take all these factors into account could improve our proposal and reveal interesting correlations we might not be aware of.
- Last but not least, users may be encouraged to connect together several narrative fragments (whether their own or other people's) to form complete narratives. This possibility opens a way to a new storytelling paradigm, *collective storytelling* [14], where users can conceive and design stories independently of each other, however contributing to the same collective story.

References

1. Bimber, O., Raskar, R.: Spatial Augmented Reality: Merging Real and Virtual Worlds. A. K. Peters (2005)
2. Bizer, C., Seaborne, A.: D2RQ - Treating Non-RDF Databases as Virtual RDF Graphs. In: 3rd International Semantic Web Conference, ISWC 2004, Poster (2004)
3. Di Blas, N., Garzotto, F., Paolini, P., Sabiescu, A.: Digital storytelling as a whole-class learning activity: Lessons from a three-years project. In: Iurgel, I.A., Zagalo, N., Petta, P. (eds.) ICIDS 2009. LNCS, vol. 5915, pp. 14–25. Springer, Heidelberg (2009)
4. Byrne, D., Jones, G.J.F.: Exploring narrative presentation for large multimodal lifelog collections through card sorting. In: Iurgel, I.A., Zagalo, N., Petta, P. (eds.) ICIDS 2009. LNCS, vol. 5915, pp. 92–97. Springer, Heidelberg (2009)
5. Cao, Y., Klamma, R., Martini, A.: Collaborative storytelling in the web 2.0. In: Proc. of the 1st International Workshop on Story-Telling and Educational Games, STEG-(2008)
6. Chiabrando, E., Likavec, S., Lombardi, I., Picardi, C., Theseider Dupré, D.: Semantic similarity in heterogeneous ontologies. In: Proc. of the 22nd ACM Conference on Hypertext and Hypermedia, Hypertext 2011, pp. 153–160. ACM (2011)
7. Console, L., Antonelli, F., Biamino, G., Carmagnola, F., Cena, F., Chiabrando, E., Cuciti, V., Demichelis, M., Fassio, F., Franceschi, F., Furnari, R., Gena, C., Geymonat, M., Grimaldi, P., Grillo, P., Guercio, E., Likavec, S., Lombardi, I., Mana, D., Marcengo, A., Mioli, M., Mirabelli, M., Perrero, M., Picardi, C., Protti, F., Rapp, A., Sandon, R., Simeoni, R., Theseider Dupré, D., Torre, I., Toso, A., Torta, F., Vernero, F.: Interacting with social netnetworks of intelligent things and people in the world of gastronomy. ACM Transactions on Interactive Intelligent Systems 3(1), 4 (2013)

8. Correia, N., Alves, L., Correia, H., Romero, L., Morgado, C., Soares, L., Cunha, J.C., Romão, T., Dias, A.E., Jorge, J.A.: InStory: A System for Mobile Information Access, Storytelling and Gaming Activities in Physical Spaces. In: Proc. of the ACM SIGCHI International Conference on Advances in Computer Entertainment Technology, ACE 2005, pp. 102–109. ACM (2005)
9. Dade-Robertson, M.: Visual scenario representation in the context of a tool for interactive storytelling. In: Cavazza, M., Donikian, S. (eds.) ICVS-VirtStory 2007. LNCS, vol. 4871, pp. 3–12. Springer, Heidelberg (2007)
10. Daemen, E., Dadlani, P., Du, J., Li, Y., Erik-Paker, P., Martens, J.-B., De Ruyter, B.: Designing a free style, indirect, and interactive storytelling application for people with aphasia. In: Baranauskas, C., Abascal, J., Barbosa, S.D.J. (eds.) INTERACT 2007. LNCS, vol. 4662, pp. 221–234. Springer, Heidelberg (2007)
11. Grillo, P., Likavec, S., Lombardi, I.: Using mobile phone cameras to interact with ontological data. In: Moreno-Díaz, R., Pichler, F., Quesada-Arencibia, A. (eds.) EUROCAST 2011, Part II. LNCS, vol. 6928, pp. 568–576. Springer, Heidelberg (2012)
12. Gruber, T.: Collective knowledge systems: Where the Social Web meets the Semantic Web. Journal of Web Semantics: Science, Services and Agents on the World Wide Web 6, 4–13 (2008)
13. Hyvönen, E., Mäkelä, E., Kauppinen, T., Alm, O., Kurki, J., Ruotsalo, T., Seppälä, K., Takala, J., Puputti, K., Kuittinen, H., Viljanen, K., Tuominen, J., Palonen, T., Frosterus, M., Sinkkilä, R., Paakkarinen, P., Laitio, J., Nyberg, K.: Culturesampo: A national publication system of cultural heritage on the semantic web 2.0. In: Aroyo, L., Traverso, P., Ciravegna, F., Cimiano, P., Heath, T., Hyvönen, E., Mizoguchi, R., Oren, E., Sabou, M., Simperl, E. (eds.) ESWC 2009. LNCS, vol. 5554, pp. 851–856. Springer, Heidelberg (2009)
14. Likavec, S., Lombardi, I., Nantiat, A., Picardi, C., Theseider Dupré, D.: Threading facts into a collective narrative world. In: Aylett, R., Lim, M.Y., Louchart, S., Petta, P., Riedl, M. (eds.) ICIDS 2010. LNCS, vol. 6432, pp. 86–97. Springer, Heidelberg (2010)
15. Melville, P., Sindhwani, V.: Recommender systems. In: Sammut, C., Webb, G. (eds.) Encyclopedia of Machine Learning. Springer (2010)
16. Nack, F., El Ali, A., van Kemenade, P., Overgoor, J., van der Weij, B.: A story to go, please. In: Aylett, R., Lim, M.Y., Louchart, S., Petta, P., Riedl, M. (eds.) ICIDS 2010. LNCS, vol. 6432, pp. 74–85. Springer, Heidelberg (2010)
17. Porteous, J., Charles, F., Cavazza, M.: NetworkING: Using Character Relationships for Interactive Narrative Generation. In: Proc. of the 2013 International Conference on Autonomous Agents and Multi-agent Systems, AAMAS 2013, pp. 595–602. International Foundation for Autonomous Agents and Multiagent Systems (2013)
18. Spaniol, M., Klamma, R., Sharda, N., Jarke, M.: Web-based learning with non-linear multimedia stories. In: Liu, W., Li, Q., Lau, R. (eds.) ICWL 2006. LNCS, vol. 4181, pp. 249–263. Springer, Heidelberg (2006)
19. Zagalo, N., Göbel, S., Torres, A., Malkewitz, R., Branco, V.A.: INSCAPE: Emotion expression and experience in an authoring environment. In: Göbel, S., Malkewitz, R., Iurgel, I. (eds.) TIDSE 2006. LNCS, vol. 4326, pp. 219–230. Springer, Heidelberg (2006)

The Youth of Today Designing the Smart City of Tomorrow

Challenges to Future Mobility, Energy, and City Climate

Simon Himmel, Barbara S. Zaunbrecher, Wiktoria Wilkowska, and Martina Ziefle

Human-Computer Interaction Center, RWTH Aachen University, Germany
{himmel,zaunbrecher,wilkowska,ziefle}@comm.rwth-aachen.de

Abstract. Sustainable energy supply, mobility concepts, a healthy city climate – the next generations will face vital urban challenges. The views of the citizens of tomorrow, today's youth, are therefore especially important when designing concepts for future urban areas that incorporate those demands. We therefore explored young pupils' attitude to these three research areas in an empirical approach. 21 students (17-24 years) participated in a workshop. First, they answered a questionnaire on their attitudes towards technology and urban environment. Afterwards, they were divided into focus groups in which they discussed and developed solutions to the three key challenges for future cities. Besides innovative ideas of how younger persons wish to live in urban environments, results reveal a rather uninformed and naïve view on the complex situation. Overall, we conclude that urban challenges should be integrated into the school education to provide a deeper understanding of the complex interaction of energy, mobility and user requirements.

Keywords: User diversity, urban development, attitude towards technology, mobility, energy, city climate.

1 Introduction

The world population is increasing exponentially, causing mankind to face enormous challenges. While diverse fields of research around the globe study today's metropolises and their development, aiming for sustainable solutions, our research focuses on small towns and urban quarters in western societies. Energy supply, mobility, ecology issues in regard to global warming, and air pollution are crucial factors for urban development worldwide. Particularly for western societies, the energy transition, electro-mobility, rural depopulation, and the demographic change play important roles in designing the city of tomorrow. The technological possibilities are tremendous, facilitating smart, integrated solutions from a technical point of view. The technological complexity can be illustrated by the following example: The electric car with its battery plugged into a smart grid can be used to store excess power from regenerative energy sources and keep the driver informed about the current battery level via a connection to a smartphone. From the user's point of view, we face challenges to gain

M. Kurosu (Ed.): Human-Computer Interaction, Part III, HCII 2014, LNCS 8512, pp. 389–400, 2014.

usability, usefulness, data security, trust, and acceptance of these complex technology developments. Not everything that is technically possible is also wanted, some wishes cannot be fulfilled, and often the distinct trade-off between personal costs and benefits leads to failure or success of technology development. Therefore, it is important to integrate the future user into the early development process.

Human-computer interaction (HCI) will play a crucial role in urban development [1]. The youth of today is linked up, all the time and everywhere. Intelligent and integrated mobile devices connect living space, urban quarter, and mobility concepts (e.g., car sharing, e-mobility). They will replace present status symbols like the own car or the first house which were dreams of an earlier generation. For the youth of today, HCI devices in combination with urban development can give solutions for not only a smarter but also a green and sustainable city of tomorrow.

In our interdisciplinary research project UFO (Urban Future Outline), we face the integrated challenges of mobility, energy infrastructure, and city climate with experts of each research field in a holistic approach from a user's perspective. The complex coupling of our research fields leads to creative solutions by integrating smart technology into city planning.

1.1 Questions Addressed

While there is some recent research on youths' attitudes towards different single aspects of future cities, e.g., energy [2, 3] and mobility [4], the holistic view on future smart cities, particularly including city climate, deserves further investigation.

Most research in the field of urban development, if user-centered at all, focuses on expert reviews and adults. The smart solutions in this work are designed by average, technology prone youths with different requirements for urban living regarding mobility, sustainable energy supply, and demands for greener cities. As a qualitative approach, 3 focus groups (n_{tot}=21, age 17-24) tried to develop intelligent solutions for mobility, energy, and ecological issues. This approach was supported by a survey to gain quantitative information about the needs and wishes for the future smart city. Furthermore, we wanted to analyze if the attitude towards technology in general plays a role for the attitude towards future energy, future mobility, and future city climate.

2 Methodology

The empirical approach followed a two-step procedure. First, participants were split into 3 focus groups. The students then all completed a questionnaire (see chapter 2.2) about their attitudes [5] towards technology, mobility, energy, and city climate before starting the discussions in the focus groups (see chapter 2.3). This way, they answered the questionnaire without being previously influenced by the other participants' opinion. Finally, the pupils presented their ideas to the other groups.

2.1 Participants

Students from a vocational school (n=18, age range 17 to 24) and a grammar school (n=3, age range 17 to 18) participated in this study. 15 students were male, 6 female. The educational level, secondary modern school degree, matched the German average [6]. The participants visited the research institution for the "Green Day 2013," a national information day on education and "green" jobs[1]. All students joined the same welcome session in order to introduce them into the research field of urban development.

2.2 Quantitative Questionnaire Study

First, all participants completed the same questionnaire. With the exception of three pupils, the participants came from the same class of the same school. Therefore, the question for their educational level was redundant. For demographic data, the students were asked for their age and gender although these data were not considered independent variables due to our homogeneous and rather small sample size.

In a second part, the participants were asked for their attitude towards technology (ATT) in general. The following 5-item set of questions targeting five attitudinal dimensions was answered on a 4-point Likert scale (total negation=1 to full affirmation=4):

1. Interest: "I am interested in technology."
2. Ease of use: "Dealing with technology is easy for me."
3. Trust: "I do not trust technology in general." (negative scale)
4. Fun: "Using technology is fun."
5. Avoidance: "I avoid technology if possible." (negative scale)

The third section of the questionnaire aimed at the environmental awareness and behavior considering attitudes in the three research fields *mobility*, *energy*, and *city climate*. The items measure the green profile, combining today's behavior and the willingness for the use of future technologies. All questions were answered using a 4-point Likert scale (total negation=1 to full affirmation=4) and tested for reliability (see chapter 3.1).

Mobility:

6. "I like to use local public transport."
7. "If the local public transport was better, I would use it more often."
8. "For short distances, I prefer walking and cycling over taking the car."
9. "I would spend more money on eco-friendly than conventional means of transportation."
10. "I can imagine using car-sharing and not buying a car."

---

[1] Information about the German Green Day:
`http://www.greenday2013.de/green-day`

Energy:

11. "Renewable energies protect natural resources and help conserve nature in its original state."
12. "Renewable energies interfere with the natural ecosystem (wind turbines, hydro-power plants, etc.)." (negative scale)
13. "We are obliged to use renewable energies, because they are the only ones which don't cause long-term damage to the environment."
14. "When choosing an energy supplier (for electricity, gas, etc.), I prefer the cheapest offer over green energy." (negative scale)
15. "We have to switch to using renewables in the long run, so that our children and grandchildren will have sufficient energy supplies."

City climate:

16. "I would like public spaces planted with fruit trees, vegetables, etc. ("Urban Gardening")."
17. "I can imagine participating in cultivating these urban gardens."
18. "I would like the whole city traffic changed to electro-mobility."
19. "I would like to have more green spaces in the city, even if this would mean less parking spaces."
20. "I imagine a city without cars, even if this would mean longer distances for me."

2.3 Qualitative Focus Groups

The students were separated into 3 focus groups (see Fig. 1). Each group had two hours to discuss one of the topics mobility, energy, and city climate. The composition of the groups was as follows (Table 1):

Table 1. Composition of focus groups

Topic	n_{group}	n_{female}	n_{male}
Mobility	7	3	4
Energy	7	0	7
City climate	7	3	4

Two scientific assistants whose research focused on the respective topic moderated each focus group. After the questionnaire study and an introduction into the respective topic, all groups followed a similar line of action. First, the groups discussed the current state of each topic regarding problems and challenges for sustainability and feasibility. In a second step, the groups were asked to develop a smart and innovative future solution for their topic in the field of urban development. They were encouraged to disregard practicability and focus instead on original ideas. This turned out to be more complicated than expected (see chapter 4.). All discussions were recorded and notes were taken to facilitate the analysis of results. In a final step, the solutions

Fig. 1. Focus groups for mobility, energy, and city climate

were compiled and presented to the other groups who evaluated the ideas regarding creativity, connection to other research fields, and originality.

3 Results

3.1 Quantitative Part: Questionnaire Study

The participants were divided into two groups, according to their ATT score (see chapter 2.3). One participant did not answer the questions on ATT and therefore was not allocated. Because overall ATT was high, participants were divided into a "high ATT" ($M > 3.5$) and a "medium ATT" ($M \leq 3.5$) group using a median-split, which was also descriptively authenticated as the sample was bimodal. The ATT scale was tested for reliability using Cronbach's alpha (α=0.795, the scale is also used in other, not yet published research by the authors).

The item blocks for environmental awareness and behavior or green profile considering attitudes in the three fields mobility, energy, and city climate (see 2.3) were also tested for reliability using Cronbach's alpha. While the questions for mobility (5 items, n=21, α=0.605) and city climate (5 items, n=21, α=0.745) were acceptable, the energy attitude (4 items (2nd was left out, because reliability significantly improved, before α =0.385), n=21, α=0.505) could not be indicated reliable for our sample. In parallel research [Zaunbrecher et al., in preparation] the scale was reliable (n=79, α=0.77). It is possible the wording of the energy questions led to misunderstandings (see chapter 4.).

The ATT groups were analyzed for significant differences in attitudes towards future mobility, future energy, and future city climate by applying ANOVAs. Fisher's Exact Probability Test was applied for gender distribution. Results are shown in Table 2.

Table 2. Descriptions of the groups based on ATT score

	Medium ATT	High ATT	Significance
n	10	10	
Gender	male= 5 female= 5	male= 9 female= 1	n.s.
Age	M= 19.6 SD= 2.6	M=18.4 SD=1.6	n.s.
Mobility	M=2.9 SD= 0.5	M=2.5 SD=0.7	n.s.
Energy	M= 3.1 SD=0.4	M=3.5 SD=0.3	$p \leq 0.05$
City climate	M=2.7 SD=0.5	M=2.7 SD=0.7	n.s.

The only significant difference between the groups was their attitude towards future energy ($F(1,18)= 8.02$, $p \leq 0.05$).

As could be seen in the focus groups (see chapter 3.1), the research fields mobility, energy, and city climate affect each other regarding urban development. The overall environmental awareness and behavior, considering all three topics and combining all 14 items, was also tested for reliability (n=21, α=0.747). This will be validated and improved in further research.

3.2 Qualitative Part: Focus Groups

The qualitative evaluation of the recorded focus groups was carried out using MAXQDA (coding software) and categories were developed with a simplified method of Mayring [7] due to the fact that all focus groups had different topics and not all subjects were comparable. Due to space restrictions, we limit this paper to the innovative and smart solutions the pupils came up with in the focus groups.

Mobility. The discussion in the focus group 'mobility' can be subdivided into 7 main categories, some with additional sub-categories. While the demand to talk about the present situation was enormous, the pupils faced huge problems considering solutions or innovative alternatives for the future.

In the first category <u>car</u>, considering 'traffic' and 'infrastructure,' the ideas for the future did not go further than reducing car traffic by switching common alternatives like bicycles, walking, and banning cars from the city. The issues of 'parking' and 'traffic jams' were also discussed intensively. However, the pupils did not develop any noteworthy solutions for these challenges.

As most of the participants did not have their own car, the *local public transit* was the second topic emphasized. In order to optimize 'capacity and frequency' of public transport, it was suggested that operators should communicate better with their users, for example by employing mobile technologies. Although the idea was mentioned, the pupils could not invent intelligent solutions for this. Instead, they started discussing pro and con arguments about public transit.

For the youths, one major problem was the insufficient *transport service at night*. A bus/taxi on-demand could be a cheap and efficient alternative to conventional taxis and busses. The cheap transportation in cities led to another big topic for the youths of our focus group: *costs*. Parking, gasoline, and taxis were considered too expensive and should be cheaper. All of the pupils have the opportunity to use public transit for free with their student tickets. Accordingly, these costs were not mentioned. One idea that was mentioned for a sustainable and greener mobility was the introduction of a financial award when disposing of a polluting car.

Eco-friendliness was only mentioned as 'not important.' Ecological improvements seemed to be considered beneficial, but they did not appear in the discussion about future mobility. All focus group members wished for more safety and preferred expanding the use of *camera surveillance* at public transit stations.

Ideas for new and *innovative means of transportation* came hesitantly and were only addressed when the moderators specifically asked for them. Nevertheless, they were not seriously discussed within the focus group. The pupils had immense difficulties disregarding practicability and being creative. They mentioned the Segway PT as a known innovative vehicle, 'personal aircrafts,' 'ropeways,' 'self-steering cars on magnetic fields,' and 'teleportation,' but they discussed neither feasibility nor usefulness for future mobility.

The wishes for future mobility were evaluated in a separate brainstorming process. The results are shown in Fig. 2.

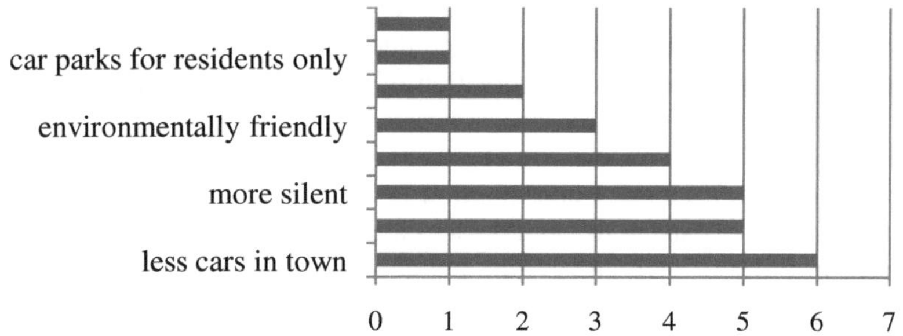

Fig. 2. Number of mentions for future mobility wishes (n=7)

Although the 'mobility' focus group had difficulties finding innovative solutions for a smart future city, all pupils agreed on the point that car traffic should be reduced in favor of a smarter, enhanced public transport system.

Energy. The 'energy' focus group started with an association process in which each participant had to write down buzzwords connected to the term 'energy' (see Fig. 3).

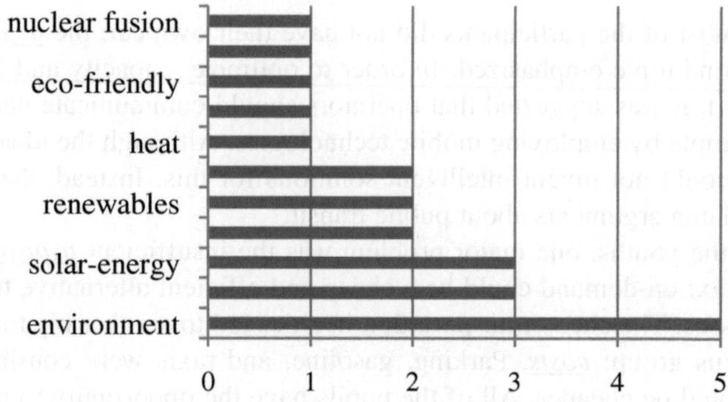

Fig. 3. Number of buzzwords for 'energy' (n=7)

As can be seen, *environment* was the most common term associated with energy. However, in the discussion that followed, the idea that the environment also plays a major role in deciding which form of energy production should be considered for the future smart city was utterly dismissed. The pupils not only associated different types of energy production or their characteristics but also the physical definition ('force'). Next, the different forms of energy production were collected and the pro and con arguments of fossil vs. renewable energies were discussed. Despite knowing that renewables are much better for the next generations, there was no evident preference for any energy transition.

The main arguments for all kinds of energy sources were their *costs.* Even though both conventional power plants and wind farms usually negatively affect the landscape, the students were more concerned with the monetary effects and managed to turn this into a positive argument: As eyesores, power plants must decrease the land's value, they reasoned, which is a benefit as rent and land acquisition would be more affordable. Innovative ideas for future cities' energy can be divided into two potential categories: 'energy savings' and 'energy production.' The ideas were not totally new, some did not even respect the conservation of energy, but the students of the focus group 'energy' were very creative.

The awareness of the importance of *energy saving* was surprisingly high. The pupils appreciate today's energy consumption labels for electronic devices, which they thought should be expanded to more devices and also mention actual costs and saving potentials. In order to save energy, the pupils wanted to have better opportunities to see which technical devices use how much electricity and, even more important, how much this electricity consumption costs. In addition, they want the option to remotely turn off these devices. This could either be put into practice by special remote controls, but it could be done even smarter by apps on their mobile devices. Intelligent systems at home could also be used to turn off devices, for example at night, or lock the front door automatically.

Most innovative were the ideas for *energy production*. Some of the examples mentioned were "doing sports, for example on a treadmill or cardio bike, to produce electricity by movement" and the integration of "little turbines in wastewater pipes as the water is flowing anyway." These smaller ideas were added to holistic ideas like "saving heat energy in summer for cold winter days" or "using thermal energy in intelligent walls with special sensors when the sun is shining."

City Climate. The focus group 'city climate' started with a brainstorming session, as their topic was less tangible compared to mobility and energy. All statements were categorized as illustrated in Fig. 4.

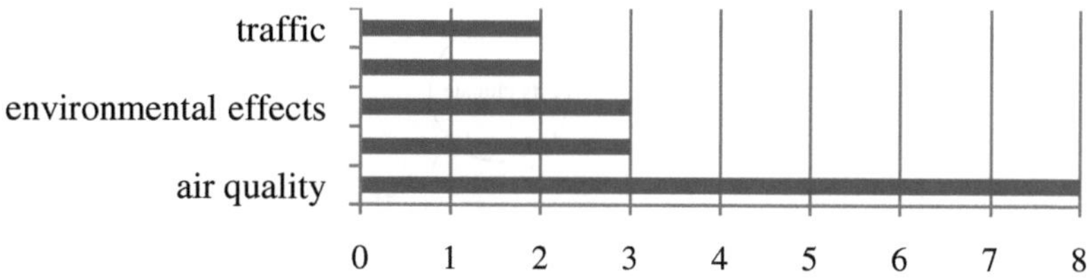

Fig. 4. Number for statements to 'city climate' categories (n=7)

The biggest concerns regarding city climate were related to air quality. The smell in rural areas was considered pleasant compared to urban areas. The stagnant air in cities makes breathing uncomfortable. There was overall agreement that future cities needed more air circulation. The group's innovative ideas for the future city from an ecological point of view can be divided into six categories.

Regarding the city *buildings*, all students agreed that their silhouette and arrangement should impact and support wind flow within the city. Industrial parks should be situated in suburban areas. Another key issue was integrating *water* into the city center. Cities located at lakes or rivers were regarded as far more attractive. Towns without natural connection to water should construct artificial canals throughout the city, leading to a central lake. *Parks* and green spaces inside the city are equally important as water. In fact, parks and water should be connected across the city. Not only the ground but also facades and rooftops could be planted and therefore positively impact the city climate - the rooftops could also be connected with sky bridges. In order to gain room for water, trees, and green spaces, cars should be banned from the city center. The students also discussed possible *payment* systems. Everyone was willing to pay small entrance fees in order to visit parks and garden rooftops. Also, inner city tolls should be implemented as well as a kind of "green seal" for cities.

The students of the city climate group also discussed how mobility could influence the city climate and wanted a city with *no cars*. To achieve this, strict bans in the city center instead of mere low-emission zones with restricted access should be implemented. The group explicitly put the focus on a car-free city center, not just on a city free of exhaust gases. In addition, the students also thought of alternatives: Deliveries to shops in the city center and all non-passenger traffic should be moved to underground means of transportation.

Further *innovative means of transport*, beside sky bridges and underground systems, are electric ground and aerial passenger tramways. The main routes should become bicycle highways with footbridges instead of traffic lights.

Thematic Linkage within the Focus Groups. The statements of all focus groups were also examined for their interdependent arguments (see Fig. 5). Most thematic intersections came up in the city climate group, particularly regarding mobility topics. However, no statements in the energy group could be linked to the city climate group. The city climate as well as the mobility group proclaimed a reduction of cars in future cities. All groups imagined a transition to electric cars.

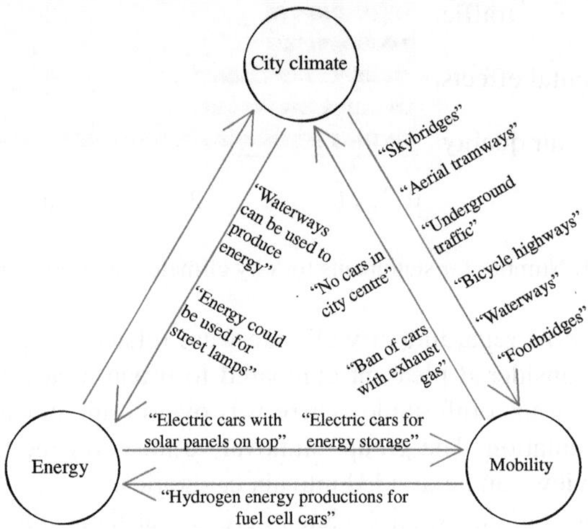

Fig. 5. Thematic linkage between mobility, energy, and city climate groups (n=21)

4 Discussion

The objective of this exploratory study was to understand the cognitive models and insights of teenagers and young adults into the dramatic changes for urban environments, which are related to energy supply, mobility requirements, and city climate. It is necessary that public information and communication seek to specifically support awareness for societal needs in combination with an environmentally friendly attitude of citizens. However, mobility, energy supply, and the diverse needs of citizens for adaptive mobility are highly complex and partly controversial. Individual needs for an adaptive and low-price mobility supply might be at the expense of a green attitude and environmentally saving behavior. Thus, individual motives and wishes might contradict societal needs, and the consequences of both are on completely different time scales. For communities and their citizens, however, it is important not only to understand the different perspectives – energy supply, mobility demands and user diversity –, but also to be aware of different norms and ethics in context of livable urban cities of the future. As found in our study, young adults and students are basically aware of the demands of modern urban environments. They stressed their wish to live in green and wealthy cities and they seem to have also a basic understanding of the shortening of fossil energy and the need to find other energy solutions that also save the environment. The wishes for green cities are consistent with prior research.

Better city climate, parks, and green spaces have a significant effect on the happiness of inhabitants [9]. All groups discussed the costs for future city improvements. While the students were not willing to pay any energy transition, they still could imagine paying entrance fees for parks. This seems counter-intuitive at first sight and raises some questions about their relation to money and income.

The quantitative results revealed no significant influence of ATT on environmental attitudes towards mobility, energy, or city climate. There was also no significant correlation between ATT and gender although this was found in latest research [8]. The overall ATT within the technology prone pupils was very high and two-thirds of the rather small sample was male so these results need validation in further research.

However, it was still striking how low the information level was as well as the ability to discuss on a more complex level. Most of their arguments were highly connected to their individual needs and they seemed unable to take a different perspective or a morality out of their individual scope [10]. Results show that a detailed information and education in dealing with complex issues is an urgent need for this age group. Especially in topical and societally relevant issues (such as the development of cities and urban environments) this seems a mandatory demand of current education policy.

5 Limitations and Future Research Duties

Finally, some limitations have to be addressed. One is the comparatively small sample size which is due to the chosen research method (focus groups). Furthermore, it could be interesting to compare different cultural views. Although the students did have different ethnic backgrounds, we did not compare the results for those groups, because the samples would have been too small. As we already have contact to several school classes in different countries, both constraints hopefully will be improved in future research.

Other limitations refer to the methodology. Answering the questionnaire before the focus group on the one hand successfully introduced participants to the topic. On the other hand, the participants might have been biased and limited in their creativity afterwards, because they might have thought that it was expected they cover the topics from the questionnaire. This trade-off will be discussed and the chronology of tasks could differ for the next focus groups. Regarding the creative process within the focus groups, the given time seemed to be insufficient. A duration of 2 hours was adequate regarding patience and concentration. As we had the impression that the students needed at least 1.5 hours to get into the topic and had just reached the discussion about innovative future solutions for sustainable cities, it could be promising to organize a continuing second meeting. In addition, as a possible reason for the presented outcomes, group dynamic processes should also be considered. Individual behavior is influenced by the presence of others [11], most likely during the teamwork in the presented focus groups. Although the questionnaire had been pretested, it became clear from the results and the questions of the students during the workshop that some items had been misunderstood. Special attention should be paid to the wording of the questionnaire for future research with groups of pupils from mixed ethnic backgrounds.

Another possible influence factor was the moderation of the focus groups. First, it is possible that speaking to an expert in the field was intimidating for the pupils and therefore they were inhibited in their creativity. Second, although all moderators received a briefing on focus group moderation, it has to be taken into account that the experts normally do not work with this method in their discipline. It is thus plausible that the influence of the experts was greater than when trained discussion leaders work with focus groups. However, this also provided the opportunity for interdisciplinary insights into the methods of other disciplines, which can be valuable for future interdisciplinary work.

Acknowledgements. Authors thank participants for their time and patience to volunteer in this study. Thanks also to Clara Erner, Chantal Lidynia, and all UFO research assistants for their support. This work was funded by the Excellence initiative of German states and federal government (Project Urban Future Outline, UFO).

References

1. Himmel, S., Ziefle, M., Arning, K.: From Living Space to Urban Quarter: Acceptance of ICT Monitoring Solutions in an Ageing Society. In: Kurosu, M. (ed.) HCII/HCI 2013, Part III. LNCS, vol. 8006, pp. 49–58. Springer, Heidelberg (2013)
2. Arkesteijn, K., Oerlemans, L.: The early adoption of green power by Dutch households. Energy Policy 33, 183–196 (2005)
3. Moula, E., Munjur, M., Maula, J., Hamdy, M., Fang, T., Jung, N., Lahdelma, R.: Researching social acceptability of renewable energy technologies in Finland. Int. J. Sustain. Built Environ (2013)
4. Cain, A.: Teenage Mobility in the United States: Issues and Opportunities for Promoting Public Transit. Transp. Res. Rec. J. Transp. Res. Board 1971, 140–148 (2006)
5. Ardies, J., Maeyer, S.D., Gijbels, D.: Reconstructing the Pupils Attitude Towards Technology-survey. Des. Technol. Educ. Int. J. 18 (2013)
6. Staat & Gesellschaft - educational background - Bildungsstand - Statistisches Bundesamt, Destatis (2013), `https://www.destatis.de/DE/ZahlenFakten/GesellschaftStaat/BildungForschungKultur/Bildungsstand/Tabellen/Bildungsabschluss.html`
7. Mayring, P.: Combination and integration of qualitative and quantitative analysis. Forum Qualitative Sozialforschung/Forum: Qualitative Social Research (2001)
8. Zaunbrecher, B.S., Kowalewski, S., Ziefle, M.: The Willingness to Adopt Technologies: A Cross-sectional Study on the Influence of Technical Self-efficacy on Acceptance (2014)
9. Chiesura, A.: The role of urban parks for the sustainable city. Landsc. Urban Plan. 68, 129–138 (2004)
10. Kohlberg, L.: Development of moral character and moral ideology. Rev. Child Dev. Res. 1, 381–431 (1964)
11. Crano, W.D.: Milestones in the psychological analysis of social influence. Group Dyn. Theory Res. Pract. 4, 68 (2000)

Evidence-Based Error Analysis: Supporting the Design of Error-Tolerant Systems*

Becky L. Hooey[1], Marco Aurisicchio[2], Robert Bracewell[3], and David C. Foyle[4]

[1] San Jose State University at NASA Ames Research Center, Moffett Field, California
becky.l.hooey@nasa.gov
[2] Department of Mechanical Engineering, Imperial College London
m.aurisicchio@imperial.ac.uk
[3] Rolls-Royce, United Kingdom
rob.bracewell@gmail.com
[4] NASA Ames Research Center, Moffett Field, California
david.c.foyle@nasa.gov

Abstract. This paper proposes an evidence-based process and engineering design tool for linking human error identification taxonomies, and human error prevention and mitigation design principles with the system engineering design process. The process synthesizes the design evidence generated and used during the design and analysis process to clearly demonstrate that credible error threats have been identified and considered appropriately in the design of the system. In doing so, it supports the designer in managing design solutions across the entire design process, leaves a design trace that is transparent and auditable by other designers, managers, or certification experts, and manages the complex interactions among other systems and sub-systems.

Keywords: error-tolerant design, human error, design rationale, designVUE.

1 Introduction

Error-tolerant systems are systems that are robust to human error, in that they guard against errors occurring whenever possible, and support efficient detection and recovery of errors when they do occur [1, 2]. The need for error-tolerant systems has long been recognized and applies to safety-critical systems such as in the aviation, space, medical, and nuclear domains, as well as to the design of 'everyday things' such as automated teller machines, consumer electronics, and home appliances [3].

1.1 Requirements for Error-Tolerant Design of Flight Deck Avionics

In 2013, The United States Federal Aviation Administration (FAA) adopted a new regulation (14 CFR 25.1302) that amends design requirements in the airworthiness standards for transport category airplanes to minimize the occurrence of design-related

M. Kurosu (Ed.): Human-Computer Interaction, Part III, HCII 2014, LNCS 8512, pp. 401–412, 2014.

flightcrew errors and to better enable a flightcrew member to detect and manage errors when errors do occur [4]. In harmony with existing European Aviation Safety Agency (EASA) regulations [5], this regulation recognizes that since flightcrew errors will occur, even with a well-trained and proficient flightcrew operating well-designed systems, system and equipment design must support management of those errors to avoid safety consequences. To the extent practicable, installed equipment must incorporate means to enable the flightcrew to manage errors resulting from flightcrew interactions with the equipment that can be reasonably expected to occur in service. The FAA Advisory Circular (AC 25.1302-1) specifies that certification will likely require multiple forms of compliance (including Statement of Similarity, Design Description, Calculation/Analysis, Evaluations, and Test) and calls for means of compliance that are methodical and complementary to, and separate and distinct from, airplane system analysis methods such as system safety assessments [4].

1.2 The Challenge of Designing Error-Tolerant Systems

Demonstrating error-tolerance of any system poses challenges for designers. Given that errors will occur, even with well-trained operators and well-designed equipment, demonstrating error-free performance in simulation or operational tests is an unreasonable goal. However, if attained, it simply shows that the specific confluence of variables tested did not combine to create an error during the observation period. Even more challenging, is demonstrating adequate design solutions that support error detection and consequence mitigation. This requires a systematic approach to comprehensively identify all potential errors and link them to related design strategies. This quickly becomes intractable when integrated across the entire design lifecycle of a complex system. Not only is it difficult for designers to ensure they have systematically and comprehensively addressed all potential for human error, it is even more difficult to demonstrate the error tolerance of the systems to outside observers.

Evidence-based safety arguments, such as Safety Cases or Assurance Cases have been gaining support as a method to demonstrate that all critical hazards have been eliminated or adequately mitigated in safety-critical systems [6]. A Safety Case is a comprehensive safety argument that communicates how evidence generated from testing, analyses, and review, collectively satisfies claims concerning safety [7]. It aims to make the rationale connecting the design process to the hazard analyses explicit [6], thus *enabling* reviewers and project engineers to understand why a mitigation is effective, see the supporting evidence, and have more confidence in the behavior of the system during operations [8].

1.3 Objective

While Safety Cases aim to identify all potential hazards, their focus tends to be on hazards related to software and hardware, and less so on human error. This paper proposes an evidence-based approach for linking human error identification taxonomies, and human error prevention and reduction design principles with the systems engineering design process. The approach synthesizes design evidence to ensure that credible error threats have been identified and considered appropriately in the design of the system. In doing so, it aims to support the designer in managing design solutions across the entire design process, and manages the complex interactions among other systems and sub-systems, while leaving a design trace that is transparent and auditable by other designers, managers, or certification experts.

2 Evidence-Based Approach for Error-Tolerant Design

The proposed evidence-based approach (see Figure 1) links Human Error Identification analyses and Human Error Mitigation techniques with design evidence (the design decisions and rationale generated during the design process) using an established engineering design knowledge capture tool known as designVUE [9, 10].

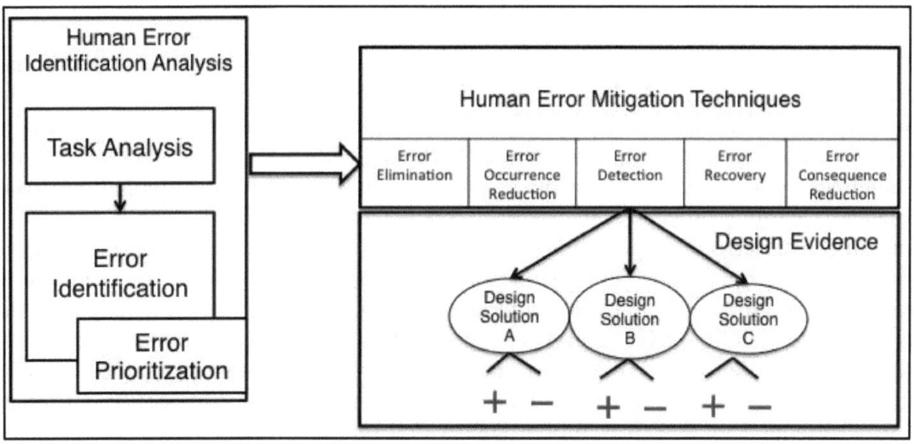

Fig. 1. Evidence-based approach for error-tolerant design

It supports the traceability of evidence-based rationale related to error identification, error prioritization, and error mitigation through design. The three components of this evidence-based approach shown in Figure 1 are described individually in sections 2.1, 2.2, and 2.3. The integration of the three is described using a case study of the design of a flight deck Data Communication (DataComm) system (Section 3.0).

2.1 Human Error Identification Analysis

Many human error identification taxonomies are available in the literature including: Systematic Human Error Reduction and Prediction Approach (SHERPA) [11], Human Error Hazard and Operability Study (HAZOP) [12], Human Error In Systems Tools (HEIST) [13] and Human Error Template (HET) [14]. See also [15] for description and examples of these and other human error identification taxonomies. The structure and dimension of the actual error taxonomy adopted depends on the system being developed as well as on the aim of the analysis [16].

In this case study, we adopted the Human Error Template (HET), as it was designed specifically for application on the aircraft flight deck. HET is a checklist that includes 12 potential error modes that were selected based on a study of actual pilot error incidence and existing error modes in contemporary human error identification methods. The HET is applied to each bottom-level task step in a hierarchical task analysis. The analyst indicates which of the HET error modes are credible (if any) for each task step. For each credible error, the analyst provides a description of the form that the error would take. The analyst then determines the outcome or consequence associated with the error. Finally, the analyst estimates the likelihood of the error (Low, Medium, High) and the criticality of the error (Low, Medium, High). If the error is given a high rating for both likelihood and criticality, the aspect of the system involved in the task step is then rated as a 'fail'.

2.2 Human Error Mitigation Techniques

The choice of suitable human error mitigation techniques depends on the system and domain under study. A large emphasis in the literature has focused on the development of design guidelines. Examples of guidelines include design strategies such as forcing functions including interlocks, lockins, and lockouts [3] and guidelines for coping with human errors through system design, including errors related to learning processes, interference among control structures, lack of resources, and stochastic errors [16]. Design techniques to avoid human error consequences in nuclear plant operations and maintenance are provided by [17]. In addition to providing guiding principles for addressing human errors (e.g., make goals and system state visible, provide a good conceptual model, make the acceptable regions of operation visible, etc.), they also provide error management strategies for the following: 1) Eliminate error occurrence; 2) Reduce error occurrence; 3) Eliminate error consequences, which is further subdivided into error detection, error recovery, and consequence prevention; and, 4) Reduce error consequence. This human error mitigation taxonomy is adapted as shown in Figure 1 and Section 3.0.

2.3 Design Evidence

Evidence-based design rationale is a representation of the reasoning behind the design of an artifact [18]. Design rationale, includes the reasons behind a design decision, the justification for it, the other alternatives considered, the tradeoffs evaluated, and the argumentation that led to the decision [19]. Sources of evidence-based rationale may range from anecdotal descriptions – either substantiated or not, to detailed data derived from analyses, experiments, or operational tests [18]. However, this information is rarely captured in a systematic and usable format because there are few tools that adequately facilitate and support the capture of these critical decisions.

One exception is a tool called designVUE [9,10], an Issue Based Information System (IBIS) derivative [20] developed for the purpose of capturing, structuring, and analyzing design decisions as they are proposed throughout the design process. Using the evolution of the IBIS notation shown in Figure 2, designVUE allows one to build directed graphs, where nodes representing issues to be resolved, alternative answers, and arguments in favor (pro) and against (con), are linked by arcs. For each issue and answer, the status can be indicated as an open answer; accepted answer; likely answer; unlikely answer; or rejected answer (see Figure 2).

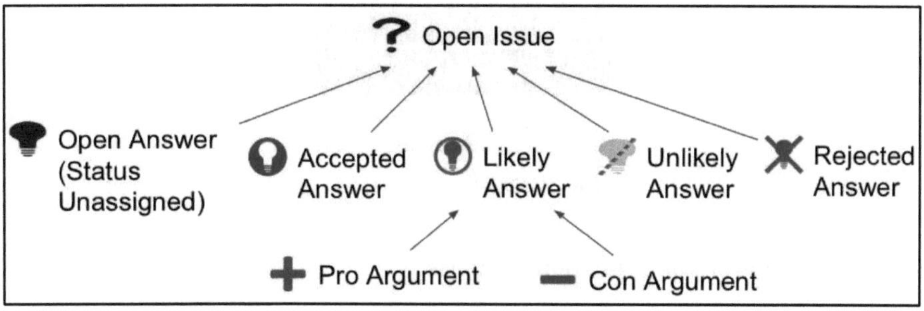

Fig. 2. IBIS notation as instantiated in designVUE

A graph generated in designVUE is captured and saved in a single file and its nodes can be linked to those of graphs in other files through a bi-directional hyperlink called a *wormhole*. In addition, the tool supports a mono-directional hyperlink to web resources as well as to files in local and shared folders. The designVUE tool was inspired by, and builds on, successful application of the Design Rationale editor (DRed) tool used by Rolls-Royce to support the capture of design rationale [21] and integrated information spaces covering product planning, specification, design and service [22].

In the case study that follows, designVUE is applied to the design of error-tolerant systems by linking human error mitigation design solutions to the human error identification analysis. It provides a context-rich digital design book that documents and links the errors that were considered and the decisions adopted to either eliminate or minimize their occurrence or mitigate the consequences.

3 Case Study: Flight Deck Data Communication (DataComm) System for NextGen Surface Operations

A case study was created for the purpose of demonstrating the design of an error-tolerant system – specifically, a flight deck Data Communication (DataComm) system used by pilots to receive and respond to Air Traffic Control taxi clearances (see Figure 3, [23]). DataComm is akin to receiving a text message from Air Traffic Control (ATC). Most simply, a taxi clearance is a single text message that lists the taxiways that the pilot must follow and the destination. For example, in Figure 3, Runway 17R is the assigned departure runway and G5, F, B, K and EG are taxiway identifiers for the assigned taxi route. A taxi clearance may include a requirement to hold short of a specified taxiway (e.g., HOLD SHORT of EL, see Figure 3). Pilots are required to indicate if they 'Will Comply' (WILCO) or if they are 'Unable to Comply' (UNABLE).

Fig. 3. DataComm System

3.1 Human Error Identification Analysis

Consistent with the HET process, the human error identification analysis begins with a hierarchical task analysis to identify the bottom-level tasks for further analysis. The task analysis for receiving and responding to a taxi clearance via DataComm is shown below in Figure 4. The human error identification analysis can be completed on each low-level subtask. In designVUE, each task box can be bi-directionally linked to the subsequent error-analyses. The case study that follows analyzes the low-level task ‘Read DataComm Message’.

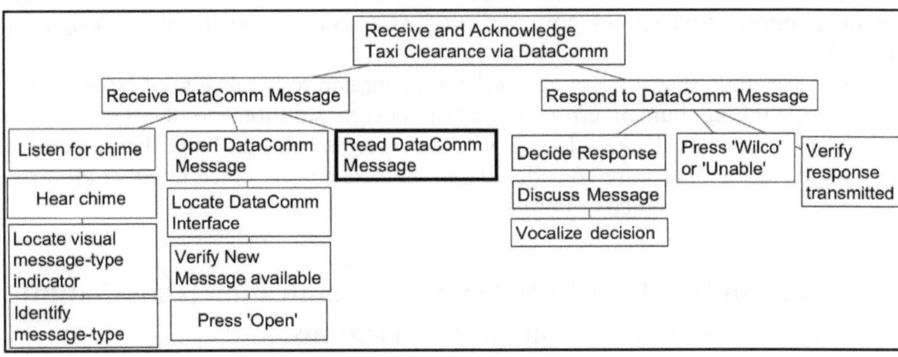

Fig. 4. Hierarchical Task Analysis

To ensure systematic and comprehensive consideration of potential errors, the HET taxonomy was implemented in designVUE as shown in Figure 5. As the starting point for the analysis, the question ‘What errors could occur?’ and the 12 possible HET error categories are provided in open status (neither accepted nor rejected).

Each of the 12 potential error categories were assigned a status to indicate that they are either credible (indicated by a green light bulb icon) or not-credible (indicted by a red light bulb icon with an X), as shown in Figure 6. Each credible error was further broken down into sub-error classifications indicating all potential error manifestations. For example, in Figure 6, the ‘Task Execution Incomplete’ error could

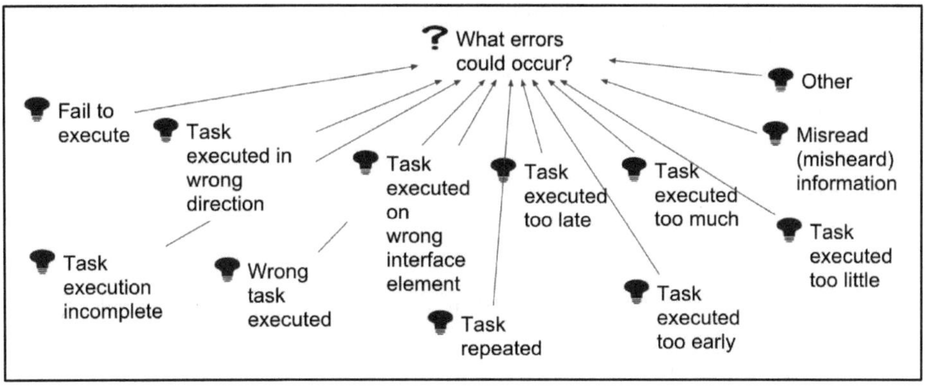

Fig. 5. Human-error Template (HET) taxonomy in designVUE

manifest such that the pilot may begin to read the taxi clearance, but not complete the entire message and miss the hold instruction. This offers the first level of traceability allowing an outside auditor to independently assess the validity of the errors selected for further design consideration.

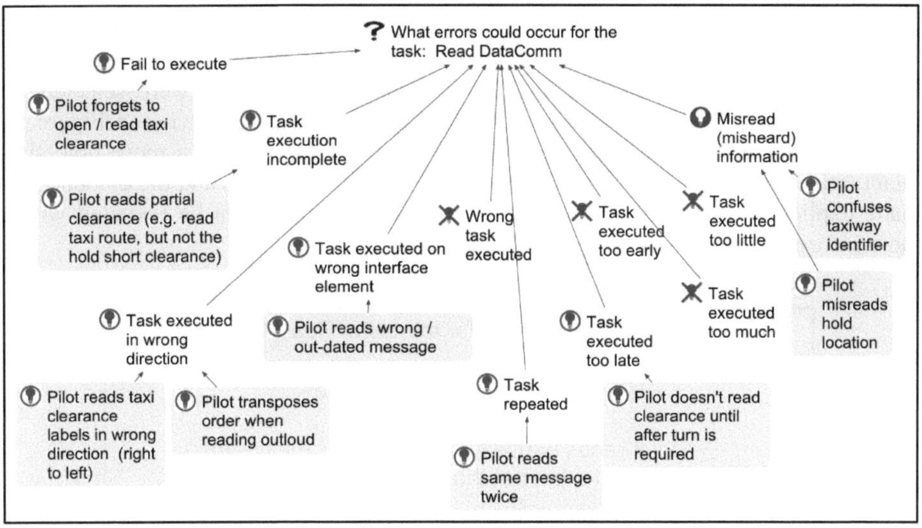

Fig. 6. Human-Error Identification for 'Read DataComm' Task

Evidence that supports the credibility of each error category can also be provided. Figure 7 shows just one branch of the Human Error Identification analysis. The error type Task Execution Incomplete is expanded to depict five arguments that justify its classification as a credible error. In this example, evidence took the form of observations of events that lead the pilots to err by reading only part of the taxi clearance during a pilot-in-the-loop simulation. Evidence for rejecting non-credible errors can also be provided to document why an error was not selected for further analysis (not shown).

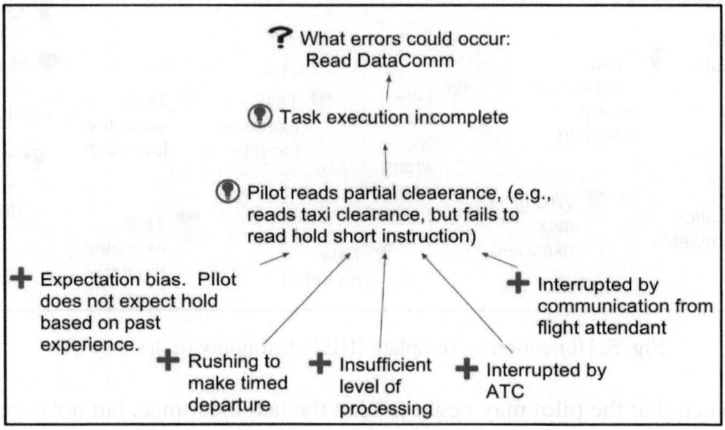

Fig. 7. Evidence to Support Error Credibility

3.2 Error Prioritization

The credible error threats were then each rated by Subject Matter Experts (SMEs) for likelihood (low, medium, high) and criticality of consequences (low, medium, high). Using the HET criteria, those that scored ‘high’ on both scales were selected for further analyses. Evidence to support the ratings was also captured (see Figure 8). Evidence may be a subjective assessment by domain experts, or a more objective, quantitative analysis of error likelihood. Because both the ratings and the evidence are made explicit in this transparent design process, the ratings can be revisited with a more informed perspective as the design proceeds.

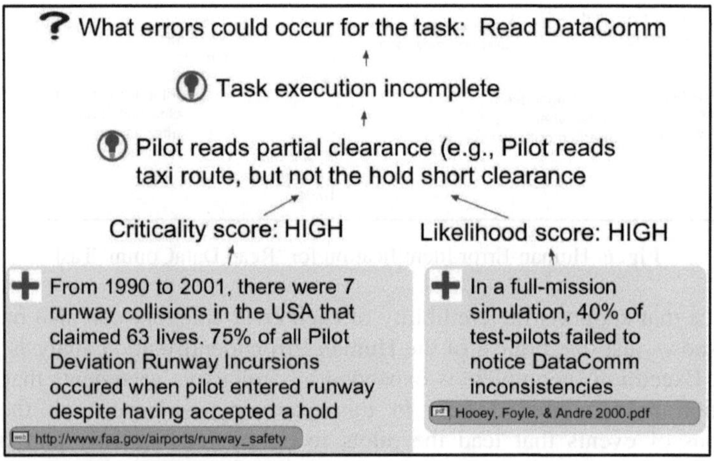

Fig. 8. Criticality and Likelihood Scores with Evidence

3.3 Design Evidence

Each prioritized error was then linked to design evidence that documents how the designers took steps to prevent or mitigate the error. A taxonomy of error prevention and mitigation adapted from [17] was implemented that includes design techniques to: 1) eliminate error; 2) reduce occurrence of the error; 3) aid error detection; 4) aid error recovery; and, 5) minimize error consequences. While designers can replace this with their own taxonomy, the use of a taxonomy serves to ensure systematic consideration of all error prevention and mitigation strategies. Typically, more than one error solution may be required. This process is demonstrated by showing the design trace for how designers incorporated features to reduce the occurrence of, and aid detection of, the 'Incomplete Task Execution' error in which the taxi clearance is read, but the hold short instruction is missed.

Error Reduction Design Evidence. Figure 9 depicts the design considerations associated with reducing the occurrence of the Task Execution Incomplete error. Four design solutions were considered to maximize the salience of the hold short taxi instruction: AllCaps, Reverse Video, Color-coding, and Blinking/Flashing. During design delibrations, 'pro' and 'con' arguments were provided to either support or refute each design solution in the form of data from simulations and tests, industry or government standards, design guidelines, or argumentation from design team members or domain experts. Hyperlinks were made to further tie the rationale statement to simulation reports or other documents spreadsheets and web URLs.

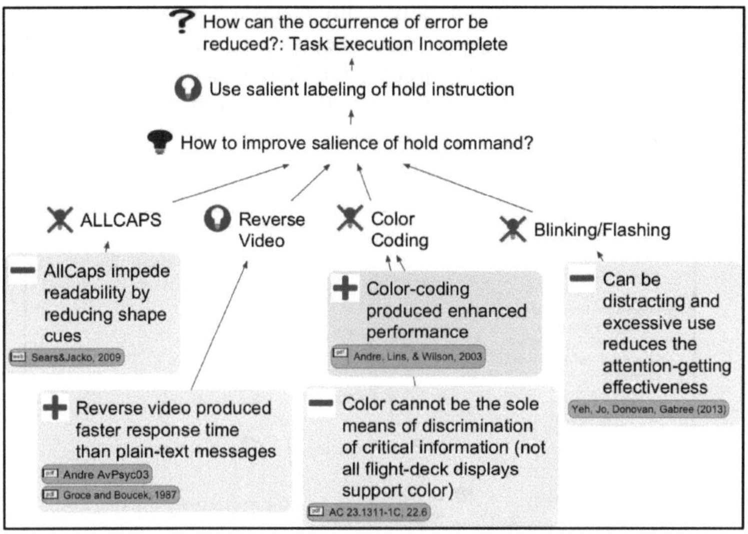

Fig. 9. Error Reduction Design Evidence

As shown in Figure 9, the use of reverse video to increase salience of the hold command was selected and supported by empirical data that showed that reverse video produced faster response time than plain, unformatted, text. A hyperlink to the document containing the simulation data is embedded. The other solutions were each refuted with evidence from empirical evaluations or flight deck design guidelines. 'Color-coding' was rejected because despite showing enhanced performance, it was noted that not all aircraft are equipped with DataComm equipage that supports the use of color embedded in DataComm text. Should this hardware constraint be removed in the future, the design solution can be reconsidered without recreating the original rationale.

Error Detection Design Evidence. Figure 10 presents the design evidence associated with aiding the detection of the error: Task Execution Incomplete. That is, if the pilot did fail to read the hold short command in the DataComm message, what features can be implemented to support the pilots' ability to detect the error before they reached their hold location? Two categories of design solutions were considered: Information Redundancy and Procedures.

The design solution, 'Information Redundancy" refers to the designers' recommendation that the hold short information embedded in the text DataComm message should also be presented redundantly, and in a graphical form, on the pilots Navigation Display. In designVUE, a graphical prototype of the design concept and hyperlinks to two empirical study reports that have tested a similar concept are embedded. This demonstrates how designVUE enables linkages across systems and sub-systems enabling information traceability. This error-mitigating design solution involves a different piece of flight deck equipment. Linking the design requirement of one to the design solution of the other reduces the risk that the graphical hold feature may be omitted from the Navigation Display leaving the DataComm system vulnerable to error. Assume, for example, that following the proposal to introduce the flight deck Navigation Display a new team is tasked to develop it. If this team captures and deliberates the system requirements in another designVUE file, the root of the requirement graph can be bi-directionally hyperlinked to the answer node in the file in Figure 10 where the solution was initially conceived. Should the team decide to capture the requirements in a spreadsheet or text document these can still be hyperlinked to the answer node in Figure 10.

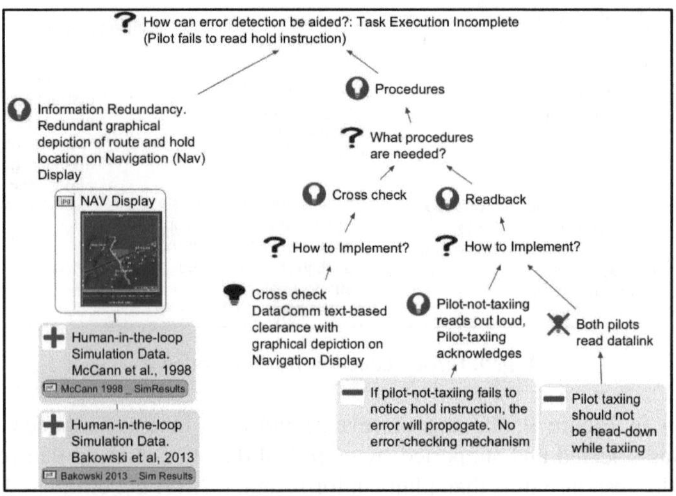

Fig. 10. Error Detection Design Evidence

Also of note is the ability to document procedural solutions (see Figure 10, right branch). Managing human error in complex systems, such as avionics, is a multi-faceted problem that includes not only physical design of multiple interacting systems, but also operations, procedures, training, and maintenance. Some [e.g., 24] have advocated for tight integration between physical design and the design of operational procedures to guard against unanticipated interactions between the procedures and the system (e.g., when the system enables tasks that are unauthorized by procedures; when information supplied by the device does not agree with information provided through procedures; or when a system is designed assuming a set of procedures, which are later changed, or vice versa). The assumptions made about procedures by the design team can be archived here, and are available for review as procedures and operations are developed and iterated in parallel with equipment design.

4 Discussion

In this paper, a process for systematically addressing and managing error in the design of complex systems was proposed. The process linked human error identification analyses and human error mitigation strategies to the system engineering design process. It supported design rationale capture for each decision using a semi-formal modeling technique. In doing so, the treatment of human error is inserted into the design process, in a manner that enables transparency, and supports integration across sub-systems, operations, and procedures. The result is a visual design logbook that synthesizes the design evidence generated and used during the design and analysis process to clearly demonstrate that credible error threats have been identified and considered appropriately in the design of the system.

Acknowledgments. This research was funded by the National Aeronautics and Space Administration (NASA) Aviation Safety Program, (System-wide Safety Assurance: Human Systems Solutions) and the United Kingdom Engineering and Physical Sciences Research Council (EPSRC) through the Pathways to Impact funding scheme.

References

1. Rasmussen, J.: Skills, Rules, and Knowledge: Signals, Signs and Symbols and Other Distinctions in Human Performance Models. IEEE Transactions: SMC-13, 257–267 (1983)
2. Rouse, W.B., Rouse, S.H.: Analysis and Classification of Human Error. IEEE Transactions: SMC-13, 539–549 (1983)
3. Norman, D.: The Design of Everyday Things. Basic Books, New York (2002)
4. United States Federal Aviation Administration, http://www.faa.gov/documentLibrary/media/Advisory_Circular/AC_25.1302-1.pdf
5. European Aviation Safety Agency, http://www.easa.europa.eu/agency-measures/docs/certification-specifications/CS-25/CS-25%20Amdt%2012.pdf

6. Denney, E., Pai, G.: A Lightweight Methodology for Safety Case Assembly. In: Ortmeier, F., Lipaczewski, M. (eds.) SAFECOMP 2012. LNCS, vol. 7612, pp. 1–12. Springer, Heidelberg (2012)
7. Denney, E.W., Pai, G.J., Habli, I.: Perspectives on Software Safety Case Development for Unmanned Aircraft. In: 42nd Annual IEEE/IFIP International Conference on Dependable Systems and Networks (DSN) (June 2012)
8. Goodenough, J.B., Barry, M.R.: Evaluating Hazard Mitigations with Dependability Cases. White Paper (April 2009), `http://www.sei.cmu.edu/library/abstracts/whitepapers/dependabilitycase_hazardmitigation.cfm/`
9. Baroni, P., Romano, M., Toni, F., Aurisicchio, M., Bertanza, G.: An Argumentation-based Approach for Automatic Evaluation of Design Debates. In: Leite, J., Son, T.C., Torroni, P., van der Torre, L., Woltran, S. (eds.) CLIMA XIV 2013. LNCS, vol. 8143, pp. 340–356. Springer, Heidelberg (2013)
10. designVUE, `http://www3.imperial.ac.uk/designengineering/tools/designvue/`
11. Rasmussen, J., Vicente, K.J.: Coping with Human Errors through System Design: Implications for Ecological Interface Design. Int. J. Man-Mach. Stud. 31, 517–534 (1989)
12. Embrey, D.E.: SHERPA: A Systematic Human Error Reduction and Prediction Approach. In: International Meeting on Advances in Nuclear Power Systems, Knoxville, Tennessee (1986)
13. Neogy, P., Hanson, A.L., Davis, P.R., Fenstermacher, T.E.: Hazard and Barrier Analysis Guidance Document. Department of Energy, Office of Operating Experience Analysis and Feedback, Report No. EH-33 (1996)
14. Reinach, S., Viale, A., Green, D.: Human Error Investigation Software Tool (HEIST). Final Report (2007)
15. Marshall, A., Stanton, N., Young, M., Salmon, P., Harris, D., Demagalski, J., Waldmann, T., Dekker, S.: Development of the Human Error Template – A New Methodology for Assessing Design Induced Errors on Aircraft Flight Decks. Final Report (2003)
16. Salmon, P., Stanton, N.A., Walker, G.: Human Factors Design Methods Review (2003). HFIDTC/WP1.3.2/1 v 1 (2003)
17. Chen-Wing, S.L.N., Davey, E.C.: Designing to Avoid Human Error Consequences. In: Second Workshop on Human Error, Safety, and System Development, Seattle (1998)
18. Buckingham Shum, S., Hammond, N.: Argumentation-based Design Rationale: What Use at What Cost? Int. J. Hum-Comput. St. 40(4), 603–652 (1994)
19. Lee, J.: Design Rationale Systems: Understanding the Issues. IEEE Expert 12(3), 78–85 (1997)
20. Kunz, W., Rittel, H.: Issues as Elements of Information Systems, Working Paper 131, Inst. Urban and Regional Dept., Univ. Calif. at Berkeley (1970)
21. Bracewell, R.H., Wallace, K., Moss, M., Knott, D.: Capturing Design Rationale. Computer Aided Design 41(3), 173–186 (2009)
22. Aurisicchio, M., Bracewell, R.H.: Capturing an Integrated Design Information Space with a Diagram Based Approach. J. Eng. Design 24(6), 397–428 (2013)
23. Bakowski, D.L., Hooey, B.L., Foyle, D.C., Wolter, C.A., Cheng, L.W.S.: NextGen Flight Deck Surface Trajectory-based Operations (STBO): Contingency Holds. In: 32nd Digit Avion Syst. Con., Syracuse (2013)
24. Pritchett, A.: Simultaneous Design of Cockpit Display of Traffic Information and Air Traffic Management Procedures. In: 17th Digit Avion Syst. Con., pp. 36/1–36/9. AIAA (1998)

Authority and Level of Automation

Lessons to Be Learned in Design of In-vehicle Assistance Systems

Anders Jansson[1], Patrik Stensson[2,3], Ida Bodin[1], Anton Axelsson[1], and Simon Tschirner[1]

[1] Department of Information Technology, Uppsala University, Uppsala, Sweden
{anders.jansson,ida.bodin,anton.axelsson, simon.tschirner}@it.uu.se
[2] Department of Informatics and Media, Uppsala University, Uppsala, Sweden
[3] Swedish Defence College, Department of Military Technology, Stockholm, Sweden
patrik.stensson@im.uu.se

Abstract. Motor vehicles and drivers' relationship with them will change significantly in the next decades. Still, most driving tasks are likely to involve humans behind the wheel, emphasizing the design of in-vehicle assistance systems. A framework for distribution of control between human beings and technology is presented, as well as a model to be used in analysis, design, development, and deployment of decision support systems. The framework and the model are applied in a project aiming for design of in-vehicle systems for future long-haul vehicles. The empirical investigations conducted support the design-as-hypotheses approach. The search for improvements of design concepts and levels of automation leads to a shift away from abstract ideas of autonomous cars to empirical issues such as how to support the driver. The need to discuss authority in relation to levels of automation is recognized, emphasizing the fact that human-machine interaction takes place on two distinct levels.

Keywords: Automation, Autonomy, Authority, Decision-making.

1 Introduction

The US National Highway Traffic Safety Administration anticipates that motor vehicles and drivers' relationship with them are likely to change dramatically in a near future [1]. Advances in automotive technology and vehicle innovations, such as self-driving cars, have the potential to improve highway safety and efficiency, mobility, and economic growth. Still, most driving tasks are likely to involve humans behind the wheel, emphasizing the design of in-vehicle assistance systems and the issue of cooperation between the human agent and the automation. In managing this threshold of significant changes in capabilities and expectations, we propose that there are lessons to be learned from application domains where automation has been around for a while, such as in aviation [2], high-speed ferries [3], and train traffic control [4].

As the first contribution of this paper we present a framework for distribution of control between humans and technology, called the Human-Machine Discrimination

M. Kurosu (Ed.): Human-Computer Interaction, Part III, HCII 2014, LNCS 8512, pp. 413–424, 2014.

(HMD) framework. A fundamental premise is emphasized: human beings and machines are categorically different [5]. This has two important implications for design of automated systems. First, technology cannot be introduced as a simple substitution of machines for people [6]. On the contrary, designers need to: (1) recognize that *design concepts represent hypotheses* or beliefs about the relationship between technology and cognition/collaboration; (2) subject these beliefs to empirical jeopardy by a *search for disconfirming and confirming evidence*; and (3) recognize that these beliefs about what would be useful are *tentative and open to revision* as we learn more about the mutual shaping that goes on between artefacts and actors in a field of practice [7, italics added]. Second, in order to fully capture and understand issues of authority, human-computer interaction research must recognize that communication between humans and machines does in fact manifest itself on two different levels.

Assuming design concepts as hypotheses, one important step is to present an approach to how this translates into practical research. Therefore, as the second contribution of this paper, we suggest the GMOC model (acronym for Goal, Model, Observability, and Controllability) that supports the division of roles between humans and machines by allocating properties between humans and automation as, for example, decision support systems. GMOC is based on Dynamic Decision Making, (DDM; e.g. [8]) an approach to human decision-making based on the premise that the very object of decision making can be regarded as that of control. With GMOC as a model for design, development, and deployment of systems, we operationalize the idea of design concepts as hypotheses by the general problem formulation:

> How can drivers' mental model development and goal formulation processes be supported by enhanced observability and augmented control functions?

We end the paper with a description of how the HMD-framework and the GMOC-model are applied in an ongoing project. MODAS (Methods for Designing Autonomous Systems; [9]) is a project that is concerned with the design of the driver environment for future long-haul vehicles. It incorporates a range of automated driving technologies assumed to be part of the driver environment in the future, including new and different forms of information displays, higher levels of automation, and forms of communication that are qualitatively different from what current systems offer. We describe how the scope of the project has changed so far as a consequence of the understanding and incorporation of the GMOC-model.

2 Autonomy/Heteronomy Distinction

As many other projects with connection to high-level automation systems, MODAS is one example of how the term *autonomous* is used to describe sub-systems with the ability to act independently. But this is not the only definition of autonomy. The concept of autonomy can mean very different things and have been found to be used in three very different ways in the literature today: (1) as a negative byproduct of automation; (2) as a desirable attribute in high-tech industry; and (3) as a differentiation in human thought and action. These different interpretations are a cause for confusion because, when a concept has multiple definitions, expectations can be maladaptive.

2.1 Autonomy as a Problematic Attribute

In the literature on automation, autonomy is described as something very problematic. The clearest example of this is Billings who brought up autonomy as one of the automation attributes that have been found in aviation mishaps [2]. According to Billings, the four most central attributes in flight accidents are: (1) complexity; (2) coupling; (3) autonomy; and (4) inadequate feedback. Autonomy was at least one of the common factors that caused the mishaps in the following accidents: A320 accident at Mulhouse-Habsheim; A300 accident at Nagoya; A320 accident at Bangalore; A310 approach at Orly; and, B737 wind shear at Charlotte. Billings continues with a definition of autonomy in [2]:

> Autonomy is a characteristic of advanced automation; the term describes real or apparent self-initiated machine behavior. When autonomous behavior is unexpected by a human monitor, it is often perceived as animate; the automation appears to have a mind of its own. The human must decide, sometimes rather quickly, whether the observed behavior is appropriate or inappropriate. This decision can be difficult, in part because of the coupling just mentioned and in part because the automation may not provide adequate feedback about its activities.

This definition is not exclusive to the work of Billings. Sarter and Woods reasoned along the same lines in [10]. Sandblad et al. and Golightly et al. use the term autonomy similar to Billings [4], [11]. They speak of autonomous algorithms in train traffic control as something very problematic. They describe how different forms of automation surprise the operators in the train traffic control centers and that the immediate effect is that the automation has to be turned off. Sandblad et al. strongly recommend not using autonomous automation [4]; they even use the term non-autonomous automation to describe their approach [11]. Another example is Balfe et al., who have labeled the "turn-it-off-syndrome", that is, the fact that automation has to be turned-off when it does not meet the requirements from the train dispatchers in specific situations [12]. They too take a clear stance when it comes to autonomous systems: they do not use the term at all, presumably because they are aware of the fact that the concept has transformed.

2.2 Autonomy as a Desirable Attribute

In the high-tech industry, the term autonomy is used for high-tech systems, particularly in the military industry. Stensson and Jansson, in their review of the literature [5], found that this view is ubiquitous, manifested by numerous organizations, research projects, and phrasings that contain the word autonomous in conjunction with technology and systems. In fact, "autonomous systems" is currently being used for systems, artefacts, and vehicles for which a high level of self-operation obviously is desirable [5]. This approach can be illustrated by a video recorded talk by Mark Campbell [13]. As can be realized from this talk, there is a chain of activities, starting with sensors followed by perception and finally planning, conveying in each step data, information, and decisions. Sensors receive input from the environment, a remote system or human operator, either in the form of signals, signs, or symbols, and deliver this as data to the perception phase. During perception, different forms of recognition and feature detection activities transform the data into pieces of information, which means that the stream of data is no longer a meaningless stream of bits, but pieces of information which means they carry with them templates or structures of meaning. These carry with them a certain amount of interpreted information structures which can be used for planning because they can be brought together in sequences which allow the system to look ahead and plan for the next sequence. The plans result in decisions suggested for implementation.

2.3 Autonomy as a Way of Thinking and Acting

Stensson and Jansson explained why concepts like autonomy and intelligence are used for artefacts even though there is no scientific basis for doing so [5]. They suggested that one way to correct this matter is to remind people of Kant's distinction between autonomy and heteronomy in human reasoning, and reintroduce it to for use in the human factors community. They suggested that this helps to signify the relevance of the division of roles between human beings and artefacts.

Kant referred to autonomy as the ability of human beings to reason as free agents without the influence of authority or inclination [14]. This statement is based on the Categorical Imperative, the basic central philosophical concept of Kant's deontological moral philosophy. Kant himself called this "the principle of autonomy of the will, in contrast with every other which I accordingly reckon as heteronomy" [14]. This view of autonomy is that of someone who is supposedly autonomous. It is about the rights and obligations that come from being an autonomous entity. Heteronomy, on the other hand, infers that thinking is constrained by previous knowledge and authorities, rules, and procedures, or biases and heuristics [15].

2.4 The Human-Machine Discrimination Framework

In a way, systems functioning all the way from sensors receiving signals to planning with decisions ready to implement can be described as something semi-autonomous. But the concept of autonomy is not just a higher order of automation. It is a qualitatively different concept. The following quote from Wood et al. in [16] illustrates very well the conceptual change currently going on:

> This Article generally uses the term "autonomous," instead of the term "automated." We have chosen to use the term "autonomous" because it is the term that is currently in more widespread use (and thus is more familiar to the general public). However, the latter term is arguably more accurate. "Automated" connotes control or operation by a machine, while "autonomous" connotes acting alone or independently. Most of the vehicle concepts (that we are currently aware of) have a person in the driver's seat, utilize a communication connection to the cloud or other vehicles, and do not independently select either destinations or routes for reaching them. Thus, the term "automated" would more accurately describe these vehicle concepts.

We agree with the final sentence in the quote above, but see no reason to accept the term autonomous for artefacts. It is an example of "lack of scientifically-based philosophy of automation" as the Air Transport Association of America wrote in their report [17]. Billings' work is the result of that call [2]. The reason for this is the following: All kinds of automation and all kinds of automatic devices can be described from a bottom-up perspective. They are built in pieces and can be broken down into the same pieces. This makes it possible to speak about different levels of automation and different levels of automaticity. Autonomy, on the other hand, is a top-down concept. It is a holistic concept, which in principle is impossible to reduce into pieces, as more or less autonomous, or a high or low level of autonomy. You are either an autonomous individual or not [5]. Kavathatzopoulos described, analogously with intelligence and the Turing-test, that if we would like to know if something is purely autonomous or not, we would expect it to be able to choose for itself whether to be autonomous or heteronomous, because this is an act we can expect from an autonomous system [18]. In a distant future, would we like a truly autonomous car to pick up our neighbor instead of ourselves?

One consequence of the fundamental premise that human beings and machines are categorically different is the fact that the interaction between these two cognitive systems manifests itself on two different levels. This fact is not explicitly recognized in human-computer interaction research to the degree we believe it deserves. Mishaps in terms of automation surprises should be evaluated differently from errors caused by non-intuitive design solutions. Figure 1 below illustrates the fundamental premise and the two levels of interaction.

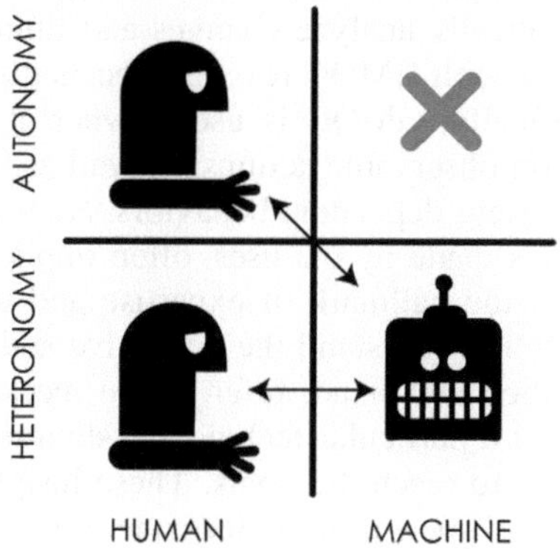

Fig. 1. Illustration of human autonomous and heteronomous decision making in contrast to heteronomous decision making of a machine. Human-machine interaction occurs on two levels.

3 GMOC: Human Decision Making in Dynamic Systems

Evaluation of the quality of human judgments requires an assessment of the predictability of the environment in which the judgment is made, and of the individual's opportunity to learn the regularities of that environment [19]. If end-users and operators can develop their mental models and formulate better goals as a consequence of augmented observability and enhanced control functions, this leads to higher predictability, thus making it easier for the human agent in such a system to predict what will happen in the close surrounding and in a near future. When humans interact with in-vehicle systems, they normally do so in order to achieve some goal. Goals can be found on different levels. They can be of a general kind, such as driving safely, deliver quality, or producing certain quantities. But goals can also be more specific, for example, a train driver brakes in order to keep the speed limit, a high-speed ferry operator navigates in order to reduce overall energy consumption while maintaining safety, and a train-dispatcher schedules incoming trains in order to avoid traffic jams. One way to understand such purposive actions is to interpret them as a way to achieve control, that is, the operator wants to reach or keep the system in some desired state. Humans interacting with complex systems need decision support systems that allow them to achieve full control in an efficient way.

Brehmer [8], [20] proposed DDM as a way to understand the activities carried out by a human operator. GMOC can be seen as the applied version of this approach. In order to achieve control, there are four prerequisites that need to be met. These are Goals, Models, Observability, and Controllability. Goals and models are properties of a human operator. Observability and controllability, on the other hand, are properties of the technical environment and are thus features of a system. The GMOC-model has been proven useful in a number of application domains (e.g. [3-4], [21-22]). Here, GMOC is proposed as a model for description, analysis, design, and evaluation of control and support systems. It gives the system designer a structure to identify connections between the four prerequisites, to analyze to what extent they are fulfilled, and how they can be further developed. It guides the system designers so that they do neither miss specific parts nor lose track of the whole picture. It provides the model needed in order to systematically analyze changes and limitations in any of the four main prerequisites. Analysis with GMOC reveals aspects that influence the efficiency of task fulfillment. Specifically, GMOC is useful when it comes to discriminating between observable and non-observable actions, as well as between behaviors related to goal-achievement and system-dependent behaviors. Non-observable actions refer to the judgments and decisions made by the user, often implicitly and with tacit knowledge. These behaviors are the hallmark of expertise and it is sometimes critical to identify them in order to fully understand the purposive actions of the users. System-dependent behaviors, on the other hand, refer to the measures taken or the actions implemented in order to get a particular technical system to carry out or execute the commands that is necessary to reach the goals. These insights, we claim, lead to design of systems that support good user performance and user experience, improve efficiency and safety as well as the overall system performance.

Let us look at an example of how GMOC translates into the work of a long-haul truck driver. The overall goal (G) for a truck driver is to transport cargo from the trailer depot and deliver it to a certain address at a specified time. This goal includes subgoals like doing so in a safe, effective, and efficient way, while also sustaining a good reputation and following regulations. Even more specific goals can be to plan ahead and in this way approach different upcoming traffic situations with appropriate speed and avoid complicated maneuvers. In order to achieve these goals, the driver needs a good understanding of the truck and its surroundings as manifested through sufficiently developed mental models (M). The driver needs to observe (O) many different states of the environment, for example, behavior of other vehicles, the truck speed and different truck states, road conditions, traffic signs, and of course, all the in-vehicle systems conveying information relevant for different situations. To be able to achieve the desired goals, the driver also controls (C) the truck, for example, in lateral and longitudinal direction (either manually or through changing settings of automated control) and by manipulating the navigator. During evaluation it is important to understand that the GMOC prerequisites are interconnected, it is not enough to consider them separately.

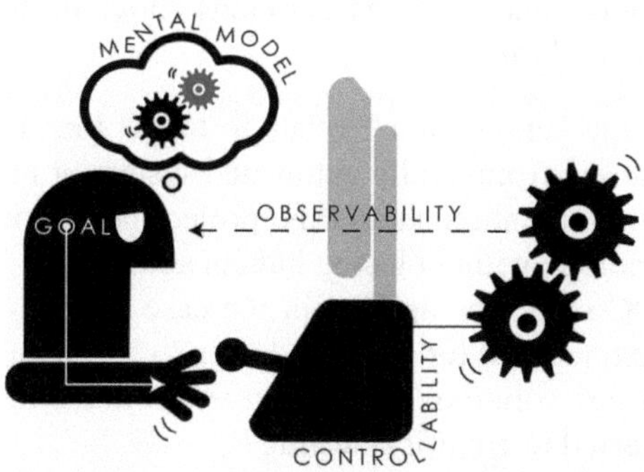

Fig. 2. The GMOC-model for design, development, and deployment systems

4 The Case Study – MODAS

MODAS [9] started out as an innovation and research project involving one of the major Swedish manufacturers of trucks for long haul driving and representatives from different Swedish universities. It started early 2013 and is expected to be completed by the end of 2014. In a way, MODAS is a project encompassing both current and future technology. It is based on current technology when it comes to all the data that are acquired in the different empirical parts. When it comes to test scenarios, it is based on models of future traffic states including models of what the future will look like in terms of complex driving environments, as well as hypotheses about what technical solutions there will be in terms of functions available in the in-vehicle driver system. Future traffic scenarios are envisaged to include a traffic environment that is high to very high in density (around 1250-1750 vehicles per hour), and with minimal vehicle separation (to sub-second separation). Further, a connected environment including vehicle-to-vehicle communication and vehicle-to-infrastructure communication is assumed.

In the first version of the project scope document – which was produced just ahead of the project start – it was stated that: From a driver perspective, the ability to operate a fully manual vehicle in the kinds of conditions described above will be difficult or impossible (or legislated against). Autonomous in-vehicle systems provide an opportunity for the driver to survive in the highly complex traffic environment of the future [23]. Thus, initially there was an expectancy that autonomous in-vehicle systems or semi-autonomous sub-systems could provide the solution to the problem of an all too complex environment for a human driver to operate and control.

But the MODAS-project also has a clear focus on human factors and the insight that design concepts represent hypotheses about the relationship between new forms of automation and human cognition/collaboration. These hypotheses need to be tested empirically and they are tentative and open to revision as long as one learns from the mutual shaping that goes on between artefacts and human actors [6]. The MODAS project time frame is too short when it comes to evaluating the final steps of this mutual shaping, but it is an example of how the scope of a project can change, as soon as design concepts and levels of automation are subjected to empirical testing and utilization of human factors competence. Once the project started, the project group realized the need to dig into some of the assumptions above in more detail. Four issues soon became important to clarify:

1. How does the concept "autonomous" relate to topics like automation? Is an autonomous system different from a fully automated system or not?
2. What philosophy of automation should the project build upon? How do we make the best out of technology without losing human authority?
3. How can the GMOC-model be applied in the case of long-haul driving and how does it translate into a method for systems design?
4. What conceptual design solutions can be derived from the initial analyses and how should they be subjected to empirical testing?

4.1 Current Empirical Investigations

The data collection in the MODAS project started with four days of observation of truck drivers driving today's trucks. The route included highway and country road driving with a variety of situations, weathers, and traffic densities. The truck drivers were well familiar with the route and had between one and thirty years of truck driving experience. To find out more about the truck driver domain, goals, strategies, and priorities during truck driving, two drivers were interviewed while watching video data collected during the observation study. During these interviews, drivers were asked to verbalize whatever came into their mind when watching both themselves and some of their colleagues driving. The method of collegial verbalization has been used before with good results [24-26]. During the interviews, the drivers were also asked for their preferences regarding level of automation. Four different types were shown to them, adapted from [27], together with a rather vivid description of what a future driver task may look like. This was close to the description above with a traffic environment that is very high in density, with minimal vehicle separation, and a lot of communication going on between vehicles and the infrastructure. The different types of automation ranged from information supporting and augmenting the perception of the environment, support for recognition and interpretation, decisions suggested for action, to actions implemented by the truck itself or its in-vehicle support systems.

From the observations and interviews, situations in which more and better information potentially could facilitate the development of the drivers' mental models were identified. Design concepts were developed based on these situations. These can be seen as design hypotheses, supposed to support the driver's information need and presenting it in a way that enhance the development of mental models sufficient for the driver to stay in control.

Two of the design concepts were included in user tests which focused on observability. The aim with the interviews was to gain information of whether the concepts support the driver's understanding of the different situations and enhance the driver's ability to regain control, for instance, in the event of automation failure. The hypotheses for design were updated using the achieved information.

4.2 The Continuation of MODAS

To further understand possible user goals, different strategies to perform the tasks will be identified. This is because different ways to perform a task can include different sub-goals (G) and therefore also different information requirements and ways to present that information (O). This might also result in different requirements of control (C). More information is also needed about how to develop highly automatic systems supporting (all) sufficient driver strategies, prevent use of less efficient strategies, and enhance the drivers' strategy development (M).

The hypotheses for design will be updated again with the information from the strategies analysis and after that, a second round of user tests will be conducted. To test if the displays developed for the future truck driver environment would develop the drivers' understanding, we need to investigate to what extent the driver can use the displays to achieve the goals and sub-goals, how well the interaction with the system works (O, C), and if this interaction support appropriate mental models.

The results coming out of the MODAS project so far show that once the empirical testing starts, that is, when the drivers are used as expert evaluators, the design concepts used to support the driver will change due to the results of the user testing. Moreover, issues of level and types of automation will also be scrutinized and subject to changes. This is not the same thing as conducting a user-oriented systems analysis, neither descriptive (how users perform the task today) nor normative (how they should complete the task). It is more of a formative approach (how the interaction could work), but in addition to this, the use of the GMOC-model helps out by making it possible to keep in mind the overall objective of human decision making in dynamic systems. By the end of the day, it is the driver that is responsible for the actions implemented during driving, regardless of all the functionality and automation that are there to help out. Level of automation is in the end an issue of authority. With the HMD-framework and the GMOC-model as a guide, the ultimate goal of the MODAS-project is to create a platform for future design, development, and deployment of future in-vehicle systems by creating a method on how to apply GMOC.

5 Discussion

Billings developed his human-centered automation approach starting with the premises that pilots bear the responsibility for safety of the flight, and flight controllers bear the responsibility for traffic separation and safe traffic flow. He then postulated the axioms that pilots must remain in command of their flight, and flight controllers must remain in command of air traffic. The corollaries following from this is: (1) the pilot and controller must be actively involved; (2) they must be adequately informed; (3) they must be able to monitor the automation assisting them; (4) the automated systems must therefore be predictable; (5) the automated systems must also monitor the human operators; and (6) every intelligent system element must know the intent of other intelligent system elements.

It is not difficult to see how these premises can be translated into the design of in-vehicle systems. Bearing in mind the HMD-framework and the division of roles between humans and artefacts, all six corollaries do also count for long-haul trucks as well as other types of self-driving cars. We suggest projects aiming for design, development and deployment of highly automated systems to consider these corollaries. In addition, we would like suggest another corollary: (7) the ability to execute authority requires actively involved operators.

As a way to transform these overall objectives into practical research, we also suggest to use the GMOC-model since it is generic enough to translate to other disciplines. Two advantages with GMOC are: (1) The four prerequisites and the division of properties between human beings and machines are the same regardless of whether the focus is on analysis, design, development or deployment; (2) GMOC helps, with its focus on goals and models, to keep in mind the two levels of communication that are one of the consequences of the HMD-framework.

6 Conclusions

The progress of the MODAS project shows that, once the empirical investigations started, the focus shifted from abstract design hypotheses to issues that focus on how to design to support the driver, and also that authority issues are relevant and need to be addressed carefully. Relocating some of the functions from the driver to automation shows that it is necessary to discuss issues of responsibility and accountability. Just substituting human operators with artefacts will not be enough. DDM is an approach well suited for understanding human decision making in dynamic systems, and it fits very well with the task to drive a long-haul truck. GMOC can be used to operationalize the design-as-a-hypothesis approach with the general problem formulation that changes in observability and controllability will affect the drivers' development of mental models and the formulation of goals. It can also be used to operationalize how the two levels of communication can be kept in mind since goal formulations are manifested on both levels.

Automation and design concepts are hypotheses about the relationship between technology and cognition/collaboration. As such they must be subjected to empirical investigations. In the case of in-vehicle systems, the design process must be open to changes as long as the mutual changes are not sufficiently well known. The HMD-framework specifies the necessity to evaluate the mutual changes along two different levels. Even though the information in the interaction and communication may be conveyed via the same interfaces, it is necessary to evaluate the content from these two separate conceptual levels. It is easy to focus on design solutions for specific situations on the heteronomy-heteronomy level of interaction. This is a natural consequence of how projects develop over time. However, it is at least as important to focus on the drivers' need to easily regain control in situations that are unfamiliar and unusual [28], that is, to utilize the ability and expertise and recognizing the autonomy of the driver. The very objective of decision making in dynamic decision tasks is that of control.

References

1. NHTSA (National Highway Traffic Safety Administration): Statement of policy concerning automated vehicles. U.S. Department of Transportation (2013)
2. Billings, C.E.: Aviation automation: The search for a human-centered approach. Lawrence Erlbaum Associates Publishers, Mahwah (1997)
3. Olsson, E., Jansson, A.: Work on the bridge: Studies of officers on high-speed ferries. Behaviour & Information Technology 25, 37–64 (2006)
4. Sandblad, B., Andersson, A.W., Kauppi, A., Wikström, J.: Implementation of a Test System for Evaluation of New Concepts in Rail Traffic Planning and Control. In: Wilson, J., Norris, B., Clarke, T., Mills, A. (eds.) People and Rail Systems: Human Factors at the Heart of the Railways. Ashgate Publ. Comp., Farnham (2007)
5. Stensson, P., Jansson, A.: Autonomous technology – Sources of confusion: A model for explanation and prediction of conceptual shifts. Ergonomics 57, 455–470 (2014)
6. Dekker, S.W.A., Woods, D.D.: MABA-MABA or abracadabra? Progress on human-automation co-ordination. Cognition, Technology & Work 4, 240–244 (2002)
7. Woods, D.D.: Commentary - Designs are hypotheses about how artifacts shape cognition and collaboration. Ergonomics 41, 168–173 (1998)
8. Brehmer, B.: Dynamic decision making: Human control of complex systems. Acta Psychologica 81, 211–241 (1992)
9. Krupenia, S., Selmarker, A., Fagerlönn, J., Delsing, K., Jansson, A., Sandblad, B., Grane, C.: The 'Methods for Designing Future Autonomous Systems' (MODAS) project. In: Ahram, T., Karwowski, W., Marek, T. (eds.) Proceedings of the 5th International Conference on Applied Human Factors and Ergonomics (2014)
10. Sarter, N.B., Woods, D.D.: Pilot interaction with cockpit automation: Operational experiences with the flight management system. International Journal of Aviation Psychology 2, 303–321 (1992)
11. Golightly, D., Andersson, A.W., Dadashi, N., Sandblad, B., Sharples, S., Tschirner, S.: A sociotechnical comparison of automated traffic control between GB and Sweden. In: Dadashi, N., Scott, A., Wilson, J.R., Mills, A. (eds.) Rail Human Factors: Supporting Reliability, Safety and Cost Reduction, pp. 367–376. Taylor & Francis, Oxford (2013)
12. Balfe, N., Wilson, J.R., Sharples, S., Clarke, T.: Development of design principles for automated systems in transport control. Ergonomics 55, 37–54 (2012)
13. Campbell, M.: Intelligent autonomous systems, `http://www.youtube.com/watch?v=Jimh-YDZNF4`
14. Kant, I.: Fundamental principles of the metaphysic of morals, `http://www.gutenberg.org/etext/5682`
15. Laaksoharju, M.: Let us be philosophers! Computerized support for ethical decision making. IT Licentiate thesis 2010-005. Department of Information Technology, Uppsala University (2010)
16. Wood, S.P., Chang, J., Healy, T., Wood, J.: The potential regulatory challenges of increasingly autonomous motor vehicles. 52nd Santa Clara Law Review 4(9), 1423–1502 (2012)
17. ATA (Air Transport Association of America): National plan to enhance aviation safety through human factors improvements. ATA, Washington (1989)
18. Kavathatzopoulos, I.: Robots and systems as autonomous ethical agents. In: Towards creative technology for the 21st century, 11th International Conference on Intelligent Technologies. Assumption University, Bangkok (2010)
19. Kahneman, D., Klein, G.: Conditions for intuitive expertise: A failure to disagree. American Psychologist 64, 515–526 (2009)

20. Brehmer, B.: Man as a stabilizer of systems: From static snapshots of judgment processes to dynamic decision making. Thinking and Reasoning 2, 225–238 (1996)
21. Jansson, A., Tschirner, S., Sandblad, B., Andersson, A.W.: Trading rigor for relevance: GMOC – a conceptual model for cognitive field studies. Unpublished manuscript (2014)
22. Tschirner, S., Jansson, A., Andersson, A.W., Sandblad, B.: GMOC – A conceptual model for analysis and design of human-work interaction. Unpublished manuscript (2014)
23. MODAS (Methods for Designing Autonomous Systems): Scope and Scenario, Deliverable 8.0. Internal project document (2013)
24. Jansson, A., Olsson, E., Erlandsson, M.: Bridging the gap between analysis and design: Improving existing driver interfaces with tools from the framework of cognitive work analysis. Cognition, Technology & Work 8, 41–49 (2006)
25. Erlandsson, M., Jansson, A.: Collegial verbalisation: A case study on a new method on information acquisition. Behavior & Information Technology 26, 535–543 (2007)
26. Erlandsson, M., Jansson, A.: Verbal reports and domain specific knowledge: a comparison between collegial and retrospective verbalisation. Cognition, Technology & Work 15, 239–254 (2013)
27. Parasuraman, R., Sheridan, T.B., Wickens, C.D.: A model of types and levels of human interaction with automation. IEEE Transactions on Systems, Man, and Cybernetics – Part A: Systems and Humans 30, 286–297 (2000)
28. Vicente, K.J.: Cognitive Work Analysis: Toward Safe, Productive, and Healthy Computer-Based Work. Lawrence Erlbaum Associates, Mahwah (1999)

Developing a Location-Aware Mobile Guide System for GLAMs Based on TAPIR Sound Tag: A Case Study of the Lee Ungno Museum

Jimin Jeon, Gunho Chae, and Woon Seung Yeo

Audio & Interactive Media Lab, GSCT, KAIST – Daejeon, South Korea
{jimin.jeon,chaegunho}@kaist.ac.kr, woony@kaist.edu

Abstract. With the emergence of new mobile media, Galleries, Libraries, Archives, and Museums (GLAMs) have paid attention to interactive context-aware mobile guide systems that can provide visitors with a customized experience based on their location and movement. However, existing location-aware guide systems using GPS, Wi-Fi, QR Code, NFC, RFID, etc. tend to overlook the special conditions of GLAM environments, often require additional hardware, and have shortcomings like inaccurate identification, high cost, and low usability. This project aims to develop a novel location-aware mobile guide system for GLAMs that can overcome such limitations and offer visitors a tailored experience. To this end, we utilize "Theoretically Audible but Practically Inaudible Range (TAPIR)" sound tag-based data communication and location detection using audio signals within the human hearing range (typically between 18 to 22 kHz). This paper describes the TAPIR sound tag-based mobile guide system, and it discusses the first user evaluation result of the guide we developed for Lee Ungno Museum.

Keywords: TAPIR, Sound Tag, Indoor Positioning, Museum, Mobile guide, Lee Ungno Museum.

1 Introduction

With the emergence of new mobile media (e.g., smartphones and tablets), Galleries, Libraries, Archives, and Museums (GLAMs) have paid attention to interactive context-aware mobile guide systems that can provide visitors with a customized experience based on their location and movement[1]. However, existing location-aware guide systems using GPS, Wi-Fi, QR Code, NFC, RFID, etc. tend to overlook the special conditions of GLAM environments, such as lighting systems, architectural structure, and exhibits. They also have shortcomings, such as inaccurate identification, high cost, and low usability, and they often require additional hardware.

This project aims to develop a novel location-aware mobile guide system for GLAMs that can overcome these limitations and offer visitors a tailored experience. To this end, we utilized "Theoretically Audible but Practically Inaudible Range (TAPIR)" sound[2] tag-based data communication and location detection using audio signals within the human hearing range (typically between 18 to 22 kHz). This paper describes the TAPIR sound tag-based mobile guide system, and it discusses the first user evaluation result of the guide we developed for Lee Ungno Museum.

M. Kurosu (Ed.): Human-Computer Interaction, Part III, HCII 2014, LNCS 8512, pp. 425–433, 2014.

2 Related Works

2.1 Mobile Guide Systems for Museums

Since the Stedlijk museum in Amsterdam developed its first audio guide–Philips radio tour (Fig. 1)–in 1952, museums have been developing their own mobile guide to provide their audience with more accessible and useful interpretations and information about their collections[3].

Early mobile guide systems for museums evolved in various ways until smart devices-smartphones and tablets-appeared on the market. One of the first mobile guides was a portable cassette player, which played a recorded audio guide. At that time, visitors passively listened to the audio guide. However, when keypad-based audio guides were developed, visitors could choose the artwork they want to know more about by choosing a number and listening to the recorded clip. This keypad-based audio guide (Fig. 1). was widely used in the 1980s and 1990s because of its interactivity[3].

After the introduction of smart devices, such as smartphones and tablets, museum mobile guide systems dynamically evolved. With new smart devices that have a camera, touch screen, and sensing and networking features, various types of new interaction were introduced in museum guides. At that time, a multitude of technologies (e.g., Wi-Fi positioning) for indoor location-aware systems (Fig. 1) were developed and applied to museums mobile guides[4]. Since the location-aware guides can provide visitors with information and content based on their position and context in museums, the indoor positioning system has attracted attention.

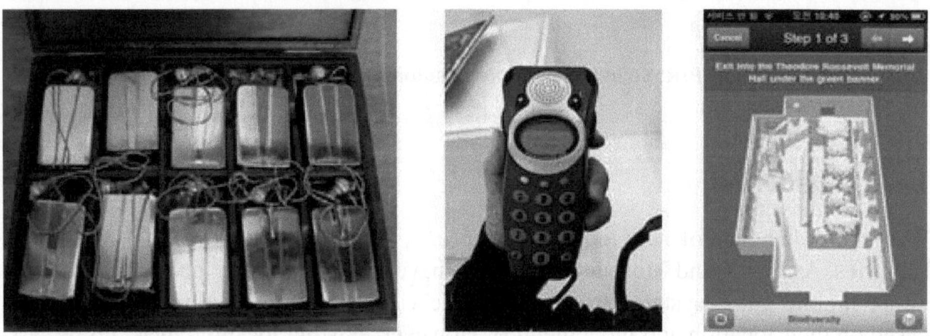

Fig. 1. Philips radio tour; keypad based; Wi-Fi positioning mobile guide app of AMNH

2.2 Indoor Positioning Systems in Museums

The head of mobile strategy initiatives at the Smithsonian Institute, Nancy Proctor, categorized indoor positioning systems for museums based on nine categories at the 2013 Museums and the Web Asia in Hong Kong[5].

- Manual Interface
- GPS
- Wi-Fi: Base station ID, Triangulation

- Bluetooth and iBeacons
- LED and IR
- RFID and NFC
- QR codes
- Visual Recognition (computer vision)
- Ultrasonic

Some of these technologies-Manual Interface, LED, IR, RFID, NFC, QR codes, GPS, and Wi-Fi-are currently available in a small number of museums and the others are in the experimental stage. The reason why these existing location-aware guide systems are not widely used in museums is because they tend to require additional hardware, and have shortcomings like inaccurate identification, high cost, and low usability. These limitations act as barriers for museum staff to actively use location aware mobile guides in museums.

2.3 Sound-Based Data Transmission

There have been many attempts to develop new techniques to utilize sound as a medium of data communication, and some of these have been commercialized in a limited way.

Normally, these techniques tend to deliberately hide the communication process using various techniques to build a seamless user experience. Although the transmission speed and stability of these systems varies depending on the techniques and algorithms they adopt, most are capable of sending a few bytes of digital data per second across a few meters.

"Shopkick[6]" is an example of a successful commercialized works. One or more speakers are arranged in specific regions in the affiliated shop. Every speaker has a unique sound ID and repeatedly emits a triggering sound, which does not disturb visitors, since it is encoded in a specific frequency band (20kHz) that is barely audible to the human auditory system (HAS). Once the app on the mobile devices is triggered by these sound signals, it downloads and provides location-specific information by detecting the ID included in the sound. This system has limitations in terms of advanced use due to its constraint of the sort of data that can be sent in its effort to maintain a simple structure. However, this limitation is also one of the main reasons why the system is stable. A similar service called Dingdong is provided in Korea.

Another example is "Yamaha Infosound[7]." This system uses an audio band above 18 kHz and has a transmission rate of 80 bps within 10 meters. Its purpose was to send additional information of TV content to audiences' devices by including the signal into the background sound. Although its usefulness is doubtful due to the emergence of IPTV technologies, Fuji TV used this system for promotional information in 2012. Its growth in TV content market and exploration of commercial uses are expected.

NTT Docomo is another organization researching data transmission using audio in a system called "Sound Barcode[8]." Its research is focused on data hiding by replacing specific bands of sound with audio signals that have a similar waveform shape as the original source[9]. This technique shows fast transmission speed and robustness against noise because it uses advanced algorithms, such as Orthogonal Frequency Division Multiplexing (OFDM), which is usually used for modern network systems, digital

TV, or cellular networks. However, commercial products and application projects using this technology have not launched yet.

3 System Design: TAPIR Sound Tag and Mobile Guide System

As mentioned above, several methods for using sound as a medium for data transmission have been suggested in recent years. These studies showed that sound can be used to transmit information to multimedia devices including Sound Barcode, Infosound, and Shopkick, which are primarily for commercial uses.

In our previous research, we focused on inaudible-high frequency sound's potential and noticed that it can be used for various purposes. Therefore, we suggested its possible application in prototypes utilizing TAPIR sound.

The most of microphones in today's mobile devices are designed to cover a wider range of sound (0 to 22-24kHz) than that of human hearing (0 to 18-20kHz). Thus, we can utilize this marginal sound band as a medium for communication between devices without human awareness[2]. This method offers a way to instantly form a kind of platform-independent local area network with a microphone but not additional hardware.

Therefore, we developed a TAPIR sound tag-based system, which is a novel acoustic data transmission system that is especially suitable for providing personalized and concrete information. We noticed that our new system is suitable for location-aware mobile guide systems for GLAMs. Transmitting information with inaudible sound is not affected by special conditions, such as lighting, and it works for every mobile device with speakers but without requiring any additional expensive hardware.

3.1 TAPIR Sound Tag

By applying advanced techniques from modern data communication system, our TAPIR sound tag system is a novel acoustic data transmission system, which shows enhanced performances and stability not found in other systems. Moreover, since we designed the system as a software framework, it is easily applicable to diverse purposes with a variety of personal mobile devices.

The new system can transmit 200 bits a second within five meters using a general small portable speaker (3W output power) in most situations. This means it can transmit one of 65,535 kinds of distinguished codes (enough for most GLAM situations) in about 0.1 sec. Thus, with our system and their own mobile devices, users can have a similar experience that of using modern tagging systems such as RFID and NFC.

3.2 TAPIR Sound Tag-Based Mobile Guide App

We designed a mobile guide app using our TAPIR sound tag system. Visitors to GLAMs can set up the app on their own devices without paying an additional fee to rent an audio guide. In GLAMs, each exhibit is assigned a sound tag, which emits its predefined unique ID information as a short-length audio stream (i.e., the TAPIR sound signal) periodically. The mobile guide app on each visitor's mobile device detects the signal from the nearest sound tag automatically (without any active response from the user) and presents the appropriate content, such as video clips or audio docent information, making it a natural, context-aware user experience.

These sequences allow users to access information on the artwork in a way similar to existing tag-based sensing technologies, such as RFID and NFC. However, the system with the sound tags does not require any special handheld device with additional wireless communication feature(s), and it can work on most smartphone platforms. This allows us to provide an interactive, location-aware mobile guide system with reliable performance and platform-independency at a lower cost.

4 Case Study: Lee Ungno Museum Mobile Guide

To test the performance of our system, we developed an exhibition application (Fig. 2a) for the Lee Ungno Museum, an art museum in Daejeon, South Korea.

This application offers an audio guide for a special exhibition named *The Silent Activists*. Visitors can use it while they are appreciating artwork in galleries. The experiment presented two methods for audio guide: (1) a list view with thumbnails of artwork, which is familiar to existing smartphone users (Fig. 2b) and (2) a TAPIR guide that we developed for this paper.

(a) The main screen view (b) The list view

Fig. 2. The developed application

On the thumbnail list view, visitors choose the artwork from their own smartphone and then listen to the recorded audio clip. However, if visitors choose the TAPIR guide, the device will catch the TAPIR sound from the speaker next to artwork (Fig. 3) and play the relevant audio clip.

Fig. 3. A participant using TAPIR sound-tag

5 Evaluation

5.1 Experiment Method

We conducted a between-group experiment to evaluate whether the TAPIR sound tag is useful as a museum mobile guide. The experiment was designed to investigate the impact of the Tapir sound tag-based guide compared to the traditional list view with thumbnails.

For the visitor (user) test, we used the Museum Experience Scale (MES) and Multimedia Guide Scale (MMGS) developed by University of York [10]. With MES, we can evaluate visitors' general museum experience based on four components-engagement, knowledge/learning, meaningful experiences, and emotional connection. With MMGS we can evaluate satisfaction with the mobile guide based on three components-general usability, learnability and control, and quality of interaction.

5.2 Procedure

A total of 20 participants were recruited for this experiment. The mean age was 29.7 with a range of 22-45; eight were male and twelve were female.

The experiment consisted of two stages. First, we put participants into two groups–A and B–randomly. We asked Group A to use the Lee Ungno Museum's mobile guide app with a list-view guide only, and we asked Group B to use only with TAPIR guide. After that, they went into the gallery to appreciate the artwork with the mobile guide for 20 minutes. After completing the tasks, participants were asked to answer survey questions about MES and MMGS based on the guide system they used. Also one open-ended question was given to know general opinion or idea of participants on each guide systems.

5.3 Result

After the participants answered questions on a scale of 1 to 5, we analyzed the results. Through MES, we knew the general satisfaction of the museum experience based on four components: engagement, knowledge/learning, meaningful experiences, and emotional connection.

The result (Fig. 4) shows that visitors, who used the TAPIR guide felt more engaged with the exhibition, knew and learned more about the museum, had a meaningful experience, and felt emotionally more connected with the museum and its exhibition compared to visitors who used the list-view guide.

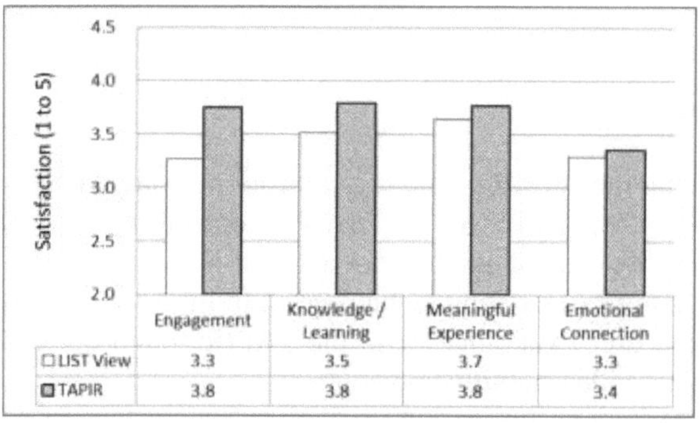

Fig. 4. Result of MES

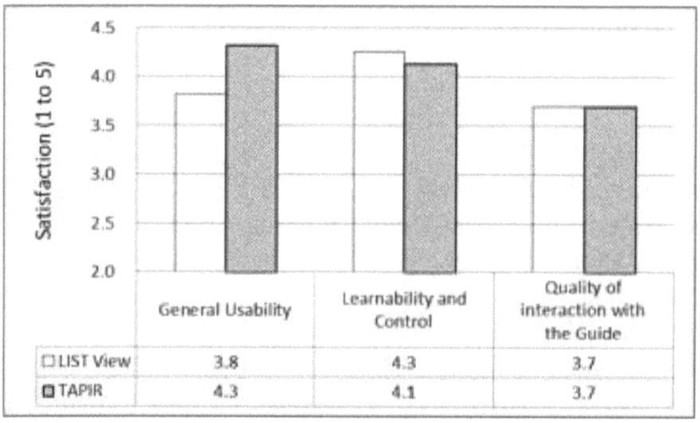

Fig. 5. Result of MMGS

However, using MMGS, the results (Fig 6.) showed visitors' general satisfaction on user experiences, such as general usability, learnability and control, and quality of interaction, and we discovered some experience-related issues with the TAPIR guide that should be improved.

When it came to general usability, the TAPIR guide received a higher score than the list-view guide. However, for learnability and control, the TAPIR guide has a lower score than the list-view guide. For quality of interaction, the TAPIR guide and list-view guide had the same score.

5.4 Discussion

After analyzing the result, we reach two conclusions.

With the TAPIR guide, visitors tend to have a better and more satisfactory museum experience. Since the TAPIR guide offers a location-based service, which does not ask visitors to play the audio guide, visitors can focus on the exhibition, and this leads to a better museum experience. After analyzing the open-ended answers on the TAPIR guide, we learned why the TAPIR guide showed a lower score on learnability and control. Even though users liked the TAPIR guide and regarded it as usable, they felt it was initially difficult to use, and they needed time to learn how to use it. Thus, we need to think about how to make this system more accessible to users, and help them learn how to use it easily.

6 Conclusion

When combined with the TAPIR sound tag, a location-aware mobile guide can provide an enhanced museum experience for visitors. We hope our research serves to convince people of the new role of sound as a tool for a location-aware guide in GLAMs that can overcome the limitations of existing technologies. In future studies, we plan to explore how to increase the user experience with the TAPIR sound tag-based mobile guide, particularly focusing on learnability and control.

Acknowledgement. We thank the members of the Lee Ungno Museum and YZ interactive for assisting our research; we are especially grateful to Geunhyoung Luke Kim and Seunghun Kim from KAIST.

References

1. Proctor, N., Burton, J.: Mobile Apps for Museums: The AAM Guide to Planning and Strategy. AAM Press, American Association of Museums (2011)
2. Yeo, W.S., Kim, K., Kim, S., Lee, J.: TAPIR Sound as a New Medium for Music. Leonardo Music Journal 22 (2012)
3. Tallon, L., Walker, K.: Digital Technologies and the Museum Experience: Handheld Guides and Other Media. Rowman Altamira (2008)
4. Roes, I., Stash, N., Wang, Y., Aroyo, L.: A personalized walk through the museum: The chip interactive tour guide. In: CHI 2009 Extended Abstracts on Human Factors in Computing Systems, pp. 3317–3322. ACM (2009)

5. Proctor, N.: Finding our way with both hands: Interior location-based systems in museums. In: Forum: Mobile Wayfinding and Location-based Solutions in Museums and the Web ASIA 2013 (2013), http://mwa2013.museumsandtheweb.com/proposals/finding-our-way-with-both-hands-interior-location-based-systems-in-museums/
6. shopkick, Inc.: shopkick (February 2014), http://www.shopkick.com
7. Yamaha Corporation: INFOSOUND (February 2014), http://jp.yamaha.com/products/soundsignage/infosound/
8. NTT DOCOMO, INC.: NTT DoCoMo Sound Barcodes (February 2014), http://www.diginfo.tv/v/09-0171-r-en.php
9. Matsuoka, H., Nakashima, Y., Yoshimura, T.: Acoustic OFDM system and its extension. The Visual Computer 25(1), 3–12 (2009)
10. Othman, M.K., Petrie, H., Power, C.: Engaging visitors in museums with technology: Scales for the measurement of visitor and multimedia guide experience. In: Campos, P., Graham, N., Jorge, J., Nunes, N., Palanque, P., Winckler, M. (eds.) INTERACT 2011, Part IV. LNCS, vol. 6949, pp. 92–99. Springer, Heidelberg (2011)

An Adaptive Semantic Mobile Application for Individual Touristic Exploration

Christine Keller, Rico Pöhland, Sören Brunk, and Thomas Schlegel

TU Dresden - Junior Professorship in Software Engineering of Ubiquitous Systems
{christine.keller,rico.poehland,soeren.brunk}@tu-dresden.de

Abstract. Expectations towards information access are rising as technology is increasingly pervasive in public spaces. Information for tourists such as on sights, transportation options or lodging is instantly available on mobile phones or public displays. However, it is still mostly up to the users to query different sources for information, find information suitable to their situation and to combine that information afterwards in order to reach their goal. In this paper, we present an approach that provides integrated and situational information on different tourism-related topics. We introduce our adaptation concept based on semantic descriptions of user context and integrated information sources and we describe the prototype implementing our concept. We evaluate our approach in a user study and discuss starting points for future work.

Keywords: Adaptation, Context-Awareness, Semantic Web, Mobile Application.

1 Introduction

Since smartphones and tablets became ubiquitous, tourists increasingly rely on them as an ad hoc information source on vacation. Most of the different tasks while visiting touristic places, for example using local transport and searching for restaurants, are served by a vast number of different applications. Users must manually search for information on the different topics, filter the information that is relevant to them and then combine the information from different sources because there is no system that integrates and adapts information from various sources into one application. Our goal is to semantically combine functionality for tourists in one mobile application and to use a continuous adaptation concept, in order to enhance the individual and explorative experience. Our prototype combines and individualizes public transport information, points of interest and dynamically planned tours. The adaptation concept considers the needs of the users, their interests and the overall situation. We provide a backend based on Semantic Web technologies to integrate different data sources and services.

2 Related Work

A wide variety of mobile applications provides information prior to or while travelling. Most of them, however, are specialized only for one task and some

M. Kurosu (Ed.): Human-Computer Interaction, Part III, HCII 2014, LNCS 8512, pp. 434–443, 2014.

additionally focus on only one region or city, like the New York City Essential Guide[1], for instance. A well-known example for an application that provides information on interesting places (points of interest) and accomodation all over the world, is the mobile application of the web site TripAdvisor[2]. It does, however, not offer whole planned tours or route planning functions, but relies on additional navigation applications for that purpose, which is true for many similar applications. Some applications also provide public transport maps of cities and regions, but still a user would have to find nearby stops and correct line numbers as well as timetables by himself. Applications that provide sightseeing tours are often specialized for one specific topic, like, for example the Audioguide Berlin Bus 100[3], that offers an audio guided predefined tour for 22 points of interest in Berlin or the application Anne's Amsterdam[4] that provides a tour of Amsterdam based on Anne Frank's story. None of these applications use linked data or Semantic Web technologies for intelligent algorithms or data integration or offers context-adaptation of its contents.

Lee et al. propose an ontology-based recommendation agent for the city of Tainan that is able to compute route recommendations [5]. The routes are based on google maps and do not take into account public transport. Their ontology is not described in a linked data compatible format, which means that it is not easily extended or linked to other ontologies. Garcìa-Crespo et al. describe their system called SPETA, "Social pervasive e-Tourism advisor" that does provide a backend based on Semantic Web technologies, recommendations of point of interest and a mobile application for pervasive usage [3]. They have a much larger database, because they link to DBPedia [6]. They do not offer any routes or tours, however, but focus on a location-based recommendation, taking into account social- and knowledge-based filtering. Castillo et al. present an adaptive system for tourists that is ontology-based [1]. They model points of interest and user context in an ontology and the system is able to compute recommended points of interest based on the preferences and context of the user. The system also provides suggestions for means of transportation, but does not take into account timetable or real-time information of public transport, as our system does. Castillo et al. write that their system is designed to deliver information on mobile phones and PDAs, but they do not provide a mobile application.

3 An Adaptive and Semantic System for Tourist Information

Our goal is to create an individual experience for tourists by providing information on sightseeing based on their interests and current situation. Our approach focuses on individualization using Semantic Technologies and utilizes deep integration of multiple information sources and services into one application. Our

[1] Available on iTunes.
[2] http://www.tripadvisor.com/apps
[3] Available on iTunes.
[4] http://www.annefrank.org/amsterdam

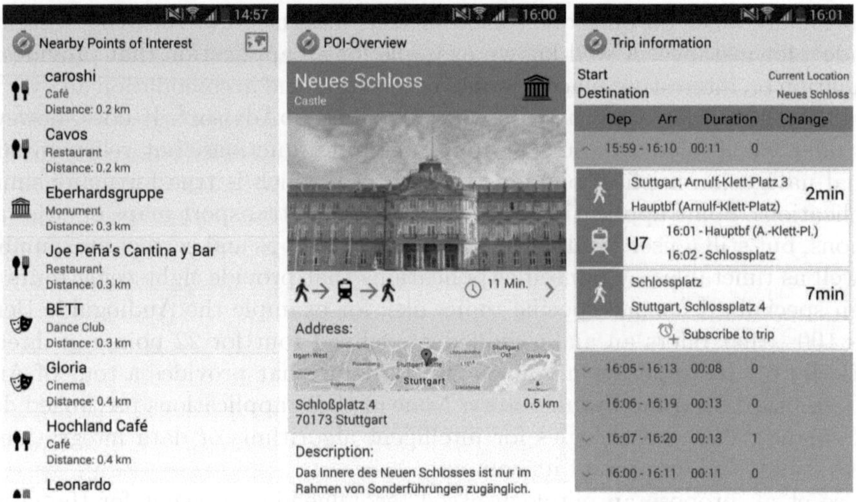

Fig. 1. Screenshots: Points of Interest and trip information

adaptation concept is designed to affect all integrated services that provide functionality in the mobile application. Context information is derived automatically where possible, but can also be supplied by the user.

Based on her current situation and timeframe, the user can search for points of interest and is then routed to them via public transport, as shown in Figure 1. The user can specify which categories of points of interest she searches for, ranging from generic categories like "shopping" or "leisure" to specific subcategories, for example "supermarket", "bakery" or "kiosk". Besides information such as description, opening hours and address, the detail view of a point of interest includes personalized public transport information. It shows, in a concise way, connections, changes and time required to reach the destination from the user's current location, which is displayed in the middle of Figure 1. By selecting the arrow to the right, a view containing more detailed information about the trip is shown.

In addition to finding points of interest, our application can also suggest individual trips of multiple interesting places and the ways in between. They are dynamically generated based on multiple context factors, such as weather information or user preferences on food. The user can specify multiple constraints about the trip, such as start time and duration, starting location and destination and if meal breaks should be considered. She can also define points of interest that should be included in the trip. Based on those constraints and automatically derived context, available points of interest and public transport connections, multiple themed trips are generated and displayed, as shown in Figure 2. Example routes are castle-tours or outdoor-tours. Each trip is computed using the optimal route, taking into account context information such as the current weather, suggestions for meal breaks and user interests as well as adapted real-time public transport information. If the user selects a trip, an ordered list

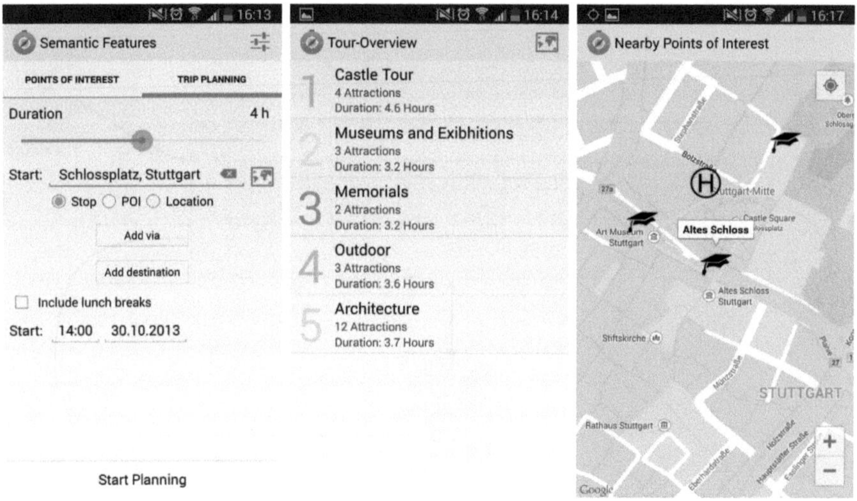

Fig. 2. Screenshots: Planning and suggestion of personalized tours

of all places that are part of trip is shown, including time information for each element. A map view of the trip is available as well. Each trip element can be selected in turn, showing the detail view as described in the previous paragraph.

3.1 Architecture

Our prototype system consists of a semantic backend system and a mobile application, as shown in Figure 3. The backend system semantically integrates data from different sources. Among others, we use data from the LinkedGeoData project [8], augmented with our own handcrafted data to describe points of interest, as a basis for the points of interest information service and the computation of sightseeing trips. Additionally, our backend integrates the different Web services we use for real-time and timetable information of public transport providers and for weather information.

The non-semantic data provided by these services is transformed into semantic data by a data conversion component that can transform data from the eXtensible Markup Language (XML) into RDF data[2] using a given ontology. The XML responses of queried Web services are converted into instances in our triple store and linked together, where necessary. A semantic context component combines the available context information and provides an interface for context data to the other components. For data on points of interest, we developed a tourism-themed ontology based on the schemas of LinkedGeoData and schema.org[5], linking it to our ontology on public transport and transformed data from the LinkedGeoData project into our triple store.

A third component combines the context data describing the situation, real-time information of public transport providers and data on points of interest with the

[5] `http://schema.org`

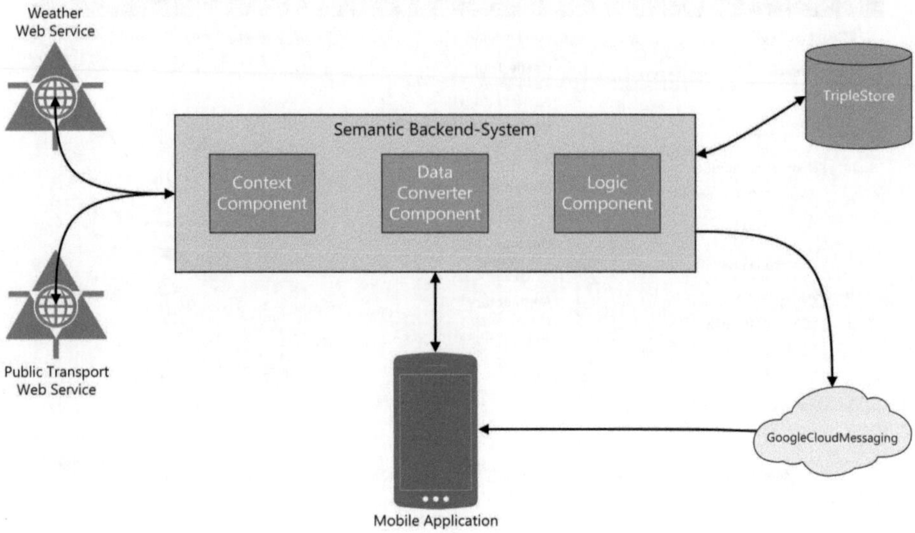

Fig. 3. Architecture of our prototype system

help of adaptive mechanisms to generate individualized information and computes personalized sightseeing trips. The synchronous request-response communication between our backend-system and the mobile application is realized over HTTP using the JSON format. For asynchronous communication, for example for polling the current location of the user's mobile device, we use the Google Cloud Messaging Services implementing a push service. The mobile application of our prototype system is implemented for the Android operating system.

3.2 Adaptation Concept

In order to personalize selection and presentation of points of interest as well as for the generation of individualized sightseeing trips, we build a semantic description of the user's situation. As a first step, we collect data from different sources of context information, as shown in Figure 4. The mobile device is a source for direct context information about the user's location and current time and it is polled by the backend using push messages as described above. The sensors of the mobile device may also be used as additional context sources, but at the moment we are only referring to location and time. Another context source are preferences of the user that are also retrieved from the mobile application. The user is able to configure her preferences regarding public transport, including preferred transportation modes, required time for interchanges or accessibility of public transport, as well as preferences regarding restaurants and meals, museums and other points of interest. In our current mobile application, the user has to enter her preferences manually and they are then synchronized with our semantic backend.

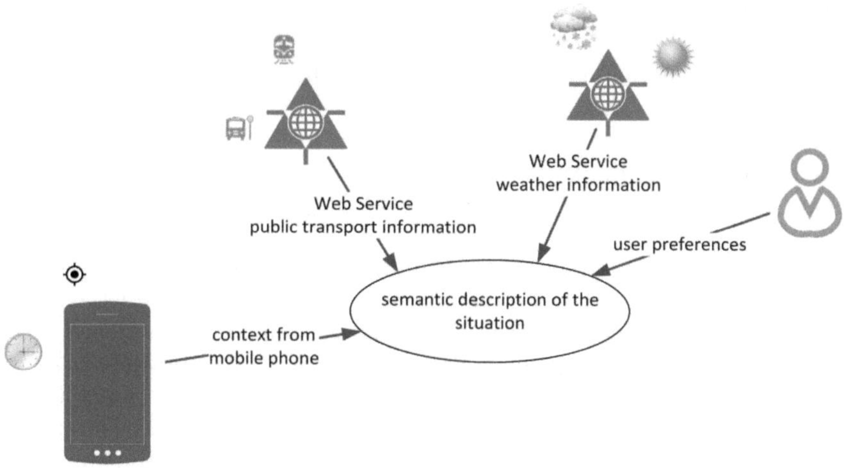

Fig. 4. Combining context sources

Additionally, we integrate external sources for context information. It is possible to add multiple Web services in our backend that contribute different context aspects. In our prototype, we query a weather Web service for information on the current weather and a weather forecast for the user's location. Furthermore, we use a Web service that provides public transport information, including schedules and realtime information on disruptions or delays. In our semantic backend, we transform the context information that comes as non-semantic data into semantic and linked data, to get an integrated description of the situation. In order to add new context sources, it is necessary to provide an ontology describing the context information, to link this description with the overall context ontology and to provide means of requesting or extracting the data. This can be done in a very modular way and therefore adding new context sources is easily done. The context data that is gathered and linked in the first step then serves as basis for different adaptation steps. It is used to specify information requests and to adapt and improve the generation of individual sightseeing tours. We query external Web services like the public transport information system and customize those requests to the customer's preferences and situation. Furthermore, we customize the selection of points of interest based on context information. Depending on weather conditions, reachability by public transport and user preferences for the different categories of points of interest, the results of a points of interest request are rated and filtered. While computing an individual sightseeing tour, the context information is used to rate the points of interest that are considered for the tour and to pick each next step in one tour. Based on the situation, some tours are only generated if they fit the situation. An outdoor tour, for example, is only calculated if the weather is dry and warm enough. The used filtering and rating steps are implemented in a modular way so that the adaptation can easily be extended with new filter and rating rules, for example, if additional context sources are added.

4 User Study

We conducted an explorative user study using the thinking aloud method, described among others by Jørgensen, to test the user acceptance of our adaptation concept and to find if and which problems users would mention using the adaptive application [4]. We evaluated the mobile application with eleven participants, following Nielsen's findings that a high percentage of problems can be found relying on 5 or more study participants [7]. The study was performed in a lab setting and took about 30 to 40 minutes per participant. We asked the test persons to fill out a questionnaire before the test and conducted an interview after the test, where we asked about the participant's experience with our application and their suggestions. While the participants performed the tasks, the mobile phone and their interaction with the mobile application was filmed. They were asked to think aloud while completing the tasks. Their statements and interactions with the mobile applications were evaluated afterwards.

Since we were not interested in testing the user interface of the application itself, but its functiontionality and adaptation behavior, we first explained the mobile application and its features to the test persons. We wanted to reduce possible usage errors due to unfamiliarity with the user interface. After the introduction, the participants were asked to perform two sets of tasks using the point of interest information and trip planning features of the mobile application. The GPS position of the mobile phone was preset to two different locations in the middle of the town that was chosen for the test setting. Each set of tasks was placed at a specific location. We used two mobile phones, identical in model and setup, each given a forged location. The test scenario for each set of tasks was explained to the test persons before they were given the assignments. The two sets of tasks were tested in two rounds, where one was performed without personalization and context-adaptation and the other was performed with given user preferences and context information taken into account. A group of five test persons performed the test without context-adaptation first and the second group of six test persons solved the tasks with personalization first and then moved on to performing the tasks without adaptation.

Without context-adaptation all participants used the pre-selection possibility to specify the categories for the point of interest search. Most of them used the categories and sub-categories to specify their request for the given task. About half of the test persons intentionally did not use the sub-category specification for some tasks, because they stated they would want to choose the points of interests from a greater variety of results. All participants were using the category specification at some point, though. Based on the given results, all of the participants then were able to solve the tasks and to find suitable points of interest.

For the task group that was performed with the context-adaptation feature, the users were asked to first set the user preferences to a given set, with the possibility to add their own preferences and then to perform the tasks. All but one test person then additionally used the selection of a sub-category of points of interest to further specify their request. The expectation of all participants was that the selection of restrictions via user preferences and sub-categories will only result in places that exactly meet these restrictions. However, since we use a rating algorithm based on the given context information, our system also provides results that do not meet all given context factors. We decided for this approach to always be able to show results, because a great variety of strict restrictions and context factors would often lead to an empty result set. This behavior was confusing to most of the probands. They obviously interpreted the given options as exclusive filters for the search results, not as a basis for rating. Many of the test persons then interpreted the results correctly and guessed that some restrictions must have been ignored to show otherwise good results. Some then suggested that they would like to see which preferences and context factors led to each result, to then decide for themselves if they considered the result or not.

Most of the test persons stated that their expectations for the sightseeing tour planning features were fulfilled. There were some interesting points on this feature, though. Most of the tours calculated by our system are a little bit longer than the trip duration a user defines in his request, some trips also are shorter. This is due to the computation of the trips, caused by the selection of points of interest that are more remote combined with their rating by context factors as well as deviations in heuristics on public transport trips and the actual given trips between points of interest. If the tour was way too long or too short than the given timeslot, all probands rejected the suggested tours. Most of the participants thought a variation of about half a hour would be acceptable. This issue again showed the conflict between the participant's expectations towards adaptations, especially of given restrictions and the difficulty of generating good adapted content, where not all given factors can be completely met.

Almost all participants rated the suggested themes for sightseeing tours positively. Many of them however stated that they would like to have the opportunity to combine the given themes and results to create a more varied tour. They also would like to be able to remove points of interest from tours and to add alternatives manually. All participants liked the idea to add meal breaks to a tour. Some of them pointed out that they would prefer a free time slot for meal breaks in the tour instead of a given location. They would rather use the point of interst search functiontionality of our system to get information about suitable food establishments nearby during their tour or tour planning. Although many participans mentioned that they would like the sightseeing tour results to be manually alterable, the majority was statisified with the results and the possibility to use context factors to improve the results. They judged the results as a good basis for manual refinement and liked the idea of being inspired by a variety of choices suitable to their context.

5 Discussion

All of our participants found the combination of different data sources and the integration of public transport and sightseeing information very helpful. Many of them suggested further integration of data sources like community-based rating of points of interest. We are currently working on the extension of our semantic data integration to include such data sources.

The main issue we found during our user study is the acceptance of the results, especially using context-adaptation. Due to the possibility of configuring their preferences and restrictions, the expectation of the probands towards the system and its results were increased significantly. If the results did not conform exactly to these expectations, they were considered not as helpful as the results without adaptation. The acceptance of the context-adaptive results depended on plausibility and traceability of the adaptivity effects. However, all but one participant stated in the interview after the test, that they would likely use such an adaptive tourism application and they considered that the application would save time getting one's bearings in an unknown town. We therefore think that the given suggestions of visualizing the effects of context factors on the chosen results in the point of interest search as well as for trip planning should be given further thought, to increase the user's acceptance by making part of the rating and choosing process more comprehensible. Also, we are planning on adding implicitly deduced user preferences in order to minimize the user interaction necessary to collect context information on the user. The issue of keeping the adaptations comprehensible will probably increase, if more context factors are unknown to the user, which is why our future work will also focus on communicating learned preferences and their impact on results to the user. Additionally, we think that giving the user more control of the results by making sightseeing tours editable and mixable, for example, would further increase the usability of our application and the usefulness of our adaptation concept.

Acknowledgments. Part of this work has been executed under the project IP-KOM-ÖV funded by the German Federal Ministry for Economic Affairs and Energy (BMWE) under the grant number 19P10003O as well as within the SESAM project under the grant number 100098186 by the European Social Fund (ESF) and the German Federal State of Saxony. We also would like to thank Steffen Huber, Andrea Mayer-Houdelet and Bianca Zimmer for their efforts during the user study.

References

1. Castillo, L., Armengol, E., Onaindía, E., Sebastiá, L., González-Boticario, J., Rodríguez, A., Fernández, S., Arias, J.D., Borrajo, D.: Samap: An user-oriented adaptive system for planning tourist visits. Expert Systems with Applications 34(2), 1318–1332 (2008)
2. Cyganiak, R., Lanthaler, M., Wood, D.: RDF 1.1 concepts and abstract syntax. W3C proposed reccommendation, W3C (January 2014), http://www.w3.org/TR/2014/PR-rdf11-concepts-20140109/
3. García-Crespo, A., Chamizo, J., Rivera, I., Mencke, M., Colomo-Palacios, R., Gómez-Berbís, J.M.: Speta: Social pervasive e-tourism advisor. Telematics and Informatics 26(3), 306–315 (2009)

4. Jørgensen, A.H.: Using the thinking-aloud method in system development. In: Proceedings of the Third International Conference on Human-computer Interaction on Designing and Using Human-computer Interfaces and Knowledge Based Systems, pp. 743–750. Elsevier Science Inc., New York (1989)
5. Lee, C.-S., Chang, Y.-C., Wang, M.-H.: Ontological recommendation multi-agent for Tainan City travel. Expert Systems with Applications 36(3, pt. 2), 6740–6753 (2009)
6. Lehmann, J., Isele, R., Jakob, M., Jentzsch, A., Kontokostas, D., Mendes, P.N., Hellmann, S., Morsey, M., van Kleef, P., Auer, S., Bizer, C.: Dbpedia - a large-scale, multilingual knowledge base extracted from wikipedia. Semantic Web Journal (2013)
7. Nielsen, J.: Estimating the number of subjects needed for a thinking aloud test. International Journal of Human-Computer Studies 41(3), 385–397 (1994)
8. Stadler, C., Lehmann, J., Höffner, K., Auer, S.: Linkedgeodata: A core for a web of spatial open data. Semantic Web Journal 3(4), 333–354 (2012)

Memory-Sharing Support Tool for Improving Local Interaction

Yusuke Kurosaki, Tomoko Izumi, and Yoshio Nakatani

Graduate School of Science and Engineering,
Ritsumeikan University, Kusatsu, Shiga, 525-8577 Japan
is0014he@ed.ritsumei.ac.jp,
{izumi-t,nakatani}@is.ritsumei.ac.jp
http://www.sc.ics.ritsumei.ac.jp/

Abstract. The goal of this paper is to improve communication between local residents. To achieve this goal, we propose a memory-sharing system for use by local residents. This system focuses on memories relating to the local area, because providing a common subject to talk about is important for the promotion of communication between people who are not acquaintances. In our system, the residents input their memories into a digital map and talk about the memories. The results of an evaluation experiment show that while awareness of connections with neighbors had been low, after using the system this awareness increased, and the residents were beginning to feel more interested in each other.

Keywords: Memory-sharing system, local communities, local area memories.

1 Introduction

This paper proposes a memory-sharing system to improve communication with users' neighbors and promote interaction between them. Establishing a close relationship with neighbors is one of the important aspects of disaster prevention, crime prevention, childcare and so on. Nevertheless, recently, there has been a reduction in intimacy in relationships with neighbors in Japan. Key reasons for this include the increase of residents who move to multi-dwelling housing in urban areas from other areas, changes in the structure of the nuclear family such as single-parent families, and large retail stores, which have caused community-based local stores to decline. According to the Heisei 19 Edition White Paper on the National Lifestyle presented by the Cabinet Office of Japan [1], it was shown that for a question about desired level of association with neighbors, the percentage of people who answered that they "want to be able talk about anything and help each other" dropped to 19.6% in 2003 from 34.5% in 1973, and the percentage of people who answered that they "want only to exchange greetings" increased to 25.2% from 15.1%. These results indicate that Japanese people now tend to prefer a distant relationship with their neighbors, in which they know only what kinds of people live nearby, rather than having a close relationship in which they and their neighbors know about each other's private lives. This trend leads to low interaction between neighbors, a situation which cannot be said to be positive.

M. Kurosu (Ed.): Human-Computer Interaction, Part III, HCII 2014, LNCS 8512, pp. 444–453, 2014.

One example that indicates the importance of association with neighbors can be seen in the comments of earthquake victims. In a questionnaire survey conducted on 240 people who suffered the Great East Japan Earthquake, 53.8% answered that they had come to prioritize communication with their neighbors after the earthquake [2]. In addition, in a Web questionnaire survey on changes in attitudes after the earthquake, 41% of 2,439 respondents said that they had a stronger awareness of communication and connections with their neighbors [3]. In this way, the reduction of intimacy in relationships with neighbors has a negative impact on community activities such as disaster and crime prevention and childcare. Therefore, it is important to understand the impact of interaction with neighbors and improve poor attitudes towards it, before problems occur which require the help and support of neighbors.

In this paper, we propose a memory-sharing system that activates communication between local residents on a regular basis, with the aim of improving community involvement.

2 Related Work

2.1 Jimoto-gaku

Jimoto-gaku, meaning "local research", is a Japanese field of research that aims to improve regional exchange [4]. Jimoto-gaku provides an ideal foundation in which anyone can participate by surveying and sharing common problems of the local area. However, there are some issues within jimoto-gaku, when we consider the increase in salaried workers and the tendency to dislike interaction with neighbors, which are factors for the reduction in relationships with neighbors. The first issue is that practicing jimoto-gaku requires forcing interaction between neighbors, to some extent. In many jimoto-gaku initiatives, local residents start by walking around the local area, learning about it, and searching for problems that exist in the local area. Connections between residents are deepened by discovering new appeal in their local area through fieldwork and sharing the same time and space with others. However, it is necessary for those that practice such activities to have a high awareness of problems in their neighborhoods; for residents with low awareness, such actions may be perceived as annoying. The second issue is that jimoto-gaku involves high costs. It is necessary to provide a place where residents can discuss common topics together anytime, anywhere when practicing jimoto-gaku. However, it is difficult to provide such a place available in both daytime and evenings, because local areas often contain a mix of residents with various occupations and consequently different lifestyle rhythms.

In this paper, we consider the provision of an arena for communication in an environment similar to social media on the Web, in which users can participate freely without being restricted by physical location. In addition to this, our goal is to realize a place where residents can freely comment upon ideas whenever they wish and share their comments with other local residents.

2.2 Collaborative Remembering

It is possible, for example, for elderly persons to interact with each other through gateball (a Japanese adaptation of croquet), and families with children can interact with other parents of similar age. Thus, persons of the same age and circumstances can interact naturally, but persons of different ages can find it difficult to interact with each other. Persons of various ages naturally live in a local area, so they need to interact regardless of age or gender. Koichi Sato states that inserting one's own experience into a conversation can raise the credibility of the conversation and enrich communication [5]. In this paper, by focusing on memories of self-experience, we use memories about the local area as a starting point for residents to interact with each other, without being conscious of differences in their ages, hobbies, etc. By recalling and sharing memories about the local area that anyone who lives in the area would possess, residents can communicate with each other by talking about things that happened a long time ago in the local area, or the differences between the present time and the past, etc.

3 System Construction

3.1 System Flow

This system was constructed as an iPhone application, because we assume that many people are familiar with using smartphones regularly, and smartphones can be used at any time and in any place, regardless of age or gender. In the application, users can input and share local memories on a digital map. The flow of the system is as follows (Fig. 1).

1. The user (local resident) inputs their memories on a digital map.
2. Other users see the memory inputted on the digital map.
3. Users input responses about the memory. At this point, users converse with each other.
4. The memories accumulate on the digital map.

Users input their memories on the digital map, following the above method. Memories inputted by users and conversations about the memories are accumulated by repeating this flow. In this way, the more memories accumulate, the more users can see other memories, and communication between local residents is naturally activated, increasing their opportunities to form relationships with other local residents through conversation.

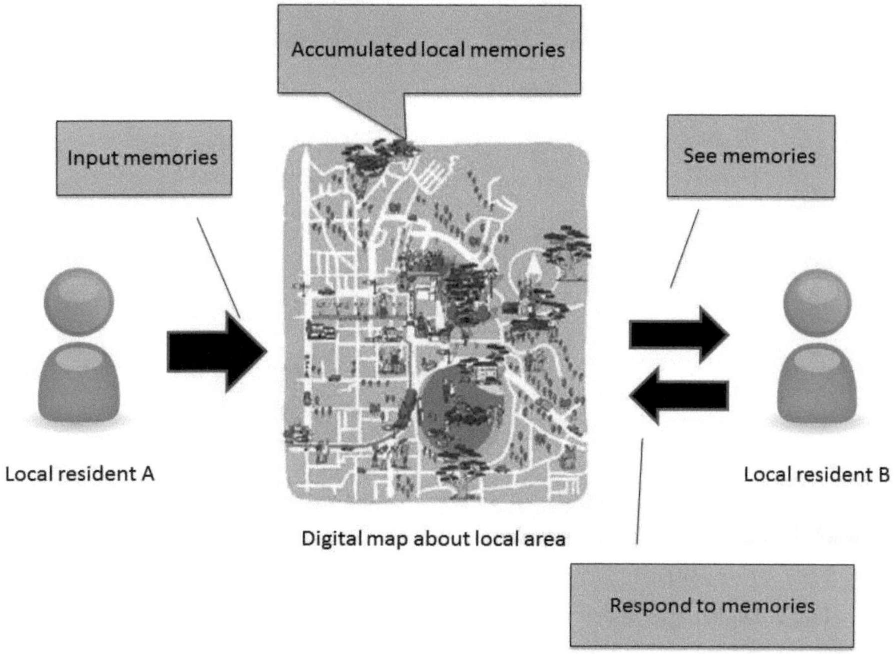

Fig. 1. Image of system

3.2 Memory-Viewing Screen

Icons that indicate types of memories are displayed at the places where local residents' memories are inputted on the digital map (Fig.2(a)). Users can see at a glance where and what type of memories were uploaded, by utilizing icons on the digital map (Fig. 3). Current social media services express all memories by only using language and pictures. However, by using a system with a digital map that has a strong connection to users and highly perceivable icons, it will be easier for users to intuitively understand what kind of memories are located in which places, and convey this information to other users. If icons were displayed for each comment, it would be difficult to see the digital map due to overcrowding of icons on the map. Accordingly, a serial conversation of comments about a single memory are compacted into a group, and displayed as a single icon. If users touch an icon that is displayed on the digital map, the first part of the most recent comment about the registered memories and the number of comments are displayed in a text balloon. When the user touches the text balloon, the system transitions to the memory's detail screen (Fig. 2(b)). At this point, the detailed memory about the place marked with the icon is displayed. By only seeing the memory's icon, location and start of the comment, without transitioning to the detail screen, it is easier for users to search for memories that interest them from among the various memories on the map.

(a) (b)

Fig. 2. Digital map screen with icons, and detail screen for an uploaded memory

Fig. 3. List of icons

3.3 Anokoro Travel

In this system, other users can see memories uploaded by a user. Although users can see various types of memories when all uploaded memories are displayed, it is difficult to recall local memories for each era, i.e. the appearance of the area at each particular time period. Thus, this system appends age information to uploaded memories. We call this function, which displays memories of a specific era when users view memories, "Anokoro Travel" ("anokoro" means "that time" in Japanese). (Fig. 4(a)). When people talk about their memories to others, it is common in Japan to say "in my junior high school days" rather than "when I was fifteen", for example. This is because Japanese people tend to talk about their recalled memories in units that mark the stages of their lives, such as the six years of elementary school or the three years of junior high school. Therefore, we provided a function in this system to search for specific ages and eras. When implementing this function, we included a screen for inputting the user's age, because this system needs to calculate the era from user's age beforehand (Fig.4(b)).

(a) (b)

Fig. 4. Selection of memories based on life stages

3.4 Memory Input Screen

The method of inputting memories is as follows.

1. Extended tap at the location on the map where the user wants to register a memory.
2. Select an icon that matches the image of the memory.
3. Input accurate age of the user for the memory, or select from a list of choices.
4. Input memory using text.
5. If using a picture, take a photograph at the location or select a picture from the user's library.

When users input a memory, they tap and hold the place on the map for the memory that they want to input. After the extended tap, a pin graphic appears at the location. Then, users select an icon that represents their category of memory (Fig. 5(a)). Next, users input the era for the memory (Fig. 5(b)). For example, the memory is registered as the period of three years of junior high school when users select a memory of their junior high school days, because the user's age has been registered beforehand. In addition, users can assign an accurate year, such as 2000 or 2002. Finally, information that cannot be conveyed with an icon alone is input using text and/or a picture. If users do not have a picture relating to the memory, they can take a photo at the location or select a picture from the user's library after uploading the memory.

(a) (b)

Fig. 5. Memory input screen

4 Evaluation Experiment

4.1 Experiment Outline

In our experiment, we communicated with a group using our system and a control group who did not use the system, and evaluated differences in the degree of intimacy in each group. One group used our iPhone application, and the control group met three times in the course of one week and spoke freely without using the iPhone application. We conducted surveys on each group's awareness about interaction with their neighbors before and after this experiment, and evaluated the changes. When neighbors meet and talk with each other, the group's degree of intimacy will obviously improve; therefore, we conducted an experiment to determine to what extent the neighborhood awareness of the group using this system (who did not meet) approached the attitudes of the control group (who met directly).

4.2 Experiment Participants

This experiment targeted people who live in the same area, and meet the following conditions.

1. People who have seen each other but have not talked.
2. People who have never talked to each other.

Accordingly, we selected two groups of five people who match the above conditions and attend Ritsumeikan university. The composition of each group of five is as follows: two males in their twenties, one male in his thirties, one female in her twenties, and one female in her thirties.

4.3 Experiment Results and Consideration

In the experiment, users answered the following questions, in consideration of the other group members as their neighbors.

1. When you meet people that live nearby, do you greet them?
2. When you have trouble or problems, do you consult your neighbors?
3. Are you interested in what kind of people your neighbors are?
4. When you have an emergency, do you ask for your neighbors' help?
5. In times of trouble, would you be able to cooperate with your neighbors?
6. Do you participate in local activities (neighborhood association, cultural/learning-based group activities, volunteering, etc.)?

In Question 1, we surveyed whether or not people conduct basic greetings. After the experiment, the degree of intimacy rose in the control group, who had met and spoken directly with each other: all members answered "I greet them voluntarily". The system-using group also gained a more positive attitude. Before the experiment, one person in the system-using group answered "I do not greet them", but after the experiment, all members answered "I greet them voluntarily" or "I greet them if they greet me first". After using the system, the users are no longer complete strangers, and it can be considered that they began to feel that they should greet people due to having a connection.

In Question 2, we surveyed the degree of neighborly association. We consider that if the neighborly relationship is one where people can always consult each other in times of trouble or problems, it is a strong neighborly association. With the exception of one participant, nine of our participants answered before the experiment that they do not consult their neighbors. After the experiment, three of the control group, and two of the system-using group, answered that they "can consult neighbors, although it depends on the type of problem". Furthermore, all of the remaining participants recognize their neighbors as desired confidants, answering that they "want to consult them, but cannot do so because we are not close". Thus, we found that an awareness of wanting to consult one's neighbors about problems, if a close neighbor exists, is generated by the act of communicating.

In Question 4, we asked whether or not consultation with neighbors in times of emergency was possible, and received similar results to Question 2. However, there was an increase in the proportion of those who answered "I want to ask them, but we are not close so I cannot" in the system-using group.

In Question 5, we asked whether or not participants could actually meet their neighbors and help each other out during times of trouble, such as a natural disaster. In the control group, all answered "I can" after the experiment. On the other hand, in the experiment group, there was no change before and after the experiment. Cooperative action in disasters or times of trouble requires mutual trust. It can be considered that the system-using group members were not able to improve mutual trust in comparison to the control group, who met directly, due to the fact that the system-using group did not meet in person.

Question 3 surveyed whether or not users are interested in their neighbors. Before the experiment, three participants in each group answered "I am not interested in my neighbors". After the experiment, all of the control group, and four of the system-using group answered "I am interested in my neighbors". Here, using the system had a broadly similar effect to meeting and talking directly. Participants were not interested in people with whom they do not have a regular chance to communicate, but after the experiment, we found that users were interested in each other due to the system's provision of an opportunity for communicating.

In Question 6, we asked about attitudes towards participation in local activities in the whole region. Two participants in the control group and one member of the system-using group answered "I do not want to participate" before the experiment, but changed their answers to "I want to participate" after the experiment. Thus, we found that using the system produced a positive attitude towards local activities.

We summarize our consideration of the above survey results as follows. The system improved basic awareness of neighborhood interaction whereby users became interested in strangers and wanted to greet them to the same degree as people whom they met directly. Generation of this awareness led in turn to an awareness that users "want to consult" with their neighbors regularly. However, regarding asking neighbors for help when emergencies such as natural disasters and personal troubles were envisaged, the control group, who met each other directly, developed better mutual trust. This result is considered to be due to the fact that trust is more greatly improved by meeting in person and communicating directly, than by using the system. Thus, it is possible to create a basic neighborly relationship and develop interest in each other using this system, and if the system acts as a trigger to develop neighborhood connections such as talking when residents pass each other in their town, essential neighborhood interaction can be regained.

5 Conclusion

It was demonstrated that the proposed method stimulated an awareness of wanting to understand one's neighbors, by recalling and sharing memories common to all residents of a local area. Henceforth, we are considering a support tool to resolve problems in regions affected by natural disasters, because we believe that utilizing memories may enable recreation of the town as it was in pre-disaster times on an emotional level, and revive the feelings of disaster victims.

References

1. The Cabinet Office of Japan: White Papers in 2007 (in Japanese), http://www5.cao.go.jp/seikatsu/whitepaper/h19/10_pdf/01_honpen/pdf/07sh_0201_3.pdf (accessed January 27, 2014)
2. Survey of the Great East Japan Earthquake (in Japanese), http://www.erc-voice.co.jp/results/pdf/H23_06_shinsai(2).pdf (accessed January 27, 2014)
3. Post-earthquake changes of awareness in residents of the metropolitan area: heightened awareness of connections with other residents "living nearby" (in Japanese), http://www.haseko-urbest.com/press/pdf/20111024.pdf (accessed January 27, 2014)
4. Yuki, T.: Departures from Jimoto-gaku, Rural Culture Association Japan (2011) (in Japanese)
5. Sato, K.: Functions and phenomenal characteristics of autobiographical memory remembering. Bulletin of Gunma University Faculty Of Education, Edited by Humanities and Social Sciences 56, 333–357 (2007) (in Japanese)

Finding Directions to a Good GPS System

A Comparative Analysis and Development of a Predictive Model

James Landy, Tatiana Lopez, Nkemjika Ndee,
Pimpisa Predaswad, Eyobin Lozano, and Patricia Morreale

Department of Computer Science, Kean University1000 Morris Ave, Union, NJ 07083
{landyj,lopezta,ndeen,predaswp,lozanoey,pmorreal}@kean.edu

Abstract. GPS devices have become commonplace today, almost as common as cell phones, especially for the developed and emerging economies. In this research paper, the development of a predictive model for selecting a GPS system for use based on the analysis of the interface design is described. The research presents subjective data from user interaction surveys, and objective data using the Keystroke Level Model (KLM). After comparison, inferences or predictions are made based on the analysis of available data. The research makes valid contributions to the GPS interface design field, and the GPS market. A higher level of accuracy can be achieved with data from a larger user survey group, and use of additional models, and an automated tool such as CogTool.

Keywords: GPS, Garmin, TomTom, Magellan, GoogleMaps, DeLorme Street Atlas, KLM, user survey, predictive model.

1 Introduction

This research was conducted determine which GPS system was the most user friendly and effective. Five GPS systems were selected for evaluation, including Garmin, Magellan, TomTom, Google Maps, and DeLorme Street Atlas. Three of the five units were well-known brand name GPS systems: Garmin, Magellan, and TomTom. These three systems are small and portable with a touch screen. Google Maps on a smartphone, and DeLorme Street Atlas, a built-in GPS system included in selected car models, were also included in the selection. With these five models serving as the research set, the GPS marketplace was well represented.

The problem which users have is determining which GPS system is best suited for them. There are many choices available, but there are no real directions or guidance on how to choose a GPS. This research will bridge the gap between what the users want and finding the most suitable device to meet their needs. The comparative analysis will also help determine how different or similar these GPS systems really are. As a result, it will be possible to predict what kind of GPS device best serves the user's need. This will provide new direction on how to choose a GPS system for the next generation of users.

M. Kurosu (Ed.): Human-Computer Interaction, Part III, HCII 2014, LNCS 8512, pp. 454–465, 2014.

2 Prior Work

Prior work, conducted on smartphones [1], identified a range of subjective factors which are used when individuals purchase new mobile phones. A survey of users was made to determine how the general public regards cell phones and identify the major design factors that prompted individuals to select their new smartphone model. The application of HCI principles such as keystroke-level modeling (KLM) and Fitts' Law to provide additional, objective data was combined with survey results. With this information, a predictive model was developed to provide consumers with more information about the different models of cell phones analyzed, as assistance help them decide on the best one for them [1].

The research presented here performs HCI and survey analysis on consumer GPS systems. All members of the research team have used and/or own a GPS.

3 Methodology

In the research methodology, five GPS units were used. Three of the five GPS were brand name units, with a touch screen and virtual keyboard. These small, thin, lightweight, and portable units have become a necessity for many users worldwide. The fourth GPS was a smartphone with the application of Google Maps. Google Maps on smartphones was included because so many users own smartphones and the widespread availability of that tool. The fifth GPS unit selected was the DeLorme Street Atlas, a built-in GPS in the car of a research team member. This range of devices provides a diversified and unbiased result.

With the five GPS units defined, a user-friendly survey was developed and used to collect data. The survey consisted of three parts: a pre-assessment, tasks, and a post-assessment. The first part, the pre-assessment script, consisted of collecting all the demographics of the sample size of 50 test subjects.

The second part of the survey included tasks that the user had to perform and rate for each GPS. All of the tasks were rated on a scale of 5 (easiest) to 1(most difficult). The third survey part, the post-assessment, was a continuation of the second part where the task results were collected and few more questions were asked of the user.

A keystroke-level model (KLM) was also used to analyze the GPS devices in this experiment. The KLM model was used to predict task execution time from the specified task scenario. The product descriptions of the five GPS systems tested follow.

3.1 Garmin

The first of the five GPS systems included in this analysis was a Garmin Nuvi 40 LM. Garmin is one of the best in the portable navigation business. This model was released in 2011 with three interesting features, which are junction view, speed limit display, and lane assistance. The layout is clear and easy to follow. It connected to the GPS satellites quickly, taking less than a minute and sometimes just a few seconds if the device has been recently used [2].

3.2 Magellan

The second of the five GPS systems included in this analysis was a Magellan Road-Mate 1212 including a QVGA 3.5" color touch screen with built-in maps of two North American countries and of Puerto Rico. The user may select six million points-of-interest, they may also select Fastest-Time, Shortest-Distance, Least-Or-Most used Motorways, or Avoid Toll-Roads. The GPS features an Address Book, Auto Day-Night view, and SD card memory.

3.3 TomTom

The TomTom GPS brand used in this research is one of the best known GPS brand names. It comes preloaded with maps of the U.S and Canada with both 2D and 3D views. Also, it has built-in turn-by-turn spoken direction, Help Me, Emergency menu, real-time traffic capability, Millions of Points Of Interest (POIs), and the MapShare instant map update.

3.4 Google Maps

Smartphones are widely available and popular in the last 10 years, so it was practical to include a GPS navigation application on a smartphone in the comparative analysis. Google Maps is a very popular app that comes standard on many smartphone models now. It is based on the Google Maps system that people can access on their computers. A new LG Escape P870 with Google Maps loaded onto it was used in this research, running Android 4.0 [3]. It has the ability to know the current location on a map, provide directions to a given address, and the Navigation part provides step-by-step voice guidance along the directed path [4].

3.5 DeLorme Street Atlas

In addition to these handheld units, a GPS system custom built into a car, the DeLorme Street Atlas in a 1997 VW Golf GTI., was included The DeLorme Street Atlas USA 2009 Plus software is known for its flexibility and powerful mapping program. Street Atlas remains one of the most popular mapping software in the carputer world [5]. Unlike other handheld GPS units, Street Atlas gives the user many options on how they would prefer to travel, what system to use it on, and routes to take. Route planning is one of the best features that the software offers as it allows users to set up a destination with only the desired highways to be used, in addition to all the points of interest to visit in between, plus directions to avoid certain tolls along the way [6-7].

4 Testing

4.1 KLM Estimations For Each Model

Keystroke-Level Modeling (KLM) uses estimations of time for actions to produce objective, numerical predictions for how easy it is to perform a given task on a device. Table 1 shows KLM value estimations used to calculate the average time per task.

Table 1. KLM Value Estimates (Seconds)

K (keystroke - type, swipe, etc.)	0.22
P (point to key)	1.1
M (mentally prepare for an action)	1.35
R(t) (system response time)	as needed

The KLM analysis showed that with these estimations it was possible to calculate and measure how long each task execution took. Some of the devices could not perform all of the functions planned to be used in the survey script, so N/A, meaning not applicable, was put down for the tasks which could not be done.

The keystrokes required and estimated completion times for each task by GPS unit tested (Table 2), considered the design usability principle of efficiency [8-10]. The data show that each of the GPS units performed differently on the two metrics of path length and time taken to complete the task. Each GPS was ranked by the shortest path length to task accomplishment and the time needed for a specific task. DeLorme, Garmin, and TomTom GPS units were highly ranked for three tasks each, while GoogleMaps appeared once.

Table 2. Keystrokes and KLM Time Estimates by Task and GPS Unit Tested

	DeLorme		Garmin		GoogleMaps		Magellan		TomTom	
Task	K	T	K	T	K	T	K	T	K	T
Get Directions to Destination (saved)	2	5.89	4	9.78	4	12.68	n/a	n/a	3	5.98
Get Directions to Destination (typing)	2	8.34	10	14.4	10	20.6	14	12.43	16	13.07
Change Routing Method	4	8.78	n/a	n/a	3	10.01	5	15.35	3	10.11
Toggle Voice Navigation	4	7.13	n/a	n/a	3	14.66	6	20.02	3	13.31
Turn On/Off Avoid Highways/Tolls	5	10.95	4	10.72	6	13.17	4	12.68	4	11.72
Create Point of Interest (visible, predefined)	3	9.31	3	10.66	3	8.66	6	19.02	3	8.31
Create Point of Interest (typing dest.)	9	9.95	11	16.6	11	22.92	18	54.06	13	20.07
Reset/Restart GPS	2	10.89	2	3.77	2	5.34	2	5.34	2	4.54
Change/Restore Time Zone	n/a	n/a	n/a	n/a	n/a	n/a	6	12.23	6	5.77
Clear Navigation History	n/a	n/a	3	4.87	4	7.98	8	23.36	4	6.49

K = Keystrokes Required **T = Calculated KLM Time Estimate (seconds)**

4.2 User Test Survey

The second part of the comparative analysis involved a user test. Each team member surveyed 10 subjects using a specific GPS model. The survey consisted of three parts. First was a pre-test assessment to gather demographic information to correlate data into user groups by age and previous experience with GPSs and similar devices. In the second part of the survey, the test subjects performed a series of preset tasks using the assigned GPS. The third part of the survey was a post-test questionnaire to capture the test subjects' impressions of the ease of use and other related factors about specific tasks and the overall experience using the GPS.

5 Results

Data from the pre-test assessment and the post-test survey was collected and analyzed according to a mix of demographics to see how various subsets of the test population responded to each of the tested GPS units.

5.1 Demographic Breakdown of the Test Subjects

One of the objectives of the GPS usability survey was to gather input from a mix of test subjects. The survey would benefit if the test group was comprised of individuals representing a variety of demographics including gender, age, race, primary language, and level of education. Tables 3, 4, and 5 demonstrate that this success.

Table 3. Distribution of Test Subjects' Age and Gender by GPS Unit Tested

	DeLorme		Garmin		GoogleMaps		Magellan		TomTom	
Age Grp	F	M	F	M	F	M	F	M	F	M
19-35	4	4	2	4	1	1	2	2	1	3
35-47			1	1	1	1	2	1	2	4
>48	1	1	1	1	4	2	1	2		

Table 4. Distribution of Test Subjects' Race and Primary Language by GPS Unit Tested

	First Language	Asian	Black	Caucasian	Hispanic	Indian
DeLorme	English		1		3	
	Japanese	2				
	Spanish				4	
Garmin	English	1		1		2
	Thai	6				
GoogleMaps	Cantonese	1				
	English			9		
Magellan	English			1	3	
	Spanish				6	
TomTom	English	1	7	1		
	Spanish				1	

Table 5. Distribution of Test Subjects' Level of Education and Gender

	DeLorme		Garmin		GoogleMaps		Magellan		TomTom	
Education	F	M	F	M	F	M	F	M	F	M
HS				1			2	3		
Some Col.		2			1	3				
2yr	2						1	1	1	1
4yr	2	2		1	3	1	2	1	1	4
Post Grad	1	1	4	4	2				1	2

In addition to these common demographics, it was important to categorize the test subjects according to some particular characteristics or experiences which could play an obvious role in how well they perform the required tasks.

Test subjects were asked what their level of experience was in using a GPS. A person with little or no GPS experience was not likely to respond to the test in the same way that someone who regularly uses a GPS would respond. Users were also asked what their level of experience was using Internet/computerized map services such as GoogleMaps or MapQuest. A person with this type of experience might have different expectations about what a GPS should do. Since most GPS units employ a touch-screen interface, test subjects were asked about their previous experience with any touch-screen devices such as smartphones, tablets, or touch-screen computers. A test subject who has never used a touch-screen device will likely have some initial discomfort with even the simplest touches and gestures. Finally, users were asked to rate themselves according to their overall technical abilities. A person who routinely delves deeply into the technical aspects of every device they use (i.e., a person who is often asked to "fix" something on someone else's computer) will probably be more successful using a new device for the first time than a person who knows or cares little about the devices they use. Table 6 shows a breakdown of the test subjects.

Table 6. Distribution of Test Subjects' Technical Experience

		Prior Electronic Map Usage								
		Few	Reg.	None	Few	Reg.	None	Few	Reg.	**Grand Total**
	Touch	Never Use GPS		Rarely Use GPS			Regularly Use GPS			
Tech Expert	-	1								**1**
	+					1				**1**
	**				9	2		1	6	**18**
Tech Intermed.	-		1							**1**
	+	3		2	1		1			**7**
	**			3	1	1	3	3		**11**
Tech Novice	+			1						**1**
	**	1			1				8	**10**
	Grand Total	**5**	**1**	**6**	**12**	**4**	**4**	**4**	**14**	**50**

Touch Screen Experience

-	None
+	Limited
**	High

As seen in Table 6, a majority of the test subjects included in this survey had regular touch-screen experience. Relatively few test subjects rated themselves as technical novices. It is not clear whether this is a true assessment or if there was a bias in the way this question was asked that caused it to skew results higher. It is interesting to note that nearly all of the test subjects that rated themselves as novices were surveyed by one member of the research team. There may have been different interpretations of this question among the members of the research team.

5.2 User Test Survey Results

The simplest and possibly most significant overall ease of use measurement is the "overall grade" that each test subject was asked to provide at the end of the test (Table 7). On this metric, the Magellan unit scored the best, DeLorme came in second, GoogleMaps and TomTom tie for third, and Garmin fourth. Breaking down that score by age group shows that Magellan's high score was primarily because of high grades from the >48 age group. Interestingly, the second place unit (DeLorme) earned its ranking by achieving higher scores in the 19-35 age group (Table 8).

Table 7. Ease of Use Average Grades (1-5) by GPS Unit

	DeLorme	Garmin	GoogleMaps	Magellan	TomTom
Overall	4.2	3.5	4	4.3	4
Task-Task	4.5	3.7	3.9	3.7	4.7
Learning	3.9	3.9	3.9	3.6	3.9
Purchase	3	3	3.3	4.4	3.9

Table 8. Ease of Use Average Grades (1-5) by GPS Unit and Age Group

	DeLorme		Garmin			GoogleMaps			Magellan			TomTom	
Age:	19-35	> 48	19-35	35-47	> 48	19-35	35-47	> 48	19-35	35-47	> 48	19-35	35-47
Overall	4.4	3.5	3.7	3.5	3.0	4.5	4.5	3.7	4.3	4.0	4.7	3.8	4.2
Task-Task	4.8	3.5	3.8	4.0	3.0	3.5	4.0	4.0	4.0	3.3	3.7	4.8	4.7
Learning	4.3	2.5	3.8	4.5	3.5	4.0	4.0	3.8	4.0	3.0	3.7	3.8	4.0
Purchase	3.3	2.0	3.2	3.0	2.5	4.0	2.5	3.3	4.5	4.0	4.7	3.5	4.2

Looking at the overall grade measurement broken down by education level (Table 9) reveals that in most cases, there was no difference in the overall score based on the test subjects' level of education. The Magellan unit did score higher among test subjects with less than a 4-year college degree, but since similar differences, positive or negative, did not appear for the other units, this is probably not a reliable factor for the predictive model.

Table 9. Ease of Use Average Grades (1-5) by GPS Unit and Education Level

	DeLorme		Garmin		GoogleMaps		Magellan		TomTom	
Education Level:	< 4yr	4yr+	< 4yr	4yr+	< 4yr	4yr+	< 4yr	4yr+	< 4yr	4yr+
Overall	4.3	4.2	2.0	3.7	4.0	4.0	4.4	4.0	4.0	4.0
Task-Task	4.5	4.5	3.0	3.8	4.0	3.8	3.7	3.7	5.0	4.6
Learning	4.0	3.8	5.0	3.8	4.3	3.7	3.6	3.7	4.0	3.9
Purchase	3.5	2.7	2.0	3.1	2.3	4.0	4.6	4.0	3.5	4.0

When looking at the test subjects' experience with touch-screen devices (Table 10), the overall ease of use grade changes for certain GPS models, but not others. For the top-scoring Magellan unit, there was no difference in the score from users who regularly use touch-screen devices when compared to users that do not. The same is true for the TomTom unit, tied with GoogleMaps for third. GoogleMaps, on the other hand, had significantly higher scores among users who routinely use touch-screen devices. If the results of this survey were limited only to users who regularly use touch-screen devices, GoogleMaps would have scored the best.

Table 10. Ease of Use Average Grades (1-5) by GPS Unit and Touch-Screen Experience

	DeLorme	Garmin		GoogleMaps			Magellan		TomTom	
Touch Experience:	**	+	**	-	+	**	+	**	+	**
Overall	4.2	3.0	3.6	4.0	3.3	4.8	4.3	4.3	4.0	4.0
Task-Task	4.5	2.0	3.9	4.0	3.5	4.3	3.3	3.9	5.0	4.7
Learning	3.9	3.0	4.0	4.5	3.3	4.3	3.3	3.7	4.0	3.9
Purchase	3.0	1.0	3.2	3.0	3.3	3.5	4.3	4.4	4.0	3.9

Touch Screen Experience

-	None
+	Limited
**	High

There are similar findings when looking at the test subjects' general technical expertise (Table 11). The overall ease of use grade changes for certain GPS models, but not others. For the Magellan and TomTom units, there was no difference in the scores from tech experts compared to intermediate test subjects. Both the DeLorme and GoogleMaps units got higher scores from test subjects who consider themselves technology experts. GoogleMaps, again, would have had the top overall score if the test subjects were limited to being technical experts.

Table 11. Ease of Use Average Grades (1-5) by GPS Unit and Technical Expertise

	DeLorme			Garmin		GoogleMaps		Magellan			TomTom	
Technical Experience:	-	+	**	-	+	+	**	-	+	**	+	**
Overall	3.0	4.0	4.4	3.6	3.0	3.4	4.6	4.0	4.3	4.3	4.0	4.0
Task-Task	3.0	4.0	4.9	3.9	2.0	3.4	4.4	4.0	3.0	4.0	4.6	5.0
Learning	2.0	3.0	4.4	4.0	3.0	3.4	4.4	4.0	3.0	3.8	3.9	4.0
Purchase	1.0	2.0	3.6	3.2	1.0	3.2	3.4	4.0	4.3	4.5	3.9	4.0

Technical Experience:

-	Novice
+	Intermediate
**	Expert

The overall grades based on the test subjects' experience with computerized map services like MapQuest (Table 12) were also examined. Based on this criterion, it was found, once again, that the overall ease of use grade changes for certain models, but not others. The most significant change was noted with the Garmin unit, which had its overall grade rise from 2.5 to 3.8 between test subjects with little experience with map services and those that use them regularly. However, the DeLorme unit performed the best among users who regularly use map services.

Table 12. Ease of Use Average Grades (1-5) by GPS Unit and Experience with Computerized Map Services

	DeLorme		Garmin		GoogleMaps		Magellan		TomTom		
Electronic Map Experience:	+	**	+	**	+	**	-	+	-	+	**
Overall	4.0	4.5	2.5	3.8	4.0	4.0	4.3	4.3	4.0	4.0	4.0
Task-Task	4.2	5.0	2.5	4.0	3.8	4.0	3.3	4.0	4.7	4.5	5.0
Learning	3.5	4.5	4.0	3.9	3.8	4.0	3.3	3.8	3.8	4.0	4.0
Purchase	2.3	4.0	1.5	3.4	4.0	2.6	4.3	4.5	3.8	4.0	4.0

Electronic Map Experience:

-	None
+	Limited
**	High

Upon examination of the average grade for likelihood of purchase in Table 7, the test subjects said they would be most likely to purchase the top-scoring Magellan unit after trying it. Interestingly, it had the lowest average rating for learning how to perform the tasks, and for navigating from task to task, tied with the Garmin unit.

The final set of questions for the test subjects asked them to rate how the units performed and whether it provided appropriate feedback and had the features they expected. They were asked if the unit produced results quickly enough, and if it provided informative feedback. They were asked if they considered the routes calculated by the GPS to be good choices or not. Responses for these three questions revealed nothing of value for the survey. All five units received perfect or near perfect scores for all three and are excluded from further discussion. Since affordance is an important concept but is not easily explained in a user survey, they were asked if they felt that the interface made all the actions and options clear to them. Users were asked if they felt that they could easily remember how to perform the tasks they just completed if they needed to do them again at a later date. The final two questions asked them to rate the completeness of the feature set relative to their expectations, and if they preferred the unit they tested over one they had used before. Table 13 shows the percentages of positive responses to these questions by GPS model.

Table 13. Percentages of Positive Responses to Post-Test Questions by GPS Unit

	DeLorme	Garmin	GoogleMaps	Magellan	TomTom
Interface Clarity	30	100	40	100	100
Step Memory	80	60	70	100	100
Feature Set	100	65	70	90	65
Unit Preferred	33	50	80	50	80

Overall, the DeLorme and GoogleMaps units scored poorly for interface clarity relative to the other units. Looking at the demographic breakdowns for these scores produced no noticeable pattern or explanation. Age, education, and previous technological experience made no difference in the scores. Responses to the question about how easy it would be to remember how to perform these tasks in the future were noticeably affected by the age of the test subjects. The Magellan and TomTom units got perfect scores, but the lower scores for DeLorme, Garmin, and GoogleMaps clearly show that scores went down as the test subjects got older (Table 14).

Table 14. Percentages of Positive Responses to Post-Test Questions by GPS Unit and Age Group

	DeLorme		Garmin			GoogleMaps			Magellan			TomTom	
Age:	19-35	> 48	19-35	35-47	> 48	19-35	35-47	> 48	19-35	35-47	> 48	19-35	35-47
Interface Clarity	38	0	100	100	100	50	50	33	100	100	100	100	100
Step Memory	88	50	83	50	0	100	100	50	100	100	100	100	100
Feature Set	100	100	75	50	50	75	100	58	100	83	83	75	58
Unit Preferred	38	0	60	50	0	100	100	50	50	33	67	100	67

An interesting anomaly in the scores for how easy it would be to remember how to perform these tasks is seen when the results are broken down by the users' experiences with online map services like MapQuest (Table 15). For DeLorme and Garmin, the test subjects who use online map services regularly gave them a higher score, but for GoogleMaps, they gave it a lower score. It is possible that a test subject's previous experience with online maps could have altered their expectations of the units they were testing, but it is not clear why this would skew results in opposite directions.

While the Garmin and GoogleMaps units' scores about their feature sets were lower than the other units' scores, there is no identifiable demographic breakdown that identifies a pattern or a reason for this.

Table 15. Percentages of Positive Responses to Post-Test Questions by GPS Unit and Online Map Service Experience

	DeLorme		Garmin		GoogleMaps		Magellan		TomTom		
Electronic Map Experience:	+	**	+	**	+	**	-	+	-	+	**
Interface Clarity	33	25	100	100	40	40	100	100	100	100	100
Step Memory	67	100	0	75	100	40	100	100	100	100	100
Feature Set	100	100	50	69	70	70	88	92	67	50	75
Unit Preferred	40	25		50	100	67	50	50	83	50	100

Electronic Map Experience:

-	None
+	Limited
**	High

For the question about which unit a user would prefer (the one they just tested or a unit they had previous experience with), there is not enough data to form conclusions about the results. Not all test subjects had prior GPS experience, and the matrix of unit tested versus unit with experience is too large a result set to satisfy with only 50 test subjects.

5.3 Predictive Model

Based on the user responses to the survey and the tasks performed on each of the GPS devices, a predictive model was developed to provide consumers with a method to improve their initial experience with a new GPS by picking one that is likely to work well for them (Figure 1). The overall scores for the GPS models tested indicate that there is no single best choice for all users. Instead, demographics such as age, technical experience and previous use of online map services can be used to predict which units are likely to be a good fit for certain users. It should be noted that there are no paths in this predictive model that suggest choosing a Garmin GPS. It is possible that another test sample or more consistent data collection procedures would produce different results, and therefore, alter this predictive model.

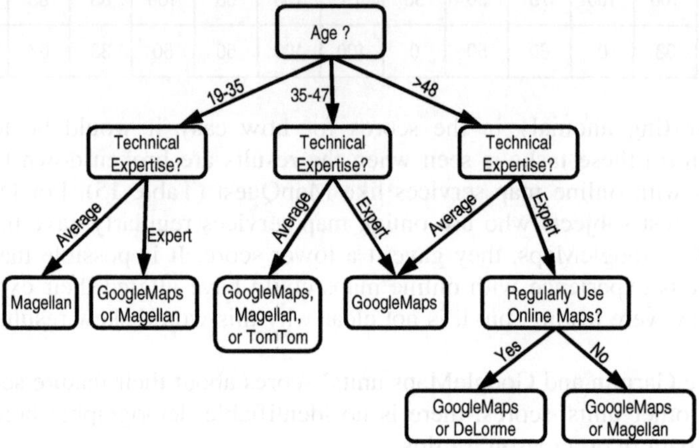

Fig. 1. Predictive Model Flowchart

6 Conclusions

In this research paper, steps taken to develop a predictive model that can be used by anyone for selecting a GPS system for use have been described. This was based on both subjective user interaction survey data, and an objective interaction measurement from a Keystroke Level Model (KLM).

The research has many practical implications. Developers can use these findings to create simple applications to help potential GPS buyers decide what suits them best. GPS interface designers can easily determine how, and where to focus their energy based on what users they are designing for.

This potential application would also serve as a cost-saving mechanism for GPS manufacturing companies, as they would know what to produce and for whom.

Additional test data from more measurement models e.g. Fitts' Law, and from a larger user sample pool, as well as using CogTool [11] to analyze the interfaces of the different GPS models could be done in the future. The results of additional analysis could serve as a tiebreaker for preliminary data from the other models, especially for tasks with no clear performance distinction. A higher level of accuracy will be guaranteed for every prediction.

7 Future Work

This work validates KLM on interfaces of GPS devices. GPS is a relevant part of daily lives. People use GPS for several reasons in their daily life and its role is increasing. The most common use for GPS remains retrieval of driving directions.

With a higher survey data sample pool, a clearer pattern should emerge, and a more consistent prediction will be possible. This could form the basis for the development of a simple web/mobile application for predicting a specific GPS choice given inputs such as ethnicity, level of education, experience with GPS and touch screen devices, computer, and experience with use of GPS device.

References

1. Jimenez, Y., Morreale, P.: Design and evaluation of a predictive model for smartphone selection. In: Marcus, A. (ed.) DUXU 2013, Part IV. LNCS, vol. 8015, pp. 376–384. Springer, Heidelberg (2013)
2. Garmin Nuvi 40 LM information from Consumer Reports. Consumer Reports (2013), `http://www.consumerreports.org/cro/cars/tires-auto-parts/gps/gps-ratings/models/overview/garmin-nuvi-40lm-d60905.html`
3. LG Escape P870 Technical Specifications. LG USA, `http://www.lg.com/us/cell-phones/lg-P870-escape/technical-specifications`
4. Google Maps for Mobile Help. Google, `http://support.google.com/gmm/?hl=en&topic=1616942&rd=1`
5. DeLorme Street Atlas Plus 2009 DVD. GPS City (2009), `http://www.gpscity.com/delorme-street-atlas-plus-2009-dvd.html#specifications`
6. DeLorme Street Atlas 2009. mp3Car (2008), `http://www.mp3car.com/delorme-street-atlas/118482-delorme-street-atlas-2009-a.html`
7. Review: DeLorme Street Atlas. Laptop GPS World, `http://www.laptopgpsworld.com/586-there-anything-better-than-delorme-street-atlas-usa`
8. Card, S.K., Moran, T.P., Newell, A.: The psychology of human-computer interaction. Lawrence Erlbaum Associates, Hillsdale (1983)
9. Holleis, P., Otto, F., Hussmann, H., Schmidt, A.: Keystroke-level model for advanced mobile phone interaction. In: CHI 2007: Proceedings of the SIGCHI Conference on Human Factors in Computing Systems, New York, NY, pp. 1505–1514 (2007)
10. Kieras, D.: Using the Keystroke-Level Model to Estimate Execution Time (2001), `http://ai.eecs.umich.edu/people/kieras/GOMS/KLM.pdf`
11. Teo, L., John, B.E., Blackmon, M.H.: CogTool-Explorer: A model of goal-directed user exploration that considers information layout. In: Proceedings of SIGCHI Conference, New York, NY, pp. 2479–2488 (2012)

A Geo-collaborative Recommendation Tool to Help Urban Mobility

Erick López-Ornelas, Rocío Abascal-Mena, and J. Sergio Zepeda-Hernández

Information Technology Department, Universidad Autónoma Metropolitana – Cuajimalpa, México
{elopez,mabascal,jzepeda}@correo.cua.uam.mx

Abstract. Geo-collaboration appears when individuals or groups work together to solve spatial decision-making problems facilitated by geospatial information technologies. In this paper we focus on current developments in geo-collaboration to help urban mobility. This work shows a collaborative mobile prototype that help people to take some decisions and share knowledge from a city. The main prototype recommends a better route to users in order to promote "walkability", in our case, Mexico City. The system not only takes on account the user profile, but the time, the date, the recommendation of other users and their spatial activity in order to give the best route.

Keywords: geo-collaborative, urban mobility, recommendation, user interface contextual design, "walkability".

1 Introduction – Urban Mobility

The past fifty years has been characterized by the explosive growth in urban sprawl and car use. Urbanization is now heavily influences by car and many households have moved out to the green suburbs and need several cars to satisfy their mobility needs. The resulting consequences of this urban sprawl are well known: the degeneration of social and neighborhood links, grater car dependence, longer journeys and increased transport costs.

Those cities that have been able to keep historic center, and maintain their commercial and cultural activities, are now threatened by the unsustainable growth of traffic and congestion. Interurban journeys are becoming quicker but cities themselves are being almost paralyzed by traffic. Unrestricted car use in towns and cities has a negative economic impact on efficiency, uses non-renewable energy sources, contributes to the greenhouse effect and their citizens suffer from high levels of noise and pollution.

Citizens today realize that their future, and that of the next generations, depends on the decision made by politicians responsible for urban planning and the mobility measures put in place by them. To ensure access to all the activities on offer, even for those without a car, and still respect the environment, car use in cities must be mastered and priority be given to public transport, pedestrians and cyclists – all measures which will improve the quality of life in urban areas.

M. Kurosu (Ed.): Human-Computer Interaction, Part III, HCII 2014, LNCS 8512, pp. 466–472, 2014.

We are all pedestrians. Walking is the most natural way to move, but requires not only legs. Requires "walkable" streets. A good walking environment has to protect pedestrians of the motorized vehicles. The speeds of circulation must be drastically reduced with free obstacles and well-illuminated sidewalks. The speed of the cars it must be reduced in the crossings streets with a good walking signals. This infrastructure must be accessible for all users, including people in wheelchairs and families with strollers. The pedestrian network must provide direct access to destinations, as schools, employment and transport stations, and it must offer diverse attractive and safe routes. The environment must be designed to attract the people who walk for pleasure safely.

With these precedents, it is important to use information technology to develop software applications in order to have a better "walkability" of the users in their environments (cities). The case of Mexico represents important "walkability" challenges and is highly contextualized.

In the next section some studies on urban mobility and geo-collaboration are shown. The section 3 we explain the designed recommendation tool with its different capabilities. The software prototype is also shown in section 3 with different interfaces. Finally conclusions are given with some further perspectives of the work in section 4.

2 State of the Art – Geo-collaboration and "Walkability"

Geo-collaboration is an emerging activity where users explore geospatial information through geo-referenced information [1], [2], in order to solve problems requiring a workspace and location components to be represented. This form of collaboration can occur in both co-located and virtually distributed settings. These systems offer co-located virtually or co-located group spatial knowledge creation for decision-making and planning support, using geographic visualizations to explore the initial available information and view intermediate results. Geo-collaborative application have been used mainly to communicate planning scenarios [1], its system design include a digital workspace for map-based analysis and visualization, multimodal interfaces for allowing interactions between participant with various roles, and databases to provide baseline data and store new information.

The system described in [3] supports synchronous and asynchronous interaction among users working in different places, providing geo-referenced localization services. The system presented in [4] uses mobile devices to provide synchronous interaction among users located in different places; The application presented in [5] uses mobile devices to support synchronous and asynchronous interaction among users in various places. In [6] the authors present a system supporting synchronous navigation of distributed users in a virtual co-located space; [7] supports the synchronous visualization of social interactions located in the same workspace through co-located mediation.

In other hand, "Walkability" is the degree to which an area within walking distance of a property encourages walking trips for functional and recreational purposes [8]. Several physical and social attributes of an area can affect walkability including street connectivity, traffic volumes, sidewalk width and continuity, topography, block size, safety and aesthetics [8].

Three known tools that evaluate pedestrian accessibility and present so-called "walk scores", or walkability surfaces to the user are WalkScore.com, Walkonomics.com, and walkshed.org. The "walk score" indices calculate a score based on facilities, such as shops, parks, restaurants, etc., that can be found within a certain distance from an evaluated location. Walkshed.org's "walkability surface" lets users select and prioritize a number of indices that are then used to derive a heat map that highlights walkable neighborhoods. The approach used in WalkScore.com has been described in detail [9], whereas the methodology applied in Walkonomics.com is only outlined generally [10].

3 Contextual Study

Mexico City is singular and therefore has unique walkability problems. Mexico City is a city with a large population and different areas of the city have different problems. A contextual study is important to identify specific problems. Our contextual study focused on the west area of the city of Mexico, where there exists a significant social inequality and where walkability index changes from one area to another. We explain the two main problems found after the contextual study.

Insecurity is the biggest problem identified in the study. People do not walk as many times because they are afraid of being assaulted and always try to avoid certain dangerous streets or routes. This insecurity feeling expands all over a specific area and the result is that the people not walk. In figure 1 we show this problem.

In Mexico, the informal trade occupies the sidewalks. The sale of food, clothing, electronics and other products is tolerated by authorities and is a source of income for thousands of families in the country. However, the occupation of sidewalks by informal trade has a negative impact on the capacity and quality of service offered by this infrastructure on pedestrian circulation. Another problem is the lack of maintenance and pedestrian infrastructure. The next figure (2) shows this problem.

Fig. 1. Insecurity, the first contextual problem found

Fig. 2. Infrastructure and sidewalks problems

Having these two main problems in mind we have decide to promote and develop a recommendation tool in order to help people walk safely on streets with a minimum of problems due to infrastructure problems.

4 The Proposed Recommendation Tool

The developed prototype is a collaborative tool for sharing some interesting and important information about a specific location, in our case the west side of Mexico City. This prototype will allow sharing some spatial knowledge recommending some urban mobility tips that will help users that are interacting with the application. This capacity to move from one place to another is very important in the Mexican context.

The collaborative tool, aims to communicate with other users some experiences when the user is walking through an urban area. In Mexico City you can walk through a pleasant park and suddenly find an unpleasant experience due to traffic, the crime, or simply to find an infrastructure problems.

The regular users interact with the recommendation tool and share this knowledge generated in order to help and recommend some pleasant an unpleasant places to other users. With this tool, the users will move and walk around in a better way. Actually, the users that interact with the mobile application have the ability to qualify, report or recommend any site of interest. These elements, displayed on the map, will help other users to move in a more comfortable way in a specific area. These elements shows how safe is an area, the state of an existing infrastructure (lighting, bridges, streets), also the user can select and recommend some attractions (parks, zoo, museums, restaurants, street). The user may then recommend and select certain areas as satisfactory spots. Other users may have access to this information.

An important feature of the collaborative application is that the user can perform a custom search of the places he wants to find. This option can be generated using its unique location based on GPS location or providing textual information. The result will be an interactive map with the satisfactory and unsatisfactory elements.

The application returns 3 different routes in order to move from one place to another: 1) the fastest, which is the traditional result of any regular navigation system, 2) the safest, which verify check and will avoid the negative recommendations identified by other users, and 3) the most pleasant, which take into account the positive and negative recommendations to define the route. The user can, then, make their own decision based on their needs.

The model used for the construction of the prototype has 3 main modules. The first input module, where the user information is stored in a database (recommended positive and negative elements). The second is the query, where the user makes the recommendation request to move from one place to another. Finally the system will display the 3 recommended option to move. It is important to say that the system will verify also the transport network database and the video monitoring network. Ideally, the 3 different options will match. The model is shown in figure 3.

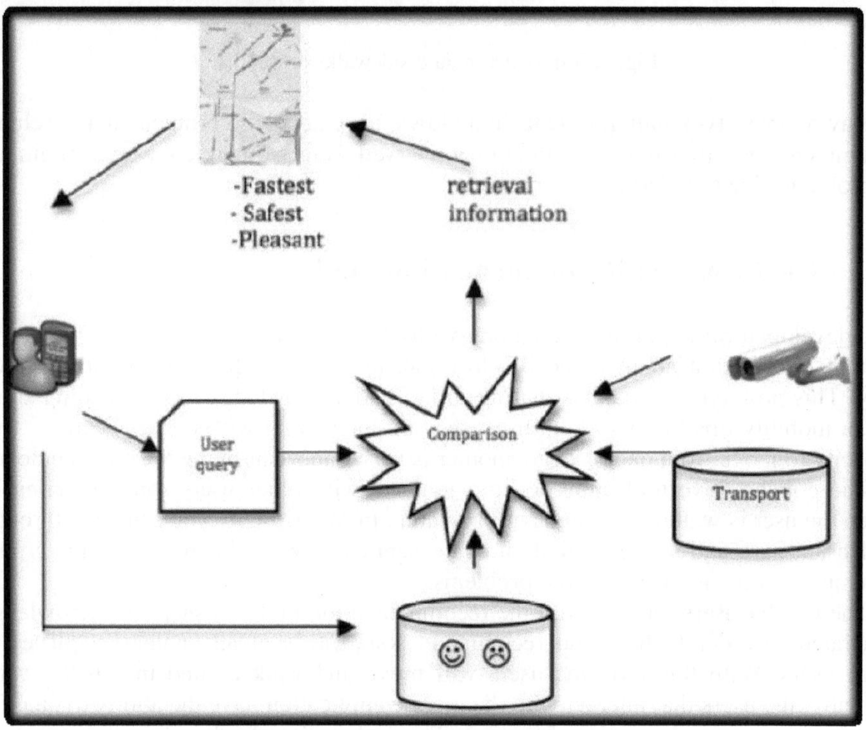

Fig. 3. Model of the recommendation tool

In the next figure (4) we shows several interfaces of the geo-collaborative tool. We show the interface where several users have reported a set of elements both satisfactory and unsatisfactory. The users that interact with the mobile application have the ability to qualify report or recommend any site of interest. These elements, green and red spots, are emoticons on the map that will help other users to move in a more comfortable way in a specific area. The result of the query will be an interactive map having the three recommended routes (fastest, safest and pleasant). The user can choose the best route in an interactive map according to their needs.

Fig. 4. Infrastructure problems and sidewalks occupied

5 Conclusion

In this article, we have presented a recommendation tool adapted to Mexico City where users directly feed the system collaboratively. Users recommend positive and negative elements in an interactive map and use some emoticons. This information is consequently used to recommend a better way to move from one place to another based on three conditions (safety, fastest and pleasant).

The tools take into account the Mexican context, which is very similar to the Latin American context and other cities could adopt it. The tool can be very useful and help "walkability" only if recommendations are accurate. The tool will work in a better way if many users use it.

This paper presents the first prototype of the recommendation tool. Further work will be the implementation of the model and the construction of the real application. An evaluation of the application has to be made in order to propose some improvements. Finally a usability study of the complete system will be a priority in order to have better results.

References

1. Derballa, V., Pousttchi, K.: Extending knowledge management to mobile workplaces. In: Proceedings of the 6th International Conference on Electronic Commerce. ACM, Delft (2004)
2. Rinner, C.: Argumentation Mapping in Collaborative Spatial Decision Making. In: Collaborative GIS, pp. 85–102. Idea Group Publishing, USA (2006)

3. Convertino, G., Zhao, D., Ganoe, C.H., Liang, J.: A Role-Based Multiple View Approach to Distributed Geo-Collaboration. In: Jacko, J.A. (ed.) HCI 2007. LNCS, vol. 4553, pp. 561–570. Springer, Heidelberg (2007)
4. Bortenschlager, M., et al.: Towards a P2P-Based GeoCollaboration System for Disaster Management. In: GI-Days 2007 - Young Researchers Forum (2007)
5. Convertino, G., et al.: Comparing Media in Emmergency Planning. In: Proceedings of the 5th International ISCRAM Conference, Washington DC, US (2008)
6. Rinner, C.: Argumentation Mapping in Collaborative Spatial Decision Making. In: Collaborative GIS, pp. 85–102. Idea Group Publishing (2006)
7. MacEachren, A., et al.: Supporting Map-based Geocollaboration through Natural Interfaces to Large-Perspectives 54(1), 4–22 (2006)
8. Pivo, G., Fisher, J.: The Walkability Premium in Commercial Real Estate Investments. Real Estate Economics 39(2), 185–219 (2011)
9. WalkScore, Walk Score Methodology. WalkScore (2011), http://www2.walkscore.com/pdf/WalkScoreMethodology.pdf
10. Davies, A.: Walkonomics - How Walkable Is Your Street? About. Walkonomics - How Walkable Is Your Street (2012), http://www.walkonomics.com/w/index.php/about

Influence of Cultural, Organizational and Automation Factors on Human-Automation Trust: A Case Study of Auto-GCAS Engineers and Developmental History

David J. Niedober[1], Nhut T. Ho[1], Gina Masequesmay[1], Kolina Koltai[1], Mark Skoog[2], Artemio Cacanindin[3], Walter Johnson[4], and Joseph B. Lyons[5]

[1] Systems Engineering Research Laboratory, California State University, Northridge, CA
{david.niedober.788,kolina.koltai.31}@my.csun.edu,
{nhut.ho.51,gina.masequesmay}@csun.edu

[2] NASA Dryden Flight Research Center
Mark.A.Skoog@nasa.gov

[3] Air Force Flight Test Center, Edwards AFB
Artemio.Cacanindin@edwards.af.mil

[4] NASA Ames Research Center
Walter.Johnson@nasa.gov

[5] Air Force Research Laboratory
Joseph.Lyons.6@us.af.mil

Abstract. This paper examines the influence of cultural, organizational and automation capability upon human trust in, and reliance on, automation in the context of an extended case study of the US Air Force Automatic Ground Collisions Avoidance System (Auto-GCAS). The paper focuses on the analyses of the system's developmental history and the perspectives of engineers involved in its development. Key findings indicate that the success of the system was a result of the innovative solutions developed; and a strong alignment between the engineering and experimental test pilot cultures. The findings suggest that the Auto-GCAS system was designed and tested in such a way as to promote effective trust calibration. A summary of the foundational lessons about how trust is influenced by cultural and organizational factors, implications of this research for adding to the body of knowledge on human-automation trust, and future research avenues, are also discussed.

Keywords: Trust, automation, reliance, F-16, military organization, engineer culture, extended case study methodology, automatic ground collision avoidance.

1 Introduction

Automation has been used in numerous applications to assist human decision making by automatically integrating and displaying information, and selecting and implementing decisions. While automation is an important asset for assisting operators,

M. Kurosu (Ed.): Human-Computer Interaction, Part III, HCII 2014, LNCS 8512, pp. 473–484, 2014.

automation-related accidents and mishaps have shown that poor designs can cause the operators to mis-calibrate their trust and reliance on automation. Common examples of inappropriate reliance on automation include misuse and disuse [1]. Misuse refers to over-reliance on, or utilization of, automation in conditions, or for purposes, that the automation was not designed. Disuse refers to the under-reliance or rejection of automation in ways that undermine the potential strength and benefits of automation

Lee and See [2] conducted a comprehensive review of the studies in the area of trust in automation, and used the review as the basis for an integrative view that links organizational, sociological, interpersonal, psychological, and neurological perspectives on inter-personal trust to the issue of human-automation trust. Specifically, they found that there is a general lack of data on, or research that examines, how cultural and organizational factors, and factors affecting automation capabilities, influence human-automation trust and reliance. Furthermore, while some studies have shown that these factors can influence human-automation interaction in unexpected ways, they have been mostly confined to experiments that examine the effects of a limited set of independent variables in a well-controlled environment. In actual operations, interactions between humans and automation usually take place in settings where there are many more variables of interest than data points available, and where the investigators do not have control over the events. Thus, to build on existing experimental data, and to lay the foundation for future research, it is essential to capture the richness of the phenomenon and the extensiveness of the real-life context in which human interacts with automation.

This paper addressed this need with a case study of an actual military automated system, identifying both practical lessons learned, and real-world perspectives on the appropriateness of reliance (i.e., where trust and use of automation matches system capabilities). Moreover, in addition to a standard approach examining how intrinsic properties of automation influence reliance, our emphasis on cultural and organizational factors allowed us to examine how human-automation reliance can be influenced in ways that are indirectly related to the characteristics of the automation. Specifically, the objectives of this case study are: 1) to reveal foundational lessons and best practices from real-world perspectives about the influence of cultural, organizational and automation capability on human trust and reliance on autonomous systems; and 2) to identify research issues critical to developing and designing more trustworthy automation.

To identify foundational lessons and best practices for appropriately calibrating reliance on automation, we conducted a case study of key Department of Defense (DOD) personnel with experience in operating and developing the Automatic Ground Collision Avoidance System (Auto-GCAS) [3]. In summary, Auto-GCAS avoids collisions by: 1) positioning the aircraft over Digital Terrain Map (DTM) with an inertial navigation system, 2) projecting the aircraft trajectory over the DTM, 3) generating a terrain profile from the local terrain map based on the aircraft's location and current maneuvering, 4) comparing the projected trajectory against the terrain profile to determine if an imminent threat exists, and 5), if the threat exists perform a last-second automatic recovery and return the control to the pilot as soon as the threat is avoided [4].

We chose Auto-GCAS for the case study for several reasons. First, it illustrates critical issues with respect to how tasks and decisions are allocated between the user and automation, in particular the issue of a system that autonomously and aggressively takes control away from the user. Second, Auto-GCAS's development spans three decades, providing a rich history from which best practices, and lessons learned can be drawn. Third, the research team has working relationships with organizations (e.g. the US Air Force and NASA) who directly lead Auto-GCAS activities, as well as with the personnel involved.

This study employed a multi-case design in which cultural, organizational, and automation capability are studied through three interrelated cases: 1) Auto-GCAS experimental test pilots; 2) Auto-GCAS engineers; and 3) management who lead and oversee the Auto-GCAS program. This paper focuses primarily on the developmental history of Auto-GCAS and the case of Auto-GCAS engineers. A previous paper has addressed experimental test pilots [5] and future papers will address the managers and leaders as well as a cross case analysis among all three groups.

In the remainder of this paper we first discuss the methodology and methods. Then we present key findings from our analysis of the historical development of Auto-GCAS, and key lessons learned from the engineers about the influence of automation capability, cultural, and organizational factors on trust development. In the last section we present conclusions and implications of this research with respect to human automation trust.

2 Methods and Methodology

2.1 Extended Case Study

Figure 1 depicts the project's extended case study methodology, in which grounded theory approach sets the framework for the project's primary sources, while the traditional research methodology provides the project's secondary sources. Using grounded theory (an inductive hypothesis generating approach), the project aimed to answer and stimulate research questions by using questionnaires, surveys, interviews with participants, field notes, and participant observations. NVivo, an ethnographic research software package, was used to code this data. The team then used the coding to help identify trends and to establish a collective story out of the key events, people, and meetings that contribute to the development of trust in Auto-GCAS. Hypotheses are generated from observing patterns that emerge out of ethnographic data.

In contrast to grounded theory, traditional research tests theories in a deductive manner. In this project, the research team immersed itself in the current literature on human automation trust development, with an emphasis on automation capability, cultural, and organizational factors. This included doing extensive literature review on the cultures and organizations involved with the development and testing of Auto-GCAS, and using the results of this review to generate hypotheses to be tested after the synthesis of the literature review was completed.

Using both primary and secondary data, comments on existing theories about trust in automation can then be posed. Once theories and hypotheses were generated from both the traditional literature review, and from the grounded theory methods, they were compared to see if they converged or diverged from each other. For an extended discussion of our methodology, methods, and lessons learned from their implementation in this project, the reader is referred to [6].

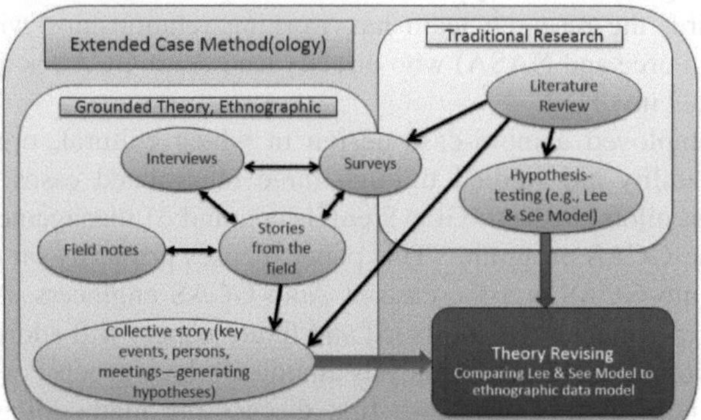

Fig. 1. Research Design Process and Strategy

2.2 Participants

15 Auto-GCAS engineers, with ages ranging between 26 and 59 (M = 38.64), completed surveys, and 12 completed follow up interviews. Of the 15 participants, only one was female; 13 were flight test engineers, whose involvement with Auto-GCAS ranges from one year to 20 years; one was responsible for all stages of the development; and one was responsible for developing the business case for Auto-GCAS.

3 Developmental History

In this section, we present a general timeline of Auto-GCAS development, and then discuss this developmental history in the context of the technical and human systems integration challenges. The information presented in this section is based on our review of the literature and analysis of surveys, interviews, and field observations with Auto-GCAS engineers.

3.1 Timeline of Auto-GCAS Development

The developmental history of Auto-GCAS spans 30 years. The initial research and development of Auto-GCAS began in 1984 [7] along with several other technologies on the Advanced Fighter Technology Integration (AFTI)/F-16 program. This first version of Auto-GCAS covered only a limited flight envelope and was based on a radar altimeter for determining terrain proximity instead of a DTM. From 1985-1997, development of Auto-GCAS continued solely on the AFTI/F-16 and only as a test support system, never being treated programmatically as a primary area of research. From 1990 to 1992, a number of variants of Auto-GCAS were developed bringing a slightly expanded envelope of capability and more importantly the use of a digital terrain map (DTM) for determining terrain proximity [7]. From 1992 to 1997 the Air Force Safety Center began to use the AFTI/F-16 team to support a number of F-16 mishap investigations where CFIT was suspected to be a contributing cause. In 1996, with USAF resources depleted for further Auto-GCAS development, the AFTI/F-16 team turned to foreign countries to solicit development interest. Sweden, just coming out of neutrality, joined the AFTI/F-16 team in further developing Auto-GCAS over the course of two test efforts. The first of these occurred in 1997 with a flight test effort to develop a nuisance criteria for the Auto-GCAS. This criteria was intended to form a core design requirement for Auto-GCAS so that there would be no adverse impacts from early recovery activations [7] (discussed later in the paper). In 1998, a full envelope system was developed and tested on the AFTI/F-16 in the first dedicated program for Auto-GCAS development. In 2000 and 2001 Auto-GCAS demonstration and evaluation tests took place with the Live Fire Test & Evaluation (LFT&E) office of OSD and Air Combat Command (ACC) [7]. A major turning point came in May 2003 with a Secretary of Defense Mishap reduction memo which set a requirement on all of the armed services to reduce mishaps by 50% [7, 8]. In 2005-06 the Defense Safety Oversight Council (DSOC) developed the Auto-GCAS fighter /attack business case [9]. This business case had two significant findings: 1) The CFIT mishap rate had remained unchanged despite the addition of numerous ground warning systems and 2) the mishap reduction goal could only be achieved in fighter aircraft by implementing Auto-GCAS. In 2006-07 the DSOC initiated the Automatic Collision Avoidance Technology/Fighter Risk Reduction Program (ACAT/FRRP) by investing $2.5 million dollars to start the program [8]. In 2008-2010, the ACAT/FRRP completed the research on Auto-GCAS and conducted an extensive test program to ready the system for production integration. This program was a collaborative effort between multiple organizations, led by the Air Force Research Laboratory (AFRL) at Wright Patterson AFB. The program not only included Auto-GCAS, but Automatic Air Collision Avoidance System (Auto-ACAS) and the Integrated Collision Avoidance System (ICAS) development. Significant advancements for DTM in terrain encoding were developed by NASA 2008-2011 for the purposes of enabling Auto-GCAS to be implemented on the F-22 platform [7]. From 2011-2014, the integration Auto-GCAS into the production USAF F-16 continued with a scheduled operational deployment in the summer of 2014.

3.2 Technical and Human-Systems Integration Context

Auto-GCAS was designed with a set of design principles meant to guide development and integration of the system. 1) Do no harm, which requires that Auto-GCAS not cause any harm to the pilot or the aircraft; 2) Do not impede, which requires the system to be nuisance free and thus does not interfere with the mission; and 3) Avoid Collision, which requires the system to avoid collision with terrain [3]. The principal goal of Auto-GCAS is to mitigate the problem of Controlled Flight into Terrain (CFIT), the number one cause of the loss of life in aviation since the beginning of manned flight. One of the most effective technological measures to mitigate CFIT to date has been Terrain Awareness and Warning Systems (TAWS), which provide the pilot warnings and directions for avoiding terrain [9]. While the development of TAWS, and the mandate for its implementation, have played a critical role in significantly reducing CFIT accidents, they also have reached a point of diminishing return due to several limitations. The first is that current TAWS are prone to nuisance warnings (leading pilots to turn them off). The second is that, because these systems require the pilot to manually respond to a warning, they are not effective when the pilot is incapacitated or spatially disoriented. The third is that the pilot may not always correctly recognize a warning or correctly make the terrain collision evasion maneuver, especially in dynamic flight conditions. Thus, the human is the limiting factor in these situations.

To overcome these limitations, Auto-GCAS was developed with a number of innovative approaches and solutions. In order to address the nuisance problem, a nuisance threshold was determined, where a warning would not be considered too early by the pilot. This was accomplished by conducting a flight test program to define what would be the maximum acceptable time to initiate a recovery maneuver so that it would not be considered a nuisance by the pilot. Just considering this problem from a temporal perspective was novel where all previous efforts had looked at distance above the ground as a metric for nuisance. To determine the time in which a fly-up maneuver would not be a nuisance, pilots flew aircraft towards terrain at different conditions and then manually initiated a recover as they reached their comfort threshold. They then rated their anxiety level at recovery initiation to capture if whether they had accidentally initiated the recovery sooner or later than they had intended to. The time period after which a recovery initiation would be considered a nuisance and the point at which the aircraft's maximum performance recovery would just clear the ground is called a nuisance budget [10].

The nuisance criteria were found to be governed by two principles for an avoidance maneuver to be acceptable to a pilot. It must be both aggressive and timely. Aggressive in the sense that the avoidance is using a significant amount of the aircraft's available maneuvering authority. And timely in the sense that it does not begin the maneuver too early such that it is deemed a nuisance or too late in that the aircraft does not have sufficient maneuverability to avoid hitting the surrounding terrain. Available maneuvering authority is driven by the unique aerodynamics of an aircraft at a given fight condition. It is presumed that each pilot has a mental model of the aircraft's ability to maneuver. Using this mental model, the pilot assesses the approaching local terrain and determines a best escape path to avoid hitting what is ahead of the aircraft. To this, it was found that the pilot applies a safety buffer based on his uncertainty of the situation (rapidly changing aircraft attitude or conditions, high turbulence, poor visibility, etc.) to determine when the "aggressive" avoidance maneuver should be initiated. Because the "aggressive" portion of the criteria imbeds within it the aerodynamics unique to a vehicle, the "timely" portion of the criteria remains the same for all aircraft. It was also found that the "timely" criterion could be approximated by a single equation with the maximum acceptable time being 1.5 seconds prior to the point where the aggressive recovery will just miss the ground.

The design of the Auto-GCAS followed the same aggressive and timely criteria.

First, the avoidance maneuver was chosen, designed and evaluated for acceptable aggressiveness in the F-16. Extensive use of flight evaluations and pilot comments were used to determine that the maneuvers were acceptable for the F-16. The maneuver chosen was an aggressive roll to wings-level, 5g pull. Next, just as with the pilot's mental model, an algorithm was developed to model that aggressive recovery and assess the near terrain proximity to determine when a timely avoidance maneuver should be initiated. Uncertainties were also used to buffer the recovery initiation by capturing the inaccuracies in the recovery model, terrain model and those sensors which are used to position the aircraft over the terrain model and used to determine the recovery trajectory. The 1.5 seconds from the nuisance criteria formed the allowable error budget for the GCAS algorithm [10].

To address the human limitations and situations in which the pilot is incapacitated or disoriented, the recovery was automated. The automatic-recovery solution eliminates the human-limit problem (i.e., different pilots have different perceptions and capabilities) by taking these out of the equation. Instead, the system makes the decision to initiate the recovery at the last second so that the perception of nuisance is eliminated.

4 Results

In this section, we report the findings of our case study on the Auto-GCAS engineers. References and comparison will be made to our case on the pilots, which is reported in another paper [5]. We then present the lessons learned and best practices.

4.1 Auto-GCAS Engineers

As part of the survey, engineers were asked to rate the highest level of Auto-GCAS automation that they would be comfortable with. The Sheridan and Verplank [11, 12, 13] taxonomy on 10 automation levels were used, where level 1 is lowest level (Human does the whole job up to the point of turning it over to the computer to implement) and level 10 is the highest level (Computer does the whole job if it decides it should be done, and if so, tells human, if it decides that the human should be told). The majority (80%) of the engineers selected level 7 (computer does whole job and necessarily tells human what it did). Additionally, engineers were asked to speculate how they believe pilots would respond to the same question. In this context, their response should show greater variation. However, the largest portion (46%) selected level 7. By way of comparison, when pilots were asked the same question the majority (65%) also selected level 7 [5]. The agreement between the engineers and pilots on Auto-GCAS automation level shows that the designer/engineers understand the needs of the users/pilots, and reinforces the decision, described in the previous section, to use an automatically executing Auto-GCAS recovery maneuver.

Further analyses included an investigation into the working relationship between engineers and their pilot and manager colleagues. The majority of the engineers reported in the surveys that they either agreed or strongly agreed that the engineers, pilots, and managers with whom they worked were competent and professional. This mutual positive regard could be a key factor contributing to the ability of the engineers to correctly predict the pilot preference of the Auto-GCAS automation levels (discussed above) and the pilot trust evolution (discussed below).

Investigations into Auto-GCAS engineers' culture yielded valuable information that illuminates the impact that engineers' trust of a system has on end-users' acceptance and trust of that system. First and foremost, engineers commented that engineers' professional duty holds them responsible for the safety and wellbeing of the operator. At the system conception and design stages, this manifests in the analysis and design of a system that meets safety requirements before conducting flight tests to refine and validating the design. At the testing and validation stages, engineers report feeling a strong sense of responsibility for protecting the lives of the test pilots, whose task is to fly and test the system at its limits. As such, the engineers indicated that they had a drive to make up for their limited first-hand experience with the system (because they do not fly), by being particularly meticulous in their data collection, analyses and reporting. This culture and interaction with test pilots has led the engineers to adopt a "healthy skepticism" attitude towards new systems, a notion reflected in the test pilot culture reported in our previous paper [5]. In this context, healthy skepticism can be described as an initial withholding of trust in the system, but one that is warranted due to their profession. It would be professionally unhealthy to immediately trust a system without vetting it first. Engineers stated that their "distrust" of the system begins to calibrate towards appropriate trust as the automation continues to work successfully and as the engineers began to ingest data to verify that the system was working as intended.

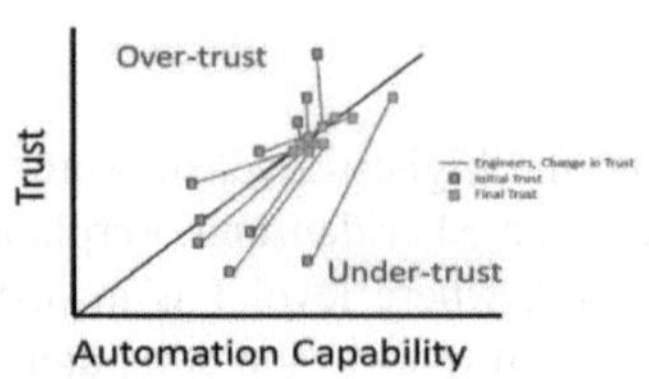

Fig. 2. Engineer Trust Evolution

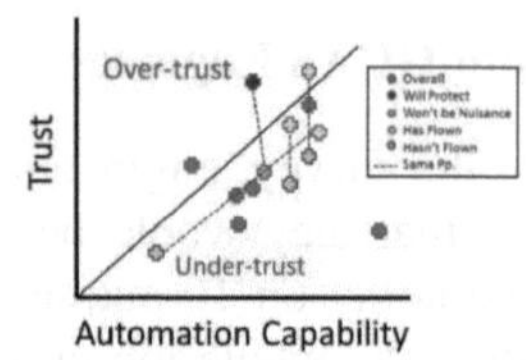

Fig. 3. Engineers' Impression of Pilots' Trust

When asked to indicate how meaningful it was to them to be involved in the Auto-GCAS development, most engineers commented that Auto-GCAS and other projects were equally meaningful. However, some of the engineers who had been highly involved in the development of the system reported feeling more strongly about Auto-GCAS, and a resultant enhanced devotion to being accurate and equitable in how they report their findings. Overall, all engineers commented that their professional culture is evidence-based, believing in what the data support, and that their trust in the system is a function of verified conclusions, rather than the degree to which they believe in the importance or value of that system. Thus, their trust that Auto-GCAS would function as it was designed only developed after having tested it thoroughly. Synonymously, they indicated that their initial perception of the system had little effect on their final trust in the system, which is based on tests that showing that it will prevent collision for 98% of all cases.

Figure 2 shows the engineers' trust evolution (in Auto-GCAS) from when they were first exposed to the system to after having tested it. The graph is a notional framework between trust and automation capability. The horizontal axis is a measure of automation capability (trustworthiness), the vertical axis is a measure of trust in the automation, and the 45-degree angle on the graph represents a line of appropriately calibrated trust, which is a 1:1 ratio between trust of a system and that system's automation capability (trustworthiness). Markings on the calibrated line would indicate that their trust in the automation appropriately reflects the automation capability. If a person marked themselves below the line, they would be indicating "distrust" and if they marked above the line, they would be indicating "over trust.' Participants were given the above graph with the diagonal line (blank of other responses) and asked to mark where they were on the graph when they first heard about Auto-GCAS to where they are now. They were also asked to indicate where they thought pilots and managers would fall on the graph. While the engineers' trust levels move toward the calibrated line, on average, they end up on the under-trust side of the line. This result is consistent with the engineer's reported sense of "healthy skeptism", and their sense of responsibility for the lives of the pilots.

In addition, the engineers were asked to predict where the pilots might place themselves on the same graph. The results are shown in Figure 3. Instead of giving a direct response, many engineers chose to dissect their prediction. As is shown in the figure, some engineers decided to place points on the graph for where the pilots might place themselves for two different situations: before and after flying with Auto-GCAS. One engineer also placed two points, but one for the pilot's trust in the system for saving the aircraft, and another point for the pilot's trust that the system does not interfere with the mission. Despite the diversity in the responses, the engineers' prediction of pilots' trust calibration is consistent with pilots' own calibration as reported in previous papers [5].

4.2 Lessons Learned

Collection, analysis, and interpretation of both the developmental history of Auto-GCAS and the data from the Auto-GCAS engineers have revealed the following valuable lessons and best practices:

- The three design principles of Auto-GCAS (1. Do No Harm, 2. Do Not Impede, and 3. Avoid Collisions) provided the framework for its success in being a trustworthy system. Most notable is the fact the "Avoid Collision" requirement is ranked lower than the other two requirements, indicating the importance of avoiding interference with the pilot. Auto-GCAS took the end-user's needs into high consideration which should help in facilitating appropriate trust on the system from the pilot community. These three principles can be considered as best practices which developers of future automated safety systems can consider.

- The primary lesson learned from the nuisance criteria was that with substantial data from previous work showing that at least 2 seconds of reaction time is required for a situationally-awared pilot to consistently begin a proper recovery, warning a pilot 2 seconds before a recovery is needed will always fail the 1.5-second nuisance criteria. Therefore, it is not possible to design a nuisance-free warning system. Thus, the designer must automate the recovery and take out the reaction time to have a nuisance free system.
- Taking the control away from the pilot (however momentarily as is in the case of Auto-GCAS), especially from a fighter pilot, appears to be a viable strategy for high pressure situations such as avoiding a collision threat. While the pilot culture [5] may shun this strategy because the pilot wants to be in control, it can be done with proper considerations of human factors. In the Auto-GCAS case, the automatic recovery can be seen as an extension of what a pilot would do in a temporally-demanding situation of a terrain threat. Successful fielding of Auto-GCAS will further reinforce the notion that this strategy is applicable for other systems and platforms.
- Healthy skepticism is an essential attitude for both designers and users to have in order to facilitate appropriate trust development. The Auto-GCAS engineers embraced this attitude because of their data-driven, and interestingly, the experimental test pilots also embraced the same attitude as reported in our sister paper [5].
- The engineers' and pilots' common preference for the automation level that Auto-GCAS should have, and engineers' accuracy in predicting the pilots' preference suggest that there is a strong potential for Auto-GCAS to be ultimately accepted by the operational pilots. However, both the engineers and the test pilots had extensive experience with the system, so pilots who are unfamiliar with the system may still be resistant to the system taking control of the aircraft. The mutual professional respect that the engineers and pilots have of each other played a key role in facilitating the common understanding and preferences.
- The Auto-GCAS engineering culture is primarily defined by meticulousness in attention to technical details and thoroughness in considering the data before making conclusions. This data-driven culture is strongly influenced by their responsibility for the safety of, respect for, appreciation of the pilots. This finding suggests that pilots who understand the motivations of the engineers might be more readily to accept automated safety systems. Additionally, the common presence of a "healthy skepticism" in the professional cultures of both the pilots and engineers again indicates further alignment of the two cultures. The data suggest that engineers' understanding of pilot culture helps them to design and test system that will be more readily accepted by pilots. It also further suggests that pilots will be more likely to accept systems if they have a better understanding of the nature of engineering culture as well as the similarities that this culture has to their own. Thus, the development of future systems can greatly benefit from the utility of user feedback and cultural variables to design trustable automation.

5 Conclusions and Future Research Avenues

The findings in this study showed: a) that there is a strong alignment between the engineering and experimental test pilot cultures, and b) that the innovative technical solutions and unique strategy adopted for Auto-GCAS development were effective. These findings indicate strong potential for appropriate trust development in operational pilots. This conclusion corroborates with the conclusion of our case study on Auto-GCAS experimental test pilots. However, these findings are based on pre-deployment data, and because trust calibration is a dynamic process, spanning from the time when the system is first conceived until it goes into operation and retirement, it would be beneficial to conduct a field study of the deployment of Auto-GCAS with operational pilots in order to collect data to validate the hypotheses and to examine the various research issues raised (e.g., potential Auto-GCAS misuse/disuse due to pilot occupational culture and/or operational circumstances, trust evolution from beginning of deployment to stages when opinions are stabilized). Such a field study would generate data and results that could influence and improve the design of the class of systems that take away control from the operator while eliminating nuisance activations and preventing interference with the mission.

The present study offers rich data related to the development of a complex form of automation that has the potential to save lives. The development, testing, and perspectives of engineers, in this case, are closely aligned to the literature on trust in automation as it relates to fostering trust. Specially, Lee and See [2] suggest that trust can be enhanced by: showing past performance of the system, showing the process (i.e., how the system works), making the technology and its algorithms understandable, communicating or visualizing the intent of the system, and using training to assess and verify the system's reliability. The auto-GCAS system exemplifies many of these recommendations, for instance: 1) it has demonstrated high reliability through extensive operational testing and this data has shaped the trust of engineers whose value system strongly emphasizes data, 2) the fly-up maneuver is consistent with a pilot's preferred behavior (e.g., wings level and 5g pull up) which helps the pilot to be familiar with the system and understand its behavior, 3) the intent of the system is to protect the pilot but also avoid interfering with the pilot by circumventing violations of the nuisance budget, this is both a unique aspect of this particular in relation to prior systems and represents an excellent factor to communicate to the pilots in order for them to understand the system's intent, and 4) the system has undergone extensive testing with test pilots receiving considerable training on the system which has supported more calibrated trust overtime. Experience with the Auto-GCAS system has moved engineers and test pilots (see [5]) toward more optimal trust strategies. It will be imperative for the trust-relevant tenants of the system to be shared with the operational pilots who will be interacting with this system for the first time. While the system was designed in such a way as to promote effective trust strategies, and past data suggests that both the engineer and test pilot communities have adopted these optimal strategies, it will be the acceptance or rejection of this system from the operational community that will determine the overall success or demise of the system.

Acknowledgments. This project was funded via NASA Dryden Research Flight Center by the Air Force Office of Scientific Research, Trust and Influence Portfolio. We'd like to thank Mark Wilkins of the DOD, members of the 416th division at Edwards AFB, and Tim McDonald and the SETP for their support; and students who have been involved in this project.

References

1. Parasuraman, R., Riley, V.: Humans and Automation: Use, Misuse, Disuse, Abuse. Human Factors 39(2), 230–253 (1997)
2. Lee, J.D., See, K.A.: Trust in technology: Designing for appropriate reliance. Human Factors 46(1), 50–80 (2004)
3. Swihart, D.E.: Automatic Collision Avoidance Technology. Wright Patterson Air Force Base: Air Force Research Laboratory (2007)
4. Skoog, M.: Digital Terrain Data Compression and Rendering for Automatic Ground Collision Avoidance Systems. NASA, Dryden Flight Research Center, Edwards (2008)
5. Koltai, K., Ho, N., Masequesmay, G., Niedober, D., Skoog, M., Cacanindin, A., Johnson, W., Lyons, J.: Influence of Cultural, Organizational, and Automation Capability on Human Automation Trust: A Case Study of Auto-GCAS Experimental Test Pilots. In: HCI-Aero 2014 (2014)
6. Koltai, K., Ho, N., Masequesmay, G., Niedober, D., Skoog, M., Johnson, W., Cacanindin, A., Lyons, J.: An Extended Case Study Methodology for Investigating Influence of Cultural, Organizational, and Automation Factors on Human-Automation Trust. In: CHI 2014 (2014)
7. Skoog, M.: Automatic Collision Avoidance Technology: Fighter Risk Reduction Report. PowerPoint presentation. NASA DFRC, Edwards, CA (August. 2012)
8. Sears, K.: Auto-GCAS ready for take-off (2007), `http://www.f-16.net/f-16-news-article2461.html` (retrieved on February 1, 2014)
9. Mapes, P.B.: Fighter/Attack Automation Collision Avoidance Systems Business Case. Air Force Research Laboratory, Wright Patterson Air Force Base (2006)
10. Prosser, K.: Nuisance Criteria Development. AFTI, Edwards (1996)
11. Sheridan, T.B., Verplank, W.: Human and Computer Control of Undersea Teleoperators. Man-Machine Systems Laboratory, Department of Mechanical Engineering. MIT, Cambridge (1978)
12. Sheridan, T.B.: Considerations in modeling the human supervisory controller. In: Proceedings of the IFAC 6th World Congress, International Federation of Automatic Control, Laxenburg (1975)
13. Sheridan, T.B., Hennessy, R.T.: Research and modeling of supervisory control behavior. National Academy, Washington, DC (1984)

Adaptive Warning Strategies from Multiple Systems: A Simulator Study with Drivers with Different Reaction Times

Evangelia Portouli[1] and Vassilis Papakostopoulos[2]

[1] National Technical University of Athens, School of Mechanical Engineering, Sector of Industrial Management and Operations Research, Ergonomics Unit, Iroon Politechneiou 9, 15773 Zografou, Greece
portouli@mail.ntua.gr

[2] University of the Aegean, Department of Product and Systems Design Engineering, Ermoupolis, Syros GR 84100, Greece
papakostopoulos@aegean.gr

Abstract. Adaptive interfaces are being developed to avoid drivers' overload and distraction. 24 drivers, assigned in two groups according to their braking reaction time, participated in a driving simulator study experiencing incidents of concurrent warnings by two support systems. Warnings were provided either independently or via an adaptive interface in which one audio warning was intensified and the other was suppressed. The driving behaviour of the two groups was different, drivers with longer reaction times should be specifically considered when designing adaptive interfaces. The employed adaptive strategy caused changes in the driving behaviour of participants with shorter reaction time, another adaptive strategy, possibly generating warnings earlier, may be more appropriate for drivers with longer reaction times. The metrics that were more sensitive in identifying changes in driving behaviour are mean speed during incident, standard deviation of speed, standard deviation of lateral position and minimum time headway to lead vehicle.

Keywords: driving support systems, adaptive interfaces, driving behaviour, evaluation, metrics.

1 Introduction

Several driving support systems are being developed [1] aiming to enhance traffic safety. Such systems usually estimate the probability of a future crash and adequately warn the driver, if needed, so that the driver can take the appropriate averting actions. Due to the growing number of such driving support but also information systems available, an acute design problem is how to integrate all the potentially concurrent warnings and information messages in an adaptive user interface in order to avoid unnecessary drivers' overload and distraction [2]. One of the objectives of the AIDE Integrated Project was to develop a methodology for quantifying the behavioural effects of driving support and information systems and their relation to road safety.

M. Kurosu (Ed.): Human-Computer Interaction, Part III, HCII 2014, LNCS 8512, pp. 485–493, 2014.

In this framework, a driving simulator experiment was performed aiming to identify which driving behaviour metrics are more sensitive for detecting changes in driving behaviour due to adaptive interfaces.

The need for adaptive interfaces to avoid overload and distraction is even bigger for drivers who are slower in perception, processing and reaction. For example, several studies report that older drivers are slower in all the facets of movement initiation and movement execution [3] and that reaction time increases with age [4]. The spare resources for a control process are related with the difference between the total time available and the total time needed to perform the control loop [5]. A thorough review of human perception-brake reaction time studies [6] conclude that factors such as age and cognitive load (either from driving or non-driving factors) are likely to reduce reaction time. Therefore, another objective of the present study was to evaluate whether drivers with longer reaction time would be equally benefited in terms of driving performance from an adaptive warning interface as drivers with shorter reaction time.

2 Method

2.1 Participants

24 persons participated in this experiment. Participants were selected among 57 people who were ranked according to their reaction time in a short test in a driving simulator. After familiarising with the simulator and while driving on a rural road, participants were asked to brake hard as soon as they would see a "STOP" message on the simulator screen. The 12 participants with the shortest reaction time were assigned in the "Early" group and the 12 participants with the longest reaction time were assigned in the "Late" group. The characteristics of the two groups are shown in Table 1.

Table 1. Characteristics of the two groups of participants

Group	Reaction time (s) mean (SD)	Gender	Age (years) mean (SD)	Annual mileage (km) mean (SD)
"Early"	0.8 (0.1)	8 males 4 females	29.8 (3.9)	19000 (9400)
"Late"	1.2 (0.2)	7 males 5 females	41.0 (17.8)	17500 (18000)

2.2 Apparatus

The experiment was performed on the dynamic driving simulator of the Hellenic Institute of Transport, built around a Smart cabin equipped with sensors. The position of all control levers, windshield wipers, blinker, ignition key and light switch is transmitted to the driving computer. All operational elements, steering wheel, accelerator pedal, brake pedal, gearshift lever and handbrake lever, provide nature-true force reactions. The gearshift functions like in the real car either as automatic or "softtip" with incrementing and decrementing the six gears and with reverse gear. The sight system includes five large-screens, each having a width of 2 m. There is on-screen projection with consumer video projectors with 2500 ANSI-lumen. The sound system generates original sounds according to the situation (starter, engine noise, horn, screeching of tires, drive wind, rain, etc.). The vibration device creates natural true vibrations of the car according to the revolvation of the simulated engine.

2.3 Experimental Design

Two support systems were simulated for the purpose of this experiment, a Forward Collision Warning (FCW) and a Blind Sport Warning (BSW) system.

The FCW was activated when the headway to the lead vehicle was less than 1.5 s. The warning was given visually in a simulated head-up display, projected on the central screen of the simulator and located under the central mirror, with a concurrent alarm sound.

The BSW was activated when the Time-To-Collision (TTC) between the rear vehicle at the left lane and the ego vehicle was less than 2 s, or when their distance was less than 5 m. This warning was given visually in a simulated visual display, projected on the left screen and located in the left external mirror, with a concurrent short beep sound.

The simulator scenario was built on a circuit route with a total length 8 km. The route consisted of a motorway with 2 lanes per direction (lane width 3.9 m), an emergency lane at the right and a central crash barrier. A lead vehicle in front of the ego vehicle was inserted at the right lane, at a steady speed of 60 km/h. If the driver overtook this, another lead vehicle was inserted at the right lane in front of the ego vehicle, at a headway of 2 s, driving also at 60 km/h. At the left lane there was a continuous flow of vehicles driving at 100 km/h with a random gap from 1 to 2 s.

The participants were instructed to closely follow the lead vehicle at the right lane.

Four times during the ride, if the TTC between the rear vehicle at the left lane and the ego vehicle was less than 3 s, in which case there would be soon a BSW activated, there was a sudden hard braking of the lead vehicle in the right lane. This would cause after a while a FCW to be generated, if the driver was indeed closely following the lead vehicle according to the instructions. In this way, there was a high chance of having concurrent warnings by the two systems. In these incidents, there were two possible reactions by the participants, either to brake in order to avoid the potential forward collision or to change lane in order to overtake the braking lead vehicle.

Two experimental conditions were used. In the "Non adaptive" condition, the two warnings were given independently of each other, namely in case of concurrent warning from the two systems, both visual warnings were displayed and both sounds were played. In the "Adaptive" condition, in case of concurrent warning from the two systems, an adaptation strategy was followed. The adaptation strategy was the extension of the duration of the audio warning of the FCW, while the audio warning of the BSW was suppressed. Both visual warnings were displayed.

2.4 Procedure

Upon arrival, participants were completing a background questionnaire with personal data and then they were asked to drive for 5 minutes the driving simulator in free traffic on a motorway, so as to get acquainted with it. The warning systems were active during the warm up scenario, so that drivers could get acquainted with their functionalities. Each subject then had to drive the whole simulator scenario in both conditions in counter-balanced order. The participants were asked to closely follow the lead vehicle and return quickly to the right lane, if they ever had to overtake.

2.5 Measures and Analysis Method

The simulator created a log file, where all dynamic variables, speed, vehicle lateral position, distance to lead vehicle, distance to cars in the left lane, brake force, lateral acceleration and other variables were stored with a frequency of 30 Hz. During post-processing of this log file, all incidents of concurrent activation of both systems were annotated. These incidents were not determined in advance; instead they were dependent on the dynamic behaviour of each participant. This is the reason why the number of incidents was not the same among participants.

From the logged data, we have calculated mean speed during the incident of concurrent activation, speed variation, lateral position variation, minimum time headway to lead car, reaction time, time headway to lead car when starting braking, time headway to side cars when initiating lane change, speed variation during lane change, maximum lateral acceleration during lane change. These were calculated for specific time windows around each incident of concurrent activation. Mean speed, standard deviation of speed and of lateral position and minimum headway to lead vehicle were calculated based on data collected in a time window starting 1.5 s before the incident and ending 4 s after the incident. The rest metrics were calculated based on data logged in a time window starting at the time of incident and ending 4 s after the incident. The reasoning for selecting the above time windows was to examine whether the adaptivity affected anticipatory driving behaviour.

Analysis of variance and t-tests were used to study effects of condition and group on the above metrics.

3 Results

In the "Early" group there were 149 incidents of concurrent warning in the "Non Adaptive" condition and 5 accidents. In 90 of the incidents the participants did not react at all, in 29 they reacted by braking, in 6 by changing lane and in 24 by exiting to the right. 20 of these reactions were early, namely they were initiated before the incident of concurrent warning. In the "Adaptive" condition there were 101 incidents of concurrent warnings, of which in 38 there was no reaction, there were 25 brakings, 10 lane changes, 28 right exists. 30 of these reactions were early. The Chi-square test has revealed that there were less cases of no reaction and more cases of early reaction in the "Adaptive" condition for the "Early" group ($p<0.01$). No difference in reactions was found between the two conditions for the "Late" group.

Table 2. Results´ overview

Events	**Early**		**Late**	
	Adaptive	*Non-adaptive*	*Adaptive*	*Non-adaptive*
Conflicts	**101**	**149**	**146**	**144**
Accidents	**14**	**5**	**24**	**15**
No reaction at all	38	90	52	64
Braking	25	29	46	34
Lane change	10	6	9	10
Exit in right	28	24	39	36
of which early reactions	30	20	42	36

In the “Non-adaptive” condition, the ”Early” group was driving at higher speed during the incidents compared to the “Late” group ($p<0.01$).

In the “Adaptive” condition, participants in the “Early” group were driving at lower speeds during the incident than in the “Non-adaptive” condition ($p<0.05$). The same trend can be seen for the “Late” group, but the difference is not significant.

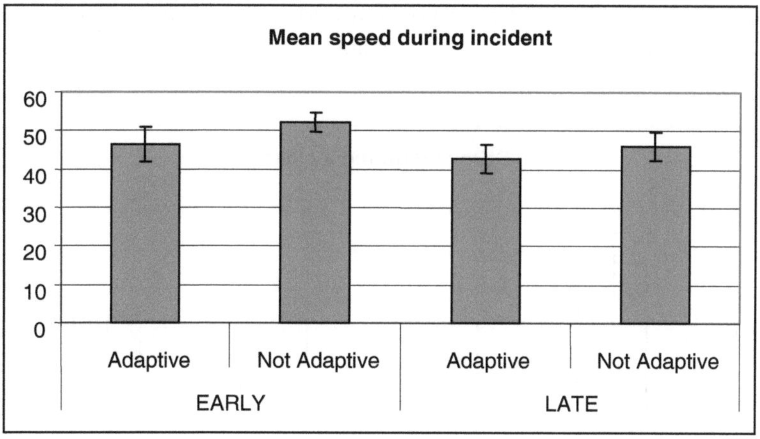

Fig. 1. Mean speed during incidents of concurrent warnings

In the “Non-adaptive” condition the standard deviation of speed of the “Early” group was lower than that of the “Late” group ($p<0.05$).

In the “Adaptive” condition, the standard deviation of speed in the “Early” group during the incident was higher than in the “Non-adaptive” condition ($p<0.01$). The same trend can be seen for the “Late” group, but the difference is not significant.

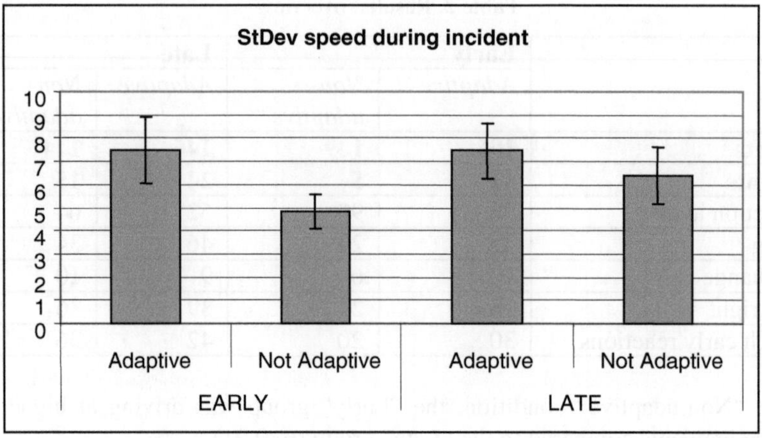

Fig. 2. Standard deviation of speed during incidents of concurrent warnings

No difference as regards the standard deviation of lateral position during the incident was found between groups in the "Non-adaptive" condition.

The standard deviation of lateral position during the incident was higher in the "Adaptive" condition than in the "Non-adaptive" condition for the "Early" group ($p<0.01$).

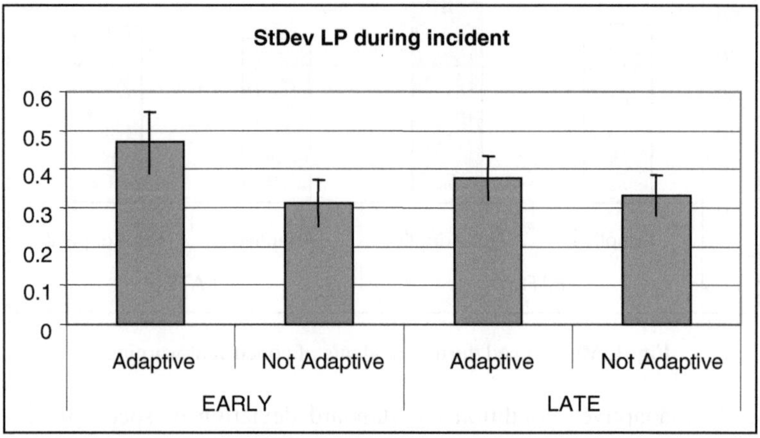

Fig. 3. Standard deviation of lane position during incidents

In the "Non-adaptive" condition the minimum time headway to the lead vehicle during the incident was longer in the "Early" than in the "Late" group ($p<0.01$).

The minimum time headway during the incident was lower in the "Adaptive" condition than in the "Non-adaptive" condition for the "Early" group ($p<0.01$).

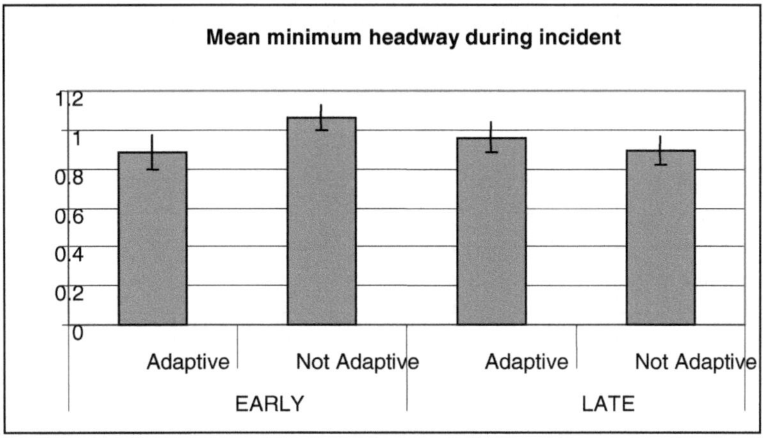

Fig. 4. Minimum headway to lead car during incidents

No difference was found either between groups or conditions as regards reaction time after an incident of concurrent warning and headway to lead car at which a reaction was initiated after such an incident.

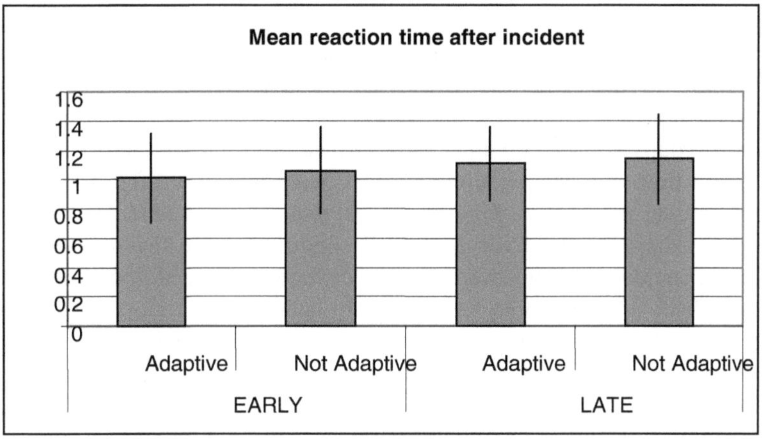

Fig. 5. Reaction time after an incident of concurrent warning

No difference was found between groups or conditions as regards the headway to the vehicle forwards or backwards in the left lane at the time point when a lane change manoeuvre was initiated.

No difference was found between groups or conditions as regards the standard deviation of speed during a lane change.

In the "Non-adaptive" condition, the maximum lateral acceleration after a lane change initiation was higher in the "Early" than in the "Late" group ($p<0.05$).

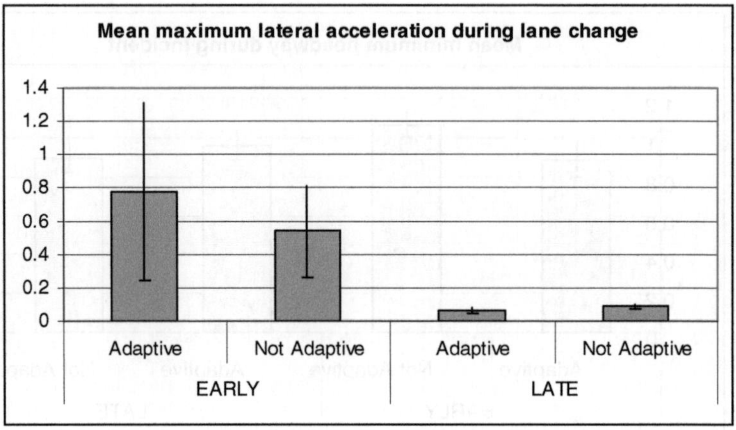

Fig. 6. Maximum lateral acceleration after a lane change initiation due to an incident of concurrent warning

4 Discussion

The results of this work will be discussed in respect to the following questions: (a) whether drivers with longer reaction time were equally benefited in terms of driving performance, from an adaptive warning interface as drivers with shorter reaction time and (b) which driving behaviour metrics are more sensitive for detecting changes in driving behaviour due to adaptive interfaces.

The two groups of drivers, which were formed according to the participants' measured reaction time in a driving simulator test, were found to differ as regards several driving behaviour parameters. Findings reveal that drivers with shorter reaction times, the "Early" group, in the "Non-adaptive" condition, were driving at higher mean speed during incidents, with lower standard deviation of speed, longer minimum time headway to lead vehicle and higher maximum lateral acceleration after a lane change initiation, than the "Late" group. No difference was found between the two groups in the "Non-adaptive" condition as regards standard deviation of lateral position during the incident, reaction time after the incident, headway to lead vehicle at which a reaction was initiated, distances to vehicles in the left lane at the start of a lane change and standard deviation of speed during a lane change. This may indicate that the brake reaction time is indicative of drivers with different driving behaviour during incidents of multiple risk. Such differences in driving behaviour should be separately studied when designing driving support systems.

Furthermore, the findings show that the adaptive interface did not affect the driving behaviour of drivers in the "Late" group. On the contrary, there were effects of the adaptive interface on the driving behaviour of participants in the "Early" group, lower mean speed during incidents, higher standard deviation of speed, higher standard deviation of lateral position, shorter minimum time headway to lead vehicle, less cases of no reaction and more cases of early reaction. These effects are contradictory as regards expected impact on traffic safety, therefore the chosen adaptivity strategy should be further examined. Since no effects of the adaptive strategy on the driving behaviour of the "Late" group were found, it seems that the chosen adaptivity strategy, namely the prolongation of one auditory warning and the suppression of the second, was not adequate for the "Late" group. Considering that the groups were formed according to braking reaction times, and that there should be a difference between the total time needed to perform the control loop [5], it seems that the chosen strategy was not appropriate for drivers with longer reaction time, since it did not increase the total time possibly needed by drivers in the "Late" group. It would have been probably better to employ an adaptivity strategy, which would provide earlier warnings to the "Late" group. Instead, in the "Early" group there is evidence that the adaptive interface induced drivers to be more alert for an anticipated multiple risk, as shown by the higher cases of early reactions.

From the studied metrics, those that were sensitive to detect changes in driving behaviour due to the adaptivity strategy were mean speed during incident, standard deviation of speed, standard deviation of lateral position and minimum time headway to lead vehicle. The metrics that were not sensitive to show changes in driving behaviour were reaction time after an incident, distance to lead vehicle at which a reaction was initiated, distances to vehicles in the adjacent lane at start of a lane change, standard deviation of speed and maximum lateral acceleration during lane change. Although our findings should be confirmed by more data and by experiments in other traffic scenarios and conditions, future studies and methodologies to evaluate the effect of adaptive interfaces on driving behaviour could focus on the more sensitive metrics.

References

1. Barnard, Y., Risser, R., Krems, J. (eds.): The Safety of Intelligent Driver Support Systems. Design, Evaluation and Social Perspectives. Ashgate (2011) ISBN: 978-0-7546-7776-5
2. Damiani, S., Deregibus, E., Andreone, L.: Driver-vehicle interfaces and interaction: where are they going? Eur. Transp. Res. Rev. 1, 87–96 (2009), doi:10.1007/s12544-009-0009-2.
3. Stelmach, G.E., Nahom, A.: Cognitive-motor abilities of the elderly driver. Human Factors 34, 53–65 (1992)
4. Cerella, J.: Information processing rates in the elderly. Psychological Bulletin 98, 67–83 (1985)
5. Hollnagel, E., Woods, D.D.: Joint cognitive systems: Foundations of cognitive systems engineering. CRC Press / Taylor & Francis, Boca Raton (2005)
6. Green, M.: How long does it take to stop. Methodological analysis of driver perception-brake times. Transportation Human Factors 2(3), 195–216 (2000)

Tourist Evacuation Guidance Support System for Use in Disasters

Toshiki Sato, Tomoko Izumi, and Yoshio Nakatani

Graduate School of Science and Engineering, Ritsumeikan University,
Kusatsu, Shiga, 525-8577 Japan
is0019ev@ed.ritsumei.ac.jp,
{izumi-t,nakatani}@is.ritsumei.ac.jp
http://www.sc.ics.ritsumei.ac.jp/

Abstract. Japan is a country that is affected by many disasters such as earthquakes, volcanic eruptions, and typhoons. The Japanese populace fears the occurrence of a major earthquake, such as an earthquake caused by the Nankai Trough and an earthquake in the Tokyo metropolitan region, which are expected to occur with a high probability within 30 years. For these reasons, seismic countermeasures have attracted considerable attention from Japanese people, and the Japanese government is taking various measures against earthquakes. Accordingly, this paper proposes a disaster information provision system using Wi-Fi access points, which gives evacuees disaster information and evacuation routes based on the user's location. We assume users of our system to be tourists, both domestic and from overseas. This system has two main functions, the first of which is to provide tourists with information about the disaster, public transportation, and evacuation areas. By using our system, it is anticipated that smooth evacuation can be realized at an early stage. In addition, as the second main function, our system aims to prevent the concentration of evacuees at the main transport terminal by guiding them to each evacuation space.

Keywords: Disaster information, evacuation support system, tourist, bus stop.

1 Introduction

Japan is known worldwide as a country prone to natural disasters, including earthquakes, volcanic eruptions, and typhoons. In particular, major earthquakes, such a Tokai Earthquake, a Tonankai Earthquake, or a Nankai earthquake caused by the Nankai Trough and an earthquake in the Tokyo metropolitan region are predicted to occur within the next 30 years. As a result, focus on seismic countermeasures in Japan is growing, and the Japanese government is taking various measures.

Meanwhile, the Japanese government is targeting the growth of tourism in Japan, and has positioned the tourism industry as a key policy [1]. Kyoto in particular has become a global tourist destination city, receiving 50 million visitors annually (130,000 per day) [2]. With the trend for increasing overseas tourists, a dramatic

M. Kurosu (Ed.): Human-Computer Interaction, Part III, HCII 2014, LNCS 8512, pp. 494–501, 2014.

increase is anticipated particularly among tourists from economically prospering Asian nations. It can be assumed that large numbers of tourists will be affected if an earthquake or other disaster occurs in such a tourist destination city. However, the disaster prevention countermeasures currently conducted by the government target local residents, and measures that apply to tourists and other irregular visitors from other regions, who are unfamiliar with the area, have only just begun in recent years. For tourist destination cities, the safety of tourists is a factor that cannot be ignored, and it can be stated that protection of their safety is the responsibility of the national and regional authorities.

During a large-scale disaster, it may be problematic for irregular visitors such as tourists and business trippers to return home, as public transport may be stopped or roads may be closed due to damage to roads and railroads and control of traffic. When huge numbers of people are stranded and unable to return home, there is a risk of secondary disaster occurring as large crowds inundate the main transport terminal in the hope of obtaining information about evacuation, moving to a safe place, and returning home. In order to prevent such a secondary disaster, attempts have been initiated to reduce the concentration of stranded persons by guiding them to temporary evacuation shelters dispersed around the city at locations such as parks. In Kyoto, a disaster response guidance method is being examined for the safe evacuation of tourists in sightseeing areas scattered over a wide area, in which tourists who attempt to converge on the central area from peripheral sightseeing areas are provisionally detained in a temporary evacuation shelter. It is important for evacuees to know about evacuation behavior and the locations of temporary evacuation shelters they should move to during a disaster, and also to correctly follow these procedures, in order for the effectiveness of such measures to be demonstrated.

Accordingly, in this study we propose a system that provides disaster information and accurate information about evacuation behavior, for which tourists are the main target. One aim of this system is to provide tourists from within Japan and from overseas with information about the disaster, public transport including status of rail transport, etc., and information on evacuation areas. Specifically, we aim to develop an interface that allows the user to ascertain the situation visually, as far as possible without relying on language. Another aim of this system is to guide evacuees away from transport hubs and towards temporary evacuation shelters such as disaster prevention broadcast bases. Since the temporary evacuation shelters are dispersed around the city, it is necessary to conduct guidance safely, and with a method in which the evacuee can follow instructions, in response to the evacuee's location. In order to conduct guidance that is adapted to location, in this study we focus on bus stops, which are installed in many cities at approximately regular intervals, and provide information related to evacuation guidance at each bus stop. Furthermore, we also propose a method to determine which evacuation shelter to move to from each bus stop, in order to provide guidance instructions that are not only safe but also can obtain the evacuee's trust.

Using this information provision system, we aim to support the initial responses of relevant persons on-site at the regional center, and also to prevent occurrence of secondary disaster and chaos caused by concentration of evacuees at the main station terminal, by providing information that contributes to the smooth evacuation guidance of tourists and other visitors.

2 Related Work

2.1 Behavioral Analysis of Stranded Persons in the Tohoku Earthquake

Although the Tohoku Earthquake, which struck on March 11, 2011, principally damaged the Tohoku region, public transport in the Tokyo metropolitan area was also severely affected, and many people became stranded and unable to return home. Behavioral analysis of victims during the 2011 Tohoku Earthquake, focusing on the Tokyo metropolitan area, is reported in [3]. Among stranded persons who walked home, around 43% visited another location before they reached their homes; the most commonly visited location was "a rail station, or station area" at 30.3%, followed by "a convenience store".

A considerable number of the stranded persons attempted to obtain information by visiting such a location. In this study, by transmitting evacuation-related information at bus stops that exist at walkable distance intervals, we aim to transmit information directed at visiting stranded persons.

2.2 Tourist Evacuation Guidance Method Evaluation Support System

An information sharing support system using WebGIS proposed by Aoyama et al. of Kogakuin University is a communication tool that targets sightseeing areas, utilizing electronic maps accessible via the Web (GIS: Geographic Information System) [4]. Outside of disaster occurrence, businesses engaged in the tourism industry can use the system to provide tourism PR information, and during disasters, each of these businesses becomes a disaster shelter for tourists and local residents and transmits information. A wide range of system users is assumed, including residents, municipal government staff, tourists and tourism-related businesses, and a key feature of the system is the potential for users to mutually convey information, whether during a disaster or in normal periods.

We will explain the system process for normal periods and during disaster occurrence, respectively. Firstly, during normal periods, the system provides information related to tourism and disaster prevention. As each business can update their own tourism information and special recommendations, it is possible for the system to maintain up-to-date information. The process of registering information updates is as follows: 1) the registrant (business, resident, etc.) selects a category icon for information related either to tourism or to disaster prevention, 2) confirms the registered location, 3) inputs detailed information. With this process, the registration operation is simplified, and it is possible for anyone to register information. Moreover, the system is also assumed to aim to have a synergistic effect on tourism PR, as the registered information can be applied as a communication tool for information-sharing between residents, municipal government staff, tourists and tourism-related businesses, etc., via the Internet.

Next, during the occurrence of a disaster, it becomes possible to aggregate information from numerous businesses dispersed over the city, such as their respective business continuation status, readiness for accepting disaster victims, the conditions of the local vicinity, and so on. By handling information appropriate for the situation, the system is envisaged to play a large role in ascertaining the local damage situation during the occurrence of a disaster.

This system has been further expanded into a system for the contribution and sharing of disaster prevention information via cooperation between residents and municipal government [4]. When the user inputs location information with disaster or damage information, a pictogram that expresses the disaster/damage status (complete destruction, partial destruction, partial collapse, fire outbreak, etc.) is displayed on the system screen in the relevant location. The advantage of the system can been found in the fact that it is possible to comprehend the information contents at a glance.

3 System Construction

In this study, we propose a system that targets tourists who are unfamiliar with the area during disaster occurrence, provides an interface that allows the user to visually perceive information about the disaster, public transport, etc., and indicates evacuation behavior in response to the tourist' location.

We envisage smartphones to be used as a device to provide this information, as their adoption has expanded, and there is a high possibility that they are carried by tourists around sightseeing areas. However, immediately after the 2011 Tohoku Earthquake, telephone and email services for cellphones were temporarily suspended due to over-congested lines caused by cellphone companies' restriction of communications. In contrast, in the case of smartphone users, it was reported that earthquake victims were able to use WiFi services and confirm their personal safety on social media. Currently, provision of WiFi spots is increasing in places visited by large numbers of people, such as shopping districts and station areas in major cities, and anyone who completes a simple registration procedure can use WiFi wireless networks in such places. For example, WiFi networks have been set up at bus stops located at various locations in the city of Kyoto, and visiting tourists are being encouraged to use them.

Accordingly, in this study, we provide useful information at bus stops that is appropriate for the area and support for evacuation guidance, on the premise that tourist evacuees will use WiFi networks at bus stops during the occurrence of a disaster. In concrete terms, the system will provide the follow information.

1. Disaster information: Disaster information for the surrounding areas, centering on the access points used by tourist evacuees, as well as information on facilities useful for evacuation, will be displayed on a map in the form of pictograms. Our reason for using pictograms is so that tourists whose native language is not Japanese will be able to easily comprehend the situation from the pictogram images. The system allows users to select the categories of displayed information, thus avoiding overcrowding of the map screen with multiple pictograms, and heightening cognition.
2. Evacuation guidance: In order to conduct smooth evacuation guidance for a huge number of evacuees, it is necessary that evacuees do not head immediately to the main transport terminal, but first evacuate to temporary shelters, and then perform a phased evacuation in accordance with the support of the authorities. Thus,

the system's evacuation guidance provides clear instructions about which temporary evacuation shelter users should go to from each bus stop location.

4 System Proposal

We aim to develop a map-based system whereby tourists can obtain useful information from WiFi access points, as a Web application that can be used by both the iOS and Android operating systems.

The system contents for the provision of disaster information and evacuation guidance are explained respectively below.

Disaster information is displayed using pictograms on GIS. First, a selection list of information assumed to be necessary immediately after the occurrence of a disaster is displayed (Fig.1). We set five categories of information that can be selected in this system: temporary evacuation shelters, public toilets, WiFi accessible spots, convenience stores, and transport information. When the user ticks the box next to their required information category, a pictogram of the selected information only is displayed on GIS (Fig. 2). The information of these pictograms is pre-registered in a database, but when a disaster occurs, the system also provides a function whereby the system administrator can omit display of data about areas that have become unusable due to the effects of the disaster.

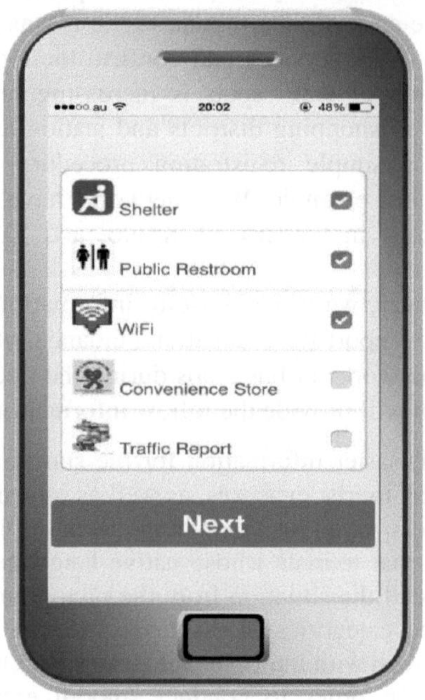

Fig. 1. List of provided information

Fig. 2. Example of evacuation guidance

The evacuation guidance function is explained as follows. It is necessary to safely guide the stranded persons who are located at each bus stop to respective temporary evacuation shelters. We specify one evacuation shelter for each bus stop, because confusion would be caused if several stranded persons at the same bus stop had different respective evacuation destinations. On the evacuation guidance screen, an appropriate evacuation route from the WiFi access point at the bus stop to the temporary evacuation shelter is displayed to the evacuees.

The location of each bus stop, the estimated number of stranded persons at each bus stop, the location of each evacuation shelter and the number of people who can be accommodated at each shelter are assumed to be known. Furthermore, with the existence of bus routes, we assume that the starting or ending point of many bus routes will be the main rail station. We propose an allocation method that takes the following points into consideration in order to safely lead stranded persons away from the main station to temporary evacuation shelters.

- The total estimated number of stranded persons at bus stops allocated to each evacuation shelter must not exceed the capacity of the evacuation shelter
- Lead the evacuees to an evacuation shelter close to the bus stop
- Evacuees from one bus stop must not overtake evacuees from another bus stop
- Where possible, guide evacuees in a direction towards the station

The allocation method is described in concrete terms below. Evacuation shelters are determined in sequence from the starting point bus stop (rail station) onwards. The system recommends evacuation shelters that are located within a circular area 50m in radius, with each bus stop at the center (Fig. 3). If an evacuation shelter with sufficient capacity for the estimated number of stranded persons at the bus stop does not exist within the circular area, the radius of the circle is widened to 100m, then to 150m. If multiple evacuation shelters with sufficient capacity exist within the circular area, the shelter with the smallest angle in a triangle consisting of the rail station, the bus stop, and the evacuation shelter is selected (Fig. 3). When an evacuation shelter is allocated to a bus stop, the estimated number of stranded persons at the bus stop is subtracted from that shelter's capacity. This method is applied to all bus stops.

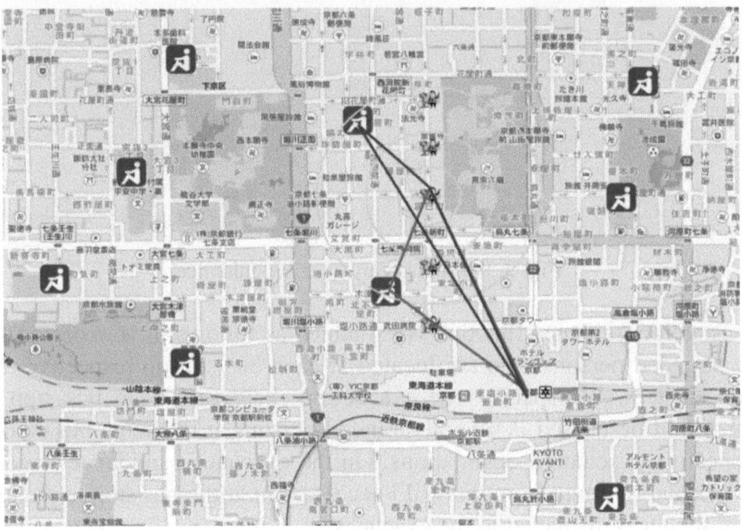

Fig. 3. Evacuation shelter recommendation method

5 Conclusion

In this paper, we proposed system construction for an information provision tool and a system that efficiently guides the evacuation of stranded persons, focusing on bus stops, in order to contribute to smooth evacuation guidance of tourists and other persons who are unfamiliar with the area during disaster occurrence.

In future, in cases when the system is unable to recommended an evacuation shelter because the nearest shelter to the station from the bus stop does not have sufficient capacity, we aim to adopt a persuasive interface and construct an effective evacuation guidance system that incorporates the current proposed algorithm.

References

1. Ministry of Land, Infrastructure, Transport and Tourism, Japan Tourism Agency. Tourism Nation Promotion Basic Law (July 01, 2012) (in Japanese), `http://www.mlit.go.jp/kankocho/kankorikkoku/kihonhou.html`
2. City of Kyoto Industry and Tourism Bureau. Annual Report of Survey on Tourism in Kyoto City for 2011 (2012) (in Japanese)

3. Cabinet Office Council for Disaster Victims Unable to Return Home during a Tokyo Metropolitan Earthquake. Results of Survey on Status of Measures for Disaster Victims Unable to Return Home: Response to 3/11 and Subsequent Initiatives (in Japanese)
4. Aoyama, T., Ichii, T., Murakami, M., Hisada, Y.: WebGIS used in Normal and Disaster Situations for Sightseeing Spot: Application for the ITO in IZU Peninsula. In: Summaries of Technical Papers of the Annual Meeting of the Architectural Institute of Japan, pp. 491–492 (2006) (in Japanese)

Evaluating Novel User Interfaces in (Safety Critical) Railway Environments

Anselmo Stelzer, Isabel Schütz, and Andreas Oetting

Railway Engineering, TU Darmstadt, Germany
{lastname}@verkehr.tu-darmstadt.de

Abstract. In this paper we present a research facility for railway operations, the Eisenbahnbetriebsfeld Darmstadt (EBD) as simulation environment. Here, new operational and dispatching software for a safety critical environment can be thoroughly evaluated. In three expert and two user evaluations it could be shown that the EBD is a well-suited environment for testing as an extension to traditional methods. On the one hand, implementing software in the EBD can be done in a timely manner and at relatively low costs. Also, it is possible to trigger certain disruptions and malfunctions at will which would be impractical in real operations. On the other hand, studies have shown that users are really keen on testing in the EBD and that their mood is constantly good all along.

1 Introduction

The domain of railway operations is in most parts a safety critical environment with special requirements regarding used technology and software. The evaluation of the software used is more complicated than in standard environments, mainly because it cannot be tested and evaluated in the real environment. As for many other safety critical domains real testing environments exist, this is not possible for the actual railway operation. For a realistic evaluation an environment which comes as close to reality as possible is needed to produce realistic results and to make the assessors act realistically.

An evaluation and testing environment is crucial to show that developed software actually fulfils its mission. But tests in environments that simplify reality by simulation or abstraction are – depending on the level of abstraction – only partially transferrable to reality.

That is why an environment is needed for the railway domain to test and evaluate new software and interfaces which comes very close to real operations. In this paper we will present a possible solution for this problem.

It has been shown in different evaluations that, concerning mental effort, testing in this environment is very demanding for the user and can therefore be estimated as very realistic. Moreover, users tend to be really enthusiastic about testing in such an environment which increases the willingness for testing as such.

M. Kurosu (Ed.): Human-Computer Interaction, Part III, HCII 2014, LNCS 8512, pp. 502–512, 2014.

In section 2 we talk about the problems and our motivation for evaluation in railway operations and in section 3 we will present a possible solution for the problem, the Eisenbahnbetriebsfeld Darmstadt (EBD). We will present three practical uses in section 4 to show the suitability of our EBD. In the following chapter we will discuss the approach and conclude in section 6.

2 Related Work

Railway operation is a critical field of application where software has to work correctly and reliably. Thus, software of railway technology in the field of control, command and signaling is subject to very high requirements. Knight [1] points out problems that arise from safety-critical applications. Functional verification by testing is also difficult due to the environment this software is used in [1].

But the safety issue not only concerns the functionality and actions of a software in this domain, but also the dispatching actions a dispatcher decides to carry out based on displayed information. Today, almost everywhere in railway operations software is used to support railway staff in their work, mostly by displaying relevant information to staff to support them in their daily tasks. Some software provides functionality different from information display such as supervision of actions (in interlocking environments) or, very rarely, decision support [2,3,4].

Changing interfaces may entail seemingly missing or misleading information either through bad implementation, but also through staff not recognizing relevant elements in the new interface. As a result dispatching decisions cannot be carried out in the same quality as with the existing system. This is one of the reasons why introducing new interfaces in a railway operation system takes an unusual long amount of time.

Thimbleby [5] faces this problem by introducing Interaction Walkthrough (IW) for safety critical interactive systems. He explains that from an existing or prototype system another system is developed in which the remarks of the assessor are considered and implemented [5]. It is further argued that the changes achieved by IW are less expensive than programming from scratch and therefore significantly more economical [5]. For this approach to work out, the assessor has to be an expert to be able to discover discrepancies or malfunctions in the evaluated system.

Our aim goes a step further in the process of introducing new software. To make new or changed software being widely used, it needs to be accepted by its future users. Moore [6] distinguishes between continuous and discontinuous innovations. While continuous innovations are generally easily accepted by the vast majority of users, discontinuous innovations need to be carefully introduced. Moore defines a set of user types to classify the degree of innovations they can bear, thus there is a spectrum between continuous and discontinuous innovation [6]. Innovators and Early Adopters can cope better with discontinuous innovations early on while the (Early and Late) Majority need a certain amount of time to adapt to new technology and the Laggard needs an unusual high amount of time. The types are distributed in a bell curve (Figure 1).

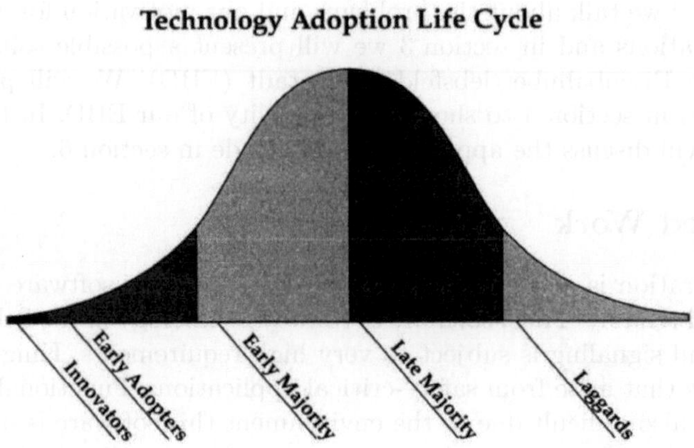

Fig. 1. Distribution of adopters for new technologies [6]

For the domain of railway operations we can assume a normal distribution for the railway staff within Moore's classification. That also means that the introduction of innovations is generally not easier than in standard user environments and the more discontinuous an innovation is, the harder for the staff to adapt.

An evaluation by an expert assessor will reveal malfunctions, badly designed interfaces and discrepancies in a system, but as an expert in the domain the assessor is rather to be classified as Early Adopter than a majority user. Accordingly, the degree of innovation he can cope with will be higher than that of the standard user. To evaluate the acceptance of average users an environment is needed where the interfaces can be evaluated without interfering with critical operations. Our aim is to create a setting in which new systems critical to railway operations can be evaluated most realistic with the future user as assessor. The evaluation is supposed to allow conclusions about the acceptance the usability of new interfaces.

3 Approach

The Eisenbahnbetriebsfeld Darmstadt (EBD) is a research facility for railway operations which embodies a very realistic simulation environment. It is operated by the Department of Railway Engineering, DB Training [7] and AKA Bahn [8]. In contrast to computer simulations the EBD comprises actual railway technology as far as possible. As a matter of fact only tracks and trains are models while the interlocking technology is real. Consisting of 13 stations, 160 main tracks and 380 points and derailers on about 90 kilometers of simulated line, the EBD offers a size in which scenarios of an adequate complexity can be created. Moreover, the EBD contains all generations of interlocking systems (mechanical and electro-mechanical signal boxes, relay interlocking systems and electronic interlocking systems) and the respective dispatchers' work areas. Beyond infrastructural dispatching (actual railway operations), there are also work places for transportation dispatchers (amongst others rolling stock and staff dispatching, connection dispatching). The EBD is further equipped with technology that is generally used for railway operations such as phones with special dialing, walkie-talkies, and railway specific printed forms. This allows providing the complete chain of railway operation and dispatching to be mapped within the EBD. The EBD contains 13 computer work places (yellow rectangles in Figure 2) which can be switched between transportation dispatcher's and infrastructural dispatcher's work place [9].

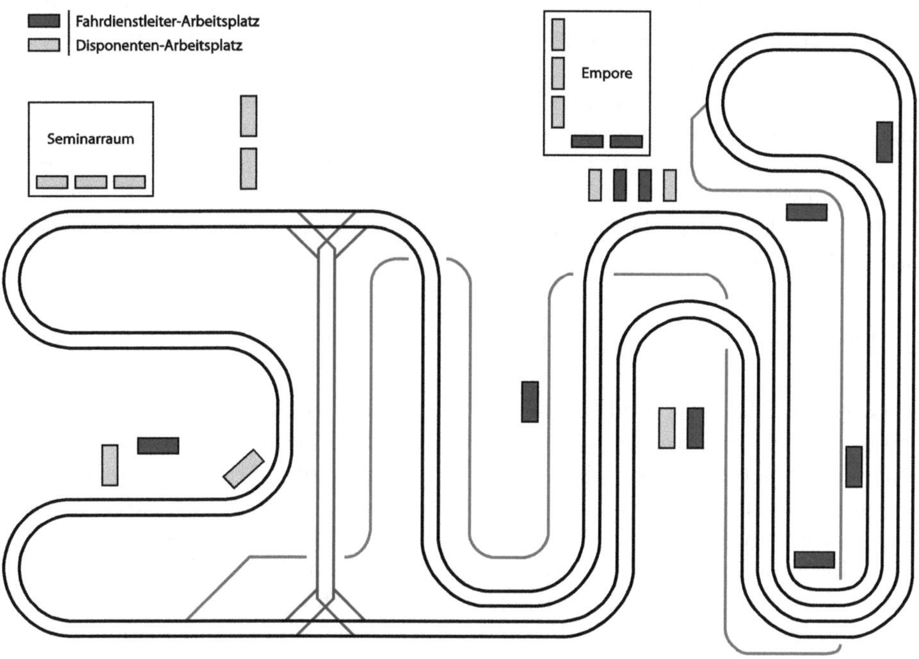

Fig. 2. Basic layout of infrastructure and work places in the EBD [9]

Beyond the working places there are seminar rooms. These are mainly used in seminars as training rooms, but they can also be used during the evaluation, i.e. for focus groups or interviews. The used software in the EBD is developed by one of the partners, AKA Bahn. With respect to the range of functions, the software corresponds to actual railway systems. Furthermore, implementation and user interface are identical to the real ones. This can be made sure on the one hand through the guidelines which were considered during the development of the software. On the other hand, among the members of AKA Bahn are traffic controllers, dispatchers, signalling technicians or employees of the Federal Railway Office who use their expert knowledge for this project. This creates an independence from manufacturers, for example of interlocking technology such as Siemens or Thales [9].

All this makes the EBD as real as it gets and apart from that there are many advantages of testing in such an environment. If new elements are required for an evaluation they can be implemented in a timely manner. New interfaces can easily be attached and tried out, either in a standalone manner or alongside the existing interface, both in real operations mode.

Since the working areas are completely identical to the ones used in real railway operations with all the equipment needed, this makes sure that dispatchers and traffic controllers act in a realistic manner. It is not possible to cheat, i.e. by watching the trains or tracks; users need to fully rely on the software. This is achieved through the special construction of the EBD which has users sit away from the stations they are responsible for. Furthermore, besides realistic surroundings, it is possible to create disruptions and malfunctions in the operation at any time and in any manner, which is not possible in real operations [9]. This facilitates triggering relevant situations as needed for the evaluation. Since testers have no line of sight to the test leader, there are no indications for an upcoming event.

All this makes the EBD a predestined area for the evaluation of new interfaces and functions in the domain of railway operations.

4 Practical Evaluation

Recently, the EBD was used to evaluate several new visual approaches and modified interfaces in railway operations. Partly, the interfaces were developed at the Department of Railway Engineering of TU Darmstadt, partly cooperation was formed to evaluate externally developed interfaces. In both cases the Department of Railway Engineering as one of the operators of EBD took part in the evaluation process and is technically supported by AKA Bahn.

Both infrastructural and transportation dispatching support software have been evaluated in the EBD. For this it is generally necessary to create operational scenarios in which the tests can be performed; however, often it is possible to reuse existing scenarios and/or to extend them. This keeps the functional effort relatively small. Technically, the new software solutions need to be interfaced with the EBD. Again, the effort is very small compared to real environments, as existing software is developed in-house, therefore extendible and accessible via open interfaces.

Subsequently, we will present three approaches of interface evaluation in the EBD. Firstly, we will talk about an expert evaluation of a new way of displaying connection conflicts to the dispatcher. Secondly, we will focus on two user evaluations of a newly developed interlocking user interface and about a redesigned interlocking user interface. Both system and evaluation methods will be shown in detail.

4.1 Evaluating an Alternative Visual Approach for Connection Dispatching

In a research project with Deutsche Bahn, a new way of displaying connections and connection conflicts was developed. Part of the project was an evaluation of the new display on real conditions.

For the visualization each connection is assigned to a category. The way of displaying a connection is based on the same. The category advices the user how to proceed with a connection (conflict). The conflicts are arranged in a matrix depending on feeders and distributors (Figure 3). The alignment of connections in the matrix format is novel compared to the interface the transportation dispatcher is used to nowadays. Connections are presented in the cells of the matrix in case a connection for the feeder and the distributor exist. The background color of the cell depends on the category. Within the cell, additional information concerning the connection is displayed [4].

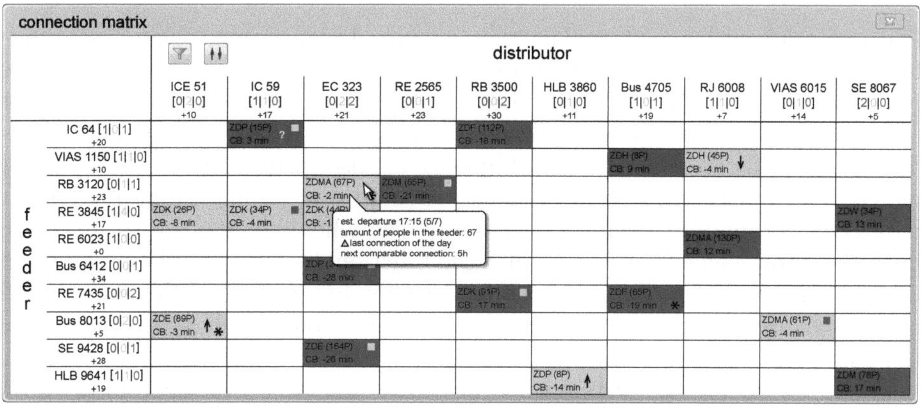

Fig. 3. Connection matrix [4]

Before implementing a prototype, several focus groups were hosted to gain input for the interface. The focus groups consisted of dispatchers which would have to work with the newly developed interface in the productive environment.

The EBD was used to proof that dispatchers are able to work with this new environment during a testing scenario with prospective users. The evaluation group consisted of dispatchers that, in addition to their daily dispatching routine, also work as trainer for quality enhancement seminars in the EBD. Therefore route knowledge was present among the participants.

To perform the evaluation of the new interface, an existing scenario was adopted and extended with connections and interchangers such that the matrix was filled with connections and information to be displayed for each of them. While running the scenario, several trains were delayed individually to provoke connection conflicts. Also, the evaluation group could choose specific trains to be delayed to try out functions for a special connection pair. Apart from existing elements such as a schedule, the scenario contained rolling stock, staff, special waiting time rules and interchange times on platforms. Using the EBD, the effect in the software if different approaches to interchange times are used could be shown.

Since an existing scenario could be used as a basis, the cost of interfacing the new interface with the EBD was comparatively low. The prototype was exclusively developed for this environment and directly interacts with existing dispatching software already available at the EBD.

The evaluation revealed some interesting results even though the opinion of the dispatchers had already been obtained within the focus groups. The evaluation within the realistic environment of the EBD showed several aspects to be improved in the interface before it could be used in real operations. These aspects have been adopted to produce a revised version of the interface.

4.2 Evaluating a Newly Developed Interlocking User Interface

In cooperation with an external partner, a newly designed interlocking user interface was tied in with the EBD for a first evaluation. The interface is a complete innovation by combining a dispatcher and a traffic controller user interface. It combines functions which are nowadays spread over multiple programs. Moreover, it contains an event triggered approach. Also, the design as such is completely new and is reminiscent of an infrastructure modelling program. Thus it is possible to zoom in from an overview of the whole country up to a specific infrastructural element. The look and the functionality are completely different from electronic interlocking systems used today. Implementing this system will cause a change in the way of working and of operation as well as an adaption of the guidelines.

While interfacing the system with the EBD, an expert evaluation in the form of a Guidelines Review was conducted. Some experts from AKA Bahn compared handling and functioning of the software with corresponding descriptions in existing guidelines for railway operations in Germany. This revealed not only bugs in the system, but also some real fundamental errors in functioning. During these expert evaluations, focus was not only on correctness of function, but also on integrating as many functions as needed to test the system in a user evaluation. Since the experts used the interface for normal railway operations missing features manifested straightforwardly. Therefore it was possible to implement these features before further user testing. Ensuring that all essential functions have been implemented and keeping the amount of errors small is important for users testing the system because immature software can be frustrating to handle and therefore can distort the results of the study. Since on one hand it is not trivial to find an adequate amount of suitable users and on the other hand testing is costly, it is crucial to ensure that all results can be used. Moreover, completing and fine-tuning functions early on can drastically reduce time pressure.

4.3 Evaluating a Redesigned Interlocking User Interface

A study comparable to the one from subsection 4.2, but more advanced was realized with a redesigned interlocking user interface. In this system, the existing interface was enhanced by a new window framework. This framework is supposed to be gradually extended by all tools a traffic controller is presently working with. So only the design of the interlocking interface was slightly modified compared to the electronic interlocking used today, while functionality and way of operations remain the same.

Before actual user evaluation, the same procedure as shown in subsection 4.2 was carried out to ensure success of the study. The aim of the user evaluation which took place after the expert evaluation assessed the usability of the user interface and the mental effort the traffic controller faces during testing. The evaluation was divided into three parts: firstly a free exploration, secondly the accomplishment of a set of tasks and thirdly a scenario the traffic controller has to handle with the prototype. Free exploration aimed at familiarizing the user with the system. Focus in the second part of the evaluation was on some basic functions like zooming, window handling and panning. The last part aimed at simulating common operations of the traffic controller with the system. The basis for this scenario was a timetable with duration of about one hour which was specially developed for this evaluation. It contains 34 trains per hour of different types, e.g. commuter and long distance trains, with different passenger stops, intervals and velocities. Through comparison with real timetables and through expert evaluations it could be ensured that the timetable is as close to reality as possible. Moreover, the scenario contains seven events within half an hour. These were chosen according to the frequency they occur in reality and with consideration of the implemented functions of the prototype. Examples for events are a defective train door, a point failure or alarm of the hot axle box detector.

At the beginning of the evaluation, users were requested to fill in a demographic questionnaire and a questionnaire assessing their current mood. After each session, users were asked to state their mental effort and their opinion about the system, also by using questionnaires. Since it was the first such user evaluation, it was aimed to keep equipment and therefore costs short, which is why the mental effort was assessed using questionnaires instead of physiological measurements. Eventually, the users were asked one more time to state their current mood by using a questionnaire and they were invited to take part in an interview to state their opinion about their experience in using the prototype. During the whole evaluation, a video camera was used. Moreover, the users were observed during the whole evaluation by the test leader. Additionally, users were encouraged to think aloud during the whole study.

On one hand, the study has revealed many facts and improvement proposals about the prototype, but it has also shown many interesting facts about testing in the EBD. It could clearly be observed that perceived mental effort measured by the "Subjective Mental Effort Questionnaire" (SMEQ) increased from "hardly demanding" after the set of tasks to "quite demanding" and even "strong demanding" after the scenario. This is the result of the realistic and demanding scenario with many events. Moreover, it was revealed that users had no positive impression of the prototype. The opinion of the users about the prototype substantially worsened during the evaluation and, as a result, enthusiasm declined drastically. Astonishingly, the mood of the users was constantly good. They felt as active, engaged, awake and attentive as before. During the interviews, it could be stated that participants rated the evaluation itself very positively. They were really keen on evaluating in the EBD and were fascinated of the infrastructure. One difficulty that manifested itself during the scenario was finding the location of events. Users had to face the difficulty that neither the prototype nor the locality where known to them. In case of an upcoming event, users had a hard time finding the respective location. Only after having located the origin, they could start dealing with the event. Then they had to look for the right software feature, so time for processing only one event was substantial. Since the time for the scenario was limited to half an hour, events were triggered in short succession. That's why during evaluation, users had to cope with many events in parallel because most of the time, events could not be processed completely before the next started. This was very demanding and sometimes confusing for the users.

5 Discussion

The EBD offers great opportunities to evaluate new functions and interfaces in a real environment. Whereas the environment is as close to reality as a simulation can be, interfacing costs are very small compared to an implementation in real operations.

Still, implementing a new interface and a scenario in the EBD is a substantial effort, as the scenarios have to be developed and new components need to be interfaced with the EBD. That is why different methods should be applied beforehand. This includes for example an Expert Evaluation, Focus Groups as performed in subsection 4.1, Guidelines Reviews as performed in subsection 4.2 and subsection 4.3 or the Interaction Walkthrough proposed by Thimbleby [5]. Heuristic evaluation as [10] can also be envisioned.

After having ensured that the evaluator faces an application that has already a certain degree of quality and a sufficient range of functions, it can be tested for practical application by common users. The comparably easy integration of new technologies also enables several evaluation sessions with an improved version of the new interface after feedback from the evaluator.

There is a broad spectrum of methods which can be used to evaluate a prototype with users. In subsection 4.3 we have performed an evaluation using video recording, questionnaires, observation and interviews. Users were highly motivated, enthusiastic und dedicated, even after having tested for about two hours, not being delighted about the prototype and facing an increasing mental effort. Larger scale studies can be conceived which facilitate psychophysiological measurements, eye- or mouse-tracking to measure mental effort much more precisely. Using these evaluation methods, it must be considered that having no route knowledge can cause the evaluator to have an increased mental effort and to look around in a confused way. For this it might be optimal to develop some sort of filter to discern glances which are looking for the right location along the track, but this might not be superficial.

One disadvantage of evaluating in the EBD is the lack of route knowledge. Finding the right location in case of occurring events may take some time and can distort the measurement of reaction or processing times. Therefore, timing processing or reaction durations is problematic because results can be misleading. In general, users in field studies need more time to perform tasks as it was observed by [11]. In reality, traffic controllers have to take route knowledge examinations and are not allowed to work independently before having passed [12]. This fact cannot be considered during testing because it is too time-consuming to teach the users before testing. Moreover, studies have shown that testing is very exhausting for the users. So the duration of tests must be limited to one or one and a half hour.

Although it is very easy to implement some form of logging every action the user executes on the prototype, results would as well be distorted because of missing route knowledge. Maybe after having conducted additional evaluations or seminars in the EBD, as for the assessors in subsection 4.1, it might be possible that more of this data be valid because the users accumulate route knowledge. Missing route knowledge should also be considered during creation of the scenario. There should be enough time between the events so that users do not have to cope with two events at the same time. This might also distort the results because mental effort increases drastically.

Summarizing, it can be stated that the EBD is a very good environment for usability tests as an extension to traditional methods which helps to achieve feedback about the quality and usability of newly developed software or interfaces.

6 Conclusion

First evaluations have revealed the possibilities the EBD offers for evaluations. Therefore much more research should be done. Fields of investigation are for example the development of suitable scenarios. It is necessary to define the adequate number of events to be scheduled within a certain amount of time. Also, some larger scale studies in the field of mental effort using psychophysiological instruments might be useful. This may confirm results obtained from a first study comprising questionnaires. A more general objective might be a comparison of the results attained in field studies, laboratory studies and simulation. Probably, a comparison with the kind of simulation being performed in the field of aviation may reveal interesting facts.

Based on the results of the evaluation presented in subsection 4.1 an implementation in a real control center is carried as the next step for this project. Thus, the EBD can help to gain knowledge about the usability of newly designed interfaces and their potential for the real environment.

References

1. Knight, J.C.: Safety critical systems: challenges and directions. In: Proceedings of the 24th International Conference on Software Engineering, ICSE 2002, pp. 547–550. IEEE (2002)
2. Fay, A.: Wissensbasierte Entscheidungsunterstutzung fur die Disposition im Schienenverkehr: Eine Anwendung von Fuzzy-Petrinetzen. VDI Verlag, Düsseldorf (1999)
3. Kurby, S.: Makroskopisches Echtzeitdispositionsmodell zur Lösung von Anschlusskonflikten im Eisenbahnbetrieb. PhD thesis, Technische Universität Dresden, Dresden (February 6, 2012)
4. Stelzer, A., Oetting, A., Chu, F.: Connection Dispatching - an Algorithmic and Visual Support for the Dispatcher. In: Proceedings WCTR 2013 (2013)
5. Thimbleby, H.: Interaction walkthrough: Evaluation of safety critical interactive systems. In: Doherty, G., Blandford, A. (eds.) DSVIS 2006. LNCS, vol. 4323, pp. 52–66. Springer, Heidelberg (2007)
6. Moore, G.A.: Crossing the chasm: Marketing and selling technology products to mainstream customers, Rev. ed., [nachdr.] edn. HarperCollins Publ., New York (2005)
7. Deutschen Bahn AG: Website of DB Training Learning & Consulting (2014)
8. AKA Bahn e. V.: Website of Akademischer Arbeitskreis Schienenverkehr e.V. (2014)
9. Streitzig, C., Stelzer, A., Schön, S., Chu, F.: TU Darmstadt – Research, Training & More Besides. EURAILmag, 152–159 (2012)
10. Nielsen, J.: Heuristic evaluation. Usability Inspection Methods 17, 25–62 (1994)
11. Duh, H.B.L., Tan, G.C., Chen, V.H.H.: Usability evaluation for mobile device: a comparison of laboratory and field tests. In: Proceedings of the 8th Conference on Human-computer Interaction with Mobile Devices and Services, pp. 181–186. ACM (2006)
12. Hausmann, A., Enders, D.H.: Grundlagen des Bahnbetriebs. Bahn Fachverlag (2007)

Identification of User Requirements for Mobile Applications to Support Door-to-Door Mobility in Public Transport

Ulrike Stopka

Technische Universität Dresden, Dresden, Germany
ulrike.stopka@tu-dresden.de

Abstract. The mobility service market has changed rapidly in the last decade. Innovative solutions like bike-, car- and ridesharing complete the classic individual car and public transport. The integration of these different transport modes to intermodal mobility solutions can be supported very effectively by the features and services of modern smartphones. The development of augmented mobility apps requires a continuous acquisition and evaluation of the public transport user needs and preferences. The paper describes the influencing factors for these demands and overviews different clustering and investigation approaches from practical projects and scientific studies. Finally the results of an own empirical study at the TU Dresden based on a focus group interview are presented. Appropriate recommendations for action are derived.

Keywords: intermodal mobility, public transport, mobility services, mobile applications, user requirements, preferences, habit, focus group, usability.

1 Motivation

Against the background of declining resources and rising energy prices, demographic changes with dramatic shifts in population density maintaining a well-functioning public transport is of particular public interest in every country. In the area of individual transport, car drivers have become accustomed to use intelligent navigation systems. Without their own activities they are continuously informed about the travel route, expected travel time, detours, accidents and any other possible disturbances on their way. These days the private car is still most convenient for door-to-door transport. Public transport is not yet able to meet these expectations in the same way. That's why it lost some of its attractiveness compared to car traffic. As reaction to this situation the initiative of the German Federal Ministry for Economic Affairs and Energy "Door-to-Door - A mobility initiative for public passenger transport of the future" was launched. The related research projects and activities focus on passenger navigation along his route from the starting point to the final destination. This includes pre-trip planning, on-trip information and dynamic guidance. The specific combination of innovative information, navigation and routing services with modern communication platforms like social media and mobile devices makes intermodal

M. Kurosu (Ed.): Human-Computer Interaction, Part III, HCII 2014, LNCS 8512, pp. 513–524, 2014.

travelling for passengers more flexible, convenient and secure. Granting ubiquitous access to all kinds of data mobile services will essentially support seamless mobility in correspondence to today's way of life.

Recent developments in mobile communication and internet computing have paved the way for a wide variety of mobile applications. Many transport companies and associations, car manufacturers and other providers of mobility services offer a significant number of apps on the market supporting effectively a particular mode of transport. But these are more or less stand-alone solutions (see Fig. 1)

The reason therefore can be seen in the complexity of coordination different transport companies' databases and in the demanding processes to build compatible interfaces and structures for data exchange. Furthermore transport companies and data owners have often only a limited willingness to share their real-time traffic data with other providers.

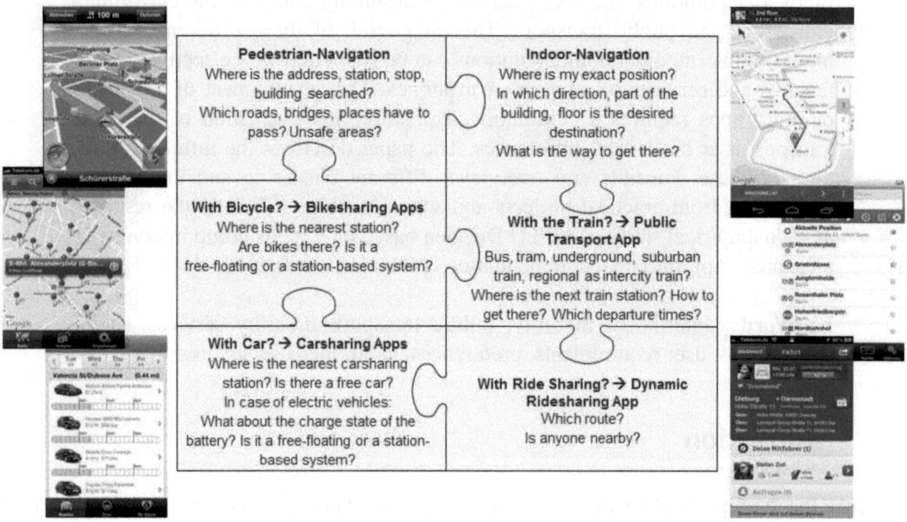

Fig. 1. Mobile applications as stand-alone solutions

Today the intermodal real-time information and travel guidance services are not yet fully taken into account. The complex door-to-door mobility covers:

- pedestrian navigation from the front door to the nearest public transport stop,
- use of rental bike to reach the next stop,
- the purchase of electronic tickets,
- information about the planned change of transport means or due to disturbances, delays or accidents,
- offering alternative routes based on real-time data,
- sending messages including authorization codes to get access to carsharing or bike-sharing services
- indoor navigation to the destination point in buildings (see Fig. 2).

That means door-to-door apps should offer intermodal information, navigation and guidance, access, online disposition and booking services including the possibility of electronic payment/ticket for users who want to switch between train, tram and bus as well as bike- or carsharing.

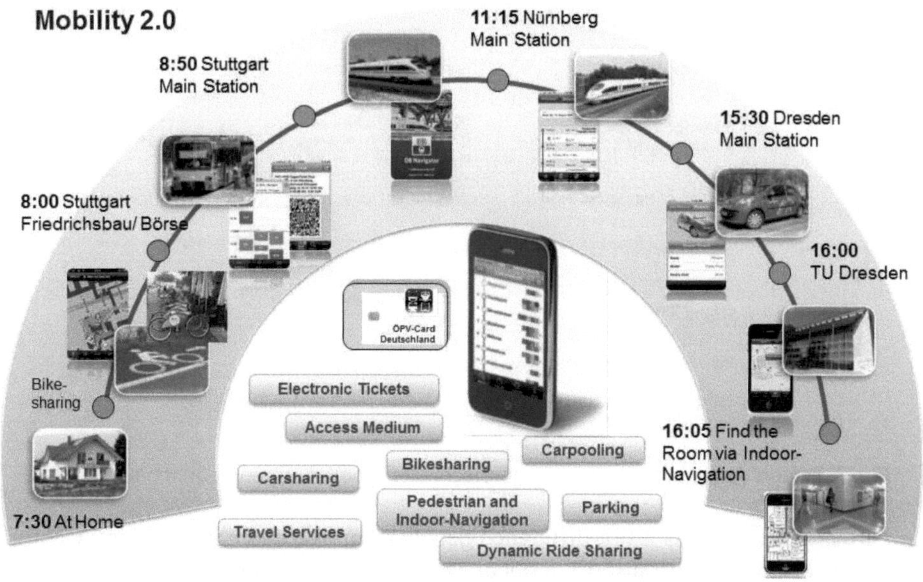

Fig. 2. Door-to-door mobility supported by mobile apps

In this context it should also be considered to what extent Crowdsourcing and Social Sensing can be used to improve the quality of intermodal apps and accompanying services as a win-win-situation for both – for transport users as well as transport companies and service providers. At least the level of personalization, up-to-dateness and accuracy of travel information and recommendations is the most important competitive advantage.

Nevertheless: in the recent past first mobile apps for public transport with intermodal approaches have been developed and piloted in Germany such as "Smart-Way" [1] (in Dresden), "Cairo" [2] as a situation-aware mobile traffic information system (in Berlin), "moovel" [3], "von AnachB" [4], "DB-Navigator" [5] and other solutions.

2 User Requirements for Mobile "Door-to-Door" Applications

2.1 Influencing Factors

The requirements for seamless dynamic mobility applications are affected by a number of different factors shown in Fig. 3.

In terms of demographics, age plays an important role because of the openness to new ideas, i.e. both for new forms of mobility as well as new technologies, skills in handling smartphones, Internet, mobile services and their features are strongly age-dependent.

demography	preferences	route	context of journey
age	technology	purpose of journey	system knowledge (network of transport routes, stations, ticketing)
income	intermodality and multimodality	social circumstances (travel alone, in company, in a group)	local knowledge
captive riders choice riders	means of transport	pressure of time	awareness of the route
restrictions	convenience	freqency of use	spatial aspects of the journey
	willingness to run	kind of ticket and ticket purchase	
	barriers to public transport use	price sensitivity	
	willigness to dynamic rescheduling		

Fig. 3. Factors influencing the user requirements for mobile door-to-door applications [6]

Furthermore, there is a big difference between captive and choice riders. Captive riders must use public transport services were as choice riders have access to own vehicles.

Regarding preferences

- the degree of enthusiasm for technology,
- willingness to change transport means during one trip from A to B (intermodal use)
- willingness to use different transport means during a given time (week, month) (multimodal use),
- the preference for own car or bike,
- the comfort,
- the willingness to accept longer walks or
- to change spontaneously routes

affect the demands on mobile apps intensively.

The combination of these numerous individual factors leads to complex scenarios of user requirements (see Fig. 4). Thereby a trade-off always exists between the simplicity and clarity of use and the degree of complexity.

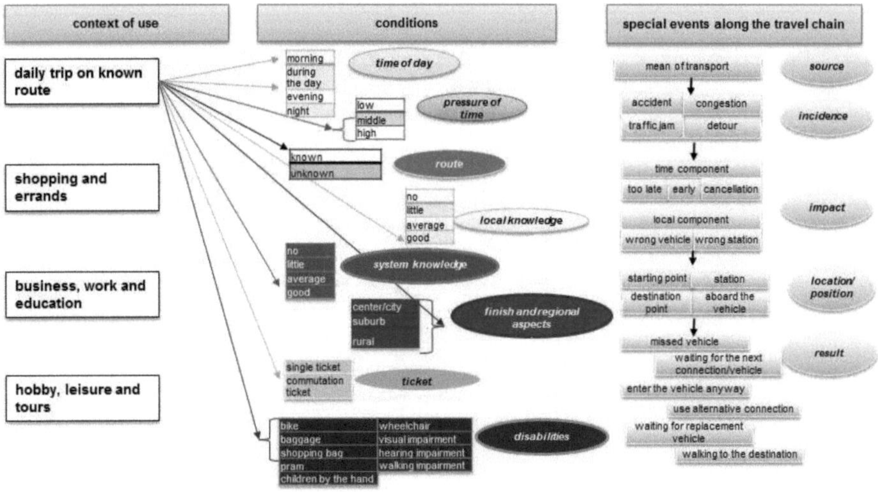

Fig. 4. Complexity of user requirements by various combinations of influencing factors [6]

3 Determination of User Demands on Mobile Apps – Results of Related Works

At the market a variety of studies on user requirements for smartphone-based mobility apps exists [6-12]. They emerged primarily in connection with development, market introduction and systematic evaluation of such apps.

The complexity of user requirements shown in the section above requires a clustering according to certain features and criteria to make them accessible for the development of new intermodal app functionalities and services. In Fig. 5 it can be seen that various projects and studies pursue very different approaches. However, the comparison reveals a certain cluster pattern for user requirements. This is mainly according to "general requirements", "technical performance" and "usability".

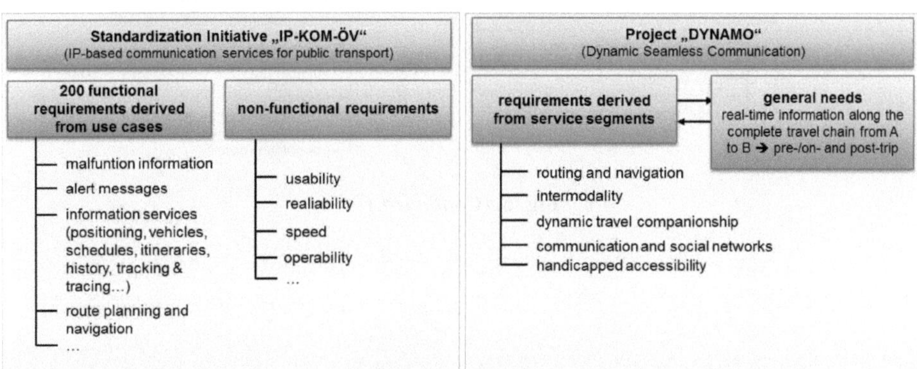

Fig. 5. Classification and clustering approaches for the determination of user demands on mobile apps [6-12]

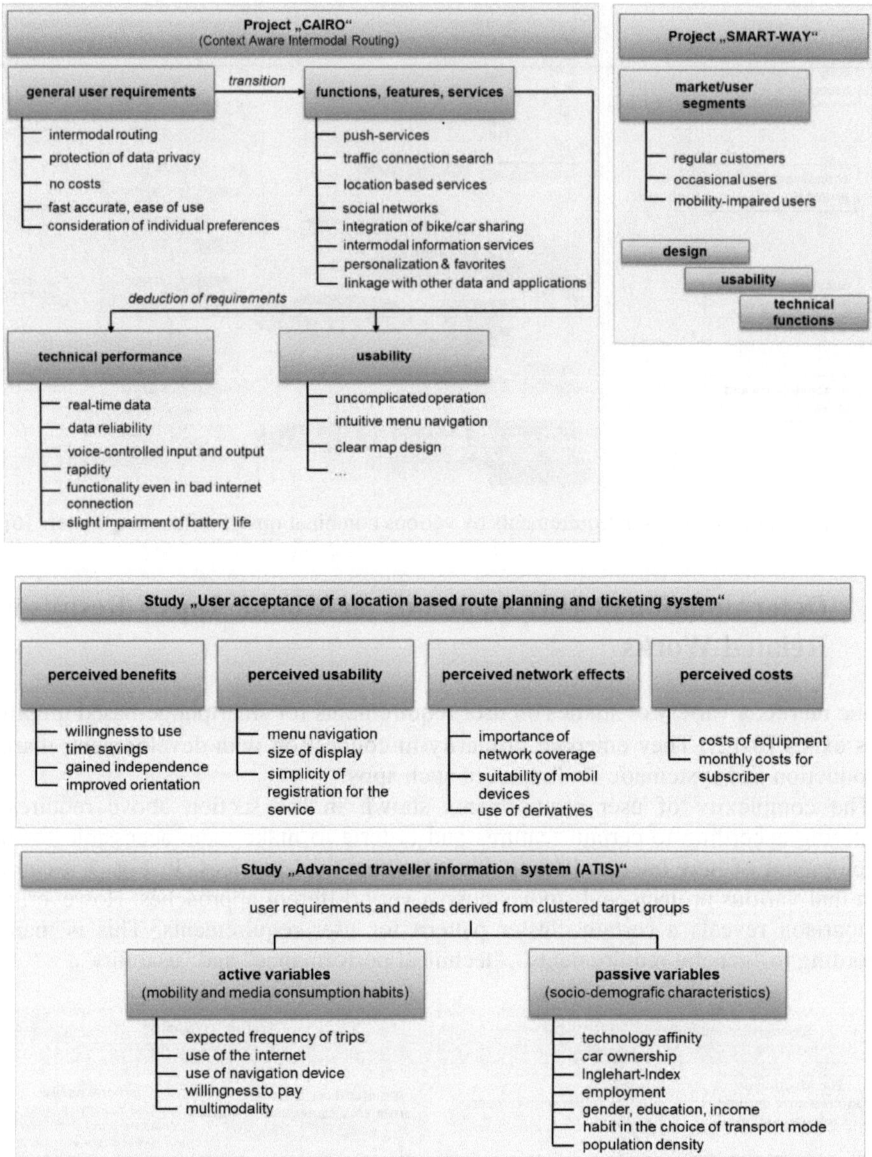

Fig. 5. (*Continued.*)

4 Results of an Empirical Study for the Determination of User Demands on Door-to-Door Mobility Apps at TU Dresden

4.1 Methodology

In preparation for the project work to provide the user and operator requirements for seamless door-to-door services and applications as part of the research project DYNAMO funded by the Federal Ministry for Economic Affairs and Energy a preliminary study at TU Dresden was conducted at the Department of Communication Economics in 2012. The investigation comprised

- a utility analysis (scoring model) of modern mobility applications and online services conducted on the methodological basis of the analytic hierarchy process and
- a focus group interview in order to determine detailed user demands on intermodal mobility apps.

This paper addresses particularly the identification of user requirements based on the focus group method.

A focus group is a carefully planned discussion designed to obtain perceptions on a defined area of interest in a permissive environment. Moderated group sessions provide the opportunity to gain an insight into the thinking and behavior patterns of the target group. Due to the open and personal character focus groups are able to reveal completely new and unexpected aspects and interrelationships. Through the mutual exchange and confrontation with the perceptions, opinions and ideas of the other panelist focus groups bring more balanced results than individual interviews [13].

The focus group in our study consisted of 8 participants, 6 men and 2 women. The average age of the participants was 28 years, with the youngest participant 19 and the oldest 46 years old. The participants had a high level of education. 50 % held a university degree. Most of the participants were owner of private cars but despite of this all were active subscribers of a carsharing provider (teilAuto). All participants had a very positive attitude toward smartphone usage, a high affinity for technology and first experiences in dealing with navigation apps [14].

In the forefront of the focus group interview the participants as well as additional ten subjects had to test and to evaluate various mobility applications in the fields of public transport, carsharing, bikesharing, pedestrian navigation as well as the electronic ticketing with respect to various criteria (see chapter 5). On the basis of these criteria the user requirements for intermodal mobility apps in the following focus group interview were discussed and summarized.

The focus group interview was conducted by a moderator on the basis of a discussion guide including five phases:

1. welcome and introduction,
2. initiatory questions about mobility concepts and the importance of apps,
3. questions to ascertain the fundamental user requirements,

4. questions for the functionality, complexity and personalization of an intermodal mobility app,
5. final questions on the outlook for future developments and derivation of recommendations for action [14].

5 Criteria for User Demands on Intermodal Mobility Apps

Based on literature studies and discussion with experts six criteria for door-to-door mobility apps (see Fig. 6) were identified and used in the app tests and focus group discussion.

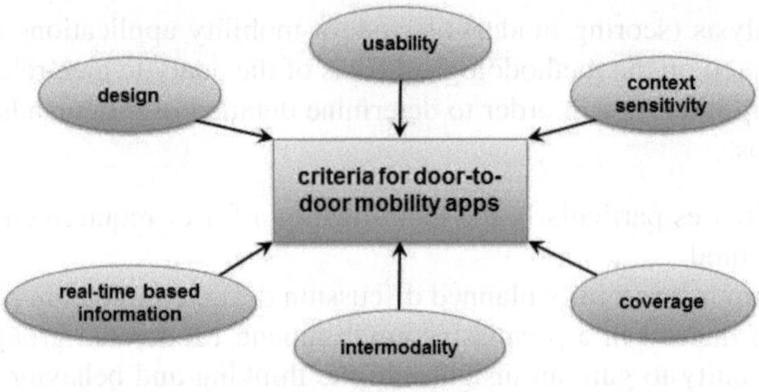

Fig. 6. Criteria for door-do-door-mobility apps [14, p. 90]

The criterion "Usability" comprises the user experience when interacting with the system or getting feedback. It is divided into five sub-categories (see Fig. 7).

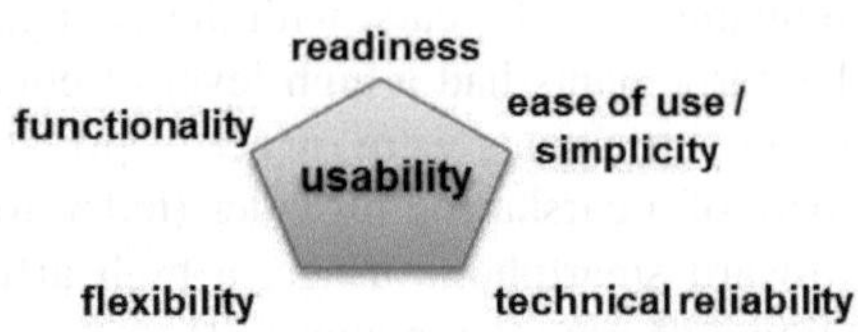

Fig. 7. Different aspects of the criterion "usability"

"Design" means the purely visual aspect of the display and information presentation. "Intermodality" comprises the use of all traditional public transport modes (bus, tram, underground, suburban, regional and intercity rail) and new innovative mobility services (bikesharing, carsharing, carpooling and dynamic ridesharing). "Context awareness" is defined as a filter taking into account the current situation of the user and makes the relevant information just at this moment available to him when it is needed. "Coverage" reflects the range of applications. A distinction is made between regional, national and international offers.

6 Presentation of the Results

The complex representation of the determined user requirements concerning all criteria shown in Fig. 6 is beyond the scope of this paper. Therefore the discussion is dedicated in particular to the user requirements with regard to the criteria "intermodality" and "usability" which are very closely interconnected. In the last consequence, the user requests of mobility apps correspond always to several criteria and can be difficult to be separated from each other. For example, the requirements with respect to intermodal route planning and travel companionship are always linked to the demand for real-time information.

Besides the already known general user requirements with regard to reliability, data security, ease of use, intuitive input and display forms (augmented reality), clear menu structures, simple call up of additional digital information etc. the most important user demands refer to the following aspects:

1. Multimodal Comparison of all Means of Transport with the Possibility of Intermodal Linkage

Users want to have a clear comparison of all possible mobility alternatives in order to go from one point A to point B. This includes information for the needed travel time, travel costs, availability of transport links or vehicles and environmental impacts. This comparison should take additionally into account besides the classic private and public transport services the increasing collaborative mobility services based on vehicle sharing. In this context an easy possibility of the transition from public transport to car- or bikesharing offerings is desired. This should be supported by real-time information about the availability of vehicles, their conditions, utility costs and their location including pedestrian navigation to go there.

From the usability point of view this user requirement is met best when the start and destination point of the searched connection can be entered directly on the first screen of an intermodal app (see Fig. 8).

Fig. 8. Appropriate presentation at the main page of an intermodal app [14, p. 134]

The starting point is determined directly via GPS. The user can enter time preferences and preferred modes of transport. With these initial data a comparison of all available options can be displayed after the query of connection. In dependence on the selected option the user will be presented all the further steps or alternatives due to the hierarchical system structure. This might be the reservation of a carsharing vehicle, the activation of a rental bike, the possibility of ticket purchase for public transport or the accumulation of points of interest for pedestrians.

2. Link-up Carsharing with Dynamic Ridesharing for the Optimal Matching between a Driver and Passenger

For instance the Carpooling platform "flinc" provides a link to vehicles of the carsharing system "DriveNow". Users can activate the "flinc" service in their app profile or use the login via the screen in the rental vehicle. By activating the navigation the ride is offered automatically on the "flinc" platform and the driver can select whether he wants to pick up an inquiring person or not (see Fig. 9). But nevertheless the focus group interview showed the existence of numerous use barriers for sharing services.

Fig. 9. Combination of carsharing and dynamic ridesharing [15]

3. Possibilities of Personalization and Efficient Administration of Favorites Include

- options for entering user settings such as "a lot of baggage," "strange city", "here I am familiar", "maximal walk distance", "required transfer time", "average speed", "attractive, fastest, cheapest route" etc.
- efficient linkage of personal defined favorite start and destination points (see Fig. 10)
- import of calendar and address data of favorites from other apps

Fig. 10. Screenshot of the shuttle app "Pendel Panda" [16]

4. Automatic Consideration of User Context Such as

- weather conditions, points of interest nearby,
- purpose of travel and deduction of related route recommendations, e.g. as automatic selection of public transport, carsharing or taxi for business trips or deactivating trouble messages for the travel to or from work on weekends,
- storage of all cross-platform settings in the cloud

5. Integration of Booking and Payment Functions in Intermodal Apps allowing a "booking through process" via all modes of transport for a selected connection and a detailed cost information for each transport mode (public transport, car-/bike-/ridesharing) [17].

6. Offering of e-tickets with Discounts for Intermodal Mobility Behavior, e.g. for bikesharing, carsharing, railway tickets or taxi trips in combination with "pay-as-you-go" or "pay-as-you-use" tariffs [17]

7. Providing Reliable Real-Time Information in any Case of Trouble and Disturbance

Users want more information and insights into the nature and causes of disturbances like the expected duration and the general options for action. In this context it is interesting to know users do not expect "precasted" alternatives. They need rather absolutely reliable forecast information when the journey can be continued or when a replacement vehicle is ready for use etc. They want to make decisions based on their own experiences and knowledge. This means user prefer reliable real-time based information giving them the freedom of choice.

Furthermore users don't want a link between their public transport use profile and social network services like Facebook. Instead they are looking for direct, quick and helpful communication with the transport company.

7 Conclusions and Outlook

User demands on mobility apps are growing. 10 years ago it was enough to be informed about schedules and departure times of public transport services. Nowadays the customer wants to know if he can park the carsharing vehicle at the station, if a rental bike is available at the destination station and how long the complete journey does it take. This information should be delivered immediately and reliably with a few keystrokes [17]. Therefore the goal of "door-to-door" apps is to support seamless "mobility on demand" solutions for the customer. Public transport should become as comfortable as car trips in terms of navigation, travelling routines and flexibility. In this context smartphones indeed facilitate the ride with public transport [17]. The integrated use of travel planning, reservation and booking, real-time information, navigation and travel accompanying as well as the access to different means of transport including billing can be controlled by the customer's personal device. But the growing variety of functions and user requirements is in some way contrary to the need for easier operation and faster information retrieval. This trade-off should be considered in future development processes of app-features and services more intensively than today. It requires a continuous acquisition and evaluation of public transport user requirements and preferences. These issues will be investigated by the further research in the Dynamo-project "Dynamic seamless mobility" in the next two years.

References

1. Smart-Way, http://www.smart-way.mobi/index.php/info-app
2. CAIRO, http://www.innoz.de/cairo20.0.html
3. moovel, https://www.moovel.com/de/
4. vonAnachB, http://www.anachb.at/
5. DB Navigator, http://www.bahn.de/p/view/buchung/mobil/db-navigator.shtml
6. DyNaMo: Meilenstein-Bericht AP 1000 im DyNaMo-Projekt Nutzer und Betreiberanalyse. Scientific Report, TU Dresden (2013)
7. IP-KOM-ÖV AK2: Meilensteinbericht, Teil Anwendungsfälle (2011)
8. Bock, B., Jahn, V., Schelewsky, M.: Cairo 2.0: Benchmark-Analyse von Mobilitätsdiensten des öffentlichen Verkehrs und intermodaler Mobilitätsprodukte. Scientific Report, Innovationszentrum für Mobilität und gesellschaftlichen Wandel (InnoZ) GmbH (2012)
9. Bock, B., Jahn, V., Jonuschat, H., Schelewsky, M.: Cairo 2.0: Begleitforschung des Feldtests eines smartphonebasierten, intermodalen Mobilitätsdiensts (AP 50). Scientific Report, Innovationszentrum für Mobilität und gesellschaftlichen Wandel (InnoZ) GmbH (2012)
10. POLITO: General conditions and users needs (2010), http://www.smart-way.mobi/index.php/project/deliverables
11. Amberg, M., Wehrmann, J.: Benutzerakzeptanz mobile Dienste – Ein Erfahrungsbericht zum Compass-Akzeptanzmodell. Scientific Report, Friedrich-Alexander Universität Erlangen-Nürnberg (2007)
12. x-sample, verkehrplus: INFO-EFFECT: Zielgruppenspezifische Wirkungen von multimodalen Verkehrsinformationen auf individuelles Verkehrsverhalten. Scientific Report, Graz, Wien (2010)
13. Haefeli, U., Matti, D., Oetterli, M.: Nutzung von multimodalen Verkehrs- und Routenwahlinformationen: Bericht zuhanden des Tiefbauamts der Stadt Zürich, Mobilität und Planung. Technical Report, Interface (2009)
14. Barthel, H.: Status und Nutzeranforderungen an Mobilitätsapplikationen. Master Thesis, TU Dresden (2012)
15. DriveNow, http://blog.drive-now.de/
16. Pendel Panda, https://play.google.com/store/apps/details?id=net.andforge.fahrplan3&hl=de
17. Schelewsky, M., Jonuschat, H., Bock, B., Jahn, V.: Einfach und komplex: Nutzeranforderungen an Smartphone-Applikationen zur intermodalen Routenplanung. Scientific Report, Innovationszentrum für Mobilität und gesellschaftlichen Wandel (InnoZ) GmbH (2013)

Fighting Technology Dumb Down: Our Cognitive Capacity for Effortful AR Navigation Tools

James Wen[1], Agnes Deneka[2], William S. Helton[1], Andreas Dünser[3], and Mark Billinghurst[1]

[1] University of Canterbury, Christchurch, New Zealand
[2] University of Twente, Enschede, The Netherlands
[3] CSIRO, Tasmania, Australia

Abstract. By overlaying virtual guidance information directly over the surrounding environment, Augmented Reality (AR) is seen as an easy alternative to maps for pedestrians navigating in unfamiliar urban environments. It is hypothesized, however, that easing navigation tasks would result in weaker cognitive maps, leaving users more vulnerable to becoming lost should their navigation device fail. We describe an outdoor navigation study that highlighted the gap between theoretical expectations and real world testing with navigation tools. We addressed the issues by creating a simulation system for testing navigation tools and report on the results of a study comparing AR with maps. We then extended the system to support simultaneous secondary tasks to assess relative workload. We present this as a way of objectively measuring relative cognitive effort expended on navigation tool use. Our findings are helpful in the design of mobile pedestrian navigation tools seeking to balance navigational efficiency with mental map formation.

Keywords: pedestrian navigation, augmented reality, maps, cognitive load, virtual environment, spatial knowledge acquisition.

1 Introduction

Rapid advances in mobile technologies coupled with the fact that many people find maps difficult to use [1] has led to the creation of a wealth of creative digital alternatives to traditional cartographic maps [7,8]. One promising technology is augmented reality (AR) where virtual information is overlaid directly upon the user's environment through a smartphone or digital eyewear [6,10]. It is assumed that users would complete navigation tasks far more efficiently with AR-based than with map-based interfaces in part because AR eliminates the lateral mental rotations as well as landmark feature associations required of map users [14]. It is hypothesized, however, that users of tools that make navigation tasks easier would do so at the expense of the user being spatially aware of their surroundings, which would leave them more vulnerable to getting lost should their navigation devices fail (e.g. due to battery depletion) [11,17]. We wish to assess the capacity of users to balance the acquisition of spatial knowledge (SK) while navigating with acceptable efficiency.

M. Kurosu (Ed.): Human-Computer Interaction, Part III, HCII 2014, LNCS 8512, pp. 525–536, 2014.

2 Background

The possible relationship between the ease-of-use of navigation tools and SK acquisition has been referred to as the "tradeoff hypothesis" where the improvement of one is at the expense of the other [11]. It has also been proposed that interfaces are becoming too easy to use and that more "effortful" interfaces need to be created so that the user will be forced to do work to help gain spatial awareness [5]. Indeed, it has been observed that users given random orientation quizzes during a navigation task performed significantly better in directional recall when compared to users not given such quizzes although it was noted that it may be unrealistic to expect users to accept having to answer random quizzes [12]. An attempt to integrate SK improvement features more tightly into the user interface by using landmark cues to encourage users to be more attentive to their surrounding environment, however, yielded no significant results [15].

Neither the notion of ease-of-use nor the nature of cognitive maps are easily quantified so it is challenging to test theories that relate the two. In our research, we seek to find objective and quantifiable measures that would provide insights for expended effort in using pedestrian navigation tools and SK acquisition for recalling routes traveled. We assume that AR is an easier interface to use than maps but hypothesize that maps would result in better SK, as shown in Figure 1. In this figure, the left half is considered *Easy* as less effort is required. This

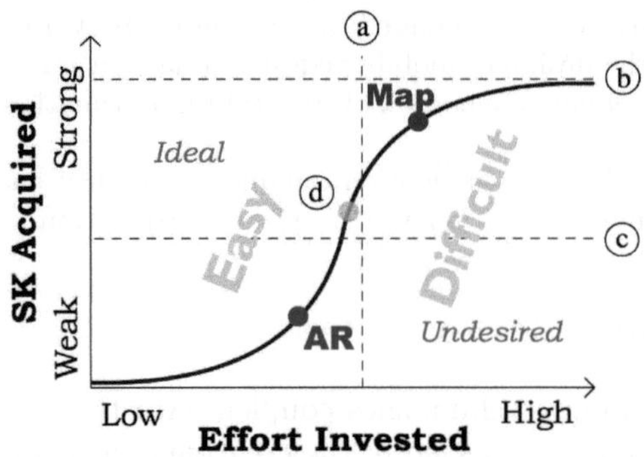

Fig. 1. The Spatial Knowledge - Effort curve

would be the desired half for interface usage. The upper half corresponds to stronger acquired SK, which would be the desired half for avoiding undesired dependencies on navigation technology. Maps would presumably reside in the upper right quadrant, being difficult to use but resulting in good SK acquired. AR, on the other hand, should be in the lower left quadrant: it is easy to use but results in weaker acquired SK.

Line ⓐ is calibrated by the tool designer and represents the maximum effort that could be reasonably imposed upon a user. To the right of this line, the interface may be considered to be too challenging to use. Line ⓑ refers to the maximum SK that can be acquired, such as a complete and thorough survey knowledge of the area. Line ⓒ corresponds to the desired minimum amount of SK the designer wishes for the user to gain. We propose a curve that passes through the AR and map positions and regard the portion of the line that passes through the *Ideal* upper-left quadrant as the interface we wish to design. Since the limits ⓐ and ⓒ are defined by the designer, the two can be adjusted so as to accommodate an ideal interface at ⓓ, which corresponds to a tool that balances effort invested with SK acquired.

In the remainder of this article, we report on our studies that sought to validate our assumption and test our hypothesis. We then describe a study measuring the capacity of users for accepting interfaces that attempt to increase user effort in order to improve SK so that an ideal interface for balancing navigation efficiency and acquired SK can be created.

3 Study 1: Performance Measurement

In order to support our assumption that AR-based pedestrian navigation tools are easier to use than map-based tools, our first study measured time-on-task performance and user perception of expended effort. A within-subjects design with three counter-balanced paths was employed on a university campus. Three smartphone interface conditions were tested: map, AR, and a combination mode that allowed the user to choose either the map or AR interface at any time (see Figure 2). Participants were asked to complete navigation tasks with a different

Fig. 2. The map (left) and AR (right) navigation interfaces

interface condition for each of the paths. At the end of each task, participants filled out a task load index (TLX) questionnaire. After completing all three paths, participants were asked to rank the interfaces in order of preference. We summarize our results and refer the reader to [2] for further details.

3.1 Results

A total of 22 participants (11 female, mean age = 31.0) completed the study. An ANOVA detected no significant differences in the time taken to navigate the

Table 1. Performance and TLX

	Time (sec)	TLX
	Mean (SD)	Mean (SD)
Map	919 (271)	39.58 (17.99)
AR	953 (344)	41.14 (17.04)
Combo	968 (275)	43.94 (15.69)

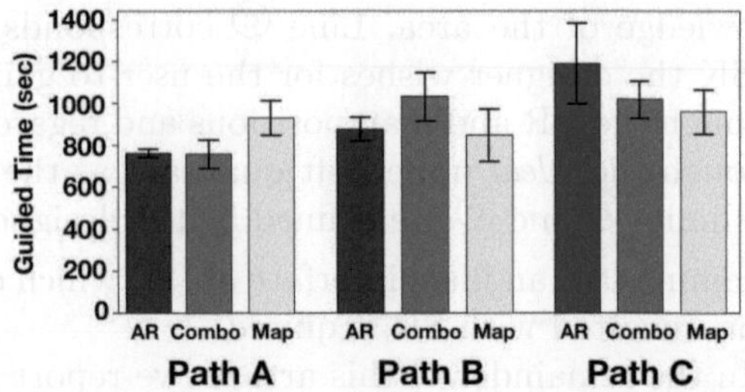

Fig. 3. Performance times for the paths

paths using the three interface conditions ($F(2,38) = .25, p = .78$), as shown in Table 1 and Figure 3.

No significant differences were detected for the combined TLX workload scores between the interfaces ($F(2,63) = .37, p = .69$). The ranking data showed that the AR interface was perceived to be significantly less useful than the Combination interface for completing the task ($\chi^2 = 10.30, df = 2, p < .01$). There was also a preference for the Map or Combination interfaces over the AR interface for use in everyday life ($\chi^2 = 6.90, df = 2, p < .05$).

3.2 Observations

Counter to our expectations, the AR interface did not offer more efficient traversal times. This, along with the results of a later independent study [13] led us to believe there may exist fundamental issues that were affecting how users perceive, use, and perform with AR-based pedestrian navigation tools. From observations, user feedback, and discussions, we suspected that outdoor tracking inaccuracies may be the primary factor causing this.

The issue of poor outdoor tracking is a known problem with considerable resources devoted to it. Since it will not likely be solved in the immediate future [9], we created a testbed within a virtual environment (VE) so that location information would be precisely defined at all times. By removing the tracking errors making AR difficult to use, we were able to focus our attention on defining the limits of how AR may affect navigational effectiveness and SK acquisition in an ideal environment.

4 Study 2: Simulating Perfect Tracking

We used the Unity3D game engine to build SPART (Simulator for Perfect AR Tracking) in order to evaluate user performance, perceived effort, and route recall in traversing a path through a desktop virtual environment. Using the mouse to change turn the direction of view and the [w] key to control forward movement, each participant was given navigation tasks that included a guided traversal followed by an unguided recall traversal of the same path. We employed a between-subjects design where each participant navigated two counter-balanced paths and was assigned one of three navigation interfaces: map (MP), map with You-are-Here marker (MY), and AR. These were activated by holding down the 1 key and displayed as shown in Figure 4. Our results are summarized here and we refer the reader to [16] for further details.

Fig. 4. The map (left) and AR (right) navigation interfaces

4.1 Results

A total of 71 participants (21 female, mean age = 19.8) successfully completed the study. There was a significant difference in guided navigation time depending on the tool being used (see Figure 5, left). MP users required the longest time and AR users needed significantly less time at the $p < .05$ level. MY users were between MP and AR users with no significant differences in performance when compared to either the MP or AR conditions.

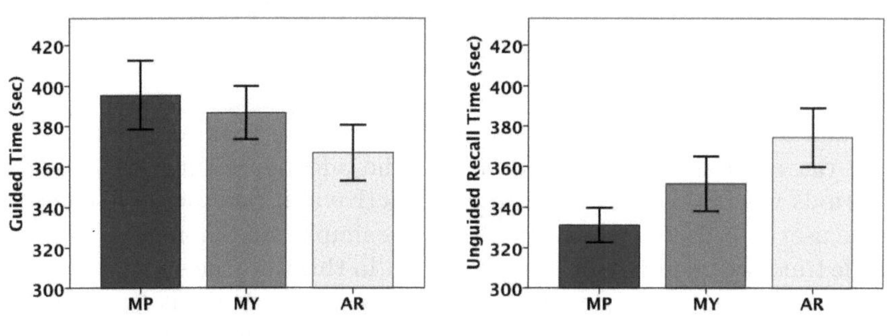

Fig. 5. Guided time (left) and unguided recall time (right)

Significant differences were also observed between interfaces for the unguided recall times (see Figure 5, right). MP users now took the least time while AR users took significantly more time at the $p < .001$ level. MY users were again between the MP and AR users; they were significantly slower than the MP users and significantly faster than the AR users, both at the $p < .05$ level.

A comparison of the unguided recall times and the initial guided traversal times is shown in Figure 6 (left). An independent t-test indicated significant differences in the average guided time and the average unguided recall time for MP users at the $p < .001$ level. Significant differences were also found for MY users in guided traversal times and unguided recall times at the $p < .001$ level. No significant differences were found for AR users between the average guided time and the average unguided time.

There was a significant difference in perceived workload between the interfaces (see Figure 6, right). A significant difference was observed between MP and AR, $(F(2,66) = 6.46, p < .01)$. MY yielded no significant differences with MP $(p = .20)$ and AR $(p = .27)$.

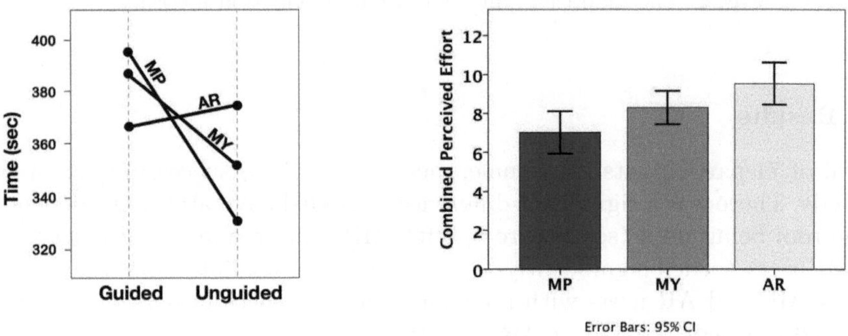

Fig. 6. Interaction (left) and TLX (right)

4.2 Observations

The results aligned with our assumptions. Map users took longer to navigate through the environment than AR users. The additional time was associated with periods where the navigation tool was active and was therefore considered to be the user interpreting the map. Given the simpler and more direct nature of AR, little time was required for interpretation. In this way, the simulation seemed consistent with the aim of AR-based navigation tools, which is to simplify the task of navigation resulting in shorter travel time. The fact that such behavior has not been observed in the real world suggests that AR is perhaps not yet ready to be used as an effective GPS-based navigation system.

The reversal of the traversal time relationship between the navigation interfaces for guided traversal times and unguided traversals for VE participants (see Figure 5) also agrees with expectations: the greater amount of time spent navigating through the environment correlated with more efficient time retracing the path at a later point. Referring back to Figure 1, this is consistent with the placement of maps in the upper half of the graph and AR in the lower half.

The results of the TLX indicated that AR users perceived greater effort was expended than map users, which is also consistent with expectations since the TLX was administered after the unguided recall navigation task, which we expected to be more difficult for AR users. The TLX is, however, a self-assessment survey and, as such, a subjective measure. To create the design parameters we seek, we would like to find a more objective measure which we describe next.

5 Study 3: Measuring Effort Capacity with Dual Tasks

We attempted to find an objective and quantitative measure that captures the ease users have with AR and map-based pedestrian navigation tools. To do this, we created a secondary task that served to distract the user from the primary task of navigation. By measuring user performance in this dual task environment, we gained insights into how the competition for cognitive resources affected both the primary and secondary tasks which, in turn, provided insights into the level of cognitive effort required.

We modified SPART to periodically display a word in the upper left hand corner of the screen. The words were taken from a standard list that has been used in studies investigating the impact of secondary tasks upon the performance of primary tasks, such as [3]. Participants were first asked to navigate through the virtual city with a navigation tool while trying to memorize as many of the words as possible. After reaching the end of the path, the participants were given two minutes to recall as many of the memorized words as possible. They were then asked to re-traverse the same path but without a navigation tool.

5.1 Results

A total of 47 participants (25 female, mean age=26.3) completed the study. Comparing interfaces, map users were significantly slower than AR users during the guided traversal ($t_{45} = 2.86, p < .05$) but, during the unguided recall traversal, map users were significantly faster ($t_{45} = -3.06, p < .05$). This is shown in Figure 7 (left).

Comparing guided and unguided recall modes, map users were significantly faster in the unguided mode than in the guided mode ($t_{470} = 3.29, p < .001$). AR users, however, did not exhibit any significant differences in time between guided and unguided recall navigation ($t_{50} = -1.79, p = .08$). These are shown in Figure 7 (right).

As a between-subjects study, we were able to compare the data from this study with Study 2. After culling out MY participants and participants who traversed Path B first, we retained 22 participants for comparison. Map users exhibited significant differences in travel times between the single-task and dual-task modes for both guided ($t_{31} = -1.75, p < .05$) and unguided recall travels ($t_{31} = -2.44, p < .05$) (see Figure 8).

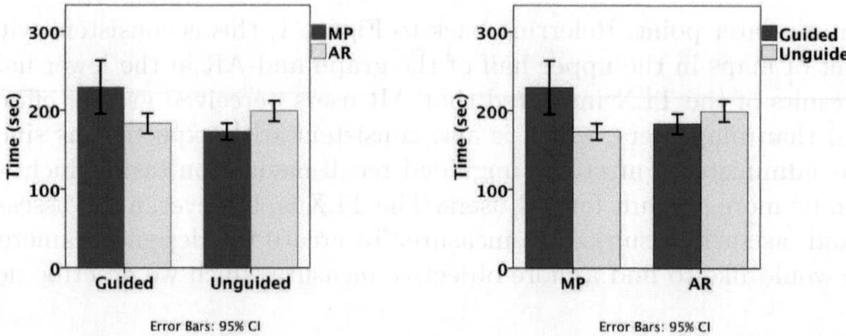

Fig. 7. Navigation performance comparisons for dual task study between interfaces and guidance modes

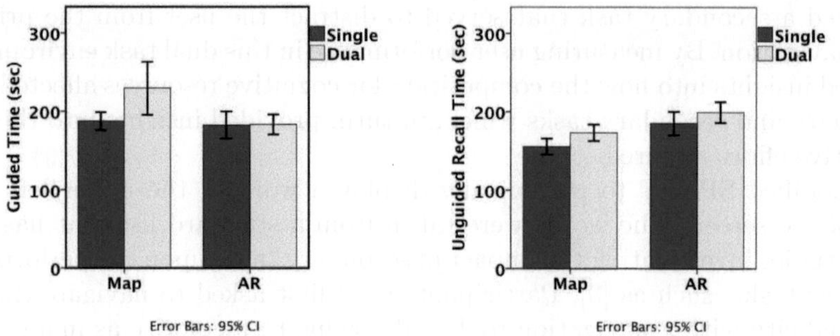

Fig. 8. Navigation performance comparisons between single and dual tasks

In contrast, AR users did not exhibit any significant differences in travel time between single-task and dual-task modes for either guided ($t_{36} = -.546, p = .59$) or unguided recall travel times ($t_{36} = -1.12, p = .27$). These are shown in the graphs of Figure 8. For the secondary task of word memorization, AR users recalled significantly more words than map users ($t_{45} = 2.08, p < .05$). A t-test conducted on the dual-task TLX results indicated that AR users perceived a significantly higher workload than map users ($t_{45} = -2.27, p < .05$).

5.2 Observations

The observation that guided performance suffered significantly for map users but not for AR users when switching from single to dual tasks suggest that the secondary task had a substantial impact on map users while it did not significantly affect AR users. A possible explanation for this is that map users had to split their cognitive resources between two tasks that were in competition. The AR condition, on the other hand, may have required so little cognitive effort that a secondary task would easily receive the attention it demanded without diminishing the performance of the primary navigation task. Users in the real world are often engaged in some secondary task—such as chatting with a friend—while finding their way in an urban environment, so the potential of AR-based navigation tools for effectively guiding such users without diminishing their secondary task is attractive.

While the secondary task slowed down map users significantly, it did not diminish the retention of a mental map for Map users since they were still significantly better than AR users in unguided travel time performance. This may suggest that the implicit retention of a mental map did not suffer as a consequence of having a secondary task. In other words, the secondary task increased the amount of time the user needed to accomplish the primary task but it did not seem to affect the mental map created.

With respect to the secondary task, AR users were able to recall significantly more words than map users without significantly increasing their guided traversal times from their single-task traversal. Map users, on the other hand, not only recalled significantly less words than AR users but also took significantly longer to follow the guided traversal when given a secondary task. As previously observed, this may show that AR users had greater spare cognitive capacity than map users to devote resources to the secondary task.

6 Discussion

Our interest in balancing navigation effectiveness with the formation of cognitive maps is challenged by a lack of objective quantitative metrics. Traditional approaches use distance and direction estimates as well as sketchmaps to build a model of cognitive maps but there are still fundamental arguments as to what actually constitute cognitive maps [4]. Instead of modeling a sophisticated concept, we chose to restrict our interest to a particular aspect of mental maps that is both more measurable and arguably of great interest: the retention of route knowledge. Our shift into a virtual setting proved advantageous since route knowledge can be tested with re-traversals but real world re-traversals of paths can be physically exhausting and not scalable on an experimental level. The difference in performance measures between the guided and subsequent unguided recall traversals gave us a basic measure for retained route knowledge.

We seek to balance SK acquisition with ease-of-use, which is another notion that is difficult to measure. Although the TLX survey is an effective measure, it is highly subjective. Our use of the dual task approach provides some basic insights in effort expended. Since our ultimate interest is in finding ways to introduce secondary tasks for improving SK, we do not need to transform effort expended into a potential ability for handling secondary tasks: the two are inversely related and so we simply interpret the results directly.

Given our focus on SK acquisition, the use of word memorization as a secondary task may lack substantial conflict with the faculties dedicated to spatial abilities. Future work should attempt to introduce secondary tasks that compete for resources more directly related to navigation.

Figure 9 illustrates how our measure can be used to guide interface design. Line ⓐ defines the minimal capacity deemed necessary for handling secondary tasks for improving SK. Line ⓑ defines the level of efficient performance. Box ⓒ defines the constraints within which pedestrian navigation tools would ideally occupy that could exploit the capacity of performing a secondary task for the sake of improving SK.

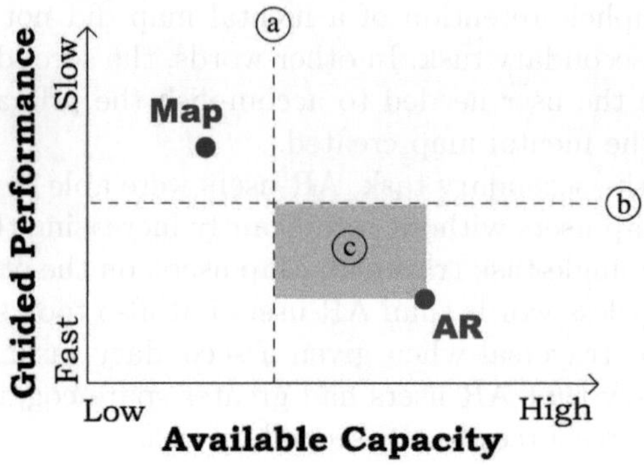

Fig. 9. Performance - Capacity Quadrants

Figure 10 illustrates how the relationship between time-on-task performance and acquisition of SK can be harnessed. The time saved by using an AR inter-

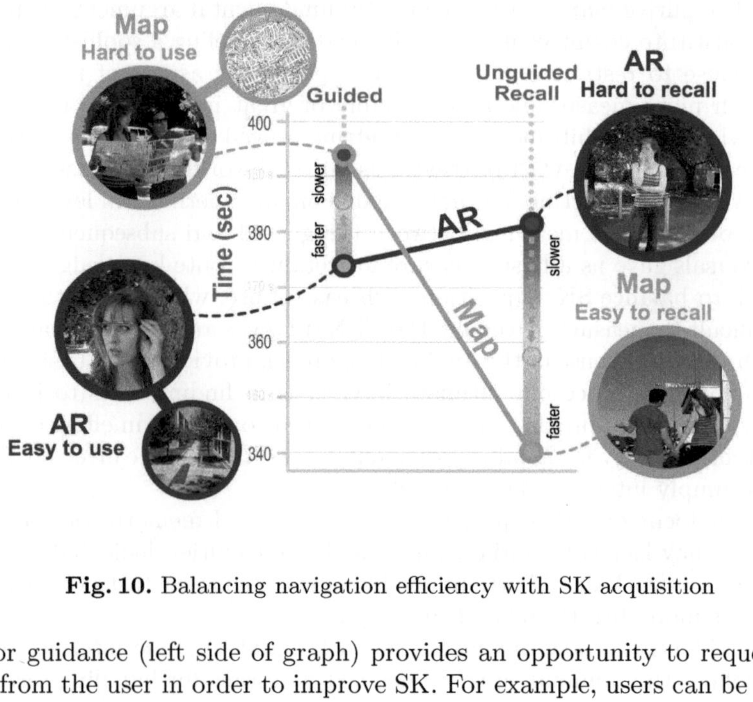

Fig. 10. Balancing navigation efficiency with SK acquisition

face for guidance (left side of graph) provides an opportunity to request more effort from the user in order to improve SK. For example, users can be asked to view a landmark briefly before receiving guidance directions. The dashed arrow indicates the time penalty caused by making AR more challenging. The benefit from the increasing the challenge is reflected in the unguided recall time (right side of graph) where the dashed arrow indicates the desired improvement in performance. The measures we presented here can help quantitatively calibrate the design of pedestrian navigation tools that employs the time saved using an AR-based navigation interface to offset the decrease in SK acquired without adversely affecting performance significantly.

7 Conclusion

There is a desire to create pedestrian navigation tools that provide efficient guidance information without sacrificing the formation of cognitive maps. To date, theoretical efforts have largely been qualitative and subjective. Experimental attempts have either yielded interfaces that would strengthen SK at the cost of usability or, they have been inconclusive. We are interested in finding an objective, quantitative measure for the factors that relate navigation effectiveness and a user's capacity to accept interfaces that require more effort for the sake of improving SK. We compared one of the newest technologies for pedestrian navigation with one of the oldest: AR with maps. We saw that AR is not quite ready for practical use although it may still, in principle, offer more efficient and better ease-of-use navigation guidance than maps. To explore this, we built SPART, a simulator that provided perfect location data for AR tracking. Our navigation testbed supported the assumption that AR-based navigation tools would be faster and easier to use than maps but offer weaker cognitive maps. By using a dual task approach, we were able to measure the capacity of users to take on secondary tasks that could be devoted to SK acquisition. We found that AR users had far greater capacity than map users to undertake a secondary task without penalizing the guided performance time. With this set of studies, further work in this area can now have a firm quantitative base upon which to design features that serve to balance the ease of navigation while improving the formation of SK.

References

1. Board, C.: Map Reading Tasks Appropriate in Experimental Studies in Cartographic Communication. Cartographica: The International Journal for Geographic Information and Geovisualization 15(1), 1–12 (1978)
2. Dünser, A., Billinghurst, M., Wen, J., Lehtinen, V., Nurminen, A.: Exploring the use of Handheld AR for Outdoor Navigation. Computers & Graphics 36, 1084–1095 (2012)
3. Green, A.L., Helton, W.S.: Dual-task performance during a climbing traverse. Experimental Brain Research 215(3-4), 307–313 (2011), `http://www.ncbi.nlm.nih.gov/pubmed/22002634`
4. Hirtle, S.C., Jonides, J.: Evidence of hierarchies in cognitive maps. Memory & Cognition 13(3), 208–217 (1985)

5. Huang, H., Schmidt, M., Gartner, G.: Spatial Knowledge Acquisition in the Context of GPS-Based Pedestrian Navigation. In: Zentai, L., Reyes Nunez, J. (eds.) Maps for the Future. Lecture Notes in Geoinformation and Cartography, vol. 5, pp. 127–137. Springer, Heidelberg (2012), http://www.springerlink.com/index/10.1007/978-3-642-19522-8
6. Liarokapis, F., Mountain, D., Papakonstantinou, S., Brujic-okretic, V., Raper, J.: Mixed Reality For Exploring Urban Environments. In: 1st International Conference on Computer Graphics Theory and Applications (2006)
7. May, A.J., Ross, T., Bayer, S.H., Tarkiainen, M.J.: Pedestrian navigation aids: information requirements and design implications. Personal and Ubiquitous Computing 7(6), 331–338 (2003), http://www.springerlink.com/openurl.asp?genre=article&id=doi:10.1007/s00779-003-0248-5
8. Millonig, A., Schechtner, K.: Developing Landmark-Based Pedestrian-Navigation Systems. IEEE Transactions on Intelligent Transportation Systems 8(1), 43–49 (2007), http://ieeexplore.ieee.org/lpdocs/epic03/wrapper.htm?arnumber=4114345
9. Mulloni, A.: Enhancing Handheld Navigation Systems with Augmented Reality. In: Mobile HCI, pp. 5–8 (2011)
10. Mulloni, A., Seichter, H., Schmalstieg, D.: Handheld Augmented Reality Indoor Navigation with Activity-Based Instructions. In: Mobile HCI 2011 (2011)
11. Münzer, S., Zimmer, H.D., Baus, J.: Navigation assistance: a trade-off between wayfinding support and configural learning support. Journal of Experimental Psychology. Applied 18(1), 18–37 (2012), http://www.ncbi.nlm.nih.gov/pubmed/22141461
12. Parush, A., Ahuvia, S., Erev, I.: Degradation in spatial knowledge acquisition when using automatic navigation systems. In: Winter, S., Duckham, M., Kulik, L., Kuipers, B. (eds.) COSIT 2007. LNCS, vol. 4736, pp. 238–254. Springer, Heidelberg (2007)
13. Rehrl, K., Häusler, E., Steinmann, R., Leitinger, S., Bell, D., Weber, M.: Pedestrian Navigation with Augmented Reality, Voice and Digital Map: Results from a Field Study assessing Performance and User Experience. In: Proceedings of the 8th International Symposium on Location-based Services, pp. 3–20 (2011)
14. Seager, W., Fraser, D.S.: Comparing physical, automatic and manual map rotation for pedestrian navigation. In: CHI 2007, pp. 767–776 (2007), http://portal.acm.org/citation.cfm?doid=1240624.1240742
15. Waters, W., Winter, S.: A wayfinding aid to increase navigator independence. Journal of Spatial Information Science 3(3), 103–122 (2011), http://josis.org/index.php/josis/article/view/43
16. Wen, J., Helton, W.S., Billinghurst, M.: Classifying Users of Mobile Pedestrian Navigation Tools. In: Oz CHI, pp. 1–5 (2013)
17. Willis, K.S., Hölscher, C., Wilbertz, G., Li, C.: A comparison of spatial knowledge acquisition with maps and mobile maps. Computers Environment and Urban Systems 33(2), 100–110 (2009), http://linkinghub.elsevier.com/retrieve/pii/S0198971509000064

Model of Mobility Oriented Agenda Planning

Tobias Wienken, Cindy Mayas, Stephan Hörold, and Heidi Krömker

Ilmenau University of Technology, Ilmenau, Germany
{tobias.wienken,cindy.mayas,stephan.hoerold,
heidi.kroemker}@tu-ilmenau.de

Abstract. Today people have a wide range of choices in their means of transportation and their mobility options that it offers. Usability and flexibility are paramount in the application to individualized lifestyles. At the same time however, the provision of information and the planning process has become more complex and the users must collect information from a wide range of different systems. In order to reduce the workload of the planning processes, the task structures of different system must be analyzed and tried to combine. This paper describes how the mobility planning process can be integrated into the agenda planning process.

Keywords: public transport, mobility information, agenda planning.

1 Introduction

Mobility is one of the key elements of a modern society, enabling citizens to go to work, use leisure-time possibilities and manage daily life activities [1]. With respect to a more ecological mobility, new means of transportation arise, e.g. car sharing and bike sharing, and public transportation take on a higher significance. At the same time, new communication behavior and information channels allow users to manage their appointments and tasks nearly everywhere [1].

Within the next century managing the personal affairs will lead to an increasing need and wish for more mobility [2]. Furthermore the number of new means of transportation will force users to choose between complex mobility offers. These facts will result in an increasing effort of mobility and daily routine planning. At the moment the market offers a variety of systems and solutions for planning to the users. For instance mobility information systems support the users in selecting the right mean of transport. Other systems offer agenda planning tools, which support users in planning and managing the appointments and tasks of their personal daily routines. All these separate systems support the planner, but in the future the effort associated with planning processes must be reduced not to overstrain the user. These developments call for kinds of combined planning systems, which do not place mobility itself into the center of interest, but rather the individual daily routine of the user.

Based on the analyzed similarities between agenda planning and mobility planning, this paper describes how mobility planning can be integrated into individual agendas. A combination of agenda and mobility planning has the potential to reduce the user

M. Kurosu (Ed.): Human-Computer Interaction, Part III, HCII 2014, LNCS 8512, pp. 537–544, 2014.

workload in an efficient way by combining tasks and using automation. As a conclusion of the studies described, a model of mobility oriented agenda planning is introduced.

2 Method

The overall aim of the study at hand is to examine the feasibility of the combination of agenda planning and mobility planning. In order to investigate the issues involved, analytical and empirical methods are selected for the four steps of the study.

A successful combination of both planning processes can improve the human performance in this setting, but any effort to carry out such an approach must initiate, based on what planners are required to do and also plan how to reach the goals [3]. The comprehension can be realized by the hierarchical task analysis (HTA). With it the tasks of mobility planning [4] and the agenda planning are analyzed by decomposing the tasks into subtasks [5]. After the analysis of the HTAs, the task structure of the agenda and mobility planning process is compared based on the result of HTA. Thus, the tasks can be identified, which are identical in both planning processes.

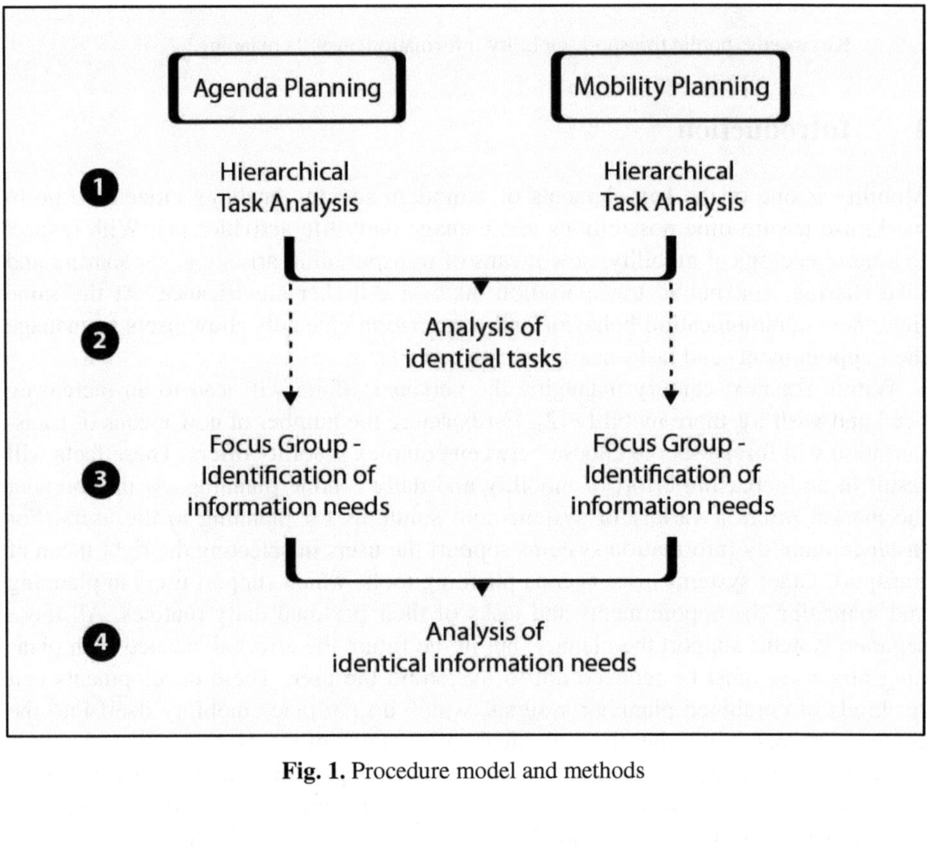

Fig. 1. Procedure model and methods

The planning tasks must be analyzed in detail in order to describe the feasibility of combination. Due to the new approach of the synthesis, the considered domain is poorly researched and therefore, a quality method would be useful for exploration and discovery [6]. Taking these aspects into consideration, the method focus group is thereby selected for the study. The focus group gathers the total information needs of the user in order to fulfill the agenda and mobility planning. These results help to identify identical information needs, which are relevant for both planning processes. Furthermore, the possibility of conversation with participants, allows to extract the influential factors of planning [7].

The composition of the focus groups is based on personas of public transportation [8]. The personas consist of different type of passengers and demonstrate their personal information, behavior, attitude and experience with the public transportation. The following enumeration shows the personas:

- Power user Maria
- Daily user Martina
- Commuter Michael
- School commuter Kevin
- Casual user Hildegard
- Ad-hoc user Bernd
- Tourist Carla

The list of the users is extended by the wheelchair user Christian to complete the different types of passengers. On average six to eight participants between 13 and 67 years took part in a group discussion.

3 Results

The results of hierarchical task analysis show, that both planning activities – agenda planning and mobility planning – are complex processes, which are related in different planning tasks. As an example of an identical task, the determination of point in time can be mentioned. In order to combine these identical tasks, the requirements of the user agenda have to match with the mobility offers. Therefore, it is necessary to know more about information needs of the tasks. Due to this fact, the presentation of the results focuses on the information demand, which must be defined during the planning processes. In order to discuss the findings, the planning information should be summarized in an abstract way. The table 1 displays the information which are relevant for the agenda and mobility planning.

An agenda element can be characterized by the following properties, in detail.

- Purpose: The purpose initiates the accruement of an agenda element and describes the reason with regards to content.
- Date and Time: The information time consists of two parts (point in time, e.g. starting point, and duration) and manages the temporal requirements.
- Location: The location shows the spatial information of an agenda element and identifies the certain place of task fulfillment.

- Sequence of agenda elements: The sequence presents information about the relationship between the agenda elements in form of the predecessor and successor arrangement.
- Social: The information, social, indicates the dependence on other persons and participants.

The information of the mobility planning process can be defined as:

- Location: The location is the origin and destination of the journey. As this includes different forms of mobility, the origin and destination can be an address, a point of interest or a stop point in public transport.
- Date and Time: This normally covers the time of departure and arrival as well as the duration when the mobility takes place.
- Sequence of mobility: Mobility is often conducted not only as a single use of one means of transportation, but as an intermodal journey, a combination of different means of transportation.
- Means of transportation: Individual and public means of transportation shape the available mobility. This includes cars, busses, trains and modern mobility concepts like car sharing or bike sharing.
- Mobility impairments and restrictions: This characteristic includes personal impairments, e.g. walking disabilities, as well as restrictions from heavy luggage.

Table 1. Comparison of information needs

Information need of agenda planning	Information need of mobility planning
Purpose	Location
Date/Time	Date/Time
Location	Sequence of mobility
Sequence of agenda elements	Means of transportation
Social	Mobility impairments and restrictions

In addition, the required information for both planning process are marked by an arrow. The similarities and combinations should be explained with an ordinary example of an agenda element, a business meeting. Within the agenda planning, the information category time is used to determine the date and the point of time of the starting point and end point. In the mobility planning, the used temporal end point of the meeting is necessary to define the departure time of the mobility offer. As an analogy to the information category time, the location fixes the place of the agenda element and the origin of next trip.

In summary, the spatial and temporal information are the precondition and initial point for the integration of mobility planning into agenda planning. The relationship shows an elementary requirement of the integrated planning approach. The spatial and temporal information of mobility planning process must be able to convert and transfer into the agenda planning process.

The information, purpose and time, are required at a minimum within an agenda to be able to begin a planning process. Further information can be fixed accordingly, depending on the kind of agenda element. However, with the increasing number of information categories, the planning flexibility of an agenda element will be reduced. As a result of the analysis of the planning process, we can state that users try to organize the tasks into different categories. Overall, two categories could be identified: appointment and to-do. These categories can be differentiated by the set of fulfilled properties.

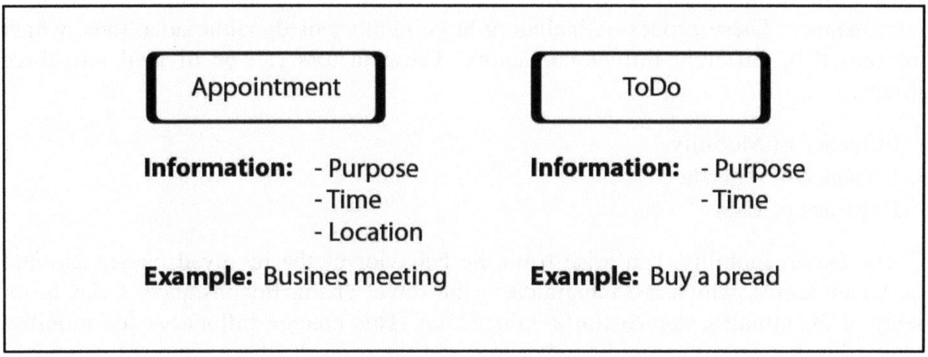

Fig. 2. Categories of an agenda element

The first category is an appointment that is defined by the properties: purpose, time and location. Naturally, the meeting has no temporal or spatial flexibility, because it starts at a certain time and at certain location. In contrast to the appointment, the flexibility plays a significant role at the category to-do. Within a to-do the fulfillment of

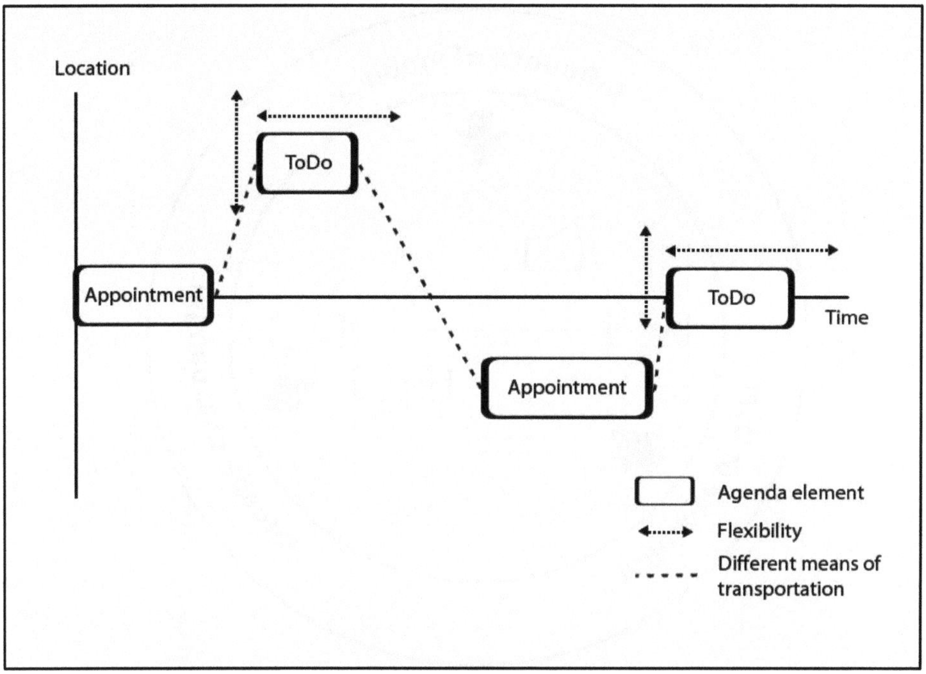

Fig. 3. Model of a personal agenda

an agenda element can vary in time and location and enable an optimization of daily routine with respect to user needs. In fact the possibilities and the benefit of optimization can be particularly visualized by displaying the whole agenda.

The model is characterized by the dynamic combination of agenda and mobility planning. With the solution, the user will be enabled to plan the daily routine and manage the resulting mobility chain between the single agenda elements in an efficient manner. These processes include a large number of dynamic adaptions, which are caused by different influential factors. These factors can be divided into three groups:

- Influence of Mobility
- Influence of Agenda
- Influence of User

The factor, mobility, can arise from the behavior of the involved passengers and the technologies, which are integrated in the travel chain. For instance, a bus has a delay of 20 minutes, due to traffic congestion. This change influences the mobility connection between two agenda elements and, as a result, the mentioned delay can disturb the start of an agenda element. However, an agenda element can also be influenced by the influential factor, agenda. This factor consists of all impacts which influence the fulfillment of tasks in the daily routine, e.g. a participant cancels a meeting. Consequentially, an agenda element must be changed in the temporal or spatial dimension or even possibly be cancelled as an element. Besides the mobility and

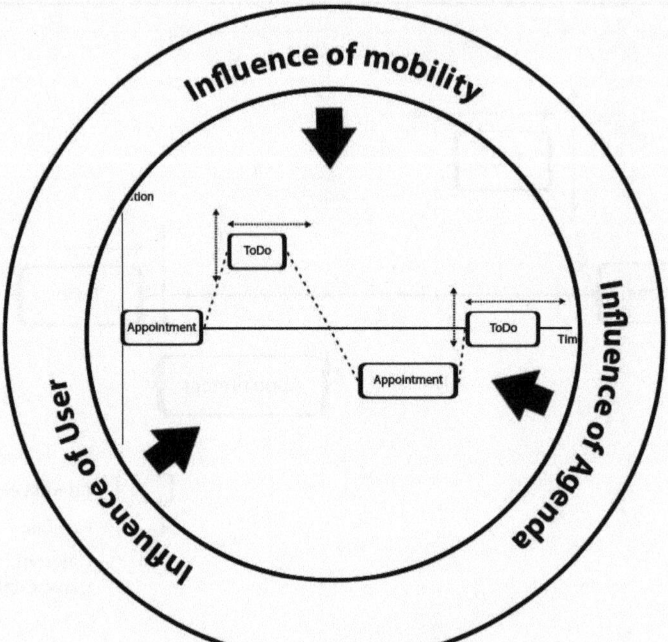

Fig. 4. Main influential factors

agenda influential factors, the attitude and preferences of the user have an effect on the planning process. These user requirements affect the usage of mobility and the fulfillment of the agenda tasks. For example, a user wants to visit only subway stations with an elevator because health reasons do not allow the user to take the stairs. In summary, every affect leads to re-planning of the agenda elements or mobility chain and can cause a modification of the daily routine.

4 Discussion

Reducing the complexity of planning processes and combining agenda and mobility planning, requires knowledge of the individual agenda, user preferences and restrictions, as well as, information of different means of transportation and mobility infrastructures. The discussed approach is a first step in this direction. But some challenges for the described approach still exist. The simplified model has to be extended by further planning properties. For this purpose, the further properties must be investigated, particularly the relationships and dependences between the already involved and new properties regarding the new challenges they provide. Also, the influential factors need to be examined further. The dependences between the different factors should especially be analyzed. Besides this issue, the strength of the factors and their consequences must be classified, in order to develop routines for managing the impacts.

5 Conclusion

The introduction of new means of transportation to the society, does not necessarily result in different forms of mobility behavior. Designing new information systems, which support new mobility behaviors and include new and traditional mobility offers, is needed. The German research projects IP-KOM-ÖV and Dynapsys already lay a foundation for these kinds of systems, defining standards for passenger information systems and developing first dynamic agenda planning systems. The Dynapsys system will feature the described combination of agenda and mobility planning from a mobility point of view, enhancing traditional personal travel assistants with a new form of planning functionality.

In future studies, the interaction concepts for the integral planning process on mobile devices and the user interface design, as well as user experience for mobility information and agenda planning processes, will be evaluated.

Acknowledgements. Part of this work was funded by the German Federal Ministry of Economy and Technology (BMWi) grant number 19P10003L and 19P12013B within the IP-KOM-ÖV und Dynapsys project. The IP-KOM-ÖV project develops an interface standard for passenger information in German public transport, with focus on the connection between personal mobile devices, vehicle systems and public transport background computer systems. The Dynapsys project develops an agenda planning system for individual task and mobility planning from "door to door".

References

1. Wirtz, S., Jakobs, E.-M.: Improving User Experience for Passenger Information Systems. Prototypes and Reference Objects. IEEE Transactions on Professional Communication 56(2), 120–137 (2013)
2. Zierer, M.H., Zierer, K.: Zur Zukunft der Mobilität: eine multiperspektivische Analyse des Verkehrs zu Beginn des 21. Jahrhunderts. VS, Verl. für Sozialwiss, Wiesbaden (2010)
3. Shepherd, A.: Hierarchical task analysis. Taylor & Francis, New York (2001)
4. Hörold, S., Mayas, C., Krömker, H.: Identifying the information needs of users in public transport. In: Stanton, N. (ed.) Advances in Human Aspects of Road and Rail Transportation, pp. 331–340. CRC Press, Boca Raton (2012)
5. Annett, J.: Hierarchical Task Analysis. In: Handbook of Cognitive Task Design, pp. 17–36. Lawrence Erlbaum, New Jersey (2003)
6. Morgan, D., Krueger, R.: The Focus Group Gudiebook. Sage Publications, Thousand Oaks (1998)
7. Krueger, R., Casey, M.: Focus Groups. Sage Publications, Thousand Oaks (2000)
8. Mayas, C., Hörold, S., Krömker, H.: Meeting the Challenges of Individual Passenger Information with Personas. In: Stanton, N. (ed.) Advances in Human Aspects of Road and Rail Transportation, pp. 822–831. CRC Press, Boca Raton (2012)

The Challenges of Developing an Online Tool to Measure the Quality of the Passenger Experience in a PanEuropean Context

Andree Woodcock[1], Panagiotis Petridis[1], Fotis Liotopoulos[2], Apostolos Georgiadis[2], and Liam Brady[1]

[1] Coventry University, Coventry, United Kingdom
{A.Woodcock,PPetridis}@coventry.ac.uk
[2] SBOING, Thessaloniki, Greece
{liotop,tolis}@sboing.net

Abstract. METPEX is a 3 year, FP7 project which aims to develop a PanEuropean tool to measure the quality of the passenger's experience of multimodal transport. Initial work has led to the development of a comprehensive set of variables relating to different passenger groups, forms of transport and journey stages. This paper addresses the main challenges in transforming the variables into usable, accessible computer based tools allowing for the real time collection of information, across multiple journey stages in different EU countries. Non-computer based measurement instruments will be used to gather information from those who may not have or be familiar with mobile technology. Smartphone-based measurement instruments will also be used, hosted in two applications. The mobile applications need to be easy to use, configurable and adaptable according to the context of use. They should also be inherently interesting and rewarding for the participant, whilst allowing for the collection of high quality, valid and reliable data from all journey types and stages (from planning, through to entry into and egress from different transport modes, travel on public and personal vehicles and support of active forms of transport (e.g. cycling and walking). During all phases of the data collection and processing, the privacy of the participant is highly regarded and is ensured.

Keywords: Adaptive and personalized interfaces, Entertainment and game user interface, Human Centered Design and User Centered Design, Internationalization and Localization, New technology and its usefulness, Qualitative and quantitative measurement and evaluation, Universal usability, transport.

1 Introduction

Public transportation improves the quality of life in communities by providing safe, efficient and economical services, and delivering a vital component necessary for a healthy economy. Thus public transport is central to people's lives and well-being, especially vulnerable groups (e.g. less mobile, elderly and disabled). The need to encourage greater public transport use is critical in achieving sustainability targets.

M. Kurosu (Ed.): Human-Computer Interaction, Part III, HCII 2014, LNCS 8512, pp. 545–555, 2014.

For many, the perception and reality of public transport does not encourage use, especially when multimodal forms of transport are needed. A holistic understanding of the passenger experience is critical to develop and support transport accessibility. Whilst previous research has focused on different aspects of passenger experience, the diversity of tools developed limits their usefulness, effectiveness and transferability. Given the maturity of research, there is a need to synthesize methods and knowledge, to produce a pan-European standardized tool for use across transport modes and with different passenger groups to focus attention away from the design of discrete elements to the whole journey experience.

Taking a holistic approach to the study of the passenger experience will provide a bridge between transport, sustainability, design, accessibility and land use; acknowledging the central importance of mobility to quality of life. To plug this gap, the authors present the work undertaken by METPEX to develop a computer based inclusive passenger experience measurement tool for European transport providers, passenger groups and municipalities validated through its use across 8 sites of varying transport complexity.

The development of such a tool is the first step in creating high quality, user-centric, integrated, accessible public transport services which are capable of attracting and retaining public transport users whilst meeting sustainability targets. Such a tool will provide reliable data which can be used by transport providers, policy makers, vehicle designers and municipalities to measure and benchmark their services and to assess where changes need to be made which will increase efficiency and effectiveness of service delivery. Enabling wider access to safe, secure, convenient, comfortable and economical public transport will in turn support the EU's carbon reduction targets as this will lead to an increase in the number of people who use public or active forms of transport. The data collected will enable the creation and dissemination of service quality and accessibility benchmark indicators.

This paper presents the initial work that has led to the development of a comprehensive set of variables relating to different passenger groups, forms of transport and journey stages. The paper will address the main challenges in transforming the variables into usable, accessible computer based tools allowing for the real time collection of information, across multiple journey stages in different EU countries.

The next section presents a brief review of data collection technologies. Section 3 presents the work conducted by the METPEX project team to develop the questions for the measurement instruments. Section 4 presents the two applications developed for the collection of data. The first application is based on GPS navigation technologies, while the second application uses gamification techniques in order to motivate the participant to fill in the questionnaires. Section 5 summarizes conclusions to date and the remaining challenges.

2 Background

The changing trends in technology have been the driving force in the evolution of surveying methods (Couper 2005). The advent of Web2.0, and the second wave of websites and applications offering a much richer experience has contributed to major innovations in survey data collection. This trend will expand with the mainstream use of new interaction devices such as Google Glasses and HMD displays.

The first travel surveys were introduced in the United States in the 1950s and were conducted by pen and paper using interviewers who went from door-to-door, interviewing survey participants in person. By the 1970s, telephone surveys became more popular, but still relied on pen and paper (PAPI Surveys). The major breakthrough in survey design was introduced in the early 90s with the introduction of Computer-Assisted Telephone Interviewing (CATI) (Taylor 2000), see Figure 1.

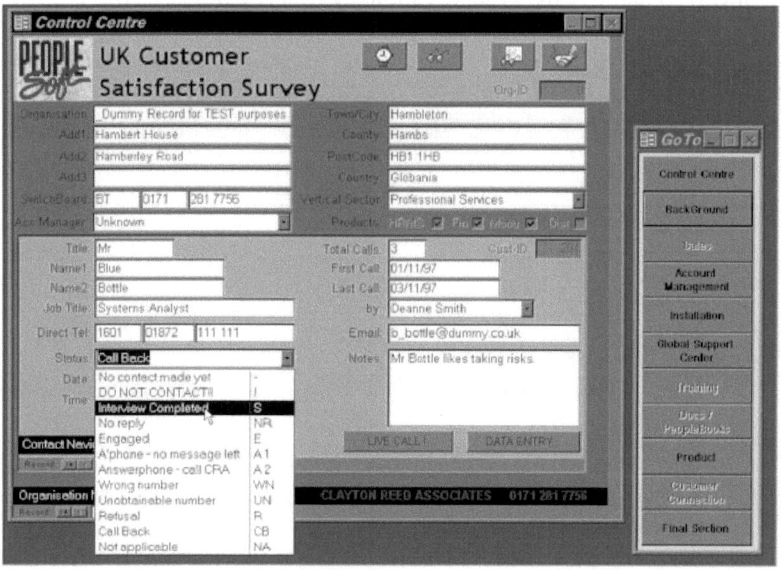

Fig. 1. CATI Survey System

At that point, travel survey methodology started a transition from a single-stage survey to multi-stage surveys which included the following steps: telephone the household/business to obtain demographic information, mail travel logs to the participants to record travel on an assigned travel day, then telephone to retrieve the details or have the participants mail them back (Sudeshna Sen 2009).

Multi-stage surveys improved the quality of the data obtained and enabled more refined data analysis. This increased demand for higher quality / finer resolution data resulted in the introduction of other technologies such as location-based tagging via Global Positioning Systems (GPS), web-based surveys, use of bar codes, and mobile phone devices.

Despite the advantages, CATI surveys are experiencing rapidly falling response rates (Owen 2002, Curtin 2005), due to the exponential increase of mobile phones and the increasing growth of mobile phone only households. This change present a challenge to the traditional household telephone surveys (Kempf 2007, Sen 2009). Through the technological improvements on the quality and speed of the WorldWideWeb two new survey systems were introduced: Computer-Assisted Personal Interviewing (CAPI), a widely used method that enables interviewers to conduct face-to-face interviews using laptops. Following the interview, the data are sent to a central computing network, either electronically via the web; or by mail (Bosley 1998)) and the Computer-Assisted Self Interviewing (CASI) in which computers take the place of interviewers in guiding respondents through the questionnaire (Tourangeau 2007). A variation of CAPI is the Computer-Assisted Survey Information Collection (CASIC), which refers to a variety of survey modes that were enabled by the introduction of computer technology. The first CASIC modes were interviewer-administered, while later on computerized self-administered questionnaires (CSAQ) appeared. A typical example of CSAQ and CASIC is survey monkey (SurveyMonkey 2013).

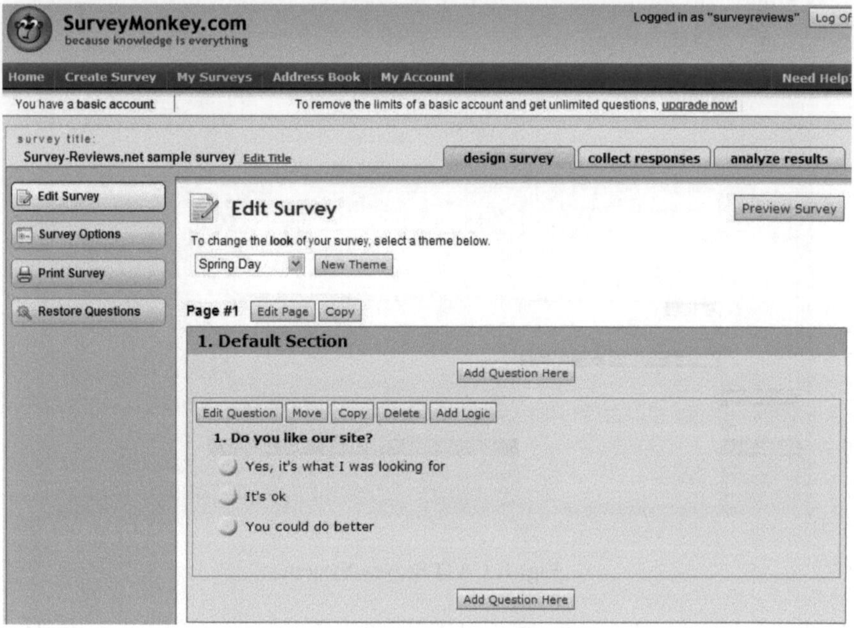

Fig. 2. A Typical CSAQ Survey tool

In addition to the advances in CASI systems mentioned above, the dramatic uptake of mobile phones in the last decade is expected to strongly influence data collection over the next decade (Sudeshna Sen 2009). The rapid growth of smartphones can be attributed to enhanced features and user interfaces, constant connectivity with the web through 3G/4G networks or through WiFi hotspots. GPS-enabled Smartphones are an emerging data collection technology that allows researchers to collect accurate information on location and travel details such as travel time, speed, acceleration, and direction of travel. Several traffic studies have demonstrated the potential of GPS-enabled Smartphones. These Smartphones provide exhaustive spatial and temporal coverage of the transportation network that help traffic monitoring and computation of reasonable estimates of travel time with GPS-level accuracy (Fontaine 2007, Sudeshna Sen 2009).

Furthermore the introduction of gamification technologies on such devices provides incentives to survey participants to complete surveys by offering them rewards on completing the survey using lessons learned from the gaming industry.

The power of games to immerse and motivate (Garris 2002, Panzoli, Peters et al. 2010) and the capabilities of games to change perceptions and views have created a more positive approach to games and new game genres (de Freitas 2009). More use of games in non-entertainment contexts such as training (e.g. Mautone 2008) are transforming everyday lives. Multiplayer and social games communities are changing social interactions, leading to greater capabilities for social learning and interactions and importantly more fun in everyday contexts (e.g. McGonigal 2011). Efficacy can be further achieved by better understanding the target audience and pedagogic perspectives, so as to make learning experiences more immersive, relevant and engaging. A recent survey by the International Software Federation of Europe (ISFE, 2010) revealed that 74% of those aged 16-19 considered themselves as gamers (n=3000), while 60% of those 20-24, 56% 25-29 and 38% 30-44 considered themselves regular players of games. However, a major challenge lies in translating interest and potential into actual adoption and use.

Deterding (2011) defined gamification as the application of game elements and digital game design techniques to non-game problems, such as business and social impact challenges. To motivate users to work toward these goals, gamification implements an accomplishment based reward system. Points, stars and badges are often "given" to users for completing important tasks. In the METPEX Game application users will be drawn in to briefly rate their journey, through their engagement in a 'game', and then to log on to the METPEX website to provide a more extensive rating and to receive a reward in the form of a downloadable content.

3 Development of the METPEX Measurement Instruments

For METPEX, the whole journey from inception to arrival is the main unit of interest. We aim to provide an inclusive set of measurement tools which can be used to assess a particular stage of a journey, or the whole journey, including modal transfers. This may include journeys made wholly or partly by active, public or private forms of transport. Providing inclusive measurement instruments, which can be used by a wide range of respondents, is key to evaluating transport service provision. Therefore METPEX is developing a suite of measurement instruments, including CASIC (on line survey using SurveyMonkey), PAPI systems (e.g. semi structured interviews) and focus groups for targeted user groups. The game app and dynamic questionnaire presented here only represent a small portion of the final suite of tools, in the understanding that these may only be used by a certain section of travelers.

In order to develop this suite of measurement instruments, the first year of the project was used to understand and consolidate previous research and research instruments, through both desk based research and interviews with stakeholders (e.g. municipalities and transport operators) in our partner countries. The subsequent analysis showed that over 400 variables would need to be considered if the whole journey was to be analysed. A pilot questionnaire, administered to over 200 people from Lithuania, UK, Greece, Ireland, Portugal, Italy, Sweden and Romania in both on-line and pen and paper formats showed the operational complexity of such a survey and the lack of appreciation of respondents who would need to fill in such a questionnaire (either in real time or retrospectively). The subsequent analysis showed the importance of some factors in determining overall satisfaction (e.g. the longest leg of the journey, overall satisfaction and mood) and the relationship between the variables.

Following this, the original categorization of variables into political, organizational, functional, environmental, technological, and social dimensions was removed (from the users perspective, although each item can be traced back to these dimensions). The variables have been recategorised to make them more respondent and journey oriented, prioritized, filtered and mapped on to different measurement instruments (on-line survey, structured interviews, diary studies and dynamic questionnaires) so that only the most useful and highly prioritized variables for each user and journey type will be presented. In this way METPEX will meet one of its objectives, i.e. to support and encourage adjustability and adaptability according to the context of use, e.g. time period, targets' framework and resource limitations. Therefore, the full list of variables can be filtered so that only the most useful and preferred variables for each condition (e.g. user, mode of transport and journey stage) are included. The filtering can be undertaken by a researcher, who can use subsets of the 'full survey' to initiate targeted campaigns, or create a set of rules to generate appropriate research instruments. The subsequent sections of the paper discuss the development of dynamic, on-line surveys which will be used for real time data collection.

4 METPEX Tool Functional Requirements

One of the major challenges that METPEX faces is the standardization of the passenger satisfaction surveys. As outlined in the previous section, the 400 variables and the items included in the pilot questionnaire have been collated into a 'full survey' database, from which subsets of questions can be drawn. One of the problems with the paper based and full on-line survey is that they may be too unwieldy to gather information on short journeys in real time. Therefore, research instruments are needed which can be used in real time, to capture the actual journey experience. In order to do this mobile phone applications and games have been created which are both adaptable and adjustable, and responsive to the information collected automatically by the device itself or user input. The smartphone applications will support:

- Multiple campaigns (i.e. according to different means of transport, participant type and location),
- Multiple questionnaires per campaign based on means of transport/location and user profile (multiple sets of questions, multiple target-groups),
- Dynamic selection of questionnaire (i.e., the app will be able to query the 'METPEX' server, identify the currently active campaign, or randomly choose one, then choose a questionnaire (randomly, or based on the user's profile, demographics, etc.) The user's profile may contain settings such as: preferred language, age/gender and will be communicated to the server strongly encrypted in order to protect the participant's privacy.

The questionnaire form, as presented to the user may contain multiple tabs, with each tab representing a different part of the passenger's journey, or a different travel mode, in a multi-modal journey. The passengers may fill in the questionnaire at their own pace, while en route, postpone doing so or cancel it. As soon as the passenger's response is uploaded to the METPEX servers, is can be processed, stored and the database updated. The management of the campaigns, surveys and responses can all be conducted via a web-based application.

4.1 METPEX Gaming Application

The proposed METPEX Gaming Application consists of two mini-games and one mobile survey tool that uses gamification elements in order to increase the motivation of participants to fill the questionnaire and to increase their engagement with the METPEX system via offering rewards, and unlocking several level of the application. The games will be available via the web and for Android and iOS (iPhone, iPad) devices.

The first two mini-games are standard memory games (e.g. memory pairs), but the items included are based on the passenger's experience at the time of playing (e.g. if the journey is being undertaken by trolleybus, icons related to trolleybus travel will be included). The games will be unlocked as the participant completes the survey so the terminology and icons will be closely related to the passenger's experience. If a respondent chooses to use the app many times, each time they log on their profile will change slightly, generating new word and icon sets. The table below shows a selection of keywords that are included in the memory game. In addition the application is fully integrated with social networking sites such as Facebook and Twitter.

Table 1. METPEX Keywords

Carbon footprint	Public transport
Reliability	Planning trip
Fares	Travel
Frequency	Quality of Passenger experience
Passenger	Performance
Quality	Bus, train and metro

As the user provides key information at the start of the game in relation to their transport mode and demographics, key, relevant questions can be asked that specifically relate to their journey drawn from the full METPEX questionnaire.

In order to increase the participants' motivation to fill in the questionnaire, we have represented the participant as a travelling musician / band member, who needs to build up tracks from musical bars created through completing the survey activity when they travel. On each trip, they unlock a one-bar looping sample by dragging notes to complete the METPEX survey. Each sample is in the same key and tempo, meaning these samples can be sequenced and layered to create original pieces of music. According to the answers, the application will create a unique music piece, representing the passenger's experience

Social mechanics are applied though a website component to the game, which allows people to upload their tracks and comment on those others have created. The motivation to play would be expected to arise from the **ownership** players develop of their content, and **curiosity** in seeing how additional samples might allow them to create more complex pieces of music. Furthermore, the **free** nature of the game, and its underlying **meaning**, that by playing the game players are contributing to improvement in public transport, can also be drivers.

A key consideration would be how a limiting factor is applied to ensure players are actually reporting on their actual journey rather than reporting fictional travel to progress the game and create different forms of music. This is a consideration in any design which will seek to motivate players to complete a survey.

The game interface will also direct the user to the METPEX website (www.metpex.eu) from which they will be able to complete a more detailed on-line survey, relating to all journey stages. The reward for this will be an entitlement to download a free game.

4.2 METPEX GPS Navigation Application

The second smartphone application that will host the METPEX surveys ("METPEX Tool") is the **SBOING GPS navigator**, called "sbNavi™", a product launched in November 2013 in Apple's app store (iTunes) and due to be launched for Android smartphones by April 2014. The SBOING GPS navigator is a satellite navigation application, developed for smartphones, which implements SBOING's crowdsourcing methodology for improved routing and faster map updates. Its community version is offered for free, together with free maps covering the entire world. The main functional characteristics of sbNavi™ include:

- Use of custom maps, based on the free and open maps of OpenStreetMap (OSM, www.openstreetmap.org).
- By utilizing historical traffic data, it leads to more accurate routing decisions, compared to existing commercial PNAs, which are based on static traffic information (i.e. the speed limit of each road),
- Distinguishes and provides better time estimates, depending on the type of vehicle (e.g., pedestrian, fast / slow motorcycle, fast / slow car, truck, bus, taxi), weather and corresponding road conditions (sun, rain, snow, etc.), time-of-day, day-of-the-week, holiday and season-of-year,
- An inherent, independent mechanism: a) to produce new maps (for uncharted areas), and b) to self-update existing maps (crowd sourcing support by entering user input about road hazards, police blocks, traffic lights, traffic signs, POIs, favorites, road network changes, etc.)
- Route simulation mode
- 2D and 3D map viewing with pan, zoom, and rotate functionality,
- User routes can be recorded and recorded routes can be managed, securely uploaded to SBOING, sent by email and replayed
- Searching: a) by free text search, b) in Favorites, c) in POIs, d) by coordinates, e) by proximity
- Easy definition of multi-waypoint lists and multi-waypoint (multi-legged) routing
- Multi-lingual support for text and voice guidance
- Ability to accommodate the maps of the entire planet in a single memory card
- Uses strong security (strong encryption) in all data uploads carried out by the user, thus ensuring the confidentiality of its private information.

The SBOING Concept. Instead of the static speed limit of a road used by today's navigators, the SBOING technology is based on a collaborative methodology, which consists of the statistical recording, for each road section, of the average travelling time for every combination of vehicle type, weather conditions, road conditions, season, day-of-the-week and time-of-day. Thus, for example, for a 100m section of road XYZ average travel time may be 40 sec., on Tuesday afternoon, or 15 sec., on Sunday morning, etc. While driving, the SBOING GPS navigator records and stores a number of parameters, including the vehicle's GPS position (GPS coordinates), velocity, altimeter and timestamp. In addition, the user may also add extra map information, such as road hazards, traffic cameras, points-of-interest (POIs), map corrections, etc. The user subsequently securely uploads its collected traces to the SBOING web-site and in return they get updated maps for its PNDs, through a "credit-debit" system (based on credit units, which are called "SBOING Credit Units", or SCUs). SCUs can then be bought/exchanged/traded as any virtual currency, i.e. with other virtual currencies (Farmville gold or Facebook currency), or for products and services at reduced prices (with targeted and location-based push advertising).

The uploaded data undergoes certain statistical validity checks, carried out by the SBOING backend (to filter out malicious or invalid data) and it is statistically integrated inside SBOING's database and world maps. Uncharted areas are updated and new roads and pathways are added to the existing maps, just by users' driving around and recording GPS traces. Based on their collected SCUs, the users can download at will maps and SBOING traffic data for any region of the world, through SBOING's web-site, which will enable them to enjoy better routing and faster map updates. The functionality and crowdsourcing methodology makes it more likely to attract a user's attention and interest and makes a passenger more motivated to respond to a survey by being given a reward (a number of SCUs) in exchange for their response.

Another advantage of using a GPS navigation application as a host application for the METPEX Tool is that the application can record and upload useful information that the passenger need not be asked about or need not be asked to provide, such as:

- User profile information, such as age, sex, demographics, etc.
- The date and time
- The place (geo-coordinates), where the questionnaire was filled in
- The route that the passenger travelled with real-time attributes.

4.3 Dynamic Surveys

Both smartphone applications aim to receive the passenger's input or feedback (i.e., responses to a questionnaire) in real time and upload it to the METPEX backend server for further processing. The back end server will hold the data derived from each measurement instrument, in each country, in a standard format enabling a variety of different queries and comparisons to be made.

Definitions: For the purposes of the following presentation,

- we define a "**survey**" to be a questionnaire of the METPEX tool,
- we define a "**campaign**" to be a class of surveys, targeted to certain user groups, or carried out for a specific purpose or goal,
- we define a "**response**" to be a passenger's response to a survey.

A survey will be defined using XML. This definition will specify each question's type (e.g. multiple choice, text, integer value, etc.), the visual components to be used in the questionnaire (e.g., checkbox, radiobutton, combobox, slider, etc.), the default response, etc.

A campaign will also be defined using XML. The definition will identify its name, type, a free-text description and the set of surveys it contains.

The surveys can be generated either statically (manually), or dynamically (e.g., with an SQL query followed by an SQL-to-XML script-based conversion). Alternatively, the XML may be replaced with JSON format messaging (more Java friendly, for Android platforms).

The passenger's response will also be formed in XML and it will be uploaded with strong encryption to the METPEX backend servers. From the application's point of view the process of dynamic survey selection will adhere to the following protocol,

Step 1: Read the active campaign (in XML / JSON format), either by calling a PHP script or by direct file retrieval. The application could place a query, based on the demographics and profile of the passenger and receive a targeted campaign.

Step 2: Choose randomly one survey, out of the class (list) of surveys defined in the campaign and load its definition (in XML / JSON format, as above). Note here that, if the passenger (based on his/her profile) is not compatible with the particular campaign, i.e., he is a Greek male and the campaign is targeted to French females, then the application should not launch the questionnaire.

Step 3: Dynamically generate the questionnaire form, from the survey description.

Step 4: When the user uploads his/her response, the application uploads / posts a response (in XML / JSON format) with a unique file ID.

5 Conclusions

This paper has presented the two applications, which are currently under development for the METPEX project, which will allow targeted data collection in real time from transport users using dynamic surveys, generated either from information automatically collected by mobile devices or from user input. The information which the user provides in real time can be later augmented through completion of the on-line questionnaire.

The development of the apps raises a number of technical and nontechnical issues including the best way to create dynamic surveys, the linking of information collected in real time with data collected from other research instruments, the demographics of the users and their motivation to participate once or many times, the ability of on-line tools to capture information about different stage of the journey using different modes of transport (e.g. cycling and walking and modal interchanges), the extent to which the information collected automatically about the journey (e.g. its speed) can be mapped on to user experience, ethical issues, the extent to which participating in a game may bias responses, and the validity /reliability and usefulness of information derived from these tools when compared to more traditional forms of data collection.

Acknowledgments. METPEX is funded under FP7-SST-2012-RTD-1, under the SST.2012.3.1-1. Research actions regarding the accessibility of transport systems work programme.

References

1. Bosley, J., Conrad, F.G., Uglow, D.: Pen CASIC: Design and Usability. Wiley, New York (1998)
2. Couper, M.P.: Technology Trends in Survey Data Collection. Social Science Computer Review 23(4), 486–501 (2005)
3. Curtin, R., Presser, S., Singer, E.: Changes in Telephone Survey Nonresponse over the Past Quarter Century. Public Opinion Quarterly 69(1), 87–98 (2005)
4. de Freitas, S., Rebolledo-Mendez, G., Liarokapis, F., Magoulas, G., Poulovassilis, A.: Developing an evaluation methodology for immersive learning experiences in a virtual world. In: Rebolledo-Mendez, G., Liarokapis, F., de Freitas, S. (eds.) Proceedings of 2009 Conference in Games and Virtual Worlds for Serious Applications, pp. 43–50. IEEE (2009)
5. Deterding, S.: Gamification: designing for motivation. Interaction 19(4), 14–17 (2012)
6. Fontaine, M., Smith, B.: Investigation of the performance of wireless location technology-based traffic monitoring systems. Journal of Transportation Engineering 133(3), 157–165 (2007)
7. Garris, R., Ahlers, R., Driskell, J.E.: Games, Motivation, and Learning: A research and Practice Model. Simulation Gamin 33(4), 441–467 (2002)
8. Kempf, A.M., Remington, P.L.: New Challenges for Telephone Surveys. Annual Review of Public Health 28, 113–126 (2007)
9. Mautone, T., Spiker, V., Karp, D.: Using Serious Game Technology to Improve Aircrew Training. In: Proc. of I/ITSEC 2008 (2008)
10. McGonigal, J.: Reality is Broken: Why Games make Us Better and how they can Change the World. The Penguin Press, New York (2011)
11. Owen, R.S.: A Matter of Trade-offs: Examining the advantages and disadvantages of on-line surveys. Quirks Marketing Research Review, 24–26 (2002)
12. Panzoli, D., Peters, C., Dunwell, I., Sanchez, S., Petridis, P., Protopsaltis, A., Scesa, V., de Freitas, S.: A Level of Interaction Framework for Exploratory Learning with Characters in Virtual Environments. In: Plemenos, D., Miaoulis, G. (eds.) Intelligent Computer Graphics 2010. SCI, vol. 321, pp. 123–143. Springer, Heidelberg (2010)
13. Sen, S., Zmud, J., Arce, C.: Evaluation of Efficiency and Effectiveness of Cell Phone Samples in Transportation Surveys. Transportation Research Record (2105), 44–50 (2009)
14. Sen, S., Bricka, S.: Data Collection Technologies - Past, Present, and Future. In: The 12th International Conference on Travel Behaviour Research, Jaipur, Rajasthan, India (2009)
15. SurveyMonkey. SurveyMonkey Website (2013), `https://www.surveymonkey.com` (retrieved February 5, 2013)
16. Taylor, H.: Does internet research work? Comparing online survey results with telephone surveys. International Journal of Market Research 42(1) (2000)
17. Tourangeau, R., Yan, T.: Sensitive Questions in Surveys. Psychological Bulletin 133, 859–873 (2007)

Interacting with games

From Screens to Devices and Tangible Objects: A Framework Applied to Serious Games Characterization

Julian Alvarez[1,2], Sylvain Haudegond[1], Clémentine Havrez[1,3], Christophe Kolski[3], Yoann Lebrun[1,3], Sophie Lepreux[3], and Aurélien Libessart[2]

[1] Play Research Lab., CCI Grand Hainaut
{j.alvarez,s.haudegond,y.lebrun}@grandhainaut.cci.fr
[2] Trigone Cirel, Lille1 University
{julian.alvarez,aurelien.libessart}@univ-lille1.fr
[3] LAMIH -UMR CNRS 8201, University of Valenciennes, France
{clementine.havrez,christophe.kolski,yoann.lebrun, sophie.lepreux}@univ-valenciennes.fr

Abstract. The accelerated progress being made with interactive devices (such as screens, cameras, joysticks and tangible objects) has triggered the development of new interaction methods for applications (e.g., body language, haptic feedback, etc.). Video games and Serious Games are being played on increasingly innovative peripherals (e.g., Kinect, Wii Balance Board). These devices have generated new, intuitive forms of Human-Computer Interaction that are completely changing our usages. The purpose of this paper is to provide an overview of gaming technologies and suggest a framework for characterizing the role that screens play in these devices. This framework differentiates between the various gaming elements (the gamers, the interactive devices and the entertaining and gamified applications). This framework is a tool to analyze the effects of device choice and configuration. This paper presents an evaluation of the characterization of 15 serious games. This evaluation will provide a glimpse of the potentialities of the framework with respect to suggested criteria as well as of the trends and potential developments in interactive media.

Keywords: Tangible objects, screens, devices, video game, serious game, characterization.

1 Introduction

We are increasingly surrounded by screens, and more generally speaking, by devices that provide various ways to interact with different types of applications (see Fig. 1). Video games, and conceivably serious video games (Serious Games [0]), regularly offer innovative technologies and usages [2, 3]. The increasing intuitiveness of Human-Computer Interaction (HCI) enables interactive devices to be more and more rapidly appropriated by users [4]. For example, households are acquiring peripherals like Kinect or the Wii Balance Board with increasing frequency [5]. We believe that the challenges to be faced in the next few years will be tangibility, and even more so,

M. Kurosu (Ed.): Human-Computer Interaction, Part III, HCII 2014, LNCS 8512, pp. 559–570, 2014.

the combination of the tangible with the virtual. The commercial success of the *Skylanders* (from Activision in 2011) and *Disney Infinity* (from Disney in 2013) tangible objects that rely on NFC technology to manage video game avatars, or games like *AppMates* (from Disney Pixar in 2012) *Apptivity toys* (from Mattel in 2013) and *Cupets* (from Giochi Preziosi in 2013), which can directly communicate with tablets, supports our hypothesis.

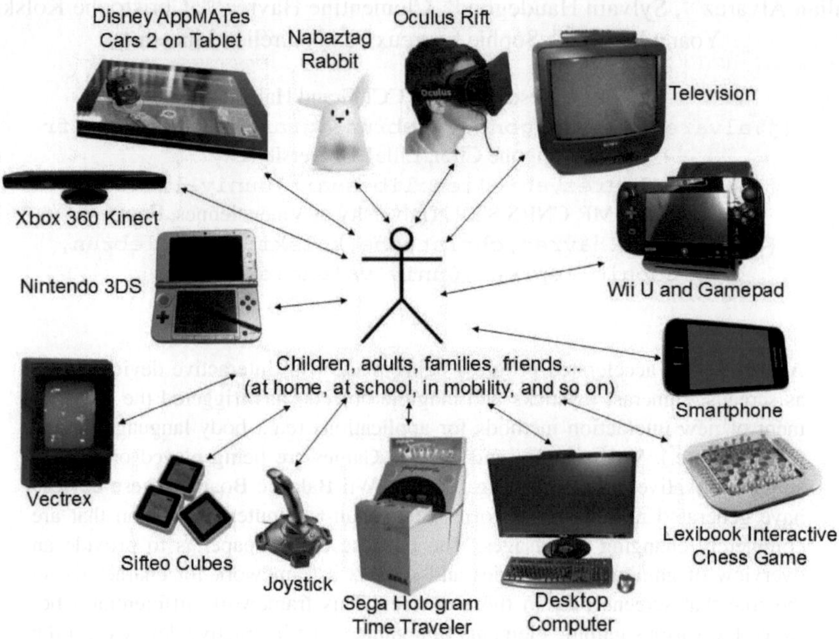

Fig. 1. What was the screen invasion has become the interactive media invasion

This is why we wanted to focus on the state of the art in video gaming (Serious or otherwise) in this paper to suggest a framework for characterizing the role of screens in such applications. This characterization focuses mainly on gaming peripherals and devices proposed by Saunders and Novak [6]. The research presented in this paper is comprised of a preliminary study whose objective was to examine the contribution made by video gaming and Serious Games in acquiring knowledge and skills, particularly in the areas of health, education and communication. We specifically refer to the potential facilitation of the skills transfer from the virtual environment to the real world that goes along with associating screens with tangible objects in a gaming context [7]. However, to conduct such research, it was appropriate first to prepare experiments to confirm or refute the hypotheses. To do this, it seemed to us that identifying the different variables that could be assembled within gaming devices through characterization represented a necessary, pragmatic approach.

The second section of this article provides an overview of current gaming technologies. This overview is not intended to be exhaustive, but rather representative of the various gaming configurations corresponding to technological breakthroughs over the years. In the third section, we suggest a framework for categorizing the games. This framework is applied in section four on 15 different Serious Games. The article finishes with a conclusion and suggestions for future research.

2 Study of Technological Developments and Breakthroughs Related to the Use of Screens and Objects in Interactive Entertainment Applications

In this state of the art section, different technological developments and breakthroughs will be reviewed and then summarized.

2.1 The Beginning: The First Display not Incorporated into a Calculator (OXO, 1952)

From the very beginning, video games have used a screen and an input interface, as illustrated in the OXO case. Created by English IT specialist Alexander S. Douglas, this tic-tac-toe game [8] was programmed into the EDSAC (Electronic Delay Storage Automatic Calculator) computer at the University of Cambridge. The EDSAC computer was able to store programs in its memory (similar to the RAM of today's computers). This device had three CRT screens displaying the current state of the memory in graphical form. Douglas's idea was to take this memory monitoring functionality and use it as a graphical display tool. As an IT student, Douglas conducted research on Human-Computer Interaction. In his academic thesis, he came up with the idea of programming a game, which illustrated the result of his work. The CRT control screen, which had a resolution of 35 x 16, was programmed to display a tic-tac-toe board as well as the signs placed by the players. The computer control panel had a rotary telephone dial. The researcher used it as a "joystick". To play, users simply needed to dial a number to indicate the box chosen for their sign.

2.2 Then Came the Joysticks... Tennis for Two (1958)

Tennis for Two, a *Pong* predecessor, was undoubtedly the first video game in history to associate potentiometers with computers to serve as joysticks. This game was designed by William A. Higinbotham. He dissected a Donner analog computer in search of ideas, and the "bouncing ball" program presented in the machine's instruction manual made him think of a tennis match. Thus, *Tennis For Two* was born. The game was improved in 1959. This new version enabled users to play with gravity settings, such as "on the Moon" or "on Jupiter", and had a larger display (increasing in size from 12 cm in the first version to 30 cm in the new version). After two years of loyal service, the game was dismantled and the famous joysticks were discarded.

2.3 Multimodal Interaction: From JoyBoard to Dataglove

It was not long after the emergence of video games that their designers began to explore different gaming modalities. The Magnavox Odyssey, which in 1972 became the first video game launched on the consumer market, offered the Light Gun peripheral (from Magnavox in 1972). This option used a rifle attached to the console. The rifle had an optics system to simulate on-screen shooting. This steering wheel enabled gamers to enjoy a heightened sensation of driving on a road at night [9]. The Atari VCS 2600 video game, which was launched in 1977, offered a wide range of peripherals throughout its life cycle, such as the Joyboard (from Amiga in 1982). It looked like a black bathroom scale and enabled gamers to guide a virtual skier using their feet. The JoyBoard may be considered the ancestor of the Nintendo Wii Balance Board, which was launched in 2007. Nintendo has also provided various video game playing methods throughout its history. FAMICOM offered a microphone on its joysticks when the console was first launched in 1983. This functionality enabled gamers to play while incorporating speech, singing or whistling. In 1989, Mattel explored motion detection with the Power Glove (from Mattel in 1989) peripheral for the NES console. In 1995, Nintendo began exploring Virtual Reality with the Virtual Boy console. This console resembled a set of binoculars placed on a tripod. The binoculars offered a red monochromatic display, endowing gamers with stereoscopic vision. Since it was suspected of causing migraines, the console did not enjoy the commercial success it was intended to have. The aforementioned examples are not an exhaustive list, but rather a representative sample of the diversity of modalities explored and developed by the video gaming industry over time. Today, this dynamic environment continues to develop with an increasing number of control methods and tangible objects (such as Kinect, Oculus Rift and the Skylanders figurines), which complete the video gaming picture.

2.4 Integrated Display Objects: Portable Electronic Games

In 1976, the American Mattel Electronics company launched what was probably one of the first mass market portable electronic games: *Auto Race*. In concrete terms, the video game device was a handheld white box. The race cars were represented by vertical red dashes that moved from the top to the bottom of the screen. In 1979, Milton Bradley launched Microvision. This was a device with interchangeable game cartridges and a 16 x 16 pixel black and white liquid crystal display. Devices were becoming more sophisticated. However, it was really the 1980 arrival of *Game&Watch*, launched by Gunpei Yokoi (from Nintendo in 1980) with a dedicated image for each object, that advances were truly made. Even though each Game&Watch only had one game, the device was a success. Nintendo revamped the Microvision concept with the 1989 launch of the Game Boy. This device had interchangeable game cartridges to be used with a single screen and command panel, in contrast to its predecessor, for which the interchangeable element was an entire block containing the command panel, the printed circuit board and the game display. The Game Boy offered a 160 x 144 pixel display with four different shades of gray. With such high resolution, the representations became more sophisticated for the players of that time: 118 million Game Boys ended up being sold across the globe.

2.5 Relationship between Input and Output Modalities: From Light Pen to Interactive Table

Two different approaches represent attempts to relate input and output modalities. Based on the first approach, Moonlander, designed by Jack Burness en 1973, invited gamers to land a space module on a lunar platform using gravity and fuel reserves.

This game was financed by the North American Digital Equipment Corporation (DEC) to promote the technical characteristics of the DEC GT40: vector graphics and a light pen. This meant that Moonlander users could guide the space module by adjusting the throttle value and the angle of the lunar lander with the light pen. Moonlander was part of a marketing campaign to demonstrate the technical qualities of a machine at commercial exhibitions.

Interactive tables represent a second approach to these new, supposedly interactive applications. Interactive tables have a surface that acts both as a screen and a detection device (with integrated or external detection mechanisms). The technical input tools for these devices can be tactile (e.g., DiamondTouch by P. Dietz and D. Leigh [10]) or tangible through the manipulation of objects on the table surface. For example, the TangiSense [11] interactive table detects objects equipped with RFID technology; the Serious Game described in [12], which is used to help teach colors and color recognition to children aged 3 to 6 years, provides learners and teachers with specific tangible objects; this Serious Game represents new tangible object applications for educational contexts.

2.6 Multiscreen Applications for Single and Multiple Gamers

There are different ways to integrate multiple screens into video games. The use of several screens can expand the standard gamer view, like in the *TX-1* racing game (from Tatsumi Electronics Company in 1983). This arcade video game has three screens to enable gamers to better immerse themselves in the gaming experience. Multiscreen gameplay can also be seen on portable devices, such as with *Donkey Kong* on the "Game & Watch Multi Screen" (both from Nintendo in 1982). A multiscreen device can also provide additional, independent visual information, like the Nintendo DS and the *Super Mario 64 DS* game (both from Nintendo in 2005). In this example, there is a 2D view on an upper screen and a third-person 3D view on the other screen. Furthermore, this console enables users to use touch control on one of the two screens.

In the preceding examples, gamers have access to several screens on a single device. However, a single player may also use several devices to play a single game. The *Tom Clancy's Splinter Cell* game (from Ubisoft in 2003), which can be used both on GameCube (from Nintendo in 2001) and Game Boy Advance (from Nintendo in 2001), is an example.

There are also multiplayer possibilities. Gamers can each have their own gaming device and screen while interacting with each other. For example, using *Cable Link* (Nintendo) two people could play the *Tetris* version released on the Game Boy (from Nintendo in 1989). Players can also interact on the same game using different devices. *Pac-Man World 2* (from Namco in 2003) offers *Pac-Man Vs.* as a bonus. *Pac-Man Vs.* enables one player to control *Pac-Man* using the GameCube and other players to control the ghosts with Game Boy Advance. Each gamer has their own view, and therefore engages in asymmetric gameplay.

2.7 The First Networked Games: Spacewar PLATO, Maze War and MUD

One of the first networked video game applications dates back as early as 1969, with a two player version on the MIT PLATO system's *Spacewar* game. The game's designer was Rick Blomme. The PLATO system gave rise to Multi-User Dungeon

(MUD) in 1978. These were textual, multiplayer networked games inspired by the traditional *Dungeons & Dragons*. However, it was in 1973 that what was undoubtedly the first client-server networked game, *Maze War*, was released. Designed by Greg Thompson, this game enabled up to eight IMLAC systems to network through a DEC-20 mainframe to play against each other. Then, through the DEC-20 mainframe's connection on the ARPANET network, access to the *Maze War* game was open to anyone with an IMLAC system using TIP and NCP protocols.

2.8 Motion and Interaction: From Mandala VR to Kinect

In 1997, the Canadian Vivid group company launched Mandala VR system that uses visual user recognition to incorporate users into audiovisual environments and enable interaction through motion sensors. Mandala VR was incorporated into games, such as *Airborne Rangers*, *City Gx*, *Meteor Storm* and *Formula Gx*. This concept mainly targeted televised games. In 1998, Nintendo launched *Game Boy Camera*, also known as *Pocket Camera*. With 256 x 226 pixel definition and four shades of gray, this device was inserted into the Game Boy cartridge slot and enabled users to take photographs that could then be incorporated into a game, if desired. This is the case, for example, with *Space Fever II*, in which the end-of-level-enemy was represented by the gamer's face. Motion detection was also used in the *Ball* game, in which users were invited to employ their hands to catch and throw balls.

EyeToy from Sony was launched in 2003, and in 2007, the "Playstation Eye" was incorporated into the Playstation 3 console, which was further improved in 2010 with the *Playstation Move* system. This system was intended to compete with the Wii motion detection system, released in 2006, and the binocular *Kinect* camera, launched in 2010 by Microsoft for exclusive use with its Xbox 360 console.

2.9 Summary

Historically examining video game state of the art from OXO in the early 50s to the present reveals various significant technological trends and breakthroughs in terms of input and output devices made available to gamers. Figure 1 provides an overview of the diversity of these devices.

This overview illustrates various concepts related to the configuration of these devices, although this list was not exhaustive. Subsequently, both single screen and multiscreen configurations have existed. Single and multiple player consoles have also existed. Today, various single and multi-user configurations are available. A single screen can be used by one gamer or be shared by several gamers. A single application can be centralized on a network for use by multiple gamers. A single gamer can stay in one place (i.e., be static) or be mobile. Gameplay can be symmetric or asymmetric. Such concepts will be used in the framework suggested in the following section.

3 Proposal for a Framework for Characterizing Entertainment and Gamified Devices

Thanks to the state of the art, we have seen different concepts for characterizing video game consoles that have evolved over time with advances in technology. The study does not aim to analyze the adaptation of devices to user needs and characteristics. Rather, it endeavors to focus on the properties of the media. These concepts are not complete, but initially, they will enable us to define the applications targeted by our study so that in future research efforts, we can draw conclusions on the impact that choice of medium and medium configuration has on learning. We chose the entity-relationship model defined by Chen [13] to represent the framework (see Fig. 2) proposed in this paper.

Entertaining and gamified applications refers to the application (software) being studied. After establishing the state of the art, we noticed that the number of players for which an application was designed, as well as the symmetry of gameplay, could influence the structure (unless the game was created for a particular structure that already defined the maximum possible number of players - it all depends on the design process [14, 15]). By symmetry, we mean the way in which gamers interact with the game, and the objectives to achieve can differ with the roles, if any, offered to gamers. In section 2.6, and especially the GameCube - Game Boy Advance interconnectivity example, we saw that symmetry can affect user experience, and we wonder about the impact that this could have on learning. Being able to play a game on a network, one of the developments discussed in our state of the art section, was added as configuration-defining element.

The interactive application is offered on at least one type of media, i.e., the Interactive device. In our model, cardinality (1, n) refers to the fact that several devices can be used for a given gaming experience, like in the aforementioned *Pac-Man Vs* example. We are not referring to the application portability concept. For each device, we specify its mobility (portable, like the Nintendo DS, or static, like the Microsoft Xbox 360 home console), the positioning of its screen(s) (whether the screen is integrated into the device or external to the device, like a television). Since some devices enable gamers to change their configuration in space, like Sifteo Cubes (from Sifteo Inc. in 2011), which can be moved relative to each other, turned and shaken, the User-adjustable parameter was added. Regarding the link between an application and its medium or media, we specify the number of screens that can or must be used by the gaming device. The *Tom Clancy's Splinter Cell* game requires gamers to use the GameCube, but can use the Game Boy Advance screen as well. This is therefore a multi-screen case.

Since games only function and make sense when they are played [16], the Gamer element is obviously crucial to our model. This is not only because gamers are the direct target of applications, but also because it is the gamers who use the device(s) to interact with a game. Gamers and devices can communicate with each other in many ways, whether through a joystick and a screen or through tangible objects, movements and sounds. This element is defined in our model as the Type of interaction. We selected gamer cardinality (0, n) since certain games, like *Tank Attack* (from CDS in 1989) do not require gamers to interact with the medium. This type of war game uses a traditional gaming platform representing a geological survey map on which gamers can move their armored military units. The computer arbitrates the game and manages the different game events, such as dice rolling and combat outcomes.

Finally, gamers are not required to play alone. They can play with other gamers in the same place (i.e., be colocated) or in different locations (networked games).

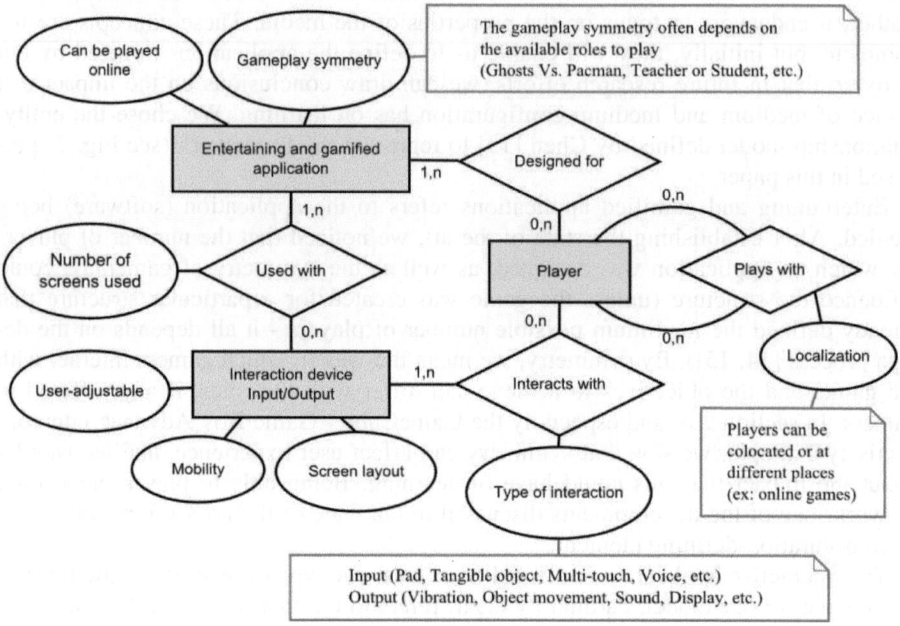

Fig. 2. Presentation of the framework in EA model

This framework enables us to characterize Entertainment and gamified devices to study the effects of their configuration on learning. In the following section, we suggest using the components of this framework to analyze the characteristics of 15 Serious Games.

4 Validation of Serious Games through Characterization

In this section, we suggest validating the framework presented in the previous section (Section 3) by characterizing 15 Serious Games. This involves identifying major trends and using the obtained results to identify possibilities for novel forms of interaction.

The table (Table 1) presents 15 Serious Games characterized according to a set of criteria. These criteria were selected using the suggested framework for defining the following aspects:

- Multi-display: indicates the presence of one or more displays in the Serious Game to provide users with different visual feedback perspectives.
- Multi-user: enables several users to interact simultaneously. The interaction can be colocated (i.e., the users are next to each other in the same room) or remote (i.e., the users are in different, distant locations).
- Display/control panel interaction: possible interactions take place in one of three different ways. Intangible mode characterizes interactions that do not provide haptic feedback to the gamer (such as through movement-related or vocal interactions). Tangible mode indicates what can be felt by touch. Immersive tangible

mode further integrates the ability to superimpose a virtual environment on the perception we have of reality (the augmented reality concept).

- Multi-device: indicates that the Serious Game can be used locally on several devices.
- Layout: refers to the layout of the display. In this context, the display can be separated from/integrated into the medium/control panel.
- Mobility: indicates whether or not the device can be easily transported.
- Gameplay: distinguishes the various roles associated with users while the game is being played.
- Networked game: refers to Serious Games that do not require any installation or that are played using an Internet connection.
- Adjustable: The device can be reconfigured in space by the user.

The Serious Games identified and numbered in the table are as follows:

(1) *Hunet Island* (form Orange in 2009) an interactive table game whose purpose is to raise client awareness of electronic invoicing.

(2) *Flee the Skip* (from Orange in 2010) is played by four people. Its purpose is to encourage solidarity among gamers confronted with a given challenge, and to do so within 20 minutes.

(3) *Thélème* (from Almédia in 2009) is a French language learning game in the form of a massive, multi-participant online adventure game.

(4) *Motion Math* (from Motion Math in 2010) is a series of several entertaining iPhone / iPad applications that teach basic math concepts.

Table 1. Characterization of the 15 Serious Games

SG / Criteria											0	1	2	3	4	5
Multi-display																
Multi-user	**Colocalised**															
	Remote															
Display/ Control Panel Interaction	**Intangible**															
	Immersive Tangible															
	Tangible															
Multi-device																
Layout	**Independent**															
	Integrated															
Mobility																
Game-play	**Symmetric**															
	Asymmetric															
Networked games																
User adjustable																

(5) *Trions et rangeons tout* (from Donuts in 2009) is a waste sorting game that uses tangible objects (waste bins and waste items) to encourage proper waste sorting behaviors.

(6) *America's Army* (from US Army in *2003)* is a multi-player tactical first person shooter game used by the US Army to improve its image and encourage people to enlist. It is available on Windows, PlayStation 2, Xbox and as an arcade video game.

(7) *Mission BRAQUO* (from Canal+ in 2011) is an interactive ARG available on several types of media (such as the Internet and mobile phones). Players must extricate themselves from difficult situations. To do so, they receive e-mails, text messages and multimedia messages at all hours of the day and night.

(8) *Dr. Kawashima's Brain Training: How old is your brain?* (from Nintendo in 2005) is a group of mini brain training games (e.g., mental arithmetic, logic and reading).

(9) *Flower Breath* (from V. Chritin, E. Van Lancker, X. Falourd and B. Bouzin in 2007) uses Positive Expiratory Pressure (PEP) devices to help pediatric Cystic Fibrosis patients have fun while performing their daily breathing exercises.

(10) *Mind Force Defense* (from Macrotellec in 2012) uses brain sensors to help children learn how to focus.

(11) *I-CARE* (from Eurocopter/University of Toulon in 2011) teaches how to manage information overflow during a flying mission. The situations are based on real cases, but the cases are staged in an entertaining way.

(12) *StoryBOX* (from Waag Society in 2011) uses technologically enhanced tangible objects to help with language learning. The players learn to express themselves by physically relying on words and concepts in their daily life.

(13) *Voracy Fish* (from Genious in 2012) is a multiplayer game that uses various peripherals for the functional rehabilitation of the upper limbs (e.g., Kinect, LEAP Motion).

(14) *Hammer and Planks* (from NaturalPad in 2013) enables hemiplegic patients regain their balance. It is a multiplayer game that can be used with the Nintendo Wii Board, Kinect, Xbox joysticks on PCs, touchscreens, tablets and smartphones.

(15) *You are blind* (http://youareblind.com/) helps educate seeing people about blind children. It uses a webcam to detect the gamer's movement's and transmit them to the game.

All the criteria in the table are associated with at least one Serious Game. Certain criteria (such as Symmetric gameplay and Independent multi-device) are used more often than others, which helps predict significant future Serious Gaming trends. It is possible to more closely examine these criteria to make them more intuitive for users and to integrate them into devices.

Moreover, Gameplay is generally characterized as symmetric, which leaves the asymmetric concept unexplored. Yet, this type of game design can help distinguish various forms of gameplay in a single Serious Game. This involves adjusting games to gamers' habits as well as adapting games to disabled gamers (in terms of mobility and concentration, for example).

Finally, we can mention the idea that the video gaming industry influences Serious Games. For example, the Kinect and Wii Balance Board have become somewhat standard in Serious Games (see SG 13 and 14 in Table 1). Conversely, Serious Games can also affect the video gaming industry by introducing modalities, like *Flutter* (the breathing device for lung vibration therapy, SG 9) and adjustable systems (see SG 12). These ideas need to be reinforced by characterizing significant and representative data.

5 Conclusion

The word is rapidly changing with the increasingly extensive introduction of all different types of screens as well as with the generalization of interactive media to the home, public spaces, the workplace, schools, universities and other learning environments. This generalization is true regardless of whether media are static or mobile, collective or individual.

Given these observations and the possibility of studying media intended mainly for skills transfer, we initially examined the technological developments and breakthroughs related to using displays and objects in interactive entertainment applications. We revealed key concepts in our summary of this study. This made it possible for us suggest an initial framework for characterizing Entertainment and gamified devices. To validate this framework, we used it to characterize a sample of 15 Serious Games using various types of devices to represent different trends. The initial results are promising, and provide us with various possibilities for future research and improvement.

It would be possible to expand this framework in future research by explicitly integrating other concepts, this time related to the type of application, and more specifically Serious Games. We could also expand the framework to incorporate gamer motivations, both in terms of learning and more generally in terms of user experience. This characterization framework should make it possible to improve Serious Games referenced in the database available at http://serious.gameclassification.com [17].

References

1. Abt, C.C.: Serious Games. The Viking Press (1970)
2. Alvarez, J., Djaouti, D.: Introduction au serious game. Questions théoriques (2010)
3. Michael, D.R., Chen, S.L.: Serious games: Games that educate, train, and in-form. Muska&Lipman/Premier-Trade (2005)
4. Swink, S.: Game feel: a game designer's guide to virtual sensation. Taylor & Francis US (2009)
5. Novak, J.: Game development essentials: an introduction. Cengage Learning (2011)
6. Saunders, K., Novak, J.: Game development essentials: Game interface design. Thomson Delmar Learning (2006)
7. Hornecker, E.: A Design Theme for Tangible Interaction: Embodied Facilitation. In: Proceedings of the Ninth Conference on European Conference on Computer Supported Cooperative Work, pp. 23–43. Springer-Verlag New York, Inc., USA (2005)
8. Triclot, M.: Philosophie des jeuxvidéo. Editions la Découverte (2011)
9. Norman, D.A.: The design of everyday things. Basic books (2002)
10. Dietz, P., Leigh, D.: Diamondtouch: a multi-user touch technology. In: Proceedings of the 14th Annual ACM Symposium on UIST 2001, pp. 219–226. ACM, New York (2001)

11. Kubicki, S., Lebrun, Y., Lepreux, S., Adam, E., Kolski, C., Mandiau, R.: Simulation in contexts involving an interactive table and tangible objects. Simulation Modelling Practice and Theory 31, 116–131 (2013)
12. Kubicki, S., Lepreux, S., Kolski, C.: Evaluation of an interactive table with tangible objects: Application with children in a classroom. In: Proceedings 2nd Workshop on Child Computer Interaction "UI Technologies and Educational Pedagogy" at CHI 2011, Vancouver, Canada (May 2011)
13. Chen, P.: The entity-Relationship model. ACM TODS 1(1), 9–36 (1976)
14. Djaouti, D., Alvarez, J., Jessel, J.P., Methel, G.: Play, game, world: anatomy of a videogame. International Journal of Intelligent Games & Simulation 5(1), 35–39 (2008)
15. Djaouti, D., Alvarez, J., Jessel, J.-P.: Concevoirl'interactivitéludique: unevued'en-semble des méthodologies de "Game Design". In: Actes du colloque "Ludovia 2010" (2010)
16. Henriot, J.: Le Jeu, Presses universitaires de France (1969)
17. Djaouti, D., Alvarez, J., Jessel, J.P., Methel, G., Molinier, P.: A gameplay definition through videogame classification. International Journal of Computer Games Technology, Volume, Article ID 470350, 1–7 (2008)

Assembling the Collective Experience of a Serious Game Mediation as an Interactional Practice

Alain Bovet and Marc Relieu

Institut Mines-Télécom, Télécom ParisTech, CNRS LTCI, Département SES, Antenne Deixis-Sophia, Sophia Antipolis, France
{alain.bovet,marc.relieu}@telecom-paristech.fr

Abstract. Public installation settings provide a great opportunity to study how various participants orient to one or several screens. In this paper, we explore how visitors use the central tactile menu of a serious game installation with the assistance of a mediator. To study this interactional organization, we conducted a video-based analysis of co-participants' practices. We focus on the close analysis of two distinct configurations of talk and bodily activities, which connect participants to the artefact through various embodied practices.

Keywords: ethnomethodology, embodied interaction, video-based studies, serious game, public interfaces.

1 Public Exhibits and Mediation

Digital interactive technologies based on distinctive interfaces are spreading across a variety of public settings. While many interfaces aim to facilitate a so-called "natural" interaction with a single user, our interest lies in installations, such as art exhibits, serious games or other performances that have been designed for a public [1]. Digital serious games have provided new resources with which to transform conventional pedagogical approaches to sustainable development and energy consumption issues, on the one hand, and, on the other hand, to public participation into urban planning.

In this area, we have a specific interest in "the work of 'professional' members of a public performance setting: *actors* -who guide participants' conduct with the interface" [2]. This paper is concerned with the mutual constitution of the sense of the artefact, the interactional conduct of the activity and the configuration of participation through the mediation of such *actors*.

2 Context

2.1 What Is Ecotype ?

Ecotype is a multi-screen installation in a dome, which has been opened to the public for ten days in Valbonne (Southern France). Ecotype has been developed as an experimental

M. Kurosu (Ed.): Human-Computer Interaction, Part III, HCII 2014, LNCS 8512, pp. 571–580, 2014.

project, partly funded by a French regional administration. Based on collaboration between several teams, Ecotype was headed by two artistic associations (Le Hublot and Scene&Act[1]). Ecotype is an innovative project which resists any attempt to describe it with a single description. It is a digital installation designed to achieve several goals in the domains of sustainable development and energy consumption, a pedagogical device aiming at understanding the interdependence between local and global planning decisions, a leverage for citizen participation in the planning decision process, a game in which participants obtain a score, an art installation with a music performance, etc. In this paper, we have chosen to put this diversity into brackets in order to focus on the actual and observable framing of the installation. In line with our interest in the co-participants' practical orientations, we examine the facticity of Ecotype as a local achievement [3].

2.2 Visiting Ecotype

The visitors of Ecotype had registered in advance for a one-hour visit, either alone or in groups ranging from 2 to 20 people. Every visit was animated by one of the two designers of Ecotype. Inside the dome, the visitors were showed a 3-minute presentation of the game. At the end of the presentation, the animator provided a number of explanations on the game and then some practical assistance.

It is on the modality of this assistance that we want to focus in this paper. We will analyse in two cases how the game itself was engaged by the visitors and the animator. An important part of this interaction was accomplished through gestures and gazes, by which the participants displayed orientations to several aspects of the installation.

2.3 The Screen as an Activity Centre

This screen is given a central position in several ways. It is the only publicly available action centre in the dome. It is set up at the centre of the dome on a floor stand. At the beginning of each visit, the animator is standing close to the screen. He invites the newcomers to gather at the same place and to adopt a postural orientation which facilitates their later gathering around the monitor. Therefore this spatial, oriented-to centrality prepares the participants to see it as a centre for action, as a public display of "where the action is" [4]. The animator demonstrates the touch-sensitive capabilities of the screen by initiating a first "blank" round in the game. Through talk, gestures and gaze, the animator highlights various components of the "interface": the colored map of the commune of Valbonne at the center of the screen; the right menu which proposes the selection of several actions.

---

[1] The two leaders, Frédéric Alemany and Benoît Colardelle, have a long-standing commitment to creating interactive exhibits. We thank Frédéric and Benoît for having launched this project and the Pacalabs Programme from the PACA Region for their financial support to Ecotype.

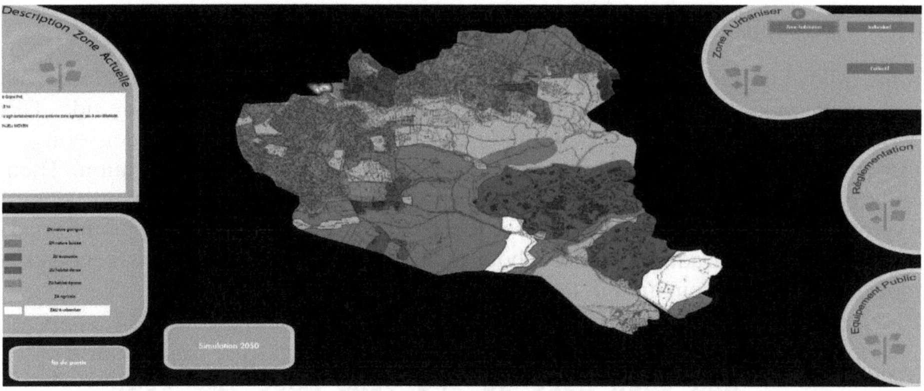

Fig. 1. Ecotype : the interface

The participants are invited to make a series of urban planning choices through this interface. But the map itself offers many opportunities for talk and action: participants are able to point towards specific areas, touch and select a particular area, or do other kinds of "spatial work" on it. Though the interface requires the assistance of an animator, it also encourages the participation of the visitor, acting as a "local planner".

3 Method and Study

A vivid and relatively new body of research has been concerned with the mutual adjustment of gesture, talk and other embodied practices through which co-participants constitute the local sense of artefacts in museums [2], [5-6]. Co-participants adjust their bodily and vocal activities to display various levels of participation and orientation towards specific features of the exhibits, which provide resources for the organization of those very activities. The focus on the social organization of participants' activities has brought a new emphasis on the embeddedness of any interaction into a material world [7-8]. This perspective has been developed through detailed analysis of video recordings. In line with theses studies, we installed three video cameras and two separate sound recorders inside the dome. This data collection process was complemented by a more traditional observational work. Our data consist in the recording and observation of more than 30 one-hour visits.

4 Results

In most cases, the task of handling the tactile interface was carried out by a single player, assisted by the animator. However, it produced a diversity of interactional arrangements. To quote Goodwin [7], "any participation framework is an ongoing contingent accomplishment, something not under control of a single party (who can at best make proposals about the structure of participation that should be operative at that moment), but rather something that has to be continuously achieved through public displays of orientation within ongoing processes of interaction."

4.1 Accomplishing the Mediation while Talking

In the following fragment[2], Tom, the animator, stands in front of the main screen with Paul, an incoming visitor. Both of them are co-oriented to the screen, side by side. This embodied formation facilitates both the orientation to the screen and the delivering of instructions. Tom frames the activity as a quasi-official political consultation. Then, Paul's participation is pre-figured, both vocally and non-verbally, as the expression of a verbal opinion. For Paul, acting as a local citizen and expressing an opinion addressed to the local administration about the planning decisions process becomes a relevant style of participation in this performance:

```
1 Tom          (.) et alors là on le plus important
       and then here we- we- the most important
2      c'est des aussi les zones blanches. (.) qui
       are also the white zones which
3      sont les zones à urbaniser.
       are the zones to urbanise.
4      (1) alors une commune elle décide de
       so a municipality decides to
5      (0.5) eu:::h de prendre les
       uh take the
6      espaces naturels, et eu:h de les ouvrir à
       natural spaces and to open them to
7      l'urbanisation,(.) et là la commune voudrait
       urbanization. and here the municipality would
8      savoir euh si vous qu'est-ce que vous sou-
       like to know if you what would you
9      haiteriez voir se développer euh comme types
       like to see develop uh as activity types
10     d'activité sur la commune.
       in the municipality
11         (0.8)
12 Tom euh de l'économique de l'habitat, de
       uh economic habitat
13     l'agriculture ou si vous voulez
       agriculture or if you want
14     conserver (.) ces
       to maintain(.)
15     ces [espaces natu]rels
       these natural spaces
16 Paul [les espaces verts]
        green spaces
```

[2] We adopt the transcription conventions of conversation analysis [9].

In the beginning of the turn, Tom highlights a series of specific areas on the visible map. This is done through the naming of the colour that singularizes these zones and through a syntactic construction by which he draws the attention of the hearer. Then, he adds a second unit (l.4) that offers a retrospective explanation for this highlighting: the white zones are also suitable to be urbanized, i.e. they are at stake for a planning decision process. This explanation is built to offer a more general remark about the kind of action which can be done by any municipality on this type of territory. More significantly, the white zones are redescribed, in this second unit of the same turn, as "natural spaces" to be urbanized (l.6). Then a third unit (l.7-10) is introduced, in which Tom focuses on *this* municipality. In this third turn constructional unit [10], Tom acts as a spokesman of the municipality of Valbonne[3]: he literally speaks on behalf of them and reports a question whose principal author is the municipality administration. Through this speech practice, he produces a local identity of mediator standing between the municipality and its citizens.

Moreover, this question is then expanded (l.12-15) so as to project four possible solutions. Tom establishes a contrast between a first collection of three possible answers and a second category, composed of a single choice. This contrastive structure provides the recipient with the possibility to anticipate what Tom says. Therefore a contrast between the three options (agriculture, habitat, economic) which were labelled as "urbanization" and a last one is introduced into the talk. The last choice has a specific stress, because it seems to be a type of choice which differs from the previous ones. It is introduced with a verb on which there is a strong emphasis: "conserver" - to maintain things as they are. Because the white zones were previously described as "natural spaces", it seems obvious, at this very moment of the turn, that this last option addresses them as such.

At the end of the turn, Paul begins to talk before Tom has completely finished his own turn. Nevertheless, this overlap is not problematic. Paul's contribution is both sequentially relevant to the previous question asked by Tom and locally relevant in relation to the termination of Tom's turn at talk [12]. Saying "green spaces" in overlap, Paul offers an answer to the question and, simultaneously, he anticipates what Tom is currently saying. For this reason, his turn is both an answer and a collaborative ending of Tom's turn.

If we re-introduce into the analysis the gestures and gazes of the parties we discover that Tom has pointed alternatively to the two main areas of the map in which the white zones are represented. This has been done with a move of his left hand, which was re-enacted three times. First, during the short pause after "savoir" (*know*); then, it takes the form of a faster move during a second brief pause after "vous " (*you*) and finally at the end of "conserver" (*maintain).* To focus on this last repeat, the first pointing component (Fig. 2) occurs while he is uttering "maintain" and the second during a short silence just after the same verb (Fig. 3). When he introduces the following noun, he gazes at Paul who then produces this terminal onset in overlap and turns toward him (Fig. 4). Through these three reiterations of the "same" hand trajectory above the screen, Tom progressively highlights a collection of the three white zones.

---

[3] Following Goffman [11], Tom is the *animator*, the party who has uttered these words, but the *principal*, the party who is socially responsible, is the municipality. Tom is putting the municipality "on stage" as a character.

Fig. 2. Tom : conserver *maintain*

Fig. 3. Tom : (.)

Fig. 4. T voc [espaces natu]rels **naturel spaces** Paul [les espaces verts]**green spaces**

This pointing gesture is oriented to two areas of the map in which there are white zones. First, Tom's hand gesture heads to the first white zone on the upper left area in the map, then it moves down to a second area at the bottom of the map where the two other white zones are situated (See Fig.1). The trajectory of this gesture is similar to the two preceding ones but its relation to the talk is different. The hand gesture immediately precedes the introduction of the deictic ("ces" (*these*)) and the category "espace naturels" (*natural spaces*). Thus the gesture can be seen not only as a referential pointing to the white zones but also as helping to project the category itself. Indeed, the white zones have been previously characterized as "natural spaces". This is exactly what the recipient does, since he produces a terminal overlap with this same category ("espaces verts" (*green spaces*)).

Tom himself quickly confirms this "invited" contribution with an acknowledgement token. Simultaneously, he begins to point to one of the three white zones on the screen. From this very moment, Tom gets involved into a course of action on the screen while uttering several affiliative displays towards Paul's turn at talk. Tom takes charge of the manipulation without inviting Paul to do it.

With emphasis, Paul expresses a general wish for the preservation of the natural space. This utterance is designed as the delivery of a personal preference for the preservation of the natural spaces in Valbonne. Because it is built as an emphatic expansion of the previous answer, the turn does not contribute to the progression of the game by itself. Therefore Tom produces several affiliative displays at relevant places while completing the selection process of the corresponding item of the menu. He maintains an orientation towards both the talk and the selection process on the screen. Through this dual orientation, he displays a minimal, positive involvement as a recipient of Paul's talk while being able to for the progressivity of the game.

Our analysis shows in detail how Tom's and Paul's vocal and non vocal contributions, their more and less direct involvement into the manipulation of the interface, and their practical understanding of what the installation is about progressively emerge as a temporal configuration of the very circumstances they produce. This configuration is created and maintained by and through their interactively achieved embodied interactional work in front of and with the central monitor. While Paul finds in the developing course of Tom's initial turn at talk an opportunity to express his opinions as a citizen, Tom becomes focused on the manipulation of the interface by which he enters Paul's verbal preferences into the system. This framing of their mutual participation, which is also a framing of the installation, is an emerging feature of the very configuration they produce rather than the output of a cognitive or deliberate choice. We will now turn to a visit where, though the animator theatrically stepped aside, he remained nevertheless close to the screen, and was thereby able to monitor the activity.

4.2 Assembling the Collective

This section will be devoted to an excerpt of the visit of Ecotype by a group of elders of the municipality. Composed of four women and one man, the group is assisted by a younger woman. The animator of the visit is Jack, the other designer of Ecotype.

Once the group has gathered under the dome, Jack starts the announcement, after which he provides numerous explanations on the game, both on the logic of the game and on practical aspects of playing. When he delivers these explanations, he stands in front of the screen, facing the visitors who are spread around in a semi-circle, the elderly women being seated on chairs. When he is finished, he says “It’s up to you” and moves to the right side of the screen, leaving the place of the player to be occupied by whoever wants to. Compared to the previous fragment, this simple move contributes to a distinct participation framework: Jack delegates the manipulation of the interface to the visitors, but stays close to it for all practical purposes.

One of the consequences of this opening is that it does not tell the visitors “what to do next”, nor which member(s) of the group should do it. A selection process must then take place: after a moment of hesitation, one of the seated women invites Ann, the younger woman, to “do it”, which she declines with laughter. Then Ann invites Tim, the elderly man standing at the left side of the screen, to go.

The analysis of this sequence will be based on the transcription below. Lines 3, 5 and 7 account for Tim's move towards the screen, which is completed at the end of line 7. Lines 10 and 13 account for Tim's hand gestures towards zones 1 and 3 on the screen (l. 10) and towards the meadow outside the dome (l. 13). These lines are simultaneous with the preceding vocal transcription lines.

1 Ann allez Tim vous êtes partis ?
come on Tim are you gone?
2 Tim je veux bien commencer ouais
I'm willing to start yes
3 Tim Mv ....
4 Tim si j'arrive à les hein ?
if i'm able to uh ?
5 Tim Mv ....
6 Tim bon alors euh euh
so then uh uh
7 Tim Mv ....screen
8 Jack donc on commence par les zones blanches
so we start with the white zones
9 Tim on le fait (.) les trois hein ?
we do it (.) the three of them right ?
10 Tim Pt ....zone1.................zone3
11 Jack voilà
that's it
12 Tim celle-là c'est le pré là-bas
this one is the meadow over there
13 Tim Pt ....meadow
14 Jack voilà
that's it

Tim replies to Ann's invitation with a guarded acceptance (l. 2). The acceptance is also made accountable by his simultaneous move to the front and centre of the screen (l. 3,5,7), where he minimally expresses his willingness to engage his task without knowing exactly how (l. 6). The accountability of Tim as the player is then acknowledged by Jack, the animator standing on the right side of the screen. Jack's turn is a mix of an instruction and an explanation (l. 8), and as such is not only addressed to Tim but to Tim as the player.

This specific address is in turn ratified by Tim who replies to Jack by asking a somewhat technical question (l. 9), thus confirming the categorial pair of player and animator. The relevance of the pair is strengthened by the tag question format adopted by Tim, which triggers an immediate ratification by Jack (l. 11).

Note that when Tim formulates the question, his right hand points to two zones of the map (l. 10). In other words, Tim uses a resource made available by his move towards the screen. Due to his position on the right side of the screen, Jack is able to see Tim's gestures, which is not the case of the elderly women who are still seated two meters behind the screen.

Tim's and Jack's body orientations display a co-involvement into a main activity. Their shoulders being oriented to the command screen, they are able to "gaze together" at the relevant zones. Through this body arrangement, they display both a common interest in the activity which takes place and a co-membershiping status in the making of this same activity.

Tim then engages in a series of three similar operations. Only the first appears on the transcript above (l. 12-13). The operation consists in pointing to one of the three zones on the screen and relating them to some items of local knowledge. In the first question, a point on the screen ("this one") is related to a point in the world outside the dome ("the meadow over there"). Both highly indexical expressions are made intelligible by accompanying pointing gestures, the first on the screen, the second outside the screen and even outside the dome. Through this "double indexicalization", Tim displays his ability not only to relate particulars of the map to his local knowledge but also to locate the whole Ecotype device in the surrounding environment. Even if it is not formulated as a question, Tim's utterance is followed by a confirmation by Jack (l. 14).

This analysis shows that Jack delegates the manipulation of the screen but remains close to the centre of the activity. It does not necessarily mean that he controls the player's behaviour. It appears that standing in front of the screen provides Tim with opportunities to exploit his extended knowledge of the territory, exhibiting thereby the relevance of his selection as the player.

This second socio-material configuration rests on a quasi face-to-face relationship which takes place over the screen. In this case, the player turns out to be the main manipulator: he selects himself the relevant menu items while being watched over by the animator. Since Tim is surrounded by other members of the group of visitors, the animator has left his usual front position to go to the other side of the screen. This configuration, which emerges from the selection process, produces specific pragmatic possibilities for the development of the visit. No one has decided to create this configuration. Nevertheless, once instantiated, it provides the participants with opportunities to act and to relate to the artefacts in certain ways.

5 Conclusion

The accountable features of the activity have been assembled by the in-situ articulation of talk, gestures and postural arrangements. How exactly the participants are acting together, as citizen trying to influence the future urban development of their municipality, as people sharing a common concern about energy consumption, and what they are doing with the artefact, playing a serious game or being involved into a democratic consultation, are not provided for by the artefact capabilities nor by some hidden social or psychological processes. The qualities of the co-participants emerge from the interactional process through which they discover what can or cannot be done with the artefact. We have shown that the animator takes part in this process without being able to fully control its trajectory. Two configurations in which humans and artefacts are both creatures and creators have been elucidated thanks to a detailed analysis of video recordings of embodied action.

References

1. Reeves, S.: Designing Interfaces in Public Settings: Understanding the Role of the Spectator. In: Human-Computer Interaction. Human-Computer Interaction Series. Springer, London (2011)
2. Heath, C., Luff, P., vom Lehn, D., Cleverly, J.: Crafting Participation: Designing Ecologies, Configuring Experience. Visual Communication 1, 9–34 (2002)
3. Garfinkel, H.: Studies in Ethnomethodology. Prentice Hall, Englewood Cliffs (1967)
4. Dourish, P.: Where the Action Is: The Foundations of Embodied Interaction. MIT Press, Cambridge (2001)
5. Vom Lehn, D., Heath, C., Hindmarsh, J.: Exhibiting Interaction: Conduct and Collaboration in Museums and Galleries. Symbolic Interaction 24(2), 189–216 (2001)
6. Vom Lehn, D., Heath, C., Knoblauch, H.: Configuring Exhibits: The Interactional Production of Experience in Museums and Galleries. In: Knoblauch, H., Kotthoff, H. (eds.) Verbal Art across Cultures: The Aesthetics and Proto-aesthetics of Communication, pp. 281–329. Gunter Narr Verlag, Tubingen (2001)
7. Goodwin, C.: Action and Embodiment within Situated Human Interaction. Journal of Pragmatics 32, 1489–1522 (2000)
8. Streeck, J., Goodwin, C., LeBaron, C. (eds.): Embodied Interaction: Language and Body in the Material World. Cambridge University Press, Cambridge (2011)
9. Jefferson, G.: Transcript Notation. In: Atkinson, J.M., Heritage, J. (eds.) Structures of Social Action: Studies in Conversation Analysis. Cambridge University Press, New York (1984)
10. Sacks, H., Schegloff, E.A., Jefferson, G.: A simplest Systematics for the Organization of Turn Taking for Conversation. Language 50(4), 696–735 (1974)
11. Goffman, E.: Footing. In: Goffman, E. (ed.) Forms of Talk, pp. 124–159. University of Pennsylvania Press, Philadelphia (1981)
12. Jefferson, G.: Notes on Some Orderlinesses of Overlap Onset. Tilburg Papers in Language and Literature (Tilburg University) 28, 1–28 (1983)

Bet without Looking: Studying Eyes-Free Interaction during Live Sports

Pedro Centieiro[1], Teresa Romão[1], A. Eduardo Dias[1,2], and David Furió[3]

[1] CITI, Faculdade de Ciências e Tecnologia, Universidade Nova de Lisboa
2829-516 Caparica, Portugal
{pcentieiro,aed.fct}@gmail.com, tir@fct.unl.pt
[2] bViva, Digital Media, Lda
Madan Parque, 2825-182 Caparica, Portugal
edias@bviva.com
[3] Instituto Universitario de Automática e Informática Industrial,
Universitat Politècnica de València,
Camino de Vera, s/n. 46022 Valencia, Spain
dafufer@upvnet.upv.es

Abstract. This paper presents a comparison study of three different interaction methods for an eyes-free interaction with a second screen application while watching a TV broadcast. These interaction methods were used in WeBet, a touch-based mobile game that prompts users to bet if a goal is about to happen during a football match. WeBet is one of the prototypes we have been developing to increase the remote users' emotional levels during live sports broadcasts, so that they feel like if they were scoring a goal with their team. However, that can only be achieved the second screen application does not require the users' attention when a goal (key moment) is just about to happen, otherwise they would be frustrated to miss that exciting moment. To this end, we conducted user tests that allowed us to determine the usage patterns and users' preferences regarding three different interaction methods, as well as to identify important refinements to be considered in future developments.

1 Introduction

Throughout the years, social scientists have studied how fans are connected with their favourite sports team. In their research, Cialdini et al [1] have introduced the definition of BIRG (Basking In Reflecting Glory). BIRG refers to one's desire to increase alliance with successful others, such as a team or player. When a team is doing well, the fans feel great, and after a team's victory people say "we won", since they feel part of the team. The closer people are identified with their favourite sports team, the more likely they are to bask in reflecting glory.

This emotional attachment that connects fans with their teams, motivated us to develop mobile prototypes that increase the entertainment and emotional levels of fans watching live sports remotely on television. Remote fans experience less satisfaction and more loneliness than when they are watching the event at the stadium [2], and

M. Kurosu (Ed.): Human-Computer Interaction, Part III, HCII 2014, LNCS 8512, pp. 581–592, 2014.

therefore we also seek to narrow the gap between the levels of thrill and excitement of watching the sports live and watching it remotely.

One of the issues to be address to accomplish this goal lies on how to provide remote users with engaging experiences without diverting their attention from the sport event being broadcasted on television. To help study this topic, we approached the second screen concept, which has become widely popular in recent years [3]. Based on it, we started by developing a multiplayer mobile game that takes users to participate in the applauses happening in the stadium during a live sports event [4]. The feedback from user tests was very positive, showing us that the idea of connecting both in-venue and remote fans to their teams, so that they can all feel part of the same community, could work. However, these kind of second screen applications can cause users to constantly shift their attention from the television broadcast to the mobile device, which may result in a disrupted experience.

Therefore, to study this issue we ended up designing and developing eyes-free interaction mechanisms, which we then used in WeBet [5]. WeBet is a mobile game that prompts users to bet if a goal is about to happen during a soccer match (it can easily be adapted to other sports), without requiring users' visual attention on the mobile phone. Results show that users got really excited when they bet that their team was going to score and they effectively did, and frustrated when they missed.

Thus, after studying the concept, we now aim to analyse what are the usage patterns and users' preferences regarding eyes-free interaction mechanisms that complement the users' experience while remotely watching a live event broadcast. We conducted a comparative evaluation study of three different interaction methods to allow the users to perform an action, on certain key moments, during a broadcast. Each one of these interaction methods uses vibration, tactile feedback and sound features to help decreasing the necessity of looking at the mobile device. We intended to determine which of these methods was the more appropriate, considering that it should be easy to perform, it should not be error prone, and it should not draw users' attention away from the live match broadcast during exciting moments.

Afterwards, in a next study, we are planning to bring this interaction mechanism to a real environment where users will be able to interact from anywhere in the world, during different kinds of live event broadcasts.

2 Related Work

The living room saw an innovative concept becoming quite popular in recent years: the possibility to interact with the content watched on television, through an additional electronic device. This concept defined as second screen, provides several functionalities that improve the viewer's experience, usually by providing additional show-related information, access to social networks and interactive experiences synchronized to program content, such as polls or quizzes. There are several examples that show the second screen rise in popularity. For instance, Nielsen data from Q1' 2010 [6] showed that nearly 60% of people were watching TV and using the Internet simultaneously, many using social media. A study conducted by Buchinger *et al* [7] presented that news, soap operas, quiz shows, and sports were the genres during which participants talk most while watching, making them most suitable for social media use.

Today, although people are used to interact with touch screen interfaces, it is necessary to have a high level of visual attention to interact with them, since the devices lack tactile feedback. Thus, when performing a task (i.e. watching TV) that requires the user's visual attention, interaction with touch screen devices becomes difficult, causing "situation impairments" [8]. This is something that happens very often in second screen applications, where users constantly shift their attention from the television broadcast to the mobile device. There are different research works that address these issues. Oakley and Park [9] present an eyes-free interaction literature review, focusing on history and scope, motivations, input and output modalities, as well as learning issues, and they also suggest a set of design principles. In the mobile domain, audio is often used for eyes-free input, as well as touch and gesture interaction, and also for feedback [10]. For example, by exploring bezel area surrounding the touch-screen display, it is possible to perform bezel-initiated gestures and interact with bezel menus that require minimum visual attention [11, 12]. When it comes to live events users want to keep focused on the TV screen, where something exciting can happen at anytime. And when it does, users do not want to shift their visual attention from the TV to the mobile screen in order to interact with it. Results from our previous study with WeBet [5] showed that participants liked to use it, stating that they would use the concept during a real match. Moreover, most of the users that usually performed parallel activities while watching a football match, stated that the WeBet concept would make them become more engaged in the match. This aspect was very positive, since one of our goals is to make users more focused on the match, in order to increase their emotional responses. The present work describes a comparison study of three different interaction methods for eyes-free interaction during TV broadcasts, in this case applied to sport events through WeBet.

3 WeBet

The goal of our overall research is to enhance remote sports spectators' experiences, so they can feel not only closer to their team but also to the in-venue fans watching the match live. This way, remote users that do not have the possibility to attend a live event, or do not have any personal relationships with other fans that share the same group affiliation, can still feel part of one worldwide community.

WeBet is one of the applications we have been developing. During a broadcasted sport event, it allows players to see information about the match, and to guess, at anytime, if a goal is about to happen. WeBet game concept can also be used for other sports where it makes sense (e.g. guess a goal on ice hockey or a touchdown on American football), while the interaction method can be applied on other kinds of events, such as contests that allow spectators to vote or answer trivia questions.

We designed and developed WeBet aiming to 1) reinforce the connection between users and their sports teams, enhancing their experience when watching a broadcasted match (WeBet allows users to score along with their team when they preview, and bet for, a goal); and 2) provide an immersive social experience, during which users can watch a live match, see real-time information, win badges, compete with their friends by bragging about who predicts more goals correctly, as well as with fans around the world battling for exclusive prizes.

To create an immersive social experience, we are exploring competition and cooperation elements that act as powerful group-level intrinsic motivators [13]. Competition is one of the most popular and powerful group-level intrinsic motivators. Take for instance fantasy football. Fantasy football is one of the most popular web games [14] about sports in the world. Thousands of friends create and join leagues, without any kind of reward, other than the simple satisfaction of beating their friends. Cooperation is a similar motivator. Many games are built around cooperation, especially MMORPGs, where players, socialize, complete quests and defeat enemies, which would be impossible to accomplish otherwise.

It is crucial to provide remote users with engaging experiences, without diverting their attention from the sport event being broadcasted on television. No one would like to miss a spectacular play just because he was looking at a second screen for a few seconds. With this in mind, we developed three different interaction methods that allow users to bet whether a goal is about to happen while watching a football match.

3.1 Current Prototype and Interaction Methods

The WeBet prototype version developed for this study presents three different interaction methods to predict a goal in the next seconds, during three different pre-recorded football matches. Once users select an interaction method and a football match on their mobile device (in this case an iPhone), a highlight video of that match is presented on the TV screen through AirPlay (using an Apple TV). While the user is watching the video, the application presents information about the match (time, result and teams), as well as a match report, which keeps users engaged during uninteresting periods of the match. Each video footage contains highlights of one match, and users are prompted to bet if each highlight or play can lead to a goal.

WeBet scoring system rewards users for predicting a goal the earlier as possible, to a maximum of 10 seconds. The challenge is on knowing a team and its players, so when a player movement occurs, you know that a goal may be imminent. Thus, when a user places a bet, the system checks if a goal occurs in the next 10 seconds. If so, the user wins 100 points, and for each second that has already passed by he wins 50 extra points. This way, a user that bets earlier will win more points. However, if a goal does not happen when a bet is made, the user loses 50 points (except when he has no points). The idea behind this rule is to prevent users from betting that a goal happens in every dangerous play.

The three different interaction methods that we implemented are described below and they can be used in various situations in which users need to interact with a touch-screen mobile device while looking at another screen (e.g. TV). Since the second screen, on the mobile device, may be displaying relevant information, we cannot just turn this screen into a big button that would be easy to press without looking at it, during the whole broadcast (besides, this would be error prone).

The first interaction method to predict a goal in the next seconds prompts users to touch on a button in the interface (iPhone screen). Here is a quick walkthrough on how this interaction technique works:

1. Users touch the button at the bottom of the interface (Figure 1a).
2. Next, the application plays a selection sound (lasting 700 ms) and the mobile device vibrates, so the user can acknowledge that the bet was made without the need to further look at the mobile device.
3. Then, a 10s countdown appears on the screen (Figure 1b).
4. If a goal happens within the 10 seconds, a cheerful sound is played, the mobile device vibrates once and an outcome screen appears to show how many points the user won. However, if no goal occurs, the mobile device also vibrates once but it plays a different sound, and displays a different outcome screen stating that the user did not win any points.

While using the second interaction method, users perform a swiping gesture to predict a goal in the next seconds:

1. Users start by doing a swiping gesture, from outside to inside the screen, to reveal a new screen that immediately places a bet once it reaches full screen (Figures 2a and 2b). A quick upwards swipe gesture can also trigger this action. As in the previous method, the selection sound is played and the mobile device vibrates once a bet is made.
2. While users are doing the swiping gesture (and have their fingers on the touchscreen) they can perform a downward swiping gesture to cancel the bet, and a downward swipe sound is played accordingly (lasting 400 ms).
3. Once a bet is made, the application plays a selection sound, the mobile device vibrates, and the 10s countdown starts like in the previous interaction method.
4. Finally, the outcome screen appears stating if users won points or not, depending on whether a goal occurred during the 10s countdown.

Lastly, we combined the previous two interaction methods to create a two-state interaction mechanism. It works as follow:

1. Like in the previous method, users start by performing a swiping gesture from outside to inside the screen, which in this case, gives access to a special bet interface (Figure 3b).
2. As soon as the special interface is full screen, an upward sound (lasting 400 ms) is played and the mobile device starts vibrating repeatedly every 500 ms, in order to inform users that they can now bet that a goal is about to happen, by touching anywhere on the mobile phone screen with no need to look at it.
3. The swiping gesture brings one big button into the screen, so users do not need to look at it to place the bet. When this happens, the mobile device stops vibrating, the selection sound is played, and the 10s countdown appears.
4. To close the special interface, and return to the game report screen (Figure 3a) without betting, users just need to do a downward swipe gesture anywhere on the screen, and the downward swipe sound is played accordingly. At this point, the mobile device stops vibrating and no bet is made.
5. Finally and as before, an outcome screen appears stating if users won points or not, depending on whether there was a goal during the 10s countdown.

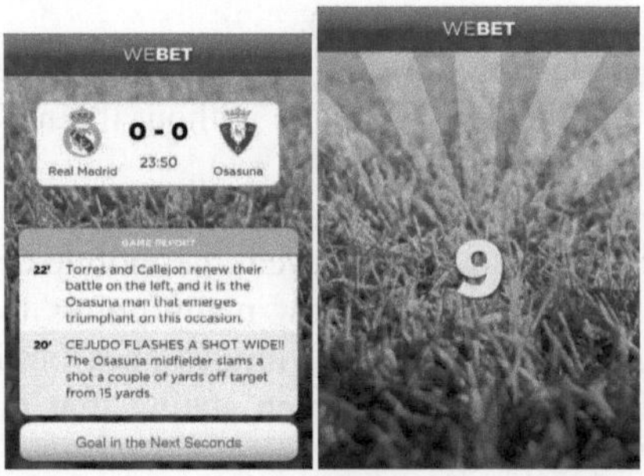

Fig. 1. First interaction method: touch a button on the bottom of the screen to place a bet (a) and the countdown screen after placing a bet (b)

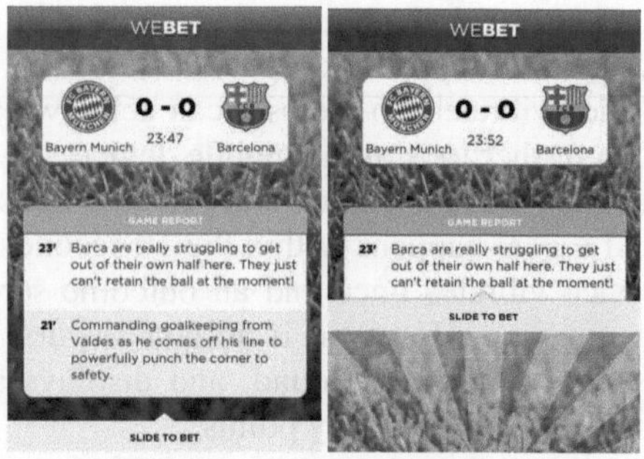

Fig. 2. Second interaction method: upward swiping gesture. The interface with the slide to bet area at the bottom of the screen (a). Performing a swiping gesture (b).

Fig. 3. Third interaction method: upward swiping gesture and posteriorly touch on the screen to place a bet. The interface with the slide to bet area at the bottom of the screen (a). The special bet interface (b).

3.2 Design Decisions

We took a lot of care in designing the three interaction methods. Allowing users to interact during critic situations without looking at the mobile device, was crucial to achieve an eyes-free interaction technique, thus prevent them from missing a key moment like a feint, a pass, or even a goal on the live TV broadcast. Otherwise, the application would annoy users, instead of enhancing their experiences. For example, in each of the different interaction methods, users do not need to worry about unlocking the iPhone from an idle state, since we force the application to stay active.

In the first interaction method, we started by placing a button at the bottom of the interface to perform an action (in this case, to place a bet). We also added sound and vibration feedback so users acknowledge when they touched the button (the bet was placed) by sensing or hearing the mobile device, even if they are not looking at it. Although this seems the easiest and fastest interaction methods of all the three, it also has its drawbacks, since users might mistakenly make a bet, and it requires visual attention to know if the user's finger is near the button. Moreover, second screen apps usually present extra interactive content related to the show being watched, thus touch screen inputs may be required for other types of interaction with the application.

With the second interaction method we wanted to present a gesture that would not be triggered inadvertently and would not require constant visual attention. Thus, we decided to have a swiping gesture starting from outside of the screen's bottom. This design decision was based on the idea that when users grab the mobile device, they have the perception of where their fingers are, and therefore they can accurately perform a swiping gesture from the bottom of the screen (e.g. by sensing the Home button on an iPhone) without looking at the device. We also wanted to use a gesture that users are familiar with, and the swiping gesture is something that iOS users perform quite often, like when they access the Notification Center (in this case, the swiping gesture starts at the top of the screen and is made downwards). But this interaction method still has one disadvantage, it lacks the ability to cancel the triggered action (in WeBet, placing a bet) in an effectively way (users can cancel it only if they do not perform the swiping gesture completely).

Therefore, we decided to create a two-state interaction mechanism, resembling a jet fighter shooting button, and enhance it with tactile and audible feedback. We combined the two previous interaction methods by having a swiping gesture starting from outside of the screen's bottom, which then reveals a special interface that only requires users to touch the device screen to confirm the action (bet in this case). Users can cancel the action by performing a downward swiping gesture to exit this interface.

Finally, we also used vibration and sound to provide users with an accurate perception of the state of the interface, without the need to look at it. Just by hearing and feeling the device, users know: a) whether the action was recognized and thus the bet was effectively placed; b) if the swipe gesture was recognized and they are ready to confirm the action (bet); or c) the outcome of the action (whether the bet right or wrong). For example, in noisy environments users may not hear the device's sound, but the vibration gives them the feedback they need. On the other hand, sound helps to create a better experience, by playing sound effects associated with the user's action. Together, vibration and sound complement each other, increasing the users' perception of the interface's state, and creating a better and more refined experience.

4 Evaluation

To study the usage patterns and the users' preferences, we conducted a comparative evaluation study of the three different interaction methods within WeBet. Results allowed us to ascertain which interaction method is the most effective in allowing the users to keep their attention on the broadcast while simultaneously playing a game.

4.1 Participants and Methodology

The user tests were conducted with eighteen voluntary participants aged 13-54, with a mean age of 31.78. Thirteen participants were male and five were female.

The tests took place in a room in our department at the University campus. An Apple TV was connected to a LED TV, and users sat in front of the TV screen. Users were free to have the iPhone (handed by the researcher) on their hands or on the table, but the majority of them held the iPhone in their hands throughout the test.

Before each test session, each user was given an initial briefing regarding what they were about to watch and the objectives of the game. Eighteen test sessions were conducted, each with an individual participant. A within-subject experimental design was used to test the three interaction methods and the sequence of interaction techniques was counterbalanced to minimize learning effects.

The videos presented were Real Madrid 4 - 2 Osasuna and Bayern Munich 4 - 0 Barcelona (both from 2013), and Denmark 2 - 3 Portugal from 2012. None of the participants had previously seen the first match, and while some had seen the second and third matches, only two participants remembered some of the footage. Each video was approximately 5 minutes long and had 7 dangerous plays, or in other words, 7 propitious moments to bet (the start and the end of the match was also shown to contextualize users). Users were not aware of the number of dangerous plays, since the videos were edited to look like typical highlight videos of a match, with the live audio commentary of the match to keep the outcome uncertain.

After watching a video and experiencing the corresponding interaction method, users were explained what they needed to do on the following interaction method. During each test session, the researcher took notes on how users reacted and interacted with the system, and he also counted the moments when users looked at the mobile device with the intention to place a bet. At the end of each test session, users were asked to answer a questionnaire to evaluate the three interaction methods.

The questionnaire started by asking users' age and gender. Next, users were asked to rate a set of five statements (Table 1) per each one of the three interaction methods, using a five-point Likert-type scale, which ranged from strongly disagree (1) to strongly agree (5). Then, users were asked what interaction method they thought was the most appropriate, taking into account the visual attention given to the broadcasted match and the fact of not betting inadvertently. Users ordered the interaction methods by preference order (1st, 2nd, 3rd), and justify their first option from a set of six possibilities: easier, faster, more reliable, less visual attention required, less tiresome or less frustrating. Users could choose more than one option. Finally, users could express any further suggestions and comments.

Table 1. Statements rated by users regarding each interaction method

Statements
S1. I have executed the betting action when I intended to.
S2. I did not lose any detail of the match during a dangerous play.
S3. I would like to use this kind of interaction during a complete match.
S4. I managed to bet without looking at the iPhone.
S5. Betting does not interfere with the visualization of the match.

4.2 Results

We performed ANOVA tests in order to compare the results gathered from the three interaction methods used. The analysis of the results showed that no significant differences were found between the methods with the exception of statement 4. The p-value in this case was below 0.01. The Tukey test (Table 2) showed that there were significant statistical differences between both the "swiping and touching" and swiping interactions, and touching interaction. Figure 4 shows the box plots of the scores given to the different interaction methods in statement 4. As we can see, both the swiping and the "swiping and touching" interaction methods had higher scores than the touching method.

Table 2. Tukey Test Table for statement 4 between the three methods

Method	diff	lwr	upr	p adj
Swiping / Touching	0.94	0.13	1.76	0.02
"Swiping and Touching" / Touching	1.11	0.30	1.93	0.01
"Swiping and Touching" / Swiping	0.17	-0.65	0.98	0.87

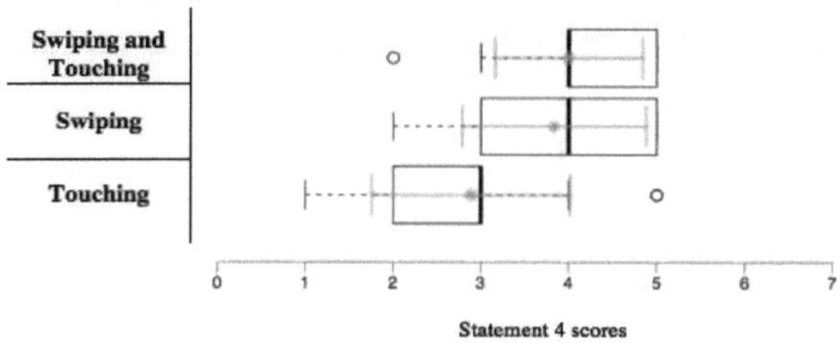

Fig. 4. Box plots of the three interaction methods for statement 4. Mean and standard deviation added in grey.

We can also observe that despite not finding significant statistical differences in statement 5, the swiping, and "swiping and touching" interactions obtained higher results than touching. The Tukey test for statement 5 in Table 3 and the Figure 5 confirm this result.

Table 3. Tukey Test Table for statement 5 between the three methods

Method	diff	lwr	upr	p adj
Swiping / Touching	0.89	-0.08	1.86	0.08
"Swiping and Touching" / Touching	0.83	-0.14	1.81	0.11
"Swiping and Touching" / Swiping	-0.06	-1.03	0.92	0.99

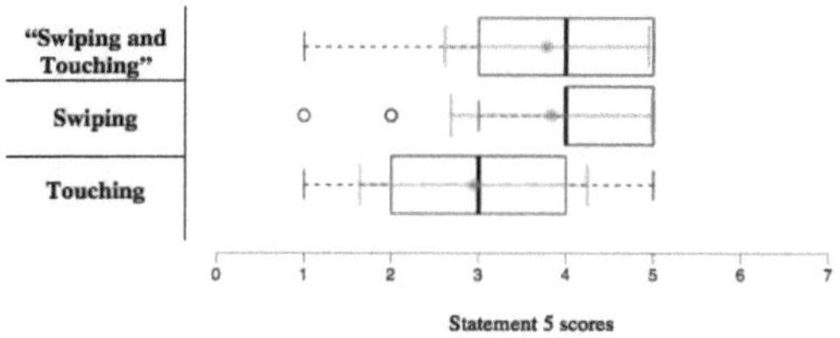

Fig. 5. Box plots of the three interaction methods for statement 5. Mean and standard deviation added in grey.

Another ANOVA test was performed in order to compare the visual attention pattern given to the mobile device while using each one of the three interaction methods. This test showed significant statistical differences between the methods. The Tukey test indicated that there were differences between the "swiping and touching" method, and the touching method (Table 5). Figure 6 confirmed these differences between the aforesaid methods in favour of the "swiping and touching" method.

Table 4. Tukey Test Table for comparing the visual attention given to the mobile device between the three methods

Methods	diff	lwr	upr	p adj
Swiping / Touching	-0.83	-1.91	0.24	0.16
"Swiping and Touching" / Touching	-1.39	-2.46	-0.31	0.01
"Swiping and Touching" / Swiping	-0.56	-1.63	0.52	0.43

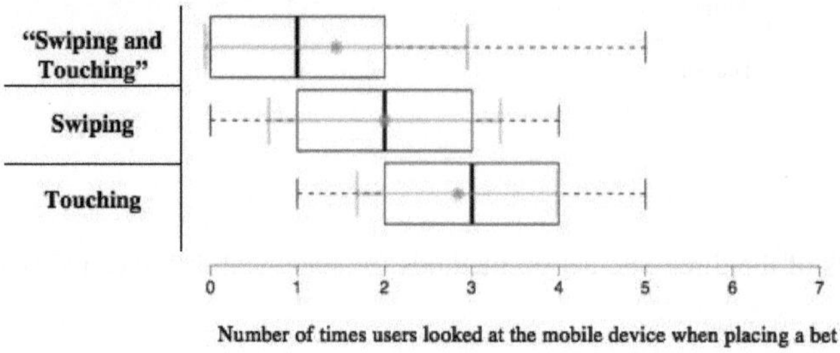

Fig. 6. Box plots of the three interaction methods for the visual attention pattern. Mean and standard deviation added in grey.

When asked about the interaction methods' preferences, 50% of the users preferred the "swiping and touching" method, 28% preferred the swiping method and 23% preferred the touching method. Users who preferred the touching and the swiping methods highlighted that they were easier to perform (50% and 40% respectively), faster (50% and 40% respectively) and required less visual attention (75% and 60% respectively). Users who preferred the "swiping and touching" method did it so because it was more reliable (89%) while also requiring less visual attention (56%).

Finally, participants made suggestions and recommendations to improve the application, such as adding vibration to the swiping gesture as soon as the finger enters the area for swiping. On the other hand, other users said that the vibration during the "swiping and touching" method distracted them, and thus they preferred the swiping gesture. Other users said that they preferred the "swiping and touching" method, because they could bring the special bet interface before a play becomes really dangerous and then when they feel that a goal may happen, they just need to touch anywhere on the screen to bet. This was consistent with our observations.

As a final remark, we can conclude from both the questionnaire results and our observations, that the "swiping and touching" and the swiping methods are better than the touching interaction method. The analysis of the questionnaire shows no significant differences between "swiping and touching" and swiping methods, so that the major factor of the difference in interaction method is swiping. The analysis of the users' preferences verifies these results, but also show that participants preferred "swiping and touching" method over both the swiping or the touching methods. Thus, we feel that the "swiping and touching" method is the one that best satisfied our goals of creating a method that would not divert users from a TV broadcast. Figure 7 shows a user interacting with WeBet, while using the "swiping and touching" method.

Fig. 7. User interacting with the "swiping and touching" method

5 Conclusions and Future Work

This paper presented a comparison study between three different eyes-free interaction methods to be used during live event broadcasts. We applied these methods in WeBet, a touch-based mobile game that prompts users to bet if a goal is about to happen during a football match. In this WeBet version, users were prompted to place a bet by touching a button; by doing a swiping gesture; and by doing a swiping gesture to access a special bet interface and then touching anywhere on the screen to place the bet. In each one of these interaction methods, we used vibration and sound features to help decreasing the necessity of looking at the mobile device.

The analysis from the results of the user tests showed that the swiping and "swiping and touching" interactions are more adequate to achieve WeBet's interaction goal (to deliver a eyes-free, non-disruptive interaction technique), than the touching interaction. Overall, users considered the "swiping and touching" interaction more reliable and requiring less visual attention than the other two methods, which makes us feel that we should proceed our studies with this interaction method in mind. Nevertheless, some improvements can still be done to this technique.

In the near future, we will expand WeBet so users can compete, in real-time during a live match, against their friends to see who can predict more goals correctly.

Acknowledgments. This work is partially funded by CITI/DI/FCT/UNL (PEst-OE/EEI/UI0527/2011). The authors thank Bárbara Teixeira for the graphic design.

References

1. Cialdini, R., Borden, R., Thome, A., Walker, M., Freeman, S., Sloan, L.: Basking in Reflected Glory: Three (Football) Field Studies. Journal of Personality and Social Psychology 34, 3 (1976)
2. Wann, D.L., Martin, J., Grieve, F.G., Gardner, L.: Social Connections at Sporting Events: Attendance and its Positive Relationship with State Social Psychological Well-being. North American Journal of Psychology 10, 2 (2008)

3. Socialnomics. TV Goes Social: The Rise of the Second Screen, http://bit.ly/1hW3FGT (accessed January 31, 2014)
4. Centieiro, P., Romão, T., Dias, A.E.: Applaud Having Fun: A Mobile Game to Cheer Your Favourite Sports Team. In: Nijholt, A., Romão, T., Reidsma, D. (eds.) ACE 2012. LNCS, vol. 7624, pp. 1–16. Springer, Heidelberg (2012)
5. Centieiro, P., Romão, T., Dias, E.A.: Enhancing Remote Live Sports Experiences through an Eyes-free Interaction. In: Proc. MobileHCI 2013, pp. 65–68. ACM Press (2013)
6. Nielsen. Americans Using TV and Internet Together 35% More Than A Year Ago, http://bit.ly/1n2qNV1 (accessed January 31, 2014)
7. Buchinger, S., Kriglstein, S., Hlavacs, H.: A Comprehensive View on User Studies: Survey and Open Issues for Mobile TV. In: Proc. EuroITV 2009, pp. 179–188. ACM Press (2009)
8. Sears, A., Lin, M., Jacko, J., Xiao, Y.: When Computers Fade: Pervasive Computing and Situationally Induced Impairments and Disabilities. In: Proc. HCI 2003, pp. 1298–1302. Elsevier Science (2003)
9. Oakley, I., Park, J.: Designing Eyes-Free Interaction. In: Oakley, I., Brewster, S. (eds.) HAID 2007. LNCS, vol. 4813, pp. 121–132. Springer, Heidelberg (2007)
10. Li, K., Baudisch, P., Hinckley, K.: Blindsight: Eyes-Free Access to Mobile Phones. In: Proc. CHI 2008, pp. 1389–1398. ACM Press (2008)
11. Jain, M., Balakrishnan, R.: User Learning and Performance with Bezel Menus. In: Proc. CHI 2012, pp. 2221–2230. ACM Press (2012)
12. Bragdon, A., Nelson, E., Li, Y., Hinckley, K.: Experimental Analysis of Touch-Screen Gesture Designs in Mobile Environments. In: Proc. of CHI 2011, pp. 403–412. ACM Press (2011)
13. Fogg, B.J.: Persuasive Technology: Using Computers to Change What We Think and Do. Morgan Kaufmann, San Francisco (2003)
14. Hollywood Reporter. Fantasy Football's $1 Billion-a-Year Business, 27 Million Players: It's a Sickness, http://bit.ly/1lpeuqk (accessed January 31, 2014)

Interface Design Strategies and Disruptions of Gameplay: Notes from a Qualitative Study with First-Person Gamers

Suely Fragoso

Federal University of Rio Grande do Sul, UFRGS – Porto Alegre, RS, Brazil
suelyfragoso@ufrgs.br

Abstract. This paper presents the results of a study about how first-person players perceive and describe their gameplay experience, what type of interface representations they consider disruptive and why. The intention to unveil fine-grained information by giving voice to players required the adoption of qualitative methods. In qualitative research, the size of the sample is less important than its adequacy. We worked with an information-rich sample of seven male volunteers, ages 16 to 40, which took part in an experiment composed by a profiling questionnaire, a two-step individual gaming session with DICE's *Battlefield 3* and semi-structured interviews. Results indicate that the integration of interface elements to the gameworld can be disruptive even when it does not compromise usability or efficiency. Smooth gameplay experience requires (a) careful balance of the level of information available at any given point and (b) aesthetical and functional coherence, internally and in relation to the gameworld.

Keywords: Entertainment and game user interface, Experience design, Graphical user interface, Interaction design, qualitative methods.

1 Introduction

Computer games shift the question of user experience from usability and efficiency to pleasure and flow, posing new challenges for interface design. Literature on the subject is growing, but much needs to be done to understand the ways in which game interfaces affect gameplay experience.

Games in first-person differ from other genres by the alignment between the points of view of the player and his representation in the gameworld. The intention of this strategy is to reinforce players' identification with the character, increasing the sense of presence and facilitating immersion [5]. However, the first-person point of view is believed to make elements that are not part of the gameworld, such as interface buttons and menus, particularly disturbing. This appears to have been the starting point of the arguments in favor of integrating interface elements into the gameworld to avoid interfering with players' immersion [15]. On the other hand, this type of strategy can compromise interface clarity or functionality unnecessarily, because it could be that explicit, superimposed interfaces do not necessarily affect immersion [4]. This debate appears to be heading towards a consensus that interface elements should be

M. Kurosu (Ed.): Human-Computer Interaction, Part III, HCII 2014, LNCS 8512, pp. 593–603, 2014.

integrated to the gameworld when possible, but not at the expense of functionality, clarity or consistency [7], [12]. This is a more balanced approach to the question, but fails to address two important assumptions behind this debate: (1) that the integration of interface elements to the gameworld is important for the experience of immersion; (2) that superimposed interface elements are disruptive of that same experience.

We addressed these points with a qualitative study that focused on how first-person players perceive and describe their gameplay experience, what type of interface representations they consider disruptive and why. In the next section, we present some theoretical understandings that guided our experiment.

2 Interfaces and Gameplay

Game interfaces tend to be understood as the buttons and menus that support user interaction with the game or "all informative elements within the game" [7]. Fagerholt & Lorentzon's understanding of the interface as "a system that provides the player with gameplay relevant information and with the right tools to interact with game" brings the user into the equation [12]. Bayliss expands this understanding by proposing that the interface is "the site or space where the interaction between the player and the game results in the particular experience we call gameplay" [1].

Our notion of interface is a development of this proposition. We understand interfaces not as a space, but as the artifact through which the player and the game interact with each other. This places the player as the most important source of information about the effects of interface design strategies on gameplay experience. On the other hand, interface features exist prior to their social use and can be discussed in terms of design strategies.

2.1 Types of Interfaces

As the mediating ground that connects the player with the gameworld, interfaces are a necessary condition for interactivity. It is debatable whether interactivity enhances immersion or makes it more difficult. On the one hand, the fact that the actions of the player interfere with the gameworld should strengthen identification with the character and increase awareness of the game environment, facilitating immersion. On the other hand, that interference takes place across two ontologically different realms: the gameworld (where the character exists) and the physical world (where the player exists). Interactivity depends on the translation of the actions of the player into the gameworld and, therefore, demands two more levels of mediation than previous media such as cinema or television. The first of these extra layers of mediation is technological: it handles the flow of information between hardware and software. The second is cognitive, and refers to the recognition of the causal link between the corporeal actions of the player and their consequences in the gameworld.

There are several possible ways to refine this basic differentiation between hardware interfaces (physical devices such as screens, controllers and speakers) and software interfaces (graphics, sound and text). In this study, we focused on software interfaces. Game software interfaces have been understood in terms of two design paradigms, as previously mentioned: interface elements are either integrated to the gameworld, or they are not [15], [4], [7]. In this study, we consider the existence of three types of interfaces, each one resulting from a different design strategy. In two of them, interface elements are integrated into the gameworld. In the first one, 'material' objects of the gameworld are used as interface elements. An example in *Battlefield 3*, the game used in our experiments, is the guns that players can collect from the floor and see in their hands. These guns 'exist' as material things in the gameworld and, at the same time, are interface elements that deliver information to the player. We call integrated interfaces that follow this strategy '**material**' interfaces. Another form of integrating interface elements is to present them as representations internal to the gameworld: for example, as images on the HUD of a helmet the user character is wearing. It is important to notice that the acronym HUD has been loosely used to refer to any representation overlaid to the gameworld. In this study, we call HUD the simulation of a 'real' HUD. Thus, the HUD is not superimposed but part of the gameworld. It respects the alignment between the point of view of the player and that of his representation in the gameworld and conveys information as visual representations within the gameworld. The images on a HUD are of a different nature than the transparent layer they are superimposed to: they are visual representations, projected light. No matter how transparent, the support upon which they are projected is a material object in the gameworld: it can be touched or broken. Thus, we understand the simulation of a HUD as a middle ground between the integration of the interface with physical elements in the gameworld and outside of the gameworld. Other examples of interfaces that follow this design logic would be images on a screen or voice instructions received through a communication device. We call integrated interfaces that follow this strategy '**semiotic**' interfaces.

A different paradigm of interface design is the enunciation of interface elements independently of the representation of the gameworld. This can be done by superimposing interface elements to the representation of the gameworld, as if they belonged to a transparent layer on top (and independent) of it. Another possibility is to use split screens, placing the representation of the gameworld and the interface side-by-side, for example. We refer to interfaces that follow this logic as **'external'** interfaces.

2.2 Immersion, Engagement and Flow

It is common to find references to the experience of gameplay as immersion, that is, as the impression of being surrounded by a fictional world and unaware of our physical surroundings. Douglas & Hargadon consider the possibility of immersion, but relate it to predictability and low levels of cognitive work. In situations that involve challenge and effort, they see a different type of involvement, that they call engagement [5]. The authors also introduce Csíkszentmihályi's notion of 'flow', i.e., "the feeling of being intensely engaged in an activity for its own sake. During flow, the passing of time seems to disappear due to the deep focus of the activity" [8]. Flow has been considered a particularly appropriate description of the involvement between players and games [1], [8], [4], [12]. It combines characteristics of immersion, such as deep and intense involvement, with the challenging and active character of engagement. It is also convergent with the idea of a state of double consciousness in which the player is fully aware of the artificiality of the game situation [14], but acts as if he believed it in order to intensify the pleasure of gameplay. "In the flow experience, the player's sense of self is not so much lost as it is expanded, such that the player can have a feeling of union or involvement with the game, whilst remaining aware of the contextual situation in which they are engaged" [1].

The development of haptic and motion-tracking controls and other similar devices is driven by the idea that approximating hardware interfaces to what happens in the gameworld can facilitate or intensify immersion, engagement or flow. The logic is similar to that behind the alignment of points of view in first-person games. However, neither of these strategies can erase the ontological difference that separates the player from game characters. To affirm this is to deny that the differences between the actions on hardware interfaces and their representations and effects are a transitory condition that is already been left behind with the popularization of motion-tracking interfaces such as Nintendo's *Wii-Remote*, Sony's *PlayStation Move* or Microsoft's *Kinect*. It must be taken into account that these are initial developments for the home market and that, in combination with multi sensorial and more responsive output systems, motion-tracking devices can reduce the mismatches between the physical actions of the player and their effects in the game. However, they cannot eliminate the additional levels of mediation that are a condition for interactivity. The dream of total alignment of hardware interfaces is akin to the idea that the ideal game interface is that in which all elements have been successfully integrated to the gameworld. We see it as the myth of representational transparency and the desire of immediacy [2] transposed to hardware interfaces. Dourish called attention to the embodied nature of our existence and, by extension, of our interactions: "we inhabit our bodies and they in turn inhabit the world, with seamless connections back and forth"[6]. No matter how advanced our interfaces, we cannot experience symbolic, immaterial worlds the same way we experience the physical world.

3 Method

Our study focused on the perception of the players about their experiences of disruptions in first-person games, especially on the identification of connections between interface representations and disturbance of the gameplay experience. Quantitative methods such as surveys and questionnaires are efficient to reveal general trends and answer broad questions [4], [5]. The detailed information we wanted to collect could only be obtained with a qualitative approach and research techniques that gave voice to the players. Previous studies have shown the power of qualitative methods to unveil fine-grained aspects of the perception and opinion of the players about their own gameplay experience [7], [9]. In this type of investigation, the size of the sample is less important than its adequacy to the research goals. Accordingly, our sampling process did not intend to identify a representative sub-set of the universe of first-person gamers, but to build an information-rich group [8].

The sample was built with a combination of purposeful choice and snowball techniques. The first three participants were chosen to maximize the probability of composing an information-rich group [13]. Two of them contributed for the snowball process. All volunteers were asked to complete the profiling questionnaire. Seven male subjects fulfilled the requirements to participate in the study, namely, to have a certain level of experience with FPS and with game consoles. Table 1 shows their age, area of expertise and previous experience with games in general, consoles (*Playstation* or *Xbox*), FPS, *Battlefield* series, BF3 in campaign mode and BF3 in multiplayer mode. All names have been changed.

Table 1. Sample Profile

Name	Age	Area of Expertise	Previous Experience with					
			Games	Consoles	FPS	BF Series	BF3 Campaign	BF3 Multiplayer
John	16	(School)	High	High	High	High	High	High
Leonard	20	Visual Design	High	High	High	Low	Low	Low
Wilson	23	Visual Design	High	High	High	Good	Good	None
Phillip	21	Automation Engineering	High	Good	High	Regular	Regular	None
Simon	40	Architecture	High	Regular	Good	None	None	None
Michael	28	Computing	High	High	Good	High	High	High
Robert	16	(School)	High	High	High	Regular	Low	Low

Data collection was composed by two-step individual gaming sessions with BF3, followed by semi-structured interviews. The reduced size of the sample allowed for longer observation and better customized interviews. The gaming sessions intended to provide a common ground for all players to refer to the same sub-genre of first-person game, the same game situations and the same interface representations. The first part of the gaming session was in single-player mode. Subjects were invited to play the campaign 'Operation Swordbreaker' for up to 15 minutes. Operation Swordbreaker presents a considerable variety of game situations and interface design strategies in a short period. As the first campaign of the game, it is not as explanatory as the tutorial, but not too difficult to compromise the chances of success of participants who were not accustomed to the specific type of controller used in the experiment or had no previous experience with this particular game. For the second part of the session, the player was positioned in 'Damavand Peak', to play in Rush Squad mode, as an Engineer equipped with an M4A1: this situation and location allowed for different types of action at a slower pace than other options and presented the user with a significant variety of interface elements. Gameplay was followed by the interviews about their general gameplay experience and, more specifically, the occasional disruptions and their possible relation to hardware input devices and graphic interface design strategies.

4 Results

The purpose of this study was to understand how FPS players perceive their gameplay experience, which type of interface representation they considered disruptive and why.

4.1 General Gameplay Experience

All participants used the word 'immersion' at some point during the interview, and explained its meaning in the broad sense of 'the feeling of being inside the game'. Five participants reported to experience immersion very often with games, and more than one affirmed to have become immersed during one or both sessions of the experiment, despite their brief duration. The intensity of the immersion of one player challenged the idea of double consciousness [14] and even the principles of embodiment [6]:

Did someone come in while I was playing? No, I didn't see or hear anything! I was totally immersed, for me you were all sat there quietly while I was playing (...) It happens at home as well, [when I play] I am out of this world (Simon)

Not all players were positive about immersion: one participant laughed at the idea, that he considered naïve, and said he never experienced anything like it, with games or other media. Another player said he does not *usually* experience immersion and referred to his experiences of gameplay in terms of engagement [5]:

...multiplayer is the one that creates tension. As you play as a team, at times someone does something wrong, gets in the way... multiplayer does not increase immersion but involvement, [due to] the difficulty, the interaction with others (Wilson)

There appears to be a relation between the description of gameplay as immersive or engaging and the preference for campaign or multiplayer mode. Subjects who played immersively tended to talk about the importance of narrative and players who prefer multiplayer referred more often to challenge and commitment. Players were unanimous about the improvement of gameplay by two other factors: the first-person point-of-view and meaningful interactivity. The first-person point of view was confirmed to facilitate identification with the character:

In these first-person games, you put yourself in someone else's shoes (Leonard)

Interactivity was as an important difference between games and other media, but pleasurable and compelling gameplay required more than feedback. Basic interactivity is not sufficient, there have to be meaningful effects on the gameworld – and evidence of them. The absence of immediate and meaningful feedback was mentioned as particularly disrupting. For example, in Operation Swordbreaker, the squad runs through a passage, at the end of which there are a gate and a door. A dog appears behind the gate as the soldiers proceed towards the door. One of our subjects turned to the gate and shot the dog, to no effect:

Narrative is very important in the offline [campaign mode] (...) There must be a range of options, with consequences, like killing the dog: you shoot the dog and it really dies. Someone could swear at you for doing that, it would increase involvement (Leonard)

Lack of meaningful feedback from hardware interfaces was also mentioned as a source of disruption.

4.2 Hardware Interfaces and Gameplay Experience

When asked about what disturbed their gameplay experience, six of our seven players first referred to the console controller. Complaints were about imprecise or delayed feedback and, in some cases, lack of familiarity with that specific hardware:

The difficulty is because I still don't know much this control[1] *so it told me to press X and I had to look to see which button was X. But I would soon get used to it and then it would become natural (Simon)*

The computer was clearly the favorite platform of those who prefer the multiplayer mode. Speed and precision were the reasons for this preference:

There is a big difference between playing with the keyboard and mouse and with controller. [With the controller] you cannot aim properly, it is troublesome (Phillip)

The mismatch between the actions required by the input devices and their effects in the gameworld was mentioned by several players. Some were of the opinion that motion-tracking interfaces are 'fun', or 'cool', but most had doubts about their real advantages. Recurring references to poor feedback suggest that technological improvements could change this scenario, but only one of our subjects mentioned a positive impact on gameplay – but at a cost:

If I play the campaign, then I would play with the rifle [CTA's Assault Rifle Controller]... because I don't worry with... it is not as complicated as the online, where you die all the time. I think I feel more inside the game with the rifle, so it does not bother much, it bothers, but immersion becomes more interesting (Robert)

The reference to the rifle 'bothering, but not much' suggests that this player, as all others in our sample, considered the quality and speed of the system's response more important than erasing the evidences of the technological and cognitive mediation between the physical world and the gameworld.

4.3 Software Interfaces and Gameplay Experience

The observations of gameplay sessions suggest that BF3's semiotic interfaces are smooth in campaign and in multiplayer mode. Sound interfaces were not mentioned in the interviews and did not appear to be a source of disruption. Contrarily to our expectations, even players accustomed to play online did not complain about the absence of a microphone. We attribute this to the fact that the conditions of the experiment did not allow for proper team play: subjects could not choose the other members of their squad and knew that the gaming session was likely to be brief. Subjects' opinions about visual interface elements were also significantly convergent.

External interfaces were not considered particularly disruptive, but most players admired the design strategies of integrated interfaces. One player disliked superimposed

[1] The player was accostumed to play with an XBox and was more familiar with its controllers, but it was not the first time he used a PS3.

elements unless he could incorporate them in the gameworld. To this end, he created sub-narratives that transformed external interface elements into semiotic interfaces, at times in spite of disagreements with the internal gameworld coherence.

...the floor is in perspective and it [an interface button] appears flat, there is nothing holding it. But the orange dots [signals indicating the location of targets] ... you can think the soldier is wearing a helmet or binoculars with points that indicate distances (Leonard)

When confronted with the fact that the behavior of the elements he considered possible to interpret as part of the gameworld behaved as inconsistently as the others, the interviewee contradicted himself. However, there was evidence that the difference between the elements he considered possible to integrate as part of a semiotic interface and the ones he could not was aesthetical.

Aesthetic coherence (use of the same color palette, related shapes, textures and levels of transparency) was decisive for the identification of different elements as part of one or other types of interface (external, semiotic or material). Transparent colors blend more smoothly but an excess of transparent elements and a repetition of the same colors can compromise clarity:

Those [superimposed transparent information boxes] didn't work. It is the colors (...) that light blue, it does not call attention. They just oblige you to concentrate more (Robert)

Independently of the mode of representation, information that the researchers had considered explicit was not noticed by several users during gameplay. Different interface elements and layers dispute player's attention at some points. Discreet interface elements and elements that are always on the screen tend to disappear from view, but elements with strong colors or that appear sporadically tend to be a source of disruption:

At times, they give you an information when you are paying attention to the game, someone can shoot you, then either you pay attention to what is written and the game stops, or you don't stop, but you can miss something important (Michael)

The solution appears to be the convergence of all information needed to the main focus of attention. One possible way of doing this is to integrate interface elements into the gameworld, but not all forms of integration are well accepted. For example, as several other FPS, BF3 interfaces do not include a health bar. Loss of health is represented by the appearance of an increasing volume of bloodstains and fading of the gameworld colors. A more abrupt color fade is used to indicate that the user has gone out of the limits of the combat area. In this case, a red warning and a counter appear on the centre of the screen, signaling the need to return.

Things like 'press R1' or whatever, these don't disturb me, not as much as any time I die and ... when there is damage, this type of thing, and the screen starts to get kind of grey, that throws me out of the game (John)

The majority of external interface elements were not considered disruptive by any of our interviewees. They convey information more clearly and were considered particularly helpful in difficult situations. On the other hand, as the game becomes more challenging it demands more attention from the player, reducing the amount of on-screen information they can handle. This optimal informational level, i.e., the balance between too much and too little information, varies from player to player and changes over time. The research team considered BF3's external interfaces highly redundant and expected players to complain about excessive repetition of commands and directions, especially in campaign mode. However, there were no complaints about external interface elements being excessive or disruptive.

BF3 has goals and has an indication there, of what you have to do, who you should follow and who you want to kill. That [orange shape indicating where to shoot] does not bother, no, it is there because it is necessary to guide the player over time (Wilson)

One particular external interface element was considered disruptive and strongly criticized by all players. At a certain point during Operation Swordbreaker a cut scene shows one of the soldiers of the players' squad being shot by a sniper and falling in front of him. The player's character advances to pull him back inside a building. The cut scene ends and a representation of the X button of the PS3 controller appears superimposed to the image of the gameworld. The X button on the screen continuously pulses to indicate that the player must press X several times to carry his companion successfully. The cut scene was considered a source of disruption, but, surprisingly, the most frequent complaints were about the inconsistency of the scene in relation to the storyline instead of the interruption of gameplay.

That guy advanced to rescue the other who was shot and I didn't even know why, I would have left him dead there and go on shooting (Simon)

One interface element of the sequence described was mentioned by all players as the most incoherent and disruptive in the gameplay sessions: the pulsing 'X' button.

That X didn't follow any pattern, it .. it was too big on the screen, it did not match anything else (Leonard)

The mismatch was not only aesthetic. The action required by the pulsing (repeatedly pressing the X button on the controller) was different from any other hardware input required by the game up to that point. Nearly all players had difficulty to change from one type of physical interaction to the other. Even those most used to the PS3 controller and who had played the game before hesitated before starting to press the X.

5 Discussion and Conclusion

Results obtained with a small sample and qualitative methods should not be generalized. Accordingly, the intention of this study was not to reveal patterns, but to gain rich, in-depth information about the way players experience gameplay disruptions and how they relate to interface design strategies. To this end, we performed a 4-phase experiment with a small sample of players and DICE's game *Battlefield 3*.

Our study indicates that most players feel immersed in the gameworld, to the point that some are not aware of their surroundings even during very brief gaming sessions.

Others, however, referred to the way they experience games in terms of engagement rather than immersion. All players confirmed that their gameplay was enhanced by the alignment of the fields of vision through the first-person point-of-view. The alignment between the actions performed by players and their effects on the game-world via motion-tracking hardware interfaces was not said to improve the gameplay experience. This can be a temporary condition, as most players said they did not like to use this type of interface due to the lack of precision. Interactivity is important but engrossing gameplay requires more than basic feedback. The effects of the player's inputs on the gameworld have to be meaningful, explicit and immediate – otherwise, interactivity can be a source of disruption.

The use of semiotic interfaces was well received. Sound, for example, was not mentioned as a source of disruption by any of our subjects. This does not mean that the integration of informational elements as sound is always a good solution, but that the way it is done in BF3 appears to be well resolved. However, not all ways of integrating information to the gameworld were so widely accepted – 'image filtering' [7], for example, is a strategy acclaimed by some authors [7], [15], but our players considered it disruptive. External interfaces were better accepted, even when the elements used were absolutely alien to the gameworld (for example, textual information above characters heads or explicit instructions like 'PRESS R1'). The relation between disruptions of gameplay and the integration of interface elements to the gameworld was weak. Aesthetic and functional interface coherence was the decisive factor for a good game experience was. Use of the same color palette, similar shapes, types of texture and levels of transparency can create a pleasant and highly informative composition. In our experiment the presence of elements that conflicted with the general aesthetic and functional pattern was reported as a main source of disruption. On the other hand, there were indications that the use of a palette that is too restricted or a library of shapes that does not allow for sufficient variation could result in excessive similarity amongst interface elements, leading to confusion.

Previous authors [4], [12], suggested that clarity and functionality are more important for game interface design than integration into the gameworld. The responses we obtained converge with their opinion that users prefer information to be explicit, easy to find and easy to monitor over time. External interfaces were not considered disruptive unless they break the aesthetical or functional coherence of the interfaces or of their relation to the gameworld. We consider this to be an important finding, which extends previous considerations about the importance of the internal coherence of the gameworld [11] to the interfaces. Coherence proved to be a major element integrating material, semiotic and external interfaces, i.e., the three types of software interfaces we had identified theoretically and according to which we organized our experiment, analysis and discussion. This conclusion also applies to the hardware interfaces considered in our study.

Acknowledgments. This work was supported by CNPq (National Council for Scientific and Technological Development, Brazil) and FAPERGS (Research Foundation of Rio Grande do Sul, Brazil). The author is grateful to her research assistant Leonidas Soares, whose help during the gaming sessions was indispensable.

References

1. Bayliss, P.: Notes Toward a Sense of Embodied Gameplay. In. Proceedings of DiGRA 2007 Conference: Situated Play, http://lmc.gatech.edu/~cpearce3/DiGRA07/Proceedings/013.pdf (accessed March 2013)
2. Bolter, J.D., Grusin, R.A.: Remediation: understanding new media. MIT Press, Cambridge (1999)
3. Bordwell, D.: Narration in the Fiction Film. Routledge, London (1995)
4. Breda, L.: Invisible Walls. In Game Career Guide, feature (August 19, 2008), http://gamecareerguide.com/features/593/invisible_.php?print=1 (accessed March, 2012)
5. Douglas, J. Y, Hargadon, A.: The Pleasures of Immersion and Interaction: schemas, scripts and the fifth business. In. Wardrip-Fruin, N., Harrigan, P.(orgs.) First Person: New Media as Story, Performance and Game. MIT Press, Cambridge (2004)
6. Dourish, P.: Where the Action Is: The Foundations of Embodied Interaction. MIT Press, Cambridge (2001)
7. Fagerholt, E., Lorentzon, M.: Beyond the HUD. User Interfaces for Increased Player Immersion in FPS Games. Master thesis. Department of Computer Science and Engineering, Chalmers University of Technology, Gothenburg (2009), http://publications.lib.chalmers.se/records/fulltext/111921.pdf (accessed April 2013)
8. Gerling, K.M., Klauser, M., Niesenhaus, J.: Measuring the Impact of Game Controllers on Player Experience in FPS Games. In: MindTrek 2011 Proceedings of the 15th International Academic MindTrek Conference: Envisioning Future Media Environments (2011)
9. Gibson, J.J.: The Theory of Affordances. In: Perceiving, Acting, and Knowing. Lawrence Erlbaum Associates, Hillsdale (1977)
10. Jørgensen, K.: I'm overburdened! An Empirical Study of the Player, the Avatar, and the Gameworld. In: Proceedings from DiGRA 2009: Breaking New Ground: Innovation in Games, Play, Practice and Theory (2009), http://www.digra.org/dl/db/09287.20429.pdf (accessed April, 2013)
11. Juul, J.: Half-Real: Video Games Between Real Rules and Fictional Worlds. MIT Press, Cambridge (2011)
12. Llanos, S. C., Jørgensen, K.: Do Players Prefer Integrated User Interfaces? A Qualitative Study of Game UI Design Issues. In: Proceedings of DiGRA 2011 Conference: Think Design Play (January 2013), http://www.digra.org/digital-library/db/11313.34398.pdf
13. Patton, M.Q.: Qualitative Research & Evaluation Methods. Sage, London (2002)
14. Salen, K., Zimmerman, E.: Rules of Play: game design fundamentals. MIT Press, Cambridge (2004)
15. Wilson, G.: Off With Their HUDs! Rethinking the Heads-Up Display in Console Game Design. In Gamasutra, Feature (February 3, 2006), http://www.gamasutra.com/features/20060203/wilson_01.shtml (accessed March 2012)

Proposal for a New Entertainment System That Connects Real Life and Net Excitement

Kazuma Hidaka[1] and Katsuhiko Ogawa[2]

[1] Graduate School of Media and Governance Keio University, Fujisawa, Kanagawa, Japan
[2] Faculty of Environment and Information Studies Keio University, Fujisawa, Kanagawa, Japan
{khidaka,ogw}@sfc.keio.ac.jp

Abstract. This paper describes a new entertainment system that enables sharing the experiences of concert halls audiences on the Web with the use of a penlight and Smartphone application. This system captures the audience's excitement and mood during a concert and then uses that data to annotate a video of the concert. Other users can relate to the audience experience in synch to the video. This system consists of a LED light stick attached to a Smartphone waved by the audience and annotates with emoticons timestamped on each particular moment. Further, the test to extract problems of usability of this system and the brief test to evaluate the user experiment of the whole system was carried out. By these test, it was suggested that this system could make a positive change to the experience of the concert.

Keywords: Annotation System, Penlight, Smartphone Application, Entertainment System.

Introduction and Background

At a concert hall, the audience shows their excitement by shaking a penlight following the music rhythm. A common penlight is a very simple device with the shape and size of a pen that emits a glowing color light. It is a very important tool for demonstrating that the audience is enjoying the music concert. However, this is an experience that is possible just on the spot and done by the audience only there, and sharing with others after the concert is difficult, and soon forgotten.

On the other hand, when watching the show on the net (such as Ustream and niconico douga [1], for example), the audience represents their excitement by adding comments on the video of the concert [2]. However, the result of the excitement that generates the show is completed only on the net, it is not tied to the experience lived in real life.

In this way, the excitement of a concert enjoyed in real life by using a penlight and the excitement of the same concert on the net shown by the comments, are isolated; and the media that fuse that excitement of real and net emotions does not exist so far.

In this paper, the system to share on the net the impression generated in the real world is built. This is made by developing an application that can be used to record the excitement in the concert hall, allowing the system to automatically add that annotation data into the concert video. The storyboard [3] of this system is shown in Fig.1.

M. Kurosu (Ed.): Human-Computer Interaction, Part III, HCII 2014, LNCS 8512, pp. 604–613, 2014.

Fig. 1. Storyboard of this System

The test to extract the user's requirement, the problem of GUI design Smartphone application, and the problem of the user interface of the entire system was carried out in the Karaoke box imitating real concerts. And the brief test to evaluate the user experience of the whole system was carried out.

Penlight Annotation on the Screen System

The purpose of this study is building a new entertainment system that share real excitement on the net by using a penlight and Smartphone application. Users use the system according to the procedure described as it follows: First, users attach our penlight device to the Smartphone, and start the application. During the concert, users touch the emoticons displayed on the screen to demonstrate whether they feel excited, bored, impressed, etc. After the concert, users watch the video and see in parallel which emoticons the audience touched, and evoke how they were feeling back then when attending the show, minute by minute. This system flow diagram is shown in Fig.2.

Implementation

In order to implement this system, three fundamental parts were developed.

- Penlight device
- Smartphone application
- Video annotation system

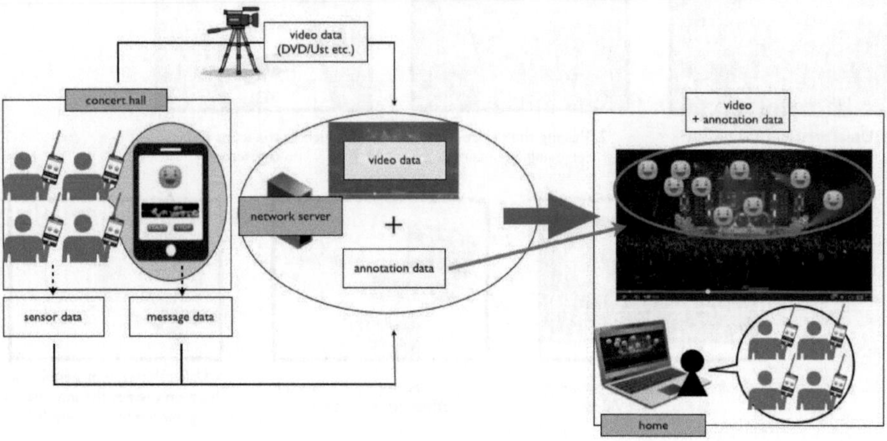

Fig. 2. System Flow Diagram

3.1 Penlight Device

Users use this system by attaching the penlight device to the Smartphone. This device, in order to omit the battery of the external device is supplied power from the headphone jack of the Smartphone. The headphone jack of the iPhone has a 2-channel L/R. The impedance of the output from each terminal is 36Ω, and maximum output voltage is 0.95Vrms(2.7V peak-to-peak). It is a low voltage as it is. It is possible to turn on the LED by going through the chopper type booster circuit (Fig.3).

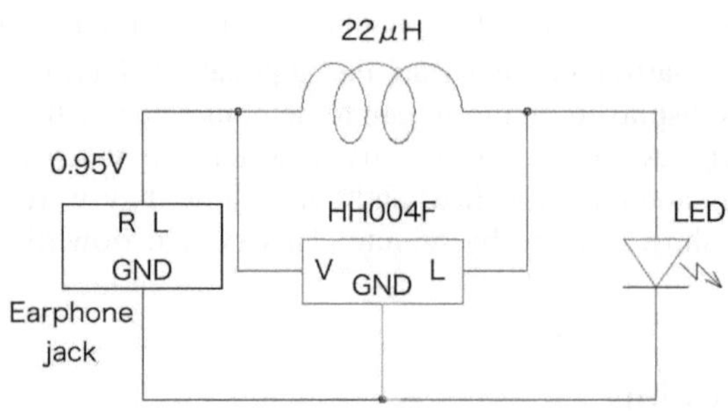

Fig. 3. Circuit Diagram of the Penlight Device

The device outputs square wave signal of frequency 440Hz from the L/R channel at the same time launch the application, and starts lighting of the LED.

3.2 Smartphone Application

In this system, this application is implemented using the iPhone terminal. This application saves three different kind of information:

- The emoticon data touched by the users
- The acceleration sensor data
- The time stamp data

Users can express the impressions of the concert in real time easily by touching the emoticon displayed on the application. The application screen recording data is shown in Fig.4. In addition, it is possible to determine when users were shaking the device by recording the acceleration sensor data. By using this, we can obtain a barometer of the excitement during concert. These data that users get offline will be collected, and transmitted to the server after the concert. This application is getting the time stamp data every 0.1 second. Later, the video and the annotation data are synchronized by the time stamp information.

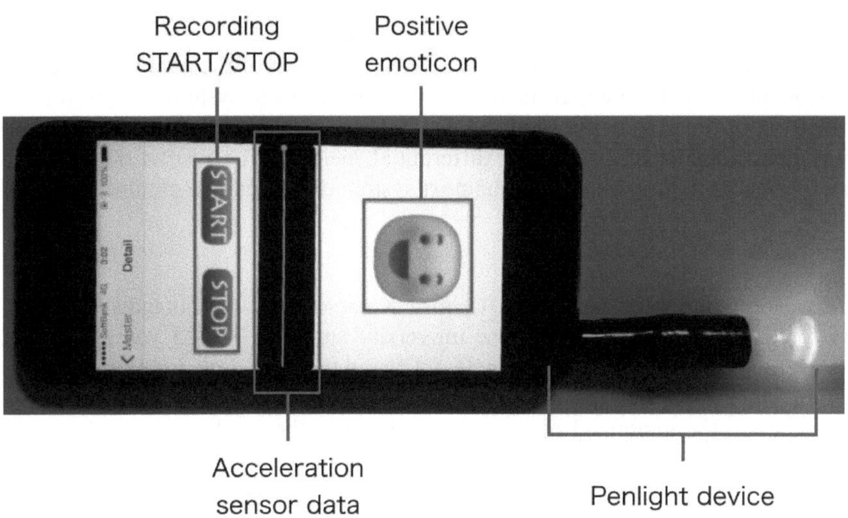

Fig. 4. The Application Screen and the Penlight Device

3.3 Video Annotation System

In this system, the saved information is synchronized with the video. The annotation data match the video and flow all over the screen from right to left. Users can see how excited the users were just by viewing the annotation data users or others recorded.

The synchronization of the video and annotation data is performed by matching the time of each device recorded with the time the concert was recorded. That is, it is necessary that the time data recording starts be set with the concert video. Because iPhone has the ability to adjust to standard time automatically, it is possible to match the time stamp data with the time of video is recorded in the area employing the same standard time.

This system employs a Japan Standard Time (JST). The device side is based on the time stamp data of the start button is pressed. The video side is based on the time 30 minutes before the concert begins (Time like always includes the time that is assumed when the user presses the start button). First, the difference between the base time of the device and the movie is calculated. Then, after playing the video, wait for the time of the difference, this system will start the display of the stamp. Since the device gets the time stamp every 0.1 seconds, deviation of the time stamp of the video is in 0.1 seconds or less. In the manner described above, two data sources are synchronized.

User Experiment and Evaluation

In order to investigate the effectiveness of this system in venues imitating real concerts, we carried out a test to verify the experience of the smartphone application and LED penlight (hereinafter, test 1) and also a brief test to observe the annotated movie (hereinafter, test2).

The purpose of the test1 was to extract the user's requirement, the problem of GUI design Smartphone application, and the problem of the user interface of the entire system. The purpose of test2 is the impression evaluation of the annotated movie. The results obtained by these experiments, we will improve the system design to the next. Verification of the effectiveness of this system was carried out by the free expression answer questionnaire and semantic differential method. The results obtained by the user experience, improvements for the next system design can be obtained.

4.1 Users

Test1 was conducted in January 2013 in a Karaoke Box in Kanagawa, Japan. The users for the test were four Japanese university students. (20-23 years of age, 21.8 years average age, 2 males and 2 females). During the test, some problems by actually experiencing the application could be discovered. In test2, we requested the same users to watch the annotated movie three days after the test1, and asked answer the impression they had of the annotated video.

4.2 Method of Test1

Steps of test1 are as follows: First, because this is a completely new entertainment system, we had a demonstration in order overview of the application, the concept and basic use. We explained how to change to stamp recording screen and how to operate the stamp-recording screen is performed, then the user has actually used. The stage of the karaoke box was assumed to be the hall of a concert, and the performer sang three songs (about 1 minute 30 seconds for each song). This was for reducing the possibility that the users know and like the songs and affect in the final result.

The songs that are registered in the karaoke were used. The first song was "God knows… / Haruhi Suzumiya", the second song was "We Are Never Ever Getting

Back Together / Taylor Swift", the third song was "Hatsukoi cider / Buono!". The users went through the experience of arriving at the concert venue, installing the LED penlight, launching the application, participation in the concert and finish.

Then, a questionnaire survey on GUI was conducted. We asked them to answer the GUI checklist [4]. GUI checklist is a checklist made on the basis of three principles of screen visualization [5] and six principles of screen interface design [6].

Next, by having them talking about feeling and troubles for each screen, protocol analysis [7] was conducted. Users were divided into two groups of two.

Finally, usability task analysis [8] was conducted. We distributed the questionnaire was to organize the six tasks when using this system; users entered in five levels (1~5) good points, bad points, and evaluation points. Because it is not a user who is familiar to this system in the test of time, it adopted the sentence completion method (with whom to answer in a style "Because (A), (B) is (C).").

Fig. 5. Users Taking the Test1

4.3 Method of Test2

Test2 was carried out 3 days after test1. We had edited the concert video that the performer sang in the test1, prepared two types. One is annotated movie; the other is not annotated movie. For each movie, the impression was evaluated by using 10 adjective pairs about affective value and arousal value [9]. The reason why movie2 was also evaluated together is in order to obtain a change in score of between movie1 and movie2 in consideration of shot cut rate, motion intensity, brightness, contrast, saturation, color energy, etc. of the movie material itself after editing.

Adjective group to be used for the impression evaluation experiment was extracted from five affective value and arousal value adjectives refer to the adjective group that is used in the Modified Mehrabian and Russell model [10]. In this experiment, adjectives that are commonly used in Japan were used. The environment for watching the movies was the laptop PC of each of them. After uploading to YouTube each movie, users viewed them in 1280*720pixel resolution. The capture video that was used is shown in Fig.6. They were divided into two groups of men and women 1; group1 viewed in the order of movie1, movie2, and group2 viewed in the order of viewing movie2, movie1. 4 users were used for this testing, and only the calculation of valance feature and arousal feature score was done Analysis of the correlation between the amounts of annotation is going to be performed in the future.

Fig. 6. Capture of Annotated Video that was used in the Test2

Result and Discussion

The problems found when the users tried to perform the tasks in the system came out after evaluating the usability task analysis and protocol analysis. The result is shown in Table 1. Answers were obtained by asking them talk freely about the good or bad points of this system and fill out a questionnaire of the sentence completion method

Table 1. The Result of Extraction of the Problems about each Task

Task	Extraction of the problems		
	Understanding and judgment	Operation	Mean score (SD)
Attaching a penlight	–	When I shake, there is a sense of anxiety that would break and come off.	3.3(1.3)
Creating a concert	If the user does not own the iPhone, there is a possibility that hard to under-stand the meaning of the button.	I want to set the image or name of the concert.	3.8(1.0)
Changing to stamp recordable state	It is difficult to check the status because the change on the display is small.	Because of gender of the size of users' hand, the easiness to press that button is different.	3.8(1.0)
Stamping a emoti-con	–	It is hard to push for a small emoti-con. The size as can push without looking at hand is good.	3.3(1.0)
Recording accelera-tion data	During the concert. It was unlikely to look at the screen.	–	4.0(0.8)
Exiting stamp record	It is difficult to check the status because the change on the display is small.	Size of the hand because of the different, such as by gender of the user, easy to press that position is different.	3.8(0.5)
Comprehensive evaluation	By looking at the hand at the time of operation, it is not possible to maintain-	Etc. add record screen, start screen and end screen, it is preferable to increase	4.3(0.5)

	ing immersive feeling.	the between screen transition.	

about the task of the operation screen. Then, users filled out scores in five levels for each evaluation. The mean and standard deviation score and the problem for each task are shown in Table1.Scores are lower, in the "Attaching a penlight", "Stamping a emoticon" tasks. It is 3.25 both. We considered that the score of “Attaching a penlight” is low, because there were some users who could not attach the penlight unless they remove the cover cases that are placed on their Smartphone.

The result of GUI checklist is shown in Table 2. "Adequacy of navigations and routes for obtaining information", "Operation error tolerance", "Flexibility, customization" score was low. As described above, it is necessary to compensate for insufficiency of navigation by addition of the operation description and increase the navigation system. Further, because the back button to the previous screen is positioned at the bottom right of screen, there was an error that would push the button by mistaking at the base of the right hand when the user have a device with the right hand. The same "Flexibility, customization" also, it is necessary to design a system that allows the user to change the position and size of the button. It is possible to operate briefly and intuitively, and, because it does not require special operations, even unfamiliar users to this system had the possibility to earn how to operate easily.

Table 2. The result of GUI checklist

Items	Mean scores (SD)
Ease of understanding items	3.8(1.3)
Emphasis of important items	3.3(1.5)
Simplicity of information and layouts	4.8(0.5)
Adequacy of navigations and routes of obtaining information	2.8(1.3)
Ease of understanding of terms	3.0(0.8)
Redundancy of information	4.0(0.8)
Adequacy of information mappings	4.23(0.5)
a visual or hearing feedback	4.0(0.8)
Adequacy of operation time	4.8(0.5)
Confirmation of the time course of the operation	3.3(1.5)
Consistency of operation	4.5(1.0)
The explicitness of the hierarchical structure	4.0(1.4)
Consistency of interface and operation image for GUI	3.8(1.0)
Ease of understanding of the whole system	3.8(1.3)
Operation error tolerance	2.3(1.0)
Flexibility, customization	2.8(1.0)

Image profiles obtained by test 2 are shown in Fig.7. The result shows a change in arousal feature is "Aroused-Unaroused". Because the amount of annotation is low, the comment that they feel rather lonely was obtained from the user who scored high on

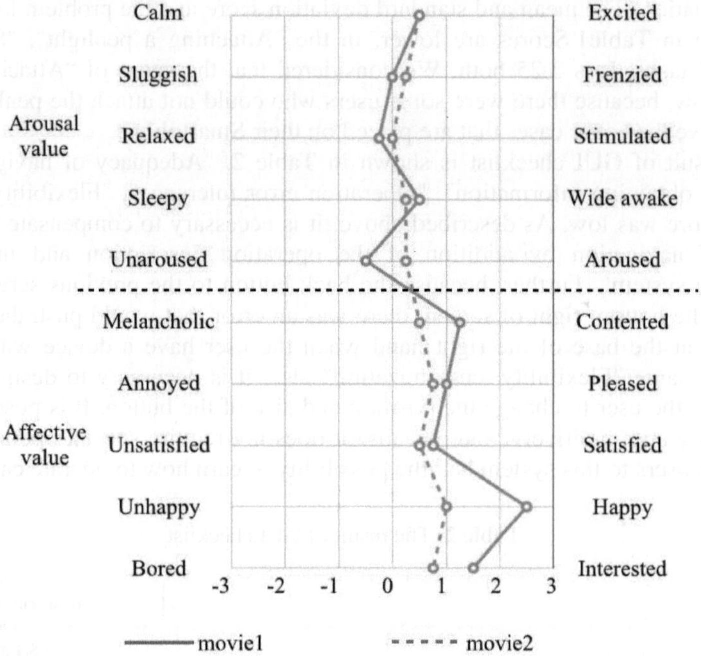

Fig. 7. Image Profiles Obtained by Test2

the Unaroused. With respect of valance feature, positive changes were obtained in every item. For example, "I did not get tired because there were changes in the screen more movie1. It was interesting not only for the performers, but also to know the audience reaction", "Without knowing the song, it is convenient to be able to know when it becomes more lively. It is fun to share that excitement.", comments such as described above were obtained. This is considered that we were able to achieve the concept in this system.

However, the opinion that feels emoticon is a nuisance when the eyes of the performer are hidden by emoticon was obtained. On the other hand, conflicting comments of "It may feel exciting so emoticon should fill the screen" were obtained. The number of times the user who answered that emoticons was getting in the way is less (9.4 times / minute), the number of times the user who answered that emoticon should fill the screen pushed is very often (37.4 times / minute).

Conclusion and Future Work

This paper described how to build this system, and prototype testing. In the user test, it is suggested that this system can make a positive change to the experience of the concert. Addition, it is necessary to examine whether two-dimensional sensitivity model of affective value and arousal value can be applied. Moreover, by obtained the causal relationship between affective value-arousal value and the amount of the annotation, it is possible to derive the amount of the appropriate annotations.

The results of test1 and test2, some problems in usability were found. It is necessary that it can be customized to suit the preferences of the user. Specifically, it is the input of basic information of the concert, and to customize the position and size of buttons. It is also possible that there is a difference by the user for the amount of the appropriate annotations. Such a function can adjust the amount of annotation is considered. That case, it is necessary that appropriate annotation amount is defined. Then, it is necessary to devise the algorithm to generate it.

In this paper, experiments with a focus on usability of smartphone applications were performed primarily; a brief experiment was performed for the user experience of the whole system. As a future work, it is necessary to evaluate the user experience by increasing the subject.

References

1. Niconico douga (February 2014), `http://www.nicovideo.jp/`
2. Hamano, S., Azuma, H., Kitada, A. (eds.): Niconico douga no seiseiryoku. NHK Publishing (2008) (Japanese)
3. Buxton, B.: Sketching User Experiences: Getting the Design Right and the Right Design. Morgan Kaufmann (2007)
4. Yamaoka, T.: The Design of GUI. Designproject, No.90 24(2), 40–43 (2011)
5. Yamaoka, T.: Human technology design Introduction, pp. 69–70. Morikita Publishing (2003)
6. Yamaoka, T.: Human technology design Introduction, pp.75–76. Morikita Publishing (2003)
7. (HANS) Kemp, J.A.M., Gelderen, T.V.: Co-discovery exploration: an informal method for the interactive design of consumer products. In: Usability Evaluation in Industry, pp. 139–146. Taylor and Francis (1996)
8. Yamaoka, T.: Proposed Methods for Extracting and Analyzing User Requirements by Usability Task Analysis. JSSD 56(6), 37–46 (2010)
9. Bradley, M.M., Peter, J.: Lang: Measuring emotion: The self-assessment manikin and the semantic differential. Journal of Behavior Therapy and Experimental Psychiatry 25(1), 49–59 (1994)
10. Mehrabian, A., Russell, J.A.: An approach to environmental psychology. The MIT Press (1974)

Distance Effect: Where You Stand Determines How Promptly You Interact with Game

Xiaolong Lou, Andol Xiangdong Li, and Ren Peng

Dept. of Digital Media, College of Computer Science, Zhejiang University, Hangzhou, China
{dragondlx68,axli,pengren}@zju.edu.cn

Abstract. Interaction efficiency is an important concern in game playing, due to that it reflects the degree of how promptly users respond and dominates user experience. To understand the relationships between interaction efficiency and distance in motion-sensing games, this paper conducted empirical studies to assess user performance (mostly hand gesture movements) at various interaction distances. The results identify the existence of 'low point' at which users responded less efficiently, the range of 'low point' values was much smaller than that of usual distances as we selected though. Beyond that, interaction efficiency recovered quickly to a steadily high level with distance increase. The results implied the distance's direct influence on interaction efficiency in motion-sensing game playing, and it also shows new avenues to address the interaction efficiency in game playing according to standing distances. Furthermore, guidelines were provided to assist game developers to fully consider the role of distance.

Keywords: Interaction efficiency, game interface, hand track, distance effect, game balance.

1 Introduction

Motion sensing technology such as hand gesture detection provides new opportunities for human-computer interaction with more natural interfaces. In the domain of game playing, it transforms traditional interaction ways into novel ones by introducing 'motion-sensing game'. To date such interaction has been gradually acquainted by game players, to whom the interaction efficiency is constantly concerned at the first place. Since interaction efficiency has overwhelmed influence on game user experience, research in how to respond promptly and precisely with the new motion-sensing technology has gained increasing interests.

This paper is aimed at investigating the relationships between interaction efficiency and the distance in motion-sensing game playing. In order to understand how the distance at which the users stand influences the general interaction efficiency in game playing, empirical studies were carried out to observe and compare users' game performances. On the basis of that, the roles of distance were analyzed and the influence was summarized. More importantly, further implications were discussed thus to provide guidelines for future motion-sensing game development, and that also provided new perspectives for considering the distance in motion-sensing interaction design.

M. Kurosu (Ed.): Human-Computer Interaction, Part III, HCII 2014, LNCS 8512, pp. 614–621, 2014.

2 Related Works

2.1 Interaction Efficiency in Motion-Sensing Game Playing

Motion sensing technologies, especially hand gesture recognition are increasingly applied in interactive video games since 3D depth cameras such as the Microsoft Kinect sensor arose [1]. As a natural and intuitive interaction measure, the gesture begins to role as one of the most primary and expressive forms of operation mode [2]. Be regarded as a mechanism for interaction [3], interaction efficiency of gesture recognition affects user's manipulation experience in motion sensing games. According to Murthy and Jadon, for making a highly effective gesture recognition system, four principles are required: Robustness, Computational efficiency, User's tolerance and Scalability. To this end a superior interactive system with high interaction efficiency for game playing are also supposed to possess such principles appropriately.

As mentioned in other studies, gesture interaction concerns complex factors, including computer vision and graphics, image processing, learning mechanism, bioinformatics and human-related psychology [3]. The interaction efficiency can be affected by any of these factors. From hand gesture recognition algorithms' perspectives, there are well developed techniques to enable accurate gesture recognition for both experimental and commercial purpose. However, research in interaction factors (such as the distance) and responding behaviors is little. Therefore, in this paper robust algorithms were adopted to investigate the relationships between interaction efficiency and the distance. Such algorithms had three main tasks, including detection, tracking and recognition, which reflected the accuracy, efficiency and robustness of motion-sensing interaction respectively [4-7].

2.2 Distance-Related Optimization in Gestural Interaction

Despite the large amount of optimization algorithms regarding to the improvement of hand gesture recognition, factors concerning interaction behaviors, such as the distance between hands and display are still implicit in the specific domain. The fact is, as a complementary influential element, distance was focused in other traditional fields.

In research work of Lee, the relationships between distance and ambient conditions (such as the display size and illumination) was evaluated, and it revealed user's tendency (preference) of distance (in TV watching) according to various sizes and illumination intensity [8]. Another research by Shieh and Lee explored the satisfied distance by user under different conditions (light sources, ambient illuminations, and character sizes) in E-reading [9]. In other studies, the distance was assessed to reflect the accuracy of Kinect depth data in [10] and thus found the random error of depth measurement increases with distance increase, which lowered the recognition accuracy. However, these studies considered distance more as an ergonomic factor, from interaction efficiency perspectives the understanding is still preliminary.

The importance of distance in previous studies is claimed as an additional and inessential factor to algorithm effectiveness. As a result, the emphasis on the role of distance in motion-sensing interaction was insufficient. To date the progress of gesture recognition techniques have made the distance not only an ergonomic factor but also (only more importantly) a factor that dominates overall user experience. The increasing popularity of virtual competition -based game is a good example of that. As Jaffe et al. discussed in their work [11], the balance amongst game factors determines the depth, fairness and engagement of game playing. When it comes to motion-sensing game, such balance has not been well gained. So via comparisons of game playing at various distances, this paper raises the awareness of the relationships between interaction efficiency and distance.

3 Method of Study

An empirical study was conducted via observing and comparing interactions at multiple distances. The laboratory-based study evaluated the differences in terms of hand gesture movement. To highlight the distance as the solo variable, the study was carried out in forms of within-subject experiment.

3.1 Independent Variable and Dependent Variable

Independent Variable. The only independent variable in our study is determined by how far the subject stood away from the interactive object, namely the distance from hand to the display, which was captured by 3D depth camera in our study. As the hand moving freely during the experiment, the depth value is changing accordingly. Thus, the depth data captured for each test per subject is floating, and average values were calculated in data analysis.

Dependent Variable. Dependent variables in the study include the cursor moving speed. By hand tracking program, subjects' hand moving was tracked and drove the mouse cursor on interface. Thus, cursor's speed was the substitution of subjects' hand moving speed. As a result, a higher moving speed means accessing targets more quickly and interacting more promptly.

3.2 Subjects

There were 27 subjects (17 male and 10 female) recruited in the study with an average age of 25. All subjects were undergraduate students and Ph.D candidates from local universities and were recruited through campus BBS. All subjects had heard about motion sensing games before, but only 3 of them had experience with motion sensing interaction. They received $5 for their participation.

3.3 Apparatus

The experiment was conducted in a lab equipped with a wall-sized large display (70 inches: 1587mm × 975mm, resolution ratio: 1920 × 1280). A motion-sensing camera (ASUS Xtion PRO LIVE) was set underneath the display. The program drove the camera to track the subjects' hand gestures and make the mouse cursor to be bounded to move on the interface with hand moving synchronously. The program was also devised to record the depth data of hand constantly and the coordinate values of moving cursor per 30 mili-seconds.

3.4 Task

Searching 9 Targets in a Geographic Map. Given many other elements might affect users' performance (i.e., pervious researches proved that immersion affects gamer performance differently), the tasks were designed without any gaming mechanism to test the merely variable: distance. We prepared a geographic visualization contained 9 targets (Figure 1) to imitate the interaction. The 9 targets were visually noticable. Subjects in the study were instructed to retrieve these 9 targets and checked them by moving the cursor over these one by one.

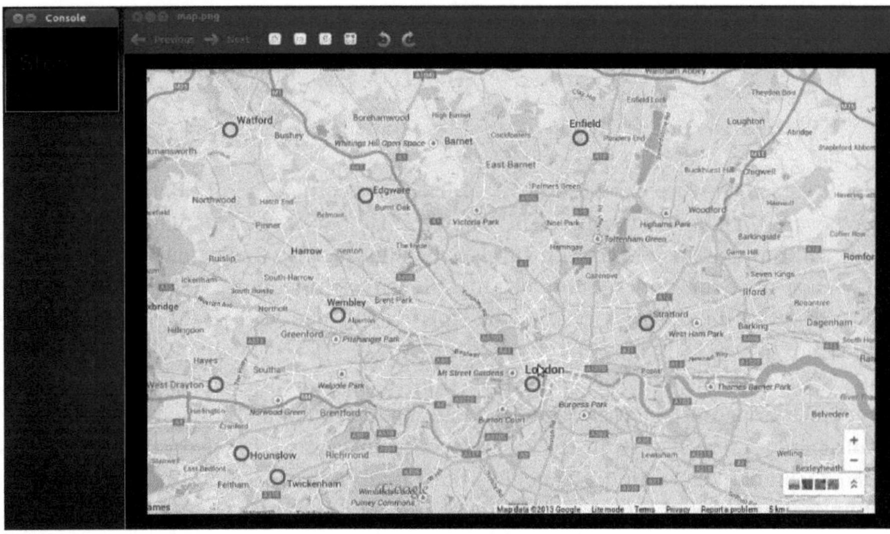

Fig. 1. Map contains 9 targets

3.5 Procedure

Subjects were asked to have a practice session after a briefly introduction of this study. Then, they were required to complete the experimental tasks. Each subject repeated the tasks three times at three distances respectively. Standing distances were limited from 800 millimeter to 2500 millimeter. Subjects were required to move the cursor to 9 targets orderly. The 9 targets were listed on the margin of the display to make subjects execute tasks more smoothly. For each subject, three standing positions were selected by themselves. Figure 2 shows a scenario of study. The study captured the hand depth and the coordinate values and saved these data to a TXT file. Our experiment collected totally 81 (27 × 3) data files. At last, 72 files were saved.

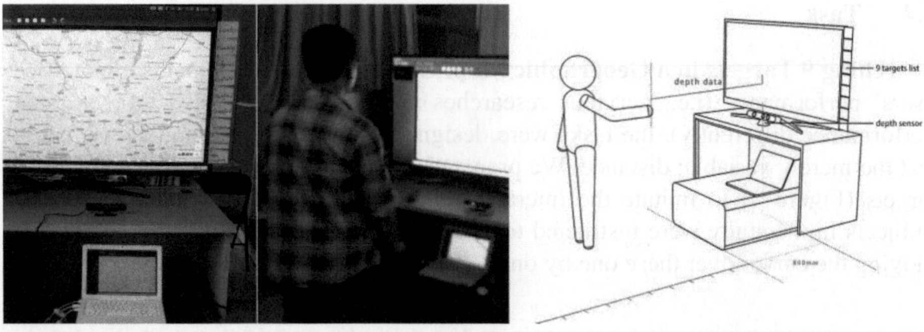

Fig. 2. Experiment scenario (the distance captured in this study is shown as 'depth data' above)

4 Results

Except 9 data files were captured or recorded incorrectly, other 72 data files from 27 subjects were maintained for analysis (Table 1). By SPSS, we calculated the distance (depth) and moving speed for each subject. For distance, it was calculated by averaging for each data file. For moving speed, the fastest forty percentage of movements were selected in the analysis, due to that this part of data directly reflected subjects' gestural moving.

As shown in Table 1, subjects performed differently at various distances, but some really tendentious implications were extracted: subjects tended to have lower interaction efficiency (slower movement) at a specific distance. The else distances corresponded to higher interaction efficiency. Statistical data from 23 subjects confirmed this implication (except for 4 subjects' data shown with gray bar chart in Table 1). As the green bars shown in the table, subjects (numbered as 03, 04, 05, 10, 16, 19, 22, 23) had relatively lower efficiency at the median distances. While other subjects (numbered as 06, 13, 20, 21, 25, 26, 27) got positive change in efficiency with distances increasing.

As shown in Figure 3, we draw a scatter diagram to visualize the statistical results. The black trend line validated the implications drawn from Table 1, there exists "low point" of distance where subjects interacted less efficiently. The "low point" lay near the value of 1000 millimeter, which is far less than distance users select in common use. This explains the difference between the subjects who were relatively less efficient under a median distance while the others got improving efficiency with increasing distances.

Besides, the distance element affected subjects' interaction efficiency differently. As shown in Figure 4, we selected 4 subjects' data randomly and calculated their trend lines. The trend lines revealed the differences among individuals. Comparing the participants numbered as 05 and 10, subjects numbered as 16, 22 performed more sensitively with distance changing.

Table 1. Distance (depth) and moving speed for each subject

Participant (Serial : Sex)	Distances (mm)	Mean Moving Speed (Pixels / Second)
01	1191.7	259.2
	1526.9	321
02	1220.9	287.5
	1481.2	215.5
03	676.9	286.4
	987.9	164.6
	1770.3	217.3
04	777.2	282.1
	1092.1	174.4
	1745	210
05	919.3	246.8
	1237.6	185.6
	1624.7	259.6
06	1156.5	191.2
	1595.2	238.2
	2180.5	279.5
07	1103	178.6
	1363.2	406.2
	1739.2	222.1
08	763.6	281.2
	1277.8	243
09	1438.5	244.8
	2003.1	605.4
10	994.5	367.9
	1334.5	324.3
	1810.3	357.4
11	1278.1	328.5
12	1108.5	205.7
	1312.4	326.1
	1704	261.7
13	1229.3	232.6
	1717.1	242.8
	2155.4	284.9
14	1139	410.3
	1531.8	319.4
	2034.5	286.1

Participant (Serial : Sex)	Distances (mm)	Mean Moving Speed (Pixels / Second)
15	1661.9	222.1
	1780.3	318.1
16	974.3	212.7
	1020.5	163.3
	1577.5	239.6
17	1369.1	288.7
	1986.6	672.7
18	1039.1	232.1
	1540.7	455.1
	2045	400.4
19	846.6	383.1
	1450.3	333.2
	1889	407
20	1061.5	278.4
	1312.2	282.7
	1528.7	345.3
21	1062.3	283.1
	1378.2	403.7
	1627.9	394.3
22	992.6	354.8
	1295.2	251.6
	1775.4	408.9
23	924.7	288.8
	1190	275.4
	1634.9	325.2
24	1247.4	209.2
	1584.9	325
	1947.5	186.7
25	656.3	381.9
	1178.6	451.2
	2286.6	560.8
26	985.9	218.3
	1590.9	230.5
	2025.6	262.8
27	910.9	195.8
	1304.8	255.2
	1642.8	307.5

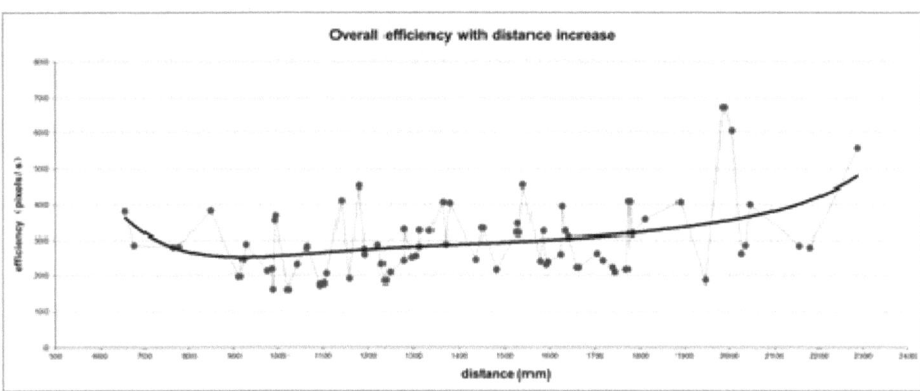

Fig. 3. Overall efficiency with distance increase

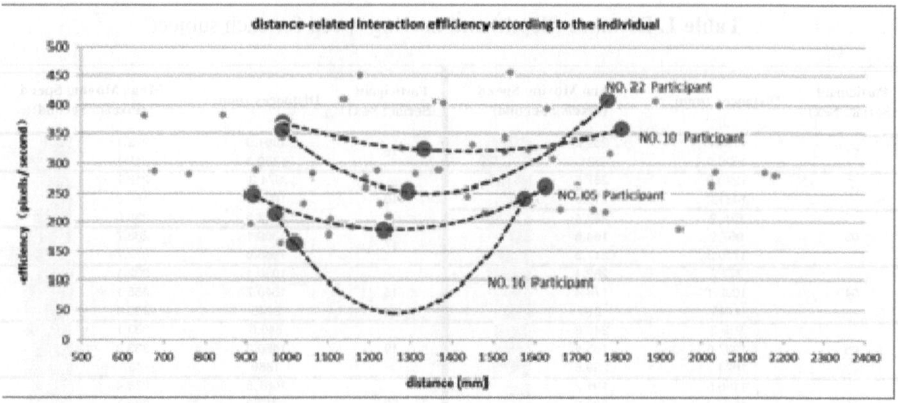

Fig. 4. Distance-related interaction efficiency according to individual subjects

Beyond the "low point", interaction efficiency improved with distances increase. This finding revealed that the distance affects interaction efficiency, greater distance helps subjects respond more promptly. This can be applied to optimize game player's interactions or to adjust the game balance when the players interact at different distances (see Figure 5). Two suggestions are provided for making equity between players or for optimizing operation agility merely.

1. A distance-adapted gestural detection algorithm can be developed to balance the distance gap. Different levels of optimization can be applied on user interface according to distance. The key of this algorithm is to connect the efficiency change mechanism with distance increase. But as Figure 4 reflects, individuals respond to distance changing with differences. Thus, the personalization determines how the distance affects interaction efficiency individually and the efficiency change mechanism should be carried out according to different users. This method balances games precisely, but individual-related optimization algorithms make the tracking program more complex. Since "personalization" exists in distance-efficiency connection, pre-test of efficiency under various distances is needed.
2. Another alternative suggestion is to supply a distance guide for game players. For instance, reminder can be presented on interface to guide players to stand at larger distance. Since the distance is changing dynamically for users may move during interaction, this method can not balance the distance factor between game players. But it can really be utilized to guide players to get better user experience by suggesting standing at a farther distance.

To sum up, these two suggestions suit for different conditions. The first offers precise balance for competitors, which is based on complex optimization algorithm recording to the individual. This will satisfy competitive game players with gestural interaction, in which there are strict requirements for game balance. As rough it is, the second suggestion can be applied to optimize interaction efficiency among the general public rather than to supply game balance, especially when game players get inferior achievements, user interface can guide them to enhance their operation agility by recommending standing farther.

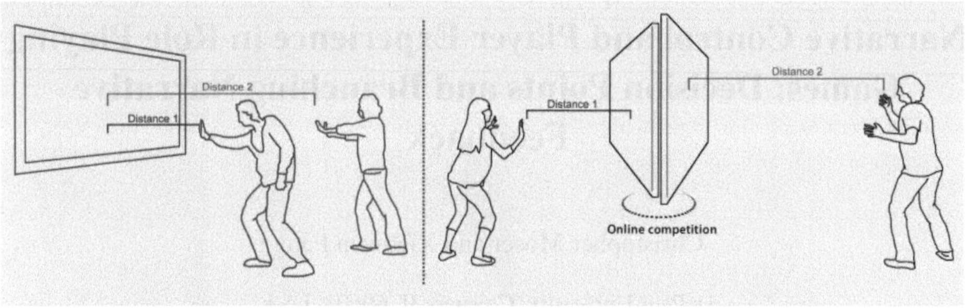

Fig. 5. Gamers compete at different distance (Distance 2 > Distance 1)

5 Conclusion

The study has explored user performance on interaction at various distances. The finding showed that the distance can be utilized to adjust game players' performances. From this root, suggestions are given to game designers that the players standing at a relatively greater distance can interact more promptly, which can be utilized to optimize players' operation agility and to supply a precise game balance mechanism for competition participants.

References

1. Zhengyou, Z.: Microsoft Kinect Sensor and Its Effect. IEEE MultiMedia 19, 4–10 (2012)
2. Wachs, J.P., Kölsch, M., Stern, H., Edan, Y.: Vision-based hand-gesture applications. Commun. ACM 54, 60–71 (2011)
3. Murthy, G., Jadon, R.: A review of vision based hand gestures recognition. International Journal of Information Technology and Knowledge Management 2, 405–410 (2009)
4. Rautaray, S., Agrawal, A.: Vision based hand gesture recognition for human computer interaction: a survey. Artificial Intelligence Review, 1–54 (2012)
5. Vo, N., Tran, Q., Dinh, T.B., Dinh, T.B., Nguyen, Q.M.: An efficient human-computer interaction framework using skin color tracking and gesture recognition. In: 2010 IEEE RIVF International Conference on Computing and Communication Technologies, Research, Innovation, and Vision for the Future (RIVF), pp. 1–6 (2010)
6. Zhu, Y., Xu, G., Kriegman, D.J.: A real-time approach to the spotting, representation, and recognition of hand gestures for human–computer interaction. Computer Vision and Image Understanding 85, 189–208 (2002)
7. Ren, Z., Yuan, J., Zhang, Z.: Robust hand gesture recognition based on finger-earth mover's distance with a commodity depth camera. In: Proceedings of the 19th ACM International Conference on Multimedia, pp. 1093–1096 (2011)
8. Lee, D.S.: Preferred viewing distance of liquid crystal high-definition television. Applied Ergonomics 43, 151–156 (2012)
9. Shieh, K.K., Lee, D.-S.: Preferred viewing distance and screen angle of electronic paper displays. Applied Ergonomics 38, 601–608 (2007)
10. Khoshelham, K.: Accuracy analysis of kinect depth data. In: ISPRS Workshop Laser Scanning, p. 1 (2011)
11. Jaffe, A., Miller, A., Andersen, E., Liu, Y.E., Karlin, A., Popovic, Z.: Evaluating Competitive Game Balance with Restricted Play. In: Proceedings 8th Artificial Intelligence and Interactive Digital Entertainment Conference, pp. 26–31 (2012)

Narrative Control and Player Experience in Role Playing Games: Decision Points and Branching Narrative Feedback

Christopher Moser and Xiaowen Fang

DePaul University, Chicago, IL 60604, USA
XFang@cdm.depaul.edu, chrismoser@outlook.com

Abstract. This paper reports an experimental study that investigated two research problems: first, how does narrative structure mediate the phenomenological experience(s) of role-playing games (RPGs)? Does branching narrative feedback heighten the experience of role-playing in terms of Flow and character identification? And second, what are the effects of salient decision points (narrative controls) on the player perception of narrative structure and complexity as well as control over the player-character? Does higher perceived complexity lead to heightened effectence and Flow? To what extent are these effects context-dependent in terms of narrative feedback mechanisms and overall structure? Two hypotheses were developed based on prior research: 1. Branching narrative in an RPG leads to improved game play experiences compared to linear narrative and 2. Presence of salient decision points in a RPG leads to improved experiences of game play. A 2x2 factorial experiment was conducted to test these hypotheses.

Keywords: role playing, RPG, interactive narrative, branching narrative, narrative structure.

1 Introduction

The development of immersive narrative experiences and the use of narrative contexts to augment interactive experiences have been the subject of research in numerous fields within digital media, including virtual reality, ludology, human-computer interaction, and the development of advanced computational narrative structures. Nasr [15] notes that there are many proposed narrative architectures and technical contributions but we know very little about the user experience within these media forms; there is a need for design lessons to guide proposals. The variety of experiential phenomena elicited by the fusion of story and interactivity poses challenges in terms of theory and measurement and requires new concept-based measures [17].

This paper presents an experiment exploring the context-dependent effects of narrative control mechanisms and feedback on the player experience of role-playing games.

M. Kurosu (Ed.): Human-Computer Interaction, Part III, HCII 2014, LNCS 8512, pp. 622–633, 2014.

2 Literature Review

Preface. This literature review contains information and analysis related to control and feedback in RPGs with a branching narrative structure. An in-depth review of RPG design paradigms and studies pertaining to related phenomena can be found at: roleplayingexperiment.wordpress.com/rpgs-history-future/

Branching Narrative and Role Play. Branching narrative structures are a distinct subset of interactive narrative structures. In computer RPGs, branching narrative structures are operationalized through pre-plotted nodes that when reached, determine the subsequent authored narrative content (story branch). Nodes have classically been comprised of cut-scenes and salient decision points, which force users to choose among specific possibilities.

The degree of user engagement within an interactive narrative lies largely with the player's perceived control over the character: the greater the sense of control over the character, the greater the sense of presence –and freedom [16]. McGonigle [13] states that the most compelling form of role-playing feedback is vividly being shown the impact of character variables on the game world. Transportation theory considers media enjoyment to be characterized by a flow-like state; particularly enjoyable forms of entertainment allow immersion and identity play as a participant in the narrative of an alternate reality [7]. We can assume some transfer of one's real-world moral decision-making into the game environment: moral disengagement was not found to be common when players were given moral agency in an RPG with a branching structure [22]; they reported making decisions as they would in real life, had high empathy for non-player characters (NPCs), and experienced emotions like those in actual interpersonal interactions.

New concept-based empirical measures reflecting the fusion of story and interactive participation [17] must center on role-play and the related concepts of Flow, identification, and control, specifically over the player-character. Interactive narrative models and related systems must be assessed by their capacity to collectively facilitate these phenomena through the determination and implementation of feedback relative to the context of interaction. RPGs work as integrated systems to emphasize user-influenced player-character variables and related feedback in order to increase identification and flow: up to 20% of total RPG game play time is delineated to character modification [1]; leveling-up of player-characters has been empirically shown as an important motivator and reward [9, 13]. RPGs are crossbreeds of games and stories [6]; even if story is the primary appeal, gaming defines the interactive relationship with the story world [6]. RPGs devote a greater percentage of total play-through time to embedded narrative content than other genres and also use the widest range of narrative delivery mechanisms [11]. The target experience of RPGs can be described as a positive feedback loop: identification with the player-character leads to higher satisfaction when goals are reached; and overcoming challenges to reach goals substantiates player-character progression and development along with abstract dimensions of heroism, etc. The overall function of branching narrative structures in the context of RPGs need to understood in terms of this feedback loop.

Causal-agency is the satisfying power to take meaningful action and see the results of one's decisions and choices [14]. Effectance refers to the phenomenological experience of causal-agency and it facilitates the perception of being in control because observation of one's own causal influence on a situation is a precondition of control. Control is bound to additional preconditions, such as the ability to influence a situation according to specific goals [12]. Two inter-dependent narrative conditions exist in games [20]: Emergent narrative (ludonarrative) arises from context-dependent interactions; Embedded narrative (pre-authored) is designed to provide motivation for game events and actions, contextualize emergent events, act as a tangible reward for achievement [20] and works to communicate abstract dimensions of causal-agency: the link between narrative progression and the immediate effectence, which is intrinsic to game-world interactions and is what qualifies such interactions as 'game-play' rather than mere activity [14].

Cinematic cut-scenes explicitly communicate effectence and changes in game state through the suspension of ludonarrative. Story nodes in RPGs typically take the form of interactive cut-scenes that give players an impression of control over story progression [12], contextualize decision points (often through dialogue with NPCs), and act as the primary feedback mechanism for player decisions; they dramatically reveal outcomes affecting both the player-character and the overall game world [13]. Salient decision points mediate the cognitive-emotional effects of subsequent cut-scenes by eliciting the experience of control over the direction of the story and story world. More decision points and higher branching complexity are likely to correlate directly with the user's perception of control [16]. Decision points increasingly allow for players to define abstract characteristics of the player-character through both words and direct actions [22]. When player decisions are made and/or acted through a character, appropriate branching (embedded) feedback allows for the experience of control over a player-character identity: feedback simultaneously affirms the player's contextual definition of the player-character and provides immediate feedback supporting immersion in terms of embodying the player-character.

Branching complexity refers to the array of unique narrative possibilities available in a story graph. Mental-models for causal-agency (system responses) are closely aligned with mental models for the overall narrative structure and thus related to perceived complexity. Experienced richness relates to complexities experienced during gameplay and is linked to the degrees of freedom to which a game can be manipulated [18]. Richness promotes engagement due to the perception of system's potential for developing human faculties; experienced control affects engagement because these potentials can be assimilated by a player. Reduced effectance produced substantially lower levels of game enjoyment [12]. Klimmt et al.[12] suggested that various states related to control have the capacity to evoke game enjoyment and should be investigated further. More available game functions has been shown to increase experienced decisional control since players can choose their goals[23] Regardless of the complexity of a branching narrative structure, a single, unbroken interactive system story run is always retroactively linear even if the path through story branches is not determined in advance [16]. Dialectically speaking, the branching structure itself potentially mediates role-play and transportation into an otherwise linear story. Mapping between player behavior and narrative response (causal-agency) is a precondition for effectence and control, which augment role-play.

The on-line construction of mental models for causal-agency and narrative complexity in branching narratives is explored through on-line realism judgments which occur as one constructs and reconstructs the mental models necessary to understand a narrative[3]. These are likely to be focused on a specific instance or moment within the narrative, are unlikely to be positive [3], and often fatally disrupt engagement. An emergent on-line realism judgment colloquially called the 'Illusion of Choice' [4], is elicited during secondary story runs in branching RPGs when alternate narrative branches do not appear to users as sufficiently dissimilar from their initial story run. This break implies: 1) perceived narrative complexity (amount/variations of possible branches and level of system responsiveness) and causal-agency are inter-dependent; 2) mental models allow perceived narrative complexity to exceed actual narrative complexity on initial story runs; and 3) mental-models for causal-agency and complexity are related to automatically imagined narrative feedback for alternative choices at decision points.

3 Hypotheses

Hypothesis 1: Branching Narrative Feedback in an RPG Leads to Increased Enjoyment and Engagement. Perceived complexities in RPGs are associated to perceived richness, engagement, and an increase of the degrees of freedom to which a game can be manipulated [23]. Richness and complexity lead to a sense of freedom, which facilitates feeling of control [13]. Narrative interactivity impacts character identification as measured through heightened cognitive-affective empathy [15].

Hypothesis 2: Presence of Salient Decision Points in an RPG Game Improves Enjoyment and Engagement. Salient decision points can elicit feelings of control the context of branching feedback as they can enable the ability to influence a situation according to specific goals [13] while facilitating immersion and role play. More decision points should correlate directly with the user's perception of control [21], which defines the degree of engagement and leads to presence [21]. Salient decision points should facilitate the automatic construction of mental models for narrative complexity and causal agency [4]. Decision points will provide mapping so that player cognitive capacity can focus on the story details [28].

4 Method

Independent Variables. There are two independent variables in the experiment: salient decision points and branching narrative structure. Narrative structure has two treatment levels: branching vs. linear. The branching treatment level refers to the viewing of mutually exclusive narrative branches in consecutive story-runs. Linear refers to the viewing of a single narrative branch in consecutive story runs. Decision points also has two treatment levels: Salient vs. No.

There are two independent variables in the experiment: salient decision points and branching narrative structure. Narrative structure has two treatment levels: branching vs. linear. The branching treatment level refers to the viewing of mutually exclusive narrative branches in consecutive story-runs. Linear refers to the viewing of a single narrative branch in consecutive story runs. Decision points also has two treatment levels: Salient vs. No.

Table 1. 2x2 Factorial Experiment Design

Variables	Salient Decision Points	No Decision Points
Branching Narrative Structure	Group 4	Group 3
Linear Narrative Structure	Group 2	Group 1

Dependent Variables. The following three dependent variables were measured as the responses of participants to different treatment conditions: enjoyment, flow, and perception of narrative structure. Game enjoyment must be considered in a valid conceptual model of interactive narrative experience [22] and is central to frameworks that examine interactions between games and players [6]. It was measured through a survey instrument developed and validated by Fang, Chan, Brzezinski, and Nair [6]. This instrument contains 11 items measuring affective, behavioral, and cognitive reactions of computer game play.

Measurement of flow allows us to understand how to induce and enhance enjoyment and engagement during game play [31]. Flow during game play was measured through an instrument developed and validated by Zhang, Fang, and Chan [31]. This instrument has 23 items related to Concentration, Autotelic Experience, Loss of Self Consciousness, Transformation of Time, and the experience of Challenge Requiring Skill, Clear Goals, and Clear Feedback.

Perception of narrative complexity and causal-agency was assessed by eight items: "The outcome of the story could not be changed."; "Players cannot influence the main character's identity."; "The other characters seem to respond intelligently to player choices."; "The story seems to respond to player actions."; "Players cannot influence the outcome of the story."; "This game seems to have multiple story paths/endings."; "Players cannot influence situations in the story."; "Players cannot change the outcome of the story." Interactive narrative systems must be assessed based on their capacity to facilitate role-play phenomena through the determination and implementation of feedback relative to the context of interaction. In addition, it is important to understand the relationship between perceived-complexity/causal-agency and Flow in various contexts. All items were combined into a single questionnaire (randomly ordered) and measured using a 7-point Likert scale.

Experimental System. In order to control for the experimental conditions, participants were presented with video recordings of play sessions rather be allowed to play the game themselves. Mental models for narrative causal-agency and narrative responses to player behavior are constructed based on observable player actions and feedback. In this context, there is no need for players to actually control a character in order to judge a game system's capacity to heighten role-play through implementation of feedback relative to the context of interaction. Moreover, it would be difficult to manipulate a single game to allow for meaningful play in all of the experimental conditions. The experiment required an RPG with a branching narrative structure operationalized by salient decision points. It was necessary to use a segment or mission within a select game that featured dissimilar branches along with an understandable, stand-alone story arc that would not be compromised when edited into 20-30 minute videos. Mass Effect 2 is a role-playing game developed by Bioware Corp. (a division of Electronic Arts) that features extensive player-character customization and salient, menu-based decision points formatted as dialogue options within cut-scenes; they are not time-constrained and contain either 2 or 3 descriptive options. The game allows players moral/ethical agency: players can make either "Paragon" or "Renegade" decisions that, in aggregate, elicit complex feedback in addition to normal branching feedback.

Video Recording and Editing. A single mission was selected for use in all experimental conditions. It includes 11 decision points spread throughout 5 interactive cut-scenes. Four play-throughs were recorded at 800 x 600 pixels. Steps were taken in both the recording and editing process to ensure that variables were properly controlled while making game-play and features appear unadulterated. The in-game cursor was not recorded. The musical score could not be recorded separately from the sound effects and was turned off to facilitate smooth editing. Two play-throughs were conducted so as to facilitate the construction of experimental videos for the salient decision point condition. Sufficient time was taken when menu-based decision points were on-screen so subjects could interpret both the mechanics of the decision point interface and the choices available. Options were highlighted in the menu for approximately 5 seconds before selection and visual augmentations were made to decision points to compensate for the modal shift from play to viewing. A translucent overlay matching the menu highlight color was placed over the selection to simulate a button-click event; this lasted 3 frames and disappeared as the menu did, appearing as a natural game element.

Two play-throughs were conducted so as to facilitate construction of experimental videos for the No Decision Point condition. Decisions were made rapidly during recording in order to present normally interactive cut-scenes as unbroken, non-interactive cut-scenes. Unexplained pauses during cut scenes when decision points would normally be apparent could potentially cue participants to our manipulation, elicit a presence break, and/or elicit negative appraisals of the game and character realism. These cut-scenes were presented with slight zoom so as to position decision point menus lower on the screen where they could be occluded by overlayed letterboxes. The default aspect ratio was maintained, simply making shots appear slightly tighter.

Videos 5 and 6 were edited to manipulate the cut-scenes (branches) that stemmed from decisions: Paragon decisions were followed by Renegade cut-scenes and vice versa. Frames were arranged so that cuts between recordings were imperceptible and cut-scenes appeared to be unaltered. Videos 2, 4, 5 (Paragon) were identical (same recording) between cut-scenes, as were videos 1, 3, 6 (Renegade). All ludonarrative/environmental interactions were retained to maintain continuity and allow for an understanding of game features and mechanics. All videos begin with the same establishing shot and end with a mission complete prompt that follows the final cut-scene. 6 videos were produced. All are between 20:35 and 23:19 in length. Differences are due to recording strategies and differences in branch (cut-scene) length.

All experimental videos can be viewed in full at:
roleplayingexperiment.wordpress.com/category/videos/
A table of videos and independent variable controls can be examined at:
roleplayingexperiment.wordpress.com/category/tables/videos-and-controls/

A table of video viewing scenarios by group can be examined at: roleplayingexperiment.wordpress.com/category/tables/viewing-scenarios

Procedure. 46 students from a large, diverse, urban university in the Midwestern U.S. were recruited and screened as participants through fliers and email. Participant data can be examined at: roleplayingexperiment.wordpress.com/category/tables/participants

The experiment was conducted one-at-a-time. Subjects were told that we were studying general game enjoyment and then given a script that introduced the characters and basic circumstances of the mission. Subjects were randomly assigned to experimental groups. Subjects were provided with headphones and allowed to set a comfortable volume and then watched two videos in succession without break. Subjects were then instructed to fill out the questionnaire while imagining that they themselves had played the game, after which they were interviewed on the game and experience.

5 Hypothesis Testing

Factor Analysis. A factor analysis was conducted to confirm the construct validity of the questionnaire. Items with loadings >.4 on a single factor were retained for analysis. Items with heavy loading on multiple factors were discarded. 8 factors were extracted. Cronbach's Alpha (α) was used to measure internal consistency. All of the 8 factors demonstrated a strong internal consistency of α = > 0.7.

Factor 1 contains 13 items (α = 0.942): 6 items from Flow instrument measuring Concentration (2 items), Transformation of Time (2 items), Autotelic Experience (1 item), and Loss of Self Consciousness (1 tem); 7 items from Game Enjoyment instrument measuring General Appraisal (4 items) and Affect (3 items). This factor represents overall engagement as evidenced by key Flow elements facilitating and enhancing overall enjoyment in a positive feedback loop.

Factor 2 contains all 8 items (α = .937) constructed to measure perception of narrative causal agency and complexity.

Factor 3 contains 4 items (α = 0.850) from the Flow instrument measuring the experience of A Challenging Activity That Requires Skill.

Factor 4 contains 3 items (α = 0.809) from the Flow instrument measuring the experience of Clear Feedback.

Factor 5 contains 2 items (α = 0.832) from the Flow instrument measuring Autotelic Experience, specifically relating to the intrinsic rewards of the experience.

Factor 6 contains 3 items (α = 0.757) from the Game Enjoyment instrument measuring Behavior, specifically related to utterances/exclamations during gameplay.

Factor 7 contains 3 items (α = 0.741) from the Flow instrument: 2 items measure the experience of Clear Goals; 1 item measures Autotelic Experience, specifically related to rewards/recognition. This factor represents the experience of external/tangible goals and/or recognition.

Factor 8 contains 2 items (α = 0.906) from the Game Enjoyment instrument measuring Cognition, specifically relating to characters.

The experience of game-play and interactive narrative cannot be measured by a single well-respected scale, especially in a role-play context. Therefore, the above 8 factors/measures were used to examine participants responses to the game play sessions.

Two-Way ANOVA. Negatively-keyed items were reverse-scored. Each participant's mean score for the total items in each factor was calculated and treated as a dependent variable for both between-group and within-condition testing. We conducted a two-way analysis of variance among two levels of Narrative Structure (Branching vs Linear) and two levels of Decision Points (Salient vs NO). An alpha of $P = < .05$ was used as criterion for significance.

The interaction effect between narrative structure and salient decision points was significant, $F(1, 42) = 5.557$, $P = .023$, on Game Enjoyment related to Cognition and characters (Factor 8). This generally supports the position that clear mapping between decisions and branching feedback facilitates the experience of control over the player-character, heightening identification. Also, clear mapping allowed for additional cognitive resources to be allotted to player-character and NPC interactions. It's important to note that decision points were delivered as dialogue options during cut-scenes. In the branching condition, salient decision points rendered cut-scenes interactive rather than passive. In the salient decision point condition, decisions were acted out by the player-character and branching feedback was intelligently acted out by NPCs; thus, NPCs played a large part in establishing the mapping necessary for experienced character control. Prior research has found that the context of interaction with NPCs mediates presence, valence, and likability but has no effect when players are told that NPCs are human avatars [16]. Future research should examine various contexts of decision point and feedback delivery in terms of this construct.

The two-way ANOVA yielded a main effect for narrative structure $F(1, 42) = 7.606$, $P = .009$, such that overall engagement and Flow (Factor 1) was significantly higher among participants in the branching condition ($M = 5.9545$, $SD = .44643$) than in the linear condition ($M = 5.1026$, $SD = 1.35431$). The main effect of salient decision points on overall engagement (factor 1) was non-significant, $F(1, 42) = .180$, $P = .673$. The two-way ANOVA also yielded a main effect for narrative structure $F(1, 42) = 32.967$, $P = .000$, such that perception of narrative causal agency and complexity (factor 2) was significantly higher among participants in the branching condition ($M = 2.0852$, $SD = .93014$) than among participants in the linear condition ($M = 4.6042$, $SD = 1.81878$). The main effect of salient decision points on narrative causal agency/complexity (factor 2) was non-significant, $F(1, 42) = .012$, $P = .915$. These findings support the position that perceived complexity and richness is correlated with overall Flow and enjoyment. The two-way ANOVA yielded no significant effects from either independent variable on factors 3, 4, 5, 6, or 7. A full table of the two-way ANOVA results can be found at: roleplayingexperiment.wordpress.com/category/tables/two-way-anova/

T-tests and One-Way ANOVA. One-way ANOVA and independent sample T-tests were conducted to measure within-subjects effects. The main effect of Decision Points was non-significant within the linear narrative condition (groups 1 and 2). The increased richness provided by decision points did not independently lead to increased enjoyment or Flow. Subjects in group 2, especially those who watched the video with appropriate feedback first, reported the experiencing the Illusion of Choice presence break and related frustration during the second video. This suggests that decision points augmented the experience until the presence break, specifically in terms of related phenomena of player-character control and perceived complexity. Interviews helped gauge the experiential function of decision points when the first video viewed included altered feedback. These subjects reported mixed experiences overall. The linked interview findings include an in-depth explanation of the topic.

In the branching narrative condition (groups 3 and 4), one-way ANOVA yielded a main effect for Decision Points, $F(1, 20) = 6.302$, $P = .021$, such that enjoyment related to characters and cognition (Factor 8) was significantly higher among participants in the Salient condition (group 4) ($M = 4.1818$, $SD = 1.60114$) than among participants in the No condition (group 3) ($M = 5.6818$, $SD = 1.16775$). This finding was supported $t(20) = -2.510$, $p = .021$, two-tailed. No other significant main effects were detected within this condition. Interviews revealed that players in group 3 did not perceive the branching structure during the first video and spent cognitive resources during the second video looking for mapping between player behavior and branching feedback. This diversion of cognitive resources likely reduced presence, along with involvement with the story and character. The lack of significant main effect on Factor 2 (causal-agency and perceived complexity) coupled with the significant main effect on Factor 8 reflects the qualitative difference between causal-agency and experienced control. Both groups experienced causal-agency, but decision points allowed for experienced control over the player-character in the context of branching feedback. However, it may also reflect the function of NPC dialogue as mentioned above.

Within the NO Decision Point condition (groups 1 and 3), one-way ANOVA yielded a main effect for narrative structure $F(1, 20) = 14.440$, $P = .001$, such that perception of narrative causal agency and complexity (Factor 2) was significantly higher among participants in the branching condition (group 3) ($M = 2.3750$, $SD = 1.08685$) than among participants in the linear condition (group 1) ($M = 4.3409$, $SD = 1.32770$). This finding was supported $t(20) = 3.8$, $p = .001$, two-tailed. No other significant main effects were found within this condition.

We can thus say that when decision points were not present, a branching structure led to higher perceived narrative complexity but did not lead to increased Flow or enjoyment. It is likely that cognitive resources were allocated to search for mapping/control, thus reducing presence and offsetting the potential increased enjoyment due to heightened causal-agency.

As expected, within the Salient Decision Point condition (groups 2 vs 4), one-way ANOVA yielded a main effect for narrative structure, $F(1, 22) = 19.569$, $P = .000$, such that perception of narrative complexity and causal agency (Factor 2) was significantly higher among participants in the branching condition (group 4) ($M = 1.7955$, $SD = .67146$) than among participants in the linear condition (group 2) ($M = 3.6154$, $SD = 1.75480$). This finding was supported $t(22) = 4.424$, $p = .000$, two-tailed. Also within the Salient Decision Points condition (groups 2 and 4), one-way ANOVA yielded a main effect for narrative structure, $F(1, 22) = 5.344$, $P = .031$, such that overall engagement and Flow (Factor 1) was significantly higher among participants in the branching condition (group 4) ($M = 6.0559$, $SD = .44468$) than among participants in the linear condition (group 2) ($M = 5.1302$, $SD = 1.25983$). This finding was supported $t(22) = -2.312$, $p = .031$, two-tailed.

Perceived narrative complexity and causal-agency was coupled with heightened Flow and enjoyment when decision points were present but not when decision points were absent. Clear mapping between decision points and feedback is required for experienced control. In addition, the clear mapping between decision points and branching feedback may have allowed for cognitive resources to be allotted to the story. Similarly, Flow was likely disrupted by the presence break was likely to have greatly diminished and control. In addition, within the Salient Decision Points condition, one-way ANOVA yielded a main effect for narrative structure, $F(1, 22) = 5.396$, $P = .03$, such that the experience of a Challenging Activity that Requires Skill (Factor 3) was significantly higher among participants in the branching condition (group 4) ($M = 5.0455$, $SD = 1.12815$) than among participants in the linear condition (group 2) ($M = 3.6154$, SD 1.75480). This finding was supported $t(22) = -2.323$, $p = .030$, two-tailed. A Challenging Activity that Requires Skill is not considered to directly measure immersion; it describes the experience of activities that require psychic investment and cannot be done without appropriate skills; [6]. Challenges go along with suspense, while established control should evoke emotional relief; both are states of enjoyment [14]. This relates to correlations between narrative interactivity and heightened intensity of positive and negative emotions [16]; heightened role-play and subsequent anxiety during moments of virtual danger could increase the attention given to controls. More research is needed to determine the extent to which presence breaks related to embedded narrative lower perceived challenge in various contexts.

Mirroring other findings, within the Salient Decision Points condition, one-way ANOVA also yielded a main effect for narrative structure, $F(1, 22) = 5.396$, $P = .03$, such that Game Enjoyment related to Cognition and characters (Factor 8) was significantly higher among participants in the branching condition (group 4) ($M = 5.6818$, $SD = 1.16775$) than among participants in the linear condition (group 2) ($M = 4.2692$, $SD = 1.67848$). This finding was supported $t(22) = -2.348$, $p = .028$, two-tailed. Full T-test and one-way ANOVA results can be examined at:

roleplayingexperiment.wordpress.com/category/tables/one-way-anova-and-t-tests/

6 Conclusions

6.1 Hypotheses

Hypothesis 1. The main effect for narrative structure was significant on Factors 1 and 2 overall; Factors 1,2,3,and 8 in the salient decision point condition; and Factor 2 in the no decision point condition; as branching structure augmented various experiential phenomena. A significant interaction effect between narrative structure and decision points was detected on Factor 8. Hypothesis 1 was supported.

Hypothesis 2. The main effect for decision points was not significant overall. However, the significant interaction effect on Factor 8 implies that salient decision points augmented experiences in the context of branching feedback. Further, decision points had a significant main effect on Factor 8 within the branching condition and augmented enjoyment related to characters and cognition. Subjects in group 2 reported the Illusion of Choice phenomenon, which suggests that salient decision points may have functioned to augment the experience during the first video. Decision points did not yield a main effect for factors containing direct measures of immersion in the Flow instrument (Factors 1 and 3) as was expected due to character control, especially in the context of branching feedback. However, branching narrative led to a significant increase in those factors within the salient decision point condition. Hypothesis 2 was partially supported.

6.2 Interviews

No participants reported difficulty imagining themselves as players when answering the questionnaire. No Participants in Group 3 reported realizing that decision points were removed. Group-specific questions were asked in order to address specific research problems. An in-depth presentation and discussion of these findings and their implications for future research and design can be found at: roleplayingexperiment.wordpress.com/category/interview-findings/

6.3 Limitations and Future Research

An explanation of limitations and discussion of future research can be found at: roleplayingexperiment.wordpress.com/category/future-research/

References

1. Bissel, T.: Extra lives: Why video games matter. Pantheon, New York (2010)
2. Brown, H.J.: Videogames and education. M.E. Sharpe, New York (2008)
3. Busselle, R., Bilandzic, H.: Fictionality and perceived realism in experiencing stories: A model of narrative comprehension and engagement. Communication Theory 18, 255–280 (2008)
4. Everett, L.: Hyperspace beacon: Illusion of choice (2011), `http://massively.joystiq.com/2011/08/02/hyperspace-beacon-illusion-of-choice/` (retrieved)
5. Fang, X., Chan, S., Brzezinski, J., Nair, C.: Development of an Instrument to Measure Enjoyment of Computer Game Play. International Journal of Human-Computer Interaction 26(9), 868–886 (2010)
6. Gottschall, J.: The Storytelling Animal. Mariner Books, Boston (2013)
7. Green, M.: Transportation into narrative worlds: The role of prior knowledge and perceived realism. Discourse Processes 38(2), 247–266 (2004)
8. Green, M.C., Brock, T.C., Kaufman, G.F.: Understanding media enjoyment: The role of transportation into narrative worlds. Communication Theory 14(4), 311–327 (2004)
9. Guo, Y., Savoy, A., Byrd, K., Salvendy, G.: Development and validation of an instrument to evaluate the content effectiveness of video games: A pilot study. Theoretical Issues in Ergonomics Science 10(2), 107–133 (2009)
10. Hartmann, T., Klimmt, C., Voderer, P.: Telepresence and media entertainment. In: Bracken, C.C., Skalski, P.D. (eds.) Immersed in Media: Telepresence in Everyday Life, pp. 137–157. Routledge, New York (2010)
11. Ip, B.: Narrative structures in computer and video games: Part 1: Context, definitions, and initial findings. Games and Culture 6(2), 103–134 (2011)

12. Klimmt, C., Hartmann, T., Frey, A.: Effectance and control as determinants of video game enjoyment. Cyberpsychology & Behavior 10(6), 845–847 (2007)
13. McGonigle, J.: Reality is Broken. Penguin, New York (2011)
14. Murray, J.: Hamlet on the holodeck. The Free Press, New York (1997)
15. El-Nasr, M., Milam, D., Maygoli, T.: Experiencing interactive narrative: A qualitative analysis of Façade. Entertainment Computing 4(1), 39–52 (2013)
16. Riedl, M., Young, R.M.: From linear story generation to branching story graphs. IEEE Computer Graphics and Applications, 23–31 (2006)
17. Roth, C., Vorderer, P., Klimmt, C., Vermeulen, I.: Measuring the User Experience in Narrative-Rich Games: Towards a concept-based Assessment for Interactive Stories. In: Entertainment Interfaces Proceedings (2010)
18. Rozendaal, M.C., Keyson, D.V., de Ridder, H., Craig, P.O.: Game feature and expertise effects on experienced richness, control and engagement in game play. AI and Society 24, 123–133 (2008)
19. Ryan, M.: Narrative as virtual reality: immersion and interactivity in literature and interactive media. The Johns Hopkins University Press, Baltimore (2001)
20. Salen, K., Zimmerman, E.: Rules of play: Game design fundamentals. M.I.T. Press, Cambridge (2003)
21. Vesterby, T., Voss, J.C., Hansen, J.P., Glenstrup, J., Hansen, D.W., Rudolph, M.: Gaze-guided viewing of interactive movies. Digital Creativity 16(4), 193–204 (2005)
22. Weaver, A., Lewis, N.: Mirrored Morality: An Exploration of Moral Choice in Video Games. Cyberpsy., Behavior, and Soc. Networking 15(11), 610–614 (2012)
23. Zhang, J., Fang, X., Chan, S.: Development of an Instrument to Measure Flow Experience in Computer Game Play. In: Proceedings of Pre-ICIS HCI/MIS Work (2011)

Prototyping for Digital Sports Integrating Game, Simulation and Visualization

Yasuto Nakanishi[1,2]

[1] Keio University, Fujisawa, Kanagawa, Japan
naka@sfc.keio.ac.jp
[2] Stanford University, Stanford, CA, USA

Abstract. Recent advances in sensor technology has made technology support for sports and physical exercise commonplace. Sports played along with mobile devices or robots are actively studied; however, most of these systems utilize only one device or robot. Iterative prototyping with several devices requires incurs additional costs for gathering test players or conducting field tests. We have proposed hybrid prototyping using both virtual and miniature spaces for prototyping spatial interactive systems to cope with problems similar to those. This paper discusses a prototyping trial for a soccer training system using physical and virtual mobile cone robots. We propose a new form of hybrid prototyping that unifies game, simulation, and visualization.

Keywords: design, hybrid, prototyping, digital sports.

1 Introduction

Within the field of human-computer interaction (HCI), there is a trend towards placing the human body at the center of the digital sports experience[1]. Motion sensing has become popular owing to advances in sensor and interactive technologies and presents new opportunities for supporting sports and physical exercise. Sports played with wearable sensors, mobile embedded devices, or robots are actively studied. Examples of digital sports utilizing robots include a flying robot accompanying joggers[2], a buddy robot following and presenting information to a swimmer[3], or a drone enabling novel sports broadcasts[4].

Most of these systems utilize only one robot and are for individual sports. To control team sports robots, their individual motion rules must be known. Each robot is expected to act naturally with responding to human players, other robots, and the environment. A developer needs to describe rules and their parameters, which are tuned through trial and error, however, since human player's behavior is sometimes based on instinct that does not conform to obvious rules, it is hard to describe appropriate rules and parameters for robots. One reason for using only one robot is that designing digital team sports with several robots or sensors increases the elements of the system and complicates prototyping. Another reason is that iterative prototyping of digital team sports incurs additional costs for gathering test players and conducting field tests with several robots.

M. Kurosu (Ed.): Human-Computer Interaction, Part III, HCII 2014, LNCS 8512, pp. 634–642, 2014.

Problems similar to those described above also occur in the prototyping of interactive system in public places. We propose to use both virtual and miniature simulations[5,6]. In this paper, we describe our hybrid prototyping process for a digital sports system that uses physical and virtual mobile cone robots. Moreover, we propose a new type of hybrid prototyping that unifies game, simulation, and visualization.

2 Prototyping of Mobile Cone Robot System

Soccer is the world's most popular sport, and players attempt to create goal opportunities by dribbling or passing the ball to another teammate and by taking shots at the goalmouth, which is guarded by the opposing goalkeeper or defender. Plastic cones are frequently used as virtual and motionless defenders and are used especially when practicing dribbling. An interactive system that consists of mobile cone robots will bring about a new experience of individual skill practice; thus, we develop a mobile cone robot based on Omni-wheel in this research.

2.1 Physical Prototyping

The mobile cone robot consists of a plastic cone and an Arduino based wheel robot. The robot receives commands from a PC via a wireless radio frequency (RF) module, XBee[1] . The PC, connected with a Microsoft Kinect sensor, tracks the cone using the ARToolkit marker[2], the soccer ball using color tracking, and the player using the OpenNI library[3]. This system is built using Processing[4] (Figure 1).

Fig. 1. Physical prototype ver.1

[1] http://www.digi.com/xbee/
[2] http://www.hitl.washington.edu/artoolkit/
[3] http://www.openni.org
[4] http://processing.org

In the first physical prototype, to represent a simple defender the robot is maintained at the middle position of the Kinect sensor and the player. In this system, the robot moves in six directions without rotation so that the maker can be easily tracked. The system sends a command to move in a direction closest to the middle position. Playing soccer with this robot was fun; however, it was too simple and its moving speed was insufficient as a defender. Thus, we developed another system to simulate playing with several mobile cones.

2.2 Virtual Prototyping

To build a simulator for several mobile cones, we utilized a physics engine, PBox2D[5], within Processing(Figure 2). We restricted the movement of the ball to be on a 2D plane in order to simplify our simulation, and we utilized the 2D rigid body simulation library.

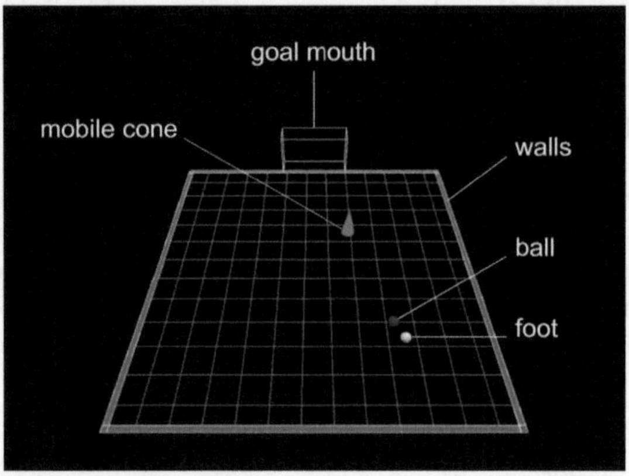

Fig. 2. Elements within the simulation of our digital sports system

Elements of the simulation include mobile cones, a ball, a goalmouth, a player's foot, and walls. Although they are drawn as 3D objects, they are defined as 2D rigid objects such as circles or rectangles. A spring is connected between the foot and the location of the mouse. One end of the spring follows the mouse location. Dragging or clicking the mouse moves the end of the spring. When the foot touches the ball, the player dribbles the ball and shoots a goal. The desirable positions of mobile cones are calculated beneath the player's position, ball, and goalmouth. Springs are connected between current and desirable positions of mobile cones; they along with the physics engine update the mobile cones' positions.

There are several methods to calculate the desirable positions of a mobile cone, even in a simulation using only one mobile cone. We implemented and compared the following methods: (1-1): the middle point of the ball and the

[5] `http://box2d.org`

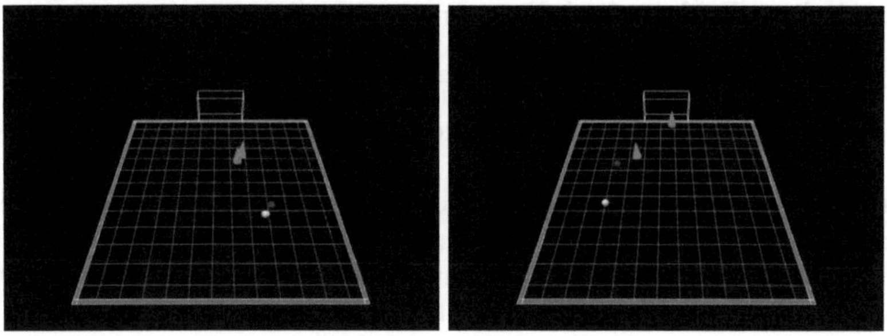

Fig. 3. Playing with two mobile cones

goalmouth; (1-2): the middle point of the foot and the goalmouth; and (1-3): the middle point of the mouse and the goalmouth.

With virtual prototyping, it is easy to increase the number of robots and compare algorithms used to move several robots. For playing with two mobile cones, we implemented the following two methods: (2-1): one cone moved according to (1-1) and the other according to (1-2) (Figure 3 left); and (2-2): one moved according to (1-2) but was slightly shifted to the near side, and the other was in front of the goalmouth but slightly shifted to the far side[6] (Figure 3 right).

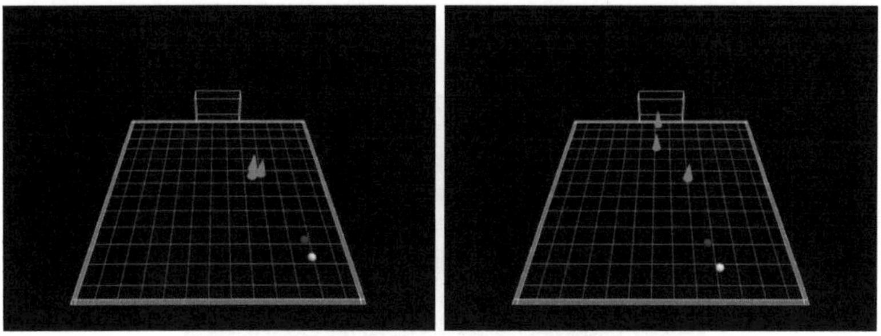

Fig. 4. Playing with three mobile cones

For playing with three mobile cones, we implemented the following two methods: (3-1: the first moved according to (1-1), the second according to (1-2), and the third according to (1-3) (Figure 4 left); and (3-2: two cones moved according to (2-2) and the third was positioned halfway between the first two but slightly shifted to the far side (Figure 4 right).

[6] When the player is on the left side of the goalmouth, the near side is the left side and the far side is the right side. When the player is on the right side of the goalmouth, the near side is the right side and the far side is the left side.

3 Studying Rules and Parameters

In order to make our virtual prototype similar to our physical prototype, it was necessary to adjust some of the parameters in the digital world. Initially, we studied physics engine parameters.

We adjusted the coefficient of restitution of the ball. When this value is close to one, the ball bounces too much making it more difficult to dribble the ball. When the spring constant of the spring between the desirable and current position of the mobile cone is small, the speed of the mobile cone becomes slow. On the other hand, when it is large, the mobile cone's speed increases making it difficult to shoot a goal. In the physical prototyping described above, the robot moves in six directions. In the simulation, the mobile cones move in any direction. Thus, we limited the movement of the mobile cones to six and twelve directions. This limit had no effect on the difficulty of dribbling the ball or making a goal.

Changing the system's degree of difficulty in the physical space results in effective practice, whereas changing it in the virtual space brings out the nature of the game in the simulation. In order to add game elements into our simulation, we implemented a dynamic view camera that chased the ball, and set virtual gravity to the physics engine that kept the ball away from the goalmouth (Figure 5).

In updating the simulation, we arrived at the following hypothesis: Intentionally expanding a simulation from hybrid prototyping into a game helps one study the virtual space parameters that should be tuned in order to perform a realistic simulation.

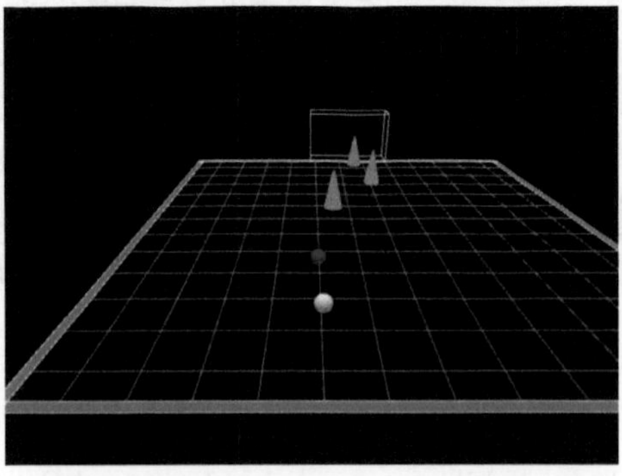

Fig. 5. A mode of the 3D space camera chasing the ball

On the other hand, simulation should be closer to the physical system visualization than to the game. For debugging purposes, we implemented a visualization of the physical system, thus updating the design to be closer to the simulation (Figure 6). However, it remains to be shown how close the operation of the physical system and the simulation actually are. In order to effectively study and tune simulation parameters, it would be helpful to import moving

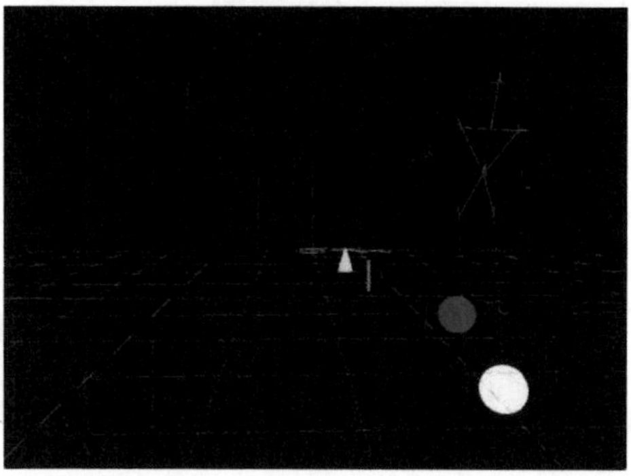

Fig. 6. Visualization for debugging the physical prototype

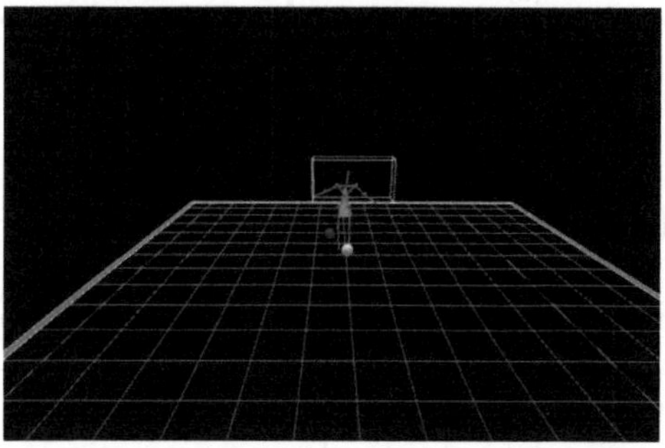

Fig. 7. Importing trajectory files into the simulator

trajectory data from the physical system to the simulator. In our current implementation, the physical system stores the depth and RGB video stream from the Kinect sensor as a recorded ONI file and the trajectory data of the mobile cone robot as a CSV file (Figure 7). The simulator imports these two files, and let the virtual mobile cone according to the tracked user's skeleton. This leads to a comparison of the movement of the virtual mobile cone and the real mobile cone.

4 Discussion

A multi-agent system of virtual soccer players has been actively studied at the international robotics competition, RoboCup[7]. Ishimura proposed a robot simulator for RoboCup in order to reduce the cost of robot strategy programming[7]. Ishimura's robot simulator unified virtual and real robots and enabled both robots to move simultaneously in the simulator. We proposed hybrid prototyping using both virtual and miniature simulation[5,6]. Carrying out a simulation in both virtual and miniature space enables one to obtain revised points of codes and tune

[7] `http://www.robocup.org`

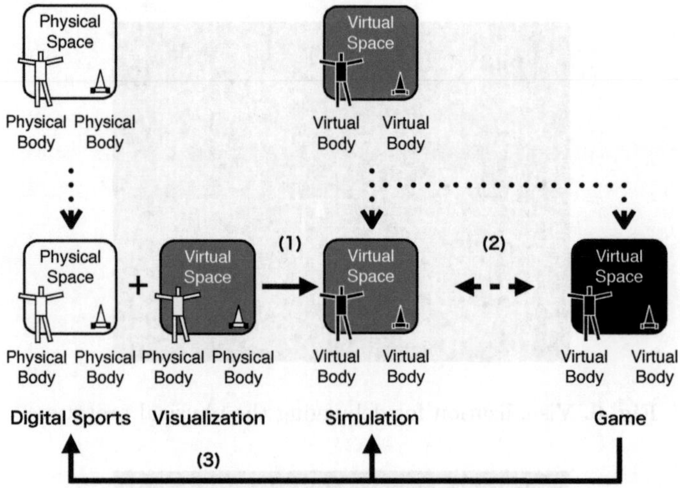

Fig. 8. A new type of hybrid prototyping that unifies game, simulation, and visualization

the parameters. Such improvements make the developed system more robust and flexible and ensure that the system is smoothly deployed in the real world.

In this paper, we propose another style of hybrid prototyping that concurrently develops game, simulation and visualization (Figure 8). In developing a complex system that consists of mechanics, electronics, and image processing, it is useful to develop a simulator to divide and conquer. Melgar and Diez introduced such a prototyping process using simulation and visualization for developing a robot controlled with using Kinect [8]. They introduced several parameters into the simulation code to move the physical robot; however, they did not mention how to find and tune these parameters. Through the prototyping described above, we arrived at the following hypothesis: Intentionally expanding a simulation into a game helps one study the virtual space parameters that should be tuned in order to perform a realistic simulation. Admittedly, we described only one of our cases; nonetheless, we suggest that developing a game different from the real world, as a branch from a simulation, may bring about an opportunity to think about the constraints in the physical space on the contrary (arrow (2) in Figure 8). There are many digital games based on sports, and it seems natural to develop digital sports systems and digital games concurrently. Furthermore, there is also potential to think of new ideas of imaginary reality games that mimic real world sports but leave behind elements of the actual games [9].

Sensors attached to sports instruments or wearable sensors has become popular, and it is common to visualize data from such sensors in a tablet PC or Smartphone. Thus, a developer of a digital sports system that plays with mobile robots also visualizes data from sensors. Model-based development based on simulations is also popular in robot programming. It would be reasonable to design a comprehensive digital sports system in which a simulator and visualization system can import data (arrow (1) in Figure 8).

In order to develop digital team sports system, it is necessary to describe many rules and tune parameters. The more human players and robotic players play together, the more complicated rules must be described. Ohsita proposed a method to learn motion rules from log in order to design non-player characters in a football game [10]. Several human-players controlled virtual-players respectively in a football game. The motion rules are learned from the control logs with a support vector machine equipped with a layered mechanism and adaptive parameters. In our study, the virtual sports system as a game was developed concurrently with a physical digital sports system. It will bring a merit to take logs under various conditions for developing physical digital sports characters (arrow (3) in Figure 8).

Role of prototypes is well established in the field of HCI and design, and researchers have attempted to identify different types of prototypes such as low- vs high-fidelity prototypes [11,12]. In our study, the physical prototype, the simulation and the game are high-fidelity prototype respectively. Lim et al. proposed an anatomy of prototypes in their generative role and two key dimensions: prototypes as filters and prototypes as manifestations, and pointed out the material, resolution and scope of a prototype as considerations of manifesting a design idea [13]. In our hybrid prototyping, between the game and the simulation, the materials are equal but the scopes are different. Between the simulation and the visualization of physical prototype, the scopes are equal but the materials are different. These equality and difference would work as filters and manifestations for prototyping.

5 Conclusion and Future Work

In this paper, we described our hybrid prototyping process for a digital sports system, and proposed a new style of hybrid prototyping for digital sports system. Developing a physical system, a data visualization system and a digital game concurrently is matter of cost. However, designing them as a system of systems will bring a new type of ecosystem in digital sports.

Our mobile cone system is still under development. In the future, we plan to add a mobile robot as a second defender. We also plan to reflect our results of examination on the determination of the robot's specifications and moving rules. Furthermore, we plan to develop another digital sports system in order to study the pros and cons of the hybrid prototype proposed in this paper.

References

1. Mueller, F., Khot, R.A., Chatham, A.D., Pijnappel, S., Toprak, C.C., Marshall, J.: Hci with sports. In: CHI 2013 Extended Abstracts on Human Factors in Computing Systems, pp. 2509–2512. ACM, New York (2013)
2. Graether, E., Mueller, F.: Joggobot: A flying robot as jogging companion. In: CHI 2012 Extended Abstracts on Human Factors in Computing Systems, pp. 1063–1066. ACM, New York (2012)

3. Ukai, Y., Rekimoto, J.: Swimoid: A swim support system using an underwater buddy robot. In: Proceedings of the 4th Augmented Human International Conference, AH 2013, pp. 170–177. ACM, New York (2013)
4. Higuchi, K., Ishiguro, Y., Rekimoto, J.: Flying eyes: Free-space content creation using autonomous aerial vehicles. In: CHI 2011 Extended Abstracts on Human Factors in Computing Systems, pp. 561–570. ACM, New York (2011)
5. Nakanishi, Y.: Virtual prototyping using miniature model and visualization for interactive public displays. In: Proceedings of the Designing Interactive Systems Conference, DIS 2012, pp. 458–467. ACM, New York (2012)
6. Nakanishi, Y., Sekiguchi, K., Ohmori, T., Kitahara, S., Akatsuka, D.: Hybrid prototyping by using virtual and miniature simulation for designing spatial interactive information systems. In: Lyons, K., Hightower, J., Huang, E.M. (eds.) Pervasive 2011. LNCS, vol. 6696, pp. 250–257. Springer, Heidelberg (2011)
7. Ishimura, T., Kato, T., Oda, K., Ohashi, T.: An open robot simulator environment. In: Polani, D., Browning, B., Bonarini, A., Yoshida, K. (eds.) RoboCup 2003. LNCS (LNAI), vol. 3020, pp. 621–627. Springer, Heidelberg (2004)
8. Melgar, E.R., Diez, C.C.: Arduino and Kinect Projects: Design, Build, Blow Their Minds, 1st edn. Apress, Berkely (2012)
9. Baudisch, P., Pohl, H., Reinicke, S., Wittmers, E., Lühne, P., Knaust, M., Köhler, S., Schmidt, P., Holz, C.: Imaginary reality gaming: Ball games without a ball. In: Proc. UIST 2013, pp. 405–410 (2013)
10. Oshita, M., Tomomasa, Y.: Learning motion rules for autonomous characters from control logs using support vector machine. In: International Conference on Computer Animation and Social Agents 2010 (CASA 2010) (2010)
11. Rudd, J., Stern, K., Isensee, S.: Low vs. high-fidelity prototyping debate. Interactions 3, 76–85 (1996)
12. McCurdy, M., Connors, C., Pyrzak, G., Kanefsky, B., Vera, A.: Breaking the fidelity barrier: An examination of our current characterization of prototypes and an example of a mixed-fidelity success. In: Proceedings of the SIGCHI Conference on Human Factors in Computing Systems, CHI 2006, pp. 1233–1242. ACM, New York (2006)
13. Lim, Y.K., Stolterman, E., Tenenberg, J.: The anatomy of prototypes: Prototypes as filters, prototypes as manifestations of design ideas. ACM Trans. Comput.-Hum. Interact. 15, 7:1–7:27 (2008)

Improving In-game Gesture Learning with Visual Feedback

Matthias Schwaller[1], Jan Kühni[1], Leonardo Angelini[2,1], and Denis Lalanne[1]

[1] Department of Informatics, University of Fribourg, 1700 Fribourg, Switzerland
{Matthias.Schwaller,Jan.Kuehni,Denis.Lalanne}@unifr.ch
[2] University of Applied Sciences and Arts of Western Switzerland, Fribourg
Leonardo.Angelini@hes-so.ch

Abstract. This paper presents a research work on gesture recognition and feedback to reduce the learning time of new gestures and to augment user performance in a game application. A Wiimote controlled space shooter game, GeStar Wars, has been developed. The player controls a spaceship through the buttons in the controller, while forearm gestures can be used to perform special actions. Gesture strokes are mapped in a 3x3 grid and are differentiated according to the path of the covered grid cells. In-game visual feedback displays to the user the current gesture path and which cells were covered after the gesture is performed. The novelty of this research resides in the correlated gesture recognition methodology and feedback which helps the user to learn and correct the gestures. The evaluation, conducted with 12 users, showed that the users performed significantly better if feedback was provided.

Keywords: Gestural interfaces, User evaluation, In-game Feedback, Accelerometer.

1 Introduction

Gesture interfaces became very popular for human-computer interaction. Gestures are very practical in some application scenarios, for instance, for entering a command or to mimic a human movement for an avatar. Although most of the gestures are somehow natural and intuitive to use, learning is still required in an initial phase, because metaphors and icons are not always sufficient to describe the gestures. Learning, however, is time consuming; therefore, some users may prefer an alternative interface if this phase takes too much time. This is a typical issue of gestural interfaces that we want to cope with in this research work. To this purpose, in this paper we explore the advantages of having visual feedback that helps the users to see which movements they have to do and where they did errors, in case they did. In today's systems, there is sometimes no additional feedback besides the action that was performed; indeed, when the command is not executed, often the user cannot understand why the system did not recognize the gesture.

Games are a very specific application domain for gestures. User skills have a very important role in games and the development of those skills is one of the most

M. Kurosu (Ed.): Human-Computer Interaction, Part III, HCII 2014, LNCS 8512, pp. 643–653, 2014.

important benefits that videogames can introduce. Subrahmanyam and Greenfield showed for example that videogames can increase spatial skills for both girls and boys [1]. The Nintendo Wii, thanks to the Wii Remote (or Wiimote), introduced a new dimension for the skills that can be developed by the user: through forearm gestures and body movements the user can improve skills that were completely ignored in classic video-games. However, a big challenge for game developers is that different people perform the same gesture in several different ways. In order to recognize gestures two strategies can be adopted:

1) the system is trained and adapted for each user with his own gestures,
2) the user learns how to correctly perform gestures.

In both cases additional time is required for the user. While a User Centered Design approach suggests designing simple gestures that can be easily learned by every user, gaming scenarios can benefit of more difficult gestures as part of the game challenge. Indeed, GeStar Wars, the game we present in this paper, adopts Wiimote gestures that are not very easy to perform for a novice user, although they can be learned with proper training.

In GeStar Wars, we implemented visual feedback that helps the user to show how the gestures are interpreted. Feedback is composed of two levels. The first level shows the smoothed accelerometer values in a snake-like visualization. The second level shows a 3x3 grid as soon as the user finishes a gesture. The grid permits to see what was wrong in a gesture, by showing which cells of the grid were covered by the gesture path and which cells were missed.

To evaluate the impact of gesture feedback, a user evaluation with 12 users was conducted. With the game we are able to measure the performed gestures that were successfully (with and without errors) and those that were not successfully. Further the game permits also to compare the scores.

The remainder of the paper is structured as follows: first a literature overview about gesture feedback is presented; then, the game application is explained. Furthermore, the gestures and feedback are illustrated. Finally, an evaluation with its results is presented, followed by conclusion and future work.

2 Related Work

Forearm gestures are very popular in many application domains and several accelerometer based algorithms exist for their recognition [2–5]. However, feedback for stroke-like gestures or metaphoric gestures is still a research topic that needs further investigations. Often, no information is provided on why a gesture was not recognized. This may be frustrating, especially for beginners.

A clever approach to help the user learn single-stroke gestures was introduced by Bau and Mackay with OctoPocus [6]. OctoPocus, combines feedback and feedforward in order to provide hints even while the user is performing the gesture. This system allows the user to know at any time in which direction s/he has to continue in order to fulfill the desired single-stroke gesture.

A more complex feedback approach was introduced for Gesture Play by Bragdon et al. [7]. The goal of Gesture Play is to help and motivate users to learn gestures through an awarding system. In their system both feedback and feedforward is provided. Gesture Play shows labels after the gesture performance in order to inform the user if the gesture was correct or not, and it shows a semi-transparent hand to help placing the hand in the correct position, as well as wheels and springs to illustrate how the action should be performed. In our application we are showing which case of the 3x3 grid has to be passed and in which order.

The GestureBar, introduced by Bragdon et al. [8], supports the users in learning pen-based gestures through a toolbar, a typical widget of many GUI applications. With the GestureBar users do not need any training or prior gesture experience to start using it, since it is always showing to the users which gestures can be performed and how they can be performed.

Li et al. presented in their second experiment a way to help the user to learn the gestures [9]. To get help, the user has to activate a widget that shows each command and the related pen-based gesture. This system allows learning a gesture again each time the user feels unsure about how to perform a command. In our system, feedback is showed immediately either after a not recognized gesture or whenever the user presses and quickly releases the gesture segmentation button.

An on-demand assistance for multi-touch and whole-hand gestures was also presented in ShadowGuides [10]. The authors showed that users remembered more gestures while learning with ShadowGuides than with video-based instructions. In GeStar Wars we introduced a tutorial level to learn the gestures; moreover, a video-tutorial was shown before the game.

Kela et al. [2] presented an accelerometer-based gesture recognizer for metaphoric 3D gestures. The gestures they presented were used to operate a VCR and to operate in the Smart Design Studio where they use gestures such as up, down, left, right, push and pull. To perform a gesture the user has to press a button at the beginning of the gesture and release it at the end. In GeStar Wars we adopted a similar technique for gesture segmentation, although gesture dimensions are limited to the x-z plane.

Several lightweight algorithms have been implemented in order to recognize accelerometer based gestures. Those algorithms require generally no or a very little training set, thus speeding up development and user adoption. A gesture recognizer for accelerometer sensors that can be quickly implemented in prototyping scenarios is presented by Kratz and Rohs [3]. Another accelerometer based gesture recognizer implemented for the Wiimote is presented by Liu et al. [4]. They also segment gestures by pressing the A-button on the Wiimote while the gesture is performed. The same segmentation technique was adopted also by Schlömer et al. [11]. To facilitate the learning phase, they introduced drawings of the gestures and demonstrated the execution of the first gesture. Another Wiimote gesture recognizer based on A-button segmented gestures was presented by Wu et al. [12]. Their system recognizes direction gestures, shape gestures and one-stroke alphabet letters. Their gesture shapes are similar to GeStar Wars one-stroke gestures.

While GeStar Wars segmentation and recognition techniques are similar to previous systems, our recognition algorithm is meant to facilitate the user understanding of the system and learning phase. Indeed, provided feedback reflects the behavior of the system and stimulate the user to increase his or her gestural skills.

3 Game Application

GeStar Wars is a space shooter game that we developed in order to assess the benefit of feedback for in-game gestures. A screenshot of the game can be seen in Fig. 1. The game was implemented using the Ogre3D[1] graphics rendering engine under Ubuntu Linux[2]. In the game, the player controls a space-ship in the 2D sky. In order to navigate the ship s/he can use the arrow buttons of the Wiimote. The player can see the obtained scores on the bottom right of the screen. To perform a normal shot the player can use the B button of the Wiimote. Furthermore, we implemented three special features that can be activated only via gestures: a shield, which protects the space-ship for 8 seconds, and two more powerful special weapons (spread shot and flame shot).

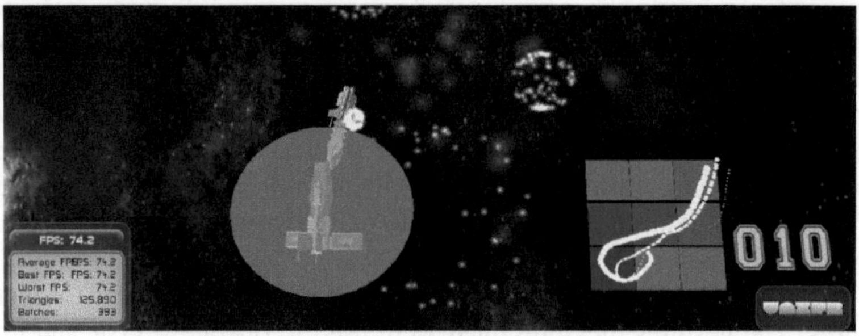

Fig. 1. Game with gesture feedback

The player has unlimited normal or special shots and can therefore perform the gestures as often as s/he wishes. The game allows for level customization in terms of duration and enemy space-ships. We implemented for our evaluation two different levels. The first level is a tutorial level, which is explained below (section 3.1), and the second one is a game level. For the game level we use 3 different types of enemies, each with different levels of difficulty. The game counts the points of the player. Indeed, the player gets points by destroying enemies and loses points when an enemy is shooting on the player's spaceship.

3.1 Tutorial Level

The tutorial level is a special level with no enemies which has the goal to help the player learning the gestures. At the beginning of the level the first gesture is illustrated (see **Error! Reference source not found.**) and the player can now test the first gesture. During this phase, the two other gestures are disabled. Afterwards, the

1 http://www.ogre3d.org

2 http://www.ubuntu.com

player can train and test the two other gestures. In the tutorial level, the player has 30 seconds to train each gesture several times.

4 Gestures

This section describes the gestures designed during the research project and those used during the evaluation. The gestures are defined through a path in the 3x3 grid and through its direction (starting and ending cells). The path is obtained by the instant vector of the filtered Wiimote x-z accelerometers. The sampling rate is 100 Hz. Gestures are segmented by the user with the A button. However, the maximum length of a gesture is 2 seconds and the first part of the gesture is truncated if it exceeds this length. The difficulty of a gesture is affected by its length, the amount of direction changes and the shape (a circle like Fig. 2. Table 1. Fig. 3g is easier to perform than a spiral like Fig. 2. Table 1. Fig. 3b). During the project we created 10 basic gestures (see Fig. 2. Table 1. Fig. 3). Since the path orientation is preserved, new gestures can be defined by simply rotating or mirroring the path of another gesture.

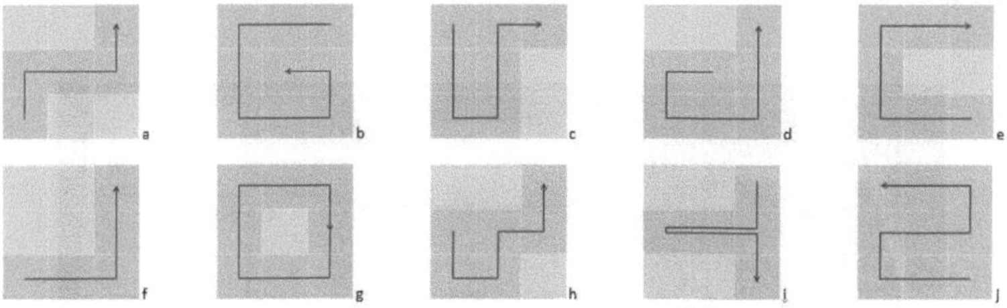

Fig. 2. Table 1. Fig. 3. Designed gestures

The gestures can be configured in GeStar Wars for special actions. As described above, in the game there are three special actions: the protection shield and two special shots (spread shot and flame shot).

For the evaluation we have chosen three of the above gestures; these three gestures are depicted with their respective actions in **Error! Reference source not found.**. We have chosen rather simple gestures in order to facilitate the learning of the gestures during the tutorial level in GeStar Wars.

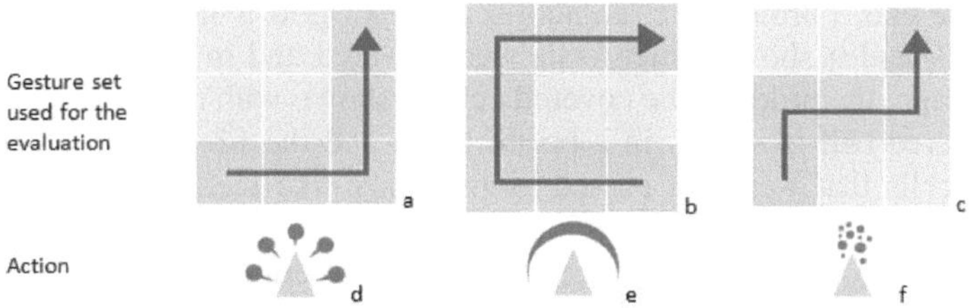

Fig. 4. The used gesture set for the evaluation *a* to *c*; the 3 gestures are illustrated from *d* to *f*

The first gesture is a horizontally mirrored "L". It permits to use the special spread shot. The second gesture is a "C" from the bottom to the top and permits to activate the shield. The third gesture is a 90° clockwise rotated "Z" and permits to activate the special flame shot.

4.1 Gesture Feedback

To support the user gesture learning, a particular multi-level gesture feedback strategy has been implemented. When the user performs a gesture which was not recognized or when the user press the A button on the Wiimote and suddenly releases it, all the possible gestures are illustrated in the top right corner. The illustrations of the gestures depict the directed path through the grid with a red arrow and highlight in green which cells of the grid has to be covered. Below the gesture illustration there is an illustration of the action that is associated to the gesture. **Error! Reference source not found.** shows the illustrations for the *a-d, b-e* and *c-f* gesture-action pairs, i.e., the three special actions of GeStar Wars. If a gesture was recognized with only one error, only the gesture illustration of that gesture is shown in the top right corner. In the tutorial level the gesture illustration that is currently learned is shown with a bigger size on the left bottom side.

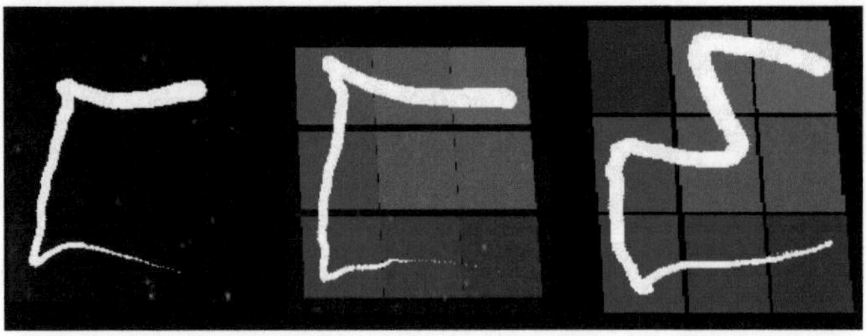

Fig. 5. Bottom right corner feedback: on the left side the gesture before its completion (A button release), in the middle the correct gesture and on the right side a gesture with an error

While the user performs a gesture, i.e., while the A button of the Wiimote is pressed, a white snake-like feedback is shown (see Fig. 4 left). This snake-like feedback represents the smoothed accelerometer values and depicts the path and direction of the ongoing gesture. Indeed, the snake-like feedback is smaller at the start and thicker at the end. Furthermore, an auto-scaled 3x3 grid is mapped under the snake-like feedback and it shows which cells were covered and in which order. Similar to the snake shape, the order of the covered cells is shown with different levels of green: the last covered cell is shown in a bright green and the first covered cell in a dark green. The cells that were not passed by the snake-like feedback are shown in gray (see Fig. 4).

In order to help users learning the gestures, our system is able to detect if there was only one cell missing by the snake-like feedback. In this particular case, the missed cell is highlighted in red in the bottom right corner feedback, in order to provide a suggestion to the user on how to correct his or her movement (see right side in Fig. 4).

To be able to give understandable feedback, the cells should be visited only once, although the gesture recognizer would allow using a cell several times in a gesture.

Furthermore, when a gesture is recognized, the Wiimote starts vibrating to give an additional non visual feedback.

5 Gesture Recognizer

The gesture recognizer was implemented in order to obtain a one-to-one mapping with feedback. This helps to give more accurate instant feedback and allows the user to understand how the system interprets his or her gestures. This gesture recognizer does not need machine learning; thus, it does not need system training and it can be quickly implemented. Due to its simplicity, this gesture recognizer is quite useful for prototypes.

The gesture recognizer exploits the Wiimote x-z accelerometer values. To facilitate the gesture segmentation, the user has to press the A button of the Wiimote while performing the gestures. In consequence, the gestures are stroke-like gestures.

While the user presses the button, the filtered values of the Wiimote are saved every 10 ms into a circular buffer. There is a predefined maximum gesture length. If this gesture length gets achieved, the system starts overwriting the oldest values. After the gesture performance, the system maps the auto-scaled 3x3 grid under the performed gesture. Because the Wiimote does not transmit a path but a series of points, a linear interpolation is performed in order to carefully check which rectangles are covered by the path. The grid auto-scaling allows the users to perform gestures as big or as small as they wish. To recognize a gesture, the algorithm compares the covered cells to the gestures in our gesture vocabulary. To accept a gesture, also the order on which the cells were covered must match. The algorithm allows having at the same time a gesture that can be contained in another gesture, for instance, a circle gesture and a double circle gesture.

With this system we are able to show to the user which cell, i.e., which part of a gesture, is not correct. This technique is helpful for learning the gestures and enables the possibility to show the error to the user and to mark with red the wrong cell in the grid (see Fig. 4). However, the designer should avoid having at the same time gestures with paths that differ by just one cell. Moreover, the current implementation is limited to two-dimensional gestures in order to map them in the 3x3 grid. An extension to three-dimensional gesture is possible but their representation in a three-dimensional cube would not be intuitive for the user.

6 Evaluation and Results

The purpose of these evaluations is to analyze if GeStar Wars gesture feedback influences the gesture learning and gesture performance of the user. We tested GeStar Wars with 12 users aged 22 – 54, 3 females and 9 males. We conducted a within subject user evaluation where all the users tested both conditions, without feedback and with feedback. In order to prevent the learning effect and the fatigue, half of the users started with feedback (group A) and half of the users started without feedback (group B).

Fig. 6. Evaluation setup: user playing game level

For the user evaluation we used both the tutorial level and the game level. The evaluation started with the tutorial level, in particular with the spread gesture, followed by the shield and finally by the flame gesture. For each gesture the user has 30 seconds to practice. Before the tutorial, we gave to the participants some explications and we showed a video-tutorial that illustrates the tutorial session. The users did not have any experience with the game or the gestures before starting the tutorial. After the two tutorial sessions, we asked the volunteers to play twice a game level. We counterbalanced also here feedback presence (with and without). After each tutorial, we gave a slightly modified version of the questionnaire in the appendix C of the ISO 9241 part 9 for non-keyboard input devices. Since we were interested in how the user learned we did not analyzed the gesture accuracy during game level sessions. In fact, the game level requires more coordination to move the ship and perform the gestures at the same time, therefore, high variation could occur between skilled users and less practiced players. Nevertheless, the in-game evaluation has been useful as observation study.

We conducted a t-test to compare the recognized gestures for all the users (group A+B), with and without feedback. There was a significant positive effect of feedback on the percentage of recognized gestures: $t(11) = 4.15$, $p = .0016$. Significant difference was also found for the not recognized gestures (without the gestures containing one error): $t(11) = -5.58$, $p = .00017$. No significant difference was found between the gestures containing one error.

By comparing the total gestures and gesture attempts for each condition, we found that there was a significant effect of feedback on the gesture attempts: $t(11) = -4.38$, $p = .0011$. The average gesture attempts while using feedback in the tutorial level of 30 seconds was 25.4 attempts and while using no feedback it was 32 attempts. Thus, when no feedback was provided, users performed more gestures than with feedback; meanwhile, fewer gestures were recognized.

Table 2. The results of the user evaluation. Group A: user 1 to 6. Group B: user 7 to 12.

	With feedback			Without feedback		
User	Recognized	With 1 error	Not recognized	Recognized	With 1 error	Not recognized
1	16.0%	4.0%	80.0%	6.9%	0.0%	93.1%
2	16.7%	20.0%	63.3%	4.9%	7.3%	87.8%
3	20.0%	0.0%	80.0%	0.0%	3.2%	96.8%
4	35.3%	23.5%	41.2%	30.4%	26.1%	43.5%
5	22.2%	11.1%	66.7%	9.1%	6.1%	84.8%
6	30.0%	20.0%	50.0%	26.1%	21.7%	52.2%
7	50.0%	7.1%	42.9%	23.1%	12.8%	64.1%
8	33.3%	22.2%	44.4%	36.0%	8.0%	56.0%
9	10.5%	10.5%	78.9%	2.6%	2.6%	94.7%
10	48.0%	8.0%	44.0%	2.8%	8.3%	88.9%
11	37.5%	12.5%	50.0%	15.8%	10.5%	73.7%
12	36.1%	22.2%	41.7%	13.0%	19.6%	67.4%
Avg	29.6%	13.4%	56.9%	14.2%	10.5%	75.2%
SD	12.7pp	8.0pp	15.9pp	12.0pp	8.1pp	18.3pp

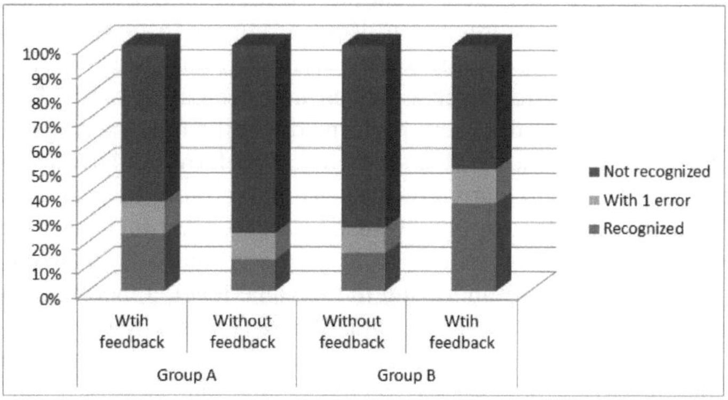

Fig. 7. Diagram showing gesture recognition rates

For both groups we found significant difference between the two conditions: with and without feedback. Comparing the two groups, we discovered that the group A was performing worse when using no feedback, even if they were already trained (first and second bar in **Error! Reference source not found.**). We suppose that this is due to the short learning time; thus, the users do not know the gestures well enough after one tutorial in order to perform them without feedback. The group B was then performing a lot better when they used feedback (third and fourth bar in **Error! Reference source not found.**). Therefore, in both cases feedback was increasing the user accuracy while learning the gestures.

In a questionnaire given at the end of the experience, all of the twelve users preferred to have feedback for the tutorial level. However, for the game level only 8 users preferred to have feedback. The 4 users that preferred no feedback during the game level explained that they had no time to look at feedback while playing the game.

Concerning the ISO 9241 part 9 questionnaire at the end of each tutorial, we found no statistical significance in terms of cognitive load. The only significant difference (Wilcoxon signed-rank test) was found for the arm fatigue. The tutorial with no feedback was found more tiring. This can be due to the fact that the user tried to make more gestures while having no feedback.

7 Conclusion and Future Work

GeStar Wars, a space shooter game with stroke-like gestures performed with a Wiimote, was presented in this article. The novelty of this game is the proposed feedback, which is directly linked to the gesture recognizer. Feedback is composed of a snake-like stroke, which represents the smoothed accelerometer values of the gesture, and an auto-scaled 3x3 grid, on which the gesture is mapped. A gesture is therefore defined by the cells of the grid and their covering order. The gesture recognizer uses the accelerometer values and therefore is not based on direct pointing.

By analyzing the results of the evaluation, we found significant difference on the percentage of recognized gestures when using or not feedback. In general the users performed better when using feedback. We were also able to show that the performance is increasing when feedback is added and decreasing when feedback is removed. We found also that the users performed significantly more gesture attempts without feedback. Besides the results, all the users preferred to have feedback for the tutorial level. The user has to learn how the system interprets the gestures and, for this purpose, feedback is helpful. In our evaluation we noticed that the training session (the two tutorials) is not long enough to learn the gestures. Even if the users were quite better at the end of the training and in the game level, a more trained person, as the authors, for instance, have still a much higher acceptance rate of the gestures. We suggest therefore training a gesture much longer. Some of the users had problems performing the gestures when several enemies came and they were under “stress”. Once the gestures are learned, feedback may distract the user from the enemies in the game. We remarked this also in the evaluation, since, after the two tutorial sessions, we let the user play the game level with the enemies. Some of the users looked more at the gesture feedback than at the rest of the game. Nevertheless, the implemented feedback works well for the tutorial level where the user has more time to look at feedback. In fact, if the user has to look at the enemies s/he has not much time to look at feedback in detail.

For future work it would be interesting to create a mixed mode in order to support the user with feedback when s/he did the gestures wrong for two consecutive times and remove feedback when s/he starts doing the gestures correctly. Moreover, it would be interesting to create other visual feedbacks to help the users learning the gestures. We could imagine to illustrate an animation of the Wiimote showing the gesture, in the case where the user did an error. It would also be interesting to extend feedback by other modalities, such as sound and/or improving the vibration feedback of the Wiimote.

References

1. Subrahmanyam, K., Greenfield, P.M.: Effect of video game practice on spatial skills in girls and boys. J. Appl. Dev. Psychol. 15, 13–32 (1994)
2. Kela, J., Korpipää, P., Mäntyjärvi, J., Kallio, S., Savino, G., Jozzo, L., Marca, S.: Di: Accelerometer-based gesture control for a design environment. Pers. Ubiquitous Comput. 10, 285–299 (2005)
3. Kratz, S., Rohs, M.: A $3 gesture recognizer. In: Proceedings of the 15th International Conference on Intelligent User Interfaces, IUI 2010, p. 341. ACM Press, New York (2010)
4. Liu, J., Zhong, L., Wickramasuriya, J., Vasudevan, V.: uWave: Accelerometer-based personalized gesture recognition and its applications. Pervasive Mob. Comput. 5, 657–675 (2009)
5. Rehm, M., Bee, N., André, E.: Wave Like an Egyptian — Accelerometer Based Gesture Recognition for Culture Specific Interactions
6. Bau, O., Mackay, W.E.: OctoPocus: A Dynamic Guide for Learning Gesture-Based Command Sets. In: Proceedings of the 21st Annual ACM Symposium on User Interface Software and Technology, UIST 2008, p. 37. ACM Press, New York (2008)
7. Bragdon, A., Uguray, A., Wigdor, D., Anagnostopoulos, S., Zeleznik, R., Feman, R.: Gesture play. In: ACM International Conference on Interactive Tabletops and Surfaces, ITS 2010, p. 39. ACM Press, New York (2010)
8. Bragdon, A., Zeleznik, R., Williamson, B., Miller, T., LaViola, J.J.: GestureBar. In: Proceedings of the 27th International Conference on Human Factors in Computing Systems, CHI 2009, p. 2269. ACM Press, New York (2009)
9. Li, P., Bouillon, M., Anquetil, E., Richard, G.: User and System Cross-Learning of Gesture Commands on Pen-Based Devices. In: Kotzé, P., Marsden, G., Lindgaard, G., Wesson, J., Winckler, M. (eds.) INTERACT 2013, Part II. LNCS, vol. 8118, pp. 337–355. Springer, Heidelberg (2013)
10. Freeman, D., Benko, H., Morris, M.R., Wigdor, D.: ShadowGuides: Visualizations for In-Situ Learning of Multi-Touch and Whole-Hand Gestures. In: Proceedings of the ACM International Conference on Interactive Tabletops and Surfaces, ITS 2009, p. 165. ACM Press, New York (2009)
11. Schlömer, T., Poppinga, B., Henze, N., Boll, S.: Gesture recognition with a Wii controller. In: Proceedings of the 2nd International Conference on Tangible and Embedded Interaction, TEI 2008, p. 11. ACM Press, New York (2008)
12. Wu, J., Pan, G., Zhang, D., Qi, G., Li, S.: Gesture Recognition with a 3-D Accelerometer, pp. 25–38 (2009)

Haptic User Interface Integration for 3D Game Engines

Gokhan Sengul[1], Nergiz Ercil Çağıltay[2], Erol Özçelik[1],
Emre Tuner[2], and Batuhan Erol[1]

[1] Atilim University Computer Engineering Department, Kızılcaşar Mahallesi,
06836 İncek Gölbaşı - Ankara – Turkey

[2] Atilim University Software Engineering Department, Kızılcaşar Mahallesi,
06836 İncek Gölbaşı - Ankara – Turkey

gsengul@atilim.edu.tr

Abstract. Touch and feel senses of human beings provide important information about the environment. When those senses are integrated with the eyesight, we may get all the necessary information about the environment. In terms of human-computer-interaction, the eyesight information is provided by visual displays. On the other hand, touch and feel senses are provided by means of special devices called "haptic" devices. Haptic devices are used in many fields such as computer-aided design, distance-surgery operations, medical simulation environments, training simulators for both military and medical applications, etc. Besides the touch and sense feelings haptic devices also provide force-feedbacks, which allows designing a realistic environment in virtual reality applications.

Haptic devices can be categorized into three classes: tactile devices, kinesthetic devices and hybrid devices. Tactile devices simulate skin to create contact sensations. Kinesthetic devices apply forces to guide or inhibit body movement, and hybrid devices attempt to combine tactile and kinesthetic feedback. Among these kinesthetic devices exerts controlled forces on the human body, and it is the most suitable type for the applications such as surgical simulations.

The education environments that require skill-based improvements, the touch and feel senses are very important. In some cases providing such educational environment is very expensive, risky and may also consist of some ethical issues. For example, surgical education is one of these fields. The traditional education is provided in operating room on real patients. This type of education is very expensive, requires long time periods, and does not allow any error-and-try type of experiences. It is stressfully for both the educators and the learners. Additionally there are several ethical considerations. Simulation environments supported by such haptic user interfaces provide an alternative and safer educational alternative. There are several studies showing some evidences of educational benefits of this type of education (Tsuda et al 2009; Sutherland et al 2006). Similarly, this technology can also be successfully integrated to the physical rehabilitation process of some diseases requiring motor skill improvements (Kampiopiotis & Theodorakou, 2003).

Hence, today simulation environments are providing several opportunities for creating low cost and more effective training and educational environment. Today, combining three dimensional (3D) simulation environments with these

M. Kurosu (Ed.): Human-Computer Interaction, Part III, HCII 2014, LNCS 8512, pp. 654–662, 2014.

haptic interfaces is an important feature for advancing current human-computer interaction. On the other hand haptic devices do not provide a full simulation environment for the interaction and it is necessary to enhance the environment by software environments. Game engines provide high flexibility to create 3-D simulation environments. Unity3D is one of the tools that provides a game engine and physics engine for creating better 3D simulation environments. In the literature there are many studies combining these two technologies to create several educational and training environments. However, in the literature, there are not many researches showing how these two technologies can be integrated to create simulation environment by providing haptic interfaces as well. There are several issues that need to be handled for creating such integration. First of all the haptic devices control libraries need to be integrated to the game engine. Second, the game engine simulation representations and real-time interaction features need to be coordinately represented by the haptic device degree of freedom and force-feedback speed and features.

In this study, the integration architecture of Unity 3D game engine and the PHANToM Haptic device for creating a surgical education simulation environment is provided. The methods used for building this integration and handling the synchronization problems are also described. The algorithms developed for creating a better synchronization and user feedback such as providing a smooth feeling and force feedback for the haptic interaction are also provided. We believe that, this study will be helpful for the people who are creating simulation environment by using Unity3D technology and PHANToM haptic interfaces.

Keywords: Surgical simulation, haptic devices, game engines, interaction.

1 Introduction

Touch and feel senses of human beings provide important information about the environment. When those senses are integrated with the eyesight, we may get all the necessary information about the environment. In terms of human-computer-interaction, the eyesight information is provided by visual displays. On the other hand, touch and feel senses are provided by means of special devices called "haptic" devices. Haptic devices are used in many fields such as computer-aided design, distance-surgery operations, medical simulation environments, training simulators for both military and medical applications, etc. Besides the touch and sense feelings haptic devices also provide force-feedbacks, which allows designing a realistic environments in virtual reality applications.

Haptic devices can be categorized into three classes: tactile devices, kinesthetic devices and hybrid devices. Tactile devices simulate skin to create contact sensations. Kinesthetic devices apply forces to guide or inhibit body movement, and hybrid devices attempt to combine tactile and kinesthetic feedback. Among these kinesthetic devices exerts controlled forces on the human body, and it is the most suitable type for the applications such as surgical simulations.

According to Robles-De-La-Torre (2006), somesthetic information is critically important for fast, accurate interaction with our environment and without adequate somesthetic feedback, achieving normal and top performance in tasks that require high levels of dexterity is extremely difficult, if not impossible [1]. Today to improve learning and skill development in several fields virtual reality and environments created in computerized environment are providing several benefits. The virtual reality environments today are being developed for education, training, entertaining, planning and future estimations as well as decision making processes. The current virtual reality based technologies are mostly designed based on the visual and auditory senses of human being. This way the user can better understand the virtual environment and get interactions with the objects designed in this computerized environment. On the other hand touch senses are another important feature of human beings for getting information from their environment. Accordingly force-feedback based haptic systems are being developed to provide touch sense for the users and researchers. It is believed that these haptic systems will greatly increase the effectiveness of simulating real-world situations [2]. Several different designs of these force-feedback haptic systems are being implemented for rehabilitation, educational and training purposes in several different areas [2]. Most common ones are surgical simulations and medical training [3-4], military applications, museum displays [5], painting, sculpting, and CAD [6], visualization [7].

Usually these haptic devices could also be customized according to the requirements of the field that the haptic interface is being provided. An example of the haptic usage in the field of surgical training environment is given in Figure 1.

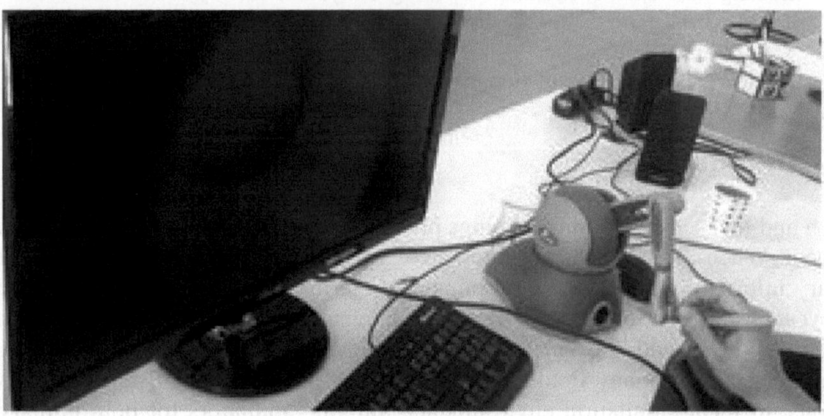

Fig. 1. Haptic Usage for Sugical Simulations

Hence several different designs of these devices with different price and performance ranges are being available. The game engines are one of the environments in which the integration of these haptic devices could provide easy development of software tools for different purposes. However, currently the haptic interfaces are mostly integrated with low-level programming environments and libraries. There are not many examples of integration models for these haptic devices with the game engines.

2 Game Engines and Their Use in Surgical Training Simulations

Creating a virtual surgical training environment requires high man-power and cost since all the parts of the environment requires individually invented and created for every time and for every application. This is the most important problem that has to be solved. All the surgical training environments need at least graphical output, capable of displaying 3D model of the human organs/tissues that needs to be visualized. Besides those, organ/tissue models need to be within a high level of realism, and they need to be able to be controlled easily with the input devices. Besides the simulation environment has to allow the physical simulations such as blood flow etc. The games engines provide high level of solutions to the aforementioned problems, and they allow us to easily generate surgical simulation environments.

A game engine is defined as a system that is used to create and develop video games. The game engines provide a software framework that allows a means to the creators to integrate the software and hardware of a system. The developed games can be run on video game consoles, desktop computers, notebooks and mobile devices.

A game engine consists of functional blocks such as 3D graphics, a physics engine or collision detection (and collision response), event handling, memory management, sound control, scripting, animation, networking, and a scene graph.

The features and details of the functional blocks of a game engine can be found elsewhere and the details are not given here. But among the functional blocks the physics engine has an important position for the surgical training simulations and it is needed to mention about it by a few words.

Distinct from a video game, a surgical training environment requires realistic behavior of the objects in the environment. The physics engine of the game engine implements mathematical models for rigid body simulations of the organs/tissues. Besides by using the physics engine simulation of soft bodies, cloths, fluids such as blood, and smoke caused by the burning of the vessels can be easily provided. So in order to effectively use the game engines in surgical simulations, it is necessary to choose a game engine that has a powerful physics engine that allows the simulations of the aforementioned requirements of the surgical training environment.

Because of the aforementioned reasons and their user friendly options, easy prototyping features, high integrity feature with the other programs, capability of programming with high-level programming languages and their visualization features we decided to use game engines in surgical training simulation environment.

There are a number of game engines available today. Some of them are free, but most of them are commercial products. In order to decide the game engine to use, we evaluated the game engines with the following criteria:

- Soft body simulation support
- Performance in real-time applications
- Visualization capacity
- Integration opportunity with the haptic devices
- License and cost
- Application capability in medical simulations

Since it is a simple and powerful game engine with high performance capability in real-time applications we preferred to use the Unity3D (www.unity3d.com). Unity3D has powerful support and it is used by many users around the world. Besides it provides programming capability by Java Script and C#, and it has high visualization capability. In Figure 2 sample visualization for integration of two haptic devices and Unity3D is given.

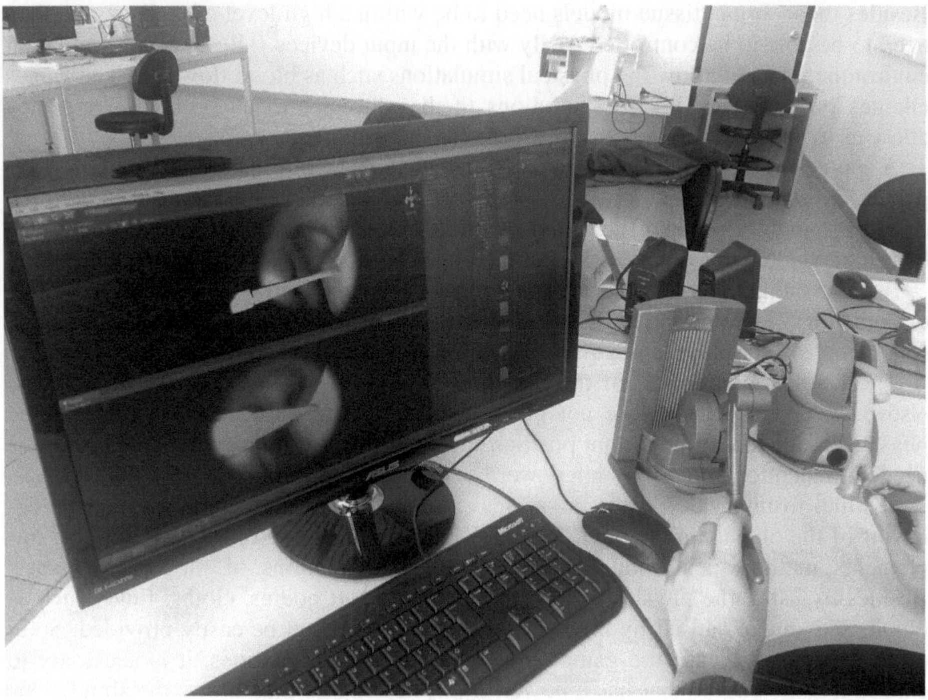

Fig. 2. Sample visualization for integration of two haptic devices and Unity3D

In the following sections we will explain the integration of Unity3D game engine and PHANToM Haptic device for creating a surgical education simulation environment. Also we will give the key points about the integration of haptic device and game engine.

3 Integration of Haptic Devices with Unity3D Game Engine

PHANToM Haptic devices provide a SDK called OpenHaptics library to users to allow easy use of the devices. OpenHaptics library provides two main APIs to programmers, Haptic Device API (HDAPI) and Haptic Library API (HLAPI). Both API can be used with C and C++. HDAPI is a low-level API that allows programmers to control device directly and it does not provide any easy haptic rendering mechanisms. So the programmer has to code the haptic rendering by calculating the force output manually. HLAPI is a high-level API which leverages OpenGL API for graphics rendering. HLAPI provides automatic haptic rendering for OpenGL geometric primitives. Since OpenGL and Unity3D integration is hard, HDAPI is preferred

HDAPI consists of two main components: the device and the scheduler. The device is the basically which haptic device(s) that is planned to use. The scheduler is basically a controller which runs on a different thread, queues and executes the functions that is added to the scheduler list. The general framework that we used for the integration of Unity3D and PHANToM haptic devices is given in figure 3. The details of the each item of the framework are given in the next paragraphs.

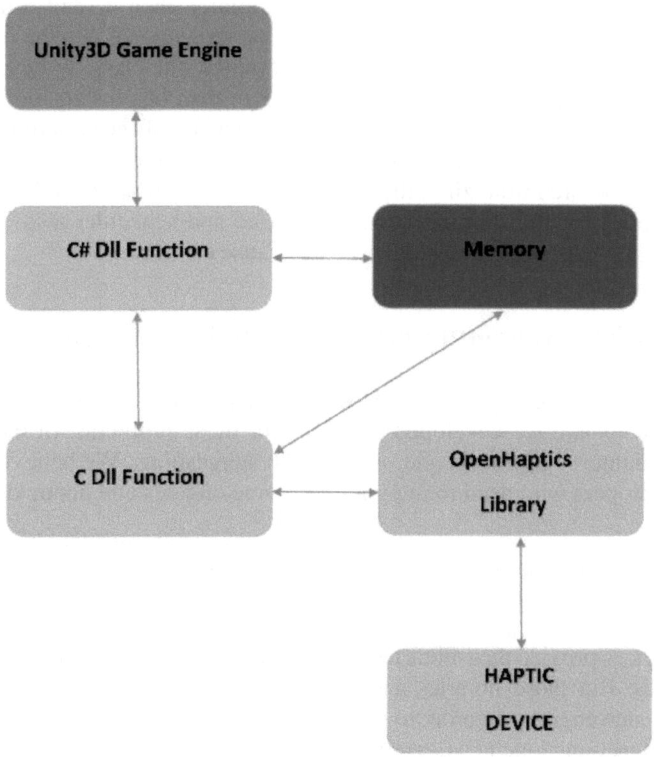

Fig. 3. The general framework for the integration of Unity3D and PAHNToM haptic devices

Since Unity3D uses C# and JavaScript for game scripts, we developed a dll in C which uses HDAPI and import the functions. We preferred to code a dll in C for HDAPI because it is easier to control the device in C than in C#. The requirements for the dll were; the position of the device, the angles of the stylus, the status of the each button on the device, and other functions to control the device and the scheduler. This dll has a structure which contains the necessary information about the device; its position, angles and the status of the buttons. It also has the functions to initialize and disable device, get the current data of the device, apply force, and scheduler functions.

After the development of the dll is completed, we tested it with another C program to see if the data from device is correct and it can apply the force correctly. After the test, we wanted to try it on Unity3D. We have created a C# script in Unity3D and imported my dll functions to that script and we were able to move the objects in game with the haptic device and apply some arbitrary forces to device. But since there will be more than one game, we developed an interface which uses dll and provides easy functions to Unity3D developer.

For this interface we followed the same structure that we did for the dll in C#. Then we created two instances of this structure in C#: one for current data and one for the previous data of the device. Then a function is coded that allocates a memory location as the size of DeviceData structure and assigns the current data instance to that memory location and marshals the structure as pointer, then it sends this pointer to one of the functions on dll. That dll function fills the structure. When the operations about the structure are done, we move forward to complete the class. We used singleton pattern for the class, because there will not be more than one instance of one haptic device. We have also hidden the initialization and starting of the structure from the Unity3D developer, because they need to be done in a specific order. For example, if scheduler is started before initializing, the device scheduler will not be able to find the device. Same applies for the shutting down the device and scheduler also. If the device is closed before stopping the scheduler, it will cause errors.

4 The Problems Encountered during the Integration

During the integration of Unity3D and PHANToM haptic devices, we have encountered many problems and we developed solutions for those problems. In this section we listed the encountered problems and our solution suggestions. We believe that this will help the developers who need to integrate the game engines and haptic devices.

4.1 The Methods Given in the Haptic Library Cannot Be Directly Used in Unity3D Game Engine

All the haptic devices provide their libraries that can be used by the users to be easily use the haptic devices. But those libraries and their methods/functions cannot be directly accessed by the game engines. In order to provide a solution to this problem, we develop two different dll functions (one is written in C and the other is written in C#) as given in the figure 3. Those dll functions include all the library functions of the haptic device. Besides those dlls have C++ library functions as well. By this way a programming environment is develop to integrate the haptic device and game engine. The functions written in C# access this dll functions first, then by using the library functions in this dlls the program is able to access the both the haptic device and game engine.

4.2 Two Haptic Devices Cannot Be Controlled and Used by the Game Engine at the Same Time

In some simulations and training environments it is necessary to use two haptic devices at the same time. Haptic device library (OpenHaptics) provides necessary integration options. Unfortunately it is not possible to connect the two haptic devices at the same with the Unity3D. In order to solve this problem we created a class in C# library and then every object defined in the class is directed to a haptic device. By this way controlling of two haptic devices is provided by the Unity3D.

4.3 Vibration Problem of the Haptic Device in Integration

There was a vibration problem of the device when it is controlled by the game engine. It is found that this was due to two reasons: the differences between the force vectors and low transfer rate of the data to the haptic. In order to solve this problem, we rescaled the force vectors and we limited the magnitude difference of the force vectors and we increased the transfer rate of the data.

4.4 Exceeding the Movement Range of the Haptic Device in Simulation Model

It is necessary to define the movement range of the haptic device in the simulations. If it is not defined, the haptic device movement commands may cause the simulation environment to move further then the available space. In order to solve this problem, we developed an interface to stop the movements when the movement range is exceeded and it also allows users to restart the simulation when the movement range is exceeded.

4.5 Unable to Measure the Force Feedbacks of the Objects That Is Moved by the Force

Unity's current surface force methods cannot allow us to measure the force feedbacks. We extended these methods to be able to measure the force feedbacks.

5 Discussion and Conclusion

The education environments that require skill-based improvements, the touch and feel senses are very important. In some cases providing such educational environment is very expensive, risky and may also consist of some ethical issues. One example to this kind of educational environments is the surgical training education. The traditional education in surgical training is realized in operating rooms on real patients, which is very risky for patients and expensive. The current trend in this education is the usage of simulators which include haptic devices. Simulator based surgical education provides safer environments education [8-10].

But on the other hand, an efficient surgical simulator design requires realistic modeling of human organs/tissues, high level of visualization capabilities and real time interaction with the haptic devices. Those are the major drawbacks of the simulators that make the design and development of the simulator difficult and it requires too much man-power and time. But efficient game engines help the developer to appropriately and easily design and develop simulators. In this study we proposed a framework to integrate the haptic devices and games engines.

We used PHANToM Haptic device and Unity3D as the game engine. We presented the game engine selection criteria as follows: real-time performance of the game engine, soft body simulation capability, flow control capability and capability of the physics engine of the game engine. We suggest that Unity3D is one of the best alternatives that can be integrated with haptic devices to be used in surgical simulator interfaces.

Besides in this study we also proposed a framework to integrate PHANToM Haptic device and Unity3D game engine. We outlined the problems encountered and we suggested our solution approaches. We believe that this work will help the developers of the simulators who need to integrate the haptic devices with the Unity3D game engine.

Acknowledgement. This study is conducted for improving the scenario designs of the educational materials which are developed for neurosurgery education project (ECE: Tubitak 1001, Project No: 112K287) purposes. The authors would like to thank the support of TÜBİTAK 1001 program for realizing the ECE project.

References

1. Robles-De-La-Torre, G.: The importance of the sense of touch in virtual and real environments. IEEE Multimedia 13(3), 24–30 (2006)
2. Bar-Cohen, Y.: Haptic devices for virtual reality, telepresence, and human-assistive robotics. Biologically Inspired Intelligent Robots 73 (2003)
3. D'Aulignac, D., Balaniuk, R.: Providing reliable virtual, echographic exam of the human thigh. In: Salisbury, J.K., Srinivasan, M.A. (eds.) Proceedings of the Fourth PHANToM User's Group Workshop. AI Lab Technical Report No. 1675 and RLE Technical Report No. 633. MIT, Cambridge (1999)
4. Mor, A.B.: 5 DOF force feedback using the 3 DOF PHANToM and a 2 DOF device. In: Proceedings of the Third PHANToM Users Group, PUG98. AI Technical Report no. 1643 and RLE Technical Report no. 624. MIT, Cambridge (1998)
5. Shulman, S.: Digital antiquities. Computer Graphics World 21(11), 34–38 (1998)
6. Dillon, P., Moody, W., Bartlett, R., Scully, P., Morgan, R., James, C.: Sensing the fabric. Paper presented at the Workshop on Haptic Human-Computer Interaction, Glasgow (2000)
7. Durbeck, L.J.K., Macias, N.J., Weinstein, M., Johnson, C.R., Hollerbach, J.M.: SCIRun haptic display for scientific visualization. In: Salisbury, J.K., Srinivasan, M.A. (eds.) Proceedings of the Third PHANToM Users Group, PUG98. AI Technical Report no. 1643 and RLE Technical Report no. 624. MIT, Cambridge (1998)
8. Tsuda, S., Scott, D., Doyle, J., Jones, D.: Surgical Skills Training and Simulation. Curr. Probl. Surg. 2009 46, 271–370 (2009)
9. Sutherland, L.M., Middleton, P.F., Anthony, A., Hamdorf, J., Cregan, P., Scott, D., Maddern, G.J.: Surgical Simulation: A Systematic Review. Ann. Surg. 243(3), 291–300 (2006)
10. Kampiopiotis, A., Theodorakou, K.: Virtual Reality in the Teaching of Motor Skills: Literature Review. Pakistan Journal of Applied Sciences 3(1), 36–39 (2003)

Business, Sustainability and Technology Adoption

Situating a Design Space for Sustainable Software Appropriation

Arman Arakelyan and David Lamas

Interaction Design Laboratory, Institute of Informatics, Tallinn University
Tallinn, Estonia
{arman.arakelyan,david.lamas}@tlu.ee

Abstract. This paper describes work in progress aimed at considering temporal aspects of the appropriation process for prolonging the use of software artifacts with enabling design choices. A model of appropriation from the Information Systems domain is applied to understand the stages of appropriation as a process. The model is complemented by proposing a design space for introducing appropriation-enabling options at each stage towards prolonged use of software solutions.

Keywords: Software Sustainability, Sustainable Software Appropriation.

1 Introduction

Research in HCI abounds in studies aiming to understand and reflect on system usage with recent stress by some authors on the temporal aspects of usage [7], [8]. Temporal aspects of usage are interesting from the perspective of design for sustainability, since the understanding of usage through time can potentially allow designers to create artifacts that are more sustainable, where "sustainable" means "designed for prolonged use". In our case, we focus on how prolonged use of software could be related to the different stages of appropriation through a model proposed in the information systems domain.

2 Related Work

Software evolution and software sustainability are research domains in software engineering. Our definition of software sustainability was formulated in software engineering by Weiss et al., as "economically sustainable software systems that cost-effectively evolve in response to changes in their environment, their usage profile, and business demands" [16]. According to this definition, sustainable software systems evolve in response to the evolution of the context (environment, usage profile, demands) in which they are based. However, SE focuses mainly on the design of tools and architectures for sustainable software development and fails to consider how interfaces can be designed to enable software evolution (an HCI agenda).

M. Kurosu (Ed.): Human-Computer Interaction, Part III, HCII 2014, LNCS 8512, pp. 665–673, 2014.

The evolution of both technology and contexts is also one of the outcomes of the process of appropriation as studied in the HCI, Information Systems and CSCW fields. With input from a recent review by Salovaara [13], appropriation can be defined as the process during which users interpret, integrate and adapt technology to make it suitable for their purposes, resulting in changes in technology use and in novel aspects of technology-related practices.

Since both appropriation and sustainability consider aspects of evolution of technology use and practices, it is natural that they would converge in HCI. The point of convergence is the discourse on "Sustainable design for appropriation" [10] in Sustainable HCI, which deals with the implications of appropriation, re-use and maintenance practices as inputs for sustainable interaction design. The studies in this discourse have mainly focused on ownership attitudes and attachment to physical artifacts (ex. [9], [14], [15]).

However, the "Sustainable design for appropriation" discourse in HCI has so far failed to employ the extensive research on appropriation in the Information Systems and the (HCI related) CSCW domains. It has also failed to address the implications of appropriation-centric software design choices on software sustainability. In this paper we address these gaps by introducing an adapted model of appropriation proposed in the Information Systems domain by Carroll [1] and complementing the model with appropriation-enabling design recommendations.

3 Approach

To understand how the use of software could be prolonged through time, we have complemented the four-stage technology appropriation cycle proposed by Carroll [1] with appropriation enabling design choices from several authors in HCI and CSCW domains. The design choices were first grouped into clusters through a card-sorting exercise and then related to the stages of the appropriation process for which they could be designed. Further, a design space analysis was conducted for a project related to the Technology Enhanced Learning domain [11]. We propose that the Design Space suggested by us can be replicated, altered and situated in other contexts for sustainability gains.

4 Technology Appropriation Cycle

The model proposed by Carroll [1] describes a process of appropriation encompassing three main stages. The process starts from an adoption decision based on initial assessment (stage 1), followed by an evaluation for suitability to needs including exploration and adaptation (Stage 2) and ending with integration into practice (stage 3). Carroll further suggests that designers should get involved in this process and design *from* and *for* appropriation (Stage 4). Below is an adapted diagram outlining the four stages.

Admittedly, the proposed cycle of appropriation is too generic to be applied to all situations and purposes. However, this approach was chosen for further exploration and enhancement, since it models a possible appropriation cycle of software artifacts that would meet our end-goal of informing design for sustainable software.

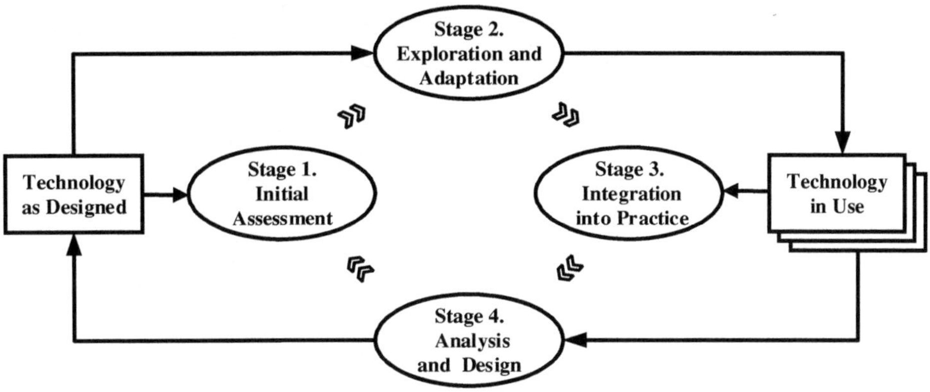

Fig. 1. The Technology Appropriation Cycle (adapted from Carroll [1])

Further, to facilitate an ongoing cycle of appropriation as depicted above, we propose to incorporate recommendations on design for appropriation from the HCI and CSCW domains. We call these design recommendations "enabling design choices". The selection and grouping of these design choices will be described next.

5 Enabling Design Choices

To determine the appropriation-enabling design choices we resorted to the literature containing design for appropriation recommendations in the HCI and CSCW domains. The guiding question for selecting the design choices was "what enabling choices have authors in HCI and CSCW domains proposed for appropriation-centric design?" A total of 27 loosely coupled proposals were drawn from the literature based on the review. These were then grouped in a card sorting activity involving four doctoral students and one professor of Interaction Design. The choice of the group was based on convenience and on the familiarity of the group members with HCI concepts. The card sorters were asked to group the choices according to similarity.

The resulting groups (see Figure 2) were then conditionally labeled into 5 categories as presented below. Admittedly, depending on contextual factors (including the grouping criteria, sorter profiles, etc.), many possible groupings are possible for these options.

5.1 Interpretability

This group included two options and was related to the possibilities of bringing individual interpretations into the designed artifacts and supporting different perspectives of information. The first choice in this group was AMBIGUITY, defined (in the card sorting activity) as allowing for different interpretations by the users. This concept is related to the *flexibility though openness* proposal by Dourish [3], according to which a system would be "simply uncommitted to particular forms of use or content". Ambiguity is also related to the *allow interpretation* proposal by Dix [2], where designers would "include elements where users can add their own meanings". Ambiguity as a

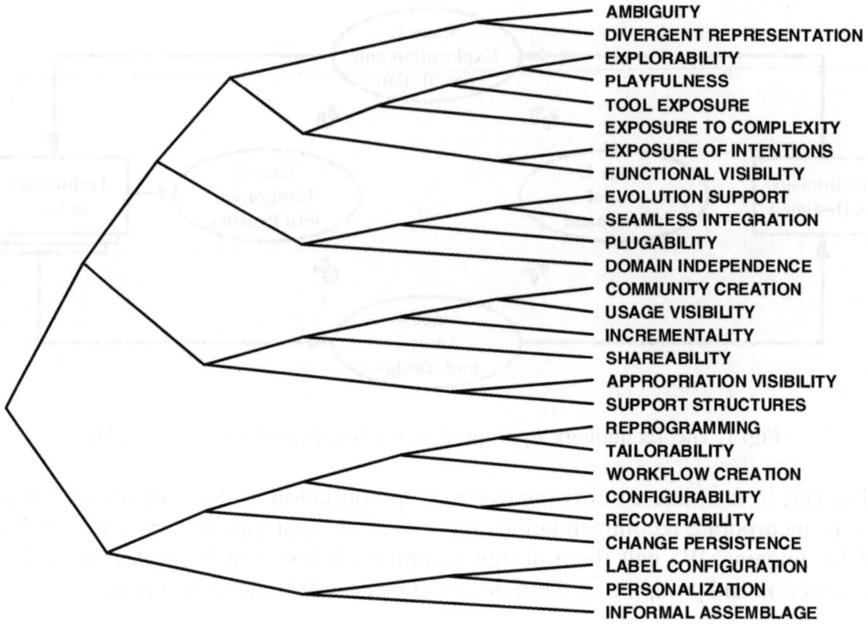

Fig. 2. Appropriation-enabling design choices clustered by card sorting activity including 5 sorters

resource in design was proposed by Gavel et al. [6], where they noted that the work done by individuals in making ambiguous situations comprehensible could lead to a deep conceptual appropriation of artifacts. The other choice in this group was DIVERGENT REPRESENTATION. This concept was used to describe the proposal by Dourish [4] on "supporting multiple perspectives on information" by separating information and structures that represent it.

5.2 Serendipity

This cluster related to choices that would allow users to assess and explore system features. The two choices in this cluster, EXPLORABILITY and PLAYFULNESS were related to creating opportunities for users to explore the system and to making the system open to play. TOOL EXPOSURE was another category aimed at exposing of system tools to users. The other choice in this group was EXPOSURE TO COMPLEXITY, related to exposing the users to the inner design of the system. Another, similar choice was EXPOSURE OF INTENTIONS, which deals with making the design intentions explicit to the users. Finally, the last choice of the cluster was FUNCTIONAL VISIBILITY, related to making functions of the system visible to the users. These highly similar choices related to the *provide visibility* and *expose intentions* proposals by Dix [2], which focused on "making the functioning of the system obvious to the users" and letting users "subvert the rules of the systems and yet still preserve the intent".

5.3 Scalability

This cluster was related to choices that would allow the systems to scale as time and changing needs necessitated evolution. The first choice was a general support recommendation, focusing on EVOLUTION SUPPORT. The second choice was SEAMLESS INTEGRATION; this would allow the systems to seamlessly integrate into the current systems, artifacts and workflows of the users. The next option in this cluster was PLUGABILITY, which would allow for plugging different system parts (modules, plugins) in different ways by the users. DOMAIN INDEPENDENCE was the last one in this cluster, which was defined as providing for the possibility to be used in different application settings and domains.

5.4 Sociability

Under the sociability cluster, the first choice was COMMUNITY CREATION defined as creating communities of system practice for learning about new features and for sharing information about appropriations. USAGE VISIBILITY was related to making usage visible to designers so that they could design instances of appropriation. INCREMENTALITY, another choice clustered in this group, related to design for graduate transformation of use for overall system stability. The next two choices, SHAREABILITY (providing the possibility to share appropriative uses with other users) and APPROPRIATION VISIBILITY (visibility of other's system states for learning about other's appropriations) related to the *Visibility* proposal by Dourish [10], which argued that “in order to share patterns of use and customization within a community, their effects have to be visible to others”. The last choice in this group was SUPPORT STRUCTURES, which was defined as creating social support structures for user appropriation. This last notion was borrowed from Draxler et al. [5] and related to supporting the social contexts of technology appropriation.

5.5 Plasticity

Choices in this group would allow the systems to evolve and change over time and were related to the concept of malleability introduced by Carroll [1]. REPROGRAMMING was the first choice in this cluster, related to allowing for the reprogramming of system functionality. TAILORABILITY stood for making the system configurable either through customization of features or coding. WORKFLOW CREATION was defined as allowing creation of workflows by the users from different system parts. CONFIGURABILITY was defined as offering ways for users to adjust system settings. Related to the notion of triability of software solutions, RECOVERABILITY was defined as supporting the recovery of system states. CHANGE PERSISTENCE was defined as allowing changes and adaptations to survive and thus provide basis for further appropriation. This option was borrowed from Dourish [10] where it was labeled as *Persistence*. Another choice was LABEL CONFIGURATION, defined as allowing for change of titles and labels for certain functions and states by users. PERSONALIZATION was defined as designing for particular user profiles. Lastly, INFORMAL ASSEMBLAGE was a concept related to providing the necessary functions, but not driving the users through consecutive steps.

These five groups of design choices were then placed by us relative to the four stages proposed by Carroll, reflecting on their general importance for each of the stages as presented in Figure 3.

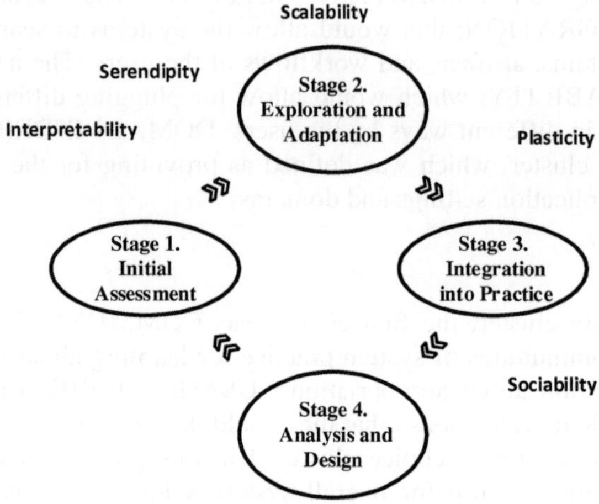

Fig. 3. Initial position of clusters of the appropriation enabling design choices in relation to the stages of the Technology Appropriation Cycle proposed by Carroll [1]

6 Selection of Stages for Appropriation-Centric Design

As depicted in Figure 3, we propose that the interaction needs and expectations for the four stages of appropriation are different. We also pose that to evolve through time, software should incorporate different enablers of appropriative interaction at different stages of this process. However, not all stages of the process can be designed for and thus we should focus our attention on those stages, appropriation enabling choices for which can be incorporated into the design of software solutions. These are highlighted in black in Figure 4, which presents a decomposed stage model of the cycle introduced in Figure 1.

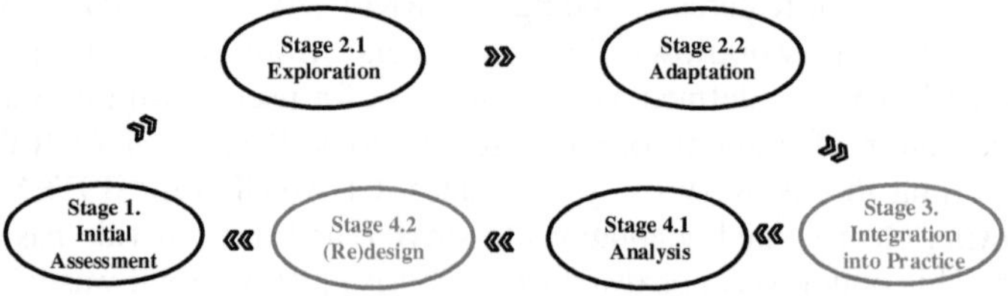

Fig. 4. Stages and sub-stages for which the enabling choices are proposed

The four stages highlighted above, namely initial assessment (by users), exploration and adaptation (by users) and analysis (by designers and developers) were chosen for the design space for sustainable software appropriation. Our Design Space currently includes the enabling design choices, viewed from a temporal perspective of usage.

Table 1. Sample of the Design Space Analysis for the first stage of the Technology Appropriation Cycle (Initial Assessment)

Q: How can we ensure that users can easily assess our solution before committing to use it?	C: Integration into existing artifact ecology	C: Sustainability	C: Providing a good user experience	C: Supporting new educational scenarios	Average	Definitions
O:DOMAIN INDEPENDENCE	1	1	2	3	1.75	Providing for the possibility to be used in different application settings and domains
O:SEAMLESS INTEGRATION	3	1	3	3	2.5	Allowing the systems to seamlessly integrate into present systems, artifacts and workflows of the users
O:EXPOSURE OF INTENTIONS	1	1	3	1	1.5	Making the design intentions explicit to the users
O:PLAYFULNESS	2	1	2	2	1.75	Making the system open to exploration and play
O:AMBIGUITY	1	2	1	2	1.5	Allowing for different interpretations by the users

7 Design Space Sample

To create the Design Space for Sustainable Software Appropriation, we resorted to the method described by MacLean et al. [12], where they propose describing questions that aim to solve a particular problem, options by which the solution could be reached and the criteria by which the choice of the options would be decided upon. Based on this approach, the dimensions of our Design Space were created. The dimensions proposed by us include the enabling choices discussed above. The Design Space Analysis (a sample of which is presented in Table 1) was applied to a design challenge related to ensuring the sustainability of a Technology Enhanced Learning solution under development at the Institute of Informatics, Tallinn University [11]. The rationale for the choices was implemented according to the criteria selected by the designers to be important for the project. The options (O) were rated according to the criteria (C) reflecting the 4 design values for the solution. The scale for rating the criteria included Not related (1point), Nice to have (2 points) and Must have (3 points). Thus a "winning" option could be selected to be elaborated for implementation.

8 Limitations

There were initial flows in the extraction and grouping of the items. First, a more comprehensive and thorough literature review process would be needed to cover an adequate number of appropriation-centric design proposals in the HCI and CSCW fields. Moreover, several items were too similar to be differentiated by the participants of the card-sorting exercise. Finally, in the Design Space analysis, the selection of the enabling choices for each stage would need to be refined and elaborated including justifications for their inclusion in each stage.

9 Closing Remarks

It is evident that successful establishment of the cycle proposed by Carroll makes the software more sustainable in terms of prolonged use. In this article we have proposed design choices that potentially enhance appropriation of the software and would allow for the cycle to flow smoothly through one stage to the other. As future steps, we aim to address the limitations of our methodology as described above.

Thus, our goal is to further refine the design space proposed by us by first undertaking a more thorough literature review process for the enabling design choices, followed by expert ratings (and inter-rater agreement analysis) for the revision and grouping of the design choices. Based on these, the proposed Design Space will be refined and implemented by us towards an evaluation of the model as implemented in real-life solutions.

This publication was made possible by the support of the Erasmus Mundus Action 2 of the European Union.

References

1. Carroll, J.: Completing design in use: closing the appropriation cycle. In: European Conference on Information Systems (2004)
2. Dix, A.: Designing for appropriation. In: Proceedings of the 21st British HCI Group Annual Conference on People and Computers: HCI..but not as we know it, vol. 2, pp. 27–30. University of Lancaster, United Kingdom (2007)
3. Dourish, P.: Evolution in the Adoption and Use of Collaborative Technologies. Presented at the ECSCW 1999 Workshop on Evolving Use of Groupware, Copenhagen, Denmark (1999)

4. Dourish, P.: The Appropriation of Interactive Technologies: Some Lessons from Placeless Documents. Comput. Supported Coop. Work 12(4), 465–490 (2003)
5. Draxler, S., Stevens, G., Stein, M., Boden, A., Randall, D.: Supporting the social context of technology appropriation: on a synthesis of sharing tools and tool knowledge. In: Proceedings of the 2012 ACM Annual Conference on Human Factors in Computing Systems, New York, NY, USA, pp. 2835–2844 (2012)
6. Gaver, W.W., Beaver, J., Benford, S.: Ambiguity As a Resource for Design. In: Proceedings of the SIGCHI Conference on Human Factors in Computing Systems, New York, NY, USA, pp. 233–240 (2003)
7. Heyer, C., Brereton, M.: Design from the everyday: continuously evolving, embedded exploratory prototypes. In: Proceedings of the 8th ACM Conference on Designing Interactive Systems, New York, NY, USA, pp. 282–291 (2010)
8. Huang, C.-C., Stolterman, E.: Capturing prolonged interactive experiences: a review of visual approaches in user research. In: Proceedings of the 6th International Conference on Designing Pleasurable Products and Interfaces, New York, NY, USA, pp. 86–95 (2013)
9. Huh, J., Nam, K., Sharma, N.: Finding the lost treasure: understanding reuse of used computing devices. In: Proceedings of the SIGCHI Conference on Human Factors in Computing Systems, New York, NY, USA, pp. 1875–1878 (2010)
10. Huh, J., Nathan, L.P., Silberman, S., Blevis, E., Tomlinson, B., Sengers, P., Busse, D.: Examining appropriation, re-use, and maintenance for sustainability. In: CHI 2010 Extended Abstracts on Human Factors in Computing Systems, New York, NY, USA, pp. 4457–4460 (2010)
11. Lamas, D., Väljataga, T., Laanpere, M., Rogalevich, V., Arakelyan, A., Sousa, S., Shmorgun, I.: Foundations for the Reconceptualization of the e-Textbook. In: Proceedings of 8th International Conference on e-Learning ICEL 2013, pp. 510–514 (2013)
12. MacLean, A., Young, R.M., Bellotti, V.M.E., Moran, T.P.: Questions, options, and criteria: elements of design space analysis. Hum.-Comput. Interact. 6(3), 201–250 (1991)
13. Salovaara, A.: Repurposive Appropriation and Creative Technology Use in Human–Computer Interaction, Aalto University and University of Helsinki, Helsinki Institute for Information Technology HIIT (2012)
14. Turner, P., Turner, S.: My grandfather's iPod: an investigation of emotional attachment to digital and non-digital artefacts. In: Proceedings of the 29th Annual European Conference on Cognitive Ergonomics, New York, NY, USA, pp. 149–156 (2011)
15. Wakkary, R., Tanenbaum, K.: A sustainable identity: the creativity of an everyday designer. In: Proceedings of the 27th International Conference on Human Factors in Computing Systems, New York, NY, USA, pp. 365–374 (2009)
16. Weiss, R., Krogmann, K., Durdik, Z., Stammel, J., Klatt, B., Koziolek, H.: Sustainability guidelines for long-living software systems. In: Proceedings of the 2012 IEEE International Conference on Software Maintenance (ICSM), Washington, DC, USA, pp. 517–526 (2012)

A Model of Web-Based Follow-Up to Reduce Assistive Technology Abandonment

Stefano Federici[1], Maria Laura Mele[1], Salvatore Agostino Romeo[2], Walter Didimo[2], Giuseppe Liotta[2], Simone Borsci[3], and Fabio Meloni[1]

[1] Department of Philosophy, Social & Human Sciences and Education, University of Perugia, IT
stefano.federici@unipg.it,
{marialaura.mele,romeo84,fa.meloni}@gmail.com
[2] Department of Engineering, University of Perugia, IT
{walter.didimo,giuseppe.liotta}@unipg.it
[3] Human Factors Research Group, School of Mechanical, Materials and Manufacturing Engineering, University of Nottingham, United Kingdom
simone.borsci@gmail.com

Abstract. The abandonment of assistive technology (AT) is strictly related to the subjective quality of the service delivery regarding the whole AT assignation process. Starting from this consideration, the aim of this work is to show the design of a Web-based follow-up model (WFM) aimed at overcoming the hearing aid abandonment in the Italian Umbria Region AT service delivery system. The WFM model described here is developed in two phases: an implementation phase, and an experimental evaluation which is still under development. The model meets the current objective of the Umbria Region's Units of Local Health Service to digitize their services in order to easily monitor the quality of the delivery service and evaluate the post-provision outcome.

Keywords: Assistive technology abandonment, assistive technology system delivery, assistive technology outcome, follow-up.

1 Background

The literature on assistive technology (AT) claims two main factors affecting AT abandonment: the perceived user interaction with the device and the quality of the AT service delivery process as experienced by the user. In particular, the first factor depends on: (i) how much the user's needs have been met; (ii) the extent of the psychomotor skills needed to use the equipment; (iii) the attributes of the AT's functioning; and/or (iv) training and support provided during and after the AT delivery. If one or more of these aspects of interaction with the AT is perceived as problematic, users tend to abandon the device. The second factor, regarding the quality of the AT service delivery as experienced by users, during and after the assignation process, was found to be strictly correlated with AT abandonment: the more the problems experienced during and after delivery, the more users are likely to abandon the AT.

M. Kurosu (Ed.): Human-Computer Interaction, Part III, HCII 2014, LNCS 8512, pp. 674–682, 2014.

In Italy, Federici and Borsci [1, 2] systematically analyzed the two factors described above, in order to estimate the rate of AT abandonment and to clarify the relationship between this rate and user satisfaction regarding the AT delivery systems in the Umbria Region local health service. Findings showed an average AT abandonment rate equal to 19.09%, which was lower than the average AT disuse, usually estimated in Western countries as being one third one year after from the device delivery [1-7].

In particular, the lowest level of abandonment (12.26%) was related to ATs delivered within a well-designed process of assignation, focused on the users' needs. In contrast, the highest level of abandonment (24.34%) concerns those devices, such as stairlifts and hearing aids, provided by those AT service delivery systems that are much more focused on reducing the costs of public spending. These latter systems are also characterized by not providing a follow-up service [1, 2].

Moving from these pivotal results, the aim of this work is to discuss a Web-based follow-up model developed to overcome hearing aid abandonment in the Umbria Region AT service delivery system (SDS).

2 Method

The overall aim of this work is (1) to analyze the Umbria Region AT delivery process and (2) formalize a Web-based follow-up model (WFM) for hearing aids and prosthetic services.

The methodology adopted involves the qualitative analysis of AT user experience by means of a user-centered web system, created in order to easily monitor the quality of use and user satisfaction. The study is structured into two phases: (1) WFM design and implementation; and (2) WFM experimental evaluation with end users. Phase 2 is still under development.

2.1 Phase 1 – The WFM Design and Implementation

Phase 1 consists of the engineering process of a WFM that is consistent with the Umbria Region AT SDS.

Phase 1 is divided into the following activities:

- Investigation on current hearing aids assignation and delivery models of the Umbria Region AT SDS, and design of a single and integrated follow-up model.
- Design and implementation of an accessible and user-centered Web-based follow-up system.

Investigation on Umbria Region Hearing Aids Assignation Models and WFM Implementation. The Umbria Region AT SDS is organized into two units of local health services (ULHS). For each one of them, the current hearing aids delivery process consists of four phases: (i) a first-user audiometric test to evaluate whether the user matches criteria for a hearing aid assignation. Then, (ii) the otolaryngologist defines a range of hearing aid models suitable for the patient's needs and initiates a trial period. In this period, (iii) the patient is given one month to test the different models suggested by the otolaryngologist in specialized centers. When the patient has identified the preferred aid, (iv) a second audiological visit is scheduled with the otolaryngologist who evaluates the appropriateness of the product selected by the patient and prescribes the AT. The prescription guarantees a full refund of the cost of the hearing aid by the ULHS.

Starting from the analysis of the current Umbria Region hearing aids assignation models, a new model was implemented to integrate them with a post-provision Web-based evaluation ideal process. The WFM proposed here uses an evaluation protocol assessing the subjective experience of both delivery process and quality of AT use by means of five questionnaires.

The questionnaires were administered immediately after the AT delivery and after three and six months. Two questionnaires measured the AT quality of use: the Assistive Technology Use Follow-up Survey (ATUFS) and the Abbreviated Profile of Hearing Aid Benefit (APHAB; [8]). Two questionnaires measured the user's perception of disability: the World Health Organization Disability Assessment Schedule 2.0 (WHODAS; [9]) and the Hearing Handicap Inventory Adult/Elderly (HHIA/E; [10]). Finally, the Quebec User Evaluation of Satisfaction with Assistive Technology 2.0 (QUEST; [11]) measured the user's satisfaction regarding both the AT delivery process and the product.

Implementation of a Follow-Up Web Portal. The implementation of a web portal called www.laregionetisente.org was carried out on the basis of a user-centered design model, which is a set of design procedures based on end users' needs. This process included (1) a prototyping phase, and (2) a system development phase. Phase 2 has been conducted alongside the iterative evaluation of the system.

1. Prototyping Phase

The web portal provides an interactive area to monitor patients with hearing impairments.

Domain Model and User Types. The main types of Web users include patients, otolaryngologists, and staff members.

- *Patient.* The interactive area allows patients to fill out a series of questionnaires aimed at monitoring the use of the prosthetic devices. Patients can fill out each questionnaire independently or with the help of a doctor or a staff member. The access to the system is limited to only authorized people. Patients may access their data at any time. The web portal can be accessed via a Web browser on any desktop computer or on any mobile smartphone or tablet.
- *Otolaryngologist.* The otolaryngologists who collaborate with the project can access the interactive area of the web portal to monitor the progress of their patients. They can enroll new patients and fill out their questionnaires. They can also view test results and data from the follow-up.
- *Administrators.* The staff members can access patient data for analysis and research, perform online tests for the follow-up process, access the patients' profiles in order to contact them directly. Administrators can also obtain some statistics and download test results in Excel format for further, more detailed analysis.

Use Cases. The use cases identified for each type of user are described below:

– *Patient*

- Homepage information reading;
- Website registration (social security number, phone or e-mail address to receive notifications, password, full name, municipality of residence);
- SMS reception;
- Mobile app download;
- Test answers insertion (APHAB, ATUFS, Base Test, WHODAS);
- Test results' visualization.

– *Otolaryngologist*

- Website registration;
- Patients' registration;
- Patients' test answers insertion (Base Test, HHIE, HHIA);
- Prosthesis data insertion;
- Patients' monitoring and test-reports printing.

– *Administrator*

- Information content modification (on the information area and the interactive area);
- Patients' registration;
- Patients' monitoring;
- Otolaryngologists' management;
- Data management and exportation;
- Test definition;
- Patients' test answers insertion (APHAB, ATUFS, HHIE, HHIA, Base Test, WHODAS) if the patient has not yet compiled it;
- Test report download;
- Database design.

The following description is a high-level overview of the database developed for the system. The UML class diagram is illustrated in Figure 1; each class represents one of the main entities in the data model.

Figure 1 shows two major categories of data: the first is to model the system's users, and the second is to handle the patients' tests. The most crucial classes of the model are described in more detail below.

Modeling Users

The high-level modeling of the user is implemented using the abstract level class VitaUser used to save the data common to all user types. The user profile (Profile class) may be of three types:

– Patient
– Otolaryngologist
– Administrator

Although at this stage of the project there are only otolaryngologists that manage patients, the system is designed to be extended in the future to all types of physicians. Notice how the administrator has the ability to enter information content into the system (Entry and Tag classes).

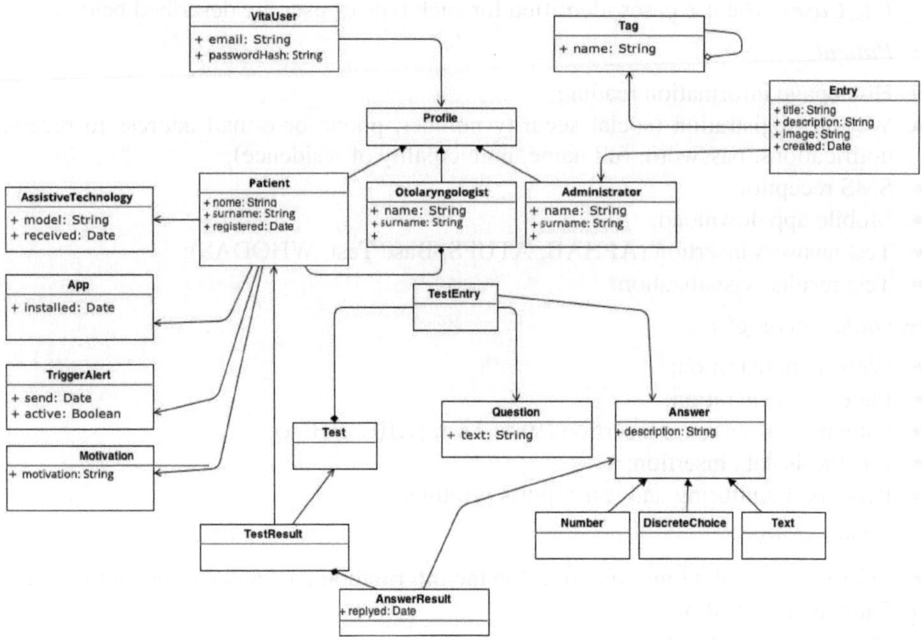

Fig. 1. The database UML class diagram

Modeling Tests

A structure that abstracts the concept of the questionnaire has been defined, so to cover all possible kinds of answers to questions, such as numerical, YES/NO, or open-ended answers. A high level of abstraction was provided to easily extend the system in the future, while still allowing the full implementation of the use cases and the questionnaires related to the management of hearing prosthesis.

Each questionnaire (Test class) consists of a pair question-answer (TestEntry) and the answers can be of different types: YES/NO, multiple choice or open. When a questionnaire is presented to the patient, an example of the test result (TestResult) is created, which contains the answers of the test (AnswerResult).

Architecture and Technology Infrastructure

The system has been designed to be easily extended in the future and to be able to handle hundreds of thousands of patients. In this section we will describe the architecture of the system and its infrastructure.

MVC Client-Server Architecture

The system was developed using well-established architecture: MVC client-server architecture (Figure 2). This architecture plans to divide the system into three levels for both the client and the server parts: the Model, which deals with persistent data in the database; the View, which displays the data; and the Controller, which coordinates the interaction between the View and the Model.

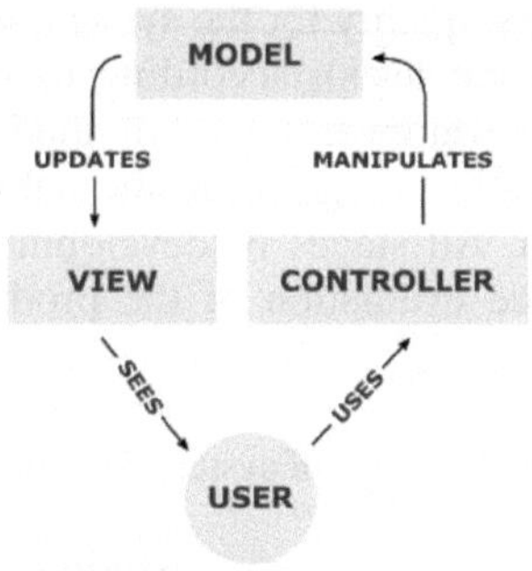

Fig. 2. MVC Client-Server Architecture

Cloud Infrastructure

In order to develop a system that can be extended in the future to monitor additional AT, the system has been designed to effectively manage hundreds of thousands of users. We decided to implement Cloud technologies to achieve a high level of scalability in the future. In particular, we opted for the Windows Azure infrastructure. The server part consists of a variable number of Worker Roles, which the load balancer, i.e. the system responsible for redirecting the requests, manages autonomously according to the load. The database has been implemented using the SQL Azure infrastructure, which supports up to hundreds of GB (gigabytes) of data with a high level of reliability. SQL Azure also directly backs up the data and secures the accesses. With such an architecture, in the future it will be possible to extend the system to support an increasing number of patients.

2. System Development Phase

The system was developed using an *Agile* methodology. The development has been divided into seven iterations, each consisting of a set of small features immediately available online. Each iteration has extended the system from time to time, up to the final version now available on the portal laregionetisente.org. The iterative method allowed us to proceed step by step, by adapting the features to the real needs of the users.

The system user-centered evaluation used the following human-computer interaction tools and methods:

- Quantitative analysis of accessibility by using the WAVE Toolbar for Firefox v. 1.1.7.
- Quantitative analysis of accessibility by using the Firefox Accessibility Extension v1.5.6.
- Cognitive Walkthrough. This is the simulation, by one or more expert evaluators, of the behavior of an inexperienced user interaction with the interface. The qualitative analysis method allows the identification of any issue that is supposed to occur in different scenarios of use.

At present, the system is implemented according to the main international standards on accessibility and following the usability principles and guidelines that are currently adopted by the international scientific community.

In order to ensure the highest quality for the system, we decided to develop the system starting from the tests (unit tests), according to the TDD methodology (Test-Driven Development). The development was divided into seven stages. The first phase focused on the information blog, while the subsequent phases addressed the design of the interactive area. All stages of development are listed in Table 1. The subjective end-user experience evaluation of the product version 1.0 will be completed by the end of 2014.

Table 1. Stages of system development

Phase	Module
1	Administrator registration module Blog Module for inserting information useful to the patients
2	Patient registration module Otolaryngologist registration module
3	Aiding device registration module Data management and exporting module
4	Notifications module
5	SMS notifications module
6	Tests definition module Test-filling module (user/administrator)
7	Smartphone mobile app Monitoring module

2.2 Phase 2 –WFM Experimentation

Phase 2 consists of the investigation of the user's needs and satisfaction regarding the prosthetic delivery service during and after the provision of the AT. This phase is conducted through the web portal that was implemented in Phase 1.

Procedure. Phase 2 is developed by the following three activities:

1. Patient recruitment and data collection. Subjects were informed about experimental purposes, procedure, and terms of the experimental process. A short interview collecting demographic information and medical history (HHIA/E) was conducted and digitized in the www.laregionetisente.org web portal by the otolaryngologists.
2. Qualitative evaluation of user's hearing aid experience. A qualitative evaluation was conducted during the AT testing and 3 and 6 months after the AT delivery. Five questionnaires were administered to assess the quality of use of AT (ATUFS and APHAB), user's perception of disability (WHODAS and HHIA/E) and the user's satisfaction of both process and product (QUEST). At any time, users are allowed to access their personal area, monitor their questionnaire results and the information on their own satisfaction in the AT use, and consult an overview of their follow-up appointments provided by the Health Service.
3. Data analysis and effectiveness investigation of the WFM.

Results. Sixty-one subjects (54% males and 46% females) were recruited. At the time of the first audiological examination, 11.4% of patients (57.1% males) were aged below 65 years and were then interviewed by using the HHIA questionnaire, while the remaining 88.6% (53.7% males) were older than 65 years and received the administration of the HHIE questionnaire. Eighteen out of the total patients enrolled required a renewal of the hearing aid license while 30 were requiring a first prescription. Data related to the outcome of the AT assigned are still being processed.

After the AT delivery, patients obtained their private login data to access their interactive profile and to fill out the subjective satisfaction and quality of use questionnaires (see activity 2). Results obtained through HHIA/E questionnaires show that 85.2% (55.7% male) of users have a "severe disability" and 14.8% (44.4% male) a "mild moderate disability." Activity 3 is currently under development.

3 Conclusion

In line with the Umbria Region's goal to digitize ULHS, WFM helps to overcome the limitations of the current hearing aid delivery process, which still follows paper-based procedure, making it difficult to monitor the quality of the delivery service and evaluate the post-provision outcome. Based on information technology, the WFM is easily manageable through a Web platform (www.laregionetisente.org): An accessible system was implemented through an interactive user-centered design process, whose usability has been constantly improved by UX methodology [12]. WFM provides a support and monitoring service, by which both professionals and patients are constantly informed about the delivery process. WFM allows otolaryngologists to easily check the patient's profile and set up and manage their appointment schedule. The patient's profile contains all related demographic information, medical history, and appointment schedule, which the physician can constantly update. Likewise, patients can read their clinical assessment outcomes and be provided with a reminder service, keeping them constantly up to date with their appointment schedule and hearing aid delivery status. Moreover, WFM returns the hearing aid perceived quality of use and satisfaction of each patient immediately after the aid has been delivered and three and six months later. This follow-up information is automatically digitally processed, based on data obtained through five questionnaires self- or interviewer-administered.

The model presented here can help to improve the appropriateness of national health-care services [13, 14] while at the same time increasing patient satisfaction. As improved training and support, and a reduction in problems experienced during and after the AT delivery process are correlated with AT abandonment, we expect that WFM might reduce the abandonment rate. In this way, our model can not only drive down costs but also avoid the economic meltdown caused by inefficient health-care systems.

Acknowledgments. The authors acknowledge support of this work through the Sanity and Social Services Department of the Umbria Region in 2013 (DGR 328/13), although the views expressed are entirely their own. None of the authors has any personal financial interests in the work undertaken or the findings reported.

References

1. Federici, S., Borsci, S.: Providing Assistive Technology: The Perceived Delivery Process Quality as Affecting Abandonment. Disabil. Rehabil. Assist. Technol. (under review)
2. Federici, S., Borsci, S.: The Use and Non-Use of Assistive Technology in Italy: A Pilot Study. In: Gelderblom, G.J., Soede, M., Adriaens, L., Miesenberger, K. (eds.) Everyday Technology for Independence and Care: AAATE 2011, vol. 29, pp. 979–986. IOS Press, Amsterdam (2011)
3. Cushman, L.A., Scherer, M.J.: Measuring the Relationship of Assistive Technology Use, Functional Status over Time, and Consumer Therapist Perceptions of Ats. Assist. Technol. 8, 103–109 (1996)
4. Dijcks, B.P.J., De Witte, L.P., Gelderblom, G.J., Wessels, R.D., Soede, M.: Non-Use of Assistive Technology in the Netherlands: A Non-Issue? Disabil. Rehabil. Assist. Technol. 1, 97–102 (2006)
5. Kittel, A., Di Marco, A., Stewart, H.: Factors Influencing the Decision to Abandon Manual Wheelchairs for Three Individuals with a Spinal Cord Injury. Disabil. Rehabil. 24, 106–114 (2002)
6. Phillips, B., Zhao, H.: Predictors of Assistive Technology Abandonment. Assist. Technol. 5, 36–45 (1993)
7. Verza, R., Carvalho, M.L., Battaglia, M.A., Uccelli, M.M.: An Interdisciplinary Approach to Evaluating the Need for Assistive Technology Reduces Equipment Abandonment. Mult. Scler. 12, 88–93 (2006)
8. Cox, R.M., Alexander, G.C.: The Abbreviated Profile of Hearing Aid Benefit. Ear Hear. 16, 176–186 (1995)
9. Federici, S., Meloni, F., Mancini, A., Lauriola, M., Olivetti Belardinelli, M.: World Health Organization Disability Assessment Schedule Ii: Contribution to the Italian Validation. Disabil. Rehabil. 31, 553–564 (2009)
10. Newman, C.W., Weinstein, B.E., Jacobson, G.P., Hug, G.A.: The Hearing Handicap Inventory for Adults: Psychometric Adequacy and Audiometric Correlates. Ear Hear. 11, 430–433 (1990)
11. Demers, L., Monette, M., Lapierre, Y., Arnold, D.L., Wolfson, C.: Reliability, Validity, and Applicability of the Quebec User Evaluation of Satisfaction with Assistive Technology (Quest 2.0) for Adults with Multiple Sclerosis. Disabil. Rehabil. 24, 21–30 (2002)
12. Borsci, S., Kurosu, M., Federici, S., Mele, M.L.: Computer Systems Experiences of Users with and without Disabilities: An Evaluation Guide for Professionals. CRC Press, Boca Raton (2013)
13. Lavis, J.N., Anderson, G.M.: Appropriateness in Health Care Delivery: Definitions, Measurement and Policy Implications. Can. Med. Assoc. J. 154, 321–328 (1996)
14. Federici, S., Scherer, M.J. (eds.): Assistive Technology Assessment Handbook. CRC Press, Boca Raton (2012)

Designing for Online Collaborative Consumption: A Study of Sociotechnical Gaps and Social Capital

Ali Gheitasy[1], José Abdelnour-Nocera[1], Bonnie Nardi[2], and Dimitrios Rigas[1]

[1] University of West London, London, UK
{Ali.Gheitasy,Jose.Abdelnour-Nocera,Dimitrios.Rigas}@uwl.ac.uk
[2] University of California, Irvine, California, USA
Nardi@ics.uci.edu

Abstract. This study attempts to investigate sociotechnical gaps in online collaborative consumption (OCC) to improve user experience and provide better design requirements. A new approach is proposed to evaluate usability and sociability of the OCC communities. The formation of social capital within OCC will also be studied to gain insights into design requirements. Due to its features as a community where OCC takes place, ETSY will be the focus of this study.

Keywords: Online Collaborative Consumption (OCC), Computer Supported Cooperative Work (CSCW), sociotechnical gap, social capital, usability, sociability and user experience (UX).

1 Introduction

Constant changes in human's social life lead to a gap between their requirements and the existing technological capabilities. The main challenge for CSCW (*Computer Supported Cooperative Work)* is to identify and ameliorate this sociotechnical gap. The problems of CSCW have been distinguished by Ackerman [1] as:

- Generalizability from small groups to a general population (social sciences)
- Predictability of affordances (HCI)
- Applicability of new technological possibilities (computer science)

Online communities that enable collaborative consumption are more than just ordinary websites. They allow users not only to consume information but also to provide and contribute to the content within a wide range of topics. They evolve in accordance with how individuals communicate, with the aid of a website or software within their social interactions. Design principles of online communities are guided by their purpose, policies, selection of technology, designing usability, and supporting sociability [1]. Sociability refers to providing "a state of being sociable" within online community, where users find it satisfying to interact with each other to achieve their goals [2].

Therefore, to approach the sociotechnical gap, it is essential to understand individuals' interaction and collaboration in online communities, the technologies supporting them, and the usability and sociability of these technologies. This could be done by investigating online communities that enable the individuals to consume collaboratively.

M. Kurosu (Ed.): Human-Computer Interaction, Part III, HCII 2014, LNCS 8512, pp. 683–692, 2014.

In doing this, we investigate users' experience, behaviours and their needs, in order to better support OCC. This research aims to answer these questions: What are the sociotechnical gaps in technologies supporting OCC? How can we better support design of OCC platforms on identifying these gaps? How is social capital formed in OCC? How to evaluate online collaborative communities?

2 Online Collaborative Consumption

OCC enables individuals to interact with each other and to exchange information, knowledge, experience, materials, support, etc. Earlier OCC mainly involved in sharing files, photos, videos and knowledge, while nowadays it engages other areas of our everyday life. Collaborative consumption provides substantial environmental benefits by increasing efficiency and reducing the waste of resources by encouraging reselling and reusing old or unwanted materials [3]. It amends our consumption habits regarding not only what to consume but also how to consume. Open collaborative projects such as open software and Wikipedia as a part of OCC inspire the collective actions, which serve the need of individuals and at the same time provide a sense of belonging to a community. It enhances the "Crowdsourcing", which is distribution of tasks between a group of networked individuals or community to solve a problem with collective intelligence and action [4]. The collaboration and interaction in the heart of OCC enables individuals to be active citizens of society, enhances their associational activities, accumulates collective actions and trust, helps to make friends, and increases their social capital.

3 Social Capital

Social capital has been defined by The World Bank [5] as "the norms and social relations embedded in social structures that enable people to coordinate action to achieve desired goals". Putnam [6] defined social capital as trust, network structures, and norms that promote cooperation among actors within a society for their mutual benefits. Therefore, it can be concluded that social capital consists of a number of core features such as: trust, associational activities and civic norms, which are closely related to the principles of OCC.

Different types of networks or groups lead to different types of social capital, which bring different advantages for individuals. Bonding social capital includes homogenous groups of individuals and close networks (sharing similar circumstances, situations or life experiences). It accumulates trust, creates shared funds, increases exchange of favour, mutual support, mobilizes solidarity, and helps to share limited resources. However, it limits the information flow and resource exchange due to its' closed networks nature [7]. Bridging social capital consists of heterogeneous groups of individuals and sparse networks (with different circumstances, situations or life experiences). It provides more informational benefits [8], due to more open and sparse network that provides actors with less redundant connections in order to easily gain non-redundant information and have new opportunities. These two types generated where there are individual ties exist. Next paragraph discusses the collective or non-tie social capital.

Social capital can also be generated within circumstances where no individual ties exist, such as online communities where individuals help each other without knowing one other. Occasionally these individuals can get to know each other after social exchange and keep in touch subsequently. Online communities enable individuals to engage in social action to achieve collective goals, facilitate social capital within social relationships, trust, and reciprocity [9-12].

Jiang and Carrol [13] theorized that most social capital studies use the SNA (social network analysis) to define and visualize community or social network. It emphases on individual gains by using an egocentric perspective and ignores the collective side of the social capital. In addition to SNA, other validated measurement scale such as Williams's survey [14] also measures individual bridging and bonding and overlook the collective side of the social capital. Therefore, this study intends to investigate the differences in the formation of social capital at collective (non-tie) and individual level, and also to discover how ties and networks can be generated within collective social capital.

4 Methodology

As one of the case studies, ETSY is the data gathering platform for this research. It is an online marketplace and community that connects buyers with craftsmen to buy and sell handmade, vintage and crafts supplies. Its diverse community features include Teams, Forums, Live chat, Offline events and online workshops. ETSY enable members with common interests to collaborate, exchange information, experience and support, and also to meet with each other. It is an appropriate platform for this study since it provides diverse collaborative tools and community features, and also it is a growing community with 30 million members in 200 countries [15]. Next, the data gathering methods for this research will be discussed.

Standard usability evaluation methods evaluate users' performance in specified tasks in a controlled context, which is not convenient for evaluating the online communities. As Preece et al. [1] argues, they are useful, but inadequate for evaluating online communities since they do not address sociability. Besides in many online communities, sociability overshadows usability. A study of Facebook users by Hart et al. [16] revealed that usability testing does not elicit all the significant aspects of social web use, such as self-expression or social pleasure. They also found that users are less concerned about the bad usability of the system when there are enjoyable aspects that compensate the usability inadequacies. In addition, they suggest a more holistic approach to evaluation in order to support the new design guidelines of modern day social websites. Likewise Malinen and Ojala [17] claim that usability heuristics concentrate on a task-oriented approach and exclude social and "hedonistic" characteristics. Regarding collaborative systems evaluation, Araujo et al. [18] identify four crucial elements; including group context, usability, collaboration, and cultural impact. These elements as part of the evaluation process distinguish the group and work context, usability strengths and weaknesses, collaboration capabilities, and investigate the impact of the system over time. Furthermore, Antunes et al. [19] suggest an "eclectic approach" in evaluation of collaborative systems to cover several factors, including the individual and group characteristics within social and organizational contexts, to assess positive and negative effects of technology.

Therefore, we can conclude that a holistic approach is needed to focus on sociability components to assess purpose, protocols, and codes of behavior in addition to usability and user experience to evaluate the ease of use and user satisfaction. A combined methodological framework is proposed in this paper to evaluate OCC, ETSY in this case. Ethnography complements predictive evaluation by considering the user at the centre of the evaluation by accompanying them in interview and surveys. (Figure 1)

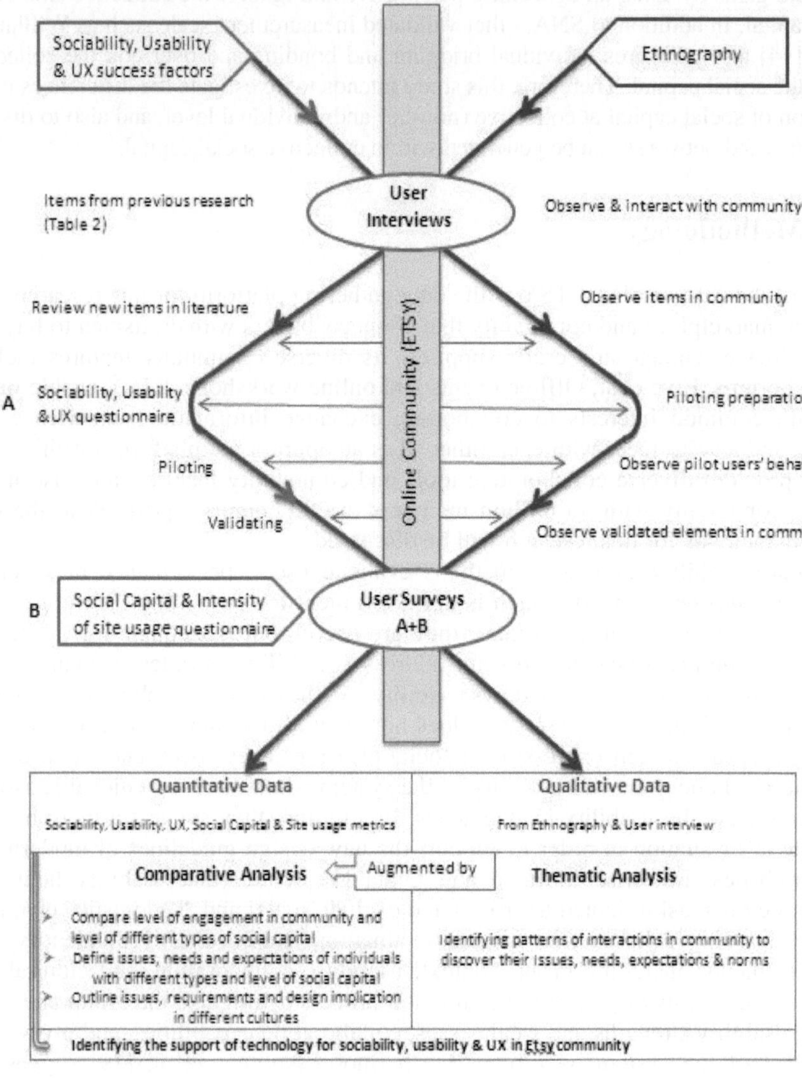

Fig. 1. User Centered Evaluation

4.1 Ethnography

Ethnography and qualitative research methods are recommended by Preece et al. [2] as suitable approaches for studying social interaction and sociability. It provides a naturalistic interpretation and understanding of human behavior within cultures and communities by providing descriptions of social structures, behaviors, symbols, and language [20]. This method helps to analyze and understand the community's interaction within their 'textual social discourse' [21]. This approach helps to understand the culture of the online community from an insider's point of view. The holistic nature of this approach, based on contextualized findings, allows the researcher to develop a deep understanding of how issues related to sociability are developed and are expressed within online community. However, we should bear in mind that for an in-depth understanding of a community and its norms and interactions, a long term commitment is essential. In addition, it is not guaranteed to be able to gain access to the relevant and suitable type of data, within existing social interaction contents. Therefore in order to increase the validity and reliability of ethnography and qualitative research methods, they need to be complemented with other methods. One of the methods which could complement ethnography can be predictive evaluation.

4.2 Predictive Evaluation

Predictive evaluation makes use of heuristics to predict the usability problems [22]. These heuristics are useful guidelines in eliciting the usability issues. But these guidelines are not always accurate in testing the interactive interfaces, such as online communities. Furthermore, like other methods, they need to be customized specifically for evaluating sociability [23]. This approach has also been criticized regarding the validity of the gathered data, as the evaluators are substitute users and it does not involve real users in the process [24]. Drawing the heuristics from the perspectives of real users of community could be a good basis for evaluating the success of the online community. Nonetheless, it has been shown that users are often not very consistent in self-reporting [25]. Thus, using the appropriate heuristics to develop surveys could be helpful in probing users in reporting their issues, needs and expectation of their online communities. Ethnography helps to understand the culture, norms and behaviours [26] of ETSY community members and facilitates selection of the relevant success factors. Considering the nature of ETSY community, the appropriate success factors or heuristics including sociability, usability and user experience (UX) drawn from previous literatures. (Table 1)

4.3 User Interviews

In this stage user interviews co-validate the above success factors or heuristics (Table 1) from the perspectives of the real users of the ETSY community. The users will be asked to rate the importance of each item by looking back on their experience using ETSY. The rating is based on 5 scale ranking, the 1 and 2 rated items will be omitted and the 3, 4, and 5 scored will be considered. They can also recommend new items. This will contribute to developing a questionnaire incorporating sociability, usability and UX constructs. In addition, the ethnography which will be carried out in the meantime, will help in developing the questionnaire by observing its' elements in the community. The final questionnaire will be piloted with the users and validated afterwards to ensure their suitability for the community.

Table 1.

Constructs	Items	Source
Social relationship	**S1:** Network creation (e.g. individuals with similar interest)	[27,2]
	S2: Face to face communication (e.g. offline meetings &events)	[29,3]
	S3: Dynamic interaction (e.g. verbal, gestural & emoticons)	[1]
	S4: Social & emotional support	[31]
Reciprocity	**S5:** Information exchange	[32]
	S6: New product & innovation	[32]
	S7: Achieving a collective goal (knowledge creation/ problem solving)	[33]
Trust (Privacy & Identity)	**S8:** Different level of anonymity (limit of privacy)	[34]
	S9: Persistent identity	[35]
	S10: Members profiles and pictures (creativity in self-presentation & identity construction)	[36, 37]
	S11: Transparency (e.g. exposing identity of content providers)	[34]
	S12: Clear establishing of self-goals for the community	[34]
	S13: Trust creation features (e.g. reputation model)	[38]
Content creation / member contribution	**S14:** Social recognition & self-expression	[39,41]
	S15: Fast & informal interaction (commenting & rating contents)	[40]
	S16: Rewards & recognition for contribution	[39,4]
	S17: Feedback to motivate (public& private)	[39]
	S18: Volunteerism	[27,4]
	S19: Self-satisfaction	[43]
Purpose, policies & procedures	**S20:** Relevant rules of behaviour & clear displayed policies	[1]
	S21: Different members' roles (e.g. contributor and reader)	[44]
	S22: Suitability & functionality of content	[28]
Information design & presentation	**SU23:** Advanced & filter search for content	[23]
	SU24: Easy information obtaining	[45]
	SU25: Discussion board organization	[1]
technology Support	**SU26:** Subgroup formation (facilitate interaction & discussion in different subtopics)	[27, 46]
	SU27: Awareness tools (e.g. calendaring tool for meeting)	Ethnography
	SU28: Social presence tools(e.g. status info, camera connection, IM, graphical presentation of activity &avatar)	[47]
	SU29: Other tools (chat, mailing list, UseNet news, etc.)	[48]
Navigation	**U30:** Consistent & easy navigation	[1, 22]
	U31: Intuitive layout	
	U32: Visibility of site (what is going on in the site…)	
User control	**U33:** Feeling in charge of system	[1, 22]

Table 1. (*Continued.*)

	U34: Error prevention & correction	
Reliability	**U35:** Access to system always to be available	[49]
	U36: Easy to remember search sequence	[44, 50]

*(**Guide**: Sociability: S / Usability: U / UX: S1-S14, S22 / Collective Social capital: S1 S13)*

4.4 User Surveys

Once the final questionnaire is validated, the user surveys will be carried out. The users will be asked to rank the support of the community for each item based on Likert scale. Ethnography will also help to finalize the questionnaire and to observe the user members' behaviours. In this stage, previously validated items for social capital and intensity of usage will be added to this questionnaire.

4.5 Intensity of Site Usage

To determine the association between the usage of OCC communities and social capital; the intensity of the usage and social capital should be measured. Intensity of site usage will be measured by using a survey in which some items will be adapted from Ellison et al's Facebook Intensity scale [28] with modified wordings to match the context of this study. This survey and interviews assess the individual's behavior and measure the engagement in OCC community. They obtain the number of friends, the amount of time spent on a day, the extent of emotional connection and the level of integration within daily activities. Defining the intensity of site usage can help in answering the formation of different social capital and possible association between the amount of site usage and the increase of social capital.

4.6 Social Capital Measures

The study of social capital will be based on three dimensions including bridging, bonding and collective. The bridging and bonding dimension will be measured by a survey adapted from the existing scales Williams [15]. He has developed and validated the survey, based on Putnam's [51] criteria to measure individuals' online social capital. According to the focus of the study some of the questions also will be modified.

4.7 Collective (Non-tie) Social Capital Measures

As discussed earlier in the literature, social relationships, trust and reciprocity are the main construct for the social capital in the online communities. These constructs will be measured within the sociability elements of the final questionnaire (Table 1, Items: S1-S13).

Results of User surveys generate quantitative data which will be augmented by qualitative data from ethnography and interviews.

5 Contribution of the Study

We hope that the results of this study will shed light on sociotechnical gaps by revealing the different social and cultural needs, requirements, and technological affordances to support OCC. The goal is to develop a framework to evaluate and support the design of OCC by revealing individuals' difficulties, needs and expectations in using OCC community. Learning about formation of social capital could inform design requirements to support development of the right type of social capital within OCC. Findings from implementing this framework will inform new and enhanced design features to support OCC in increasing collective and non-tie social capital. Furthermore they will expose the individuals' collaboration and social interaction patterns in and across different cultures.

References

1. Preece, J., Abras, C., Maloney-Krichmar, D.: Designing and evaluating online communities: research speaks to emerging practice. International Journal of Web Based Communities 1, 2–18 (2004)
2. Phang, C.W., Kankanhalli, A., Sabherwal, R.: Usability and sociability in online communities: A comparative study of knowledge seeking and contribution. Journal of the Association for Information Systems 10, 721–747 (2009)
3. Botsman, R., Rogers, R.: What's mine is yours: how collaborative consumption is changing the way we live. Collins, London (2011)
4. Howe, J.: Crowdsourcing: Why the Power of the Crowd is Driving the Future of Business (2008)
5. The World Bank, World Development Report. Washington, DC: The World Bank (1985)
6. Putnam, R.: Bowling alone: America's declining social capital. J. Democr. (1995)
7. Portes, A.: Social capital: Its origins and applications in modern sociology (1998)
8. Burt, R.S.: The social capital of structural holes. New Directions in Economic Sociology. Russell Sage Foundation (2001)
9. Blanchard, A.L., Horan, T.: Social capital and virtual communities (1998)
10. Chaboudy, R., Jameson, P.: Connecting families and school through technology. Book Report 20(2), 52–57 (2001)
11. Hampton, K.N.: Grieving for a lost network: Collective action in a wired suburb (2003)
12. Iriberri, A.: Building online community: An action research project. In: Romano, N. (ed.) Proceedings of the Eleventh Americas Conference on Information Systems. AIS, Atlanta (2005)
13. Jiang, H., Carroll, J.M.: Social Capital, Social Network and Identity Bonds: A Reconceptualization. ACM 978-1-60558-601. University Park, Pennsylvania, USA (2009)
14. Williams, D.: On and off the Internet: Scales for social capital in an online era. Journal of Computer-Mediated Communication 11(2), article 11 (2006)
15. Etsy. Notes from Chad: 30 Million Members Strong (2013), `http://www.etsy.com/blog/news/2013/notes-from-chad-10/` (accessed December 11, 2013)
16. Hart, J., Ridley, C., Taher, F., Sas, C., Dix, A.: Exploring the facebook experience: A new approach to usability. In: 5th Nordic Conference on Human-Computer Interaction: Building Bridges, pp. 471–474 (2008)

17. Malinen, S., Ojala, J.: Applying the heuristic evaluation method in the evaluation of social aspects of an exercise community. In: Proceedings of the Conference on Designing Pleasurable Products and Interfaces, p. 15 (2011)
18. Mendes de Araujo, R., Santoro, F.M., Borges, M.R.S.: The CSCW lab for groupware evaluation. In: Haake, J.M., Pino, J.A. (eds.) CRIWG 2002. LNCS, vol. 2440, pp. 222–231. Springer, Heidelberg (2002)
19. Antunes, P., Herskovic, V., Ochoa, S.F., Pino, J.A.: Structuring dimensions for collaborative systems evaluation. ACM Computing Surveys (CSUR) 44, 8 (2012)
20. Patton, M.Q.: Qualitative Research and Evaluation Methods. Sage Publications, Inc. (2002)
21. Abdelnour-Nocera, J.: Ethnography and hermeneutics in cybercultural research accessing IRC virtual communities (2002)
22. Nielsen, J.: Usability inspection methods. In: Proceedings of the Conference on Human Factors in Computing Systems, pp. 413–414 (1994)
23. Preece, J.: Sociability and usability in online communities: determining and measuring success. Behaviour & Information Technology 20, 347–356 (2001)
24. Kanter, L., Rosenbau, M.S.: Usability Studies of WWW Sites: Heuristic Evaluation vs. Laboratory Testing (1997)
25. Kim, A.J.: Community Building on the Web. Peachpit Press, Berkeley (2000)
26. Boellstorff, T., Nardi, B., Pearce, C., Taylor, T.L.: Ethnography and Virtual Worlds: A Handbook of Method. Princeton University Press, Princeton (2012)
27. Iriberri, A., Leroy, G.: A life-cycle perspective on online community success. ACM Computing Surveys (CSUR) 41, 11 (2009)
28. Väänänen-Vainio-Mattila, K., Wäljas, M., Ojala, J., Segerståhl, K.: Identifying drivers and hindrances of social user experience in web services. In: Proceedings of the SIGCHI Conference on Human Factors in Computing Systems, pp. 2499–2502 (2010)
29. Wellman, B.: Community: From neighbourhood to network. ACM 48(10), 53–55 (2005)
30. Blanchard, A.L., Markus, M.L.: The experienced "sense" of a virtual community: Characteristics and processes. Data Base Adv. Inform. Syst. 35(1), 65–79 (2004)
31. Ridings, C.M., Gefen, D.: Virtual community attraction: Why people hang out online. J. Comput. Mediat. Commun. 10(1) (2004)
32. Millen, D.R., Fontaine, M.A., Muller, M.J.: Understanding the benefit and costs of communities of practice. ACM 45(4), 69–73 (2002)
33. Hampton, K.N.: Grieving for a lost network: Collective action in a wired suburb. Inform. Soc. 19, 417–428 (2003)
34. Leimeister, J.M., Ebner, W., Krcmar, H.: Design, implementation, and evaluation of trust supporting components in virtual communities for patients. J. Manage. Inform. Syst. 21(4), 101–135 (2005)
35. Kollock, P.: Design principles for online communities. In: Proceedings of the Harvard Conference on the Internet and Society (1996)
36. Hummel, J., Lechner, U.: Social profiles of virtual communities. IEEE Computer Society Press, Los Alamitos (2002)
37. Zhang, Y., Hiltz, S.R.: Factors that influence online relationship development in a knowledge sharing community. In: Galleta, D., Ross, J. (eds.) Proceedings of the Ninth Americas Conference on Information Systems, Tampa, FL, AIS, Atlanta (2003)
38. Sabater, J., Sierra, C.: Regret: A reputation model for gregarious societies. In: Fourth Workshop on Deception Fraud and Trust in Agent Societies (2001)

39. Tedjamulia, S.J.J., Olsen, D.R., Dean, D.L., Albrecht, C.C.: Motivating content contributions to online communities: Towards a more comprehensive theory. IEEE Computer Society Press, Los Alamitos (2005)
40. Malinen, S.: Heuristics for supporting social interaction in online communities. In: Proceedings of IADIS International Conference WWW/INTERNET, Rome, Italy, November 19-22, pp. 327–334 (2009)
41. Hart, J., Ridley, C., Taher, F., Sas, C., Dix, A.: Exploring the facebook experience: A new approach to usability. In: Proceedings of the 5th Nordic Conference on HCI: Building Bridges, pp. 471–474 (2008)
42. Andrews, D.C., Preece, J., Turoff, M.: A conceptual framework for demographic groups resistant to online community interaction. IEEE Computer Society Press, Los Alamitos (2001)
43. Wang, Y., Fesenmaier, D.: Towards understanding member's general participation and active contribution to an online travel community. Tour. Manage. 25, 709–722 (2004)
44. Preece, J.: Online Communities: Designing Usability, Supporting Sociability. Wiley, New York (2000)
45. Phang, C.W., Kankanhalli, A., Sabherwal, R.: Usability and Sociability in Online Communities: A Comparative Study of Knowledge Seeking and Contribution. Journal of the Association for Information Systems 10(10), 721–747 (2009)
46. Maloney-Krichmar, D., Preece, J.: A multilevel analysis of sociability, usability, and community dynamics in an online health community. ACM Trans. Comput.-Hum. Interaction 12(2), 201–232 (2005)
47. Malinen, S., Ojala, J.: Applying the heuristic evaluation method in the evaluation of social aspects of an exercise community. In: Proceedings of the Conference on Designing Pleasurable Products and Interfaces, p. 15 (2011)
48. Preece, J., Maloney-Krichmar, D., Abras, C.: History and emergence of online communities. Encyclopedia of Community: From Village to Virtual World, pp. 1023–1027. Sage Publications, Thousand Oaks (2003)
49. Palmer, J.W.: Web Site Usability, Design, and Performance Metrics. Information Systems Research 13(2), 151–167 (2002)
50. Hornbæk, K.: Current Practice in Measuring Usability: Challenges to Usability Studies and Research. International Journal of Human-Computer Studies 64(2), 79–102 (2006)
51. Putnam, R.D.: Bowling Alone: The Collapse and Revival of American Community. Simon & Schuster, New York (2000)

Getting the Most from CRM Systems: Data Mining in SugarCRM, Finding Important Patterns

Qamir Hussain

Aveclabs, Dublin, Ireland
qhussain@aveclabs.com

Abstract. An automated approach to business intelligence can help improve key performance indicators (KPIs) for businesses using SugarCRM. Data mining techniques will be used to analyze and present recommendations in a meaningful way to users of SugarCRM. One of the important outputs of the data mining process will be recommendations made to the user that effect KPIs of the business. Data mining can also be used to give users a better understanding of the dynamics of their own business and industry as predictable patterns can emerge from CRM datasets. While the approach and conclusions are general, the proposed strategies in this paper and the implementation are based on a SugarCRM installation. Predictive analytics in conjunction data mining has the potential to further improve reporting mechanisms from SugarCRM.

Keywords: CRM, Data mining, Patterns, Predictive Analytics.

1 Introduction

With larger resources large organizations are familiar with using data mining techniques to improve and simplify decision-making by analyzing data for business intelligence purposes. It often forms an important function of business development and strategy. This generally isn't the case with SMEs, however, there is nothing that should prevent small and medium sized enterprises (SMEs) from using data mining for the same reasons and gaining the same benefits. It is important, regardless of size of the business to analyze business data and make sense of underlying patterns.

It is arguable that it is even more important for SMEs to use data mining techniques and to perform analysis on the output of these data mining processes as with less resources SMEs are often stretched from personnel point of view. Often working 'on the business' is neglected or dealt with too late to save difficult situations. Additionally it is often an implicit assumption that small businesses have small amounts of data and therefore mining the data is easy or can be done manually.

This is a blind spot. Even in a one-person business, patterns in the data can easily be overlooked and misinterpreted when reviewed manually when simply relying on reporting functions. Automatic non-biased data mining technology has the advantage of objective review of data.

M. Kurosu (Ed.): Human-Computer Interaction, Part III, HCII 2014, LNCS 8512, pp. 693–699, 2014.

2 The Importance of Predictive Analytics and Data Mining

Data mining is becoming more and more necessary. The need to transform data into business intelligence is commonplace. Large organizations have lead the way in defining techniques terms of making sense of large datasets. It is now the turn of SMEs to make use of the same power of data mining.

In any modern business, data are present and scattered among multiple data stores. This includes customer relationship management (CRM) applications, calendars, documents, websites, spreadsheets etc. Therefore even small businesses have data that is disparate enough to demand an automated approach to gather and analyze the data in favor of a manual approach. Without mining these data can be treated flat in the sense that it is created and then archived until required, this passive approach to data can be a disaster for business intelligence as the motivation for analysis, even manually, can arrive too late for the data to save something serious from happening.

Data mining advocates a more active approach in dealing with data. By automatically clustering, classifying, regressing and associating rules between data.

2.1 Data Mining Processes

Data mining processes is broadly made up of three categories: discovery, predictive modeling, and forensic analysis. [1]

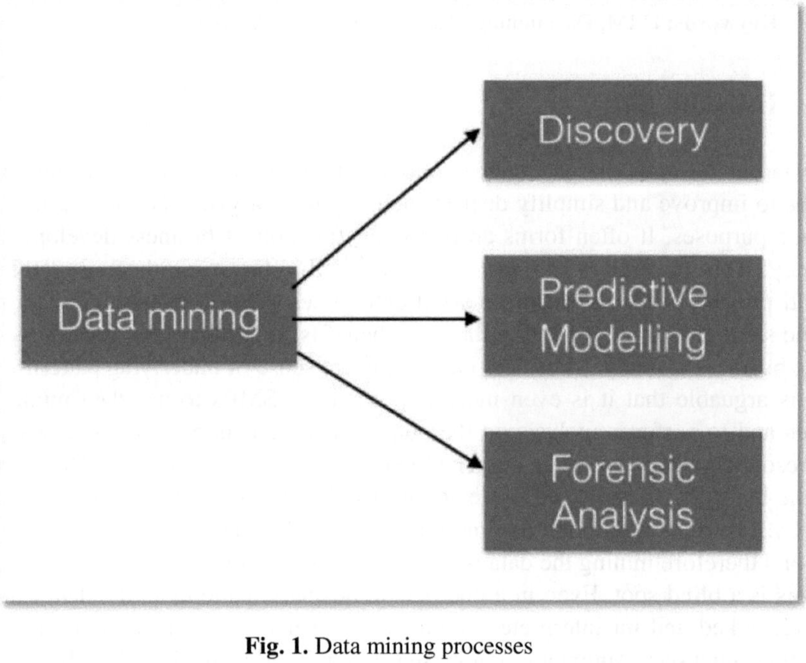

Fig. 1. Data mining processes

Discovery. This is the process of searching through a database to find hidden patterns. No a priori assumption is made as to the patterns underlying the data.

Predictive Modeling. This is the process of taking patterns that were discovered while searching the database, and to use these patterns to predict future events.

Forensic Analysis. This is the process of applying the extracted patterns in finding anomalous or unusual data elements.

Each stage in the data mining process serves an important purpose that help greatly in describing the underlying nature of the information as found within any datasets. This is especially true for seemingly unstructured datasets. The discovery phase is the initial phase and will outline patterns within the data without any assumptions regarding predetermined hypotheses on what these patterns might be. The predictive modeling phase will use what's discovered to show how the overall KPI's may be affected. At this point a comparison should be drawn between two options:

1. If current activity and behaviors remain the same, i.e. if recommendations aren't followed.
2. The performance of the same KPI's if the recommendations are followed

These 2 options provide important motivation to the user when more than gut instinct is required in decision-making.

Finally forensic analysis will show the user any unusual activity or behavior in the system. These will be key in eliminating wasteful behavior, and also identifying those elements within the system that have the greatest effect on KPIs.

3 Actions Are Needed in Addition to Data Mining

While data mining itself is a very important process it is not enough to present output data. Getting the user to perform actions based on the output from the data mining process is the most important step. The critical parts are the decisions the user makes based on the recommendations that result from the data mining.

It is not enough to have in depth analysis of datasets. The crucial part is to use those analyses to improve KPIs in a CRM system. The presented results and recommended actions should furthermore not overwhelm the user. Doing so risks the user becoming demotivated and not trusting the system. This would result in the user potentially abandoning the system and thus the key benefits from data mining can be lost. What we want to achieve is a way for the user to have a dialogue with the data, where each recommended action is given at the time where it is most appropriate and useful. Not too early and not too late.

4 An Approach to Use Data Mining in SugarCRM

To illustrate the approach to data mining, I will use, as an example, the marketing role in SugarCRM.

The author proposes to use a Data mining Plugin that will provide the necessary technology to perform both the data mining and recommendations.

Figure 3 below describes and illustrates the model proposed in this paper. Marketing data is found and used by the data-mining engine. The data is used to provide a

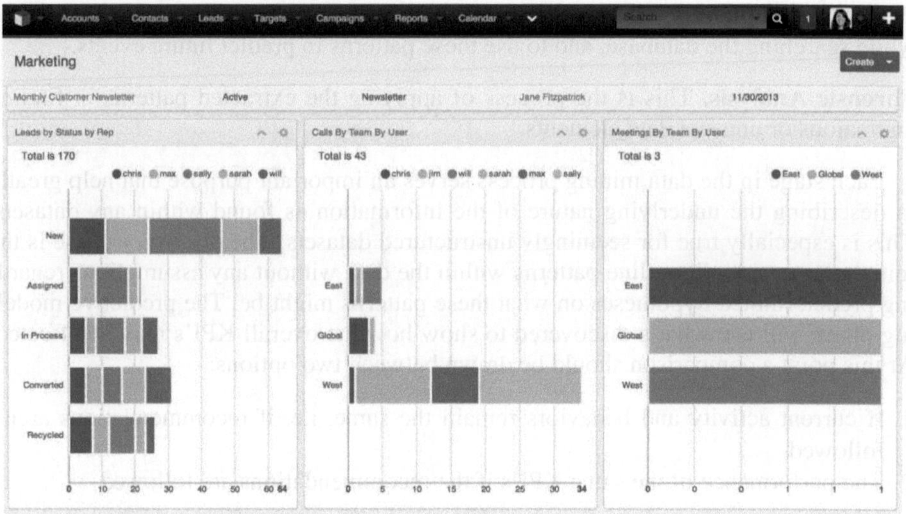

Fig. 2. SugarCRM Marketing

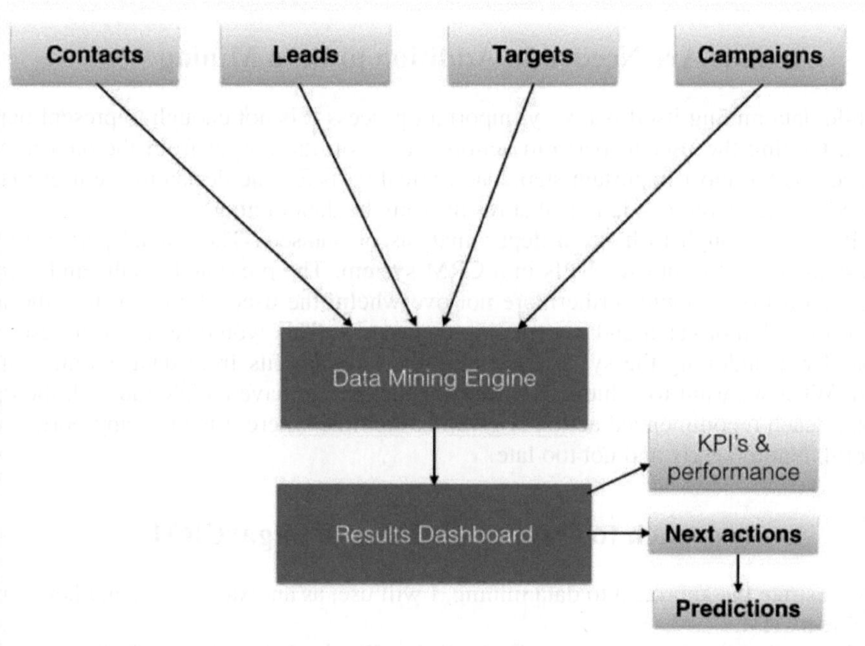

Fig. 3. Architecture of the Data Mining Plugin targeted of marketing data

dashboard outlining KPI performance along with a list of predictions and recommendations. Recommendations are provided as a list of "next actions", and the predictions are provided as a list that outlines how KPIs should perform.

The most important part of the user interface and user experience is to show only the most salient data to the user on the results dashboard. The user also needs to be presented with the option to drill down into the result set should that be required for tracking and highlighting results and causality.

The goal here is to present the user with timely advice and predictions. At all cost we must about bombarding the user with too many statistics and analyses, but instead to show data that need and can be acted on at every step along the course of the marketing process.

4.1 Enticing Users to Note Important KPIs

Extracting the data and calculating next actions and predictions only provide one part of the solution. The other part, equally as important, is getting the user to take note of and also to perceive and understand the presented data. Finally, the user also needs to take action as proposed by the presented data.

It is therefore important to present the minimal amount of information that will influence the user to take the appropriate action. The visualization needs to be clear and concise so that the user can perceive intended action in a single glance. It is furthermore important that the user feels in control. The user needs to be an active participant and part of the process and given timely feedback on taken actions and consequences.

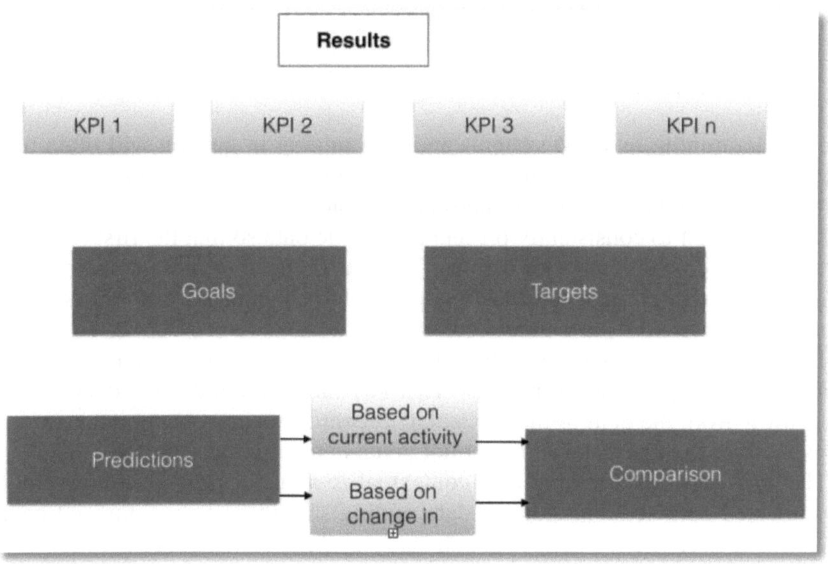

Fig. 4. Results Schematics

4.2 Encourage the User to Follow Recommendations

The system should always encourage the user to follow recommendations. Regardless of action taken by the user, the system should always state and visualize taken action and consequences in terms of recommendations and predictions.

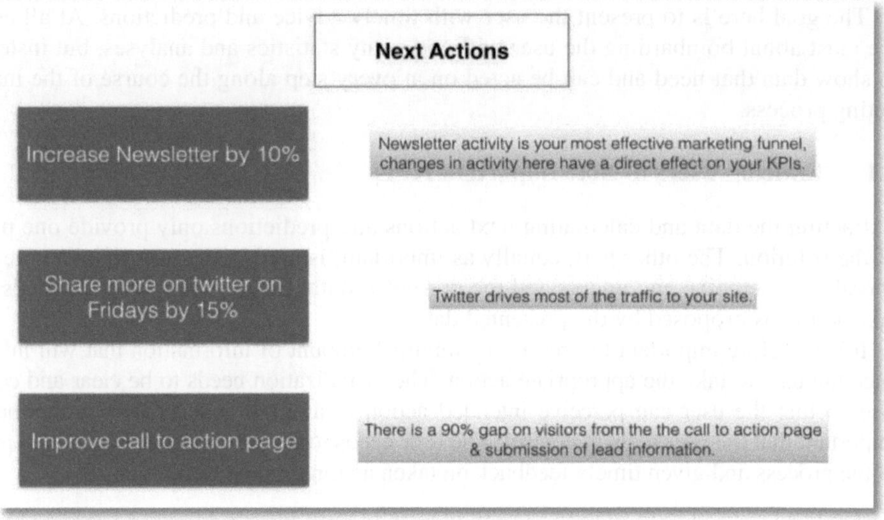

Fig. 5. Recommendations, next actions

5 Conclusions

Use of data mining in CRM systems and data mining in general will often turn what the user sees on its head, often data mining presents surprising and sometimes unexpected recommendations for next steps and actions.

It is important to consistently present actionable data so that the first things the user will see are the next courses of actions. There is no need to present summaries of the data mining process, unless the user is particularly interested in the process that the system used to reach a particular conclusion.

The enterprise sector is littered with software showing too much to the user and hence overwhelming the user. This often has the unwanted consequence of taking focus away from the goal of the particular software. Business support software should focus the user to either take action or not given in a particular context.

The purpose of data mining is to contextualize a businesses' most powerful asset – the collected data set. The goal of data mining should be to recommend courses of action to the user and to back it up with analyses done on the data store.

Given that the average business user is time constrained, this proposed strategy and approach should give the user a list of concrete actions to perform so the user feels real value in the in process. Should the user wish, the user can drill down to inspect and investigate the path to decision and potentially also get a list of contemplated but discarded actions.

As the more data is presented to the data mining process the predictions and recommendations will become better and more accurate thereby increasing the value in using data mining in CRM and indeed in any business process.

Regardless of there being sets of actions or a single action recommendation, these actions are always backed up with decision trees and data. The user should at all times be made confident that the recommendations are given due to solid research and analysis done using the systems internal data.

While the data mining process was used on marketing data, further improvements can be made with further incorporation of other functions within SugarCRM and thereby giving a richer view of the dynamics of the users customer data.

References

1. Rygielskia, C., Wangb, J.-C., Yena, D.C.: Data mining techniques for customer relationship management. Technology in Society (November 2002)
2. Teng, C.-I., Huang, L.-S., Jeng, S.-P., Chou, Y.-J., Hu, H.-H.: Who be loyal? Personality, flow experience and customer e-loyalty. 20 Int. J. Electronic Customer Relationship Management 6(1) (2012)
3. Nguyen, B., Mutum, D.S.: Customer relationship management: advances, dark sides, exploitation and unfairness. Int. J. Electronic Customer Relationship Management 6(1) (2012)
4. Farquad, M.A.H., Ravi, V., Bapi Raju, S.: Analytical CRM in banking and finance using SVM: a modified active learning-based rule extraction approach. 48 Int. J. Electronic Customer Relationship Management 6(1) (2012)

Humanization of Work and Environmental Protection in Activity of Enterprise

Aleksandra Kawecka-Endler and Beata Mrugalska

Faculty of Engineering Management, Poznan University of Technology, Poznan, Poland
{aleksandra.kawecka-endler,beata.mrugalska}@put.poznan.pl

Abstract. Industrial production is an integrated process where a human plays the most crucial and vital role. The employees' ability to perform tasks at shift contributes to a significant loading of health. Thus, providing them good working conditions is necessary. In order to achieve it, safe and environmental friendly systems of work should be assured. In this paper the results of the survey considering safety work and working conditions in Polish enterprises are shown. They indicate that respect for safety and health regulations is essential and in most cases poor working conditions are due to the lack of safety supervision and control.

Keywords: green job, humanization, safety, working conditions.

1 Introduction

Dynamic and difficult to anticipation changes, which appear in the surrounding of enterprises, require continuous acquiring and actualization of knowledge which is related to production or service activities. Fast and flexible reaction to these changes in the surrounding is the basis for survival and shaping competitive advantage of the enterprise.

One of the most important factors of the competitiveness of enterprises is quality of their products and services offered on national and international markets. On the other hand, quality does not only decide about efficiency and productiveness of the enterprise and its success. It is a human who plays a decisive role in the realization of all processes.

The results of investigations conducted in Polish and foreign enterprises confirm the existence of huge reserves connected with broadly-taken humanization of work environment and embedded in so called human factor (Butlewski & Tytyk, 2012). However, in order to benefit from this potential it is necessary to apply solutions encompassing humanization aspects, demands and ergonomic requirements in design work processes (Kawecka-Endler & Mrugalska, 2011; Kawecka-Endler & Mrugalska, 2012).

The design processes should be integrated with the whole production (or service) activity of the enterprise.

Achieving this goal guarantees several benefits:

M. Kurosu (Ed.): Human-Computer Interaction, Part III, HCII 2014, LNCS 8512, pp. 700–709, 2014.

- improvement of quality and competitiveness of products and services to customers (price, modernity, attractiveness, security, variety),
- systematic and consequent withdrawing of technologies harmful to men and environment which will force implementation of solutions compatible with ergonomics and environment protection standards,
- development and spread of ergonomic design methods (or ergonomic verification) of products and processes, as well as technical objects, machines, equipment and tools,
- gaining detailed knowledge about the influence of production processes on work conditions (micro scale) and environment (macro scale) in order to efficiently diminish them (to meet the requirements stated in standards) or totally eliminate them,
- improvement of general awareness among the enterprise workers (and entire society) of quality aspects, meaning of good and safe working conditions which should be the base of all integrated actions aiming at environment protection.

2 Humanization of Work

The notion of humanization of work is defined as a common system of all rules and practical activities which lead to such a shaping of work system that human work is more productive but also adjusted to his psychophysical possibilities and needs of a certain human.

The requirements of work humanization point out the existing range of problems, which in reality require detailed solutions for particular line of business or even for particular work group. The most important of these problems are:

1. Health losses caused by accidents at work and work related illnesses (they can be caused by noise, working with harmful materials and dangerous tools etc.) Most frequent work related illnesses are: loss of hearing, respiratory system illnesses, and skin diseases.
2. Working conditions, not necessarily harmful, can be unpleasant and hardly acceptable (can be caused by high or low temperature, noise, unpleasant smells, working outside regardless to season and in extreme climate, etc.)
3. Activities requiring hard physical labour (ex. assembly of big and heavy elements, loading and unloading), constant concentration (ex. product control, sight quality control) or uncomfortable and not physiological body position (ex. assembly or over-head welding)
4. Monotony, especially while actions repeated in short cycles (ex. manual assembly and disassembly), activities in ordered sequence and beat (forced work beat) and activities without necessary work space and without possible cooperation (planning and shaping own work)
5. Social isolation and (or) little communication during work as an effect of separation of work stands, which require certain conditions (ex. materials examining with UV beams, work stands equipped with protection screen) or working at home (new, developing forms of work in western countries)

6. Organizational conditions regarding social relations after work, work time-offs and unfavourable time of work for human (nights, weekends, work shifts). Apart from these social life domains in which unfavourable work time is stipulated by the nature of the work (ex. public transport, health care, power plants) there are also situations where shifted work and weekend work are used for economic reasons, allowing better use of very expensive means of production (ex. engineers work at manager's work stands) (Luczak 1991).

3 Safe System of Work

Designing a work system, not only the rules of ergonomics and health protection of employees should be taken into consideration, but also a well-known maxim of German philosopher – Schopenhauer: "Health is not everything, but without health, everything is nothing"(European Agency for …, 2010).

The performance of tasks at shift requires a lot of efforts from employees what contributes to a significant loading of health. In order to understand the notion „health" as a whole, it is necessary to analyse framework conditions and factors influencing a human at first. To shape work system in an ergonomic way one should start with understanding of the rules of health protection and then apply appropriate methods of work shaping, which will enable work and production organization in the enterprise (Bullinger et al. 2003).

This aim is possible to achieve thanks to system, rational and integrated activities guaranteeing achievement of ergonomic working and production conditions which are a basis for better quality, more efficient and safer work. As a result, an improvement of quality and profitability (economic efficiency) in the enterprise is achieved.

In Poland a multiyear program entitled „Improvement of safety and working conditions" has been introduced in 2008. Its main goal is to reduce the number of work accidents and occupational diseases. Thus, in the last years causes and circumstances of accidents became the subject of numerous researches and analysis. They are conducted in order to determine the causes of accidents and introduce preventive measurements. There is no question that the accidents are compound and result from the combination of events which have technical, environmental, human and organizational background (Kawecka-Endler & Skulska, 2011). For example, safety is not perceived as a matter of particular importance in machinery design in spite of the fact that the number of new regulations regarding machine safety has been enlarged considerably (Mrugalska & Kawecka-Endler, 2011; Mrugalska & Arezes, 2013).

The analysis of statistics of accidents at work allowed to distinguish their most often occurring causes. As it was investigated, one of the most crucial factors having an impact on rate of accidents is work organization at a work stand. Working conditions, which are often determined by a significant number of different factors, can also influence accident-threatening situations on a varied degree and scope. In practice the probability of occurrence of accident situations is often the result of one specific factor.

The number of accidents at work is undoubtedly the result of change of life model, technological change, transformation of economic systems, pursuit of job, fast life pace, and lack of time for rest and bad working conditions related to it. Each year the accidental risk increases in all areas of human activities (Kawecka-Endler & Skulska, 2011).

4 Safety in Green Economy

The assumptions of the Europe 2020 Strategy underline the necessity of focusing on sustainable, high-employment and knowledge and innovation based economy (European Commission, 2010). In order to achieve it, a rapid growth is expected in the “"green economy” leading to over 1 million new jobs. Particularly, such areas as: solar power, wind energy, biomass technology and waste recycling are supposed to expanse very rapidly (European Agency for..., 2010).

According to the study carried out by PLANET SA and Danish Technological Institute it is shown that European companies which actively promote actions to reduce their environmental impact or the "green segment" account for:

- 3-4% of the micro companies,
- 7-8% of the small companies,
- 6-7% of the medium-sized companies,
- 16-17% of the large companies.

But, the data are much lower when the green segment is only understood as companies which use certified environmental management systems (EMS) such as EMAS, ISO 14001 or national or sector-specific systems. In the EU27 approximately 80,000 companies of the 20 million companies are registered users and belong to the green segment what encompasses about 0.4% of all the companies in the EU (Constantinos et al., 2010).

Leading to “green economy” means to create “green jobs” and “greening” current industries, production processes and jobs. However, it is noticed that if certain jobs are considered to be “green”, the used technologies used may protect the environment but the employees may be put at greater risk. For example, efforts to reduce the use of the ozone-depleting, chlorofluorocarbons, have led to the promotion of substitute such as 1-bromopropane (1-BP) the exposure to which causes reproductive and neurologic effects on human (Schulte et al. 2010). Moreover, in “green economy” new hazards are supposed to appear as contemporary knowledge may not be able to deal with new technologies or working processes associated with green jobs. The skill gaps can also appear as the workers have not been trained before in new areas which often combine skills of a few jobs (for instance, the installer of a solar water heater must be qualified as a roofer, a plumber and an electrician). Thus, it is necessary to integrate safety and health at work into green jobs policies. It will result in integrating risk assessment and management measures in the life cycle analysis of all green jobs (European Agency for..., 2010).

5 Organization of Work Process and Rate of Accidents

International Labour Organization estimates, out of 2.34 million occupational accidents and diseases per year, about 321,000 are due to fatal accidents what corresponds to a daily average of 800 per day (International Labour Organization, 2013). In 2009-2012 data about accidents in Poland, reported by the Central Statistical Office, are presented in Table 1.

Table 1. Accidents at work (CSO et al., 2013)

Accidents	2009	2010	2011	2012
Total number of accidents	87 052	94 207	96 136	91 000
Fatal accidents	406	446	404	350
Serious injuries	780	645	683	627

The analysis of the most common causes of accidents at work indicates that in the last years inappropriate organization of work and work post are quite a large group of reasons causing accidents (ca. 11%). Such numbers result mainly from a low level of knowledge regarding safe work practices, not only among employees but also employers (CSO et al., 2013). Moreover, it appears that almost 90% of accidents take place while performing five activities. Most accidents (ca. 30%) are deviations such as slipping, stumbling, and falling of a person while walking at work stand or between work stands. They also result from manipulation of work objects (17%), hand transport (14%), work with non-mechanized hand tools (13%) and machinery operation (12%) (Studenski, 2009).

In many Polish enterprises occupational health and safety rules are still not restricted and risk assessment is performed inadequately or is not carried out at all and employees are not informed about occupational risks and protection to hazards (Przenniak, 2006).

Many employers are not aware how difficult it is to predict consequences of dangerous, burdensome and harmful working conditions. They are not mindful that direct losses (destroyed or damaged machinery, downtime, stoppage of the whole enterprise or its part) will be increased by costs of medical treatments and rehabilitation of injured parties and other benefits related to it (Zakrzewska-Szepańska, 2008).

6 Results and Discussion

As it was mentioned (see Introduction) contemporary enterprise acts in dynamic changing conditions in the surrounding and its success depends on innovations, flexibility (rapid adjustment to changes) and entrepreneurship. However, the basic and most important factor in every activity is so called human factor and humanization of work environment. For an employee, who is the performer of all processes, appropriate working conditions and health protection should be assured.

The activities, which intent to improve safety and working conditions, are necessary not only due to national and European Union legal requirements (Mrugalska, 2013). They are crucial and vital because they lead to reduction of the number of accidents at work. Among entrepreneur the awareness of assuring safety working conditions and their influence on company's economic results is increasing.

Knowledge is the determinant of right solutions in safety and working condition. In this case, it is engineering knowledge – gained during studies, necessary to design workplace and its organization and further applied it in practice. Such knowledge allows to identify abnormalities which can be diagnosed by the observation of workplaces in the enterprise.

Taking an attempt to obtain information how work safety and working conditions are understood and how they are assessed in practice a questionnaire survey was carried out in November 2013.

In the survey 71 students (diploma semester) of Safety Engineering participated. Firstly, they were asked how they understand such notions as: safety work and working conditions. Afterwards, they verified the defined terms which described the real state in the enterprises. In the research the students described the following types of enterprises where they had training or/and worked:

- 6 micro enterprises (fewer than 10 persons employed),
- 11 small enterprises (10 to 49 persons employed),
- 29 medium-sized enterprises (50 to 249 persons employed),
- 19 large enterprises (250 or more persons employed),

what constitutes 65 enterprises.

The results of the investigation concerning work safety are illustrated on Figure 1.

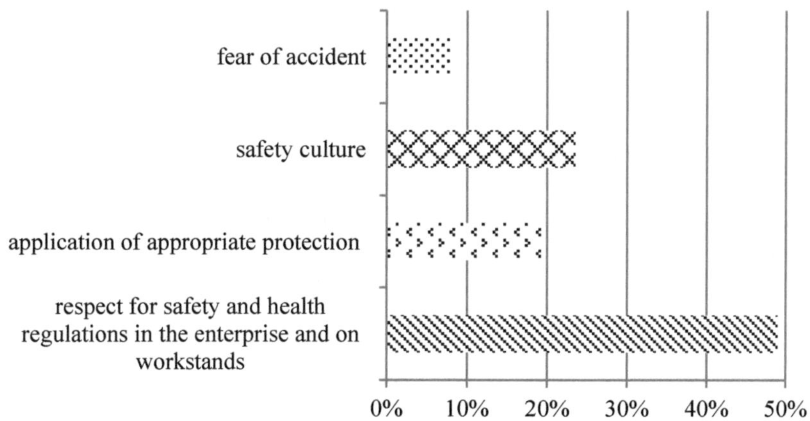

Fig. 1. Issues connected with work safety in theory

As it can be noticed in the theoretical considerations of work safety almost half of the respondents pointed out the respect for safety and health regulations in the enterprise and on the work stands. Moreover, it is worth to emphasize that only 23% of them perceived work safety as safety culture and 19% as use of appropriate protection means. 8% of the students indicated fear of accident as the factor connected with occupational safety. The perception of work safety in industrial environment is depicted on Figure 2.

The respondents less often indicated the significance of safety and health regulations in the enterprise and on the work stands with respect to the enterprises where they had training or/and worked. On the other hand, more attention was paid to the application of appropriate protection (30%). Safety culture was perceived on the same level (23%) in practical and theoretical considerations. The similar approach to work safety was identified for fear of accident (7%). Furthermore, the respondents indicated the need of implementation of a safety management system in the investigated companies. They explained the existing lack of protection as the result of inadequate penalties in companies. Moreover, it was noticed that protective means should be used in clerical work and field work and bonus payment should be planned for health and safety specialists.

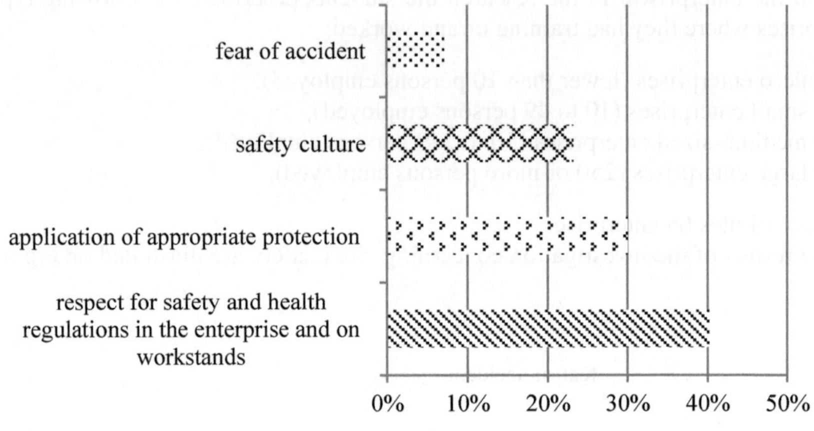

Fig. 2. Issues connected with work safety in practical applications

The second part of the questionnaire concerned working conditions and its results are presented on Figure 3.

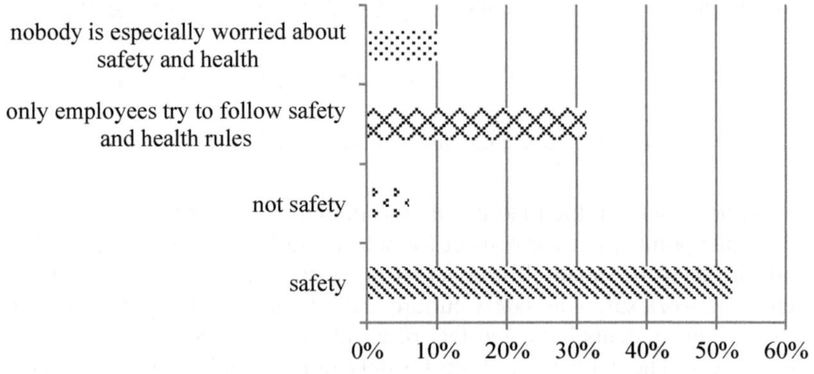

Fig. 3. Working conditions in enterprises

As it can be seen more than half of the respondents assessed working conditions in the enterprises as safety. However, it is worth to emphasize that one-third noticed that only employees tried to follow safety and health rules at work. 10% of the respondents stated that nobody was especially worried about safety and health at work. In 7% of cases the students defined working conditions as not very safety indicating the lack of determined actions in the scope of occupational safety and health. The explanation of the existing state of working conditions in the enterprises is shown on Figure 3.

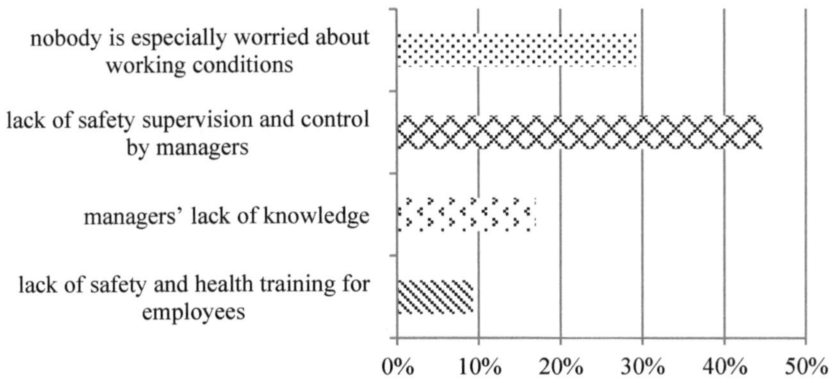

Fig. 4. Causes of working conditions in enterprises

The analysis of the results of the research shows that the lack of safety supervision and control by managers is the most often cause of poor working conditions. Furthermore, 29% of the students noticed that it may result from the fact that nobody was especially worried about working conditions in these enterprises. It was also revealed that managers' lack of knowledge (17%) and safety and health training were not carried out (9%). It was also mentioned that in order to improve working conditions the following actions should be introduced:

- regular safety controls,
- regular safety trainings for employees and health and safety specialists,
- planned financial assets,
- employees should be cautious at work,
- introduction and adherence of safety procedures,
- restriction of regulations and completion of tasks in a timely manner.

Moreover, in the analysed companies working conditions were not satisfactory what resulted from:

- lack of financial possibilities,
- lack of qualification of safety specialists from outside companies,
- not restriction of safety regulations,
- too low budget for health and safety departments,
- lack of managers' willingness to introduce new solutions.

Among the 65 analysed enterprises, working conditions were assessed as very good three times and two times as good and sufficient.

7 Conclusions

Production of modern, technologically advanced and high-quality products is the basic requirement which must be fulfilled by the enterprise to on the market. It is also a main criterion of social usability.

In cases of increasing significance of knowledge and information about innovation processes, which enable development and improvement of products, more and more often a question about costs arise – both cost of production activity and achieved quality of products and operations.

In these considerations a human – an employee, who is a direct performer of production processes, is not always taken into account. A basis of human protection in work environment is just knowledge how to shape a work system which can guarantee good and safety working conditions assuring good health. The costs of accidents at work, occupational diseases and all kinds of benefits paid out for health care are also social costs.

References

1. Bullinger, H.J., Warnecke, H.J., Westkämper, E.: Neue Organisationsformen im Unternehmen, pp. 421–461. Springer, Heidelberg (2003)
2. Butlewski, M., Tytyk, E.: The Assessment Criteria of the Ergonomic Quality of Anthropotechnical Mega-systems. In: Vink, P. (ed.) Advances in Social and Organizational Factors, pp. 298–306. CRC Press, Taylor & Francis Group, Boca Raton (2012)
3. Constantinos, C., Sørensen, S.Y., Larsen, P.B., Alexopoulou, S.: SMEs and the Environment in the European Union. PLANET SA and Danish Technological Institute. European Commission: DG Enterprise and Industry (2010)
4. CSO, Demographic Surveys and Labour Market Department. Accidents at Work in 2012. Central Statistical Office, Warsaw (2013)
5. European Agency for Safety and Health at Work. Workplace Health Promotion for Employees (2010), https://osha.europa.eu/en/publications/factsheets/94
6. European Agency for Safety and Health at Work. Workers' Safety and Health in Green Jobs, https://osha.europa.eu/en/topics/green-jobs
7. European Commission. Communication from the Commission Europe 2020: a Strategy for Smart, Sustainable and Inclusive Growth (2010), http://eur-lex.europa.eu/LexUriServ/LexUriServ.do?uri=COM:2010:2020:FIN:EN:PDF
8. International Labour Organization. The Prevention of Occupational Diseases (2013), http://www.ilo.org/public/english/region/eurpro/moscow/areas/safety/docs/2013/wd_report2013_en.pdf
9. Kawecka-Endler, A., Mrugalska, B.: Contemporary Aspects in Design of Work. In: Karwowski, W., Salvendy, G. (eds.) Advances in Human Factors, Ergonomics and Safety in Manufacturing and Service Industries, pp. 401–411. CRC Press, Taylor & Francis Group, Boca Raton (2011)
10. Kawecka-Endler, A., Mrugalska, B.: Analysis of changes in work process. In: Vink, P. (ed.) Advances in Social and Organizational Factors, pp. 672–681. CRC Press, Taylor & Francis Group, Boca Raton (2012)

11. Kawecka-Endler, A., Skulska, M.: Wpływ Projektowania Ergonomicznego Stanowisk Pracy na Zmniejszenie Liczby Wypadków przy Pracy. In: Kawecka-Endler, A., Mrugalska, B. (eds.) Praktyczne Aspekty Projektowania Ergonomicznego w Budowie Maszyn, pp. 71–90. Wydawnictwo Politechniki Poznańskiej, Poznań (2011) (in Polish)
12. Luczak, H.: Arbeitswissenschaft (Konzepte, Arbeitspersonnen), T. 2, Technische Universität Berlin, 3. Auflage, Berlin (1991)
13. Mrugalska, B.: Environmental Disturbances in Robust Machinery Design. In: Arezes, P., et al. (eds.) Occupational Safety and Hygiene, pp. 229–236. Taylor and Francis Group, London (2013)
14. Mrugalska, B., Arezes, P.: Safety Requirements for Machinery in Practice. In: Arezes, P., et al. (eds.) Occupational Safety and Hygiene, pp. 97–102. Taylor and Francis Group, London (2013)
15. Mrugalska, B., Kawecka-Endler, A.: Machinery Design for Construction Safety in Practice. In: Stephanidis, C. (ed.) Universal Access in HCI, Part III, HCII 2011. LNCS, vol. 6767, pp. 388–397. Springer, Heidelberg (2011)
16. Przenniak, W.: Uświadamiać Konsekwencje Wypadków, Atest – Ochrona Pracy. 12 (2006) (in Polish)
17. Schulte, P.A., Heidel, D., Okun, A., Branche, C.: Making Green Jobs Safe. Industrial Health 48(4), 377–379 (2010)
18. Studenski, R.: Jak Obniżyć Wypadowość o 25%? Elementy Strategii dla Polski, Atest - Ochrona Pracy. 3 (2009) (in Polish)
19. Zakrzewska-Szepańska, K.: BHP w Polsce 2007: Nie Jest Dobrze, Służba Pracownicza. 9 (2008) (in Polish)

The Gap between What a Service Provider Shows Off and What Users Really Watch

Dongjin Kim[1] and Jaehyun Choi[2]

[1] UX Development Center, LG U+, Seoul, Republic of Korea
danielkim@lguplus.co.kr
[2] U2 System, Gyung-gi do, Republic of Korea
choi2000@u2system.co.kr

Abstract. We identified watching behaviors on the first IPTV established with Google OS in the world. Log analysis method was taken because actual usage behaviors could be understood. Log data that forty eight users used the IPTV service were collected by the application embedded in the IPTV. As a result of the log data analysis, the frequency of zapping channels by channel up & down button was more than that of changing channels by recommendation or searching. It was indicated that users did not access VOD contents by recommendation. However, a search was used to find Youtube contents.

Keywords: watching behavior, IPTV, U+ tv G, Google OS, log analysis.

1 Introduction

There are several ways to define "Smart TV", but generally it is either a television set with integrated internet capabilities or a set-top box for television that offers more advanced computing ability and connectivity than a contemporary basic television set [1]. At the beginning that smart TV had been launched, there was full of optimistic outlook for it as an innovative service followed by smart phone. Approximately 2 million units of smart TV would be shipped in 2015 (Figure 1). Also smart TV was predicted as a main demanding channel of SNS like Facebook [2]. Besides, smart TV alliance by LG Electronics Inc., TP Vision and Toshiba was founded in 2012 for expanding ecosystem of smart TV [3]. Lately, android or web OS has emerged as a main platform, which affects as a factor to strengthen the ecosystem of smart TV.

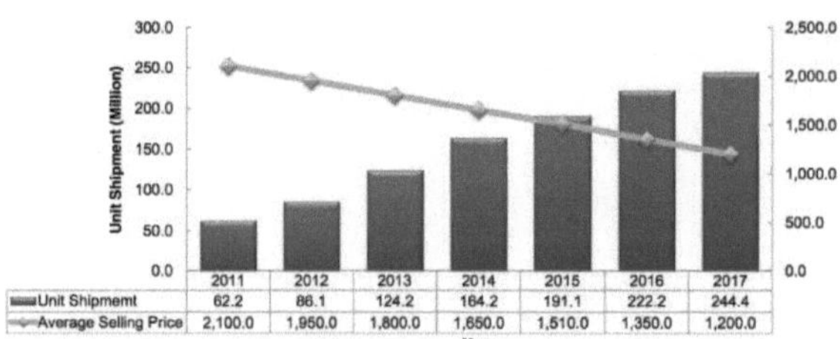

Fig. 1. Smart TV segment – unit shipment and ASP forecast (Source: Frost & Sullivan, 2012)

M. Kurosu (Ed.): Human-Computer Interaction, Part III, HCII 2014, LNCS 8512, pp. 710–720, 2014.

In reality, however, the usage behavior on smart TV doesn't correspond to an optimistic outlook anticipated in the beginning. It shows that the ecosystem of smart TV doesn't have a powerful influence compared to that of smart phone. According to data from NPD group, usage rate of most contents has stayed under 10%, except watching OTT video contents like Netflix or Hulu (Figure 2). In case of Korea, it is clear that usage frequency of unique function of smart TV is very low except watching a broadcast program [4] (Table 1). There are various interpretations about this status. For example, they are lack of contents, absence of smart UI, failure of differentiation, limitation as a lean back viewing condition.

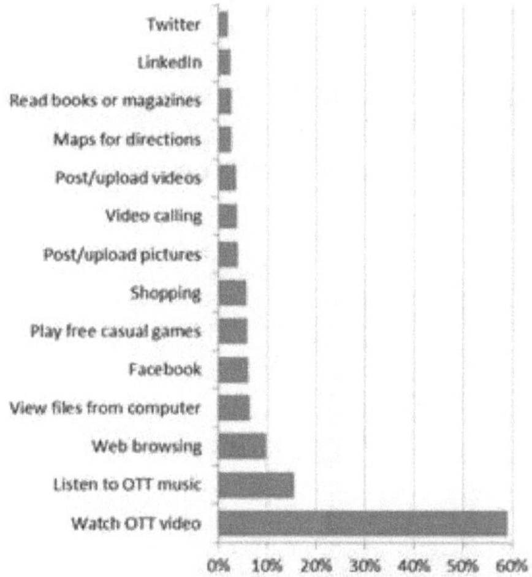

Fig. 2. TV screen application usage (Source: NPD Group, 2012)

Table 1. Comparison of share of time to use contents by each of smart devices (Source: KISDI, 2013)

	Smart phone	Tablet PC	Smart TV
TV/Radio broadcast program	1.8%	40.7%	99.6%
Movie/Music/Picture	6.2%	5.0%	0.3%
Newpaper/Book/Magazine	1.6%	15.9%	0.0%
Call/Message/email	79.0%	4.6%	0.0%
Online search/SNS/commerce	8.3%	15.5%	0.1%
Game	2.9%	6.2%	0.0%
Document/Graphic work	0.1%	12.1%	0.0%

Nonetheless, there is little research which grasps usage behaviors on smart TV and finds out why the main function of smart TV doesn't appeal to consumers. Wilfinger et al. evaluated an interaction concept in the field but overall behaviors to use interactive TV were not investigated [5]. Vinayagamoorthy et al. conducted the user experience research for connected TV but quantitative data are not enough to reveal actual usage behaviors on connected TV [6].

This research analyzes actual usage behaviors on smart TV through a log analysis on U$^+$ tv G which loads Google OS first in the world, and suggests points to be considered when designing an user experience of smart TV from the result. Smart TV and IPTV can be differentiated in composition of hardware and software. However, in this research a log analysis on IPTV service was conducted since the definition of smart TV is included to the definition of IPTV and these are judged as a similar service in researching a usage pattern.

2 The Introduction of U$^+$ TV G

2.1 Google Search

Because the device equipped with Google OS supports Google search function, users can search live TV program, VOD contents, Youtube contents and web page, etc altogether at a time by pressing 'search' button on remote control (Figure 3).

Fig. 3. Remote controller of U$^+$ tv G

2.2 TV Application

Youtube service optimized for the condition of watching TV is supported and people can use an internet on TV through chrome browser. Also, they can use some of the applications used in smartphone or tablet PC on TV.

2.3 The Rest of Services

In the living room, it is difficult for users to watch the TV program they would like to without handling remote control. Using '2nd TV' service gives a solution to this shortcoming. Users can watch some of live TV program or VOD contents wherever they want in the house by tagging their smartphone on U$^+$ tv G NFC sticker or using '2nd TV' application. Users can watch contents by 'phone to TV' service on TV screen in case that they want to see contents on big screen, not on smartphone. Family members can share their pictures, videos at smart phone as well as at TV by ‘Family Album’ service.

3 Evaluation of Usage Behavior

3.1 Subject

It was analyzed on usage behaviors of forty eight families who used U^+ tv G. Subjects were recruited according to criteria which included styles from a single household to a family of four and to have economically productive members in family or not, etc. The violation of privacy was prevented in advance by getting subjects’ consent to provide personal information.

Table 2. Subjects

Number of members	Type	Number
1	Male	4
	Femail	2
2	Couple	5
	Father & son	1
3	Couple with child	12
	Couple with a twenties	5
	Mother with two twenties	1
4	Couple with two children	8
	Couple with teenager and twenties	2
	Couple with two twenties	8

3.2 Log Analysis

Although there are many ways to evaluate usage behaviors of a service, it is easy to analyze usage frequency and has an advantage to collect detail usage behaviors automatically if log analysis is utilized [7]. In this research, log analysis is used to evaluate actual behaviors of TV viewers. After registering subjects to log analysis system who would participate in this evaluation, the application to collect log data was delivered via Gmail. Subjects accessed Gmail through chrome browser in U^+ tv G and installed the application delivered. Then, the data of usage behaviors from each family were delivered to data server automatically. The application was installed as an embedded type to prevent subjects from the application. By monitoring the application on a regular basis, the data server restored it immediately even if the problem had been occurred (Figure 4).

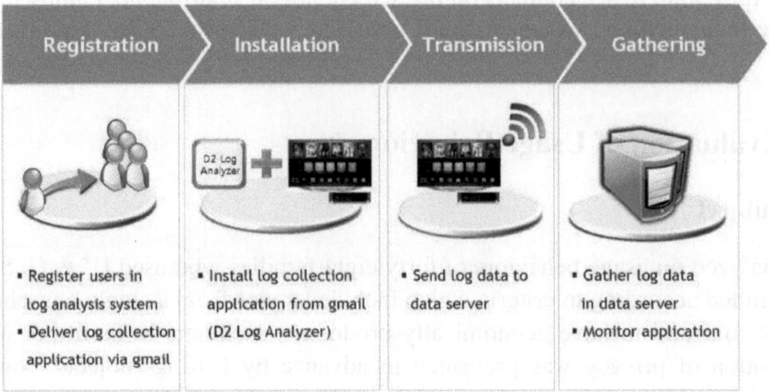

Fig. 4. The system of analysis

3.3 FGD (Focus Group Discussion)

The advantage of log analysis is to figure out service use pattern objectively. However, it is hard to understand the cause of usage pattern. Because of this, FGD was conducted for systematical research (Figure 5).

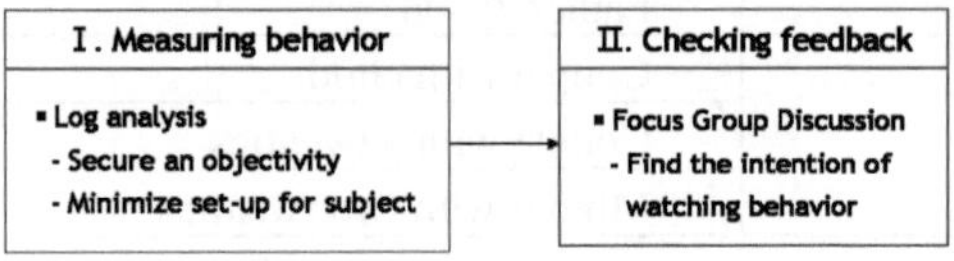

Fig. 5. Research system

3.4 Period of an Evaluation

From March 31th to April 16th in 2013, log data that subjects had used U+ tv G service were collected from forty-eight houses. And FGD was conducted from eight houses among forty eight houses for May 28th and 29th to understand the intent of their usage behaviors.

4 Results

The time to watch U^+ tv G was increased after getting up in the morning and also increased after coming from work until about 9:00 p.m. Considering a number of household members, three members household had more time to watch U^+ tv G than another household (Figure 6).

The type of contents was classified to live TV program, VOD contents, and TV applications and the time to watch live TV program was much more than others. The time to view VOD contents like drama or movie, and TV application like Youtube or Google service accounted for thirteen percent (Table 3).

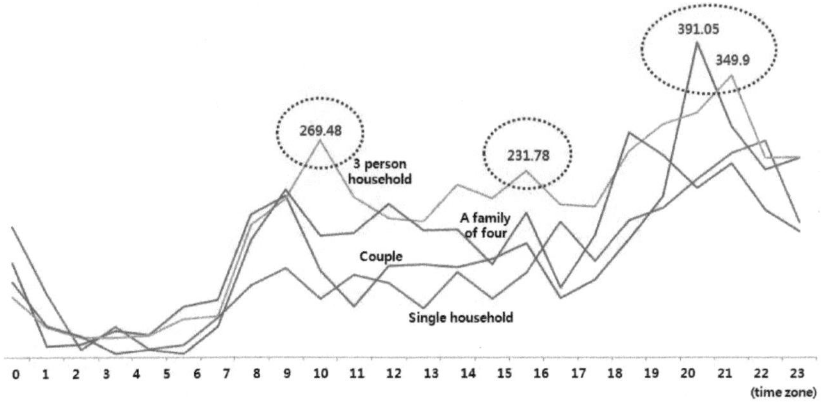

Fig. 6. Average watching time by the type of household

Table 3. The rate of viewing time by the type of content

Type of content	Rate
Live TV program	87.0%
VOD contents	8.0%
TV applications	5.0%

Users usually changed channels by channel UP, DOWN or number button on a remote control when watching live TV program (Figure 7). Though a channel could be changed by smart EPG (Electronic Program Guide) (Figure 8) after OK button had been selected, OK button was not used frequently. The case of guide button was similar to that of OK button. Users were able to change channels by selecting one of buttons on on-screen-display (OSD) after pressing OK or guide button. Therefore, in case of OK or guide button, the rate to switch channels could be calculated. The rate of switching channels by guide button was relatively higher than others like number or OK button.

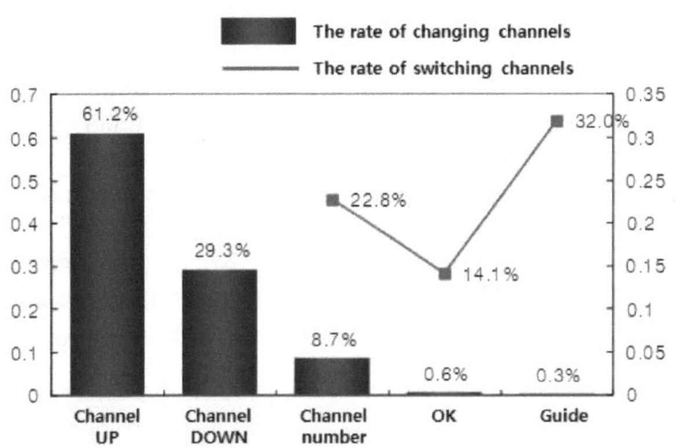

Fig. 7. The rate of changing and switching channels by each of buttons

Fig. 8. Smart EPG

After access to home menu screen by pressing home button on remote control, users could get various contents through upper recommendation area or middle category area on screen (Figure 9). There were five category menus that contained EPG and VOD contents which were 'EPG', 'replaying TV program', 'movies/animation', 'kids/education', and 'documentary'. Users were able to have an access to detail screen from home menu screen after they had controlled to move screens between menu depths. They could get a content to select "watch immediately". The rate of access to contents and the conversion rate to get contents could be calculated based on this usage flow. There were few times for users to have an access to detail screen and nothing to get contents from upper recommendation area (Figure 10).

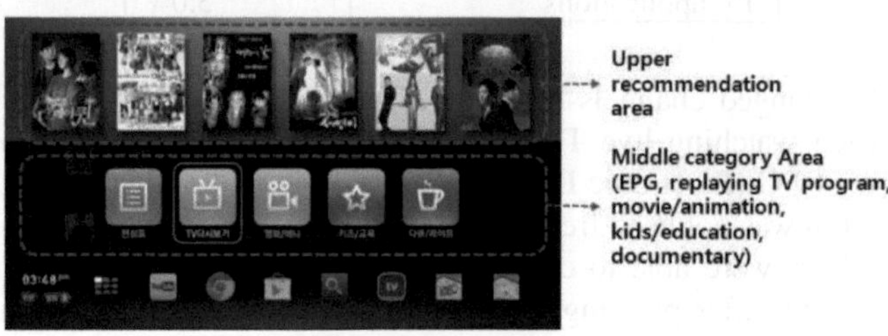

Fig. 9. Home menu screen

There were many routes to access to VOD contents. For example, if users pressed 'replaying TV program' on remote control or selected 'replaying TV program' button on home menu screen, they could get 'replaying TV program' contents on 'replaying TV program' menu screen. The conversion rate to get contents of 'replaying TV program' was slightly higher when users got contents from home menu screen than by pressing 'replaying TV program' (Figure 11). The conversion rate to get contents of 'kids/education' was considerably high.

Users got VOD content through various routes because of many attributes in content. For example, "I live by myself" was one of entertainment and amusement programs broadcasted on MBC, Friday. So, users were able to get content through flow (1) as well as flow (2).

'Replaying TV program' > 'Entertainment and amusement' > 'Weekly entertainment' (1)

'Replaying TV program' > 'MBC' > 'Entertainment and amusement' (2)

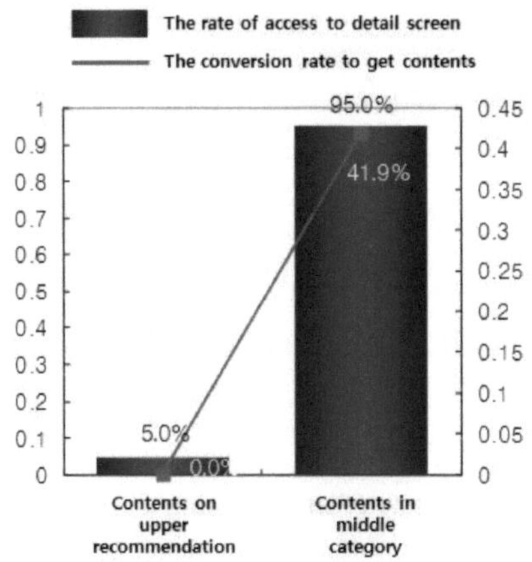

Fig. 10. The access and conversion rate from contents on upper recommendation and middle category

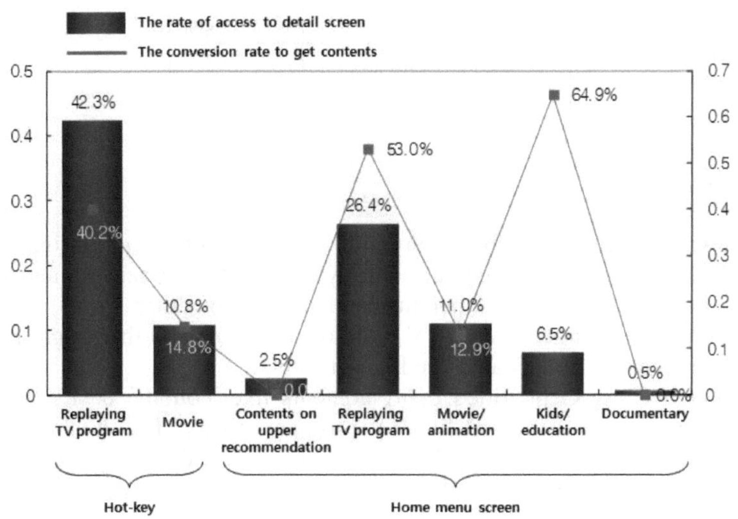

Fig. 11. The access and conversion rate from hot-keys and home menu screen

It was possible for users to reach LG U$^+$ or Google service by selecting one of icons or 'all applications' icon on launcher bar at the bottom of home menu screen. Among these, users spent most time to watch Youtube service (Figure 12). They could watch contents from the list after they entered keyword, or to have an access to menu like 'recommended'. It was dominant to watch Youtube service by predictive input (Table 4).

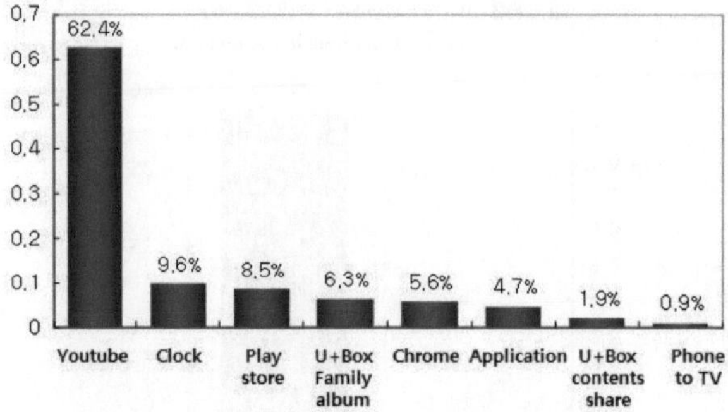

Fig. 12. The rate of time of using TV applications

Table 4. The rate of time of watching contents by searching methods

Methods	Rate
Predictive input	96.8%
Best menu	2.8%
Recommeded menu	0.3%
Fully input	0.1%

5 Discussion

Since families with three members were almost just a couple with an infancy, VOD contents for kids were mostly seen at noon by housewife and her kid, and news was seen at night by housewife and her husband mostly. In other words, it was three members family who turned on the TV with longest hours and that might be the reason why their watching time was at the highest level.

Even though U^+ tv G provided many contents like Youtube or TV applications from Google play, users watched live TV program mostly. This is similar with the result of research which found out that even with smart TV, what people mainly use was to watch live TV program [8]. Users changed channels simply though there were many different ways to search it. Although channel recommendation on EPG which could be reached by OK button was supported for users, usage frequency of it was not much. It could be understood as a feature of lean back viewing condition.

According to log analysis, users changed channels for thirteen times on average and switched channels for three times except with channel UP or DOWN button. Channels on U^+ tv G are divided by each of genre such as terrestrial broadcast from five to thirteen, news from twenty three to twenty seven, movie from twenty nine to thirty eight, and sport from fifty to fifty nine. So, it could be deduced that users controlled to move a channel by number button and then switch channels for three times with channel UP or DOWN button. This was verified by FGD (3).

"Since sport channels are from number fifty to fifty nine, I first reach there and then search channels up and down." (3)

Users did not concentrate on recommended contents on upper area of home menu screen. In case of contents of 'replaying TV program', they had already set to watch content before searching it. This was also checked by FGD (4).

"I have already set to watch a soap opera, so the important thing is to be sure what the last episode is." (4)

It might be right decision to provide various routes to access to VOD contents because the route of VOD content that each of users recognized was different.

People used to choose Youtube contents from the list after predictive input had been worked. It seems that this has no big difference with the case of smartphone. However, once a user had chosen content from the list, it kept showing next content automatically after chosen one had been over. This could be considered that user experience had been designed to optimize viewing contents on TV. Anyway, users spent most time to watch Youtube contents among whole services except live TV program and VOD contents.

From the result of research, some of the guidelines were drawn to consider designing user interface on the viewpoint of users. First, it was considered for users to change channels easier than before. With the list of start channels by genres, users could control to go to a channel in one of genres without pressing number button. Then, they were able to control to change channels easily by pressing channel UP or DOWN button. Second, it would be needed to replace contents on upper recommendation area of home menu screen because users had already set VOD contents in their mind and recommended contents was not noticeable to them.

6 Conclusion

This study has focused on viewer's usage behavior through log analysis on U^+ tv G. Although it was an IPTV which has attributes of smart TV, the time to watch live TV program accounted for ninety percent of total watching time approximately. Users just tried to change channels by pressing channel UP or DOWN button even though there were various ways to transfer channels by recommendation. People had an access to home menu screen after they had already set to view VOD contents and reached content in various routes. As a result, there were few cases to get contents on upper recommendation area of home screen. Users spent most time to watch Youtube contents except live TV program and VOD contents. And they searched contents by predictive input.

In this study, there is a limitation to comprehend viewers' actual usage behavior as the study was conducted for only nine days. However, the problem was supplemented by utilizing log analysis and FGD systematically. Additional research will be needed to find actual usage behavior for longer period by a qualitative research approach.

References

1. Wikipedia, http://en.wikipedia.org/wiki/Smart_TV
2. Thomas, N.: Making TV social. In: The future of TV: Strategies for Becoming Connected, Social, and in the Cloud, pp. 13–15. IP&TV World Forum (2012)

3. Smart TV Alliance, http://www.smarttv-alliance.org/default.aspx
4. Kim, M.: Comparison of usage pattern of contents by each of smart devices, KISDI stat report (2013)
5. Wilfinger, D., Pirker, M., Bernhaupt, R., Tscheligi, M.: Evaluating and investigating an iTV interaction concept in the field. In: Euro ITV 2009, pp. 175–178 (2009)
6. Vinayagamoorthy, V., Hammond, M., Allen, P., Evans, M.: Researching the user experience for connected TV - A case study. In: CHI 2012, pp. 589–604 (2012)
7. Nielsen, J.: Usability engineering. Morgan Kaufmann, San Francisco (1993)
8. Park, Y., Kim, M., Lee, K.: Analysis of proof of smart device usage behavior, Basic research. Korea Information Society Development Institute (2011)

Design Artefacts as Business Decision Prompts: Tackling the Design and Business Values Gap

Joanna Kwiatkowska[1], Agnieszka Szóstek[2], and David Lamas[1]

[1] Tallinn University, Narva Mnt 25, 10120 Tallinn, Estonia
[2] Academy of Fine Arts, Krakowskie Przedmiescie 5, 00-068 Warsaw, Poland
{joan.kwiatkowska,aga.szostek}@gmail.com, david.lamas@tlu.ee

Abstract. This paper focuses on ways of supporting business in staying focused on the identified design values throughout the entire product or service development process. Based on literature review we propose design artefacts as business decision prompts. This consideration is used to structure and discuss probes artefacts as business decision prompts.

Keywords: design artefacts, probes, User-Centered Design, prompts, design values, business values.

1 Introduction

It is undoubted that design is of great importance for companies at present [28, 14, 10]. It is source of innovation, competitiveness, problems solving approach as well as mean for differentiation. Design supports development of products and services, and, as stated by the ICSID (International Council of Societies of Industrial Design, 2005), "it is the crucial factor of cultural and economic exchange". Furthermore, it assists management in organizations [14].

1.1 Approaches

There are several ways that designers might apply to tackle design problems, e.g. User-Centered Design (UCD), Activity-Centered Design, Systems Design or Genius Design [25]. User-Centered Design is perceived as a dominant approach, thus it is often accepted as the only right method while elaborating a new product or service [23, 4]. Therefore, an increasing number of companies outside of the IT domain value more and more the user-centered approach in the development process of their products and services [1, 2]. Some of these companies decide to establish User Experience (UX) departments with the goal to align their offerings with user needs and desires and deliver recognized design values in final products or services.

1.2 Roles and Values

The role of the UX department in the company is to understand users, create concepts of products or services which will bring real value to target users, monitor the

M. Kurosu (Ed.): Human-Computer Interaction, Part III, HCII 2014, LNCS 8512, pp. 721–730, 2014.

development process so that the design values will remain in the final product or service (embed design values in designed solutions) and, finally, indirectly bring money for the company [12, 13]. On the other hand, the role of business is to deliver profitable products or services, which bring return or investment as well as meet other company requirements (e.g. fit corporate culture).

The presented roles of UX and business teams determine values appreciated by them as well. The UX departments promote design values which cover user needs, desires, concepts that meet user requirements, functionality and usability aspects that are favourable for users [12]. Business values, by contrast, regard *"creating products for which a good business case can be made"* [12] (ratio of invested money to the return on investment).

These two systems of values (design vs business values) are competing and there is a gap between design and business values (see: Fig. 1).

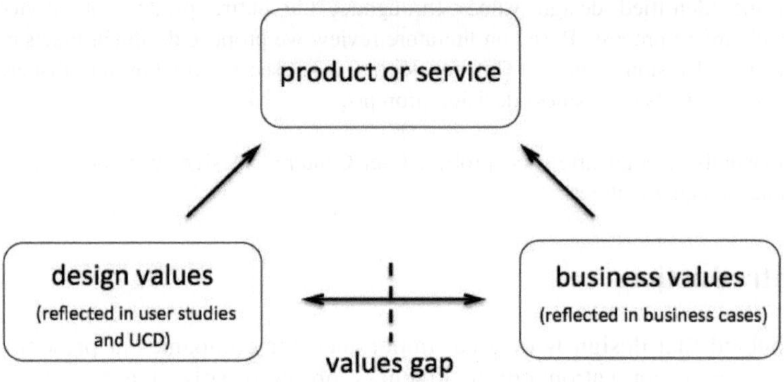

Fig. 1. The user and business values relations

1.3 Outcomes and Consequences

Although a high interest in UX department's deliverables might be distinguished [1, 2], in practice User-Centered Design values tend to fall behind business decisions and an overall low awareness of user needs can be observed throughout the company [15, 16].

UCD places users at the centre of design decisions and engages them into design process within design research activities [29]. However, according to Cockton UCD is: *"strong on problems, but weak on solutions"* [6]. Therefore, instead of definite products or services, the UCD activities might bring outcomes in the form of artefacts defined as information which let us imagine how a design would appear or behave [6]. Thus, since the form of such information is not precise, there is a risk that UCD deliverables might be misinterpreted by business teams members, e.g. they might support immediate business decisions instead of guiding the whole design and development process. In consequence, it causes unbalance between business and design focus in the resulting solutions, often to the disadvantage of the user [15, 16]. Therefore, the gap between design and business values is strengthened.

2 Problem Statement

Even if the results of user research are viable, currently business teams are unable to effectively utilize them in the development process. Henderson et al. recognized the following problems resulting from the design and business value gap (see: Fig. 2):

- the implications from user studies and UCD are not included in final products or services (not included early enough or in enough depth),
- design values are lost in development (misunderstood, cost-reduced),
- design values never reach final use [12, 13].

Therefore, we argue that there is an increasing need to provide effective tools or solutions to support stakeholders in paying attention to the discovered user needs in order to deploy products and services which use of knowledge generated by research. This article focus on exploring possible ways to support business teams in staying focused on the identified user needs and design values throughout the entire development process.

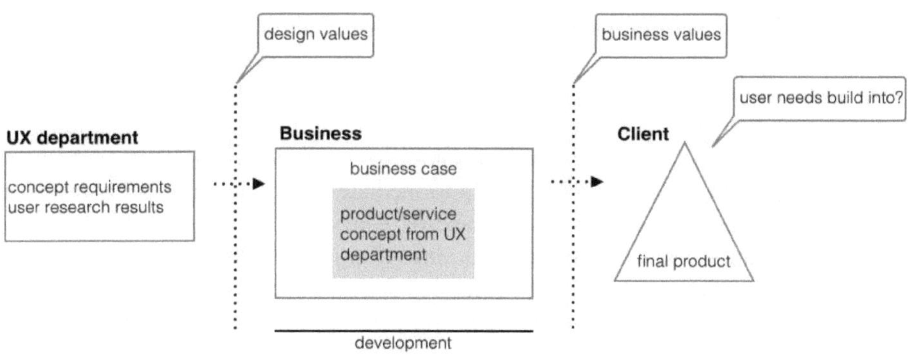

Fig. 2. Research problem

Development in the context of the given article means the overall process of creating new products or services: idea generation, strategy, product creation, marketing as well as evaluation.

3 Related Work

The topic of transferring user data to business has been discussed since the dawn of the HCI domain. The problem has traditionally been approached from two angles: organizational and communicative. In the first approach both the teams and processes are created within the company to support UCD process throughout business development [18]. In the second approach various communication tools and artefacts are developed to remind the teams about design values, motivations and goals. The most known artefact is probably persona [7] widely used in various types of business from marketing agencies to software houses. Yet personas seem to be insufficiently successful in what they aim to convey [25]. It may be due to the fact that personas are quite complex and one needs to be trained to use them properly [22]. We argue that simpler tools and artefacts could prove to increase the overall sensitivity to user-centered insights outside of the UX teams.

4 Design Artefacts as Business Decision Prompts

The term artefact comes from Latin *arte factum*, which means something made with skill [8]. Primarily artefacts indicate something made or given shape by human, e.g. tools or works that might be of archaeological or cultural interest. Furthermore, artefacts might be perceived as symbolic higher-order tools of the designers [11], e.g. prototypes, sketches, user stories, probes, etc. Artefacts provide different design perspectives as well as communicate values while conducting design activities [3]. According to Vyas et al. [30] design artefacts improve efficiency, bring quality and richness to people performance by supporting their creativity and invention. In line with Zimmerman et al., "design *artefacts (...) can transform the world from its current state to a preferred state*" [31]. Particularly, material artefacts are likely to play an important role in cooperative work. Vyas et al. [30] showed an experiential role of artefacts, particularly physical ones, to be used as prompts supporting collaboration among designers. They help to mediate design activity, i.e. conception, communication and cooperation during the design process.

What we want to bring into question is since design artefacts are quite effective in communicating values within design activities and prompting designers, would they act similarly within business teams and support application of design values in developed products or services? Thus, we propose design artefacts as business decision prompts, where term *prompt* comprises anything that serves to remind: spur, cue, hint or stimulus.

To address the posed question, the literature review has been conducted with the goal to verify the possible applicability of design artefacts as business decision prompts. The artefacts qualities and characteristics have been identified where on the basis of the conducted affinity diagramming the four clusters have emerged representing the dimensions where artefacts might influence:

- **personal** dimension defines how artefacts influence individuals who interact with an artefact,
- **group** dimension describes the intermediary artefacts qualities,
- **design activity** dimension characterizes how design artefacts mediate design activities,

– **outer** dimensions presents what are the prospects of further design artefacts application – beyond the design activity.

The parameters of the particular dimensions have been presented in Figure 3.

personal	group	design activity	outer activity
• improve development [5] • bring quality and richness to people performances [30] • support creativity and innovation • provoke insights [11] • provoke reflection [11]	• improve social development [5] • align collaborative efforts [3] • evoke empathic relations [3] • enable divergent and convergent thinking [24] • support discussions [5] • provoke insights [11] • provoke reflection [11]	• frame design even in specific way [3] • applied in participatory design, co-design, HCI research, collaborative activities • support goal-oriented actions [5] • provoke design changes [11] • enable rapid transformation [11] • document, e.g. discussion [11] • support communication among designers and usurers	• support discussion [5] • support goal-oriented activities [5] • provoke reflection [11] • act as boundary objects [24] • play important role in stakeholders understanding [3]

Fig. 3. The artefacts dimensions

In the design artefact as business decision prompts context, the emergence of the outer activity dimension is crucial. Particularly the *support goal-oriented activities* as well as *act as boundary object* parameters bring the opportunity for a solution which facilitate embedding design values into products or services throughout the development process.

4.1 Probes

To address the research problem, the literature review aimed as well at finding research methods, which by its nature provide the results in the form of design artefacts and deeply engage users. Such assumption guarantees that the given artefact would act as design values carrier. Therefore, the probe research methods have been indicated as a first approach for further design and business gap investigation.

The understanding of the term *probe* might be associated with a solution, where a given object is sent to the areas where human researchers cannot go, so data might be collected automatically. The probe approach has been proposed by Gaver et al. [9]. Probes in this context are specifically designed toolkits applied in user research based on self-documentation and self-reflection. Such toolkits (material packages) are given to users to provoke them to reflect and document their experiences, emotions, feelings, needs, values, thoughts as well as to inspire them to visualise their actions or ideas [19]. The probing approach enables users to become active participants of the design process. The main goal of probes is to create dialogue between the designer and user. Further purposes of the probe research method application and its role have been presented in Table 1.

Table 1. Probes' characteristics

	Probes
role	- inspire - provoke - collect data - explore new opportunities - ask open questions - reveal future needs - study users in their own environment - orient the design - with exploratory goal - document the present - predict future; look for future possibilities - self-documentary
purpose of application	- communication medium for ideation - stimulate imagination - empower users as well as designers creativity - support reflection - collect information about users - create insights - capture design ideas - facilitate participatory workshops - support non verbal thinking - support dialogue between the designer and user - gather ethnographic information - gather empathetic data - get data on usability issues - understand the potential for new technologies
critical issues	- ambiguous and fragmented data - no guidelines for designing probes - lack of formal analysis

The context of the method application determines the probe form:

- cultural probes –applied to explore users cultural setting (Gaver et al. (1999): "designed objects, physical packets containing open-ended, provocative and oblique tasks to support early participants' engagement with the design process"),
- design probes – aim to provide inspiration for designers and gather insights,
- empathy probes – enable to collect the data concerning experiences, attitudes, life-styles. The self-documented material is discussed with users in personal interviews after the probing task to support its understanding (Mattelmaki (2006)),

– technological probes – introduces technologies to collect self-documented data from users (Hutchinson (2003))
– mobile probes – the method applies mobile device to probe users actions in mobile contexts (Hulkko et al. (2004))
– urban probes – applied to find new opportunities for technology in urban spaces (proposed by Paulos and Jenkins (2005)) [14],
– informational probes (Crabtree 2003) – collect information about users: their experiences, needs, etc.,
– reflective probes (Loi 2004) – enable users to reflect around the examined experience,
– primitive probes (Loi 2004) – this approach assumes that we enable users to design probe kits for themselves or for other users.

4.2 Business Decision Prompts

The goal of the given research was to provide effective tool or solution to support business in staying focused on discovered design values throughout entire product or service development process. On the basis of the results from the literature review on artefacts' and probes' characteristics, the following working hypothesis has been formulated:

The result of the probe research method in the form of design artefact constitutes an effective business decision prompt, where effective refers to high applicability of design values into product or service development (see: Fig. 4).

Fig. 4. The artefacts dimensions

To test if probe artefacts might serve as business decision prompts, their identified characteristics have been mapped on artefacts dimensions proposed in section 4 (see: Fig. 3).

On the personal dimension, probe artefacts support mainly the creation of insights as well as reflection. Group dimension qualities support dialogue between designers who work in the same team (e.g. work on the same project and analyse the data coming from probes' artefacts). Within the framework of design activity, probes' artefacts facilitate dialogue between users and designers. Furthermore, they evoke designers' empathy for probe activity participants [21]. However, the most essential is the emergence of overlapping characteristics in outer activity dimension where probe artefacts might be a mean of user-centered dialogue promotion [20] (e.g. probes' artefacts as promotion of research results in companies) as well as empathy tool (the probes artefacts could evoke empathy among business representatives).

Therefore, we propose probes' artefacts as business decision prompts to address the following areas:

- promotion of user-centered dialogue in companies,
- tool for evoking empathy with participants of design activities.

Probes' artefacts as a tool for promoting user-centeredness would:

- act as *in-house marketing* tool for research results promotion [20],
- increase the engagement in design activities through the fresh approach of user studies,
- orient business towards user context,
- increase commitment to the research results.

On the other hand, probes artefacts as empathy tool could:

- build up a discussion,
- support dialogue: *involve organization into dialogue* [19],
- support learning and understanding users,
- create interaction among different groups of stakeholders.

5 Closing Remarks

The article discusses the notion of design artefact and probe artefact as related concepts. The probes' characteristics and context of their application have been presented as well. Furthermore, article attempts to define the unique properties of design artefacts that determine their success in supporting business teams in staying focused on the discovered user needs.

Finally, on the basis of the literature review, probes artefacts properties applicable as business decision prompts are indicated: probes artefacts as a tool for promoting user-centeredness and evoking empathy towards design values in companies.

In the next study we aim to analyse further types of artefacts and concepts with respect to their potential for engaging business in the product or service design process, e.g. boundary objects or generative tools. Furthermore, a case study would be conducted to test the effectiveness of probes' artefacts as business decision prompts.

References

1. Bannon, L.: Reimaginig HCI: Toward a more human-centered perspective. Interactions 18, 50–57 (2011)
2. Bevan, N.: Quality in use: Meeting user needs for quality. Journal of Systems and Software 49, 89–96 (1999); Bodker M.: Performative artefacts: Users "Speaking through" artefacts in collaborative design. In: Proceedings of the 21st Annual Conference of the Australian Computer-Human Interaction Special Interest Group: Design: Open 24/7. ACM (2009)

3. Breitenberger, P.: Probes in Design Research. Frameworks and guidelines for designing, applying and evaluation probes. Akademiker Verlag (2012)
4. Brown, J., Lindgaard, G., Biddle, R.: Stories, sketches and lists: Developers and interaction designers interacting through artefacts. In: Proceedings of the Agile 2008. IEEE Computer Society (2008)
5. Cockton, G.: UCD: Critique via Parody and a Sequel. In: CHI EA 2012: Proceedings of the 2012 ACM Annual Conference on Extended Abstracts on Human Factors in Computing Systems Extended Abstracts. ACM (2012)
6. Cooper, A.: About Face 3: The essentials of interaction design. Wiley (2007), Dictionary.com – artefact: `http://dictionary.reference.com/browse/artifact`
7. Gaver, W., Dunne, T., Panceti, E.: Cultural Probes. Interactions 6(1), 21–29 (1999)
8. Gomes, A., Branco, V.: How to measure design contribution to the competitiveness of companies: models for analysis tool. In: DPPI 2011: Proceedings of the 2011 Conference on Designing Pleasurable Products and Interfaces. ACM (2011)
9. Hansen, N., Dalsgaard, B., The, P.: productive role of material design artefacts in participatory design events. In: Proceedings of the 7th Nordic Conference on Human-Computer Interaction. ACM (2012)
10. Henderson, A., Anderson, L., Ashley, J., Heuman, P., Rohn, J.: The route to the sea for user value. In: CHI 2006: Proceedings of the SIGCHI Conference on Human Factors in Computing Systems. ACM (2006)
11. Henderson, A., Bradt, A., Hammontree, M., Heuman, P.: Building user value into the business case. In: CHI 2006: Proceedings of the SIGCHI Conference on Human Factors in Computing Systems. ACM (2006)
12. Kronqvist, J., Salmi, A.: Co-designing (with) organizations – human-centeredness, participation and embodiment in organizational development. In: DPPI 2011: Proceedings of the 2011 Conference on Designing Pleasurable Products and Interfaces. ACM (2011)
13. Lindgaard, G.: Making the business our business: One path to Value-Added HCI. Interactions 11 (2004)
14. Lindgaard, G., Millard, N.: The business value of HCI: How can we do better? In: CHI 2002 Extedned Abstracts on Human Factors in Computing Systems, pp. 928–929. ACM (2002)
15. Loi, D.: Reflective probes, primitive probes and playful triggers. In: Ethnographic Praxis in Industry Conference, pp. 233–246 (2007)
16. Lund, A.: User Experience Management: Essential skills for leading effective UX teams. Morgan Kauffman (2011)
17. Mattelmaki, T.: Applying probes – from inspirational notes to collaborative insights. CoDesign 1(2), 83–102 (2005)
18. Mattelmaki, T.: Design probes. University of Art and Design Helsinki (2006)
19. Mattelmaki, T., Battarbee, T.: Empathy probes. In: Proceedings of PDC 2002, pp. 277–271 (2002)
20. Matthews, T., Judge, T., Whittaker, S.: How do designers and user experience professionals actually perceive and use personas? In: CHI 2012. ACM (2012)
21. Norman, D.: Human-Centered Design Considered Harmful. Interactions 12(4) (2005)
22. Pennington, D.,, D.: The dynamics of material artifacts in collaborative research teams. Computer Supported Cooperative Work 19(2) (2010)
23. Saffer, D.: Designing for Interaction: Creating Smart Applications and Clever Devices. Peachpit Press (2006)

24. Sanders, E., Westerlund, B.: Experiencing, exploring and experimenting in and with co-design spaces. In: Nordic Design Research Conference (2011)
25. Sanders, E., William, T.: Harnessing people's creativity: ideation and expression through visual communication. In: Focus Groups: Supporting Effective Product Development. Taylor and Francis (2001)
26. Thenint, H.: Design as a tool for innovation. Innovation Policy Report, Global Review of Innovation Intelligence and Policy Studies. A PRO INNO Europe project (2008)
27. Williams, A.: User-centered design, activity-centered design, and goal-directed design: a review of three methods for designing web applications. In: SIGDOC 2009: Proceedings of the 27th ACM International Conference on Design of Communication. ACM (2009)
28. Vyas, D., Heylen, D., Nijholt, A., Veer, G.: Experiential role of artefacts in cooperative design. In: Proceedings of the Fourth International Conference on Communities and Technologies, C&T 2009, pp. 105–114. ACM (2009)
29. Yoo, D., Huldtgren, A., Woelfer, J., et al.: A value sensitive Action-Reflection Model: Evolving a co-design space with stakeholder and designer prompts. In: CHI 2013: Proceedings of the SIGCHI Conference on Human Factors in Computing Systems. ACM (2013)
30. Zimmerman, J., Forlizzi, J., Evenson, J.: Research through design as a method for interaction design research in HCI. In: Proceedings of the SIGCHI Conference on Human Factors in Computing Science, pp. 493–502. ACM (2007)

Home Networking: Smart but Complicated

Abbas Moallem

College of Engineering, San José State University,
One Washington Square, San Jose, CA 95192-0085
abbas.moallem@sjsu.edu

Abstract. Internet connection at home has fundamentally changed the way that appliances are designed in the same way that the invention of electricity did. Having efficient and reliable home networking is the key to any modern home. The number of devices that need to be connected to a home networking system increases every day. Computers, televisions, tablets, gaming devices and sound systems are just some of the many appliances that need that connection. Despite the improvements to the hardware of networking devices, re-search shows that the software to set up networking devices along with their configuration are extremely complicated. This paper presents the results of several usability investigations on home networking devices including: a comparative study of different product brands, two series of user surveys, and empirical observations. The results of these investigations show that all of the major brands of home networking appliances use a complex, feature-oriented, rudimentary user interface (UI) design with terms that are understood by a very small percentage of people.

Keywords: Smart Device, Home Networking, Routers User Interface, Wi-Fi Network.

1 Introduction

With the growing number of smart appliances at home [1] that need to connect to the Internet efficiently and with the security to operate successfully, the Internet and Internet-based technologies have become a basic utility, like electricity, gas, or water. Thus the need for wireless connections at home to allow all devices to be connected and interconnect is an essential feature of a modern home. There exists a need for a high-speed Internet connection, a reliable and high-speed router/modem, device interconnectivity and discoverability in a network, and the ability to enable users to easily manage this network, set security criteria and most importantly, troubleshoot any issues [2], [3] & [4]

Not long ago, Internet connection was limited to one or more computers at home. Now, gradually within a "smart home" [5] a multitude of computerized devices are interconnected and interact with each other. Users should be able to not only configure them but also monitor them on a daily basis, while interacting with them and, more importantly, problem-solving any and all network issues.

Despite progress in the hardware of these devices, improvements in the usability of their software are still insufficient. Users commonly agree that managing home

M. Kurosu (Ed.): Human-Computer Interaction, Part III, HCII 2014, LNCS 8512, pp. 731–741, 2014.

networks is a tedious, difficult task that is out of reach for most users with limited networking experience.

Some research points out a variety of usability issues for home networking technologies [6] [7] [8].

The expansion of the smart home concept adds even more complexity to home networking. Pairing the devices with routers, selecting the right channels, conflicts, ranges, incompatibility of signal are some of the most common issues that users are confronted with [8], [9] & [10].

It is still believed that home networking should benefit elder adults who also tend to have an overall positive attitude towards this technology. A good example of how people benefit from this technology is the usage of health monitoring sensors or security devices in the home that enhance their lives [11]. Yet the ease of use of these applications is crucial for successful usage by elder adults.

Home network devices should make it easy to add computers or any other smart appliances to the home network, and establish interaction by offering users an easy to use and intuitive method of centralized management and monitoring of devices.

The results of a survey on home wireless usage reveal that currently 22% of people surveyed bought their wireless router based on speed, followed by 17% that based it on low price, and 1% for ease of use. However when participants were asked about purchasing a new wireless router, speed remained the top factor but its importance increased to 37%, and ease of use moved up to second priority with 17% [1].

Consequently, making home networking smart is not achievable unless the usability of the devices (software and hardware) along with their configurations, is extensively improved and accessible to all types of users. [12 &13)

The goal of this study was to first identify the most important issues in usability and then to investigate how usability can be improved.

2 Method

After completing a comparative study of user interfaces of several networking router brands, two groups of participants were surveyed through two different online questionnaires: one on terminology and a second on home networking. Some participants participated in both studies.

In the terminology study, 84 participants (mostly college students and former graduate students in software engineering, human factors, and psychology) completed an online survey. 54% of participants were male, 45% female, with 54% under age 25, 24% ages 26 to 35, 12% ages 36-45 and 8% over 46 years. There were 54% with a formal education of college, 26% graduate schools and 14% with other. It is important to underline that 86% of the respondents owned a rout-er at their place of living.

In the networking study, 67 participants (mostly college students and former graduate students in software engineering, human factors, and psychology) completed the online survey. 67% of the participants were male, 33% female, with 55% ages 18-25, 19% ages 26-35, 6% ages 36-45, and 19% over age 45. 6% of the participants self-evaluated their level of expertise in computer usage as "Expert", 25% as "Advanced", 52% as "Intermediate", and 16% as "Beginners." 30% of the participants had a graduate level education, 60% college and 9% high school.

3 Results

3.1 Comparative Study of Router User Interfaces

Comparing the user interfaces of four major brands of devices illustrated the similarity of the design among the different brands. (Basic screens of router interfaces for these brands are shown in Figure 1a, b, c and d). A quick review of the screens, despite some differences in color palette or layout, reveals that the UIs are built using the same terminologies. Each UI displays a number of parameters that are required for users to understand and set or configure without knowing the context, what the settings do, and the relationship among the parameters. All four UIs evaluated use a feature-based design approach targeted to advanced users with IT background.

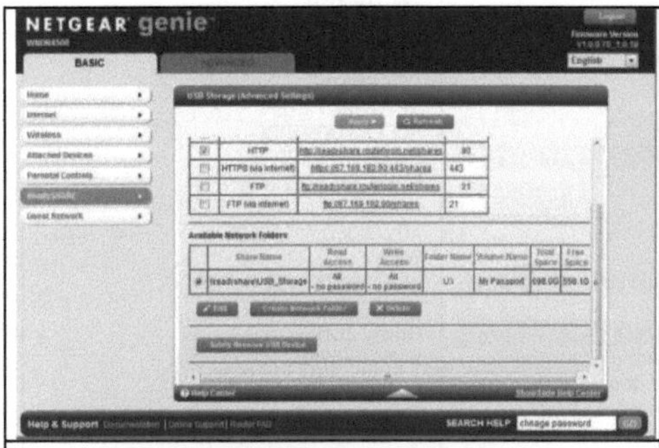

Figure 1.a: NETGEAR- Field Labels

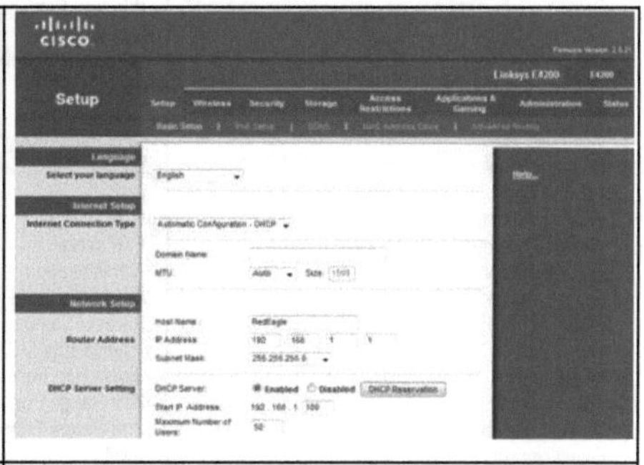

Figure 1.b: 2:Cisco-Linksys-Field Labels

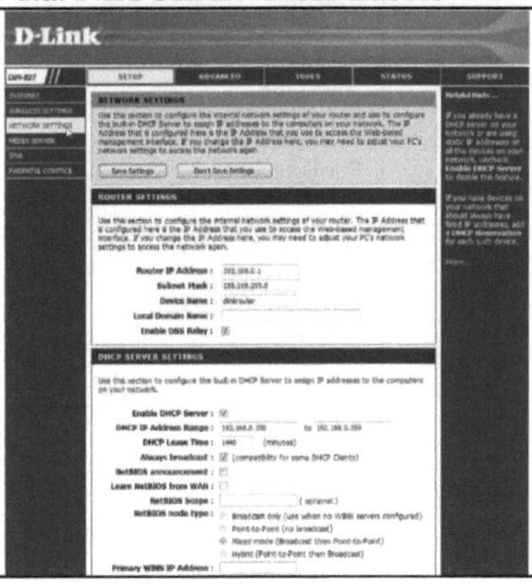

Figure 1.c: D-link- Field Labels

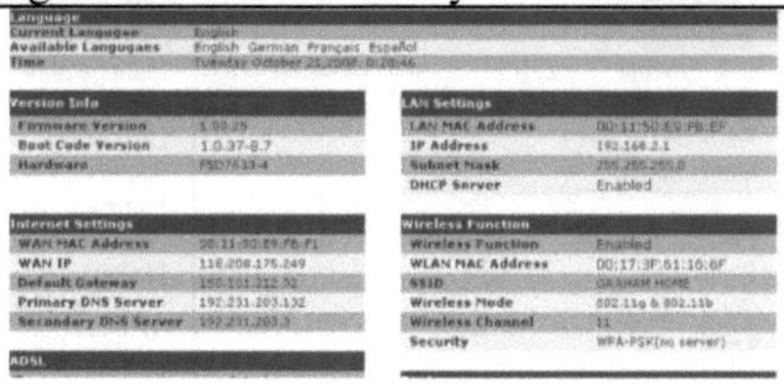

Figure 1.d:Belkin Modem Router

Fig. 1. 1a, 1b, and 1c, show UI screens of the four router brands evaluated. The field labels and terminology seem very similar if not identical.

Figures 1.a to 1.d show the main page UIs of the four router brands. The field labels and terminology seem very similar if not identical.

Figures 2.a, b, and c show the information architecture of the left hand navigation. Terminology and concept again stay similar for all the three compared brands.

All of the major brands of home networking appliances use a complex feature-oriented rudimentary user interface (UI) design. Among other things, we notice a tremendous amount of text, very technical terminology, complex labeling and difficult navigation. The situation is not very different from one product to an-other among major brands.

a. NETGEAR	b. Linksys	c. D-Link
Home	**Setup**	**SETUP**
Internet	Basic Setup	IINTERNET
Wireless	iPv6 Setup	WIRELESS SETTINGS
Parental Controls	Mac Address Clone	MEDIA SERVER
ReadySHARE	Advanced Routing	IPV6
Guest Network	**Wireless**	PARENTAL CONROL
Home	Wireless Settings	ADVANCED
Internet	Guest Access	VIRTUAL SERVER
Wireless	Wireless Mac Filter	APPLICATION RULES
Parental Controls	Security	QOS ENGINE
ReadySHARE	Firewall	NETWORK FILTER
Guest Network	VPN Passthrough	ACCESS CONTROL
Router Information	**Storage**	WEBSITE FILTER
Internet Port	Disk	FIREWALL SETTINGS
Wireless Settings (2.4GHz)	Media Server	ROUTING
Wireless Settings (5.0GHz)	FTP server	ADVANCED WIRELESS
Guest Network (2.4GHz)	Administration	WISH
Guest Network (5.0GHz)	**Access Restriction**	WI-FI PROTECTED SETUP
Setup Wizard	Parental Control	**ADVACNED** NETWORK
WPS Wizard	**Applications & Gaming**	GUEST ZONE
Wireless	Single Port Forwarding	IPV6 FIREWALL
Internet Setup	Port Range Forwarding	IPV6 ROUTING
Wireless Setup	Port Range Triggering	**TOOLS**
Guest Network	DMZ	ADMIN
WAN Setup	iPV6 Firewall	TIME
LAN Setup	QoS	SYSLOG
QoS Setup	**Administration**	EMAILSETTINGS
USB Storage	Management	SYSTEM
ReadySHARE	Log	FIREWARE
Advanced Settings	Diagnostics	DYNAMIC DNS
Media Server	Factory Default	SYSTEMCHECK
Security	Firmware Upgrade	SCHEDULES
Parental Controls	**Status**	**STATUS**
Block Sites	Router	DEVICE INFO
Schedule	Local Network	LOGS
E-mail	Wireless network	STATISTICS
E-mail	Ports	INTERNET SESSIONS
Administration		ROUTING
Router Status		WIRELESS
Logs		IPV6
Attached Devices		IPV6 TOUTING
Backup Settings		SCHEDULES
Set Password		
Firmware Update		
Advanced Setup		
Wireless Settings		
Wireless Repeating Function		
Port Forwarding / Port Triggering		
Dynamic DNS		
Static Routes		
Remote Management		
USB Settings		
UPnP		
IPv6		
Traffic Meter		

Fig. 2. Left hand navigation in the three major router brands

Table 1. Labeling terms used in most router user interfaces

Cable Modem, Channel, DNS Servers, Domain Name, DSL Modem, Enable SSID Broadcast, FTP (via internet), Gateway IP Address, Guest Network, HTTP (via internet),Hitter, Internet IP Address, IP Address, IP Subnet Mask, IP Subnet Mask,IPv6,Media Server, Modem, Passphrase, Primary DNS, Router, Router MAC Address, Secondary DNS, Static IP Address, USB Settings, WEP, WPA/WPA2 Enterprise, WPA-PSK [TKIP],WPA-PSK [TKIP] + WPA2-PSK [AES],WPA-PSK WPA2-PSK [AES],

3.2 Terminology

If you have a home networking device, there is a good chance that you have experienced a variety of home networking user interfaces. You might have even asked someone with technical knowledge to help you with installing, connecting, and configuring the device that you acquired or had problems with. This might have happened for any type of device from a Wi-Fi router to more advanced de-vices such as storage, security systems, and interactive TV or sound systems.

The poor usability of these user interfaces (UIs) is not noticeable with only one or two brands of products. A simple comparison among the most common brands on the market reveals that all brands suffer to some degree from the same usability issues.
Table [1] shows the 30 common terms used in configuration and setting of major Wi-Fi router brands.

The results of a survey with 84 potential users show that a very small percentage of people know the meaning of the terms used in these devices' user interfaces (UIs). Many users do not understand even the more common terms shown in Table 2, such as DSL modem or IP address. For example, 41% of participants could not be certain of the meaning of the words "Passphrase", 37% for "Media Server", 46% for "WEP", and even 4% for "Router". (Chart 1 and Table 2).

Even for terms like "Modem", "Router, and "IP address", while the percent-age of participants who were "not sure at all" is low (3%, 4% and 6%), those who "know what it means but not sure" was very high (44% for Modem, 37% for Router and 43% for IP Address) (Chart 2, Table 2).

It is important to underline that 86% of the respondents own a router at their place of living.

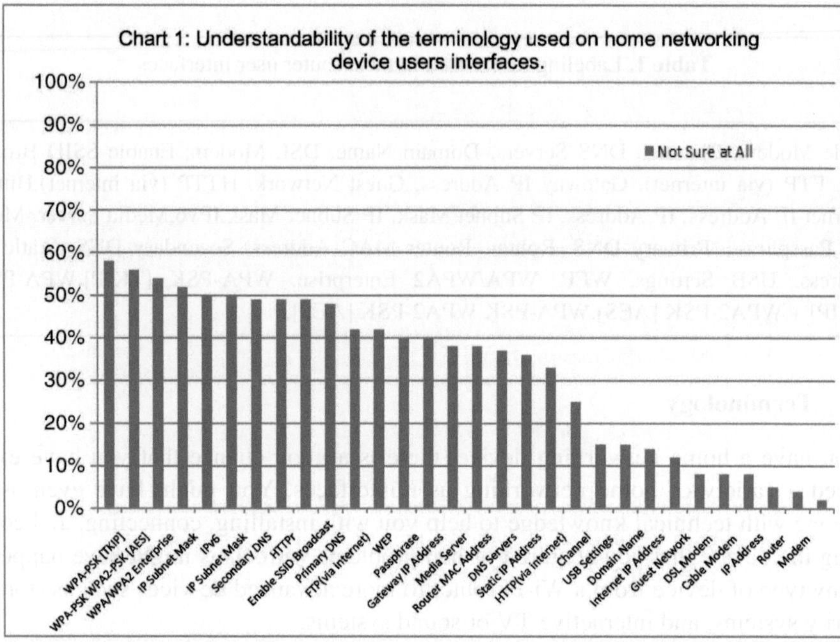

Chart 1. Understandability of the terminology used on home networking device users interfaces

Considering that 80% of the participants have a formal education of college or higher and 54% are under the age 25, the assumption of this level of computer knowledge and understanding of terminology used is interesting to note, especially in consideration of the design of user interfaces for networking products. However, seeing as this survey was conducted out of the context of the UI it is hard to draw a global conclusion (Chart 1 & 2).

Empirical observations also support the extent to which users are unfamiliar with all terms used. Knowledge of terms and their meanings requires education, training and the reading of many pages of documentation and online help, which is another hard task for the average user. To underline the unfamiliarity with these terms, the readers of this article can check to see which ones they themselves are familiar with.

Table 2. Understandability of selected networking terminologies used in field labeling of router UI

Term	No sure at all	Know what it means but not sure.	Definition Provided
WPA-PSK [TKIP]	59%	9%	33%
WPA-PSK [TKIP] + WPA2-PSK [AES]	59%	14%	30%
WPA-PSK WPA2-PSK [AES]	56%	14%	30%
IPv6	56%	19%	26%
Secondary DNS	53%	20%	27%
IP Subnet Mask	53%	24%	23%
IP Subnet Mask	51%	24%	24%
Enable SSID Broadcast	50%	21%	29%
HTTPr	49%	26%	26%
Primary DNS	47%	23%	30%
WEP	46%	23%	31%
FTP(via internet)	41%	21%	37%
Passphrase	41%	27%	31%
DNS Servers	40%	24%	36%
Gateway IP Address	40%	36%	24%
Router MAC Address	39%	29%	33%
Media Server	37%	27%	36%
Static IP Address	36%	33%	31%
WPA/WPA2 Enterprise	36%	23%	26%
HTTP(via internet)	21%	54%	24%
Domain Name	16%	40%	44%
Channel	16%	50%	34%
USB Settings	16%	50%	34%
Internet IP Address	11%	50%	39%
Guest Network	10%	46%	44%
Cable Modem	8%	49%	42%
DSL Modem	7%	54%	39%
IP Address	6%	43%	51%
Router	4%	37%	59%
Modem	3%	44%	53%

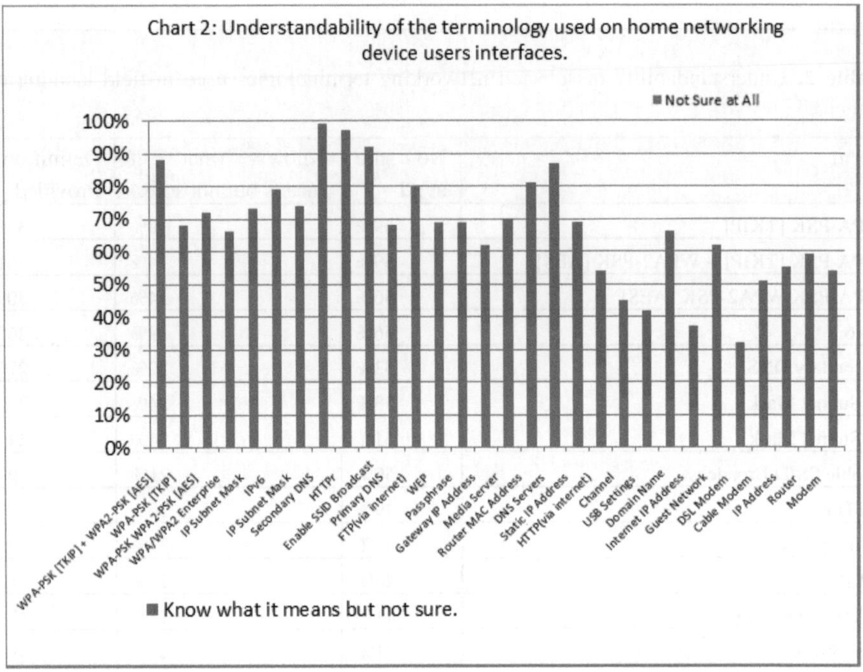

Chart 2. Understandability of the terminology used on home networking device UI

3.3 Networking Survey Results

The second survey consisted of more detailed questions about networking usage and needs. In this section we will review a number of responses related to this survey.

One of the questions regarded how many people among the respondents handle their networking issues such as disconnected Internet. The result indicates that 64% of the respondents would handle it themselves, 10% their wives/spouses or partners, and 26% used another method. When they were asked who had installed their home networking, again 60% respondents reported themselves, 9% their wives/spouses or partners, 10% had it done by technicians, 4% by their friends, 11% another method, and finally 4% who were not sure who did it. Considering the demographic of the participants, 10% seems like a large number of people who chose to use a technician.

The results also indicate that 64% believe only 1 to 2 persons should have the ability to fully access the device and modify it versus 55% who believe 1-2 persons in the household should have limited access to the device for modifications.

In another series of questions, we tried to see what major tasks users would like to accomplish with their devices if they were easy to perform. Both Table 3 & Chart 3 show the main results. Overall, of the tasks asked about, all were rated over 5, showing a wish to do such tasks such as 'Block', 'Test and Measure your network connectivity', and most importantly 'Use the printer remotely' were high.

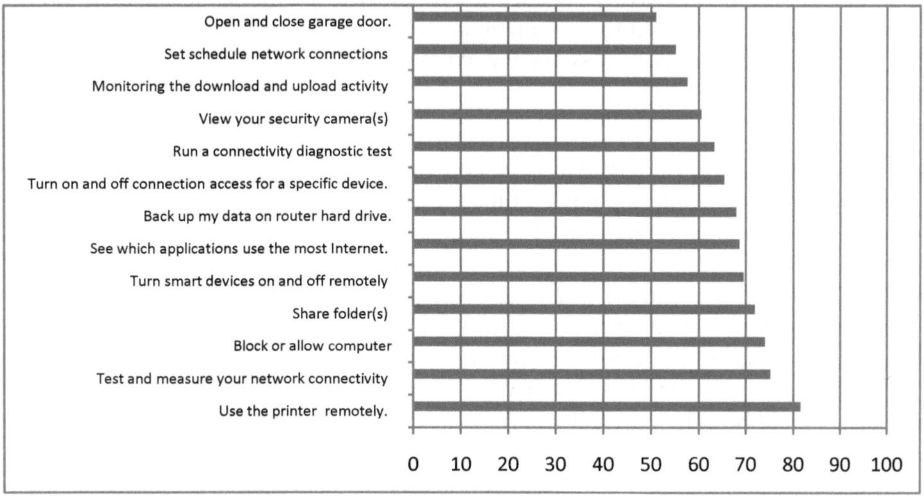

Chart 3. The main tasks that users would like being able to accomplish with their devices

4 Conclusion

The results of this study suggest that the user interfaces in all home networking devices are not built with users in mind. Most of the terminology used seems to be unfamiliar to most users while the user interface itself is complex. However users themselves feel that they would like to be enabled to accomplish some important tasks using their home networking devices if the interfaces were built in an easy-to-use manner.

Table 3. Ranking of the tasks that users would like to do on a router.

#	Task Raking	Ratio*
1	Use the printer connected to your network to print document remotely.	0.81
2	Test and measure your network connectivity speed in different locations of your home.	0.75
3	Block or allow computer/ devices access to your network.	0.74
4	Share folder(s) (picture, music or files) stored on your router storage with your social networking friends, such as Facebook.	0.72
5	Turn smart devices on and off remotely such as: lighting, sprinkler system and so on.	0.70
6	See which applications use the most Internet connection.	0.69
7	Back up my data on router hard drive.	0.68
8	Turn on and off connection access for a specific device.	0.65
9	Run a connectivity diagnostic test of your network remotely.	0.63
10	View your security camera(s) installed at home remotely.	0.61
11	Monitoring the download and upload activity within the billing cycle.	0.58
12	Set schedule network connections of specific computers or devices to your network.	0.55
13	Open and close garage door.	0.51

Ratio is established based on the total score given by the responds to each items divided by total possible score.

In an attempt to extensively enhance the usability of the home networking device, user interfaces (UIs) should focus on making common tasks of installing, configuring, and monitoring the network easy for the average home user according to each user's needs.

Based on this study the following concepts were identified that impact usability:

- Users' needs are different. All users don't need all the functionalities offered by devices. Consequently, the device functionalities should be scalable. The interface should not complicate the task of average users who need to complete only a few basic tasks
- The UI should use common and easy to understand terminology and avoid complex and technical language.
- The UI should offer a task-based interface in terms of what users want to achieve rather than a combination or a variety of features or parameters.
- Users should be able to install, configure, and monitor their network devices in the shortest time possible.
- The UI should let users install, set and monitor the application with the least number of navigation clicks.
- The UI should be appealing and not distracting when users have the application open for long periods of time.
- The UI should be built with minimal objects, the simplest behavior, general rules, understandable terminology, and should be consistent.
- The UI should use the most common paradigm that users are familiar with to reduce learning and remembering the design pattern.
- Comparison of several home networking device brands illustrates that most, if not all, target advanced users with some knowledge of IT networking.

Today's market is not about focusing on more features and functionalities. We are moving towards a situation where comparable products often offer the same functionality. The example of the mobile smart phone illustrates that despite the complex functionalities among smart phones, people will prefer the phone that is the easiest to use and operate rather than the one that offers the most functions. This philosophy is applicable to all types of technology. With the expansion of smart home appliances, success will fall to the home networking enterprises that offer a simple product, satisfying the most common users.

Acknowledgments. The author would like to thank all participants in the surveys and Nassim Moallem for her assistance all along this study.

References

1. TMC News. Cisco Home Networking Issues Consumer Survey [Professional Ser-vices Close - Up], August 31, 2011 TMC News (2011), `http://www.tmcnet.com/usubmit/2011/08/31/5741669.htm`
2. Grinter, R.E., Ducheneaut, N., Edwards, W.K., Newman, M.: The Work To Make The Home Network Work. In: ECSCW, pp. 469–488. Springer/Kluwer, Paris (2005)

3. Poole, E.S., Chetty, M., Grinter, R.E., Edwards, W.K.: More Than Meets the Eye: Transforming the User Experience of Home Network Management GVU Center, School of Interactive Computing. Georgia Institute of Technology, Atlanta, GA, USA (2008)
4. Yang, J., Edwards, W.K.: ICEbox: Toward Easy-to-Use Home Networking Graphics, Visualization and Usability Center, College of Computing, Georgia Institute of Technology (2007), `http://www.cc.gatech.edu/~keith/pubs/icebox-interact` (accessed on December 2011)
5. Cheng, J., Kunz, T.: A Survey on Smart Home Networking Inside the smart home, Springer. Carleton University, Systems and Computer Engineering, Technical Report SCE-09-10 (September 2009)
6. Edwards, W.K.: Before building the network or its components, first understand the home and the behavior of its human inhabitants. Communications of the ACM 54(6) (June 2011)
7. Shehan, E., Edwards, W.K.: Home Networking and HCI: What Hath God Wrought? In: CHI 2007 Proceedings, San Jose, CA, USA, April 28-May 3 (2007)
8. Rashidi, P., Cook, D.J.: Keeping the Resident in the Loop: Adapting the Smart Home to the User. IEEE Transactions on Systems Man & Cybernetics. Part A
9. Yang, J., Edwards, W.K., Haslem, D.: Eden: Supporting Home Network Management Through Interactive Visual Tools. In: UIST 2010, New York, USA, October 3-6 (2010)
10. Brush, A.J.B., Lee, B., Mahajan, R., Agarwal, S., Saroiu, S., Colin Dixon, C.: Home Automation in the Wild: Challenges and Opportunities. In: CHI 2011, Vancouver, BC, Canada, May 7–12 (2011)
11. Demiris, G., Rantz, M., Aud, M.D., Marek, K.D.: Inform H.M., Older adults' attitudes towards and perceptions of 'smart home' technologies: a pilot study 29(2), 87–94 (2004)
12. Moallem, A.: Why should home networking be complicated? In: Advances in Usability Evaluation. CRC Press (2013)
13. Moallem, A.: Location, location, location: About home networking devices location and features. In: Marcus, A. (ed.) DUXU 2013, Part I. LNCS, vol. 8012, pp. 107–114. Springer, Heidelberg (2013)

A Systematic Review of Sustainability and Aspects of Human-Computer Interaction

Vânia Paula de Almeida Neris, Kamila Rios da Hora Rodrigues, and Renata Firmino Lima

Department of Computer Science,
Federal University of São Carlos/UFSCar, São Carlos, Brazil
{vania,kamila_rodrigues,renata.lima}@dc.ufscar.br

Abstract. Sustainability is the term employed for the practice of ensuring that goods and services are produced in ways that do not use resources that cannot be replaced. This practice has been in focus on several different research agendas. In the area of Human-Computer Interaction, studies devoted to works investigating this matter began to appear eight years ago. It is a timely moment to look back and see how much the community has achieved. This paper provides the results of a Systematic Review carried out in four scientific databases. The selected papers were grouped considering the topics they present, the methodological approach adopted and the kind of outcomes that emerged. The results suggest that among the different methodological approaches adopted, literature reviews and criticism still form the main basis to underpin the outcomes. Moreover, climate change and energy savings were found to be the specific areas that were most researched. The results obtained make it possible to suggest opportunities for further research.

Keywords: Sustainability, Systematic Review, Human-Computer Interaction.

1 Introduction

Sustainability is the term employed for the practice of ensuring that goods and services are produced in ways that do not use resources that cannot be replaced. Its application entails defining human practices in a way that prevents our needs from causing harm to future generations. Sustainability is currently an issue of global concern and has thus been highlighted in several different research agendas.

As well as being concerned with environmental factors, regarding the adoption of measures that do not degrade the environment, (for example a reduction in fossil fuel consumption), the concept of sustainability also involves social and economic issues. The social questions concern human rights, respect for differences and the spread of values that support the maintenance of society for future generations. The economic questions involve taking measures that are financially viable, yield a profit and support income distribution.

Computers play a central role in sustainability issues. On the one hand, computers are increasingly present in daily life and allow the dissemination of information on a

M. Kurosu (Ed.): Human-Computer Interaction, Part III, HCII 2014, LNCS 8512, pp. 742–753, 2014.

large scale. They can thus be used as a tool for awareness, mobilization and the encouragement of behavioral changes in favor of sustainability. On the other hand, computing solutions, which include both hardware and software, are a commodity and hence affect sustainability issues, and require new ideas about our design, developmental policies and consumer practices.

Some large companies have already begun developing hardware solutions that require less energy, reduce the amount of heavy materials or use recyclable materials in their manufacture, such as PET bottles. In the implementation of software, there has also been the development of open source solutions, architectures that facilitate the reuse of software and technical data storage that uses less memory, to name a few.

Researchers in the field of Human-Computer Interaction (HCI) have pondered on this issue. Studies that were devoted to this issue began to appear eight years ago. Since then, there has been an increase in the number of HCI researchers concerned with this issue; workshops have been set up and meetings held to discuss it. In his summary, Blevis [1] states that research into HCI can assist in two key complementary areas: (i) sustainability through design or, as we prefer to call it, design for sustainability, i.e. how interactive systems can lead to more sustainable behavior, such as games that teach the principles of sustainability or clothing that interacts with nature by fostering environmental awareness and (ii) sustainability in design, i.e. how sustainability can be used as a critical lens to reveal the design of interactive technologies themselves.

In this paper, we examine the results of a Systematic Review (SR) which was carried out to determine how the HCI community has contributed to research into the question of sustainability. Four databases of scientific knowledge were examined: ACM, IEEE, Scopus and Google Scholar. The searches returned 200 papers, and after the exclusion criteria defined in the SR protocol were applied, 51 were chosen to represent the research that has been carried out in HCI with a focus on sustainability. The selected papers were grouped considering the topics they present, the methodological approach adopted and the different types of outcomes. In the light of the SR results, seven key groups for analysis have emerged: a)Design for Sustainability, b)Sustainability in Design, c)Living with Technology, d) Specific topics including climate change, peace, feminism, energy saving and hunger, e)Methodological aspects and approaches, f) Persuasion and g) Implications for Design.

The paper is structured as follows: Section 2 clarifies the concept of sustainability; Section 3 describes how the SR was carried out in this work; Section 4 outlines the chosen papers according to the formed groups; Section 5 conducts a critical analysis; and Section 6 summarizes the conclusions and draws attention to gaps in the research.

2 The Concept of Sustainability

In 1987, the Norwegian chairman of the World Commission on Environment and Development (WCED) of the United Nations, Gro Harlem Brundtland, issued the report "*Our Common Future*". In this he argued that humanity is capable of an appropriate development to meet the needs of the present without adversely affecting the needs of future generations. This report also seeks to reconcile economic growth with environmental issues and thus attain a balanced development. The combination of three pillars (social, economic and environmental), gives rise to a database that can be analyzed to ensure that a practice is sustainable.

The environmental pillar concerns all the wealth that sustains natural ecosystems and the benefits that they produce, including the flora, fauna and all the products derived thereof. The social pillar addresses the question of human rights, but also includes broader measures of health and education that can ensure the continuity of life in society. The economic pillar is linked to profit. Its main objective is to analyze questions such as the return on investments, market share, profitable activities that increase the return on investment for shareholders and increasing business growth [2].

3 The Research Approach

An SR is a research technique that aims to carry out an evaluation of a research question, by employing a review methodology that is reliable, accurate and allows auditing [3]. This technique involves gathering and collating a large amount of research data, answering research questions that have been previously defined and using systematic and clear methods to identify, select and critically evaluate research material [4]. The SR carried out in this work seeks to help the authors to determine how the HCI community has conducted research by examining the question of sustainability. The application of this technique occurs in three phases: Planning, Execution and Results Analysis [3].

3.1 Planning

Planning is designed to determine the research objectives, the way in which the SR will be carried out and which criteria will be applied to the studies [3]. The main purpose of this investigation is to examine works that show the state- of- the- art in HCI research on sustainability.

The research questions defined for this work are as follows: Q1) What topics in Sustainability and HCI have been addressed by researchers? Q2) What methodological approaches have been adopted? and Q3) What outcomes have been formalized, especially those which support the design?

Four databases were used for the analysis and selection of primary studies: IEEE, ACM, Google Academic and Scopus. The Papers had to be written in English. The following inclusion criteria were chosen to provide guidelines for each of the research questions: I1 - The work should address the sustainability issue; I2 - The work must be related to IT; I3 - The work should approach aspects of HCI. Exclusion criteria were defined to refine the search, find works that were appropriate for the context and address the research questions. These criteria are as follows: E1 - The work does not take account of aspects of IHC; E2 - The work is not related to IT; E3 - The work does not address issues related to sustainability; E4 - The work is not available on the Internet; E5 – The work has the same author(s), results and methodological approach as that of another paper which is already included.

3.2 Execution

The SR was carried out over a period of 4 months. The search string defined was:

(("Sustainable Interaction Design") OR ((design) AND (HCI) AND (sustainability)))

The searches in the Google Academic database returned 73 works. The ACM database returned 48 works, the Scopus database returned 56 works and the IEEE database returned 23 works, making a total of 200 related works. After the exclusion criteria were applied, 51 papers were chosen to represent the research that has been carried out in HCI with a focus on sustainability.

3.3 Results Analysis

Following the objectives of this systematic review, 51 key primary studies were read again and classified according to the main issue or problem investigated. The methodological approach and the outcomes were analyzed in a way that took account of the implications for the design. Figure 1 illustrates the main phases of this SR.

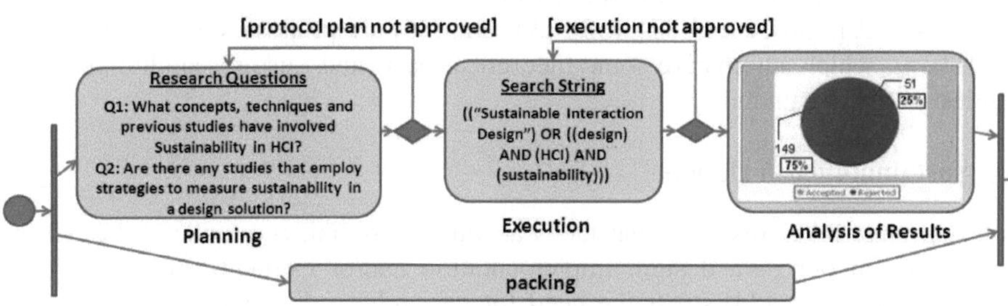

Fig. 1. Instantiation of SR. Source: [3] adapted.

4 Sustainability and HCI

After studying the 51selected papers, seven major thematic groups emerged. These are: a) Design for Sustainability, b) Sustainability in Design, c) Living with Technology, d) Specific Topics including climate change, peace, feminism, energy saving and hunger e) Methodological factors and approaches, f) Persuasion and g) Implications of SR for Design.

4.1 Design for Sustainability

This group is concerned with studies on how to design software and hardware that fosters or supports sustainability and/or a more sustainable behavior in humans. In other papers, this is called sustainability through design. The papers conduct investigations mainly into human behavior, design principles and software systems.

[5], [6], [7], [8] investigate people's attitudes and critical thinking about sustainable practices. [9] and [10] argue in favor of supporting the collective and collaborative aspects of sustainability. In [11] and [12], Piccolo and Baranauskas explore motivational

factors. [13] analyses the complexity of sustainable choices and emphasizes the need for simplicity and reliable information. [14] and [15] defend flexible and adaptive informatics, to deal with a possible world collapse.

In [1], Blevis sets out several principles to guide Sustainable Interaction Design and in [16], Wakkary and Tanenbaum give examples of Blevis' principles and expand the concept of the user, as forming a part of a sustainable identity. [17] analyses a set of design techniques that can be used to support design for sustainability. Pereira et al. [18] argue in favor of sustainability as a value for the design of software applications. [19] illustrates some model design concepts that are related to sustainability and [20] give an overview of the research approaches adopted in Information Technology and sustainability.

The design of software systems is discussed in several papers. [21] outlines an eco-feedback system and [12] describes a residential energy feedback system. [22] carried out routines to keep computer machines off for a longer time. [23] discusses sustainable factors in an environmental management system. Sourcemap [24] represents sustainability factors in supply chains and the Climate Change Habitability Index [25] presets diagrams of climate change. Coralog and Timelog [26] are systems to ambient displays that represent metrics of sustainability.

[27], [28], [29], [30], [31], [32], [33], [34] and [35] are proposals for events, mainly workshops, which summarize some theoretical basis and raise research challenges in the design for sustainability.

4.2 Sustainability in Design

This group undertakes research that takes account of social, economic and environmental issues in our own design, implementation and/or evaluation practices. Although Mankoff et al. [34] stress the need for research on this area; from the works returned in the SR, only [36] treats this question as a central issue. Mann et al.[36] underline the need for the invisible to be made visible in a sustainable approach to software development, as well as he need to think about scalability.

However, it is possible to highlight some features of the returned papers that can be explored in greater depth to improve sustainability in the design. [21] and [22] investigate attitudes regarding the reduction of the energy consumption of the computerized machines which are used in our daily professional practices. Issues of collaboration [9], information complexity [13] and (un)sustainable materials [5] can be explored for the design process. [16], examines the question from the perspective of a sustainable identity, and discusses some possible sustainable design features from the user to the designer. [19] explores the prospect of applying pedagogical practices in design courses to prepare professionals for sustainability in design as well. In [37], Arieff and Casey discuss the role of designers in sustainability and also encourage changes in design firms.

4.3 Living with Technology

The studies on this question are concerned with fashion consumption. [38] and [39] discuss the role of fashion and luxury when a customer is choosing personal electronic devices. The main idea in these papers is that if we can better understand how fashion affects consumer attitudes and behavior, we may be able to use fashion as a positive force for changing behavior with regard to sustainability. Especially in the digital domain, fashion can persuade people to adopt new technologies or new devices. This can lead to premature technological obsolescence and raises the question of what to do with so many devices that are left unused or needlessly disposed of for reasons of fashion and consumption. [1], [13] and [40] discuss the concept of reuse of devices.

4.4 Specific Topics

Since it is a multidisciplinary area, HCI can address different aspects of sustainability. This category examines some specific topics that appeared in the SR:

Hunger. According to [41], one imminent consequence of global warming is its effect on food supply, which is the basis of human sustenance. Essentially, sustainability in this sense is concerned with "securing" food: ensuring supplies are stable and available and that the food is of an acceptable quality. In helping to encourage the sustainable use of food, Blevis and Morse [42] propose a set of practices such as the "monitoring of food" - interactive technologies can trace the origin of food, and provide information that can ensure that that the food is organic or has "sensors for gardens" - which can be linked to computer applications that provide advice on what can be planted and when, and other useful information.

Energy Saving. The works related to this category focus on areas that can assist in the reduction of energy consumption by outlining new technologies that foster awareness among users and encourage them to change their behavior. [11], [12], [21] and [22] provide eco-feedback systems, which are interactive devices that reveal energy use. In [43], Froehlich maps ten design dimensions for feedback systems. In [44], the focus is on designing strategies for eco-visualizations by "offering behavioral cues as indicators".

Peace. Hourcade et al. [45] propose combining other disciplines in researching the areas of peace and human conflict. Subjects such as neurology, political science, behavioral economics, and sociology should be included to support the development of interactive technologies. The advent of Internet connectivity, mobile devices and social media, provides a powerful cocktail that allows computing and HCI to be key components in peaceful change, at both an individual and social level.

Feminism. Bardzell and Blevis [46] suggest researchers to think differently about gender lead, considering, for example, to conduct user research in a way that is sensitive to gender-identity practices i.e. when interacting with users, one should be mindful of the cultural conventions of gender, and focus user research acknowledging different standpoints and experiences.

Climate Change. [24] proposes a carbon footprint calculator that measures each life stage of a product: raw material extraction, production, transport of goods, use and end-of-life. [25] shows diagrams to enable ordinary individuals to understand the state of the world in terms of habitability at particular places, in the face of climate change. In [14],

Tomlinson et al. consider the possibility of an imminent global change, mainly caused by climate change, and emphasize the need for HCI research in crisis scenarios. [47] speculates on some actions that the interaction design community can take to "prepare for the worst".

4.5 Persuasion

It is apparent that most of the works on sustainability seek to educate people and persuade them to make changes in their daily-life practices. By analyzing environmental discourses in papers about sustainability, [48] classifies the design of persuasive applications as a key objective.

In [22], Hanks et al. see a behavioral change in IT professionals regarding energy savings, through the GoGreen sidebar gadget. They have made use of mass email services to inform people about the changes and provide other communication tools to report problems and disseminate instructions. Kim et al. [26] analyze the effects of Coralog and Timelog on fifty-two participants. The results suggest that ambient displays can help bring about alterations in behavior.

Piccolo and Baranauskas [11] study motivational factors and one of the design strategies outlined in their study relies on credibility as a key factor in the persuasiveness of energy feedback systems. In [49], the same authors provided evidence of a lack of intrinsic motivation for people to make savings in the consumption of electricity. [41] proposes a design framework to encourage a sustainable food culture in urban environments. They examine behavioral changes through engagement, which they believe should take account of people, places and technology. In [50], DiSalvo et al. highlight the need for a debate regarding sustainability and HCI and point out concerns about ethical issues when persuasion begins to border on coercion.

4.6 Methodological Aspects and Approaches

This section aims to answer the second question defined in the SR and the studies have been grouped considering the main methodological approach they mentioned. Interviews were conducted in [38] with a sample of 30 participants to assess their consumer behavior. Odom [40] carried out 22 in-home contextual interviews and [13] interviewed 11 people about the complexity of information. Surveys were undertaken in [5] with 435 participants who gave their opinions about the material effects of information technologies. In Australia, 216 business men took part in a survey on their attitudes toward environmental issues [23]. In [49], 280 participants were involved in a structured interview about the reasons to save energy.

Case studies were undertaken with 4 families to find out about sustainable everyday design practices [16]. [7] investigated the motivating factors, practices and experiences of 35 environmentally responsible households. [39] analyses design decisions in several technologies and [51] design decisions regarding technology in several places. [10] studied the deployment of PreHeat, a home heating system, in 5 homes in USA and 2 in UK. A participatory design was introduced with students for a residential energy feedback system [12], and [8] records some participatory practices with 19 residents of an eco-house college with "ethnographically-inspired" methods. Organizational Semiotics was applied as a theoretical reference in [11] and Goodman [48] employed a discourse analysis technique in 3 different literature sources.

User tests were performed with an eco-feedback system [21], and the GoGreen gadget [22]. [26] conducted online surveys, analyzed logs in a period of two weeks and held semi-structured interviews with users of Coralog. [24] supplies some data on the use of Sourcemap in different situations. Several other papers employed literature reviews and/or criticism as their main methodological approach such as [1], [6], [9], [14], [17], [18], [20], [36] [41], [43], [44], [45], [47], [50], [52], [53] and [54].

4.7 Implications for Design

This section attempts to answer the third question in the SR and the papers were grouped considering the main implications for the design they formalized. We did our best to keep the terms as those adopted by the authors. Requirements were set in a few papers. In [11], they include, for example, publish global results of individual attitudes to motivate users. In [26], there are design requirements for persuasion and in [49], there are requirements for residential eco-feedback systems. [5] classifies four personal profiles for sustainable use and discusses some strategies to deal with them.

Principles were formalized in [1] and consisted of linking invention and disposal, and promoting renewal and reuse. In [16], there are principles for design-in-use. In [40], the principles include symbolism, material qualities, engagement and augmentation among others. [52] defines several principles for sustainable design that are based on social theories. Some speculations for design are made in [38] and for research questions as pointed out on [47]. Singhal [17] speculates on how some methods and techniques can be employed for eco-feedback technology.

Sohn and Nam [6] formalize a framework based on four attributes of unconscious everyday human behavior. [39] proposes an informal design critical framework for luxury and sustainability. [19] establishes a framework for teaching strategy design planning which can include sustainability concerns in the design. Pereira et al. [18] postulate sustainability as a value for design and [14] emphasizes the need for adaptation in technology. Froehlich [43] defines ten design dimensions for feedback systems, including data granularity and social sharing. [7] defines design directions which include encouraging individuals to make personal choices and identity expression. Key points [41] and lessons for sustainable design, with an emphasis on collaboration [9] were also formalized. Goodman [48] recommends participatory design and moving beyond human-centered computing as promising directions for future work.

5 Critical Analysis

The information obtained from the SR was plotted in a Bubble Chart with two quadrants [55], as illustrated in Figure 2. In the first quadrant (left), there is information about the groups (classification) and the amount of works in each of them per year. It should be noted, for example, that in 2011 we detected 8 works classified in the Design for Sustainability group, 3 works in Sustainability in Design and so forth. The studies can be labeled in more than one classification.

In the second quadrant (right), the studies for each group were classified in accordance with the methodology used. It was possible to notice that 7 different kinds of methodologies were employed in the collected works. These are as follows: user tests, literature review and/or criticism, case studies, discourse analysis, surveys, participatory design and interviews. In Specific Topics, for example, 6 studies were considered as forming a Literature Review/Criticism. Some studies used more than one type of methodology or assessment instruments, and thus, were also classified in more than one methodology in the chart above.

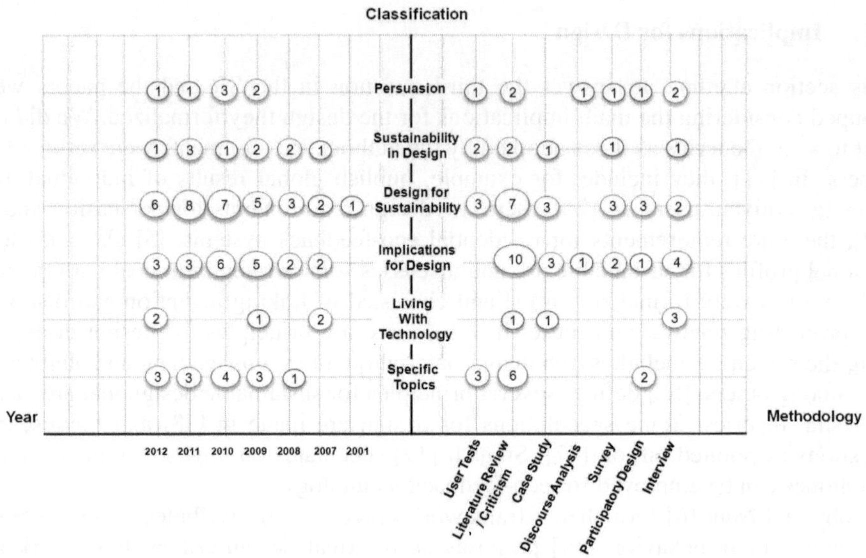

Fig. 2. Distribution of works about sustainability and HCI over the years and the main methodologies employed. Numbers in the balls represent quantity of works.

From Figure 2, it can be observed that there was an "upsurge" in the volume of works on sustainability from 2010 onwards. However, apart from that, there has been a progression of works over the years which suggests that the authors in this area have consistently been publishing new papers. We also observed that most of the studies, in most of the classifications, have adopted literature reviews and pure criticism. This applies, for example, to the works classified in the 'Implications for Design' category. Although this category contains several works, few of them provide guidelines or specifications for design which have been validated with users.

6 Conclusion

Research on how we can live in a sustainable manner is essential for future generations. Computers play a central role in this issue, and hence, the HCI area can contribute to research that addresses this complex issue. In the last seven years, several important achievements have been made by the HCI community with regard to sustainability, and a few research groups have been focusing on different issues.

In the light of the results of the SR, some gaps in research can be detected, or in other words, there are research opportunities with regard to sustainability in the HCI.

These include the following: (1) Other methodological approaches can be used to support the outcomes, including long-term studies and ethnography. (2) The users should be included in different stages of the design process, not only when requirements are being elicited (mainly through questionnaires). Participatory design or action-research can be more employed. (3) Research on specific (and important) topics such as peace and hunger need interdisciplinary and intercultural collaboration. Geographically-separated research groups can be formed. (4) The solutions generally take account or the environmental, or the social or the economic aspect of sustainability. Until now, few studies have examined two of them in combination. Research on sustainability should focus on the three pillars together. (5) We need to rethink our design practices in the light of sustainability and create artifacts, tools, techniques, models etc, which can support both the design for sustainability and sustainability in the design.

References

1. Blevis, E.: Sustainable interaction design: invention & disposal, renewal & reuse. In: Proceedings of the SIGCHI 2007. ACM, New York (2007)
2. Estender, A., Pitta, C., Moreira, T.T.O.: Concept of Sustainable Development - The Third Sector (2008) (in Portuguese), `http://revistas.ung.br/` (accessed on: September 2012)
3. Kitchenham, B.: Procedures for Performing Systematic Reviews. Technical Report, TR/SE-0401, Australian (2004) ISSN: 1353-7776
4. Clarke, M., Oxman, A.D.: Cochrane Reviewers' Handbook 4.1; Section 7. In: Review Manager (RevMan) [Computer program]. The Cochrane Collaboration (2001), `http://www.cochrane.dk/cochrane/handbook/handbook.htm` (accessed on: November 2012)
5. Hanks, K., et al.: Sustainable millennial: attitudes towards sustainability and the material effects of interactive technologies. In: Proceedings of the CHI 2008. ACM, New York (2008)
6. Sohn, M., Nam, T.: Design Method for Sustainable Interaction. In: Proceeding of the IASDR 2009 (2009)
7. Woodruff, A., Hasbrouck, J., Augustin, S.: A bright green perspective on sustainable choices. In: Proceedings of the CHI 2008. ACM, New York (2008)
8. Davis, J.: Participatory design for sustainable campus living. In: Proceedings of the CHI 2010. ACM, New York (2010)
9. Mann, S., Smith, L.: Collaboration in sustainability vision. In: International Conference on Collaboration Technologies and Systems (CTS) (2011)
10. Hazas, M., Brush, A.J.B., Scott, J.: Sustainability does not begin with the individual. Interactions 19(5), 14–17 (2012)
11. Piccolo, L.S.G., Baranauskas, M.C.C.: Motivational aspects in energy feedback systems design. In: Proceedings of the IHC+CLIHC 2011 (2011)
12. Piccolo, L.S.G., Baranauskas, M.C.C.: Energy, environment, and conscious consumption: making connections through design. In: Proceedings of the IHC 2012 (2012)
13. Remy, C., Huang, E.M.: The Complexity of Information for Sustainable Choices. In: Proceedings of the CHI 2012, Austin, TX, USA, May 5-10 (2012)
14. Tomlinson, B., et al.: What if sustainability doesn't work out? Interactions 19(6), 50–55 (2012)

15. Tomlinson, B., et al.: Collapse informatics: augmenting the sustainability ICT4D discourse in HCI. In: Proceedings of the CHI 2012. ACM, New York (2012)
16. Wakkary, R., Tanenbaum, K.: A sustainable identity: the creativity of an everyday designer. In: Proceedings of the CHI 2009 (2009)
17. Singhal, H.: Eco-Feedback Technology: Road to Sustainability. In: Proceedings of Nordchi 2010, pp. 178–187. ACM, Iceland (2010)
18. Pereira, R., Lima, M., Baranauskas, M.C.C.: Sustainability as a value in technology design. In: Proceedings of the IWCSC 2010. ACM, New York (2010)
19. Blevis, E.: Designchallenge based learning (DCBL) and sustainable pedagogical practice. Interactions 17(3), 64–69 (2010)
20. Hilty, L., Lohmann, W., Huang, E.: Sustainability and ICT – An Overview of The Field. Notizie Di Politeia Xxvii, 104, 13–28 (2011) ISSN 1128-2401
21. Heras, D.B., Otero, D., Arguello, F.: An eco-feedback system for improving the sustainability performance of universities. In: Proceedings of the VECIMS 2011 (2011)
22. Hanks, K., et al.: SUSTAINABLY OURS: Small change, big result. Interactions 16(6), 24–27 (2009)
23. Wilmshurst, T.D., Frost, G.R.: The Climate Change. Business Strategy and the Environment 10(3), 135–147 (2001)
24. Bonanni, L.: Sourcemap: eco-design, sustainable supply chains, and radical transparency. XRDS 17(4), 22–26 (2011)
25. Pan, Y., Cheong, C.M., Blevis, E.: The climate change habitability index. Interactions 17(6), 29–33 (2010)
26. Kim, T., Hong, H., Magerko, B.: Design requirements for ambient display that supports sustainable lifestyle. In: Proceedings of the DIS 2010 (2010)
27. Haakansson, M., et al.: Simple, sustainable living. In: Proceedings of CHI 2012 Extended Abstracts on Human Factors in Computing Systems (2012)
28. Khan, A., et al.: Sustainability community invited panel: challenges ahead. In: CHI 2011 (2011)
29. Busse, D.K., et al.: Designing for a sustainable future. In: Proceedings of the Seventh ACM Conference on Creativity and Cognition. ACM, New York (2009)
30. Bonanni, L., et al.: Visible - actionable - sustainable: sustainable interaction design in professional domains. In: Proceedings of the CHI EA 2011 (2011)
31. Pierce, J., et al.: Everyday practice and sustainable HCI: understanding and learning from cultures of (un)sustainability. In: Proceedings of the CHI EA 2011, New York, NY, USA (2011)
32. Nathan, L.P., et al.: Beyond the hype: sustainability & HCI. In: Proceedings of the CHI 2008. ACM, New York (2008)
33. Huh, J., et al.: Examining appropriation, re-use, and maintenance for sustainability. In: Proceedings of the CHI 2010. ACM, New York (2010)
34. Mankoff, J.C., et al.: Environmental sustainability and interaction. In: Proceeding of the CHI 2007. ACM, New York (2007)
35. Huang, E.M., et al.: Defining the role of HCI in the challenges of sustainability. In: Proceedings of the CHI 2009. ACM, New York (2009)
36. Mann, S., Smith, L., McGregor, G.: A research framework for sustainable software. In: Proceedings of the CITRENZ 2011, CITRENZ, NZ, pp. 167–180 (2011)
37. Arieff, A., Casey, V.: (P) REVIEW: Merging design, Business, and sustainability: the designers accord. Interactions 15(3), 61–66 (2008)
38. Pan, Y., et al.: Re-conceptualizing fashion in sustainable HCI. In: Proceedings of the DIS (2012)

39. Blevis, E., et al.: Luxury & new luxury, quality & equality. In: Proceedings of the DPPI 2007. ACM, New York (2007)
40. Odom, W., et al.: Understanding why we preserve some things and discard others in the context of interaction design. In: Proceedings of the CHI 2009. ACM, New York (2009)
41. Choi, J.H., Blevis, E.: HCI & sustainable food culture: a design framework for engagement. In: Proceedings of the NordiCHI 2010. ACM, New York (2010)
42. Blevis, E., Morse, S.C.: Sustainably Ours: Food, dude. Interactions 16(2), 58–62 (2009)
43. Froehlich, J.: Promoting Energy Efficient Behaviors in the Home through Feedback: The Role of Human Computer Interaction. In: HCIC 2009, Winter Workshop (2009)
44. Pierce, J., Odom, W., Blevis, E.: Energy aware dwelling: a critical survey of interaction design for eco-visualizations. In: Proceedings of the OZCHI 2008. ACM, New York (2008)
45. Hourcade, J.P., et al.: HCI for peace: beyond tie dye. Interactions 19(5), 40–47 (2012)
46. Bardzell, S., Blevis, E.: The lens of feminist HCI in the context of sustainable interaction design. Interactions 17(2), 57–59 (2010)
47. Blevis, E., Blevis, S.: Hope for the best and prepare for the worst: interaction design and the tipping point. Interactions 17(5), 26–30 (2010)
48. Goodman, E.: Three environmental discourses in human-computer interaction. In: Proceedings of the CHI 2009. ACM, New York (2009)
49. Piccolo, L.S.G., Baranauskas, M.C.C.: Basis and prospects of motivation informing design: requirements for situated eco-feedback technology. In: Proceedings of the IHC 2012. Brazilian Computer Society, Porto Alegre (2012)
50. Disalvo, C., Sengers, P., Brynjarsdóttir, H.: Navigating the terrain of sustainable HCI. Interactions 17(4), 22–25 (2010)
51. Blevis, E., Blevis, S.: Sustainably Ours: Images of sustainable interactions: seeing with the lens of sustainability. Interactions 15(3), 27–29 (2008)
52. Fuchs, C.: HCI and Society: Towards a Typology of Universal Design Principles. International Journal of Human-Computer Interaction 26(6), 638–656 (2010)
53. Huang, E.M.: Building outwards from sustainable HCI. Interactions 18(3), 14–17 (2011)
54. Mankoff, J.: HCI and sustainability: a tale of two motivations. Interactions 19(3), 16–19 (2012)
55. Tufte, E.: The Visual Display of Quantitative Information, 2nd edn. Graphics Press, Cheshire (2001) ISBN 0-9613921-4-2

Issues of ERP Upgrade in Public Sectors: A Case Study

Tanja Scheckenbach[1], Fan Zhao[2], Erik Allard[2], Jermaine Burke[2], Kevin Chiwaki[2], and Sean Marlow[2]

[1] College of Business, Wuerzburg University
tscheckenbach@wiinf.uni-wuerzburg.de
[2] College of Business, Florida Gulf Coast University
fzhao@fgcu.edu

Abstract. As more organizations seek to upgrade their ERP systems to take advantage of continuing technological innovations, effective technology implementations are increasingly important. This study tried to provide a deeper understanding of ERP upgrade in public sectors industry. Three issues were found in the study: problems left from ERP implementation, choice between customization and fully adoption, and organizational culture related issues. Lessons and implications were discussed.

Keywords: ERP Upgrade, Public Sectors, Case Study.

1 Introduction

ERP systems are commercial software packages that attempt to integrate all departments, functions, and business processes in an organization into a single computer system/application. The reasons that companies implement an ERP system vary, but overall, most companies state that they implement an ERP system for seamless flow of company information, to improve and streamline business processes, and to increase cost savings.

ERP upgrades are mainly intended to take advantages of new technologies and business strategies to ensure that the organization keeps up with the latest business development trends. Therefore, the decision to upgrade ERP is usually not driven by code deterioration or anticipated reduction in maintenance costs alone, but by different purposes. According to an AMR research [1], 55% of upgrades were voluntary business improvements triggered by the need for new functionality, expansion or consolidation of systems; 24% of upgrades were triggered by technology stack changes; 15% of upgrades were forced by de-support of the running version of software to avoid vendor support termination [2]; and 6% of upgrades were triggered by bug fixes or statutory changes. The cost of ERP upgrades is high [3]. Swanton [1] mentioned that the costs of each upgrade include: 50% of the original software license fee and 20% of the original implementation cost per user, which means over 6 million dollars for a 5,000-user system. Typically, each ERP upgrade requires eight to nine months of effort with a team the equivalent of one full-time employee per 35 business users. The ERP-adopting organization does not have to develop and re-write the ERP system itself but rather it replaces (or upgrades) the old version with a readily

M. Kurosu (Ed.): Human-Computer Interaction, Part III, HCII 2014, LNCS 8512, pp. 754–763, 2014.

available new version from the ERP vendor. However, a lack of experience may cause the costs and length of the upgrade project to approach or even exceed those of the original ERP implementation effort. Collins [4] listed some general benefits for organizations from ERP upgrades:

- Eligibility for Help Desk Support: Most of ERP software vendors stop providing technical support 12 to 18 months after the next version becomes available. Therefore, keeping upgrade with the pace of ERP vendors will guarantee the support for the system from the vendors.
- Solutions for Outstanding "Bugs" or Design Weaknesses: It is impossible to guarantee spotless and error-free ERP systems after the implementations even though vendors will conduct many different testing processes to eliminate the happenings of errors in the system before the leasing time. "The majority of software bugs are resolved and delivered either fix-by-fix, or all-at-once as part of the next release version of the ERP package". In this case, upgrades will be beneficial to the organizations in problem solving.
- New, Expanded, or Improved Features: ERP software provides organizations the knowledge and strength (i.e. best practices) from the vendors. ERP upgrades provide organizations future enhancement from the vendors to give the organizations better opportunities to catch up the current business development, improve their processes and build more efficient business models with new functions, new features and new processing styles provided in the upgraded ERP versions.

Regarding the research of ERP, more lessons were learned on optimizing ERP implementations after more and more companies completed their initial ERP implementation. For years, ERP acceptance models, such as TAM [5], DoI [6], attract many researchers. Recently, researchers began to notice the importance of post-implementation studies [7]. ERP maintenance and upgrade are two major activities in ERP post-implementation. However, only a few studies were found in ERP upgrade and there is no empirical or case study focused on ERP upgrade in public sectors. Therefore, this paper focus on a public sector case to study the issues of ERP upgrade in a certain industry.

2 Literature Review

System upgrades occur in the post-implementation stage after the initial ERP implementations. Similar to ERP implementations, an ERP upgrade is deceptively complicated and could be a disaster to those organizations ignoring the massive efforts required by the project [8]. Ng et al. [9] demonstrated a software upgrade stage model for ERP upgrade (see Table 1 for details). By following this upgrade stage model, some benefits are obtained by the organization. Stage 1 minimizes upgrade risk by identifying risks at an early stage. Stage 3 allows the organization to justify all the benefits and costs of an upgrade to ensure a successful activity. Stages 6 to 11 are recommended by consultants and practitioners for best practices in ERP upgrade process. Visibility and facilitating management and control are also provided by this upgrade stage model.

Table 1. Upgrade stage model by Ng et al. [9]

Stage Number	Upgrade Stages	Description
1	Design an upgrade project methodology	Identify the best method to apply ERP upgrade and tailor it for internal use and gather the information about tools and services available from the vendor to the customer
2	Research for upgrade options available	Analyze different upgrade options available; analyze pros and cons, and the stability of each option; and identify the support window for the versions to ensure the chosen upgrade version is the optimal solution based on the organization's business objectives
3	Develop a business case	Identify the factors influencing the upgrade decision by developing a business case, such as planning for the upgrade data, evaluating costs for the upgrade, developing a plan for budget allocations, evaluating the benefits of the upgrade, and evaluating the personal requirements
4	Make full assessment of modifications in the current version and technical environment	Analyze current system from both management and technical perspectives to investigate the number of modifications on the existing system and identify which modifications are still required and which are not
5	Make full assessment of the new functionality, and technical requirements in each (potential) upgrade option	Analyze each upgrade option from both management and technical perspectives to assess the new features/functionality in each option for each ERP module of interest and the technical requirement in each option to evaluate benefits of the functionality to the organization
6	Conduct impact analysis between the new upgrade version and the existing version	Gap analysis of current system and new upgrade version to examine the impacts of the new version on the organization and minimize future maintenance cost and ensure that requirements for the project are identified so that budget, time, and staff allocations can be made accordingly
7	Install the new version onto the development system	Apply all the previous patches onto the new ERP system to ensure that the new version is up-to-date by incorporating all the earlier bug fixes and enhancements
8	Construct the new system	All previous development (reporting capability, interfaces, and modification) overwritten during the new version upgrade will be redeveloped or re-applied on the new system to ensure that all competitive business processes remain in the new

Table 1. (*Continued.*)

9	Conduct a thorough testing of the upgrade system	Verify accuracy of the system functionality and data conversion to ensure that the new system still meets the user requirements and is aligned to the business objectives
10	Carry out the trial upgrades	Conduct the trial upgrades to exercise the upgrade process and identify errors or potential problems that would happen during the actual upgrade
11	Conversion (or go live)	Deliver the well-tested system into the production system

The decision to upgrade an ERP system is usually influenced by both internal and external factors [8-10]. Upgrades should be coincided with business needs and expansion, such as greater ROI, expanded system capabilities, integration of new modules, and so on. However, sometimes, companies are "forced" into upgrading their system by their vendors. ERP vendors encourage their clients to upgrade their systems to newer versions or business suites. They do this by setting "de-support dates" – this means that at a certain date, the ERP vendor will stop support on old versions of their systems. This forces organizations to make the decision to either risk the responsibility for maintenance of their ERP system or to upgrade the system [8-10].

Wenrich [10] suggests that treating system upgrades as a new system implementation is a critical factor for post-implementation success. The same processes that were used for the system implementation must be used for the system upgrade, although importance will be varied [8]. Companies may underestimate the importance of some critical success factors during a system upgrade. This could easily cause a failure upgrade project. Therefore, a successful ERP implementation does not mean a successful upgrade later. To further understand the issues of ERP upgrade, in this study, we focus on an ERP upgrade of a local school district.

Many school districts have moved from standalone system applications to fully integrated ERP systems with one central database. School districts face a unique challenge of being in a niche market due to the fact that most legacy systems need to have enough customization in place in order to carry out the various tasks they face on a daily basis. Most notably school districts with a well-defined project plan, a well-informed project team, and a culture that understands the benefits and risks associated with the implementation of a new ERP system, have achieved success within their school district at getting an ERP system up and running in a timely matter and close to their projected budget. Though many small and medium-sized school districts have reported price savings and an improvement to their budget, other school districts have experienced difficulties in failing to implement a new ERP system due to budget constraints and organizational and corporate culture issues experienced in their school district. This paper describes a case study for a school district who are facing too many challenges in order to upgrade a working ERP system. Lessons such as having a well-defined project plan, a qualified project team, proper data testing, and an organization and corporate culture who understands the risks and benefits associated with

ERP projects are discussed in order for other school districts to discover the benefits of upgrading their ERP systems all while helping them to avoid issues that may be experienced during their implementations.

3 Case Description

Collier County Public Schools (CCPS) is a preK-12 educational institution serving Collier County Florida. CCPS administrates 48 schools with an enrollment of approximately 45,000 students. CCPS administration depends on ERP software to manage their rather large organization and a relatively small IT department in proportion to the size served to get the job done. This division is known as the Division of Administrator Technology, and the head is the coordinator of software selection.

CCPS is a government entity that falls under the local county government category. It is a sub entity of the state government and the Florida Department of Education. Any ERP system the district would want to implement or has implemented not only must follow the strict standards and needs of CCPS but also the laws of Collier County, Florida. These laws include record keeping, privacy laws, protecting students, budget constraints, and the disposal of discharged hardware. The ERP system has to follow several laws pertaining to how data is handled, and must also do it at a level where the rules/laws are well integrated into the system at a near unnoticeable status. Though these laws are implemented for the protection the students and staff, they have added an extra hurdle in selecting and customizing software. For example, it adds difficulty in the selection process of new software, as well as maintaining the system and adding additional code. The supervisors of CCPS are the superintendent and five board members, who were elected into office. Board members serve five-year terms that are staggered so that there is some continuity in the board's voice but also a sense of progressiveness due to constant change of each seat. The district is home to 29 elementary schools, 10 middle schools, 8 high schools, and one PreK-thru-12 school. CCPS spans a large and diverse population necessitating a strong and effective ERP system to efficiently govern the student-body and other enterprise administrative tasks commonly found in ERP systems.

Currently, the district is using an older version of EDR platform on IBM AS400 mainframe system where the system is housed. The system was upgraded to its current form during the Y2K upgrade phase to become Y2K compliant. EDR software was specifically developed for education industry and further specialized in Florida law pertaining to education and record keeping.

The Division of Administrator Technology acts as a development team when lack of resources call for it. Since the 2007 economic recession, most government entities have had to scale back their budgets due to overall budget cuts, and the CCPS district is no exception. The budget cuts have deterred the district from truly upgrading their software and instead the team is faced with the task of developing their own "bolt-on" software, which has been described to have the "look-and-feel" of the overall ERP system. The ERP and mainframe server run on a COBOL based language, making the daunting task of in-house development even more impressive. One prime example is the food-service section of the ERP system. The current version of SR4 did not support foodservice in their software. The Division of Administrator Technology developed their own code for handling this side of the ERP. It was then "attached" to the ERP so that it was accessible from EDR ERP.

CCPS does have a decent recovery plan to back up data in the event of an emergency. In this aspect, the biggest threat to Collier County is hurricanes, and so out-of-area backup is necessary to make recovery realistically possible. Currently, all data is backed up at a site in Miami, FL. The data is replicated using the hot-backup method. The data can then be recovered and accessed in neighboring Lee County, which uses the same mainframe system but a different ERP. Alternatively, the data can also be recovered at a site in Jacksonville, FL. The Jacksonville site is useful if a region-wide emergency occurs, which would affect neighboring Lee County too.

ERP systems used in education industry differ slightly from a traditional ERP. The overall system is familiar including components such as HR, food service revenue, payroll, and accounting. There is also, however, the education side, which contains student's records, scheduling forms, and discipline issues. The student section is the main focus of an education based ERP, and helps integrate data across the many schools of Collier County. The student records section particularly is of interest because it is accessed by many end-users. This section is not accessed directly through ERP but a web-based application that acts as a user interface and bridges the two together. For all intents and purposes, it can be described as middleware.

The Division of Administrator Technology appears to be in the midst of a wind of change, at least from an outsider's perspective. They currently do not have successor plans for any of their key positions, and so positions are not filled when personnel move-on. Instead, positions are consolidated and the duties are simply passed around to the staff left behind. Another indication of a change is that all personnel are older and very close to retirement, about a decade or less. As technology has matured, specifically ERP, the need for a full IT staff such as the one CCPS house may no longer be necessary and this is a division being phased out or at least moving in a very different direction. Additionally, with the emergence of cloud computing and its many variations, the outsourcing of an ERP system (at least to the extent of having a full-blown division/department dedicated to it) may be a thing of the past. Of course, this is speculation from the point of the researchers and might merely be the effects of government budget cut especially in a state that is not famous for its Department of Education.

4 Case Analysis

In this case study, the manager and staffs in The Division of Administrator Technology were interviewed with a semi-structure interview format to explore key issues of ERP upgrade. Some documents related to ERP upgrade were also reviewed to complement the findings from the interviews to finalize the discussion and conclusions.

For our case study, we focused on key issues in three main areas: the need for short of special IT staff and proper planning, the customization aspect of software, and organizational and corporate culture. The first key issue referred to the implementation phase. While the initial implementation was ten years, the team members working on upgrading their legacy system were only part-time members. The second issue was customization of the current ERP. It is likely that problems will arise during the implementation phase of upgrading the current legacy ERP systems to newer ERP systems. The final issues we focused on are organizational and corporate culture. This includes the level of comfort users feel with the system, and how news including new ERP systems, upgrades, and other important announcements are made aware to the employees of the organization.

5 Case Discussion

When the Collier County School District faces to the ERP upgrade request, there were several issues seen throughout the case. The first problem that was made aware to us was that the staff members working on the project were part-time. Bingi et al. [11] argues that "companies intending to implement an ERP system must be willing to dedicate some of their best employees to the project for a successful implementation." Schiff [12] agrees with this assessment and states "many organizations focus on getting executive approval, instead of gathering key participants from across the organization, from finance, operations, manufacturing, purchasing, and the warehouse, in addition to IT."

The problem with the Collier County School District's implementation team was the fact that they were only part-time members. Since the project members were part-time, no one was dedicated to the project. Ultimately choosing the right team will help the ERP project by having key team members involved throughout the implementation process and avoiding any unnecessary delays since everyone involved will have a common interest, and help to curtail any additional implementation costs. Another issue that occurs under poor planning is not having a solid project plan in place to help throughout the ERP implementation. The Collier County School District failed to have a strong project plan in place which leads to them not having any hard deadlines. This resulted in them taking ten years to complete the implementation of the ERP system, which became a legacy system right after the implementation was completed.

Second key issue that Collier County School District faced relates to the customization aspect of the ERP system. According to Kimberling [13], the two main disadvantages of ERP customization are "upgrades become more complex, costly, and risky, and customization may be a symptom of organizational change management issues." As the organization continues to perform more customization on ERP system, the costs associated with the customization will continue to increase. Aldrich [14] argues that although customization can be costly and time-consuming, it can bring a great deal of benefit to a company. One thing that the Collier County School District did was cater to the users in the individual departments. The manager of the Division of Administrator Technology introduced that users in the Collier County School District would want little features added here and there to make their jobs easier. Eventually more people called the IT department up to request features. During the ten-year's implementation, Collier County School District developed many customized functions and features in EDR ERP systems. Overall, this is a disadvantage for a school district during the upgrade. The disadvantages of the influx of requested changes may have outweighed the potential benefits of customization. Aldrich [14] argues that "if an organization customizes software in order to cater to the comfort of employees, the organization may end up ignoring inefficient business processes that need reengineering." In order to correct this mentality at the school district, the school district should have evaluated their business processes in order to see which processes actually required additional customization. This reevaluation could potentially save the organization time and money during the ERP upgrade.

The last key issues that we found through the interviews are organizational and corporate culture mentalities in the Collier County School District. According to Kappos [15], an organizations culture "can be defined by a number of constructs, such as symbols, language, ideology, beliefs, rituals, and myths that affect an individual's behavior." Organizational culture refers to patterns of behavior in organizations. It is a wider and deeper concept than corporate culture. Corporate culture, on the other hand, refers to beliefs and behaviors that determine how a company's employees and management interact and handle outside business transactions. Generally a corporate culture is implied and develops organically over time from the cumulative traits of the people the company hires.

In the case of the Collier County School District, this may be due to the fact that staff and management are set in their ways regarding how they perform their daily tasks. Kappos [15] argues that the organization's culture change is influenced by the organization's ability to assimilate to the ERP by allowing a sufficient amount of time to pass in order for members to get used to the changes. In other words, while users get set in their ways for the daily tasks they perform at work, they will need to adapt to the changing conditions in the workplace. This includes their daily routine, training on new software they will have to use to perform their tasks, and any new employees or superiors that will join the organization.

According to Cook [16], changing organizational culture isn't as simple as issuing a memo or calling a meeting. Corporate culture takes steady effort directing and making people realize that things are changing. Change management in the ERP context can be thought of as involving all human, social-related and cultural change techniques needed by management to ease the transition to and minimize organizational resistance of the new ERP environment [17]. ERP projects bring a massive change in an organization's structure and affect the way people work and interact. Therefore the introduction of ERP systems can cause resistance, confusion, redundancies, and errors. It is estimated that half of ERP projects fail to achieve expected benefits because organizations significantly underestimate the efforts involved in change management [18]. To overcome the corporate culture change, organizations need to make sure the employees are aware of the new ERP system by making them feel welcome in the new ERP system. This is vital to the newly released ERP system so the adoption rate in the company is high. Since most of the IT staffs are close to retirement and most of the users in EDR ERP systems used the current system for years, it will be hard for them to accept a new ERP system. This could be a vital issue even the upgrade project is successful. In this case, integrating proper management support, information, communication and training should be a good way to smooth the change derived from an ERP upgrade project. In addition, Norris et al. [19] argued that leadership, communication, training, planning and incentive systems can be tools to help organizations manage the change.

6 Conclusions

As more organizations seek to upgrade their ERP systems to take advantage of continuing technological innovations, effective technology implementations are increasingly important. This study tried to provide a deeper understanding of ERP upgrade in public sectors industry.

We have examined the school district CCPS, and found several issues in their current ERP system and concerns for their upcoming ERP upgrade. District administration's view of IT, like many companies, is as an expense and not as the key asset in ensuring the functionality of the organization as a whole. CCPS must take their next ERP upgrade project more seriously and tackle it head on. They must use a dedicated staff for implementation and not treat it as mini side projects. If they don't they are guaranteed to end up with another out of date system by the time they finish implementation.

Additionally, CCPS needs to decide what their IT department's role will be in the future. Will they still house and maintain their own mini-development team, or will they downsize to a simple IT department that maintains workstations? If this is the case, outsourcing is the best option but has consequences. If not, they need to dedicate more resources. ERP technology has matured enough to be treated with more importance. Only when they figure this out CCPS will be able to move ahead completely and successfully.

After carefully analyzing the data and all of the problems experienced in the Collier County School District, we have come to the conclusion that the school district failed to have a strong project plan in place throughout their implementation. Not having a well-defined project plan in place caused them to experience the issues that we have discussed. For public sectors, they need to clearly outline all of the goals and objectives they need from an ERP upgrade. This includes having team members that are dedicated to the project. In the past they had part-time members working on the team. This will no longer be the case. They need to think of the project as a vital part of their organization instead of the traditional view of an extensive and time consuming endeavor. They should also make sure the project plan has objectives for assessing their current ERP system. This will enable the school district to see what areas meet their requirements and what areas need improvement.

Another important view that the school district needs to understand is the time aspect of the project. This should be made aware to all members of the team, upper management, and finally to the end users. They need to work on their mentality of being able to perform changes to the software at will in the future. Their new ERP application may not be as conducive to this way of thinking and they must adapt to this going forward. This may be able to be accomplished by spending additional time to carefully select the correct ERP application. This can be accomplished by considering multiple vendors and even have the vendor demo the product to the school district. If the district needs to hire outside consultants in order to help them improve their change management mindset, then they must outline these objectives in their project plan in order to accomplish the goals. Once they have a well-defined project plan in place, and an overall different perspective in the school district, they should be able to achieve great success in upcoming ERP upgrade.

References

1. Swanton, B.: Build ERP upgrade costs into the business change program – not the IT budget. Computer Weekly, 28–28 (September 21, 2004)
2. Craig, R.: Laurier enterprise system upgrade. In: Proceedings of International Conference of Information Systems, Charlotte, USA, pp. 654–662 (1999)
3. Montgomery, N.: Build your business case for upgrades by adding functionality. Computer Weekly, 16 (2004)
4. Collins, K.: Strategy and execution of ERP upgrades. Government Finance Review 15(4), 43–47 (1999)
5. Zviran, M., Pliskin, N., Levin, R.: Measuring user satisfaction and perceived usefulness in the ERP context. Journal of Computer Information Systems 45(3), 43–52 (2005)
6. Bradford, M., Florin, J.: Examining the role of innovation diffusion factors on the implementation success of enterprise resource planning systems. International Journal of Accounting Information Systems 4(3), 205–226 (2003)
7. Yu, C.: Causes influencing the effectiveness of the post-implementation ERP system. Industrial Management Data Systems 105(1), 115–132 (2005)
8. Beatty, R.C., Williams, C.D.: ERP II: best practices for successfully implementing an ERP Upgrade. Communications of the ACM 49(3) (2006)
9. Ng, C., Gable, G., Chan, T.: An ERP maintenance model. In: Proceedings of the 36th Hawaii International Conference on System Sciences (HICSS 2003), USA (2003)
10. Wenrich, K., Ahmad, N.: Lessons learned during a decade of ERP experience: a case study. International Journal of Enterprise Information Systems 5(1), 55(19) (2009)
11. Bingi, P., Sharma, M.K., Godla, J.K.: Critical Issues Affecting an ERP Implementation. Information Systems Management 16(3) (1999)
12. Schiff, J.: 13 Common ERP Mistakes and How to Avoid Making Them. CIO Magazine (2012), http://www.cio.com/article/702989/13_Common_ERP_Mistakes_and_How_to_Avoid_Making_Them (retrieved)
13. Kimberling, E.: The Case For – and Against – ERP Customization. Panorama Consulting Solutions (2012), http://panorama-consulting.com/the-case-for-and-against-erp-customization/ (retrieved)
14. Aldrich, J.: Customization vs. Organizational Change Management: Which is Easier? Panorama Consulting Solutions (2013), http://panorama-consulting.com/customization-vs-organizational-change-management-which-is-easier/ (retrieved)
15. Kappos, A.: Organizational culture and the achievement of ERP strategic advantages and BPR performance improvements (2000), http://spectrum.library.concordia.ca/1240/1/MQ54302.pdf (retrieved)
16. Cook, R.: ERP and Corporate Culture (June 7, 2013), http://it.toolbox.com/blogs/inside-erp/erp-and-corporate-culture-56342 (retrieved)
17. Somers, T., Nelson, K.: A taxonomy of players and activities across the ERP project life cycle. Information & Management 41, 257–278 (2004)
18. Motwani, J., Subramanian, R., Gopalakrishna, P.: Critical factors for successful ERP implementation: exploratory findings from four case studies. Computers in Industry 56, 529–544 (2005)
19. Norris, G., Hurley, J., Hartley, K., Dunleavy, J., Balls, J.: E-Business and ERP: Transforming the Enterprise. John Wiley & Sons, New York (2000)

The Willingness to Adopt Technologies: A Cross-Sectional Study on the Influence of Technical Self-efficacy on Acceptance

Barbara S. Zaunbrecher, Sylvia Kowalewski, and Martina Ziefle

Human-Computer Interaction Center, RWTH Aachen University,
Campus-Boulevard 57, 52062 Aachen, Germany
{Zaunbrecher,Kowalewski,Ziefle}@comm.rwth-aachen.de

Abstract. Possible explanations for the acceptance or rejection of technological innovations have become a crucial topic in research. Depending on the type of technology, a variety of factors affect acceptance motives. This paper looks into the influence of technical-self efficacy (TSE) on acceptance of technology infrastructure. An empirical study (n=137 participants) was conducted to study effects of TSE on approval, discomfort, and resistance towards technology infrastructure, using electricity pylons, mobile phone masts, and wind power plants as examples. Overall, it was corroborated that TSE is a key variable for explaining users' acceptance of technology infrastructure. The individual technical self-confidence contributed to the explanation of approval and discomfort, whereas resistance was largely based on place of residence. Acceptance differences between technologies were based on different influential user factors. Our research provides valuable insights for stakeholders and contributes to the research on acceptance of energy infrastructures by providing a cross-sectional view.

Keywords: energy infrastructure, technology acceptance, technical self-efficacy, user diversity, renewable energies.

1 Introduction

The ongoing diffusion of technical innovations in many parts of daily life is an important prerequisite for the wealth of modern societies. Information and communication technologies, as well as industrial production systems and energy technologies, represent essential facilities providing innovations, job security, and electronic services for citizens.

However, with the increasing presence of technology people are confronted with, the acceptance of those technologies and the extent to which citizens are willing to adopt and tolerate these technologies are serious issues and not to be neglected [1],[2]. This is especially true facing the diversity of users who usually not only lack domain knowledge and technical expertise but who also do not possess detailed knowledge regarding the factual consequences of these technical developments.

M. Kurosu (Ed.): Human-Computer Interaction, Part III, HCII 2014, LNCS 8512, pp. 764–775, 2014.

The issue of technology acceptance has been researched from multiple perspectives for quite a long time now. It describes the approval, favorable reception, and ongoing use of newly introduced devices and systems.

The majority of theoretical models of technology acceptance refer to the acceptance of information and communication technologies in a mainly job-related context [3]. According to traditional acceptance theories, users' decision to use a novel technology is mainly determined by the perceived ease of use of the technical system and its perceived usefulness [4]. The success of these theoretical models was shown in many studies, but they are restricted to single small devices (e.g., computer, mobile phone) in the working context [5],[6]. It is highly reasonable that technology acceptance and the willingness of citizens to accept large-scale technologies in their living environment is much more complex [7].

Another shortcoming of traditional technology acceptance models is that mostly younger and technology-experienced persons were studied, a group not representative of today's technology users [8]. Beyond age, technology generation, and gender, the technical self-efficacy was found to considerably influence the way and the extent to which persons are willing to accept a (new) technology. Technical self-efficacy refers to the individual confidence in one's capability to use technical devices [9]. Studies have shown that computer self-efficacy is an influential factor for the performance and the ease of use in small screen devices [1], [6], [10]. However, it is unclear to what extent technical self-efficacy has an effect when dealing with large-scale technologies instead of small screen devices.

2 Acceptance of Infrastructure of Different Technologies

Recent technology acceptance research is directed at large scale technologies and infrastructure systems of different technology fields such as base stations [11], [12], Carbon Capture and Storage [13], heating systems [14], geothermal energy [15], photovoltaic systems [16], wind farms [17], renewable energy [18], and biogas [19].

In this context, technology acceptance is predominately related to persons' risk perceptions, i.e., the subjective assessments of the perceived probability and possible outcomes of expected negative events (e.g., natural hazards or environmental threats [20]). Characteristically, risk perceptions are a complex combination of perceived benefits, perceived barriers, and the perceived thread brought by technology interwoven with the individual bias for refusal or resistance.

While recent research considerably augmented the knowledge about technology acceptance in large-scale technologies, so far it is still insufficiently understood in how far risk perception and technology acceptance of infrastructure technologies are impacted by individual characteristics such as technical self-confidence.

In this study, we use an empirical approach to explore the influence of technical-self efficacy on approval, discomfort, and resistance towards technology infrastructure, taking electricity pylons, mobile phone masts, and wind power plants as examples.

3 Methodology

For an online survey, a questionnaire was designed to collect data from respondents on their TSE and their perception of different types of technology infrastructure. For this, electricity pylons, mobile phone masts, and wind power plants were chosen, as they share certain characteristics: all are vertical, lathy constructions that have a vital purpose in daily life. Additionally, they are all associated with health risks that have been widely discussed in the literature: radiofrequency emissions from mobile phone masts, electric and magnetic fields from electricity pylons, and infrasound from wind power plants. Lastly, they are all perceived as visual obtrusions and thus often subject to debate in citizen groups.

Questionnaire Design. The questionnaire included items on demographic information, living area, and proximity to the investigated infrastructure. Furthermore, six questions from the New Environmental Paradigm (NEP) scale [21] were used to measure attitude towards the environment. TSE was measured using selected items from Beier's TSE-questionnaire [9]. Both scales were shortened to assure a manageable length of the questionnaire. Acceptance of electricity pylons, mobile phone masts, and wind power plants was measured using the following seven items (with "x" respectively standing for "an electricity pylon," "a mobile phone mast," and "a wind power plant"). All questions, with the exception of the demographic information, were answered on a six-point-Likert scale ("1=do not agree at all" to "6=fully agree"). Finally, participants were invited to leave comments on the topic.

Table 1. Items used to measure discomfort, resistance, and approval of electricity pylons, mobile phone masts, and wind power plants. The items "unhappy," "controversial," and "protest" were adapted from [22].

Factor	Item name	Label
discomfort	unhappy	I would be unhappy if x was built nearby.
	danger	I think x is dangerous.
	health risk	I fear that x poses health risk.
resistance	controversial	It would be controversially discussed in my neighborhood.
	protest	I would protest against the building of x.
approval	acceptance	I would accept seeing x from my house.
	useful	I find x useful.

Reliability of Scales. To measure reliability of the scales used, a reliability analysis was performed for items used to quantify environmental attitude, TSE, discomfort, resistance, as well as approval of the three technologies (electricity pylons, mobile phone masts, and wind power plants). For the six items used to measure NEP, Cronbach's alpha was 0.72, respectively 0.90 for the eight items on TSE.

Because the scales to measure attitude towards technology infrastructure had not been used before, a factor analysis with Promax rotation was carried out on the items for each technology to verify the separation into the factors "discomfort," "resistance," and "approval." Results of the factor analysis are shown in Table 2.

As can be seen in Table 2, the total explanation of variance for electricity pylons was 78.33%, for mobile phone masts 79.97%, and for wind power plants 83.08%.

The three factors for each technology were also tested for reliability by applying Cronbach's Alpha as a measure of internal consistency. For electricity pylons, CA was reported between 0.48 and 0.85. For mobile phone masts, CA resulted between 0.59 and 0.88. The CA for factors on attitude towards wind power had a CA between 0.66 and 0.84. All factors were thus considered sufficiently reliable.

Table 2. Means, SD, and factor loadings for items on infrastructure acceptance

Factor	Variable	M	SD	Loading	Explanation
electricity pylons **discomfort**	unhappy elec	3.9	1.4	0.82	50.13%
	danger elec	3.0	1.2	0.91	
	health risk elec	3.3	1.3	0.96	
electricity pylons **resistance**	controversial elec	4.3	1.4	0.88	10.67%
	protest elec	2.9	1.3	0.18	
electricity pylons **approval**	acceptance elec	3.8	1.3	0.92	17.54%
	useful elec	4.1	1.2	0.68	
mobile phone masts **discomfort**	unhappy mobile	4.0	1.4	0.89	55.01%
	danger mobile	3.6	1.3	0.98	
	health risk mobile	3.7	1.3	0.97	
mobile phone masts **resistance**	controversial mobile	4.2	1.4	1.03	9.95%
	protest mobile	3.1	1.3	0.30	
mobile phone masts **approval**	acceptance mobile	3.6	1.3	0.62	15.00%
	useful mobile	4.0	1.2	1.00	
wind power plant **discomfort**	unhappy wind	2.9	1.5	0.38	57.22%
	danger wind	2.0	1.1	1.02	
	health risk wind	2.1	1.2	1.04	
wind power plant **resistance**	controversial wind	4.0	1.5	1.08	14.22%
	protest wind	2.2	1.3	0.57	
wind power plant **approval**	acceptance wind	4.3	1.4	0.69	11.64%
	useful wind	5.0	1.2	1.09	

Data Collection. A pretest was arranged with n=5 participants to ensure comprehensibility of the tasks. Their answers were not included in the analysis. After the evaluation of the pretest and minor modifications to the original questionnaire, data were collected in an online survey in Germany, between December 2013 and January 2014. The poll took approximately 15 minutes to complete.

3.1 Sample

137 participants took part in the study (47% women, 53% men). The mean age was 34.2 years (SD=13.3). Half of the sample reported to hold a university degree, 16% had completed vocational training. 44.5% lived in the city center, 37.5% in the

outskirts, and 19% in a village. To control for regular exposure to the investigated infrastructure, we asked if respondents lived within view of electricity pylons, wind power stations, or mobile phone masts (Fig. 1).

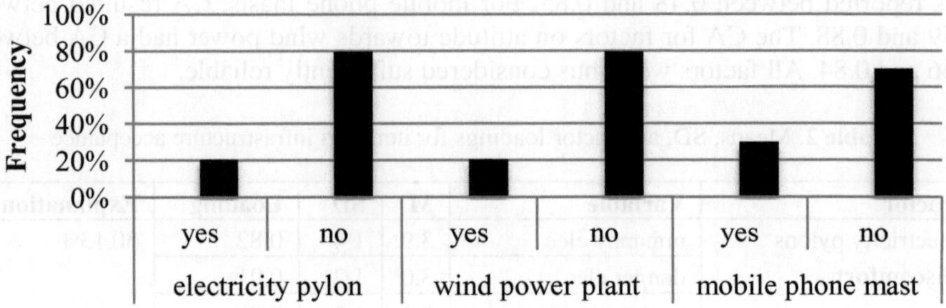

Fig. 1. Do you live within view of...? (n=137)

The mean score for TSE for the sample was M=4.7 (out of 6 points maximum) (SD=0.9). TSE correlated significantly with age ($r=-0.20$, $p \leq 0.05$). A significant gender difference for TSE between male (M=5.1, SD=0.6) and female participants (M=4.2, SD=1.0) was revealed ($F(1,135)=36.5$, $p \leq 0.01$). The mean score for environmental attitude was M=4.8 (6 points maximum) (SD=0.7), with no significant gender differences. Further analyses revealed no significant differences for TSE or environmental attitude. However, a significant age effect occurred ($F(2,134)=17.47$, $p \leq 0.01$): The further participants lived outside the city center, the older they were.

4 Results

In a first step, mean scores for the factors discomfort, resistance, and approval were calculated for each technology. Results are shown in Fig. 2. Resistance was almost

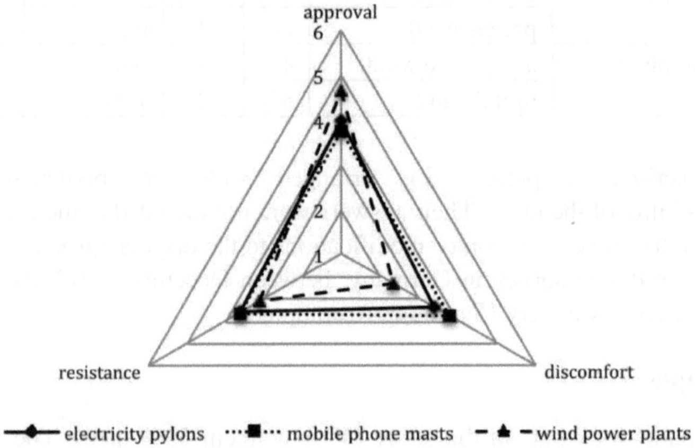

Fig. 2. Mean scores for factors resistance, discomfort and approval for electricity pylons, mobile phone masts, and wind power plants (1= do not agree at all, 6= fully agree)

identical for mobile phone masts (M=3.6, SD=1.2) and electricity pylons (M=3.6, SD=1.1), while wind power plants scored slightly lower (M=3.1, SD=1.2). Discomfort was also similarly high for mobile phone masts (M=3.8, SD=1.2) and electricity pylons (M=3.4, SD=1.1), but it scored considerably lower for wind power plants (M=2.3, SD=1.1). Accordingly, approval was the highest for wind power plants (M=4.7, SD=1.2), with lower scores for electricity pylons (M=4.0, SD=1.0) and mobile phone masts (M=3.8, SD=1.1).

Next, the influence of user characteristics on the three different factors was analyzed for all three technologies. First, correlations (Pearson's r) were run for continuous variables (age, TSE, environmental attitude) to identify possible influence factors on resistance, discomfort, and approval. Figures 3 to 5 show the significant correlations.

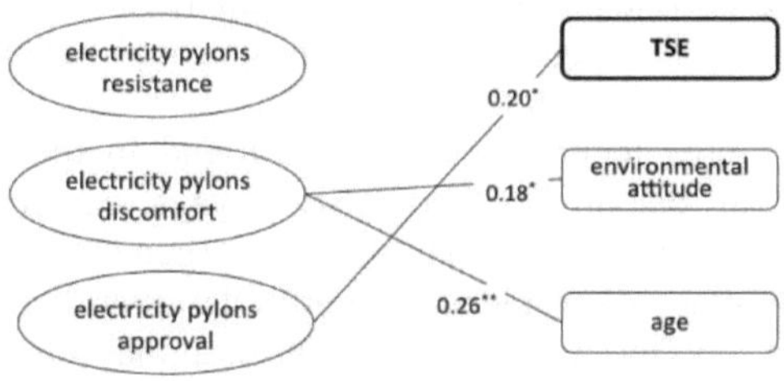

Fig. 3. Significant correlations between attitude towards electricity pylons and user characteristics (Asterisks indicate significance: * p≤ 0.05, ** p≤ 0.01)

It was found that electricity pylons and mobile phone masts show a similar pattern with regard to significant correlations, not only for the variables involved but also for the direction of the correlations. For both technologies, environmental attitude correlates positively with discomfort and TSE correlates positively with approval. Age, in both cases, is correlated positively with discomfort. Additional significant correlations for mobile phone masts were age and approval (negatively correlated) and environmental attitude and resistance (positively correlated).

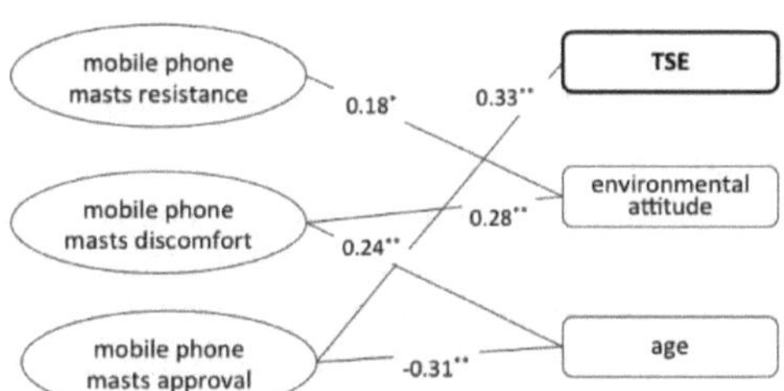

Fig. 4. Significant correlations between attitude towards mobile phone masts and user characteristics (Asterisks indicate significance: * p≤ 0.05, ** p≤ 0.01)

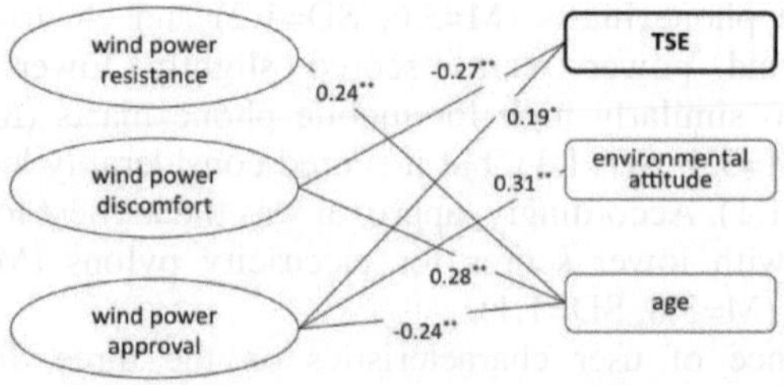

Fig. 5. Significant correlations between attitude towards wind power plants and user characteristics (Asterisks indicate significance: * p≤ 0.05, ** p≤ 0.01)

The pattern for wind power plants presented a direct contrast to this. Here, environmental attitude correlated positively with approval and not with discomfort. TSE did not merely correlate significantly with approval but also with discomfort. Age correlated significantly with all three factors.

Similarities for all three technologies can be found in the fact that age always correlated positively to discomfort and TSE always correlated positively with approval. Significant effects of nominal variables (gender, living within view of respective technology, place of residence) on attitude towards the three technologies were calculated using AVONAS by defining the nominal variables as independent (IV) and the attitude factors as dependent variable (DV). No significant differences between groups were reported for gender and participants who lived within or out of view of the respective technology infrastructure. No significant differences in attitude towards mobile phone masts were detected for groups based on the place of residence. For the attitude towards wind power plants and electricity pylons, however, place of residence played a significant role (Table 3): People who lived closer to the city center show less resistance and more approval towards wind power plants and less discomfort and resistance towards electricity pylons. This tendency is also supported by the non-significant factors for electricity pylons and wind power values.

More than one user factor showed to be influential for attitude towards the different technologies. Therefore, step-wise multiple regression analyses were performed for resistance, discomfort, and approval to identify the factor that predicts each mindset the best. Results are shown in Fig. 6 (electricity pylons), Fig. 7 (mobile phone masts), and Fig. 8 (wind power plants).

TSE significantly contributed to the prediction of approval for mobile phone masts and electricity pylons. For mobile phone masts, TSE ($\beta = 0.27$, $p<0.01$) and age (β =-0.25, $p<0.01$) contributed almost equally ($F(2,134)=13.41$), whereas for electricity pylons, TSE was the sole variable with significant contribution ($F(1,135)=5.62$) to approval. Furthermore, it was found that age significantly predicted discomfort for electricity pylons ($\beta = 0.28$, $p<0.01$), as did environmental attitude ($\beta = 0.21$, $p<0.05$) ($F(2,134)=8.37$). Age and environmental attitude combined also explained 15% of the variance for discomfort in the context of mobile phone masts ($F(2,134)=11.92$), both variables contributing similarly (age: $\beta = 0.28$, $p<0.01$, environmental attitude: $\beta = 0.31$, $p<0.01$). In addition, environmental attitude was identified as the single predictor for mobile phone mast resistance ($F(1,135)=4.43$). Resistance against electricity pylons, in contrast, was predicted solely by place of residence ($F(1,135)=6.52$).

Table 3. ANOVAS for place of residence (IV) and attitude towards wind power plants (DV)

Place of residence	Dependent variable	M	SD	df1	df2	F	Level of significance
city center	wind power plant **approval**	4.9	1.1	2	134	3.73	p≤ 0.05
suburbs		4.6	1.2				
village		4.2	1.2				
city center	wind power plant **resistance**	2.9	1.1	2	134	4.56	p≤ 0.05
suburbs		3.1	1.3				
village		2.6	1.1				
city center	wind power plant **discomfort**	2.1	0.9	2	134	3.01	n.s.
suburbs		2.5	1.2				
village		2.6	1.1				
city center	electricity pylons **approval**	4.1	1.1	2	134	1.86	n.s.
suburbs		3.9	0.9				
village		3.7	1.0				
city center	electricity pylons **resistance**	3.4	1.1	2	134	3.43	p ≤ 0.05
suburbs		3.6	1.1				
village		3.9	1.2				
city center	electricity pylons **discomfort**	3.2	1.1	2	134	3.86	p ≤ 0.05
suburbs		3.5	1.1				
village		3.9	1.4				

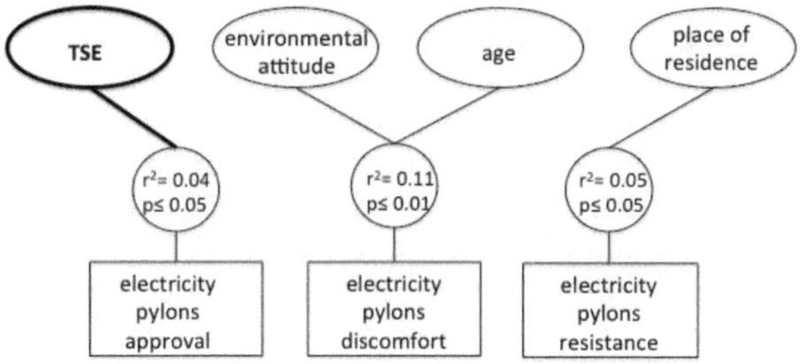

Fig. 6. Regression analysis for attitude towards electricity pylons

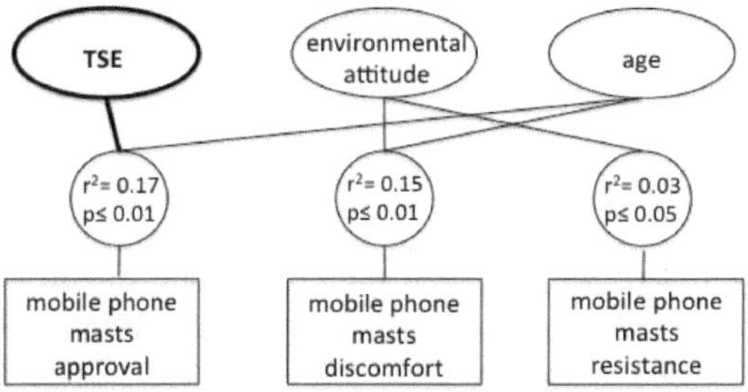

Fig. 7. Regression analysis for attitude towards mobile phone masts

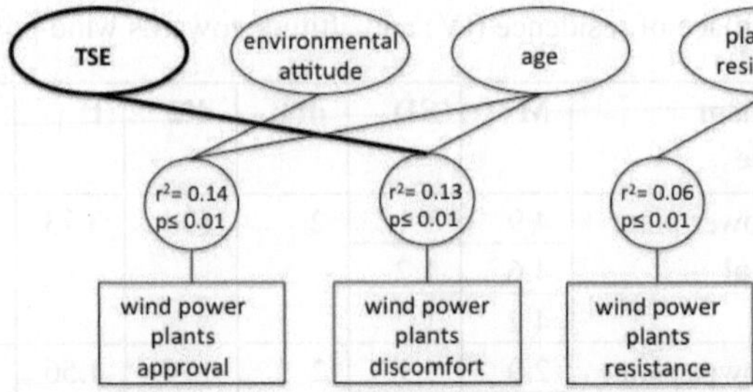

Fig. 8. Regression analysis for attitude towards wind power plants

Contrary to the findings for electricity pylons and mobile phone masts, TSE was found to be a predictor for discomfort for wind power plants ($\beta = -0.22$, $p<0.01$), as was age ($\beta = 0.24$, $p<0.01$) ($F(2,134)=9.70$). Another difference is the fact that environmental attitude ($\beta = 0.28$, $p<0.01$) in combination with age ($\beta = -0.21$, $p<0.05$) was found to predict approval for wind power plants, not discomfort. As it was for electricity pylons, place of residence was the only predictor for wind power plant resistance ($F(1,135)=8.68$).

TSE significantly contributed to the prediction of approval for mobile phone masts and electricity pylons. For mobile phone masts, TSE ($\beta = 0.27$, $p<0.01$) and age ($\beta =-0.25$, $p<0.01$) contributed almost equally ($F(2,134)=13.41$), while for electricity pylons, TSE was even the only single variable with significant contribution ($F(1,135)=5.62$) to approval.

It was found that age significantly predicted discomfort for electricity pylons ($\beta = 0.28$, $p<0.01$), as did environmental attitude ($\beta = 0.21$, $p<0.05$) ($F(2,134)=8.37$). Age and environmental attitude combined also explained 15% of the variance for discomfort in the context of mobile phone masts ($F(2,134)=11.92$), both variables contributed similarly (age: $\beta = 0.28$, $p<0.01$, environmental attitude: $\beta = 0.31$, $p<0.01$). Additionally, environmental attitude was identified as the single predictor for mobile phone mast resistance ($F(1,135)=4.43$). Resistance against electricity pylons, in contrast, was predicted solely by place of residence ($F(1,135)=6.52$).

Contrary to electricity pylons and mobile phone masts, TSE was found to be a predictor for discomfort for wind power plants ($\beta = -0.22$, $p<0.01$) besides age ($\beta = 0.24$, $p<0.01$) ($F(2,134)=9.70$). Another difference is the fact that environmental attitude ($\beta = 0.28$, $p<0.01$) in combination with age ($\beta = -0.21$, $p<0.05$) was found to predict approval for wind power plants, and not discomfort. Place of residence, like for electricity pylons, was the only predictor for wind power plant resistance ($F(1,135)=8.68$).

5 Discussion

In this empirical approach, we explored the acceptance of infrastructure systems in the context of renewable energy technologies, using electricity pylons, mobile phone masts, and wind power plants as examples.

Connecting to outcomes in other studies which corroborate the considerable impact of user characteristics on the extent to which users are willing to adopt novel technologies [1] ,[5], [8], we looked into the influence of technical-self efficacy (TSE) on acceptance of technology infrastructure in terms of individual approval, discomfort, and resistance towards said infrastructure. We also looked into the effects of the participants' age and their levels of environmental awareness: age, we found out, was also connected to their TSE levels.

The discussion section first focuses on how TSE influences attitudes towards electricity pylons, mobile phone masts, and wind power plants, then turns to other variables that have been identified to play a key role. Next, the results will be discussed, comparing the three different technologies.

Across the three technologies under study, it could be shown that TSE played a significant role for acceptance: the higher the levels of technical self-confidence, the higher the approval of infrastructure technologies (electricity pylons, mobile phone masts). Also, TSE was found to impact the discomfort regarding wind power plants (the lower TSE, the higher the discomfort ratings). Apart from place of residence, TSE was the only user factor that served as a single predictor for explaining technology acceptance for large-scale technologies. Beyond TSE, the participant's age was also an important factor. The fact that age affected approval and discomfort for mobile phone masts could be due to belonging to different technology generations [23]. Technology generation means the mental model of technology of a respective time and its influence/availability during the upbringing of the participants. From the voluntary comments given by participants, one (by a 57 years old male person) reflects the technology-generation related attitude towards mobile phone masts:

> "Pull down as many masts as possible. Imagine that I have survived my childhood and youth without any mobile phones. True emotions can much better be transmitted without electronic devices, but face to face. And (…) I have managed to start my family, even without any smartphones." (m, 57 y)

The study also revealed interesting differences across the three infrastructure technologies. While electricity pylons and mobile phone masts received almost comparable ratings for participants' resistance, discomfort and approval, wind power plants were overall perceived as much more positive. The difference between the large-scale technologies could be explained by the fact that wind power plants are a symbol of an environmentally friendly generation of electricity and thus evoke (mostly) positive associations. This is supported again by the comments that were given at the end of the questionnaire. It is striking that, in contrast to electricity pylons and mobile phone masts, wind power plants are connected with more positive associations: They are perceived as "beautiful" and "elegant," as "useful," "ecologically friendly," and as "the future" or "modern." Even though there were, of course, also negative associations ("infrasound," "dangerous for birds"), it is evident that its overall evaluation is more positive in comparison to the other two large-scale technologies. On the basis of the present data, this difference cannot be conclusively resolved. In future studies, we will have a look into mental models and images of those technologies. One assumption is that persons might be more affirmative towards wind power plants because they are perceived as successors of "windmills" which carry a positive connotation and reflect the good old days [24].

Acknowledgements. Thanks to Clara Erner and Chantal Lidynia for research support. This work was funded by the Excellence Initiative of German federal and state government.

References

1. Arning, K., Ziefle, M.: Different Perspectives on Technology Acceptance: The Role of Technology Type and Age. In: Holzinger, A., Miesenberger, K. (eds.) USAB 2009. LNCS, vol. 5889, pp. 20–41. Springer, Heidelberg (2009)
2. Gaul, S., Ziefle, M.: Smart Home Technologies: Insights into Generation-Specific Acceptance Motives. In: Holzinger, A., Miesenberger, K. (eds.) USAB 2009. LNCS, vol. 5889, pp. 312–332. Springer, Heidelberg (2009)
3. Davis, F.D.: Perceived Usefulness, Perceived Ease of Use, and User Acceptance of Information Technology. MIS Q. 13, 319–340 (1989)
4. Venkatesh, V., Davis, F.D.: A Model of the Antecedents of Perceived Ease of Use: Development and Test. Decis. Sci. 27, 451–481 (1996)
5. Arning, K., Ziefle, M.: Understanding age differences in PDA acceptance and performance. Comput. Hum. Behav. 23, 2904–2927 (2007)
6. Wilkowska, W., Ziefle, M.: Which Factors Form Older Adults' Acceptance of Mobile Information and Communication Technologies? In: Holzinger, A., Miesenberger, K. (eds.) USAB 2009. LNCS, vol. 5889, pp. 81–101. Springer, Heidelberg (2009)
7. Kowalewski, S., Arning, K., Minwegen, A., Ziefle, M., Ascheid, G.: Extending the engineering trade-off analysis by integrating user preferences in conjoint analysis. Expert Syst. Appl. 40, 2947–2955 (2013)
8. Wilkowska, W., Ziefle, M.: User diversity as a challenge for the integration of medical technology into future home environments. In: Human-Centred Design of eHealth Technologies. Concepts, Methods and Applications, pp. 95–126. IGI Global, Hershey (2011)
9. Beier, G.: Locus of control when interacting with technology (Kontrollüberzeugungen im Umgang mit Technik). Rep. Psychol. 24, 684–693 (1999)
10. Melenhorst, A.-S., Rogers, W.A., Bouwhuis, D.G.: Older Adults' Motivated Choice for Technological Innovation: Evidence for Benefit-Driven Selectivity. Psychol. Aging. 21, 190–195 (2006)
11. Dohle, S., Keller, C., Siegrist, M.: Conjoint Measurement of Base Station Siting Preferences. Hum. Ecol. Risk Assess. Int. J. 16, 825–836 (2010)
12. Arning, K., Kowalewski, S., Ziefle, M.: Health Concerns vs. Mobile Data Needs: Conjoint Measurement of Preferences for Mobile Communication Network Scenarios. Hum. Ecol. Risk Assess. Int. J. (2013), doi:10.1080/10807039.2013.838127
13. Wallquist, L., Seigo, S.L., Visschers, V.H.M., Siegrist, M.: Public acceptance of CCS system elements: A conjoint measurement. Int. J. Greenh. Gas Control. 6, 77–83 (2012)
14. Michelsen, C.C., Madlener, R.: Motivational factors influencing the homeowners' decisions between residential heating systems: An empirical analysis for Germany. Energy Policy 57, 221–233 (2013)
15. Kubota, H., Hondo, H., Hienuki, S., Kaieda, H.: Determining barriers to developing geothermal power generation in Japan: Societal acceptance by stakeholders involved in hot springs. Energy Policy 61, 1079–1087 (2013)
16. Jager, W.: Stimulating the diffusion of photovoltaic systems: A behavioural perspective. Energy Policy 34, 1935–1943 (2006)

17. Jobert, A., Laborgne, P., Mimler, S.: Local acceptance of wind energy: Factors of success identified in French and German case studies. Energy Policy 35, 2751–2760 (2007)
18. Arkesteijn, K., Oerlemans, L.: The early adoption of green power by Dutch households. Energy Policy 33, 183–196 (2005)
19. Emmann, C.H., Arens, L., Theuvsen, L.: Individual acceptance of the biogas innovation: A structural equation model. Energy Policy 62, 372–378 (2013)
20. Kasperson, R.E., Renn, O., Slovic, P.: The social amplification of risk: A conceptual framework. Risk Anal. 8, 177–187 (1988)
21. Dunlap, R.E., van Liere, K.D., Mertig, A.G., Jones, R.E.: Measuring Endorsement of the New Ecological Paradigm: A Revised NEP Scale. J. Soc. Issues. 56, 425–442 (2000)
22. Sustainable Energy Ireland: Attitudes towards the Development of wind farms in Ireland (2003), http://www.sei.ie/uploadedfiles/RenewableEnergy/Attitudestowardswind.pdf
23. Sackmann, R., Winkler, O.: Technology generations revisited: The internet generation. Gerontechnology 11, 493–503 (2013)
24. Joffe, H.: Risk: From perception to social representation. Br. J. Soc. Psychol. 42, 55–73 (2003)

The Impact of Culture Differences on Cloud Computing Adoption

Fan Zhao[1], Hans-Jürgen Scheruhn[2], and Mark von Rosing[3]

[1] Department of ISOM, Florida Gulf Coast University
fzhao@fgcu.edu
[2] Department of Automation and Informatics, Hochschule Harz University
hscheruhn@hs-harz.de
[3] University Research & Enterprise Standards, Global University Alliance
mvr@GlobalUniversityAlliance.net

Abstract. To cut cost, while increasing competitiveness, more and more small and medium-sized enterprises (SMEs) are considering cloud computing technology for supporting their business processes. However, initial cost, possible long term cost, security, accessibility and transformation issues are concerned by the organizations. By adopting LEADing Practices and Hofstede [16] national culture dimensions, this study provides substantive conclusions about the transformation effects of national culture dimensions on cloud computing acceptance in organizations.

Keywords: Cloud Computing, National Culture, Acceptance, ERP.

1 Introduction

During the last decade, many small and medium-sized enterprises (SMEs) have tried to adjust their business operations to cope with dramatic changes in the market. Over the past few years, many initiatives have come to life for organizations: Initiatives from service–oriented architecture (SOA), business process management (BPM), value management (VM), enterprise resource planning (ERP), and with this not only the enablement of technology and information to put it into the cloud. SMEs are trying to adopt a better solution to improve the effectiveness, efficiency and quality of their business processes. Benefits from ERP systems are obvious. Gattiker and Goodhue [1] describe the ERP benefits in following aspects: (1) improving the integration of information flow between sub-units; (2) centralizing the administrative activities, such as accounts payable and payroll; (3) reducing costs of system maintenance; (4) increasing the ability to deploy new IS functionality; (5) enabling transformation from inefficient business processes to accepted best practices. In this case, an ERP system seems to be one of the best to SMEs [2]. Since the majority of large companies have already implemented ERP systems, today ERP vendors are shifting their focus towards SMEs. Several reasons have encouraged the interest of ERP vendors towards SMEs. These include the saturation of the market, as most large enterprises have implemented ERP software, the supply chain integration between large and small

M. Kurosu (Ed.): Human-Computer Interaction, Part III, HCII 2014, LNCS 8512, pp. 776–785, 2014.

enterprises, the high number of SMEs compared to the number of large enterprises, and the technologies development together with the availability of relatively cheap hardware. However, to compete in the new economy, SMEs are now facing challenges to become more responsive and agile. Most SMEs operate in a highly dynamic world, where both internal and external requirements may change [3]. Changes may come from the need to be more cost-effective, from customers in the form of requirements for new products and product variants, from government agencies in the form of regulations, or by advances in technology. Often the SME is the weaker part in a supply chain and thus the ability to adapt to changes imposed by customers or suppliers will be an important competitive factor. Most SMEs have utilized the flexibility that comes from having a lower number of orders, customers, employees, etc. when changing processes and practices. It is therefore important that this flexibility is retained when new IT systems are implemented. [4] Scheruhn et al developed an agile Information Reference Model Framework for large and small enterprises exemplified by comparing case studies of different demo companies using SAP ERP and SAP Business byDesign. The use of commodity software, such as ERP systems, may force a more rigid structure on a SME and thus weaken their competitive advantage. It is critical to launch an investigation about the firm performance after SMEs adopted ERP systems.

In recent years, after many SMEs adopted various ERP packages from different ERP vendors, there is a new technology/concepts available in ERP adoption for SMEs called Cloud Computing. Cloud computing is an emerging business and technology concept to support an on-demand delivery of computing, storage and applications for executing business processes over the Internet. A recent IDC report shows global revenue in cloud software market reached to $22.9 billion and it will grow to $67.3 billion in 2016 [5]. This projection includes revenue generated by the shift from on-premise to on-demand providers as well as by the planning and architecture behind the shift. Comparing to ERP, cloud computing seems like intangiable because both hardware and software are not under control by the business who adopted this technology. Therefore, what are the key factors that may impact the acceptance of this technology by business will be a good research question.

2 Literature Review

The usage of the word "cloud" in cloud computing implies the architecture taking the form of a cloud which is easily accessible for business and users from anywhere in the world on demand [6]. It has important links to management aspects and also helps in cost reduction and driving innovation in a firm. In this sense, cloud computing means that instead of IT departments hosting data centers on the premises of companies themselves, this hosting is outsourced to third parties and made available via per-usage subscription fees that typically scale, along with the underlying infrastructure, with demand. Cloud Computing refers to a large, abstract pool of dynamically scalable on-demand infrastructure and on-demand software provided and /or accessed over the Internet.

Customers (= IT users) can access IT-capacity /services that is/are available in the Cloud. Cloud computing is a term used to describe both a type of application, platform and infrastructure. Cloud computing involves the delivery of hosted or virtualized services via the internet. Cloud computing is different from traditional hosting in several ways. Cloud services are flexible and can provide as much or as little of a particular service as a user needs at a given time. Cloud services are managed completely by the provider. The user needs only a computer and access to the internet to take advantage of these services. A cloud computing platform dynamically provisions, configures, reconfigures, and deprovisions servers as needed. Cloud computing also describes applications that are extended to be accessible through the Internet. These cloud applications use large data centers and powerful servers that host Web applications and Web services [7].

For enterprises, Cloud Computing can be adopted as one of the following services [8-12]:

- Software as a service (SaaS): providing software subscription services
- Storage as a service: providing remote storage resource services
- Database as a service (DaaS): providing remotely hosted database services
- Information as a service (INaaS): providing remotely hosted information services
- Business Process as a service (BPaaS): providing business processes based on remote resources
- Application as a service: also known as SaaS
- Testing as a service: providing testing services for local or remote systems
- Platform as a service (PaaS): providing a complete platform to support application development, interface development, database development, storage, information and testing
- Infrastructure as a service (IaaS): providing a service to access computing resources remotely
- Security as a service: providing core security services remotely over the Internet
- Integration as a service: providing a complete integration stack service

According to Beaubouef [13], there are three Cloud Models of ERP adoption:

- Software as a service: a subscription model for small customers who share hardware.
- Hosted ERP: a typical solution for large customers who have separate hardware and instances.
- Hybrid ERP: a combination solution that maintains on-premise software as well as integrated a degree of on-demand services.

Additionally, according to Gartner's report [13], more and more companies are considering on-demand services in different applications (Figure 1).

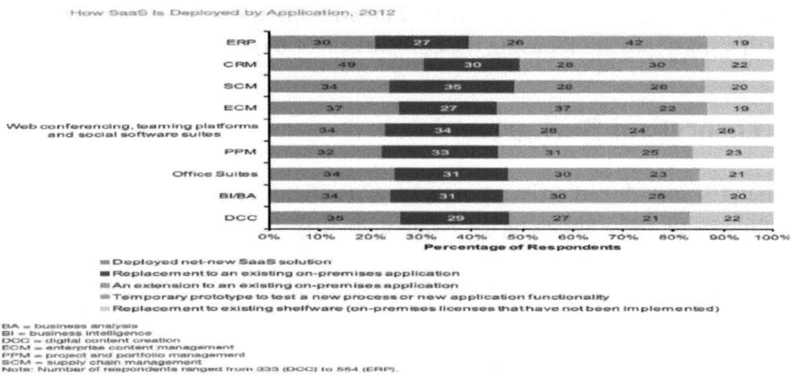

Fig. 1. How SaaS Is Developed by Application

2.1 Aspects of Cloud Computing

For years, researchers focus their cloud computing studies on advantages, disadvantages, acceptance procedures. [14-15]. The most evident advantage of Cloud Computing is the possibility to outsource processes in the way that somebody else might do this service at a low cost. More broadly, cloud computing can be thought of as the urge to stop worrying about how a process weakness cluster you might have or an unproductive, inefficient and ineffective process or flow in an organization should be resolved in order to focus on how the process can cut cost or done better (value potential).

There is no need to invest in infrastructure for platforms. Furthermore the Cloud provider is in charge of the professional management of the IT-solution, which reduces the need of human and technical resources. The total IT cost (TCO = Total Cost of Ownership) of Cloud Services are and remain low. The time requirements for the implementation of new IT systems can be massively reduced. By using Cloud services companies have resources at their disposal, which are easily accessible, highly scalable, flexible and location-independent. "On demand" infrastructure is – as its name says it – accessed on demand and charged by utilized units.

While calculation of costs for an individual Cloud Computing solution depends on numerable things, basically it is based on the six following factors:

1. Initial cost: depending on type of cloud solution
2. Computing Resources: number of CPUs & size of memory
3. Occupied disk space
4. Duration of use / operation
5. Number of Cloud Management User
6. Number of licenses (optional)

Many researchers adopted case studies to study cloud computing issues in different countries [16-17]. However, limited studies paid attention to the role of national culture in explaining cloud computing acceptance across countries. According to Waarts and Van Evaerdingen [8], national culture is one of the key factors influencing IS innovation adoptions founded by an empirical study of firms across Europe. Therefore, this paper tries to explain the relationship between cloud computing and national culture. United

States and China are two countries with dramatic differences in national culture. Therefore, in this study, we are focusing the comparison of these two countries.

3 Theoretical Background

Hofstede [19] introduced a five dimension classification of cultures based on a survey of employess in IBM subisdiaries located in fifty courtries: power distance, individualism/collectiveism, masculine/feminine, uncertainty avoidance, and long versus short-term orientation. He argues that national cultures can be differentiated in values. Therefore, we can identify and describe national cultures quantitively in difference categories.

There are five dimensions in Hofstede's model. Power distance index (PDI) is more about social structure rather than personalities. It identifies how societies under different cultures regulate the behavior of their members. In large power distance countries, the less powerful members expect and accept the unequality of power distribution. Lower power members are required to be obedient and respectful to higher power members. For example, employees are rarely encouraged to challenge their superiors. In countries with lower distance power, children are allowed to contradict their parents or challenge their teachers. In ERP usage, power users are a special group of people who have especially strong computer systems aptitude, provide a "first-call" options for other users, and answer most basic user questions within a department, division or other working group before escalating those calls to help desk or experts. According to Hofstede [19], organizations in countries with high power distance are often characterized by centralized decision structures, authority, and formalized rules. High level of centralization, authority and formalization will give more power to higher level users in ERP systems under the constrained hierarchical organizational structure. Therefore, adopting cloud computing may decrease the managerial control of the organization Hence, we suggest the following hypothesis:

H1: The higher the country's PDI score, the more likely companies in that country are NOT to adopt cloud computing.

According to Hofstede [19], uncertainty creates anxiety and people feel threatened by uncertain or unknown situations, for example, knowledge of a life after death. Uncertainty Avoidance Index (UAI) describes how people adapt or cope with these uncertain or unknown situations. In high UAI cultures, people tend to adopt technology, law, rules, and religion to decrease the ambiguity of situations by making events clearly interpretable and predictable. Organizations in high UAI cultures will not take unnecessary risks and only plan and complete those projects with enough value that they can explicitly approve in the market.

Since cloud computing is still a quite new technology to most of the organizations, there are uncertain issues that may cause problems to the business in the future. Therefore, to avoid uncertain issues of cloud computing, organizations in high UAI cultures are inclined to stay in mature technologies. Hence, we suggest the following hypothesis:

H2: The higher the country's UAI score, the more likely companies in that country are NOT to adopt cloud computing.

Individualism and collectivism index (IDV) represents the relationship between the individual and collectivity or the group in a certain society. Individualism and collectivism impact the decision making of a person in the society. Individualism culture is more toward personal decision making with less influence from the surrounding collectivity or group. For example, converting oneself from believing one religion to another is a highly individual activity in the countries with high individualism score while, in high collectivism countries, it is more reasonable that people tend to change their views together with their surrounding groups. In organizations with high individualism culture, employees are more likely to get more freedom in controlling ERP systems and follow their own pace and schedule in completing business processes. Hence, we suggest the following hypothesis:

H3: The higher the country's IDV score, the more likely companies in that country are to adopt cloud computing.

The fourth dimension in Hofstede's model is Masculinity (MAS) and Femininity. Basically, Hofstede [19] argues that gender differences come from the natural differences between men and women. Culture could be more Masculinity or more Femininity according to how the societies define and follow norms in different ways. From his survey, Hofstede found two basic facts. First, historically, masculine cultures tend to be more militaristic; second, masculine cultures tend to be more competitive while feminine cultures try more to encourage cooperation. Masculine cultures focus more on ambition, competition, and material values. Therefore, to increase the competition, organizations with higher MAS scores tend to adopt new technologies. Hence, we hypothesize the following:

H4: The higher the country's MAS score, the more likely companies in that country are to adopt cloud computing.

In his second edition of Culture's Consequences, Hofstede [19] defines a new dimension of national cultures: Long- Versus Short-Term Orientation. This Long-Term Orientation Index (LTO) score is based on a Chinese Value Survey (CVS) conducted in 1985 from students in 23 different countries. Cultures with high LTO scores tend to persist for a longer time with higher perseverance. The key words in LTO connotations summary are persistence, perseverance, personal adaptability to different circumstances, and believe of the happening of the most important events in life in future. On the contrary, people in Low LTO cultures expect quick results, prefer personal steadiness and stability, and believe that the most important events in life occurred in past or occur in present instead of future. Therefore, we expect that organizations in high LTO cultures are more likely to focus on future results with long strategy and operations planning, and more receptive to changes which may offer better results in the future, while as companies in low LTO cultures tend to emphanize short term benefits and are resistant to change. Obviously, cloud computing will lower the IT-related cost immediately by just paying monthly fee instead of the large amount initial investment of IT. However, the cost of cloud computing eventually will be larger than a typical ERP system. Therefore, organizations in high LTO cultures will prefer the lower cost system rather than a cloud computing system.

H5: The higher the country's LTO score, the more likely companies in that country are NOT to adopt cloud computing.

In the following sections, we will focus on the five hypotheses we mentioned above to explain the method of our ERP usage analysis and discuss the analysis results.

4 Research Method and Results

To exam the research model, a survey was conducted. The survey was sent to 547 SMEs in three US cities (one large city, one mid-size city and one small town) and 783 SMEs in three Chinese cities with similar city size pattern. A total of 246 surveys were completed and 235 (141 from US and 94 from China) were used in the analysis. Table 1 shows the industry distribution of the companies.

Table 1. Industry Distribution

Industry	Number	Percentage
Industrial Manufacturing	51	28%
Public Sector	9	8%
High Technology	68	25%
Education	15	6%
Healthcare	44	13%
Utilities	9	4%
Agriculture	11	4%
Others	28	12%

The items used in this survey were adapted from Hofstede's IBM and China survey questionnaires. The reliability of the items was evaluated using Cronbach's alpha [19]. The coefficient alphas for the PDI, UAI, IDV, MAS, and LTO were 0.76, 0.82, 0.83, 0.71, and 0.86, respectively. Pearson's correlation coefficients were also determined to assess the convergence validity. Since all the attribute coefficients were somewhere from high to moderate ranges, they were all retained for future analysis. Additionally, there were no concerns about multi-collinearity because none of the coefficients was extremely high.

The data were analyzed using multiple linear regression analysis. The purpose of a regression analysis is to relate a dependent variable to a set of independent variables. Regression analysis, therefore, was the most appropriate analytical technique in this study to determine the relationship between customer commitment and innovation characteristics, between customer attitude and innovation characteristics, and between customer commitment and customer attitude. Table 1 shows the hypothesis testing results along with the conclusions whether the hypothesis is supported by the statistical analysis at $a<.05$.

Table 2. Summary of Regression Analysis Results

Hypothesis	Independent Variable	t-value	Significance	Support
H1	PDI	-2.370	0.025	Yes
H2	UAI	-2.876	0.011	Yes
H3	IDV	5.205	<0.001	Yes
H4	MAS	1.098	0.276	No
H5	LTO	-4.341	<0.001	Yes

5 Discussion and Conclusions

As demonstrated by the data analysis above, this empirical study supports hypothesis 1, 2, 3, and 5, while hypothesis was not supported. Consequently, we can answer the research question in our study. First, national cultural variables, such as PDI, UAI, IDV, and LTO are related to acceptance of cloud computing in SMEs; Secondly, national culture should be added to the acceptance framework in cloud computing studies. Table 3 shows the summary of hypotheses testing of this study.

Table 3. Summary of Testing the Hypotheses 1 to 5

Culture Variable	Hypothesized influence on Cloud Computing Adoption	Results
Power Distance Index (PDI)	Negative	Confirmed
Uncertainty Avoidance Index (UAI)	Negative	Confirmed
Individualism Index (IDV)	Positive	Confirmed
Masculinity Index (MAS)	Positive	Not Confirmed
Long-Term Orientation Index (LTO)	Negative	Confirmed

The findings indicate that level of MAS is not an issue related to cloud computing acceptance. The possible reason to explain this result may be because US and China have a similar culture in this dimension. According to Hofstede [19], the MAS score of US and China are 62 and 66, which are very close. Therefore, the results may not show a significant difference between these two countries under a limited sample size.

Our study provides substantive conclusions about the effects of national culture dimensions on cloud computing acceptance in organizations. We formulated a number of hypotheses regarding the influences of various national culture dimensions, such as PDI, UAI, DVI, MAS, and LTO. According to our data analysis, we found evidence to support most of our hypotheses. We can conclude that national culture does influence the cloud computing acceptance in organizations. Hofstede dimensions appeared to be a good theoretical background for cloud computing acceptance study. Higher level of the individualism positively influenced the cloud computing acceptance, while higher level of the Power Distance, Uncertainty Avoidance, and

Long-Term Orientation has a significant negatively influence on decision making of cloud computing adoptions.

This research is the first study distinguishing cloud computing acceptance differences between different national cultures by adopting Hofstede's cultural dimension model. Our findings suggest that attention should be paid to differences between different areas, such as China and US. According to different culture and regulations, Chinese and US companies have different management styles and decision-making strategies. Additionally, the results from this study can help global organizations to adjust their strategies regarding to the information systems acceptance policies according to each country's cultural traits.

This empirical study would also provide theoretical background to researchers who are working on cloud computing research. This is the very first paper discussing cloud computing acceptance under cultural circumstances. This research not only provides substantive conclusions about the effects of national culture dimensions influencing cloud computing acceptance, but also emphasizes the importance of culture differences in cloud computing acceptance in SMEs. Culture issue could be an additional dimension in many other cloud computing acceptance studies. Researchers therefore can further expend their research models to more generalized applications.

The empirical findings would be beneficial in the theoretical understanding of the adoption behavior of cloud computing technology. It may also help in driving the development and execution of a better acceptance framework in cloud computing research.

In this study, we only focus on two different cultural areas in the cloud computing acceptance research. In the future, we are planning to expand to other nations, such as European countries [19] to further test the relationship between the cultural differences and cloud computing acceptance. Furthermore the authors plan to integrate information objects of cultural aspects into existing Enterprise Information Reference Model Frameworks [4,21] .

References

1. Gattiker, T., Goodhue, D.: Understanding the plant level costs and benefits of ERP: will the ugly duckling always turn into a swan. In: Proceedings of the 33rd Hawaii International Conference on System Science, Hawaii (2000)
2. Olson, K., Satre, P.: ERP for SMEs – is proprietary software an alternative? Business Process Management 13(3), 379–389 (2007)
3. Branzei, O., Vertinsky, I.: Strategic pathways to product innovation capabilities in SMEs. Journal of Business Venturing 21, 75–105 (2006)
4. Scheruhn, H., Sicorello, S., Weidner, S.: Repository-based ERP case studies: A study about chances and benefits of agile case study development. In: Abramowicz, W., Domingue, J., Wecel, K. (eds.) BIS 2012 Workshops. LNBIP, vol. 127, pp. 186–197. Springer, Heidelberg (2012)
5. Mahowald, R., Sullivan, C.: Worldwide Saas and Cloud Software 2012-2016 Forecast and 2011 Vendor Shares. International Data Corporation, IDC (2012), http://www.idc.com/getdoc.jsp?containerId=236184#.USTXoh3kseB (retrieved)

6. von Rosing, M., Hendrickx, H., Daley, K., Mahakena, M.: Defining the Architecture Profession. Published by: IEEE Commerce and Enterprise Computing, 325–332 (September 2011) ISBN: 978-0-7695-4535-6
7. Hove, M., von Rosing, M., Presten, T.: Combining Enterprise Architecture in Complex IT Projects. Published by: IEEE Commerce and Enterprise Computing, 271–278 (May 2011)
8. Bhardwaj, S., Jain, L., Jain, S.: Cloud Computing: A Study of Infrastructure as a Service (IaaS). International Journal of Engineering and Information Technology 2(1), 60–63 (2010)
9. Kim, W.: Cloud Computing: Today and Tomorrow. Journal of Object Technology (January/February 2009)
10. Linthicum, D.: Cloud Computing and SOA Convergence in Your Enterprise. Addison Wesley, Boston (2010)
11. Velte, A., Velte, T., Elsenpeter, R.: Cloud Computing, A Practical Approach. McGraw-Hill (2010)
12. Wang, L., von Laszewski, G., Younge, A., He, X., Kunze, M., Tao, J., Fu, C.: Cloud Computing: A Perspective Study. New Gneration Computing 28, 137–146 (2010)
13. Beaubouef, B.: Cloud ERP – New Dog, Same Fleas (May 22, 2011), `http://gbeaubouef.wordpress.com/2011/05/22/cloud-erp/` (retrieved Febraury 5, 2013)
14. Gartner, Inc. Stanford, Connecticut, USA. Press release: Global IT Spending Forecast (June 20, 2012), `http://www.gartner.com/newsroom/id/2055215` (retrieved)
15. Lorraine, S.: Understanding the role of managerial agency in achieving business benefits from ERP systems. Inforation Systems Journal 20(3), 213–238 (2010)
16. Nortan, A., Yvette, C., Coulson-Thomas, C., Ashurst, C.: Ensuring benefits realization from ERP II: the CSF phasing model. Journal of Enterprise Information Management 26(3), 218–234 (2013)
17. Pan, K., Nunes, M., Guo, P.: Risks affecting ERP post-implementation. Journal of Manufacturing Technology Management 22(1), 107–130 (2011)
18. Waarts, E., Van Everdingen, Y.: The Influence of National Culture on the Adoption Status of Innovations: An Empirical Study of Firms Across Europe. European Management Journal 23(6), 601–610 (2005)
19. Hofstede, G.: Culture's Consequences. Sage Publications, Housand Oaks (2001)
20. Cronbach, L.: Essentials of Psychology Testing. Harper and Row, New York (1970)
21. LEADing Practice: Artifact Description: Business, Information & Data Object Modelling (February 7, 2014), `http://www.leadingpractice.com/wp-content/uploads/2013/10/LEADing-Practice-Object-Modelling.pdf` (retrieved)

Just Rate It! Gamification as Part of Recommendation

Angelina de C.A. Ziesemer, Luana Müller, and Milene S. Silveira

Faculdade de Informática — PUCRS
Avenida Ipiranga 6681, 90619-900, Porto Alegre - RS, Brazil
{angelina.ziesemer,luana.muller}@acad.pucrs.br,
milene.silveira@pucrs.br

Abstract. In attempt to help users in filtering available products, recommender systems are being used by e-commerce systems to try to predict users' preferences and suggest them new products. Some recommender systems are based in previous ratings and evaluations provided by users to purchased items. When new users or new items join in recommender systems they can suffer by the so called cold-start problem. However, do you rate the products that you bought? This question and other ones were made to 367 participants by an online survey that aims to identify customer profiles and motivations. Also, we investigated user engagement in gamified systems and the effects of tangible and intangible rewards in their behavior. This work presents a theoretical framework that provides basis for defining how gamification can be used to encourage ratings and improve user engagement in tasks that benefit user reputation, item reliability and to overcome cold-start problem.

Keywords: gamification, recommendation, e-commerce.

1 Introduction

E-commerce systems have growth in the quantity of users and content available for searching and due to this, Recommender Systems (RS) become essential to help users find relevant products. The purpose of recommendation algorithms on e-commerce is to filter products according to users' preferences. There are distinct approaches [3, 4, 16, 17, 22] for recommending content and one of the most popular technique is the Collaborative Filtering (CF) [19] that uses ratings/reviews from users on items.

Ratings and reviews are known as explicit feedback [21] and using this technique the user is the one who informs the content relevance. Amazon[1] has used ratings and reviews for years and a well known problem caused by this is that CF can face the cold-start problem. The cold-start problem occurs when recommendations are required for users that have no activity (ratings, reviews) or there are items in the dataset that no one has yet rated [18]. To understand this

[1] https://www.amazon.com/

M. Kurosu (Ed.): Human-Computer Interaction, Part III, HCII 2014, LNCS 8512, pp. 786–796, 2014.

problem we performed a survey with 367 participants. We asked users about their consumer routine, their behavior related to rating/reviews on e-commerce systems and whether users are familiar with gamification [10]. Based on the results we propose a theoretical framework to overcome the cold-star problem using gamification approaches.

The term gamification consists in the use of game design elements in a non-game context to motivate and increase user activity [9], and many services like Foursquare[2], LinkedIn[3], Stackoverflow[4] have adopted this technique.

We did not find any research related to the use of recommendation with gamification, so this motivated us to develop directions to use the best of the two approaches to engage users in the rating and review tasks using game elements on e-commerce systems.

In the next section we present an overview about Recommender Systems and Gamification. Next, we present the results from the survey performed with 367 participants and after a theoretical framework proposing the use of gamification in order to engage users to rate products on e-commerce systems. Finally, we present the conclusion about the survey and future research prospects.

2 Background

2.1 Recommender Systems

Due to the amount of information available on the Internet, recommender systems have become an efficient alternative for helping users find relevant content and are being widely deployed on the web in many domains including large e-commerce powerhouses such as Amazon [15]. Regardless of the approach, recommender algorithms use information about the users preferences to try recommend items that people with similar tastes and preferences liked in the past [1].

A Likert' five-point response is a popular technique of explicit feedback and it is widely used in CF approaches. This kind of feedback is used internally to measure the similarity among items/products and increase the quality of recommendations [11]. However, explicit feedback requires additional effort from users and sometimes they might not be willing to provide it. Thus, the number of available ratings explicitly, might be too small and can result in a poor recommendations quality [3]. Further, new products in an e-commerce dataset do not have evaluations, which exclude them from the recommendation item-based algorithm and the same occurs with users that are new in the system.

One of the most challenging key questions in recommender systems is: "how to provide recommendations at the initial stage of the system when available data about users, items and ratings is extremely sparse?" [15]. Recently, users are willing to contribute to their community knowledge (a direct reflection from the Web 2.0 and the role of online communities). Still, recent researches are focusing

[2] http://foursquare.com
[3] http://www.linkedin.com/
[4] http://stackoverflow.com/

on developing techniques that can help to persuade the users to provide more ratings [11].

However, when it is necessary to deliver content to new users or deliver recommendation items that were not rated in the system, one of the recommender systems' problems can appear: the cold-start problem.

Beyond the Cold-Start Problem. Pure CF methods base their recommendations on users' preferences ignoring user and item attributes as demographics and product descriptions. The cold-start problem can occur in the following situations: recommendations for existing items for new users, recommendations for new items for existing users and recommendations for new items for new users [15]. To try overcome these problems, recommender systems try to get users to rate items at the beginning of their profile creation, asking them to answer questions about their preferences or using stereotypes (e.g. elderly people usually enjoy classical music) [14].

Another approach is to use content information to infer similarities from existing items compared to new items. Content recommendations can be made for new items that seem similar to others. However, the cold-start problem is only one of the problems related to new users and new items. In [13] users reported that customer reviews played a role in deciding whether or not to buy a product, but the reviews are not the only factors. Users are also concerned about reviewers' expertise and reputation, and products that have five stars might be attractive, but if it is based only on one or few reviews it is possibly not very interesting. Some systems can rank reviews and products based on the author's reputation, but if a new product is rated by new users some recommendation will possibly fail in quality.

Therefore, user engagement in the rating task is needed to improve recommendation. In the next section we present the gamification definition and the elements that are involved to motivate users.

2.2 Gamification

The term gamification refers to the use of game elements and concepts within systems and applications. It has recently increased and triggered a buzz in the academy, mainly for those trying to better define, understand and explore its effects. One of the major reasons to use gamification approaches is to motivate people to become more involved in an activity, environment or any task that requires user engagement.

According to the Self Determination Theory [6] (SDT), people are intrinsically or extrinsically motivated. Intrinsic Motivation (IM) is related to activities that people do because they have an internal aspiration, such as personal development, or because it is the right thing to do or just because it is enjoyable. On the other hand, Extrinsic Motivation (EM) is related to activities that people do because they have a reward or status and it is all about its value. SDT examines people life goals or aspirations, showing the variations regarding intrinsic versus extrinsic life motivation to perform [8] a task, activities etc.

The goal of implementing game elements in the way that users can interact with a system is to motivate them through rewards. Rewards in a gamified system are generally related to badges, leaderboards, status and reputation, whereas their structure is related to progress, cooperation, feedback, etc. Moreover, Deci and Ryan [7] conceptualize the Cognitive Evaluation Theory (CET) to categorize the type of rewards that can influence behavior [20]. Rewards in CET are categorized as tangible or intangible, expected or unexpected, or contingent rewards. We are particularly interested in tangible vs. intangible rewards and contingent rewards to understand users motivation regarding products evaluation and their behavior:

- Tangible rewards are related to prizes/rewards that are material, real or physical. They are related to money or prizes that people can have.
- Intangible rewards are related to prizes/rewards that are not material. They are game elements that can be used in a gamified system, like users reputation, digital badges or leaderboard position etc.

In the other hand contingent rewards are related to the rewards structures:

- Task non-contingent: users will win this reward every time e.g. they logon.
- Engagement-contingent: users will win when they start a new task.
- Completion-contingent: users will win this reward when they complete a task.
- Performance-contingent: reward based on the quality of the task performed.

3 Case Study and Data Analysis

To analyze users of e-commerce websites, their product evaluation behavior and their use of gamified applications or systems, data was gathered through an online survey. A total of 367 individuals completed the survey, 221 (60%) male and 146 (40%) female, with an average age of 30. From this sample, we used 356 (97%) responses, that represent only those participants who usually buy on e-commerce systems.

The focus of the survey was to identify and compare users behavior on e-commerce systems and understand users motivation for rating products.

The data obtained from the survey is composed by categorical and qualitative variables. We use the Chi-square test and Z-Test of Proportion to gauge the comparative frequency of variables obtained from this survey and also a qualitative analysis from the participants answers.

Next, we present an analysis of the qualitative responses obtained during the survey. The answers show that although users tend to express more interest in tangible rewards, they have other motivations to evaluate products.

3.1 Users' Behavior and the Cold-Start Problem

In a previous section we explained the cold-start problem and its causes. According to [13], those users that intend to buy e.g. a book in the Amazon website, claim for expertise reviewers. It is possible for Amazon costumers say whether a rating and a review are helpful or not, and this action can increase the reviewers reputation and also improving the quality of recommendation.

However, what are the kind of ratings expected by websites and recommender systems? All kind of rating play a role in recommendation, even those ratings that do not represent high or low level of satisfaction because the item was even the way that the consumer expected.

For the 356 (97%) participants that are used to buy online, 210 (58%) said that they do not usually return to the website for rating products. Here we have the first point: the longer the products wait for ratings, the longer the cold-start problem will persist.

We asked participants an open question with the purpose of understanding why they evaluate products. 119 participants explained when and why they would return to the website to rate a product. 104 respondents said that they usually rate their purchased products when an item does not meet their expectations. However, 64 respondents also said that they rate products for the opposite reason, when it positively exceeds their expectations. This action can difficult the recommender system to recognize the real user feelings about new products that they could possibly purchase. Also, future buyers can be influenced by these opposite reviews.

Only 48 participants reported that they always rate a product regardless of the situation, even when the products are consistent with the description available on the website and other ratings. Also 30 participants stated that they only go to the website to rate products when the website or the seller (on websites like eBay[5]) send to them an email asking for a review. Another reasons that participants pointed for evaluating products were:

- When he/she has being a website user since a long time.
- When his/her opinion is different from other buyers.
- When the system provides to him/her some points or advantages.
- When the website is a C2C[6].
- When the product presents problem.
- When the customer service was not satisfactory.
- When he/she intends to return to the website to make more purchases.

Product ratings are important to e-commerce and users need to feel that ratings are necessary and indispensable. When this is not established in users minds, it is necessary to develop and improve tools that encourage them to perform this task. A good product rating (not only in the extremists cases) can improve recommendations, and consequently increase sales, users loyalty and their online shopping experience.

[5] http://www.ebay.com/
[6] Customer-to-customer

3.2 Rewards and Motivations

To try understand users motivation regarding the type of rewards discussed in this paper, we asked participants two similar questions related to tangible and intangible rewards.

First we asked them: "Would you feel motivated to return to an e-commerce website and evaluate a purchased product if this task would help you to improve your reputation or points in the system?". We analyzed the proportion of participants that care about intangible rewards (IR). The results show that the proportion of users that use gamification and those who not, do not differ significantly ($Z = -0.55, p = 0.57$) as described in Table 1. The participants motivation to rate products if the system give them a reputation or points is not related to the previous use of gamification.

Table 1. Individuals behavior related to tangible and intangible rewards and those who use and not use gamified systems

Motivation	Not Use Gamification	Use Gamification	Overall	Proportion
IR	41 (54%)	161 (58%)	202 (56%)	$Z = -0.55$
TR	71 (93%)	252 (90%)	323 (90%)	$Z = 0.91$

Furthermore, we observed the same behavior for the second question. Participants were asked about their motivation regarding tangible rewards (TR) and the rating/review task. The proportion of users that would return to evaluate products from those that use and do not use gamification are similar ($Z = 0.91$ $p = 0.36$).

However from the overall participants, 90% said that they could evaluate products if it would give them tangible rewards and only 56% would do this if the rewards were intangible. Then, the motivation for users keep doing a gamified task could not be just related to the rewards it offers, users can have a intrinsic motivation to keep them engaged. In the next section we investigate why users rating products and their motivation for keeping rating items.

3.3 Rating and Motivation

In this section we intend to analyze the motivations for users to rate products. The results shown here are related to qualitative and a quantitative analysis and helped us to evaluate issues related to intrinsic and extrinsic motivation.

Regarding the question "Why would you feel motivated to return in a website and evaluate a purchased product if you received some type of reputation or points in the system?", 172 participants answered this question. Each answer was read, analyzed and categorized according to the motivations reported by them. Some respondents had more than one motivation, but the answer was categorized according to the strongest one.

Fifty-four users stated that their motivation is related to virtual economy. For them, reputation or points need to provide a discount, benefit or reward. One user reported: *"I would return to the website if it generates points or reputation that could be useful for new acquisitions, also discounts or improvement in payment methods."* Another user stated, *"Indirectly I would be contributing with the seller. Thus, I would like to receive some benefit. Even if the benefit takes a long time to bring me a credit I like the simple fact of knowing that the benefit is mutual."* These are examples of extrinsic motivation for rating products and it is all about virtual currency or virtual economy.

Another 34 respondents said that their mainly motivation is to have their loyalty recognized by the website. These users would like to be recognized as "good buyers" and consequently improve their reputation in the system.

For 28 participants, simply to be encouraged to do something is a motivation. One of them stated: *"Beyond winning points, you are helping other people to know about the product reputation. I believe it would be a motivation"*. Moreover, 11 users reported that they usually rate their purchased products because it is the right to do. For them, gamification will be an additional motivation to keep them doing something that they already do. This behavior is related to intrinsic motivation, in other words, people complete tasks because they think it is important and the right to do.

Moreover, regarding intrinsic motivation, the game feeling and the possibility to compete with friends were one of the motivations reported by 7 respondents. One of them reported: *"the simple fact that it seems like a competition is the necessary motivation to keep me busy performing some task"*.

For three participants the motivation is the loyalty promoted when the user feels stimulated to always return to the same website to do their purchasing. According to one of them, *"the company gives to you a reason to return and buy again"*. The main motivation to use a gamified system is to keep users engaged with the business objectives through the tasks provided by the system. Also, other 35 remaining participants did not know how to explain their motivations.

Moreover, we asked participants if they usually rate products on the internet. Overall, less than a half (41%) participants responded that they rate products in the internet. We used the Pearson Chi-square to gauge the relationship between the use of gamification and the rating task on e-commerce systems. Results show that those who use gamified systems and those who not, tend to rate products with equal frequency ($X^2 = 1.32$, $p = 0.24$). However, 98% of participants answered that they read product reviews online before purchasing an item and more than a half (55%) evaluate reviews left by other users in products that they intend to buy.

According to the results, users have mainly intrinsic motivation for rating products, although they think that tangible rewards could lead them to more frequently rate and review items.

4 Theoretical Framework

Explicit feedback is a common approach for creating recommender systems and there are several works trying to improve recommendation by algorithms to treat rating accuracy [2, 5, 12]. However, ratings and reviews are feedbacks given by humans and it is also necessary to motivate users engagement to complete these tasks and to try to overcome the cold-start problem.

Moreover, individuals are also concerned about the quality and reliability of recommendations that they have received. It was reported by [13] that those users who receive recommendations also analyze the reviews and ratings and they take into account not only the rating but the quantity of users that evaluate the product and their expertise about the subject.

Figure 1 shows the effect of new ratings on new items from new users. Those users that are new in the system have low/no reputation because they do not have too much interaction/ratings in the systems and consequently the recommended item may fail in reliability because it has received a new evaluation from a new user. The same occurs with new items and new users, users can have weak or no recommendations until items have a x number of reviews by "trusted users". Also, new items reviewed only few times could be considered with low reliability.

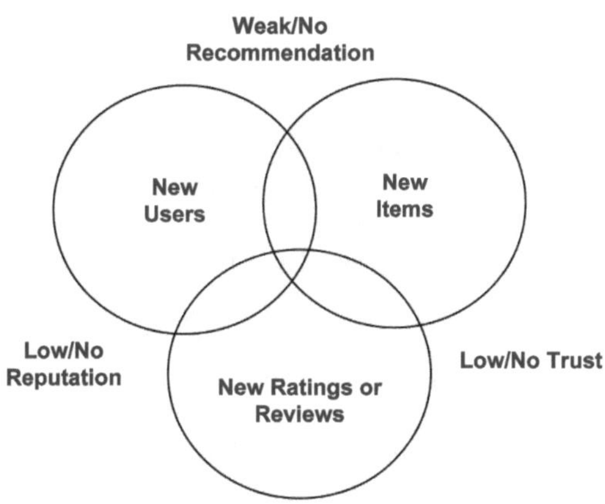

Fig. 1. Beyond the cold-start problem, new items may fail in trust if new users with low reputation rate it

In order to gather as much information as necessary to improve recommendation, recommender systems typically ask users to rate a diverse set of items, especially those users that are new in the system [2]. We propose the use of gamification to improve recommendation, explicit feedback, items and users reputation. Gamification is the way to design systems that motivate people to do things and using the right approaches it could succeed as many success stories recently reported by [20]. The main purpose of using gamification on e-commerce systems is to promote user engagement in those tasks that result in better recommendation for themselves.

To better recommend content to new users and also to improve their reputation, an e-commerce system may be designed to call the user's attention by intrinsic motivation and offering rewards for each task completed by users.

Users that are new in the system can be motivated to complete a task by intrinsic reasons. For example, Netflix[7] encourages users to evaluate movies that were already seen by them to improve recommendation. However, Netflix has no game elements involved to keep users doing the rating task.

The use of intangible and engagement-contingent rewards can keep users involved with the results as they receive a feedback about their journey through the tasks, using badges and leaderboard to motivate them. Also, tasks that have a Fixed Ratio [20] (every x number of times a user performs a task he/she will receive a reward) can engage users in tasks such as reviews evaluation.

For those users that have high reputation, gamified system can encourage them to evaluate (new) products if they have already used or bought it. For this task, it is interesting to stimulate the users by intrinsic and extrinsic motivation by the use of performance-contingent rewards given users tangible and intangible rewards when they perform good reviews. In addition, other users can evaluate the review and it can also be gamified. Users can be encourage to evaluate reviews from other users to ensure the quality of recommended items and users reputation.

5 Conclusion

This work began by thinking about how gamification could help to fix the cold-start problem present in recommender systems. Through an online survey, we have gathered information in order to understand how users behave on e-commerce websites, when it is required for them to evaluate purchased products.

We asked participants questions about their purchase routine and their motivations to evaluate products. We investigated and presented the results from two perspectives. First, we investigated the reasons why users rate products, results show that most users usually rate their purchased products when it is not according to their expectations (positively and negatively). This action can result in a poor recommendation because the recommender system needs to work only with extreme ratings.

Second, we investigated the motivations for users to return to the website to rate products if the e-commerce website provides them points or reputation. Most part of the participants showed that they are moved by tangible rewards, however, they have intrinsic motivations to perform this action.

We developed a theoretical framework that supports the use of game elements on e-commerce websites to improve product ratings. The framework was developed based on the results of the survey presented here.

We intend to implement this framework and compare the user engagement before and after the use of game elements. We have also observed that users

[7] http://www.netflix.com/

are using gamification without noticing it and this could be an interesting point for future research. This paper provides the initial elements to start a deeper investigation about the subject. We showed how users are motivated, why users usually rate products, how gamification can improve the ratings, and mainly, which problems are related to the lack of (good) ratings.

References

1. Adomavicius, G., Tuzhilin, A.: Toward the next generation of recommender systems: A survey of the state-of-the-art and possible extensions. IEEE Trans. on Knowl. and Data Eng. 17(6), 734–749 (2005)
2. Amatriain, X., Pujol, J.M., Tintarev, N., Oliver, N.: Rate it again: increasing recommendation accuracy by user re-rating. In: Proceedings of the third ACM Conference on Recommender Systems, RecSys 2009, pp. 173–180. ACM, New York (2009)
3. Balabanović, M., Shoham, Y.: Fab: content-based, collaborative recommendation. Commun. ACM 40(3), 66–72 (1997)
4. Bostandjiev, S., O'Donovan, J., Höllerer, T.: Tasteweights: a visual interactive hybrid recommender system. In: Proceedings of the Sixth ACM Conference on Recommender Systems, RecSys 2012, pp. 35–42. ACM, New York (2012)
5. Choi, S.M., Han, Y.S.: Identifying representative ratings for a new item in recommendation system. In: Proceedings of the 7th International Conference on Ubiquitous Information Management and Communication, ICUIMC 2013, pp. 64:1–64:6. ACM, New York (2013)
6. Deci, E.L., Ryan, R.M.: Self-Determination Theory: A Macrotheory of Human Motivation, Development, and Health. Canadian Psychology 49(10), 182–185 (2008)
7. Deci, E.L., Cascio, W.F., Krusell, J.: Cognitive Evaluation Theory and Some Comments on the Calder and Staw Critique. Journal of Personality and Social Psychology 31(1), 81–85 (1975)
8. Deci, E.L., Ryan, R.M.: Intrinsic and Extrinsic Motivations: Classic Definitions and New Directions. Contemporary Educational Psychology (25), 54–67 (2000)
9. Deterding, S., Dixon, D., Khaled, R., Nacke, L.: From game design elements to gamefulness: defining "gamification". In: Proceedings of the 15th International Academic MindTrek Conference: Envisioning Future Media Environments, MindTrek 2011, pp. 9–15. ACM, New York (2011)
10. Deterding, S., Khaled, R., Nacke, L., Dixon, D.: Gamification: Toward a definition. In: CHI 2011 Gamification Workshop Proceedings, Vancouver, BC, Canada (2011)
11. Jannach, D., Zanker, M., Felfernig, A., Friedrich, G.: Recommender Systems: An Introduction, 1st edn. Cambridge University Press (September 2010)
12. Kwon, Y.: Improving top-n recommendation techniques using rating variance. In: Proceedings of the 2008 ACM Conference on Recommender Systems, RecSys 2008, pp. 307–310. ACM, New York (2008)
13. Leino, J., Räihä, K.J.: Case amazon: ratings and reviews as part of recommendations. In: Proceedings of the 2007 ACM Conference on Recommender Systems, RecSys 2007, pp. 137–140. ACM, New York (2007)
14. Masthoff, J.: Group recommender systems: Combining individual models. In: Recommender Systems Handbook, pp. 677–702 (2011)
15. Park, S.T., Chu, W.: Pairwise preference regression for cold-start recommendation. In: Proceedings of the Third ACM Conference on Recommender Systems, RecSys 2009, pp. 21–28. ACM, New York (2009)

16. Rashid, A.M., Albert, I., Cosley, D., Lam, S.K., McNee, S.M., Konstan, J.A., Riedl, J.: Getting to know you: learning new user preferences in recommender systems. In: Proceedings of the 7th International Conference on Intelligent User Interfaces, IUI 2002, pp. 127–134. ACM, New York (2002)
17. Said, A., Fields, B., Jain, B.J., Albayrak, S.: User-centric evaluation of a k-furthest neighbor collaborative filtering recommender algorithm. In: Proceedings of the 2013 Conference on Computer Supported Cooperative Work, CSCW 2013, pp. 1399–1408. ACM, New York (2013)
18. Schein, A.I., Popescul, A., Ungar, L.H., Pennock, D.M.: Methods and metrics for cold-start recommendations. In: Proceedings of the 25th Annual International ACM SIGIR Conference on Research and Development in Information Retrieval, SIGIR 2002, pp. 253–260. ACM, New York (2002)
19. Su, X., Khoshgoftaar, T.M.: A survey of collaborative filtering techniques. Adv. in Artif. Intell., 4:2–4:2 (January 2009)
20. Werbach, K., Hunter, D.: For the Win: How Game Thinking Can Revolutionize Your Business. Wharton Digital Press (2012)
21. Ziesemer, A., Oliveira, J.: How to know what do you want? a survey of recommender systems and the next generation. In: Proceedings of the Eighth Brazilian Symposium on Collaborative Systems, SBSC 2011, pp. 104–111 (October 2011)
22. de C.A. Ziesemer, A., de Oliveira, J.B.S.: Keep querying and tag on: Collaborative folksonomy using model-based recommendation. In: Antunes, P., Gerosa, M.A., Sylvester, A., Vassileva, J., de Vreede, G.-J. (eds.) CRIWG 2013. LNCS, vol. 8224, pp. 10–17. Springer, Heidelberg (2013)

Author Index

FSC
www.fsc.org
MIX
Papier aus verantwortungsvollen Quellen
Paper from responsible sources
FSC® C105338

If you have any concerns about our products, you can contact us on
ProductSafety@springernature.com

In case Publisher is established outside the EU, the EU authorized representative is:
Springer Nature Customer Service Center GmbH
Europaplatz 3, 69115 Heidelberg, Germany

Printed by Libri Plureos GmbH
in Hamburg, Germany